Counseling, Psychology, and Children

Counseling, Psychology, and Children

A Multidimensional Approach to Intervention

William G. Wagner
The University of Southern Mississippi

Upper Saddle River, New Jersey
Columbus, Ohio

Library of Congress Cataloging-in-Publication Data

Wagner, William G.
Counseling, psychology, and children : a multidimensional approach to intervention / William G. Wagner.
p. cm.
Includes bibliographical references and index.
ISBN 0-13-084814-X
1. Child psychotherapy. I. Title.
RI504.W24 2003
618.92′8914--dc21

2002032592

Vice President and Publisher: Jeffery W. Johnston
Executive Editor: Kevin M. Davis
Editorial Assistant: Autumn Crisp
Production Editor: Mary Harlan
Production Coordination: Sondra Greenfield, UG / GGS Information Services, Inc.
Design Coordinator: Diane C. Lorenzo
Cover Design: Bryan Huber
Cover Image: SuperStock
Text Design and Illustrations: UG / GGS Information Services, Inc.
Production Manager: Laura Messerly
Director of Marketing: Ann Castel Davis
Marketing Manager: Amy June
Marketing Coordinator: Tyra Cooper

This book was set in Palatino by UG / GGS Information Services, Inc. It was printed and bound by Courier Westford, Inc. The cover was printed by Phoenix Color Corp.

Pearson Education Ltd.
Pearson Education Australia Pty. Limited
Pearson Education Singapore Pte. Ltd.
Pearson Education North Asia Ltd.
Pearson Education Canada, Ltd.
Pearson Educación de Mexico, S.A. de C.V.
Pearson Education—Japan
Pearson Education Malaysia Pte. Ltd.
Pearson Education, *Upper Saddle River, New Jersey*

10 9 8 7 6 5 4 3 2 1
ISBN:0-13-084814-X

I dedicate this book to my parents, J. Frank and Lois Wagner,
who taught me to love learning,
and to my wife, Diane, who continues to help me live my dreams.

Preface

Counseling, Psychology, and Children: A Multidimensional Approach to Intervention describes a practical method for remediating common childhood problems, preventing their occurrence in at-risk children, and facilitating optimal development in all children. Designed for mental health and school counselors, psychologists, family therapists, and social workers, the book is more than a review of the extensive literature on child interventions of the past 100 years. Significant theoretical contributions and empirical findings on child therapies are discussed, but in the context of a four-factor treatment model that requires consideration of developmental and cultural influences as they relate to the collaboration of therapists and significant other adults (e.g., parents, teachers) who deliver remedial, preventive, and educational/developmental services to children.

Contemporary psychosocial treatments for children are very different from the method that Sigmund Freud used with Little Hans at the beginning of the 20th century. These changes are addressed here, first as basic concepts and issues (Part 1), and then in terms of the theory and practice of commonly used treatments (Part 2), and other intervention methods for children and families (Part 3). Individual chapters progress from a description of the four-factor multidimensional model (Chapter 1) to the ultimate goal of this book, the use of integrated treatments in everyday practice (Chapter 16). Other topics include ethical and professional issues (Chapter 2), and brief and empirically supported treatments that can be used in an era of managed mental health care (Chapter 3). In Chapter 4, special attention is given to assessment methods for collecting treatment-related information from children, parents, and teachers. Therapy as an art and a science is discussed in Chapter 5, which contains a model based on the work of John Dewey, and a description of quantitative and qualitative research methods that can be used to study the process and outcome of treatment. In Part 2, there is a review of the most commonly used psychosocial treatments for children: psychodynamic, child-centered, behavioral and cognitive-behavioral, and family systems therapies. For each approach, one chapter is devoted to theoretical issues and a second to related treatment methods. Part 3 contains information on other interventions, such as consultation, psychopharmacotherapy, and narrative therapy.

Case vignettes are included throughout the book to illustrate the application of the theoretical constructs and empirical findings presented in the text. A novel feature of the book is its use of empirical research on child development in a multicultural society. This material is presented throughout the book as it relates to clinically relevant topics. Developmental and multicultural influences are also addressed in Contemporary Issues Boxes that contain recent findings on important topics related to children.

As stated above, the ultimate goal of this book is the use of integrated treatments for children. As the field of child therapy has matured, authors have begun to describe and study these methods, which often represent the combination of more than one theoretical orientation. Integrated treatments are based, in part, on the assumption that individual methods have both strengths and limitations. Therapists who select this approach must be skilled in the treatments that are commonly used with children. In other words, before they can integrate based on the strengths of different theories, therapists must have a thorough understanding of the principles and techniques of each method. This book is offered as a step toward this goal.

Acknowledgments

Although my name appears as the author, many other people were involved in the preparation of this book by being there when I needed them. I appreciate the administrative support that John Alcorn and Stan Kuczaj provided during the years I devoted to this project. I am indebted to the University of Southern Mississippi and its Cook Library, including Karolyn Thompson and her helpful staff in Interlibrary Loan who obtained many of the materials I used in the preparation of this book.

During more than 20 years in academia, I have had the opportunity to work with scores of talented students who expanded my knowledge of counseling and psychology. Sections of this text will sound very familiar to my research assistants, especially William Fowler, Desiree Kilcrease-Fleming, Ramona Mellott, Rita Porter, Lisa Moon, Marci Burroughs, Melinda Dale, Charmain Jackman, Keith and Valerie Crabtree, Jennifer Knight, Natalie Gaughf, and Michael Davidson. I want to thank Elliott Brown, whose countless trips to the library and detection of typographical errors in early reference lists allowed me to stay focused on my writing.

I also appreciate the time and effort of the colleagues and students who reviewed individual chapters and offered recommendations for revisions. These include Mark Leach, Deborah Heggie, Joe Olmi, Terence Tracey, Daniel Randolph, Larry Gates, Pernella Singleton, Yolanda Crump, Heidi Nelson, William Lyddon, and Lillian Range. Special thanks go to those colleagues who reviewed the manuscript for Merrill: Christopher Brown, Southwest Texas State; Barbara L. Carlozzi, University of Central Oklahoma; Merith Cosden, University of California, Santa Barbara; Julie A. Dinsmore, University of Nebraska at Kearney; Maria Gutierrez, University of Missouri; Donna A. Henderson, Wake Forest University; Margaret A. Herrick, Kutztown University of Pennsylvania; Richard James, University of Memphis; Peggy Kaczmarek, New Mexico State University; David Lawson, Texas A&M University; Robert Myrick, University of Florida; and Lee A. Rosen, Colorado State University.

I am indeed fortunate to have worked with the talented staff at Merrill/Prentice Hall. These include Kevin Davis, who was there to support me from the beginning; Christina Tawney, who patiently provided the structure I needed as a neophyte author of textbooks, and Mary Harlan, whose production expertise was invaluable. And I am indebted to Sondra Greenfield and the staff at UG/GGS who were indispensable during the final stage of production on this book.

About the Author

William G. Wagner is a professor in the Department of Psychology at The University of Southern Mississippi (USM). Before receiving his Ph.D. in Counseling Psychology from the University of Florida in 1981, Dr. Wagner was a teacher in the public schools of Vermont and a case worker and regional administrator for Youth Programs, Inc., a court alternative program for juvenile offenders in Florida. Since joining the faculty at USM, he has studied developmentally appropriate treatments for children with nocturnal enuresis, child survivors of sexual abuse, and children of divorce. He also maintained a part-time private practice in which he treated children and families with a broad range of presenting problems, such as attention-deficit hyperactivity disorder, enuresis, oppositional defiant disorder, and adjustment to divorce and the death of a significant other. His current research interests include the development of forgiveness in children, gender- and ethnic-related influences on children's development, and the application of the multidimensional model described in this text. Dr. Wagner is a licensed psychologist and is listed on the National Register of Health Service Providers in Psychology. He is also a National Certified Counselor and is a member of the American Counseling Association, the American Psychological Association, and the American School Counselor Association. He has published more than 40 articles in a variety of journals, including *The Counseling Psychologist*, the *Journal of Counseling Psychology, Child Abuse and Neglect*, the *Journal of Counseling and Development*, *The Journal of Pediatrics*, and the *Journal of Pediatric Psychology*. He has served as a consulting editor for the *Journal of Counseling Psychology* and is currently a member of the editorial board of *Child Abuse and Neglect*.

Discover the Companion Website Accompanying This Book

THE PRENTICE HALL COMPANION WEBSITE: A VIRTUAL LEARNING ENVIRONMENT

Technology is a constantly growing and changing aspect of our field that is creating a need for content and resources. To address this emerging need, Prentice Hall has developed an online learning environment for students and professors alike—Companion Websites—to support our textbooks.

In creating a Companion Website, our goal is to build on and enhance what the textbook already offers. For this reason, the content for each user-friendly website is organized by topic and provides the professor and student with a variety of meaningful resources. Common features of a Companion Website include:

FOR THE PROFESSOR—

Every Companion Website integrates **Syllabus Manager™**, an online syllabus creation and management utility.

- **Syllabus Manager™** provides you, the instructor, with an easy, step-by-step process to create and revise syllabi, with direct links into Companion Website and other online content without having to learn HTML.
- Students may logon to your syllabus during any study session. All they need to know is the web address for the Companion Website and the password you've assigned to your syllabus.
- After you have created a syllabus using **Syllabus Manager™**, students may enter the syllabus for their course section from any point in the Companion Website.
- Clicking on a date, the student is shown the list of activities for the assignment. The activities for each assignment are linked directly to actual content, saving time for students.
- Adding assignments consists of clicking on the desired due date, then filling in the details of the assignment—name of the assignment, instructions, and whether it is a one-time or repeating assignment.
- In addition, links to other activities can be created easily. If the activity is online, a URL can be entered in the space provided, and it will be linked automatically in the final syllabus.
- Your completed syllabus is hosted on our servers, allowing convenient updates from any computer on the Internet. Changes you make to your syllabus are immediately available to your students at their next logon.

FOR THE STUDENT—

Counseling Topics—17 core counseling topics represent the diversity and scope of today's counseling field.

Annotated Bibliography—includes seminal foundational works and key current works.

Web Destinations—lists significant and up-to-date practitioner and client sites.

Professional Development—provides helpful information regarding professional organizations and codes of ethics.

Electronic Bluebook—send homework or essays directly to your instructor's email with this paperless form.

Message Board—serves as a virtual bulletin board to post—or respond to—questions or comments to/from a national audience.

Chat—real-time chat with anyone who is using the text anywhere in the country—ideal for discussion and study groups, class projects, etc.

To take advantage of these and other resources, please visit the Counseling, Psychology, and Children: A Multidimensional Approach to Intervention Companion Website at

www.prenhall.com/wagner

Brief Contents

Contents

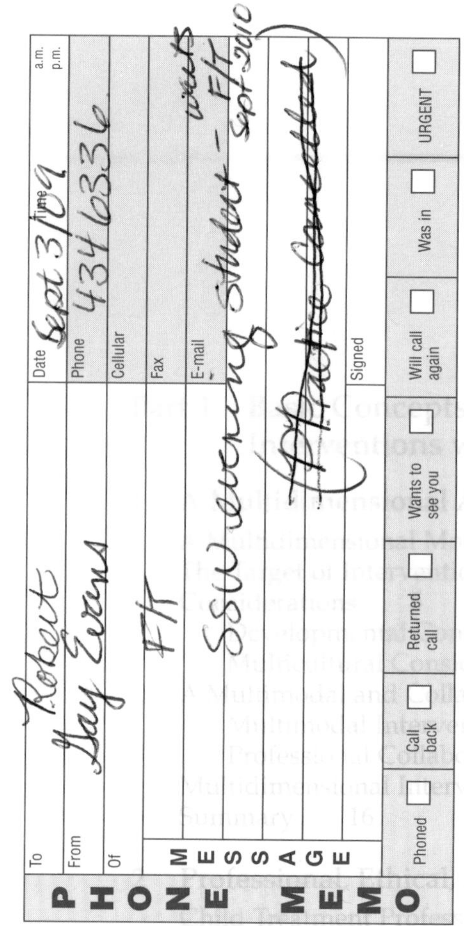

Part 1

Basic Concepts and Issues for Multidimensional Interventions with Children

■ ■ ■

Six-year-old Samuel refuses to separate from his mother when they arrive at school. Ms. Ward, the boy's teacher, meets Samuel and his mother in the parking lot every morning to walk him from the car to the classroom. Yesterday he bit her arm when she took his hand and asked him to go with her.

Eleven-year-old Marisa is the only Asian American child in her elementary school. Adopted as an infant into an upper middle-class European American family, she is socially adept, artistically talented, and academically advanced for her age. Her teacher recently encouraged the parents to enroll Marisa in enrichment activities after school.

At age 8, Joseph is the youngest of five children in a lower socioeconomic, single-parent family living in a high-crime inner-city neighborhood. The boy's two oldest siblings are currently in a juvenile detention center after their conviction for the robbery of three local businesses. Joseph's mother describes him as "a good boy," and his teacher says he is an excellent student.

■ ■ ■

Which of these children can benefit from mental health services? If you are like most people, you probably picked Samuel. After all, he is the one who is currently having problems. But all three children have psychosocial needs worthy of intervention. Samuel, of course, represents the traditional client who is placed in therapy to remediate difficulties that interfere with everyday life. Although most people would describe Marisa and Joseph as "normal" children, they too can benefit from treatments designed to enhance optimal functioning and prevent problems in the future. Marisa, for example, is a gifted child in need of after-school developmental activities to capitalize on her artistic abilities. She also might benefit from educational services to facilitate development of her ethnic identity. Joseph is doing well at home and in school, but he lives in a neighborhood that places him at risk for the delinquent behaviors of his siblings. To avoid this unfortunate outcome, prevention programs at school or in the community should be established for him and other children to counteract the negative effects of their environment.

Helping children like Samuel, Marisa, and Joseph requires the use of a multidimensional approach that includes the selection of appropriate educational/ developmental, preventive, and remedial interventions. Multidimensional treatment also involves the collaboration of therapists and significant other adults in the child's life. For example, if Marisa is to develop her artistic abilities, she will need a teacher who has the specialized skills and experience in this area. The prevention program for Joseph might be established as a daily after-school activity that involves neighborhood children in arts, crafts, and sports. No therapist can fulfill all of these responsibilities, so clinicians must work with other professionals to implement comprehensive treatment services for children.

Therapists are constantly reminded of the uniqueness of every child. Therefore, multidimensional treatment requires consideration of each client's developmental level and cultural background. To understand a child's needs, the therapist must view the client's behavior in relation to others of his or her age and in the context of what we will term the child's *cultural surround*. Preschoolers and older elementary school students, for example, think and process information in different ways, so clinicians must individualize treatment to each client's developmental level. Therapists also need to consider such factors as the child's gender, ethnic background, sexual orientation, and disability status.

When we combine intervention modality (i.e., education/development, prevention, remediation) and professional collaboration with children's developmental level and cultural background, we have a four-factor multidimensional approach to intervention. In this book, you will explore how this model can be used to assess and treat children. We begin with an in-depth discussion of the model (Chapter 1) followed by an examination of ethical, legal, and professional issues as they relate to the treatment of children (Chapter 2). We explore contemporary issues in child therapy (Chapter 3), as well as the first step to effective intervention—the assessment of the child (Chapter 4). We conclude Part 1 with a discussion of the art and science of therapy and an examination of the process and outcome of treatment with children (Chapter 5).

1

A Multidimensional Approach to Intervention with Children

■ ■ ■

Seven-year-old Thomas is the only child of John and Mary Jamison. He recently told his African American father and European American mother that his classmates were teasing him about his appearance. When Mr. Jamison telephoned Thomas' teacher to discuss the matter, he learned that his son had been fighting with the other students and not completing his classwork. The teacher said she had not observed the other children teasing Thomas in class but acknowledged that it could be occurring on the playground during recess.

At home, Thomas disobeys his mother, has temper tantrums, and does not finish his homework without parental supervision. He has no friends in the neighborhood, in part because most of the other children are junior and senior high school students. As a result, he spends much of his time watching television and playing alone in his room.

■ ■ ■

Thomas is similar to many children who are in need of therapeutic services. He is having difficulty functioning in more than one environment. His development is being hampered in different areas as he experiences problems with social relationships and academic performance. He influences and is influenced by significant others through daily interactions with parents, teachers, and peers at home and at school. Therapists who want to help clients like Thomas must appreciate the importance of these factors as they try to understand how children develop in the context of their cultural surround.

This chapter examines a multidimensional approach to mental health services for children. It considers the role of developmental and multicultural factors as they relate to therapeutic interventions with children, ages 12 years and younger. The chapter also explores a treatment model that is multimodal and multidisciplinary because it is designed to prevent and remediate problems while facilitating optimal development in children through a collaborative effort by therapists, parents, and significant other adults in a child's life. At the end of the chapter, we examine how this multidimensional approach is used in treatment with the Jamisons.

A MULTIDIMENSIONAL MODEL FOR THERAPEUTIC INTERVENTION WITH CHILDREN

Morrill, Oetting, and Hurst (1974) described a three-dimensional model of therapy based on the target, purpose, and method of intervention. As shown in Figure 1-1, the authors' target of treatment included the individual client and sig-

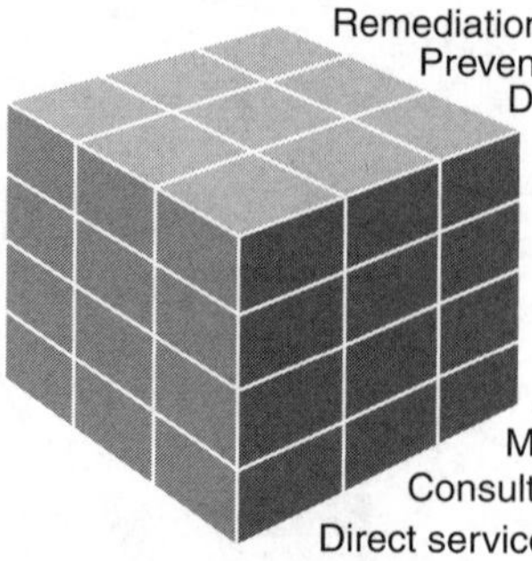

Purpose of intervention
Remediation
Prevention
Development
Target of intervention
Individual
Primary group
Associational group
Institution or community
Method of intervention
Media
Consultation and training
Direct service

Figure 1–1. The Three-Dimensional Model of Therapy Developed by Morrill, Oetting, and Hurst (1974) From "Dimensions of Counselor Functioning," by W.H. Morrill, E.R. Oetting, and J.C. Hurst, 1974, *Personnel and Guidance Journal, 52,* p. 355. Copyright 1974 by the American Counseling Association. Reprinted with permission of the author.

nificant others, such as the family, peer group, school, and community. They believed that the purpose of therapy varies, from eliminating and preventing problems to fostering positive development in individuals and institutions. The third dimension of their model, the method of intervention, involves both direct services, including individual or group therapy for clients, and indirect techniques, such as consultation, that can be used to effect change in a child's environment.

Wagner (1994) adapted the Morrill et al. (1974) model for use with children. He retained the authors' purpose of intervention but divided the original target dimension into two interacting elements: lifespan development and cultural diversity. The innate tendency toward physical and psychological growth that exists in all children constitutes development. But a child's growth and development are shaped by social, political, and economic forces in the cultural surround. Who a child is at a given point in time is a result of developmental and cultural factors. A 12-year-old client is very different than that same child at age 5 years, when his or her cognitive, emotional, and moral development were less sophisticated. Therapists must remember that children live in a multicultural environment where others' expectations can differ significantly from culture to culture and from one family to the next. A precocious child of college-educated African American or European American parents will require treatment services that are different than those provided to an average youngster in a recently immigrated Hispanic American or Asian American family.

Wagner (1994) expanded the Morrill et al. (1974) method of intervention to include research and practice activities, but he did not describe how therapists should actually treat children. The multidimensional model presented here is intended to address this limitation. Therapists' attitudes regarding the nature and scope of intervention are very important. Many clinicians believe their role is limited to remediation, or the elimination of children's problems. This perception is understandable, given evidence suggesting that approximately 1 in 5 U. S. youths has a mental or substance abuse problem that interferes with daily functioning (Costello, 1989). But therapists who focus on eliminating problems or treating psychopathology often overlook opportunities for facilitating optimal development in children. Likewise, clinicians who limit their practice to troubled children miss the chance to prevent problems and enhance development among the majority of young people who do not require remedial interventions. To accomplish this, clinicians must embrace a multimodal approach to intervention that can be used with all children, not just those having psychosocial problems.

Using a multimodal approach with children of different developmental levels and cultural backgrounds can overwhelm both novice and experienced therapists. Implementation of this method requires the collaboration of significant adults in a child's life. All too often, clinicians see themselves as independent practitioners rather than members of a multidisciplinary team that provides integrated therapeutic services. For example, to effectively treat a socially isolated child who is having academic problems, a therapist must think beyond the traditional, 50-minute treatment hour and establish working relationships with at least the client's parents, teachers, and school counselor. By collaborating with these adults, the clinician becomes a contributing member of a treatment team that works together on behalf of the child.

In summary, a multidimensional approach with children requires consideration of developmental and multicultural influences. It involves the use of interventions whose purpose can be education/development, prevention, remediation or a combination thereof. This collaborative method brings together significant other adults who coordinate their efforts to benefit children. Applying this model in practice requires that therapists experience a conceptual shift from an individual and isolated approach to treating troubled clients toward a more inclusive framework for helping all children, regardless of age, cultural background, or psychosocial adjustment. The following sections examine this model in more detail, beginning with the developmental and multicultural components of the intervention target identified by Morrill et al. (1974).

THE TARGET OF INTERVENTION: DEVELOPMENTAL AND MULTICULTURAL CONSIDERATIONS

All clinicians face the challenge of identifying the target for intervention. Will it be the child, the family, or the child's school or community? Because children depend on adults for their basic needs, treatment typically involves more than one target. A child who exhibits problems at home and school probably requires interventions for the child, family, and school. Treatment for the child may include strategies to improve self-esteem, decision-making skills, and anger control. To address family-related problems, the therapist might work with the parents and child to foster better communication and problem-solving skills. School-based interventions could include consultation with teachers and the school counselor to improve the learning environment or establish a home-based reinforcement program to reward appropriate classroom behavior.

Anna Freud, the renowned child psychoanalyst, once wrote that "children of all ages are unfinished human beings" (A. Freud, 1956/1969, p. 305). She was referring to the ever-changing content, structure, and process of children's thoughts, feelings, and behaviors. As young people mature and interact with their cultural surround, they revise earlier views of themselves and the world and begin to develop an adult perspective that was previously beyond their level of understanding. This transformation of meaning making defines the childhood years and gives parents, therapists, and other child care professionals their greatest challenges and rewards.

Regardless of the intervention target, clinicians must consider the role of developmental and cultural influences. Figure 1-2 illustrates how these factors interact when the target of intervention is a child. The developmental domains listed are those identified by Wagner (1996) and represent the general areas that have received considerable attention from developmental psychologists. Also included are four sociocultural influences that have been studied relative to children's development. This section briefly reviews developmental and multicultural considerations when the child is the target of intervention. Later

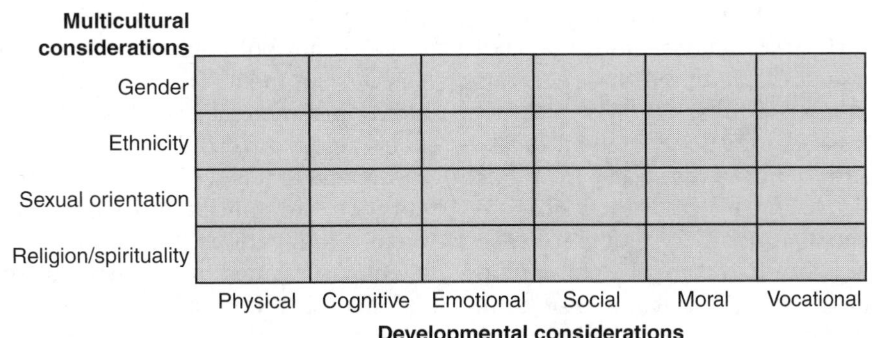

Figure 1–2. Developmental and Multicultural Considerations when a Child is the Target of Intervention

chapters examine these factors in more detail, including their application to other intervention targets.

Developmental Considerations

Forehand and Wierson (1993) described how courses in developmental psychology and child interventions are separate entities in most counseling and applied psychology graduate programs. Many students are exposed to the theoretical and empirical foundations of child development in classes taught by nonclinical instructors. They learn to integrate the theory and practice of child treatments from clinical faculty in specialized courses, practica, and internships. But as Forehand and Wierson warned, "The result of these two parallel sequences is that the developmental aspects of children and their problems are never integrated into clinical and research activities" (p. 118). The developmental component of the multidimensional model provides the opportunity to correct this deficit, allowing students to examine the work of developmental psychologists as they acquire the therapeutic skills needed to work with children.

Johnson, Rasbury, and Siegel (1997) contrasted child and adult clients and concluded that the two groups differ most in terms of their developmental level. The rate of growth or development in childhood is rapid, especially when compared with the relative stability observed in adults. A 10-year age difference during childhood or adulthood, for example, can have dramatic effects. The average 32-year-old person processes information, talks with others, and distinguishes right from wrong in a manner similar to the way the person functioned at age 22. But a 10-year difference in childhood has remarkable effects. Consider the cognitive, language, and moral development of the average 11-month-old. Then imagine how that youngster will think, speak, and make choices when he or she is 11 years old. Clearly, therapists who work with children must be more aware of developmental differences than clinicians who limit their practice to adults.

Developmental psychologists have given considerable attention to the changes that occur from birth to puberty. Jean Piaget and his colleagues observed that elementary school students were able to reason using concrete objects but had difficulty thinking on an abstract level using concepts that were not immediately visible to the eye (Piaget & Inhelder, 1969). An average 8-year-old child can be expected to recognize that identical balls of clay continue to have the same quantity regardless of their shape, but this same child has difficulty applying the concept of partial vacuum to explain why we are able to drink liquids through a straw. Therapists must appreciate these developmental differences if they are to design and implement effective interventions with clients. Treatment for the average 8-year-old child is more likely to involve the use of concrete materials, such as toys or art supplies, rather than the manipulation of abstract concepts that characterizes the traditional talk therapies used with adults.

Developmental differences also play an important role in deciding whether a client's behavior is normal or abnormal. A behavior that is considered appropriate at one stage of development may be viewed as a problem at a later age. MacFarlane, Allen, and Honzik (1954) provided some direction in this regard with their analysis of data collected as part of the Berkeley Growth Study, a longitudinal study of human development initiated in 1928. MacFarlane et al. found that certain problem behaviors, such as disturbing dreams and excessive activity, were relatively common in childhood but infrequent during early adolescence. Other behaviors were either uncommon regardless of age (e.g., soiling), declined significantly during the elementary school years (e.g., lying), or increased as children approached adolescence (e.g., nail biting).

Wenar (1982a) contended that "an understanding of development is essential" (p. 195) if therapists are to correctly discriminate normal from abnormal behavior in children. But development itself is a multidimensional phenomenon that includes biological, cognitive, social, emotional, moral, and vocational domains (Wagner, 1996). The complex nature of this process becomes clear when we realize that development typically occurs at different rates across these domains. For example, a gifted child with average physical development may be advanced in the cognitive domain but below average in emotional and social development. The therapist who works with this child must remember that the client's adultlike vocabulary and conversational skills mask an emotional awareness that is typical of less mature children. To be effective, the clinician must assess the child's development across various domains and not assume that the client has attained the same maturity level in all areas.

Therapists must also consider the developmental differences that exist between the clinician and child. Of course, the most obvious of these is physical size. Consider the potential impact of height. Compared with the average man of 5 feet, 10 inches or woman of 5 feet, 4 inches, the typical 6-year-old boy or girl is noticeably shorter at 3 feet, 10 inches or 3 feet, 9 inches, respectively (Needlman, 1996). Although the difference is less dramatic with older children, 12-year-old children are still, on average, shorter than their clinician regardless of whether the child is a boy of 4 feet, 11 inches or a girl of 5 feet (Needlman, 1996). This height differential is rarely observed with adult clients and therefore represents a unique influence on the therapist–child relationship. Imagine how comfortable you would feel if, at your present height, you were expected to share personal life experiences with a stranger who is 10 feet tall.

The two points when physical development is most rapid are the first 12 months of life and the transition that occurs during puberty (Berndt, 1992). Interestingly, the average boy reaches half of his adult height by the age of 24 months, 6 months later than the average girl (Tanner, 1978). Girls and boys grow at comparable rates through their childhood years, but the average girl begins her adolescent growth spurt at age 11 or 12 years, 2 years ahead of the average boy (Malina, 1990). Therapists encounter interesting challenges as they adapt their interventions to each child's developmental level. One hour may be spent sitting on the floor in play therapy with a sexually abused 6-year-old girl, but the next hour may be devoted to traditional talk therapy in which the clinician is seated in a chair helping a precocious and physically advanced 11-year-old boy adjust to the changes associated with his parents' recent divorce.

A significant time in a child's physical development is during the onset of puberty. Therapists are likely to encounter children, particularly girls, who experience this major life transition during the late elementary school years. Malina (1990) reported that girls now enter puberty approximately 3 years earlier than their counterparts did during the second half of the 19th century. Malina noted that the average onset of menarche was approximately age 16 years among girls in 1860, a figure that has dropped to about age 13 years. The physical changes associated with puberty, such as the growth of body hair and the development of wider hips in girls and broader shoulders in boys, have been associated with gender-based psychological changes that are apparently related to the timing of puberty. Compared with girls who enter this transition at a later age, early maturing girls appear to be more prone to adjustment problems such as emotional difficulties and concerns surrounding body image (Brooks-Gunn, 1988). In contrast, early maturing boys seem to fare better, have more self-confidence and are more satisfied with their physical appearance than their peers who mature later (Brack, Orr, & Ingersoll, 1988).

Flexibility is the guiding principle for therapists who work with children. Clinicians must adjust their interactional style and treatment strategies to suit their clients' physical size, thought processes, social skills, emotional awareness, moral understanding, and plans for the future. The younger the child, the more important it is that therapists consider these developmental differences. The changes that occur during childhood also pose a significant challenge for clinicians' selection of intervention techniques, most of which were originally conceived for adults. Because certain developmental factors are more relevant to particular theories of therapy, these considerations are examined in chapters devoted to the major theoretical approaches to child treatments.

Multicultural Considerations

Pedersen (1991) identified multiculturalism as a "fourth force" (p. 6) in counseling, one that is generic to all therapeutic relationships and complements the psychodynamic, behavioral, and humanistic perspectives that have been the theoretical foundation for the helping professions for decades. Despite a dramatic increase in theoretical and empirical inquiry on multiculturalism, the field is in its infancy. Its young age is reflected in the diverse terminology that experts have used to describe key constructs. Pedersen and Carey (1994), for example, observed that more than 150 definitions have been proposed for "culture" alone. For our purposes, we will use the words of Carter and Qureshi (1995), who described culture as "a learned system of meaning and behavior that is passed from one generation to the next" (p. 241). Because each child's experience of the world is unique, culture could be interpreted on a highly personal level. But the traditional view is that it represents the "shared values, shared perceptions of reality, shared symbols" (Smith & Vasquez, 1985, p. 532) that members of a group use in their everyday life.

Cultural groups have been identified using various criteria, including race and ethnicity. Traditional definitions of race are based on the categorization of people according to biological or physical differences, such as skin color and facial features. Unfortunately, labeling someone as a member of a specific race is not as easy as it might appear. Zuckerman (1990) noted that variability within racial groups often exceeds the differences between them, and Baruth and Manning (2003) observed that commonly used racial labels are not distinct categories. Accordingly, Baruth and Manning adopted a socially derived definition of race as "the way a group of people defines itself or is defined by others as being different from other groups because of assumed innate physical characteristics" (p. 9). A very important term here is "assumed." That is, people erroneously categorize others based on biological differences that do not exist.

Phinney (1996) recommended that race be subsumed under ethnicity, which she described as "broad groupings of Americans on the basis of both race and culture of origin" (p. 919). Although other writers have questioned Phinney's position (see Helms & Talleyrand, 1997), children born to interracial unions have made it impossible to categorize people solely on the basis of biological differences. For our purposes, we will adopt Phinney's position and use the term *ethnicity* to refer to socially constructed groups that have common religious practices, language, cultural symbols, and history. Categorization by ethnicity in the United States has often involved the distinction between "majority" and "minority" groups. Although this approach has some appeal, defining people according to their representation in the total population fails to take into consideration local and regional differences. This method also overlooks political and economic influences, which are the basis for an alternative method that identifies ethnic groups as either dominant or nondominant. The historical role of European Americans has established their position as the dominant group in the United States. Nondominant ethnic groups are people of color, such as Americans of African, Asian, and Hispanic heritage as well as Native Americans, who preceded all others on this continent.

Another important construct in the field of multiculturism is *acculturation*, or the process by which people identify with the beliefs, values, and behaviors of the dominant culture (Lee, 1995). Acculturation is sometimes measured by the length of time an individual has lived in a country. But length of residence is not an accurate indicator of this important process. Consider two individuals. The first has resided in the United States for 20 years and continues to rely on his native language and follow the cultural practices of his country of origin. The second person immigrated to this country only 5 years ago but now uses English and makes decisions based on dominant group values. If these individuals were in therapy, their clinicians would have to look beyond the number of years spent in the United States to develop a treatment plan that meets each client's needs.

Acculturation can be illustrated using the model proposed by Vontress (1986). Vontress believed that we live within five concentric and intermingling cultures: the universal, ecological, national, regional, and racio-ethnic. As a human being, each of us has characteristics, such as cardiovascular and digestive systems, that are universal. We relate to an ecological culture based on the natural environment that surrounds us, live within a national culture that is defined by a common language and governmental structure, and are simultaneously influenced by regional differences and characteristics of our ethnic group. Let us consider two families living in the Southwestern United States. One is a fourth-generation Italian American family, and the other is a Mexican American family that has recently emigrated from the Yucatan Peninsula. Both share characteristics at two cultural levels: the universal, such as physiological functions, and the ecological, which includes residence in a suburban setting with a semi-arid climate. Although the families share a common allegiance to state and federal laws, their national culture also differs, with one family proficient in English only and the other bilingual in English and Spanish. Because of their recent immigration to this country, members of the Mexican American family are being introduced to the regional culture of the Southwest. Consequently, their day-to-day experiences are similar to those of the Italian American family to the extent that Southwestern culture reflects Mexican beliefs and practices. The families differ most at the racio-ethnic level. Contrasts in physical features may result in others' attributions of superiority or inferiority, attitudes that represent vertical (i.e., better than or less than) rather than horizontal (i.e., different from) beliefs. And although both families have common holidays, such as Christmas, they celebrate these events with different foods and activities.

In 1998, the U.S. Census Bureau estimated that approximately one in four citizens was a member of a nondominant ethnic group, but the statistics for children reveal even greater diversity (U.S. Bureau of the Census, 1999). Table 1.1 contains a comparison of the

Table 1–1
U.S. Census Bureau Percentage Estimates of the Ethnic Composition of the Total Population and Children Under the Age of 13

	ETHNIC GROUP				
	European American	African American	Hispanic American	Asian American	Native American
Total population	72	12	11	4	1
Children (birth–age 12 years)	64	15	16	4	1

Note: Hispanic Americans may be of any race.

U.S. Bureau of the Census. (1999). *Statistical abstract of the United States: 1997* (119th ed.). Washington, DC: Author.

ethnic breakdown for the total population and children. If the higher representation of African Americans and Hispanic Americans in the youngest segment of our population continues, the demographic makeup of the United States will be dramatically different in coming decades. Will mental health professionals be prepared for this change? Are they currently able to address the needs of all children? One way of answering these questions is to examine the ethnic backgrounds of practicing clinicians.

Most therapeutic relationships involve European Americans in the role of clinician. Representation of people of color in the mental health professions is such that most children, regardless of their ethnicity, will be treated by a European American therapist. Although it is unclear how many child treatment specialists are members of nondominant ethnic groups, Wohlford (1991) estimated that fewer than 10% of all clinicians are of African American, Hispanic American, or Native American descent. He indicated that representation was best among social workers (12%), with lower rates reported for psychiatrists (8%), psychologists (4%), and psychiatric nurses (4%). These figures are clearly at odds with the ethnic background of U.S. children, as presented in Table 1.1.

Therapists must appreciate the impact of cultural influences on children. In session, they need to consider how these factors affect client self-disclosure and the development of the helping relationship (Forehand & Wierson, 1993). They must remain alert for culture-based differences in children's values, feelings, and career aspirations. This requires an understanding of how child development is both the same and different across cultures (see Sue, 1998). To untangle this complex interaction, therapists need to assess variables such as social values, acculturation, and socioeconomic level (Baruth & Manning, 2003). Sue recommended that practitioners function as scientists and study the extent to which client problems are the result of culture-specific causes or factors common to all groups. Baruth and Manning warned that relatively little research is available on the relationship between culture and development in children, and they encouraged investigators to explore areas such as ethnic groups' attitudes about parenting and their effects on children.

Clinicians must consider the questions raised by the cultural compatibility hypothesis that posits three attitudes toward treatment: the culturally specific perspective, the two-type alternative, and the universalistic attitude (Tharp, 1989). Proponents of the culturally specific perspective believe that therapists must tailor their interventions to the needs of specific ethnic groups. Those who favor the two-type view endorse the use of one set of treatments for European American children and a separate set of strategies for clients of color. Advocates of the universalistic attitude believe that the same form of treatment, with minor adjustments, can be used with all children, regardless of their cultural background. Which of these attitudes is correct? Although little research is available on culturally sensitive therapies for children (Kazdin, 1993), Tharp (1991) recommended that clinicians use contextualized treatments that take into consideration the impact of a child's cultural surround.

Tharp (1991) acknowledged the benefits of traditional individual therapy, but he believed this approach was the treatment of last resort for children of color because it tends to overlook environmental influences. For these clients, he recommended that clinicians first consider community-based services to address the sociopolitical causes of a child's behavior. On a continuum of decreasing contextualization, interventions in the community are followed by network therapy that includes extended family and significant others in the child's life, home-based treatments, family therapy, educational programs for children, group therapy, and finally individual therapy. Elsewhere in this book we will explore these treatment methods. For now, we can conclude that clinicians must become skilled at culturally sensitive interventions if they are to serve all children, regardless of ethnic background.

A MULTIMODAL AND COLLABORATIVE APPROACH TO INTERVENTION

As discussed previously, mental health services for children represent more than the remediation of existing problems. Clinicians also provide education/development and prevention services intended to foster optimal development and to prevent problems in at-risk children. Figure 1-3 illustrates how any or all of these services can be directed at the child, family, school, and community. When viewed from this perspective, treatment is a complex process that requires therapist collaboration with significant other adults in the child's life. These individuals include parents and the professionals who typically provide mental health services to children and their families (see Chapter 2). This section discusses a multimodal and multidisciplinary approach with children. Later we will examine how this method can be used to address the challenges encountered by the Jamison family.

Multimodal Interventions

Other authors have used the term *multimodal* to describe therapeutic interventions for children and adults. In the multimodal therapies of Lazarus (1976) and Keat (1990), the clinician is expected to assess and treat different components of a client's presenting problem (see Chapter 16). For our purposes, *multimodal* refers to the three classes of intervention that clinicians use with children: education/development, prevention, and remediation. Professionals and laypeople alike often define mental health services as the therapies used to help troubled children. But these methods represent only one treatment modality, remediation, which is intended to eliminate existing problems. If this is the case, why do so many of us have such a restricted view of our role? One answer can be found in the historical development of these services in the United States.

During much of the 20th century, most of the mental health services provided to children were remedial in nature and designed to address the client's intrapsychic or individual problems. Despite the popularity of this perspective, we would be wrong to assume that individually oriented interventions were always the treatment of choice. Levine and Levine (1992) described an era of social reform in the United States, from the late 1800s to the early 1900s, when mental health professionals were more interested in environmental influences on children's development. Settlement houses, juvenile courts, and public schools of this time period conducted community-based interventions to improve the everyday living conditions of children and families. Unfortunately, interest in this approach waned during the 1920s, when community reform gave way to the intrapsychic problem-oriented perspective that prevailed during the remainder of the century. Despite intermittent calls (e.g., Albee, 1990, 1992) for proactive, community-based education/development and prevention, remediation continues to be the preferred modality for treating children's problems.

There are many reasons why therapists have devoted considerable time and energy to remediation.

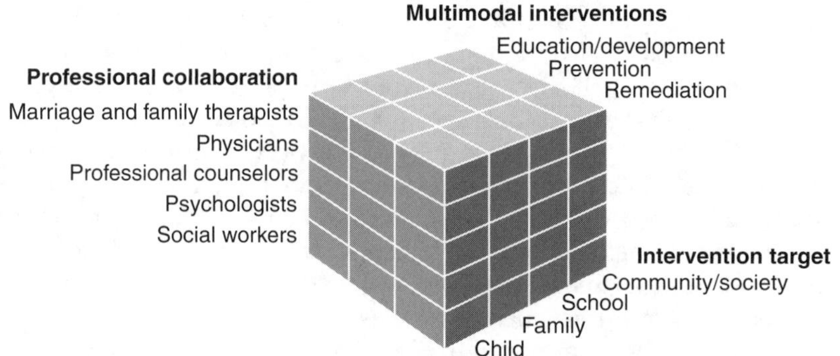

Figure 1–3. A Multidimensional Model for the Delivery of Children's Services

First, there is a demand for these services. The social consequences of a child's misbehavior are sometimes significant enough that failure to intervene in this manner causes negative consequences for the child and others. Consider a suicidal client who intends harm to herself, or a conduct disordered student who repeatedly disrupts the classroom learning environment. Failure to remediate either of these problems can have a detrimental outcome for all involved. Another reason for therapists' use of remedial interventions is the third-party reimbursement system that currently supports much of the nation's mental health care system and rewards clinicians who provide these services (Gelso & Fretz, 1992). If alternative modalities are to survive, monetary inducement is needed to encourage therapists to offer education/development and prevention services for children.

Another limiting factor has been clinicians' passion for psychopathology. Therapists who enjoy helping young clients with problems may gain little satisfaction from educational programs for so-called "normal" children. Fascination with the nature and causes of psychological disorders has also contributed to a problem-oriented perspective in research and professional training. When compared with their studies of remedial interventions for childhood problems, researchers have given little attention to other modalities. And most graduate programs offer limited training in education/development and prevention, possibly because the faculty do not have the knowledge and experience required to teach these methods. Elsewhere in this book we will examine education/development and prevention strategies based on different theoretical principles. For now, we review selected methods that have been designed and tested with children.

T. Berry Brazelton, a respected pediatrician, has written extensively about programs and techniques that parents and professionals can use to foster healthy development in children. His classic "child-oriented approach" (Brazelton, 1962, p.121) to toilet training is an excellent example of an education/development technique. Brazelton encouraged parents to conceptualize toilet training as a milestone that occurs as part of normal development. With this straightforward and proactive intervention, he hoped to reduce parents' anxiety about toilet training and thereby decrease the rate of enuresis in children. Of the 1170 preschoolers whose parents participated in his program, fewer than 2% were still wetting the bed at 5 years of age. This figure is well below that reported by Oppel, Harper, and Rider (1968) who found that 19% of 5-year-old children were incontinent.

Education/development programs have also been used in settings other than the physician's or therapist's office. A popular site has been public schools. Dubow, Schmidt, McBride, Edwards, and Merk (1993), for example, designed a 13-session program to teach problem-solving and coping skills to fourth grade students. The authors' I CAN DO program included stories, films, roleplay exercises, and group discussions to teach students how to handle stressful events. Results revealed that when compared with children not enrolled in the program, participants were better able to devise solutions to environmental stressors and were more confident in their ability to handle these events. An important component of this program was the authors' collaboration with classroom teachers. Based on feedback received from teachers and students, Dubow and his colleagues modified their program to make it more "child friendly" by replacing didactic instruction with games that were more interesting to the children.

Prevention programs are based on the assumption that it is important to identify at-risk children and intervene before problems arise. An excellent example of this approach is the Primary Mental Health Project (PMHP), another school-based program in continuous operation since its inception in 1957 (Cowen et al., 1996). Originally designed for children in the primary grades, PMHP and variants of the program, such as the Children of Divorce Intervention Program, have been expanded to the upper elementary and junior high school grades. Central to PMHP is the early detection and screening of students for the program. A team approach is used in which teachers and school administrators, mental health professionals (e.g., school psychologists, elementary school counselors), and paraprofessionals collaborate to serve children in need. Paraprofessionals are carefully selected and trained to provide individual and small group services in a playroom located within the school. They establish a supportive relationship with each child using developmentally appropriate activities, such as reading or telling stories and playing board games. Cowen et al. reviewed the results of PMHP evaluation research and concluded that the program has been successful in enhancing students' learning, social competence, and behavioral adjustment.

Intervention programs are sometimes designed to offer more than one mode of service. MacGregor,

Nelson, and Wesch (1997) described a multifaceted program that school counselors can use to create a positive learning environment for students. The counselor addresses education/development and prevention goals by having teachers and administrators establish a code of acceptable behavior for students. Through consistent application of these standards, school personnel create a climate in which children work to fulfill their academic potential. In the MacGregor et al. program, counselors also provide remedial services through individual or group therapy for problem children and serve as case managers for treatment teams composed of the child's parents, teachers, and relevant school staff.

Gelso and Fretz (1992) observed that the difference between education/development and prevention is "often subtle" (p. 6). Distinguishing all three modalities from each other can be especially difficult when the target of intervention is a child. Because of the rapid changes associated with normal development in children, the remediation of problem behaviors may subsequently have additional benefits for child clients. Consider a 6-year-old with encopresis who has normal self-esteem but soils his pants on a regular basis. Successful remediation of the child's encopresis may also prevent behavior problems at a later age while laying the foundation for the development of a positive view of self.

Education/development and prevention programs are sometimes designed to produce long-term benefits. Recent efforts to reduce tobacco use among children and adolescents are one such example (Contemporary Issues Box 1-1). In these programs, youths are taught the health risks of tobacco to prevent them from becoming users. The long-term goal of these interventions is a decline in the rate of tobacco use among adults. Many of these projects include smoking cessation programs; therefore, they span all three treatment modalities because they are designed to educate children and adolescents about tobacco, prevent its use among at-risk youth, and remediate smoking and related behaviors in current consumers. Later chapters examine how clinicians can incorporate the principles of different systems of psychotherapy to implement multimodal treatments for children.

Professional Collaboration

As they age and develop, children become less dependent on their parents for basic needs. Contacts with their cultural surround increase, and they begin to rely on other adults, including teachers, school counselors, and social workers. Therapists need to consider how these and other professionals influence children's development. They must collaborate with others in a multidisciplinary team effort that encourages each member to participate in the planning and delivery of services. This method is significantly different from the remedial therapies used with adults in which most clinicians only interact with the client. Therapists who work with children must cooperate with other professionals to design and implement comprehensive treatments that are appropriate to each client's needs.

Multidisciplinary interventions are practical because members of different professions sometimes offer similar or overlapping services despite their recognized expertise in a particular area. Teachers characteristically focus on students' academic growth, Children's Protective Services workers strive to ensure a child's right to a non-abusive environment, physicians treat or prevent common childhood diseases, and therapists attend to clients' social and emotional well being. But overlap among professions sometimes makes it difficult to delineate the lines of responsibility (Hoagwood & Rupp, 1994). For example, a teacher may intervene to improve a student's self-esteem, and a therapist may teach the child more effective study skills. Overlap can have negative and positive outcomes, from territorial disputes that compromise professionals' ability to help children to cooperative efforts that facilitate the planning and delivery of services.

For a collaborative approach to work, professionals must appreciate their colleagues' contribution to the treatment process. Awareness can enhance cooperation, so therapists must have a working knowledge of their colleagues' areas of expertise. A clinician who treats a child diagnosed as having a severe case of attention-deficit hyperactivity disorder must consider the benefits of psychopharmacotherapy. To be successful with this client, the therapist must consult the child's physician to determine whether medication is needed. A therapist who learns that a child is being sexually abused must report this information to the appropriate authorities and establish a working relationship with the client's caseworker at Children's Protective Services to stop the abuse and ensure access to treatment.

Professionals who work with children do so, for the most part, in either school- or community-based settings. Teachers, school counselors, and school

Contemporary Issues Box 1–1

Tobacco Education/Development, Prevention, and Cessation Programs for Children

In July 1997, the major tobacco producers in the United States reached a $3.4 billion settlement with the State of Mississippi in the nation's first Medicaid-related lawsuit to recover the costs of treating smoking-related illnesses ("Acting alone," 1997). Although other states reached similar agreements, relatively few have used their monies for anti-smoking campaigns to prevent tobacco use among children and adolescents ("Anti-smoking funds," 2001). Mississippi has been one of the exceptions.

As part of its tobacco education, prevention, and remediation efforts, Mississippi initiated programs for elementary school students. The Partnership for a Healthy Mississippi conducts Reject All Tobacco (RAT) for children in grades kindergarten to 3 and Students Working Against Tobacco (SWAT) for students in grades 4 to 6. These programs include presentations in schools and the use of award-winning websites for children, parents, and teachers (www.gorat.com and www.getswat.com). Since its inception in 1998, the Partnership has trained more than 5500 teachers who have provided tobacco education to approximately 140,000 students in grades kindergarten to 12. The group also developed nationally recognized television, radio, and billboard advertisements on tobacco-related illnesses. Through grants to law enforcement agencies, the Partnership has gained commitments from more than 85% of the retailers in the state to not market tobacco products to minors. Community-based programs also have been implemented. These include a faith-based initiative in more than 275 houses of worship, primarily rural African American churches, where the project has reached more than 15,000 children in grades 4 to 7.

An important part of the Partnership's activities is program evaluation and outcome research. In a study of children in grades 4 to 6, Carver, Reinert, Range, and Campbell (2000) found a significant but small increase in students' tobacco awareness. At posttest, for example, significantly more students indicated that they would "walk away" if a friend offered them a cigarette. Whether these changes in attitude will translate into healthy behaviors in the future remains to be seen. But the Partnership points to a recent decrease in tobacco use among middle school students as early evidence of the program's success. Specifically, the Mississippi 2000 Youth Tobacco Survey (Mississippi State Department of Health, 2000) revealed that 18.5% of eighth graders reported smoking one cigarette or fewer in the previous 30 days compared with a rate of 29% in 1999. Although this change was statistically significant, the overall decline of 23% to 18.1% among middle school students was no better than would be expected by chance. Clearly, additional research is needed to evaluate the long-term effects of the program in preventing tobacco use in children.

psychologists typically work with students to facilitate their educational and psychological development and to prevent and remediate behavior and learning problems. Community-based professionals, such as marriage and family therapists, mental health counselors, psychologists, psychiatrists, and social workers, use a variety of interventions to resolve problems and promote the development of children and families. Chapter 2 examines in more detail the training, work environments, codes of ethics, and services provided by these individuals. Clinicians can use this information to develop collaborative relationships with other professionals for the benefit of their clients.

MULTIDIMENSIONAL INTERVENTIONS FOR CHILDREN: A CASE EXAMPLE

It is difficult to illustrate all aspects of the multidimensional model in one case, especially in the limited space available here, but case vignettes do provide the opportunity to apply abstract concepts to real-life situations. We now examine a therapist's first session with John and Mary Jamison and their only child, 7-year-old Thomas,[1] who was described

[1] The information contained in the Jamison vignette and others presented in this book are fictitious in nature and do not represent actual children or families.

at the beginning of this chapter. Mr. Jamison, the oldest of seven children in an African American family, and Mrs. Jamison, the younger child of European American parents, have conflicting views on child rearing. This difference, combined with everyday stressors, has compromised the couple's ability to guide and nurture their son. As you read the following vignette, consider how developmental and multicultural factors will affect the therapist's use of a multimodal and multidisciplinary approach to intervention.

▪ ▪ ▪

When Dr. Miller, a licensed psychologist, asks the Jamisons to discuss their reasons for seeking professional help, Mr. Jamison answers, "Thomas is having all kinds of problems, and my wife just can't control him anymore."

"I don't think my husband really understands the situation," Mrs. Jamison argues. She describes her son's frequent temper tantrums that sometimes involve incidents of head banging and running into traffic on the busy street in front of the family's home.

"I've never seen Thomas do any of these things," the father interrupts. "Sometimes I think my wife is making up all this stuff. Thomas doesn't act like that around me, probably because he knows I'll punish him if he gets out of line."

While the parents describe their concerns, Thomas stares at the floor and remains quiet, despite the therapist's attempts to involve him in the discussion. Dr. Miller learns that Mr. and Mrs. Jamison frequently disagree about child-rearing techniques and have never used a consistent method of parenting their son.

When the therapist asks about the boy's performance at school, Mrs. Jamison reports that he received mostly A's in first grade but has gotten C's and D's on his first two report cards in second grade. She also mentions that Thomas was recently sent to the principal's office for fighting with a classmate. Mrs. Jamison adds, "I think Thomas needs some friends his own age." She elaborates by saying that he has no playmates in their neighborhood, where the youngest child is a 13-year-old who lives five houses down the street.

Mrs. Jamison believes that Thomas is having problems because she works outside the home. She identifies her decision to accept a job 3 years ago as the point when his behavior began to deteriorate. The temper tantrums were of gradual onset and followed an initial period when Thomas would cling to her legs as she was about to leave every morning.

"How do you feel about working away from home?" Dr. Miller asks.

"Very guilty," she answers, "but what can I do about it unless we want to starve?" The parents then spontaneously volunteer information about their financial situation, which Mr. Jamison describes as "terrible."

The therapist decides to question the parents without Thomas present. She leads the boy to a reception area where other staff members can provide supervision. She returns to her office and asks the parents to elaborate on their current living arrangements, including family finances. Mrs. Jamison says that after they pay rent and utilities, grocery expenses, and the loan on their newly purchased automobile, they have less than $200 remaining to cover all other expenses during the month. Mr. Jamison adds that he and his wife were planning to contact a finance company to discuss consolidation of their auto loan and various credit card accounts, which currently have a combined balance in excess of $5,000.

Mr. Jamison says that he and his wife have arranged their work schedules so at least one of them is always home with Thomas. Mrs. Jamison works from 8 A.M. to 5 P.M. as a legal secretary for a small firm located approximately 2 miles from home. Mr. Jamison works from midnight to 8 A.M. at a local manufacturing plant, where he is a technician apprentice. To help ease the family's financial problems, Mr. Jamison often works additional shifts during weekends. When the therapist asks the couple what they do for fun, they respond almost in unison, "Work, sleep, and look after Thomas."

Mrs. Jamison then admits, "I think all of this is starting to affect our relationship."

After her interview with the parents, Dr. Miller meets individually with Thomas. She and her client sit on the floor in a corner of the office, where she has arranged an assortment of toys, puppets, and art materials. "How do you feel about coming here today?" she asks.

"OK, I guess," the boy responds as he places a puppet on his hand. "Ah!" he shouts, opening the puppet's mouth as far as it will go. "I don't like it," the puppet continues.

"You don't like it?" Dr. Miller asks the puppet.

"No," he answers.

As her client quietly manipulates the puppet, Dr. Miller asks, "Did you hear what Thomas' Mom and Dad said?"

"Thomas is a bad boy," he answers.

"A bad boy," she says.

"Uh-huh. Nobody likes him because he's a bad boy."

Thomas uses the puppet to describe events at home and school when he was reprimanded for his behavior. During her 20-minute interview with him, Dr. Miller hears themes of loneliness, hopelessness, and anger. She begins to develop an intervention plan that will include individual meetings with the boy, parent and family sessions, and consultation with school personnel.

At the conclusion of her meeting with Thomas, Dr. Miller smiles and says, "I think it would be a good idea for the three of us to meet here in my office again next week."

She is surprised and pleased when Thomas looks at her, removes the puppet from his hand, and quietly says, "OK."

▪ ▪ ▪

In a vignette as brief as this, much important information is missing. For example, we know very little about the parenting techniques that Mr. and Mrs. Jamison actually use with their son. We have only indirect reports of Thomas' behavior at school. And aside from our interpretation of his comments with the puppet, we have limited information about his view of the situation. Still, this case report can be used to illustrate a multidimensional approach to intervention.

First, Dr. Miller was aware of developmental factors that merited consideration in this case. The family format used here may not be the most appropriate intervention for Thomas. Some children actively disclose their thoughts and feelings in family sessions, but others are more reticent to do so, at least during the initial phase of therapy. During her individual interview with Thomas, the therapist learned that he would participate when she combined play with traditional talk therapy. Dr. Miller also demonstrated an awareness of developmental issues when she asked Thomas to go to the reception area while she talked with Mr. and Mrs. Jamison. The parents' spontaneous discussion of family finances was a spousal issue that is best left to the adults involved. Having Thomas present during this portion of the session may cause increased anxiety for a child who has little understanding of the mechanics of financial planning and virtually no control over the outcome of his parents' corrective actions.

The Jamisons present an interesting multicultural consideration—the child of an inter-ethnic marriage. Sometimes referred to as biracial children, the offspring of inter-ethnic unions are best understood from a multigenerational perspective. If we limit our view to the parent's generation, Thomas would be the bi-ethnic son of African American and European American parents. But from a multigenerational perspective, he is multiethnic because of the African American and Hispanic American heritage of his paternal grandparents.

The number of children born to inter-ethnic unions in the United States has increased in recent decades, in part because of revisions in the nation's immigration laws and *Loving v. Virginia* (1967), the U.S. Supreme Court decision that struck down anti-miscegenation statutes (Root, 1992). To better serve these children, therapists must understand the needs of their clients and the prevailing beliefs about multiethnic individuals. According to Kerwin, Ponterotto, Jackson, and Harris (1993), these children have traditionally been viewed as at risk for various psychological problems, including poor self-esteem, identity confusion, and cultural conflicts and marginality. Although little research is available, what does exist suggests that these children are not destined to experience such problems (Johnson & Nagoshi, 1986; Kerwin et al., 1993). Still, peers sometimes tease them, using derisive terms such as "mutt," "zebra," or "chocolate chip" (Shackford, 1984, p. 4). Based on the information contained in our case report, we cannot determine whether Thomas got into a fight at school because his classmate was calling him names or because he was angry with the child for other reasons. In her work with the Jamisons, Dr. Miller will need to consider how these factors are related to the boy's behavior and development.

A second cultural consideration is the therapist's inquiry regarding Mrs. Jamison's feelings about working outside of the home. This question does seem clinically relevant because the mother associated the onset of Thomas' problems with her entry into the labor force. But the same question apparently was not asked of the father and may therefore constitute gender bias on the part of the therapist. Always viewing fathers as "providers" and mothers as "nurturers" represents a counterproductive gender stereotype. These beliefs frequently translate into other discrepancies in a marriage, including parents' participation in domestic tasks, which are typically handled by mothers, even in dual income families such as the Jamisons (Aldous, Mulligan, & Bjarnason, 1998; Barnett & Shen, 1997; Lamb, 1987).

Dr. Miller has the opportunity to integrate different treatment modalities in this case. Based on the information available, it would appear that remedial interventions are needed to decrease the frequency of Thomas' temper tantrums and life-threatening behavior. Likewise, similar efforts should be considered to help the boy regain his academic performance in first grade. But the therapist should go beyond these problems to envision ways in which treatment can be structured to enhance the boy's development. To do this, she will want to include education/development and prevention strategies in her treatment plan.

Mr. and Mrs. Jamison are candidates for prevention designed to ensure the stability and quality of their marriage. We know very little about their relationship as husband and wife, but Mrs. Jamison expressed concern that the everyday pressures of parenting and providing for the family's needs were harming the marriage. The therapist could encourage the couple to contrast their roles as husband and wife from their roles as father and mother. This might include having them set aside daily private time after Thomas is in bed and before Mr. Jamison leaves for work to share their experiences of the day. Dr. Miller could help them examine the effect that the family's schedule is having on the marital relationship.

The Jamisons described the difficulties they were having with family finances. In fact, Mr. Jamison mentioned that he and his wife had thought about contacting a finance company to consolidate their debts. Therapists are not trained as money managers or financial planners, so Dr. Miller could help the parents process the decision to consult an advisor and facilitate implementation of the expert's recommendations. The long-term benefits of this action would include a less stressful home life for a couple that is at risk for serious marital problems.

Treatment could also include an education/development strategy designed to enhance Thomas' ethnic identity. According to Jacobs (1992), multiethnic children develop a more integrated identity of self between ages 8 and 12 years. To facilitate this process, the therapist might use portions of individual meetings with Thomas to have him draw a family tree or create a collage to illustrate his family (Gibbs, 1989). She could encourage the parents to introduce Thomas to their cultural customs, including ethnic holidays, and to include him in the creation of new family traditions based on both parents' cultural backgrounds (Gibbs, 1989; Winn & Priest, 1993). By combining education/development and prevention strategies with remedial interventions, Dr. Miller has the opportunity to facilitate Thomas' development in a healthy family while addressing the behavioral problems that prompted the parents to enter therapy.

Different treatment modalities are frequently provided in collaboration with other professionals. The starting point for any collaborative effort is the parents' informed consent for allowing the therapist to contact these individuals (see Chapter 2). With the Jamisons, Dr. Miller could work with a number of other professionals. To design and implement her remediation plan, she would collaborate with Thomas' teachers and the school counselor to collect information and use a school-based intervention as part of treatment. Because a significant change has occurred in the boy's school work between first and second grade, Dr. Miller should consider a referral to the family's physician to determine whether organic problems, such as visual or auditory impairment, have caused the decline in academic performance.

If Thomas' fight with a classmate was ethnically oriented, the therapist should collaborate with the school counselor to implement an education/development program to enhance students' appreciation for cultural diversity and individual differences. This school-based intervention could include classroom presentations to increase other students' awareness of cultural differences as well as in-service programs for teachers to improve their communication with troubled students and to develop diversity-based initiatives, such as classroom celebrations of ethnic holidays and special library collections about multiethnic children and their families (Benedetto & Olisky, 2001). By improving children's acceptance of peers, regardless of their ethnic backgrounds, these programs can foster the development of a school environment that would enhance self-esteem in Thomas and other children of color.

SUMMARY

In this chapter, we examined a multidimensional approach to intervention in which clinicians consider developmental and multicultural influences on children. The model also highlights the importance of the format and scope of treatment. Therapists are best known for the remedial interventions they provide, but they also help children through the use of education/development and prevention programs designed to foster optimal growth in all youths and to avoid problems for those at risk. Clinicians must remember that children rely on adults for guidance and fulfillment of their basic needs. Effective intervention requires a collaborative effort by the therapist, parents, teachers, and other adults in the child's life.

2

Professional, Ethical, and Legal Issues

▪▪▪

When Mrs. Baldwin attends the last parent–teacher conference of the school year, she learns that her son, 9-year-old Kevin, may be retained in the third grade because he is failing math and reading. Mr. Stitt, the boy's teacher, says that Kevin refuses to complete class assignments and frequently annoys the other students. He encourages Mrs. Baldwin to read with her son in the evenings and check the accuracy of his homework. Although Mrs. Baldwin has heard many of these problems and suggestions before, she becomes increasingly concerned about Kevin's having to repeat the third grade.

Ms. Stinson, the school counselor, arrives midway through the conference to discuss Kevin's problems with the other children. "I don't believe Kevin has any friends in class," she says. "When I see him on the playground, he's usually by himself or fighting with some of the other students." The counselor encourages Mrs. Baldwin to seek professional help. When the mother agrees, Ms. Stinson gives her a list of therapists to consider and then adds, "I really encourage you to get help for Kevin soon."

▪▪▪

Collaboration between school- and community-based professionals requires consideration of both ethical principles and the laws that apply in the jurisdiction of practice. Rae and Fournier (1999) described the ethical and legal aspects of child treatments as "the greatest responsibility of any psychotherapist" (p. 67). Regardless of their preferred treatments, clinicians must follow the law and comply with the ethical principles of their profession. Children are more dependent on others for their health and safety, so therapists must remember the words of Ross (1980): "The ethical implications of treating an individual's psychological problems increase in magnitude as an inverse function of that individual's freedom of choice" (p. 62). Children represent a special treatment population because they have relatively little choice in everyday matters and are at greater risk of having undesirable or inappropriate limits imposed on them.

Therapists face increasingly complex legal issues in their work with clients. Sometimes ethical-legal conflicts arise, such as the ethical obligation to ensure the privacy of client information when statutes mandate disclosure to others. In these situations, the limits imposed by the law supersede the therapist's professional ethics. The complex interaction of ethical and legal issues is especially complicated when the focus of treatment is a child. The vulnerability of the young client and variations in local laws create a terrain that therapists must navigate with caution. If clinicians are to effectively serve their clients, they must conduct their practice in a manner consistent with prevailing ethical, legal, and professional standards of care.

This chapter examines ethical issues that different helping professions have identified as important for child therapies. It also discusses legal limits unique to child treatments, including state reporting statutes for suspected cases of child abuse and neglect. Clinicians who adopt the collaborative approach described in Chapter 1 must be aware of the training and expertise of other professionals who work with children. We begin with a discussion of these professions and their role in a multidimensional approach to treatment.

CHILD TREATMENT PROFESSIONALS

Multidisciplinary interventions involve the collaboration of professionals from a number of different fields. To overcome the artificial boundaries that separate these specialists, therapists must understand how others contribute to the process and outcome of treatment. No individual holds all of the keys to effective therapies for children. Likewise, no single profession has the magic wand needed to solve the diverse and often complex problems that young people encounter. A multidisciplinary approach to treatment requires an understanding of the history, training, and characteristic services of the child treatment professions. This section examines how the professionals listed in Table 2-1 work with children and their families.

Family Therapists

Family therapists conceptualize a child's behavior within the context of the family system, and they formulate their interventions based on that model. The emergence of family therapy in the 1940s and 1950s occurred as a result of the work of pioneers such as Gregory Bateson, Nathan Ackerman, and Murray Bowen, who were independently studying family dynamics (Kolevzon & Green, 1985; Okun, 1990). Broderick and Schrader (1981) noted that family therapy developed within the field of psychiatry, but the authors identified John Bell, a psychologist, as the person most deserving of the title "father of family therapy" (p. 18). Bell's contribution to the field was his decision to set aside one-on-one therapy with individual members and treat the family as a unit.

An important step in the development of any discipline is its struggle for identity. Family therapy has not been immune to this challenge. As Goldenberg and Goldenberg (1991) noted, some have questioned whether family therapy is "a profession, an orientation to human problems, or simply another modality of psychotherapy?" (p. 290). This uncertainty is reflected in the training opportunities and professional organizations that currently exist. In 2002, there were approximately 60 universities, institutes, and seminaries in the United States and Canada that offered COAMFTE-accredited programs leading to master's or doctoral degrees in this specialty (Commission on Accreditation of Marriage and Family Therapy Education, 2002). But training in family theory and techniques is not limited to these programs because students preparing for careers in other disciplines (e.g., psychiatry, psychology, social work) can obtain instruction in family interventions as part of their course plan. As indicated in Table 2-1, the most visible professional organization for family therapists is the American Association for Marriage and Family Therapy (AAMFT). But members of other disciplines can affiliate with family therapy divisions or special interest groups within their respective professional group. Psychologists, for example, are able to join the Division of Family Psychology, which is part of the American Psychological Association.

Another significant step in the development of any profession is public recognition of its status as a specialty. This often occurs through the passage of state laws that define the limits of practice for service providers. Many states' legislatures have decided that family therapy merits this official designation. As Lee and Sturkie (1997) reported, at least 37 states have adopted laws that govern the practice of family therapy. When family therapists participate in a multidisciplinary treatment, they help other professionals conceptualize a child's presenting problem within the context of the family system. Chapters 12 and 13 examine the work of family therapists in more detail.

Professional Counselors

The field of professional counseling encompasses a number of specialty areas. We focus on two groups that are directly involved with children: mental health counselors and elementary school counselors. Although both share a common history in the vocational guidance and mental hygiene movements,

Table 2–1
Traditional Practice Settings, Primary Organizational Affiliations, Representative Journals, and Training of Child Treatment Professionals

Professionals	Practice Settings	Organizational Affiliations	Journals	Training
Family Therapists	Community mental health centers, private practice	American Association for Marriage and Family Therapy	*Journal of Marital and Family Therapy*	Master's and doctoral programs
Professional Counselors				
Mental Health Counselors	Community mental health centers, private practice	American Mental Health Counselors Association	*Journal of Mental Health Counseling*	Master's and doctoral programs
Elementary School Counselors	Elementary schools	American School Counselor Association	*Professional School Counseling*	Master's and doctoral programs
Social Workers	Department of Public Welfare, hospitals, community mental health centers, private practice	National Association of Social Workers	*Social Work*	Undergraduate, master's, and doctoral programs
Physicians				
Child and Adolescent Psychiatrists	Hospitals, community mental health centers, private practice	American Academy of Child and Adolescent Psychiatry	*Journal of the American Academy of Child and Adolescent Psychiatry*	M.D. plus a residency in the specialty
Pediatricians	Hospitals, private practice	American Academy of Pediatrics	*Pediatrics*	M. D. plus a residency in the specialty
Family Physicians	Hospitals, private practice	American Academy of Family Physicians	*American Family Physician*	M.D. plus a residency in the specialty
Psychologists				
Clinical Child Psychologists	Hospitals, community mental centers, private practice	American Psychological Association	*Journal of Clinical Child and Adolescent Psychology*	Doctoral programs
Pediatric Psychologists	Hospitals, medical clinics, private practice	American Psychological Association	*Journal of Pediatric Psychology*	Doctoral programs
Counseling Psychologists	University counseling centers, community mental health centers, private practice	American Psychological Association	*The Counseling Psychologist*	Doctoral programs
School Psychologists	Schools, private practice	American Psychological Association, National Association of School Psychologists	*School Psychology Quarterly; School Psychology Review*	Master's and doctoral programs

each has developed unique characteristics that qualify it as a specialty.

Mental Health Counselors. Weikel and Palmo (1989) described the mental health counselor as a "hybrid, born from an uneasy relationship between psychology and education counseling, but with family ties to all of the core mental health care disciplines" (p. 17). Mental health counselors draw on their knowledge of human growth and development, counseling skills, and personality characteristics to serve a broad array of clients, including those with severe and chronic psychological problems (Vacc & Loesch, 1994; West, Hosie, & Mackey, 1987).

In its model licensure act for this specialty, the American Counseling Association (Glosoff, Benshoff, Hosie, & Maki, 1995) identified the training and experience that states should require for a clinician to become a licensed professional counselor. At the present time, almost all states have passed counselor licensure acts (Remley & Herlihy, 2001). Although model legislation specifies the criteria for practice as a licensed clinician, it also sets the standard for the training programs that prepare future professionals (Glosoff & Rockwell, 1997). Graduate-level instruction in mental health counseling; community counseling; and marriage, couple, and family counseling/therapy is available in the United States and Canada. Training programs in these areas are accredited by the Council for Accreditation of Counseling and Related Educational Programs (CACREP). In 2002, there were over 180 CACREP-accredited master's programs and an additional 43 doctoral programs in counselor education and supervision (CACREP, 2002).

Mental health counselors provide a significant amount of the treatment services delivered in community settings. Unfortunately, all of these clinicians have not been adequately trained to work with children and families. Professionals who pursue a multidisciplinary approach should seek out mental health counselors who are interested in children and have completed course work and supervised practica or internships specific to this population.

Elementary School Counselors. According to Hardesty and Dillard (1994), elementary school counselors attempt to foster students' academic, social, emotional, and vocational development. This is truly a challenge, especially when a school counselor is often responsible for hundreds of children at any point in time. In contrast to their counterparts in community-based settings, school-based counselors are more involved in promoting learning for their students (Neukrug, Barr, Hoffman, & Kaplan, 1993). They accomplish this in many ways, including the development of positive learning environments for children (Paisley & Peace, 1995).

School counseling for elementary school students first appeared at the beginning of the 20th century (Dimick & Huff, 1970), but relatively few programs existed in the United States until the 1950s, when the nation responded to technological advances that were occurring in the Soviet Union (Kaczkowski & Patterson, 1975). Passage of the National Defense Education Act (NDEA) in 1958 resulted in the expansion of counseling programs in secondary schools. In fact, Myrick (1997) identified this legislation as "perhaps the single most important event in the history of the school counseling profession" (p. 6). Federal support for guidance and counseling for elementary school students followed, with the adoption of the Elementary and Secondary Education Act of 1965 which supported comprehensive programs in both elementary and secondary schools.

Early school counseling programs were designed to help students with problems, but the 1960s witnessed a more comprehensive developmental model intended to make education/development, prevention, and remediation services available to all students (Gerstein & Lichtman, 1990; Gysbers, 1990). Counselors moved from a reliance on individual interventions with children to a more complex function that included consultation and coordination of services for teachers, parents, administrators, and mental health clinicians outside of the school (Cole, 1988). Elementary school counselors now perform a range of services in addition to individual and group counseling with students. These activities include classroom presentations on relevant topics (e.g., study skills, personal safety, and wellness), the organization and supervision of peer helper programs, staff development, and workshops for parents on a variety of child-rearing issues (e.g., development of positive self-esteem) (Gerstein & Lichtman, 1990; Martin & Baldwin, 1996; Otwell & Mullis, 1997).

Lockart and Keys (1998) observed that U.S. schools have recently become a more important source of remedial services because of changes in family demographics (e.g., divorce and remarriage, socioeconomic level) and national health care policy (e.g., managed care systems). In areas where therapeutic services are limited, elementary school counselors find themselves in what Lockhart and Keys called "the critical position of being the only accessible mental health service provider for many students and families" (p. 4). Zahner, Pawelkiewicz, De Franceso, and Adnopoz (1992), for example, found that 37% of the troubled 6- to 11-year-old children in their study received counseling services through their school; only 13% were treated at medical clinics and 11% at community mental health facilities.

One method of handling this problem is to train counselors so they are prepared to deliver remedial interventions. As an alternative, Ponec, Poggi, and Dickel (1998) suggested collaboration between school- and community-based service providers.

Many therapists in the community have resisted this idea, even though the presenting problems they routinely encounter are reflected in or exacerbated by a child's experiences and behaviors in school. A collaborative approach also requires cooperation among school-based professionals. For example, Osborne and Collison (1998) stated that school counselors must work with outside clinicians who are employed part time or full time in the schools. The authors described how mutual respect and organizational procedures intended to enhance collaboration can transform what they termed a "hostile coexistence" (p. 8) into an integrated service delivery system.

Counseling in the schools has had its critics, such as the American Family Association, who contend "school counseling programs usurp parental authority" (Glossoff & Rockwell, 1997, p. 33). Glossoff and Rockwell described how budget cuts and personnel shortages have threatened the existence of these programs. These challenges to program integrity are unfortunate, given the important function that school counselors serve in meeting the educational and psychological needs of children.

Training in school counseling is available at many colleges and universities, including 142 programs that were CACREP-accredited in 2002 (Council for the Accreditation of Counseling and Related Educational Programs, 2002). School counselors are not licensed to practice in the same way as community-based therapists. Instead, they are certified by their state department of education to provide counseling services to students in the schools.

Social Workers

Popple and Leighninger (1996) highlighted the relationship between children and the social work profession when they stated that "child welfare is clearly social work's field" (p. 296). Social workers attempt to protect children from negative social influences, such as poverty and poor parenting. They conceptualize a child's behavior within the context of family, neighborhood, and community. Social workers also offer a range of services, which include locating financial assistance for families who are economically deprived, offering protective services to ensure the safety of children who are at risk of being abused or neglected, and providing counseling to those in need (Popple & Leighninger, 1996).

Social workers have historically conceptualized a client's experiences within the context of the person's cultural surround. A child's problems are interpreted relative to the family, the community, and the nation's political and economic conditions (Mather & Lager, 2000). Social workers do not limit themselves to remedial interventions. They are also active in preventing the environmental challenges that compromise healthy growth and development in children. These activities include reorganizing the child welfare system to improve its response to children in need, teaching parents to use more effective child rearing skills, and developing support networks in the community to facilitate families' access to financial assistance programs (e.g., Aid to Families with Dependent Children).

Unlike other professionals described in this section, social workers are trained across a broad educational spectrum, from 2-year community college programs in human services to Ph.D. programs designed to enhance research and advanced clinical skills. Of the social workers practicing in the field, most have graduated from university or institute-based programs that offer the bachelor's of social work (BSW) or master's of social work (MSW) degrees. Although Popple and Leighninger noted some confusion regarding the practice implications of the BSW and MSW, Hoffman (1992) described the former as the entry-level degree for community-based practice and the MSW as the "terminal practice degree" (p. 9). In 2002, there were 430 BSW and 146 MSW accredited programs in the United States (Council on Social Work Education, 2002). The professional practice of social work is regulated by the individual states, which require applicants to provide proof of their training, supervised experience, and knowledge of the discipline (Dial et al., 1992).

Physicians

According to Chamberlin (1987), physicians are in "a particularly strategic position to provide emotional support and instruction about family and child development" (p. 148). In their role as mental health providers, physicians assess and—in varying degrees—treat children's emotional and behavioral problems. Bray and McDaniel (1998) observed that physicians vary in their understanding of children's psychosocial development and related problems. They also differ in their awareness of the child therapist's role and function, so clinicians should educate physicians about these matters in language that is easy to understand (Evers-Szostak, 1998). Bray and McDaniel (1998,

p. 316) emphasized physicians' roles in contemporary mental health practice when they stated that "managed care companies usually respond" when physicians request psychological services.

The three areas of medicine most commonly involved with the mental health needs of children are child and adolescent psychiatry, pediatrics, and family practice. Although child and adolescent psychiatrists are involved primarily in the delivery of mental health services, family physicians and pediatricians also address these needs as part of their delivery of comprehensive health care. Although differences exist among the specialties, all three are distinguished from the other mental health professions by training requirements and practice activities, including the prescription of psychopharmacotherapeutic agents. Clearly, therapists must establish and maintain collaborative relationships with physicians if they hope to provide comprehensive treatments for children.

Child and Adolescent Psychiatrists. According to the American Academy of Child and Adolescent Psychiatry (1994), child and adolescent psychiatrists are "trained to promote healthy development and to evaluate, diagnose, and treat children and adolescents and their families who are affected by disorders of feeling, thinking, and behavior" (3. Description of AACAP section). Historically, child and adolescent psychiatrists served as treatment team leaders for psychologists and social workers in child guidance clinics (Levine & Levine, 1992). Today, they are better known for their expertise in pediatric psychopharmacology. Although other physicians may prescribe and supervise the use of these medications with children, child and adolescent psychiatrists are specially trained to provide these services.

To become a member of this specialty, physicians must first be certified in general psychiatry and then complete a 2-year residency in child and adolescent psychiatry (Phillips, Sarles, & Friedman, 1987). Although training requirements are well-defined, regulatory limits on practice are less clear. Hershenson and Power (1987) warned that physicians in the United States may limit their practice to child psychiatry without first obtaining board certification. Therefore, therapists should investigate the training and experience of psychiatrists before referring children for services.

Pediatricians. According to Behrman (1992), pediatricians are responsible for children's "physical, mental, and emotional progress from conception to maturity" (p. 1). This immense task is one that requires knowledge of the biological aspects of the growth process as well as an understanding of the developmental impact of family, community, and culture. During its more than 100 years of existence, the field of pediatrics has undergone dramatic changes because of technological advances in immunization and antibiotic therapies for childhood illness (Reisinger & Bires, 1980). The profession's early focus on the treatment of infectious diseases has given way to a more preventive health-oriented model. Garrison et al. (1992) emphasized pediatricians' role in identifying children in need of psychological services. They estimated that approximately one of every four children brought to pediatric clinics for well-child care exhibit behavioral, developmental, or family interaction problems. The authors found that pediatricians responded to these problems in different ways, including reassurance, brief interventions during the clinic visit, and referral for therapeutic services.

The pediatrician's ability to identify and treat children with psychosocial problems is complicated by the limited amount of time available to address these concerns. For example, Reisinger and Bires (1980) studied 305 well-child visits with 23 pediatricians and found that although the average visit lasted approximately 10 minutes, only 37 seconds of that time were devoted to anticipatory guidance for behavioral and emotional concerns. Although pediatricians are unable to routinely offer mental health services for children, they hold an important position as a referral source for these treatments. They also have the expertise needed to rule out the physiological causes of certain problems, such as enuresis and encopresis, so they are valuable participants in a multidisciplinary approach to treatment.

Training for pediatricians resembles that of other physicians, except the residency is specific to pediatrics. Again, pediatricians are licensed as physicians but can receive certification from the American Board of Pediatrics after successful completion of an approved pediatric residency and a comprehensive written examination (American Academy of Pediatrics, 1995).

Family Physicians. According to Taylor (1994), the field of family medicine was officially recognized in 1969 to foster the development of "a single specialist physician who could counter the fragmentation in medicine and serve America in an integrationist role" (p. 1). Family physicians adopt a community-based approach to coordinated, comprehensive, and ongoing health care services. They see patients of all ages, not just young people (as is the case for pediatricians). Through regular contact with children and in response to parents' requests for help, family practitioners provide a broad array of services, which include the assessment and treatment of behavioral problems (Kimmel & Chessare, 1994). Because they are typically "the doctor of first resort" (Roberts, 1994, p. 1017), family physicians play vital roles in the identification of children in need of psychosocial therapies. To become certified in family practice, a physician must have completed a 3-year residency in the specialty. Residency programs are available in settings such as hospitals, medical schools, and community clinics (American Academy of Family Physicians, 1996).

Psychologists

Psychologists from a variety of specialties (e.g., developmental psychology, educational psychology) have contributed to what we currently know about children. This section focuses on four applied areas: clinical, pediatric, counseling, and school psychology. Most applied psychologists share a training experience that is based on the scientist-practitioner model, which requires mastery of "both the helping practitioner roles and the methods of investigative science" (Gelso & Fretz, 1992, p. 44). Trained in this manner, psychologists are constantly engaged in the study of human behavior, whether they are providing therapy to children and families or conducting formal research on the treatment of childhood problems.

To become licensed as a clinical, counseling, or school psychologist, a person must successfully complete a doctoral degree, a period of postdoctoral supervision specified in the state's licensure statute, and a written and oral examination. No special licensing requirements exist for psychologists who specialize in services to children, so therapists should consider the training and experience of individual clinicians before referring clients for treatment.

Clinical Child Psychologists. The characteristic most often associated with clinical psychology is its focus on abnormal or maladaptive behavior (Garfield, 1965). Contemporary clinical psychologists, however, work in a variety of settings with clients who present a full range of problems, including those of a less serious nature. The association between clinical psychology and children dates back to the early work of Lightner Witmer, who has been called the father of clinical psychology (Garfield, 1965). In fact, Ross (1985) noted that because of Witmer's work, "clinical psychology began as clinical child psychology" (p. 31), although the latter term did not appear in print until 1951 (Ross, 1959).

Clinical child psychologists have traditionally focused on the diagnosis and treatment of troubled children, conducted research on various aspects of child psychopathology, and trained future professionals to serve children (Ross, 1959). La Greca (1985) observed that clinical child psychologists have expanded their roles and responsibilities in reaction to the challenges of contemporary society. Although they continue to offer traditional assessment and treatment services, many now consult with public schools or juvenile justice agencies, advocate for children, and develop and administer multidisciplinary interventions (Glenwick & Neuhaus, 1985).

Clinical child psychologists complete a doctoral program in clinical psychology that includes a year of predoctoral internship. As part of their training, they typically research child-related concerns and obtain supervised clinical experience with children. In 2001, there were 209 accredited programs in clinical psychology (American Psychological Association, 2001).[1] As participants in a multidisciplinary approach to intervention, clinical child psychologists draw on their training in psychological assessment and treatment to provide therapeutic services to children and their families. With their traditional focus on psychopathology, they can advise other professionals on the nature and severity of a child's behavior.

Pediatric Psychologists. Pediatric psychology developed as a result of the collaboration of pediatricians and psychologists, most often clinical psychologists. Proposed by Kagan (1965), this specialty is intended to foster more comprehensive delivery of health care services to children and their families (Roberts, 1986). Duff, Rowe, and Anderson (1973) highlighted the need for pediatric psychology when they found that only 12% of the patients examined in pediatric practices were presenting with problems of a purely phys-

[1]In of 2001, the American Psychological Association also accredited 12 programs in combined professional-scientific psychology (e.g., counseling/school, clinical/counseling/school), which are not included in the numbers reported in this chapter for accredited programs in clinical, counseling, and school psychology.

ical nature. In fact, 36% of the problems were judged to be psychological and 52% were thought to represent a combination of physical and psychological needs. Since the field's inception, pediatric psychologists have used a variety of intervention strategies, including consultation, psychological assessment, and therapy.

Because of the limited amount of time that pediatricians are able to devote to individual patients, pediatric psychologists are asked to treat children with behavior disorders. Based on her practice experience, pediatric psychologist Evers-Szostak (1998) reported that approximately three fourths of clients referred to her were children with disruptive behaviors, attention problems, and school-related concerns. Pediatric psychologists also assist in the treatment of children with medical problems, including chronic childhood illness (Wallender, 1993). They work with these clients to enhance treatment compliance, develop coping skills, and foster psychological adjustment in children with illnesses ranging from asthma and diabetes to cancer and spina bifida. When they collaborate with other professionals, pediatric psychologists bring a knowledge of the emotional and behavioral aspects of childhood diseases that can be used to design child- and family-based interventions provided in conjunction with traditional medical services. Unlike the other applied areas of psychology, training programs for pediatric psychology are not accredited as such by the American Psychological Association. Students interested in this specialty should investigate educational opportunities provided as part of accredited programs in other areas.

Counseling Psychologists. Historically, the focus of counseling psychology has been the needs of relatively normal people who are experiencing problems of everyday living. When counseling psychologists treat more disturbed individuals, they retain this positive orientation by attending less to psychopathology and more to the client's strengths and assets (Gelso & Fretz, 1992). This approach seems ideally suited to the treatment of troubled children whose healthy development is often compromised by environmental events, such as a dysfunctional family system or child abuse and neglect. Counseling psychology also can be traced to Lightner Witmer, who adopted a growth-oriented approach with children and viewed educational interventions as a means of developing a child's potential (Levine & Levine, 1992).

Most counseling psychologists have worked with adults, especially college students, but some have addressed childhood concerns (see Wagner, Stern, & Kaczmarek, 1994). Those who work with children use individual and family treatments to eliminate negative environmental influences and enhance the child's development. In 2001, there were 72 APA-accredited programs in this specialty (American Psychological Association, 2001). Kaczmarek and Wagner (1994) found that more than half of the 48 programs they surveyed had at least one faculty member who was interested in working with children. Many of these programs offered child-related course work and practicum experiences for their students. If counseling psychology is to fulfill its potential with children, more programs must expand their historical focus on adults to include the needs of young people. As participants in a multidisciplinary treatment, counseling psychologists bring an understanding of development across the lifespan and the benefits of focusing on a child's potential in the context of a multicultural society.

School Psychologists. The traditional roles of school psychologists have been assessment, treatment, and consultation intended to facilitate children's learning (French, 1990). The primary place of employment for members of this specialty is the nation's public schools, where their most common function remains the psychological assessment of individual children (D'Amato & Dean, 1989). Because of its long-standing relationship with elementary and secondary students, the field has been described as "American psychology's ambassador to the school" (Fagan, 1986, p. 859).

Lightner Witmer also represents an important figure in the history of school psychology. His work with public school students referred for learning problems is consistent with the defining characteristics of this specialty. Reschly and Wilson (1997) estimated that approximately 200 colleges and universities offer graduate programs in school psychology. In 2001, 54 of these programs were approved by the American Psychological Association (2001). Separate state policies for certification and licensure have evolved to regulate practice within and outside of the public schools. Typically, the former is by the state board of education and the latter by the state board of psychological examiners. School psychologists can be an invaluable addition to collaborative interventions. They are able to facilitate community–school contacts and assist in the development and coordination of school-based treatment programs. With their training in child assessment techniques, school psychologists also can identify causes and solutions for behavioral, emotional, and learning problems in children.

PROFESSIONAL ETHICS

An important function of any professional organization is defining and monitoring the ethical practice of its members. All of the associations discussed in this chapter have developed codes of ethics to offer direction to their members. Many of these codes contain two sections: ethical principles and ethical standards. Whereas ethical principles are ideals to which members should aspire in their everyday professional practice, standards are broadly stated rules that organizations can enforce in monitoring their members' ethical behavior (American Psychological Association, 1992). Some associations also have developed guidelines for practice that are intended as recommendations rather than enforceable standards. Examples include the *Guidelines for Psychological Evaluations in Child Protection Matters* (American Psychological Association, 1999) and the *Guidelines for Child Custody Evaluations in Divorce Proceedings* (American Psychological Association, 1994a).

Our discussion of professional ethics codes is not intended to be a thorough treatment of this important area. Rather, we will focus on ethical considerations that are relevant to the treatment of children. Specifically, we will examine child-related principles and standards that appear in the ethics codes of the American Association for Marriage and Family Therapy (2001) (see http://www.prenhall.com/wagner), American Counseling Association (1995) (Appendix A), American Psychological Association (1992) (Appendix B), American School Counselor Association (1998) (see http://www.prenhall.com/wagner), and National Association of Social Workers (1999) (Appendix C). Therapists are held accountable to the code of ethics of each professional association where they hold membership. But clinicians should be familiar with the ethics codes of other organizations, especially when they adopt a multidisciplinary approach to intervention. This includes an understanding of common beliefs and contradictions or ambiguities that exist across professional groups.

The ethics codes share many elements. For example, all contain principles and standards related to the competence of the clinician, responsibility to the consumer, confidentiality, and multiple relationships. There has been an increased amount of attention given to the role of cultural diversity in the delivery of treatment services. All codes include direct or indirect references to children. The American Association for Marriage and Family Therapy (2001, Responsibility to Research Participants section, 5.2), American Counseling Association (1995, A. 8 Multiple Clients), and American Psychological Association (1992, p. 1605) make limited reference to "children," but the American School Counselor Association (1998) refers to "students" (A.1. Responsibilities to Students section). Of course, children are included in any ethical principle or standard that refers to therapists' use of language appropriate to "the client's level of understanding" (National Association of Social Workers, 1999, 1.03 Informed Consent (c) section).

Despite their common features, ethics codes differ in the attention given to psychological testing, consultation, and forensic activities. Another important difference is the identification of the client who is the focus of treatment. Because parents and other family members often participate in a child's treatment, clinicians must carefully assess each situation at the outset of therapy and determine who the client is. Professional organizations in counseling and psychology, whose historical focus has been the individual, have tended to define the client from an individual perspective. Associations that have a more sociological foundation have tended to adopt a broader point of view, such as the National Association of Social Workers' (1999) definition of the client as "individuals, families, groups, organizations, and communities" (Preamble section, paragraph 2).

As family systems therapies and community-based interventions have become more common, counseling and psychological associations have expanded their earlier focus on the individual. Both the American Counseling Association (1995) and the American Psychological Association (1992) have included standards for therapists to follow in their work with families. The American Counseling Association endorsed the following:

> When counselors agree to provide counseling services to two or more persons who have a relationship (such as husband and wife, or parents and children), counselors clarify at the outset which person or persons are clients and the nature of the relationships they will have with each involved person. If it becomes apparent

> that counselors may be called upon to perform potentially conflicting roles, they clarify, adjust, or withdraw from roles appropriately. (A. 8. Multiple Clients section)

In its 1992 Code of Ethics, the American Psychological Association addressed its oversight of family-based treatments by adopting similar standards for psychologists who work with children and families.

The American Association for Marriage and Family Therapy (2001) recognized the rights of the individual while describing the family therapist as an advocate for both the family and its members. Clinicians who use family treatments encounter what the association called "unique confidentiality concerns because the client in a therapeutic relationship may be more than one person" (Principle II Confidentiality section). The American Counseling Association (1995) was more specific when it cautioned that "information about one family member cannot be disclosed to another member without permission" (B. 2. Groups and Families b. Family Counseling section). The association also stated that therapists should maintain and control access to client records in a manner that ensures the privacy of information disclosed to the therapist during individual therapy. Later in this chapter, we will examine this issue in more detail as it relates to children in family therapy.

A different situation exists when the child is a pupil in a school setting. The American School Counselor Association (1998) addressed the unique nature of the school when it described the responsibilities that counselors have to students, parents, the school, and the community. In its ethical standards, the association stated that the school counselor's primary obligation is to the student. But the counselor also is expected to be sensitive to parents' needs and responsibilities and to provide information about a child without violating the student's right to privacy. Complying with this standard can be a difficult task that often involves educating parents about the importance of privacy in therapy and helping them feel comfortable with very general descriptions of information discussed in sessions with the child.

The school counselor is also responsible to the school that students attend. When counselors become aware of factors that compromise the educational goals of the school, they communicate this information to the appropriate parties, such as the principal, and assist in the design and implementation of education/development, prevention, and remediation programs to address the problem. When counselors learn about a problem from a client, they present the information to others in a manner that maintains the privacy of the counseling relationship and protects the identity of the child. School counselors are expected to follow the same standards when they address problems detected in the community.

Associations have adopted ethics codes containing standards that have special meaning for child treatments. The National Association of Social Workers (1999), for example, provided the following standard to help therapists use techniques, such as developmental play (see Brody, 1997), that involve physical contact between clinician and child.

> Social workers should not engage in physical contact with clients when there is a possibility of psychological harm to the client as a result of the contact (such as cradling or caressing clients). Social workers who engage in appropriate physical contact with clients are responsible for setting clear, appropriate, and culturally sensitive boundaries that govern such physical contact. (1.10 Physical Contact section)

The association also adopted standards for multidisciplinary approaches to treatment by emphasizing the need for professionals to compare and contrast their codes of ethics to identify potential obstacles and avenues for resolving ethical conflicts before treatment is initiated. In a related standard, the American Counseling Association (1995) stated that clients who receive services that are coordinated and reviewed by a multidisciplinary team must be told this information, including the identification of team members. Additionally, the clinician must ensure that all team members follow policies and procedures to protect the privacy of client data.

The American School Counselor Association (1998) established a standard for school-based peer helper programs. Myrick (1997) described how these programs can be used to expand the scope of services provided by elementary school counselors. Peer facilitators learn basic communication and attending skills before being supervised in a helping role with other students. Because they are not professionally trained clinicians, the purpose and nature of their role must be clearly identified. The school counselor is responsible for the services that helpers provide to their peers. As a result, counselors must provide proper training and supervision for the student facilitators involved in these programs (American School Counselor Association, 1998).

ETHICAL AND LEGAL ISSUES IN CHILD THERAPY

The application of abstract ethical principles to everyday clinical situations requires careful consideration of the potential consequences of treatment for the child and other members of the family. Rae and Fournier (1999) identified important ethical principles that therapists must consider in their work with children and families. The first is competence. Before clinicians treat children, they must be adequately trained and supervised in the delivery of services to young clients. They must adapt all interventions to the child's developmental level and the family's cultural background. Therapists must always have the welfare of the client as their foremost concern. With children, this requires the use of treatment techniques that have been identified as appropriate for the presenting problem. It also means that clinicians must intervene in an appropriate manner when they suspect that a child has been abused or neglected or is at risk for harm to self or others. Finally, Rae and Fournier stated that therapists must treat children and their families in a professional manner, conveying respect and being honest when presenting their credentials and recommendations in treatment. To this list, we should add that clinicians must be aware of emerging therapeutic techniques and consider the ethical implications of these methods before using them with children and families (see Contemporary Issues Box 2-1).

As noted at the outset of this chapter, codes of ethics are superseded by the laws that apply in the therapist's jurisdiction of practice. The distinction between legal and ethical issues is no minor concern. Therapists who treat children encounter complex dilemmas that are the result of conflicting ethical and legal standards. For example, a clinician who learns that a child is being molested by a caregiver is required to report the abuse to the appropriate authorities despite an ethical commitment to protect the privacy of client information. To resolve these conflicts, therapists must understand the relevant laws that apply in their area. Summaries of state statutes that relate to children can be found online at http://www.calib.com/nccanch/services/statutes.htm. This section examines issues that therapists encounter in their work with children and families: informed consent and assent, confidentiality and privileged communication, the parents' and child's rights in treatment, the proper maintenance of client records, handling suicidal behaviors, children's testimony in court, and child custody litigation.

Informed Consent and Assent

As Pope and Vasquez (1991) cautioned, "Nothing blocks a patient's access to help with such cruel efficiency as a bungled attempt at informed consent" (p. 74). If children and families are to benefit from therapy, clinicians must provide a developmentally appropriate explanation of the nature, potential outcomes, and limitations of treatment. With this knowledge, parents and children can decide whether therapy is a possible solution for their problems. Any discussion of informed consent as it relates to children must include consideration of two related terms, consent and assent.

Informed consent involves a number of related elements. First, a person must be told the information needed to make a decision. In therapeutic settings, this typically involves the therapist's describing the nature, duration, possible outcomes, and cost of treatment. Clients should also be informed of the limits to confidentiality, including legal mandates regarding the reporting of suspected cases of child maltreatment. Informed consent requires that the person making the decision be competent to make a choice. Although defined in different ways, competence often includes the person understanding the situation, using a reasonable process of decision making, and stating a preference (Melton & Ehrenreich, 1992). Informed consent also requires that the person's decision be a voluntary act that was not forced on him or her by others. The final element of informed consent is that the decision maker be of the legal age required to make such a choice.

Although certain adolescents in some states are allowed to give informed consent, this right does not extend to elementary school students, who are typically viewed as lacking at least one of the elements described above. Instead, children give informed assent, which Schouten and Duckworth (1999) described as a "general agreement to treatment" (p. 171) that does not have a minimum legal age. The American Academy of Pediatrics Committee on

Contemporary Issues Box 2–1

Teletherapy, Children, and Families

Van Horn and Myrick (2001) observed that the growth of computer technology in the schools has enhanced counselors' access to information, facilitated their communication with parents and other professionals, and provided an additional avenue for education/development and prevention activities with children. The availability of computers, special software, and telecommunication links has also affected the delivery of mental health services in the community. Aymard (1999), for example, described computerized drawing and storytelling programs that clinicians can use with children in therapy. And telehealth services provided via interactive televideo and the Internet are emerging, especially in rural areas where practitioners and clients are located at great distances from each other (Sammons, 2001).

To date, very few studies have been conducted on the process and outcome of telehealth services or teletherapy. This is unfortunate because there are a number of issues that merit investigation. These include the individuals involved in therapy (e.g., client, clinician, insurance company), the financial costs, regulatory policies and clinician liability, and professional standards of practice (Sammons, 2001). An example of a telehealth service is the telepsychiatry program that Ermer (1999) described between the University of Kansas Medical Center and a mental health center located 120 miles away in Pittsburg, Kansas. Children are assessed and selected for the program by the staff at the local mental health center. A clinic nurse typically sits with the child and parents as they are being interviewed by a university psychiatrist through interactive teleconferencing. Ermer reported that the program was successful, but he relied on anecdotal evidence to support his conclusion.

Stephenson (1995) described an interesting approach to telehealth services called "Starbright World," which allows videoconferencing among children hospitalized for complex medical procedures, such as chemotherapy and bone marrow transplants. Funded by the Starbright Foundation under the leadership of film director Steven Spielberg, this multimedia network is being evaluated at various hospitals in the United States. For example, Holden, Bearison, Rode, Kapiloff, and Rosenberg (2000) conducted a meta-analysis of single-case experimental data collected from 44 patients, ages 7 to 18 years, at Mount Sinai Medical Center in New York City. When compared with an alternative condition of traditional interventions (e.g., individual or group play, family visits, reading), Starbright World was found to produce lower self-reported ratings of pain and anxiety. Additional research is needed, including studies of developmental and cultural influences, as well as controlled treatment trials to evaluate process and outcome data collected from children, parents, and hospital staff.

How common is teletherapy? The answer depends on the definition of telehealth services. In their survey of practicing psychologists, VandenBos and Williams (2000) found that only 2% of the respondents provided teletherapy via closed-circuit television, the Internet, and satellite communication. This rate jumped to 98% when services delivered by telephone were included, with 69% of respondents reporting the use of this tool for individual therapy and 23% for group or family therapy. The telephone has been found to have other applications in the delivery of therapeutic services. Ritterband et al. (2001), for example, conducted a preliminary evaluation of their "telecommunication monitoring system" (TMS) (p. 636) to collect daily information for children diagnosed with encopresis. Simply stated, parents were instructed to use the telephone to submit daily records of their child's toileting behaviors and other problems. Similar to the daily written diaries or records used by many therapists to collect information about clients' behaviors, TMS holds possibilities that are not available in the traditional approach to data collection. For example, Ritterband et al. suggested that their method could be combined with the use of the Internet to prompt parents and to collect and store client data. As they stated:

> Clinicians would be able to track symptom improvement over time by having an automated phone call placed to a patient every day. This information would then be

stored in a secure database on an Internet server, which could then be viewed by the clinician from any computer connected to the World Wide Web. (p. 640)

Because of the paucity of research on teletherapy, clinicians must exercise special caution to ensure that clients are treated in an ethical manner. The Ethics Committee of the American Psychological Association (1997) cited therapist competence with the technique, confidentiality, and the therapeutic relationship as possible concerns. In their discussion of multidisciplinary applications of telehealth services, Reed, Mclaughlin, and Milholland (2000) stated that "the basic standards of professional conduct governing each health care profession are not altered by the use of telehealth technologies" (p. 172). In other words, clinicians must adhere to the ethical principles of their professions, regardless of whether therapeutic services are provided in a traditional or technological format.

In its Ethical Standards for Internet On-line Counseling, the American Counseling Association (1999) addressed these and other issues. The Association indicated that appropriate technology, such as e-mail encryption, must be used to ensure confidentality of information exchanged online. Therapists must know the limits and potential hazards of teletherapy so they can inform clients of these risks (e.g., threats to confidentiality) before the outset of treatment. Clinicians must also assess each client to determine whether teletherapy is the proper method and to refer for traditional treatments clients who are deemed inappropriate or choose to reject online services. The American Counseling Association (1999) cited special concerns in the use of teletherapy with children and adolescents. As stated in the Ethical Standards, "Professional counselors must verify that clients are above the age of majority, are competent to enter into the counseling relationship with a professional counselor, and are able to give informed consent" (Establishing the On-Line Counseling Relationship section (e) Minor or Incompetent Clients). The standards do allow for teletherapy with children if a parent or guardian provides written consent before treatment is begun. But Internet-based therapy may have limited applications for younger clients, many of whom lack the writing and keyboarding skills currently required for online interactions.

Bioethics (1999) indicated that assent should include the following:

1. Helping the patient achieve a developmentally appropriate awareness of the nature of his or her condition.
2. Telling the patient what he or she can expect with tests and treatment(s).
3. Making a clinical assessment of the patient's understanding of the situation and the factors influencing how he or she is responding (including whether there is inappropriate pressure to accept testing or therapy).
4. Soliciting an expression of the patient's willingness to accept the proposed care. (p. 315)

Children are usually considered to be incompetent to make treatment decisions, so their parents or guardians are expected to act in their best interests. This includes the decision to initiate treatment services and release therapeutic information to others. When children and parents disagree on these matters, the parents' wishes are often followed. As Melton and Ehrenreich (1992) stated, "As a matter of law, consent or refusal by the child is considered to be not only insufficient but irrelevant, for once the parent has consented, treatment can be provided even over the child's objection" (p. 1039).

Many parents request professional help for what they perceive to be adjustment or behavior problems in a child. As adults, therapists are at risk of affiliating with parents and overlooking the child's point of view. Johnson, Rasbury, and Siegel (1997) acknowledged the difficulties that clinicians encounter when they assess parent–child conflicts about participation in treatment. The authors believed that therapists can solve these predicaments through serious consideration of the child's age and developmental level, the nature and severity of the child's problems, and the parents' overall adjustment. Clinicians factor this information into their assessment of the need for treatment services. In some cases, therapy for the troubled child is warranted. In others, a family-based intervention to improve family functioning is appropriate. Or the therapist might opt for couples therapy to address marital problems or to give parents information about child development.

The growth of managed mental health care has introduced another factor that therapists must consider in regard to informed consent. Clinicians must know the limits of a family's mental health insurance policy and ensure that clients understand any restrictions on the length or nature of therapy at the outset of treatment (Sauber, 1997). Although therapists direct much of this discussion to parents, they must also give the child a developmentally appropriate explanation of the number and nature of treatment sessions. The clinician then assumes responsibility for providing therapy within the context of preauthorized sessions, advocating for reauthorization when additional services are needed and appealing all denials of these requests. Poynter (1998) recommended that therapists provide clients with a description of the insurer's role in monitoring treatment progress, the number of preauthorized sessions, and the types of service that will not be reimbursed (e.g., growth-oriented therapy).

An important consideration in children's participation in therapy is the client's understanding of the nature and purpose of treatment. Adults often assume that children are unable to make decisions about the purpose and direction of therapy, but experts who studied this issue have suggested otherwise. In the 1980s, researchers began to investigate developmental factors related to treatment decisions. Although much of this work was conducted with adolescents, the results are relevant to children's participation in treatment.

In their study of clinicians' attitudes, Taylor, Adelman, & Kaser-Boyd (1984) found that approximately half of their respondents did not seek assent from children and adolescents, presumably because these clients were thought to be incompetent to make treatment decisions. When Sigelman and Mansfield (1992) studied knowledge and acceptance of therapy among students enrolled in grades 2 to 3, 6 to 7, and 10, they found that students' understanding of the clinician's role improved with age. Middle and high school students were more aware of therapists' activities and seemed to have a better understanding of the types of problems that merit treatment. Kaser-Boyd, Adelman, Taylor, and Nelson (1986) studied clients between ages 10 and 19 years. They found no significant age-related differences in participants' ability to weigh the risks and benefits of therapy. When presented with a hypothetical treatment situation, many of the 10- and 11-year-old children in the study "were surprisingly good at weighing risks and benefits" (p. 170). The decision to involve children in treatment decisions must be made on an individual basis, involving young clients consistent with their decision making skills and understanding of therapy.

Confidentiality and Privileged Communication

Therapists who work with children must understand two important and related constructs: confidentiality and privileged communication. Confidentiality is an ethical principle that is essential to the development of trust in the therapeutic relationship. It pertains to the clinician's protection of client information learned during treatment. This includes test results and all comments made by the child and other family members during the course of therapy. It also includes the mere acknowledgment that a child or any other family member is receiving treatment services.

Privileged communication is a statutory right that limits a therapist's disclosure of client information in court proceedings. Under these laws, it is the client, not the clinician, who holds the right to invoke the privilege and restrict disclosure by the therapist. Each state identifies the relationships, such as husband and wife or attorney and client, that qualify for this protection. Some states have included the therapist–client relationship in their laws, but the mental health professionals covered by these statutes differ from state to state. For this reason, clinicians must review the law that applies in their locale before they begin work with clients.

When the client is a child, clinicians must handle disclosure in a different manner than is done with adults in therapy. First, therapists are required to get informed consent from a child's parents or legal guardian before clinical information is disclosed to others. Clinicians must document this decision by having the parents or guardians sign a written release to disclose information before contacting the others specified in the agreement. Therapists should also obtain informed assent from the child. Young clients are sometimes reluctant to have the therapist contact their teacher to inquire about events at school. When the clinician believes it is important to speak with the teacher and when parents have consented to this contact, the therapist should encourage the child to discuss his or her reservations. Often this approach provides valuable information about school personnel that the therapist can use during contacts with teachers and the school counselor. Consider a client who describes how a teacher notified his class that another student was in counseling "because he's having problems." During contacts with this person, the therapist should emphasize the need for confidentiality, limit disclosure of therapeutic information, and focus on data the teacher can provide to facilitate the integration of treatment into classroom activities.

Levine et al. (1993) stated that a child "does have the moral if not legal rights to have some information kept confidential" (p. 93). Therapists frequently find themselves balancing children's moral right to privacy with parents' legal right to access clinical materials. A child who is suspicious and distrusts the clinician is unlikely to disclose information that he or she wants to keep private. Parents, on the other hand, are typically entitled to review their child's records, whether held by a school, a physician, or a mental health professional (Melton & Ehrenreich, 1992). Although parents do not often ask to see a child's treatment record, many do question the therapist about their child's progress in treatment. The reasons for these requests vary, from a sincere interest in the child's welfare to a desire to control the direction of therapy to the fear that a child will disclose what is perceived to be sensitive family information. Experts have proposed various ways of handling intrafamilial challenges to confidentiality with child clients. Hendrix (1991) cited four: complete confidentiality, limited confidentiality, no guarantee of confidentiality, and forced informed consent.

Ross (1958) described complete confidentiality as the therapist's not disclosing anything shared by the child or parents to other members of the family. Ross proposed this approach because he assumed that all children would distrust their clinician, thereby compromising development of the therapeutic relationship. The limitations to complete intrafamilial confidentiality are numerous, including the clinician's obligation to report suspected cases of child maltreatment. Complete confidentiality and limited confidentiality are the same in terms of the therapist's disclosure of information obtained from the child. They differ in regard to the clinician's disclosure of comments made by the parents. Unlike complete confidentiality, in which no such disclosure occurs, clinicians who adopt a limited approach to intrafamilial confidentiality share parents' comments with the child. Limited confidentiality also has its problems. For example, parents who understand that the content of their sessions may be communicated to their child may not disclose certain events, such as the decision to file for divorce, which could significantly affect the therapist's work with the child.

Another method of handling intrafamilial confidentiality with child clients is no guarantee of confidentiality. Here the therapist decides what information is to be shared and when. The content of disclosures is not limited to mandated exceptions to confidentiality. Clinicians who adopt this method must inform their clients at the outset of treatment that any information disclosed during individual sessions may be communicated to other family members, at the discretion of the therapist. Clinicians who restrict their contacts with children to family sessions avoid issues related to intrafamilial confidentiality because the entire family is present during all discussions. Of course, this assumes that no one will initiate individual contact with the therapist outside of session, and that individual meetings with the child or parents are unwarranted.

Although Hendrix (1991) used the term "forced, informed consent" in his article, "forced, informed assent" is probably the more appropriate descriptor for our purposes. In this approach, the therapist has flexibility in the types of information about a child that are shared with parents. This includes legally mandated disclosures, such as suspected maltreatment and danger to self or others. Johnson et al. (1997) added that clinicians may provide parents with a general description of what transpires in session with the child, without reference to specific information. An example of this approach would be the session with a child who describes various contacts with friends at school, including games during recess, peer tutoring with a student in a lower grade, and collaborative work with peers on a group science project. If a parent were to request information about the session, the therapist could reply, "We talked about friends and school today."

The use of forced, informed assent does not have to compromise the child's relationship with the therapist. Taylor and Adelman (1989) recommended a proactive approach in which the clinician identifies the information to be disclosed, informs the child of this decision, and then assesses the child's reaction. In cases in which the response is positive, the therapist might help the client assume responsibility for disclosing the information to his or her parents.

Preparing a child for this task involves asking the client to imagine how the parents will react to the disclosure. Likewise, the therapist must determine whether encouraging the child to take the lead is a therapeutic intervention or the clinician's attempt to avoid an uncomfortable responsibility. When a child does not agree with the therapist's decision to disclose information, Taylor and Adelman recommended that the clinician help the child to consider the benefits and liabilities of disclosure. If the client continues to resist, the therapist should explain the rationale for disclosure, examine potential consequences, and disclose the information to parents in a manner that is least traumatic for all involved.

When a client is thought to be a danger to self or others, the therapist must take the appropriate steps to prevent the client from engaging in these behaviors. This often requires breaking confidentiality, as articulated in the ethics codes of the mental health professions. For example, the American Psychological Association (1992) stated that one of the reasons for disclosing confidential information without the client's agreement is "to protect the patient or client or others from harm" (p. 1606). Similarly, the American School Counselor Association (1998) permits disclosure without a client's assent or consent when "required to prevent clear and imminent danger to the counselee or others or when legal requirements demand that confidential information be revealed" (A. 2. Confidentiality b. section). Later in this chapter, we will examine recommended procedures for handling a child's risk of harm to self.

The most publicized court case involving a therapist's duty to warn others in danger is *Tarasoff v. Board of Regents of the University of California* (1976). In this case, Dr. Moore, a psychologist, had reason to believe that one of his adult clients, Prosenjit Poddar, represented a threat to a woman, Tatiana Tarasoff, who had previously rejected the client's amorous advances. Although Dr. Moore notified the police, he did not contact Ms. Tarasoff. The police questioned Mr. Poddar, concluded he was not dangerous, and warned and released him. The client did not return to therapy, and 2 months later he killed Ms. Tarasoff. When her parents' suit was heard by the California Supreme Court, the judges ruled that the psychologist had a duty to warn the intended victim. Although the Tarasoff decision was a California case, it has had nationwide impact, resulting in the passage of duty-to-warn statutes in a number of states and similar rulings in other jurisdictions throughout the United States (Reaves & Ogloff, 1996).

Clinicians who practice in elementary schools must be aware of the special limits to confidentiality that exist in these settings. The federal Family Educational Rights and Privacy Act (FERPA) (1974), sometimes referred to as the Buckley Amendment, specifies that if a school system is receiving federal funds, parents and students of majority age are allowed to review a child's educational files. The law does not apply to records that are "kept in the sole possession of the maker, are used only as a personal memory aid, and are not accessible or revealed to any other person except a temporary substitute for the maker of record" (34 C. F. R. § 99.3) According to Sealander, Schwiebert, Oren, and Weekley (1999), this includes private notes that a therapist or school counselor maintains for individual treatment sessions with a student. But to qualify for this exemption, the counselor must keep the client's progress notes separate from the student's other educational records and in a secure location to which only the clinician has access (Remley & Herlihy, 2001).

An interesting question that sometimes arises with children of divorce is whether noncustodial parents are allowed to access their child's school records. Fischer and Sorenson (1996) stated that both FERPA regulations and case law permit either parent to review the student's educational file, unless this right has been revoked by state statute or a court decree. School officials have been found to restrict noncustodial parents' access to these records (see Fischer & Sorenson, 1996). Such was the issue in *Page v. Rotterdam-Mohonasen Central School District* (1981), in which the biological father of a fifth grade boy was not permitted to inspect his son's school file. Mr. Page was separated from his wife, who had requested that the school not allow the father to review the boy's educational records or participate in parent–teacher conferences. The court found on behalf of the father, citing FERPA and State of New York provisions that allow parents to review their child's school records and to participate in the student's education.

Therapists should describe the limits to confidentiality at the outset of treatment. This includes informing clients, especially parents, of any records the family's insurance company expects from the clinician. The emergence of managed mental health care has heightened therapists' concerns about client confidentiality. Authorization and review of treatment sessions is conducted in the offices of the client's insurance company. Therapists are asked to provide sensitive information about their clients for case management purposes, so clinicians and insurers share the responsibility of maintaining the privacy of client records (Edmunds et al., 1997). Unfortunately, clinicians cannot guarantee that insurance companies will follow the same ethical standards they uphold in their practice. For this reason, Sauber (1997) recommended that therapists have clients review all case reports that are submitted to an insurer and sign a form indicating that they have read the records. Cooper and Gottlieb (2000) warned clinicians to never transmit client information via e-mail, to fax records with caution, and to rely on written notification by regular mail whenever possible. These steps seem to have merit, given Ackley's (1997) accounts of insurance companies' sharing clinical information with third parties, such as clients' employers.

The Rights of Children

In 1989, the General Assembly of the United Nations ratified its Convention on the Rights of the Child (United Nations Convention on the Rights of the Child, 1989). According to Melton (1991), this 54-article document emphasizes "the significance of liberty, privacy, equality, and nurturance as rights essential to preservation of children's integrity as individuals" (p. 343). The United States has delayed in ratifying the Convention, and the rights granted to children in this country are based on two related and somewhat contradictory attitudes (Stein, 1998). Although children are entitled to certain rights granted to adults, they are also treated as a special population that needs legal protections to ensure their safety. When used in a legal sense, the term "rights" means "claims that are enforceable in a court of law" (Stein, 1998, p. 139). During the latter half of the 20th century, significant court decisions outlined these claims, including childrens' rights to due process and free speech.

Before the U.S. Supreme Court's *In re Gault* (1967) decision, it was unclear whether children were entitled to the same rights afforded to adults under the Fifth and Sixth Amendments of the Constitution. This landmark case involved Gerald Gault, a 15-year-old boy who was accused of making obscene telephone calls. When found guilty, Gault was sentenced to incarceration until age 21 years. Had he been an adult at the time of his crime, the penalty would have been a fine of $5 to $50 or imprisonment for a maximum of 2 months (Stein, 1998). The Court ruled in Gault's favor, thereby recognizing children's rights to due process that were previously limited to adults. As a result of the Gault decision, children now have the right to receive written notice of the charges brought against them, representation by an attorney, and protection against self-incrimination.

In *Tinker v. Des Moines Independent Community School District* (1969), the U.S. Supreme Court recognized children's right to free speech. This case involved two high schoolers and one junior high student who wore black arm bands to school as a symbolic protest against the Vietnam War. The students were suspended because they refused to comply with a recently approved policy prohibiting the wearing of arm bands at school. The court ruled in favor of the students. Writing for the majority, Justice Fortice stated that school officials had violated the students' First Amendment rights to free speech by restricting a behavior that did not disrupt the daily operation of the school.

The second theme identified by Stein (1998) is the belief that children are a vulnerable group that requires special protections under the law. A crucial right for any child is protection from abuse and neglect. According to the United Nations Convention on the Rights of the Child (1989), governments are responsible for protecting children from maltreatment and establishing procedures for reporting, treating, and monitoring cases of abuse and neglect when they do occur. In the United States, states have passed mandatory reporting laws to minimize the harm of child abuse and neglect. Legislatures have adopted these statutes under the authority of *parens patriae*, or the state's right to assume the role of parent when children are mistreated. Included as part of these laws is the identification of the state agencies authorized to remove a child from a parent's custody when the child is believed to be in danger.

In 1963, the United States Children's Bureau provided the model that was used to develop mandatory reporting laws for child maltreatment in all 50 states during the 1960s (Besharov, 1985). These statutes were later revised, following creation of the National Center on Child Abuse and Neglect as part of the federal Child Abuse Prevention and Treatment Act (CAPTA) (1974). Besharov indicated that as a result of this statute, states were required to expand their existing laws to mandate reporting of all types of child abuse and neglect. The eventual outcome was a dramatic increase in the number of maltreatment cases reported to authorities.

An important consideration in the passage of mandatory reporting laws is the accurate and practical definition of relevant terms. For example, how are socially sanctioned child-rearing practices distinguished from a parent's abusive and neglectful behaviors? Although statutes vary in their definition of the different types of child maltreatment, Stein (1998) offered the following descriptors: physical abuse; sexual abuse; neglect; and a fourth category that is sometimes used, emotional neglect or abuse. Specifying the nature and practical limits of these categories is no easy task. Stein, for example, described physical abuse as "a physical injury caused by other than accidental means that causes or creates substantial risk of death, disfigurement, impairment of physical health, or loss or impairment of function of any bodily organ" (p. 83). Specifying what is meant by "substantial risk" in this definition is a challenge that hinders the identification of a clear-cut dividing line between abusive and nonabusive behaviors.

Mental health professionals have incorporated the rights of clients, including children, into their ethics codes. For example, the American School Counselor Association (1998) stated that students are entitled to respect, dignity, self-determination, privacy, freedom, and responsibility in achieving personal goals. Therapists' attitudes about children's rights to privacy or confidentiality in treatment have undergone considerable change, in part because of statutory and other limits imposed on clinicians. Such is the case when a therapist has reason to suspect that a child has been abused or neglected. Therapists who do not follow their state's mandatory reporting statute may contribute to continued child maltreatment and make themselves vulnerable to legal penalties. As a result, ethics codes have been revised to allow disclosure of information, without client assent or consent, "when legal requirements demand that confidential information be revealed" (American Counseling Association, 1995 B. 1. Right to Privacy c. section).

Prout, DeMartino, and Prout (1999) described the case of *Phillis P. v. Clairmont Unified School District* (1986) in which school officials were held accountable for their failure to report suspected child abuse. In this case, an 8-year-old girl was being sexually molested by another child at school. Although her teacher, the school psychologist, and the principal were made aware of the abuse, they did not file a report as mandated by state law. The mother filed suit against the district, and the court found on her behalf by agreeing that the school had failed to protect the child.

Therapists must be aware of the nature and scope of the mandatory reporting statute that applies in their practice jurisdiction. Although state laws follow the federal model, they differ in their specification of who is required to report cases of child maltreatment as well as how and under what conditions these reports must be filed. In addition, state legislatures routinely review and revise their statutes, so clinicians must monitor these changes to ensure that they are in compliance with the current law. Therapists can obtain information about state statutes online from the National Clearinghouse on Child Abuse and Neglect Information at http://www.calib.com/nccanch/services/statutes.htm. The revision of only a few words in a multi-paragraph statute can have significant implications for a therapist's obligation to report. For example, consider a change that requires reporting when the clinician has "reasonable cause to suspect that a child is an abused or neglected child" rather than "reasonable cause to suspect that a child brought before him or her for examination, care, or treatment, or of whom he or she has observation is an abused or neglected child." The new law no longer specifies that the therapist have contact with the child, so a parent's disclosure of abuse by another adult may require that a report be filed, even if the clinician had never seen the child.

So who is required to report suspected cases of child abuse and neglect? Although statutes vary, Stein (1998) observed that, as a general rule, educational and mental health professionals in all states are considered mandated reporters. Some legislatures have adopted very broad standards. A number of states including Florida, Idaho, Indiana, and New Jersey, require that any person who suspects abuse must file a report (National Clearinghouse on Child Abuse and Neglect Information, NCCANI, 2001a). These states have codified the responsibilities that all citizens have in protecting children from maltreatment. Preventing child abuse and neglect involves the entire community, not just therapists, child welfare workers, teachers, and physicians.

Other states have adopted less inclusive laws. Pennsylvania, for example, required the following individuals to report suspected cases of maltreatment:

> Licensed physicians, osteopaths, medical examiners, coroners, funeral directors, dentists, optometrists, chiropractors, podiatrists, interns, registered nurses, licensed practical nurses, hospital personnel engaged in the admission, examination, care or treatment of persons, Christian Science practitioners;

Members of the clergy, school administrators, school teachers, school nurses, social service workers, day-care center workers or any other child-care or foster-care workers, mental health professionals, peace officers or law enforcement officials. (NCCANI, 2001a, p. 39)

In states where the phrase "any person" has not been included in the reporting statute, the list of mandated reporters can be quite lengthy. In a recent version of the California law, more than 50 individuals were identified, including psychologists, counselors, paramedics, and firefighters (NCCANI, 2001a).

When is a therapist required to report child maltreatment to the proper authorities? As a general rule, states require that a report be filed when a person has what is often referred to as "reasonable cause to suspect" that a child has been abused or neglected. The therapist's challenge is determining what constitutes "reasonable cause." In some cases, the answer to this question is clear, such as a child who says that a parent inflicted the lacerations or burns that the clinician observes on the child's body. But in many instances, the signs are less obvious or the child gives a different explanation, such as accidental injuries that occurred during play. California tried to clarify the meaning of "reasonable" by including the following definition in its reporting statute.

> Reasonable suspicion means that it is objectively reasonable for a person to entertain a suspicion, based upon facts that could cause a reasonable person in a like position, drawing, when appropriate, on his or her training and experience, to suspect child abuse or neglect. (NCCANI, 2001b, p. 14)

In the absence of clear evidence, a therapist in California would be expected to rationally process the available information as other clinicians "in a like position" would do.

Stein (1998) observed that the criteria used to define abuse and neglect vary from state to state. One point is clear: mandated reporters are only required to suspect maltreatment, not to investigate or substantiate the existence of child abuse and neglect. State legislatures have assigned these responsibilities to other professionals, typically Child Protective Services workers and law enforcement officials (Stein, 1998). Clinicians must understand the statutory penalties for failing to report suspected cases of child maltreatment. Once again, the consequences for not reporting differ across states. The penalty can be a fine, incarceration, or both. For example, recent revisions to the Mississippi statute specified that "anyone who willfully violates any provision of the reporting law shall be, upon being found guilty, punished by a fine not to exceed $5000, or by imprisonment in jail not to exceed 1 year, or both" (NCCANI, 2001c, p. 9). Of course, the most serious consequence that can result from the failure to report is continued abuse or neglect of the child.

Parents are not the only people who abuse children. Bajt and Pope (1989) surveyed a group of experienced psychologists to determine whether they were aware of sexual intimacy between therapists and child or adolescent clients. Approximately one fourth of the respondents reported a total of 81 incidents, 56% of which involved girls. The ages of these clients ranged from 3 to 17 years for girls and 7 to 16 years for boys. Of course, these results are based on respondents' reports of inappropriate behavior by other therapists, so we must not conclude that one in four clinicians sexually abuses young clients. Still, Bajt and Pope have identified a significant area for concern. If children are to benefit from therapy, their clinicians must be trustworthy individuals who do not violate the clients' rights, which include a therapeutic relationship in which the welfare of the client is the foremost concern.

Kalichman, Craig, and Follingstad (1989) described the conflict that therapists experience as they juggle their ethical responsibilities to maintain confidentiality and their legal duty to report suspected cases to protect young clients from maltreatment. Clinicians must prepare for the inevitable by having in place a framework for reporting cases of abuse and neglect. When a therapist learns this information during an individual meeting with a child, the clinician should collect the data needed to determine whether there is reasonable cause to suspect maltreatment. This includes specific information about the alleged perpetrator, abusive episodes, and trustworthy caregivers. After the clinician has sufficient reason to suspect abuse, the child should be reminded of the exceptions to confidentiality that were discussed at the outset of treatment. When the perpetrator is someone other than the parent who accompanied the client to treatment, the therapist should inform the child of the need to disclose details about the abuse to that parent in session.

Alternative arrangements are usually required when the alleged abuser is the adult who brings the child to therapy. The clinician's primary concern in these situations is the welfare of the child. The therapist may decide to meet individually with the parent to discuss the child's allegations of maltreatment. Some parents, when confronted with a detailed description of events, will acknowledge responsibility for their actions. In these cases and those in which the parent is not the alleged perpetrator, therapists can adopt the decision-making tree formulated by Stadler (1989) (Fig. 2-1). This approach allows the parent to assume different levels of responsibility for reporting, without compromising the therapist's ultimate responsibility to ensure that the proper authorities are notified.

Before terminating a session when reporting is required, the clinician must ensure the child's safety. This includes consideration of potential threats, such as family pressures on the client to recant abuse allegations and the risk of physical harm to the child for betraying family secrets. With nonabusing parents, therapists often use anticipatory guidance to help family members examine possible future events and develop alternative responses to each. These include discussion of the upcoming investigative interview with authorities, support services available in the community, and the steps parents can take to prevent further maltreatment of the child. Therapists should communicate their concern for the child and their desire to support the client during the investigation and prosecution of the abuse. When an abusing parent becomes angry in session and represents a danger to the child, the clinician must collaborate with Child Protection Services workers to secure a safe, out-of-home placement for the client.

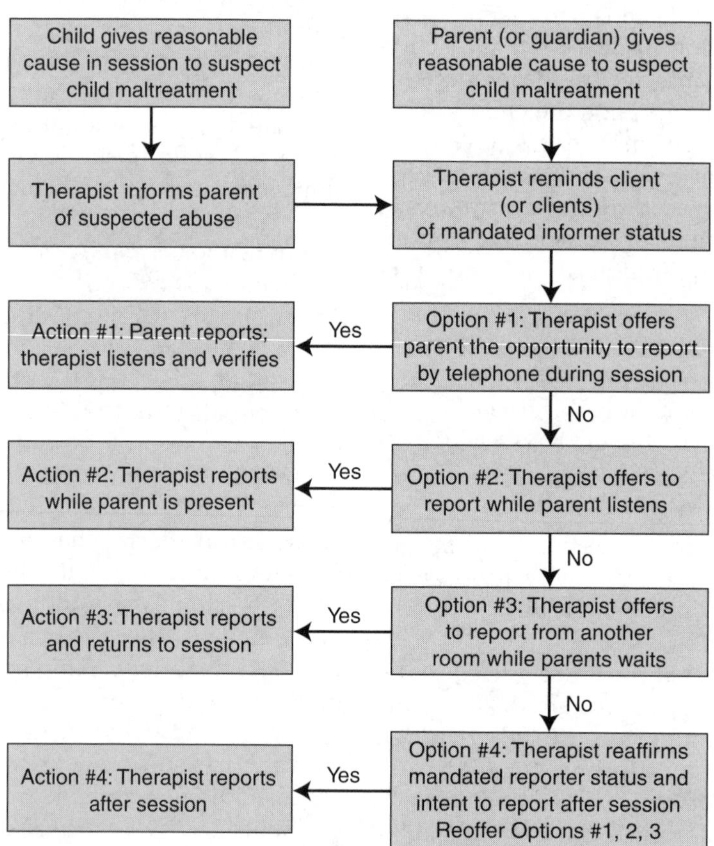

Figure 2–1. An Adaptation of Stadler's (1989) Decision-Making Tree for Reporting Suspected Cases of Child Maltreatment. Adapted from "Balancing Ethical Responsibilities: Reporting Child Abuse and Neglect," by H. A. Stadler, 1989, p. 107. Copyright 1989 by Sage Publications, Inc. Adapted with permission of the author.

The Rights of Parents

State laws that limit the child-rearing techniques parents may use are exceptions to the general view that parents should have the authority to discipline their children as they choose (Pagliocca, Melton, Weisz, & Lyons, 1995). For example, parents are given considerable latitude in the procedures they use to raise their children. As long as their methods are within socially sanctioned limits, parents are permitted to use a variety of disciplinary techniques without outside interruption. This includes the use of physical punishment with a child. Not until this method exceeds social limits and is thought to be abusive does the community challenge the parents' rights to raise their children as they wish. When a court determines that a parent is guilty of child maltreatment, the state may proceed to terminate parental rights, but not without consideration of the parents' right to due process. For example, parents have the right to have their case heard in a court of law, where the state must present evidence to indicate that they are a danger to the child. In *Santosky v. Kramer* (1982), the Court ruled that a state must present clear and convincing evidence that a child is in danger before parental rights may be terminated. In *Stanley v. Illinois* (1972), the U.S. Supreme Court ruled that an unwed father had the right to file for custody of his children after the death of the biological mother. The Court found that the father's Fourteenth Amendment rights had been violated because he was not given the same access to a custody hearing that is afforded to other parents.

As already discussed, parents have the right to consent to medical and psychological treatments for their children, even in cases in which a young client objects. In many states, parents also have the legal right to reject treatment based on religious grounds and to use spiritually based interventions in place of traditional therapies. These laws often specify that the decision to rely on spiritual methods does not constitute child abuse or neglect. For example, a 1995 version of the Kansas statute permitted the following:

> Nothing under the definition of child endangerment shall be construed to mean a child is endangered for the sole reason the child's parent or guardian, in good faith, selects and depends upon spiritual means alone through prayer, in accordance with the tenets and practice of a recognized church or religious denomination, for the treatment or cure of disease or remedial care of such child. (NCCANI, 2000a, p. 5)

As is the case in other states, certain conditions must be met for these laws to apply, including the parents' use of practices that are consistent with the principles of a recognized religious group.

Maintenance of Client Records

Therapists must maintain organized records of their contacts with children and families. The information contained in a client's case file is there for the benefit of the client. Therapists document their work with clients for a variety of reasons. First, the case file is a source of information about the intervention techniques used in therapy and the client's response to treatment. This record is particularly valuable in cases in which there is a change of clinician when clients seek services elsewhere or therapy is terminated because of the clinician's retirement, relocation, disability, or death. The information contained in the case file also can benefit the therapist. As the American Psychological Association (1993a) noted, the case record facilitates treatment planning and evaluation because it contains information that may otherwise be forgotten during the course of therapy. Organized files in which treatment services are well documented also can be helpful to the clinician in cases involving malpractice litigation.

The American Psychological Association (1993a) described the information that should be included in a client's case file. For young clients, the record should contain identifying information about the child, parents, and others involved in treatment. The dates and nature of each contact with the client, including telephone conversations with parents and significant other adults, should also be noted in the case record. All documentation of clients' informed consent and assent to treatment should be included. The case file should also contain notes regarding the fees charged for services as well as copies of all measures completed by the child and family, assessment reports, treatment plans and summaries, and assent and consent to release information forms obtained during treatment.

Case files must be stored in a safe and secure location to ensure confidentiality of client information. Clinicians must comply with legal and agency restrictions regarding others' access to client records. They should inform family members of these limits and their implications at the outset of treatment. Therapists must also adhere to statutory guidelines regarding the retention of a client's case records. As a minimum, the

American Psychological Association (1993a) recommended that the entire file for adult clients be held for at least 3 years after termination of treatment and the file or a summary of records retained for an additional 12 years. When the client is a child, the complete case file should be kept for at least 3 years after the client reaches the age of majority.

Poynter (1998) described the therapist's clinical and record keeping responsibilities with clients who are reimbursed for the cost of treatment by managed mental health insurance companies (see Chapter 3). He described what he called "clinically integrated paperwork" (p. 20), or therapist documentation of treatment-related matters, such as intake and assessment results, treatment and aftercare plans, client satisfaction data, and all information required for authorization of treatment. He provided examples of forms that therapists can adopt, including a treatment planning chart, a client satisfaction questionnaire, and a procedures list to facilitate compliance with the requirements of each insurer. The procedures chart can be especially helpful when a therapist serves customers from various insurance companies, each of which has its own policies for documenting services.

Suicidal Behavior in Children

Contrary to popular opinion, children do exhibit suicidal ideation, threats, and attempts, some of which result in death (Milling & Martin, 1992). Experts who studied this problem have found suicidal ideation, threats, and attempts in 7 of 10 children admitted to an inpatient psychiatric unit (Pfeffer, Conte, Plutchik, & Jerrett, 1979), 1 in 3 young clients from an outpatient clinic sample (Pfeffer, Conte, Plutchik, & Jerrett, 1980), and 1 in 8 "normal" school children (Pfeffer, Zuckerman, Plutchik, & Mizruchi, 1984). Fortunately, the rate of completed suicides among U.S. children, ages 5 to 14 years, is less than 1 per 100,000 (see Pfeffer, 2000; Stillion & McDowell, 1996). But therapists who encounter suicidal children must carefully and seriously consider all client disclosures about self-destructive behavior. Failure to do so can result in the child's serious injury or death.

Negligence on the part of the therapist also can result in litigation initiated by the child's family. Clinicians have been found liable in cases in which death occurred as a result of suicide. Consider *Tabor v. Doctors Memorial Hospital* (1990) in which a young man was denied emergency room services for financial reasons after he attempted suicide. The following day, the man shot and killed himself. His parents subsequently sued, and the Louisiana Supreme Court ruled that the emergency room physician was negligent and that his decision to not hospitalize the patient contributed to the young man's death. When the suicidal client is a child, therapists must exercise special caution to prevent the child from engaging in self-destructive behavior. This typically involves breaking confidentiality to inform parents of the client's risk to self and to develop a collaborative suicide prevention plan.

When a client discloses suicidal thoughts or intentions, the clinician must assess for lethality, or the likelihood that a child's actions will result in death. Lethality would be high for a client who describes in detail how he plans to take a loaded handgun from his parents' bedroom, go into the backyard that night, place the weapon to his head, and pull the trigger. By contrast, lethality is relatively low for the child who says, "I guess I'll just run away from home and spend the night with my grandmother." Although leaving home without adult supervision is potentially dangerous, this plan is not as lethal as the first, especially if the grandparent lives next door. Children are less likely to consider the long-term consequences of their behavior, and they are relatively unskilled at determining the lethality of their actions. After all, cartoon characters jump from high buildings and are unharmed, so children might assume they can do the same without hurting themselves. Therapists must be especially careful when working with suicidal children to ensure that an impulsive act does not cause serious negative consequences.

Pfeffer et al. (1979) described five levels of suicidal behavior in children that can be of help in determining lethality. The most benign of these is no suicidal ideation, in which the child does not represent a threat to self. More serious is suicidal ideation, or the thoughts that children have about harming themselves. Therapists must listen for client comments such as, "I wish I wasn't here" or "I wish I was dead." Even more serious are a child's threats to engage in suicidal behaviors. Therapists sometimes learn about these statements from parents, who report incidents at home where children verbalize an intent to engage in a self-destructive act. An example of such a threat is the child who tells a parent that he is going to jump into a river and kill himself because no one loves him.

The next level in the Pfeffer et al. (1979) model is the mild suicidal attempt, which is potentially harmful but not sufficiently serious to be life threatening. A child who ingests two aspirins to end his life is an example of a mild suicidal attempt. More dangerous is the serious attempt that involves self-destructive behaviors which could result in physical impairment or death. A child who stands by a busy highway and then runs in front of an oncoming car may suffer life-threatening injuries that require medical attention. We can add a sixth level to the five-stage model proposed by Pfeffer et al. The most dangerous form of suicidal behavior is the completed suicide, in which a child's actions result in death. Although clinicians are obviously unable to treat these children, they must remember that the completed suicide represents the ultimate level of the self-destructive behaviors they are trying to prevent. Therapists can use the Pfeffer et al. model to assess lethality, with suicidal attempts viewed as more serious than threats, which are of more concern than ideation only. But therapists must seriously consider all incidents of suicidal behavior in children. Because the research in this area is limited in scope, quantity, and methodological rigor (Milling & Martin, 1992), it is currently impossible to predict when and under what conditions a child's thoughts of suicide might become a threat, an attempt, or death.

Therapists must be competent to handle suicidal behaviors before they arise. Clinicians must understand the dynamics of childhood suicide, legal and ethical obligations, techniques for assessing harm, and client management procedures. Pfeffer (1986), Milling and Carey (1994), and Milling and Martin (1992) described principles and guidelines that therapists should follow when assessing suicidal behavior in young clients (Table 2-2). Because suicidal behavior in children is more common than previously believed, clinicians must include this area as part of their initial assessment of the client. Milling and Martin (1992) recommended that therapists introduce the topic by asking, "Have you ever thought about hurting yourself or killing yourself? Have you ever tried to do it?" (p. 334). Interview questions can be coupled with child-report inventories that provide a global assessment of suicidal behavior (see the Children's Depression Inventory in Chapter 4).

When a child discloses suicidal behavior, the clinician must seek answers to a variety of questions. For example, how long has the client been considering suicide? Has she attempted to harm herself in the past? How serious were these attempts? Does the child currently have a plan for suicide? How detailed is the plan? How depressed, impulsive, or hopeless is the client? Does he have access to the instruments or location needed to harm himself? What does he hope will happen as a result of his suicide? With younger

Table 2–2
Principles for Interviewing a Suicidal Child

1. The therapist must have the knowledge and training required to handle suicidal behaviors in children.
2. The clinician must be aware of his or her own conscious and unconscious feelings about suicide and death. To achieve an awareness of unconscious feelings, the therapist should consult with a colleague or in some cases, seek therapy.
3. The clinician should assess for suicidal behavior in all children and not limit his or her attention to clients who volunteer this information.
4. All suicidal behavior, regardless of lethality level, must be taken seriously.
5. The therapist must use developmentally appropriate language when interviewing the child.
6. The clinician must assess the child's suicidal thoughts and fantasies, knowledge of death concepts and the outcomes of suicide, prior attempts and current plan, potential for immediate action, and motivations for engaging in suicidal behaviors.
7. The therapist must identify and evaluate protective factors in the child's family, school, and community.
8. The clinician must obtain a commitment from the child to not engage in self-destructive behavior between the interview and the next scheduled appointment with the client. With some clients, this involves the use of a no-suicide agreement.
9. The therapist must inform parents or caregivers of the child's suicidal behavior and involve them in treatment to identify causal factors and ensure proper supervision of the child outside of the therapy hour. In cases in which the family is unwilling or unable to protect the child, the therapist must consider the use of alternative services, including hospitalization.
10. The therapist primarily uses a developmentally appropriate verbal approach to interviewing to highlight the seriousness of suicidal behavior and to collect the details needed to assess lethality.

Adapted from Milling and Carey (1994, pp. 398–399), Milling and Martin (1992, p. 334), and Pfeffer (1986, pp. 173–178).

children and those who have language impairments, therapists sometimes use play techniques to assess for suicidal behavior. Readers are encouraged to consult Pfeffer (1986) for a discussion of this approach and the author's observations that suicidal children are more likely than their nonsuicidal peers to persist in reckless, destructive, or dangerous behaviors and play related to themes of loss and separation.

After lethality has been determined, the therapist moves from the assessment stage to intervention. Milling and Carey (1994) highlighted two important concerns for case management: ensuring the child's safety and changing the factors that precipitated the suicidal behavior. When lethality is high, hospitalization is usually required to protect the child from self-destructive acts. If lethality is low, outpatient treatment combined with careful monitoring from parents is often appropriate. In these cases, therapy sessions are scheduled more frequently than once a week. Parents must agree to secure or remove all items, such as guns, knives, and poisons, that a child could use to enact a suicidal plan. If the parents are unwilling or unable to provide adequate supervision, the clinician must consider hospitalization or placement in a supervised setting, even when lethality is moderate or relatively low.

Two important steps that link assessment to intervention are parent notification and obtaining a commitment from the child to not engage in self-destructive behavior. Whenever children report suicidal behavior, therapists must notify the parents or caregivers. This should be done in a careful and supportive manner by reminding the child of the limits to confidentiality discussed at the outset of treatment and explaining that the parents are being notified to ensure the child's safety. The therapist might say, "I'm concerned about you, and I don't want anything bad to happen to you. I'm going to ask your parents to join us so we can talk about what you have said. How do you feel about that?" The answer to this question can be very helpful in preparing the parent notification plan. Some children will respond, "Oh, they already know. I've told them before, and they didn't care." In these situations, the therapist must be ready to respond to the parents' anger or apathy before disclosing the child's suicidal behavior. Some clients will trust the clinician and willingly agree to notification, but others will strongly resist breaking confidentiality because they fear the parents' reaction. Regardless of the child's response, the therapist must inform the parents and elicit their support to protect the child.

Clinicians must also obtain the child's commitment to not engage in self-destructive acts. Sometimes this is done by having the client sign a no-suicide agreement. This approach is commonly used with adults, but relatively little is known about its use with children. Davidson and his colleagues investigated this sensitive topic when they studied developmentally based no-suicide agreements with children. Davidson, Wagner, and Range (1995) found that therapists believed this technique was more appropriate for adolescents and adults than for children between the ages of 6 and 11 years. Davidson and Range (2000) asked psychologists to rate the appropriateness and effectiveness of agreements specifically developed for children, ages 6, 9, and 12 years. Respondents believed these agreements would be more appropriate and effective with 9- and 12-year-old children than with 6-year-old clients, even when the content and reading level of the agreement had been adjusted to the child's grade level.

The no-suicide agreement is not a panacea for self-destructive behaviors in children. As you might expect, it is very difficult to systematically research this technique with children who are exhibiting these behaviors. For this reason, Goldman and Beardslee (1999) cited two reservations that therapists should have when using no-suicide agreements. First, the focus of an agreement is usually the child's behavior, not the environmental factors that precipitated these actions. To prevent childhood suicides, clinicians must ensure that the family is capable of providing guidance and support for the child. Goldman and Beardslee also warned that suicidal clients may have difficulty establishing a trusting relationship with a therapist. The child may appear committed to living while in session but engage in self-injurious behaviors soon thereafter. Consequently, the therapeutic relationship must be considered a necessary but not sufficient condition for preventing suicidal behavior.

Still, therapists must obtain a commitment from the suicidal child to not behave in a self-destructive manner. Despite their limitations, no-suicide agreements are part of a comprehensive approach to assessment and intervention for suicidal children (Miller, 1999). As Goldman and Beardslee (1999) stated, therapists can use this technique to establish specific boundaries and concrete expectations for clients and their families. When a child is unwilling to enter into a no-harm agreement, the clinician must consider hospitalization to ensure the child's safety. No-suicide agreements provide a focus for an ongoing assessment of the client's suicidal behaviors.

They also specify the therapist's commitments, which often include 24-hour availability in case of emergency during the acute stage of treatment. As lethality declines, agreements can be used in conjunction with interventions designed to remediate personal, familial, and other factors related to the client's suicidal behaviors.

During follow-up sessions with these children, therapists must not overlook the client's potential for suicide. The clinician should reassess lethality each session, especially with children who have attempted to kill themselves. According to Milling and Carey (1994), there are numerous causes for suicidal behavior in children and at least as many approaches to intervention. If the child is depressed, the therapist should consider individual therapy and referral for psychopharmacotherapy (see Chapter 15). When parent–child problems are identified, the clinician should consider family therapy or parent training. Therapists usually discover that more than one causal factor is involved. In these cases, the clinician must develop an integrated treatment designed to address these causes. For a depressed and suicidal 12-year-old child who lives in a conflicted family environment, treatment might include psychopharmacotherapy and regular individual sessions for the child, couples therapy with the parents, and family sessions to address systemic issues. The therapist might also work with the child's school counselor and teachers to effect a more positive learning environment. By identifying and reinforcing the child's "reasons for staying alive" (Linehan, Goodstein, Neilsen, & Chiles, 1983, p. 276), the clinician can help the child replace suicidal acts with more positive, growth-oriented behaviors.

It is worth noting that children are not the only family members who engage in self-destructive behaviors. Therapists must be prepared to handle suicidal ideation, threats, and attempts in parents. Clinicians can obtain a global assessment of suicidality and depressive symptoms by administering the Beck Depression Inventory (Beck & Steer, 1987) to parents at the outset of treatment. When parents disclose suicidal behaviors, the therapist must assess for lethality, use a no-suicide contract, and intervene in an appropriate manner to ensure the parent's health and safety.

Children's Testimony in Court

Stein (1998) stated that criminal prosecution of adults who abuse children is a difficult and complex process. The conviction of an accused perpetrator requires sufficient evidence to convince a judge or jury that a crime was committed. Children are sometimes called to testify in court, especially in cases involving sexual abuse in which the perpetrator and the young survivor are the only witnesses to the crime. A district attorney's decision to prosecute is mainly based on the evidence that is available. As Wagner (1987a) stated, inadequate evidence hampers the prosecution's efforts to convict a perpetrator and has the potential for traumatizing the child a second time through an unnecessary court appearance.

Two important considerations for the child as witness are competency and the procedures used to present a child's evidence in court. Kramer (1994) identified criteria commonly used to determine whether a child is competent to testify. The young witness must be sufficiently intelligent to provide meaningful testimony, capable of distinguishing truth from falsity, and able to understand the need to testify truthfully. Kramer added that intelligence is usually determined based on the child's ability to observe, remember, and describe the events at issue in the case. Stein (1998) observed that states generally assume that children are competent to testify, unless determined otherwise. Age alone is not a criterion for determining competency. In fact, children as young as age 4 years have been allowed to give testimony (e.g., *State v. Brotherton*, 1986; *Reyna v. State*, 1990).

Before a young witness testifies, the court must determine whether the child understands the difference between the truth and a lie. Defendants have challenged guilty verdicts based on evidence provided by children. In the case of *Chambers v. State* (1982), an adult male friend of the family was convicted of forcing a 6-year-old girl to perform fellatio. The perpetrator appealed, claiming that the child should not have been allowed to testify. The Supreme Court of Arkansas affirmed the lower court's decision and permitted the girl's testimony, in part because "the victim stated that she had learned about telling the truth from Bible stories read to her, and that if she told a lie she would be put in jail." (Opinion section)

In another case involving the sexual assault of a 6-year-old girl, the perpetrator appealed his conviction. Although the child had given examples in court to support her competency, her abuser challenged a statement she made regarding the Easter Bunny. In their affirmation of the lower court decision, the Supreme Court of New Hampshire in *State v. St. John* (1980) wrote as follows:

> The defendant makes much of the fact that the victim, when asked about Easter, said that was the time when the Easter Bunny comes and brings her eggs. He claims that this testimony shows unreliability as to recollection. That there might not be an Easter Bunny, however, does not in any way reflect on the ability of the victim, who undoubtedly had been told that the Easter Bunny leaves eggs, to recall events. Rather, it demonstrates her ability to recall events and to associate them with specific holidays. (Opinion section)

The New Hampshire courts considered the child's developmental level and treated her belief in the Easter Bunny as the recollection of significant events rather than evidence of her inability to distinguish fact from fantasy.

Sometimes there is a rather lengthy delay between the occurence of a crime and a child's appearance in court. Therefore, children's memory and susceptibility to suggestion is a significant developmental issue (see Contemporary Issues Box 2-2). In the 1980s and 1990s, researchers devoted more attention to the accuracy of children's memory and its relationship to court testimony. Interest in this developmental topic grew, in part, because of well-publicized reports of children's accounts of maltreatment in settings such as the McMartin Preschool in Los Angeles (Garven, Wood, Malpass, & Shaw, 1998).

Wolfe, Sas, and Wilson (1987) emphasized the importance of preparing children for their court appearances. Preparation does not include telling children what they are to say. Rather, it serves as an introduction to the setting and procedures of the courtroom. Therapists can rely on victim advocacy experts for assistance in preparing and supporting child witnesses. These services are available in many communities, where they often receive funding through the federal Victims of Crime Act. Children are frequently given a tour of the courtroom in advance of the trial, and they are introduced to the representative from the district attorney's office who will be responsible for examining them. Wolfe et al. recommended that clinicians work with children and their families to prepare them for the anxiety that often arises before and during the trial. The authors suggested that therapists teach clients relaxation techniques that can be used to counter their fears and anxiety (see Chapter 11).

Therapists must also advocate for change in the court procedures used with young witnesses (Wolfe et al., 1987). A number of states have adopted laws to provide additional protections for children. These include speedy disposition of cases in which child witnesses are involved, the right to have the courtroom closed during a child's testimony, and the opportunity to be accompanied by a trustworthy adult during the proceedings. Approximately half of U.S. states have adopted statutes mandating speedy disposition. The 1998 California statute allowed for the following:

> Criminal actions in which a minor is a victim or a material witness shall be given precedence over all other criminal actions on the trial calendar. The court shall grant continuances only after a hearing and determination of the necessity of the continuance. If a continuance is granted, the court must state the basis for its determination of good cause on the record. In any event, the trial shall commence within 30 days after arraignment unless a continuance is granted. (NCCANI, 2000b, p. 22)

As discussed earlier, the Sixth Amendment guarantees a defendant the right to a speedy trial. The accused has the right to request a continuance and, when granted, obtain a delay in the court's hearing of the case. Continuances pose special problems when child witnesses are involved. For example, repeated delays in child abuse cases can be emotionally taxing for young survivors, who face the uncertainties of their court appearance and the outcome of the case.

States such as California, Illinois, and Georgia have adopted laws to permit the use of closed hearings when young witnesses testify. Illinois adopted the following in 1998:

> In a prosecution for certain sexual crimes, where the alleged victim of the offense is a minor under 18 years of age, the court may exclude from the proceedings, while the victim is testifying, all persons, who, in the court's opinion, do not have a direct interest in the case, except the media. (NCCANI, 2000b, p. 4)

In 1995, Delaware allowed that "a 'friend' or other person in whom the child trusts" accompany the witness and advise the judge regarding the child's ability to comprehend the court proceedings, including the questions being asked (NCCANI, 2000b, p. 4).

A number of states, including Alabama, New Hampshire, and New York, have taken into consideration the developmental level of the child witness and allowed the use of anatomically detailed dolls. These dolls contain age-appropriate external body parts and are available in child and adult models for

Contemporary Issues Box 2–2

The Child Witness: The Interviewer's Role in Suggestibility

Increasing numbers of children have been asked to provide court testimony. Bruck and Ceci (1999) attributed this change to the increase in child sexual abuse cases and the revision of legal standards pertaining to children's testimony. Questions about the accuracy of testimony given by child witnesses have prompted a growing body of research in the area of suggestibility, which Ceci and Bruck (1993) defined as "the degree to which children's encoding, storage, retrieval, and reporting of events can be influenced by a range of social and psychological factors" (p. 404). These influences include but are not limited to the types of questions used to interview children, event-related information that is given to them either directly or indirectly, and any incentives or rewards that are offered to children to respond in a particular manner.

Older children and adults have been found to be less suggestible than preschoolers, but even adults' descriptions of life events are not always accurate (Bruck & Ceci, 1999). Still, age should not be the sole criterion for determining whether a witness is able to provide accurate testimony in court. As Bruck and Ceci (1999) stated, "It is clear that children—even preschoolers—are capable of accurately recalling much that is forensically relevant" (p. 436). Although the amount of detail that children disclose improves with age (Peterson & Bell, 1996), the accuracy of their statements has been found to be related to the format and methods used by clinicians and forensic interviewers. Poole and White (1991), for example, reported that when open questions were repeatedly asked to adults and 4-, 6-, and 8-year-old children, there was no age-related difference in the content of respondents' answers. When closed questions of a specific nature were repeated, 4-year-old children answered in a more inconsistent manner and were likely to respond "in ways that raise further concern about the usefulness of specific memory probes" (p. 983). It is worth noting that adults in the Poole and White study disclosed significantly more information, both accurate and inaccurate, but the rate of inaccurate answers was relatively low and was similar for children (6.5%) and adults (5.5%).

Interview style has also been found to have an important influence on the accuracy of children's description of life events. Lepore and Sesco (1994) studied the effects of what they called "neutral" and "incriminating" interview methods with children, ages 4 to 6 years, who had been exposed to a brief encounter between two adults. The neutral approach involved the use of open questions and other facilitative techniques but did not include interpretations of the child's statements about the event. In the incriminating condition, the interviewer followed open questions with interpretations and misleading information. When interviewed later using closed questions, children in the second group were more likely to give an inaccurate description of the adults' encounter. Consistent with the results of Poole and White (1991), Lepore and Sesco found no significant deterioration in respondents' accuracy during free recall. The results of these studies suggest that interviewers must be cautious in their use of closed and specific questions that have the potential to increase inaccuracy in children's report of events.

Clinicians have adopted a number of techniques to adjust traditional interview methods to the child's developmental level. One technique has been the use of drawings, which Bruck, Melnyk, and Ceci (2000) studied with preschoolers, ages 3 to 6 years. Two weeks after they participated in a brief magic show, children were interviewed at approximately 2-week intervals on three different occasions. During the first and second interviews, participants were asked to describe the magic show. Then they were presented with true and false reminders of the performance. Children were then asked to draw pictures or answer questions about these reminders. During the final interview, participants were asked to describe the magic show through free recall and in response to specific closed questions. Results revealed that drawing facilitated preschoolers' report of true reminders. Unfortunately, the children were also more likely to incorporate false reminders into their description of the magic show. Children's drawings, similar to any other interview technique, are susceptible to misinformation provided by others, so therapists must use this method with care, es-

Contemporary Issues Box 2–2 *(cont.)*

pecially when they have prior information about an event and are at risk for leading the child's self-report.

The interviewer's personal opinion and a priori conclusions about an event have been found to compromise the accuracy of children's description of life events (Bruck & Ceci, 1999). When clinicians have information obtained from other sources, they must not allow this knowledge to dictate the direction of the interview. For example, a therapist who has been led to believe that a child was sexually abused is at risk for asking questions that will confirm this "fact" rather than exploring alternative explanations. The legal implications of interviewer bias can be found in the McMartin Preschool case in California. Garven, Wood, Malpass, and Shaw (1998) described different methods that were used with these children. One technique is what Garven et al. (1998, p. 348) labeled the "suggestive question" in which interviewers introduce new information that the child has not discussed previously. This would include the interviewer asking, "Did he touch your private parts?" when a child never alledged this act. Other inappropriate techniques include reinforcing certain statements given by children, telling them about events or information described by others, and asking clients to imagine or pretend that certain events happened.

Garven et al. (1998) interviewed preschoolers, ages 3 to 6 years, 1 week after a graduate student named Manny Morales told the story of *The Hunchback of Notre Dame* to the children during story time at their day care center. A week later, the children were assigned to one of two interview groups. Suggestive questions (e.g., "Did Manny tear the book while he was reading it?") (p. 351) were used in both conditions. However, children in one group also received information reportedly received from other sources (e.g., "Well, I already talked to the big kids and they said that Manny did some bad things") (p. 351) and were praised for their agreement with these probes. Participants who received suggestive questions and were praised for their agreement with information supposedly obtained from other children made significantly more false allegations than did children given suggestive questions only. The authors concluded that even brief periods of praise and misinformation "can have a strong, immediate impact on children's accuracy" (p. 354).

Garven et al. (1998) reported equivocal findings for children's age, but it is tempting to hypothesize that older children would be less likely to succumb to the interview techniques used in the study. Garven, Wood, and Malpass (2000) used the story time procedure with children, ages 5 to 7 years, and found that praise for inaccurate answers—but not information obtained from other witnesses—increased the rate of false allegations. In this study, Garven et al. (2000) examined children's agreement with closed questions regarding extraordinary allegations similar to those reported by some children at the McMartin Preschool (e.g., being kidnapped from their school). Again, praise for inaccurate responses, not information from others, resulted in a significantly higher rate of agreement to fantastic allegations. Children who were initially praised for agreeing with closed questions about fantastic events were more likely to report these events than were children who did not receive reinforcement.

The Garven et al. (1998, 2000) findings for the closed-question format raise additional concerns about the use of these questions in forensic interviews with children. Therapists must be trained to use procedures that facilitate accurate responses from child witnesses. Leading or misleading clients and reinforcing them to respond in a manner consistent with the interviewer's a priori decision about the case are clearly inappropriate. Although nonverbal techniques, including drawings, are developmentally appropriate for children, clinicians must remember that any method is prone to elicit inaccurate information when used improperly. Many preschoolers and elementary school children appear able to correctly describe events, although they might differ in the amount of detail they provide. Responsibility for the accuracy of a child's testimony is shared by the interviewer and interviewee, so clinicians must use empirically tested methods with children to avoid introducing or reinforcing information that provides the foundation for false allegations.

each sex. Different manufacturers produce dolls of varying quality. To facilitate clear communication between the child and therapist, Boat and Everson (1993) recommended that clinicians purchase dolls that contain openings for the mouth, vagina, and anus. The adult models should contain pubic hair, and all dolls must have separate digits to represent fingers rather than a single paw for the hand. Therapists who use anatomically detailed dolls must be properly trained in the procedures and limitations of these interview tools. They should use the dolls in conjunction with a standard interview protocol, such as the step-wise procedure described by Yuille, Hunter, Joffe, and Zaparniuk (1993) (Table 2-3). When dolls are properly used, judges have allowed the child survivor's account of the abuse to be used as evidence in court.

In *Reyna v. State* (1990), a man found guilty of sexually assaulting two sisters, ages 4 and 8 years, appealed his conviction, in part because the girls were allowed to use anatomically detailed dolls during their testimony. A Texas court of appeals upheld the lower court ruling when it found that the dolls were used:

> as a tool to aid the jury with the witness' testimony, in the same manner as a map, sketch, or diagram would be used. Moreover, the record reflects that the dolls were used in a neutral, non-suggestive manner; each child used the dolls to illustrate the areas of the body relevant to her testimony. (Opinion section)

The court recognized that anatomically detailed dolls can be used for visual clarification of a child's verbal testimony.

California, Iowa, and North Dakota considered the special needs of children when they decided to limit the length of time that young witnesses are permitted to testify in court (NCCANI , 2000b). A version of the Iowa statute reads as follows:

> A court *may*, upon its own motion or upon the motion of a party, order the court testimony of a child to be limited in duration in accordance with the developmental maturity of the child. The court *may* consider or hear expert testimony in order to determine the appropriate limitation on the duration of a child's testimony. However, the court *shall*, upon motion, limit the duration of a child's uninterrupted testimony to one hour, at which time the court *shall* allow the child to rest before continuing to testify. (NCCANI, 2000b, p. 16)

Table 2–3
A Step-Wise Approach to Interviewing Sexually Abused Children

1. Develop rapport with the child.
2. Ask the child to describe two specific and memorable events from the past that are unrelated to the abuse.
3. Assess the child's ability to distinguish truth from falsity and get his or her agreement to tell the truth during the interview.
4. Carefully introduce the topic of abuse, beginning with open-ended questions or drawings.
5. Allow the child to give a free narrative of the abuse by keeping questions to a minimum and avoiding interruptions or corrective statements.
6. Ask general questions based on information contained in the child's narrative.
7. If necessary, ask specific questions to clarify or expand on certain aspects of the narrative.
8. If necessary, use interview tools (e.g., drawings or dolls) in a step-wise manner that begins with the child's disclosure of events.
9. Thank the child for participating in the interview and then conclude the session.

Adapted from "Interviewing Children in Sexual Abuse Cases," by J. C. Yuille, R. Hunter, R. Joffe, and J. Zaparniuk, 1993, p. 99 and pp. 104–110. In G. S. Goodman & B. L. Bottoms (Eds.), *Child victims, child witnesses: Understanding and improving testimony* (pp. 95–115). New York: Guilford. Copyright 1993 by Guilford Press.

More than 10 states have adopted legislation to limit the number of interviews that may be conducted with child survivors of abuse and neglect. By imposing these restrictions, the states have given official support to the multidisciplinary team approach to the management of these cases. A 1997 version of the Hawaii law specifies that "one purpose of the children's advocacy program within the judiciary is to reduce to the absolute minimum the number of interviews of child sex abuse victims so as to minimize revictimization of the child" (NCCANI, 2000b, p. 18). To avoid multiple interviews with abuse survivors, some treatment teams have used specially trained investigators whose interviews with the children are videotaped and made available to other team members.

Many states have passed laws that permit the use of videotaped testimony in court with children in cases of maltreatment. To avoid traumatizing the witness through direct contact with the alleged perpetrator in court, states have developed procedures that allow either a videotape of the child's testimony to be shown in the court or the simultaneous transmission of testimony obtained in a different setting via closed-circuit television. State laws on this matter differ in the age of child covered by the law. Although some states, such as Illinois and Iowa, have set the maximum age at 17 years, others have limited the use of closed-circuit testimony to children under the age of 10 years (e.g., Washington) or 11 years (e.g., Delaware, Georgia) (NCCANI, 2000c).

Criteria for the admissibility of this testimony also varies from state to state, with some attending to the quality of the evidence and others considering the child's reaction to an appearance in court. In a recent statute, Alaska allowed the use of closed-circuit television when "the testimony by the child under normal court procedures would result in the child's inability to effectively communicate" (NCCANI, 2000c, p. 4). Mississippi has permitted the use of this method after "a finding based on expert testimony that there is a substantial likelihood that the child will suffer traumatic emotional or mental distress if compelled to testify in open court" (NCCANI, 2000c, p. 17).

Videotaped and closed-circuit television testimony have been challenged in court, usually because they are thought to violate a defendant's Sixth Amendment right to confront his or her accusers. In *Maryland v. Craig* (1990), the U.S. Supreme Court upheld closed-circuit television coverage of a child's testimony in cases in which direct contact with the defendant would be emotionally stressful for the child. In this case, the child witness was examined and cross-examined in a separate room while the testimony was shown in the courtroom. Because the defendant was able to maintain electronic communication with counsel, the Court ruled that the method used in this case was not in violation of the Sixth Amendment. When these rights are not protected, a conviction based on videotaped testimony may be overturned on appeal. Such was the outcome in *Lowery v. Collins* (1993) in which a U.S. Court of Appeals overturned the state conviction of a Texas man found guilty of sexually assaulting his stepson. In the original case, the state included the 6-year-old boy's videotaped description of the abuse. The interview with the child had been conducted by a social worker and did not include questioning by the defendant's attorney. The appeals court ruled that this use of videotaped testimony violated the stepfather's Sixth Amendment right to confront his accuser.

Child Custody Evaluations

Divorce and remarriage have become common events in the lives of many U.S. families. Although parents often divorce because of a conflicted spousal relationship, most seem to eventually agree on custody and visitation arrangements for their children. Approximately 90% of divorcing couples settle their differences out of court, and the majority of parents who seek judicial intervention for child custody disputes do not present testimony from a mental health professional (Melton, Petrila, Poythress, & Slobogin, 1997). When mental health professionals are involved, they conduct evaluations of children and parents, provide mediation services, and sometimes recommend custody and visitation arrangements they believe are in the child's best interests.

Therapists who want to conduct custody evaluations must become competent to provide this very specialized service (American Psychological Association, 1994a). Unfortunately, many clinicians have not obtained the requisite training and have found themselves unprepared for the complex legal and psychological challenges they encounter. Koocher and Keith-Spiegel (1998) offered the following caution for clinicians to consider before prematurely expanding their practice to include child custody evaluations.

> It is very difficult to predict what will happen as a result of custody decisions. Unfortunately, however, it can be reliably predicted that a contested custody situation will have an adverse effect on the children. . . . They are subjected to the whims of the legal system and too often are cast as pawns in the struggle between sets of angry combatants for custody. Into this void rides (or are tossed) too many unwary would-be psychological Solomons ready to share their wisdom with the courts to resolve these agonizing cases. (p. 368)

The courtroom is very different from the therapy room. A major distinction is the adversarial quality of the courtroom. Child custody evaluations are difficult because parents do not always accept the clinician's opinion and a judge's subsequent decision regarding the placement of a child. When done properly, the evaluation can facilitate the handling of these cases. When performed incorrectly, the evaluation can result in actions that are of little benefit to the child.

As a point of beginning for their entry into child custody litigation, clinicians must possess the knowledge and supervised experience required to conduct a psychological assessment and diagnosis; individual and family approaches to treatment; and the clinical application of research on child, adolescent, and family development. Therapists must then acquire additional preparation in child custody litigation by attending appropriate classes and workshops. Clinicians must have a thorough understanding of the differences between traditional assessment and therapeutic services and the practice of forensic psychology. The American Psychology-Law Society of the American Psychological Association developed its *Specialty Guidelines for Forensic Psychologists* (Committee on Ethical Guidelines for Forensic Psychologists, 1991) to assist clinicians, especially those who regularly provide psycholegal services within the judicial system.

The American Psychological Association (1994a) addressed issues specific to the custody evaluation in its *Guidelines for Child Custody Evaluations in Divorce Proceedings* (Appendix D). The clinician must ensure that all participants understand the nature and purpose of the evaluation. This includes an explanation of all limits to confidentiality, including the purpose and recipients of the evaluation report. The case file must contain documentation of informed consent and assent for participants as well as copies of all release of information forms required to disclose information to others involved with the case. To obtain a comprehensive view of a family's situation, the clinician should involve both parents in the evaluation process. When this is not possible, the evaluator must avoid conclusions about the psychological adjustment and child-rearing capabilities of the nonparticipating parent. Clinicians must avoid dual relationships and not conduct custody evaluations with families they have treated previously. Likewise, they should not provide therapy to family members after an evaluation.

Therapists must understand the legal aspects involved in the awarding of child custody in their jurisdiction of practice. As you might expect, the criteria that apply in these cases vary from state to state. For example, West Virginia courts usually award custody to the parent who has served as primary caretaker for the child (Pagliocca et al., 1995). This standard was adopted from *Garska v. McCoy* (1981), in which specific criteria were given to identify the primary caretaker. The list included items such as the parent who is primarily responsible for bathing the child, preparing meals, cleaning clothes, and transporting the child to after-school activities. Pagliocca et al. acknowledged that some individuals will criticize the West Virginia standard because it seems to favor mothers, who typically assume many of these responsibilities. But the authors argued that parenting is more than just providing financial support for a child. It includes daily involvement with children, fulfilling basic needs and fostering their development.

When a therapist is contacted to schedule an appointment for a child custody evaluation, it is relatively easy for the clinician to refer elsewhere if he or she is not competent to provide this service. When this request arises during the course of treatment with a family, the unwary Solomon described by Koocher and Keith-Spiegel (1998) can have a more difficult time taking the proper action and referring the family to a professional who has the requisite training and experience. Although difficult, referral in these situations is the correct decision that can eliminate unnecessary turmoil for the child, parents, and therapist.

ETHICAL AND LEGAL ISSUES FOR GROUP TECHNIQUES

Clinicians are responsible for ensuring the safety of children in group therapy (Vernon, 1999). In their role as the adults in loco parentis, therapists must protect clients from physical and psychological harm. This means establishing group rules to prohibit fighting and verbal abuse among members. It also means setting limits for risky behaviors, such as throwing play materials and jumping from tables or other furniture. Therapists must address these threats before treatment begins, when they are planning the group's goals and procedures. Groups will not be therapeutic for children who experience injury, physical impairment, or psychological stress. Clinicians can guard against these problems by establishing and implementing appropriate limits on children's behavior (see Chapter 5).

Confidentiality represents a unique concern in group therapy. Unlike individual treatment in which the clinician assumes responsibility for maintaining confidentiality, group interventions involve other children who may or may not comply with this cornerstone of therapy. Clinicians must address this ethical consideration with children during the very first meeting of the group. For many young clients, this discussion is educational because they do not understand the purpose, format, benefits, and limitations of group therapy. If clients are to discuss thoughts and feelings that are personally meaningful, they must have some assurance that their fellow members will not share this information with others outside of the group. Clinicians can introduce this topic using a statement similar to the following:

> Whatever is said in group must stay in group. We must not tell other people what anyone else

says in our meetings. I may talk with someone else only if you tell us that someone has abused you, that you plan to hurt yourself or another person, or a judge tells me that I must talk about our sessions.

The therapist should add that parents are entitled to a general description of what occurs in therapy but are given specific information only when the child gives the clinician reason to suspect abuse or neglect or when the client indicates a desire to harm self or others. Peled and Davis (1995) recommended that children be told they are allowed to talk with their parents about what they disclose in group therapy but may not share comments made by other members. If the group is conducted in an educational setting, the therapist must understand school policies that apply to treatment confidentiality (Corey & Corey, 2002).

The Association for Specialists in Group Work, a division of the American Counseling Association, developed practice guidelines for therapists to follow when conducting groups (Rapin & Keel, 1998). An issue that all clinicians must consider is the proper selection of children for group therapy. Clinicians should meet individually with each candidate and his or her parents to obtain consent and assent to treatment and to determine whether the child can benefit from individual treatment, group therapy, or both. Clients in need of individual services should be monitored to determine if group therapy is warranted at a later time. When a client is deemed appropriate for group treatment, the therapist must select an experience that is consistent with the child's presenting problem. Whereas shy and withdrawn children may benefit from friendship groups, students who mistreat their peers are candidates for social skills training groups. Clinicians must consider the client's age and gender when dealing with certain problems. For example, a group for child survivors of sexual assault is likely to have either girls or boys, but not both, who are similar in age and developmental level to facilitate discussion of abuse-related thoughts and feelings.

A PROCESS MODEL FOR ETHICAL DECISION MAKING

On paper, ethical principles and standards seem to be a straightforward guide for action. But applying a professional code of ethics in real clinical situations can be a complex and perplexing matter. Simply knowing the information contained in an ethics code is inadequate preparation for the dilemmas that therapists encounter in their work with children and families. Clinicians also need a method for applying that code in treatment. Canter, Bennett, Jones, and Nagy (1994) described a seven-step process that can be used to handle ethical concerns with clients (Table 2-4). Steps 1 through 4 in this model can be considered a preparation stage for ethical decision making. Clinicians must know their code of ethics as well as current state and federal statutes and regulations related to the delivery of mental health services. Therapists who endorse a multidisciplinary approach to intervention must also know the ethics codes of other professionals who work with children. When clinicians understand each other's ethical perspective, they are more likely to avoid conflicts that might impede the effective delivery of services.

Therapists must also comply with the policies and procedures of the agency or institution where they are employed. This includes specific standards for maintaining client records and documenting the release of information. Clinicians must also participate in continuing education activities on ethical matters by attending workshops or classes and reading ethics articles in professional journals. As Canter et al. (1994) stated:

> In these days of rapidly expanding databases, innovative services, new health care delivery systems, new research interests, novel education and training experiences, ubiquitous lawyers, litigious consumers,

Table 2–4
A Process Model for Ethical Decision Making

1. Know the code of ethics for your profession.
2. Understand the current federal and state laws that apply to psychological interventions with children and families.
3. Know and understand the policies and procedures of your place of employment.
4. Participate in continuing education activities to become better informed about ethics and ethical practice.
5. Anticipate and identify potential ethical conflicts.
6. Use a systematic approach to analyzing ethical dilemmas when they arise.
7. Seek professional consultation if you have difficulty selecting the ethical response to a dilemma.

Adapted from *Ethics for psychologists: A commentary on the APA Ethics Code* (pp. 3–7), by M. B. Canter, B. E. Bennett, S. E. Jones, and T. F. Nagy, 1994, Washington, DC: American Psychological Association. Copyright 1994 by American Psychological Association.

> and ever changing ethical rules, there is much opportunity to lose sight of the rules and the subtleties of ethics unless one persists with ongoing efforts at continuing education. (p. 4)

The last three steps recommended by Canter et al. (1994) can be thought of as the implementation stage of ethical decision making. Clinicians must consider whether the problems they encounter are caused by a lack of competence. A therapist with no training in biofeedback who is asked to provide this service to a child must refer elsewhere rather than offer this treatment. Clinicians need to anticipate the consequences of their actions by asking themselves, "What could happen next?" (Canter et al., 1994, p. 6). By scrutinizing treatment decisions, therapists can avoid the negative outcomes that result from unethical behavior.

Canter et al. (1994) stated that clinicians must establish a method for analyzing the difficult choices that arise in therapy. Some dilemmas, such as a child's disclosure of suicidal ideation, are clear-cut events that require immediate action. Therapists must enter these situations with a method for collecting and evaluating relevant information, choosing a course of action, and responding in an ethical manner. Koocher and Keith-Spiegel (1998) recommended that clinicians avoid impulsive reactions to therapeutic dilemmas by carefully analyzing each event to determine which, if any, ethical principles and standards are relevant. When the situation is ambiguous and does not require immediate action, the therapist may need to research the matter outside of session, consider all issues in an objective manner, and then respond. As a general rule, ethical decision making requires that clinicians identify possible actions and their consequences, eliminate less appropriate choices, and then act in a way that is consistent with their code of ethics and the law. Remley and Herlihy (2001) added that therapists must consider their emotional reaction to ethical dilemmas and how these feelings affect the analysis of relevant information and the implementation and evaluation of the response.

Some ethical dilemmas are so complex that they represent a challenge for even veteran therapists. In these cases, the word to remember is *consult*. When a clinician has followed the outlined steps but is still unsure of the most appropriate response, Canter et al. (1994) recommended that the therapist review the facts of the case with an experienced colleague. The authors also recommended that therapists contact their professional associations' ethics committee or a university professor who specializes in ethical issues. Of course, any discussion of case material with an external expert must be done in a manner that protects the identity of the child and family in treatment.

DEVELOPMENTAL CONSIDERATIONS

In their work with clients, therapists discriminate between appropriate and inappropriate behaviors by using legal statutes and ethics codes such as those described in this chapter. We assume that as adults, they have reached the level of moral development required to make professional decisions. To understand how children acquire the ability to distinguish right from wrong, we must consider a complex interaction of cognitions, emotions, and behaviors that occurs in the context of the child's cultural surround. This section briefly reviews three models of moral development that are relevant to child therapies: Lawrence Kohlberg's cognitive model, Nancy Eisenberg's work on prosocial behavior, and Lawrence Enright's model of forgiveness.

Table 2-5 contains a summary of Kohlberg's (1976) cognitive-developmental model. This is a theory of moral reasoning in which a person's motivation for action is thought to progress from external to internal controls on behavior. According to Kohlberg, most children younger than age 9 years reason at the preconventional level, most adolescents and adults are conventional thinkers, and relatively few individuals use postconventional reasoning. When Colby, Kohlberg, Gibbs, and Lieberman (1983) conducted a 20-year longitudinal study of moral development in boys, they found that most of the 10-year-old boys used stage 1 or stage 2 moral reasoning. None of these children were found to be in stage 4, which was first observed in approximately 3% of 13- to 14-year-old boys.

If we assume that the Colby et al. (1983) results are valid for today's children, we can consider their implications for the therapist–client relationship. First, clinicians might expect many elementary school students to approach moral decisions with the hope of avoiding punishment, obtaining rewards, or fulfilling previous agreements with others. It is unlikely that young children will solve moral dilemmas to benefit society or remain consistent with an internalized moral code. But adults frequently consider societal effects or internal consistency when solving moral dilemmas. These

Table 2–5

The Levels of Moral Reasoning According to Kohlberg's Cognitive-Developmental Model of Moral Development

Level I: Preconventional: A lack of understanding of societal rules and expectations

Stage 1: Heteronomous Morality: Avoid punishment from authorities (e.g, parents)

Stage 2: Individualism, Instrumental Purposes, and Exchange: Fulfill personal needs and deals or agreements made with others

Level II: Conventional: An understanding of societal rules and expectations

Stage 3: Mutual Interpersonal Expectations, Relationships, and Interpersonal Conformity: Be "the good person" who meets the expectations of others; maintain interpersonal relationships through qualities such as trust and respect

Stage 4: Social System and Conscience: Follow social laws in order to benefit society and prevent the breakdown of social order

Level III: Postconventional: An understanding of the principles underlying societal rules and expectations

Stage 5: Social Contract: Recognize that social rules are changeable, with the exception of the rights to life and liberty

Stage 6: Universal Ethical Principles: Follow a personal ethic based on the principles of justice, equality, and respect for the individual

Adapted from "Moral stages and Moralization: The Cognitive-developmental Approach," by L. Kohlberg, 1976, pp. 302–307. In T. Lickona (Ed.), *Moral developmental and behavior* (pp. 31–53). New York: Holt, Rinehart and Winston. Copyright 1976 by Holt, Rinehart and Winston.

differences create misunderstandings when parents or therapists assume that children are able to use a stage of moral reasoning that is beyond their developmental level. Convincing a young client that stealing is wrong because it interferes with the daily functioning of society, not because it can result in punishment, is likely to be ineffective as well as frustrating for both the therapist and the child.

Other writers have criticized Kohlberg's model for various reasons, including possible gender biases (see the Multicultural Considerations section in this chapter), and the weak relationship between moral reasoning and behavior. Even Kohlberg (1976) acknowledged that a person's level of moral reasoning does not always translate into the corresponding level of moral behavior. A preadolescent who is able to solve moral dilemmas based on expected reactions from significant others (i.e., Stage 3) might actually resist stealing candy from a store because of the punishment that could result from this act (i.e., Stage 1). Nancy Eisenberg has contributed to our understanding of the relationship between moral reasoning and behavior through her research on prosocial behaviors in children.

Eisenberg and Fabes (1998) described prosocial behavior as "voluntary behavior intended to benefit another" (p. 701). These acts have been observed in children as young as age 2 years and appear to increase with age (Eisenberg & Fabes, 1998; Robinson, Zahn-Waxler, & Emde, 1994). Most parents and teachers encourage children to share and help others, and these efforts seem to have a positive impact. For example, Stockdale, Hegland, and Chiaromonte (1989) reported that preschoolers often exhibit prosocial behaviors when told to do so by an adult. Researchers have also found a relationship between children's use of prosocial behaviors and their ability to adopt another's perspective and empathize with that person (Eisenberg, 1988; Roberts & Strayer, 1996). Society benefits when children learn to exhibit prosocial acts; therefore, teaching these behaviors represents an important responsibility for parents, teachers, and therapists.

Spaide (1995) described techniques that parents can use to enhance prosocial behaviors in children. These include membership in clubs whose purpose is helping others, volunteer work with charity organizations, and participation in fund-raising efforts for community groups. When children voluntarily help others without expectation of rewards or immunity from punishment, they are exhibiting a special class of prosocial acts called *altruistic behavior*. Wagner (1996) offered an example when he described the work of Amber Coffman, who as a child founded an organization to feed the homeless in her community. Although later recognized by others for her efforts,

Ms. Coffman's initial reason for volunteering appears to have been a concern for the welfare of others.

Therapists are rarely consulted to enhance a child's prosocial behaviors. It is far more common for clinicians to be asked to remediate antisocial or aggressive behavior in children. Although boys are more likely than girls to be aggressive with peers, Hektner, August, and Realmuto (2000) found that aggression and other inappropriate acts, such as teasing, accounted for less than 5% of the behaviors that children exhibited during unstructured play. Fortunately for all involved, the overall rate of aggression in young people declines during the elementary school years (see Nagin & Tremblay, 1999). But aggressive behavior in children is a clinically significant issue that merits intervention because young people who exhibit this problem are at greater risk for aggression later in life. As Huesmann, Eron, Lefkowitz, and Walder (1984) found in their 22-year longitudinal study, children who were aggressive at age 8 years were more likely to exhibit this behavior at age 30 years.

Enright, Santos, and Al-Mabuk (1989) observed that developmental psychologists have given relatively little attention to the concept of forgiveness, possibly because of the religious overtones frequently associated with this construct. Enright and his colleagues have studied forgiveness to determine how children, adolescents, and adults resolve experiences when they were harmed or offended by others. According to Enright, Gassin, and Wu (1992), forgiveness is an affective, behavioral, and cognitive phenomenon that represents:

> the overcoming of negative affect and judgment toward the offender, not by denying ourselves the right to such affect and judgment, but by endeavoring to view the offender with compassion, benevolence, and love while recognizing that he or she has abandoned the right to them. (p. 101)

Enright et al. (1989) described a six-stage model of forgiveness that parallels Kohlberg's (1976) cognitive-developmental approach (Table 2-6). When Enright et al. examined the relationship between age and forgiveness, they found that fourth graders scored significantly lower on the authors' forgiveness scale than did college students or adults, but similar to seventh and tenth grade students in the study. Overall, fourth graders clustered in stage 2 (i.e., Restitutional or Compensational Forgiveness), and adolescents were primarily in stage 3 (i.e., Expectational Forgiveness). Based on these findings, clinicians can anticipate that 10-year-old children will forgive another's transgressions if they receive something from the offender. This might involve the return of a stolen item, replacement of a broken toy, or an apology for the wrongdoing. In contrast, children whose forgiveness is less developed may forgive another's physical attack only after they punish the other child in return.

Table 2–6

Enright's Stages of Forgiveness and the Corresponding Stages of Moral Reasoning

Stages of Forgiveness Development	Stages of Moral Reasoning
1. Revengeful Forgiveness: I can forgive only if I make the other person feel the same pain that he or she caused me.	Heteronomous Morality
2. Restitutional or Compensational Forgiveness: I can forgive if I get back what was taken away from me.	Individualism, Instrumental Purposes, and Exchange
3. Expectational Forgiveness: I can forgive if others pressure me or expect me to forgive.	Mutual Interpersonal Expectations, Relationships, and Interpersonal Conformity
4. Lawful Expectational Forgiveness: I forgive because my religion demands it.	Social System and Conscience
5. Forgiveness As Social Harmony: I forgive to reduce social conflict and to restore social harmony.	Social Contract
6. Forgiveness As Love: I forgive unconditionally because I love the person who hurt me and because forgiveness promotes a true sense of love.	Universal Ethical Principles

Adapted from "The Adolescent as Forgiver," by R. D. Enright, M. J. D. Santos, and R. Al Mabuk, *1989 Journal of Adolescence, 12*, p. 96. Copyright 1989 by Academic Press/Harcourt. Adapted with permission of the author.

MULTICULTURAL CONSIDERATIONS

This section continues the discussion of moral development by examining Carol Gilligan's criticism of Kohlberg's cognitive-developmental model. More specifically, was Gilligan correct when she proposed that boys and girls process moral dilemmas in distinctly different ways? We also discuss gender-based differences in aggressive and prosocial behaviors in children. Of course, the ethical treatment of multicultural issues extends beyond gender, so at the end of this section, we consider the knowledge and skills a therapist must have acquired in order to be considered a culturally competent clinician.

Recent writers have questioned whether all children follow the stages of moral development outlined by Kohlberg (1976). The foremost criticism of his model has been Gilligan's challenge regarding gender-based differences in children's acquisition of moral reasoning skills. Gilligan (1982) stated that Kohlberg's developmental criteria are based on male values and offer an incomplete picture of girls' moral reasoning. She expanded his stages of moral development with her description of two moral orientations, one based on justice and the other on care. The former is reflected in Kohlberg's model and involves moral judgments characterized by the use of logic and the principle of fairness. Gilligan stated that a justice orientation might adequately describe moral reasoning in boys, but she contended that it does not explain how girls learn to distinguish right from wrong. For this purpose, she proposed her ethic of care in which "morality is conceived in interpersonal terms and goodness is equated with helping and pleasing others" (Gilligan, 1982, p. 18).

Research on Gilligan's model has raised questions about the existence of gender-based differences in moral reasoning. In their work with adolescents and adults, Gilligan and Attanucci (1988) found that 69% of the male and female participants in their studies used a combination of both orientations. Women were significantly more likely to draw on a morality of care, and men were more likely to approach moral dilemmas from a justice orientation, but many participants used both methods. Walker (1991) tested Gilligan's model in 80 families with a son or daughter enrolled in either first, fourth, seventh, or tenth grade. Based on individual interviews with each father, mother, and child, Walker found "a considerable mix" (p. 344) of Gilligan's two orientations. Although gender-based differences in moral reasoning are not as clear-cut as Gilligan initially proposed, boys and girls do not travel an identical path of moral development. Support for this statement can be found in studies of prosocial behaviors and aggression in children.

Gender-based differences have been reported in children's use of prosocial behaviors. Eisenberg and Fabes (1998), for example, indicated that girls are more likely to exhibit these acts, possibly because of their lower rate of aggressive behaviors and their planful approach to solving problems. But gender alone does not account for all of the variability observed in children's prosocial and aggressive acts. Their behavior has also been related to cultural influences and their parents' approach to child rearing. Stevenson (1991), for example, found prosocial behaviors to be more common among children raised in cultures in which cooperation and trust are emphasized. Children are more likely to exhibit prosocial acts when parents exhibit these behaviors, provide guidance by prompting helping and sharing behaviors, and help children understand the effects of these actions on others (Eisenberg & Fabes, 1998). Parents also represent significant change agents for developing moral reasoning in children. Walker and Taylor (1991), for example, found that parents were most effective in helping their children resolve real-life moral dilemmas when they were supportive, active listeners who adopted a style of moral reasoning slightly more advanced than that of the child. For this reason, therapists should consider parent-focused interventions when they attempt to increase prosocial behavior in their young clients.

When clinicians are consulted to remediate a child's aggressive behavior, the client is more likely to be a boy because aggression is more common in boys (Eisenberg, Martin, & Fabes, 1996). As mentioned previously, these behaviors seem to decline with age, so therapists have reason to be concerned about older boys who continue to exhibit verbal and physical aggression toward others (Maccoby, 1998). Treatment for these clients should involve consideration of the child's ability to self-regulate feelings and behaviors and his or her attributions about the intent of other people's behavior. When compared with "normal" children, for example, unpopular students were more likely to interpret teasing by others as a hostile behavior and to choose an aggressive response (Feldman & Dodge, 1987). Likewise, Eisenberg et al. (1996) noted that boys tend to exhibit less self-control than do girls, who are more likely to approach problems by collecting relevant information and then devising a solution. Based on these findings, it appears that treatment for aggressive clients should include cognitive interventions intended to alter negative expectations of others and teach more effective decision-making skills (see Chapter 11 for relevant techniques).

During the last decades of the 20th century, greater attention was given to cultural influences as they relate to the delivery of therapeutic services. As professional organizations revised their ethical principles, they placed greater emphasis on cultural considerations (Bass, 1996). Some developed separate guidelines for clinicians to follow when working with members of underrepresented groups. For example, the Association for Assessment in Counseling, a division of the American Counseling Association, prepared its *Multicultural Assessment Standards* (Prediger, 1994), and Arredondo et al. (1996) presented competencies for therapists' work with culturally diverse clients. To better prepare its members to serve clients of underrepresented groups, the American Psychological Association (1993b) published its *Guidelines for Providers of Psychological Services to Ethnic, Linguistic, and Culturally Diverse Populations* (Appendix E).

All of the ethics codes reviewed in this chapter contain principles, standards, or both related to cultural diversity. According to the American Psychological Association (1992), clinicians should view diversity as a multidimensional construct that includes factors such as "age, gender, race, ethnicity, national origin, religion, sexual orientation, disability, language, and socioeconomic status" (p. 1599). Other groups have cited additional characteristics, such as marital status (e.g., American School Counselor Association, 1998), culture (American Counseling Association, 1995), color (e.g., American School Counselor Association, 1998), and political beliefs (National Association of Social Workers, 1999). Considering the differences that exist between a therapist, a child, and other family members, only rare therapeutic relationships do not contain at least one of these elements.

How is a therapist judged to be culturally competent? The answer to this question can be found in models of multicultural competence, including traditional (Sue, Arredondo, & McDavis, 1992) and alternative (Sue, 1998) approaches. Common to the traditional methods are the clinician's multicultural awareness, knowledge, and skills (Lee, 1999). Therapists are multiculturally aware to the extent that they understand their own attitudes and values regarding client characteristics such as ethnicity, sexual orientation, age and gender, and disability status. Aware clinicians appreciate and respect cultural differences and are cognizant of the effect that personal attitudes can have on therapeutic relationships.

Multicultural competence also requires knowledge of the ever-expanding body of theory and research on the impact that diversity has on children's development and the delivery of treatment services. For example, therapists must recognize the risks of using tests with children of color when these instruments were normed with European Americans. They must know that traditional interventions, such as individual therapy, may not be the treatment of choice for all clients (Tharp, 1991). Therapists must not be naive about the historical roots of racism and oppression of politically nondominant groups, nor the sociopolitical forces that can compromise a child's development. Multicultural knowledge also includes an understanding of diverse family structures and hierarchies, expectations of children, and child-rearing attitudes.

Multiculturally skilled clinicians have acquired the interviewing techniques needed to work with clients of different cultural backgrounds. This includes the ability to adapt verbal and nonverbal behaviors, including eye contact and tone of voice, to the interpersonal style of the client. As we discussed in Chapter 1, therapists who treat children must develop the special skills required to interact with clients who are of much smaller physical stature. Chapter 5 examines the use of interpreters with clients whose primary language is different from that of the therapist. Culturally competent clinicians also possess the skills needed to develop school- and community-based interventions and advocacy programs to foster the development of children from underrepresented groups. Culturally skilled therapists interact with people of different cultural backgrounds outside the treatment room (Sue et al., 1992). These interactions enhance clinicians' awareness and knowledge of life from a different point of view, which serve as the foundation for a more meaningful way of relating with others.

Sue (1998) presented an alternative model to multicultural competence. He described a culturally competent clinician as someone who uses the scientific method in therapy. This requires the development and testing of treatment hypotheses to study the impact of intervention techniques with clients of different cultural backgrounds. Clinicians must be flexible by focusing on culture-specific issues when appropriate or adopting a more inclusive perspective that includes consideration of issues common across children and families when this approach is warranted. For example, a culture-specific approach could be used with a Hispanic American child who is ridiculed by other students for her facial features and the color of her skin. A therapist might opt for the inclusive perspective with an anxious African American student who is having difficulty handling the daily pressure imposed by a domineering teacher who expects every child in the class to submit perfect tests and assignments. The flexible approach enables therapists to avoid overgeneralization and stereotyping of their clients and presenting problems.

Sue (1998) also stated that culturally competent clinicians have developed the expertise needed to work with clients of a particular cultural heritage. This requires an understanding of indigenous treatments, many of which contain religious or spiritual elements. An example of an indigenous method is the native Hawaiian practice of *ho'oponopono,* which Mokuau (1990) described as a "highly systematic and ritualized" (p. 610) approach to therapy. Conducted by a faith healer, *ho'oponopono* involves the assessment and discussion of a child's problems, a resolution phase in which family members acknowledge responsibility and seek or offer forgiveness, and affirmation of the family's bonding with each other and to the spiritual powers. The approach typically includes prayers to God, family spirits, or both followed by a meal during which the family offers food to the spirits. Therapists who are experts in the unique practices of a given group are better able to relate to these clients and understand the belief systems that impact their behavior.

In its *Guidelines for Providers of Psychological Services to Ethnic, Linguistic, and Culturally Diverse Populations,* the American Psychological Association (1993b) warned that clinicians who are not competent to work with members of underrepresented populations must refer these clients elsewhere. Because of the increasingly diverse nature of contemporary society, therapists need to remediate multicultural deficits rather than avoid contact with clients of different backgrounds. As they become more aware, knowledgeable, and skilled, these clinicians will be better prepared to help an increasing array of clients learn more effective ways of living in a culturally diverse society.

PROFESSIONAL, ETHICAL, AND LEGAL ISSUES: A CASE EXAMPLE

The ethical principle of competence requires that therapists have the training, skills, and supervised experience needed to deliver treatment services. It also involves an awareness of personal and professional deficits. When clinicians are asked to offer interventions that are outside their area of competence, they must consider referral to a professional who has been trained to provide the service. Sometimes these limits are mandated by state statutes. For example, therapists who are not medically trained are prohibited from prescribing medications, so they must refer clients to a physician when psychopharmacotherapy is needed. Most clinical decisions are not regulated by law, so clinicians are responsible for assessing their competence with a therapeutic technique and determining whether referral elsewhere is appropriate.

All therapists must be competent to handle certain situations, such as suicidal behaviors and mandated reporting of suspected child maltreatment. They must have the knowledge and skills needed to interview children and families, conduct assessments of presenting problems, and deliver and evaluate therapeutic interventions that are appropriate to the needs of each client. But the broadening scope of available treatments combined with the emergence of therapeutic subspecialties means that no clinician can be competent to provide all services to all clients. Some therapists are trained to provide behavior therapy, hypnosis, family therapy, eye movement desensitization and reprocessing, or child-centered play therapy. But only rare individuals are competent to offer all of these treatments to children and families. Clinicians who want to use a treatment that is beyond their scope of competence must first obtain the training needed to become proficient with that technique. Obviously, the time to develop competence is well in advance of the point when the therapist decides to use a treatment in session with a client.

We now examine the principle of competence by following the case of Kevin Baldwin presented at the beginning of this chapter. The case also includes consideration of informed assent and consent and a therapist's responsibilities with suicidal clients. The Baldwin case provides a general description of treatment, with a more detailed view of three sessions to illustrate the application of ethical and legal issues in therapy. As you recall, the school counselor advised

Kevin's mother to seek professional help to remediate the child's oppositional behaviors at school. Within a week of the parent–teacher conference, Mrs. Baldwin scheduled an appointment for her son to see Mary Murphy, a licensed professional counselor whose specialty is children and families.

▪ ▪ ▪

When the Baldwins arrive for their first appointment, Ms. Murphy greets them in her waiting room and asks them to join her in her office. There she describes the therapeutic process, including confidentiality and the limits to privacy. "Sometimes all four of us will meet. Other times I will want to see Kevin alone. When he and I talk, it will be important that what we talk about stays between the two of us."

"My wife and I understand," Mr. Baldwin interrupts. "Kevin has to know that we won't be pressuring you for information about him."

"But you are his parents, and I believe you are entitled to a general idea of what we discuss in session. For example, if Kevin tells me that he finished his math papers in school today and played kickball during recess, I could tell you that we talked about school."

Kevin listens as his parents agree to these conditions. Ms. Murphy turns to him and asks, "Is that OK with you, Kevin?" When he nods his head in agreement, she continues, "But I must break this rule if you tell me that someone has hurt you. Or if you say you are thinking about hurting yourself or someone else. If we talk about any of these things, we must tell your Mom and Dad because I don't want anything bad to happen to you. Is that OK?"

When Kevin agrees, Ms. Murphy gives each parent a consent to treatment form containing a more detailed summary of the conditions she just described. Included on this form is information about the scheduling and fees for therapy sessions, a reference to the state's mandatory reporting law for suspected cases of child maltreatment, and a statement indicating that the parents agree to have Ms. Murphy treat their son. While Mr. and Mrs. Baldwin read their consent form, Ms. Murphy gives Kevin an assent to treatment form on which she has typed his name (Fig. 2-2). "Would you like to read it out loud?" she asks.

"Yes," he answers and then reads the form without difficulty.

"Do you have any questions?" Ms. Murphy asks. Kevin shakes his head, so Ms. Murphy asks him to write his name on the assent form. When he finishes, she adds her signature and the date. She asks Mr. and Mrs. Baldwin if they have questions about the consent to treatment form. Both say they understand the conditions for treatment, and each signs the form.

During the remainder of the session, Ms. Murphy collects information about the nature and duration of Kevin's problem behaviors. She asks the parents to complete a set of questionnaires about the boy's behavior and development before the next appointment. Ms. Murphy also asks them to sign consent forms allowing her to contact Kevin's teacher and school counselor to discuss the boy's academic progress and classroom behaviors. When the parents agree, she asks Kevin to assent to her contacts with the school. He immediately shakes his head and says, "No."

"You don't want me to talk with your teacher and Ms. Stinson, the counselor?" she asks.

"You can talk to Ms. Stinson but I don't want you talking to my teacher," he answers.

"So it sounds like it's OK with you if I call Ms. Stinson, but. . . . "

"Don't talk to my teacher," he demands. "He's just gonna make fun of me."

I, Kevin Baldwin, will see Ms. Murphy to make my life better. I will talk to her about my problems. She will not tell anyone what I say, unless I tell her:

1. Someone else hurt me, or
2. I want to hurt myself, or
3. I want to hurt someone else.

____
(Child's Signature)

____
(Therapist's Signature)

Date: ____________________

Figure 2–2. Ms. Murphy's Assent to Treatment Form for Kevin.

"Make fun of you?"

"Uh-huh, just like he always does."

"Maybe I could talk with Mr. Stitt about that and ask him to not make fun of you," Ms. Murphy suggests.

Kevin hesitates and then agrees, "OK, but don't forget to tell him."

Ms. Murphy assures Kevin that she will ask the teacher to refrain from chastising him in front of the other children. She takes a blank piece of paper and prepares an assent statement for him to sign (Fig. 2-3). Although she is under no legal obligation to obtain written assent from the boy, Ms. Murphy routinely does this to empower her young clients in therapy. Immediately before she ends her session with the Baldwins, she schedules next week's meeting, an individual session with Kevin.

The next day when she telephones the school, Ms. Murphy learns that Kevin's behavior has deteriorated during the current school year. The counselor states that the parents refused to seek professional help for their son until recently, when Mr. Stitt and the counselor told Mrs. Baldwin that Kevin would fail the third grade if his academic work did not improve during the last 6 weeks of school. Ms. Murphy learns that Kevin refuses to complete classwork, frequently loses his temper with the other children, and seems to enjoy annoying the students who sit near him in class."We've tried everything we know," Ms. Stinson admits. "We hope you have some suggestions for us." When the therapist speaks with Mr. Stitt, he acknowledges reprimanding Kevin in front of the other students. After a brief discussion about this matter, he agrees to respond to the boy's misbehavior by walking to Kevin's desk and quietly correcting him there.

Ms. Murphy maintains contact with the school during the next 4 weeks. During this time, she has two individual sessions with Kevin and two additional meetings with the Baldwin family. The parents' responses to the child behavior and development questionnaires presented a picture of an angry boy with severe academic and social problems. During the final weeks of the school year, Kevin continues his angry outbursts with other students. His school work improves somewhat, but not enough to compensate for earlier deficits. His teacher decides that he must either attend summer school in math and reading or remain in the third grade for another year. When Kevin and his mother arrive for his third individual session with Ms. Murphy, he is reluctant to discuss Mr. Stitt's decision. Instead, he complains in a harsh tone, "Nobody likes me. Sometimes I wish I was dead."

Ms. Murphy calmly responds, "Dead?"

"Uh-huh."

"You're saying that you've thought about dying?"

"Uh-huh."

When Ms. Murphy asks Kevin to elaborate, he acknowledges that he has considered different methods of harming himself. Although some are less serious, such as skipping school and going to the park, other approaches are significantly more lethal. When she asks him how he would hurt himself, he describes the loaded pistol his father has hidden in a bedside table.

"It's there," he says. "I've seen it."

"Have you touched it?" Ms. Murphy asks.

"Yes."

"When?"

"Oh, different times when my Mom and Dad aren't home. I get it out and hold it."

Kevin tells Ms. Murphy that he has thought about taking his father's gun into the backyard, where he would shoot himself. When she asks if he has ever removed the gun from his parents' bedroom, he says, "One time. When my parents were at work, I took it out on the back porch." As she collects more detailed information, Ms. Murphy decides she has sufficient reason to believe Kevin is a danger to himself. He has expressed suicidal ideation, has a plan, and has access to the means needed to carry out his plan. She reminds him of their discussion of confidentiality during their very first session.

I, Kevin Baldwin, agree to let Ms. Murphy talk with Ms. Stinson and Mr. Stitt. She will ask Mr. Stitt not to make fun of me at school.

____
(Child's Signature)

____
(Therapist's Signature)

Date: ________________

Figure 2–3. Ms. Murphy's Assent Form to Contact Others about Kevin.

"Kevin, do you remember when we talked about what I will tell your parents about our sessions?"

"Uh-huh, you said you won't tell them what I say."

"That's right. What we talk about in here is between the two of us, except when?"

He shrugs his shoulders and says, "I don't know."

"What we talk about is private unless you tell me that someone has hurt you. Or you tell me that you want to hurt yourself or someone else. Remember?"

Kevin looks down at the floor and nods his head.

"I think this is one of those times. We need to tell your Mom what you told me today."

Kevin squirms uneasily in his chair, "But she's gonna get really mad at me."

"Mad at you?"

"Yes, she's gonna say, 'You shouldn't say things like that.'"

"Well, I'm glad you talked to me about it. I want to help make life better for you." When Ms. Murphy decides that her client is ready to proceed, she asks, "Do you want to tell your Mom or do you want me to tell her?"

"You tell her," he answers. Ms. Murphy agrees and then asks Mrs. Baldwin to join them. She reminds the mother of the exceptions to confidentiality before she says, "Kevin has told me that sometimes he wishes he were dead."

"No, Kevin. Please don't say that," his mother pleads.

"Ms. Murphy continues, "Yes, Kevin said that he has thought about using the pistol his Dad has in your bedroom."

"Kevin, I didn't think you knew that gun was there," Mrs. Baldwin responds.

Ms. Murphy describes the rest of Kevin's plan and then says, "Kevin has even touched the gun and taken it outside when you and your husband were at work."

"No, Kevin," his mother says as she begins to cry.

"I understand how upsetting this can be," Ms. Murphy responds, "but I wanted to share this information with you so we can work together to help Kevin."

"I told you she'd be mad," he quietly says to Ms. Murphy.

"I'm not mad; I'm upset," his mother answers. "I don't want anything bad to happen to you. I want you to grow up and be happy."

"I think there are some things we need to do," Ms. Murphy intervenes. "First, I need you and your husband to unload the pistol and lock the gun and the bullets in separate locations. Will you do that?"

"Yes, of course," Mrs. Baldwin answers.

"Next, we need to have your husband join us again to discuss how all of us can help Kevin."

"I'm sure he'll do that."

Ms. Murphy continues, "I understand Kevin has been by himself after school when you and your husband were at work. What are your plans for the summer months?"

"I've been thinking about that," Mrs. Baldwin replies. Turning to her son, she says, "Kevin, I think it would be a good idea for you to go to Grandma's house when your Dad and I are at work." Ms. Murphy listens as mother and son discuss the arrangements. When Kevin reluctantly agrees to this plan, Ms. Murphy introduces the no-suicide agreement she plans to use with the boy (Fig. 2-4). With Mrs. Baldwin observing, she discusses the details of the agreement with Kevin. When she is certain that he understands all of the conditions, she lets him sign the form. She then asks the mother if she has any questions about the agreement or the intervention plan they discussed.

"No," Mrs. Baldwin answers, "but I'd really like for Kevin to see you before next week. All of this really worries me."

Ms. Murphy indicates that she wants to meet with Kevin, his parents, and his maternal grandmother in 2 days. She gives her telephone number to Kevin and his mother, and she asks Mrs. Baldwin to telephone her the

I, Kevin Baldwin, will not hurt myself before I see Ms. Murphy again. If I think about hurting myself, I will tell my Mom, my Dad, or my Grandma. I want to live a happy life. I will talk to Ms. Murphy so we can make life better for me.

____
(Child's Signature)

____
(Therapist's Signature)

Date: ____________________

Figure 2–4. Mrs. Murphy's No-Suicide Agreement for Kevin.

next morning to discuss the progress made in implementing the intervention plan. At the close of the session, Ms. Murphy again thanks Kevin for telling her about his suicidal thoughts. She emphasizes her desire to help him. Kevin smiles for the first time during the meeting when she tells him she looks forward to seeing him in 2 days. "You have my telephone number," she reminds him and his mother. "Please call me if you have any questions or if you need me."

The telephone is ringing when Ms. Murphy arrives at her office early the next morning. It is Mrs. Baldwin calling to say that her husband refused to remove the loaded pistol from their bedroom. "I tried to tell him how serious this is, but he just wouldn't believe me. He thinks Kevin told you all those things just to get attention and that you are overreacting. I don't know what to do."

Ms. Murphy checks her schedule and finds an open hour after lunch. "I take all suicidal thoughts seriously, especially with children," she says. "I would like to meet with you and your husband today. I have an opening at 1:00. Would that be OK for the two of you?"

Mrs. Baldwin says that she will check with her husband and call back soon. Within minutes the phone rings and Ms. Murphy learns that Mr. Baldwin is not willing to continue treatment. "He said you haven't helped Kevin, so why should we spend more time and money for counseling? I told him I thought you have been good for Kevin. After all, we never would have found out about these horrible thoughts if it weren't for you. If you still have that 1:00 appointment, I'd like to come by myself."

Ms. Murphy schedules the session because she is concerned that the parents have been unable to work together on the suicide intervention plan. When Mrs. Baldwin arrives, Ms. Murphy greets her and immediately focuses on her young client, "Where is Kevin today, and how is he?"

"He's at my mother's. I think he feels a little better after talking with you yesterday. I spent some extra time with him last night. He seemed to enjoy that."

"Please tell me about the discussion you had with your husband."

Mrs. Baldwin describes the late night argument the couple had about the loaded gun. For about the next 15 minutes, she describes how she and her husband disagree about many issues, especially their parenting of Kevin. Then she informs Ms. Murphy that she and Kevin will be living with her mother in a nearby town. "I've decided that we'll stay there for awhile," she says. "My mother has plenty of room at her house, and she's been rather lonely since my father died last year. I know she'll let us stay as long as we want."

Ms. Murphy helps Mrs. Baldwin process this decision. When they discuss Mr. Baldwin's reaction, the mother says, "I don't think he'll really care. Anyway, I have to make sure Kevin is safe, and I don't think being in a house with a loaded gun is a good idea right now. I'd like you to call my husband today and see if you can convince him to change his mind. I don't want you to tell him we might leave, but I think he needs to hear from you how serious the situation is."

"Would you like me try to reach him now?"

"Sure. I think he's probably in his office."

Ms. Murphy reaches the father on the second ring. As she begins to describe her meeting with Kevin, Mr. Baldwin interrupts and informs her that he has no intention of securing his gun and is no longer interested in participating in therapy. Despite repeated attempts to convince the father of the seriousness of the situation, Ms. Murphy is unable to get Mr. Baldwin to cooperate with her suicide intervention plan. When she realizes that he is about to hang up, she thanks him for his time and encourages him to contact her if he changes his mind.

"See what I mean?" Mrs. Baldwin says when Ms. Murphy hangs up the phone. "Can Kevin and my mother and I see you tomorrow at the time we had scheduled?" Ms. Murphy agrees and then reviews the intervention plan in the context of the impending move to the grandmother's house.

The next day, Ms. Murphy begins with a brief family meeting to introduce the grandmother to therapy and to obtain her written consent to participate in treatment. She then meets individually with Kevin to assess his suicidal behaviors. He reports that he has not thought about hurting himself since their last meeting and that he did not look at or touch his father's pistol. When she determines that he is adjusting to his temporary home, Ms. Murphy prepares a new no-suicide agreement for Kevin to sign. This time he agrees to not hurt himself before their next appointment, which she plans to schedule 4 days later. Kevin signs the new agreement without hesitation.

Ms. Murphy asks the mother and grandmother to join them. Together, they discuss the change in living arrangements and special precautions that should be taken to ensure Kevin's safety. Mrs. Baldwin asks that future appointments be scheduled in the late afternoon because Kevin begins summer school next week. As the end of the hour nears, she asks if she can see Ms. Murphy alone for a few minutes.

When Kevin and his grandmother have left the room, Ms. Baldwin discloses, "I've decided to file for divorce, but I haven't told Kevin. How do you think he's gonna react?"

Ms. Murphy hesitates as she tries to process this new and significant piece of information. "How long have you been considering this?" she asks.

"Oh, Don and I have been having troubles for years, but I thought it was better for us to stay together for Kevin," she answers. "The gun did it for me. If he really cared about Kevin, he'd get rid of that thing. The other night when we had that fight he said he was more afraid of someone breaking into our house and killing us than he was of Kevin shooting himself."

As Ms. Murphy listens, she reminds herself that Kevin is her client. Mrs. Baldwin has not asked for individual or marital therapy, so she returns to the mother's original question. "I'm not sure how Kevin will respond to this decision," she says, "but I'll do whatever I can to help him. I would not involve him in your decision-making process. Once you and your husband decide to part, it would be best if the two of you sat down with him and explained your decision, making sure you let him know that he did not cause this to happen."

During the following weeks, Ms. Murphy sees Kevin alone and with his mother and grandmother. She continues to use no-suicide agreements until she determines that he is no longer a danger to himself. He does well enough in summer school to be promoted to the fourth grade. Every afternoon when Mrs. Baldwin is at work, his grandmother takes him to a local park, where he develops a friendship with a boy who lives in the neighborhood. Mrs. Baldwin decides to separate from her husband rather than file for divorce. Mr. Baldwin continues to have a loaded gun in the house, so his contact with Kevin is limited to out-of-home activities, such as coaching the boy's baseball and soccer teams.

In mid-August, Ms. Murphy decides that Kevin has made sufficient progress in therapy. When she raises the issue of termination with him and his mother and grandmother, all agree that treatment has been very helpful but that two or three more sessions would be appropriate to help Kevin through the beginning of the school year. Ms. Murphy sees Kevin for the last time in September. In contrast to the angry boy of last spring, she sees a happy child who is doing well at his new school and developing friendships with other students.

Ms. Murphy does not hear from the Baldwins until the following February, when Kevin's mother calls to schedule an appointment to talk about Kevin. "He's doing fine at school," she tells Ms. Murphy on the telephone, "but I want to schedule an appointment to talk with you about the future."

During the initial minutes of her session with Ms. Murphy, the mother describes how well her son is doing at home and school. She reports that the two of them are still living with her mother and that Kevin continues to see his father two or three times a week. "In fact, that's why I came to see you today," she says. "I've decided to file for divorce, and I want to get custody of Kevin. I told his Dad this and he said he was going to fight me all the way. I don't believe it. He's the reason we left to begin with, and now he wants Kevin to live with him."

Ms. Murphy listens as the mother describes a recent visit to her attorney, who advised that she obtain a child custody evaluation. "When I told him that we saw you for a number of months and that Kevin really likes you, he suggested that I ask you to do the evaluation. Will you help us out?"

"Mrs. Baldwin," she begins, "I really appreciate your thinking of me. But I'm not trained to do this type of work, so I'm going to have to say no."

"But you know all of us. You're the perfect person to do it," the mother protests.

Ms. Murphy calmly and assertively responds, "We need to find a specialist who is trained to perform child custody evaluations. If you want, I'll give you a list of names that you and your husband can consider."

"But Kevin might not talk to a new person," Mrs. Baldwin continues. "Anyway, you have all those tests my husband and I did when we first came to see you. Why don't you just send them to my attorney so he can decide if we can use them?"

"Well, when judges and attorneys talk about child custody evaluations, they usually mean a different process in which the child, both parents, and other important adults in the child's life are interviewed, tested, and asked to sign consent or assent forms to release all information to the court. The evaluation should be performed by a neutral person who has not treated the child and family before."

"I just thought it would be a lot easier if you did it," the mother says as she begins to realize that alternative arrangements must be made. Ms. Murphy provides the list of qualified evaluators practicing within a 50-mile radius of town. She offers to provide additional names if the parents are unable to schedule an appointment with someone on the list.

Ms. Murphy never hears from Mr. or Mrs. Baldwin after that February meeting. One year later while reading the local newspaper, she sees a picture of a fifth grade class on field trip to the local art museum. In the front row is Kevin, smiling with his arm around the boy standing next to him.

▪ ▪ ▪

In this case, the therapist demonstrated the use of an assent form with the child, consent forms with parents, a no-suicide agreement that was adjusted to the boy's developmental level, and the use of referral when the clinician was not qualified to provide an intervention. When clinicians work with troubled children and their families, it is not unusual for conditions to change during the course of treatment. In some cases, parents will decide to separate or divorce in the middle of therapy, presenting ethical and legal challenges for the clinician. For example, the limits of confidentiality present a unique dilemma for the therapist who treated the entire family at the outset of treatment but continues to see the children and one parent after an intervening marital transition. Before therapists release information about a nonparticipating parent, they must ensure that the person is still willing to have this material disclosed to others.

Ms. Murphy was fortunate that Mrs. Baldwin removed her son from what appeared to be a dangerous situation. When her husband refused to lock his loaded pistol in a secure place, the mother moved the child to the maternal grandmother's house. Sometimes a therapist is confronted with two parents who are unwilling to recognize the lethality of their child's suicidal behavior. These cases require careful consideration of all factors affecting the welfare of the client because they have complex ethical and legal implications. Ms. Murphy handled the mother's request for a child custody evaluation in an appropriate manner. Some clinicians could be convinced that they were qualified to assume this responsibility. Through her actions, Ms. Murphy did more to help Kevin and his parents than she would have had she agreed to perform an evaluation whose results would have been clouded by her lack of competence and her previous interactions with the family in therapy.

The consent and assent forms and the no-suicide agreement presented here are only examples that therapists might consider adapting to the individual needs of a child and family. They should not be viewed as models that are to be routinely used with all clients. Research on the effectiveness of developmentally appropriate assent forms and no-suicide agreements with children simply does not exist. As such, we have no empirical evidence on which to base decisions regarding the use of these techniques in therapy. Neither method by itself is likely to guarantee a child's commitment to participate in treatment or avoid self-destructive behavior, so clinicians who use these techniques should combine them with other interventions within the context of the therapeutic relationship.

SUMMARY

This chapter explored various professions that are involved in the care and treatment of children. When clinicians understand the perspective and expertise of each group, they are better prepared to collaborate in a multidisciplinary approach to intervention. This includes being aware of the commonalities and differences that exist across the ethics codes of these professions. Therapists also need to understand and comply with the laws that apply in their jurisdiction of practice. With this understanding of the ethical and legal limits to treatment, clinicians are prepared to take the first step to therapeutic intervention: the assessment of the child's problems.

3

Contemporary Issues: Managed Mental Health Care, Brief Therapies, and Empirically Supported Therapies for Children

■ ■ ■

On his third day of first grade, 6-year-old Charles soils his pants in class. When his parents, Paul and Louise Trimble, learn about the incident from the teacher, they schedule an appointment with their pediatrician, Dr. Maurice Shipley. Dr. Shipley is very aware of the problem, having treated Charles for encopresis on three previous occasions. Although prior interventions produced short-term benefits, the child always resumed soiling within months after termination of treatment. This time, Dr. Shipley decides to use a different approach. He refers the Trimbles to Dr. Rebecca Faller, a pediatric psychologist, who conducts her practice through his clinic.

■ ■ ■

Encopresis is a troublesome behavior that is believed to occur in approximately 1.5% to 7.5% of children (Doleys, 1989). Many of these clients are initially treated by their pediatrician or family physician. When faced with difficult cases that do not respond to traditional medical interventions, physicians sometimes refer families for mental health services. McGrath, Mellon, and Murphy (2000) described a number of medical and behavioral treatments that have been found to be useful in controlling childhood encopresis. Supported by empirical evidence, these methods are typically brief therapies that can be used in the context of a managed mental health care environment.

Before returning to the case example of Charles Trimble and his parents, this chapter examines three important influences on the contemporary practice of child therapy. First, we explore the role of managed mental health care in the treatment of troubled children and their families. We then turn our attention to the characteristics of brief therapy and discuss this approach relative to treatment compliance and managed care guidelines. Our third influence, empirically supported therapies, represents an important development in clinicians' attempts to document their accountability with children and families. Therapists are expected to give more and more attention to these factors, which are central to the current evolution of child treatments.

MANAGED MENTAL HEALTH CARE

Ollendick and Russ (1999) identified the emergence of managed mental health care as one of the dramatic changes in child therapy that occurred during the last two decades of the 20th century. When combined with developments in empirically supported therapies and brief interventions, the transformation of the U.S. health delivery system has changed the way that clinicians work with children. External monitoring of therapists' treatment decisions by managed health care companies has become a common part of everyday practice. More than ever before, clinicians are expected to consider the financial aspects of treatment and provide time-limited and cost-effective services. In order to survive in this environment, therapists must understand the structure and procedures of managed care, provide evidence for their accountability, and revise the traditional time frame for the delivery of treatment.

Fox (1996) noted that managed health care began in the early 20th century, but its use in mental health treatments is of more recent origin. Thomas and Cummings (2000) stated that in the 1950s, no insurance companies reimbursed clients for mental health services. Lobbying efforts by professional groups brought about expanded coverage, first for services provided by psychiatrists and eventually those offered by psychologists, social workers, and counselors. However, the movement toward third-party reimbursement for mental health services did have its critics. For example, Meltzer (1975) suggested that reimbursement for psychologists' services could have a number of negative consequences. Interestingly, these included increasing health care costs for consumers and clinical decisions based on financial rather than psychological principles.

The 1990s witnessed a dramatic increase in the use of managed mental health care. Experienced practitioners at the time were familiar with a fee-for-service system, also known as indemnity plans, with which clients were allowed to select their provider, enter therapy of a nature and duration determined by the client and clinician, and have their insurance company provide "unquestioned reimbursement for most therapists' bills that fell within reasonable guidelines" (Poynter, 1998, p. 3). As the cost of treatment rose, insurers started to manage care in accordance with the benefit limitations specified in the client's insurance plan. It is important to remember that customers or employers select insurance plans, and the plans differ in terms of the number and type of allowable treatment sessions. The nation's mental health care system was revolutionized as more and more attention was given to therapist accountability, cost containment, brief-term remedial interventions to restore normal functioning rather than foster personal growth and development, and case management procedures such as preauthorization and reauthorization for treatment.

Models of Managed Mental Health Care

To succeed in this practice environment, clinicians must understand the vocabulary of managed health care. Table 3-1 contains a sample of the terminology that has been used. Four important terms on this list represent the methods used to deliver health care services: fee-for-service plans, health maintenance organizations (HMOs), preferred provider organizations (PPOs), and point-of-service (POS) plans (The Health Insurance Association of America, 1999). The fee-for-service approach represents the traditional method of funding health care before the emergence of managed care systems. An alternative is HMOs, in which comprehensive services are offered using the "gatekeeper" system. In this system, a primary care physician coordinates evaluation and treatment for policy holders who pay a fixed prepayment for these services. Clients encounter no additional costs as long as they obtain their care from a provider associated with the HMO. As managed care evolved, insurance companies have moved away from the gatekeeper model and given consumers more direct access to mental health clinicians (D. Heggie, personal communication, November 12, 2001).

The Health Insurance Association of America (1999) described PPOs and POS plans as hybrid methods. Companies that offer PPOs negotiate fees with providers, who become part of panels or networks that offer services to clients. The association described the PPO as a combination of fee-for-service plans and HMOs. For example, policy holders are allowed to receive treatment from an out-of-network provider, but they must assume a larger share of the cost for these services. The POS method combines

Table 3–1
The Terminology of Managed Health Care

Capitation	Payment for service based on a fixed amount per client, regardless of the actual cost of treatment
Fee-for-service	The traditional method of reimbursement for treatment used before the emergence of managed health care
HMO	The acronym for health maintenance organization, which was originally meant to describe care for individuals who voluntarily enrolled in a capitated health care plan
MCO	The acronym for managed care organization that is now used as a generic term for managed health care plans
Member	A client who receives services through an MCO
POS	The acronym for point-of-service plans, which permit access to outside providers but with a higher copayment or deductible for the client
PPO	The acronym for preferred provider organization, which refers to a form of managed health care in which the insurance company either offers an incentive or limits clients' access to certain clinicians; therapists typically contract with the insurance company to deliver services at a discount rate
Preauthorization	The requirement that therapists receive insurance company approval before initiating treatment
Provider	A therapist who treats clients who are members of a managed health care plan
Reauthorization	The requirement that therapists receive insurance company approval before continuing treatment after the completion of previously authorized sessions
Utilization Review	A managed care company's monitoring of the need, appropriateness, and outcome of treatment

aspects of HMOs and PPOs. Insurance companies that offer these plans use provider networks and ask policy holders to select a primary care physician to function as gatekeeper for services. Similar to policy holders in HMOs, clients who receive care from a POS network provider do so at little or no out-of-pocket expense. Similar to those enrolled with PPOs, clients must pay a portion of the cost of care when treated by an out-of-network provider.

Unlike the fee-for-service system in which clients enter treatment on their own volition, managed care companies require preauthorization for services before therapy begins. Insurers typically authorize clinicians to provide a set number of sessions in a specified period of time. Companies then review treatment and monitor cases that involve more than the preauthorized number of sessions (Poynter, 1998). When additional treatment is needed, clinicians must provide evidence that these services are necessary. Companies vary in their definition of "necessary," but Poynter (1998, p. 15) noted that "psychosocially necessary" or "medically helpful" treatments are usually not covered under managed care policies. Table 3-2 contains the criteria for outpatient treatment currently in use at the nation's largest managed mental health care company.

Definitions for medical necessity and the benefits contained in a family's insurance plan pose challenges for the therapist who wants to integrate education/development and prevention with treatments designed to remediate diagnosable mental disorders. Although managed care companies are unlikely to reimburse parents for the first two components of a multimodal approach to treatment, therapists must not overlook these services. As discussed in Chapter 1, remediation of a child's problems can involve interventions that capitalize on the client's normal developmental tendencies to foster healthy growth while reducing the risk of future difficulties. Consider the 6-year-old client with encopresis described at the beginning of this chapter. The therapist who provides brief-term behavioral treatment for the child can teach his parents to use more effective child management skills that will prevent the occurrence of other maladaptive behaviors in the future. By encouraging the parents to enroll the child in enrichment activities, the clinician introduces experiences designed to enhance the child's growth and psychosocial development. When we continue with this case, we can observe how the therapist combined education/development, prevention, and remediation to eliminate the client's soiling behavior and establish a foundation for healthy development.

The emergence of managed mental health care has facilitated the growth of empirically supported treatments and brief therapies for children. Buchanan (1997) observed that, on average, children in therapy are more likely to improve and in a

Table 3–2

An Example of Medical Necessity Criteria for Outpatient Treatment

Criteria for Initial Treatment Status Review

The specified requirements for severity of need and intensity and quality of service must be met to satisfy the criteria for the initial treatment review.

I. Initial Review—Severity of Need

Criteria A, B, and C must be met to satisfy the criteria for severity of need.

A. The patient has a DSM-IV diagnosis on Axis I and/or Axis II.

B. The patient has DSM-IV psychiatric/substance-related disorder symptoms, intrapsychic conflict, behavorial and/or cognitive dysfunction consistent with the diagnoses on Axes I and II.

C. Either 1, 2 or 3 below must be met to satisfy criterion C.

1. The patient has a least mild symptomatic distress and/or impairment in functioning due to psychiatric symptoms and/or behavior in at least one of the three spheres of functioning (occupational, scholastic, or social), that are the direct result of an Axis I or Axis II disorder. This is evidenced by specific clinical description of the symptom(s) and/or impairment(s) consistent with a GAF (DSM-IV Axis V) score of less than 71.
2. The patient has a persistent DSM-IV illness for which maintenance treatment is required to maintain optimal symptom relief and/or functioning.
3. There is clinical evidence that further therapy is required to support termination of therapy, although the patient no longer has at least mild symptomatic distress or impairment in functioning. The factors considered in making a determination about the continued medical necessity of treatment in this termination phase are the frequency and severity of previous relapse, level of current stressors, and other relevant clinical indicators. Additionally, the treatment plan should include clear goals needing to be achieved and methods to achieve them in order to support successful termination.

II. Initial Review—Intensity and Quality of Service

Criteria A, B and C must be met to satisfy the criteria for intensity and quality of service.

A. There is documentation of a DSM-IV diagnosis on Axis I and/or Axis II, and there are completed assessments on Axes III, IV, and V.

B. There is a medically necessary and appropriate treatment plan, or its update, specific to the patient's impairment in functioning and DSM-IV psychiatric/substance-related disorder symptoms, behavior, cognitive dysfunctions and/or intrapsychic conflicts. The treatment plan is expected to be effective in either:

1. Alleviating the patient's distress and/or dysfunction; or
2. Achieving appropriate maintenance goals for a persistent illness; or
3. Supporting termination.

C. The treatment plan must identify 1–6 to satisfy criterion C:

1. The status of target-specific DSM-IV psychiatric/substance-related disorder symptoms, behavior, and cognitive dysfunction being treated.
2. The current, or anticipated modifications in, biologic, behavioral, psychodynamic or psychosocial framework(s) of treatment for each psychiatric symptom/cluster and/or behavior.
3. The status of specific, achievable and measurable goals for treatment specified in terms of symptom alleviation, behavioral change, cognitive alteration, or improvement in social, occupational, or scholastic functioning.
4. The current, or anticipated modifications in, treatment methods in terms of:
   - treatment framework or orientation
   - treatment modality
   - treatment frequency
   - estimate of treatment duration
5. Status of measurable, target criteria used to identify both interim treatment goals and end of treatment goals (unless this is a maintenance treatment) to substantiate that: a) treatment is progressing, and/or b) goals have been met and treatment is no longer needed.
6. Description of an alternative plan to be implemented if the patient does not make substantial progress toward the given goals in a specified period of time. Examples of an alternative plan are a second opinion or introduction of adjunctive or alternative therapies.

Criteria for Continued Treatment

III. Continued Stay

Criteria A and B must be met to satisfy the criteria for continued outpatient treatment.

A. The patient's condition meets the Severity of Need Criteria (I above).

B. The treatment plan meets the Intensity and Quality of Service Criteria (II above).

shorter period of time than are older clients. Although there are exceptions to this rule, the therapeutic needs of many children appear to be treatable within a managed care system. Buchanan recommended that clinicians adopt a multisystemic approach that resembles the multidisciplinary method described in Chapter 1. If treatment is to be both brief and effective, therapists must collaborate with parents, teachers, and significant other adults. By changing pertinent systems, such as the home, school, and community, therapists can create a more consistent and supportive environment for the child.

Brief treatments have been found to be appropriate for a broad range of presenting problems, but they are not appropriate for every child. When a client requires longer-term treatment, the therapist becomes an advocate for the child with the family's insurance company. Warren and Messer (1999) endorsed this role when they warned that economic concerns should not limit a child's access to a range of appropriate treatments. Clearly, the growth of managed mental health care has required clinicians to consider the finances of therapy to a greater extent than was true under the traditional fee-for-service system. Authors such as Ackley (1997) and Poynter (1998) have written about the business of therapy and described the practice management skills that therapists must acquire.

Case Management Procedures

Poynter (1998) described two processes that characterize the delivery of mental health treatment in a managed care environment. The first—and more important—one relates to the therapist's traditional role as service provider. This process involves a number of stages, from the initial assessment of the client's presenting problem to the evaluation and termination of therapy. But the emergence of managed mental health care has brought more attention to a second process: case management and documentation of treatment services. Although this change has resulted in increased paperwork for therapists (Davis & Meier, 2001), there is reason to believe that the quality of clinical record keeping has actually improved under managed mental health care because insurance companies are required to follow standards established by accrediting organizations, such as the National Committee for Quality Assurance (www.ncqa.org). In the fee-for-service system, client files were kept primarily for clinical and legal purposes. In a managed care environment, written records are also maintained for administrative purposes.

All insurance companies are unlikely to cover the cost of treatment unless therapists document their work with clients. Poynter (1998) recommended that clinicians include in a client's file the paperwork used in a fee-for-service system: intake summary forms, documentation of clients' consent to treatment, and release of information forms allowing the therapist to contact the client's insurance company and others directly involved in the case. He also emphasized the need for including materials specific to managed mental health care, such as a summary of managed care procedures, the insurer's assessment and billing forms, questionnaires and rating forms relevant to the presenting problem, and a termination or discharge summary at the end of treatment.

Poynter (1998) stated that the first form clinicians should give to clients is a written summary of managed mental health care. He suggested that the description include a statement regarding plan limits on the initial number of sessions allowed. The following example contains information about the preauthorization and reauthorization of treatment:

> Your medical insurance company endorses the concept of brief therapy, which researchers have found to be helpful in treating a variety of childhood problems. We can expect your insurer to cover the cost of 6 to 12 therapy sessions. Although the company may authorize additional treatment, we must consider this limit on the number of sessions as we discuss your goals for therapy and develop our plan for treatment.

Insurance companies vary in their procedures and individual plans provide different levels of coverage, so therapists must adapt their introductory summaries for each provider panel and the client's insurance plan.

Most clinicians are familiar with the billing or service reimbursement forms that insurers require. A commonly used document is the Health Insurance Claim Form prepared by the Health Care Financing Administration (www.hcfa.gov), which provides fee-for-service and managed care benefits through such programs as Medicare, Medicaid, and the State Children's Health Insurance Program. In his text on managed care, Poynter (1998) recommended that clinicians complete a symptom index to document the specific characteristics of the client's presenting problem. Therapists who work with children and families are fortunate because they can select from a number of child-, parent-, and teacher-report questionnaires and rating forms that have good psychometric properties. Chapter 4 provides examples of measures that clinicians can use in place of the symptom index provided by Poynter.

Preauthorization for service usually includes specification of the number of therapy sessions the insurance company will cover before further review is necessary. According to Poynter (1998), there is no perfect formula for determining the length of treatment required for a presenting problem, so preauthorization often involves "only an educated guess" (p. 119) by insurance companies. For this reason, clinicians and clients often discover that additional treatment is needed. When this occurs, the therapist must contact the client's insurer and provide evidence for reauthorization of additional therapy sessions. This step is an example of the convergence of clinical and procedural processes described by Poynter. As a clinician, the therapist makes a professional judgment regarding the need for additional treatment. As a record keeper, the therapist monitors the delivery of preauthorized services to determine when a reauthorization request must be submitted. As Poynter warned, failure to obtain preauthorization and reauthorization means that insurers are not required to reimburse for a child's therapy.

The documentation that Poynter (1998) described as necessary for reauthorization of treatment sessions includes traditional fee-for-service records and forms required by managed care companies (Figure 3-1). Not all insurers require a treatment plan as part of the reauthorization process, but clinicians should prepare this document at the outset of therapy as part of standard clinical practice. The plan should indicate who will participate in therapy, as well as the presenting problems, treatment goals, and interventions that will be used with the child. Information on this form should be organized in a manner that clearly illustrates the connection between problems, goals, and treatment. Table 3-3 contains the treatment plan the therapist intends to use in our case example.

An essential record-keeping activity is the progress note the therapist enters in the client's file after each session and after every outside contact related to the case. Although therapists vary in their approach to writing progress notes, Moline, Williams, and Austin (1998) indicated that all session-related entries in a client's file should contain the session date and length, the type of therapy (e.g., individual play therapy, family therapy), a statement of progress relative to the treatment plan, and a behavioral description of any psychological impairment. Moline et al. recommended that clinicians summarize each session by recording their observations of the client's behavior, the topics discussed in therapy, recent significant events in the client's life, and the homework assigned for the next week. Again, therapists should note the participants in each session because significant other adults and siblings are frequently involved in a child's treatment (see Table 3-4 for a progress note on the second session with the Trimbles).

The termination or discharge summary is intended to provide information that can be used to evaluate treatment and plan follow-up services. Although an insurance company may not require a termination summary, clinicians should prepare this document in case treatment collaborators or future service providers request the information. Poynter (1998) indicated that summaries usually include outcome data, pretreatment and posttreatment diagnoses, and the therapist's assessment of prognosis. Clinicians should specify any services that children and families will need after discharge from treatment. These may include information about self-help and support groups for parents, enrichment activities for children, and school-based educational programs. Poynter also recommended that therapists collect consumer satisfaction data from clients to evaluate their opinions of therapy. He provided a form that clinicians can use for this purpose.

The Therapist in Managed Care

Many clinicians have criticized the changes brought about by managed care. In a recent survey of psychologists, approximately 80% of the respondents reported that managed care had a negative impact on their work, and only 10% believed its effects were positive (Phelps, Eisman, & Kohut, 1998). Dislike for the system is so strong that one author chose to remain anonymous when writing about its benefits because he was "fearful of reprisals from his colleagues for speaking positively about managed care" (Anonymous, 1995, p. 235). One of the benefits that Anonymous cited is the "free supervision" (p. 235) provided by the case reviewers employed by managed care companies. Koocher (1995) questioned this point and others made by Anonymous, citing possible conflicts of interest for case reviewers who offer clinical advice while being held accountable for their company's cost containment efforts. Other writers,

Magellan Behavioral Health
and its affiliated entities Human Affairs International, Inc., Green Spring Health Services, Inc., CMG Health, Inc. and Merit Behavioral Care Systems Corporation

TREATMENT REQUEST FORM (TRF)

Use black pen. Make block letters and numbers.
Dates need to be in the MM/DD/YYYY format.

PATIENT INFORMATION

PATIENT'S FIRST NAME

PATIENT'S DATE OF BIRTH ___ / ___ / ___

MEMBERSHIP NUMBER

AUTHORIZATION NUMBER

PRACTITIONER INFORMATION

PRACTITIONER ID#

PHONE NUMBER

PRACTITIONER NAME & ADDRESS

Date Patient First Seen For This Episode Of Treatment ___ / ___ / ___

Is the patient on mental health or chemical dependency short-term or long term disability? O Yes O No

Have you communicated with the PCP/other relevant health care practitioners about treatment? O Yes O No

DSM-IV MULTIAXIAL DIAGNOSIS (PLEASE COMPLETE ALL FIVE AXES)

AXIS I Dx Code ___ . ___ Dx Code ___ . ___

AXIS II Dx Code ___ . ___

AXIS III Does the patient have a current general medical condition that is potentially relevant to the understanding or management of the condition(s) noted in Axis I or II? O No O Yes

AXIS IV Severity of current psychosocial stressors
O None O Mild O Moderate O Severe

AXIS V: GAF Score Highest Past Year ___ At first Session ___ Current ___

Current Medications (if not applicable, no response is required)

O Anti-psychotic O Anti-anxiety O Anti-depressant O Psycho-stimulant O Injectibles
O Hypnotic O Non-psychotropic O Mood stabilizer/Anti-convulsant O Antabuse O Other

Symptoms

Please rate the patient's current status on these symptoms, if applicable. If not applicable, no response is required.

	Mild	Mod	Severe		Mild	Mod	Severe
Self-injurious behavior	O	O	O	Homicidal ideation	O	O	O
Suicidal ideation	O	O	O	Substance use problems	O	O	O

Concurrent Auth Request (number of sessions)

Length of time for requested sessions: O 1 month (or less) O 2 months O 3 months O 6 months

	1	2	3	4	5	6	7	8	9	10	11	12
90804	O	O	O	O	O	O	O	O	O	O	O	O
90805	O	O	O	O	O	O	O	O	O	O	O	O
90806	O	O	O	O	O	O	O	O	O	O	O	O
90807	O	O	O	O	O	O	O	O	O	O	O	O
90847	O	O	O	O	O	O	O	O	O	O	O	O
90853	O	O	O	O	O	O	O	O	O	O	O	O
90862	O	O	O	O	O	O	O	O	O	O	O	O
96100	O	O	O	O	O	O	O	O	O	O	O	O
Other	O	O	O	O	O	O	O	O	O	O	O	O

How many times have you seen the patient to date? **(01-99)?**

0	O	O
1	O	O
2	O	O
3	O	O
4	O	O
5	O	O
6	O	O
7	O	O
8	O	O
9	O	O

Other CPT Code ___

Signature of provider: ______________________ ___ / ___ / ___ Date

My signature attests that I have a current valid license in the state to provide the requested services.

 Version TRF 09/06/01

Figure 3–1. A Sample of a Treatment Reauthorization Form. From "Treatment Request Form," by Magellan Behavioral Health, Inc. Copyright 2001 by Magellan Behavioral Health, Inc. Reprinted with permission from Magellan Behavioral Health, Inc.

Table 3–3
The Treatment Plan Form for the Trimble Family

Client's Name: Charles Trimble Parents' Name: Paul & Louise Trimble Client #: 2001089 Date: 09-10-02
Diagnosis: Encopresis With Constipation and Overflow Incontinence (DSM-IV-TR 787.6)
Substance Abuse: Yes (No) Danger to Self: Yes (No) Danger to Others: Yes (No)
Current Medications: None Allergies: None

CLIENT	PRESENTING PROBLEM	TREATMENT GOAL	INTERVENTION
Charles	Encopresis	To permanently eliminate soiling behavior	Enemas, high-fiber diet, scheduled toilet sitting, cognitive-behavioral play therapy, contracting, positive reinforcement
Parents	Inconsistent parenting	To increase use of child management skills	Behavioral parent training, anticipatory guidance

such as Cooper and Gottlieb (2000) and Daniels (2001), have described the ethical dilemmas created by managed care, but Belar (2000) suggested that many of these problems existed for decades but were never adequately addressed. Whether therapists practice under a fee-for-service or managed care system, they must uphold the ethics of their profession. As discussed in Chapter 2, these ethics include being competent, maintaining confidentiality of client information, and obtaining informed consent before contacting others outside the therapeutic relationship.

With the growth of managed care, the clinician's role has changed from therapist to a combination of therapist and businessperson. Of course, survival in independent practice always required a certain degree of business acumen, but therapists must now possess the procedural skills that Poynter (1998) identified as necessary for justifying and documenting clinical services. Therapists also need to prepare themselves for the ethical dilemmas they will encounter as they attempt to balance the expectations of families and their insurance companies. Clinicians can acquire these skills by attending workshops and reading the works of authors such as Ackley (1997), Bagarozzi (1996), Davis and Meier (2001), Kongstvedt (1997), and Poynter (1998). As competent therapists, they are prepared to address the

Table 3–4
Progress Note for Session #2 With The Trimble Family

Client's Name: Charles Trimble Parents' Name: Paul and Louise Trimble Client #: 2001089
Date: 09-17-02 Session Number: 2 Session Length: 55 minutes
Diagnosis: DSM-IV-TR 787.6

I. Participants: Charles and his parents
II. Type of Therapy: Family therapy with cognitive-behavioral play therapy
III. Psychological Adjustment: Parents and child were active participants and in contact with reality.
IV. Behavioral Observations: Family well groomed and appropriately dressed. Charles was verbal and well-behaved in session. Parents submitted monitoring chart with soiling episodes, scheduled sittings, and proper BMs (see attachment #091002). No data for fiber diet.
V. Discussion Topics/Significant Events: Parents said Charles soiled 6x at home and 2x at school. Mother very worried about school "accidents." Parents used scheduled sitting for 10 minutes each morning; Charles had one BM. Discussed need for high-fiber diet.
VI. Intervention: Charles used toy dog in play to describe what might have been a scary toileting experience at school. Discussed using rewards for appropriate behavior. If Charles has at least 4 days of scheduled sitting and fewer than six soiling episodes, the family will go on a picnic.
VII. Homework: Parents will continue to monitor Charles' behaviors. Parents will take Charles on a picnic if he meets criteria for scheduled sitting and soiling episodes.
VIII. Treatment Plan: Contact teacher re: Charles' play; evaluate charts and assess parents' use of reward; address dietary issues.

needs of clients who expect both quality care and monetary reimbursement from insurers committed to managing treatment costs (Rodwin, 1995).

Most people associate managed care with the services provided in community settings, but its impact is also being felt elsewhere. House (1999) described how the nation's public schools have begun to seek third-party reimbursement for psychological assessments and treatment. School psychologists are being asked to provide formal diagnoses for troubled children so districts may access this alternative source of funding. With the development of school-based mental health clinics (see Dryfoos, 1997), the growth of managed care in the schools is likely to continue. Clinicians must prepare themselves for this change so they are prepared to handle the sometimes conflicting needs of students and families, schools, and insurance companies.

BRIEF THERAPIES FOR CHILDREN

Traditional views of therapy have held that effectiveness is positively correlated with the length of treatment (Garfield, 1989). Brief therapies were viewed with suspicion. Treatment must not be hurried, it was assumed, because the longer a person remains in the therapy, the better the outcome. Although it is true that some clients require extended treatment, others can benefit from brief interventions. The nature and duration of a client's presenting problems are two factors that can affect the length of treatment. On average, we might expect that less time is required to remediate recently developed symptoms or situational difficulties with a motivated client than is needed to resolve long-standing intrapersonal conflicts for someone who questions the value of therapy. The question is not whether brief therapies have merit, but which problems of what duration can be treated using brief-term interventions.

What qualifies a therapy as brief? A number of characteristics have been cited, including the use of circumscribed treatments in which specific problems are targeted for intervention (Wachtel & Messer, 1997). Koss and Shiang (1994) observed that clients are both selected and excluded based on how appropriate their presenting concern is for a brief intervention. This approach should not be adopted with every child. Shapiro (1994) cautioned against its use with young clients who have been severely traumatized, those with pervasive developmental disorders such as autism, and those who are experiencing difficulty adapting to repeated life transitions such as frequent changes of residence. Brief therapy also is defined by the role of the clinician, who is actively involved in treatment and functions as a "teacher, expert, and facilitator" (Shapiro, 1994, p. 25). For example, at the beginning of therapy, the clinician strives to develop rapport with the client while simultaneously conducting a quick assessment of the problem and developing goals that can be achieved in a limited number of sessions. But it is the length of time required for treatment that is the most obvious characteristic of this approach.

How long is brief therapy? Writers have differed in the maximum number of sessions used to distinguish brief from traditional methods. O'Malley (1998) offered a very subjective criterion when he described brief therapy as "no more treatment than is necessary" (p. 94). Koss and Shiang (1994) were more specific in noting that many writers have considered 25 sessions as the maximum limit for brief interventions. Many clinicians would question the practical benefits of such a high number. As proof, they might offer the more restricted time limits imposed by clients' health insurance plans as an indication that brief therapy is much shorter in duration. Indeed, a number of factors have contributed to greater use of brief interventions. Messer and Wachtel (1997), for example, observed that an increase in the number of dual-income families means that people have less discretionary time to devote to therapy. But a very important consideration is the actual number of treatment sessions that clients typically attend.

Garfield (1994) reviewed the results of therapeutic outcome studies conducted during the second half of the 20th century. He concluded that the median number of sessions that clients attend ranges from 5 to 8, significantly fewer than the figure cited by Koss and Shiang (1994). Although many of these studies involved adults in therapy, the results for children are no more encouraging. For example, Sowder, Burt, Rosenstein, and Milazzo-Sayre (1981) found that 70% of approximately 130,000 outpatient clients, ages 9 years and younger, completed fewer than 6 sessions. The similar outcome for child and adult clients is no surprise because most young clients rely on their parents for access to therapy. Clinicians must realize that treatment is a time-limited endeavor and must revise their expectations for therapy. The purpose of treatment is no longer that of transforming a child's personality. Rather, brief therapy is designed to effect change in a client's environment and capitalize on the child's inherent potential for development. It is for this reason that therapists providing short-term therapy are likely to involve parents in treatment and collaborate with teachers to remediate specific problems.

Although the process of brief therapy is compressed into a relatively short period of time, treatment does progress through different stages. Shapiro (1994) described four stages: establishing the therapeutic relationship, diagnosis, treatment implementation, and generalization. Although the development of therapist–client rapport is important, Shapiro noted that it is not essential. Some children are reluctant or unwilling to engage in treatment. The time needed to establish a working relationship with these clients is simply not available, so clinicians tend to rely on parents and others to restructure the child's environment. Although Shapiro labeled his second stage as a diagnostic period, he was not referring to the traditional categorization of behaviors (see Chapter 4). Rather, this is the time when the therapist develops a treatment plan that includes the most appropriate interventions for the child's presenting problem.

Implementation of brief therapy is a collaborative effort between the therapist, child, parents, and significant other adults. As part of the treatment plan, the clinician must specify who is responsible for each component of therapy and then coordinate the efforts of this treatment team. For individual therapy sessions with the child, Shapiro (1994) recommended that clinicians use games. Chapter 15 discusses some commonly used therapeutic board games for children. But Shapiro suggested that traditional childhood games, such as Simon Says, can be used with young clients. Treatment is effective to the extent that the therapeutic gains generalize to the child's everyday life. This final stage in Shapiro's model must be on the clinician's mind from the outset of treatment because the end of brief therapy occurs so soon after the first visit to the clinic. As Shapiro stated, "From the moment that the child walks in the door, the therapist must also envision him or her walking out the door at the end of treatment" (p. 30).

Brief therapy appears to be an effective method for treating a variety of presenting problems (Koss & Shiang, 1994; Messer & Wachtel, 1997). Although much of the research on these interventions has been conducted with adult clients, the approach seems to have merit for children.

Selected chapters of this book explore the use of brief therapy with children. Although behavioral interventions are typically brief, proponents of other theoretical approaches have developed brief versions of their methods. Clinicians must realize that brief treatments are used for reasons other than the restrictions implemented by managed health care companies. For example, brief therapists are able to serve more children than are their colleagues who use traditional approaches. To successfully use the brief-term model, clinicians must recognize that all troubled children do not require extensive individual therapy to overcome their problems. For many clients, brief therapies targeted to specific problems can be effective and efficient interventions.

EMPIRICALLY SUPPORTED THERAPIES FOR CHILDREN

A relatively recent addition to the field of child treatments is the concept of *empirically supported therapies* (ESTs), which were originally called *empirically validated therapies* by the American Psychological Association's Division of Clinical Psychology, Task Force on Promotion and Dissemination of Psychological Procedures (1995). Chambless et al. (1996, 1998) described the standards used to qualify a treatment as empirically supported. Lonigan, Elbert, and Johnson (1998) adapted these criteria for use in identifying *well-established* and *probably efficacious* therapies for children (Table 3-5). When Chambless et al. (1998) updated their list of ESTs, they cited two well-established treatments for children: (1) behavioral conditioning for nocturnal enuresis (Houts, Berman, & Abramson, 1994) and (2) parent training for oppositional behavior (Wells & Egan, 1988). They also listed five probably efficacious treatments: (1) behavioral treatment for childhood obesity (Epstein, Valoski, Wing, & McCurley, 1994; Wheeler & Hess, 1976), (2) behavior modification for encopresis (O'Brien, Ross, & Christophersen, 1986), (3 & 4) cognitive-behavioral treatment and family anxiety management training for anxiety disorders in children (Kendall, 1994; Barrett, Dadds, & Rapee, 1996), and (5) exposure for phobias (Menzies & Clarke, 1993).

Messer and Wachtel (1997) questioned the original decision to describe these treatments as "empirically

Table 3–5

The Criteria for Empirically Supported Therapies

WELL-ESTABLISHED TREATMENTS

1. At least two well-conducted group-design studies, conducted by different investigatory teams, showing the treatment to be either
   a. superior to pill placebo or alternative treatment, OR
   b. equivalent to an already established treatment in studies with adequate statistical power.
   OR
2. A large series of single-case design studies (i.e., $n > 9$) that both
   a. use good experimental design, AND
   b. compare the intervention to another treatment.
   AND
3. Treatment manuals used for the intervention preferred.
   AND
4. Sample characteristics must be clearly specified.

PROBABLY EFFICACIOUS TREATMENTS

1. Two studies showing the intervention more effective than a no-treatment control group (e.g., a wait-list comparison group).
   OR
2. Two group-design studies meeting criteria for well-established treatments but conducted by the same investigator.
   OR
3. A small series of single-case design experiments (i.e., $n > 3$) that otherwise meet Criterion 2 for well-established treatments.
   AND
4. Treatment manuals used for the intervention preferred.
   AND
5. Sample characteristics must be clearly specified.

From "Empirically Supported Psychosocial Interventions for Children: An Overview," by C. J. Lonigan, J. C. Elbert, and S. B. Johnson, 1998, *Journal of Clinical Child Psychology, 27,* p. 141. Copyright 1998 by Lawrence Erlbaum Associates, Inc. Reprinted with permission of the author.

validated" because they believed this phrase instilled an undeservedly high level of confidence in these therapies. Researchers, practitioners, and insurance companies may incorrectly assume that the interventions included in a list of these treatments should be used routinely with all children who exhibit a certain problem. Kendall (1998) agreed, cautioning that evidence is available to support the use of ESTs but not to justify the confidence warranted by a "validated" therapy. Investigators have found that ESTs work when tested under laboratory conditions, but these results may not generalize to the real world of clinical practice. Chambless et al. (1996) encouraged therapists to consider the many factors that influence a child's response to treatment. As they stated, "We have made no recommendations about what is the best treatment for a particular problem" (Chambless et al., 1996, pp. 5–6). What they have attempted to do is consolidate the existing research on child therapies to offer better guidance to clinicians.

Weisz and Weiss (1989) and Weisz, Weiss, and Donenberg (1992) described how child therapies, as evaluated in research settings, differ from treatments used in clinics (Table 3-6). In general, research therapies are more prescribed and focused on a particular problem. Because clinic therapies are designed to meet the unique needs of each child, their actual form and content differ from client to client. To successfully use ESTs in clinical practice, therapists must adapt research therapies to the individual needs of the child. As Messer and Wachtel (1997) stated: "Practitioners typically cannot be as choosy as researchers about whom they treat, nor do—or should—they limit their treatment efforts to one isolated characteristic of what troubles the individual" (p. 24). The brief treatments we discussed earlier offer an interesting opportunity to bridge the gap between research and clinic therapies for children. The time-limited approach and problem-focused orientation of research therapies are also criteria used to define brief treat-

Table 3–6
A Comparison of Research and Clinic Therapies

Research Therapies	Clinic Therapies
1. Children are recruited to participate in a focused treatment program	Children are referred for the treatment of comorbid disorders.
2. Treatment samples are homogeneous and share a common problem.	Each child has a unique set of problems.
3. Treatment addresses the common problem.	Treatment addresses a variety of problems.
4. Therapists are specially trained to use specific treatment techniques.	Therapists rely on previous training to use a range of treatments.
5. Therapy sessions are prescribed in a treatment manual.	Therapy sessions are based on the clinician's judgment.
6. Therapists are monitored in their use of the treatment program.	Therapists function without external monitoring.

Adapted from Weisz and Weiss (1989) and Weisz, Weiss, and Donenberg (1992).

ments. Because brief interventions are used in real-life settings, they resemble the clinic therapies used with everyday clients. With the continued development of empirically supported treatments for a broader range of presenting problems, therapists will be able to select from a list of interventions to treat specific problems in the context of brief therapy.

Another factor that merits consideration is the information used to identify an intervention as an EST. A review of the criteria cited in Table 3-5 reveals that treatments are chosen based on studies that have been reviewed and selected for publication in the professional literature. Although this sample includes reports of child therapies that were found to work, it probably does not include studies in which ESTs were not helpful to clients. Reviewers and editorial boards tend to publish articles that contain significant results. This bias against nonsignificant findings limits the data pool available to qualify a treatment as empirically supported. For this reason, therapists must remember that designation as an EST does not guarantee that a treatment has been or will be successful in all cases.

Messer and Wachtel (1997) observed that ESTs tend to be behavioral and cognitive behavioral interventions. In fact, most of the treatments that meet the Chambless et al. (1998) criteria are behavioral or cognitive-behavioral in nature. This does not mean that interventions based on other theoretical principles are ineffective. Rather, it reflects the limited amount of empirical research currently available about other child therapies. The number of controlled studies on psychodynamic, child-centered, and family systems interventions pales in comparison with published research on behavioral and cognitive-behavioral treatments. Considerable effort is needed to rectify this imbalance, or therapists will have increasingly fewer options available. As Russ and Ollendick (1999) warned, proponents of other treatments must provide empirical support for their methods if these techniques are to remain viable. We can safely assume that therapists will be held accountable for their work. Increasing the number and nature of ESTs will provide a broader selection of interventions for children and their families.

Ollendick and Russ (1999) observed that controlled treatment studies for specific childhood problems have contributed to the establishment of clinics that provide services tailored to an individual problem. For example, children with encopresis may receive treatment in clinics staffed by medical and mental health specialists with expertise on this problem. Although the specialized approach to intervention has merit in areas in which there is a sufficient number of children with a given problem, it is less appropriate for rural communities where therapists are expected to be generalists who treat a broad range of presenting problems. If ESTs are to be used with a wider range of problems and treatment settings, researchers and practitioners must bridge the artificial divide that has separated them. Hibbs and Jensen (1996) agreed, citing the limits implemented by managed health care providers as evidence that "there has never been a time in which these professionals were so dependent on one another for survival" (p. 5). The conditions of the market place have emphasized the need for clinicians and researchers to collaborate and capitalize on the methodological skills and clinical knowledge of each group to bring research therapies into the everyday world of clinical practice (Weisz et al., 1992).

BRIEF AND EMPIRICALLY SUPPORTED THERAPY IN MANAGED MENTAL HEALTH CARE: A CASE EXAMPLE

Encopresis is a problem behavior that many children and adults have difficulty discussing. McGrath, Mellon, and Murphy (2000) described the disorder as "defecation in inappropriate places over a given time span" (p. 226). Although Easson (1960) differentiated between children who have never achieved bowel control (i.e., primary encopresis) and those who were continent and resumed soiling at a later point (i.e., secondary encopresis), encopresis is typically classified as either retentive or nonretentive. Children with retentive encopresis have a history of constipation followed by fecal compaction. Their soiling results from seepage or overflow around this blockage in the bowel. Children with nonretentive encopresis are not constipated and are likely to pass fully formed stools. As McGrath et al. (2000) and Christophersen and Mortweet (2001) indicated, both forms of encopresis must be differentiated from constipation itself, which involves the difficult and often painful passage of hard or large stools without fecal incontinence.

Unless they have personally experienced elimination problems, adults typically give little time and attention to this behavior. But McGrath et al. (2000) described the many steps that children must learn in order to defecate in an appropriate manner. First, they need to consume a diet that contains sufficient fiber and water to permit passage of feces through the lower intestinal tract. Unfortunately, many of the foods that children enjoy have low amounts of fiber. Examples of foods with a moderate to high level of dietary fiber are fruits, vegetables, wheat breads, and cereals (American Academy of Pediatrics, 1998). Williams, Bollella, and Wynder (1995) highlighted the relationship between age and daily fiber intake when they suggested that children consume one gram of fiber for each year of life, plus 5. This means that the recommended amount for Charles, the 6-year-old boy in our case example, would be 11 grams, one for each year of his life plus 5. Information on the dietary fiber content of foods can be obtained from *Bowes and Church's Food Values of Portions Commonly Used* (17th ed.) (Pennington, 1998).

Children must also recognize and respond to the physical cues that signal the need to void, and they must be sufficiently motivated to seek an appropriate place for toileting. A child who is happily playing in the backyard may sense these cues but remain outside and subsequently soil his pants. Children who make the trip to the bathroom must be able to undress themselves, engage in the abdominal muscle movements to initiate voiding, and clean themselves after elimination of feces. Therapists need to be alert for any breakdown in this sequence of behaviors that can cause elimination problems. For example, children who are constipated are likely to experience pain as they try to void and may resist their parents' attempts to have them engage in proper toileting activities.

When asked to treat children with encopresis, therapists must conduct a thorough assessment of the behavior. Christophersen and Mortweet (2001) provided a form that clinicians can use to collect information about a child's diet, toileting behaviors, and elimination problems (e.g., constipation). The authors observed that parents often assume that the child who is going to the bathroom each day is not constipated. But Christophersen and Mortweet described how children who void small amounts on a daily basis can become constipated as feces accumulates in the bowel. An important component of any treatment program for encopresis is a medical assessment designed to identify children whose incontinence is caused by organic problems. After physiological causes have been eliminated, therapists should assess the behavioral aspects of the soiling. This involves consideration of the nature and duration of the encopresis, the time and location of soiling episodes, and the caregivers' response to these events. Additionally, information on the outcome of previous treatments can provide insight on parenting practices (e.g., rewards, punishment) and techniques that should be modified or avoided. Therapists must not limit their assessment to the encopresis. Parent-, teacher-, and child-report measures can be administered to obtain a general view of the client's psychosocial development (see Chapter 4 for examples). Treatment for a child whose soiling is only one of a number of inappropriate behaviors is different from the treatment given to a client whose development is normal except for the encopresis.

In their review of treatments for childhood encopresis, McGrath et al. (2000) described medical interventions, psychotherapy, biofeedback, and behavior therapy. Of these, the most common methods appear to be medical and behavioral treatments, which are often used in combination. Medical interventions include laxatives and purgatives to eliminate fecal compaction, increased fiber intake, and brief periods of sitting on the toilet after a meal to take advantage of the gastro-ileal reflex associated with the normal passage of feces (see Young, 1973). Behavioral interventions involve the use of positive reinforcement, punishment (e.g., requiring the child to wash soiled clothes), and educational programs on the benefits of a high-fiber diet. The medical and behavioral methods used to treat children with encopresis require the active and consistent involvement of parents. Collecting data on a child's soiling behavior and proper toileting, following dietary recommendations each day, and scheduling toilet sitting after meals takes considerable time and effort. But researchers have found that families who are willing to implement these interventions can control a child's encopresis.

Houts and Peterson (1986) used a combination of medical and behavioral strategies with a 7-year-old boy diagnosed as having retentive encopresis. At the outset of treatment, the parents were instructed to reward the child for bowel movements he had in the toilet and days when he did not soil his pants. After 4 weeks, these procedures were terminated and the parents implemented a high-fiber diet and scheduled toilet sitting (i.e., 10 minutes) about 15 to 20 minutes after the family's evening meal. The two methods were combined 4 weeks later. This treatment was used for 5 weeks, when the boy was toileting appropriately and not soiling his pants. Houts and Peterson contacted the family 1 year later and found that the child was successful in maintaining these behaviors.

Stark, Owens-Stively, Spirito, Lewis, and Guevremont (1990) developed a six-session treatment that included the use of enema clean-out to eliminate compaction, a high-fiber diet, a 10-minute toilet session at the same time each day, and rewarding the child for treatment compliance and appropriate toileting behavior. An interesting aspect of the Stark, Owens- Stively, et al. combination of medical and behavioral techniques is the authors' use of group sessions for parents and children. Each week, groups of parents met to learn about the relationship between diet and encopresis, the use of child behavior management techniques, and the importance of a consistent approach to parenting. In their groups, children had the opportunity to interact with other clients in treatment for encopresis. They also learned about the connection between diet and encopresis and about relaxation techniques they could use when administering an enema. Stark, Owens-Stively, et al. found that the clients in their study exhibited a significant increase in fiber intake and appropriate bowel movements. They also reported a significant decline in soiling episodes, with approximately 90% of the children symptom free at the end of treatment. These findings were later replicated by Stark, Opipari, et al. (1997).

Clinicians have incorporated play into their treatment of young children with encopresis. Knell and Moore (1990), for example, used a bear puppet in cognitive-behavioral play therapy with a 5-year-old boy diagnosed as having nonretentive encopresis. When it became apparent that the child was afraid of the toilet, the clinician used the puppet to model appropriate behaviors and to teach the child that these acts would not cause any negative consequences, such as getting flushed down the toilet. The boy's parents also participated in treatment when Knell and Moore instructed them to use behavior management skills to encourage appropriate toileting. The authors found that after 12 sessions, the boy was using the toilet regularly. After his fourteenth session, he was no longer soiling his pants. Similar to Houts and Peterson (1986), Knell and Moore reported a positive long-term outcome for the child. At 45-month follow-up, he was continent and toileting appropriately.

Geroski and Rodgers (1998) recommended a multidisciplinary approach to treating children with encopresis. We have discussed the role of the therapist and physician, but some children, such as Charles in our case example, soil themselves at school. When this occurs, teachers and school counselors are important participants in a collaborative treatment. Geroski and Rodgers indicated that school counselors can identify children with incontinence problems, contact parents to arrange a medical referral, and provide supportive services for clients and their families. With informed consent from parents, counselors can collect and provide information to community-based service providers to use in developing an effective intervention. When a child is being teased by other students, Geroski and Rodgers suggested that counselors implement classroom programs to encourage classmates to be more caring and tolerant of others. School counselors are also important sources of individual treatment, especially when these services are not available elsewhere.

We now return to the case of Charles, whose encopresis has returned despite three previous trials of medical treatment. When Dr. Shipley treated the boy before for this problem, he prescribed enemas and laxatives, a high-fiber diet, and scheduled sitting on the toilet. When he reviews his notes from previous visits, he recognizes a recurring pattern: fecal continence and constipation followed by encopresis. Charles' parents initially complied with treatment but returned to the family's regular diet and ceased using daily toileting sessions after the child had stopped soiling. Dr. Shipley realizes that the Trimbles require a more comprehensive treatment of medical and behavioral strategies designed to remediate and prevent the occurrence of this behavior. The brief intervention described here represents a combination of strategies that were empirically tested by Houts and Peterson (1986), Knell and Moore (1990), and Stark and her colleagues (Stark, Opipari, et al., 1997; Stark, Owens-Stively, et al., 1990). Treatment is described in the context of the case management procedures that Poynter (1998) recommended for managed mental health care services.

▪ ▪ ▪

During his brief visit with the Trimbles, Dr. Shipley learns that Charles became constipated about 1 month ago. He recently developed retentive encopresis and is now soiling his pants at least once a day. When Dr. Shipley asks about the parents' response, Mrs. Trimble admits that her husband and she did not continue the prescribed treatment after Charles became continent approximately 4 months ago. Mr. Trimble adds that it is difficult to implement Dr. Shipley's recommendation every day. Despite their attempts to keep Charles on a high-fiber diet, he refuses to eat the foods prepared for him. Instead, he prefers processed meats, dairy products, and snack foods.

"How often is Charles having a bowel movement in the toilet?" Dr. Shipley asks.

"I'm not sure. I don't think it's very often," the father answers. "Actually, my wife and I have been real busy lately, so we haven't had a chance to keep up with that."

Dr. Shipley concludes that the family has returned to its normal routine and the parents have been inconsistent in their use of the prescribed medical procedures. Controlling his frustration, he asks whether the current episode of encopresis is different in any way from previous incidents.

"Yes," Mrs. Trimble answers, "Charles is having accidents at school. His Dad and I are really concerned."

The parents agree to schedule an appointment with Dr. Faller. They sign release of information forms allowing Dr. Shipley to speak with the therapist and to contact their medical insurance company. As he had done during previous visits with the Trimbles, Dr. Shipley instructs the parents to give Charles an enema on each of the next 3 days, to increase the fiber content in his diet, and to resume scheduled sittings on the toilet. As in past visits, the parents agree to immediately implement these interventions.

Later that afternoon, Dr. Shipley confers with Dr. Faller regarding a combined treatment of medical and behavioral procedures. "Here's written documentation on the referral," he says. "We've notified the family's insurance company about the referral, so they shouldn't have any problems getting authorization to see you." As part of the referral materials, Dr. Shipley provides a copy of the parents' signed release of information form allowing the two professionals to communicate regarding treatment.

"It sounds like you've been able to control the boy's soiling for brief periods, but the parents haven't followed through on your recommendations. I think I need to see them without Charles, at least for the first session." Dr. Faller returns to her office and opens a case file for the Trimbles. In the file, she places Dr. Shipley's referral information and then records her conversation with him as her first progress note.

When Mr. Trimble calls the next morning to schedule an appointment, Dr. Faller realizes that the family is eager to begin treatment. "I'm really worried about school," the father says. "Yesterday, I found out that the other kids are making fun of Charles and calling him names." Although she prefers group treatment for children with encopresis, Dr. Faller decides to see the Trimbles as a family rather than wait until she starts her next group.

"Can you and your wife meet with me on Friday?" Dr. Faller asks.

"That's 4 days from now!" the father answers. "Can't we do it earlier?"

"Well, Friday is my first opening, and I understand that Dr. Shipley has asked you to give Charles an enema each day for 3 days."

"Yes, we haven't done it yet." He hesitates and then adds, "But we will."

"I think that's where we need to begin. Let's do what Dr. Shipley suggested between now and Friday. I'd like to see you and your wife first so we can discuss the situation in detail. Before we meet, you should contact your insurance company to get approval for therapy."

"Yes, my wife's already done that," he answers. "The guy she talked to said it was okay to start. He just wanted to know what the problem was and whether Charles had been treated for it before."

Immediately after the telephone conversation, Dr. Faller documents the date and content of the contact as a progress note in the case file. She then adds other materials she will need when she meets with the parents. These include an intake form and blank consent to treatment and release of information forms. She also inserts a description of the insurer's treatment authorization and case management policies, which include coverage for eight initial sessions over a 2-month period. Dr. Faller serves on provider panels for different insurers, so she maintains up-to-date summaries of commonly used plans for each company. During her first session with the parents, she gives this information to them along with a pamphlet describing her assessment and therapy services, billing procedures, and limits to confidentiality.

As she is describing the insurance company's procedures, Mr. Trimble interrupts, "I didn't know we could only see you for eight sessions."

"How are we going to keep Charles from having these accidents if we only have eight sessions?" the mother asks.

"That's a very good questions," Dr. Faller answers. "I understand that you've been able to control Charles' soiling before, if only for a brief time. I think we can get the same results again if we follow Dr. Shipley's procedures. But the three of us also need to come up with a plan to permanently eliminate the encopresis."

The parents seem to feel more comfortable as Dr. Faller describes her goals for therapy. After they sign the consent to treatment form, the parents complete the therapist's intake form, which contains sections for demographic information about family members, the child's developmental history, a brief description of the presenting problem and previous treatments, and the family's insurance company and policy number. The parents also sign a release of information form allowing Dr. Faller to contact their insurer for billing purposes. Although clients who sign company reimbursement forms endorse a brief statement permitting communication between the insurer and therapist, Dr. Faller uses a more detailed release form so families understand the nature of the information to be disclosed.

Dr. Faller discusses Dr. Shipley's referral summary with the parents. She then listens as they describe Charles' soiling history and the family's attempts to remediate the behavior. Mrs. Trimble admits that she and her husband have been inconsistent in using Dr. Shipley's interventions. Similar to her colleague, Dr. Faller detects a recurring pattern of intense parent interest in treatment followed by poor compliance when the child's encopresis subsides. She turns to Mr. Trimble and says, "On the phone, we talked about Dr. Shipley's prescription of three daily enemas for Charles. How did that go?"

"I think they've helped, but he's still having accidents," he answers. Although Charles dislikes the enema clean-outs, the parents report that the procedure seems to be relieving the compaction in his bowel. "He's gone to the bathroom some each time we've given him one," the father says. At the end of the session, Dr. Faller asks the parents to visit briefly with Dr. Shipley, who advises them to use a brief trial of laxatives with their son.

Dr. Faller's treatment goal is the permanent elimination of the boy's encopresis. She decides to motivate the parents by capitalizing on their school-related concerns. "I share your concerns about the soiling incidents at school," she says. "What do you think we can do so Charles will never soil again?" The parents recite what Dr. Shipley has told them about the benefits of a high-fiber diet and scheduled toileting, but they admit that they are not using either of these interventions. Dr. Faller collects specific information about the parents' previous attempts to follow a high-fiber diet and scheduled toileting. Then she says, "It's going to be very important that you keep daily records of these behaviors because we will use that information to decide if treatment is working." She shows the parents how to record these data and then explores potential obstacles with them. She gives them a chart for reporting soiling incidents, the timing of scheduled sittings, appropriate bowel movements in the toilet, and the daily fiber content of Charles' diet.

Dr. Faller asks the Trimbles to identify steps they can take to become more consistent with Charles. As part of this discussion, she asks them to describe the boy's strengths and interests. The parents mention that he likes to swim and that the two of them had thought about taking him to swimming classes at the local YMCA. Dr. Faller reinforces this idea, which she believes to be an education/development strategy for enhancing the boy's self-concept. At the conclusion of the session, she has the parents complete a questionnaire to provide an overall assessment of his behavior. The Trimbles sign consent forms allowing her to communicate with Dr. Shipley and to maintain contact with Charles' teacher and school counselor.

Between sessions, Dr. Faller telephones Ms. Wilson, the school counselor, to ask her to participate in a collaborative treatment. The counselor reports that Charles' teacher, Ms. Blackstone, requested help after the boy first soiled his pants in class. "Some of the other students are making fun of him, calling him 'baby' and other names," Ms. Wilson says. "I'm meeting with his class twice a week to conduct activities about individual differences. His teacher has spoken to some of the kids who are giving Charles a rough time."

When she contacts Ms. Blackstone, Dr. Faller confirms that the other students have been teasing Charles. The teacher agrees to keep a record of his soiling and to reward him for appropriate behavior in class. She also reports that Charles refuses to use the bathroom at school. "I think he's afraid but I'm not sure why," she says.

During the second session, Dr. Faller meets with the family but initially focuses her attention on Charles, who presents as talkative and engaging. When she mentions his encopresis, he hesitates and then acknowledges the behavior, adding that he wants to stop soiling his pants.

"What's that?" he asks, changing the topic and walking toward the therapist's play area. Dr. Faller follows him to a corner of her office, where she has placed plush toys, a miniature chair, and an infant's toilet. Charles sits on the floor and begins playing with a toy dog. Dr. Faller joins him, taking the plush cat in her hand. "What's your name?" she has the cat ask Charles.

"Max." Charles has the dog answer. "What's yours?"

"Priscilla," the cat says.

"Priscilla? That's a funny name," the dog replies. As the therapist and child are engaged in free play, Charles places the dog on the toilet. "Watch out!" the dog yells. "They're gonna get you." He grabs a toy bear and places it in front of the dog. "Hey, you. Get outta here," the bear says. Charles throws the bear on the floor and removes the dog from the toilet. As Dr. Faller watches him at play, she wonders whether he is portraying a significant event from school.

During the latter part of the session, Dr. Faller reviews the parents' charts and discusses how they can reinforce Charles' appropriate behaviors. The family decides that they will go for a picnic at a nearby park if Charles engages in scheduled toileting on at least 4 days and soils himself fewer than six times during the week. At the end of the session, Dr. Faller provides another chart for the parents to use in recording Charles' behaviors.

Between sessions, she contacts Ms. Blackstone and describes the scene Charles portrayed in session. "Do you think something happened in the bathroom at school?" she asks. Ms. Blackstone is not aware of any such episode but says that she will allow Charles to use the bathroom when other students are not there. During the following weeks, the teacher is unable to obtain evidence to support Charles' story, but he starts to use the bathroom, first alone and eventually with his classmates.

In the third session, the family reports that Charles only soiled his pants three times at home. The parents also state that Charles' swimming lessons will begin this week. When Dr. Faller and Charles move to the play area, they use the plush dog to act out appropriate toileting behaviors. Dr. Faller praises the toy for its behavior and has Charles make positive self-statements, such as, "I'm a good dog. I used the potty." During the same visit, she uses the plush toy to explain the relationship between diet and successful toileting. "So if Max eats the right food," she says at one point, "he won't have an accident. Maybe we should try that."

"Huh?" Charles asks.

"Maybe we should pick the foods you can eat so you won't soil your pants." Dr. Faller invites the parents to join the discussion about the boy's diet. She asks Charles to list his favorite foods and is glad to hear him mention items that contain moderate to high levels of fiber. These include apples, oranges, oatmeal and raisin bran cereal, whole wheat bread and crackers, peanuts and peanut butter, and baked beans. The parents agree to have these foods available and to award a sticker on each day that Charles eats at least three portions of them. The family decides that when he has accumulated six stickers, they will take a trip to the local zoo.

Dr. Faller meets with the parents only during the fourth session to continue their earlier discussion of a consistent approach to child rearing. At the outset of the session, the mother reports that Charles did not soil his pants during the past week. "He used the bathroom every day," she says, "and he's eating the foods we talked about last week." Mr. Trimble describes the special activities they do with Charles each day, regardless of how tired they feel after work. These include reading bedtime stories and taking him to swimming lessons. Dr. Faller uses the parents' earlier experiences in therapy to discuss various child management skills, including charting and positive reinforcement. She gives them a pamphlet about these techniques and has them discuss how they can use these skills to prevent a relapse of the encopresis and to facilitate Charles' psychosocial development.

Each week, Dr. Faller gives Dr. Shipley a brief written summary of the boy's progress. She reports data on appropriate toileting, his soiling episodes at home and school, and his dietary fiber intake. She also describes the parents' compliance with treatment as well as any relevant information she obtains from the school.

When the Trimbles arrive for their fifth session, they report that Charles has not soiled his pants at home or school for the past 2 weeks. Dr. Faller praises the boy and then asks him what he has done to remain continent. "I use the bathroom," he answers, "and I eat the stuff we talked about." She congratulates the family for their hard work and asks them to discuss their plans for maintaining success.

"We're not going to get off track this time," Mrs. Trimble answers. "I mean, we're so proud of Charles. We are going to work hard to make sure he eats the right foods and goes to the bathroom every day." Because the parents have complied with treatment so far, Dr. Faller suggests a 3-week interval before the family's next appointment. This visit will occur 1 week before the 2-month termination date set by the family's insurance company during the preauthorization process.

During the intervening time period, Dr. Faller contacts the school and learns that Charles has not soiled his pants again. Ms. Blackstone mentions that he is using the bathroom and has begun to make friends in class. One of these students also attends swimming lessons with Charles and has spent the night at his house. The teacher says that the school counselor's presentations on individual differences appear to have had a positive effect. She reports a noticeable decrease in the amount of teasing, in general, among the students in her class.

When the Trimbles return for their sixth visit, the parents report that Charles has been continent for 5 weeks. During this session, the parents actually spend more time talking about Charles' progress at the YMCA and his new friends at school than they devote to his encopresis. Aware that this change of attitude preceded relapse in the past, Dr. Faller asks the family to again discuss the possible obstacles to long-term success. Both Mr. and Mrs. Trimble say that for Charles to remain continent, they must consistently follow the high-fiber diet and use the child management skills learned in therapy.

To further reduce the likelihood of relapse, Dr. Faller schedules two follow-up appointments at 1-month intervals. Because this will require more than the 2 months initially authorized by the Trimble's insurer, Dr. Faller telephones the company to request an extension. Because she has not completed the eight preauthorized sessions, she receives verbal approval for an additional 3 months without having to submit a treatment reauthorization form. During the eighth session with the family, she tells the parents that she will contact them at 6-month intervals over the next 2 years to discuss their posttreatment progress. She also asks them to notify her if Charles becomes constipated and begins to exhibit encopretic symptoms.

After her last session with the Trimbles, Dr. Faller prepares a treatment summary for Dr. Shipley. She describes her treatment program and the family's progress in controlling the encopresis, increasing fiber intake, and encouraging appropriate toileting. Because the parents were noncompliant in the past, she lists the prognosis as guarded and describes her plan to monitor the family's progress during the next 2 years. Dr. Faller incorporates this same information into the discharge summary she sends to the Trimbles' insurance company. This report also contains the dates and length of therapy sessions, pretreatment and posttreatment diagnoses, and summary charts containing the weekly soiling, dietary, and appropriate toileting data reported by the parents.

During follow-up telephone conversations with the Trimbles, Dr. Faller hears encouraging news. The parents report that Charles has not relapsed and is toileting appropriately every day. For health reasons, the entire family decided to follow the high-fiber diet, and the parents continue to use the child management techniques with their son. Charles has joined the YMCA swim team and has become friends with two of his teammates. He reportedly enjoys school and is doing well academically.

▪ ▪ ▪

Brief therapy was effective in treating Charles' encopresis for a number of reasons. First, the parents had medical insurance that covered the cost of a collaborative intervention provided by the pediatrician and psychologist. Had the family not had access to third-party reimbursement for services, it is possible that the child's soiling would have continued and become an obstacle to his psychosocial development. It is also important to note that Mr. and Mrs. Trimble were motivated to remediate and prevent their son's encopresis. This important element was missing from previous treatment attempts and probably accounted for the boy's poor long-term response to medical intervention. Although the parents attributed this lack of commitment to their employment status, they appeared to have a healthy marital relationship and were willing to work together to help their son. Dr. Faller focused on the parents' inconsistent use of medical interventions by teaching them more effective child management skills. The positive outcome in this case is no doubt related to the fact that Charles' problems were limited to a single behavior. His compliance with therapy may have been different had he exhibited behaviors that would compromise the treatment process. Finally, the Trimbles and Dr. Faller benefited from the empirical studies that researchers, such as Stark and her colleagues, had conducted on medical-behavioral treatments for encopresis. With this information, the therapist used an intervention designed specifically for children with retentive encopresis.

Dr. Faller was able to obtain an extension of the preauthorized time for therapy without submitting a treatment reauthorization form. Had it been necessary for her to request additional sessions, she would have been prepared to document the outcome of her work with this family. Given the Trimbles' history, the therapist was wise to schedule follow-up visits to ensure treatment compliance. Bernard-Bonnin, Haley, and Nadeau (1993) suggested that the unsuccessful outcome of Dr. Shipley's earlier interventions is not unusual. In their follow-up study of children treated for encopresis, Bernard-Bonnin et al. found that only 36% of the clients did not experience relapse during the 3.5 years after termination of treatment. For this reason, therapy for children with encopresis should be of a multimodal nature. Sometimes the same intervention will fulfill more than one purpose. In our case, continuation of the high-fiber diet initially used to control the soiling was part of the long-term plan to prevent the return of this behavior. Helping the parents to become more consistent was a significant component of the treatment program. Modifying their behavior also prevented this and other problem behaviors from occurring in the future. Elimination of the soiling behavior was itself a remedial, preventive, and educational/developmental event. Charles is less likely to experience psychosocial problems because of encopresis-related rejection by other students. And we might expect that this change, in combination with enrichment activities and classroom presentations on individual differences, will facilitate the development of positive self-esteem and healthy peer relationships.

SUMMARY

The practice of child therapy in a managed care environment requires the use of effective, time-limited treatments. Brief and empirically supported therapies offer a starting point for designing interventions that meet the unique needs of each child and family. Compared with what was asked of therapists in the traditional fee-for-service system, clinicians now are more likely to find themselves balancing clinical and business considerations in their everyday work. Documentation of assessment, diagnostic, and treatment activities has become even more important because managed care companies use this information to authorize treatment and make reimbursement decisions. Having medical necessity as a precondition for therapy means that clinicians must integrate the three components of the multimodal approach into a single treatment. Therapists can no longer follow a stage model in which presenting problems are remediated before prevention and education/development activities are implemented.

4

Assessment: The First Step

▪ ▪ ▪

Mr. and Mrs. Morris request professional help for their 7-year-old son, Joseph, at the insistence of his teacher. The teacher is concerned that the boy's inconsistent grades and lack of friends at school are caused by attention-deficit hyperactivity disorder (ADHD). Mr. Morris states that Joseph often loses his school work and is unable to complete homework assignments without parental supervision. According to Mrs. Morris, none of the children in the neighborhood play with Joseph because he does not follow the rules in organized games and sports. As the parents describe their concerns during the clinical interview with Dr. Anne Pellegrini, Joseph repeatedly interrupts by getting out of his seat and walking around the room. Every time this occurs, Mrs. Morris asks him to sit down or Mr. Morris threatens to punish the boy.

▪ ▪ ▪

The first step to effective treatment is a thorough assessment of the child within the context of his or her cultural surround. As Kaplan (1986) stated, "The more accurate the assessment, the better the treatment; if assessment is inaccurate, the subsequent treatment will be inappropriate" (p. 27). The assessment techniques that clinicians select differ according to their theoretical orientation and the purpose of the assessment. This chapter explores methods that are commonly used to assess childhood problems. It also examines developmental and multicultural issues that therapists must consider when assessing children. At the end of the chapter, we continue with the case of Joseph and review a multidimensional assessment for ADHD.

THEORETICAL PERSPECTIVES

The assessment of children involves the use of a variety of theoretical perspectives, each with its unique strengths and limitations. Briefly stated, the psychodynamic approach is based on the belief that psychological disorders in children are the "manifestation of underlying or unconscious conflicts or forces" (Knoff, 1986, p. 9) related to early childhood experiences (see Chapter 6). Learning theory serves as the foundation for behavioral assessment, in which attention is focused on the relationship between a child's actions and environmental antecedents and consequences (see Chapter 10). Family assessment is a systems-based approach in which behavior is interpreted relative to its function within the family unit (see Chapter 12). Another approach that is important but not addressed elsewhere in this book is the biological approach to assessment.

The Biological Approach to Assessment

Most therapists are trained by nonphysicians in nonmedical settings. Consequently, they are less likely than physicians to consider physical abnormalities as possible causes for psychological problems in children. Often referred to as the medical model, the biological approach involves a search for the organic factors believed to be at the root of a child's difficulties (Konarski & Spruill, 1987). Therapists so infrequently encounter children with organic problems that they tend to overlook physical causes in cases in which referral to a physician is needed. Strayhorn (1987) described what he called "horror stories" (p. 50) in which organic disorders in children were incorrectly diagnosed as psychological problems. The following is an example in which psychostimulant medication was used to treat a suspected case of ADHD:

> A child is treated with psychotherapy for 2 years because of worsening peer relationships, poor school performance, and problems paying attention. She is given a trial of methylphenidate as well, and this drug seems to help. She complains of headaches, but these are felt to be side effects of the methylphenidate. It is only when her legs develop weakness and incoordination that she is taken to a neurologist. The diagnosis is a meningioma, a brain tumor that would have been curable with no residual damage if operated on earlier. (p. 50)

Strayhorn noted that because of the incorrect diagnosis, this child was likely to have permanent brain damage. To avoid situations such as this, therapists must learn to recognize possible organic causes of psychological problems in children. They should also develop working relationships with competent physicians they can consult when needed.

Table 4-1 contains five rules that Strayhorn (1987) provided as a guide for therapists to use in determining whether a child's problems are the result of physical causes. Particular attention must be given to rule #2. That is, therapists must never totally discount the possibility that what appears to be a psychological problem is actually organic in nature. Strayhorn described 21 physical causes of behavioral problems in children. Because of our limited space, we will briefly examine three of these: prescription drugs, vitamin deficiencies, and physical abnormalities.

Prescription Medications. It is not unusual for children to be in therapy while they are taking a medication prescribed by a physician. As part of the initial assessment, therapists must identify any concurrent treatments the child is receiving. For example, from 7% to 10% of youths may have asthma at some point in their childhood years (Behrman, Kliegman, Nelson, & Vaughan, 1992). Asthmatic children are sometimes treated with theophylline, a drug that has been found to cause nausea, irritability, and insomnia at therapeutic levels (Bukowskyj, Nakatsu, & Munt, 1984). Although less common than asthma, epileptic seizures are thought to affect approximately 8 of 1000 children (Lechtenberg, 1984). A drug that is used with these children is phenobarbital, which can produce irritability, temper tantrums, or behaviors that resemble those characteristic of ADHD (i.e., attention problems, hyperactivity) (Behrman et al., 1992). Even medications prescribed to treat childhood psychological problems can produce behavioral side effects. For example, the psychostimulant medications used to treat children with ADHD can cause irritability, insomnia, or decreased appetite (Behrman et al., 1992).

Vitamin Deficiencies. Approximately 16% of U.S. children are living in poverty (U.S. Bureau of the Census, 2000) (see Contemporary Issues Box 4-1). Therapists must be alert for the behavioral symptoms of vitamin deficiencies in these children. Young people who lack sufficient levels of vitamin B1, or thi-

Table 4–1

Strayhorn's (1987) Guidelines for Assessing Organic Causes for Childhood Problems

1. Organic causes for childhood problems are more likely when:
   a. A child's impairment in functioning is more severe.
   b. A child experiences a deterioration of previous cognitive abilities.
   c. Therapists are unable to identify psychosocial causes for these problems.
   d. A child is experiencing physical symptoms in addition to psychosocial problems.
2. Therapist must never reject the possibility that a child's problems are organic in nature.

Adapted from "Medical Assessment of Children with Behavioral Problems," by J. M. Strayhorn, 1987, p. 52. In M. Hersen & V. B. Van Hasselt (Eds.), *Behavior therapy with children and adolescents: A clinical approach* (pp. 50–74). New York: John Wiley. Copyright 1987 by John Wiley.

Contemporary Issues Box 4–1

Poverty and Children: Poverty Thresholds and the Living Wage

Living in poverty has been found to have direct and indirect effects on the lives of children. McLoyd (1998) described how economically disadvantaged youths are more at risk for academic and psychosocial problems than their peers from higher-income families. Although poverty is often equated with income level alone, Huston, McLoyd, and Garcia Coll (1994) cautioned that the duration and context (e.g., rural vs. urban) of a family's economic status are also important. For example, children who live in poverty for extended periods of time are more likely to have problems than are their peers whose exposure is either brief or nonexistent (McLoyd, 1998). The relationship between children's development and the duration, context, and level of poverty appears to be mediated by other factors, including the parent–child relationship and parents' psychological adjustment. McLoyd (1989), for example, identified the behavioral and psychological distress experienced by unemployed fathers as an important and compromising influence on their children's development. In other words, fathers' reactions to job loss mediated the effect of decreased family income on children.

The U. S. Census Bureau annually determines poverty thresholds based on family size and the number of members younger than age 18 years. Dalakar (2001) reported that in 2000, the criterion for a four-person family with two members under 18 was $17,463. He also described how poverty declined during the 1990s. Between 1993 and 2000, the rates for families in which no member was employed decreased from 42.9% to 28.7%. In families with at least one employed adult, the poverty rate was lower and declined from 9.6% to 7.6%. Although the rate in 2000 for youths younger than age 18 years was the lowest since 1979, a total of 16.2% of children and adolescents were still living in poverty. This figure increased to 39.8% in families in which children were living with a single female head of household.

Although employment reduces the poverty rate in families, the Dalakar (2001) figures reveal that children of working parents are not immune to economic hardships. Many of the parents in these families likely have jobs that pay at or slightly above the federal standard for a minimum wage. The hourly rate for these jobs was $5.15 at the beginning of 2002, the level established by Congress on September 1, 1997. A full-time worker employed at this wage would earn approximately $10,700 annually, well below the poverty threshold for a family of four with two children. Although many parents have chosen to pursue dual careers in order to compensate for this discrepancy, this option is not available to single mothers living alone with their children.

Community activists and others concerned about the welfare of children and families have proposed the living wage, an alternative approach for determining the minimum wage that employers pay their workers. As the name implies, the living wage is a standard designed to raise family income above the poverty threshold while adjusting for the cost of living in different geographical areas. Pollin and Luce (2000) described the rationale for this approach: "Anyone in this country who works for a living should not have to raise a family in poverty" (p. 1). Since the movement to establish a living wage began in Baltimore in 1994, the approach has been adopted in different forms in communities as diverse as Los Angeles; Barre and Montpelier, Vermont; New York City; and Orange County, North Carolina (Pollin & Luce, 2000). Pollin and Luce contended that living wage programs can be adopted without having negative effects on the economy. Although they lauded the potential benefits of local efforts, the authors recommended the establishment of a living wage on the national level. They indicated that raising the wages of low-income workers to the poverty threshold would be "a substantial step forward" (p. 163), but the long-term goal should be to provide full-time workers with a wage that allows them to move their families out of poverty.

amin, may exhibit fatigue or apathy, nausea, irritability, or concentration problems during the early stages of the deficiency (Behrman et al., 1992). Behrman et al. also noted that children who lack niacin, another member of the vitamin B complex, may experience depression, insomnia, or disorientation. According to Strayhorn (1987), therapists can assess for vitamin deficiencies by questioning parents and children about their diet. When it appears that a client is not receiving adequate nutrition, the clinician should consider referral for support services, such as food assistance from local social service agencies.

Physical Abnormalities. Included under this category are brain tumors, epilepsy, and visual or hearing impairment. Behrman et al. (1992) noted that weeks or months before a tumor is diagnosed, children may exhibit irritability, lethargy or overactivity, forgetfulness, and poor academic performance. Fortunately, brain tumors in children are uncommon. Unfortunately, their low rate of occurrence means that most therapists will never treat a child whose behavioral problems are tumor related and will therefore overlook this organic cause in their assessment. Childhood seizure disorders assume many forms, including infantile febrile seizures, petit mal and grand mal epilepsy, and psychomotor seizures. Infantile febrile seizures, the most common form, affect 3% to 4% of children, typically remit spontaneously, and do not develop into other seizure types (Behrman et al., 1992). Whereas children with petit mal epilepsy experience an absence of consciousness, sometimes for periods of 5 to 15 seconds (Njiokiktjien, 1988), those with grand mal epilepsy have a sudden loss of consciousness followed by alternating muscular contraction and relaxation (Behrman et al., 1992). The behavioral manifestations of psychomotor epilepsy mimic psychiatric symptoms. During a psychomotor seizure, a child may exhibit rage, hallucinations, anxiety, panic, or confusion; between seizure episodes, these children may be depressed or aggressive, display temper tantrums, or experience sleep disorders (Njiokiktjien, 1988).

DEVELOPMENTAL CONSIDERATIONS

Kamphaus and Frick (1996) identified three important issues that therapists must consider when assessing children: developmental norms, development processes, and temporal and contextual stability. The significant developmental changes that occur from birth through adolescence are accompanied by constant redefinition of the criteria that clinicians use to distinguish normal from abnormal behavior in children. As Kamphaus and Frick noted, "The same behavior may be developmentally appropriate at one age but indicative of pathology at another" (p. 49). Consider anxiety in children. Although it is relatively common to observe separation anxiety in 14-month-old infants (Feldman, 1998), this response is the exception among elementary school children. An infant's reluctance to separate briefly from its caregiver is considered normal, but the same behavior in a 10-year-old child is thought to be problematic. Reed, Carter, and Miller (1992) noted other age-related changes in childhood anxiety. Although 2-year-old children tend to be anxious of imaginary creatures (e.g., monsters), death, and robbers, 4-year-old children are more likely to fear the dark, and 6-year-old children are understandably more prone to school-related anxiety.

Straightforward interpretation of test scores based on age-appropriate norms actually provides a rather simplistic view of a child. Both Wenar (1982b) and Kamphaus and Frick (1996) noted the importance of developmental processes in this regard. Kamphaus and Frick, for example, described how test results should be viewed within the context of the child's environment using models such as Erikson's (1968) psychosocial theory of development (see Chapter 6). Consider a 5-year-old abused girl who has not met Erikson's challenge of trust versus mistrust. Although the child's social anxiety may exceed that of her peers, the meaning of her behavior becomes apparent when viewed in the context of the mistrust she has learned to associate with her family environment.

Another important assessment issue is the temporal and contextual stability of a child's psychological adjustment. Kamphaus and Frick (1996) cautioned therapists against concluding that a child's behavior at any point in time is an enduring sign of his or her personality. As we have already discussed, behaviors undergo considerable change during childhood. Contextual stability is another matter. Children's behavior may differ across settings (e.g., home, playground, classroom) simply because of situation-specific contingencies. In the classroom, students are expected to exhibit on-task behavior, but they are allowed to engage in free play activities during recess. An observer's interpretation of a child's behavior will differ from setting to setting. The actions of a mildly depressed student may seem normal in a classroom, where remaining quiet and following instructions are viewed as healthy. The observer may have a different interpretation when the same child isolates himself on the playground.

In recent decades, researchers have given increased attention to the development of abnormal behavior in children. The result has been the emergence of a new area of study, *developmental psychopathology*, which Achenbach (1990) described as "a framework for organizing the study of psychopathology around milestones and sequences in physical, cognitive, social-emotional, and educational development" (p. 3). Because it involves theoreticians and researchers from different fields of study, developmental psychopathology represents a mechanism for communication between scientists and practitioners who are experts on genetic, neurological, psychological, and philosophical influences (Toth & Cicchetti, 1999). Different models have been proposed for studying the development of psychopathology in children, including the medical model, the environmental perspective, and the interactional or transactional model.

The principles of the medical model have been applied to behavioral genetics, in which consideration is given to genetic, nongenetic organic, and behavioral genetic influences on children's development (Phares, 1996). Genetic and nongenetic organic (e.g., prenatal exposure to teratogens) factors are thought to directly affect development. Eaves et al. (1997), for example, found support for "a widespread influence of genetic factors" (p. 977) in the abnormal behavior of 1412 twins, ages 8 to 16 years. But genetic factors alone do not account for all of the variability found across children's behavior, so more recent work in behavioral genetics has focused on the interaction between children's genetic predisposition and their environment (Phares, 1996).

The environmental model is based on the principles of behavior theory (see Chapter 10). It proposes a unidirectional relationship between external influences and a child's development. Here the cause of a 5-year-old child's misbehavior is thought to exist in the child's cultural surround, such as ineffective parenting techniques. Family systems and ecological theorists expanded on this model and identified interacting levels at which problems can occur: the individual child, the marital dyad, the family, and extrafamilial social systems (Phares, 1996). When this transactional model is integrated with the principles of behavioral genetics, psychopathology is conceptualized as the interaction of a child's physiological predisposition, psychological characteristics, and familial and social factors.

Researchers have studied developmental influences on psychopathology in different ways. Cross-sectional designs have been used to distinguish between normal and abnormal behaviors at various ages or stages of development. Longitudinal studies are conducted to identify early predictors of adjustment during childhood, adolescence, and adulthood. In many of these studies, researchers have adopted a multiaxial approach in which different domains of child development (e.g., cognitive, emotional) are examined based on information obtained from multiple informants (e.g., child, parents). When applied to clinical practice, the multiaxial approach offers a "standardized normative-developmental" (Achenbach, 1990, p. 13) assessment that can be used to obtain a more complete picture of the child by assessing physical development, behavior, thought processes, and emotional adjustment based on information collected from the child, parents, and teachers. Later in this chapter, we discuss two examples of multiaxial assessment systems for childhood problems.

Achenbach, McConaughy, and Howell (1987) highlighted the role of different informants in the assessment process. The authors found that agreement between teachers and parents (r = .27) regarding children's behavior was less than that observed between mother–father (r = .59) and teacher–teacher pairs (r = .64). Agreement was also low between children and parents (r = .25) and students and their teachers (r = .20). If cross-informant agreement of children's behavior is, on average, greater within rather than across settings, disagreement among informants from the same setting must be considered clinically significant. For example, a difference in parents' ratings of their child may indicate that one parent is more disengaged from family life and less aware of the child's behavior. It may also reflect conflict between the parents regarding the definition of normal development and appropriate child-rearing techniques.

Lack of interrater agreement can have positive implications for the treatment of troubled children. Therapists should always search for variability in a child's behavior, because with variability comes hope for improvement. A student who is rated as outstanding by her art and music teachers but a problem child by her math and reading instructors presents the therapist with the challenge of identifying the constructive aspects of the positive learning environments and designing a strengths-based intervention to remediate problems in the others. For example, an observer might discover that art and music instruction involves the use of an individualized approach in which the child is praised for her accomplishments. Consultation with the girl's math and reading teachers might include recommendations to increase their one-on-one interaction with the student and their use of positive reinforcement for appropriate behaviors.

Johnson (1994) observed that "we seem to know a substantial amount about the abnormal to normal continuum and very little about the other end of the spectrum, the continuum between adjustment and mastery or between surviving and thriving" (p. 459). Indeed, researchers and clinicians have given considerable time and effort to the study of childhood disorders, but they have paid little attention to optimal development in young people. A related concept that has received some consideration is resilience, which Wolin and Wolin (1993) defined as the "capacity to bounce back: to withstand hardship and repair yourself" (p. 5). We might consider resilience to be a preventive drive that enables some children to thrive amid very dysfunctional conditions. Resilience does not appear to be a resource that a child has or does not have, which is equally applied across adverse situations. Freitas and Downey (1998, p. 267) described resilience as the application of six "psychological mediating units" that are appropriate to the situation: expectancies or beliefs, biases, goals, values, affects, and competencies. How mediating units are used in a given situation will determine whether a child responds to adversity in a socially appropriate manner.

A student's academic performance is influenced by beliefs regarding the benefits of education for achieving personal goals. When the goals and the values that children hold match those of school and society, students can be expected to put forth effort in the classroom. If a child has developed biases against societal values or institutions or his or her self-worth is based on membership criteria for dysfunctional groups (e.g., street gang), academic performance suffers. Finally, the nature of a child's response to environmental stressors will be influenced by the individual's application of "self-regulatory competencies" (Freitas & Downey, 1998, p. 271). A student who decides to complete homework and study for an upcoming test rather than watch television or play with friends will exhibit greater resilience than a child who opts for nonacademic activities. According to the Freitas and Downey model, resilience represents the interaction of psychological mediating units in response to environmental contingencies. Consequently, two children of comparable academic potential and from the same troubled neighborhood can travel different life paths, one that leads to a graduate degree and a professional career and the other to an eighth-grade education and incarceration after multiple felony convictions.

MULTICULTURAL CONSIDERATIONS

Dana (1993) warned that adopting a European American world view with clients from politically nondominant groups can place these individuals "at risk of having their presenting problems inadequately identified or entirely obscured" (p. 92). The assessment of these children has typically involved the use of theory, procedures, and measures designed for European Americans and assumed to be clinically appropriate for all children, regardless of their cultural backgrounds. Recent work on multicultural aspects of psychological assessment and treatment has given us reason to question this assumption. For example, do behaviors diagnosed as pathological in a child from an affluent suburban family merit the same label in a youth from a poor family living in a dysfunctional urban environment?

Sattler (1998) described the complexity of a multicultural approach to assessment when he stated that interviewing and assessing children requires consideration of the following: "ethnic and racial identity, acculturation, language, changing family patterns, sex roles, religious and traditional beliefs, customs for dealing with crisis and change, racism, poverty, social class, health care practices, and the interactions among these factors" (p. 270). When considered in this context, a child's behavior may constitute psychopathology or it may represent what Dana (1993) described as "problems-in-living that are not necessarily pathological but are derived from specific and unique cultural experiences" (p. 95). How therapists conceptualize a child's behavior affects the choice of intervention for the presenting problem. With a European American, suburban child, the clinician might select individual or family therapy, but a community-based intervention designed to improve safety in the neighborhood could be used with a troubled urban youth (see Tharp, 1991).

The American Psychological Association's Board of Ethnic Minority Affairs developed *Guidelines for Providers of Psychological Services to Ethnic, Linguistic, and Culturally Diverse Populations* (American Psychological Association, 1993b) (Appendix E). When applied to assessment, these guidelines indicate that therapists must educate clients about the assessment process, consider the influence of culture and language, and adopt a contextual perspective regarding the child's presenting problem. Overall, the guidelines serve as notice that therapists, teachers, and other child care professionals must consider the contribution of cultural influences in their work with children. This includes each professional's self-examination of stereotypic attitudes and biases regarding the psychosocial development of children from nondominant groups and the impact these beliefs have on psychological assessment and treatment.

The Association for Assessment in Counseling developed standards that clinicians should follow when using educational and psychological tests with people from nondominant ethnic groups (Prediger, 1994). These criteria include an evaluation of the language, item content, and norms for each test to ensure that the instrument is appropriate for all clients. Test developers have tried to meet these standards in a number of different ways, including the development of "culture-free" or "culture-fair" measures. Of the tests currently available for children, very few have been promoted as being culture free. An example of these exceptions is the Culture-Free Self-Esteem Inventories (2nd ed.) (CFSEI-2) developed by Battle (1992).

Two child-report forms of the CFSEI-2 are available: Form A, which contains 60 forced-choice items, and Form B, which has 30 items of the same format. According to Battle (1992), the measure is appropriate for students who have at least a second or third grade reading level. Each form of the CFSEI-2 yields scores for four domains of self-esteem: General, Social/Peer-Related, Academic/School-Related, and Parent/Home-Related. Subscale scores are summed to produce a Total Self-Esteem score. The inventory also contains a Lie scale, which is designed to measure defensiveness, or a child's attempt to present self in an overly positive manner. Battle normed his measure on students enrolled in grades 2 through 9 in the United States and Canada, but he did not provide ethnic group data for the sample. He reported subscale internal consistencies ranging from .66 to .76 and test-retest reliabilities of .81 to .89 across an unspecified period of time. The concurrent validity between the CFSEI-2 and the Self-Esteem Inventory (Coopersmith, 1967) ranged from .71 to .80.

In her review of the CFSEI-2, Brooke (1995) questioned whether the inventory is really culture free. She stated that Battle (1992) failed to provide adequate empirical evidence to show that his measure was not culturally biased. Holaday and her students (1996) evaluated this concern when they administered Form A to students, ages 8 to 20 years, enrolled in four U.S. schools, two in Canada, and one in Venezuela. Participants represented a variety of ethnic groups, including Inuit, Hispanic, and Hispanic American. If the CFSEI-2 were truly culture free, one would expect to find no significant between-group differences in respondents' scores. Holaday et al. found the reverse to be true and concluded that Battle's (1992) measure "is certainly not culture free" (p. 552).

The limitations of the CFSEI-2 are not surprising, given previous attempts to construct culture-free or culture-fair intelligence tests. Cohen and Swerdlik (1999) described the difficulties that test developers have encountered in designing these measures. As Cohen and Swerdlik observed, the content and format of these tests are reflections of the cultural surround in which they are developed, administered, and interpreted. Despite the use of such features as oral and pictorial response formats, test designers have been unable to eliminate cultural biases in these measures. As a result, clinicians must evaluate the cultural content of both test items and the questions posed to clients during the clinical interview. When selecting standardized measures, they must determine whether test norms are appropriate for assessing behavioral and emotional adjustment in children of color. Clearly, additional research is needed to develop tools that will minimize the risk of culturally biased assessments.

THE CLINICAL INTERVIEW

Wenar (1982b) warned that therapists should "never assume that within the space of a few hours they will be able to understand the nature and origin of the problems which bring a particular child to their attention" (p. 355). Therefore, the clinical interview represents the therapist's initial step that is used in conjunction with the administration of standardized questionnaires or rating scales and contacts with significant others in the child's life. The purpose of the interview varies from case to case. Sometimes the therapist who conducts the clinical interview continues in treatment with the child. In other cases, the child is referred to another clinician for intervention services. The clinical interview is not always integrated with treatment. For example, therapists sometimes interview children and significant family members to assist in the determination of child custody arrangements after parental divorce (Weithorn & Grisso, 1987). Or a child is assessed in conjunction with an ongoing investigation regarding allegations of child abuse or neglect (Sattler, 1998).

Hughes and Baker (1990) identified three theoretical approaches to the clinical interview: structured diagnostic, psychodynamic, and behavioral. A structured diagnostic interview is what the name implies, a standardized method for collecting relevant information (e.g., nature of the presenting problem, developmental history) from the child and parents for the purpose of clinical diagnosis. In the psychodynamic interview, the therapist focuses on the relationship with the child, often incorporating play activities to facilitate disclosure of thoughts and feelings. A behavioral interview involves the functional analysis of a presenting problem, including its antecedents and consequences.

The therapist's theoretical orientation has an impact on the approach selected, but the purpose of the interview is also an important consideration. For example, a clinician who conducts admissions interviews at an inpatient treatment facility is likely to adopt the structured approach to obtain relevant information from the child and parents for diagnostic purposes. But a therapist who interviews a young and withdrawn child after her mother's recent death may opt for a psychodynamic approach and use play to facilitate the child's self-disclosure within a supportive relationship. For clients who present with more specific problems, such as nocturnal enuresis, the clinician may conduct a behavioral interview to assess the nature of the target behavior (e.g., wetting frequency), antecedent events (e.g., excessive consumption of fluids before bedtime), and consequences (e.g., the child's responsibility for clean-up activities).

An important practical consideration is the therapist's preparation for the clinical interview. This includes having a general plan to follow during the course of the session. For example, a therapist may begin by meeting with the family unit before interviewing the parents and then meeting alone with the child. When case information is available, the therapist reviews this material before the interview to become familiar with basic demographic data and the clients' reasons for seeking professional help. Thompson and Rudolph (2000) emphasized the need for an interview setting where children will feel comfortable. The room should not be overly stimulating (e.g., cluttered, noisy), and furniture should be arranged to avoid physical barriers between the therapist and clients. Clinicians must be prepared to conduct interviews while seated on the floor with the child. They should also have developmentally appropriate toys and other manipulatives to facilitate client participation during the assessment.

The clinical interview may involve the child, the child and the parent (or parents), the child and the nuclear family, or the child and members of the social network (e.g., teachers). Who participates is often determined by who is available. Sometimes with children of divorce, for example, only the child and the custodial parent are present because the noncustodial parent is either unable or unwilling to attend. The nature of the presenting problem also has an influence on who participates. For a preschool child who misbehaves in a variety of settings, the interview might include the child, the parents and siblings, the preschool teacher, and the grandparent who cares for the child after school when the parents are at work. A common characteristic of all clinical interviews, regardless of the individuals present, is the special manner in which the therapist interacts with the child. As Garbarino (1989) stated, "Interviewing is an adult form of inquiry" (p. 170). Therapists must adapt their method to the child's developmental level. This typically involves adjustments in interviewing style and the topics discussed during the session.

The clinician's initial face-to-face contact with the child typically occurs in the therapist's waiting room. Children's waiting room behavior is quite variable, so therapists must be flexible in their response to clients' verbal and nonverbal messages (Barker, 1990). Observant clinicians assess whether brief physical contact (e.g., a handshake) is appropriate, if bending forward to equalize the level of eye contact is needed, or whether humor might help the child feel more comfortable. Therapists should observe how children are dressed. Genuine comments such as, "Wow, I really like the color of your shirt" might help a young client feel more at ease and willing to disclose relevant information to the interviewer. If the therapist notices a logo or picture on an article of clothing, a comment such as, "It looks like we have a baseball fan with us today" might prompt a brief discussion of the child's favorite team or recent experiences in youth sports activities.

At the outset of the interview, the clinician's primary task is to develop rapport with the child, not to collect facts pertinent to the case (Barker, 1990). Again, the purpose of the interview will determine the depth of the relationship a therapist establishes with a child (Hughes & Baker, 1990). When a young client is to be interviewed once and then referred elsewhere for services, the clinician should provide a supportive environment but avoid developing an emotionally close relationship that will end abruptly at the close of the interview. As Goldman, Stein, and Guerry (1983) stated, "The clinician should not encourage greater attachment and emotional dependence than is appropriate or the child will feel deserted and resentful when the contact terminates" (p. 93). In cases in which the interviewer continues as the child's therapist, the clinical interview is the starting point for developing a trusting and supportive relationship in which the child feels comfortable and safe.

Chapter 2 discussed how various authors have handled confidentiality with children in treatment. Another topic that requires consideration early in the clinical interview is the chain of the events that preceded the appointment, including the child's involvement in the decision to seek professional services. Children rarely refer themselves to treatment (Adelman, Kaser-Boyd, & Taylor, 1984; Johnson, Rasbury, & Siegel, 1997). Unlike adult clients, who perceive a need for help and schedule an appointment for therapy, children enter treatment at the recommendation or insistence of their parents or other adults (e.g., teachers, physicians, juvenile court counselors). It is not unusual to encounter children who are not aware of the reasons for the interview, are anxious because they understand the purpose but are reluctant to discuss sensitive topics (e.g., child abuse) in the presence of a stranger, or feel angry because they believe the interview indicates that they are "bad" or even "crazy." In some cases, children simply feel disappointed that they are unable to play with their friends when the interview is scheduled after school.

One method of handling these reactions is to give children information about the nature and scope of the interview, especially when therapy is to follow the assessment. This material must be presented in a developmentally appropriate manner, especially with younger children who seem most in need of this information (Sigelman & Mansfeld, 1992). When therapists have the opportunity to speak by telephone or in person with parents before the interview, they can encourage them to talk with their child about the upcoming session. Children's fears are sometimes relieved when they hear a brief explanation, such as, "Dr. Smith talks with lots of boys and girls, so we're going to see her to make things better for us at home." For children who are particularly inquisitive, therapists can offer written materials (e.g., Nemiroff & Annunziata, 1990) that parents can read with their child.

In many cases, clinicians have no prior contact with parents, so information is provided during the interview itself. In the case of a girl whose parents have requested an assessment for the child's oppositional behavior, an interviewer who would also provide subsequent therapeutic services might share the following explanation:

> Today we are going to talk about some of the things that have been happening at home. I don't live at your house, so I will need you to tell me what it's like for you there. Sometimes I will ask questions. Other times, I will listen. My job is to help you and your parents discover things that all of you can do to make life better at home.

Early in the interview, the therapist should briefly state his or her understanding of the reasons for the appointment. This can be accomplished in a number of ways, including a statement such as, "I spoke with your dad on the telephone, and he said that he and your teachers want to help you do better at school." This global summary of an earlier conversation with the father will sometimes encourage a child to discuss the situation. Other children will object or withdraw, signaling the therapist to postpone collection of factual information in favor of continued rapport development by discussing such nonproblem areas as the child's hobbies, friends, or favorite television programs. Clinicians must remember to individualize their description of the purpose of therapy to "the child's age, culture, and cognitive, social, and emotional development, as well as the type of presenting problem" (Thompson & Rudolph, 2000, p. 35).

Hughes and Baker (1990) correctly described the therapist's job of questioning children as "a subtle art" (p. 35). Barker (1990) suggested that interviewers rely on simple questions and avoid negatively phrased terms (e.g., unpopular), multiple-choice questions, and the chaining of more than one question in a single interrogative statement (e.g., "What do you like best about your teacher, and what would you change about your school?"). Therapists should also avoid "why" questions, which closely resemble the accusatory remarks that adults sometimes use with children (e.g., "Why did you do that after I told you not to?"). Skilled interviewers combine minimal encouragers (e.g., "I see," "Uh-huh") and open questions (e.g., "What do you like best about school?") with carefully placed closed questions (e.g., "Did you go to school today?"). Open questions, which begin with interrogatives such as "how," "what," "when," or "where," are generally preferable because they give the child more flexibility in formulating an answer. Although these questions tend to elicit more information, closed questions can be answered with a nod of the head or a simple "yes" or "no" response. Closed questions are sometimes used to engage withdrawn children or young clients who have difficulty answering open questions. Interviewers also conduct play interviews with these and other children to facilitate client self-disclosure in a developmentally appropriate manner.

The Play Interview

Play represents an important mode of expression for children, so clinicians must be prepared to integrate this activity into the clinical interview. In order to do this, they must first understand and appreciate the value of play in the assessment of children. Many clients who lack the verbal skills needed to verbally communicate complex thoughts and feelings are able to express this information through play. For communication to occur, the interviewer must be able to translate the child's behavior into data that are clinically meaningful. A 6-year-old boy whose father has abandoned him after the parents' divorce could express his frustration and anger by repeatedly kicking and throwing a male puppet. An 8-year-old girl who believes she must be perfect might exhibit this attitude by drawing a picture, erasing it because "it's not right," and then making another attempt. In order to understand what these children are saying through play, interviewers should try to remember what it is like to communicate in the concrete and nonverbal manner of a young child. This requires that the clinician make an imaginary journey to his or her own childhood to recollect favorite play activities and the personal meaning of each.

Morrison and Anders (1999) described how play can be used to engage children in clinical interviews. As we discussed earlier, therapists should sit on the floor with the child or take other measures to ensure that they are on the same eye level with their client. Clinicians frequently adopt an unstructured approach by inviting children to use whatever play materials they choose. Minimal encouragers as well as open and closed questions are used to facilitate client self-disclosure in connection with play activities. A child who has one puppet tease another might be asked, "What are their names?" and "How does Tom feel when John makes fun of him?" Morrison and Anders advised clinicians to be alert for dramatic changes in a child's play that could reflect an uncomfortable topic or theme. In treatment, therapists might interpret these events in hopes of remediating a child's problems. But the clinical interviewer is unlikely to adopt this approach, preferring instead to focus on the collection of information that can be used to develop treatment hypotheses and plans.

Johnson and Schwartz (2000) observed that play enables children to address significant life issues through fantasy, which helps them avoid the emotional distress frequently associated with talking about these events. A similar process sometimes occurs in therapy with adults who use metaphor to explore anxiety-producing issues (see Chapter 16 for information on the use of metaphor with children). According to Morrison and Anders (1999), children who are comfortable while at play during the clinical interview are likely to be experiencing and expressing thoughts and feelings similar to those of everyday life. Therefore, the content and process of their play represent valuable pieces of information about the client's view of him- or herself and the world. The format for the play interview varies from an individual interview with the child to family-based sessions in which parents and their children are observed at play (see Chapter 13 for more information).

Structured and Semistructured Interviews

Many therapists use a structured or semistructured method of interviewing children and families. Sattler (1998) provided 43 semistructured interview protocols that clinicians can use with children, parents, and teachers to collect information about a variety of presenting problems, including child custody disputes and suicidal ideation. Sattler warned that the reliability and validity of these protocols have not been established, so therapists should consider them as guidelines to be adapted to the needs of each client. Psychometric results are available for other methods, such as the Semistructured Clinical Interview for Children and Adolescents (McConaughy & Achenbach, 2001), which is part of the multiaxial assessment system developed by Achenbach and his colleagues (see Multiaxial Assessment Systems later in this chapter).

Designed for use with clients between the ages of 6 and 18 years, the Semistructured Clinical Interview for Children and Adolescents (SCICA) (McConaughy & Achenbach, 2001) contains a Protocol Form, Observation Form, and Self-Report Form, and requires from 60 to 90 minutes to complete. The clinician conducts the interview using the Protocol Form, which contains open questions on different topics, such as school, friends, and family. With younger clients, SCICA questions are incorporated into play activities. Children also are asked to draw and describe a picture of their family. On the Protocol Form, the interviewer records observations of the child's interview behavior and the client's responses to the SCICA items. After the interview is concluded, the therapist uses a 4-point scale to rate Observation Form items about the intensity of the child's behavior and the Self-Report Form to record information disclosed by the child.

The interviewer's ratings on the Observation and Self-Report Forms are scored for two age groups, 6 to 11 years and 12 to 18 years, as Observation and Self-Report total problems, two broad-band groupings (i.e., Internalizing and Externalizing), and eight syndromes, five of which (i.e., Anxious, Withdrawn/Depressed, Language/Motor Problems, Attention Problems, Self-Control Problems) are obtained from the Observation Form and three (i.e., Anxious/Depressed, Agressive/Rule-Breaking, Somatic Complaints [ages 12 to 18 years only]) from the Self-Report Form. The SCICA also provides scores for six scales related to diagnostic criteria for childhood problems contained in the DSM-IV-TR (American Psychiatric Association, 2000) (see Diagnosis section later in this chapter). These scales are Affective Problems, Anxiety Problems, Somatic Problems (ages 12 to 18 years only), Attention Deficit/Hyperactivity Problems, Oppositional Defiant Problems, and Conduct Problems. With the exception of Somatic Problems which is based on the SCICA Self-Report Form only, the DSM-oriented scales were constructed using Observation Form and Self-Report Form items.

McConaughy and Achenbach (2001) collected normative data from a sample of 381 children, ages 6 to 11 years, and 305 youths, ages 12 to 18 years, who were referred for psychoeducational evaluations. The inventory was found to have good psychometric properties. The authors reported that SCICA scores were stable over a brief period of time (i.e., 5 to 29 days). Internal consistency was lower for the Somatic Complaints and DSM-oriented scales (.32 to .79) than for the other SCICA scales (.58 to .90). When McConaughy and Achenbach examined the validity of the instrument, they found that compared with a nonreferred sample, children referred for psychoeducational services scored significantly higher on all but two SCICA scales, Anxious for both ages groups and Anxiety Problems for 6- to 11-year-old children.

In the hands of a skilled therapist, the clinical interview can provide a tremendous amount of information about the history and nature of a presenting problem, the child's and others' interpretation of the problem, and family members' styles of interacting with the therapist and each other. But the clinical interview also has certain limitations, the most important of which is the restricted amount of time the therapist has to collect relevant data from the informants who are present. To overcome this problem, clinicians often use psychological tests, questionnaires, or rating forms in addition to the interview to obtain a more comprehensive picture of the child and the presenting concern.

ASSESSMENT MEASURES FOR CHILDREN

A number of child- and adult-report inventories have been developed to assess childhood problems. These include broad-based measures that are part of multiaxial assessment systems as well as instruments intended to assess specific aspects of a child's psychological adjustment, including self-concept and depression. Before we examine these instruments in more detail, we must consider the two properties—reliability and validity—that are used to determine whether an inventory is psychometrically sound.

The *reliability* of a psychological measure refers to its consistency across time (i.e., test-retest reliability), raters (i.e., interrater reliability), different versions of the same test (i.e., alternate forms reliability), and items on the inventory (i.e., internal consistency). If a measure is not reliable, therapists can expect to obtain inconsistent results even when a psychological construct, such as IQ, is relatively stable. Reliability is statistically calculated using a correlation coefficient. Although no absolute criteria exist for identifying a measure as reliable, commonly accepted minimum standards are .70 for internal consistency, .50 for test-retest across at least 3 months, and .70 for interrater reliability (Whiteley, 1996).

Validity is the accuracy of a measure, or the extent to which scores on a test represent the construct of interest. For example, we expect an intelligence test to assess native intellectual ability, a self-concept inventory to tap a child's view of self, and a depression instrument to measure negative affect. A statistically oriented approach to determining the validity of a measure is construct validity. Similar to reliability, *construct validity* is calculated using a correlation coefficient to determine the relationship between the instrument and a previously validated measure of the same construct. Another method is the statistical comparison of test scores obtained from two or more groups known to differ on the construct of interest. For example, we would expect the scores on a measure of depression to be significantly higher for children diagnosed as being depressed than for children labeled "normal."

A child's score on an instrument has little interpretive value unless the therapist can compare the score with normative data for the measure. Because of the impact of development and diversity in children, the norms for child measures should permit interpretation of a child's scores by age, gender, and ethnicity. Unfortunately, very few child inventories have such comprehensive norms. Another important consideration when selecting a psychological measure for children is the reading level of the instrument. To collect self-report data from children, therapists must choose measures that are consistent with the child's reading skills. Although this is less of a concern when parent-report measures are used, clinicians must remember that some adults do not have the literacy skills needed to answer these inventories; therefore, alternative test administration procedures (e.g., reading the measure to the parent) are required.

The inventories used for child assessment can be categorized as child-report measures, parent-report measures, and multiaxial assessment systems. The most comprehensive of these is the multiaxial approach which permits the assessment of a child's development across different areas (e.g., academic performance, psychological adjustment) as described by different informants (e.g., child, parents, teachers). Although this method includes the use of child-, parent-, and teacher-report measures, individual child- and parent-report inventories also are available for specific aspects of psychological adjustment in children. The measures presented in this chapter are only a sample of those currently available, so readers are encouraged to consult other sources (e.g., Kamphaus & Frick, 1996; Merrell, 1999) for information on additional instruments.

CHILD-REPORT MEASURES

The inventories reviewed in this section were developed to obtain an understanding of children's views of themselves in the world. Included are a number of self-report inventories that therapists use to assess anxiety, depression, self-concept, and self-esteem in children. In addition to these objective paper-and-pencil measures, clinicians sometimes use projective techniques that are based on the principles of psychodynamic theory. We begin with three of these.

Projective Measures

A traditional approach to assessment is the projective technique in which a child's responses to ambiguous stimuli are believed to provide information about "underlying personality processes and social-emotional functioning" (Merrell, 1999, p. 179). In this section we review three methods that have been used with children: the Children's Apperception Test (Bellak & Bellak, 1949), Tell-Me-A-Story (Costantino, Malgady, & Rogler, 1988), and the Draw-A-Person: Screening Procedure for Emotional Disturbance (Naglieri, McNeish, & Bardos, 1991).

Children's Apperception Test. An adaptation of Murray's (1971) Thematic Apperception Test, the Children's Apperception Test (CAT) (Bellak & Bellak, 1949) was developed to assess the psychological adjustment of children, ages 3 to 10 years. The CAT consists of 10 black-and-white cards containing drawings of animals which are individually presented to a child, who is to report what happened before, during, and after the picture. Children's responses are often interpreted as themes that emerge regarding personal and interpersonal needs and challenges. Although the use of animal pictures with children has intuitive appeal, human figures appear to be as or more effective stimuli (Levitt & French, 1992). An example of this approach is the Tell-Me-A-Story (TEMAS) technique that Costantino et al. (1988) developed to measure the psychological functioning of children from nondominant groups.

Tell-Me-A-Story. The TEMAS is a multicultural inventory designed for use with children between the ages of 5 and 13 years. The measure consists of two sets of 23 standardized color pictures: one set for European American children and a second for Hispanic and African American youth. The TEMAS pictures contain "ethnically and racially relevant and contemporary stimuli" (Costantino & Malgady, 1996, p. 95) that are intended to measure cognitive, affective, intrapersonal, and interpersonal aspects of a child's development. Similar to the CAT procedure, children are asked to describe what is happening in each picture, what occurred previously, and what will happen in the future. Although the 23-card measure requires approximately 2 hours to administer, a nine-card version can be completed in about 45 minutes (Costantino et al., 1988).

Costantino et al. (1988) developed a scoring system that includes 18 Cognitive Functions (e.g., Reaction Time), 9 Personality Functions (e.g., Sexual Identity), and 7 Affective Functions (e.g., Happy). The authors reported normative data for three age groups (i.e., 5 to 7, 8 to 10, and 11 to 13 years) from mostly lower- to middle-class families in the New York City area. Costantino et al. reported coefficients of internal consistency ranging from .31 to .98 for Hispanic American and African American children, so therapists must cautiously interpret the results for certain functions (e.g., Delay of Gratification, Anxiety/Depression). In a validation study of the European American version of the TEMAS, Costantino, Malgady, Colon-Malgady, and Bailey (1992) were successful in distinguishing between groups of referred and nonreferred children. More importantly, significantly different TEMAS scores were reported when the alternate version of the inventory was administered to referred and nonreferred Hispanic American and African American children, ages 5 to 14 years (Costantino, Malgady, Rogler, & Tsui, 1988).

Draw-A-Person: Screening Procedure for Emotional Disturbance (DAP:SPED). A very popular projective technique for children has been the interpretation of human figure drawings (Lubin, Larsen, & Matarazzo, 1984). A variety of drawing techniques are available, including the House-Tree-Person (Buck, 1948), Kinetic Family Drawing (Burns & Kaufman, 1972), and Human Figure Drawing Tests (Koppitz, 1968). Common to all three is the child's use of paper and pencil to draw the objects of interest. There are advocates and critics for all projective techniques, including children's drawings. As Koppitz (1983) noted, "Few psychologists are neutral about the utility of projective drawings with children and adolescents" (p. 421). Therapists who question this approach typically do so for psychometric reasons. In defense of children's drawings, Koppitz (1983) noted the following:

> Drawing is a natural mode of expression for boys and girls. It is a nonverbal language and form of communication; like any other language, it can be analyzed for structure, quality, and content. In the hands of a skilled clinician, drawings can provide a great deal of information and insight into youngsters' self-concepts, attitudes, concerns, and wishes. (p. 426)

Consequently, proponents of this technique have developed qualitative and quantitative methods for scoring and interpreting children's drawings.

Qualitative or symbolic interpretation requires careful consideration of the child's developmental level (e.g., fine motor control and artistic abilities), part-whole relationships in the drawing, and the real life experiences of the child. Although symbolic interpretations often have intuitive appeal, O'Leary and Johnson (1979) warned that clinicians "cannot conclude from a child's responses to projective material that the kinds of events that go on in his/her fantasies necessarily go on in his/her real world" (p. 239). For example, attributing symbolic meaning to the animals that appear in a child's drawing may be unwise if the youngster recently visited the local zoo with his or her family. Although it may be significant that a child selected a particular life experience as the subject for a drawing, the therapist and child may differ in the meanings they attribute to that creation.

Quantitative scoring methods (e.g., Koppitz, 1968) have been developed for interpreting children's drawings, but Martin (1988) recommended that therapists use these "with great caution" (p. 274) because of psychometric limitations. To address the problems in existing scoring systems, Naglieri et al. (1991) developed the DAP:SPED as a more objective method for scoring the drawings of children between the ages of 6 and 17 years. In the DAP:SPED, clients use separate standardized record forms to draw pictures of a man, woman, and self. Therapists then rate and score each drawing using 55 criteria for content (e.g., body parts omitted) and dimension (e.g., figure size). A point is awarded for each scorable criterion, and points are summed across the three drawings. Raw scores are translated into standard scores and interpreted based on gender by age group (i.e., 6 to 8, 9 to 12, and 13 to 17 years) norms provided by Naglieri et al.

Interrater reliability is an important consideration for the DAP:SPED because raters are expected to apply standard scoring criteria to children's drawings. Naglieri et al. (1991) reported that the DAP:SPED has very good interrater reliability (.84), as well as internal consistencies that range from .67 to .78 for girls and boys in the different age categories. Bruening, Wagner, and Johnson (1997) found the inventory's scoring criteria to be sufficiently objective, so raters' knowledge of a child's presenting problem (i.e., sexual abuse vs. non-abuse concerns) did not affect DAP:SPED scores. Naglieri and his colleagues examined the validity of the measure and found that the DAP:SPED distinguished between normal children and those with psychological problems (McNeish & Naglieri, 1993; Naglieri & Pfeiffer, 1992).

Measures of Anxiety

According to Hagopian and Ollendick (1997), anxiety is "a response to a stimulus perceived as threatening" that "may include behavioral avoidance, cognitions of impending harm and danger, increased physiological arousal, and feelings of dysphoria or terror" (p. 431). Anxiety can be either adaptive or maladaptive. For example, fear represents a normal physiological reaction to threatening stimuli, but phobias constitute a maladaptive response to an event or object that is nonthreatening for most individuals. Anxiety disorders in children assume different forms, including separation anxiety disorder, generalized anxiety disorder, and obsessive-compulsive disorder. Researchers have designed assessment measures to reflect different models, including those based on state versus trait and global versus specific factors.

State-Trait Anxiety Inventory for Children. Spielberger (1973) developed the State-Trait Anxiety Inventory for Children (STAIC) to assess the first of these models. State anxiety is a transitory event that occurs in reaction to an identifiable stressor, and trait anxiety is an enduring phenomenon that is independent of external events. Spielberger (1973) developed the STAIC as a downward extension of the State-Trait Anxiety Inventory (Spielberger, Gorsuch, & Lushene, 1970) that is used with adolescents and adults. This 40-item inventory contains an equal number of items designed to measure how children feel at a "particular moment in time" (i.e., state anxiety) and how they "generally" feel (i.e., trait anxiety). Clients rate each item using a 3-point scale, with higher scores representing more anxiety. Individual state and trait anxiety scores are calculated by summing the child's responses for each 20-item scale. Although Spielberger (1973) designed his inventory for children, ages 9 to 12 years, Walker and Kaufman (1984) noted that STAIC items have a seventh grade reading level. Therefore, therapists should consider using oral administration of the measure with elementary school children, especially those who are reading at or below grade level.

Normative data for the STAIC have come from a variety of sources. Spielberger (1970) reported gender by grade norms for a sample of 1554 children enrolled in fourth, fifth, or sixth grade. Despite the size and ethnic diversity (35% to 40% of the children were African American) of this group, all children were enrolled in Florida public schools, which raises concerns about the generalizability of the STAIC norms. Although subsequent researchers (e.g., Cross & Huberty, 1993; Papay & Hedl, 1978; Papay & Spielberger, 1986) have reported additional norms for the inventory, therapists should be cautious when using the results reported in the manual. As Merrell (1999) observed, "A current and nationally representative standardization of the STAIC would be of great use in increasing the confidence of obtained test scores, and in ensuring the continued use of the test, which is deserved" (p. 267). Spielberger (1970) found the STAIC to be internally consistent for both the state (boys = .82, girls = .87) and trait (boys = .78, girls = .81) sections. As we would expect, 6-week test-retest reliability for the state section (boys = .31, girls = .47) was lower than that obtained for the trait portion of the inventory (boys = .65, girls = .71). As support for the instrument's validity, Spielberger reported that children's STAIC trait scores were found to correlate

(.75) with those obtained on the Children's Manifest Anxiety Scale (Castenada, McCandless, & Palermo, 1956).

Revised Children's Manifest Anxiety Scale. Manifest anxiety is traditionally associated with emotions (e.g., worry) and behaviors (e.g., attention problems) related to physiological arousal, but latent anxiety is considered an underlying cause for other behaviors (e.g., aggression). Reed et al. (1992) indicated that the distinction between manifest and latent anxiety may not be relevant with children, so we will limit our discussion to the assessment of manifest anxiety.

The trait portion of the STAIC and the Revised Children's Manifest Anxiety Scale (RCMAS) (Reynolds & Richmond, 1978) are two of "the most frequently used self-report measures of global anxiety and fearfulness in children" (Hagopian & Ollendick, 1997, p. 442). Based on the Children's Manifest Anxiety Scale (Castaneda et al., 1956), the RCMAS contains 37 forced-choice items (i.e., Yes/No) that can be used with children, ages 6 years and older. The RCMAS contains 28 anxiety items and a nine-item Lie Scale that is intended "to detect acquiescence, social desirability, or faking of responses" (Gresham, 1989, p. 695). Reynolds and Richmond wanted to make the reading level of the Castaneda et al. measure more appropriate for elementary school children, but they later found the RCMAS to have a third grade reading level (Reynolds & Richmond, 1985). Consequently, clinicians who use the inventory with younger children should orally administer the measure.

Total Anxiety and Lie scores for the RCMAS are computed by summing the number of positive responses (i.e., Yes) on each scale. In addition to the global measure of anxiety, therapists can calculate scores for the following subscales: Physiological Anxiety (10 items), Worry/Oversensitivity (11 items), and Social Concerns/Concentration (7 items). Reynolds and Paget (1983) provided age by gender by ethnicity norms for the five RCMAS scales based on results collected from 4972 children, ages 6 to 19 years. Normative data are presented in the RCMAS manual by gender and ethnicity (i.e., European American & African American) at 1-year intervals, from ages 6 through 16 years and as a combined age group for young adults ages 17 to 19-years.

Based on studies of the internal consistency of the RCMAS, therapists can be most confident using the Total Anxiety score (Reynolds & Richmond, 1985). The lower coefficients obtained for the anxiety subscales have raised questions regarding their interpretation as individual measures (Gresham, 1989). The Lie Scale has been found to be internally consistent (Reynolds & Richmond, 1985), but Rabian (1994) observed that this scale may be less appropriate for younger children for whom alpha coefficients were lower. Reynolds (1981) studied the stability of the RCMAS across a 9-month period and reported test-retest coefficients of .68 for Total Anxiety scores and .58 for the Lie scale. Reynolds (1980) provided evidence for the validity of the instrument as a measure of chronic anxiety when he found that Total Anxiety scores were significantly correlated with STAIC trait scores (.85) but not STAIC state scores (.24).

Revised Fear Survey Schedule for Children. A revision of an earlier measure by Scherer and Nakamura (1968), the Revised Fear Survey Schedule for Children (FSSC-R) (Ollendick, 1983) is intended to measure a specific aspect of anxiety in children, ages 7 to 18 years. This 80-item inventory contains a 3-point response format (i.e., None, Some, A Lot) that children use to rate various fear stimuli, such as burglars and being struck by a car. Responses are summed to produce a total fear score and five subscale scores: Failure and Criticism, The Unknown, Minor Injury and Small Animals, Danger and Death, and Medical Fears (Ollendick, King, & Frary, 1989).

Ollendick et al. (1989) reported FSSC-R normative data by gender and by age group (i.e., 7 to 10, 11 to 13, and 14 to 17 years) based on results collected from 1185 children in the United States and Australia. Ollendick (1983) reported coefficients of internal consistency above .90 in two samples of elementary school students, ages 8 to 11 years. Test-retest reliability for groups of children selected from these samples revealed high stability (.82) over a 1-week interval and moderate stability (.55) across a 3-month period. In a validation study, Ollendick found that a group of elementary school students entering treatment for school phobia received higher FSSC-R total scores than did a sample of nonreferred children matched by age, gender, and school grade.

The measure appears to have good psychometric properties when used with children from different cultures, but Fonseca, Yule, and Erol (1994) cautioned that the 80 FSSC-R items may not account for all childhood fears. Based on others' work in different cultures, Fonseca et al. suggested that future revisions of the FSSC-R contain additional items (e.g., nuclear assault) and greater specificity on the item pertaining to death (i.e., death of father, death of mother). Still, the FSSC-R appears to be a psychometrically sound measure that can be used to assess the presence and intensity of specific fears in children and to compare the level of a child's overall fears with those reported by a normative sample.

Measures of Depression

Despite considerable debate regarding the presence of depressive symptomatology in children, researchers have now concluded that "depression does indeed exist in children" (Milling & Martin, 1992, p. 319). From 2% to 5% of children in the general population are thought to be depressed (Kashani & Simonds, 1979; Lefkowitz & Tesiny, 1985), but more than 30% of those in therapy may qualify for this diagnosis (Lobovits & Handal, 1985). Children who are depressed may present with a variety of concerns, including sadness, hopelessness, low self-esteem, and lack of energy. Based on their study of 1030 children and adolescents, Weiss et al. (1991) emphasized the importance of development when they found that an affective component (i.e., sadness, loneliness) was common in both children and adolescents, but oppositional or aggressive behavior was more likely to occur in children. Kovacs (1992) noted the variable nature of depression in children when she reported that some researchers observed that girls were more likely to be depressed, others found boys to be more at risk, and still others reported no gender difference. Although various measures are available for assessing depression in children, we will limit our discussion to the Children's Depression Inventory (CDI) (Kovacs, 1992).

Children's Depression Inventory. First developed in 1977, the CDI is a downward extension of the Beck Depression Inventory (Beck, 1967) which is used with adults. Designed for youths between the ages of 7 and 17 years, the CDI contains 27 items that children answer by selecting one of three answers that best describes their feelings during the previous 2 weeks. For younger children or those with reading problems, the examiner should read aloud the instructions and items on the inventory. A child's responses to all items are summed to produce a Total Score. Therapists also can calculate five factor scores: Negative Mood (five items), Interpersonal Problems (four items), Ineffectiveness (four items), Anhedonia (eight items), and Negative Self-Esteem (five items).

The CDI contains one item designed to assess suicidal ideation in children. Because of the implications of a child's response to this item, therapists should check each client's answer before the assessment session is terminated. When children indicate that they either think about killing themselves or actually want to kill themselves (Kovacs, 1992, p. 8), the therapist should conduct a more thorough investigation to assess lethality. If it is determined that a child is a potential danger to him- or herself, the clinician has reason to break confidentiality, consult with the child's caregivers, and take appropriate steps to ensure the client's safety (see Chapter 2).

Kovacs (1992) provided CDI norms based on a geographically limited sample of 1266 students from racially and ethnically diverse school districts in Florida. Girls ranged in age from 7 to 15 years, and boys were between 7 and 16 years old. Various psychometric studies of the CDI have revealed coefficients of internal consistency ranging from .71 to .89. Kovacs presented the results of 16 test-retest reliability studies as support for the stability of the CDI, but she warned that scores tend to decrease with repeated administrations of the measure. Therapists must consider this characteristic when using the CDI as a measure of progress in treatment. Kovacs (1992) reviewed the results of different validation studies and concluded that the CDI is a "reasonably valid measure of depression in children" (p. 43). Still, she warned that the inventory must be combined with data obtained from other sources, such as the clinical interview, when the CDI is used for diagnostic purposes.

Measures of Self-concept and Self-esteem

The two most common terms used to describe a child's view of self are self-concept and self-esteem. Although *self-concept* is the manner in which children "conceive of themselves in relation to other people" (Cole & Cole, 2001, p. 375), *self-esteem* is children's positive or negative "evaluations of their worth, value, and competence" (Berndt, 1997, p. 522). Piers (1984) combined these constructs when she defined self-concept as "a relatively stable set of self-attitudes reflecting both a description and an evaluation of one's own behavior and attributes" (p. 1). As an alternative, Harter (1983a) described a self-system that is composed of three interacting components: self-concept, self-esteem, and self-control.

According to Harter (1983a), self-concept is a child's multidimensional description of self, which includes physical characteristics (e.g., "I have brown hair"), activities (e.g., "I play the piano"), and likes and dislikes (e.g., "I like to go to school"). The qualities that children use to define themselves are related to the different roles (e.g., athlete, student) they assume in their environment. A child's view of self is therefore based on an integration of self-concepts rather than a single concept of self (Gergen, 1971; Wells & Maxwell, 1976). The number and nature of self-concepts differ from one child to the next. The salient self-concepts for a third grader may be daughter, student, and pianist, but a classmate relies more on his roles as grandson and class comic.

Therapists tend to be more interested in children's self-esteem, or the evaluation of self-concepts. Harter (1982) challenged the traditional view that self-esteem is a single construct that represents the summation of children's self-evaluations across different domains, such as behavior, popularity, and physical appearance. In her research, she found that children, ages 8 years and older, evaluated themselves relative to individual domains, including cognitive competence and physical competence, that were different from their perception of "general self-worth" or how well the child "likes himself or herself as a person" (Harter, 1982, p. 88). In order to assess self-concept and self-esteem in children, therapists must consider a child's evaluation of self in various roles (e.g., student, friend, athlete). Two measures that are often used for this purpose are the Piers-Harris Children's Self-Concept Scale and the Self-Perception Profile for Children.

Piers-Harris Children's Self-Concept Scale. Piers and Harris (1969) developed the 80-item Piers-Harris Children's Self-concept Scale for students in grades 4 through 12. The inventory was once called "the best children's self-concept measure currently available" (Jeske, 1985, p. 1170). The measure contains a forced-choice response format (i.e., Yes/No) and has a third grade reading level (Piers, 1984), although therapists may need to define certain words (e.g., "pep") for children regardless of age. Piers and Harris (1969) also stated that the measure can be used "for clinical purposes with a bright child" (p. 9) below the fourth grade level if it is individually administered. Likewise, Piers (1984) recommended that examiners read the instructions and test items to elementary school children to eliminate confusion and error.

The Piers-Harris inventory was designed to provide an indication of global self-concept in children. A total self-concept score is computed based on a child's response to all 80 items, with higher scores thought to indicate a better concept of self. Piers and Harris (1969) also identified six clusters that can be scored: Behavior, Intellectual and School Status, Physical Appearance and Attributes, Popularity, Anxiety, and Happiness and Satisfaction. Again, higher scores are thought to reflect better self-concept, with the exception of the Anxiety cluster, in which higher scores are thought to indicate less anxiety. Although some confusion can arise regarding the interpretation of this cluster, therapists should remember that higher scores on the inventory reflect a more positive self-concept. Therefore, higher scores on the Anxiety cluster are best thought of as indicating an absence of anxiety.

Martin (1988) described the Piers-Harris scale as "the most widely used and researched measure of self-concept for children" (p. 244). Unfortunately, the normative data presented in the revised manual (Piers, 1984) are based on 1183 children from a single school district in Pennsylvania who were tested in the 1960s. Therefore, therapists must exercise caution when interpreting an individual child's score relative to these norms. Based on a number of psychometric studies, Piers (1984) reported coefficients of internal consistency ranging from .88 to .93 for the total score and .73 to .81 for the seven clusters. Test-retest reliability for the inventory has also been found to be acceptable. In 13 studies with test-retest periods ranging from 2 weeks to 1 year, coefficients for total scores ranged from .42 to .96, with coefficients above .70 reported in eight studies. Considerable variability has been found for the validity of the Piers-Harris. For example, Piers (1984) cited coefficients ranging from .34 to .85 for eight studies in which Piers-Harris total scores were correlated with results obtained on other measures of self-concept.

The Self-Perception Profile for Children. The Self-perception Profile for Children (SPPC) (Harter, 1985) is a 36-item inventory designed for use with elementary and junior high school students. The SPPC contains the following six-item subscales: Scholastic Competence, Social Acceptance, Athletic Competence, Physical Appearance, Behavioral Conduct, and General Self-Worth. The most obvious difference between the SPPC and the Piers-Harris is the ingenious "structure alternative" (p. 89) response format that Harter used to construct her items. A child is first asked to select one of two categories to describe him- or herself. This choice could be represented by "Some kids remember to do their homework" and "Other kids forget to do their homework." The child then indicates whether the characteristic is "sort of true for me" or "really true for me." Having children make two dichotomous choices provides a final response based on a 4-point scale. Because of the uniqueness of this approach, therapists must ensure that children understand the response format, especially when the SPPC is administered to children in groups.

The SPPC and the Piers-Harris scales also differ in their overall design. The SPPC General Self-Worth subscale is composed of items related to a child's satisfaction with self and life in general and is designed to provide a global assessment of the child's perception of self as a person. Unlike the Piers-Harris total score, which is the sum of all items on the inventory, General Self-Worth scores on the SPPC are calculated based on the six items contained on this subscale. The other five SPPC subscales are intended to assess children's beliefs about their competence in academic and athletic domains and their adequacy in social relationships, behavior, and personal appearance. Harter (1985) provided SPPC normative data for a geographically limited sample of girls and boys in grades 3 through 9. Coefficients of internal consistency across different samples ranged from .71 to .86 for the six SPPC subscales (Harter, 1985).

ADULT-REPORT MEASURES

Adults are an important source of information in the assessment of childhood problems. Parents, for example, are frequently asked to provide a developmental history that children are unable to report. Although it appears that children are better sources of information about internal mood states, including depression and anxiety, adults have been found to be more reliable reporters of overt behaviors. O'Leary and Johnson (1986) underlined the importance of adult-report data when they stated that parents' and teachers' behavioral ratings and direct observation of a child constitute "the most common and most methodologically rigorous methods" (p. 445) of assessing overt behavior problems, such as oppositional-defiant disorder and ADHD.

Factor analytic studies of various parent-report measures have revealed the presence of what Achenbach and Edelbrock (1983) called "broad-band groupings of behavior problems" (p. 31). Although researchers have used different terminology, two consistent factors have emerged from these studies. Achenbach and Edelbrock (1983) described these as Externalizing behaviors, characterized by aggression or opposition-defiance, and Internalizing behaviors, such as withdrawal, depression or anxiety. Others have labeled these two groupings as Conduct Problem versus Personality Problem (Peterson, 1961), Aggression versus Inhibition (Miller, 1967), and Undercontrolled versus Overcontrolled (Achenbach & Edelbrock, 1978), but the nature of the behaviors involved remains the same.

Researchers and clinicians have recently given considerable attention to the Internalizing versus Externalizing distinction proposed by Achenbach and Edelbrock (1983). Although each factor has its defining characteristics, therapists must avoid dichotomous categorizations of children's behavior because the two are not mutually exclusive domains. Achenbach and Rescorla (2001a), for example, reported a mean correlation of .53 for Internalizing and Externalizing scores on the Child Behavior Checklist for Ages 6 to 18, Teacher's Report Form, and Youth Self-Report (see description in the following section). This suggests that children scored as having more problems in one grouping are more likely to have higher scores on the other. Although some children have a preferred mode of responding to environmental stressors, others may exhibit both or vacillate between internalizing and externalizing behaviors depending on the situation or setting.

Similar to the inventories designed for children, parent-report measures have been developed to obtain global and specific ratings of a child's psychological adjustment. For example, the Personality Inventory for Children (Lachar, 1982; Wirt, Lachar, Klinedinst, & Seat, 1977, 1990) is a global measure that can be used to obtain parent ratings of a number of clinically significant issues, including depression, anxiety, and social skills. The Parenting Stress Index (Abidin, 1995) is a more focused inventory that was designed to measure child, parent, and situational influences on the process of child rearing. Information about these and other instruments can be obtained by consulting the respective manuals and test reviews published by others (e.g., Kamphaus & Frick, 1996; Merrell, 1999). Chapter 13 reviews another specific measure, the Family Environment Scale, which is used to collect information about family structure, relationships, and goals. Later in this chapter, we examine the ADHD Rating Scale-IV (DuPaul, Power, Anastopoulos, & Reid, 1998) as part of our case example for child assessment. At this point, we turn our attention to the parent-report measures that are part of two multiaxial assessment systems: the Achenbach System of Empirically Based Assessment and the Behavior Assessment System for Children.

MULTIAXIAL ASSESSMENT SYSTEMS

In a multiaxial assessment, therapists examine different aspects of a child's development from the perspective of the child and significant other adults. This comprehensive approach typically involves the use of five axes: (1) parent report; (2) teacher report; (3) an assessment of the child's cognitive functioning (e.g., intelligence and achievement tests); (4) an evaluation of physical functioning; and (5) data collected from the child through interviews, behavioral observations, and self-report measures (Achenbach & McConaughy, 1997). Collecting information from parents, teachers, and the child requires empirically derived instruments that share common content and normative data. The results obtained from these respondents are compared with each other to identify similar views of the child and to isolate significant differences. In the past, therapists who attempted to perform a multiaxial assessment were hampered by a lack of appropriate measures. With the development of programs like the Achenbach System of Empirically Based Assessment (ASEBA) and the Behavior Assessment System for Children (BASC), clinicians can now obtain a more comprehensive picture of a child's psychological adjustment based on information collected from the child and significant others.

Achenbach System of Empirically Based Assessment

Earlier in this chapter, we discussed McConaughy and Achenbach's (2001) Semistructured Clinical Interview for Children and Adolescents. We now consider other measures that are part of Achenbach's assessment system. The Child Behavior Checklist for Ages 6 to 18 (Achenbach & Rescorla, 2001a) and the Child Behavior Checklist for Ages 1½ to 5 (Achenbach & Rescorla, 2001b) are parent-report inventories that are used to rate the behaviors of children, ages 6 to 18 and 1½ to 5 years respectively. In this section, we also examine three other components of the Achenbach System of Empirically Based Assessment: the Youth Self-Report (Achenbach & Rescorla, 2001a), Teacher's Report Form (Achenbach & Rescorla, 2001a), and Direct Observation Form (Achenbach & Edelbrock, 1983).

Child Behavior Checklist for Ages 6 to 18 (CBCL/6-18). Achenbach and Edelbrock (1983) designed the Child Behavior Checklist to collect parent or primary caregiver ratings of maladaptive and prosocial behaviors in children. Although Achenbach (1991a) retained the inventory's original items, he developed new scoring procedures and norms for the measure. In their latest revision of the measure, Achenbach and Rescorla (2001a) changed the age range for the inventory, made minor changes to items, and introduced the scoring and interpretation of scales related to diagnostic criteria in the DSM-IV-TR (American Psychiatric Association, 2000).

The CBCL/6–18 (Achenbach & Rescorla, 2001a) contains two sections: Competence and Problem Scales. Parents rate their child's prosocial behaviors using the Competence scales, which contain items pertaining to academic performance; social relationships; and participation in sports, activities, clubs, and household tasks. The Problem Scales section of the CBCL/6–18 consists of 113 items pertaining to various behaviors (e.g., disobedience, feelings of guilt) that parents endorse as either "not true," "somewhat or sometimes true," or "very true or often true" of their child during the previous 6 months. To aid therapists in the diagnosis of childhood problems, Achenbach and Rescorla (2001a) developed the procedures for scoring the same DSM-oriented scales contained on the Semistuctured Interview for Children and Adolescents (McConaughy & Achenbach, 2001). These are Affective Problems, Anxiety Problems, Somatic Problems (ages 12 to 18 years only), Attention Deficit/Hyperactivity Problems, Oppositional Defiant Problems, and Conduct Problems.

Factor analysis of the behavior problem items on the CBCL/6–18 revealed eight syndromes and two broad-band groupings: Internalizing and Externalizing. The Internalizing grouping contains the Anxious/Depressed, Withdrawn/Depressed, and Somatic Complaints syndromes. The Externalizing grouping is composed of Rule-Breaking Behavior and Aggressive Behavior. Three additional syndromes (i.e., Social Problems, Thought Problems, Attention Problems) are considered separately because their relationship with the broad-band groupings was not as clear as the other syndromes on the CBCL/6–18. Analysis of the Competence items revealed three factors, which were labeled Activities, Social, and School.

Based on a diverse normative sample of 3098 boys and 1896 girls, Achenbach and Rescorla (2001a) reported Problem Scales norms for boys and girls in two age groups, 6 to 11 and 12 to 18 years. Gender-based Competence scale norms were collected from a smaller sample of 1753 boys and girls, ages 6 to 11 and 12 to 18 years. Responses to Problem Scales items are summed to produce a Total Problems score and scores for the broad-band groupings and eight syndromes. Competence items are used to generate a Total Competence score and scores for the three scales: Activities, Social, and School. High scores on the Problem Scales are thought to indicate difficulties, but low scores suggest the same for the Competence scales. When interpreting a child's CBCL/6–18 profile, therapists should explore score differences between and within syndrome groupings because significant discrepancies have been associated with different behavioral styles (McConaughy, Achenbach, & Gent, 1988).

Achenbach and Rescorla (2001a) reported reliability and validity results for the CBCL/6–18. In general, internal consistency has been found to be higher for syndromes on the Problem Scales. Specifically, coefficients alpha for scores on the four Competence scales ranged from .63 to .79, in comparison with .72 to .91 on the DSM-oriented scales and .78 to .97 for the Problem Scales, including the Total Problems score. Test-retest reliability over an average of 8 days was also found to be very good for the Competence, Problem, and DSM-oriented scales. Interrater agreement is an important consideration on a measure such as the CBCL/6–18. When Achenbach and Rescorla (2001a) examined interparent agreement on their inventory, they found significant mean correlations on the Competence (r = .69), Problem (r = .76), and DSM-oriented (r = .73) scales. But mothers were found to report significantly more problems on a number of the Problem and DSM-oriented scales. Achenbach and Rescorla (2001a) reported validation results indicating that children referred for mental health services scored significantly lower on the Competence scales and significantly higher on the Problem Scales, compared with a group of nonreferred children. Scores on the DSM-oriented scales were compared to clinicians' ratings on the DSM-IV Checklist for Childhood Disorders (Hudziak, 1998), which can be used to diagnose various childhood problems. Results revealed significant correlations ranging from .43 to .80 on the five DSM-oriented scales.

Child Behavior Checklist for Ages 1½ to 5 (CBCL/1½–5). The CBCL/1½–5 (Achenbach & Rescorla, 2001b) contains 100 items with the same response format used on the CBCL/6–18. Unlike the CBCL/6–18, the CBCL/1½–5 does not contain a Competence section, and parents are asked to rate their child's behavior during the previous 2 months. The inventory also contains five DSM-oriented scales: Affective Problems, Anxiety Problems, Pervasive Developmental Problems, Attention Deficit/Hyperactivity Problems, and Oppositional Defiant Problems. Based on a national sample of 700 children, Achenbach and Rescorla (2001b) developed norms for Total Problems, the Internalizing and Externalizing broad-band groupings, and individual syndromes. The Internalizing syndromes are Emotionally Reactive, Anxious/Depressed, Somatic Complaints, and Withdrawn. The Externalizing grouping contains Attention Problems and Aggressive Behavior. One additional syndrome, Sleep Problems, is not included as part of either broad-band grouping.

Achenbach and Rescorla (2001b) reported reliability and validity results for the CBCL/1½–5. Internal consistency was high for Total Problems (.95) and the Internalizing (.89) and Externalizing (.92) groupings. Results for the syndromes were more variable (.66 to .92), which was also true for the DSM-oriented scales (.63 to .86). The CBCL/1½–5 was found to be stable, with 8-day test-retest reliabilities ranging from .68 to .92. The results for interparent agreement revealed a significant mean correlation of .61, with significant syndrome and DSM-oriented scale correlations ranging from .48 to .67. Unlike the significantly higher scores for mothers on the CBCL/6–18, Achenbach and Rescorla (2001b) found no significant difference in mothers' and fathers' scores on the CBCL/1½–5. Achenbach and Rescorla (2001b) also reported the results of a validation study in which nonreferred children were rated significantly lower on all

CBCL/1½–5 Problem Scales, compared with children referred for clinical services. Achenbach and Rescorla (2001b) described two additional ASEBA measures designed for use with preschoolers: the Language Development Survey and the Caregiver-Teacher Report Form. Readers who are interested in learning more about these inventories are encouraged to consult the Achenback and Rescorla (2001b) manual.

Youth Self-Report. The Achenbach and Rescorla (2001a) revision of the Achenbach (1991b) edition of the Youth Self-Report (YSR) is designed to assess problem and prosocial behaviors during the past 6 months in older children and adolescents, ages 11 to 18 years. The measure shares a common response format and many items with the CBCL/6–18. The YSR items have been found to have a fifth grade reading level. Based on normative data collected from 1429 boys and 1122 girls, children's responses to items on the Problem Scales are scored as Total Problems, Internalizing and Externalizing groupings, and the eight CBCL/6–18 syndromes. Competence items are scored as Total Competence, Activities, and Social scales based on a normative sample of 1047 youth.

Achenbach and Rescorla (2001a) reported reliability and validity results for the YSR. Internal consistency for the YSR scales ranged from .55 to .75, with 18 of the 20 scales having coefficients at or above .70. Included in this group of 18 are coefficients alpha for Internalizing (.90), Externalizing (.90), and Total Problems (.95) scores. Competence scales ranged from .55 to .75, and the syndromes were from .71 to .86 and DSM-oriented scales were from .67 to .83. The YSR was found to be relatively stable, with 8-day test-retest reliabilities from .67 to .91. The YSF also has been found to discriminate between nonreferred children and those referred for psychological services (Achenbach & Rescorla, 2001a).

Teacher's Report Form. The Teacher's Report Form (TRF) (Achenbach & Rescorla, 2001a) is a revision of an earlier version (Achenbach, 1991c) that is designed to measure prosocial and problem behaviors in a school setting. Designed for use with students between the ages of 6 and 18 years, the TRF has the same response format and 97 of the Problem Scales items that appear on the CBCL/6–18. In place of the CBCL/6–18 Competence scales, the TRF contains the Adaptive Functioning section that is used to assess school-related domains, including standardized test scores. Similar to the CBCL/1½– 5, the TRF is designed to assess a child's behavior during the previous 2-month period. Based on a normative sample of 2430 boys and 2007 girls, the Problem Scales are again scored as Total Problems, Internalizing and Externalizing groupings, and the eight CBCL/6–18 syndromes. Norms for the Adaptive Functioning section were collected from 2319 students and are used to interpret teachers' ratings for a Total Adaptive Functioning scale and four individual scales: Working Hard, Behaving Appropriately, Learning, and Happy. This section also includes norms for an Academic Performance scale. The DSM-oriented scales on the TRF are the same as those contained on the CBCL/6–18 and the YSR, with the exception of the Attention Deficit/Hyperactivity Problems scale, which is reported as a total score and separate scores for Inattention and Hyperactivity-Impulsivity.

Coefficients of internal consistency for the scales on the TRF Problem Scales section ranged from .72 to .97, including scores for Total Problems (Achenbach & Rescorla, 2001a). Coefficient alpha for the Total Adaptive Functioning scores was .90, and results ranged from .73 to .94 for the DSM-oriented scales. The TRF also appears to be stable over short periods of time. Sixteen-day test-retest coefficients ranged from .60 to .96, with 28 of 30 above .70. Teachers' agreement with each other varied considerably, with mean correlations for teacher dyads of .49 for the Adaptive Functioning scales, .60 for the Problems Scales, and .58 on the DSM-oriented scales. These findings could be caused by students' being observed and rated in different academic subjects or by teachers with different styles of instruction and discipline. Agreement was highest for Conduct Problems (.76) and Hyperactivity-Impulsivity (.72), scales that are designed to measure overt behaviors which are more disruptive and easily observed in a classroom setting. Compared with nonreferred peers, children who had been referred for mental health services were more likely to have lower scores on Adaptive Functioning and higher scores on the Problems and DSM-oriented scales (Achenbach & Rescorla, 2001a).

Direct Observation Form. The Direct Observation Form (DOF) (Achenbach & Edelbrock, 1983) provides a means of assessing the actual behavior of children between the ages of 5 and 14 years. Using a 4-point scale, observers rate 96 behavior problems, of which 72 are common to the CBCL/6–18 and 83 to the TRF (Achenbach, 1991c; Achenbach & Rescorla, 2001a). The DOF also contains a narrative section where observers describe "the child's behavior and interactions over a 10-minute interval" (Achenbach, 1991a, p. 218). Normed on 287 nonreferred children, the DOF is scored for Total Problems, the Internalizing and Externalizing groupings, and six syndromes: Withdrawn-Inattentive, Nervous-Obsessive, Depressed, Hyperactive, Attention Demanding, and Aggressive. Observers can also compute a score for on-task behavior based on the child's performance on assigned tasks.

Therapists who use the DOF must first select a clinically relevant setting in which to observe the child's behavior. For a student who is failing math but doing very well in reading, the clinician would assess the child's on-task behavior in both classes to identify factors related to the performance discrepancy. When using the DOF, the rater observes the child for a 10-minute period and notes significant information in the DOF narrative section. At the end of each minute during the observation period, the rater specifically attends to the child's on-task behavior for a 5-second period. If the child is "mainly on task" (Achenbach & Edelbrock, 1983, p. 160), the observer awards one point, creating an on-task score range of 0 to 10. At the end of the 10-minute period, the observer rates the child's performance using the 97 DOF items. Achenbach (1991a) recommended that clinicians collect from three to six 10-minute samples of a child's behavior along with one sample for two other children, one before and another after the DOF rating periods, to permit comparison of the student's behavior with others in the same setting. Achenbach and Edelbrock (1983) recommended that a child's total score on the DOF be computed by averaging across the scores obtained for the three to six samples. When observations are conducted at different locations and times, such as math class in the morning, and afternoon reading class, therapists also should check for meaningful differences in these variables.

Reed and Edelbrock (1983) reported high interrater reliability for individual 10-minute ratings using the DOF, with Total Problems score coefficients ranging from .81 to .92, and on-task coefficients from .56 to .87. In their validation study of the measure, the authors found that boys referred for psychological services had significantly lower on-task scores and significantly higher behavior problem scores than did their nonreferred peers.

Summary. Achenbach (1991a, 1991b, 1991c, 1992) cautioned that repeated administrations of the various ASEBA inventories may result in significant declines in scores for certain scales, the broad-band groupings, and the Total Problems composite. Achenbach and Rescorla (2001a) recommended that clinicians use a test-retest interval of at least 1 month. They also suggested that therapists revise the specified timeframe (e.g., "the past 6 months") contained in the instructions for individual inventories. Clinicians who use the ASEBA measures to evaluate treatment effectiveness must be aware that better scores may not indicate an actual improvement in the child's behavior. The information collected using these inventories must be compared with and interpreted in the context of results obtained from other assessment techniques.

Achenbach's multiaxial system represents a significant step forward in the assessment of prosocial and problem behaviors in children. With the instruments provided, therapists can obtain a more comprehensive view of a child by comparing information obtained from different informants. When discrepancies are identified, clinicians should investigate the extent to which these differences reflect informant bias or actual variability in the child's behavior. Based on the outcome of this analysis, the therapist can tailor treatment to the needs of the child, parents, and the child's school.

Behavior Assessment System for Children

The Behavior Assessment System for Children (BASC) (Reynolds & Kamphaus, 1992) is another multiaxial approach for assessing children and adolescents, ages 4 to 18 years. It includes child-, parent-, and teacher-report forms; a survey for assessing developmental history; and an observation form that can be used to record a student's classroom behavior. Similar to the ASEBA, the BASC provides information about children's prosocial behavior and behavioral problems. Reynolds and Kamphaus also collected normative data from large samples of children, parents, and teachers, enabling therapists to compare results obtained from these informants to develop a broader view of the child.

Parent Rating Scales. The BASC Parent Rating Scales (PRS) (Reynolds & Kamphaus, 1992) was designed to assess problem and prosocial behaviors in youths between the ages of 4 and 18 years. To address developmental differences, the authors devised three age-appropriate forms: preschool (4 to 5 years), child (6 to 11 years), and adolescent (12 to 18 years). The structure of these forms, which contain approximately 130 items, is basically the same from one level to the next, but item content differs to reflect the behaviors that characterize children of different ages. For parents who have reading problems but understand spoken English, the authors have provided audiotapes that can be used to administer the PRS. Parents answer PRS items using a 4-point scale (i.e., Never, Sometimes, Often, Almost Always). Responses are scored according to an *F* index, or validity scale designed to identify extreme negative responses (i.e., "faking bad"), an overall Behavioral Symptoms Index, four broad-based composites (i.e., Externalizing Problems, Internalizing Problems, School Problems, Adaptive Skills), and from 10 to 12 behavior scales for children of different ages. Table 4-2 contains a breakdown of the four composites by age for the PRS scales. Reynolds and Kamphaus also identified critical items (e.g., suicidal ideation, psychopharmacotherapy) that merit individual examination because they constitute important areas for investigation.

Reynolds and Kamphaus (1992) reported PRS normative data for two groups: parents of children in the general population (i.e., General) and those whose child was receiving psychological services (i.e., Clinical). To obtain a representative sample, the authors collected General norms from 3483 parents at 116 testing sites and Clinical norms from 401 parents at 39 different locations. In the BASC manual, Reynolds and Kamphaus reported their PRS General scale norms by gender (i.e., male, female, combined) and age group (i.e., 4 to 5, 6 to 7, 8 to 11, 12 to 14, and 15 to 18 years). They also provided combined norms for the Clinical scales and the General and Clinical composites.

Internal consistency for the PRS composites ranged from .84 to .94, and above .65 for virtually every PRS scale across age and gender groups in the General and Clinical samples. Based on the General norms, Reynolds and Kamphaus (1992) reported very good test-retest reliability across a 2- to 8-week period for the PRS composites and scales in the

Table 4–2
Composites and Scales for the Parent Rating Scales and the Teacher Rating Scales of the Behavior Assessment System for Children

Composite or Scale	Teacher Rating Scales			Parent Rating Scales		
	Preschool	Child	Adolescent	Preschool	Child	Adolescent
Externalizing problems	•	•	•	•	•	•
Aggression	•	•	•	•	•	•
Hyperactivity	•	•	•	•	•	•
Conduct problems		•	•		•	•
Internalizing problems	•	•	•	•	•	•
Anxiety	•	•	•	•	•	•
Depression	•	•	•	•	•	•
Somatization	•	•	•	•	•	•
School problems		•	•			
Attention problems	•	•	•	•	•	•
Learning problems		•	•			
Other problems						
Atypicality	•	•	•	•	•	•
Withdrawal	•	•	•	•	•	•
Adaptive skills	•	•	•	•	•	•
Adaptability	•	•		•	•	
Leadership		•	•		•	•
Social skills	•	•	•	•	•	•
Study skills		•	•			
Behavioral Symptoms Index	•	•	•	•	•	•

From *BASC: Behavior Assessment System for Children manual*, by C. R. Reynolds and R. W. Kamphaus, 1992. Copyright 1992 by American Guidance Services, Inc.

preschool and child samples, although stability was somewhat lower for adolescents. Although the authors found that the PRS composites and scales correlated with related dimensions on the Child Behavior Checklist, they indicated that additional research is needed to support the validity of the PRS.

Self-Report of Personality. The BASC Self-Report of Personality (SRP) is a forced-choice inventory that can be used with children between the ages of 8 and 18 years. Because of the significant changes that occur across this age span, the authors developed two forms of the SRP, one for children (ages 8 to 11 years) that contains 152 items and another for adolescents (ages 12 to 18 years) with 186 items. Responses are scored as an overall Emotional Symptoms Index, three composites (i.e., Clinical Maladjustment, School Maladjustment, and Personal Adjustment), and 12 individual scales for children and 15 for adolescents (Table 4-3). The SRP also contains three validity scales. In addition to the *F* index, there is a *V* index that is used to detect children who give unusual responses as a result of "poor reading comprehension, failure to follow directions, or poor contact with reality" (Reynolds & Kamphaus, 1992, p. 27). The adolescent version of the inventory also contains an *L* index to identify respondents who appear to be denying problems (i.e., "faking good"). Similar to the PRS, the SRP contains critical items that require individual inspection and follow-up assessment when endorsed by the child. Again, audiotapes of the SRP are available for children who understand English but are unable to read the inventory.

Table 4–3
Composites and Scales for the Self-Report of Personality of the Behavior Assessment System for Children

Composite or Scale	Child	Adolescent
Clinical maladjustment	•	•
Anxiety	•	•
Atypicality	•	•
Locus of control	•	•
Social stress	•	•
Somatization		•
School maladjustment	•	•
Attitude to school	•	•
Attitude to teachers	•	•
Sensation seeking		•
Other problems		
Depression	•	•
Sense of inadequacy	•	•
Personal adjustment	•	•
Relations with parents	•	•
Interpersonal relations	•	•
Self-esteem	•	•
Self-reliance	•	•
Emotional Symptoms Index	•	•

From *BASC: Behavior Assessment System for Children manual*, by C. R. Reynolds and R. W. Kamphaus, 1992. Copyright 1992 by American Guidance Services, Inc.

General norms for the SRP were collected from a representative sample of 9861 U.S. children and adolescents, ages 8 to 18 years, while SRP Clinical norms are based on 411 youths of the same age range (Reynolds & Kamphaus, 1992). In the BASC manual, Reynolds and Kamphaus reported their SRP General scale norms by gender (i.e., male, female, combined) and age group (i.e., 8 to 11, 12 to 14, and 15 to 18 years). They also provided combined norms for the Clinical scales and the General and Clinical composites. Internal consistency for the SRP composites ranged from .85 to .97, and above .70 for most of the SRP scales across different ages and genders in the General and Clinical samples. Using the General norms, the authors reported very good test-retest reliability for the SRP composites and scales. Support for the validity of the measure is limited. Although Reynolds and Kamphaus described two studies in which 8- to 12-year-old children were administered the SRP and other child-report measures, the results of these investigations were inconsistent and highlight the need for additional research in this area.

Teacher Rating Scales. The BASC Teacher Rating Scales (TRS) can be used to assess prosocial and problem behaviors that occur in school. Similar to the PRS, the TRS uses a 4-point response format on three forms: preschool (ages 4 to 5 years), child (ages 6 to 11 years), and adolescent (ages 12 to 18 years). The forms differ in length, from 109 items on the preschool version to 148 on the child inventory. Responses are scored relative to an *F* index, an overall Behavioral Symptoms Index, four broad-based composites (i.e., Externalizing Problems, Internalizing Problems, School Problems, Adaptive Skills), and from 10 to 14 behavior scales for children of different ages (see Table 4-2). The TRS also contains critical items that should be individually examined and compared with results obtained from the parents and child.

General norms for the TRS were collected from 2401 preschool, elementary, and secondary teachers, but TRS Clinical norms are based on the responses of 693 teachers of students receiving psychological services (Reynolds & Kamphaus, 1992). In the BASC manual, Reynolds and Kamphaus presented their TRS norms in the same format used for the PRS: General scale norms by gender (i.e., male, female, combined) and age (i.e., 4 to 5, 6 to 7, 8 to 11, 12 to 14, and 15 to 18 years), along with combined norms for the Clinical scales and the General and Clinical composites. Internal consistency for the TRS composites ranged from .82 to .97, and above .70 for almost every TRS scale across different age and gender groups in the General and Clinical samples. Using the General norms, Reynolds and Kamphaus reported very good test-retest reliability over a 2- to 8-week period for the TRS composites and scales. The authors also described the results of a validation study in which TRS scores for students were compared with those obtained using Achenbach's (1991c) Teacher's Report Form. As was reported for the PRS, correlations were best for scales intended to measure similar dimensions of children's adjustment, such as the TRS Aggression scale and the TRF Aggressive Behavior scale.

Structured Developmental History. Reynolds and Kamphaus (1992) designed their Structured Developmental History (SDH) to offer "a thorough review of social, psychological, developmental, educational, and medical information about a child that may influence diagnosis and treatment" (p. 33). Parents may complete the SDH by themselves or with the therapist as part of the clinical interview. The inventory contains items regarding family history and relationships, the parents' decision to seek professional help, and the child's development history. The results obtained using the SDH are not compared with normative data. Instead, clinicians use relevant information, such as the age of onset for the presenting problem, to determine appropriate diagnoses and design interventions that are consistent with the needs of children and their families.

Student Observation System. Reynolds and Kamphaus (1992) designed their Student Observation System (SOS) to record prosocial and problem behaviors in the classroom. The SOS is intended to complement other BASC inventories with its detailed assessment of the child "whose emotional or behavioral problems are significant enough to impede academic progress" (Reynolds & Kamphaus, 1992, p. 37). The measure is used to obtain a 15-minute sample of a child's classroom behavior. The rater repeatedly observes the child for 3-second intervals followed by 30-second recording periods when behavior is coded according to 14 behavioral categories, such as Response to Teacher/Lesson, Peer Interaction, and Inappropriate Vocalization.

Before using the SOS, the observer must learn the 65 behaviors that are used to define the behavioral categories. The rater then completes the three sections of the SOS: a time sampling of classroom behavior, a checklist of behaviors observed during the rating period, and a summary of the teacher–student interaction. During the 15-minute sampling of behavior, the rater marks the behavioral categories the child exhibits during each 3-second observation interval. Raters then complete the checklist by indicating whether the specific behaviors were never, sometimes, or frequently observed over the course of the entire 15-minute period. Finally, the observer describes how the student and teacher interacted with each other.

To obtain a representative picture of a child's classroom behavior, the SOS should be administered on different days, times of the day, or classes. The results can be interpreted in a number of ways. First, within-student comparisons can be made by examining the same child's behavior across times and settings. Because normative data are not available for the SOS, between-student comparisons are made by simultaneously completing measures for the target child and another student of the same gender (e.g., a child identified as a model student). Results for both children are compared in terms of the type, frequency, and disruptiveness of their behavior. The SOS also can be used as an outcome measure that is completed before and after treatment to evaluate the effectiveness of an intervention.

Summary. Of more recent origin than the ASEBA, the BASC is another valuable multiaxial method for assessing childhood problems. Similar to its predecessor, the BASC provides a means of collecting and comparing clinically relevant information from children, parents, and teachers. Reviews of the Reynolds and Kamphaus (1992) measures have been positive. Merrell (1999, p. 80), for example, described the BASC as an "extremely impressive" system, especially the PRS and the TRS. He also called the SRP an "exemplary" (p. 162) child-report measure.

DIAGNOSIS

Measures such as the ones we have reviewed are often used to diagnose or classify a child's presenting problem. Although diagnostic systems are imperfect and sometimes controversial, they provide a common language that professionals can use to discuss the developmental status and therapeutic needs of clients. Through a process of differential diagnosis, the therapist must determine whether a child's behavior is normal or abnormal and then select the most appropriate diagnosis based on a comparison of the child's behavioral adjustment and relevant diagnostic criteria (Merrell, 1999). Although different diagnostic systems are available (e.g., *International Statistical Classification of Diseases and Related Health Problems*, World Health Organization, 1991, 1996), therapists in the United States rely on the *Diagnostic and Statistical Manual of Mental Disorders* (DSM), which is now available in a revised text version of its fourth edition. Published by the American Psychiatric Association (2000), the DSM-IV-TR provides a standardized method for classifying psychological disorders, including those observed in children.

Diagnostic systems such as DSM-IV-TR do have their limitations, including the need to fit complex multidetermined behaviors into discrete categories (Sonuga-Barke & Edmund, 1998). Herlihy (1998) suggested that diagnosis can restrict the clinician's conceptualization of a child's problem by encouraging a focus on psychopathology rather than the client's potential. In addition, confusion results when professionals endorse different diagnostic systems. Feminists have criticized standard diagnostic systems as examples of the politically dominant group's use of power. Through the process of "naming and norming" (Ballou, 1995, p. 42), clinicians label clients' behavior according to a standard that the dominant group believes is right or healthy for everyone. Behaviors that do not comply with this standard are considered inappropriate or abnormal. Critics of the DSM have observed that certain adult diagnoses, such as major depressive disorder and borderline personality disorder, are more likely to be used with women. The situation is apparently reversed with children, when many DSM diagnoses, including ADHD and oppositional defiant disorder, are more often used with boys. Ballou challenged clinicians to consider contextual factors when formulating a diagnosis. This would appear to be especially important when naming and norming women and children, who tend to hold less power than men in society.

Despite its widespread use in community settings, the DSM has until recently received little attention in the nation's public schools, where children in need of special services are identified using different criteria, such as the Education of the Handicapped Act of 1977. Conoley and Conoley (1991) described the confusion that sometimes develops between clinic- and school-based service providers who rely on different classification systems. Community-based therapists routinely diagnose children for the presence of psychological disorders, but professionals in the schools are more likely to assess students for remedial educational services, including special reading instruction. Conoley and Conoley indicated that bridging the gap between clinic and school can be accomplished by determining whether a child requires services based on both clinic and school criteria. The authors gave the example of a student who had both a learning disability and behavior problems. The child met the criteria for educational and psychological diagnoses, thereby permitting a collaborative approach to intervention.

The value of any diagnostic system depends on the skills and integrity of the professionals who use it. Cooper and Gottlieb (2000) described the practice of *downcoding* and *upcoding* that is sometimes used to either avoid labeling clients or to facilitate reimbursement for treatment costs. Upcoding involves the use of a more serious diagnostic category than the client's behavior warrants. If an insurance company does not reimburse for adjustment disorders, a clinician might upcode from adjustment disorder with disturbance of conduct to oppositional defiant disorder if the insurer pays for that diagnosis. Downcoding, as the term implies, refers to the use of a less serious but incorrect diagnostic category. If a diagnosis of adjustment disorder is considered less severe than oppositional defiant disorder, the therapist might choose the former category to avoid labeling the client. Unfortunately, upcoding and downcoding are not unusual in clinical practice. In their survey of mental health counselors, Mead, Hohenshil, and Singh (1997) found that 7 of 10 counselors were aware of clinicians who engaged in downcoding and 6 of 10 counselors were aware of clinicians who upcoded with their clients.

In the previous chapter, we learned that managed mental health care is entering the nation's public schools. As House (1999) stated, school districts are seeking insurance company reimbursement for psychological assessments and treatment as an alternative to traditional tax revenues. To obtain this external funding, schools are expected to provide a formal diagnosis for each student as a precondition for payment of services. According to House, school psychologists are the most appropriate people for this job. Power and DuPaul (1996) offered another reason why school psychologists should understand diagnostic systems. They stated that school psychologists who know the language and procedures of the DSM-IV-TR are better prepared to communicate with community-based clinicians and to overcome the school-community divide described by Conoley and Conoley (1991).

Sattler (1998) emphasized the need to consider parents' reactions to the results of the assessment and diagnostic process. Even when they suspect that their child has a problem, when some parents hear the clinician's diagnosis, they respond as Fortier and Wanlass (1984) described in their stage model of families in crisis. Professional confirmation that a problem exists can cause increased anxiety, sadness, denial, and even grief. According to Fortier and Wanlass, parents must resolve these feelings before they can take constructive action. The authors acknowledged that no single intervention is effective with all families, but Sattler recommended that therapists "always show warmth, understanding, and respect" (p. 198) when sharing diagnostic impressions. Of course, parents sometimes have conflicting reactions to the clinician's diagnosis. For example, a mother might accept the therapist's professional opinion, but the father might reject it. The outcome of treatment will depend, in part, on both parents' willingness to acknowledge the existence of a problem. We will explore this important issue in greater detail in Chapters 5 and 16 when we examine how clients' readiness for treatment—what Prochaska and Norcross (1994) described as the stages of therapeutic change—affect the delivery of mental health services for children and families.

ASSESSMENT: A CASE EXAMPLE

Attention-deficit hyperactivity disorder is a relatively common reason for referral among children in the United States. Those who present with this disorder exhibit a general pattern that involves problems with "behavioral inhibition, persistence, and overactivity specifically, and self-regulation more generally" (Barkley, 1997a, p. 89). According to the American Psychiatric Association (2000), 3% to 7% of school-age children are thought to have this disorder. Although therapists and educators have recently become more interested in this problem, ADHD is not a new disorder. Previously referred to as minimal brain damage syndrome and hyperkinetic impulse disorder (Jordan, 1998), this complex of behaviors was officially labeled as ADHD in the DSM-III:R (American Psychiatric Association, 1987). Further revisions in the DSM-IV (American Psychiatric Association, 1994) resulted in the current categorization of three types: predominately inattentive, predominently hyperactive-impulsive, and combined. Table 4-4 contains the diagnostic criteria for these types, which were retained in DSM-IV-TR.

Based on the results of recent studies, Barkley (1997a) reported that the predominantly hyperactive-impulsive type has been found to appear during the preschool years. He suggested that the combined type is more likely to be used with children of elementary school age when inattention appears in combination with hyperactive-impulsive behaviors. Barkley questioned whether the predominately inattentive type is a form of ADHD or a different disorder that merits a separate diagnostic category. He also described the challenge therapists face when diagnosing ADHD in a child who also meets DSM-IV-TR criteria for other childhood disorders, such as oppositional defiant disorder. If treatment is to have a chance of succeeding, clinicians must consider the possibility of comorbidity and design their interventions accordingly.

According to DSM-IV-TR criteria, a comprehensive assessment for ADHD requires consideration of the symptoms, duration, and age of onset for the disorder; the situational nature of the child's behavior problems; and how appropriate these behaviors are for the child's developmental level. Barkley (1997a) indicated that the ADHD assessment should include a developmental history of the child, a broad-based assessment for other disorders, testing specific to ADHD symptoms, and the study of parent- and teacher-related influences. Clinicians should also assess for the child's strengths, which can be used to facilitate progress in treatment. To collect these data, the therapist must interview the child, parents, and teachers; administer rating scales to the parents and teachers; observe the child in different

Table 4–4
DSM-IV Diagnostic Criteria for Attention-Deficit Hyperactivity Disorder

A. Either (1) or (2):

(1) six (or more) of the following symptoms of **inattention** have persisted for at least 6 months to a degree that is maladaptive and inconsistent with development level:

Inattention

(a) often fails to give close attention to details or makes careless mistakes in schoolwork, work, or other activities
(b) often has difficulty sustaining attention in tasks or play activities
(c) often does not seem to listen when spoken to directly
(d) often does not follow through on instructions and fails to finish schoolwork, chores, or duties in the workplace (not due to oppositional behavior or failure to understand instructions)
(e) often has difficulty organizing tasks and activities
(f) often avoids, dislikes, or is reluctant to engage in tasks that require sustained mental effort (such as schoolwork or homework)
(g) often loses things necessary for tasks or activities (e.g., toys, school assignments, pencils, books, or tools)
(h) is often easily distracted by extraneous stimuli
(i) is often forgetful in daily activities

(2) six (or more) of the following symptoms of **hyperactivity-impulsivity** have persisted for at least 6 months to a degree that is maladaptive and inconsistent with developmental level:

Hyperactivity

(a) often fidgets with hands or feet or squirms in seat
(b) often leaves seat in classroom or in other situations in which remaining seated is expected
(c) often runs about or climbs excessively in situations in which it is inappropriate (in adolescents or adults, may be limited to subjective feelings of restlessness)
(d) often has difficulty playing or engaging in leisure activities quietly
(e) is often "on the go" or often acts as if "driven by a motor"
(f) often talks excessively

Impulsivity

(g) often blurts out answers before questions have been completed
(h) often has difficulty awaiting turn
(i) often interrupts or intrudes on others (e.g., butts into conversations or games)

B. Some hyperactive-impulsive or inattentive symptoms that caused impairment were present before age 7 years.
C. Some impairment from the symptoms is present in two or more settings (e.g., at school [or work] and at home).
D. There must be clear evidence of clinically significant impairment in social, academic, or occupational functioning.
E. The symptoms do not occur exclusively during the course of a Pervasive Developmental Disorder, Schizophrenia, or other Psychotic Disorder and are not better accounted for by another mental disorder (e.g., Mood Disorder, Anxiety Disorder, Dissociative Disorder, or a Personality Disorder).

Code based on type:

314.01 Attention-Deficit/Hyperactivity Disorder, Combined Type: if both Criteria A1 and A2 are met for the past 6 months

314.00 Attention-Deficity/Hyperactivity Disorder, Predominantly Innattentive Type: if Criterion A1 is met but Criterion A2 is not met for the past 6 months

314.01 Attention-Deficity/Hyperactivity Disorder, Predominantly Hyperactive-Impulsive Type: if Criterion A2 is met but Criterion A1 is not met for the past 6 months

Coding note: For individuals (especially adolescents and adults) who currently have symptoms that no longer meet full criteria, "In Partial Remission" should be specified.

From *Diagnostic and statistical manual of mental disorders* (5th ed.), Text revision, by the American Psychiatric Association, 2000.

settings; and administer parent-report measures designed to assess the parents' functioning (Barkley, 1997a). Although laboratory measures, such as continuous performance tests, have been used to assess ADHD in children, Barkley recommended that clinical use of these procedures be delayed pending completion of additional psychometric studies.

Therapists can select from a number of ADHD-specific parent- and teacher-report measures. These include the ADHD Rating Scale-IV (DuPaul et al., 1998), Home Situations Questionnaire (Barkley, 1997b), School Situations Questionnaire (Barkley, 1997b), Academic Performance Rating Scale (APRS; DuPaul, Rapport, & Perriello, 1991), and ADD-H Comprehensive Teacher Rating Scale (Ullmann, Sleator, & Sprague, 1984). Here we focus on the ADHD Rating Scale-IV and the Academic Performance Rating Scale.

The ADHD Rating Scale-IV (DuPaul et al., 1998) is an 18-item measure based on DSM-IV criteria that was designed for use with children, ages 5 years and older. Parents or teachers use a 4-point scale to rate the frequency of nine items that parallel the diagnostic criteria for Inattention and another nine items for Hyperactivity-Impulsivity. Responses are summed to produce a Total score; separate Inattention and Hyperactivity-Impulsivity subscale scores are also calculated. DuPaul et al. reported normative data collected from parents and teachers in two different national samples, each containing 2000 students in grades K to 12. The authors have provided separate parent and teacher norms for boys and girls in four age groups (i.e., 5 to 7, 8 to 10, 11 to 13, and 14 to 18 years).

DuPaul et al. (1998) reported very good coefficients of internal consistency for total and subscale scores on the parent (.86 to .92) and teacher (.88 to .96) versions of the inventory. Four-week test-retest reliabilities were .78 to .86 for the parents and .88 to .90 for teachers. Parent-teacher agreement was lower, between .40 and .45, possibly caused by different target behaviors and the settings in which children were rated. The authors also reported the findings of various validation studies in which scores on the parent and teacher versions correlated with results on another hyperactivity rating scale. DuPaul also found that parent and teacher ratings discriminated between students diagnosed with ADHD and control children. The ADHD Rating Scale-IV appears to be a psychometrically sound measure for assessing ADHD symptoms in children. The measure is based consistent with DSM-IV-TR diagnostic criteria and can be used to rate children's behavior at home and school. Although designed for use as an independent measure, a minor revision of the inventory has been included as part of the Barkley and Murphy (1998) Disruptive Behavior Rating Scale, which is intended to provide parent and teacher ratings of ADHD symptoms as well as those characteristic of oppositional defiant disorder and conduct disorder.

The Academic Performance Rating Scale (APRS; DuPaul, Rapport, & Perriello, 1991) was not designed to measure specific ADHD symptoms, but this 19-item teacher-report inventory provides important information about a child's classroom behaviors. Teachers rate students' academic skills, accuracy, and output using a 5-point response format. Responses to all items are summed to produce a total score. Ratings also are scored according to three factors: Academic Success (7 items), Impulse Control (3 items), and Academic Productivity (12 items).

DuPaul et al. (1991) reported high coefficients of internal consistency for the APRS: Total = .95; Academic Success = .94; Academic Productivity = .94; and Impulse Control = .72. Two-week test-retest reliability was also high for all factors and the total scale (.88 to .95). The authors examined the validity of the APRS and found that total and subscale scores were significantly correlated with teacher ratings of ADHD symptoms and students' performance on standardized tests. The measure appears to be a valuable addition to the ADHD assessment battery because it offers a psychometrically sound method of measuring children's performance in the classroom.

We now return to the case of Joseph Morris to examine the use of selected measures reviewed in this chapter. The procedure adopted here is based, in part, on examples that Achenbach and McConaughy (1997) used to illustrate a multiaxial assessment of attention problems in children. Table 4-5 contains a list of the instruments used in this case. The younger of two children, Joseph attends a neighborhood elementary school, where his brother is a sixth grader. When Mrs. Morris called the local mental health center to schedule an appointment with Dr. Pellegrini, she indicated that her son's teacher, Mr. Johnson, had encouraged the parents to seek professional help and that Dr. Rahmed, their family physician, also recommended that Joseph receive therapy. Mrs. Morris stated that her son was tested at school about a month ago after he received failing grades on his first report card. Dr.

Table 4–5
The Measures Used in the Assessment Case Example

Child-report measure
- Semistructured Clinical Interview for Children and Adolescents

Parent-report measures
- Child Behavior Checklist for Ages 6 to 18
- ADHD Rating Scale-IV
- Beck Depression Inventory
- Structured Developmental History

Teacher-report measures
- Teacher's Report Form
- ADHD Rating Scale-IV
- Academic Performance Rating Scale

Behavioral observation measure
- Direct Observation Form

Pellegrini asked her to bring this information to the clinical interview, where she would have the parents sign release forms allowing her to speak with school personnel and the family's physician. "We'll do anything you ask," Mrs. Morris replied.

▪ ▪ ▪

During the early minutes of the interview with Joseph and his parents, Dr. Pellegrini attempts to clarify the purpose of the appointment. While Mr. and Mrs. Morris describe their concerns, Joseph stands up and walks across the room.

"Joseph, will you please come here and sit down?" Mrs. Morris asks.

When the child fails to respond, Mr. Morris warns, "You heard what your mother said. Now sit down, or you're gonna get a spanking." Joseph returns to his chair but immediately begins to fidget as he glances around the office. Mrs. Morris continues her description of the presenting problem, but Joseph interrupts, "How much longer do we have to be here?"

"Joseph, your Mom was talking about your school work," Dr. Pellegrini says, "Please tell us what you think about school."

"I don't like school," he answers. "The kids make fun of me, and nobody wants to play with me."

Dr. Pellegrini notices that when she directs her attention to Joseph, he engages in one-on-one conversation with her. But when she turns and questions the parents, he gradually becomes more active and distracted by sights in the room and the sounds of cars passing on the nearby street. After she obtains a general description of the situation, she terminates the family interview so she can meet with Joseph alone. She asks the parents to return to the waiting room and independently complete the Child Behavior Checklist for ages 6 to 18, ADHD Rating Scale-IV, and Beck Depression Inventory.

Joseph has no difficulty separating from his parents when they leave the office. Dr. Pellegrini introduces him to the toys in her storage cabinet and then begins to question him using the Semistructured Clinical Interview for Children and Adolescents. As he briefly plays with one toy after another, Joseph describes his reasons for disliking school (e.g., mean classmates, difficult school work) and feeling mistreated by his parents.

"They let my brother do anything," he complains, "but I'm the one who gets in trouble." Joseph talks incessantly throughout the interview, often skipping from one topic to the next. Ten minutes into the interview, Dr. Pellegrini realizes that she will be unable to complete the SCICA with Joseph because of his inattention and overactive behavior. For example, when she asks him to draw a picture of his family, he immediately begins the task but quickly becomes distracted by the street sounds and walks around the room and inspects various objects in her office.

When she concludes the interview with Joseph, Dr. Pellegrini asks the parents to return. She checks to ensure that all parent-report measures are completed, and then she describes her reasons for wanting to contact Dr. Rahmed, Joseph's teacher, and the school psychologist. The parents sign the appropriate consent forms, and Joseph writes his name on the corresponding assent forms. She schedules a second session for only Mr. and Mrs. Morris to discuss the results of the school testing and the parents' questionnaires. She gives each parent a copy of the BASC Structured Developmental History and asks them to independently complete sections she has selected before they return for their next appointment.

The parents' CBCL/6-18 results are consistent in that both rated Joseph within the normal range on the Internalizing and Externalizing broad-band groupings. They gave their son significantly high scores on the Attention Deficit/Hyperactivity Problems scale and the Social Problems and Attention Problems syndromes. They also gave him significantly low scores on the Activities, School, and Social scales. Both parents, for example, reported that Joseph assumes no responsibility for household chores, has no friends, and does poorly at school. On the ADHD Rating Scale-IV, they indicated that during the past 6 months, he exhibited a clinically significant number of inattention and hyperactivity-impulsivity symptoms. A difference was found on the parents' responses to the Beck Depression Inventory, with the father scoring in the normal range and the mother in the mild to moderate range of depression.

During the week after the clinical interview, Dr. Pellegrini contacts Dr. Rahmed and discovers that Joseph has been a healthy child despite a number of accidental injuries. When he was 5 years old, for example, Joseph fell from a tree in his backyard and broke his right arm. Last year, Dr. Rahmed treated the boy for a sprained ankle he received when he climbed onto the roof of his front porch and jumped to the sidewalk below. Dr. Rahmed describes Joseph as "an active child." He once discussed psychopharmacotherapy with the parents, but they were unable to make a decision. "Mrs. Morris seemed to be in favor of the idea," he says, "but her husband told me he didn't want Joseph taking medication if he didn't have to."

When she reads the testing report written by Dr. Tom Shuttersworth, the school psychologist, Dr. Pellegrini learns that Joseph scored in the average range of intelligence and below grade level on a test of academic achievement. To assess his classroom behavior, Dr. Shuttersworth trained the teacher's aide to use the Direct Observation Form with Joseph. Across four different classes, the child was rated significantly high on the Hyperactive and Attention Demanding syndromes and was off-task (e.g., out of his seat, daydreaming) an average of 80% of the time. By contrast, the aide's ratings of two comparison students, one before and another after her 10-minute observations of Joseph, were within a normal range. During a fifth observation, when Mr. Johnson was instructed to randomly place tokens on the child's desk as he worked on class assignments, the rate of off-task behavior decreased to 50%. In his report, Dr. Shuttersworth recommended that Mr. Johnson use behavioral conditioning to increase compliance in the classroom and that Joseph be evaluated for psychostimulant medication.

During a telephone conversation with the school psychologist, Dr. Pellegrini obtains additional information to support a diagnosis of ADHD. Dr. Shuttersworth cautions that the boy's intelligence and achievement scores might underestimate his abilities. "Joseph was a difficult child to test because he kept getting up and walking away from the testing table," he says. "When I asked him to sit down, he would listen, but I got the impression that he had to exert extra effort to stay on task." Joseph's hyperactive and off-task behaviors during the aide's observations of him did not appear to be a direct response to environmental factors. "The other children in class were at work on their assignments, and there were no extraneous noises that would account for Joseph's noncompliance." Although the teacher's behavioral intervention was of some help, Dr. Shuttersworth tells Dr. Pellegrini that he believes psychological services alone will not remediate Joseph's problems.

When she contacts Mr. Johnson by phone, Dr. Pellegrini learns that Joseph rarely submits his homework but will finish class assignments if the teacher stands beside him and keeps him on task. "Joseph's grades fluctuate from A's to F's," he says. "A lot of times, he doesn't pay attention to what he's doing, so he makes silly mistakes or just doesn't finish his work." Mr. Johnson describes a child who seems to be in constant motion. "Even when he sits in his seat, he's usually bouncing his feet on the floor or tapping his fingers on his desk. And he has a difficult time getting along with the other kids. In class, he talks a lot and interrupts others. When we go to lunch, he always has to be first in line. This really irritates the other students, so they just try to ignore him."

At Dr. Pellegrini's request, Mr. Johnson completes the Teacher's Report Form, ADHD Rating Scale-IV, and Academic Performance Rating Scale. Similar to the parents, Mr. Johnson gives the boy significantly high scores on the TRF Attention Deficit/Hyperactivity Problems scale, including both the Inattention and Hyperactivity-Impulsivity subscales, and the TRF Social Problems and Attention Problems syndromes. He also gives significantly low ratings on the inventory's Academic Performance and Adaptive Functioning scales. On the ADHD Rating Scale-IV, Mr. Johnson reports that Joseph has often or very often exhibited seven symptoms of Inattention and six characteristics of Hyperactivity-Impulsivity. His APRS responses are consistent with that of a child who is having academic problems.

When the parents arrive for the second assessment session, Mrs. Morris submits her completed Structural Developmental History. Mr. Morris immediately says, "I didn't get a chance to finish mine. We really were busy at work this week." To herself, Dr. Pellegrini interprets the father's lack of action as a possible sign of his limited commitment to treatment. She decides to proceed using only the mother's SDH results. Mrs. Morris indicated that Joseph's birth was normal and that he achieved developmental milestones (e.g., walking alone, speech) at or before the normal age. She also reported that her son was very active since birth, was easily frustrated as a toddler, and required less sleep each night than his older brother did at the same age. On the inventory, she had written, "Joseph is the first person up each morning, and he goes to sleep at night later than his brother does." Mrs. Morris also reported problems with the boy's development of adaptive behaviors, including everyday manners, completion of household tasks, and self-care activities (e.g., bathing).

During her interview with the couple, Dr. Pellegrini learns that both parents hold college degrees and were employed outside the home until Mrs. Morris quit her job as a computer programmer after the birth of the couple's first child. To compensate for the lost income, Mr. Morris spent extra time at work and was eventually promoted to manager of a local department store. The long hours on the job have continued, so Mrs. Morris has assumed primary responsibility for rearing the children. "It was easy with my older boy" she says, "but Joseph has been a different story. I just don't know what to do with him."

"You just need to be firmer," the father insists.

"That's easy for you to say," she says to her husband. "You're never home when it's time to help him with his homework. Or in the afternoons when he comes home crying because the kids on the bus make fun of him. He always says he hates school and never wants to go back. And he's constantly losing things." She turns to Dr. Pellegrini and adds, "I've bought him pens, pencils, and markers for school, but he never holds onto them for more than a day."

"I can imagine how difficult it must be for each of you to handle your responsibilities," Dr. Pellegrini intervenes. "Parenting children and supporting a family are challenging, even in the best of situations." When she asks about their preferred parenting techniques, Mrs. Morris states that she tries to reason with her sons so they understand why she is asking them to behave in a certain manner. Before her husband has a chance to respond, she points to him and says, "But he thinks you teach children by punishing them, just like his parents did with him."

"You never set any limits for the boys. How are they going to know right from wrong if there are no consequences for their behavior?" He looks at Dr. Pellegrini and says, "I think you can see my wife and I disagree about how to handle Joseph. I know I'm not around the house very much, but I don't think it's too much for me to expect her to be able to get the kids dressed, fed, and ready for school each day. I'm not home when Joseph has to finish his assignments, but he's only in second grade. How much homework could he possibly have to do each night?" Mr. Morris describes how he sometimes arrives home after closing the store and finds his wife crying at the kitchen table. "I put in a long day, and then I have to come home to that."

Dr. Pellegrini asks if they have consulted Dr. Rahmed about medication for Joseph. Mr. Morris answers, "That's what the psychologist at school told my wife we needed to do, but I'm not sure I want Joseph taking drugs. He's only 7 years old. What does that teach him? That the solution to his problems is in a pill?"

"I don't have the same concerns my husband has about medication," Mrs. Morris adds. "If Joseph can't help himself without drugs, then we need to see Dr. Rahmed and get a prescription."

▪ ▪ ▪

Based on the information available to her, Dr. Pellegrini determines that Joseph meets the criteria for a diagnosis of Attention-Deficit/Hyperactivity Disorder, Combined Type (DSM-IV-TR 314.01). His clinically significant number of Inattention and Hyperactivity-Impulsivity symptoms are not of recent origin. He is currently exhibiting these behaviors at home and in school, causing impairments in his academic and social development. Data to support these conclusions were obtained from a number of sources. The parents and classroom teacher rated Joseph's behavior in different settings, but their CBCL and TRF scores were in basic agreement as were their responses to the ADHD Rating Scale-IV. The description of a child with significant attention problems was supported by the aide's DOF ratings of the boy's behavior in class and Dr. Pellegrini's and Dr. Shuttersworth's observations.

Other than the SCICA, Dr. Pellegrini did not include any child-report measures in her assessment. She probably considered a number of factors when making this decision. First, there are few standardized self-report measures that have a reading level appropriate for children of Joseph's age. Second, adults are likely to be more reliable reporters of the overt behaviors used to define ADHD. Finally, Joseph's inattention and hyperactivity-impulsivity during the abbreviated semistructured interview suggest that he is probably a poor candidate for traditional paper-and-pencil child-report inventories. Still, Dr. Pellegrini was able to collect important information from Joseph during the clinical interview. Specifically, she learned that he dislikes school and believes his parents and other children do not like him.

Notice how the therapist handled her contacts with other informants. Instead of having face-to-face meetings with the teacher, school psychologist, and physician, Dr. Pellegrini contacted each person by telephone to discuss their impressions of the child and to request their help in completing questionnaires when needed. Although electronic communication results in the loss of important information (e.g., personal observation of the quality of the learning environment), it is an efficient method of collecting relevant data and establishing contact with other professionals who interact with the child. Based on the information available to her, Dr. Pellegrini developed an overall impression of a child who was experiencing significant problems related to his ADHD symptoms. In Chapter 16, we will return to this case to examine how these assessment results can be used to design a multidimensional treatment for Joseph within the context of his family and school environments.

SUMMARY

Thorough assessment of the presenting problem is a prerequisite for effective treatment. By combining the clinical interview with paper-and-pencil measures completed by different informants, therapists collect data that are essential for diagnosis and treatment planning. Recent advances in the field of developmental psychopathology and multiaxial assessment have given therapists the concepts and tools needed to perform more objective and comprehensive studies of troubled children. The information obtained during this process provides the basis for determining the direction of therapy and evaluating the effectiveness of treatment services.

5

Therapeutic Interventions with Children: Art and Science, Process and Outcome

▪ ▪ ▪

Jan Hilder, a case worker for North County Children's Protective Services, is called to Jackson City Elementary School to investigate a report of sexual abuse involving two sisters, 7-year-old Maria and 12-year-old Consuelo Martinez. When Mr. Hilder meets with the school principal, he learns that Maria told a teacher that her mother's boyfriend was molesting the girls. He then interviews the child, who describes in detail how the man enters the sisters' bedroom at night and fondles them. Mr. Hilder also meets individually with Consuelo, but she neither confirms nor denies Maria's account of the boyfriend's behavior.

▪ ▪ ▪

The sexual abuse of children is an unfortunately common event. Finkelhor, Hotaling, Lewis, and Smith (1990), for example, found that 27% of women and 16% of men in a national survey reported being molested as a child or adolescent. Abuse survivors do not exhibit a characteristic pattern of behavior (Conte & Schuerman 1987), so therapists must individualize treatment to the unique needs of the child. This requires consideration of both the process and expected outcome of therapy as clinicians select and evaluate interventions that are appropriate for each case.

The end of this chapter discusses the Martinez children and their experiences in therapy. But first we consider therapeutic interventions with children from a broader perspective. We examine how child therapies are a combination of art and science. As part of this discussion, we review selected research designs, quantitative and qualitative, that have been used to study children's development and therapeutic interventions for young clients. After we explore the process and outcome of therapy, we will return to the Martinez sisters to examine how a standardized treatment is adapted for two clients who differ in age and willingness to participate in therapy.

CHILD THERAPIES: ART AND SCIENCE

Professional disputes over the nature and benefit of child treatments have frequently centered on the question of whether therapy is an art or a science. The simple answer is that therapy is both, but a more detailed response requires clinically relevant definitions for these terms.

The Art of Therapy

For our purposes, we will employ John Dewey's description of art as experience. This prominent American philosopher and psychologist is known for his contributions to the field of progressive education during the early decades of the 20th century. Dewey was born in Burlington, Vermont on October 20, 1859. He graduated from the University of Vermont in 1879 and taught high school for three years in Pennsylvania and Vermont before pursuing a graduate degree in philosophy at Johns Hopkins University. There he had the opportunity to study under G. Stanley Hall, who introduced Dewey to the laboratory approach to psychology. After he completed his Ph.D. in 1884, Dewey taught at the University of Michigan, briefly at the University of Minnesota, the University of Chicago where he directed the Laboratory School, and finally at Columbia University. His productive career includes significant work in the fields of education, philosophy, and psychology. Active in all three, he was recognized by his fellow psychologists in 1899 when he was elected president of the American Psychological Association (Campbell, 1995).

The layperson's view of art is typically a finished product composed of paint and canvas, wood, or stone. But the arts also include forms such as dance, music, and drama that unfold over time. Dewey (1934) incorporated this temporal perspective into his definition of art as the experience a creator has across time with his or her medium. As he stated, "The act of expression that constitutes a work of art is a construction in time, not an instantaneous emission" (p. 65). But Dewey believed that art is more than the simple passage of time required for an artist to produce a preconceived idea in the concrete form of a painting, a sculpture, or a musical score. Rather, environmental limits force the artist to continually revise the original idea to adapt to the characteristics of his or her medium of expression. The sculptor who wants to create the human face in wood will encounter unexpected changes in grain that require revisions of the artist's initial plan. A composer must ensure that a melodic line is within the range of the instrumentalists or vocalists who will perform the work. Likewise, the tempo or speed of the piece must be within the musicians' technical proficiency.

Therapy can be conceptualized in Dewey's terms of art as experience. First, each therapist-client relationship involves two unique human beings whose interaction with each other is unlike any other. While the traditional arts involve a person with a nonliving object, therapy is the dynamic encounter of at least two living beings. Clinician and client enter treatment with expectations about the nature and outcome of the therapeutic endeavor. Unlike the piece of marble or wood that does not self-initiate change during the artistic process, therapist and client are continually changing as they interact with each other in session and with significant others outside of treatment. Because of the dynamic nature of therapy as experience, both clinician and client are constantly revising earlier attitudes and expectations to develop working cognitive models for the present direction of treatment.

The therapist as artist enters treatment with a plan that is based on prior training and clinical experience. Because each client is different from the next, the clinician is forced to adapt this plan to the individual needs of the child and family. These changes occur throughout treatment, beginning with the first therapist-client encounter. For example, the clinician is continually revising the working model to adapt to the child's developmental level, cultural background, and changes in the client's everyday experiences. As the therapist becomes more aware of the client's unique and ever changing needs, the treatment plan is revised in order to achieve the ultimate goal of treatment—the successful termination of therapy.

Prochaska and Norcross (1994) provided a view of the complex nature of therapy in their discussion of the stages, levels, and processes of therapeutic change (Table 5-1). Later in this chapter we will discuss the authors' processes of change. Here we examine their stages and levels of change and how these provide a framework for conceptualizing therapy as an artistic experience. Prochaska and Norcross recognized that each client is a unique person who enters therapy with different motivations, expectations, and developmental characteristics. The authors' transtheoretical approach has been used to plan and evaluate therapy for adults, especially clients in treatment for addictions. The model has not been applied to children but it seems to have promise for developing treatments for young clients and their families. The clinician's first consideration in this regard is the stage at which families members enter therapy.

Prochaska and Norcross (1994) identified six stages of therapeutic change: precontemplation, contempla-

Table 5–1
The Prochaska and Norcross (1994) Model of the Stages, Levels, and Processes of Therapeutic Change

Stages of Change	Levels of Change	Processes of Change
Precontemplation	Symptom/Situational problems	Consciousness Raising
Contemplation	Maladaptive Cognitions	Catharsis/Dramatic Relief
Preparation	Current Interpersonal Conflicts	Self-reevaluation
Action	Family/Systems Conflicts	Environmental Reevaluation
Maintenance	Intrapersonal Conflicts	Self-liberation
Termination		Social Liberation
		Counterconditioning
		Stimulus Control
		Contingency Management
		Helping Relationship

Adapted from *Systems of psychotherapy: A transtheoretical analysis* (3rd ed.), by J. O. Prochaska and J. C. Norcross, 1994, pp. 458, 461-465, and 470. Pacific Grove, CA: Brooks/Cole. Copyright 1994 by Brooks/Cole.

tion, preparation, action, maintenance, and termination. Precontemplators fail to recognize that a problem exists and tend to see little purpose for therapy. Individuals in the contemplation stage are aware that problems exist but have difficulty articulating possible causes and solutions for their difficulties. Clients in the preparation stage understand that a problem exists but have been unsuccessful in bringing about change before they entered treatment. The transition from precontemplation to preparation means that clients are more likely to recognize that a problem exists and to view therapy as a solution for their difficulties. Clinicians who provide individual treatment to adults must identify the client's stage of change and adapt therapeutic interventions accordingly. The situation is more challenging when the client is a child whose parents also participate in treatment.

Clinicians must remember that adults are able to independently enter therapy, but children are typically referred by others and brought to sessions by their parents. Unlike the adult in individual therapy who occupies a single stage of change at any point in time, the parents and child who enter the clinician's office may be at three different stages simultaneously. Consider the Dunlap family who enters therapy because 6-year-old Janine is anxious and socially withdrawn. Mrs. Dunlap has been concerned about her daughter for more than a year and made repeated attempts to involve the child in church and after-school activities. Mr. Dunlap recognizes that Janine is having problems but he is more involved with the couple's older son and has made no attempt to help his daughter. The situation is further complicated because Janine does not realize that there is a problem and cannot understand why her parents have interrupted her after-school television shows for therapy sessions. The clinician in this case faces the challenge of developing a treatment plan that meets the needs of a mother in the preparation stage, a father in the contemplation stage, and a child who is a precontemplator.

Many parents are at the preparation stage when they enter treatment with their children. They may view the clinician as an expert who can cure their child, or they seek help in becoming more effective change agents for the child. Therapists must assess each family member's stage of change and then encourage movement into the action stage to help clients resolve their presenting problems. Notice that the action stage is the fourth step in the Prochaska and Norcross (1994) model. Many clinicians and clients erroneously assume that treatment is characterized by action from beginning to end. This misunderstanding may account for many of the unsuccessful outcomes in child treatment. Therapists who assume that every family member is ready to confront and solve problems at the outset of treatment are at risk of employing a one-intervention-fits-all approach that fails to meet the needs of the clients.

During the maintenance stage, regularly scheduled sessions end as the focus turns to continuing the progress made in treatment. Clinicians sometimes employ follow-up sessions during this period to prevent relapse and to help the child and family move toward termination, the final stage of change. Therapists must consider termination issues, such as a client's feelings of abandonment, to ensure that the therapeutic experience has a positive ending and is not a repetition of prematurely terminated relationships from the past. When the behaviors that prompted treatment are no longer functional because family members have acquired more effective solutions for their problems, therapy sessions are formally terminated.

Applying the Prochaska and Norcross (1994) model to a multidimensional approach to treatment requires additional considerations. Therapists must assess the stages of change for significant other adults in the child's life. For example, parents may be at the precontemplation stage while the child's teachers and school principal have been in the action stage for many weeks. Clinicians should also consider developmental influences on the maintenance and termination of children's problems. As their cognitive, emotional, social, and moral perspective expands, children may recycle through previous stages of change as they revisit important life events. Chapter 9 discusses one such case when we examine the impact of development on a child's adjustment to the death of her brother.

The growth of managed mental health care has raised concerns regarding external pressures to limit the length of treatment. As discussed in Chapter 3, insurance companies typically preauthorize a certain number of therapy sessions but will consider reauthorization of additional treatment based on the clinician's justification of need for these services. Therapists must be prepared for the case in which an insurer does not approve additional sessions. Cooper and Gottlieb (2000) offered a number of recommendations for clinicians to consider. As discussed in Chapter 3, therapists should inform clients at the outset of treatment of their insurance plan's limits on the number of sessions. The authors stated that clinicians must anticipate reauthorization and arrange for appropriate referrals in cases where an insurance company denies additional therapy sessions. To avoid client abandonment through the abrupt termination of treatment, Cooper and Gottlieb stated that therapists must conduct an exit interview with all clients before terminating treatment.

The second dimension of the Prochaska and Norcross (1994) model is the level on which therapeutic change occurs. The authors identified five interrelated levels: symptoms or situational difficulties, maladaptive thoughts, interpersonal conflict, systemic conflicts, and intrapersonal conflict. Prochaska and Norcross recommended that clinicians initiate treatment at the symptomatic/situational level because change can occur most quickly here. This suggestion seems appropriate for children whose problems are of relatively recent origin and likely to respond to environmental manipulation. If 5-year-old Terisa and her parents agree that the goal of therapy is the elimination of a learned behavior such as thumb sucking, then this behavior becomes the initial focus of treatment. But parents and children do not always agree about the purpose of treatment, possibly because family members are at different stages of change when they enter therapy. Clinicians must therefore assess the contribution of different levels of change when they develop their treatment plan. In Terisa's case, this might include attention to the child's thumb sucking behavior, maladaptive parent beliefs such as, "I'm afraid Terisa is never going to be like the other kids," teasing from other children, systemic conflicts associated with ongoing marital discord, or psychopathology in one or both of the parents.

The clinician's challenge is to devise a treatment that addresses the family's presenting problem, thumb sucking in the case of Terisa, while directly or indirectly intervening on related levels of change. If it is determined that the child's behavior is a response to marital discord or parent psychopathology, the therapist might intervene directly with the parents. Rather than treating the child's thumb sucking using accepted methods, the clinician could employ couples therapy to address spousal conflicts or refer a parent for individual therapy or psychopharmacotherapy to treat personal problems. Therapists usually rely on indirect interventions to remediate a client's relationship problems with other children. Terisa's therapist might address the teasing by remediating the thumb sucking, which is the focus of peer attacks, or consulting with teachers to eliminate the peers' inappropriate behavior at school. Or the clinician could combine direct and indirect methods to change the parents' maladaptive cognitions. Treatment might involve the direct use of cognitive techniques to eliminate the parents' catastrophizing as well as behavioral interventions with Terisa to eliminate the thumb sucking and indirectly challenge the parents' beliefs about the child.

The Science of Therapy

Clinicians are expected to document the effects of treatment as more attention is given to therapist accountability and brief-term interventions. Therapists who have basic research skills know how to collect this evidence and present it to others. Historically, there has been a separation between the clinical practitioner and the experimental researcher. This is often reflected in a person's place of employment, with therapists treating clients in the community and researchers working in universities or research institutes. As a result, practitioners have rarely conducted controlled studies of clients in therapy and few researchers have regular clinical contacts with children and families. This is an unfortunate situation because each of these professionals has insight and experience that would prove valuable were both to collaborate on the study of children in therapy.

Chapter 2 discussed ethical and legal issues related to therapeutic interventions with children. Ethics and the law are also important considerations when conducting research with children and families. To protect the rights of participants, investigators must design and conduct research in a manner consistent with the ethics code of their respective profession. Because children constitute a vulnerable population, researchers must take special precautions to ensure the welfare of young participants. Before they are allowed to conduct a study, investigators must obtain approval from an Institutional Review Board (IRB), sometimes referred to as the Human Subjects Committee. Institutions that receive federal funds are required to have an IRB that reviews research proposals and protects the rights of participants. Researchers must take special steps to ensure participants' safety when a study involves children. This includes obtaining assent from each child, when he or she is capable of giving assent, and consent from parents or guardians prior to enrolling a child in a research project (Protection of Human Research Subjects, 1991).

Although most therapists complete a graduate-level course in research methods, and some complete a data-based thesis or dissertation, relatively few clinicians conduct formal research after graduation. But the material covered in that methods course offers a variety of designs that can be used to evaluate the process and outcome of treatment. Here we briefly review a sample of quantitative and qualitative research methods that have been used to study child development and therapeutic interventions with children.

Quantitative Research Methods. Most therapists are taught to use quantitative methods that involve the administration of tests or questionnaires to collect numerical data that can be statistically analyzed. Quantitative methods include survey, correlational, causal comparative, longitudinal, quasi-experimental, and experimental designs (Mertens, 1998). The choice of design depends on the nature of the research question under consideration. These approaches vary in the amount of control that an investigator exerts over the variables of interest and the participants in a study.

Most people are familiar with the survey approach to research. This method typically involves the development of a questionnaire which is administered to a sample of people to collect demographic information and respondents' knowledge or attitudes about a topic or issue. Survey data can be analyzed in different ways. A relatively simple approach is the calculation of means and standard deviations or the frequency of responses for each survey item. This method provides a picture of the nature of the sample and participants' views. Researchers will sometimes use statistical procedures to study relationships among the responses to survey items.

As discussed in Chapter 2, Bajt and Pope (1989) found evidence of sexual contact between therapists and their child and adolescent clients. The authors collected their data in a mail survey to 100 psychologists who were randomly selected from the membership list of the American Psychological Association's Division of Child, Youth, and Family Services or had published in the area of therapist-client sexual intimacy. The authors' response rate was excellent, with 90% of the psychologists submitting a completed survey. As noted in Chapter 2, about a third of the respondents had either personal or indirect knowledge of cases involving sexual contact. While the Bajt and Pope figures are not accurate estimates of the prevalence of this problem, the results of their survey give clinicians reason to question whether the adult who sexually abused a child may have been a former therapist whom the child trusted.

Researchers employ the correlational design when they are interested in studying the strength of a relationship between two variables. This method often involves the administration of two or more measures at the same point in time. A researcher who wants to examine the relationship between depression and self-esteem in children could recruit a sample of fifth graders and ask them to complete the Children's Depression Inventory (CDI) (Kovacs, 1992) and the Self Perception Profile for Children (SPPS) (Harter, 1985). The students' scores would be analyzed using an appropriate statistical test, such as a Pearson correlation coefficient. If there was no relationship between these variables, the value for this coefficient would be zero. The stronger the relationship, the more the coefficient would approach its maximum value of either −1.00 or +1.00. Negative values mean that higher scores on one measure correlate with lower scores on the other. Positive values indicate that the two scores rise or fall in tandem with each other. In our example, we would expect to find a negative relationship in which high CDI scores correlate with low SPPC results.

Stormshak, Bierman, McMahon, Lengua, and Conduct Problems Prevention Research Group (2000) used a correlational design to study the relationship between parenting practices and behavior problems in a sample of first graders. The authors conducted home interviews to assess parents' child rearing techniques and behavioral ratings of their child. When Stormshak et al. analzyed these scores, they found that behavior problems were related to parents' use of punitive techniques such as spanking. They also found that low parental warmth and involvement were correlated with aggressive and oppositional behaviors in children. Because the researchers employed a correlational design, we are unable to determine causality. Although there was a relationship between parent and child behaviors, it is impossible to conclude whether parenting techniques were the cause or result of the children's problems.

Mertens (1998) described the causal comparative design as a method that can be used to study differences between groups. Researchers sometimes want to know more than the strength of a relationship. They are interested in studying whether groups of parents or children differ in their behaviors, attitudes or feelings. Investigators who employ this design recruit participants from each group, administer relevant measures, and then compare these results by using statistical procedures such as a t-test or an analysis of variance. The researcher who wants to study gender differences in depression and self-esteem could recruit boys and girls and have each child complete the CDI and the SPPC. Participants' scores would be analyzed to determine whether there is a statistically significant difference between the two groups. If so, the researcher would conclude that the difference observed is beyond what constitutes a predetermined level of chance. If no statistically significant difference is found, the investigator would decide that there was no gender-based difference in depression and self-esteem for the boys and girls in the study.

Daly and Glenwick (2000) employed a causal comparative design in their study of caregiver adjustment and perceptions of children's behavior among custodial grandmothers seeking treatment for their grandchildren, nonclinic custodial grandmothers, and mothers requesting therapy for their children. The authors administered measures of depression, parental stress and satisfaction, and perceptions of child behaviors. While there were no significant differences between the two clinic samples, the clinic grandmothers reported higher levels of depression and stress and more negative views of children's behavior than did grandmothers in the nonclinic group. These women also felt less competent in their role as parent and were less satisfied with the relationship they had with their grandchildren. The results of the Daly and Glenwick study suggest that grandmothers of troubled children have special needs that therapists must consider when treating these families.

Researchers who are interested in the developmental process in children often adopt the longitudinal design, which requires the study of the same individuals across time. When compared with the cross-sectional design that involves children of different ages tested at the same point in time, the longitudinal approach is more complex and costly because it typically requires a number of years to complete the repeated assessments employed in these studies. Of course, the advantage of this method is that statistical comparisons are conducted on results collected from the same children tested at different ages. These data enable researchers to analyze changes that occur within individuals over the course of the study period. Because of this characteristic, Seifert and Hoffnung (1997) concluded that longitudinal studies are considered "more truly 'developmental' because they show the steps by which individuals actually change" (p. 19).

Mertens (1998) described quasi-experimental designs as " 'almost' true experimental designs" (p. 77) that do not include the random assignment of children to treatment conditions. This approach is often used in educational settings where existing classes of students are compared with each other. A quasi-experimental design might be used to test the benefits of two programs intended to prevent tobacco use, with one program employed in Teacher A's class and the other intervention provided to the students of Teacher B. In this study, practical limitations prohibit the researcher from reorganizing class membership through randomized assignment of students to the prevention programs. In order to conduct the study, the investigator must employ a design that does not interrupt the daily operation of the school.

In a true experimental design, children are recruited and then randomly assigned to one of two or more conditions, which often include what is called a "waiting list control" where participants receive no treatment during the time of the study. Researchers have used this method to study the outcome of child therapies. For example, an investigator could employ an experimental design to study the benefits of a new intervention for childhood depression versus no treatment. In this case, children identified as depressed would be randomly assigned to either the treatment or waiting list condition. Any change that occurs in clients' depression scores between the therapy and waiting list groups is then statistically determined using procedures such as an analysis of variance.

The quasi-experimental and experimental designs share the use of independent and dependent variables. Simply stated, an independent variable is the condition or treatment a researcher manipulates during the study. In the quasi-experimental design mentioned above, the independent variable is the tobacco prevention program given to students. In this case, the independent variable has two levels, the different programs administered in the two classrooms. Some studies involve more than two levels of the independent variable. Children enrolled in an experimental treatment study for depression could be randomly assigned to either 10 weeks of child-centered play therapy, behavioral conditioning, or a treatment waiting list. The researchers would study the effects of these interventions by examining the dependent variables, which in this case could include scores on the Children's Depression Inventory (Kovacs, 1992).

Researchers who employ experimental designs must decide whether they will test children after treatment only or before and after their intervention. In a posttest-only, control group design, children are treated and then tested using the dependent measures. When the pretest-posttest, control group design is selected, participants are tested before and after treatment. The standard for quantitative studies of treatment outcome is the pretest-posttest, control group experimental design in which children are randomly assigned to a specified period of either treatment or waiting list, or one of two or more treatments. The treatment conditions represent the independent variable, while the dependent measures are the tests or rating scales administered at the beginning and the end of the study. Data can be analyzed to assess for changes in the dependent variables over time (i.e., pretest vs. posttest), between the treatment conditions, as well as interactions between time and treatment.

Barrett (1998) employed a pretest-posttest, control group design in her experimental study of cognitive-behavioral therapy for childhood anxiety. She randomly assigned clients to either 12 weeks of cognitive-behavioral group therapy (CBGT), cognitive-behavioral and family-based group treatment (CBFGT), or a clinical waiting list. Clients in the CBGT condition met each week for a 2-hour group session with other children to learn anxiety management techniques. Children who received CBFGT participated with their parents and other families in 2-hour weekly sessions where children were also taught anxiety management skills and parents learned to reward their child for effective use of these strategies. Parents were also taught cognitive-behavioral methods for handling their own anxiety and everyday problems. When she retested participants at the end of treatment and 12-month follow-up, Barrett found that both interventions were better than waiting list, although the family-based intervention was somewhat better than children's group therapy only.

All of these quantitative designs require the participation of groups of children. But most therapists treat individual children and their families. The typical clinician sees many clients each week, but these children are treated for different problems using uniquely crafted interventions instead of the prescribed treatments used in most between-groups experimental studies. An experimental method that is viable for individual clients is the single-case experimental design (Hersen & Barlow, 1976). Described as "the best kept secret in counseling" (Lundervold & Belwood, 2000, p. 92), the single-case design originated in clinical settings and is a practical method for conducting research as part of everyday practice.

The single-case approach involves the operational definition of a child's presenting problem, repeated measurements across time, and the systematic introduction and removal of treatment. The therapist's first task is helping the child and family to define the presenting problem in a manner that lends itself to objective measurement. The parents who describe their 10-year-old son as "impossible to handle" must be asked to specify what they mean by this phrase.

With the therapist's assistance, the parents might indicate that the boy never performs assigned household tasks, fails to comply with family rules, and rarely finishes his homework. After the presenting problem has been operationally defined in this manner, clinicians often ask parents to report the frequency of individual behaviors. Because post hoc report tends to be unreliable, therapists instruct parents to collect information called *baseline data* by having them record the number of times the behavior occurs each day. Formal application of the single-case design would require that the child not realize he is being observed. Otherwise, monitoring alone may produce a reactive effect in which his behavior changes simply because he knows his actions are being recorded. To reduce the reactive effect in practice, therapists sometimes schedule their first meeting with the parents only, instructing them to interact with their child as they have in the past and to record behaviors without the child's knowledge.

The baseline period represents the first of repeated measurements taken over the course of therapy. Figure 5-1 contains a record of the weekly data for the 10-year-old boy we have been discussing. The parents in this case selected homework as the starting point for treatment. The therapist asked them to record in column "B" (i.e., baseline), the number of nights the boy finished his assignments by the bedtime hour. When the family returned for the next appointment, treatment was initiated in which the child had to complete all of his homework correctly before he was allowed to engage in his favorite activities of watching television and playing video games.

The single-case experimental design offers a flexible approach to treatment evaluation that can be incorporated into any intervention, regardless of its theoretical foundation (Hayes, 1981). By collaborating with clients to specify treatment goals and measure therapeutic outcomes, clinicians are able to recognize when their interventions are appropriate and when different treatments are needed. Unlike some traditional approaches in which evaluation occurs at the end of therapy, single-case methodology offers weekly reports of the mini-outcomes of therapy. These data often prove to be invaluable in other ways. Consider the pattern of behavioral change presented in Figure 5-1. Obviously, the child is becom-

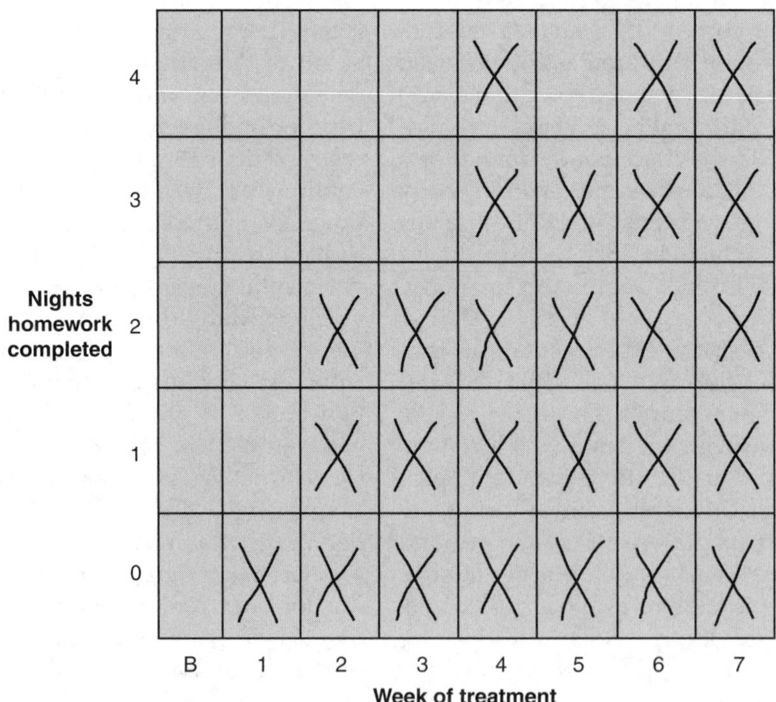

Figure 5–1. Application of the Single-Case Experimental Design in the Treatment of a 10-year-old Boy.

ing more compliant over the course of therapy. If after the third week, the parents were to report that treatment was not having any effect, the therapist would have data to challenge this belief. Without this information, the clinician may discover that the family prematurely terminates therapy when, in fact, treatment was having a positive effect. Based on what they learn from this initial intervention, the therapist and family could apply their treatment to other aspects of the presenting problem.

Ashbaugh and Peck (1998) used a single-case design to evaluate their behavioral treatment of a 2-year-old girl with sleep problems. The authors began by collecting baseline data for 11 days when the parents recorded whether the child was asleep or awake during each 15-minute interval of a 24-hour period. The parents indicated that their daughter's ideal sleep times were from 9:00 P.M. to 7:00 in the morning and during naptime from noon until 1:00 P.M. Ashbaugh and Peck discovered that during baseline, the child averaged about 18 intervals of disturbed sleep per day when she was either awake during ideal sleeping hours or asleep when she should have been awake. The authors also found that the parents allowed their daughter to sleep with them when the child would awaken at night and enter their bedroom.

The authors' intervention involved daily adjustments to the child's bedtime. If she fell asleep within 15 minutes after going to bed, her parents would put her to bed 30 minutes earlier the next night. If she was not asleep within 15 minutes, the parents would keep her awake by playing with her for 30 minutes. They repeated this response each time the child did not fall asleep within a 15-minute period. In addition, the parents would delay her bedtime by 30 minutes the next night. If the child fell asleep during ideal waking hours, the parents would arouse her and play with her to prevent her from falling asleep. If she entered the parents' bedroom at night, they took her to her room and put her back to bed.

Figure 5-2 is a graph of the child's episodes of disturbed sleep during baseline, treatment, a return to baseline, and the reinstatement of treatment. Ashbaugh and Peck (1998) were able to improve the child's sleep behaviors and achieve their goal of having the girl fall asleep at 9:00 each night. There was one additional benefit of treatment. The authors noted that the parents no longer had their sleep interrupted each night so their sleep–wake cycle stabi-

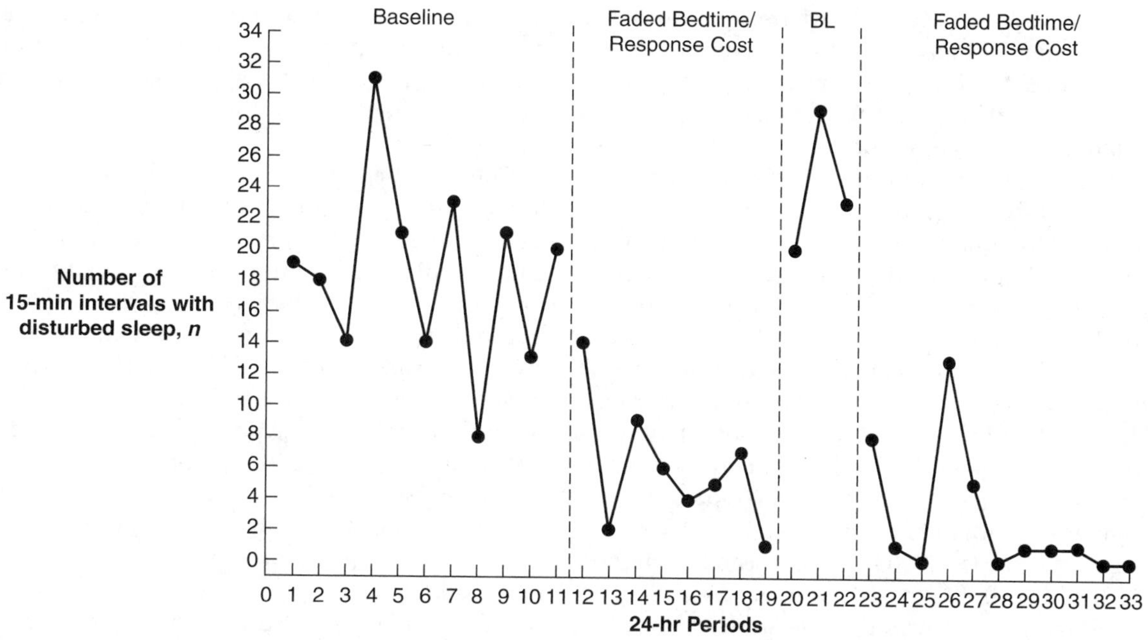

Figure 5–2. Frequency of 15-minute Intervals of Disturbed Sleep for a 2-year-old Girl. Asbaugh, R., & Peck, S. M. (1998). Treatment of sleep problems in a toddler: A replication of the faded bedtime with response cost protocol. *Journal of Applied Behavior Analysis, 31,* p. 129. Copyright 1998 by the Society for the Experimental Analysis of Behavior, Inc. Reprinted with permission of the author.

lized. From a researcher's perspective, notice how this study did not require large numbers of children who presented with the same problem. Ashbaugh and Peck were able to use the single-case design to evaluate the effectiveness of their intervention strategy. Therapists can do the same by using this method with clients.

A recent development in outcome research for child therapies is the use of meta-analyses, a quantitative approach to the review and analysis of existing studies. Whitley (1996) compared meta-analyses with traditional literature review techniques. The latter represent a more subjective approach in which the authors provide a narrative summary of the results of previous studies. In a meta-analysis, previously reported data are statistically analyzed to compare, for example, the outcomes for child therapies and no treatment. The statistical test that is often used in meta-analyses is the Pearson correlation coefficient, which provides a measure of the magnitude of effect, or effect size, an independent variable (e.g., treatment condition) has on the dependent variables (e.g., treatment outcome). Later in this chapter, we will discuss meta-analyses of treatment outcome, with special attention given to the work of John Weisz and his colleagues.

Qualitative Research Methods. Mertens (1998) stated that qualitative designs are used to obtain "an in-depth description of a specific program, practice, or setting" (p. 159). Consequently, the decision to use a quantitative or qualitative design is made in accordance with the research questions under investigation. Patton (1990) described a number of topics that are appropriate for qualitative analysis. These include the therapeutic process, the outcome of empirically supported treatments adapted to the needs of the individual, and developmental changes that occur across the lifespan. Qualitative designs are a viable option in practice settings where the number of participants is often limited and the focus of attention is therapeutic change in the individual child. Unfortunately, relatively few clinicians are trained to use these methods with their clients.

Of the seven types of qualitative research identified by Mertens (1998), the most commonly used method with children in therapy is the case study. In fact, Edwards (1996) called the case study "the cornerstone of theory and practice" (p. 10). Often criticized by quantitative researchers as lacking empirical rigor, this method does provide a systematic way of obtaining an in-depth look at a child in treatment through the use of therapist observations and client self-reports. Yin (1993, 1994) described how the case study can be used as a qualitative research method. The first step is the development of research questions to be investigated in the study. A researcher who wants to study the behavior of sexually abused girls in treatment might ask: "What factors contribute to sexually abused girls' participation in treatment?" Yin (1994) indicated that the investigator must then develop propositions, similar to hypotheses, to describe the reasons for a client's behavior. The researcher might propose that girls' therapeutic involvement may be related to the gender of their therapist. That is, clients treated by male clinicians may approach the therapeutic relationship in a different manner than girls treated by a female therapist.

The next step in the Yin (1994) model is identification of the unit of analysis that will be used. In the abuse study, the unit could be 2 girls and 2 female adolescents who had received no prior treatment for their recent abuse. The unit of analysis also would include a male therapist and a female therapist with training and supervised clinical experience with sexually abused girls. Yin recommended that researchers describe how the data collected during the study will be related to the propositions. This might involve repeated analyses over the course of treatment through the use of therapist observation summaries after each session, weekly self-report data from the client, and observer ratings of therapy videotapes.

The statistical procedures used to analyze quantitative data are usually not incorporated into qualitative studies. Rather, results are compared and contrasted to determine consistency with the stated propositions or alternative propositions. The results of the sexual abuse treatment study might reveal different interactional patterns for girls treated by the male or female therapist. These could include the male clinician's observations of lower therapeutic involvement by his clients, combined with higher client reports of anxiety and raters' descriptions of withdrawn behaviors. Based on these findings, the investigator might recommend follow-up studies, either qualitative or quantitative, to determine whether the results of this study generalize to other therapists and abuse survivors.

A few researchers have attempted to combine quantitative and qualitative methods in their studies of therapeutic interventions with children. Kush and

Cochran (1993) used this approach in their investigation of a 5-week career planning program for high school students. The authors trained parents in the treatment group to use a career planning workbook with their teenager, but participants assigned to the waiting list control condition received no formal intervention. The quantitative component of the study was a statistical comparison of pretest-posttest results for the treatment and control groups. The qualitative analysis involved posttreatment interviews with 12 participants: the 3 students who were most improved and the 3 who were least improved in the treatment group as well as the 6 most improved students in the waiting list group.

Quantitative results revealed that the parent treatment was better than assignment to a waiting list. But the qualitative findings revealed within-group variability and similarities between the groups. Most interesting was the fact that waiting list interviewees actually engaged in career guidance activities during the 5-week study. They used computer-assisted guidance programs, met with career counselors, and discussed career-related issues with their parents. These qualitative findings provide important information for researchers who use no-treatment conditions in their studies. Children and families assigned to waiting lists might receive some form of treatment, regardless of the investigator's attempt to control this important independent variable. If a sufficient number of waiting list participants seek services, quantitative analyses indicating no significant between-group differences may actually underestimate the impact of the treatment under investigation.

Most of the research on child development and children in therapy has been quantitative in nature. But qualitative designs and quantitative-qualitative combinations represent important methods for expanding our current knowledge base. Readers who are interested in learning more about qualitative research and its use in clinical settings are encouraged to consult Edwards (1996), Marshall and Rossman (1999), Mertens (1998), and Patton (1990).

THERAPEUTIC PROCESS AND OUTCOME

Child therapies involve two important components: process and outcome. Garfield and Bergin (1994) defined therapeutic process as the "variables that account for the changes secured in psychotherapy" (p. 10). These include factors such as the gender and race of therapist and client, the clinician's in-session behaviors, and the client's motivation for therapy. Therapeutic outcome constitutes the client changes that occur during the course of treatment and is the dependent variable that researchers typically measure to evaluate the impact of their intervention. The bulk of the empirical research on child therapies involves studies of treatment outcome. As Kazdin (1993) stated, there have been relatively few attempts to study the process of therapy with children. In this section, we consider selected examples of work in this area.

Therapeutic Process

The traditional focus of process research is the relationship between the therapist and client. Often referred to as the working alliance or therapist–client rapport, this relationship is the context for the fundamental activities of therapy. An essential component of the working alliance is client involvement in treatment (Greenberg & Pinsof, 1986). Involved clients participate in therapy by setting goals, engaging in self-disclosure, and examining themselves in relation to others. With adults, client involvement usually occurs through verbal discourse. But children are more likely to use a combination of words and actions in therapy. The younger the child, the more likely it is that he or she will express thoughts or feelings through play.

Based on research with adults in therapy, Morris and Nicholson (1993) discussed client factors that may affect the development of the working alliance with children. These include the child's expectations for therapy. As discussed earlier, children often enter treatment at the precontemplation stage of therapeutic change. Most have had considerable experience handling requests and instructions from adults. These experiences are likely to have an effect on the child's expectations of the therapist. Children who have been criticized by their parents and teachers are likely to expect the same from their clinicians. Clients who are expected to comply with adult directives may anticipate similar demands from the therapist.

A child's presenting problem also affects the therapist–client relationship. For example, the in-session behaviors of an oppositional or defiant child may cause the therapist to spend more time setting limits for the client than would be done with a depressed child. Likewise, a clinician may use family therapy to treat a disruptive child but select individual play therapy for a sad and withdrawn client. Of course, a child's age and developmental level also have an impact on the therapeutic alliance. Again, whereas individual treatment for younger clients is more likely to involve play techniques, pre-adolescents and more developmentally advanced children may participate in traditional talk therapy.

Smith-Acuna, Durlak, and Kaspar (1991) suggested the presence of three child dimension in the working alliance: affective experiences in treatment, perceptions of the therapist's feelings, and perceptions of the clinician's actions. Shirk and Saiz (1992) conceptualized the working alliance with children as having two dimensions: the clients' affective experience of therapy and the child's participation in treatment activities. The authors developed child and therapist versions of their Therapeutic Alliance Scales for Children that contain positive affect, negative affect, and therapeutic tasks subscales. Based on an initial study with 7- to 12-year-old clients, Shirk and Saiz found that children who had more positive feelings about the therapeutic relationship were more likely to talk about their problems in treatment. The reverse was true for clients' ratings of negative affect, with more negative feelings related to less active participation in therapy.

Therapists' thoughts, feelings, and behaviors also contribute to the development and maintenance of the working alliance. Carl Rogers (1957) described what he believed to be the necessary and sufficient conditions for therapeutic change (see Chapter 8). Briefly stated, the clinician's function is to accept the client and attempt to view the world from the child's perspective. This obviously requires a perceptual and conceptual shift for most therapists, who are accustomed to interpreting life events from an adult viewpoint. Clinicians must behave in a manner that communicates interest, acceptance, and understanding of the child. Freedheim and Russ (1983) agreed when they described a positive therapist–client relationship as "a basic requirement of all forms of individual therapy with children" (p. 983).

Very little is known about the relationship between a therapist's qualities and his or her working alliance with young clients. Early work by Truax and his colleagues (e.g., Truax, Altmann, Wright, and Mitchell, 1973) on the effects of therapists' empathy, warmth, and genuineness has not been continued. It is difficult to explain this unfortunate situation, especially because of the importance that clinicians of all theoretical orientations have placed on the therapeutic relationship with children. Morris and Nicholson (1993) described a number of therapist variables that have been studied with adult clients, but they noted the absence of similar studies with children in therapy. One factor that has received recent attention is the effect of the gender of therapist on young clients' participation in therapy. Later in this chapter, we will briefly examine the therapeutic process studies that Wagner and his students conducted to examine the impact of male and female clinicians with sexually abused girls.

Earlier we examined the stages and levels of therapeutic change described by Prochaska and Norcross (1994). The third dimension of the authors' model is the processes of change that represent "the covert and overt activities that people engage in to alter affect, thinking, behavior, or relationships related to a particular problem or more general patterns of living" (p. 12). Prochaska and Norcross identified 10 change processes that have received empirical support: consciousness raising, catharsis/dramatic relief, self-reevaluation, environmental reevaluation, self-liberation, social liberation, counterconditioning, stimulus control, contingency management, and the helping relationship (p. 458). As mentioned previously, the authors developed their transtheoretical model based on research with adults in therapy. Although clinicians might expect to observe these processes with parents, they must revise their expectations when the focus of attention is a child client.

Although no empirical studies exist to permit an enlightened selection, we might assume that the helping relationship is an important change process for children. As we have discussed, therapists of all theoretical orientations have identified the working alliance as an important factor in child therapy. We might also assume that individual treatment for young clients also involves catharsis/dramatic relief, whether it occurs through play or talk therapy. Clinicians could expect a child's developmental level to limit the client's ability to experience consciousness raising, self-reevaluation, environmental reevaluation, self-liberation, and social liberation. But when parents are actively involved in treatment, especially when behavioral techniques are used, we can anticipate that counterconditioning, stimulus control, and contingency management will be part of the therapeutic process. When clinicians work with families, they can anticipate that whereas parents may benefit from any or all of these change processes, children are limited to certain categories.

Additional research is needed on the process of child therapy. This includes studies on the application of the Prochaska and Norcross (1994) model to children and families in treatment. Current videotaping and audiotaping technologies provide opportunities for recording and coding treatment sessions that Carl Rogers and his colleagues never had available. Our studies of the therapeutic process should have improved since the 1950s, but the limited number of investigations conducted with child clients indicates that there has been little progress. Researchers must develop psychometrically sound measures of the therapeutic process with children and then conduct treatment studies to assess the relationship among client and therapist demographics, in-session behaviors, and treatment outcomes. Investigators should not limit themselves to the study of individual therapy, which represents only one of a number of interventions commonly used with children (Freedheim & Russ, 1983). They must also examine the therapeutic process in family-based treatments, parent training, and group therapies for children.

Therapeutic Outcome

The outcome of therapy can be measured in three ways: efficacy, effectiveness, and efficiency (Messer & Wachtel, 1997). Treatment efficacy is associated with research therapies that are used with clients who meet specified criteria for admission and are randomly assigned to manualized treatment for a specific problem. For an intervention to be effective, it must work with children and families in the everyday world of clinical practice, where treatment is individualized to the client's needs. Lonigan, Elbert, and Johnson (1998) discussed the relationship between these measures of treatment outcome when they described efficacy as "a necessary but not sufficient condition for demonstrating the effectiveness of psychosocial interventions" (p. 139). If a treatment does not work under the controlled conditions used to study research therapies, there is little reason to believe the method will be effective in the everyday world of clinical practice.

Another important measure of therapeutic outcome is efficiency, or the cost of services provided. For example, if treatments A and B are equally effective and treatment A can be provided at half of the cost of treatment B, then intervention A is more efficient. Cost containment efforts in the mental health field have made therapists more aware of the efficiency of the treatments they offer. Consequently, clinicians must be aware of the outcome research on different techniques if they are to provide treatments that are both effective and efficient.

Hoagwood, Jensen, Petti, and Burns (1996) proposed five domains or criteria for measuring therapeutic outcome with child clients. As we might expect, these include the traditional focus on the remediation of presenting problems or symptons. But Hoagwood et al. believed that an evaluation of treatment outcome should also include consideration of the client's adaptive functioning, such as the positive qualities or skills that enable a child to move toward optimal development. Therapists must evaluate the progress made in remediating negative influences in the child's environment, such as school violence and parents' marital strife, as well as systemic changes, including the development of community-based collaborative interventions for children. The final component of the authors' model is clients' perception of treatment, which includes their satisfaction with the services received. Clinicians can collect consumer satisfaction data by interviewing children, parents, and other adults involved in treatment to determine their views on the effectiveness and efficiency of therapy.

Studies of treatment efficiency often involve an evaluation of the number of sessions provided and the dollar cost per client served. Selecting outcome criteria for treatment efficacy and effectiveness can be more difficult. Early investigators used rather subjective measures, such as clinician progress notes in client case files. Researchers eventually used more rigorous methods, including the analysis of results obtained from standardized instruments administered before and after treatment. But the measures used in these studies vary according to the investigator's theoretical orientation. Proponents of behavioral principles have studied change in clients' observable actions. Psychodynamic researchers opted for global measures of personality development, including ego strength, anxiety, and intrapsychic conflict. Family systems theorists examined changes in communication style and subsystem boundaries. Researchers' theoretical allegiance is also reflected in the treatment techniques they evaluate. These include procedures as diverse as individual talk therapy, behavioral conditioning based on operant principles, play therapy, and family interventions.

Researchers have studied child treatments by using the same designs used with adults in therapy.

Although there are similarities, including examination of the therapist–client relationship, studies of child interventions pose unique methodological challenges. For example, outcome research with adults is usually limited to an evaluation of the individual in therapy, but studies of child treatments can include data collected from the child, parents, and teachers. The setting for therapy is also different because treatment may be implemented in the home or the classroom rather than being restricted to the clinician's office. Fortunately, considerable progress has been achieved in the design and implementation of these studies since their inception in the 1930s.

Barrett, Hampe, and Miller (1978) observed that much of the early work on treatment outcome was conducted for the purpose of program evaluation. For example, Helen Leland Witmer and her colleagues found that 79% of the youth in treatment at the Institute for Child Guidance in New York City were either "successfully adjusted" or "partially adjusted" (Witmer and Students, 1933). Therapeutic outcome in this study was evaluated through a review of case files, and success was defined by what "the clinic says is successfully adjusted" (p. 341). When Witmer (1935) expanded her research to include child guidance clinics in four different cities, she found similar effects across these samples. As part of this study, Witmer conducted an early analysis of the predictors of treatment outcome. Interestingly, she found that parents' attitudes toward their children were more important than child-related factors and the type of treatment used.

From the early 1930s until the late 1950s, clinicians were confident that child therapies were effective (Barrett et al., 1978). But Levitt (1957) challenged this belief after he reviewed 18 studies of child treatments. Although he found that 67% of the clients improved by the end of therapy, Levitt also reported a 73% improvement rate for children who did not receive treatment. Levitt, Beiser, and Robertson (1959) followed with a comparison of children who completed treatment and those for whom therapy was prematurely terminated. Based on information obtained from children and their parents, the authors found no significant difference in outcome for the two groups. But Levitt et al. cautioned that the type of treatment differed across clients, with only 10% of the cases involving only the child and more than 40% having only the mother in therapy. This led Barrett et al. (1978) to state that "in more than one-half of all cases that might be offered as evidence for the lack of effectiveness of *psychotherapy with children*, the child himself was not 'treated'!" (p. 418)

During the following decades, researchers studied therapeutic outcome for a variety of child interventions. When Casey and Berman (1985) analyzed the treatments used in 75 studies, they found that the majority (56%) were behavioral interventions, including cognitive-behavioral treatments, with less consideration given to client-centered (29%), dynamic (9%), and what the authors called "mixed or unclassifiable nonbehavioral techniques" (9%). Outcome results seem to support the use of behaviorally oriented treatments. In their meta-analysis of 150 outcome studies, Weisz, Weiss, Han, Granger, and Morton (1995) found that behavioral therapies were significantly better than nonbehavioral treatments. This imbalance between behavioral and nonbehavioral therapy differs from the theoretical orientations and practices of clinicians. When Tuma and Pratt (1982) surveyed clinical child psychologists, they found that 59% identified themselves as eclectic, 22% said they were psychodynamic, 12% cited a preference for behavioral techniques, and 7% endorsed humanistic-existential or other orientations. When the authors took a closer look at their eclectic participants, they found that approximately 50% of them claimed either psychodynamic, behavioral, or both as their primary approach to treatment.

A clinician's professional affiliation may also have a significant influence on the types of treatment used. Kazdin, Siegal, and Bass (1990) found that whereas psychiatrists were more likely to use psychoanalysis and psychodynamic therapy, psychologists preferred behavior modification and cognitive therapies. No differences were found for respondents' ratings of family interventions. In a more focused study of treatment preference, Wagner and Hicks-Jimenez (1986) surveyed members of the Association for Advancement of Behavior Therapy (AABT) and the American Association for Marriage and Family Therapy (AAMFT) regarding their therapy of choice for childhood nocturnal enuresis. Although behavioral conditioning with a urine alarm has been identified as the treatment of choice for this problem (Hours, Berman, & Abramson, 1994), AAMFT members were significantly more likely to select family therapy, but AABT members preferred behavioral conditioning. The AABT respondents were also more accurate in their estimates of the average cure rate for behavioral treatment. These results are especially troubling because members of both groups were as likely to treat clients experiencing this relatively common problem. The gap between child therapy research and practice appears to exist even when the weight of empirical evidence supports a particular intervention strategy.

Chapter 3 contrasted research and clinic therapies. The differences between these treatments are important to any discussion of therapeutic outcome for child clients. Because most empirical studies of child interventions involve research therapies, we might question the relevance of these findings for child therapy as practiced in clinic settings. Weisz et al. (1992) reviewed studies on child treatments and concluded that the positive outcomes reported for research therapies may not generalize to everyday clinical practice. Analyses of anywhere from 75 to 223 studies of research therapies have revealed that after treatment, the average client functions better than 76% to 81% of the children assigned to a control condition (Casey & Berman, 1987; Kazdin, Bass, Ayers, & Rodgers, 1990). But when Weisz and Weiss (1989) analyzed the outcomes of different types of clinic therapies, they found no significant difference between children assigned to behavioral, nonbehavioral, or no-treatment conditions.

Weiss, Catron, Harris, and Phung (1999) conducted a controlled evaluation of the effectiveness of traditional therapies with children whose average age was 10 years. The authors' study is noteworthy because it was not an efficacy study of research therapies. Treatment was provided in school-based clinics by professional therapists who were permitted to select interventions based on the needs of the child. In addition, therapy was not time limited; rather, it extended over a 2-year period. Weiss et al. randomly assigned children to one of two conditions: traditional therapy or an attention control group in which participants received regular sessions of academic tutoring. A review of therapists' treatments indicated that clinicians used individual, group, and family therapies as well as consultation with parents and teachers. Although a comparison of pretreatment and posttreatment results revealed some improvement for all children over the course of the study, no significant difference was found between the treatment and control conditions.

To achieve the results for research therapies in clinic settings, practitioners need to approximate the treatment conditions used in efficacy studies. Weisz and Weiss (1989) echoed the recommendations of Beutler (1979) when they advised that:

> child and adolescent psychotherapy can be effective when conditions of therapy are carefully arranged, as when specific targets of treatment are clearly delineated, when these are well matched to the type of therapy provided, and when the therapists included are well trained in the approach they use. (p. 746)

Researchers can facilitate the transfer of treatment techniques from the laboratory to the clinic by controlling for factors that distinguish child therapies from those used with older clients. A list of these conditions includes client characteristics, such as the age and developmental level of the child. With the exception of Casey and Berman (1985), the cited efficacy studies included both children and adolescents. But clinicians have designed interventions that are developmentally appropriate for child clients. Of particular importance are the various play techniques commonly used with children. Although these methods are not appropriate for most adolescent clients, they offer children in therapy a means for self-expression and communication with the clinician. Researchers can address developmental differences by recruiting only child clients to receive age-appropriate treatments or evaluating a sufficient number of children and adolescents to determine age-related outcomes with the same intervention strategy.

Therapists often become frustrated or disappointed when clients prematurely terminate treatment. If they knew the factors that cause early withdrawal from therapy, clinicians could intervene in advance to prevent a child's departure from treatment. Unfortunately, there is no formula that can be used to reliably distinguish between therapy completers and defectors. Unlike adult clients, who typically decide whether to continue treatment, children depend on their parents for transportation to therapy sessions and the payment of treatment fees. As a result, clinicians must recognize characteristics of both children and parents that increase the probability of early withdrawal from therapy.

Weiss et al. (1999) found that children withdrawn from treatment were likely to have more serious problems at the outset of therapy. They also observed that these clients were less likely to live with both biological parents and more likely to reside in a home headed by a single mother. Venable and Thompson (1998) studied the relationship between parents' psychological adjustment and children's early removal from treatment. They found that primary caregivers who prematurely terminated therapy for their child were more likely to express hostility toward themselves, which included self-criticism as well as excessive and unrealistic feelings of guilt. Venable and Thompson cautioned that successful treatment for young clients "is not dependent solely on the relationship between the child and counselor" (p. 292). In addition to a child's level of functioning, clinicians must consider family structure and parents' psychological adjustment to decrease the chances of a child's early withdrawal from therapy. Premature termination is an important concern for all therapists, but it is of particular concern to clinicians who treat children whose participation in treatment is so dependent on others. Because of the problems caused by early termination, clinicians have developed treatments that can be delivered within a limited time frame and at less expense to the family (see Chapter 3).

PLAY: A THERAPEUTIC TECHNIQUE FOR CHILDREN

Most therapeutic interventions used with children have been adapted from techniques commonly used with adults. An exception to this rule is play therapy, which Nystul (1993) identified as one of the few methods specifically developed for children. All therapists, regardless of their theoretical orientation, must be able to incorporate play into their work with young clients. Clinicians trained in such diverse methods as child-centered, cognitive-behavioral, psychoanalytic, Gestalt, and family systems therapy have used this technique with children (O'Connor & Braverman, 1997). Play is undoubtedly popular because it offers young clients a developmentally appropriate medium for the expression of clinically relevant thoughts and feelings. It is appropriate for young children with limited verbal skills and older clients who are reluctant to talk in session.

Children who have difficulty expressing their feelings in words may find their voice in play. Virginia Axline (1950) described the play of Mitt, a 4-year-old girl whose mother complained about the child's many problems.

> During one of Mitt's play therapy sessions she put on the "dress-up" clothes and became the mother. Her voice became cross and scolding. "Hurry! Hurry! Don't be so slow. And look at that dress. Clean just five minutes ago. I'll spank you, that's what I'll do. And you can go to bed and have *bad dreams*. Maybe the bad man will come and take you away and I can get another good little baby!" (p. 71)

An average 4-year-old child would have difficulty expressing these thoughts and feelings in traditional talk therapy. But in play, Mitt was able to communicate with the clinician and provide a view of the world as seen through her eyes. In this example, the therapist was able to collect valuable data about the relationship between the mother and daughter and the girl's expectations of others' reactions to her behavior.

Although play is a commonly used technique, controlled studies of its process and outcome with children are rare. Kazdin (1994a) noted the dearth of research on play treatments but acknowledged that the few studies available suggest therapeutic play can bring about positive change in troubled children. It is difficult to explain why researchers have not given more attention to an intervention that is used so often. One answer can be found in the theoretical foundations for this method. As discussed in Chapters 7 and 9, play therapy was developed by psychodynamic and child-centered therapists who have been less active in researching their techniques. Because so little is known about this popular intervention, researchers and practitioners must collaborate to expand on a literature base composed mostly of descriptive reports of children in treatment.

Therapists must realize that play is more than a simple leisure activity. They must accept it for what it is: an important and natural form of expression for children. By combining play and traditional talk therapies, clinicians can develop interventions that are more closely matched to the developmental levels of young clients. Skilled therapists are proficient with a variety of techniques, including art activities, psychodrama, and constructive play. These clinicians also feel comfortable using these interventions with children; comfortable with the clutter the child creates in the playroom; comfortable with the seemingly slow pace of therapy with a client who vacillates between "clinically meaningful" activities and those observed in any child at play; and comfortable setting aside the traditional approach to interviewing clients in favor of a developmentally appropriate technique.

GROUP TECHNIQUES

The process of group therapy differs from that of individual therapy because of the larger number of interpersonal relationships that result from having more than one client in the treatment room. Clinicians can use these interactions as a fulcrum for clients' development of social skills, self-esteem, and an understanding of their cultural surround. Group methods are an efficient form of treatment because they enable therapists to treat more than one child during a single session. In this section, we discuss issues that clinicians must consider when planning and conducting therapeutic groups for children.

Begin (1999) identified developmental issues that therapists must address when using groups with children. As is true in individual therapy, the younger the child, the more important it is to integrate play into treatment. With older children who have the linguistic and listening skills needed to communicate with others, clinicians can rely more on verbal discussions about clinically relevant topics. But age and developmental level are not the only issues that therapists must consider when conducting groups with children. Clinicians must also select members whose needs are consistent with the goals and procedures of the group. Inviting a child with attention-deficit hyperactivity disorder to join a friendship group for withdrawn, socially isolated students is likely to compromise group cohesion, frustrate the clinician, and limit the therapeutic outcomes of all members.

Therapists must also decide the number and length of sessions and how many children will be allowed to participate. Although group size is related to members' age and presenting problems, Begin (1999) recommended having three to four participants in primary school groups and from six to eight members for groups of older children. As a general rule, groups for clients with externalizing behaviors should be smaller because of the difficulties involved in maintaining order and ensuring each child's safety. Begin stated that the frequency and length of group meetings vary, with some therapists using weekly or twice-weekly sessions, ranging from 30 to 60 minutes each. Again, this decision involves consideration of the members' ages and presenting problems. By addressing group size, length, and frequency at the outset, clinicians can avoid complications that result from an ill-conceived format or structure for the group.

Therapists who conduct groups sometimes adopt the co-facilitator model because of its advantages in working with children. Corey and Corey (2002) described how co-therapists can draw on each other's knowledge and experience when planning group sessions. During group meetings, they are able to observe the therapeutic process from different perspectives and collect unique information that can be shared during post-session reviews. These conferences also provide opportunities for the co-therapists to explore the significant thoughts and feelings they experienced during group sessions. The co-facilitator model is also appropriate for children with externalizing behavior problems because two clinicians are better able to monitor clients' disruptive acts and intervene when needed. An effective co-therapist relationship begins with clinicians' selection of a colleague they respect, trust, and enjoy having as a treatment partner (Corey & Corey, 2002). Again, with proper planning, two therapists can work together to provide a therapeutic experience for children.

Chapter 2 discussed confidentiality in group therapy along with procedures for informing clients about this important issue. Therapists establish other limits appropriate to the age and developmental level of the children in group therapy. Generally speaking, the younger, more cognitively naive, and socially immature the members, the more responsibility the therapists must assume for establishing limits on clients' behavior. In order to reduce clients' anxiety and lay the foundation for group cohesion, clinicians should devote a portion of the first session to the development of group rules. These include necessary limits, such as being kind to other members, and rules pertaining to social conventions, which include listening when others talk. Corey and Corey (2002) suggested that therapists enter the first session with specific limits in mind but encourage clients to discuss the rules that will apply in their group. The authors found that children usually recommend the same limits chosen by the clinician. If clients overlook rules the therapist deems necessary for a safe and therapeutic experience, the clinician should suggest these limits and provide a rationale for their use in group.

Rules should be written on a poster that can be brought to each session and displayed for clients' reference. To involve children in this process, Smead (1995) recommended that clients who have the necessary skills be allowed to write group rules on the poster. All rules should be clearly stated in a concrete, positive, and developmentally appropriate format. Examples include, "Keep my hands to myself," "Stay in my seat," and "Listen when other people talk." When children lack the requisite reading and writing skills, rules can be placed on the poster using appropriate pictures or symbols. Schaefer, Jacobsen, and Ghahramanlou (2000) recommended that clinicians use six rules or fewer so children can remember them. Therapists must give careful consideration to the limits that are established at the outset of group therapy because they will be responsible for implementing these rules in a consistent manner during later sessions.

Kernberg and Chazan (1991) described how group therapists encourage socialization and group cohesion. Through their interactions with each other, children receive peer feedback about their behavior. When members identify with the group and support each other, they are more likely to offer constructive comments and practice socially appropriate behavior with other members. To achieve these goals, Kernberg and Chazan recommended that clinicians combine play with verbal statements, including encouragement and directing clients' attention to events as they occur in session. They also suggested the use of interpretive statements to help children understand the reasons for their behavior in group. The authors provided the following example of a therapist's interpretation in response to clients' in-session behavior:

> You are all angry at me for having stopped the game. Rather than telling me about how you feel, Sam and Bob are fighting with each other, Dick is pretending I don't exist by turning his back to me, and Ronald is throwing chalk all over the place. (p. 203)

The timing of such statements is extremely important. Kernberg and Chazan, for example, recommended that interpretation be used only during the middle or toward the end of therapy when group cohesion exists and clients are more comfortable with the group process.

DEVELOPMENTAL CONSIDERATIONS

Therapy is a linguistic endeavor whose process and outcome typically occur as a result of verbal communication between the therapist and child (Lester, 1975). Even play techniques, such as developmental play during which nonverbal interventions are emphasized, involve verbal interactions between the clinician and child. Therefore, clients' language development represents an important consideration in child therapies.

Between the ages of 9 and 12 months, infants usually say their first words, such as "Mama" or "Dada" (Haslett, 1997). This initial collection of words related to objects and people in the environment grows to a speaking vocabulary of more than 8000 words by age 6 years (Santrock, 2000). Children begin to combine words into simple sentences called two-word utterances at about age 18 to 24 months (Santrock, 2000). These include statements containing people and action, such as "Mommy run," and those expressing a relationship between action and objects, such as "Eat cookies." But it is during the elementary school years that children become more skilled at communicating the meanings of their messages as they expand their vocabulary, develop grammatical skills, and use language in a socially appropriate manner that includes taking turns when talking with others.

Therapists must consider children's linguistic development when they interview young clients. Garbarino and Stott (1989) cited a number of mistakes that clinicians make, including the use of too many questions, sophisticated terminology, and complex sentences. Boat and Everson (1986) offered recommendations for interviewing clients, ages 5 years and younger, but many of these suggestions merit consideration with other children:

1. Use sentences containing only three to five more words than the child uses in an average sentence.
2. When the child does not understand a question, rephrase it rather than repeating it to avoid giving the impression that the client gave an incorrect answer.
3. Be patient and communicate interest in what the child is saying, even when the client "rambles" through relevant and irrelevant details of an event.
4. When talking about other people, use their name rather than pronouns.
5. Use the child's terminology for people, objects, and events. (pp. 27-28)

Hughes and Baker (1990) encouraged clinicians to connect their questions to activities occurring in session. Notice how the therapist in the following interview uses a child's dollhouse play to facilitate client self-disclosure.

THERAPIST: What is the girl doll doing?
CHILD: Playing in her room.
THERAPIST: Mmmm.
CHILD: Her Mommy and Daddy are downstairs. (Child places the mother and father dolls in the kitchen.) They are fighting.
THERAPIST: The Mommy and Daddy are fighting.
CHILD: Uh-huh. My Daddy hit my Mommy. (Pause.) She cried.

By following the client's lead, the clinician was able to use her play as a stimulus for verbal communication.

Hughes and Baker (1990) provided other examples of the use of play and concrete referents with children. Instead of asking a client how she feels about her parents' divorce, a clinician might show the child:

> a picture of a mother and a father on one side of a door and a girl on the other side. The interviewer says, "Here are a mother and a father. They are talking about getting a divorce. What do you think they are saying?" (p. 38)

As the therapist and client discuss the event, the clinician might ask the child to describe how she thinks the girl in the picture feels about the divorce. In this way, a visual stimulus is used to encourage the client to express her thoughts and feelings related to a personal experience.

MULTICULTURAL CONSIDERATIONS

Language is a particularly important consideration when working with children from nondominant groups, especially those reared in bidialectal or bilingual environments. African American children, for example, are often exposed to standard English and what has been termed "black English," or Ebonics. Choney, Berryhill-Paapke, and Robbins (1995) estimated that more than 150 languages can be found among Native American populations. Bee (1997) stated that "the great majority" (p. 423) of Hispanic Americans either speak only Spanish or are bilingual. Regular exposure to more than one language characterizes the daily experience of many children from underrepresented populations and poses a significant challenge for therapists who treat these children and their families.

Black English is a complex dialect that differs from standard English in the speech sounds that are used, the ways that word units are linked to each other, how words are combined to produce sentences, and the social rules that govern appropriate discourse (Cole & Taylor, 1990). In Ernest Gaines' (1993) novel, *A Lesson Before Dying*, young Louis Washington begins the pledge of allegiance as follows, "Plege legen toda flag" (p. 56). During therapy with a father and child, the parent might instruct the child, "Ax da doctah what he want chew ta do." Obviously, the clinician's understanding of and appreciation for this dialect can have a significant impact on the process and outcome of therapy.

Black English has traditionally been viewed as an inferior or deficient version of standard English (Bountress, 1980). This attitude has sometimes resulted in prejudicial treatment, including the misdiagnosis of speech articulation disorders in African American students (Cole & Taylor, 1990). Many of these children have become proficient in two dialects. For example, at school a child uses standard English but switches to black English at home or when talking with African American peers (Seymour & Ralabate, 1985). Because most therapists are of European American descent, a child's bidialectal experience has implications for the therapeutic process. Smith (1981) suggested that some African American clients are reluctant to talk in therapy because they fear clinicians will negatively evaluate their speech. Whether this explains the reticent behavior of every young client is uncertain, but therapists should at least consider a child's language history when the client remains silent or offers only brief responses in session.

Rogler, Malgady, Costantino, and Blumenthal (1987) contended that the "lowest common denominator of cultural sensitivity with Hispanics is generally that of linguistic accessibility" (p. 566). Many Hispanic American children become bilingual by speaking English at school and using Spanish at home. This is particularly true in recently immigrated families in which children, because of formal and informal learning at school, become more proficient than their parents in the use of the English language (Gushue & Schiarra, 1995). Conflict can develop in these families when children adopt the language, values, and practices of the dominant culture and the parents strive to maintain their culture of origin. Similar problems have emerged in recently immigrated Asian American families in which children adopt English and parents continue to use their native language (Huang & Ying, 1989).

Therapists who are proficient in more than one language are a valuable addition to any school or clinic staff. For example, Sue, Fujino, Ho, Takeuchi, and Zane (1991) found that matching Mexican American clients with therapists based on language and ethnicity resulted in a lower rate of premature termination and a greater number of sessions attended. Bilingual clinicians have the ability to communicate with and engage family members who speak different languages (e.g., a bilingual child, a Spanish-only mother, and a Spanish-primarily father) and thereby use the family structure (e.g., the father–child dyad) for therapeutic gain (Gushue & Schiarra, 1995). When language matching of clients is not possible, therapists must consider using a trained interpreter (American Psychological Association, 1993b). Although bilingual children are sometimes asked to serve in this role, clinicians should avoid this practice because it challenges the traditional parent–child hierarchy in these families (Gushue & Schiarra, 1995; Ho, 1987).

The use of interpreters in therapy is a complex endeavor that involves the translation of words as well as the "intended meaning of the message" (Vasquez & Javier, 1991, p. 164). Because interpreters provide the crucial connection between clinicians and clients, they must be adequately trained to understand the terminology, knowledge base, and interpersonal dynamics of therapy (Acosta & Cristo, 1981). Vasquez and Javier (1991) noted the problems that can result when untrained interpreters are used. They described an interview with the Hispanic American mother of a mildly retarded boy who had recently been hospitalized for an acute psychotic condition. During the session, the therapist has the interpreter ask the mother if she is depressed. The following interchange results.

INTERPRETER (SPANISH): The doctor wants to know if you feel sad.

PATIENT (SPANISH): Yes, I feel like crying almost every night. Sometimes I wonder if it is better to be dead. I have not been able to sleep for two nights because of my son. I just need to sleep for a while.

INTERPRETER (ENGLISH): She said yes and has thought that it was better killing herself. She said that only in this way she was going to be able to rest. (pp. 164–165)

As Vasquez and Javier (1991) indicated, the untrained interpreter distorted communication by paraphrasing statements rather than translating the exact words of the therapist and client. The interpreter actually became the interviewer and conveyed inaccurate information to the clinician.

Accuracy of translation is one of the factors that Acosta and Cristo (1981) addressed in their training program for interpreters. The authors recruited bilingual-bicultural individuals from the Hispanic American community in Los Angeles and provided weekly training designed to enhance interpreters' proficiency in both English and Spanish. Trainees were taught basic psychological principles and psychotherapeutic terminology. Interpreters who translate for children should also receive instruction in child development and family dynamics. Acosta and Cristo trained their interpreters in the behaviors of therapy, such as maintaining an even tone of voice, giving exact translations, and encouraging the therapist or client to rephrase statements when the meaning was ambiguous. Again, interpreters who translate with children should receive specialized instruction in the techniques used to establish rapport with young clients.

Acosta and Cristo (1981) described the triadic relationship of the therapist, client, and interpreter. For an interpreter to be effective, both the clinician and client must adjust to the presence of this third party. The therapist should inform clients that the clinician, not the interpreter, is the professional to whom they should "direct all of their gestures, eye contact, and dialogue" (Acosta & Cristo, 1981, p. 480). Likewise, clinicians must use direct statements (e.g., "Please tell me more about your son" vs. "Please ask her to tell me more about her son") and maintain nonverbal communication with the client. Therapists need to adjust the pace of their intervention style to the indirect and slower verbal interaction that occurs when an interpreter is used. This includes avoiding the use of long sentences spoken at a rapid pace in a third-person format (Vasquez & Javier, 1991).

THERAPEUTIC PROCESS AND OUTCOME: A CASE EXAMPLE

Kazdin (1993) described the need for research about the relationship between therapeutic process and outcome for children in treatment. As a step toward this goal, Wagner and his colleagues (e.g., Fowler & Wagner, 1993) examined the use of a psychoeducationally oriented program of individual therapy for sexually abused girls. In a series of studies intended to evaluate the process and outcome of treatment, the investigators considered the effects of girls' age and the gender of therapist on clients' therapeutic involvement and psychological adjustment after an incident of sexual assault. Research with this population is important because sexual abuse is an unfortunately common experience that many therapists encounter in their work with children.

There is no single description that adequately represents the behavioral and emotional adjustment of all sexually abused children (Conte & Schuerman, 1987). Therapists must be prepared to treat symptoms of depression, suicidal ideation, anxiety, and low self-esteem in these clients (Blumberg, 1981; Mannarino & Cohen, 1986; Tong, Oates, & McDowell, 1987; Wagner, 1991). Of course, the presence of these behaviors does not mean that a child has been sexually abused. Nonabused children also enter therapy for these problems, so there is considerable overlap in the therapeutic techniques used with all of these clients. Still, the treatment of sexually abused children involves special considerations, including the selection of therapists for these cases.

According to Finkelhor and Russell (1984) and Sedlack and Broadhurst (1996), girls are more likely to be abused by a male perpetrator. This has led some to conclude that female survivors should be treated by female therapists (Blick & Porter, 1982; Cole, 1985; Mogul, 1982). Although Hazzard, King, and Webb (1986) suggested that sexually abused girls are more likely to trust and disclose with a female clinician, recent evidence suggests otherwise. When Wagner and his colleagues treated girls abused by a male perpetrator, they found that clients treated by a male or female therapist became equally involved in therapy and exhibited comparable improvement in their psychosocial adjustment.

The research team used six sessions of manualized treatment designed by Fowler and Wagner (1993). The first and last sessions in this protocol were 20-minute meetings that the therapist conducted after the pretreatment assessment and before the posttreatment evaluation. The intervening sessions were 50 minutes in length and involved the use of The Ungame (The Ungame Company, 1983) during the second session and the authors' Sexual Abuse Board Game in the third through fifth sessions. In both games, the therapist and client roll a die, move a game piece, and respond to questions on cards that correspond to spaces on the board.

The researchers used these games so they would have a degree of control over the topics discussed in treatment. A limited number of questions was selected for each session to ensure that the same information would be discussed with all clients. Questions in The Ungame are intended to facilitate general sharing about self, but cards used in the Sexual Abuse Board Game are equally divided between questions about self and those specific to abuse-related topics (Table 5-2). The questions used in this game are phrased in a third-person format to allow both the therapist and client to respond to the cards.

During the pretreatment assessment, girls were administered a battery of self-report measures, including the Counselor Preference and Comfort Survey (Fowler, Wagner, Iachini, & Johnson, 1992) to assess clients' preference for and anticipated comfort with male and female therapists. Clients were informed that "we cannot always give people the counselor that they would like, but it is important for us to know who you would like to have as a counselor if you could pick." Immediately after the assessment, girls were assigned to either a male or female therapist who delivered the Fowler and Wagner (1993) treatment protocol. When the authors evaluated girls' actual comfort with their therapist after the sixth session, they found no significant difference between girls treated by a man and those treated by a woman. This finding is noteworthy because every girl stated a preference for a female clinician at the outset of therapy. Fowler and Wagner believed this change in attitude was a result of clients' in vivo interaction with a caring and supportive male therapist who did not mistreat the child as her abuser had.

When Wagner, Kilcrease-Fleming, and Fowler (1993) studied girls' in-session behaviors, they found that clients' participation in therapy improved across the six meetings. Again, there was no significant dif-

Table 5–2
Session Topics and Sample Questions for the Sexual Abuse Board Game

Session Number	Topic	Sample Questions
3	The child's disclosure of the abuse; significant others' reactions; legal issues	"Why is it against the law for people to sexually abuse children?"
4	The child's thoughts and feelings about sexual abuse; damaged goods syndrome	"What would you say to a friend who said that a sexually abused girl did something to make the abuse happen?"
5	Review of topics discussed during previous sessions.	"What have you learned about sexual abuse that you didn't know before we played this game?"

Adapted from "Preference for and Comfort with Male vs. Female Counselors Among Sexually Abused Girls in Individual Treatment," by W. E. Fowler and W. G. Wagner, 1993, p. 68. Copyright 1993 by the American Psychological Association. Reprinted with permission of the authors.

ference in the therapeutic involvement of girls treated by a male or female clinician. The research team questioned whether the nature of girls' participation (i.e., their verbalization in session) might have been different depending on the gender of their therapist. So Porter, Wagner, Johnson, and Cox (1996) examined girls' responses to the questions used as part of the Sexual Abuse Board Game. The authors found that clients seen by a male clinician were as likely to discuss abuse-related topics as were girls treated by a female therapist. In their study of clients' psychological adjustment, Wagner et al. found a significant increase in girls' self-esteem and a significant decline in depressive symptoms and suicidal ideation from the beginning to the end of treatment. Again, there was no significant effect for the gender of the therapist.

Moon, Wagner, and Kazelskis (2000) found limited evidence to suggest that the gender of the therapist may have some influence on older abuse survivors' participation in treatment. When the authors compared 7- to 11-year-old and 12- to 17-year-old girls, they observed that the two groups differed during the fourth session of the Fowler and Wagner (1993) protocol. Compared with the younger girls, adolescent clients treated by a man became less involved when molestation topics were presented in this session. These findings suggest that therapists must consider the needs of each client when selecting a clinician for the child. The overall impression gleaned from research conducted by Wagner and colleagues is that clinical recommendations regarding the assignment of therapists to sexually abused children were too restrictive. But the Moon et al. findings suggest that the routine use of male therapists with all female abuse survivors, regardless of age, is unwarranted.

Some children probably respond better if treated by a man. Others are likely to show more improvement if treated by a woman. Some children will benefit from treatment, regardless of the gender of their therapist. Additional research is needed to examine the outcome of therapist–client matching across the broad range of problems that bring children to treatment. This can include a pretreatment assessment of the child's preference and anticipated comfort with a male or female clinician. At the beginning of this chapter, we learned about the sexual abuse of two sisters, ages 7 and 12 years. The appropriate method for handling cases of abuse and neglect is a multidisciplinary approach to intervention, which is discussed in Chapter 13. For now, we turn our attention to the process and outcome of therapy for Maria and Consuelo Martinez.

After he completed his interviews with the children, Mr. Hilder travels to the mother's place of employment. There he learns that Mrs. Martinez speaks very little English, so he interviews her in Spanish. When Mr. Hilder describes Maria's account of the abuse, the mother initially denies that her boyfriend could have molested the children. But as she listens to the case worker's detailed description of nighttime events in the home, Mrs. Martinez begins to cry as she realizes that her daughter is telling the truth. When she asks what will happen to her boyfriend, Mr. Hilder indicates that the police have gone to Mr. Martinez's work place to interview him. "I expect they will detain him and recommend that he hire an attorney," he explains.

The next morning, Mrs. Martinez and her daughters meet with Mr. Hilder at his office. The caseworker recommends that the girls receive individual therapy at a local clinic specializing in the treatment of sexually abused children. Mr. Hilder describes how all cases of child maltreatment in North County are handled by a team of professionals from the district attorney's office, law enforcement, Children's Protective Services, and the local mental health clinic and trauma treatment center. Mrs. Martinez agrees to bring her daughters to therapy and to participate in sessions when necessary. Mr. Hilder schedules intake appointments with Mr. Morris Sempler, a child treatment specialist at the community mental health center. He informs the therapist that an interpreter will be needed for all sessions involving Mrs. Martinez.

Mr. Sempler decides to collaborate with his colleague, Dr. Rita Diaz, who is proficient in Spanish. As part of the initial assessment of the Martinez children, Dr. Diaz administers the Counselor Preference and Comfort Survey to each girl. Results reveal that 7-year-old Maria seems to have no clear preference for a male or female therapist, but 12-year-old Consuelo indicates that she would feel more comfortable talking with a woman. The therapists decide that Maria will see Mr. Sempler and Consuelo will meet with Dr. Diaz. The therapists meet with Mrs. Martinez and her daughters to present their treatment plan.

▪ ▪ ▪

Dr. Diaz begins by saying that she will serve as interpreter during family meetings. In Spanish, she briefly describes her background and her bilingual upbringing. She discusses confidentiality and its limits, including the therapists' contacts with members of the child abuse multidisciplinary team. The mother and daughters agree to these conditions and sign the appropriate assent and consent to treatment and release of information forms.

Mr. Sempler establishes eye contact with Mrs. Martinez and says, "We have a copy of Mr. Hilder's report, but . . ."

Consuelo interrupts, "Tenemos una copia del informe del Sr. Hilder, pero . . . "

Mr. Sempler turns to the child and smiles, "Consuelo, thank you for wanting to help. I just realized that I'm the only person here who does not speak Spanish. That's one reason why Dr. Diaz is with us today. She will help your mother and me understand each other. Is that OK with you?"

Consuelo nods her head, and Dr. Diaz begins, "Tenemos una copia del informe del Sr. Hilder, pero . . . "

Mr. Sempler adds, "We want to hear how we can help Maria and Consuelo."

Dr. Diaz continues, "Queremos oír cómo podemos ayudar a María y a Consuelo."

"No quiero que se hieran de lo que pasó. Espero que Uds. puedan ayudarles a darse cuenta que todo esto no es su culpa y que Terry no debió hacerlo."

"I don't want them to be hurt by what happened," Dr. Diaz translates. "I hope you can help them realize that all of this is not their fault and that Terry should not have done it."

"Has either Maria or Consuelo been in counseling before?" Mr. Sempler asks.

"¿María o Consuelo ha estado bajo consulta antes?" asks Dr. Diaz.

"No."

"As Dr. Diaz and I meet with the girls, we may want you to participate. How do you feel about that?"

"Al tener consulta con las señoritas, es posible que el Dr. Díaz y yo queramos que Ud. participe. ¿Cómo se sentiría?" Dr. Diaz asks.

"El Sr. Hilder me dijo que talvez Uds. quieran que yo me reuna con Uds. Haré lo que me pidan," Mrs. Martinez hesitates for Dr. Diaz to respond.

"Mr. Hilder told me that you might want me to meet with you. I will do whatever you ask."

"Voy a consultar con nuestro sacerdote. Me ha ayudado antes con las muchachas. Ahora le pido que me ayude a mí." (Translation provided by Dr. Giovanni Fontecchio, Department of Foreign Languages, University of Southern Mississippi, Hattiesburg, MS.)

"I am going to consult with our priest. He has helped me before with the girls. Now I am asking him to help me," Dr. Diaz says.

Mr. Sempler turns to the children and asks how they feel about being clients in therapy. Maria and Consuelo demonstrate their bilingual skills by responding in English to Mr. Sempler's questions and using Spanish when they talk with their mother. The therapists avoid asking specific questions about the abuse, delaying these topics until later in therapy and focusing instead on the girls' friendships and academic progress. At the end of the session, they schedule an individual appointment for each child.

During his first meeting with Maria, Mr. Sempler is struck by the child's openness. A very talkative youngster, Maria explores the therapist's office and comments on the play materials she finds placed about the room. "What's in here?" she asks as she opens the door to a storage cabinet.

"Those are games we can play, if you want," Mr. Sempler answers.

"I like games," Maria says. She pulls out a number of boxes before selecting the checker game. "Can we play checkers?"

"Sure," the therapist replies. They sit down at a small table in the middle of the office and proceed to play the game. During the next 15 minutes, Maria talks as she moves her checkers about the board. When she tires of this activity, she says, "What can we do now?" Before the therapist is able to answer, Maria points to the easel and colored markers nearby. "Is that for drawing pictures?" she asks.

"Yes," Mr. Sempler answers as the child walks to the easel and begins to draw a picture of a house with flowers in the garden and a bright yellow sun in the sky. Again, she talks as she draws for the remainder of the session. At no point does Maria or Mr. Sempler mention the topic of sexual abuse. When the child returns for her next session, she uses hand puppets to volunteer the story of a family on vacation. She also talks about her friends at school and the day care center where she and her sister spend the late afternoon hours while their mother is at work. Even though Maria is reading at a second-grade level, Mr. Sempler decides that during the next session, he will introduce a board game designed to facilitate discussion of abuse-related topics.

When the child returns for her third session, she immediately sees the game on the table in the middle of the room. "What's that?" she asks.

"It's a game I thought we could play today," Mr. Sempler responds.

"OK. What do we do?" Maria asks as she sits at the table and examines the game board.

The therapist joins her and describes how he uses this special game with children who have been hurt by other people. As Maria listens, he reads the instructions for the game. (The instructions were adapted from Fowler and Wagner [1993] with the authors' permission.) "You are a world famous expert on child sexual abuse and you have written 10 books about it. Because you are so famous, a school has asked you to come to talk to its students. Some kids will want to ask you questions about yourself, like what you like to do, so they can get to know you better. Other kids will want to ask your opinion about sexual abuse. When you answer a question, you are the teacher and I am the class, so I may ask you more about your answers, just like kids do in class." He explains how each of them will roll a die and move a game piece on a path of blue and green spaces. "If we land on a blue space, we draw a blue card from this stack. When we are on a green space, we draw a green card from here."

Maria eagerly rolls the die. She counts her move, lands on a blue space, and pulls a blue card from the center of the board. She gives the card to Mr. Sempler, who reads it for her.

"What is the funniest thing you ever saw?" he asks.

"My dog chases its tail," she laughs. "He goes around and around. He can't stop."

Mr. Sempler smiles and then moves his game piece, draws a green card, and reads the question aloud. "What is the best thing that can happen if you tell someone that you are being sexually abused? I think the best thing would be for the abuse to stop."

Maria nods her head before taking her turn. She gives Mr. Sempler the green card she selects.

"What is the best thing that someone in your family could do if you told that someone abused you?"

Maria thinks for a few seconds and then answers, "Know that I'm telling the truth."

"So you want them to believe you?"

"Uh-huh," she responds. "My Momma believes me."

"Your Momma believes you."

"Uh-huh, you know, about what Terry did to me and Consuelo." Maria picks up the die and begins to roll. "Oops, it's your turn," she says.

This time, Mr. Sempler draws a blue card. "What was the happiest time in your life?" He hesitates and then answers, "I think the happiest time for me was when my son graduated from college. I was so proud of him. How about you, Maria? What was the happiest time in your life?"

"When we moved into our new house and I got my own room," she answers.

"You got you own room?"

"Uh-huh. I have my own bed and a place for my dolls."

Mr. Sempler and his client play the game for the rest of this session and during their next three meetings, each time with a different set of questions. Based on Maria's answers, Mr. Sempler concludes that she does not blame herself for the boyfriend's behavior and is happy her mother believed her. Maria's level of therapeutic involvement is markedly different from her sister's participation in treatment. Dr. Diaz had planned to follow Mr. Sempler's treatment plan, but during her first individual meeting with Consuelo, she discovers that changes will be needed in the timing of her interventions.

"I'm glad to see you again, Consuelo," Dr. Diaz begins. "How do you feel about coming to see me today?"

"Oh, it's OK," she answers.

"It's OK?"

"Yes."

"How was school today?" Dr. Diaz asks.

"It was OK."

Dr. Diaz realizes that by asking repeated questions, she is assuming too much control in session and impeding the development of rapport with the child. She decides to postpone her inquiry and comment on everyday issues. "I really like that necklace you're wearing," she says.

"My Momma bought it for me," Consuelo answers as she holds the pendant forward for Dr. Diaz to see.

"That's really pretty," the therapist says as she looks at the small gold figure of a dancer in the child's hand. "It's a dancer, isn't it?"

"Yes, that's what I want to be when I grow up."

"A dancer."

"Yes, my Momma is teaching me to do all kinds of dances."

Dr. Diaz feels the mood of the session change as Consuelo talks about her favorite hobby. At one point, the child asks if the therapist would like to see one of her dances. Dr. Diaz agrees, so Consuelo performs a series of steps she recently learned. When she finishes, the therapist applauds and congratulates her. Consuelo is now maintaining better eye contact with Dr. Diaz, and she is volunteering information about school and her friends in the neighborhood.

The therapist decides to delay the use of the sexual abuse game. During the next two sessions, she and Consuelo continue their discussion of the child's plans for the future. Consuelo performs more dances in session and eventually talks about Tonya, her best friend who is moving out of town.

"It sounds like you are going to miss Tonya," Dr. Diaz says.

"She's my best friend."

"How did you become best friends?" she asks.

"I don't know. We just did," Consuelo responds. "We've gone to school together since first grade. She's the only one who knows about Terry."

"Tonya is the only person you told about Terry?"

Consuelo nods her head, then looks down at the floor and remains quiet.

Dr. Diaz patiently waits for the child to continue. She recognizes the significance of this moment. Her client had voluntarily introduced the topic of sexual abuse. After about 10 seconds of silence, which seemed like an hour, she intervenes. "I can understand how difficult it is to think about what happened with Terry. But I think it might help if we talk about it." Consuelo does not answer. Only 15 minutes remain in the session, so Dr. Diaz adds, "I have this game that sometimes makes talking about these things a little easier. Maybe we could use the game when we get together next week."

Although Consuelo does not commit to this plan, she appears less troubled as she glances around the office. "What's that picture?"

"That's my brother when he was about your age." Dr. Diaz says.

"I always wanted a little brother," she says. The therapist and client spend the final minutes of the session discussing how life at home would be different if Consuelo had a younger brother. By the end of the hour, the child is smiling as she talks about her family.

When she returns for the next session, Consuelo finds that Dr. Diaz has arranged the sexual abuse game on her office table. After a brief discussion of the preceding week, Dr. Diaz asks the child if she wants to play the game, and Consuelo agrees. The two of them move to the table, where the therapist introduces the game by reading the directions.

For her first move, Consuelo draws the card containing the question, "Whose fault is it when a girl gets sexually abused?"

"I think it's the girl's fault," she answers.

"The girls' fault?" Dr. Diaz asks.

"Yes, for letting it happen."

"Well, I know that some people think that, but I believe that the adult is always responsible when sexual abuse happens."

"That's not what Terry says," Consuelo answers.

"What does Terry say?" the therapist asks.

"He told me that he touched me because I was pretty."

"You are pretty. But you didn't make him touch you."

"That's what my Momma says. She told me that Terry was wrong."

"What do you think?" Dr. Diaz asks.

"I don't know." Although Consuelo is beginning to question her interpretation of the abuse, she continues to blame herself for Terry's actions. Dr. Diaz gently challenges this belief every time the child mentions it in therapy.

Every week when they meet and play the game, Consuelo appears more willing to discuss her abuse and the problems it has caused. During a later session, Dr. Diaz draws the question, "How hard would it be for a girl to stop a man from abusing her?"

"I think it could be really hard to do that," she answers. "A man is a lot bigger and stronger. And some men tell girls that if they talk to someone about the abuse, something bad will happen to them."

"Terry told me that Momma wouldn't believe me," Consuelo volunteers. She describes how the boyfriend told her he would deny any reports of the abuse and her mother would agree with him. "So I didn't tell," she says.

"How about Tonya, your best friend?" Dr Diaz asks.

"Tonya?"

"Yes, a few weeks ago you said that you told Tonya about Terry."

"Uh-huh. She said I should tell the teacher," Consuelo says, "but I was afraid."

Dr. Diaz accepts the child's feelings and then says she is glad Consuelo is talking about the abuse with her. As therapy progresses, the clinician and client rely less and less on the game as a stimulus for discussion. In their seventh individual meeting, for example, they sit before the game board but never roll the die as Consuelo describes specific episodes of abuse and Dr. Diaz helps her explore thoughts and feelings associated with these events. Because Consuelo was more reluctant to participate at the outset of treatment, she attends more sessions than Maria does. Although her sister was verbally active throughout treatment, Consuelo's level of participation improves from one session to the next. Both girls respond well to treatment, but Consuelo requires a patient therapist who is willing to adapt a prescribed intervention to the unique needs of her client.

▪ ▪ ▪

The case of the Martinez girls illustrates two paths of client involvement in therapy. Mr. Sempler was able to follow a manualized treatment with Maria because she responded well to each intervention. Although Dr. Diaz initiated therapy according to the prescribed protocol, she immediately realized that she needed to change her treatment plan if she wanted to help Consuelo. It is worth noting that the older Martinez child was the client who required special consideration. Although this pattern is consistent with the results of Moon et al. (2000), there is no reason to assume that all older survivors of sexual assault will be less willing to engage in therapy. Obviously, other factors merit consideration. In the case of the Martinez sisters, it appears that the perpetrator threatened Consuelo and told her that other people would not believe her account of the abuse. We might expect the effect of these warnings to generalize to the therapeutic relationship, increasing the child's reluctance to disclose abuse-related information for fear of adult retaliation or disbelief.

Another interesting aspect of therapy with the Martinez children was the potential barrier posed by an English-speaking clinician and a Spanish-speaking mother. The use of an interpreter in this case affected the therapeutic process, slowing the pace of interactions between Mr. Sempler and Mrs. Martinez. Clinicians and clients alike were fortunate that Dr. Diaz was bilingual and could interpret for her fellow therapist and the mother. The benefits of having a skilled interpreter probably extended beyond the simple transfer of information that occurred in session. Based on the findings of Sue et al. (1991), we might anticipate that the mother felt more comfortable with a Spanish-speaking therapist and was therefore more likely to participate in treatment and less likely to prematurely terminate therapy for her daughters.

SUMMARY

Therapy with children is both an art and a science that involves the creative adaptation of empirically supported treatments to the specific needs of the client. Clinicians are held accountable for their work, so they must select a method, such as the single-case experimental design, to document the effectiveness of therapy. Child interventions, including those based on play, share a common linguistic foundation, so clinicians must possess the interviewing skills required to communicate with young clients and facilitate their involvement in treatment. Special efforts, such as the use of trained interpreters, are needed when clients speak a different language from the therapist. Researchers and practitioners must become more attentive to the effect that factors such as language, gender and race of the therapist, and clinician behaviors have on the process and outcome of child therapies. Through their collaborative efforts, professionals who work in the research laboratory and the community clinic can expand the number and theoretical diversity of empirically supported treatments for children.

Part 2

Therapeutic Interventions with Children:

Theory and Practice

An important part of any multidimensional treatment is the actual therapeutic strategy the clinician uses with a child. It is in this realm where much of the debate about child therapies has occurred. Proponents of individual schools or methods of treatment have challenged the theoretical and technical aspects of other systems while emphasizing the benefits of their own approach. This has led to divisive disputes about the comparative merit of individual methods, such as classical analysis, child-centered therapy, and behavioral interventions. It has also contributed to the formation of professional organizations (e.g., Association for Advancement of Behavior Therapy, American Association for Marriage and Family Therapy) to advocate for particular treatments.

Clinicians must have a working knowledge of the principles and techniques of the therapies commonly used with children. Although many treatment approaches are available, we will focus our attention on four important categories: psychodynamic, child-centered, behavioral/cognitive-behavioral, and family systems. Each school of thought is characterized by a certain theme or belief system, but it is not unusual for a particular approach to include diverse theoretical principles and treatment methods. For example, proponents of the psychodynamic approach share a belief in the importance of early childhood experiences, but they have developed intervention techniques based on classical drive theory, ego psychology, object relations theory, analytical psychology, and individual psychology.

This book's ultimate goal is to discuss integrated treatments for children. Effective use of these interventions requires an understanding of the theoretical principles and the techniques of therapies that were developed for children during the 20th century. The informed clinician recognizes the contributions and limitations of each method and is able to combine different theoretical approaches into integrated treatments that are appropriate to the needs of individual clients. Chapters 6, 8, 10, and 12 review the theoretical foundations for each school of therapy. These chapters continue the discussion of developmental and multicultural issues that clinicians must consider in their work with children. Chapters 7, 9, 11, and 13 examine intervention techniques that have been developed based on these theories. These chapters discuss the multimodal and multidisciplinary components of our multidimensional model through a review of relevant literature and case examples designed to illustrate the use of each approach with a common childhood problem.

6

Psychodynamic Theory

Psychodynamic interventions for children can take many forms, including those based on classical drive theory, object relations theory, ego psychology, analytical psychology, and individual psychology. Proponents of these theories share a common interest in the role of early life experience, but they vary in their description of personality development. Psychodynamic theorists also differ in their emphasis on instinctual and sociocultural influences. This chapter considers the theoretical bases for variants of this approach. We examine selected research on infant development, attachment theory and social development, and children's play. In our discussion of multicultural considerations, we explore childhood friendships and ethnic identity development. But first, we review the historical development of this important theoretical perspective.

HISTORICAL BACKGROUND

Contemporary psychodynamic therapies can be traced to early psychoanalytic theory (Okun, 1990). Psychoanalytic interventions with children originated with Sigmund Freud (1856–1939) and his work with Little Hans, a 5-year-old boy who had developed a phobia of horses and other large animals. Although this case is the first recorded use of psychoanalytic theory with children, Freud actually had little direct contact with Hans. His face-to-face interaction with the boy was limited to one session, "a short one" (Freud, 1909/1956, p. 184) with the child and his father. Freud's principal role in this case was that of consultant to the father, who implemented treatment based on Freud's theory of psychosexual development (e.g., Oedipal complex, castration anxiety).

Freud worked with Hans and his father at a time when the use of psychoanalysis with children was a very controversial matter. Freud (1922/1956) discussed the professional reaction to his treatment of the child, noting that the case

> caused a great stir and even greater indignation, and a most evil future had been foretold for the poor little boy, because he had been "robbed of his innocence" at such a tender age and had been made the victim of a psycho-analysis. (p. 288)

Interestingly, Little Hans visited Freud when he was 19 years old. Freud (1922/1956) described the young man as "perfectly well" (p. 288) and stated that Hans did not recognize himself when he read Frued's account of his treatment. In fact, he had no recollection of the experience. Although some might say that Hans was repressing what had been a very frightening event, others would point to his healthy development and conclude that treatment was not destructive, as Freud's critics had predicted.

A pioneer in the field of child interventions is Hermine Hug-Hellmuth, whom MacLean (1986) called "the world's first child psychoanalyst" (p. 580). An associate of the Vienna Psychoanalytic Society, Hug-Hellmuth was an elementary school teacher before receiving her Ph.D. in philosophy from the University of Vienna (Young-Bruehl, 1988). Her work spanned educational and clinical applications, including the use of play as a developmentally appropriate form of analysis for children. Unfortunately, Hug-Hellmuth's career was abruptly terminated in 1924, when she was murdered by her nephew, who had been one of her patients (Luck, 1997).

Another important figure in the history of child psychoanalysis is Melanie Klein (1882–1960), who is considered the founder of the British school of object relations (Okun, 1990). Born in Vienna, Klein was encouraged to become a child analyst while she was an adult analysand of Sandor Ferenczi (Money-Kyrle, 1975). Likierman (1995) described her as a "passionate, spontaneous, and imaginative" (p. 318) person who had little interest in the systematic inquiry that characterizes the scientific method. Klein was not formally trained to work with children, but she applied what she learned from Ferenczi in rearing her son. She presented a paper about this experience to the Hungarian Psychoanalytic Society, which subsequently invited her to become a member (Likierman, 1995). In her work with 5-year-old Fritz, Klein (1921/1975) first tried and then abandoned Freud's consultation model in favor of individual analysis with the young boy using her technique of "Play Analysis" (Klein, 1932/1959, p. 40). Chapter 7 examines this method in which the clinician observes and interprets a child's play based on psychoanalytic principles.

D. W. Winnicott (1896–1971), an English pediatrician and psychoanalyst, was also a proponent of object relations. Winnicott (1965) believed in the importance of maternal care in a child's development, and he coined the term "good-enough mother" (p. 57) to denote the parent's ability to fulfill an infant's physical and psychological needs. The concept of the good-enough mother reflects object relations theorists' interest in early childhood experiences, which more contemporary writers like Mary Ainsworth (1979) have explored in their studies of mother–infant attachment. During a pediatric career that spanned approximately 4 decades, Winnicott became increasingly interested in psychoanalytic theory. He wrote about and lectured on topics related to child psychoanalysis, including what he called "on demand" (Winnicott, 1977, p. 2) treatment in which children are seen intermittently rather than on a daily or once-a-week schedule.

Freud (1933/1964a) noted that child psychoanalysis was initially "the domain of women analysts" (p. 148). Included in this group was Anna Freud (1895–1982), the youngest of six children born to Sigmund and Martha Freud. Anna Freud was devoted to her father and his cause. Young-Bruehl (1988) described their truly unique relationship as father and daughter, teacher and student, and analyst and analysand. She began her professional career as an elementary school teacher in Vienna and later became a lay analyst and a member and officer in the Vienna Psychoanalytic Society. In 1938, she and her parents fled Nazi-occupied Austria and relocated in London, where she studied and practiced developmental/educational, preventive, and remedial applications of psychoanalytic principles with children. During World War II, she obtained funding to open the Hampstead Nurseries, which provided day treatment and residential care to children whose lives had been disrupted by the war (A. Freud & Burlingham, 1943). Later she helped organize the Hampstead Child Therapy Clinic and Course to provide psychoanalytic treatment and professional training (Mishne,1993). Whereas Melanie Klein focused on the use of play analysis with preschoolers, Anna Freud developed a play approach that could be used with elementary school children (A. Freud, 1927/1965). The age of the client was only one of a number of factors that distinguishes the work of these two pioneers in the field of child analysis. In fact, Likierman (1995) noted that Melanie Klein and Anna Freud "could agree on very little" and were "lifelong professional protagonists" (p. 314) for their methods. This chapter and Chapter 7 explore these differences as well as Anna Freud's work in establishing ego psychology as a recognized derivative of classical drive theory.

Erik Erikson (1902–1994), a student of Anna Freud, was also influential in the development of ego psychology. Born near Frankfurt, Germany, he arrived in the United States in 1933 and eventually joined the faculty at Harvard University, despite never having completed a college degree (Coles, 1970). In his most significant work, *Childhood and So-*

ciety, Erikson (1950) described his eight-stage model of psychosocial development in which he expanded the scope of psychoanalytic theory across the lifespan, from birth to old age. In addition to this important theoretical advance, he contributed directly to the practice of child analysis with his work on identity development in children and adolescents (Mishne, 1993). Erikson was another theorist who recognized the importance of play in the analysis of young clients. Paraphrasing Freud's reference to dreams, he stated, "We have called play the royal road to the understanding of the infantile ego's efforts at synthesis" (Erikson, 1950, p. 182).

The son of a Protestant minister, Carl Jung (1875–1961) was trained in medicine and dedicated his career to the practice of psychiatry. Jung was a close associate of Freud for approximately 6 years, but his interests in the spiritual aspects of human development and the transgenerational nature of consciousness (i.e., the collective unconscious) led to the termination of this relationship in 1913 (Crain, 2000). Freud and Jung differed on other matters, including their use of "the couch," which Freud adopted and Jung did not. Clark (1953) described a conversation he once had with Jung regarding this disagreement. Jung reportedly told Clark that Freud and he discussed the role of the couch in analysis and that Freud protested, "What do you expect me to do, have these people look at me all day long?" (Clark, 1953, p. 4). Although Jung is not recognized for his work with children, his fascination with the meaning of symbols has stimulated others to develop creative interventions, such as serial drawing and sandplay, that are used with young people.

Alfred Adler (1870–1937), another early associate of Freud, was interested in the development of educational and therapeutic interventions for children. According to Sharf (2000), Adler was instrumental in developing school-based child guidance centers where clinicians conducted family education programs that included instruction in child-rearing techniques. This work eventually resulted in schools based on democratic principles and pedagogical methods designed to facilitate learning (Mosak, 1995). It is worth noting that the German word Adler used for his clinics was *Erziehungsberatungsstellen*, which translates as "centers for advice in rearing children" (Dreikurs, 1948, p. 283). Because of the importance he attributed to parenting, we should not be surprised to discover that Thompson and Rudolph (2000) described Adler as being "50 years ahead of his time" (p. 275) in his work on family-based treatments.

With the rise of Nazism in the 1930s, Adler moved his family to the United States, where he was joined by others, including Rudolf Dreikurs (1897–1972). Dreikurs was trained as a physician at the University of Vienna and eventually became the Director of the Alfred Adler Institute in Chicago. He specialized in the application of Adlerian principles to the psychological treatment of children and families. With books such as *Children: The Challenge* and *The Challenge of Parenthood*, Dreikurs (1964; 1948) translated Adler's theory into everyday terminology and practical techniques that parents and teachers could use with children.

The historical development of psychodynamic thought involves a change in focus, from the intrapsychic and biological drive theory of Freud to the more interpersonal perspective of ego psychologists and object relations theorists. Whereas Freud emphasized the psychosexual development of the child, many of his followers were more interested in psychosocial factors, such as the infant's relationships with the primary caregiver and the child's adaptation to his or her cultural surround (Okun, 1990). But the history of psychodynamic theory is more than a transition from an intrapsychic orientation to one based on interpersonal relationships. Jung, for example, explored how symbols in artwork and literature may reveal significant information about the unconscious. Adler developed a socioteleological approach in which behavior was viewed as purposive or goal directed. Psychodynamic theory has also been the touchstone against which many theories, including behavioral and person-centered theories, were developed. Its basic concepts continue to play an important role in therapeutic interventions with children.

THEORETICAL FOUNDATIONS

This section examines the writings of prominent psychodynamic theorists whose work has had a significant impact on treatment services for children. We begin with a discussion of Freud's classical drive theory and then move to the more interpersonal models presented by object relations theorists and ego psychologists. We then consider the contributions that Jung and Adler have made to the field of child psychology.

Classical Drive Theory

As Okun (1990) stated, "No one can dispute the dominant influence of Freud on the development of Western thought" (p. 21). His work has shaped not only the practice of therapy but the fields of literature, art, philosophy, and the social sciences. Freud's training as a physician is reflected in the biological model he adopted for classical drive theory. He explored the role of innate drives in human development, devoting particular attention to psychosexual needs, which he believed unfold through oral, anal, phallic, latency, and genital stages. His theory is considered to be deterministic because early childhood experiences are thought to affect how individuals function later in life. Freud's approach is also structural in the sense that personality represents the competitive interaction of the id, ego, and superego, and consciousness is composed of three mental processes: unconscious, preconscious, and conscious. Finally, Freud discussed the developmental implications of anxiety and the ways humans attempt to minimize feelings of emotional distress.

Instincts and Drives. Jones (1955) discussed the difficulty of translating the German word *Trieb* into English. He favored the word "instinct" because the word "implies an inborn and inherited character" (p. 317), but Sharf (2000) observed that more often the term is translated as "drive." Freud (1915/1953) formulated his concept of *Trieb* in biological terms using physical sensations such as hunger, thirst, and sexual arousal. He believed that each of us strives to satisfy these drives when they arise. Consider an extended hike in the mountains on a hot, sunny day. Halfway through your journey you become thirsty, a sensation that worsens until you experience the pleasure of a cool drink from a mountain stream. A similar drive would arise on a day when you skip breakfast, miss lunch because of a meeting, and experience hunger late in the afternoon.

Freud believed that drives are characterized by their source (e.g., stomach) and their aim, which is the cessation of the organic sensation (e.g., hunger). He developed his "pleasure-unpleasure principle" (Jones, 1955, p. 317) in which unpleasure is viewed as the organic sensation and pleasure represents its cessation. Freud acknowledged the existence of numerous drives, including play and destruction, but he was most interested in two variants of what he termed "primal instincts": ego instincts, such as hunger, whose purpose is to preserve the individual, and sexual drives which are intended to preserve the species (Freud, 1915/1953, p. 67). Of these, he focused on the latter (Jones, 1955) and developed his concept of libido. Although Freud (1922/1953) initially used the term to describe "the dynamic manifestations of sexuality" (p. 131), this concept was expanded to include all life instincts that serve to seek pleasure and avoid pain (Sharf, 2000).

Psychosexual Stages. Freud's model of psychosexual development was to have a significant impact on the theoretical principles of psychoanalysis. He described a sequential progression across five stages: oral (birth to 18 months), anal (18 months to 3 years), phallic (3 to 6 years), latency (6 to 12 years), and genital (12 years through adulthood). Early stages involve a change in the physical focus of sexual pleasure, from the mouth (oral stage), to the anus (anal stage), and then the penis or clitoris (phallic stage). When pleasure is exaggerated or frustrated during these psychosexual stages, fixation occurs and the child is predisposed to problems later in life as libidinal drives are repressed (Freud, 1922/1953). Consider the following example. In infancy, we rely on our sucking reflex to gain nourishment from our mother or primary caregiver. Babies who are fed on demand or neglected and not fed when needed are believed to be at risk for eating disorders or problems with excessive alcohol consumption at a later age. During the anal period, attention is turned to toilet training and the development of bowel control. If conflicts develop here between the parent and child, the youngster is believed to be at risk for developing anal retentive or anal expulsive tendencies, which are reflected in a concern for cleanliness or destructive behaviors (Sharf, 2000).

During the phallic stage, the child becomes focused on the genital area and the pleasure derived from rubbing the penis or clitoris. The Oedipus complex is thought to develop during this psychosexual stage. Named after Oedipus, the mythical Greek king, the complex involves a son's love for his mother and jealousy of his father's relationship with her. Freud observed that the Oedipus complex is manifested when a young boy "shows the most undisguised sexual curiosity about his mother, if he wants to sleep with her at night, insists upon being present while she is dressing, or attempts to caress her" (Freud, 1920, p. 288). Boys and girls have different experiences during the phallic stage. Freud (1925/1953) stated that as girls become aware of the anatomical differences between the sexes, they discover that they lack a penis. Their resulting penis envy is transformed into a wish for a child of their own. They choose the father as the object of their love and become jealous of the mother's relationship with him. Much has been written about penis envy and the Oedipus complex. Nancy Chodorow (1989, p. 204), for example, offered a feminist alternative, "womb envy" (p. 204), in which men feel inferior because they are unable to give birth. Children who experience phallic stage difficulties are thought to be predisposed to later difficulties with sexual identity and interpersonal relationships with same- or opposite-sex peers (Sharf, 2000).

Freud (1920) believed the oral, anal, and phallic stages were extremely important to a child's development, but he cautioned that the experiences of this early period are often forgotten during the latency stage. During this period, children focus their energies on activities at school, relationships with friends, and hobbies (Sharf, 2000). The latency period in life may actually constitute what Freud (1920, p. 282) described as a "pause" or "reversion" of sexual development, although earlier psychosexual experiences are thought to provide the foundation for the emergence of the genital stage. The final period in Freud's developmental model, the genital stage, begins with the onset of puberty when young adolescents are thought to develop an interest in heterosexual relationships.

Personality Structure. To understand Freud's model of personality, we must first examine his work on the levels of consciousness. Although he was not the first writer to address this topic, Freud integrated the concepts of unconscious, preconscious, and conscious into a systematic theory. These mental processes are distinguished from each other by a person's awareness of the elements involved. For example, we are aware of conscious phenomena, such as the warmth of the sun shining on our face or the pain experienced when we place our hand on a hot burner. Some mental processes, including memories, are not in our immediate awareness but can be retrieved relatively easily. If you mentally retrace your day, you will recapture images of events retained in your preconscious. Unconscious phenomena, on the other hand, are different in the sense that they are "quite inaccessible" (Kline, 1984, p. 15) to us. Consider a man who was physically abused as an infant and is not aware of unconscious anxiety associated with this experience. Although he is unable to explain why he has repeatedly postponed the decision to have children, the possible impact of this unconscious material is apparent.

Freud's concept of consciousness is important for understanding his structural model of personality, which is composed of the id, ego, and superego. The id is the "dark, inaccessible part of our personality" (Freud, 1933/1964b, p. 73) whose purpose is the satisfaction of instinctual needs. As a balance to this irrational dimension, Freud (1933/1964b) described the superego, which represents the values of parents, teachers, and other individuals who are significant to a child's development. The third component of Freud's triad, the ego, serves as the "mediator with the outside world" (Mishne, 1993, p. 15). The ego controls the id impulses by bringing behavior in line with the expectations of society. Freud (1933/1964b, p. 77) used the analogy of a horse and rider to describe the relationship between the id and ego: The id provides the energy, and the ego supplies the direction needed to function effectively in society. Meanwhile, the superego is watching this performance and supplying the moral standards for evaluating behavior. If the person fails to meet these criteria, he or she can experience what Mishne described as "intense feelings of guilt and inferiority" (p. 16).

Although the id is present at birth, the superego develops later in life. Freud (1933/1964b) believed that children are naturally "amoral" (p. 62) and that behavioral restraint comes not from self-regulation but from the authority that parents exercise when they use love and praise for appropriate actions and punishment for inappropriate behaviors. The superego gradually develops as the child internalizes the expectations of parents and other caregivers. As children mature, they develop the ability to express their needs and wants relative to the reactions they have learned to expect from significant others. Their egos emerge, and they become increasingly able "to test reality, to plan, to think logically, and to develop plans for satisfying needs" (Sharf, 2000, p. 31).

Anxiety constitutes an important concept for psychoanalytic theorists. Defined as "all forms of emotional anguish" (Chapman, 1978, p. 41), anxiety arises when there is conflict among the id, ego, and superego. To relieve this psychic discomfort, Freud (1904/1956) believed we use what he called *defense mechanisms*, such as repression and regression, to deny or distort everyday experiences to make them more consistent with our unconscious thoughts and feelings. When used excessively, defense mechanisms interfere with a person's ability to function normally. Consider again the man abused as an infant. His maltreatment was extremely uncomfortable, so he repressed the experience into his unconscious and has no conscious recollection of the abuse. When questioned about his childhood, the man might deny any maltreatment and describe his parents as loving and caring individuals. But as he watches a movie or television show depicting child abuse, he regresses to an earlier stage of development and exhibits behavior (e.g., sucking on his fingers or chewing his nails) characteristic of that period (e.g., oral stage). The more often he unknowingly uses these defense mechanisms, the less realistic his perception and interpretation of the world around him are and the more difficult it is for him to maintain a semblance of normalcy. Freud's developmental interpretation of defense mechanisms has significant implications for therapists who treat children and families. By fostering healthy parent–child relationships, clinicians establish the foundation for a children's psychosocial development.

Object Relations Theory

Freud introduced some of the terminology used by object relations theorists, but he never developed this material as part of his ongoing revision of psychoanalytic theory (Blanck & Blanck, 1986). Compared with Freud's biological model, object relations theory is more interpersonal in nature. People are thought to be socially active beings from birth who meet their needs through interactions with significant others. Accordingly, an infant is "an active partner seeking to develop relationship with its mother, responding to and modifying her ways of relating, in the course of which needs for food, warmth, entertainment, and rest are met" (Scharff & Scharff, 1987, p. 43). As might be expected, object relations theorists have expanded the focus of psychodynamic theory beyond the structural components and psychosexual stages proposed by Freud. Their interpersonal model involves greater attention to the role of early relationships, especially mother–infant interactions.

What do the terms *objects* and *object relations* actually mean? When classical drive theorists discussed an object, they were referring to "a thing, a person, or a part of a person or goal" (Okun, 1990, p. 32) to which the individual directs instinctual needs. Within a Freudian framework, objects are conceptualized developmentally. For example, an infant first relates to his or her mother's breast, then with the mother as a person, and eventually to other caregivers who satisfy the child's needs (St. Clair, 1996). Contemporary object relations theorists have expanded the meaning of objects beyond these external objects, such as the mother, to include others, "both external and internal, both real and imagined" (Okun, 1990, p. 32). Although external objects continue to refer to environmental stimuli, such as the infant's caregiver, internal objects represent the child's mental representations of external objects. For example, the parent constitutes an external object, and the child's mental representation or image of the parent is the internal object. In other words, the child develops an internal mental representation (i.e., internal object) of the real person (i.e., external object), an image that may or may not accurately represent that person.

Therapists are usually more interested in a client's internal objects because they reflect the child's view of the world. Consider a client whose parents adopted an authoritarian approach to child rearing, which Baumrind (1971) described as involving firm control of the child, low expression of warmth, and little encouragement of independence in the child. The client's internal object of these parents might include such characteristics as distant, controlling, and cold. Contrast this child with a peer raised by authoritative parents who also exercise firm control but exhibit warmth and encourage independence in their children (Baumrind, 1971). This child's internal object of parent is more likely to involve attributes such as loving, consistent, and trusting. The internal objects that each of these children develops serve as a "blueprint" for interactions with parents and significant others, including teachers and therapists.

Object relations theorists are particularly interested in the internal objects that children form of their primary significant others, the mother and father. These objects are important to the formation of a child's *object relations*, the internal representations of interactions with other people that develop based on early interpersonal relationships. Object relations are socially significant because they constitute the "inner residues of past relationships" (St. Clair, 1996, p. 1) on which all subsequent social interaction is based. Consider again the children of authoritarian and authoritative parents. As the youngster's social world expands beyond the family, relationships with others are formed based on the "blueprint" of object relations the child developed with the parents. According to object relations theory, the child enters interpersonal relationships by anticipating that others will interact in either a distant, controlling, and cold manner or a loving, consistent, and trusting way that is similar to the style of the primary significant others. Object relations theory is relevant to the therapeutic relationship because a child of authoritarian parents is likely to expect the clinician to be formal and distant, and the child of authoritative parents will anticipate a warm and loving relationship with a trusting and trustworthy adult.

How do children develop object relations? D. W. Winnicott described this process using the concepts of *good-enough mother*, *holding environment*, and *transitional objects*. According to Winnicott (1965), object relations develop as an infant gradually moves from total dependence on his or her mother to the relative independence of adulthood. Winnicott believed that the mother–infant relationship serves as the foundation for this transition. He introduced the phrase "good-enough mother" (Winnicott, 1965, p. 57) to refer to caregivers who fulfill their infant's instinctual needs, such as hunger and thirst, and foster the baby's inherited potential for the emergence of his or her sense of self or ego development. An important aspect of good-enough mothering is the warm and secure holding environment a mother provides for her infant. According to Winnicott (1987), holding is "all that a mother is and does" (p. 7) and therefore consists of psychological and physiological elements. It involves the mother's physical touching and caressing of the child (i.e., physiological) as well as her empathy for the infant (i.e., psychological). In this holding environment, the baby's instinctual needs are met, object relations first develop, and ego organization begins. Although Winnicott referred to the good-enough mother in much of his writings, he later used "good-enough parents" (Winnicott, 1993, p. 123) to describe mothers and fathers who are consistent and real with their children.

As Winnicott (1987) stated, "From the baby's point of view there is nothing else but the baby, and therefore the mother is at first part of the baby" (p. 11). This merging of the infant and mother is gradually transformed into a mother–child relationship in which the child has a sense of self that is separate from his or her mother. Winnicott (1965) believed that an important component of this change is what he called "transitional objects" (p. 110). Although he believed that newborns and young infants are too immature to acquire transitional objects, they eventually select and relate to these objects as stepping stones to greater independence and self-awareness. Most of us are familiar with the transitional objects that babies select. Some choose a doll or stuffed toy and repeatedly play with this item. Others have a favorite blanket they carry with them wherever they go. Although some parents are embarrassed to take along their child's favorite object on visits with friends or to the grocery store, Winnicott (1957) advised that transitional objects are a normal and important part of human development. I remember one young boy's relationship with his "Bubba," a stuffed rabbit he was given as a baby gift. As Winnicott (1957) suggested, Bubba had become a "part of the family" (p. 190) who was always with the boy at bedtime and accompanied the child on trips away from home. Children often resist parents' attempts to "retire" their transitional objects (Winnicott, 1957). In the case of Bubba, the rabbit was constantly in need of repair, but the boy steadfastly refused to accept the replacement his mother had bought for him.

Winnicott (1957) believed that children develop "a very primitive form of loving—a mixture of affectionate caressing and destructive attack" (p. 184) with their transitional objects. An infant lying in a crib may cuddle an object one minute, throw it onto the floor the next, and immediately cry to have the object returned. Transitional objects are thought to facilitate infants' individuation from their mother. For example, when a mother is physically absent for a brief period of time, the transitional object fulfills the child's need for support and security until the mother returns. Winnicott believed that transitional objects also serve as the basis for children's participation in play activities. As their interest in play develops, children eventually set aside transitional objects and replace them with playmates.

A child's relationship with transitional objects can have long-term consequences, as illustrated in the following example:

> A boy baby became very early interested in a colored woolen covering. Before he was a year old he had become interested in sorting out according to their colors the threads of wool that he had pulled out. His interest in the texture of wool and in colors persisted and, in fact, never left him, so that when he grew up he became a color expert in a textile factory. (Winnicott, 1957, p. 186)

Although the impact of transitional objects is usually less dramatic than in this case, they are important because they help the child shift from experiencing "himself as the center of a totally subjective world to the sense of himself as a person among other persons" (Greenberg & Mitchell, 1983, p. 195).

To develop this sense of self, an infant must distinguish between self and nonself (e.g., mother, father, sibling). This process involves the discrimination of pleasant and unpleasant feelings. A baby who experiences pleasure when fed by his mother and does not distinguish self from nonself internalizes this pleasurable feeling as a part of self, what object relations theorists term a good internal object. Likewise, when an infant is hungry and her mother does not offer immediate nourishment, the unpleasant feeling is integrated into self as a bad internal object. As the infant matures, she becomes increasingly able to distinguish between self and nonself and to more correctly attribute feelings to their appropriate sources. The child is able to view his parents as being nurturant at one point (e.g., feeding the hungry child) and restrictive at another (e.g., placing the child in a car seat during a drive to the grocery store). During this developmental process, errors can occur. External objects are not treated as *whole objects* that have both positive and negative qualities; rather, they are treated as *part objects* that are experienced as only good or only bad (St. Clair, 1996). An example of this phenomenon is a girl of authoritative parents who develops a part object of her father based on the frustration she feels when he sets limits, rather than a whole object that is composed of his good (i.e., warmth, affection) and bad (i.e., limit setting) characteristics.

Ego Psychology

Anna Freud studied the mental processes that human beings use to defend the ego against the discomfort of anxiety. She expanded on her father's writings on the id, ego, and superego to address "the defensive function of the ego" (Blanck & Blanck, 1986, p. 3). Her perspective on human development is more interpersonal and less deterministic than her father's instinct-oriented theory. Okun (1990) attributed this difference, in part, to Anna Freud's work with children, which led her to conclude that human beings are "active and efficacious, not merely victims of internal conflicts" (p. 26). As discussed earlier, Anna Freud initially trained and worked as a teacher before she committed to a career as a child analyst. Based on her observations of children, normal and abnormal, she concluded that ego defenses can be adaptive or maladaptive, depending on the function they serve within a child's cultural surround (Sharf, 2000).

Blanck and Blanck (1986) described how Anna Freud integrated the sexual and aggressive drives that captivated her father's attention with the psychosocial influences that foster an infant's awareness of the existence and needs of other people. She concluded that "the proper field for our observation is always the ego" (A. Freud, 1936/1966, p. 6), which provides a view of the id and the superego. Based on her studies of ego development in normal and abnormal children, she proposed the concept of *developmental lines* to refer to various aspects of a child's progression from the "state of infantile immaturity and dependence to the gradual mastery of his own body and its functions, to adaptation to reality . . . and to the building of an inner organization" (A. Freud, 1962/1969, pp. 32–33). Lines of development include physiological aspects, such as the progression from instinctive sucking in infants to the selective intake of food in adults. Infants initially depend on others for the care of their bodies (e.g., diapering), but they gradually learn the skills required for self-care (e.g., bowel and bladder control). In the process, they progress from a state of infantile dependence on others to greater autonomy in adulthood. Psychologically, there is a change in the individual's view of self in the world, from infantile egocentricity toward empathy and interdependence. Anna Freud related ego development to children's play. The infant progresses from the exploration of his or her body and that of primary caregivers to the manipulation of toys and participation in games and team sports.

Correspondence across developmental lines may be irregular, with more progress in one area (e.g., participation in games or sports) than another (e.g., bladder control). Anna Freud (1965) believed that lack of correspondence is caused by the interaction of dispositional and environmental factors. Consider her example of a musically gifted child whose mother sings to him as an infant and encourages his development of musical talents. The same child raised by parents who have little interest in music would probably fail to develop these abilities unless he receives encouragement from others. Likewise, a child with limited musical aptitude raised by musical parents is unlikely to become proficient in music. Anna Freud believed that lack of correspondence across developmental lines does not imply pathology. Rather, intrapersonal variability is normal and accounts for a child's unique qualities.

Anna Freud (1962/1969) described how children's developmental levels are revealed in their responses to significant environmental challenges, such as separation from the mother, the birth of siblings, and entry into preschool or kindergarten. When confronted with these challenges, children sometimes become frustrated and temporarily regress to behaviors that are viewed as normal for an earlier stage of life (e.g., thumb sucking). Development is not a unidirectional process. It is typical for children to progress normally, regress during periods of stress and then regain their path of normal development after stress is overcome (A. Freud, 1965). In fact, we might hypothesize that relatively brief periods of regression followed by growth are functional because children learn that they can overcome life's challenges.

Therefore, normal development is characterized by periods of growth, temporary regression, and renewed growth. But some children fail to rebound, so regression no longer represents an opportunity but a sign of pathology (A. Freud, 1965). In these cases, intervention is needed to restore the healthy interaction of dispositional and environmental factors to enhance the child's development. Anna Freud (1962/1969) and her colleagues studied the lines of development in children and developed a tool, the Developmental Profile, for therapists to use with clients. This measure is examined in Chapter 7 when we consider psychoanalytic approaches to assessment.

Erik Erikson (1950) devised a theory of human development based on a series of eight psychosocial stages rather than the five psychosexual stages described by Freud. Freud described development from birth to adolescence, but Erikson considered the entire lifespan. For each of the stages, Erikson described the developmental task or crisis a person must address. For example, in the Trust vs. Mistrust stage of infancy, a baby must adjust to new and strange surroundings after the relatively safe and secure experience in utero. Likewise, Erikson believed that resolving the Integrity vs. Despair crisis is relevant to older adults who are most likely to reflect on and assess the value of their life.

Erikson (1950) integrated aspects of Freud's psychosexual model into his own theory of psychosocial development. For example, the Autonomy vs. Shame and Doubt stage was described as a time of social "holding on and letting go" (p. 222) that emerged concurrent with the development of anal muscular control. Similar to Freud, Erikson believed that failure to successfully handle the developmental challenges associated with a stage contributes to problems later in life. An infant who fails to achieve the first task of the ego (i.e., Trust vs. Mistrust) will view the world as an unsafe place and the self as untrustworthy and will be unable to handle the everyday challenges of life. Similar to Winnicott and others, Erikson emphasized the importance of the mother–infant relationship. He also cited the benefits of having parents who are well adjusted psychosocially.

Analytical Psychology

As noted earlier, Jung questioned Freud's emphasis on sexuality. He rejected the concept of the libido as sexual energy in favor of a more holistic description of the psyche as "a combination of spirit, soul and idea" (Douglas, 1995, p. 95). His writings on personality theory provide a new perspective on topics related to ego development, levels of consciousness, and psychological types.

Jung (1928/1954) believed that the psychic energy of childhood is mostly instinctual in nature. When a child begins to recognize that she is an individual, usually between the ages of 3 and 5 years, the ego emerges and the child starts to use pronouns such as "I" and "me." According to Jung, ego development is a gradual process that constitutes the challenge of the first half of life. Parents are crucial here because they have the responsibility of directing and focusing the psychic energies of their children. Failure to do so results in misbehavior from the child, which parents can correct after they assume their proper roles and responsibilities (Jung, 1928/1954).

Jung described three levels of consciousness, two of which are similar to those proposed by Freud. Jung (1935/1976), similar to Freud, believed we have a conscious awareness of certain thoughts and feelings. His "personal unconscious" (Jung, 1954/1969, p. 3) resembles Freud's concept of the unconscious and is composed of life experiences that are not readily available to us. But Jung's third level of consciousness, the "collective unconscious" (Jung, 1954/1969, p. 3), separates his theory of personality development from that of other psychoanalytic theorists. The collective unconscious is transgenerational because it represents "the mighty deposit of ancestral experience accumulated over millions of years" that "acts upon us in a timeless present, from the deepest and apparently most subjective recesses of the psyche" (Jung, 1931/1969, p. 376). The collective unconscious draws from our ancestors' experiences across the millenia and represents our predisposition to think, feel, or behave in a certain manner. It contains instincts, such as our inherited tendency to act (e.g., flee when we are in danger), as well as archetypes, which enable us to perceive and structure our experiences in meaningful ways (Jung, 1948/1969). Jung (1954/1969) described a number of archetypes, including the mother; father; shadow; persona; and self, which organizes our personality into a whole. Archetypes are important because they are the basis for symbols we create in dreams, fantasies, artwork, and literature (Scharf, 2000). Chapter 7 explores the important function that symbols serve in Jungian analysis.

Jung is also known for developing the concept of psychological types to describe how people process information and behave in their cultural surround. Psychological types are composed of attitudes and functions. Jung (1921/1971) described two attitudes: introversion and extraversion. Attitudes reflect an individual's orientation to self or others. For example, whereas introverted individuals tend to make decisions based on their own thoughts and feelings, extraverts draw energy from others and seek the opinions of others before making decisions. The concept of psychological type also includes two mental functions: thinking and feeling, and sensing and intuition (Jung 1921/1971). Thinking types are likely to process information based on logic, but feeling types are more focused on fostering satisfaction among the individuals affected by their decision. Sensing types are interested in the details of the choices at hand, but intuitive types adopt a more abstract perspective.

Attitudes and functions are combined to form eight different psychological types (e.g., introverted-thinking, extraverted-sensing). Each type is thought to reflect a person's preferred mode of thought and action. For example, extraverted-intuitive individuals tend to succeed in situations that involve interaction with other people and the processing of abstract ideas. Psychological types are probably best conceptualized as preferences, similar to our tendency to prefer one hand or the other. Although some of us are right handed and others are left handed, our overall performance is enhanced if we are skilled in using both hands. The same can be said for our functions and attitudes. Consider the functions of thinking and feeling. Balanced individuals have refined their preference for logical thinking while developing an awareness of others' feelings. These people are likely to make decisions that "make sense" and foster satisfaction among those directly affected by their actions. With his description of psychological types, Jung provided a framework for appreciating the diverse—and normal—ways that children relate to their world. In cases in which a child's style is extreme, the therapist's task is to help the client develop more balance in his or her attitudes and mental functions.

Individual Psychology

Alfred Adler shared Freud's interest in early childhood experiences. He believed these events are the basis for what he called our "style of life," the largely unconscious map we use to chart our path in life (Ansbacher & Ansbacher, 1956, p. 1). Developed during the preschool years, each person's style of life is unique, in part because of the idiosyncratic nature of the child's place and experiences in the family. Adler was particularly interested in the family constellation, which is the structural elements (e.g., family size) that influence the psychosocial dynamics within a family (Adler, 1927). One element that Adler's followers have examined in detail is birth order. Adler believed that the situation into which a child is born affects the youngster's relationships with parents and siblings. As he stated, "It is a common fallacy to imagine that children of the same family are formed in the same environment" (Ansbacher & Ansbacher, 1956). Consider two siblings who are 6 years apart in age. In this family, the older child might teach the younger sibling how to play a game or provide supervision in the parents' absence. Because these children assume different positions and roles in the family, Adlerians believe they will develop different styles of life.

Adler expanded on Freud's and Jung's theories by introducing the future-oriented concept of purposive or goal-directed behavior. Adler believed that human beings are "creative, choosing, self-directed decision makers" (Mosak, 1995, p. 53), so he focused on where individuals want to go rather than attending to the past they try to overcome. The purpose of behavior becomes apparent in the context of a person's cultural surround. A child's concern for cleanliness and order is not the result of anal stage difficulties as much as it reflects a desire to please a parent and gain recognition for completion of household tasks.

When Adler was young, he was very ill with rickets and pneumonia and survived two life-threatening accidents. These experiences were probably helpful to him when he formulated his concept of inferiority, which he believed to be an inherent and normal part of everyone's life (Ansbacher & Ansbacher, 1956). Adler believed that inferiority is functional when it precipitates purposive behavior whose goal is success or superiority. But life is a subjective experience, and we often make decisions based on our personal interpretation of events and conditions. Adlerians believe that children are more likely to make subjective decisions because they lack the cognitive skills and life experiences of adults (Mosak, 1995). Children who are convinced they are inferior, despite contrary evidence, may develop what Adler termed an *inferiority complex* which "permeates the whole personality" (Ansbacher & Ansbacher, 1956, p. 257). The inferiority complex compromises movement toward psychological health, leading instead to a failure mentality in which children believe they are unable to solve everyday problems (Ansbacher & Ansbacher, 1964).

Adler's theory offers a social perspective on human development, and his concept of *social interest* is central to it. He defined social interest using the words of an English author: "To see with the eyes of another, to hear with the ears of another, to feel with the heart of another" (Ansbacher & Ansbacher, 1956, p. 135). To develop this potential, a person must contribute to the welfare of others and society in general. Adler believed that human beings are psychologically healthy to the extent that they exhibit social interest (Mosak, 1995). His concern for the welfare of society is not surprising when we remember that he fled his native Austria after the rise of Nazism in Germany.

Rudolf Dreikurs drew upon this same experience to develop his democratic approach to child rearing. He shared Adler's concern for social interest and believed that children "learn to become independent by recognizing that *contributing* and not *receiving* is the effective instrument for obtaining social status" (Dreikurs, 1948, p. 194). Similar to Adler, Dreikurs (1948) emphasized the importance of family. In fact, he recommended that clinicians turn their attention from the problems of children to the actions of parents. Dreikurs believed that effective parenting involves maintaining order, avoiding conflict, and providing encouragement within a climate of respect for the child, respect for order, and respect for the rights of others (Dreikurs, 1964).

Dreikurs (1964) used Adler's concept of purposive behavior to describe how children misbehave when they are discouraged and have adopted mistaken goals. He described four of these goals (Dreikurs, 1948), the least serious of which occurs in children who are seeking attention. To achieve this goal, a child may choose constructive or destructive means and behave in an active or passive manner. A "model" student might excel in school and behave in an appropriate manner (i.e., active-constructive). Although the child appears to be well-adjusted, his attention-seeking behavior suggests that he has not achieved the desired place in the family. Other children may seek attention by "showing off" (i.e., active-destructive), working extremely hard to be loved by others (i.e., passive-constructive), or exhibiting no effort in relationships and doing nothing to contribute to the welfare of others (i.e., passive-destructive).

A more serious mistaken goal is that of demonstrating power. These children have observed adults and learned to use power to get what they want by doing what they are not supposed to do and not doing what is expected of them (Dreikurs, 1948). If demonstrating power proves to be unsuccessful, a child may resort to the third mistaken goal of seeking revenge by attempting to punish or get even with parents and teachers. These children sometimes engage in delinquent behavior or become physically abusive with significant others. According to Dreikurs, the fourth and most serious mistaken goal is demonstrating inadequacy. Children who demonstrate inadequacy are not just giving up; they are determined to not comply with others' wishes, regardless of the amount of external pressure used. Fortunately for adults, this goal is rarely observed because it is these children who, in Dreikurs' (1948) words, "drive parents—and teachers even more—to utter despair" (p. 271).

DEVELOPMENTAL CONSIDERATIONS

Pioneers in the field of child psychoanalysis recognized that children are developmentally different from adults. Psychodynamic theorists have written about infants' dependence on parents, the infant–caregiver relationship as the foundation for children's social development, and play as a therapeutic technique. In this section, we discuss a collection of studies that developmental psychologists have conducted on these topics.

Infant Development

Okun (1990) stated that many psychodynamic theorists have underestimated infants' abilities to function in their cultural surround. Researchers have found that during the third trimester, fetuses can distinguish between male and female voices as well as different syllables (i.e., "ba" vs. "bi") (Lecanuet, Granier-Deferre, & Busnel, 1995). At 2 to 4 days of age, newborns have been found to prefer musical and speech patterns that were presented to them in utero (Lecanuet et al., 1995). And Karen Wynn (1995) observed that infants possess mathematical abilities that enable them to distinguish between numbers (e.g., 2 vs. 3) presented to them either visually or auditorily. Wynn (1992) also reported fascinating findings that suggest babies have arithmetic abilities previously thought to be nonexistent at such a young age.

Based on her work with 4- to 6-month-olds, Wynn (1992) concluded that infants are able to add and subtract. Using an ingenious experimental procedure, she studied the length of time that babies stare at a miniature stage on which toy animals are either added or removed. For example, an animal is placed on the stage in full view of the child. The researcher closes a stage curtain and has the baby observe the addition of a second animal. This animal is then retained on stage or removed through an opening at the rear of the apparatus. Wynn found that when the curtain was opened and infants viewed the animal(s) on stage, those who expected two animals and discovered only one stared longer, on average, than when the correct number was present. Wynn concluded that, "infants possess true numerical concepts—they have access to the ordering of and numerical relationships between small numbers, and can manipulate these concepts in numerically meaningful ways" (p. 750). If she is correct, early psychodynamic descriptions of an instinct-driven, socially passive infant merit closer scrutiny because babies may be more aware and innately able than was previously recognized.

Infant–Caregiver Attachment

Object relations theorists have emphasized the importance of the mother–infant relationship, which developmental psychologists have investigated in their studies of infant–caregiver attachment. Santrock (1995) defined attachment as "a close emotional bond between the infant and the caregiver" (p. 225). Numerous researchers have investigated the nature and developmental implications of this phenomenon. Ainsworth, Blehar, Waters, and Wall (1978), for example, studied infants during brief periods of separation and reunion with their mothers. The authors identified three attachment patterns: secure, insecure-avoidant, and insecure-resistant. Although Main and Solomon (1986) proposed a fourth category for infants who could not be classified into one of these groups, we will limit our discussion to the attachment triad described by Ainsworth and her colleagues. Securely attached infants prefer close proximity with their caregiver, become distressed during separation periods, and are happy when they are reunited. Insecure-avoidant babies do not appear distressed during their caregivers' absence and tend to avoid or ignore the caregiver when reunited. Insecure-resistant infants may become angry or "conspicuously passive" (Ainsworth et al., 1978, p. 62) when the caregiver is absent and often resist contact or appear ambivalent about reuniting with the caregiver.

Most attachment researchers have examined the mother–infant relationship, although some have studied babies' attachment to their fathers. Cox, Owen, Henderson, and Margand (1992), for example, found that infants exhibit clear attachment to fathers who are actively involved in child rearing. The authors observed that the quality of father–infant attachment at age 1 year was affected by fathers' attitudes about their infant and their perceived roles in the parenting process. Parent attitudes are only one factor that seems to influence infants' attachment to their caregivers. Isabella and his colleagues (Isabella & Belsky, 1991; Isabella, Belsky, & von Eye, 1989) found that attachment patterns were affected by the synchrony of the mother's response, or how closely her reaction fit the child's behavior. Mothers of securely attached babies were found to be more responsive to their infants than were mothers of insecure-avoidant babies, who tended to overstimulate their infants, and mothers of insecure-resistant babies, who were more inconsistent and underinvolved. We might ask whether infant temperament plays a role in the development of attachment patterns. Does the behavior of an active or colicky baby prompt a different attachment pattern than would be observed with a quiet infant? Although Bukatko and Daehler (1995) warned against concluding that child temperament is a contributing factor, various researchers (e.g., Calkins & Fox, 1992) have suggested that infants and caregivers influence each other and thereby contribute to their attachment patterns. Another interesting consideration in regard to infant–caregiver attachment is the possible impact of recent developments in reproductive technology that provide infertile parents with alternatives other than adoption for having children (Contemporary Issues Box 6-1).

Contemporary Issues Box 6–1

Reproductive Technology and the Family

Infertility is thought to affect 10% to 12% of couples of childbearing age, which represents more than 5 million couples in the United States (Leiblum, 1997). Technological advances in reproductive medicine have provided alternative methods for having children. Although recent developments in the cloning of animals have increased public awareness of reproductive technologies, two of these methods, artificial insemination and in vitro fertilization, are not of recent origin. According to Leiblum, artificial insemination was first performed in 1866 by J. Marion Sims, a U.S. gynecologist. In a 1937 editorial in the *New England Journal of Medicine*, the authors contemplated human applications of in vitro fertilization, which had been used successfully in animals ("Conception," 1937). Interestingly, the first successful case of in vitro fertilization in humans did not occur until July 25, 1978, in Great Britain, when Lesley Brown gave birth to Louise Brown, "the first test-tube baby" (Andrews, 1999, p. 4).

Physicians have used artificial insemination and in vitro fertilization through various combinations of parent, surrogate, or donor egg and sperm (see Holt, 2001). Kleinpeter and Hohman (2000) described a method of artificial insemination in which a father's sperm are used to impregnate a surrogate mother, who bears the child and signs over custody to the father. The father's wife then adopts the infant. In vitro fertilization differs in that parent, surrogate, or donor sperm and egg are fertilized in the laboratory and the resulting embryo is implanted in the uterus of the mother or a surrogate. Both procedures can result in a newborn with multiple parents. As Andrews (1999) stated, a child could have five parents: "a sperm donor, egg donor, surrogate mother, and the couple who intended to raise the child" (p. 18). Consequently, the legal and psychosocial implications of technological approaches to human reproduction are many and varied.

Dolgin (1997) described early questions about legal parenthood for children born through artificial insemination. She cited a 1964 Georgia statute as the first in the United States to recognize offspring conceived with donor sperm as "the legitimate children of their mother's husband" (p. 9). Other legal questions have arisen in connection with reproductive technologies, including the use of surrogate mothers. Chesler (1988), for example, described the well-known case of Baby M, whose biological father and his wife, Bill and Betsy Stern, had contracted with Mary Beth Whitehead to be artificially inseminated with the father's sperm. The courts were asked to decide legal parenthood when Ms. Whitehead chose to keep the child rather than give her to the Sterns. More recently, a California couple contracted with a surrogate mother to deliver a child conceived using in vitro fertilization with the husband's sperm and donor eggs chosen by the couple (Glionna, 2001). When they discovered that the birth mother was pregnant with twins, the couple instructed her to abort one of the fetuses because they wanted only one child. The surrogate mother refused, and the courts became involved.

Susan Golombok and her colleagues have studied the psychosocial impact of reproductive technology in British families. Golombok, Cook, Bish, and Murray (1995) evaluated children's psychosocial development and the quality of parenting for 4- to 8-year-old children genetically related to both parents through in vitro fertilization, linked to their mother only as a result of donor insemination, or having no genetic relationship with the parents because they were adopted. These groups were compared with each other and with families of same-age children who were conceived naturally. Mothers who used assisted reproduction described themselves as warmer and more emotionally involved with their offspring than did mothers of naturally conceived children. This difference did not translate into adjustment discrepancies among the children in the four groups, which were not significantly different from each other. Golombok, MacCallum, and Goodman (2001) reevaluated three of the Golombok et al. (1995) samples (i.e., in vitro fertilization, adoptees, and naturally conceived children) at age 12 years. Both mothers and fathers in the reproductive technology group reported significantly higher warmth for their children than did parents of adoptees, but their warmth was comparable to that of parents of naturally conceived chil-

Contemporary Issues Box 6–1 *(cont.)*

dren. As was the case in the original study, no significant group differences were observed in children's psychosocial development.

Reproductive technology is not a panacea for all couples experiencing infertility. For example, Andrews (1999) described the relatively low success rate for in vitro fertilization. When infertility problems persist, some couples enter therapy to explore other methods, such as adoption, or to process their thoughts and feelings associated with remaining childless (Braverman, 1997). The psychosocial adjustment of children in families in which reproductive technology has been successful appears to be positive. Based on the findings of Golombok et al. (1995, 2001), therapists are no more likely to encounter troubled children conceived using assisted reproduction than they are those adopted as infants or conceived naturally. When these children do experience problems that warrant therapeutic intervention, clinicians should not focus excessively on the child's conception history. Rather, this factor should be considered as one of a number of possible factors related to the child's behavior.

How important is infant attachment to clinicians who work with school-age children? In other words, how stable across time are the attachment patterns observed in infancy? Main and Cassidy (1988) examined this question and found that 84% of the 6-year-old children in their study exhibited the same attachment pattern with their mother that was displayed at age 12 months. Sroufe and his colleagues (e.g., Egeland, Carlson, & Sroufe, 1993; Sroufe, Carlson, & Shulman, 1993) observed that infant attachment patterns even predicted social relationships into middle childhood and adolescence. The results of these longitudinal studies are consistent with object relations theorists' belief that early caregiver–infant interactions influence social interactions later in life. Therapists should consider the potential impact of early attachment patterns in their work with children and families. But they must remember that research by Sroufe and others does not prove that early life experiences determine a child's subsequent development. As you will recall from our discussion of resilience in Chapter 4, children have been found to overcome very difficult beginnings and to thrive later in life. If this were not the case, we would have little reason to expect that educational and therapeutic interventions could remediate problems or prevent difficulties in at-risk children.

To what extent do environmental factors affect infants' attachment to their caregivers? Vaughn, Egeland, Sroufe, and Waters (1979) found that family stressors, such as financial hardship and a parent's loss of employment, negatively affect attachment patterns. The authors observed that securely attached 12-month-old infants were more likely to exhibit insecure/avoidant or insecure/resistant patterns at age 18 months if their families had experienced turmoil during the intervening 6-month period. Fortunately, Jacobson and Frye (1991) found that providing support to stressed mothers of newborns contributed to more secure attachment in their babies. These findings support the use of prevention programs with at-risk children. They are also consistent with the beliefs of various psychoanalytic writers (e.g., Adler, Dreikurs, Winnicott) who recommended that clinicians help parents provide growth-enhancing environments for their children.

Childhood Friendships

Peer friendships are an important part of a child's social development. Damon (1977) described three developmental stages of friendship, which progress from what Berk (2000, p. 468) called the early "handy playmate" period to childhood friendships based on trust and helping others and the more psychologically intimate relationships of adolescence. Damon observed that some children simultaneously exhibit characteristics of more than one stage, so movement from one level to the next is not a clear-cut change. Researchers have provided evidence to support Damon's developmental model. Bigelow (1977), for example, studied Scottish and Canadian youth, ages 6 to 14 years, and found that younger children described a best friend in superficial terms, such as a peer engaged in a common activity, but older respondents were more likely to emphasize loyalty, acceptance, and intimacy. Keller and Wood (1989) reported similar findings in their longitudinal study of Icelandic children at ages 9, 12, and 15 years. As they grew older, respondents were more likely to view closeness and the resolution of conflict as important to a friendship.

An important element in the development of friendships is a child's ability to assume the point of view or social perspective of another person. Selman (1976) described what has become a popular five-stage model of this developmental process (Table 6-1). The qualitatively different levels in Selman's model represent changes in the structure and content of a child's understanding of another's point of view. A preschooler who assumes that other children see the world as he or she does gradually comes to realize that others can have different thoughts and feelings about events. The child eventually interprets the actions of self and others in the context of society. Selman and Byrne (1974) tested an earlier three-stage version of Selman's model with children, ages 4, 6, 8, and 10 years. The authors found age-related changes in perspective taking, from the more egocentric view of preschoolers to the self-reflective and "spectator" perspective of 8- and 10-year-old children.

Perspective taking appears to be related to the quality of childhood friendships. Kurdek and Krile (1982) found that popular students were more likely to understand other children's points of view. This relationship was age related, with a stronger correlation observed in students from grades 6 to 8 than among third to fifth graders. But elementary perspective-taking abilities have been found to play a role in the peer relationships of young children. Hudson, Forman, and Brion-Meisels (1982), for example, observed second graders tutoring kindergarten children and found that students proficient in perspective taking were more likely to help others by offering assistance with troublesome tasks.

A very early development in childhood friendships is the imaginary friend, which can be an invisible companion, a role that children assume (e.g., a superhero), or an object that is given personal qualities (Gleason, Sebanc, & Hartup, 2000). It is unclear why children create imaginary friends. One explanation for personified objects is that children develop pretend relationships with a doll or a toy animal that previously served as a transitional object during the primary caregiver's absence (Singer & Singer, 1992). It is not unusual for children to have pretend companions. When Gleason et al. interviewed mothers of preschoolers, they found that approximately one in five children had invisible human friends and personified objects that tended to be animals. Mothers also reported a difference in the nature of children's relationships with their imaginary friends. With personified objects, children were more likely to assume the role of parent and have the object portray a child. With invisible companions, the relationship was more typical of everyday childhood friendships.

What criteria do children use when selecting real friends? A common method of studying childhood friendships is the peer nomination technique in which children are asked to give the names of their

Table 6–1
Selman's Developmental Model of Perspective Taking in Children and Adolescents

Stage	Approximate Age Range in Years	Description
Egocentric role taking	4 to 6	Children do not differentiate between the thoughts and feelings held by themselves and others; they cannot describe the reasons behind another person's actions
Social-informational role taking	6 to 8	Children understand that people can have different thoughts and feelings about the same event, but are unable to assume the other person's social perspective
Self-reflective role taking	8 to 10	Children understand that people interpret events differently because they hold different beliefs and values; they are able to interpret their own behavior from another person's perspective
Mutual role taking	10 to 12	Children are able to view actions by self and other from the perspective of a third party or average spectator in the cultural surround.
Social and conventional system role taking	12 to 15 and older	Adolescents realize that effective communication is based on group members' understanding of the consensus or shared perspective of society

Adapted from "Social-cognitive Understanding: A Guide to Educational and Clinical Practice," by R. L. Selman, 1976, pp. 302–307. In T. Lickona (Ed.), *Moral development and behavior: Theory, research, and social issues* (pp. 299–316). New York: Holt, Rinehart and Winston. Copyright 1976 by Holt, Rinehart and Winston.

best friends. When Hundley and Cohen (1999) studied the friendships of children in grades 1 through 6, they found that students were most likely to select classmates who had included them on their list of friends. In other words, childhood friendships appear to be mutually established relationships. Hektner, August, and Realmuto (2000) provided additional support for the reciprocal nature of early friendships when they studied aggressive and nonaggressive 7-year-old children enrolled in a summer school program. The authors found that children, in general, preferred to play with peers who were less aggressive. In addition, the number of mutual friendships that highly aggressive students had declined by 40% over the course of the 6-week program. Children exposed to intrafamilial conflict at an early age appear to be more at risk for conflicted peer relationships. In their longitudinal study of boys at ages 3.5, 5, and 6 years, Ingoldsby, Shaw, and Garcia (2001) found that preschoolers who experienced more than one type of family conflict, such as spousal dispute and parent–child problems, were more likely to have difficulties in peer relationships during their early school years.

Do children benefit from having friends? The answer to this question is more complex than it first appears. In many ways, children who have friends seem to function better than their friendless peers. Ladd and his colleagues examined the relationship between childhood friendship and students' performance in school. Ladd (1990) found that kindergartners who entered school with friends were more likely to have positive attitudes about school and that success in school was related to maintaining existing friendships and developing new friends in class. The opposite was true for socially isolated children, who were more likely to experience problems adjusting to school. When Ladd, Kochenderfer, and Coleman (1996) studied kindergarten children with a "best friend," they found that conflict in these relationships was associated with school adjustment problems, especially among boys. Conversely, the authors reported more positive attitudes and feelings about school among children who perceived their best friend as someone who provided assistance to them.

Hartup (1996) agreed that children with friends seem to function better, but he cautioned that friendships vary in quality and the identity of each friend. As Hartup stated, some children are good role models, but others are not. Friendships differ in the number of activities and amount of time that children spend together. Some friends engage in constructive pursuits, but others spend their time together in destructive or predelinquent acts. Decisions can be made through negotiation between equal partners or by one friend's domination or power over the other. And some friendships are a source of emotional support, but others are characterized by stress and ongoing conflict. Because of the importance of these factors, researchers and practitioners alike must determine not only if a child has friends but must assess the behavioral adjustment of these children and the quality of their peer relationships. Given the developmental significance of childhood friendships, it is not surprising that specific interventions have been devised to remediate peer relationship problems. An interesting example is Pair Play Therapy, which involves weekly pairings of children in sessions designed to foster positive interpersonal understanding, effective social skills, and the willingness to make an emotional investment in friendships (Selman, Watts, & Schultz, 1997).

Play as a Therapeutic Technique

As already discussed, child psychoanalysts such as Melanie Klein and Anna Freud established play as a therapeutic medium for young clients. Play is a complex phenomenon that assumes different forms across the lifespan (Bergen, 1988). Between the ages of 3 and 5 years, children continue the exploratory play of infancy to investigate their surroundings. They develop motor skills by manipulating toys and other objects in practice play. Although the frequency of practice play declines during the preschool years (Rubin, Fein, & Vandenberg, 1983), all of us continue to engage in this activity to some degree as we refine various skills (e.g., musical, athletic).

Preschoolers are most likely to exhibit constructive play as they create products and attempt to solve problems (Hetherington, Cox, & Cox, 1979). Children build houses with wooden blocks, form roads in a sand tray, or draw pictures of themselves and their world. Therapists can use constructive play to help young people reproduce their world as they perceive it or as they want it to be. Symbolic play, which emerges between 9 and 30 weeks of age (Santrock, 1995), also has therapeutic potential. Here children use objects (e.g., wooden blocks) to represent something else (e.g., cars, trucks). As children become more socially aware, develop imagination, and become verbally fluent, their symbolic play takes the form of pretend, make-believe, or dramatic play (Smilansky, 1968). Singer and Singer (1992) noted that elementary school children engage in various types of symbolic play, including storytelling, fantasy thinking, and drama. This type of play has therapeutic value in helping children devise strategies for handling problems, including fear of the dark, anger toward parents, and concerns related to peer rejection (Bretherton, 1989).

An important development that occurs during the elementary school years is the emergence of a form of play called "games with rules." These include hide and seek, hopscotch, video games, group sports activities, and board games. Although some preschoolers experiment with rule-governed play, they have difficulty assuming the perspective of another person, which is crucial to games with rules (Berndt, 1997). According to Harris and Liebert (1991), children's play becomes very competitive around age 10 years. Therapists who work with elementary school students should use interventions that take into consideration a child's interest in competitive play. In their work with these clients, clinicians must determine whether a child's desire to win is within normal limits or if it represents a problem behavior that will impair psychosocial development. Chapter 15 examines competitive and noncompetitive board games that are available for this purpose.

The next chapter considers the debate that Melanie Klein and Anna Freud had regarding the symbolic interpretation of children's play. Simply stated, Klein contended that therapists should interpret the symbolic representation of unconscious conflicts in clients' play. Anna Freud believed otherwise and suggested that children's play may have symbolic meanings or may simply be portrayals of recent life experiences. Based on the empirical evidence available about symbolic play, we can reframe the Klein–Freud debate as a question of symbolic referrants. According to Anna Freud, a child who crashes two wooden blocks together may simply be reenacting an auto accident observed en route to the clinician's office. But pretense in children's play may reflect more than a single event and may therefore provide important thematic material about ongoing life experiences. Hetherington et al. (1979), for example, observed that the play of preschoolers of divorced parents was more disrupted than that of peers from intact families. The authors found that negative effects were most prominent within 1 year of the divorce and that the children of divorce, especially boys, engaged in less make-believe play than did children whose parents were married. Clinicians can expect children to engage in various forms of symbolic play during therapy. They must carefully evaluate each situation to determine whether the play is in reference to a specific event; an ongoing life experience; or as Klein has suggested, unconscious thoughts and feelings.

MULTICULTURAL CONSIDERATIONS

Carl Jung and Erik Erikson had a special interest in the cultural aspects of personality development. Therapists who integrate psychodynamic theory into their work must consider the relevance of this orientation in a multicultural society. Two areas that merit consideration are cultural influences on childhood friendships and the role of religion or spirituality in child therapy. We now look at some of the empirical research that has been conducted on these multicultural issues.

Gender, Ethnicity, and Childhood Friendships

How do children pick their friends? Recent evidence suggests that an important part of this process is a child's perceived similarity with peers. As a general rule, children tend to select friends who resemble them in a personally significant way. Two criteria that have been found to be important in children's selection of a best friend are gender and ethnicity (Kupersmidt, DeRosier, & Patterson, 1995). Of these, gender appears to be the more salient factor. Children usually select friends of their same gender, and boys and girls seem to have different reasons for having friends. When Rose and Asher (1999) studied fourth and fifth grade students, they found that girls placed a higher value on emotional closeness with friends. When children were asked to describe how they would handle hypothetical examples of relatively benign conflict with a friend, girls were more likely to report prosocial goals and strategies, including compromise and attempts to maintain the friendship. Boys were more likely to endorse a hostile response and a desire for control or revenge in the relationship. When asked about their actual friendships, boys and girls reported having a similar number of best friends and comparable levels of conflict with these children. But when Rose and Asher examined students' responses to the hypothetical examples used in the study, they found that children who reported high levels of revenge were less likely to have a best friend and more likely to report conflict when they had a friend.

Researchers have found that boys and girls differ in their behavior with friends. Zarbatany, Van Brunschot, Meadows, and Pepper (1996) experimentally grouped fifth and sixth graders into same-gender triads, each containing two friends (identified as hosts) and a third child who was either another friend or a nonfriend (identified as a guest). Based on their observations of students' behavior during a competitive board game, the authors found that female hosts were more likely to invite their guest to participate in the game. Zarbatany et al. stated that boys appeared to be more interested in winning the game than attending to the needs of their guest. It is important to note that the authors also found friendship history to be an important factor. Boys and girls were more likely to ask a friend, rather than a nonfriend, to play with them.

Lansford and Parker (1999) observed triads of same-gender friends, grades 3 to 5, as they engaged in group discussion, puzzle making, a competitive activity, and snack time. Boys were found to exhibit more aggression, and girls were more likely to disclose personal information with their friends. Lansford and Parker cautioned that despite these differences, the boys and girls in their study were similar in many ways, including the apparent social hierarchy within each triad and students' willingness to cooperate and respond to each other. Based on the results of these studies, it appears that the friendships of boys and girls differ in significant ways but that they also share common characteristics. Clearly, more research is needed to examine both main and interaction effects on children's selection of friends and their everyday interactions with them.

The role of ethnicity in children's selection of friends is less clear. Graham and Cohen (1997) and Kupersmidt et al. (1995) found that gender was a more important consideration among elementary school students. The effects of ethnicity appear to interact with other factors, including age and gender. For example, Graham and Cohen found that the older African American and European American first to sixth graders in their cross-sectional study had less positive attitudes about cross-ethnic relationships. Graham, Cohen, Zbikowski, and Secrist (1998) found similar results in their 3-year longitudinal study of first through third graders. When they retested students in grades 4 to 6, the authors found that children were more likely to select each other as friends if they were of the same gender and ethnic background. An important exception was the higher number of same-gender, cross-ethnic mutual friends reported by older boys, a change that was not observed in girls.

For many young people, school provides the chance to interact with children of different ethnic backgrounds, an opportunity that might not be available in their neighborhoods. The demographic composition of the school classroom has been found to be related to students' social development. Kistner, Metzler, Gatlin, and Risi (1993) examined the relationship between childhood friendships and the ethnic makeup of the classroom in their study of African American and European American students in grades 3, 4, and 5. Of their sample, 532 children were in classes where the majority of students were of the same ethnic background. The remaining 127 children were from classrooms where most of the students were of the opposite ethnic group. Kistner et al. found both ethnicity and gender to be important factors in students' nomination of peers as their most and least preferred playmates. Being in the minority, regardless of actual ethnicity, was associated with fewer positive nominations. Karcher and Nakkula (1997) described how cross-ethnic friendships can enhance a child's understanding of others from different cultural backgrounds. Because of the homogeneous nature of many residential neighborhoods, the nation's schools seem to be the ideal environment for interventions designed to enhance cross-ethnic relationships.

Religion and Spirituality

Despite Jung's interest in spirituality and religion, therapists have traditionally separated psychological and spiritual matters. As a result, they have often overlooked an important developmental influence for many children, including those from nondominant ethnic groups. Specific practices vary from one group to the next. Cervantes and Ramirez (1992) described how Hispanic American families are involved in formal groups, particularly the Roman Catholic Church, or practice *curanderismo*, a multigenerational form of folk healing in which supernatural powers are thought to influence health and well-being. The practices of Asian Americans include Christian and Buddhist faiths; worship of their ancestors; and no formal affiliation in emigrants from Communist countries, where religious activities were illegal (Lee, 1997). Native American children have been exposed to a belief system that involves "a loving respect for nature as well as independence and self-discipline" (La Fromboise & Low, 1989, p. 121). Therapists must appreciate these beliefs and be open to treatments that include the use of folktales or children's books, such as *Children of the Sun* (Carew, 1980), in which spirituality and family are integrated to teach a lesson of altruism to Native American twin boys.

The Roman Catholic faith is deeply embedded in the Hispanic American culture, which Deck (1995) described as "permeated by a kind of Catholic ethos that revolves around a rich collection of rites and symbols" (p. 466). Therapists must understand how these practices affect family structure and members' interactions with others within and outside of the family system. They must also consider the importance of spirituality, which Elkins, Hedstrom, Hughes, Leaf, and Saunders (1988) defined as:

> a way of being and experiencing that comes about through awareness of a transcendent dimension and that is characterized by certain identifiable values in regard to self, others, nature, life, and whatever one considers to be the Ultimate. (p. 10)

This definition resembles the description that Cervantes and Ramirez (1992) gave for *mestizo*, a Mexican American practice that emphasizes "harmony, interdependence, and respect for the sacredness of one's place in the world" (p. 109). Cervantes and Ramirez described how these beliefs can be incorporated into family therapy by having family members go beyond day-to-day matters and address their relationships with extrafamilial systems, acceptance of all human beings, and deference to God or a higher power.

Richardson (1991) emphasized the central role of religion in the lives of African Americans when he wrote, "No other institution claims the loyalty and attention of African Americans as does the church" (p. 65). Clinicians have made surprisingly little effort to incorporate interventions into this key institution. This is an unfortunate oversight because Dressler (1991) found that two of the four coping resources used by members of a Southern African American community were religious in nature. That is, respondents identified the social support of the church and their belief in God as tools for handling everyday problems. Richardson (1989) reported that members of the black clergy generally have positive attitudes about the mental health professions. Because of the central role of the church in the lives of many African American families, therapists should collaborate with the clergy to establish church-based outreach and prevention programs designed to address psychosocial concerns (e.g., depression, family communication problems), developmental issues (e.g., teenage sexuality), and living skills (e.g., time management) (Thomas & Danby, 1985).

SUMMARY

According to Wolitzky and Eagle (1997), no one theory defines psychodynamic formulations on human development. As we have seen in this chapter, the psychodynamic umbrella covers a diverse set of beliefs, from Freud's interest in instincts or drives to object relations theorists' focus on interpersonal dynamics, Adler's interest in goal-directed behavior, and Jung's transgenerational model of personality. Despite these differences, psychodynamic theorists share a belief in the long-term effects of early childhood experiences. Recent studies about caregiver–infant attachment seem to support this viewpoint and suggest that concepts such as "good-enough parenting" have merit. Chapter 7 explores how psychodynamic principles have been applied to therapeutic interventions with children.

7

Psychodynamic Interventions

■ ■ ■

Seven-year-old Jeanne is the only child of Tom and Toni Harris. When she was 5 years old, her parents divorced after a 9-year marriage that was wrought with ongoing spousal conflict. Before their divorce, the parents separated for approximately 2 years when they argued about custody arrangements for their daughter. During this time, Jeanne lived with her mother, who was eventually awarded custody. Although Mr. Harris was granted regular visitation rights, he rarely contacted Jeanne, failed to make child support payments, and typically "forgot" to send cards or presents on holidays. To support the family, Ms. Harris became more involved with her career and relied on family and friends for child care. Now a second grader, Jeanne is aggressive with other children and is doing poorly in her schoolwork.

■ ■ ■

The spousal conflict that occurs before, during, and after divorce can be stressful for a child. Although a number of therapeutic interventions have been used with children such as Jeanne, we will consider a treatment based on psychodynamic theory. Before we continue with our case example, we begin with a discussion of different psychodynamic approaches that are used to assess children. We then explore psychodynamic methods of education/development, prevention, and remediation. We also consider the role of the parent, child, therapist, and school in the treatment of children. Before returning to the case of Jeanne, we examine the contributions and limitations of this popular approach to child therapy.

ASSESSMENT

The psychodynamic approach involves the study of traits or characteristics that are thought to be relatively stable across settings, activities, and time. Assessment results are interpreted as a sign of underlying problems that originated early in childhood and have impeded normal development. Proponents of the psychodynamic approach have incorporated play into the assessment process. This technique is especially useful with children who have limited verbal skills and verbally proficient clients who "find self-expression easier through play than words" (Scharff & Scharff, 1987, p. 307). The format for play assessment ranges from an unstructured approach during which the child engages in free play, to more structured methods in which the interviewer introduces specific stimuli, such as family puppets or dolls, to elicit information relevant to the child's presenting problem. Parents are sometimes interviewed to obtain information that children are unable or unwilling to provide. This includes a history of the child's physical and psychological development and significant life events, such as the birth or adoption of a sibling.

When psychodynamic therapists use psychological tests, they tend to select measures that tap global constructs, such as the ego or self. Because of their interest in the unconscious, they frequently use projective measures, such as the Rorschach Inkblot Test (Rorschach, 1921), the Children's Apperception Test (CAT) (Bellak, 1954), or Tell Me A Story (TEMAS) (Malgady, Costantino, & Rogler, 1984). The underlying assumption of these techniques is that children unconsciously project negative feelings onto a less threatening object, such as an inkblot or a picture, and reveal their underlying conflicts (DiLorenzo, 1987). Although psychodynamic therapists have traditionally focused on intrapsychic features of the individual child, those who adopt an object relations perspective attend to both intrapsychic and interpersonal aspects of a child's development. Winnicott (1971), for example, believed that an important component of any child assessment is a review of family, school, and community influences in the child's environment.

Anna Freud (1962/1969) adopted a multidimensional approach to assessment with her concept of developmental lines. She and her colleagues designed their Developmental Profile as a systematic method for conducting assessments with children, monitoring treatment progress, and conducting follow-up evaluations to measure the long-term impact of therapy. The profile is designed to assess the developmental process rather than pathological symptoms, so it can be used with normal children as well as those having problems. In order to avoid paying undue attention to only one area of development, Anna Freud included a variety of domains, such as intellectual functioning and social development, so clinicians would be able to assess "all parts of the child's personality" (A. Freud, 1962/1969, p. 28). The profile is to be used within a multidisciplinary setting in which teachers, psychologists, psychiatrists, and child development specialists contribute relevant information based on their contacts with the child and significant others. Information is collected through the use of appropriate tests, including a battery of intelligence and academic achievement tests, as well as interviews with the child and parents.

The results of a Developmental Profile are organized according to the child's drive and ego development, developmental lines, fixations and regression, conflicts, and prognosis (A. Freud, 1962/1969). Drive development is assessed relative to the child's progression through the psychosexual stages and the expression of aggression toward the self and others. Ego development is measured by the child's ego functions (e.g., contact with reality, personality integration), ego defenses (e.g., repression, displacement), and superego development (e.g., moral standards). To assess developmental lines, the counselor must examine the correspondence across contrasting dimensions (e.g., egocentricity and empathy, play and work) and the child's mastery of certain developmental tasks (e.g., responsibility for personal cleanliness activities and care of the body).

Development is an uneven process that includes movement forward as well as periods of regression resulting from conflicts in the child's life. As part of the Developmental Profile, clinicians determine whether a child has regressed from a mature level of functioning (e.g., bowel continence) to more infantile behavior (e.g., soiling). They also attempt to identify the conflict (or conflicts) that may have precipitated these problems. Conflicts may be either external (e.g., child vs. parents, child vs. teachers) or internal (e.g., id vs. ego). Anna Freud (1962/1969) believed that external conflicts may respond to environmental manipulation but that resolution of internal conflicts requires psychoanalysis. The last category of the Developmental Profile is prognosis. Here clinicians are asked to assess the child's tolerance for frustration and anxiety, resources for handling anxiety, and developmental direction (i.e., growth vs. regression) to provide a basis for predicting treatment outcome and long-term development. Although the profile is similar to most traditional forms of assessment (e.g., pretreatment-posttreatment assessment of functioning), it clearly reflects the principles of psychoanalytic theory with its focus on ego and drive development and the child's ability to manage anxiety.

EDUCATION/DEVELOPMENT AND PREVENTION

Early writers noted the educational value of psychoanalysis, but they were apparently referring to more than what occurs in the traditional school classroom. The ambiguity here may have its origins in the English translation of the German term *Erziehung*. As Strachey suggested in his translation of Freud's works, this word has a broader meaning that "includes 'upbringing' in a general sense" (Freud, 1933/1964, p. 147). In fact, formal education is only one aspect of *Erziehung*, which refers to the overall rearing of children within their culture (personal communication, William Odom, November 24, 1997). When considered from this perspective, psychodynamic theory offers a means of delivering comprehensive mental health services that incorporate education/development, prevention, and remediation.

According to Hug-Hellmuth (1921), child analysts are "both analyst and educator" (p. 287). She believed that child psychoanalysis is actually "character-analysis" in which difficulties are remediated concurrent with the development of "moral and aesthetic values" (p. 287). Freud overlooked the educational benefits of psychoanalysis but recognized his daughter Anna for her development of psychoanalytic techniques intended to foster "the upbringing of the next generation" (Freud, 1933/1964, p. 146). Anna Freud designed interventions that could be used with normal and disturbed children in a variety of settings, including schools, residential treatment centers, and clinic therapy rooms. Her interest in alternative modalities is no doubt a reflection of her early training and professional experience as a teacher (Peters, 1985).

Of the psychodynamic theorists, Alfred Adler and his followers have probably contributed the most to education/development and prevention strategies for children. Chapter 6 discusses the parent education programs of Adler and Dreikurs. Frequently used to remediate children's misbehavior, these programs also provide a method for preventing future problems and enhancing the development of normally functioning children. Two contemporary figures who have contributed to this area are Donald Dinkmeyer and Donald Dinkmeyer, Jr. In this chapter, we discuss three programs developed by this father and son team. Here we examine Systematic Training for Effective Parenting (STEP) (Dinkmeyer & McKay, 1976), which the authors developed to teach more democratic methods of child rearing. Later when we discuss the school's role in helping children, we examine a program designed for children, Developing Understanding of Self and Others (DUSO) (Dinkmeyer & Dinkmeyer, 1982), and a STEP equivalent for teachers, Systematic Training for Effective Teaching (STET) (Dinkmeyer, McKay, & Dinkmeyer, 1980).

Dinkmeyer and McKay (1976) designed STEP to teach parents how to become more effective with their children. Participants in this nine-session program learn to use encouragement, natural and logical consequences, and basic communication skills. Instruction is provided in a small group format, so parents can practice skills before they apply them at home. Clients are taught to set aside autocratic methods, such as punishment, in favor of techniques based on democratic principles. Clinicians who conduct STEP groups must "practice what they preach" by incorporating encouragement into their teaching style instead of treating parents as failures. As Dinkmeyer et al. (1987) noted, "It is not that parents lack ability, but that they lack skills and models" (p. 328). STEP groups incorporate both and can be used to pursue remedial, preventive, and educational/developmental goals.

Dinkmeyer, McKay, and Dinkmeyer (1990) reviewed studies on the effectiveness of STEP and concluded that the program changes parents' child-rearing attitudes. For example, Nystul (1982) found that parents who participated in STEP developed a more democratic perspective on parenting and were more likely to encourage verbalization in their children than were parents who had not participated in the program. Researchers have generally reported success when using STEP, but specific findings have varied from study to study. The latter may be the result of the flexibility that STEP leaders are given in running their groups. Dinkmeyer and Dinkmeyer (1979), for example, stated that experienced leaders "may want to use their own innovations of the STEP material" (p. 49). This approach may result in a lack of standardization across studies, thereby limiting the conclusions that can be drawn about the effectiveness of the program.

REMEDIATION

Classical Drive Theory

As discussed in Chapter 6, Freud's treatment of Little Hans is often identified as the birth of child psychoanalysis. Before their only meeting, the boy's father had been keeping a record of Hans' development since about age 3 years to assist Freud in his study of childhood sexuality. As we might expect, these notes reflect the principles of Freud's psychosexual theory of personality development. The father's account contains repeated reference to the boy's questions and comments about his "widdler" (Freud, 1909/1956, p. 151). At one point, Hans asked whether his mother had a widdler; at another time, he commented on the penis of a lion he saw at the Vienna Zoo. He also described his sister's widdler as "quite small," but said he expected it to "get bigger all right" when she was older (p. 155).

When Hans was almost 5 years old, his father wrote a letter to Freud saying that his son "is afraid *that a horse will bite him in the street*, and this fear seems somehow to be connected with his having been frightened by a large penis" (p. 165). Theoretically, the boy's fear is an expression of his unconscious and has nothing to do with horses, except that the horse functions as the external object onto which he projects anxiety. The father attempted to explain the child's fear by suggesting that Hans' earlier observation of large penises on horses caused him discomfort. Interestingly, he also blamed his wife, whom he described as excessively affectionate with Hans and permissive in allowing the boy to sleep with her.

Freud's initial response in this case was psychoeducational in nature. Before he ever met with the child, he recommended that the father teach Hans various facts about human sexuality (e.g., his sister and his mother do not have penises). Although this seemed to be of some help in reducing the boy's fears, the benefit was short lived and the anxiety returned. At that point, Freud conducted his one session with Hans and the father in the consulting room at his home at Bergasse 19 in Vienna. During the brief visit, Freud asked Hans about the appearance of his "anxiety-horses" (Freud, 1909/1956, p. 184), which the boy described as being black around their mouths. Freud interpreted the child's fears as symptomatic of the Oedipal complex:

> I asked Hans jokingly whether his horses wore eyeglasses, to which he replied that they did not. I then asked him whether his father wore eyeglasses, to which, against all the evidence, he once more said no. Finally, I asked him whether by "the black round the mouth" he meant a moustache; and I then disclosed to him that he was afraid of his father, precisely because he was so fond of his mother. It must be, I told him, that he thought his father was angry with him on that account; but this was not so, his father was fond of him in spite of it, and he might admit everything to him without any fear. (pp. 184–185)

After this meeting, the father continued to provide regular reports of his son's progress. Freud served as a consultant, helping the father interpret Hans' behavior from a psychoanalytic perspective.

Object Relations Theory

Hug-Hellmuth (1921) contended that psychoanalysis could not be conducted with very young children. Melanie Klein believed otherwise and became a pioneer in the field of child psychoanalysis through her work with preschoolers. In the case of 5-year-old Fritz, Klein first tried Freud's consultative approach by meeting with the boy's mother and recommending that she encourage her son to talk about "the many unspoken questions which were obviously at the back of his mind" (Klein, 1955/1975, p. 123). This approach was not as effective as Klein had hoped, so she made a significant step in the history of child interventions when she set aside consultation and engaged in direct analysis with the boy (Pick & Segal, 1978). Klein (1932/1959) called her method "Play Analysis" (p. 40), and she believed her approach to be more appropriate for children than the talk therapy commonly used with adults. At first, Klein conducted her sessions in children's homes where they could play with their own toys. Later, she dropped this practice and conducted analysis elsewhere so the client would realize "that the consulting-room or the play-room, indeed the whole analysis, is something separate from his ordinary home life" (Klein, 1955/1975, p. 125).

Klein described the setting in which play therapy is to occur. The treatment room should be equipped with "a washable floor, running water, a table, a few chairs, a little sofa, some cushions and a chest of drawers" (Klein, 1955/1975, p. 126). Clinicians must have a variety of play materials available for young clients. Klein (1932/1959) offered the following examples:

> On a low table in my analytic room there are laid out a number of small toys of a primitive kind—little wooden men and women, carts, carriages, motor-cars, trains, animals, bricks and houses, as well as paper, scissors, and pencils. (p. 40)

She emphasized that toys should be small and nonspecific in nature, thereby facilitating the child's expression of unconscious thoughts and feelings (Klein, 1955/1975). She also recommended that clinicians provide clients with their own drawers where they can store the toys that will be used during play sessions.

Klein's approach to treatment was very intense. Her play analysis could be very lengthy, which in the case of 9-year-old Egon was 425 hours (Klein,

1932/1959, p. 110). Her focus in session was also more complex. Klein (1927/1975) believed that children exhibit the transference neurosis with the therapist, so she suggested that clinicians engage in direct and deep interpretation early in treatment. She also believed that children exhibit transference earlier than do adult clients, in part because children's unconscious is still close to consciousness and therefore "much simpler to find" (Klein, 1932/1959, p. 30). Klein integrated Freud's theory of psychosexual development into her method. She regularly interpreted sexual symbolism in a client's play and recommended that therapists enlighten the child regarding sexual matters by offering "as much sexual information as the growth of its desire for knowledge requires, thus depriving sexuality at once of its mystery and of a great part of its danger" (Klein, 1921/1975, pp. 1–2).

An example of this practice is her work with Richard, a 10-year-old boy who entered analysis because of war-related anxiety (e.g., school truancy, hypochondriacal symptoms, social ineptness). During his first session, Richard described how he feared for his mother's safety at night and worried that a "tramp" might break into her room and harm her. Klein (1984) first interpreted the tramp as a symbol for Adolf Hitler. She suggested that the tramp might represent Richard's father, who could hurt the mother when the parents were in bed at night and "something could happen between them with their genitals that would injure Mummy" (p. 21).

Klein believed that psychoanalysis with adults and children differs only in technique, not in principle. She contended that play is a child's equivalent of free association in adults and represents symbolic expressions of a child's "fantasies, wishes, and actual experiences" (Pick & Segal, 1978, p. 432). During her twentieth session with Richard, she watched as he arranged toy ships and submarines according to their size. Klein interpreted the ships and submarines as symbols of the boy's family. Richard first declared that one of the submarines, "the smallest of all but the straightest" (Klein, 1984, p. 90) represented him. Later he asked Klein to read to him from one of her books, "the largest volume" (p. 90), but when he decided that the text was "too grown-up" (p. 90), he returned to his play with the boats, this time selecting a destroyer to represent himself.

As Richard moved his toys around the floor, Klein interpreted the meaning of his play as it related to both her and his mother. She recorded the following in her case notes.

> Mrs. K. interpreted that Richard first decided to be the smallest but the straightest, which expressed his thought that it was safer to remain a child with a small but undamaged genital. Then he wished to explore Mrs. K. (and Mummy) represented by the big book. "Too grown-up" for him meant not only that it was too advanced but also that Mrs. K. (and Mummy) was too big; that he was not capable of putting his small penis into such a vast genital . . . (and) was afraid of losing his penis inside the grown-up Mrs. K and Mummy. (p. 91)

Here we also have an example of Klein's interpretation of transference. According to Langs (1981), Klein expanded on Freud's concept of transference to include the client's complete relationship with the therapist, some of which is distorted and based on early interactions with primary significant others. The remainder is directly related to the analyst as a participant in the present therapeutic encounter. Although psychoanalysts' definitions of *transference* can vary, they all share the belief that this dynamic is an important aspect of treatment. Analysts differ in the importance they give to the transference neurosis, which Sandler, Holder, Kawenoka, Kennedy, and Neurath (1981) described as "that intensification of the transference in which the patient's major conflicts become centered around the person of the analyst" (p. 39). Klein (1927/1975) believed that children develop a transference neurosis just as adult clients do. The analyst's role is one of identifying and interpreting the unconscious material that is the basis of the transference neurosis. To achieve this goal, the analyst must follow a path of discovery that leads to the child's internal object relations with primary significant others.

Klein acknowledged children's dependence on their parents; however, in analysis, she focused on the child and had limited contact with parents. D. W. Winnicott, another proponent of object relations, emphasized the importance of parents and the family environment. In fact, he believed that the problems of children are a reflection of either "illness in one or both of the parents" (Winnicott, 1971, p. 8) or problems in the child's cultural surround. Winnicott (1971) believed that the more dysfunctional the family environment, the more involved and lengthy the treatment must be. Winnicott (1977) was somewhat unconventional in his method of child analysis with his "on demand" (p. 3) approach to scheduling sessions. Unlike other analysts, who met with their young clients five times each week, Winnicott might see a child only once or for a limited number of sessions scheduled over an extended period. In his work with Gabrielle, for example, he scheduled 14 meetings with the child from when she was 2 years old until she was 5 years old (Winnicott, 1977). The clinician who uses the on-demand method can serve as a developmental consultant to parents when difficulties arise. Although Winnicott (1977) acknowledged that some children require regularly scheduled meetings, he contended that therapeutic change can occur with only one therapy session when a "sacred" (Winnicott, 1971, p. 4) interaction develops between the child and a caring and understanding adult.

Winnicott believed that child analysis does not require lengthy interpretation of unconscious conflicts. Although he used interpretation with children, his approach was more flexible than that of his predecessors. He viewed the timing and wording of an interpretation as critical, and he evaluated each by the child's response. If a client rejects an interpretation, it could mean that the therapist was incorrect, intervened at the wrong time, or used words the child did not understand. Whatever the reason, Winnicott (1971) recommended that clinicians withdraw "incorrect" interpretations because failing to do so gives the child only two choices: accept what the clinician has said, regardless of its accuracy, or reject the interpretation. Unfortunately, choosing the latter option also means that the child is rejecting the therapist and the therapeutic relationship.

To establish rapport with children, Winnicott (1971) often used his Squiggle Game. The therapist begins by drawing a squiggly line on a piece of paper and saying: "I shut my eyes and go like this on the paper and you turn it into something, and then it is your turn and you do the same thing and I turn it into something" (Winnicott, 1971, p. 12). Clinician and client alternate, drawing a squiggle and finishing the squiggle into a meaningful picture. This nonverbal activity is typically coupled with verbal comments that serve as the basis for the therapeutic relationship. The Squiggle Game can be particularly helpful with clients who are shy and withdrawn or have difficulty communicating their thoughts to the therapist.

Winnicott (1971) used his the Squiggle Game with 9-year-old Iiro, who was scheduled to receive surgery for syndactyly, a congenital condition that results in "webbing" of the fingers and toes. When Winnicott drew his first squiggle, Iiro responded, "It's a duck foot" (p. 12), which Winnicott believed was the boy's desire to discuss his disability. Later in the session, Iiro seemed to intentionally draw what appeared to be a deformed hand. As Winnicott and Iiro squiggled, the boy talked increasingly about his disability and his plans for the future, which included playing the flute. To counter the child's belief that only surgery would make him whole and lovable, Winnicott said, "The first thing is to be loved as you are and as you were born" (p. 22). Winnicott met with Iiro's mother, who also had syndactyly. During their interview, the mother disclosed that she felt guilty about giving the disorder to her son and was obsessed with obtaining surgical correction for the boy. Based on his brief contact with mother and child, Winnicott helped both of them become more accepting of Iiro as a person and less compelled to base their opinion of the boy on changes that might occur as a result of surgery.

Winnicott (1971) cautioned that no two children, no two sessions, and no two clinicians are alike. He presented his Squiggle Game as a flexible option that therapists can adapt to the needs of the child. Winnicott recognized the significant role that parents play in their children's development, so he sometimes showed clients' drawings to parents. It is important to note that Winnicott made his decision to share these materials based on the facts of the case. With some parents, he showed the drawings because they contained important information that parents could use to help their child. With others, he refrained because he feared the parents would use the information against the child.

Ego Psychology

Anna Freud (1946) acknowledged Melanie Klein's contribution to child psychoanalysis when she described Klein's play technique as "almost indispensable for familiarization with small children, who are not yet capable of verbal self-expression" (p. 28). But these pioneers are usually remembered for their differences in the treatment of young clients. Johnson, Rasbury, and Siegel (1997) identified two of these as their use of symbol-based interpretation of children's play and their position on the existence of the transference neurosis in child analysis.

Anna Freud believed that children's play does not always merit the symbolic interpretation that Klein recommended. For example, a child who crashes two cars together during a play session may be reproducing an event observed on television or on the way to therapy, rather than symbolically describing his or her parents performing sexual intercourse. As noted previously, Klein's belief in the symbolic meaning of children's play was based on her assumption that play is the equivalent of free association in adults. But children may be unable to freely associate because this therapeutic activity requires that a client have the ability to suspend logical connections between thoughts, permit the emergence of unconscious thoughts and feelings, and develop insight based on the analyst's interpretation of clinical material (Harter, 1983b).

Anna Freud believed that children do not form a transference neurosis with their clinician because of the nature of the therapist–client relationship and children's continued dependence on their parents. Unlike psychoanalysis with adults in which the clinician remains neutral, even detached from the client, successful psychoanalysis with children requires that the therapist establish a positive relationship with the client. As Anna Freud stated, "The child in fact will only believe the loved person, and it will only accomplish something to please that person" (A. Freud, 1946, p. 31). Because the therapist is actively involved in establishing a positive relationship with the child, the conditions (i.e., passivity, detachment) that facilitate the transference neurosis with adults do not exist. In other words, the client's transference onto the analyst does not intensify to the point where the client's conflicts with others are focused on the analyst.

Anna Freud (1946) offered an additional reason why she believed the transference neurosis does not occur with child clients. Adults are thought to form a transference neurosis based on their unconscious conflicts with primary significant others. The source of these conflicts is believed to exist in early parent–child interactions, experiences that, by their very nature, are no longer a part of the adult's everyday life. When the conflicts arise during analysis, they are directed at the clinician and then resolved within the therapeutic relationship. Anna Freud contended that children do not experience this emotional reliving of a conflicted parent–child relationship because they continue to have daily contact with their parents and depend on them for their basic needs.

Although she argued against the emergence of the transference neurosis, Anna Freud believed that children do exhibit positive or negative transference with their therapists. Upon entering treatment, a 10-year-old child can be expected to relate to the clinician in a manner consistent with his or her past experiences with significant other adults. Anna Freud (1928) highlighted the value of positive transference when she stated that success in therapy "will always go hand in hand with a positive attachment" (p. 34) between the child and therapist. Positive transference is therapeutic, but negative transference, including projection of hostility onto the therapist, compromises the working relationship between the clinician and child and is something the analyst "must seek to weaken and destroy" (p. 34).

Erik Erikson is best known for his lifespan approach to developmental theory, but he also wrote about the therapeutic benefits of play, which children use to work through psychological insecurities in the presence of a supportive adult. Erikson (1950) believed that a child's transference onto the clinician can at times become so intense that the client displays a "sudden and complete or diffused and slowly spreading inability to play" (p. 196). He illustrated this point in his account of 4-year-old Ann, whose mother was distressed about the child's nightly soiling episodes and her refusal to have normal bowel movements.

Ann was initially reluctant to engage in treatment, so Erikson did not question her. Instead, he sat quietly on the therapy room floor and constructed a wooden block house for a family of dolls. As he did this, Ann watched and sucked her thumb before reacting.

> Our patient, increasingly fascinated with this wordless statement of a problem, suddenly goes into action. She relinquishes her thumb to make space for a broad and toothy grin. Her face flushes and she runs over to the toy scene. With a mighty kick she disposes of the woman doll; she bangs the bathroom door shut, and she hurries to the toy shelf to get three shiny cars, which she puts into the garage beside the man. (pp. 45–46)

A likely interpretation for this response might be that the child used the toys to express resistance or anger toward her mother and a desire to please her father. At the close of this play episode, Ann transferred her conflicted feelings onto the therapist. She began to cry, asked for her mother, and ran from the room to reunite with her mother in the waiting area. Freud might have interpreted the child's behavior as having its origin in the oral (i.e., thumbsucking) or anal (i.e., soiling) stage. Erikson (1950) preferred to conceptualize Ann's behavior within the context of her interactions with significant others. As he noted, "A child's loves and hates cannot be evaluated without an inquiry into the loves and hates of those around her" (Erikson, 1950, p. 49). He believed that Ann communicated her conflicted feelings to the parents by soiling and holding feces, resisting her mother's requests, and trying to please her father. In therapy, she exhibited these feelings by vacillating between a pleasing child who quietly watched the clinician and an angry youngster who destroyed the therapist's creation.

Analytical Psychology

Jungian therapists focus on the meaning of symbols that children create. They are particularly interested in clients' artwork, including drawings, paintings, and sandtray pictures. Jung (1956) described two kinds of thinking. The first, directed thinking, is logical, expressed in words, and intended to represent the events that occur in the outside world. The second form of thinking is more fantastic in nature, which Jung (1956) described as "effortless; working as it were spontaneously, with the contents ready to hand, and guided by unconscious motives" (p. 18). The clinician's challenge is to unleash the healing qualities inherent in the child's fantasy world. To accomplish this, Jungian therapists use art activities to enter the client's unconscious.

Jung (1963) described a time in his life when he drew every morning. He studied his drawings and observed what he described as "psychic transformations from day to day" (p. 195). Allan (1988) capitalized on Jung's discovery when he developed his serial drawing technique in which the child is asked to draw a picture each session. As Jung did with his creations, the therapist studies the themes that emerge across the child's drawings. Allan described three stages that seem to develop in serial drawings. Initially, the activity offers a means of establishing rapport with the child, and the drawings are thought to provide a peek at the child's internal world, which frequently includes negative emotions. As treatment progresses, the drawings provide stimuli for the child to talk about experiences, thoughts, and feelings. During the middle stage, Allan observed that children begin to address conflicting feelings by separating them into "good" and "bad." Drawings created during the last stage, termination, reflect a greater sense of self and mastery over the problems the child was experiencing at the outset of therapy.

Allan (1988) offered concrete suggestions for using serial drawing, including the following introduction:

> Often children like to draw and talk when they come to see me. Drawing and talking seem to help children feel better, overcome problems, and enjoy life more . . . You can draw or talk about whatever you wish . . . I will keep your pictures here in my office in this file . . . When life goes better and when you and I have finished seeing each other, then I will give the file, with all of the pictures, back to you. (p. 27)

Allan observed that some children do not require these instructions. They arrive at the first therapy session, see the drawing materials, and spontaneously begin their work. For these clients, he recommended that clinicians use a nondirective approach. For more withdrawn or reluctant children, clinicians can be more directive and ask the child to draw a particular picture (e.g., his or her family). Allan described a third approach, which he labeled "partially directive," that can be used with children who spontaneously draw an image that is relevant to the client's presenting problem. Every 4 to 6 weeks, the therapist asks the child to draw this image. Each new drawing is compared with the quality and content of previous images. Allan warned that clinicians should be cautious when interpreting children's drawings. He recommended that the symbols in a child's artwork be considered within the context of available case material, which includes the client's comments about the drawings. Some children are not interested in drawing or painting, so therapists must be prepared to use other creative activities, such as psychodrama, storytelling, and sandplay.

Dora Kalff (1980), a Swiss Jungian, described the therapeutic value of sandplay. Children choose from hundreds of miniature figures to create pictures in a sandtray that measures 57 × 72 × 7 cm. Kalff believed that a child's sand creation is a "three-dimensional representation of some aspect of his psychic situation" (p. 32). Clients select from miniatures that represent people from ancient and modern times, as well as an assortment of "wild and domestic animals, houses of different styles, trees, bushes, flowers, fences, traffic signals, cars, trains, old carriages, boats; in short everything which exists in the world as well as in fantasy" (p. 38). Collecting a varied assortment of miniatures can be both challenging and expensive. Therapists interested in using sandplay can follow the example of one of my students, who built her large collection of figures by visiting garage sales, flea markets, and toy and department stores when sales were advertised.

Jungians believe troubled children construct sand pictures to represent unconscious conflicts that originated in the early mother–infant relationship. Consequently, the therapeutic relationship is a crucial aspect of sandplay. Therapists help their clients develop by providing the trust and care that characterizes a healthy mother–infant relationship. Clinicians facilitate this relationship by being flexible and setting limits. As Kalff (1980) noted, "The child has absolute freedom in determining what to construct, which figures to choose and how to use them" (p. 39). Limits are provided in the form of the dimensional boundaries of the sandtray and the limited number of miniatures available to the child.

When a client has completed a sand picture, the therapist sometimes offers a symbolic interpretation that is appropriate to the child's developmental level. The Jungian approach to symbol interpretation is quite complex and is beyond the scope of our discussion. Students who are interested in learning more about the interpretation of sand pictures should consult Kalff's (1980) text, *Sandplay: A Psychotherapeutic Approach to the Psyche*. In this book, the author provides case materials and interpretations for nine clients, including 12-year-old Daniela, who entered treatment as a withdrawn, lonely child who was having social and academic problems at school. In her work with the child, Kalff combined sandplay, dream interpretation, and drawing with traditional talk therapy. Kalff (1980) described a series of six sand creations, starting with Daniela's first picture.

> During her first counseling session, Daniela created the following picture. She started, as she said, by letting cows graze in a fenced pasture. In front of the pasture was a coach that was pulled by two horses whose hooves were stuck deep in the sand. Directly in front of the horses a street was marked off, leading to an inn on the opposite side. A man was walking towards the inn. By the street, under a tree was a bench for resting. (p. 74)

Kalff believed the coach represented the child's life, which was at "a standstill" (p. 74). Interestingly, the horses' hooves were stuck near the cows, which Kalff described as a motherly symbol associated with Daniela's home life. The man in front of the inn was thought to represent the child's outer world. Because the inn was on the opposite side of the sandtray from the coach, Kalff interpreted this placement as meaning that the child's "path into the world seemed long and tiring" (p. 74).

Now let us compare Daniela's first sand picture with her last.

> On an airfield, airplanes were standing ready to take off, ships rode at anchor ready to sail away, a mail coach and a car stood ready to start and a train was on a point of beginning to move. (p. 82)

Here impending movement suggests that the child is ready to grow and individuate from her family. Jungians would view this movement as the emergence of Daniela's control over her psychic development. Kalff integrated multiple sand pictures into Daniela's treatment similar to the way that Allan uses children's artwork in his serial drawing technique. As noted previously, therapists must acquire specialized training before they offer Jungian interpretations of children's drawings and sandplay creations. This includes having a thorough understanding of Jungian theory and obtaining supervised experience with these methods.

Individual Psychology

Adlerian therapists intervene using individual and group interventions with children, family approaches designed to help parents become more effective in rearing their offspring, and school-based programs designed to enhance learning. Clinicians select their interventions after considering a number of factors, including the age and developmental level of the child. Dinkmeyer et al. (1987) noted that Adlerians tend to treat the problems of younger children by interviewing parents or teachers, and they typically reserve individual or group work for young clients who have the requisite verbal skills. A common focus of treatment is the child's mistaken goals. In their work with significant others, therapists foster awareness of these goals and encourage parents and teachers to use encouragement as a means of redirecting discouraged, misbehaving children. When they counsel children, Adlerians facilitate awareness of mistaken goals by helping clients "see that it is to their benefit to operate with, rather than against, their parents (or teachers)" (Dinkmeyer et al., 1987, p. 138).

Similar to other proponents of psychodynamic theory, Adlerians use children's play as a therapeutic tool (Yura & Galassi, 1974). Therapists are interested in the purpose of children's behavior, and they believe that play offers important information about children's goals. For example, a client whose goals are mistaken might strike or throw toys at the clinician (i.e., seeking revenge), passively resist engaging in play activities (i.e., demonstrating inadequacy), or test the limits in therapy (i.e., demonstrating power). Play is thought to represent the expression of a child's style of life; therefore, it provides insight into a client's preferences later in life (Adler, 1927/1954). A child who plays endlessly with toy cars and trucks may become a mechanic, truck driver, or mechanical engineer. A student who organizes play during group games may work in management as an adult. Play also provides a glimpse into children's social interests. For example, how children play with each other reveals their "capacity to give and take" (Dinkmeyer & McKay, 1973, p. 29) and their willingness to consider the welfare of others.

Yura and Galassi (1974) described how Adlerians use play materials with young clients. In their work with an aggressive 5-year-old boy, the authors used puppets to enact disagreements. Having the child role-play classmates who were the recipients of his aggression seemed to give him a new appreciation for their points of view and helped him behave more appropriately with his peers. In another case, Yura and Galassi used a miniature dollhouse and doll family to learn about a 6-year-old boy's family constellation. The youngest of three children, Michael enacted a "helpless and dependent child" (p. 198) in play. During treatment, the boy used the dolls to explore new ways of interacting with members of his family. For example, he had the doll portraying him "do some things for himself—for instance, pretend mamma is busy and the other children are out" (p. 198). According to the authors, Michael became less dependent on others as he began to work toward goals that he set for himself.

Rudolf Dreikurs (1948) believed that children's problems are really "problems of a disturbed parent-child relationship" (p. 289). He wrote extensively about techniques that parents can use to become more effective in guiding and encouraging their children. Dreikurs' approach is psychoeducational, with the therapist functioning as the teacher who helps parents become more objective observers of their child's behavior and more astute at interpreting the purpose of that behavior. Dreikurs recommended a variety of democratic child-rearing methods, including the use of encouragement, logical consequences, and the Family Council.

To be effective, parents must encourage discouraged children. Dreikurs (1964) described this task as "more important than any other aspect of child-raising" (p. 36). Parents can encourage a child through what they say and how they say it. By repeatedly communicating respect for the child's ability to accomplish developmentally appropriate tasks, parents facilitate self-confidence and growth-enhancing purposive behavior in the child. They can accomplish these goals by using a developmental approach to child rearing in which age-appropriate challenges are given to children and success is acknowledged.

Consider the message that the parent communicates in the following example:

> Ethel, five, was happily struggling to make her bed. Pulling the covers this way and that, she finally got them up where she wanted them. Mother came into the room, saw the imperfectly made bed, and said, "I'll make the bed, honey. Those covers are too heavy for you." (Dreikurs, 1964, p. 47)

This parent failed to focus on the child's accomplishments and applied a success criterion that is probably more appropriate for an adolescent or adult. If this interaction is repeated, we might expect Ethel to become discouraged and decide to leave bed making to her mother, who happens to be more competent with such tasks.

Dreikurs believed that parents must establish age-appropriate limits and consequences for their children. He presented his concepts of natural and logical consequences as alternatives to the reward and punishment that parents often use (Dreikurs, 1964). A natural consequence is based on the laws of nature and is the result of what Dreikurs and Grey (1968) called "ill-advised acts" (p. 63). The natural consequence of losing your footing while climbing a tree is that gravity will cause you to fall. A child who refuses to eat dinner will later experience hunger. Logical consequences, on the other hand, are those that parents or significant others arrange to provide limits for children. The outcome is not simply the result of a child's actions (e.g., losing one's footing), but can be found in the "if A, then B" relationships that caregivers establish for children.

Consider a family in which the parents tell their child they will launder her dirty clothes only if these items are placed in the clothes hamper. The child who is informed of this relationship in advance and who decides to not comply will experience the logical consequence of not having clean clothes to wear. According to Dreikurs (1964), the use of logical consequences requires "a reorientation of our thinking" (p. 84) because the parents' function is no longer that of punishing the child. A democratic approach to child rearing requires that the parent help the child understand the relationship between behavior and consequences. As children learn this connection, they become better prepared to make the increasingly complex decisions they will encounter as adolescents and adults.

Dreikurs (1964) described Allen, a 10-year-old boy who loses his baseball mitt. Although some parents might respond by yelling or lecturing the child about responsibility, Dreikurs recommended the following as a way of helping the boy understand how he could appropriately exert personal power to bring about change (i.e., obtain a new mitt):

> Daddy can say, "I'm awfully sorry you lost your mitt, Allen." "But, I've *got* to have a mitt," Allen explodes. "Do you have the money for a new one?" "No—but you could give it to me." "You will get your regular allowance at the regular time." "But that's not enough!" "Sorry, but there is nothing I can do." Daddy must remain firm, although friendly. (pp. 83–84)

Allen learns that his behavior is important. Although he did lose his baseball glove, he is able to overcome this failure by saving his allowance and maybe doing extra work around the house to earn the money needed to buy a new mitt.

Dreikurs, Gould, and Corsini (1974) described the Family Council as a way for family members to meet at regularly scheduled times to openly discuss issues relevant to their day-to-day lives. Dreikurs (1964) recommended that families set aside 1 hour every week when all members convene to address concerns in an egalitarian interaction where "the parents' voices are no higher or stronger than that of each child" (p. 301). A chairperson is chosen to coordinate the meeting and to ensure that all members have the opportunity to express their opinions. The role of chairperson rotates among the family from one meeting to the next, so no individual develops greater control over the group. During each meeting, participants discuss family matters that concern them. Decisions regarding family rules are made based on consensus agreement, not simply majority opinion, and the entire family agrees to follow whatever rules are adopted for the upcoming week. Rules may not be changed until the next Family Council, when members can express their dissatisfaction with previous decisions and discuss revisions to existing rules.

Dreikurs et al. (1974) offered the following dialogue from a Family Council meeting during which a mother expresses concern that her children walk in the front door wearing muddy shoes. She recommends that everyone enter the house by the kitchen door. The family then discusses her suggestion:

> DAVID But other people come in the front door. They might have mud on their shoes. Would you say "Go around to the back" to them?
>
> GAIL And the same thing for you or Daddy?
>
> MOTHER You mean guests?
>
> GAIL Right. And they may have muddier feet than we do.
>
> DAVID Yeah—they might by accident have mud all over them.
>
> FATHER I think we might be able to solve part of the problem by putting a piece of carpet down there to wipe our feet on.
>
> DAVID Until they get clean.
>
> GAIL I think we can take off our shoes.
>
> MOTHER Alright, I'll tell you what. I'll be willing to try it for one week, and we'll discuss it next week if it seems to be a problem. Is that OK with everybody? (pp. 39–40)

In this example, all family members contributed ideas and agreed to follow their plan until the next meeting, when they could discuss changes to the rule. The benefits of Family Council meetings often extend beyond the weekly rules that members adopt. In some families, the Family Council is the only time when all members are together and focused on a common task. The meetings provide opportunities to build relationships, communicate concern and understanding for others, and learn group decision-making skills.

PLAY TECHNIQUES

As discussed previously, play therapy for children originated with the work of Melanie Klein and Anna Freud. Each of these master clinicians entered the playroom with a distinctly different view on therapy. For example, Klein (1927/1975) believed that children's play is similar to free association in adults and should be used to address clients' negative transference. Anna Freud (1946) held a different view on these matters and chose to emphasize the therapeutic benefits of a positive therapist–client relationship. Although they disagreed on important matters related to the treatment of children, these pioneers in the field of play therapy established the foundation on which proponents of other theories of therapy would devise developmentally appropriate interventions for children.

Early writers treated children in a practice environment that was very different from what clinicians now encounter. As discussed, Klein (1932/1959) used lengthy treatment with clients. Although many psychodynamic therapists adopted this model, there are such exceptions as Winnicott's (1977) on-demand method. If psychodynamic play therapy is to remain a viable option for children, brief and effective methods are required. Warren and Messer (1999) cited three reasons why brief psychodynamic interventions are needed. As discussed in Chapter 3, relatively few clients continue in therapy past the tenth session. The economic constraints imposed by managed health care companies also limit the number of sessions that most clients can receive. Additionally, Warren and Messer described how brief treatments are appropriate for many children because the normal developmental process is a therapeutic ally for the remediation of less severe problems.

Chapter 3 discussed the selection of clients and the identification of treatment goals in brief therapy. Warren and Messer (1999) observed that candidates for these treatments should have less severe problems, supportive family and social environments, and life histories devoid of abuse and neglect. Children must also be able to establish working relationships with their therapists in a timely manner. Clients whose parents are exhibiting psychopathology and are themselves displaying significant problems related to childhood trauma that are impeding their child's development are less likely to benefit from a brief intervention. Warren and Messer emphasized the role of parents in brief psychodynamic therapy. Because of the limited number of contacts with the child, therapists must involve parents to ensure their commitment and to offer information, support, and encouragement throughout the treatment process.

Psychodynamic therapists have developed play techniques that are appropriate for time-limited interventions. For example, Warren and Messer (1999) described a brief psychodynamic therapy for anxious children. The authors developed an unstructured play technique that incorporates Winnicott's (1965) concepts of the holding environment and transitional objects. The therapist functions as "an optimal parental figure" (p. 229) in play sessions with the child, providing emotional support for the child, who is permitted to explore anxiety-related topics without fear of adult punishment. Warren and Messer used their treatment with a 4-year-old girl who was wetting the bed, overeating, and being resistant at bedtime. Important elements in this case were the parents' separation and the father's absence from the home. In session, the child was allowed to engage in free play with materials (e.g., human figures, a play house) the clinician had previously selected to facilitate the exploration of family issues. The authors noted significant improvement after about 10 play sessions with the child and consultation with the mother.

Sloves and Peterlin (1993) described a structured play method in which clinicians impose limits by selecting play materials and planning the content of each session "to hurry the therapy along without frightening the child into passivity, active resistance, or flight" (p. 304). At the outset of treatment, families are asked to sign a contract in which they agree to attend a specified number of sessions. The contract also contains a brief and concrete description of the clinician's formulation of the central theme for the presenting problem. Therapeutic play is structured around this theme. For example, before session, the clinician arranges toys in a theme-related scene to facilitate the exploration of relevant issues. In their account of structured play with a 9-year-old boy, Sloves and Peterlin described how children sometimes reject the prepared scene. In these situations, the therapist must follow the client's lead and adopt alternative methods for integrating thematic material. This includes having children bring favorite toys from home that can be used to explore the central theme. Sloves and Peterlin identified a more important obstacle to treatment when they acknowledged that clinicians who prefer extended, unstructured therapeutic contacts with children may have difficulty using the authors' method.

GROUP TECHNIQUES

Kernberg and Chazan (1991) described a therapeutic play group based on ego psychology and object relations theory. The authors used this method so clients could develop self-regulation, understand that other children have different views, and practice more effective social skills with their peers. Their group also gave clients the opportunity to receive emotional support from other children. Acceptance from peers and the therapist contradicts a child's dysfunctional object relations and requires revisions of these early mental representations of interpersonal relationships. During weekly sessions with three to six children, co-therapists work with same-gender groups of similar-age elementary school students in treatment for different behavior problems. Kernberg and Chazan used co-therapists for two reasons. First, they wanted to have sufficient leadership to ensure the safety of children in the group. The authors also used this approach because they believed the co-therapists could model a healthy interpersonal relationship for clients who were having problems interacting with their peers.

Prout and Brown (1999, p. 136) described Adlerian principles as a "natural" for group therapies with children. Interactions with peers that foster constructive attitudes and behaviors are consistent with Adler's concept of social interest (Ansbacher & Ansbacher, 1970). Wick, Wick, and Peterson (1997) used Adlerian principles in an adventure therapy for fifth grade students. Their action-oriented method included cooperative and noncompetitive play activities designed to improve clients' self-esteem and develop their sensitivity to the needs of others. For example, the authors used the trust fall, in which a child falls backwards into the arms of group members, and the trust walk, in which a child is blindfolded and led through an obstacle course by other members. Wick et al. conducted a pretest-posttest evaluation of their six-session program and found significant improvement in children's self-esteem. Their results suggest that group play based on Adlerian principles can be therapeutic when children are asked to work together and help each other.

RESEARCH

Fonagy (1999) described the conflicting results that researchers have reported on the outcome of psychodynamic therapies for children. He observed that the results of existing studies have been compromised by methodological problems, such as the lack of randomization in treatment assignment and the use of small samples and measures with questionable psychometric properties. If psychodynamic treatments are to be accepted in an era of managed mental health care and empirically supported brief therapies, investigators must study these methods using research designs that control for extraneous variables and isolate the therapeutic components of these interventions. A popular focus in studies on psychodynamic therapies with children is the impact of the length of treatment. We now consider three examples of this work.

Heinicke and Ramsey-Klee (1986) examined the outcome of treatment length in their study of 7- to 10-year-old boys in psychoanalytic therapy for different problems, including anxiety and attention-deficit hyperactivity disorder (ADHD). Clients were seen either once a week or four times a week for periods of time ranging from 19 to 42 months. The authors reported that children who were seen more frequently exhibited better academic and psychosocial adjustment after treatment. Unfortunately, the Heinicke and Ramsey-Klee study contains a number of methodological problems that limit the interpretation and generalizability of the results. The most obvious limitation is the sample size. The authors treated only 12 boys, with 4 clients in each of three therapy conditions. Critics might also question the length of treatment used in this study and the relevance of these findings in a practice environment where brief therapies are common.

Smyrnios and Kirkby (1993) compared two lengths of psychodynamic therapy with a minimal contact condition that involved one to three assessment interviews, a feedback session, and a follow-up interview. Psychodynamic therapy was either brief (M = 10.5 sessions) or unlimited (M = 27.7 sessions) and included a follow-up session. The authors randomly assigned children, ages 5 to 9 years, to one of the three conditions. Treatment involved weekly play therapy for the child clients and less frequent psychodynamic- and family systems–oriented sessions for parents. When Smyrnios and Kirkby examined their results, they found that longer therapy was not necessarily the more effective intervention. In general, the brief therapy, unlimited therapy, and minimal contact conditions were all found to produce similar improvement in children's behavior.

Chapter 5 discussed the work of Weiss, Catron, Harris, and Phung (1999), who conducted a controlled evaluation of unlimited therapy that lasted an average of 60 sessions. This clinic-based study involved 132 children who were randomly assigned to either traditional psychotherapy or an attention-control condition of academic tutoring that involved an average of 53 sessions. When the authors compared clients' scores on various standardized measures (e.g., Child Behavior Checklist, Teacher Report

Form), they found pretreatment-posttreatment improvement regardless of treatment condition. Although it is possible that tutors engaged in informal therapy with students and contributed to the lack of between-group differences, Weiss et al. found no evidence for this based on ratings of audiotapes from randomly selected tutoring sessions.

Compared with other treatments (e.g., behavioral), relatively little data-based research has been conducted on psychodynamic interventions. A number of reasons have been cited for the dearth of empirical support for these methods. Here we consider three: the diverse nature of psychodynamic interventions, theorists' and therapists' interests in abstract concepts, and limited diversity in research methodologies.

One impediment to research has been the number of variants that are available on the psychodynamic theme (Marans, 1989). Consider the theoretical and practical differences between Freud's psychosexual stages and Jung's archetypes, as well as Winnicott's concept of good-enough parenting and Adler's description of purposive behavior. Researchers must set aside the unrealistic goal of studying the psychodynamic approach in general in favor of more focused investigations of specific interventions. A particularly important area for study is the therapeutic process and outcome of psychodynamic strategies for children of diverse cultural backgrounds. The results of these studies could expand the applicability of psychodynamic theory beyond its traditional focus on "the white, middle-class norm of a nuclear family" (Okun, 1990, p. 107).

A second impediment to data-based studies of psychodynamic therapies is the attention that theorists and practitioners have given to abstract concepts, such as the superego and archetypes. Critics have questioned the value of these constructs because they are difficult to define in a manner that permits empirical investigation. A related limitation is the different ways that practitioners have applied these concepts in clinical practice (Wachtel & Messer, 1997). How therapists define *ego*, for example, influences their selection of intervention strategies. Researchers face the challenge of selecting and studying treatments they believe to be most appropriate for a particular theoretical construct.

Research on these therapies suffers from a lack of methodological diversity. As Wachtel and Messer (1997) stated, the study of therapeutic interventions requires the use of different research methods. Proponents of psychodynamic treatments for children have relied more on the case study approach than traditional experimental designs. Although in-depth descriptions of individual cases can provide enlightening information about the process and outcome of therapy, controlled comparisons of psychodynamic treatments, therapies based on other theories, and no-treatment and attention-control conditions are sorely needed. In the future, researchers must capitalize on the strengths of different research designs to achieve a more balanced study of psychodynamic interventions with children.

INTERVENTION TARGET

Role of the Parent

Beginning with Sigmund Freud, psychodynamic theorists and therapists have recognized the important role that parents play in their children's development. Obviously, Freud relied on Little Hans' parents, particularly the father, in his consultative approach with the boy. Hans' father was uniquely qualified to work with his son because he understood psychoanalytic principles, having previously been in analysis himself (Freud, 1909/1956). He also had a working relationship with the boy and was knowledgeable of the child's past. Hug-Hellmuth (1921) recommended therapist–parent interaction to prevent premature termination of a child's treatment. She believed that parents sometimes "expect a 'miraculous cure' which shall remedy in the course of days the mistakes of years" (p. 302). Through their contacts with parents, clinicians can obtain relevant information about the child and convince parents that they have a significant influence on the therapeutic process and the child's development.

Melanie Klein (1932/1959) believed that the amount of contact with parents should vary according to the needs of the client. She described how some parents are ambivalent about having their child undergo therapy. For example, a father may recognize the need for professional help but postpone treatment because it constitutes an acknowledgment of his failure as a parent. We must remember that Klein abandoned the role of parent consultant in favor of child analyst. She believed analysis is "a purely personal matter between myself and my patient" (p. 118), so she avoided giving parents information about what occurred during the child's analytic hour. When she did interact with parents, her purpose was usually that of obtaining reports about the child's behavior outside of therapy.

Anna Freud (1946) stated that clinicians "must know the people in (the child's) environment and be sure to some extent of what their reactions to the child are" (p. 36). This is especially true at the outset of treatment, when it is the parents, not the child, who are able to provide a detailed developmental history and pertinent information regarding the problems that prompted treatment. A unique aspect of Anna Freud's work at the Hampstead Nurseries during World War II was her observation of mothers' contacts with their children and the nursery staff. Under the extreme conditions of wartime, she and her colleagues observed parents' ambivalence about seeking professional assistance. For example, a mother may view leaving her child at the nursery:

> as a fulfillment of her unconscious desire to get rid of her child. In that case she will be unable to stand the situation. She will disregard all reasons against it, will use the slightest pretexts to explain her decision to herself and will enforce re-union with the child so as to be re-assured about her own love for it. (A. Freud & Burlingham, 1945, p. 174)

Although the conflict between conscious and unconscious feelings may be less pronounced in outpatient settings, therapists must recognize parents' ambivalence as a potential obstacle to treatment.

Alfred Adler and his disciples emphasized parents' role in children's development. Adlerians treat children individually and in groups, but they are also recognized for their work in parent education. In their contacts with parents, clinicians strive to foster "the relationship between parent and child by making more alternatives available and by promoting greater understanding and acceptance" (Dinkmeyer et al., 1987, p. 319). As the name implies, therapists who provide parent education may have little or no contact with the child. Instead, they conduct group sessions to teach mothers and fathers to understand the goals of their child's behavior. After this is accomplished, parents are encouraged to identify and facilitate alternative and more appropriate behaviors the child can use to achieve these goals.

Clearly, psychodynamic writers have viewed parents in different ways. Some have focused their attention primarily on the parents by serving as consultants (e.g., Freud) or instructors (e.g., Adler) for parent education groups. Others (e.g., Klein) were more child focused and chose to limit their contacts with parents consistent with the needs of the client. As a general rule, therapists must remember that children depend on their parents for many things, including food, shelter, and emotional support. Therefore, the question is not if parents will be contacted, but how often, for what purpose, and in what context.

Role of the Child

Psychodynamic interventions for children cover a broad spectrum that involves different forms of client participation. Little Hans had very limited contact with Freud, who consulted with the father about the boy's treatment. The play techniques described by Klein (1932/1959) and Anna Freud (1946) allow children to participate in therapy without saying a word. The creative strategies developed by Kalff (1980), Winnicott (1971), and Allan (1988) provide stimuli for client verbalization. With these techniques, psychodynamic therapy can be adjusted to the needs and disposition of the child. A shy and withdrawn client can communicate with the therapist through play. Verbal clients can share thoughts and feelings during one-on-one conversations with the clinician or in conjunction with play or creative activities.

Psychodynamic writers have described how children transfer their feelings onto clinicians. Transference can be either nonverbal, such as resisting eye contact with the therapist, or verbal, which can include angry comments directed at the clinician. As discussed earlier, psychodynamic therapists often use interpretation with children. For this to be helpful, clients must listen and integrate interpretive material with their view of themselves and the world. Children can enhance the therapeutic benefits of interpretation by discussing recent experiences from home, school, and the neighborhood. They also provide relevant information about past experiences and their goals for the future.

Role of the Therapist

Children rarely initiate treatment on their own, so the clinician's first challenge is to engage the child in the therapeutic process. As Anna Freud (1946) noted, therapists must foster positive transference from young clients as "the prerequisite for all later work" (p. 31). Although the best method for achieving this goal varies from one child to the next, clinicians are more likely to succeed if they imagine themselves as children and picture an adult who would have helped them feel comfortable in sessions. This person probably has a sincere smile, a caring voice, and eyes that communicate interest. Therapists can foster this therapeutic image by joining the child in a modification of what Parten (1932) called parallel play. The clinician and client play separately using similar toys while the therapist poses questions or makes comments to encourage the child's disclosure of significant thoughts and feelings.

As Hug-Hellmuth (1921) cautioned, clinicians should avoid prohibitive statements with young clients. First, such statements do little to create a supportive and caring environment for therapy. Second, these statements foster the emergence of negative transference from the client, who then responds to the clinician as punitive parent. When therapists interpret children's play, they are wise to remember Winnicott's (1971) comment that it is the child who determines the validity of any interpretation. How and when the clinician shares an impression is probably as important as its content or meaning. A therapist who interprets a child's play and then defends this statement in response to the client's objections does little to enhance the therapeutic relationship. Instead, the clinician should withdraw the interpretation, revise the wording, and deliver the thought at a more appropriate point in treatment.

Role of the School

As we discussed earlier, there is a long-standing connection between psychodynamic theory and educational methods. Freud (1933/1964) appreciated this relationship, but his daughter Anna actually adapted his model for the classroom. Alfred Adler was another advocate for educational applications of psychodynamic theory. Since the 1920s, Adler's principles have been used to develop democratic classrooms and enhance students' social interest and skills (Kelly, 1999). Adlerians believe that educators should expand their vision beyond academic goals to include the overall psychosocial-educational development of the child. Because of their overlapping responsibilities, teachers and therapists are able to collaborate on behalf of troubled children; therefore, the atmosphere in the democratic classroom complements the work done in therapy.

Sweeney (1998) described the steps that educators should take to transform an autocratic classroom into a democratic learning environment. These include involving students at an appropriate developmental level in the design and implementation of disciplinary systems in schools. Teachers must strive for mutual trust, respect, and cooperation in the classroom to prepare students for adult life in a democratic society. These qualities are also important characteristics for effective therapist–teacher collaboration on behalf of students. All children, including those in therapy, can benefit from supportive learning environments in which the development and pursuit of goals are encouraged. Adlerians have developed methods and materials that teachers and clinicians can use for this purpose. We previously discussed the STEP program, which Dinkmeyer and McKay (1976) developed as an instructional tool for teaching democratic child rearing. We now examine two related programs, one for children and another for teachers: Developing Understanding of Self and Others (DUSO) (Dinkmeyer & Dinkmeyer, 1982) and Systematic Training for Effective Teaching (STET) (Dinkmeyer et al., 1980).

Dinkmeyer and Dinkmeyer (1982) designed DUSO for individual and group work with children. The program contains pictures and stories that serve as concrete stimuli for enhancing students' awareness of themselves and their relationships with others. Clinicians use DUSO to help children become more proficient in basic communication skills, such as empathy and the expression of feelings (Dinkmeyer, Dinkmeyer, & Sperry, 1987). Dinkmeyer et al. (1980) developed their STET program to train teachers in the use of Adlerian principles in democratic classrooms. The STET program typically involves 14 sessions with small groups of teachers who practice democratic educational strategies, such as encouraging students. Although the STET techniques are appropriate for students who misbehave, they also offer a method for establishing a more student-centered learning environment in which children are motivated to develop their innate abilities.

A major concern for many teachers is maintaining discipline in the classroom. Dreikurs, Grunwald, and Pepper (1982) approached this issue from a student's point of view by developing techniques to encourage self-discipline. The authors recommended that teachers encourage children to respect themselves and others and to cooperate with those around them. Defined in this way, discipline is very different from the aversive techniques used to control children. The benefits of engaging a child in the disciplinary process is illustrated in the case of 10-year-old Mason, who was placed in a special learning environment because of inappropriate behavior. Although he improved significantly, he continued to speak out in class without raising his hand. When the teacher asked him to recommend a solution for this problem,

Mason suggested, "Each time I talk out loud without raising my hand, I will have to leave the room for two minutes and make up my time later" (Dreikurs et al., 1982, p. 85). His behavior improved within 1 week. By having Mason participate in decisions about classroom disciplinary procedures, the teacher communicated respect for him and was successful in remediating the disruptive behavior.

Clark (1995) described the program he developed to enhance social interest in children. This school-based intervention is designed to encourage problem solving, helping others, and nonviolent resolution of interpersonal conflict. Students participate in class discussions designed to enhance mutual support and encouragement in schools. Children volunteer in the community and raise funds for charitable organizations, and they help at school by cleaning or decorating their classroom and becoming peer tutors for other students. Therapists who endorse the multimodal approach described in Chapter 1 can use programs such as Clark's to help clients accomplish educational/developmental and preventive goals in treatment. Without the active participation of teachers and other school personnel, democratic classrooms and social interest programs will not exist. When these Adlerian techniques are implemented, clinicians can incorporate them into a collaborative intervention with the school.

CONTRIBUTIONS AND LIMITATIONS

The most important contribution from early proponents of psychodynamic therapies for children is their successful adaptation of the principles of adult analysis for young clients. Instead of being the dangerous experiment that some had predicted, child analysis became the foundation for decades of progress in individual, group, and family treatments. Hug-Hellmuth, Klein, and Anna Freud recognized that children are not miniature adults, so they set aside traditional talk therapy in favor of developmentally appropriate techniques that could be used with preschoolers and elementary school students. The breadth of the psychodynamic school is reflected in the work of others, such as Adler and Winnicott, who emphasized the role of parents in the lives of children.

Another contribution of psychodynamic theory is its emphasis on early childhood experiences. If the problems of adolescence and adulthood are rooted in the earliest years of life, then childhood represents an important time for multimodal and multidisciplinary interventions. Therapists can offer education/ development, prevention, and remediation for children, parents, teachers, and significant others in the child's life. Some writers have used nontraditional settings for the delivery of these services. Adler and Anna Freud, for example, expanded the boundaries beyond the confines of the therapist's office to include the school classroom and residential facilities for children. Adler also expanded clinicians' temporal perspective when he refocused attention from problems in the client's past to the child's goals for the future.

Although psychodynamic theorists have recognized the importance of the parent–child relationship, they have given little attention to systemic influences. Children are indeed their parents' offspring, but they are also members of a family, residents of a neighborhood, students of a school, and members of an ethnic group. If psychodynamic theory is to be relevant for children in a multicultural society, theorists must consider how young people develop in the context of their cultural surround. Practitioners and researchers must work together to design interventions that address systemic factors that are important to children's development.

We have already discussed how the lack of empirical research represents a major limitation for the psychodynamic approaches. It is crucial that investigators collect such evidence, especially in the current practice environment where therapists are held accountable for the outcome of their work. Contemporary practitioners are expected to be effective and efficient, which often requires therapeutic results in a relatively brief period of time. If psychodynamic approaches are to remain viable options for children, researchers must examine the process and outcome as well as the efficacy and effectiveness of these interventions when delivered in a time-limited format.

A significant limitation of psychodynamic theory is the sexist constructs that writers have used, such as the good-enough mother, and their endorsement of a male model of normal development (e.g., "penis envy"). One example of the restrictive aspects of these stereotypes is Freud's (1933/1964) belief that women are somehow better suited than men for the field of child psychoanalysis. Fortunately, he was wrong, but other psychoanalytic writers have reinforced sexist beliefs, especially in the area of child rearing, in which mothers are often portrayed as the parent responsible for what children are and what they become. Greater attention must be given to the father's role as parent. As Cox, Owen, Henderson, and Margand (1992) reported, infants can attach to either parent if he or she is caring and sensitive. Psychodynamic interventions with children must endorse an expanded view of parenting in which fathers and mothers are seen as important participants in the child-rearing process. As Luepnitz (1988) stated, "The father must be a real member of the family, neither its head nor its foot soldier, neither its backup nor its shadow, but a lover of children, a person capable of both work and friendship" (p. 24).

PSYCHODYNAMIC INTERVENTIONS: A CASE EXAMPLE

Every year, millions of parents separate, divorce, or remarry. Many writers have focused on the negative reactions (e.g., depression, anxiety, conduct problems) that children sometimes exhibit in response to these changes, but marital transitions are stressful for both parents and children (King, 1992). Therapists and others often focus on the divorce itself without considering the experiences that precede and follow the event. Clinicians who have this restricted view tend to conceptualize a child's post-divorce adjustment as a reaction to a single incident rather than the response to a sequence of experiences. Of course, divorce is a distinct point in time when a husband and wife legally end their marital relationship, but many children anticipate this change after observing months or years of overt spousal discord. Others are surprised, even shocked, to learn that their parents are separating after what appeared to be a happy marriage.

The events that occur after a divorce also affect the lives of parents and children. Hetherington, Stanley-Hagan, and Anderson (1989), for example, reported that 80% of fathers and 75% of mothers remarry and that remarried couples are more likely to divorce than are first-marrieds. As a result, many children are expected to adjust to marital transitions other than their biological parents' divorce. Another complicating factor is that divorce does not necessarily bring an end to spousal discord. The post-divorce period sometimes involves continued conflicts, which can have a greater impact on a child's adjustment than do the structural changes (e.g., parents living in separate homes) related to divorce (Emery, 1988).

Therapists who work with these children must consider a number of clinically relevant issues. First, they must remember that no two children, even in the same family, will react to marital transitions in the same manner. Clinicians also need to understand the custody arrangements that legally define where children live and the conditions under which they have contact with their noncustodial parent. Although judges have often awarded custody to mothers, based on the "tender years doctrine" (i.e., young children belong with their mother), this has not always been true. Until 1839, children were automatically placed in the father's custody because they were considered to be his property (Blau, 1984). More recently, judges in many states have chosen to award joint custody, which allows mothers and fathers to share in the rearing of their children. Joint custody is also intended to give children more equal access to their parents.

Any discussion of child custody must include mention of the difference between *de jure* and *de facto* custody. The former constitutes "the official legal assignment of decision-making responsibility for the child" (Depner, 1994, p. 101). *De facto* custody represents the actual division of time and labor that parents adopt in raising their children. The legal distribution of child-rearing responsibilities is not always identical to what parents actually practice. The hypothetical case of Jeanne described at the beginning of this chapter is one example. Although the child's father was awarded regular visitation with his daughter, he failed to exercise this privilege. *De facto* custody can change during the post-divorce years. The shifting family structures (e.g., living arrangement, rules) associated with these changes can affect a child's development and should be a focal issue in therapy.

We now examine the case of Jeanne to illustrate the use of psychodynamic principles and techniques with a child of divorced parents. The client's interactions with her therapist, Mr. Thompson, and his responses to her are based in part on case descriptions that Oclander (1993) provided for her brief-term psychoanalytic counseling with children of divorce. As you read this case, notice how the clinician integrates object relations theory (Winnicott, 1971) into treatment. He hypothesizes that during infancy, Jeanne lacked the warm and secure holding environment that children need for healthy development. The therapist provides psychological holding by establishing a supportive, consistent, and predictable environment for the child. One aspect of this approach is his use of Allan's (1988) serial drawing technique to help the client visually portray her world. Notice how the clinician strives to develop a therapeutic relationship by fostering positive transference from the child (A. Freud, 1946) and accepting her reactions to his interpretations (Winnicott, 1971). After rapport is established, he uses the therapeutic relationship to help Jeanne work through feelings of anger, frustration, and guilt (Erikson, 1950). Although he addresses past and present concerns, Mr. Thompson also relies on Adlerian theory to explore the purposive nature of the child's behavior and help her plan for the future.

▪ ▪ ▪

Mr. Thompson conducts his assessment session with the mother alone so he can collect background information about the family and the presenting problem. Although he wanted to have the father present, this was not possible because Mr. Harris had told his ex-wife that he did not want to participate in treatment. During the interview, the mother reports that she and her husband "fought about something, usually sex or money, almost every day" of their married life. "We still argue a lot," she adds, "mostly on the telephone when I try to get him to spend time with Jeanne." She states that Mr. Harris has never developed a relationship with his daughter. Although he lives and works within 15 miles of Jeanne's house, he has not seen her for at least 6 months. Parenting appears to have been inconsistent, both before and after the divorce. Mr. Harris had an erratic work history throughout the 9-year marriage, so Ms. Harris always held at least a part-time job to help support the family. "My parents usually watch Jeanne when I'm at work," she says, "but I've also had friends and an aunt who've helped out when I needed them."

"How did you decide to get treatment for Jeanne at this time?" the therapist asks.

"Oh, the school recommended it months ago, but I guess I didn't want to admit that she was having problems." Ms. Harris describes how Jeanne's teacher, Mr. Lenson, and the school counselor, Ms. Kellner, encouraged her to seek professional help for the child. "Mr. Lenson says that Jeanne doesn't have any friends at school. I think it would be a good idea for you to talk with him to find out what's going on."

"I agree but I would like to meet with Jeanne first," Mr. Thompson answers. "I'd also like to talk with her father and encourage him to join us in session. How do you feel about that?"

"That's fine. I hope you have better luck with him than I have," she answers. Ms. Harris signs consent forms allowing the therapist to contact Mr. Harris, Jeanne's teacher, and the school counselor. Then she schedules an appointment for her daughter the following week.

When Jeanne enters Mr. Thompson's office, she walks around the room and inspects the play materials. She sees the artist's easel and says, "I'm a good drawer." She picks up a marker and asks, "What should I draw?"

"Whatever you want," the therapist answers.

Jeanne proceeds to sketch a doll, which she describes as the birthday gift she recently received from her grandparents. She immediately describes the party her mother and maternal grandparents gave her. When Mr. Thompson asks her to draw a picture of her family, she complies without hesitation. She sketches carefully and then identifies her mother, her maternal grandparents, and herself. When the therapist asks where her father is, she says, "He's not home because he has to work." During subsequent meetings, Jeanne offers a variety of reasons for her father's absence from her drawings and his lack of contact with her: "He lives far away," "He's busy," and "He forgets things a lot."

At the end of the session, Mr. Thompson says that he will save her drawings in a folder and that Jeanne and he will meet next week to draw and play. She assents to his plan to talk with her teacher and school counselor.

When Mr. Thompson telephones the school, he learns that Jeanne is having academic and social problems. Mr. Lenson describes her as "a quiet but angry child" who sometimes bites or hits other students without provocation. He volunteers to assist with her treatment and agrees to keep a daily log of her behavior. Ms. Kellner reports that Jeanne had similar problems in first grade, but her teacher, a woman with 24 years of classroom experience, was able to manage the situation. "I'm glad Ms. Harris contacted you," the counselor says. "You must talk with the grandparents. They'll help out in any way they can." Unfortunately, the same is not true for Jeanne's father. When Mr. Thompson speaks with him by telephone, he corroborates the mother's report about his attitude toward therapy.

At the outset of Jeanne's second session, she walks to the easel and spontaneously draws a large house with trees in the yard, flowers by the front door, and a big yellow sun in the sky. "That's no good," she says and abruptly tears off the sheet of paper and throws it on the floor.

"You don't think your picture was good enough for me?" Mr. Thompson asks. Jeanne ignores this question and begins to draw a second house. "Who lives in this house?"

"Nobody," Jeanne answers. "They didn't have any money, so they had to move."

When the therapist asks her to draw her family, she again draws her mother, her maternal grandparents, and herself. This time she volunteers that her father is "not home." Mr. Thompson interprets the drawing as a symbol of Jeanne's confusion about her relationship with her father. "No, He's just not home!" she shouts. The therapist accepts this response and encourages her to draw other pictures.

Over the course of 10 weekly sessions, Jeanne draws many pictures with diverse content. During her third session, for example, she sketches what appears to be an angry child who is screaming and holding her arms above her head. When the therapist asks if this is a picture of Jeanne, she responds, "No, it's my cousin. She's a cheerleader. She's gonna teach me to be one." The first time she includes her father in a family drawing is in the fourth session. The picture contains figures representing

Jeanne, her mother, and her grandparents grouped together on the left side of the page. Ms. Harris is pointing to the father, who is standing at the far right of the picture. "My Mommy and Daddy are fighting," she explains.

"About what?"

"Me." Jeanne then says that if she had not been a "bad girl," her parents would have never argued and divorced. When Mr. Thompson challenges this statement, Jeanne becomes visibly upset. "That's why my Dad doesn't come to see me," she says, "because I'm a bad girl." She tears her drawing from the easel, crumples it in her hands, and throws it at the therapist.

"It's OK to be angry, Jeanne," Mr. Thompson responds. "I think you're angry at your Dad." He pauses and then adds. "And sometimes maybe you're angry at your Mom or your grandparents or your teacher." Unlike her response to previous interpretations, Jeanne does not reject this idea.

When she returns for her fifth session, Jeanne is noticeably upset. Rather than walking to the easel, she stands in the center of the room and announces, "I don't want to come here anymore." She explains that because of her weekly trips to therapy, she is unable to watch her favorite afternoon television programs. Mr. Thompson remains silent as she recites a list of activities that would be "more fun than coming here." When she finishes, he interprets the wish to discontinue therapy as her fear that he cannot help her. He suggests that she is unsure about what to say in session because she does not want to anger him the way she believes she has upset her parents. Again, he reminds her that she is not to blame for her parents' divorce or her father's absence from her life. He tells her that he believes she wants him to become a part of her family but is afraid he will become angry and leave just as her father has done.

Jeanne listens intently and then walks to the easel and draws what appears to be an incomplete picture of her family. She stares at the drawing, mumbles, "I'm not coming here anymore," and leaves the room.

At one point during the next session, Jeanne says, "I like it here." Mr. Thompson interprets her previous wish to terminate therapy as an attempt to overcome the guilt and fear she experiences when she finds herself looking forward to therapy sessions. He elaborates by saying that Jeanne is afraid her mother will become jealous of the therapeutic relationship, feel rejected, and abandon her. "It's really confusing, isn't it?" he asks. She nods her head in agreement. "If we could wave a magic wand and make your life perfect, what would happen?"

"Have my Mommy and Daddy back home," she answers. Based on what he knows about the parents' relationship, Mr. Thompson recognizes this as a mistaken goal. He reflects how angry she must sometimes feel when her parents argue and give no sign of reconciling their relationship. He then says that he believes Jeanne abuses her classmates not because she is angry at them but because she is angry at her parents for getting divorced and at her father, specifically, for deserting her.

A very important part of the therapist's work in this case is preparing the child for the inevitable termination of treatment. Throughout therapy, Mr. Thompson strives to provide the safe and secure holding environment that Jeanne lacked as an infant. During the sixth session, he introduces the topic of termination by exploring the mistaken goals she adopts in her relationships with other children. He suggests that Jeanne may hurt other children so they will avoid her, thereby sparing her the pain of separation that accompanies the termination of a meaningful relationship. In the seventh session, the therapist and client talk more specifically about the end of therapy. Termination seems appropriate because Jeanne's academic work and her interactions with other students have improved. For example, the entries in Mr. Lenson's diary reveal that she has not struck or bitten anyone for approximately 1 month. In session, Jeanne talks more positively about herself and describes more realistic hopes for the future. She seems to understand that her parents will never reconcile and that she is not responsible for their decision to divorce. Although she continues to hope that her father will eventually play an active part of her life, she has begun to realize that it is "not fair" to project onto others the anger she feels toward him.

During the eighth session, Mr. Thompson reminds his client of an early discussion they had about the brief nature of therapy, which is intended to help children solve their problems. She immediately stops drawing, turns to him, and says, "I like coming here."

"I really look forward to seeing you each week," he answers, "and I feel good when I think about how well you are doing and how much happier you are. The saddest part of my job is getting to know kids, helping them, and then saying good-bye because they no longer need to see me."

Jeanne stares uncomfortably at him, then abruptly changes the topic by announcing, "I'm going to get a puppy." She approaches the easel and draws a picture of her family that includes a puppy standing beside her.

At the end of the session, Mr. Thompson meets with Jeanne and her mother. "Things seem to be going very well," he says. "Let's skip a week and schedule our next appointment for 2 weeks from today." Because he had previously addressed termination with Jeanne and her mother, both agree that skipping a week is a good idea. During the ninth session, Mr. Thompson learns that Jeanne continues to do well, so he recommends another 2-week interval and suggests that the tenth session be their last.

During the termination session, Jeanne talks about her new puppy as she draws pictures of the dog running in the yard. Her family drawing includes her, the new puppy, and her mother and grandparents taking a walk on the beach. When Mr. Thompson asks about her father, Jeanne says that she has not seen him and does not expect him to contact her soon. She mentions that she and her mother have been reading *The Boys and Girls Book About Divorce* (Gardner, 1970), which the therapist had given them earlier in treatment.

"That book says it's not my fault," Jeanne says.

"Not your fault."

"The divorce."

"That's right," Mr. Thompson says before they continue their discussion about the end of therapy.

Mr. Thompson has three additional "on demand" sessions with Jeanne and her mother. Two of these meetings occur during the weeks immediately before and after her eighth birthday. During the first session, Jeanne draws a picture of her upcoming birthday party. In it, she includes herself and five of her classmates, but no adults. The therapist interprets this drawing as a symbol of the child's anxiety about her father's role in the event. "Do you think he'll buy me a present?" she asks. Again, Mr. Harris does not send a gift or a card. When she returns the next week, Jeanne's behavior suggests that her anxiety was caused more by uncertainty about her father's response than it was his actual rejection of her. She describes the presents she received from her friends, her mother, and her grandparents, and she draws a picture depicting what she called a "really fun" party.

Months later Ms. Harris calls to schedule what she terms as "an insurance session" the week before the new school year. She was trying to get Jeanne excited about returning to school but was worried about her daughter's first day in class. During his session with the child, Mr. Thompson concludes that the mother has been successful in her efforts because the first picture Jeanne draws is of her walking into school. As she draws, she says, "I made all A's on my report card last year. I'm gonna do it again this year."

▪ ▪ ▪

In this hypothetical case, we focused on the clinician's interactions with Jeanne. We did not examine other aspects of his multidimensional intervention. For example, Mr. Thompson collaborated with the child's teacher and school counselor to address Jeanne's academic and behavioral problems. His efforts on the child's behalf included prevention and education/development strategies. When he learned that other students at school were the children of divorcing or divorced parents, he helped Ms. Kellner design a small-group intervention similar to the program described by Pedro-Carroll, Cowen, Hightower, and Guare (1986). As a result of her participation in this group, Jeanne realized that she was not the only child of divorced parents and that other children sometimes think they are responsible for their parents' marital turmoil. She was able to discuss divorce-related feelings with other students and to learn more effective methods for handling stressful situations.

Mr. Thompson also served as an advocate for children of divorce when he conducted a workshop for teachers and school administrators to make them more aware of children's perspectives on marital transitions (Cantor, 1982). This program helped Jeanne's teacher to understand that when she challenged him in the past, she was displacing her anger toward her father onto a convenient significant other man in her life. Mr. Thompson followed Ms. Kellner's suggestion and met with Ms. Harris and her parents to introduce them to an Adlerian approach to parenting. As a result of this intervention, he was able to establish a more consistent environment based on logical consequences and democratic child rearing (e.g., weekly Family Council meetings) that encouraged Jeanne to develop her innate talents and abilities.

Not all children will respond as well to the interventions used in this case. Some require more treatment sessions and others need fewer. Some children are less verbal than Jeanne, so clinicians need to rely more on therapeutic play and creative techniques. In some cases, both biological parents are interested in participating actively in treatment. In others, only one caregiver or a combination of biological parents and stepparents is involved. The case of Jeanne illustrates how various psychodynamic methods can be combined to form an integrated treatment. Other children require different combinations of techniques, including those based on other theories of therapy (see Chapter 16), that are designed to meet the unique needs of each child.

SUMMARY

Psychodynamic interventions with children represent a diverse set of techniques that are based on classical drive theory, object relations theory, ego psychology, analytical psychology, and individual psychology. These methods include therapeutic play and creative activities as well as traditional talk therapy for verbal children. Clinicians who embrace the psychodynamic orientation work with children, parents, and significant others in the child's life. The therapist's focus ranges from an interest in early life experiences to the child's goals for adolescence and adulthood. The long history and diverse nature of psychodynamic treatments provide the basis for educational/developmental, preventive, and remedial interventions for children.

8

Child-Centered Theory

In the middle of the 20th century, proponents of humanistic, or client-centered, theory were challenging the dominance of the psychodynamic model. This chapter examines how the transactional world view (Altman & Rogoff, 1987) that is reflected in the work of Carl Rogers and others has influenced both pedagogical and therapeutic techniques. It also discusses research findings on children's drawings, emotional awareness, and understanding of death concepts. Our review of relevant research also includes an examination of studies on the development of self-concept and self-esteem in children. In our discussion of multicultural considerations, we explore the role of gender and ethnic identity development. We begin with a brief review of the history of child-centered theory.

HISTORICAL BACKGROUND

Carl Rogers (1942a) traced the origins of his theory to psychoanalysts such as Otto Rank, Jesse Taft, and Frederick Allen. According to Lieberman (1985), Rank (1884–1939) was Sigmund Freud's "devoted helper and most creative student" (p. xxv) who emigrated from Vienna to Paris in 1926 and eventually moved to New York. A major force in the field of psychoanalysis, Rank was often criticized by his colleagues for beliefs that subsequently were the basis for other forms of psychotherapy. He was particularly interested in the therapeutic relationship, which he believed to be the mechanism for clients' creative "unfolding and enrichment of the self" (Rank, 1936, pp. 5–6). For him, the focus of treatment was the present relationship, not events from the client's past. When Lieberman interviewed some of Rank's former clients, one woman described him as follows:

> With Rank there was no dogma. . . . Everything was open from minute to minute. Nothing was imposed on you. Rank was not looking for disease, he was not trying to eradicate anything. He wanted you to open up and be as you might want to be but didn't dare to. He had an overwhelming force but it did not take away from anything else—it gave you a force of your own. (Lieberman, 1985, p. xxxvi)

Jesse Taft (1882–1960) was a patient, student, colleague, and biographer of Rank (Lieberman, 1985). After earning her Ph.D. in social work at the University of Chicago, she assumed a position as "mental hygienist" in Philadelphia in 1918 (Taft, 1933/1962, p. vi). There she worked with troubled children at the Children's Aid Society of Pennsylvania and developed what she called "relationship therapy." Taft (1927/1962) believed that therapeutic growth occurs in the context of the therapist–client relationship. To be effective, clinicians must adopt a child-centered viewpoint and realize that children have the potential to change. Her focus on the client's ability to resolve everyday problems within the context of a supportive therapeutic relationship is a theme that later appears in the writings of Carl Rogers.

Californian Frederick Allen was a colleague of Taft who cofounded the Philadelphia Child Guidance Clinic in 1925 and served as its director. In his presidential address to the American Orthopsychiatry Association, Allen (1934) described the role of the therapist. He emphasized the importance of helping each child develop as a unique person, without imposing external controls on the client. When he talked about the clinician's function in treatment, Allen described the therapist as another unique individual with personal qualities that affect the development of the therapeutic relationship.

Carl Rogers (1902–1987) developed the theoretical foundation for child-centered therapy. In the first chapter to *On Becoming A Person*, Rogers (1961) described the life experiences that led to his creation of a new approach to theory and practice. Born the fourth of six children, Rogers described his home life as "marked by close family ties, a very strict and uncompromising religious and ethical atmosphere, and what amounted to a worship of the virtue of hard work" (p. 5). He described himself as a socially isolated child whose parents restricted him and his siblings from typical youth activities, such as dancing, attending movies and theater, and drinking carbonated beverages. He entered the University of Wisconsin to study agriculture but changed his major to history, which he believed to be better preparation for his newfound career goal—the ministry. When he completed his undergraduate studies, Rogers entered Union Theological Seminary, where course work in psychology brought about another and lasting change of career.

The man who would eventually create a new method of conceptualizing and treating troubled adults was initially drawn to the psychosocial needs of children. This chapter and Chapter 9 examine Rogers' early work with children, which was important in his transition from the seminary to doctoral study in clinical and educational psychology.

> I began to take more courses at Teachers College, Columbia University, across the street from Union Seminary. . . . I began practical clinical work with children under Leta Hollingworth, a sensitive and practical person. I found myself drawn to child guidance work, so that gradually, with very little painful readjustment, I shifted over into the field of child guidance, and began to think of myself as a clinical psychologist. It was a step I eased into, with relatively little clearcut conscious choice, rather just following the activities which interested me. (Rogers, 1961, p. 9)

While a student at Columbia, Rogers acquired the research skills required of a social scientist. During his internship at the Institute for Child Guidance, he developed a practitioner's clinical skills. Before he completed his degree in 1931, Rogers accepted a position as one of three psychologists in the Child Study Department at the Society for the Prevention of Cruelty to Children in Rochester, New York. There he began to challenge the principles and techniques he was taught in graduate school, entering the first stage of a career that produced the theory and therapy that bears his name (Sharf, 2000).

During his 12 years of practice in Rochester, Rogers gradually moved away from the traditional psychodynamic approach he was taught at Columbia. He found that psychosexual interpretations of a client's behavior did not necessarily lead to effective treatments. He questioned traditional approaches to interviewing, which he believed were likely to direct clients to respond as the therapist wanted. He also learned to appreciate clients' views of their presenting problems and individuals' capacities for self-growth. As he stated, "It is the *client* who knows what hurts, what directions to go, what problems are crucial, what experiences have been deeply buried" (Rogers, 1961, pp. 11–12). Rogers' ideas were initially ignored by other psychologists. When the Psychology Department at the University of Rochester rejected his requests for a teaching position, he turned to the social work profession, which "seemed to be talking my language" (p. 12) and taught courses in the university's Department of Sociology and Department of Education.

In 1939, Rogers published *The Clinical Treatment of the Problem Child* based on his experiences in Rochester. He discussed topics such as the use of personality tests with children, family-based treatments, the school's role in changing a student's behavior, and the therapeutic potential of foster care and summer camps. Rogers (1961) believed that it was the publication of this book that got him a faculty appointment at Ohio State University in 1940. His 5 years in Columbus represent the beginning of what is often referred to as his nondirective period (1940–1950) when he emphasized the skills of counseling (Ivey & Simek-Downing, 1980). During his client-centered (1950–1961) and person-centered (1961–1987) periods, Rogers turned to the study of the clinician as a person with unique attitudes and experiences that impact the therapist–client relationship (Ivey & Simek-Downing, 1980). His interests eventually extended beyond the therapy room to include community-based concerns such as dispute resolution and political activism (Sharf, 2000).

Rogers presented his ideas in a wealth of articles and books, some of which were considered controversial at the time. For example, his publisher and he worried that *Counseling and Psychotherapy* (Rogers, 1942a) would not sell the 2000 copies needed to cover the costs of preparing and printing the book. They were obviously pleased when more than 70,000 copies were sold (Rogers, 1961). Rogers published many other books, including *Client-centered Therapy* (Rogers, 1951); *Freedom to Learn: A View of What Education Might Become* (Rogers, 1969); and *On Becoming a Person* (Rogers, 1961), which brought the master "more fame and influence than he could ever have hoped for" (Thorne, 1992, p. 17).

His academic career also took him to faculty positions at the University of Chicago (1945–1957) and the University of Wisconsin (1957–1963). In 1963, Rogers left Wisconsin to join the Western Behavioral Sciences Institute (WBSI) in La Jolla, California. There he became involved in the adult encounter group movement and published *Carl Rogers on Encounter Groups* (Rogers, 1970). During the person-centered stage of his career, he and some of his WBSI colleagues founded the Center for Studies of the Person in 1968. Despite their early rejection of his ideas, other professionals eventually recognized Rogers' contributions to the field of psychotherapy. This included numerous honors, including the American Psychological Association's Distinguished Professional Contribution Award, which he received in 1973.

The best known figure in the field of child-centered treatments is Virginia Axline, a student of Rogers who used his model to develop child-centered play therapy. Axline relied on her clinical experiences with children to develop case material for her books and articles. She joined Rogers at the University of Chicago, where she wrote her classic text, *Play Therapy* (Axline, 1947). This book contains the fundamental principles for her approach along with excerpts from play sessions with children. Axline later moved to Columbia University Teachers College and wrote *Dibs: In Search of Self* (Axline, 1964), a moving account of a young boy in child-centered treatment. In this wonderful book, she described how a troubled client emerges as a healthy child through the process of client-centered play therapy.

Other contributors to the development of child-centered treatments are Elaine Dorfman and Clark Moustakas. A graduate of the University of Chicago, Dorfman studied under Rogers, who served as chairperson for her doctoral dissertation committee. Although she conducted empirical research on child-centered treatments (Dorfman, 1958), she is probably best known for her chapter on play therapy that appears in Rogers' (1951) *Client-centered Therapy*. Clark Moustakas was a staff member at the Merrill-Palmer School in Detroit who was introduced to child-centered methods by Axline (Moustakas, 1953). Similar to Taft, he called his approach "relationship therapy" (Moustakas, 1959, p. 1), which he used with normal and troubled children. Moustakas believed that training in play techniques should not be restricted to professional therapists but should be available for parents, teachers, social workers, and family therapists. As he stated:

> It takes a long time for a person with concentrated, formal training to stop trying to act like the professor in the classroom or clinic, to stop repeating the abstract concepts in the book and the dictates of a preconceived expert, and to start living the fresh, unique experience of a relationship in child therapy. (Moustakas, 1959, p. 317)

Moustakas published many theoretical and data-based articles and books, including *Children in Play Therapy: A Key to Understanding Normal and Disturbed Emotions* (Moustakas, 1953) and *Psychotherapy with Children: The Living Relationship* (Moustakas, 1959).

An important figure in the contemporary field of child-centered play therapy is Garry Landreth, whose career transitions have taken him from high school teacher to guidance counselor to play therapist and university professor. Landreth received his Ph.D. from the University of New Mexico and joined the University of North Texas in 1966 as a faculty member in the Counselor Education Department. Since then, Landreth has been an active contributor to the professional literature, including his book *Play Therapy: The Art of the Relationship* (Landreth, 1991), which has been translated into Chinese, Russian, and Korean. At the University of North Texas, he founded the Center for Play Therapy to promote training, practice, and research activities on this important intervention strategy. The Center regularly publishes the *Play Therapy Training Directory* (Landreth, 2000), which contains a listing of professional associations for play therapists as well as universities and colleges that provide graduate-level training in play techniques. Readers interested in learning more about the Center's work are encouraged to contact Dr. Landreth and his staff by mail at P.O. Box 311337, Denton, TX 76203-1337 or online at www.coe.unt.edu/cpt/.

Another resource for play therapists is the Association for Play Therapy, which Charles Schaefer and Kevin O'Connor founded in 1982 to promote the development of play-based interventions. The association conducts various educational activities, including annual conventions and publications such as the *International Journal of Play Therapy*. The group has encouraged research on play therapy and offers a review of these works online at www.iapt.org.

THEORETICAL FOUNDATIONS

Rogers (1961) believed that human beings are basically good by nature and that within each of us is the tendency toward positive and creative action. Maslow (1954) agreed when he wrote that human nature is not "*primarily, biologically, fundamentally* evil, sinful, malicious, ferocious, cruel, or murderous" (p. 118). Unlike the Freudian model in which the socially-derived superego is thought to restrict the drives of the id, client-centered theory represents a more optimistic view of humankind in which the tendency toward growth is present from infancy (Rogers, 1959). This positive view does not mean that people never exhibit bad behavior. They do, but the cause of these actions cannot be found in an inherently evil inner core of being. Instead, the source of negative behaviors is believed to be a restrictive environment that limits a person's natural tendency toward healthy development.

As Okun (1990) noted, Rogers and other humanistic writers have focused on the inner subjective experience rather than external observable events. As a result, considerable attention has been given to the development of the self, including concepts such as self-awareness, self-concept, self-esteem, and self-actualization. Because an understanding of the self is critical to child-centered theory, we begin by examining this construct. Later we discuss Maslow's hierarchy of basic needs to explore what humanistic writers believe motivates our behavior. Finally, we consider Rogers' concept of the necessary and sufficient conditions for client change that have had a significant impact on the empirical study of the therapeutic process.

The Self

Rogers (1951) described how human beings develop within the phenomenal field that is their conscious and unconscious experience of the world around them. Because this experience is personal and unique, Rogers believed that each individual's phenomenal field is a "private world" (p. 483) that is unknowable to anyone else. Similar to contemporary proponents of constructivist theory (see Chapter 16), Rogers believed that reality is not an external absolute; rather, it is the individual meaning a person makes of everyday life events. He offered as an example the reactions that two people have to the same political speech. Although both hear the same words delivered in the same manner, one person concludes that the candidate is trying to destroy the existing quality of life, but the other interprets the speech as a blueprint for a more caring and understanding society.

According to Rogers (1951), people respond to their perception of reality (i.e., the phenomenal field) as a whole person in a "total, organized, goal-directed" manner (pp. 486–487). Furthermore, there is a health-oriented focus to these actions. That is, the individual "*has one basic tendency and striving—to actualize, maintain, and enhance the experiencing organism*" (p. 487). As already discussed, the belief that human beings are inherently good is a central principle in Rogers' theory of personality development. The capacity for growth that exists within each of us is the central tendency that therapists attempt to unleash as they help clients move beyond their problems. Because of the personal and subjective nature of this tendency toward health, clinicians cannot assume to have a priori knowledge of the beliefs and feelings that are unique to the individual. As Rogers learned in his work with troubled children in Rochester, "*The best vantage point for understanding behavior is from the internal frame of reference of the individual himself*" (p. 494).

An important component of the developmental process is the affect or feelings related to what Rogers (1951) called the person's seeking and consummatory behaviors. He believed that unpleasant or excited feelings accompany approach or seeking behaviors, and calm or satisfied feelings are associated with the related consummatory or outcome experiences. As children repeatedly perform these behavioral sequences in the context of their cultural surround, they each develop a conscious concept of self (i.e., "I," "me"), which to Rogers was "an awareness of being, of functioning" (p. 498) The development of self-concept in children is accompanied by the acquisition of self-esteem, which comprises a young person's beliefs and feelings about self that are related to others' evaluations of the child.

Children respond to the messages they receive from other people in one of three ways (Rogers, 1951). First, they sometimes ignore unrelated or irrelevant messages. A student who walks across the playground and disregards classmates' comments about the games they are playing does not integrate this information into his concept of self. At other times, children integrate new information into their existing view of self. Consider a child who uses a perfect score on a test to strengthen her belief that she is an excellent student. Rogers believed that his third response category is of greatest interest to therapists. Here children deny or distort information that conflicts with their concept of self. The successful student who fails one test might blame the teacher for administering a very difficult examination. Or he might overlook his previous perfect scores, focus on the failure, and experience excessive anxiety every time the teacher gives a test in class.

A child's response to other people's messages is important because Rogers (1951) believed that we behave in a manner that is consistent with our self-concept. In other words, our actions reflect our view of self. The child who believes she is an honest person is likely to tell her parents the truth about her recent misbehavior. Every time she misbehaves and believes she must hide her transgressions from the parents, her view of self as an honest person is challenged. The more inconsistent these experiences are, the more her self-concept is threatened and the more rigid her self-structure must become in order to maintain itself. As Rogers stated, "She can and will defend her self against this threat of inconsistency. If the self cannot defend itself against deep threats, the result is a catastrophic psychological breakdown and disintegration" (p. 516).

Self-concept and self-esteem develop within the context of the child's cultural surround. Dorfman (1951) believed that the inherent tendency toward health is manifested when a child is genuinely accepted as a person by at least one significant other. In this relationship, she has the opportunity to examine her self in a nonthreatening manner. The significant other can be a parent or other relative, a teacher, or a therapist who accepts, respects, and listens to the child. As she accepts inconsistencies and contradictions as part of her self, the child also becomes more accepting of others, including their behaviors, beliefs, and values. Through this process of becoming, she moves closer toward what Rogers (1969) believed is the goal of human development: "the fully functioning person" (p. 278).

According to Rogers (1969), the fully functioning person approaches life in an open and nondefensive manner, feels a broad array of emotions, and treats life as an exciting progression of new and fascinating experiences to be lived in the moment. The person is self-confident and trusts his ability to handle each challenge in life as it arises, without reverting to ineffective strategies from the past. Rogers observed that becoming a fully functioning person is not a trivial task. Some approach this level of psychological being through growth experiences, such as education and therapy. Regardless of the method used, the process "involves the stretching and growing of becoming more and more one's potentialities. It includes the courage to be. It means launching oneself fully into the stream of life" (p. 196).

Maslow's Hierarchy of Basic Needs

Abraham Maslow (1968) also believed that human beings have an inherent tendency toward psychological health. Normal development occurs when a child is able to exercise free choice because "*he* 'knows' better than anyone else what is good for him" (p. 198). According to Maslow, children behave in socially inappropriate ways when they become frustrated by environmental limits that restrict their tendency toward health. He developed a hierarchy of human needs as a model for discussing the motivation to act in social contexts. Maslow (1954) described levels of motivation, beginning with basic physiological needs, such as hunger and thirst, and progressing to higher levels related to safety, love and affection, self-esteem, and self-actualization.

Maslow (1954) organized his model in a hierarchical manner because he believed that higher-order needs are not pursued until more basic needs are met. A physically neglected and malnourished child is primarily concerned with the physiological needs of hunger and thirst. A well-fed but severely ill youngster whose daily routine is interrupted by hospitalization wishes for the return of a predictable and safe environment. For children whose physiological and safety needs are met, attention turns to the desire for parental love and friendships with peers. When these needs are met, the child strives to fulfill the need for self-respect and the respect of others.

The highest level in Maslow's (1954) hierarchy is self-actualization, which he described as a person's "desire for self-fulfillment. . . . to become everything that one is capable of becoming" (p. 46). When more basic needs have been met, striving for self-actualization becomes the salient issue. Because it sits at the pinnacle of Maslow's hierarchy, this highest of needs has the most preconditions, offers the best chance for positive subjective experiences (e.g., happiness), and involves greater individuation of the person's unique sense of self. Achieving self-actualization requires an optimal environment that encourages the person's development of a self. For children, the most significant figures in this environment are typically their parents.

Parents play an important role in meeting children's basic needs. They are responsible for providing for a safe and secure home in which basic needs such as hunger and thirst are met. The love and affection they offer is the foundation for children's sense of belonging in the family and the development of positive self-regard. Parents also provide the social, emotional, and educational experiences from which self-actualization can emerge. An artistically precocious child is unlikely to achieve an optimal level of development without adequate art instruction, exposure to the work of famous artists, and access to the supplies needed to acquire and refine the requisite skills. The child's parents also must offer emotional support and communicate a belief in the value of art to society.

As children mature, they assume more responsibility for meeting their basic needs. Although it is true that parents continue to purchase food for the family, most elementary school children have learned to address their hunger needs by walking to the kitchen and preparing a simple snack. When a child's social environment extends beyond the family, significant other adults assume responsibility for meeting basic and higher level needs. Acting in loco parentis, teachers ensure that students eat lunch at the assigned hour, and they are responsible for children's safety during the school day. To help students achieve higher-level needs, teachers must provide the proper psychological climate. This includes a classroom environment where children are treated as human beings who have the potential for self-actualization. Therapists assume the same responsibilities when children enter treatment to remediate everyday problems. Rogers emphasized clinicians' role in helping clients progress toward self-actualization when he developed his necessary and sufficient conditions for therapeutic change.

Rogers' Necessary and Sufficient Conditions

Drawing on his clinical experience and that of others, Rogers (1957) described what he called the "necessary and sufficient conditions of therapeutic personality change" (p. 95). His model contains the six qualities that he identified as central to a facilitative or therapeutic relationship (Table 8-1). Rogers believed these conditions are "*necessary* to initiate constructive personality change" and when considered collectively, they are "*sufficient* to inaugurate that process" (p. 95). If these conditions are present over time, psychological growth will occur.

Rogers' (1957) first condition, the psychological contact, is the foundation for all others. He believed that without this relationship between the therapist and client or teacher and student, personal growth will not occur. When clients seek help in therapy, they must be experiencing discrepant or conflicting thoughts and feelings. This second condition is particularly relevant with children, who rarely refer themselves for treatment. On a superficial level, young clients sometimes offer little evidence of their inner conflicts. By establishing rapport with the child, the clinician can facilitate the client's expres-

Table 8–1
Carl Rogers' Necessary and Sufficient Conditions for Client Change

1. Two persons are in psychological contact.
2. The first, who we shall call the *client*, is in a state of incongruence, being vulnerable or anxious.
3. The second person, who we shall call the *therapist*, is congruent or integrated in the relationship.
4. The therapist experiences unconditional positive regard for the client.
5. The therapist experiences an empathic understanding of the client's internal frame of reference and endeavors to communicate this experience to the client.
6. The communication to the client of the therapist's empathic understanding and unconditional positive regard is achieved to a minimal degree.

Adapted from "The Necessary and Sufficient Conditions of Therapeutic Personality Change," by C. R. Rogers, 1957, *Journal of Consulting Psychology*, *21*, p. 96. Copyright 1957 by the American Psychological Association.

sion of feelings and begin to understand the problem situation from the child's point of view. For example, a third grader who initially seems unaffected by her parents' complaints about her academic performance and social relationships eventually discloses feelings of sadness and guilt arising from the parents' unrealistic demands.

Rogers (1957) stated that the clinician must be "a congruent, genuine, integrated person" (p. 97). Therapists must be aware of their personal thoughts and feelings and the effects these have on their interactions with clients. This includes an understanding of cognitive and emotional reactions to the child and how these relate to different presenting problems, such as depression and suicide, oppositional defiant disorder, and adjustment to divorce. A lack of genuineness compromises a therapist's ability to communicate unconditional positive regard for a child. By accepting each client as a "beautiful and noble person" (Landsman, 1974, p. 349) without setting conditions for that acceptance, therapists can communicate a belief in the child's ability to solve problems. The therapist who accepts an oppositional defiant child only when he complies with directions and behaves as he "should" in session is not offering this important therapeutic condition. It is common and appropriate for child-centered clinicians to set behavioral limits in session (see Role of Therapist in Chapter 9), but they should do so in a way that communicates a belief in the child's potential for growth. This sometimes involves the difficult task of accepting the child as a noble human being in the face of negative behaviors. Clients such as this highlight Rogers' opinion that experiencing unconditional positive regard is not an absolute but an ideal that clinicians constantly try to achieve.

According to Rogers (1957), empathy is the sensing of "the client's world as if it were your own" (p. 99) while at the same time recognizing that a person's inner self is unique and therefore never truly knowable to others. A client of an empathic therapist might say, "She understands me." The client's awareness of the clinician's empathy and unconditional positive regard is the last of Rogers' six conditions. Through their words and actions, therapists communicate understanding and acceptance to the child. Fulfilling this particular condition is especially challenging across the developmental divide that separates adult therapists from young clients. For a child to understand, a clinician must phrase all messages in a form that is appropriate to the client's developmental level. Likewise, the therapist must be a skilled listener who is able to understand the child's message, which is often disclosed in a nonverbal and indirect manner.

As Rogers (1957) stated, the therapist–client contact is essential for the other five conditions, which exist in varying degrees in the therapeutic relationship. He suggested that by enhancing these conditions in treatment, clinicians can improve the client's chances for experiencing positive personality change. A therapist's use of such interview techniques as open questions and reflection of feeling is helpful in this regard. But technical skill in the absence of a child-centered frame of reference does not ensure the presence of these necessary and sufficient conditions. The therapist must also believe in the child for treatment to be effective.

Axline (1947) reformulated Rogers' client-centered theory to make it more developmentally appropriate for children. She translated Rogers' six necessary and sufficient conditions for therapeutic change into her eight theoretical principles for child-centered play therapy (Table 8-2). Similar to Rogers, Axline believed that children possess the ability to find

Table 8–2
Virginia Axline's Eight Basic Principles of Client-Centered Play Therapy

1. The therapist must develop a warm, friendly relationship with the child in which good rapport is established as soon as possible.
2. The therapist accepts the child exactly as he is.
3. The therapist establishes a feeling of permissiveness in the relationship so that the child feels free to express his feelings completely.
4. The therapist is alert to recognize the *feelings* the child is expressing and reflects those feelings back to him in such a manner that he gains insight into his behavior.
5. The therapist maintains a deep respect for the child's ability to solve his own problems if given an opportunity to do so. The responsibility to make choices and to institute change is the child's.
6. The therapist does not attempt to direct the child's actions or conversation in any manner. The child leads the way; the therapist follows.
7. The therapist does not attempt to hurry the therapy along. It is a gradual process and is recognized as such by the therapist.
8. The therapist establishes only those limitations that are necessary to anchor the therapy to the world of reality and to make the child aware of his responsibility in the relationship.

From *Play Therapy* (pp. 73–74), by V. M. Axline, 1947, New York: Ballantine Books. Copyright by V. M. Axline.

solutions to everyday problems. She and other child-centered theorists have focused on children's expression of feelings and their awareness of self. As Moustakas (1953) stated, child-centered writers have emphasized the importance of the therapeutic relationship for helping children experience emotional growth so they can "gain faith in themselves as feeling individuals" (p. 2).

Chapter 9 examines how the theoretical beliefs of Rogers, Axline, and Moustakas have been translated into child-centered interventions. The principles described here are the theoretical foundation for a variety of treatment techniques used to develop a working alliance with child clients. The result of this effort has been the creation of developmentally appropriate strategies, including play techniques, that clinicians can use in their work with children.

DEVELOPMENTAL CONSIDERATIONS

Child-centered treatments involve the consideration of a number of developmental issues. As discussed previously, the emotional life of the client is central to child-centered therapy. Children who enter treatment often have difficulty understanding, regulating, and expressing their feelings (Denham, 1998). A child's anger, for example, is sometimes manifested in negative behaviors that impede their relationships with their peers and caregivers. Chapter 9 discusses how child-centered therapists use techniques, such as reflection of feeling, to facilitate clients' emotional awareness. To effectively use these strategies, clinicians must know how children acquire an understanding of their feelings. This section examines relevant research on this important area of development, including children's acquisition of the feeling vocabulary needed to communicate their emotions to others.

Child-centered therapists have given considerable attention to the development of self-concept and self-esteem, so we review selected theory and research on the self. We then turn to the development of children's artistic abilities. Child-centered therapists often use art activities with young clients, so we examine children's acquisition of drawing skills. The sample case in Chapter 9 involves a child's response to the sudden death of a sibling, so we complete our review of developmental issues with a discussion of children's understanding of death concepts. Therapists who help families through the bereavement process must understand how children of different ages respond to the loss of a loved one. As we will see, the interventions used with grieving adults are not necessarily the appropriate techniques for children.

Emotional Awareness

According to Santrock (2000), an emotion is a *"feeling or affect that involves a mixture of physiological arousal (a fast heartbeat, for example) and overt behavior (a smile or grimace, for example)"* (p. 198). Emotions are central to human development and constitute a basic form of communication that precedes our use of speech (Maccoby, 1992). For example, smiling serves an important role in the infant–caregiver relationship. Babies learn the social implications of smiling and increase their use of this behavior when reinforced by others (Etzel & Gewirtz, 1967). Likewise, parents are more likely to engage in play behaviors and infant-directed speech when their baby responds with a smile.

Fundamental emotions, such as anger and sadness, are thought to exist by age 4 months, but others, including shame and guilt, seem to emerge between 12 and 18 months of age. As children mature, they develop more complex emotions (e.g., hostility) that represent combinations of fundamental feelings (i.e., anger, contempt, disgust) (Izard & Malatesta, 1987). They also experience conflicting emotions, which appear to follow a developmental sequence. Harter and Buddin (1987) examined 4- to 12-year-old children's understanding of multiple and conflicting emotions in their cross-sectional study of similar and contradictory feelings toward the same or different people or events (Table 8-3). The authors found a significant stage-related increase in children's level of emotional awareness. Preschoolers in the study could explain how two feelings would occur one after the other, but they had considerable difficulty describing the simultaneous occurrence of these emotions. By contrast, many 11- and 12-year-old children understood simultaneity, even when the feelings were conflicted and directed at the same target.

The Harter and Buddin (1987) results are important for child-centered therapies when a goal of treatment is client awareness of conflicting feelings (e.g., love and anger) for a significant other (e.g., a parent). Clinicians can expect younger children to experience more difficulty in this regard. A 6-year-old child who fails to acknowledge both pleasant and unpleasant emotions for a parent or peer may do so, not because of denial of feelings, but for normal developmental reasons. Another interesting outcome of the Harter

Table 8–3
The Harter and Buddin (1987) Model of Children's Understanding of Similar and Conflicting Emotions Directed at the Same and Different Targets

Stage	Mean Age in Years	Children's Response to Combinations of Emotions
0	5.2	Unable to express similar feelings toward the same target
1	7.3	Able to express similar feelings toward the same target (e.g., "I was upset and mad when my brother messed up my stuff.")
2	8.7	Able to express similar feelings toward different targets (e.g., "I'd be happy I got a motorcycle and glad I got a race car.")
3	10.1	Able to express conflicting feelings toward different targets (e.g., "I was scared my mom was going to punish me for not cleaning my room, and happy I was watching TV.")
4	11.3	Able to express conflicting feelings toward the same target (e.g., "I was glad my grandmother was visiting but mad because she didn't bring me a present.")

Adapted from "Children's Understanding of the Simultaneity of Two Emotions: A Five-Stage Developmental Acquisition Sequence," by S. Harter and B. J. Buddin, 1987, *Developmental Psychology, 23*, pp. 389 and 393. Copyright 1987 by the American Psychological Association. Adapted with permission of the author.

and Buddin study is the authors' finding that the youngest children in their sample were the least likely to express negative emotions. Again, therapists should exercise caution when interpreting the limited variability in a preschooler's or kindergartner's verbalization of positive affect.

By observing and studying everyday experiences, preschoolers learn the causes of their feelings and the emotional states of others, especially their parents (Denham, 1998). In order to develop meaningful interpersonal relationships, it is important for children to understand how other people feel. The awareness of others' emotions begins early in life when infants focus on the facial expressions of their caregivers. Although babies do not understand the social and emotional significance of these expressions, even newborns are able to discriminate and reproduce the happiness, sadness, and surprise they observe on the faces of adults (Field et al., 1983; Field, Woodson, Greenberg, & Cohen, 1982).

Children's understanding of others' feelings appears to improve with their developing awareness of personal emotions. During the elementary school years, students begin to realize that different people can have different emotional reactions to the same event. Harter (1986) observed that children's understanding of their parents' feelings seems to follow by about 1 year their level of awareness for personal affective states. This delay exists in both the structure of emotion, as described by Harter and Buddin (1987), and the content of the parents' feelings.

Harter (1986) reported that very young children believe their parents derive the same enjoyment from different events and activities as they do. For example, a child who likes to play checkers or hide-and-seek assumes that parents feel the same about these games. Between ages 6 and 10 years, children begin to understand that their parents and they can have different feelings. Although Harter reported that children of this age tend to see themselves as "the primary source of a parent's emotional life" (p. 137), not all children identify their behavior as the cause of their parents' feelings. Dunn and Hughes (1998), for example, found that only one third of the 4-year-old children they studied cited themselves as the reason for their mother's anger. Some of these preschoolers identified external causes, such as marital conflict, for the mothers' sadness. Although it is true that children sometimes behave in ways that anger, frustrate, or please their parents, they are not always the source of these feelings, a fact that even some young children seem to understand. A therapist's challenge is to determine the accuracy of each client's attributions of responsibility and to select interventions appropriate to the cause of the parent's feelings. Individual therapy might be used with children whose self-blame is unfounded, but couples therapy is appropriate when marital discord exists.

Verbal communication of affective states requires an awareness of personal feelings and a command of the vocabulary needed to label these emotions. Because of the linguistic nature of psychotherapy, including most child-centered strategies, a child's feeling vocabulary represents an important developmental consideration. When Ridgeway, Waters, and Kuczaj (1985) surveyed parents of 3-year-old children, they found that most children correctly used words such as "happy," "sad," "afraid," "angry," and "mad." By the time they enter first grade, children have typically acquired the language needed to express feelings in a culturally appropriate manner (Haviland-Jones, Gebelt, & Stapley, 1997). Therapists must select feeling words that are appropriate to the client's developmental level. Younger children tend to draw broad comparisons, such as "good" versus "bad" or "happy" versus "sad," but older clients are more likely to make finer discriminations, such as "worried" versus "excited." Cultural differences also emerge. For example, children whose parents have emphasized self-control of emotions and forgiving others may acknowledge feeling "upset" or even "mad" at a peer but deny being "angry."

Self-concept and Self-esteem

Developmental psychologists have studied the formation of self-concept in children. This dynamic construct involves a transition from an initial awareness of self as a being to more complex verbal self-descriptions using physical and psychological terminology. Lewis and Brooks-Gunn (1979) found that by age 2 years, most infants are able to recognize themselves in a mirror. They can tell you their name and whether they are a boy or a girl (Bee, 1997). Preschoolers, ages 3 to 5 years, tend to describe themselves in concrete terms, such as day-to-day activities (e.g., "I wash my hair myself") and body image (e.g., "I have eyes") (Keller, Ford, & Meacham, 1978). But therapists sometimes encounter children in this age group who use psychological characteristics to describe themselves. Eder (1989), for example, found that approximately a third of the 3.5-year-old children in her study referred to internal states, such as feelings and beliefs, in their descriptions of themselves or others. These children demonstrated the ability to integrate their thoughts and feelings and to relate emotions to specific behaviors. For example, one child described "scared" in a metaphorical manner by saying it was "like running away" (p. 1226). Eder also found that between the ages of 3.5 and 7.5 years, children made greater use of internal or psychological states in their descriptions of self. Based on these results, clinicians should remain alert for precocious preschoolers who refer to internal states when describing themselves.

As discussed in Chapter 4, researchers have studied the self from at least two perspectives, self-concept and self-esteem. The toddler who looks in a mirror and touches the spot of rouge a parent placed on its nose is demonstrating an awareness of self (Lewis & Brooks, 1974). Self-recognition is an early stage in the child's development of her concept of self. With maturation, of course, comes a more complex understanding of self that follows a developmental pattern. The preschooler's use of externally visible characteristics to describe herself (e.g., "I play baseball," "I have black hair") gradually expands during the elementary school years to include social comparisons and psychological attributes (e.g., "I'm better at baseball than my brother," "I am good at math") (Damon & Hart, 1982).

As children develop, the structure of the self becomes more complex. In her studies of children and adolescents, Susan Harter documented the emergence of new and personally meaningful domains. Physical appearance and athletic competence have been found to be important domains for children, but romantic appeal and job competence do not appear until adolescence (see Harter, 1998). Based on data collected using the Self-Perception Profile for Children (see Chapter 4), Harter (1985) found that children construct an image of self based on their academic and athletic performance, appearance, peer acceptance, and behavior. Clinicians must consider the relative importance of each of these domains for a child to help the client develop a more complex awareness of self.

With elementary-age children, therapists can facilitate self-understanding by encouraging clients' self-reflection and consideration of others' opinions of the child (Harter, 1983b). With younger clients, therapists might use puppets or dolls to have children enact clinically significant scenes. Harter described a variation of this technique in which clients provide the narrative for both child and adult dolls:

> The strategy I employ involves my stepping back from the play, and as Dr. Harter, I whisper to my child client, K, "What should I have Sissy say?" K willingly whispers back, "She says she doesn't want to go to school today." We then both move back into the play, at which point I whine: "Ah, Mom, I don't want to go to school today. Do I have to?" (pp. 118–119)

If we assume that "Sissy" actually represents the client in this situation, Harter has skillfully used her technique to facilitate the child's self-disclosure.

Harter (1985) observed that self-esteem in children involves two constructs: self-worth and competence in specific domains. Self-evaluations in these dimensions emerge during the elementary school years as children begin to make global judgments about themselves and evaluate their performance in individual areas, such as behavior and academic achievement. The validity of self-evaluations also changes with age as children become more accurate in their perceptions of self. Although individual differences do exist, preschoolers and kindergartners typically have a positive view of themselves and believe they have a relatively high level of physical and cognitive competence (Harter & Pike, 1984). A child who describes herself as skilled in soccer also tends to have a positive view of herself in the classroom. But during elementary school, children's self-ratings become more accurate and remain relatively consistent until the transition to junior high school, when there is a significant but temporary drop in self-esteem (Harter, 1998) (see Multicultural Considerations later in this chapter).

A child's view of self is not independent of environmental influences. Even 2-year-old children have been found to recognize behaviors that adults consider inappropriate (Cole, Barrett, & Zahn-Waxler, 1992). Consequently, the criteria that parents and significant others use when responding to a child's performance are important and merit serious consideration in treatment when these expectations are developmentally unrealistic. The self-esteem of elementary school children has been related to their classmates' opinions of them. Cole (1991), for example, found that fourth graders' evaluations of their academic and social competence were influenced by their peers' ratings of the students' performance in these domains. These findings highlight the need for school-based interventions to enhance children's self-esteem. Harter (1998) described how early programs intended to enhance students' general self-worth have given way to skills-based interventions to develop competence in specific areas. Children with low self-esteem related to poor academic competence are candidates for tutoring intended to improve performance in subjects where deficits exist. As these students acquire the necessary skills and receive better grades and praise from their teachers and parents, their opinions of self change and self-esteem improves. Harter emphasized the role of significant others in this equation. Self-worth depends, in part, on others' recognition of the child's potential, effort, and achievement. As Kaplan (2000) noted, "Every child has some areas of competence that can be reinforced" (p. 424). By capitalizing on these abilities, clinicians and teachers can help students build on their strengths, become more competent, and feel better about themselves.

Children's Drawing Skills

As discussed in Chapter 4, drawings have been a popular strategy for assessing children's psychosocial adjustment. Therapists who use drawings as part of treatment must consider developmental variations in clients' artistic creations. An important factor is the child's drawing ability, which is first revealed in the scribbles of children as young as age 2 years (Kellogg, 1955). Di Leo (1977) described children's artistic development using the stages identified by G. H. Luquet, who studied 1700 drawings that his daughter produced between the ages of 3 and 8 years. According to Di Leo, 3- to 4-year-old children are likely to draw an object based on their mental image of that object. For example, a child is likely to draw a person in a standing position, regardless of whether the actual model is standing, sitting, or reclining. At about age 4 years, children begin to draw what Light and Barnes (1995) described as "tadpoles" (p. 244), human figures that contain only a large head with lines attached for arms and legs. It is not until about age 7 years that children draw objects as they see them in the environment. As Di Leo stated:

> The drawings reflect to an increasing degree the actual appearance of objects. Transparencies gradually disappear. Men are no longer visible through the hull of a ship. Legs are no longer seen through trousers. . . . Heads will no longer dominate bodies by their size. (p. 48)

Light and Barnes (1995) described how drawing skills develop during the elementary school years. As is true for all artists, a child's biggest challenge is to represent the three-dimensional world in a two-dimensional space. This requires the ability to portray distance and occlusion, the placement of one object behind another. Light and Barnes described how this skill appears to emerge around age 8 years, when children draw a full object in front and a partial figure of the second object behind. At about the same age, they also begin to draw in perspective by including the height, width, and length of objects. But elementary school children have difficulty incorporating convergence into their drawings. They often represent a road by drawing parallel lines rather than lines that meet on the horizon to introduce depth into the picture.

In her study of drawings produced by 4-, 6-, 8-, and 10-year-old children, Dennis (1991) observed some of the qualitative changes described by Light and Barnes (1995). Specifically, children chose different settings for their drawings. Dennis found that preschoolers did not include a background in their drawings, but 6-year-old children incorporated primitive details, such as a line across the bottom of the paper to represent the ground. The 8-year-old children in this study also used a bottom line or strip for the ground, but they added depth by differentiating near and far objects in the picture. But as we might expect, the 10-year-old children incorporated the most detail in the setting for their drawings. As Dennis stated, "a sporting field or arena might be depicted, rather than just a general outdoor scene (i.e., sky and grass)" (p. 233). The detail in children's drawings often contains information that is relevant to treatment. For example, therapists can use the activities, the number and placement of people, and the location for a picture as stimuli to facilitate a child's disclosure of meaningful events. Chapter 9 discusses how child-centered clinicians have incorporated art activities into therapy.

Children's Understanding of Death Concepts

Chapter 9 examines how a therapist uses child-centered treatment with a 5-year-old girl whose brother was recently killed in an automobile accident. Clinicians who treat young survivors must consider the client's understanding of death. Piaget (1926, 1929) believed that before age 7 or 8 years, children engage in animistic thinking and have difficulty distinguishing between living and nonliving things. But other researchers (e.g., Bullock, 1985; Gelman, 1989; Richards & Siegler, 1984) have found that many children younger than this age can discriminate between animate and inanimate objects, although some children as old as age 11 years sometimes consider an object's ability to move when classifying it as living or nonliving.

Harris and Liebert (1991) observed that children's understanding of death involves more than the differentiation of animate and inanimate objects. When therapists treat young clients who have lost a significant other to death, they must consider the child's awareness of the concepts of irreversibility, causality, inevitability, and cessation (Lazar & Torney-Purta, 1991). Simply stated, irreversibility involves recognition of the finality of death; causality involves an understanding of the actual reason for a person's death; and inevitability is the awareness that all living things will eventually die. Cessation is more directly linked to Piaget's concept of animism because it represents a child's understanding that with death go "all biological, sensational, emotional, and cognitive functions" (Lazar & Torney-Purta, 1991, p. 1322).

According to Carey (1985), children's understanding of death develops in three stages. Those younger than age 6 years do not understand the four characteristics of death, so they often describe the deceased person as asleep or on a trip away from home. Between ages 6 and 8 years, children develop an understanding of irreversibility and cessation, although they emphasize external causes (e.g., guns, disease) that "happen to" people rather than internal biological changes (Carey, 1985, p. 63). Lazar and Torney-Purta (1991) found that children in this age group also become aware of the inevitability of death, but it is not until about age 9 or 10 years that they begin to view the cessation of life as a biological process (Carey, 1985). A fourth developmental stage occurs during adolescence when teenagers start to conceptualize death in a more adultlike manner based on the philosophical, religious, or spiritual beliefs of their cultures (Corr, 1995).

The transitions that occur in children's conceptualization of death require developmentally appropriate interventions. Therapists who treat preschoolers should not be surprised if these clients fail to exhibit the "normal" signs of bereavement observed in adults. After all, people who are sleeping will eventually awaken, and those away on a trip usually return. Treatment in these cases often involves educating parents about developmental issues and recommending that caregivers provide a secure and supportive environment for the child. With younger elementary school children, therapists can focus on the client's feelings about the permanence of the loved one's death while being alert for any suicidal ideation related to the child's desire to join the significant other. As children approach adolescence and begin to conceptualize death in a more adultlike manner, therapists can incorporate the client's religious beliefs into the treatment process.

Goldman (2000) described specific techniques for therapists to use with children after the death of a loved one. Consistent with the cognitive development of these clients, her methods involve concrete activities intended to stimulate memories and facilitate disclosure of thoughts and feelings about the deceased. She recommended that children be allowed to collect objects that remind them of the loved one and to save these in a special place. Goldman also suggested art and writing activities. These include the creation of collages and pictures, which can serve as stimuli for poems or creative writing projects. An example of the latter is what Goldman called a "memory book" (p. 23). If the deceased person is a family member, this biographical account could have chapters devoted to significant events, including summer vacations and special holidays. With clients who do not possess the requisite writing skills, the therapist can record the information as the child narrates the text. The clinician can help the child enrich these stories through questions (e.g., "How did you feel when you were fishing with your Dad that day?") designed to introduce feelings into each chapter.

MULTICULTURAL CONSIDERATIONS

The study of the development of the self in children requires consideration of cultural influences, including ethnicity and gender. Numerous researchers have investigated how these factors affect a child's identity, self-esteem, and attitudes toward others. This section examines selected studies on ethnic identity, prejudice, and gender identity development.

Ethnic Identity

An important component of a child's development of the self is the formation of an ethnic identity. Research in this area has included studies of ethnic awareness, preference, and stereotypes (Katz & Kofin, 1997). Phinney (1990) observed that early empirical work in the area concentrated on children, but more recent studies have focused on adolescents and adults. Phinney (1989), for example, presented a three-stage developmental model that she tested with high school students. The rationale for this and related studies can be found in the work of Erikson (1968) and Marcia (1980), who viewed adolescence as the significant life stage for identity formation. But the foundation for this change can be found in the meaning that children make of their early life experiences.

Theories of ethnic identity development have been proposed for specific groups, including African Americans (Cross, 1978) and Asian Americans (Ibrahim, Ohnishi, & Sandhu, 1997). These models are important contributions to the literature, but their use can divert attention from the similarities that exist across ethnic groups. Atkinson, Morten, and Sue (1993) recognized these limitations and proposed a generic theory that takes into consideration characteristics and experiences common to members of nondominant ethnic groups. Atkinson et al. described five ways that ethnic identity relates to a person's view of self, others of the same and different nondominant groups, and members of the dominant culture. These views vary from an acceptance of the dominant culture and concurrent devaluation of self and one's own and other nondominant groups to an identity that is accepting of self as an individual, a member of a nondominant group, and a participant in a culture in which European American values prevail. Phinney, Romero, Nava, and Huang (2001) provided support for this model when they studied the ethnic identities of Armenian American, Vietnamese American, and Mexican American adolescents. Although between-group differences existed, ethnic identity in all three groups was associated with participants' proficiency in the language of their native cultures, social interactions with same-group peers, and parents' efforts to maintain their cultural beliefs and practices.

Atkinson et al. (1993) offered their model as a framework for understanding therapist–client relationships. It is not intended to be a theory of personality development because every individual does not experience all five views, and the stages do not occur in a predetermined sequence that reflects movement toward more appropriate ethnic attitudes or behaviors. Researchers who have studied ethnic identity development in children focused on what might be considered the pre-adolescent issues of ethnic awareness, preference, and stereotypes. In a longitudinal study of infants and young children, Katz and Kofkin (1997) found that awareness of color differences preceded children's identification of self and others, their preferences in playmate selection, and the stereotyped attitudes they developed about members of the same and other ethnic groups. Aboud (1988) observed that children become aware of between-group differences according to the same timetable. But the age when they develop their own ethnic identity varies, with European Americans achieving this goal before African

American and Hispanic American children, followed by Asian Americans and Native Americans.

Bernal, Knight, Ocampo, Garza, and Cota (1990) proposed a model of ethnic identity for Mexican American children that has five stages: ethnic self-identification, constancy, role behaviors, knowledge, and feelings and preferences. According to this framework, children select an "own-ethnic-group category" (p. 33) to identify themselves as members of that group (i.e., ethnic self-identification). They learn that characteristics of their ethnic group remain constant across time and setting. That is, if children see themselves as Mexican Americans today in their neighborhood, the same identification will apply next week at school. Bernal and her colleagues also believed that children exhibit behaviors, acquire knowledge, and develop preferences consistent with the beliefs (e.g., values) and practices (e.g., language, customs) of their ethnic group. When they tested their model in a cross-sectional study of 45 Mexican American children, ages 6 to 10 years, Bernal et al. found age-related differences on four of their five stages. There was no difference in children's report of the use of ethnic role behaviors (e.g., speaking Spanish at home), but older children were better at choosing and explaining their ethnic self-identification. They were also more aware of the constancy of their ethnic identity, had greater knowledge of Mexican practices (e.g., celebration of *Cinco de Mayo*), and were more likely to prefer Mexican traditions (e.g., breaking the *pinata* at a birthday party).

Chapter 1 referred to Jacobs' (1992) model of identity development for multiethnic children born to African American and European American parents. Based on his work with 3- to 12-year-old children, Jacobs identified three developmental stages (see Table 8-4). Children who are in what he called the Pre-color Constancy stage do not use skin color as a standard for evaluating themselves and others. This viewpoint changes during the Post-color Constancy stage, when children experience ambivalence as they search for an ethnic identity label to describe themselves. Jacobs observed that parents play an important role in this process by helping children acquire a label that reflects their multiethnic heritage. Children in this second stage classify themselves and others based on skin color. It is during Jacobs' third stage when children begin to understand that skin color alone does not account for socially sanctioned assignments to ethnic groups. They learn that ethnic labels result from society's classification of their parents. As Jacobs stated, a child is not multiethnic because her father is black in color and her mother is white, but because the child's father belongs to the social class known as African American and her mother is socially classified as European American. It is uncertain whether the Bernal et al. (1990) and Jacobs models explain the development of children from other nondominant groups. Additional research is needed to examine the unique characteristics of these groups and the commonalities described by Atkinson et al. (1993) and Phinney et al. (2001).

Studies of ethnic identity development in children span more than 5 decades. Katz and Kofkin (1997), for example, found that the 6-month-old infants in their study were able to distinguish between pictures of African American and European American faces. A classic work in the area is the doll study conducted

Table 8–4
Jacobs' (1992) Model of Multiethnic Identity Development

Stage	Approximate Age Ranges in Years	Characteristics
Pre-color constancy	Under 4.5	Children are typically aware of their own skin color but do not use this criterion when classifying others.
Post-color constancy	4.5 to 8	Children understand that skin color is a permanent characteristic as they begin to develop a label for their multiethnicity.
Multiethnic identity	8 to 12	Children realize that their multiethnic identity is based not on skin color but on society's ethnic classification of their parents.

Adapted from "Identity Development in Biracial Children," by J. H. Jacobs, 1992, in M. P. P. Root (Ed.), *Racially mixed people in America*, pp 199–203. Newbury Park, CA: Sage. Copyright 1992 by Sage Publications, Inc.

by Clark and Clark (1947), whose results were given as evidence in the U.S. Supreme Court case of *Brown v. Board of Education* (1954). Clark and Clark presented white and brown dolls to a sample of African American children, ages 3 to 7 years. Although more than 90% of these children correctly identified the two skin tones, only one third chose the white doll as the one that looked like them. Children in the Clark and Clark study were also more likely to choose this doll to identify their preferred playmate, the nice doll, and the one that had nice color. Katz and Kofkin found a similar preference in playmates when the participants in their study were 3 years old. Although 82% of the European American children indicated a same-group preference, only 32% of the African Americans preferred someone from their own ethnic group.

Parents play a significant role in their children's development of ethnic identity. Thornton, Chatters, Taylor, and Allen (1990) found that parents of color emphasize cultural, minority, or mainstream issues. The least popular of these appears to be the cultural approach, in which mothers and fathers educate their children about their ethnic heritage and traditions. Parents seem to give more attention to the "minority" experience, including the challenges that members of nondominant ethnic groups encounter in a European American society. Or they focus on their child as an individual and provide what Thornton et al. described as a mainstream experience in which educational achievement and moral development are highlighted.

Marshall (1995) examined the relationship between parents' attitudes and ethnic identity in her study of African American mothers and their children. She found that parents emphasized mainstream values such as education, religion, self-worth, and industry (e.g., hard work). Although 89% of the mothers considered ethnicity to be an important issue, only 2% of them considered ethnic identity development to be a priority in raising their children. It is worth noting that the more attention parents gave to the attitudes of the dominant culture, the more likely their children were to question European American values. Clearly, more research is needed in this area before therapists are able to encourage parents to use one orientation or another. For now, we must assume that parents do play a significant role in socializing their children to life in a multicultural society. Clinicians must therefore consider parental influences when designing education/development, prevention, and remediation programs for these children.

Prejudice in Children

The formation of personal attitudes about members of other ethnic groups is related to the development of ethnic identity. These attitudes are the basis for prejudice, which Aboud (1988) defined as "an organized predisposition to respond in an unfavourable manner toward people from an ethnic group because of their ethnic affiliation" (p. 4). Prejudice has been observed in some children, even those of a young age. Daniel and Daniel (1998), for example, found that African American preschoolers revealed no significant preference when selecting traditional African American personal names to represent positive and negative attributes. But the European American children in this study were more likely to choose an African American name for negative behaviors, such as physical aggression and laziness. Doyle and Aboud (1995) conducted a longitudinal study of prejudice in European American kindergartners and third graders. They found that prejudice against African American and Native Americans was high among kindergartners but significantly lower by the time these children reached the third grade. With age, students seemed to become more aware of the differences within a given race and the commonalities across races. This change in attitudes is a promising finding for educational programs intended to promote cultural harmony.

Quintana and Vera (1999) questioned second and sixth grade Mexican American children and found that the younger students believed other people were prejudiced against Mexican Americans because of their physical appearance, language, or customs. By contrast, sixth graders used less obvious criteria. They were more likely to say that prejudice resulted from parents' and peers' comments or more subtle influences, such as the portrayal of Mexican Americans in the media. These age-related differences in the use of physical and social criteria parallel what others have reported for the development of the self in children (e.g., Damon & Hart, 1982). Both sets of criteria can be incorporated into education/development and prevention programs designed to reduce or eliminate prejudice in children. Clinicians should adopt a broad-based approach and design interventions that can be used in school classrooms, presented to community organizations, and disseminated to the public through the media.

Gender Identity in Children

Skin color is not the only physical characteristic that children use to classify themselves and others. As Kaplan (2000, p. 347) stated, gender represents "one of the first and most obvious distinctions" used by children to categorize people. Even 6-month-old infants have been found to discriminate between pictures of male and female faces (Katz & Kofkin, 1997). Gender awareness is an important factor in a child's identification of self. Commonly referred to as gender identity, this aspect of the self relates to a child's sense of being male or female and is often reflected in the play of young children. For example, many 3-years-old children have developed gender-stereotyped preferences for toys, with boys choosing cars and trucks and girls selecting dolls and pretend cooking utensils (Huston, 1983). Between ages 3 and 4 years, children begin to segregate into same-gender play groups and engage in different types of activities (Maccoby, 1998). For most children, these patterns continue through elementary school, although boys have been found to be more stereotyped in their toy selection and play (Huston, 1983).

Numerous theories have been proposed to explain children's development of gender identity. A recent model is gender schema theory in which consideration is given to the mental representations of maleness and femaleness that influence children's behavior and interpretation of life events. Based on their observation of others, children develop schemas regarding socially sanctioned expectations for boys and girls and women and men. These include the activities and clothing that are deemed acceptable for a child. An important factor in the development of gender schemas is a child's awareness that he or she is a girl or boy (Ruble & Martin, 1998), which includes an understanding of the socially sanctioned criteria for gender. Martin, Eisenbud, and Rose (1995), for example, found that 4- and 5-year-old children believed others of their gender had the same preference in toys but that those of the opposite gender would choose different toys. Children's beliefs about maleness and femaleness can change in response to new information. Bigler and Liben (1990, 1992) found that gender-based career stereotypes in elementary school students could be altered if children were taught to classify occupations using nongender schemes, such as workers' actual preference for different jobs and the skills required to perform these jobs.

An important consideration for children in therapy is the relationship between gender schemas and behavior. More specifically, how do these attitudes affect clients' actions in play therapy? Researchers have suggested that a child's understanding of gender typing in toys affects the client's choice of play materials. For example, Carter and Levy (1988) found that preschoolers' gender schemas were positively related to their selection of same-gender toys and negatively related to the choice of opposite-gender toys. When clinicians use play techniques with children, they should anticipate the impact of clients' gender schemas. Some boys resist using dolls or puppets in treatment because they believe these objects are for girls. Conversely, some girls avoid blocks and toy vehicles because these items are supposed to be for boys. Therapists can prepare for these reactions by having a varied collection of materials in the playroom. When gender stereotypes emerge in session, clinicians can avoid encouraging reluctant children to use certain toys because alternative play materials are available.

Various authors have found age-related differences in the self-esteem of boys and girls. As stated previously, children's evaluations of themselves are relatively consistent during the elementary school years, but a gender-based decline in self-esteem has been observed when students enter junior high school (Wigfield & Eccles, 1994). In their meta-analysis of 82,569 children, adolescents, and adults in 226 samples, Major, Barr, Zubek, and Babey (1999) found that with increasing age, girls were more at risk for low self-esteem. The authors found no significant relationship between gender and the self-evaluations of 5- to 10-year-old children, but older girls, especially those between the ages of 14 and 18 years, were more likely than boys to report lower self-esteem. The 11- to 13-year-old period seems to be a transition stage for this change. Consequently, clinicians and educators should consider the use of education/development programs for elementary school students, especially girls, to better prepare them for the transition to adolescence.

Gay, Lesbian, and Bisexual Youth

According to Fontaine (1998), gay, lesbian, and bisexual youths are one of the last minority groups "who can be victimized with few social consequences" (p. 8).

They routinely encounter teasing and harassment from peers, pressure from parents, and socially sanctioned acts based on homophobic attitudes. Most of the research on homosexuality in children has involved retrospective studies with adolescents and adults who are asked to report childhood recollections and memories. Savin-Williams (1996) conducted one such study when he interviewed homosexual and bisexual young men, ages 17 to 23 years. He found that this predominantly European American sample presented three identifiable histories. About two thirds of the respondents described same-gender attractions that occurred early in life, frequently before the first grade. A smaller group reported that as children they spent more time playing with girls in traditionally feminine activities. Although their parents may have encouraged or forced them to participate in sports, these men reported a preference for other activities, such as reading and artistic pursuits. An even smaller group in the Savin-Williams sample was composed of individuals who reported no childhood memories of same-gender attractions. For all three groups, puberty was a critical period when they became more aware of the sexual nature of their attraction to other boys.

Interviewing children about their sexual orientation presents significant ethical and practical limitations. Parents who are informed of the purpose of such a study are sometimes hesitant to allow their child to participate because of the sexual nature of the investigation. If parent consent and child assent are obtained, researchers face the challenge of designing developmentally appropriate questionnaires or interview protocols for these children. With few exceptions (e.g., Green, 1987), investigators have limited their samples to adolescents and adults. Despite the methodological problems associated with post hoc self-report, these studies have been helpful in identifying factors associated with the development of gay, lesbian, and bisexual youths. The results of this research can be used to design programs to counter the increased risk of emotional distress, drug use, and early sexual relationships observed in these individuals during adolescence (Resnick et al., 1997).

Two important developmental constructs that have been studied and are believed to originate early in life are gender identity and sexual orientation. As described earlier, gender identity is a child's awareness of being male or female. Sexual orientation is a physical-erotic attraction to others, which can be heterosexual, homosexual, or bisexual (Ryan & Futterman, 1998). Most of the research with children has been conducted on cross-gender preferences and behaviors related to gender identity. These are commonly labeled "sissy" behavior in boys and "tomboy" behavior in girls and reflect socially sanctioned limits on children's preference for different activities. Girls are typically reinforced for traditionally feminine behaviors, including ballet and painting, but boys who engage in these activities are likely to be criticized or encouraged to pursue what are viewed as more masculine interests, such as competitive sports and games. Green (1987) observed that girls are given more latitude in their use of cross-gender behaviors, including the selection of clothing. For example, wearing pants to school is considered acceptable behavior for both girls and boys, but only girls have the option of wearing dresses.

Green (1987) presented evidence for a relationship between sexual orientation and childhood gender preferences and behaviors. He conducted a 15-year longitudinal study, beginning with boys between the ages of 4 and 12 years who engaged in a significant amount of cross-gender behaviors. More than 80% of this group had expressed the desire to be a girl, almost 70% frequently engaged in cross dressing, and more than 80% had best friends who were girls. It is worth noting that parents indicated these behaviors were present at an early age. Green compared this group with a sample of similar-age boys who exhibited traditionally masculine behaviors and significantly lower rates of cross-gender preferences and behaviors. When he interviewed both groups 15 years later, he found that 75% of the traditionally feminine group self-identified as homosexual or bisexual compared with only one member of the traditionally masculine group.

When a child's cross-gender preferences are accompanied by persistent discomfort with his or her own gender and there is significant impairment in general functioning, including social and academic development, therapists must consider the presence of a gender identity disorder (American Psychiatric Association, 2000). A controversial topic (see Neisen, 1992), this diagnostic category is more likely to be used with boys, which probably reflects greater societal discomfort with cross-gender behavior in boys and men. Although the prevalence of the disorder is unknown, therapists can expect to encounter more boys than girls with this problem. Zucker (2000), for example, reported a 6:1 ratio of boys to girls, ages 3 to 12 years, in his sample of children referred for gender identity concerns. The signs of gender identity disorder often are evident in toddlers and preschoolers, and some parents and teachers initially reinforce cross-gender behaviors but alter their response as these children age (Zucker, 2000). Treatment for these children must be preceded by a thorough assessment to distinguish between children with the disorder and those exhibiting what Rekers, Kilgus, and Rosen (1990, p. 150) called "episodic and flexible exploration of masculine and feminine sex-typed behaviors" that are part of normal development (see Rekers & Kilgus, 1998, for examples). Chapter 11 discusses the behavioral play therapy that Rekers (1983) developed for children diagnosed with gender identity disorder.

Most therapeutic interventions for gay, lesbian, and bisexual youths have been designed for adolescents (see Reinert, 1998). Fontaine (1998) suggested that similar services are needed for children with gay, lesbian, and bisexual parents or siblings and the small number of elementary school students who have questions about their own sexual identity or have identified themselves as gay, lesbian, or bisexual. Clinicians who work with these children should consider the stages of lesbian or gay identity development described by Troiden (1989). He identified childhood as a sensitization period in which children recognize that they have different thoughts and feelings than their same-gender peers but do not see themselves as sexually different. With the onset of puberty, adolescents become aware of same-gender physical and erotic attractions and experience identity confusion as they try to understand these thoughts and feelings in the context of a heterosexually biased cultural surround. In treatment, therapists should strive to facilitate horizontal (i.e., "different from") rather that vertical (i.e., "better or worse than") interpretations of these children. This sometimes involves the use of educational interventions for parents and children as well as anticipatory guidance to prevent identity confusion and to foster optimal development later in life (Ryan & Futterman, 1998). A valuable resource in this regard is the Federation of Parents and Friends of Lesbians and Gays (www.pflag.org), a national organization that provides educational and support services for gay, lesbian, and bisexual individuals and their families.

SUMMARY

Child-centered theory has had a profound impact on the development of child therapies. With its positive view of human beings and its emphasis on the therapeutic relationship, this transactional model has alerted clinicians to children's roles in determining the development and direction of treatment. By capitalizing on each client's inherent potential for growth, therapists can facilitate the process of self-actualization and help the child move toward the goal of becoming a fully functioning person. Based on his early work with children and subsequent process and outcome studies with adults in therapy, Rogers described the conditions that all clinicians, regardless of theoretical orientation, must consider as they establish and maintain therapeutic relationships. Child-centered theorists discussed the importance of emotions and the self, but developmental psychologists have conducted the research to help us understand how these emerge during childhood. Although Rogers articulated the principles for his method, others adapted his theory for the treatment of children. Chapter 9 examines these applications, including play interventions that can be used to remediate problems, prevent future difficulties, and encourage growth in all children.

9

Child-Centered Interventions

▪▪▪

Mr. and Mrs. Jackson request therapy for 5-year-old Joanne. The parents are worried about their daughter's reaction to the recent accidental death of her 16-year-old brother. Both parents are concerned that Joanne has shown no emotional response to their son's death. "She acts as if nothing has happened," Mrs. Jackson says. They, on the other hand, are very distraught about their loss and intend to do everything possible to help their daughter adjust to this family tragedy. As Mr. Jackson says, "My wife and I don't want Joanne to be harmed by all this. We want her to be a normal kid and just accept what's happened."

▪▪▪

The loss of a loved one is a significant event in the life of a family. Survivors often call on each other for emotional support and understanding. When these resources are inadequate, families sometimes seek therapeutic help. These cases are especially challenging when one of the survivors is a child whose developmental level is very different from that of parents and older siblings.

This chapter discusses education/development, prevention, and remediation techniques that are based on the theoretical principles presented in Chapter 8. It explores the therapeutic role of the child and adult caregivers as well as the contributions and limitations of child-centered treatment. At the end of the chapter, we continue with the case of 5-year-old Joanne to discuss how this method can be used with children who have experienced the death of a loved one.

ASSESSMENT

Most child-centered therapists do not use formal assessment and diagnostic procedures with clients. As Rogers (1946) stated, the traditional use of tests can alter the therapeutic relationship because clients are treated as subordinates of the expert therapist. Rogers was not always so reluctant to use formal measures in treatment. For his dissertation at Columbia University, he developed an objective measure of personality adjustment for 9- to 13-year-old children (Rogers, 1931). This paper-and pencil inventory, the Test of Personality Adjustment, was designed to assess children's views of themselves and their families. Although the instrument has its limitations, including the reading level for younger children, it represents an important step in the development of objective child-report measures of psychological adjustment.

In *The Clinical Treatment of the Problem Child*, Rogers (1939) devoted an entire chapter to personality assessment and diagnosis. He described a number of objective and projective measures that offer "one means of determining 'what's wrong' with a misbehaving or delinquent child" (p. 17). He believed that tests should be used in combination with other techniques, such as the clinical interview, to identify the causes of a client's problems and to obtain a comprehensive view of the child. Rogers' interest in assessment waned when he was a faculty member at Ohio State University and concluded that the diagnostic use of tests was inconsistent with his theoretical principles (Ellinwood & Raskin, 1993).

Unlike traditional approaches to assessment in which the clinician collects information and determines the client's problem, child-centered therapists are more likely to use the therapeutic relationship to understand the child from the client's point of view. Psychological tests are thought to impede the development of the very relationship that provides this information and serves as the foundation for therapeutic growth. Although some Rogerians have used assessment instruments for research purposes, most tend to avoid their use in clinical settings (Sharf, 2000). But the advent of brief therapies has meant that clinicians have less time to form hypotheses about client problems. For this reason, child-, parent, and teacher-report measures merit consideration in child-centered therapies. The administration of psychometrically sound and clinically relevant instruments at the outset of treatment can be helpful in identifying the family member (or members) who will be the focus of therapy. Assessment results also provide information about a child's preferred mode of expression (e.g., internalizing and externalizing behaviors). By combining these data with observations made during the clinical interview, therapists can obtain a more complete picture of the child and develop a treatment plan in a timely manner.

Ellinwood and Raskin (1993) stated that child-centered clinicians perform assessments in a way that communicates care, understanding, and respect for the client. Test results are shared with parents and sometimes with older children, so clients can use this information to decide the direction of treatment. But therapists must remember Rogers' warnings and recognize that a formal pretreatment assessment can alter the therapeutic relationship if the child views the clinician as an expert. Ellinwood and Raskin observed that some children have difficulty making the transition from the structured assessment protocol to the less restrictive atmosphere of therapy that often includes play activities. Clinicians can facilitate this change by attending to their behavior during the assessment stage to ensure that child-centered principles, such as respect and empathy, are used.

EDUCATION/DEVELOPMENT AND PREVENTION

Rogers was interested in educational and therapeutic applications of his theoretical principles. In *Freedom to Learn* (1969), he described learning as a self-initiated act of discovery in which the student is personally involved and aware of the changes that are occurring in different developmental domains. An extremely important factor in this process is the teacher, who has the responsibility of facilitating the learning process (Rogers, 1951). Child-centered teachers accept students as they are and strive to facilitate their self-awareness. Instead of being forced to conform, students are encouraged to express their feelings and gain personal insight in the presence of a supportive adult (Axline, 1944).

Students in child-centered classrooms acquire information and skills that are of interest to them and relevant to their developing self-concept. When a teacher presents information that is inconsistent with a student's view of him- or herself, the child typically rejects or distorts this threat to the self. Learning occurs when threats are minimized and the student can experience different perspectives on relevant issues. Child-centered teachers create classroom environments where students have access to resource materials on topics of interest to them. Teachers trust students and recognize the importance of children's feelings in this idiosyncratic journey of self-discovery. The "open classroom" movement of the 1960s and 1970s was an example of a child-centered learning environment. In these schools, children progressed at their own rates of speed, consistent with their interests and abilities.

Child-centered theory was developed in the United States, but A. S. Neill (1960) applied its principles at Summerhill in Leiston, England. The purpose of this coeducational boarding school was "*to make the school fit the child*—instead of making the child fit the school" (Neill, 1960, p. 4) Neill believed that children have the capacity and desire to learn. If adults can refrain from imposing restrictions and demands, students will develop their innate abilities and grow up to become teachers, sanitation workers, or whatever interests them so they can enjoy a fulfilling life. As Neill stated:

> The function of the child is to live his own life—not the life that his anxious parents think he should live, nor a

> life according to the purpose of the educator who thinks he knows what is best. All this interference and guidance on the part of adults only produces a generation of robots. (p. 12)

Class attendance was optional at Summerhill. In fact, relatively few restrictions were placed on the students. A schedule of daily events was posted, but children could choose whether to follow it. Throughout his text, Neill provides interesting and humorous examples of students' adjustment to Summerhill. He believed that his school was successful because his teachers and he tried to avoid interfering with their students' natural tendency toward healthy and fulfilling lives.

Gordon (1974) developed Teacher Effectiveness Training (TET) to help educators use child-centered techniques in the classroom. Rogers and others highlighted the importance of the therapist–client relationship. Gordon described how the teacher–student relationship affects the educational process. He believed that teachers can enhance the learning environment by exhibiting an open and caring manner that facilitates the development of students' creativity and individuality. Teachers who use TET principles in the classroom listen to students and encourage them to share their thoughts and feelings. Teachers model appropriate feedback by replacing threats and accusatory "you" statements (e.g., "Thomas, you are acting really dumb") with "I" messages that more accurately reflect the instructor's thoughts and feelings (e.g., "Thomas, when you throw your pencil, I get very upset because I worry that someone will get hurt"). The principles that Gordon used to develop TET are similar to those presented in Parent Effectiveness Training (Gordon, 1970), which is examined in Chapter 13.

Child-centered principles have also been incorporated into preventive play techniques for children. Hoffman (1991), for example, described how individual or small group play sessions can be used to facilitate preschoolers' development of self-esteem and interpersonal skills. Moustakas (1953) used child-centered play therapy with normal nursery and elementary school children. In session, clients were offered a safe place to express and explore thoughts and feelings. Moustakas believed this experience helped children process minor difficulties before serious problems developed. Another preventive application of play is filial therapy, which has been used to foster healthy parent–child relationships. Guerney (1964) developed filial therapy to teach parents to play with their children. Similar to later interventions such as parent–child interaction therapy (Eyberg, Boggs, & Algina, 1995; see Chapter 16), Guerney's method involves the application of child-centered principles to foster more effective interactions between parents and children. Instructors conduct small group sessions to explain and demonstrate the use of play techniques. They also use client-centered methods to facilitate parents' disclosure of their thoughts and feelings regarding the at-home use of play with their children. Guerney (1997) stated that numerous studies have been conducted on filial therapy and that the approach appears to decrease negative behaviors in children and improve the relationship between parents and their children.

REMEDIATION

Child-centered principles have been the foundation for talk therapies, play-based interventions, and combinations of the two. Common to all is a belief in the importance of the therapist–client relationship, including its affective component. As Rogers (1951) stated, "The words—of either client or counselor—are seen as having minimal importance compared with the present emotional relationship which exists between the two" (p. 172). This does not mean that child-centered therapists have no interest in the facts they collect during their sessions with children. But the therapeutic potential of this information is thought to be less significant than the relationship that develops between the clinician and child. Moustakas (1959) described the process of client-centered play therapy as follows:

> A relationship between the child and therapist in the setting of a playroom, where the child is encouraged to express himself freely, to release pent-up emotions and repressed feelings, and to work through his fear and anger so that he comes to be himself and functions in terms of his real potentials and abilities. (p. 227)

Child-centered therapists believe that it is the therapist–client relationship that provides the opportunity for personal growth.

Child-centered treatments are based on the same theory that Rogers espoused for therapy with adults. Clinicians emphasize the child's potential for growth, respect the client's integrity, and attempt to minimize the effects of developmentally restrictive environmental influences (Rogers, 1943). Rogers (1951) believed that treatment facilitates the organization of the client's self-system. With adult clients, this often involves overcoming the accumulation of negative interpersonal experiences from the past in pursuit of a positive self-concept. When the client is a child whose self-system is developing, clinicians are able to remediate current interpersonal conflicts and promote positive views of self and others.

In their work with young clients, child-centered therapists have devoted considerable time and effort to the development of play-based interventions. Although these treatments are based on Rogerian principles, their techniques vary from one clinician and client to the next. One factor that can be used to distinguish child-centered treatments is the amount of structure the therapist imposes on play sessions. Some clinicians prefer a more structured approach in which they direct the child's play through the use of materials that are relevant to the client's presenting problem. With children of divorce, for example, therapists sometimes provide family puppets for clients to explore their relationships with parents and siblings. Moustakas (1959) and Axline (1947) preferred an unstructured approach that gives children greater latitude in their choice of therapeutic activities. Proponents of the structured and unstructured methods agree that clinicians must focus their attention on the child's verbal and nonverbal behavior in therapy sessions. This requires the use of skills typically referred to as *active listening*.

Table 9–1
Active Listening Skills for Child-Centered Therapists

1. Minimal encouragers: Verbal (e.g., "Uh-huh") and nonverbal (e.g., leaning forward, a nod of the head) behaviors designed to communicate acceptance and facilitate client self-disclosure
2. Closed questions: Typically begin with "do," "is," or "are," and tend to limit client self-disclosure; can be used to focus discussion or collect information about a specific topic
3. Open questions: Usually begin with "how," "what," "when," or "where," and encourage clients disclosure of thoughts and feelings
4. Reflection of feeling: A statement intended to identify or describe the affect in a client's message and to facilitate the exploration of feelings
5. Paraphrase: Rewording a client's statement or recent statements to communicate understanding and to encourage discussion of a clinically relevant issue
6. Summarization: An integrative restatement of the thoughts, feelings, and behaviors described by a client during part or all of the therapeutic hour or across therapy sessions
7. Confrontation: The presentation or juxtaposition of conflicting messages to address inconsistencies in a client's statements
8. Self-disclosure: A therapist's sharing of personal experiences that are related to those of the client
9. Silence: The avoidance of verbal and nonverbal interruptions so both the therapist and child can contemplate significant issues

Active Listening

Child-centered therapists use active listening and basic attending skills in therapy sessions to facilitate the process of discovery for children. Table 9-1 contains a summary of these skills. Verbal and nonverbal minimal encouragers communicate interest in a client's message and facilitate disclosure of thoughts and feelings. By saying "I see" or "Uh-huh" in response to clients' comments, therapists can encourage children to explore clinically relevant topics. The same outcome can be pursued using such nonverbal behaviors as leaning toward the client to communicate interest in what the child is saying, using a nod of the head to acknowledge a client's self-disclosure, or smiling as the child engages in therapeutic play. Of course, clinicians must always consider differences in physical size between themselves and children when using nonverbal minimal encouragers. By sitting on the floor during play sessions, for example, therapists can minimize height discrepancies that might impede the development of eye contact with children.

Chapter 4 discussed the use of open and closed questions in clinical interviews. Therapists can encourage client self-disclosure during treatment sessions by using open questions that begin with "how," "what," "when," or "where." Clinicians who use these questions with young clients must remember that children are probably more familiar with the closed questions that adults use in everyday discourse. When a therapist asks a closed question, such as "Did you have fun at school today?", the child can respond with a simple "yes" or "no" answer. The use of an open question, such as, "What did you do at school today?", encourages the client to elaborate and provide more than a one-word response. Clinicians who make creative use of open questions can help children explore thoughts and feelings about significant events and issues. Therapists should limit their use of closed questions to situations in which brief answers are desired. They also should avoid "why" questions, which clients might interpret as accusations because adults often use these questions to criticize children (e.g., "Why did you do that?").

Child-centered therapists use a variety of techniques to encourage client disclosure of thoughts and feelings. Reflection is intended to facilitate disclosure of feelings, and paraphrase and summarization are designed to encourage discussion of content. Moore, Presbury, Smith, and McKee (1999) indicated that with children, reflection is used in response to overt disclosure of affect and the expression of feelings that appear to be "under the surface or implicit in what the child is saying" (p. 167). In *Dibs: In Search of Self*, Axline (1964) used this technique with a very intelligent but troubled young boy. When Dibs refused to leave a play session, Axline acknowledged his desire to remain but informed him that it was the end of the therapy hour. She then offered to help him get dressed for his trip home:

> I waited while he thought this over. He sat down on the little chair, whimpering. I put on his shoes and then his boots—without much cooperation from him. Tears rolled down his cheeks as he sat there.
>
> "You are unhappy, now," I said. "I understand how you feel, Dibs." (p. 30)

In this brief interchange, Axline verbalized the negative affect the boy was expressing through his noncompliant behavior. Axline (1947) warned that clinicians must be prepared to accept "any feeling" (p. 149) from a child. In this way, they communicate that therapy is a safe place where both positive and negative feelings may be shared without fear of reprisal.

Child-centered therapists focus on the present in their interactions with clients. This involves reflecting feelings that clients express in therapy sessions. For this technique to be effective, clinicians must attend to momentary changes in the child's tone of voice, play behaviors, and verbal statements. Moustakas (1953) described how reflection was used with an aggressive 7-year-old boy.

C: I'll drill the whole place full of lead! Do you hear me? I'm gonna dirty this place up so far that I don't think you'll be able to clean this stuff up with all the water in the world. I'm gonna really fix this stuff, I'm telling you. I'm gonna mess this room up like a coyote. And then I'll take this jackknife and cut everything up. Then I'll try it on you next!

T: You want to show me how very angry you can be. (p. 61)

Notice how the therapist did not respond to the client's specific comments. Instead, the child's threats were interpreted as a here-and-now statement of his feelings.

Therapists use paraphrase to communicate understanding of the content and meaning of a client's message. Significant words from the client's statement are integrated into this response. Paraphrase is used to reword either a single comment or a limited number of related statements made by the child. Axline (1964) used this technique with Dibs in the following manner:

> "Finger paints," he said. "They are not of interest to me. I will paint a picture."
>
> "Think you would rather paint a picture?" I said.
>
> "Yes," he replied. "With the watercolor." (p. 37)

Notice how Axline's paraphrase ended with a question mark. Whenever therapists use reflection or paraphrase, they are never completely certain that their response accurately describes the child's thoughts and feelings. Axline could have used a declarative sentence, but she appropriately paraphrased Dibs' words in a questioning manner. In this brief example, she happened to be correct.

Therapists use summarization to restate the information that clients share over a longer period of time in session. Consider a child who devotes 30 minutes to conflicted peer relationships and possible solutions for this problem. In this case, the therapist could summarize the content of the client's remarks as follows:

> It sounds like the other kids at school have teased you an awful lot. You've thought about telling the teachers, but you're not sure that's the best idea.

Clinicians sometimes use summarization to bring together related topics. The therapist in our example uses the following intervention to combine material from different sessions:

Last week you told me how you stopped the neighborhood kids from teasing you. I'm wondering if you ever thought about doing some of those things at school.

Confrontation involves the presentation of two conflicting ideas or choices to the child. Some clinicians are reluctant to use confrontation because they believe it is a negative intervention that can harm the therapist–client relationship. But Moore et al. (1999) stated that when done in a caring manner, confrontation "invites children to examine their behavior and decide if they want to change" (p. 167). Axline (1964) used this technique with Dibs when he resisted leaving therapy at the end of the treatment hour. Consider how she juxtaposed the time limits of therapy with Dibs' desire to remain in the playroom.

> "Your time in the playroom for today is almost up," I said. "There are only five more minutes left."
>
> Dibs ignored me. He continued to make squares of painted color in the same rigid sequence—red, orange, yellow, green, blue, black, white, violet.
>
> Finally, the fifth minute came and went. I stood up. "Our time is up now, Dibs," I said. "It is time to go."
>
> But Dibs did not want to go.
>
> "No!" he shouted. "Dibs not go! Dibs stay!"
>
> "I know you don't want to go, Dibs," I said again. "But our time is up for today and you will have to go home now. You may come back again next week. And the week after that. And the week after that. But each time, after our hour is up, you will have to go home." (p. 30)

Therapy is a time-limited endeavor, so clinicians must prepare young clients for the end of the therapy hour as Axline did with Dibs. Many children respond to the clinician's intervention by making preparations for their departure. Therapists who experience resistance from a client can use gentle confrontation similar to Axline's intervention.

Child-centered clinicians make limited use of self-disclosure with their clients. Still, it is sometimes appropriate for a therapist to share personal experiences that are clinically relevant. Clinicians must assess each situation to determine whether self-disclosure will be therapeutic. If a client asks, "Did anybody tease you when you were a kid?" the therapist must determine whether self-disclosure will facilitate the child's exploration of this significant area or focus attention on the needs of the clinician. Therapists disclose personal experiences to expand clients' awareness of an issue or problem. They do not use this technique to tell children what to do. Consider a clinician who learned in third grade that ignoring students' teasing and name calling can eliminate these behaviors. Sharing this experience to expand a client's perspective is an appropriate use of self-disclosure. Recounting how it felt to be teased as a child facilitates development of the therapeutic relationship because the client learns how the therapist reacted to this experience.

Effective use of silence is very difficult for many clinicians. Therapists are trained to question clients, conceptualize children's behaviors, and respond using the verbal methods described. Most clinicians receive very little training in the therapeutic uses of silence, possibly because the standard for everyday interpersonal relationships is the verbal exchange of information. Being silent in the presence of others who are also quiet is an exceptional experience. Whether a therapist uses silence with a quiet child depends on the quality of the therapeutic relationship and the stage of treatment when silence occurs. Rogers (1942a) believed this technique tended to have a negative effect during an initial interview but was useful during later sessions when therapist–client rapport had developed.

To effectively use silence with children, therapists must determine why the client is quiet in session. Anxious or uncomfortable silence typically merits supportive or redirective statements from the clinician. When a child's silence represents boredom, a change in activity is warranted. Another type of silence that is observed in therapy can be described as contemplative. When this occurs, the therapist should remain quiet to avoid interrupting the client's thought process. After a sufficient period of time, the clinician could encourage disclosure by saying, "Sounds like you've got something on your mind," or asking, "What kind of thoughts are going through your head right now?" Of course, the therapist's challenge is to correctly identify the reason for a child's silence and to select the most appropriate intervention.

Dorfman (1951) described the quiet child in therapy. She believed that the clinician's acceptance of a child's silence can itself be therapeutic as the client realizes that silence is one of many behaviors that are appropriate during the therapy hour. Dorfman provided the following example of a 9-year-old boy who had quietly painted throughout the session:

DICK: How much time do I have left now?

THERAPIST: Five more minutes, Dick.

DICK: (SIGHS VERY DEEPLY) Ah, five minutes more *all to myself*.

THERAPIST: (VERY SOFTLY) Five more minutes *all your own*, Dick?
DICK: Yes! (p. 246)

For the remainder of the session, the child closes his eyes and quietly rocks back and forth in a rocking chair. The therapist is silent until the end of the hour, when she reflects the boy's feelings.

THERAPIST: It feels good just to sit and rock.
DICK: (*Nods.*)
THERAPIST: That's all the time we have for today, Dick.
DICK: O.K. (*He gets up immediately and goes to the door with the therapist. They say good-bye, and he goes out.*) (p. 246)

Treatment Stages

Axline (1947) warned that clinicians must not hurry the process of child-centered play therapy. But the duration of treatment is a significant consideration in the world of contemporary practice. Limits imposed by managed mental health care companies combined with the number of troubled children in need of therapeutic services restrict the use of lengthy interventions. Fortunately, play therapists have adjusted to these limits. Phillips and Landreth (1995), for example, found that the median number of sessions used by play therapists ranged from 11 to 20. Landreth and Sweeney (1997) described studies in which positive outcomes were achieved in fewer than 10 sessions.

Clinicians can improve the efficiency of play therapy if they consider how clients tend to respond at various points in treatment. Moustakas (1955) observed that children seem to progress through five different stages of emotional growth. At the outset of therapy, disturbed children are likely to express negative feelings in a pervasive and unfocused manner. In fact, it is usually the intensity and frequency of the client's expression of these feelings that has prompted significant others to seek treatment for the child. In the following example, Moustakas described how June exhibited her anxiety through a series of confusing responses:

J: Where is it?
T: Where is *it*?
J: What?
T: Whatever it was you were looking for.
J: I'm not looking for anything.
T: You're not looking for anything.
J: Yes, now I am.
T: You *are* looking for something.
J: Yes. (*Laughs.*) (p. 85)

Play therapists must be prepared to respond to different levels of client anxiety during their first session with the child. Landreth and Sweeney (1997) recommended that therapists introduce the child to the play setting, help the client feel comfortable and safe, and lay the foundation for a trusting therapeutic relationship. The clinician must not dominate the interaction. Instead of providing lengthy explanations of playroom activities and behavioral limits, therapists should offer succinct statements and permit the client to assume the leadership role in treatment. For most children, this meeting is their first therapy experience, so the clinician's behavior influences clients' expectations for later sessions.

During the second stage of treatment, the client's expression of negative feelings becomes ambivalent. Moustakas (1955) described changes that occurred in one child's puppet play. Initially, the client stated that she did not like any of the puppets in the playroom. She then indicated that she liked one of the puppets, but she immediately contradicted herself by saying, "No. I don't like him either" (p. 87). Moustakas observed that the ambivalence of the second stage becomes more focused during the third stage, when clients symbolically express negative feelings toward significant others. Young Vera exhibited anger toward her parents and newborn sibling as follows:

V: (*Picks up group of family dolls.*) Bang. Bang-bang . . . what I'm thinking. There. I'm gonna shoot the baby. They're Indians. I'm an Indian.
T: You're going to shoot them.
V: Yeah. Bang. Shoot her. All of them. (p. 88)

A different form of ambivalence appears during the fourth stage when the child's play behavior vacillates between positive and negative emotions. Moustakas (1955) described how Mary struggled with her attendance at sessions.

M: Well, I don't like this playroom anyway, with all these dirty old puppets and that old thing. (*Walks to shelves, picks up a puppet and throws it down, slaps Bobo in passing.*)
T: You really don't like these things.
M: (*Anxiously.*) But I can come here again, can't I?
T: Are you afraid that maybe you can't?

M: I can still come here, can't I?
T: Yes, if you want to come again. (p. 91)

Notice how the therapist gave a direct answer at the end of this interaction to reduce the client's anxiety.

During the last stage of play therapy, children exhibit insight and express negative and positive feelings in a clearer manner. Moustakas (1955) stated that at this point in treatment, clients are more likely to discuss positive thoughts and feelings. When negative emotions are expressed, they are less frequent and intense than at the outset of therapy. Moustakas' five-stage model offers a general framework for therapists to use when evaluating clients' behavior in play therapy. Although empirical support for the nature and sequence of these stages is unavailable at this time, clinicians can expect that disturbed clients will typically become more focused over the course of treatment as their diffuse expression of negative feelings is gradually replaced with a more normal balance of positive and negative emotions.

PLAY TECHNIQUES: THE PLAYROOM AND PLAY MATERIALS

Throughout this chapter, we have discussed child-centered therapists' use of play with children. When clinicians use therapeutic play with young clients, they must have access to the proper setting and materials required to conduct this special type of treatment. Axline (1947) described the playroom as "good growing ground" (p. 16) where children are free to express their thoughts and feelings in therapy without fear of adult recrimination. Landreth (1991) suggested that playrooms should be located where the noise of children's play does not interrupt other clinicians in their work with clients. The room needs to be about 12 feet by 15 feet in size, have no windows that would distract the child (and therapist), and contain a vinyl floor and enamel painted walls for easy cleaning. It should also have a one-way mirror or closed-circuit videotaping system to allow observation of therapy sessions. Landreth indicated that the room should be equipped with a cold-water sink, a chalkboard, and shelves and storage space for play materials. When new construction is planned, he recommended that therapists design their playrooms to include a bathroom. This eliminates clients' requests to leave the therapy room to use the bathroom during treatment. Finally, the room should be furnished with a child's table and chairs and one adult chair for the clinician.

Similar to their psychodynamic counterparts, child-centered play therapists equip the therapy room with selected toys, manipulatives (e.g., wooden building blocks), puppets, competitive and noncompetitive board games (see Chapter 15), and art supplies. Play materials are central to the process of therapy because "toys are children's words and play is their language" (Landreth, 1991, p. 116). If control of these words is to be left to the child, then toys should be arranged in an unstructured manner in the playroom so clients can choose the materials they will use during therapy sessions. This approach facilitates client self-disclosure across a broad range of issues and concerns. When a more focused discussion is desired, therapists select toys that are appealing to the child and provide a means of exploring specific issues. A sexually abused child, for example, might have access to family puppets or dolls and a dollhouse, art materials, and therapeutic board games.

When therapists purchase play materials, they must consider each item's purpose in treatment. As Landreth (1991) warned, "Toys and materials should be selected, not collected" (p. 117). Landreth recommended that clinicians choose toys that are durable, appropriate for clients of different ages, and useful in solitary play and parallel or cooperative play by the therapist and child. To these criteria we might add that play materials should stimulate children's creativity. For example, wooden building blocks can be used for a number of purposes. When combined, they symbolically represent buildings or bridges; individually, they can be used as a car or truck traveling on a pretend highway. The creative potential for items such as these is significantly greater than a battery-powered remote-controlled vehicle that offers fewer expressive options for the child. Therapists sometimes involve children in the creation of play materials. This includes the design and construction of puppets that represent a client's unique personality (James & Myer, 1987).

Therapists who conduct play sessions must become skilled and comfortable with play materials, including puppets, before they actually use them with their clients (James & Myer, 1987). To capture the child's attention, therapists must continuously manipulate the puppet and create a unique voice for each character. In child-centered therapy, puppets should not be used as an indirect way of interrogating the child. Instead, they are an integral part of the therapist's active listening and are used to express open questions, paraphrase, and reflection of feelings. Clinicians must overcome the initial anxiety that often accompanies a novice's use of puppets in treatment. James and Myer (1987) recommended that therapists observe competent clinicians and practice with normal children before using puppets with clients. Of course, this is also good advice for becoming competent with the broad array of play materials that are used with children.

James and Myer (1987) stated that therapists must pace themselves and follow the child's lead when developing a puppet's character. The authors offered the case of Dennis to illustrate how a clinician can begin a puppet session and use puppets to help children examine clinically relevant topics.

COUNSELOR: I have a number of puppets in here who are my friends. This is Uncle Zach. He's a special friend of mine and talks to kids a lot for me when I'm too shy to do it myself. Say "Hello" to Dennis.

ZACH: How y'all doing thar youngun? How'se 'bout find'n a puppet that'd shoot the breeze with old Zach? (*Dennis looks over the puppets and picks up a shark.*)

DENNIS: I'm Jaws and I can do anything I want! I can eat everything, even you, Uncle Zach!

ZACH: Shore do sound like you madder 'n wet hen today, Jaws.

DENNIS: It's not just Jaws, but I'm mad today, too.

ZACH: Gee whilikers, Dennis, how'se about telling me what yer so mad about?

DENNIS: You know, Bobby and all those other kids just keep calling me names.

ZACH: So, if you had all them thar teeth and were jest as big and powerful as Jaws, you wouldn't have to take none ah that thar slack jaw from Bobby and his bunch. (pp. 295–296)

In this case, Dennis was a good candidate for puppet play because he readily engaged the clinician in the role of Zach. Notice how the therapist reflected the child's feelings while portraying Zach and refocusing the client from Jaws to himself. As an alternative intervention, the therapist could have assumed the role of clinician and interacted directly with Zach as follows: "Wow, Zach, Dennis is really angry today. Somebody's done something that he's really mad about" (James & Myer, 1987, p. 296). Through skillful transitions from the puppet's fantasy world to the reality of the present, therapists can help children explore their emotional world and facilitate problem solving.

GROUP TECHNIQUES

Child-centered group therapy involves the use of structured and unstructured formats. Axline (1947) adopted the latter in her application of child-centered principles to groups. Therapists who conduct unstructured groups prefer to follow the lead of the child but are directive to the extent needed to ensure the safety of all members. Clinicians in these groups attend to the therapeutic process using the same active listening skills that child-centered therapists use in individual treatment. Axline offered the following transcript of a group for five boys, ages 7 to 9 years, who were referred for the treatment of behavior problems.

TIMMY: I'll mash your head in. (*Bobby pouts.*)

THERAPIST: You certainly don't like the way Timmy treats you sometimes.

BOBBY: No!

TIMMY: Well!

BOBBY: Next time I'll put on a puppet show and one of them will be Timmy and I'll beat him up.

THERAPIST: You can beat up the puppet, and get the best of it when you feel like that. (p. 245)

The clinician in this case used reflection of feeling in response to Bobby's nonverbal behavior and paraphrase to describe the child's plans for puppet play. These interventions provided emotional support for the child, defused the boys' conflict, and maintained a safe therapeutic environment.

Moore et al. (1999) observed that contemporary child-centered groups for children are more likely to have a thematic structure, such as the development of friendships and self-esteem. Therapists in these groups also use active listening skills, but they plan and implement activities for each session to address their treatment goals. A common setting for structured groups is public schools. An example of this approach to group treatment is "The Go For It Club," which Boutwell and Myrick (1992) developed to facilitate academic performance in low-achieving elementary school children. The authors used a variety of structured activities with groups of 6 to 10 students who met once or twice a week for 30 minutes. One technique was "Rhythm Sticks" during which children sit in a circle and pass a stick while music is playing. When the music stops, the child holding the stick is asked to talk about the topic for the session, which might be a successful school experience or the best way to study for a test. Based on informal evaluations of their method, Boutwell and Myrick reported that approximately 80% of the students were exhibiting better classroom behavior and academic performance by the end of the 6-week program.

Child-centered principles have been integrated with other theories to design and implement structured group therapies for children. Boutwell and Myrick (1992), for example, used operant conditioning in "The Go For It Club" by rewarding students for their weekly participation and classroom performance. In their group for adopted children, Kizner and Kizner (1999) combined self-esteem enhancement and exploration of feelings with a psychoeducational component to introduce members to the process of adoption. Additionally, Peled and Davis (1995) included client self-disclosure and self-esteem development in a group for children of abused mothers that also contained a unit on self-protection to teach members how to use conflict resolution and assertiveness skills.

Many group methods that are used with children are based, at least partly, on child-centered theory. For example, therapists often use active listening in session and have self-enhancement as their treatment goal for children. Increased interest in brief therapies has translated into greater use of structured methods, which are more likely to involve child-centered techniques combined with behavioral and psychoeducational interventions. Vernon (1999), for example, described the format for an eight-session group for children of divorce. Her program contains the psychoeducational, child-centered, and cognitive-behavioral goals of facilitating clients' understanding of divorce, expression of feelings, and acquisition of coping skills. She combined art, drama, and roleplay activities with an informational videotape and a group interview with a divorced parent to address members' thoughts, feelings, and behaviors.

RESEARCH

Research on child-centered treatments is relatively limited, especially compared with the number of empirical studies conducted on behavioral interventions for children. Early in the development of client-centered therapies, pioneers in the field investigated the process and outcome of this novel approach. A result of these efforts is *Psychotherapy and Personality Change*, which contains Rogers and Dymond's (1954) compilation of results from studies conducted during Rogers' tenure at the University of Chicago. Also in this text is Gordon, Grumman, Rogers, and Seeman's (1954) description of two impediments to the scientific study of psychotherapy: the complexity of the therapeutic process and clinicians' opposition to controlled treatment studies. Since the publication of *Psychotherapy and Personality Change*, various researchers have confronted these challenges and conducted data-based studies on the process and outcome of client-centered therapies.

Lebo (1951) reviewed the empirical literature on child-centered play therapy and concluded that it was "meager, unsound, and frequently of a cheerful, persuasive nature" (p. 177). Early efforts in the area were hampered by a lack of adequate measures of play process, small samples, and poor research designs. The number of controlled studies on child-centered therapy is still very limited, and the gap between this work and the research on behavioral and cognitive-behavioral treatments continues to widen. This discrepancy is an unfortunate result of the philosophical differences between data-oriented behavioral approaches and experiential child-centered interventions. If these treatments are to thrive in a managed mental health care environment, investigators must expand on the process and outcome studies currently available on child-centered play therapy.

Early work in the area was devoted to studies of the behavior of therapists and children in therapy sessions. Landisberg and Snyder (1946) analyzed the content of clinicians' interactions with their clients and reported results that are consistent with Rogers' principles. Specifically, the authors observed that children made approximately 60% of the responses during the therapy hour, and clinicians accounted for the remainder. Therapists were most likely to give nondirective responses, such as clarification and reflection; children tended to disclose information or engage in play behaviors. Landisberg and Snyder offered support for the use of active listening when they found that 85% of clients' responses were preceded by a nondirective intervention from the therapist.

Landisberg and Snyder (1946) studied the therapeutic process using response categories originally designed for adult clients. To overcome this methodological limitation, researchers have developed rating scales that specifically target children's behaviors in play therapy. One of the most comprehensive is the Moustakas and Schalock (1955) play process scale which contains 82 therapist and 72 child response categories. Although some researchers have used measures such as this to analyze the behavior of young clients in treatment, others have conducted process studies with normal children at play. For example, Lebo (1952) studied the in-session behavior of 4- to 12-year-old clients and found that older children were less likely to test limits and request information from the therapist. They were also more likely to make comments, both positive and negative, about their playroom experiences and significant others in their life.

Truax and his colleagues asked whether the therapist-offered conditions of empathy, warmth, and genuineness that are significant with adult clients are also important for children in therapy. Traux, Altmann, Wright, and Mitchell (1973) trained observers to rate 16 clinicians in their work with children. They found that high levels of empathy, warmth, and genuineness appeared to have a positive impact on clients' improvement in therapy. Although these results are encouraging, it must be noted that interrater reliabilities on the scales used to measure these conditions were typically lower than previously reported for adults in treatment (Wright, Truax, & Mitchell, 1972). Additional work is needed in this area, especially with children of different ethnic backgrounds, to determine the effect of therapist conditions on treatment process and outcome.

Myrick and Haldin (1971) conducted a formal case study of child-centered play therapy with a disruptive, first-grade boy. The authors collected pretreatment observational data on the child's negative acts in class, teacher ratings of his behavior, and the boy's report of self-concept. Treatment involved 30-minute sessions of child-centered play therapy that were delivered in school on 15 consecutive class days. Results revealed a marked decline in disruptive behavior as well as pretreatment-posttreatment improvement in the teacher's behavioral ratings and the child's descriptions of himself. Unfortunately, others have not followed the example set by Myrick and Haldin. By incorporating a formal evaluation into their treatment of a single child, the authors were able to collect and report interesting findings on the outcome of therapy. Researchers and practitioners alike should expand on the work of Myrick and Haldin by adopting the single-case experimental design to conduct controlled analyses of play techniques with children in therapy.

Contrary to the common assumption that child-centered play therapy is a lengthy process, numerous researchers have reported positive outcomes for brief-term interventions intended to address psychological and educational problems. Bills (1950), for example, found that a sample of third graders with reading deficits exhibited significant improvement in their reading ability after a maximum of six individual and three group sessions of play therapy. In their case study of a 4-year-old girl who had pulled out all of her hair, Barlow, Strother, and Landreth (1985) reported that the child's behavior was more appropriate and her hair had begun to grow back after eight sessions of child-centered play therapy and biweekly consultations with her parents.

More recently, Burroughs, Wagner, and Johnson (1997) assigned children of divorce to five sessions of either structured play therapy or therapeutic board game treatment using *My Two Homes* (The Center for Applied Psychology, 1992) (see Chapter 15). The authors found a significant pretreatment-posttreatment decline for both interventions in parents' ratings of clients' internalizing behaviors and children's self-report of state and trait anxiety. Play therapy in this study included having children draw pictures to represent different emotions (in the second session); construction of a collage to represent self (in the third session); and writing stories for the front page of a pretend newspaper that contained blank columns with labels such as Headline, Hobbies/Sports, and School (in the fourth session). Burroughs et al. did not use a control condition in their study, so they were unable to determine whether their interventions were better than no treatment. But Rae, Worchel, Upchurch, Sanner, and Daniel (1989) addressed this limitation in their study of child-centered play therapy.

Rae et al. (1989) treated children, ages 5 to 10 years, who were admitted to a hospital pediatric ward for surgery (e.g., tonsillectomy) or treatment of infectious diseases. The authors compared child-centered play therapy with diversionary play (i.e., nontherapeutic play with various toys), supportive talk therapy without toys, and a waiting list control condition. Treatments were limited to two 30-minute sessions delivered in the child's hospital room. Rae et al. found that children who received play therapy reported a significantly greater decline in hospital-related fears than did children in the other three conditions. Interestingly, the authors' play intervention was more effective than a talk therapy condition based on child-centered principles. This appears to support traditional claims that children respond better to play-based interventions than the verbal therapies used with adolescents and adults.

The Rae et al. (1989) investigation is another model that clinicians can use to develop their own studies of child-centered therapy. Of particular importance is the authors' decision to conduct their controlled comparison in a real-life setting where children were being exposed to a stressful experience. Additional research on child-centered interventions is sorely needed to expand on the relatively limited number of studies now available. This includes studies of integrated treatments, such as parent–child interaction therapy (Eyberg, Boggs, & Algina, 1995) (see Chapter 16), in which child-centered interventions are combined with techniques based on other theoretical approaches.

INTERVENTION TARGET

Role of the Parent

Dorfman (1951) indicated that child-centered therapists were initially reluctant to treat children without also having therapeutic contact with parents. As she stated, the child's problems were thought "to spring at least partially from the emotionalized attitudes of his parents" (p. 238). Axline (1947) also recognized the important role that parents play in children's psychological development. She described how the behaviors of parents and children influence and are influenced by each other and the actions of other family members. For example, parents' use of more effective child-rearing techniques causes a decline in the child's oppositional defiant behavior, which results in a more positive response from parents and siblings and additional improvement in the child's actions. Given these interactional effects, therapists face the difficult challenge of selecting the starting point for intervention. Should treatment involve individual therapy with the child, parent training, a family-based treatment, or a combination of these methods?

Axline (1947) stated that therapy for both parents and children merits consideration when families are receptive to the idea. In fact, she described this approach as "much simpler and complete" (p. 67) than therapy with either the child or the parents. But she also believed that play therapy alone can be helpful for a child, even when the parents do not receive concurrent treatment. Consider her detailed account of therapy with Dibs, who benefited from treatment despite his parents' limited involvement. Axline also found that individual work with children in schools and residential facilities offered therapeutic benefits without the active participation of parents.

Many child-centered therapists have asked parents to participate in treatment. Gordon (1970), Guerney (1964), and Eyberg et al. (1995), for example, trained parents to use child-centered techniques with their children. But parents have also been involved in other ways. When a child is reluctant to separate from his or her parents and walk to or remain in the playroom, therapists typically accept the child's request and have both the child and parent attend the play session (Moustakas, 1953). Many parents are willing to participate in therapy. Moustakas recommended that therapists treat parents with the same respect, acceptance, and faith they offer children. By accepting a parent's view of the presenting problem at the outset of therapy, clinicians communicate understanding and a belief in the parent's concern for the child's welfare. Child-centered therapists also recognize that parents are sources of important information about the child, family, and presenting problem. Through the use of active listening, they help parents to assume a leadership role in describing the family's reasons for seeking professional help.

Moustakas (1953) did not pressure parents to attend treatment sessions beyond the initial interview. But he found that many parents continued to participate in therapy when the clinician communicated a belief in the parents' concern for the child. When young clients are seen in individual play therapy, it is not unusual for parents to request information about their child's progress in treatment. Moustakas recommended that clinicians maintain confidentiality in these situations by offering a brief and general description of the course of treatment without sharing personal information that is irrelevant to the child's health and safety. He also suggested that therapists respond by focusing on the parent's feelings, as the clinician does in the following example:

MOTHER: My husband and I wanted to know whether Marcia ever talks about the other kids at school and how they make fun of her.

THERAPIST: How the other kids make fun of her.

MOTHER: Yes. She sometimes comes home crying about the horrible things the girls say about her.

THERAPIST: And you are concerned about how to handle these situations when they arise.

MOTHER: Uh-huh. It just tears me up when she comes home crying like that.

THERAPIST: It really hurts to see her in so much pain.

MOTHER: Uh-huh. I really don't know what to do. I was hoping you would have some suggestions for me.

Although the mother in this case requested information about the child, her primary concern was the girl's behavior at home. The therapist focused on the parent's feelings about her daughter's reaction to the unfortunate incidents at school. Whether the client had discussed these events in therapy was less important to the therapist than the mother's feelings and her request for help. Whatever recommendations the clinician might offer, the parent would assume responsibility for evaluating each suggestion and selecting her course of action. The mother in this case had direct contact with the clinician, but many parents adopt child-centered techniques without being clients in therapy. Some acquire this information through the media, and others use less formal methods.

Natalie Fuchs (1957) described how she conducted play therapy at home with her daughter who was exhibiting fears related to toilet training. When Ms. Fuchs wanted information about child-centered techniques, she wrote a letter to her father, Carl Rogers.

> Dear Dad,
>
> I wish you had time to visit us and to see your cute, blonde granddaughter, Janet. At the age of one-and-a-half she is running circles around me (literally), has quite a large vocabulary, and is beginning to put some of her big words together into short sentences. But she does have one rather overwhelming difficulty about which I would like to ask your advice. She is terrified at having to do her bowel movements and does everything she can to hold them back. She fusses and cries every time she has any peristaltic action . . . When she thinks she does have to eliminate, she strains, turns red-and-blue in the face and obviously gets all upset about it. (p. 89)

In a return letter, Rogers suggested that his daughter reread *Play Therapy* (Axline, 1947) and collect appropriate play materials, such as dolls and a potty chair, which she could use with Janet. Fuchs reported that her home-based play treatment was effective, and she concluded that "reasonably intelligent, sensitive parents can help their children over some of the rough spots of growing up by using the techniques and attitudes of a play therapist" (p. 89).

Some might question whether Rogers entered into a dual relationship with his daughter by assuming the role of clinical consultant in Janet's treatment. Obviously, therapists must be cautious when responding to requests for help from family and friends. They must also recognize that parents learn about child-rearing methods from a number of sources other than therapy. The clinician's role in facilitating dissemination of this information includes giving presentations or workshops for community groups, informed interviews to the media, and parenting classes through community adult education programs. With the knowledge and skills gained from these experiences, parents can create a more supportive, child-centered atmosphere for their families.

Role of the Child

As Axline (1947, p. 16) stated, "The *child* is the most important person" in the therapeutic relationship. The child client sets the direction for therapy. The client's feelings are the avenue to self-awareness. The child's view of the presenting problem provides essential information that can be used to remove environmental limits to healthy development. Additionally, it is the "curative forces within the child" (p. 69) that provide the energy to foster personal growth.

The child's role is to experience the therapist–client relationship and gain a greater awareness of self. Clients who feel accepted by the clinician begin to believe in their self-worth and significant other adults' acceptance of them. Axline (1950a) described how child-centered therapy enabled one young client to gain this insight:

> It used to be I thought everybody was out to get me but I guess I been wrong. All people aren't bad people. *Some* people are *good*. You're good. Sometimes I'm good. Maybe—Say, listen—Maybe *all* people are some good and some bad just like me. Maybe you are. Maybe *even* Mom. (p. 55)

Rogers (1942a) stated that recipients of client-centered therapy are more active in the therapeutic process than are clients in other treatments. They have the opportunity to explore and revise their perception of themselves. They take advantage of the freedom in the therapeutic relationship to express emotions that are typically controlled in the presence of significant others. Clinicians must remember that children's understanding of emotions is less sophisticated than that of adults. Young clients are also less skilled at verbal expression of emotion, so therapists must be prepared to construe clients' communication of feelings through action, such as play behaviors.

Child-centered therapy is grounded on the belief that children possess an inherent potential for growth. Consequently, the answer to the problems a young client encounters are to be found within the child. The therapist's challenge is to listen and empathize with the child by following the client's tempo and direction in treatment. Instead of giving interpretations and solutions for problems, child-centered therapists patiently follow clients through the process of self-discovery. The outcome of this joint effort is reflected in statements that Axline (1950a, p. 58) reported based on her 5-year follow-up of children in child-centered therapy. Clients remembered the activities and materials they used in session. For example, one child commented, "I remember the family of dolls and our doll house." Children also recalled the therapist's behavior and their feelings in treatment. As one client stated, "You were good to us. You let us do what we wanted to do." And as another noted, "I lost my feeling of being lonesome and I felt that I wasn't all bad and that some people liked me and didn't shove me away."

Role of the Therapist

Axline (1947) also recognized the importance of the clinician when she wrote, "Successful therapy begins with the therapist" (p. 66). The actual treatment a clinician provides is shaped by the therapist's training, theoretical orientation, clinical experience, and personal attributes. Rogers (1942a) contrasted a clinician's role in traditional and client-centered approaches to therapy. In the former, a clinician "discovers, diagnoses, and treats the client's problems, provided that the counselee gives his active cooperation in the procedure" (p. 115). The therapist is viewed as the expert who possesses the knowledge and skills needed to solve the client's difficulties. The role of a traditional therapist is markedly different from that of the client-centered therapist who accepts the client as a human being and believes in the client's ability to solve his or her problems.

Some children have a difficult time understanding the role of child-centered clinicians. Axline (1964) described how Dibs wrestled with this issue during his last therapy session:

> "I can't figure this all out," he said.
> "What can't you figure out?" I asked.
> "All this. And you. You're not a mother. You're not a teacher. You're not a member of mother's bridge club. What are you?" (p. 171)

Axline's method apparently helped the boy resolve his confusion because he later announced that she was "the lady of the wonderful playroom" (p. 172).

Axline (1947, 1950b) described an effective child-centered therapist as a friendly, relaxed, and dependable person who sets aside personal thoughts and feelings and focuses attention on the child. Clinicians must also adopt three important attitudes toward their child clients: faith, acceptance, and respect (Moustakas, 1953). A therapist who has faith believes that "children have within themselves capacity for self-growth and self-realization" (Moustakas, 1953, p. 4). Accepting a client means being actively involved in the therapeutic process and committed to the child as a person. And clinicians respect children for who they are in the moment, not the individuals they should or ought to be in the future.

Dorfman (1951) described how a therapist communicated respect to a 9-year-old boy.

JACK: I think I'll paint something. What should I paint?

THERAPIST: You want me to tell you what to paint? (*The therapist fails to respond to the first half of Jack's statement, and thus inadvertently focuses attention on the second half.*)

JACK: Yes. What do you want me to paint? You tell me.

THERAPIST: Jack, I know you want me to decide for you, but I really can't, because I don't want you to paint any particular thing.

JACK: Why not, don't you care about what I do?

THERAPIST: Yes, Jack, I care, but I think that what you feel like painting is really up to you. (p. 240)

When children are accustomed to responding to adults' directives, they are likely to approach the therapist–client relationship with the same expectations in mind. Clinicians must be aware of this attitude and avoid interacting with the child as others typically do.

Dorfman (1951) also described how therapists must offer a safe and accepting environment where clients can explore their personal thoughts and feelings. Accepting the child as a person does not mean acceptance of each and every behavior exhibited in session. Child-centered therapists do set limits for their clients. By establishing and consistently maintaining these boundaries in session, clinicians help clients to achieve greater self-awareness and to make decisions within the predictable limits of the therapeutic relationship. Various authors have studied clinicians' use of limits and found consistent patterns among child-centered therapists.

Ginott and Lebo (1961) and Rhoden, Kranz, and Lund (1981) found that play therapists of different theoretical orientations establish common behavioral limits, such as ending the session on time and not allowing clients to destroy play materials. Rhoden et al. reported that 35 of the 54 1imits they included on their survey were used by at least 61% of the respondents. Relatively few differences were found based on therapists' theoretical orientation (i.e., psychoanalytic, child-centered, other). When the authors grouped their limits into six categories, they found that therapists were most likely to restrict clients' physical aggression toward the clinician and play equipment as well as behaviors that were threats to health and safety, such as climbing on high places in the playroom. These restrictions on children's behavior seem appropriate. Therapists function in loco parentis, so they must be alert for threats to a child's safety in session. Likewise, budgetary restrictions in most clinical settings make it difficult for therapists to replace damaged play equipment.

Hoffman (1991) described how the limits used in therapy should be appropriate to the child's developmental level. Although health and safety limits must be used with all children, regardless of age, these restrictions are especially important for clients who fail to consider the long-term consequences of their behavior. Clinicians must also attend to the child's presenting problem. Limits on physical aggression are usually more relevant for a hostile, oppositional defiant child whose divorcing parents are ignoring him than they are for a shy and withdrawn client who has recently transferred to a new school and is trying to make friends. Landreth (1991) recommended that clinicians use total rather than conditional limits. As he described, not allowing a child to pinch the therapist in any manner is a clearer guideline than a conditional limit that permits this behavior "if it doesn't hurt" the clinician.

Beginning therapists must acquire the attitudes and skills needed to establish behavioral limits for children in therapy. They should examine their thoughts and feelings about limits, conduct a review of relevant literature, and obtain supervised practice using limits with young clients. Child-centered therapists should not restrict clients' verbal expression of feelings, but they should limit behavioral manifestations of certain emotions (Dorfman, 1951). These include anger-based responses, such as the destruction of play materials and physical aggression directed at the therapist. As Dorfman noted, it is important to remember that the limits established in a therapy room provide a connection to the child's everyday life.

Another important role for child-centered therapists is the dissemination of information about child development theory and research (Rogers, 1942b). As discussed in Chapter 1, clinicians must have a working knowledge of the child development literature in order to determine whether a child's behavior is within normal limits. Because of recent advances in developmental psychopathology (see Chapter 4), skilled therapists can identify potential causes of a child's maladaptive behavior, intervene accordingly, and prevent problems later in life. Likewise, clinicians are better prepared to address parents' pathologizing of a behavior that is considered normal for children of a similar demographic background.

Role of the School

Earlier in this chapter we discussed how child-centered theory has been applied in the classroom. These methods are valuable because school-age children spend a significant part of their time in this setting. Classroom teachers are important influences on the development of children's sense of self. In an early study in the schools of Columbus, Ohio, Rogers (1942c) found that teachers rated one third of their students as problem children, although personality test results suggested the figure was approximately half that number. A teacher's view of students has been related to their classroom behavior, which can have a significant and lasting impact on children's academic achievement and feelings of self-worth. Aspy and Rosebuck (1977) studied the effects of a child-centered approach to education with 500 public school teachers and 10,000 students. The authors found that students of teachers who used empathy, genuineness, and unconditional positive regard in the classroom had fewer absences from school, greater scholastic achievement, and better self-esteem than did the students of teachers who did not use these skills.

Landreth (1991) described how the emergence of counseling and guidance programs in elementary schools during the 1960s contributed to the development of child-centered play therapy. This technique has been combined with other behavioral and educational interventions to help troubled students. Johnson, McLeod, and Fall (1997), for example, provided child-centered play therapy as an adjunct to classroom-based behavioral treatments for six disruptive boys, ages 5 to 8 years. They used a qualitative design to study the effects of six 30-minute, weekly play sessions with the students who were diagnosed with various childhood disorders (e.g., attention-deficit hyperactivity disorder, autism). Results revealed that play therapy facilitated clients' expression of feelings in session and seemed to help them cope with everyday challenges.

CONTRIBUTIONS AND LIMITATIONS

Clinicians who adopt other theoretical approaches are indebted to client-centered therapy for its emphasis on the therapeutic relationship. The facilitative conditions of congruence, unconditional positive regard, and empathy that are the method's philosophical base have been incorporated into many other treatment approaches. Proponents of other therapies have recognized that effective intervention requires a healthy therapist–client relationship, which child-centered clinicians foster through active listening. This involves the use of minimal encouragers and open questions to facilitate clients' self-disclosure. Therapists gently confront children so they can consider conflicting views on relevant issues. And clinicians use reflection of feeling to help clients become aware of affective elements in the presenting problem. If these techniques were unavailable, therapists would have a more difficult time understanding the client's point of view, and they would be at greater risk of imposing their own beliefs on the child.

The emphasis on feelings represents another contribution of the client-centered approach. Young clients' display of emotion sometimes appears confused, inconsistent, or ambivalent (Moustakas, 1953). Child-centered therapists have developed innovative play and artistic techniques that can be used in combination with active listening to facilitate clients' emotional development. Moustakas (1959) observed that a therapist's behavior can sometimes stimulate negative affect (e.g., anger, fear) in a child. When this occurs, clinicians must be aware of their own feelings so they can react in a therapeutic manner. A common response in these situations is reflection of the child's feeling, which Moore et al. (1999) divided into two categories. When a client verbally expresses feelings, the therapist responds using different words to describe the emotion. When a child indirectly expresses affect through play, the clinician verbalizes the underlying emotion and communicates acceptance of the child, regardless of the nature of these feelings.

The most important contribution of the child-centered approach is the belief in a child's capacity for growth and the resolution of everyday problems. This health-oriented perspective differs from the psychopathological view that characterizes many other approaches to intervention. It also seems very appropriate for children, who are in the process of developing and learning about themselves and the world around them. A therapist who capitalizes on a child's inherent ability to grow and solve life's challenges is able to encourage the child's development of the self and movement toward Rogers' (1969) "fully functioning person" (p. 278).

A major limitation of child-centered theory is its focus on the individual child. Relatively little attention has been given to the impact of the child's cultural surround. The belief in a child's potential for growth without consideration of environmental limits can lead to less effective and efficient treatments. Consider a third grader who is performing poorly at school because her teacher lacks the class management skills required to provide a proper learning environment for his students. Child-centered play therapy would be less appropriate in this case than school-based consultation designed to help the teacher learn and confidently use appropriate limits in the classroom (see Chapter 14). A focus on the child as an individual has also contributed to blaming clients for their problems. If the therapist fails to consider the teacher's skills and focuses solely on the child's behavior, responsibility for poor grades could be erroneously attributed to inadequate effort by the child. Oversight of environmental influences can be especially critical with children who live in abusive or neglectful homes.

Another limitation of child-centered therapies is the lack of attention that clinicians have given to observable behaviors and consequences. Therapists are less likely to use behavioral methods that have been found to be effective in remediating certain childhood problems (see Chapter 11). They tend to overlook the function of a client's behavior in the context of the family, school, or neighborhood. Consequently, the focus on a child's development of the self can result in more lengthy treatments in which little attention is paid to the antecedents and consequences of problem behaviors within the context of surrounding systems.

Child-centered therapists have given relatively little consideration to the developmental impact of early childhood experiences. Their emphasis on the here-and-now interactions of the therapist and client tends to focus attention away from past events, such as trauma and loss, that are sometimes related to a child's presenting problem. Proponents of the child-centered approach have also avoided formal assessment and diagnosis of children's behavior. But the emergence of brief therapies and managed mental health care has increased the need for these activities. As discussed earlier in this chapter, Rogers offered a rationale for formal assessment in his early writings. The question is not whether therapists adopt psychometrically sound assessment procedures. Rather, the issue is how child-centered therapists can transform the assessment process in a way that incorporates the principles espoused by Rogers, Axline, and Moustakas.

CHILD-CENTERED INTERVENTIONS: A CASE EXAMPLE

The process of normal development involves continual adjustment to events in the child's environment. Some children encounter significant challenges, such as parental divorce, and require therapeutic intervention. When clinicians design treatment plans for these clients, they must consider the child's developmental level. This is particularly true for a young client who has recently experienced the death of a loved one. As discussed in Chapter 8, children's understanding of death undergoes important changes between the preschool and adolescent years. Therefore, clinicians must determine a child's awareness of irreversibility, causality, inevitability, and cessation before they begin treatment.

Preschoolers have a limited understanding of death concepts, so therapy often involves greater parent involvement and less individual contact with the child. When children understand irreversibility, cessation, and causality, more attention is directed to the client's thoughts and emotions regarding the loved one's death. For children who understand the inevitability of death, treatment can include consideration of personal beliefs and feelings about the end of life. But more adultlike discussions of death from a philosophical or spiritual perspective are typically reserved for adolescent clients.

Developmental changes in children's understanding of death sometimes results in therapy that resembles Winnicott's (1977) "on demand" (p. 3) approach to treatment. A 4-year-old child whose behavior is unchanged after a grandparent's death receives a brief therapeutic contact but returns at age 7 years to explore unresolved concerns regarding irreversibility and cessation. The parents of that same child might request therapy a third time when the client is an adolescent struggling with inevitability issues and the spiritual aspects of death. Some might challenge this treatment plan, charging that therapy at age 4 years must have been ineffective because subsequent services were needed. But this criticism fails to take into consideration important developmental issues. If the grandparent's death is a significant life event, we can expect the child to interpret this loss in an increasingly complex manner, depending on her understanding of death. Addressing irreversibility and inevitability with a very young child is premature and would seem to have little therapeutic value.

We now return to the Jackson family described at the beginning of this chapter. Joanne's reaction to her brother's death appears to be consistent with that of the average preschool child who lacks an adequate understanding of death concepts. Likewise, the parents' emotional response reflects their awareness of death and its implications for the deceased and the surviving family members. When Mr. Jackson contacted Dr. Charlene Howard to schedule an intake appointment, he reported that his son James was the couple's older child who excelled both academically and athletically. The parents had always been involved in their son's life, coaching his youth soccer team and serving as officers in the parent–teacher organization at school. Mr. Jackson described how difficult it was for his wife and him to even drive by James' high school and the playground where their son had played soccer. When Dr. Howard requested that the parents come by themselves to the first appointment, Mr. Jackson agreed. "I think that might be helpful for all of us" he said.

▪ ▪ ▪

At the outset of the clinical interview, Dr. Howard welcomes the parents and reinforces their decision to meet with her regarding Joanne's reaction to James' death. "The loss of a child is a very difficult experience," she says. "Please tell me about James and his relationship with Joanne." When the parents struggle to respond, Dr. Howard uses open questions and minimal encouragers to facilitate disclosure. As she listens to the parents describe their son and his recent death in an automobile accident, she realizes that both parents have been profoundly affected by this unforeseen event in their lives.

About midway through the session, Mr. Jackson says, "I keep thinking there is something we could have done to prevent this. I mean, if I hadn't let him take the car to practice that day, he'd still be alive."

Mrs. Jackson tries unsuccessfully to convince her husband that he is not responsible for James' death. She turns to Dr. Howard and says, "It's been like this ever since that horrible day. We've been meeting with our priest, and he's helped us talk about our feelings. But both of us keep thinking we'll walk into the kitchen some morning and find James sitting there."

At no time during the first half of the session do the parents mention Joanne. When Dr. Howard asks them to talk about their daughter, both state that the child is not reacting normally to James' death. Mrs. Jackson says, "I would expect her to be sad or maybe cry every now and then. I'm afraid she's trying to cover up her feelings because she knows how upset we are." When questioned further, the parents report that Joanne is a well-behaved child.

Based on the information obtained during this session, Dr. Howard schedules an individual meeting with the child. Before she terminates the parent interview, she asks each of them to complete the Child Behavior Checklist for Ages 1½–5 and the Beck Depression Inventory. Mr. and Mrs. Jackson also sign release forms allowing her to contact Father Michael, the family's priest. Dr. Howard tells the Jacksons that she will meet with them together after she sees Joanne and speaks with Father Michael.

During the week when Dr. Howard contacts Father Michael, she learns that the Jacksons are active in the church and have always seemed to be a close family. During their six sessions with him, the parents expressed guilt about not preventing the accident. They also described considerable anger toward God for letting their son die. Father Michael indicates that the couple has made progress in both areas, but then adds, "They continue to worry a lot about the effect James' death will have on Joanne." It was for this reason that he encouraged them to meet with a specialist to determine whether the child could benefit from therapy. Father Michael and Dr. Howard agree to collaborate on the case, with Father Michael providing counseling for the parents and Dr. Howard intervening with Joanne.

Mr. and Mrs. Jackson's responses to the Child Behavior Checklist supported their benign description of Joanne. Neither parent reported a significant level of internalizing or externalizing behaviors in the child, but both scored in the "mild to moderate" range on the Beck Depression Inventory. Although they did not indicate any suicidal ideation, both parents reported feeling sad much of the time.

The next week when Joanne arrives for therapy, she readily separates from her parents and walks with Dr. Howard to the playroom. There she carefully examines the toys and art materials placed around the room. "Can I play with this?" she asks as she picks up a hand puppet.

"You may play with anything you want," the therapist responds.

Joanne giggles and selects two puppets, one for each hand. "Hi, my name is Joanne. What's yours?" the right puppet asks. "Mary," the left puppet answers. Joanne continues this fantasy interaction for a brief period of time before she turns to Dr. Howard and says, "Here, you take this one. Let's play house. You be the girl. I'll be Momma. She's sad."

"Mary's sad," Dr. Howard responds.

"No, Momma's sad," Joanne answers. "Mary makes her laugh." The client grabs the therapist's puppet to demonstrate how Mary acts silly to help the mother feel happy.

"Here, you do it," Joanne says as she gives the puppet to the therapist. Dr. Howard follows the instructions, and the two of them enact various scenes in which Mary comforts the mother puppet.

At an appropriate point in the session, Dr. Howard chooses another puppet to be a child friend who asks the Mary puppet, "What can Daddy do to help Momma feel better?"

"Oh, nothing," Joanne interrupts. "He's sad, too."

"What are they sad about?" the friend asks.

"Somebody went away. But he'll come back," Joanne answers in a positive tone of voice. Throughout the session, the child provides no evidence of being distressed by her brother's death. She is concerned about her parents' feelings surrounding their loss and seems to believe she can help them feel better. Dr. Howard combines her observations of the child with the information obtained from significant others. She conceptualizes Joanne's behavior as a normal response for a child who does not comprehend the concepts of irreversibility and cessation. She decides to focus on the parents' understanding of the child's reaction and to encourage them to continue their work with Father Michael.

During the week after the play session, Dr. Howard telephones Father Michael to share her conclusions about the Jacksons. She informs him that she would meet with the parents to discuss Joanne's behavior in a developmental context. Father Michael agrees to continue providing grief counseling for Mr. and Mrs. Jackson. He says he would also ask the parents to join his weekly bereavement group. When Dr. Howard meets with Mr. and Mrs. Jackson, she praises them for their commitment to Joanne and explains how children develop an understanding of irreversibility, causation, inevitability, and cessation. She encourages them to continue their sessions with Father Michael and to contact her if Joanne exhibits any significant behavioral changes as she matures and begins to understand death concepts. Dr. Howard concludes by saying, "We want to prevent problems before they happen so Joanne can continue to be a normal, happy child." The parents agree to this plan.

Dr. Howard does not hear from the parents until the summer before Joanne enters third grade. When Mrs. Jackson telephones to arrange an appointment, she says, "My husband and I remember you saying that Joanne might have some problems when she's a little older. Well, she has recently become rather moody and seems to spend a lot of time alone in her room." As Dr. Howard listens, she decides to schedule another session with the parents to determine whether Joanne is actually experiencing problems at this time.

During her interview with the parents, she finds that Mr. and Mrs. Jackson still miss their son, but they have accepted his death and no longer blame themselves for his accident. Unlike the first session, the parents spend most of the hour talking about Joanne. Mrs. Jackson says that she first noticed a difference about a week or two after her daughter's birthday in early July. Mr. Jackson agrees, adding that Joanne enjoyed day camp in June and seemed to be a happy child until recently. Neither parent can identify a cause for this change. "She had a wonderful birthday party," Mrs. Jackson says, "All of her friends were there, and she got plenty of gifts." At the close of the interview, Dr. Howard again asks the parents to complete the Child Behavior Checklist for Ages 6 to 18 and the Beck Depression Inventory.

Because the change in Joanne's behavior occurs during the middle of the summer, Dr. Howard does not contact her second grade teacher. Likewise, no collaborative contact is made with Father Michael, who had been transferred to another church about a year after the parents finished counseling with him. The results of the parent inventories were informative. Both parents now score in the "normal" range on the Beck Depression Inventory, but their responses to Child Behavior Checklist items suggest that Joanne is exhibiting a significant level of internalizing behaviors. Specifically, Mr. and Mrs. Jackson describe their daughter as exhibiting behaviors characteristic of the Withdrawn/Depressed syndrome and the DSM-oriented Affective Problems scale. Both parents indicate that Joanne has not reported any suicidal ideation.

When Dr. Howard sees Joanne the next week, she encounters a far more serious child than the cheerful 5-year-old girl who had eagerly played with puppets years earlier. As they enter the playroom, Dr. Howard smiles and says, "Joanne, I'm so glad to see you again. The last time you and I met, we played with puppets, didn't we?"

Joanne gives a brief smile and answers, "Yes, ma'am."

Therapist and client reminisce about their earlier visit before Dr. Howard says, "Your Mom and Dad tell me you've been kind of sad recently. And it seems like you're a bit sad today."

Joanne shrugs her shoulders but then says, "I guess."

"Let's talk about it."

Again, Joanne shrugs her shoulders, but this time she remains quiet. Dr. Howard becomes aware of her own discomfort. She finds herself wanting to hurry the treatment process by getting the child to talk about her feelings, but she realizes that this intervention could create an adversarial relationship with the client. In her head, she hears the session's valuable seconds ticking away, but she reassures herself that patient timing is crucial to her success with this child. Aware of her body language, Dr. Howard remains physically calm while she allows her client to assume control of the therapeutic interaction. After less than a minute of silence, which seemed like hours to the therapist, Joanne responds, "James isn't coming back, is he?"

"It sounds like you've been thinking about your brother?"

"Yes, ma'am. Momma and I were looking at birthday pictures the other day. We saw pictures of his birthday parties. Momma cried."

"How did you feel when you looked at the pictures?"

"Sad."

"Sad," Dr. Howard responds.

"Yes, ma'am. Sad because I knew he wasn't going to come back."

"It sounds like you feel sad because you know you won't see him again."

"Yes, ma'am."

Dr. Howard asks Joanne to talk about her brother. The child gives vivid descriptions of happy memories. She talks about a Christmas morning when James and she opened presents, a summer trip to their grandparents' farm, and an afternoon playing hide-and-seek in the family's back yard. Dr. Howard is struck by the positive and detailed nature of the child's stories. In contrast to the client's serious attitude at the outset of the session, she is noticeably happier as she remembers her interactions with James.

"It sounds like your brother has been a very important person in your life," Dr. Howard summarizes.

Joanne's mood becomes more somber when she responds, "Yes, ma'am, but I won't see him again."

Dr. Howard says that even though James is physically absent from Joanne's life, her memories of him are still alive. She adds, "It sounds to me like you want to remember your brother just the way he was when you were little." When Joanne nods her head in agreement, Dr. Howard suggests that the two of them use therapy to write a book about James. "We can write down your memories so you'll always have the book to help you remember him."

The therapist and client discuss the procedures they will use. Dr. Howard asks Joanne if she wants to write and illustrate the book herself, but the child decides to have the therapist transcribe her stories about James. "I'll draw the pictures," she says, "but I want you to write down the words."

As the end of the session approaches, Dr. Howard asks Joanne to help her by completing the Children's Depression Inventory. The client agrees and completes the questionnaire with little assistance from the therapist. Before Dr. Howard terminates the session, she quickly checks the measure and learns that Joanne did not express any suicidal ideation. She then meets with the child and her parents to briefly review the treatment plan. Dr. Howard describes the book as similar to a child's confidential diary or journal. Mr. and Mrs. Jackson accept the plan and agree that the book will remain Joanne's personal property.

After the session, Dr. Howard reviews the Children's Depression Inventory and discovers that Joanne endorsed a variety symptoms characteristics of childhood depression. Two days later, she receives a telephone call from Mrs. Jackson. "Are you sure this book is a good idea?" the mother asks. "I mean, my husband and I are trying to help Joanne put James' death behind her. We're worried that digging up these memories might make things worse. You know, getting her to think more and more about James rather than forgetting that horrible time and getting on with her life."

"I understand your concern about Joanne's welfare," Dr. Howard responds. "Developmentally, she's a very different child than when she was 5 years old. Children her age understand that when people die, they are not going to return to life as we know it. But even though loved ones are gone, they continue to be an important part of our lives through the memories we have of them." Dr. Howard capitalizes on the parents' fears about Joanne's future. "I typically use a memory book with children to help avoid problems later in life. Joanne probably remembers things about James that she will forget by the time she reaches adolescence or adulthood. Her book will provide a concrete record that she can use to recall the special times she spent with him, regardless of how old she is."

When Dr. Howard finishes, Mrs. Jackson replies, "I see what you mean. I guess I want to forget about that day when James was taken from us, but I don't want to lose my special memories of him either. I'll explain this to my husband. I'm sure he'll understand."

When Joanne returns for her next appointment, she says she is ready to begin work on her book. She agrees with Dr. Howard that it would be a good idea to devote a chapter to each of her memories about James. The therapist says that it is usually helpful to include feelings in the chapters, so she will sometimes ask questions while Joanne is telling her story.

"Where would you like to begin?" she asks.

"Christmas!" Joanne answers.

"Christmas it is," Dr. Howard responds. "It sounds like you have a particular Christmas in mind. How old were you?"

"5."

"Where did you have Christmas?"

"At home."

"When do you want to start your chapter? On Christmas Eve or Christmas morning or...?"

"Christmas morning," Joanne interrupts.

"OK. Let's start the chapter this way, 'It was Christmas morning when I was 5 years old.' " As Dr. Howard writes this sentence on the paper Joanne had selected for her book, the child begins to describe that special morning.

"I woke up, and it was light outside. Everybody else was sleeping. I went to the living room and saw all the presents under the tree. I ran back to James' room and woke him up. 'Santa Claus came,' I said. I still believed in Santa Claus back then."

"How did you feel right then?" Dr. Howard asks.

"Excited."

"So would you like to say, 'I felt excited'?"

"Yes, ma'am," she answers and then resumes her story. "James told me I'd better not open any presents until Momma and Daddy were awake. I said, 'You get them up so we can see what Santas Claus brought me.' He said, 'OK,' and he did it."

"How did you feel when James said 'OK' and woke up your parents?" Dr. Howard asks.

"Really happy," Joanne responds before rewording the sentence for her book, "I mean, I felt really happy that he got them up."

As the child describes the events of the morning, the therapist records her story verbatim. At appropriate points, Dr. Howard intervenes to have the client reflect on her feelings about the events of the day. Throughout the session, she attempts to focus Joanne's attention on her brother by using sentence stems such as "My brother . . . " or "James . . . ." Joanne responds to one of these stems to describe his gift to her. "James gave me his present. He smiled and said, 'I think you're going to like this one.' It was the baby doll I wanted, the one that talks to you when you touch its belly." Without being prompted, Joanne adds, "I was really happy. That was the best present I got that Christmas."

When she finishes her Christmas story, Joanne draws a picture to illustrate that morning. In front of the family's tree are James and Joanne giving gifts to each other. Their parents are seated nearby. As she draws, the child continues to talk about this important day in her life.

During the next five meetings, Joanne describes and illustrates other memories of her brother. At her last session, she seems pleased with the results of her work as she and Dr. Howard review her eight-chapter book. "Can we read it to my Momma and Daddy?" she asks. The therapist agrees and asks the parents to join them in the playroom. As Joanne reads chapters from her book, Mr. and Mrs. Jackson are moved by the child's vivid memories of her experiences with James. When she finishes, Mr. Jackson says, "Joanne, that was beautiful. It's how I remember your brother, too."

Posttreatment results on the child- and parent-report measures reveal normal functioning on all scales, so Dr. Howard terminates therapy for the Jacksons. She will receive one additional request for treatment when Joanne is 15 years old. After the accidental drowning of a classmate, Joanne becomes oppositional and refuses to complete her school work and household tasks. During 10 weekly sessions with Dr. Howard, she expresses considerable anger at God for letting her classmate and her brother die at such young ages. To address these concerns, Dr. Howard collaborates with Joanne's priest, who is very active with the youths in his church. In her meetings with Joanne, Dr. Howard helps the client explore conflicting emotions about her brother. During a very important session, Joanne wrestles with these feelings.

"Why did he do it?" she asks.

"Do what?" Dr. Howard responds.

"Why did he go out and kill himself like that? He should have been more careful." Joanne pauses and stares at the floor for what seemed like minutes before she looks at Dr. Howard. "Why am I blaming him?" she asks. "He wasn't the one who ran that stop sign. He tried to get out of the way. I guess I'm angry at him, but I shouldn't be."

"Shouldn't be."

"I mean, it wasn't his fault."

"It sounds like you're saying you are both angry and not angry at James."

"Yes, ma'am. I keep thinking that if he was still here, we could do fun things together." She hesitates and then adds, "I just wish he had just stayed home from soccer practice that day."

During this and subsequent sessions, Dr. Howard helps Joanne explore her anger and love for James. The therapy room becomes a safe place for the client to express negative feelings that her parents and others would find objectionable. As she begins to resolve these contradictory emotions, Joanne becomes more at ease with herself and is again more productive at school and home.

▪ ▪ ▪

The case of Joanne is an example of one child's developing awareness of emotions and death concepts. As an elementary school child, she used only positive feelings to describe her brother. By the time she returned to therapy as a 15-year-old young woman, her emotional understanding had reached the Harter and Buddin (1987) stage when she was able to express conflicting feelings toward the same target. During these sessions, she confronted the guilt and anxiety that is often associated with contradictory emotions for a significant other. When viewed from a developmental perspective, Joanne's behavior was normal at ages 8 and 15 years, despite the differences in her expressions of emotions.

This case also illustrates the continuing care that therapists can offer as children face life's challenges at different stages of development. Individual therapy for the child involved 18 sessions spread across a 10-year period. As a 5-year-old girl, Joanne's reaction to her brother's death was consistent with her naivete regarding the concepts of death. At age 8 years, her depressed affect was consistent with her understanding of irreversibility. At age 15 years, her reaction to a classmate's drowning was consistent with a more sophisticated religious interpretation of death. Through repeated therapeutic contacts over the decade, the clinician interacted with the same and different child who had attended previous treatment sessions.

Dr. Howard used education/development, prevention, and remediation interventions in her work with the Jacksons. When Jeanne was 5 years old, the therapist informed the parents about the normal development of death concepts in children. She chose this approach instead of a remedial intervention after she learned that the child was not exhibiting significant behavior problems at home or school. During her meetings with the parents, she normalized Joanne's response to the brother's death while preparing Mr. and Mrs. Jackson for possible changes in the future. To prevent problems and facilitate the child's development, Dr. Howard encouraged them to be alert for these changes and to contact her so appropriate steps could be taken. As a result, the family returned for additional sessions when Jeanne began to experience developmentally normal questions and concerns at ages 8 and 15 years.

Notice how Dr. Howard collaborated with the family's priests to help Joanne and her parents explore religious issues related to James' death. At the outset of treatment, this meant having relatively few therapeutic contacts with the Jacksons while the parents continued their sessions with Father Michael. Dr. Howard established no collaborative contacts when Joanne was 8 years old and was exhibiting symptoms of depression related to her increased understanding of death concepts. When the client entered treatment as an adolescent, the therapist again collaborated with the girl's priest, who helped Joanne explore her religious concerns.

During therapy sessions with the Jacksons, Dr. Howard permitted her clients to assume the leadership role in therapy. She was an active listener who used open questions, clarification and summarization, and reflection of feelings to facilitate discussion of topics that were relevant to the family. But there were times when she intentionally directed the course of treatment. During her second meeting with the parents, for example, Dr. Howard assumed the expert role when she offered child development information and presented what she believed was the appropriate treatment plan. When Joanne and she engaged in puppet play in their first meeting, Dr. Howard introduced a puppet friend as a means of facilitating client disclosure about the father and his response to James' death. During the second phase of treatment, she presented the memory book as an option for therapy. Crucial to both of these interventions was Dr. Howard's focus on the child's reaction. If Joanne had rejected either method, the therapist would have accepted the child's decision rather than insisting that her choice of action was the correct direction for treatment.

Dr. Howard always tried to be aware of her own feelings in session. When Joanne returned to see her at age 8 years, Dr. Howard felt uncomfortable with the child's initial silence. Her awareness of this feeling enabled her to pace the timing of her interventions so Joanne could assume leadership in therapy. Dr. Howard gradually realized that her anxiety was related to other factors: Joanne's dramatic change of mood and the child's use of "ma'am" to refer to the therapist. Although Dr. Howard was prepared to meet an older and developmentally different child, she had not expected the somber client who arrived at her office. She realized that she was expecting to resume treatment with the cheerful youngster who had attended one therapy session at age 5 years. Her discomfort with "ma'am" was another matter. She did not want Joanne to see her as the expert, but she heard this message every time the child referred to her in this manner. It was not until later that day when Dr. Howard realized her discomfort was caused by cultural differences. Unlike Dr. Howard's parents, Joanne's mother and father expected children to display respect by using "sir" and "ma'am" when interacting with adults. In session, Dr. Howard restrained her initial reaction to tell Joanne it was unnecessary to use this term with her. After further consideration, she decided this would have been therapeutically inappropriate and culturally insensitive. Her anxiety subsided when she realized that accepting Joanne as a person also meant accepting this behavior.

Finally, Dr. Howard used developmentally appropriate techniques with her client. She used puppets when the client was 5 years old, narrative and illustration of a memory book when she was 8 years old, and traditional talk therapy when she was an adolescent. Regardless of the technique used, Dr. Howard always focused on her client's affect in session. She consistently offered a safe environment where the child could express and explore her feelings. In this way, her treatment reflects the theoretical principles of child-centered therapy in which the client is thought to possess an inherent potential for growth.

SUMMARY

Child-centered therapy involves empowerment of the client and the development of each child's potential. Compared with other methods described in this book, child-centered interventions involve greater attention to the emotional world of the child. Similar to their psychodynamic counterparts, proponents of child-centered treatments emphasize the role of the therapist–client relationship. They believe that a clinician's faith, acceptance, and respect for a child are basic attitudes that facilitate the client's growth. Child-centered principles have been applied in educational and mental health settings. When used in therapy, they serve as the foundation for the active listening skills that clinicians use to facilitate the child's process of self-discovery.

10

Behavioral and Cognitive-Behavioral Theory

Over the course of the 20th century, writers expanded the boundaries of learning theory beyond its early focus on overt behaviors toward an integration of behaviors, cognitions, and feelings. Although traditional behavioral theory constitutes an interactional worldview, more recent formulations have included trait (e.g., the physiological component of some cognitive theories) and organismic (e.g., behavioral-family systems theory) features (Fishman & Franks, 1997). What began as the application of the scientific method to observable behaviors has become a form of quantitative inquiry into the development of human beings in the context of their cultural surround.

This chapter examines the development of behavioral and cognitive-behavioral theories as they relate to therapeutic interventions with children. It begins with a brief historical review of the major theorists followed by a more detailed examination of the principles of each theory. The Developmental Considerations section investigates Piagetian, information processing, and sociocultural models of cognitive development. The chapter also includes a discussion of developmental and multicultural considerations for children's narrative style and vocational development.

HISTORICAL BACKGROUND

Child behavior therapy has its origin in early 20th century studies of classical conditioning conducted by John B. Watson, Rosalie Rayner, and Mary Cover Jones. The work of these early pioneers was basically overlooked for more than 2 decades as clinicians rejected behavioral interventions in favor of psychodynamic and child-centered treatments (Meyers & Craighead, 1984). B. F. Skinner's research on operant conditioning in the 1950s provided the impetus for new work on behavioral interventions with children when reinforcement and punishment paradigms were studied in educational and mental health settings. In the latter half of the 20th century, cognitive theorists, such as Albert Bandura and Albert Ellis, established the foundation for later developments in cognitive-behavioral treatments for children.

In 1913, John B. Watson (1878–1958) delivered a lecture at Columbia University that was to become known as the "behaviorist manifesto" (Wozniak, 1997, p. 198). In this talk, later published in *Psychological Review*, Watson separated himself from psychodynamic theorists when he declared:

> Psychology as the behaviorist views it is a purely objective experimental branch of natural science. Its theoretical goal is the prediction and control of behavior. Introspection forms no essential part of its methods, nor is the scientific value of its data dependent upon the readiness with which they lend themselves to interpretation in terms of consciousness. (Watson, 1913 p. 158)

Watson was criticizing the unobservable nature of psychodynamic constructs, such as ego and superego, and recommending that psychologists select behavior as the basis for scientific inquiry.

When he enrolled in doctoral study at the University of Chicago, Watson studied philosophy, psychology, neurology, and biology and physiology (Watson, 1978). He graduated in 1903, remained at the university to teach, and continued his research on animal psychology. In 1908, Watson joined the faculty at Johns Hopkins University, where he began his research with children through an affiliation with the Phipps Clinic in Baltimore. Watson was a proponent of classical conditioning, which he believed provided the framework for understanding human development. In a frequently cited quote, he wrote:

> Give me a dozen healthy infants, well-formed, and my own specified world to bring them up in and I'll guarantee to take any one at random and train him to become any type of specialist I might select—doctor, lawyer, artist, merchant-chief and, yes, even beggar-man and thief, regardless of his talents, penchants, tendencies, abilities, vocations, and race of his ancestors." (Watson, 1925 p. 104)

Watson's interests in environmental determinants of behavior is reflected in his *Psychological Care of Infant and Child*, which he dedicated to "the first mother who brings up a happy child." In this text for parents, Watson (1928) described how effective child-rearing techniques can be used to eliminate children's fears, temper tantrums, and bedtime problems.

Watson's most important contribution to child therapies is his collaboration with Rosalie Raynor and their classic study with Little Albert, an 11-month-old infant who was conditioned to fear a white rat and other furry objects (see Theoretical Foundations later in this chapter). Although they never treated Albert's fears, Watson and Raynor (1920) suggested that deconditioning could be used to eliminate fearful behaviors in children. Mary Cover Jones (1924) did just that in her work with Little Peter, a 2-year-old boy who "seemed almost to be Albert grown a bit older" (p. 309). This comment is indeed interesting, given the nature of Peter's fear objects: "a white rat, a rabbit, a fur coat, a feather, cotton, wool, etc., but not . . . wooden blocks and similar toys" (p. 309). But Peter apparently was not Albert because Jones stated that her study was conducted approximately 3 years after Watson and Raynor reported their findings. Historian Robert Watson (1978) also noted the similarity between Albert and Peter but emphasized that Peter's fears were "homegrown, not produced in the laboratory" (p. 459).

Burrhus Frederic Skinner (1904–1990) was born and lived the first 18 years of his life in the small railroad town of Susquehanna, Pennsylvania. The older of two sons to an attorney father and a musical mother, young Skinner was a child inventor who found the parts for his creations among piles of debris near his house, including abandoned cars parked alongside a nearby blacksmith shop (Bjork, 1993). His brother and he were reared in an environment where "prohibitions and habits were elevated to a code of behavior that, when violated, was said to result in dire consequences to moral and physical health" (Bjork, 1993, p. 14). This professed relationship between behavior and consequences would later serve as the foundation for operant conditioning.

After completing an undergraduate degree in English at Hamilton College, Skinner was unsuccessful in his attempts to become a short-story writer (Coleman, 1997). According to Bjork (1993), Skinner followed his developing interests in psychology and entered Harvard University, where he completed all requirements for his doctoral degree in 1931 but remained, with the support of fellowships, to continue his studies of animal behavior, which included "a study of ant locomotion on slanted surfaces" (Coleman, 1997, p. 208). Later in his career as a professor at Harvard, Skinner explored the application of his operant model to human behavior. In *Science and Human Behavior* (1953), for example, he discussed the use of operant conditioning in therapeutic and educational settings. In *Walden Two*, Skinner (1948) described a utopian community based on the operant principles he studied in his Harvard laboratory.

Skinner's childhood inventive interests continued into adulthood. In addition to the Skinner box he designed to study animal behavior, he invented a number of devices that could be used with children. These included teaching machines (see Chapter 11), a special crib for infants, and a musical toilet seat he used with his daughter Deborah and found to be helpful for developing sphincter control (Bjork, 1993). Skinner had high expectations for his "baby tender," which was "a thermostatically controlled, enclosed crib with a safety glass front and a stretched-canvas floor" (Bjork, 1993, p. 129). This special crib was intended to be a space where infants could move around freely while they were simultaneously protected from the dangers of the surrounding environment. It also permitted parents to handle other responsibilities in the home without having to worry about their baby's safety.

According to Bjork (1993), Skinner tried to popularize his invention with an article titled "Baby Care Can Be Modernized," which he sold to *Ladies Home Journal*; however, it was published in 1945 under the title "Baby in a Box." Although many readers liked Skinner's invention, Bjork suggested that the title change "gave the impression that the author was as much a crackpot inventor as a progressively minded scientist" (p. 132). For whatever reasons, the public never accepted the baby tender despite Skinner's attempts to market the device. Although reports circulated that Skinner mistreated his daughter by placing her in his baby tender, Deborah later countered these rumors by saying, "My father is a warm and loving man. He was not experimenting on me" (Bjork, 1993, p. 133).

Albert Bandura (b. 1925), a native of Canada, completed his Ph.D. in clinical psychology at the University of Iowa in 1952 (Nordby & Hall, 1974). While a faculty member at Stanford University, Bandura collaborated with his first graduate student, Richard Walters, on what was to become his pioneering work on social learning theory. An active researcher, Bandura demonstrated that children learn by observing others, without immediately exhibiting and receiving reinforcement for the newly acquired behavior. These findings provided the foundation for later work on the effects of television viewing on children and the impact that aggressive role models can have on children's behavior. Concerns about violent behavior in children existed when Bandura and his colleagues initiated their work on observational learning. In the introduction to their classic article, Bandura, Ross, and Ross (1963a) described an incident reported in the *San Francisco Chronicle* in which "a boy was seriously knifed during a reenactment of a switchblade knife fight the boys had seen the previous evening on a rerun of the James Dean movie, *Rebel Without a Cause*" (p. 3). During his career, Bandura has published many articles and books, including *Social Learning Theory* (1977) and *Self-efficacy: The Exercise of Control* (1997).

Albert Ellis (b. 1913) was born in Pittsburgh but grew up in New York City, where he completed his undergraduate studies at City College of New York and received a Ph.D. in clinical psychology from Columbia University (Nystul, 1993; Sharf, 2000). Ellis had a rather stressful childhood. He contracted nephritis and pneumonia around age 5 years and was frequently hospitalized as a child. His father was usually away from home on business, and Ellis described his mother as "a neglectful woman in her own nice way" (Dryden, 1989, p. 539). When he was 12 years old, his parents divorced (Dryden, 1989). Ellis was an excellent student and possessed an optimistic view of life, which was later reflected in the principles of his rational emotive behavior therapy (REBT) (Weiner, 1988). At the beginning of his professional career, he used psychoanalytic techniques but developed REBT when he became disenchanted with the analytic approach (Sharf, 2000). Unlike Watson and Skinner who conducted much of their work in the laboratory, Ellis devised his approach based on clinical experiences (Meyers & Craighead, 1984). Although he published a wealth of articles and books (e.g., *Reason and Emotion in Psychotherapy*, 1962), most of these works are about adults and the problems they face. Some exceptions are his *Rational-Emotive Approaches to the Problems of Childhood* (Ellis & Bernard, 1983), *Case Studies in Rational Emotive Behavior Therapy with Children and Adolescents* (Ellis & Wilde, 2002), and his early writings on emotional education with children (e.g., Ellis, 1972). Ellis has actively promoted his approach through publication of the *Journal of Rational-Emotive Behavior and Cognitive-Behavior Therapy* and establishment of the Institute for Rational-Emotive Therapy.

THEORETICAL FOUNDATIONS

This section explores the writings of various behavioral theorists as their work relates to personality development and the etiology of childhood problems. Specifically, it examines the principles of classical and operant conditioning, observational learning, and cognitive-behavioral theories.

Classical Conditioning

Behavioral conditioning techniques for children have been designed using classical and operant principles. Classical or respondent conditioning is based on Pavlov's work in which the pairing of a conditioned stimulus (CS) with an unconditioned stimulus (UCS) produces a conditioned response (CR). Of the laws related to classical conditioning, Ollendick and Cerny (1981) cited three that are significant to clinical applications of this model. The more frequent the pairing of CS and UCS, the stronger the learned association is between these stimuli. The more intense the UCS, the stronger the learning. Combined, these laws suggest that repeated exposure to more pleasurable or traumatic stimuli can be expected to result in stronger emotional ties to these stimuli. The third law identified by Ollendick and Cerny is that repeated exposure to a CS in the absence of the UCS results in extinction of the learned association. This is a significant consideration in any discussion of the therapeutic benefits of classical conditioning. A child might develop a fear of dogs after repeated contacts with a neighborhood dog (CS) that always barks and growls (UCS) at passersby. The child learns to overcome a general fear of dogs through gradual exposure to dogs (CS) that are friendly. Watson and Raynor (1920) and Jones (1924) demonstrated both applications of classical conditioning with young children.

Watson and Raynor (1920) trained 11-month-old Albert to fear a white rat by striking a steel bar when the rat was present. With repeated pairings of the rat and the loud sound of the bar, Little Albert became conditioned to fear the rat as well as other furry animals and objects, including a rabbit and a Santa Claus mask. He did not exhibit fear when exposed to non-furry items, such as wooden blocks, so Watson and Raynor demonstrated that children can learn emotional responses to environmental stimuli. Specifically, the infant was exposed to a CS (i.e., a rat) concurrent with the presentation of the UCS (i.e., a loud noise). With repeated trials, Albert learned to fear other furry objects that were presented without the noise of the steel bar.

Mary Cover Jones (1924) used classical conditioning as one component of her treatment to extinguish Little Peter's fear of rabbits. To eliminate the boy's fears, Jones (1924) initiated twice-daily and eventually once-a-day sessions of "direct conditioning" (p. 312). She gave Peter food, which he ate as a caged rabbit was gradually placed closer and closer to him. After more than 20 sessions, he overcame his fear of the rabbit and exhibited "fair adjustment" (p. 314) in his fear of other furry objects. But the principles of classical conditioning may not completely explain the boy's progress in treatment. Peter was seen in group meetings with three other children who exhibited no fear of the rabbit during play. When he observed this behavior, he began to hold the animal. Therefore, it is possible that the elimination of his fears was caused partly by observational learning, which Albert Bandura studied decades later.

Operant Conditioning

The classical conditioning model has been useful in explaining how children learn simple actions, such as reflexes, but it does not account for the acquisition of more complex behaviors. The operant conditioning model described by Skinner (1953) has been more helpful in this regard and is the basis for many of the behavioral treatments used with children. Skinner's description of the importance of behavioral consequences has lead to the development of interventions based on reinforcement, punishment, and extinction paradigms. The important consideration for identifying an operant procedure is the child's response. Skinner (1953) justified this criterion when he wrote: "There is nothing circular about classifying events in terms of their effects; the criterion is both empirical and objective" (p. 73). Therefore, operant procedures are defined in terms of their effect on a target behavior after the presentation or removal of an environmental contingency or stimulus event.

Reinforcement. Reinforcement occurs when the presentation or removal of a contingency or consequence increases the rate of a target behavior. In positive reinforcement, the presentation of a consequence, known as a positive reinforcer, increases the occurrence of the behavior. A withdrawn student raises his hand, is routinely recognized and praised by the teacher, and becomes a more active participant in class discussions. In this example, the increase in the target behavior (i.e., the child's class participation) is likely caused by the teacher's response (i.e., attention and praise). It is important to remember that a consequence is a positive reinforcer only when its presentation results in an increase in a child's behavior. This principle sometimes leads to rather unusual examples of positive reinforcement. Consider a child whose misbehavior intensifies despite repeated reprimands from a parent. In this case, parent reprimands, which are usually assumed to be a form of punishment, appear to be reinforcing the child's misbehavior and increasing the likelihood that he will act in this manner.

Negative reinforcement occurs when the probability of a behavior increases after removal of a contingency. Skinner (1953) described how the removal of a noxious stimulus, such as a bright light or a loud noise, can result in an increase in a target behavior. Imagine yourself in the supermarket check-out lane watching a parent buy candy for a crying child. As soon as the child receives the candy, the crying ceases. When your return to the store each afternoon, you watch the child begin to cry when he enters the check-out lane. When the parent provides the candy, the child stops crying. If our target is the parent's behavior (i.e., giving candy to the child), we are watching an example of negative reinforcement in which the parent learns that giving candy terminates an unpleasant event. That is, the removal of a noxious stimulus (i.e., the child's crying) increases the probability that the target behavior will occur in the future.

The supermarket example can be used to illustrate an interesting characteristic of operant conditioning. When applied in therapeutic settings, operant principles are often discussed in terms of their effect on a child's behavior. But operant conditioning is an interactional phenomenon that involves more than one person, such as a parent and a child or a teacher and a student. In real-life situations, the behavioral mechanisms that influence the actions of one participant may differ from those affecting the other person's behavior. To understand these interactions, clinicians must consider four elements: the target behavior, the environmental contingency, the perspective or point of view of the person who controls the contingency or stimulus event, and the behavioral changes that occur after repeated pairings of behavior and event. We discussed our supermarket example in terms of the parent's behavior as the target, crying as the stimulus event, the child as the person who controls the environmental contingency, and the consistent behavioral pattern that emerges.

Another way of analyzing this interaction is to have the child's crying serve as the target behavior, the candy as the environmental contingency, the parent as the person in control of the stimulus event, and the parent's pattern of administering the contingency to the child. What we then have is an example of positive reinforcement in which the probability of the child's crying in the check-out lane increases with the parent's repeated use of candy as a reinforcer for this behavior. If the parent were to seek help in remediating this problem, the therapist would need to identify the stimulus events that are reinforcing for both the parent (e.g., a well-behaved child, silence) and child (e.g., love and attention, candy). The clinician would use this information to identify each client's needs or wants and to craft a treatment plan that helps the parent and child obtain desired reinforcers in a mutually fulfilling manner. By limiting the focus to one person or the other, the clinician has an incomplete picture of how reinforcement maintains the child's and the parent's behaviors.

The benefits of an interactional analysis are not limited to inappropriate behaviors. A studious child who receives a perfect score on an important test is positively reinforced for her preparation with an "A" grade and the teacher's praise. The teacher is also reinforced by the child's smile when she reviews the test and the self-statements he makes about his instructional skills. Failure to consider the interactional nature of behavioral conditioning can cause confusion. One individual describes the supermarket incident as an example of positive reinforcement, but another argues that it demonstrates the principles of negative reinforcement. Of course, both are correct depending on the target behavior and stimulus event that are the focus of attention. The implications for therapeutic interventions with children are many. By focusing on only one person in an interaction, therapists fail to identify the antecedents and consequences that affect the behavior of both participants.

The Nature of Reinforcers. Positive reinforcers can be classified as either primary or secondary. Primary reinforcers are stimuli that are naturally reinforcing, such as food to a hungry child. Secondary reinforcers "are not automatically reinforcing" but acquire this characteristic "through learning" (Craighead, Kazdin, & Mahoney, 1976, p. 114). School grades are an example of secondary reinforcers because children learn that grades translate into reinforcing events such as praise from parents and promotion to the next grade level. Generalized conditioned reinforcers, a special class of secondary reinforcers, involve the pairing of more than one reinforcer in response to a child's behavior and are "extremely effective in altering behaviors" (Craighead et al., 1976, p. 114). Attention, approval, affection, and tokens (e.g., money, stickers) are generalized reinforcers because they involve more than one reinforcer. Affection, for example, is typically displayed through positive physical contact, caring behaviors (e.g., assistance during crises), and acknowledgment of a person's self-worth, all of which can be reinforcing to a child.

Reinforcers have also been classified as tangible, social, token, or activity (Spiegler & Guevremont, 1998). Tangible reinforcers are concrete entities that a child can hold and manipulate, such as toys and foods, and social reinforcers include the recognition, attention, and praise children receive from others. Although tangible and social reinforcers are part of everyday life and children respond to both, social reinforcers offer the advantages of being readily available and easy to deliver (Spiegler & Guevremont, 1998). Birnbrauer (1978) identified several characteristics of effective reinforcers, the first of which is immediacy or the close proximity between a target behavior and its consequence. Unfortunately, reinforcers cannot always be administered immediately after a behavior, so tokens (e.g., stars, stickers, money) are often given to the child who accumulates and exchanges them for back-up reinforcers (e.g., toys, a trip to the zoo). Chapter 11 discusses the use of tokens in the behavioral treatment of childhood problems.

The last category of reinforcers described by Spiegler and Guevremont (1998) is activities, such as watching television, that increase the rate of a target behavior. Premack (1959) provided the rationale for using reinforcing activities. According to his Differential Probability Principle, activities that a child frequently engages in are preferred behaviors and therefore constitute reinforcing experiences. As Premack stated, "*Any response A will reinforce any other response B, if and only if the independent rate of A is greater than that of B*" (p. 220). In other words, for two behaviors, one infrequent (presumably unattractive) and the other frequent (presumably attractive), making access to the more frequent behavior contingent upon performance of the less frequent behavior will result in an increase in the latter. When parents make frequent activities, such as television viewing or playing with friends, contingent on completion of a less appealing behavior, such as successful completion of homework, they are rearing their children according to the Premack Principle. Therapists can also incorporate this principle into treatment by helping families identify privileges that will serve as reinforcers for appropriate behavior.

Differential Reinforcement. Behavioral change has been found to occur in response to different types of reinforcement. We have already discussed one form: the direct application of reinforcers for a target behavior. If a child exhibits a certain behavior, a reinforcer is administered. Another type is differential reinforcement, which Kazdin (1994b) defined as "reinforcing a response in the presence of one stimulus and not reinforcing the same response in the presence of another stimulus" (p. 49). Skinner (1953) illustrated this principle when he described how a mother's behavior differentially reinforced her son's whining behavior:

> If she is busy with other matters, she is likely not to respond to a call or request made in a quiet tone of voice. When the child raises his voice, she replies. This is differential reinforcement. The average intensity of the child's vocal behavior rises. When the mother has adapted to the new level, again only the louder instances are reinforced. Further differentiation in the direction of loud responses follows. (p. 97)

Spiegler and Guevremont (1998) described four types: differential reinforcement of incompatible behaviors, competing behaviors, other behaviors, and low response rates.

Differential reinforcement of incompatible behaviors, competing behaviors, or other behaviors is based on the premise that increasing the frequency of positive behaviors reduces the rate of the negative target behavior. Incompatible behaviors are those that "cannot be performed with the undesired behavior" (Kazdin, 1994b, p. 158). A child who is seated at her desk finishing her classwork cannot simultaneously walk around the classroom. But this student would be able to memorize multiplication facts while pacing around the room, two competing behaviors that can be successfully performed at the same time. As Spiegler and Guevremont (1998) pointed out, some behaviors, such as self-mutilation, are so inappropriate that "it may be necessary to reinforce *any other* behavior in order to decrease the target behavior quickly" (p. 137). In these situations, children are sometimes reinforced for less than ideal behaviors, such as physical or play activities (e.g., computer games, building puzzles) that restrict performance of the maladaptive behavior. Reinforcement of low response rates differs from other types because the child is reinforced not for exhibiting an alternative behavior but for declining rates of the inappropriate behavior. Kazdin (1994) described how the criterion for reinforcement is changed as the undesirable behavior decreases. A child who is talking in class would be reinforced for talking less than five times in a 30-minute period, then with improvement three times during the same interval, and eventually after no occurrences. Or the child would be reinforced for talking out less than twice in a 15-minute period, then less than twice over 30 minutes, with gradual increases in the time interval as improvement occurs.

Reinforcement Schedules. The changing criteria (e.g., frequency of the behavior, time interval) that are used to administer reinforcers constitute the reinforcement schedule for modifying the target behavior. Reinforcement schedules vary according to the regularity at which a consequence is paired with a behavior. When a continuous schedule is used, the consequence is applied every time the behavior occurs. In everyday life, continuous schedules are the exception rather than the rule. Most day-to-day experiences involve intermittent schedules in which a behavior is reinforced on some but not all occasions. For example, sometimes the teacher calls on a child who raises her hand in class; at other times, another child is selected.

The reinforcement schedules that operate in everyday life are far more complex than the continuous-intermittent dichotomy indicates. Intermittent reinforcement is sometimes delivered based on the number of times a behavior is exhibited (i.e., ratio schedule). Under other schedules, reinforcement occurs based on the amount of time that elapses between the administration of reinforcers (i.e., interval schedules). Reinforcement under these schedules occurs at either a fixed or variable rate (Table 10-1). As the term implies, fixed schedules involve the administration of reinforcers at a set rate. For example, a child receives a token every time she correctly answers 10 math questions (i.e., fixed ratio) or after she finishes at least one problem during a 10-second interval (i.e., fixed interval). In a variable schedule, reinforcers are delivered around an average rate. Over a course of five learning trials, for example, the child on a variable ratio schedule is reinforced after completing 13, 8, 10, 12, and 7 math problems (i.e., M = 10 completed problems). The child on a variable interval schedule has to wait for varying lengths of time, such as 12, 8, 11, 9, and 10 seconds (i.e., M = 10 seconds).

When the reinforcement schedules that appear in Table 10-1 are used for therapeutic purposes, they are to replace the random reinforcement schedules that children often encounter with a more structured and consistent use of reinforcers at home and in the classroom. A child's response differs depending on the reinforcement schedule introduced. For example, Craighead et al. (1976) stated that continuous and intermittent schedules have different effects depending on when they are used. If a child is learning a new behavior, continuous reinforcement is preferable. Crossman (1991) indicated that if high rates of a behavior are desired, a ratio schedule should be used; if moderate rates are preferred, an interval schedule is more appropriate. Parents who want an underachieving child to finish homework on time would attend to and reinforce completion of assignments in every subject during each night's homework session. After the child is performing well, the parents could maintain this behavior by intermittently reinforcing the

Table 10–1
A Description of Intermittent Reinforcement Schedules

	BASIS FOR REINFORCEMENT	
Reinforcement Rate	Ratio	Interval
Fixed	Reinforcer delivered after behavior occurs a specified number of times	Reinforcer delivered after behavior occurs after a specified period of time
Variable	Reinforcer delivered after behavior occurs around an average number of times	Reinforcer delivered after behavior occurs around an average period of time

child's completion of homework in some subjects and not others (e.g., math and science on one evening, English and math on the next). This does mean the child is to be ignored. As Crossman (1991) stated, "*Any behavior on any schedule will eventually disappear if it is not reinforced frequently enough*" (p. 136).

Chaining and Shaping. Most of the behaviors that children learn are complex and require the orderly combination of simpler behaviors or responses. A behavioral chain is "a combination of the individual responses ordered in a particular sequence" (Kazdin, 1994b, p. 43). Even what appear to be simple activities, such as brushing your teeth, are an involved sequencing of behaviors. A very brief section of the chain includes holding the toothbrush in one hand, picking up the toothpaste with the other, opening the tube, squeezing the tube to put toothpaste on the bristles of the brush, closing the tube, and returning the tube to the bathroom cabinet. The behavioral complexity of this daily routine pales in comparison with driving a car to work, building a house, or pursuing a graduate degree.

Behavioral chains occur when a behavior introduces or modifies "some of the variables which control another response" (Skinner, 1953, p. 224). Removing the cap from a toothpaste tube is impossible if the toothpaste is still in the cabinet. The links in a behavioral chain are often overlooked because many of the behaviors that we engage in every day are grouped together and labeled as one response (e.g., brushing your teeth). Craighead et al. (1976) described chaining as a backward process in which behavior C reinforces behavior B, which in turn reinforces behavior A. Consider a sleepy child who is on her way to bed. The final reinforcer is falling asleep, which follows crawling into bed, which in turn served as a reinforcer for walking into the bedroom. Each link in a behavioral chain also serves as an antecedent, or discriminative stimulus, for the next behavior. As the child crawled into bed, she set the stage for going to sleep. When they analyze complex behaviors, therapists must remember to assess the antecedent and consequent functions of each link in the chain.

Skinner (1953) said that "operant conditioning shapes behavior as a sculptor shapes a lump of clay" (p. 91). The artist's interaction with the medium gradually unfolds through a process of successive approximations to the final product, which has limited resemblance to the raw artistic materials, such as the individual containers of paint used to fresco the ceiling of the Sistine Chapel. Children also learn complex behaviors through successive approximation as small steps toward the final behavior are reinforced, thereby shaping the behavior. A child's acquisition of speech and language is an example of a complex behavior that is gradually shaped through reinforcement from significant others. The babbling of a 6-month-old infant bears little resemblance to the language that individual will later use in her high school valedictorian address. The opposite is true for chaining, in which individual links are retained and performed in an orderly sequence. Every time a child brushes his teeth, for example, an observer could recognize the links in this behavioral chain.

Punishment. Punishment is characterized by a decline in the rate of a target behavior after the presentation of an aversive stimulus or the temporary application of a condition in which positive stimuli are removed. When punishment by presentation is used, aversive stimuli can be categorized as either primary or secondary (Melamed & Siegel, 1980). Primary aversive stimuli are naturally unpleasant, such as the physical pain associated with an electric shock. Secondary aversive stimuli gain their negative effects after repeated pairing with stimuli that are already unpleasant to the child. An example of a secondary aversive stimulus is a verbal reprimand, such as "Stop," which was previously paired with physical punishment. Punishment also occurs when the rate of a behavior declines after the temporary removal of stimuli that are pleasant for the child. Common examples of this paradigm are restriction of a child's privileges (e.g., "grounding"), response cost procedures in which tokens are lost as the result of inappropriate behavior, and time out from reinforcement (Kazdin, 1994b).

Craighead et al. (1976) described how the effect of punishment is enhanced when it is consistently applied immediately after a child exhibits the target behavior. The authors stated that punishment is more effective when it is introduced at its most intense level, rather than at increasing levels of severity. Punishment of misbehavior should be linked with reinforcement of appropriate behaviors, including those that are incompatible with the target behavior. Reprimanding a child for fighting with classmates should be coupled with praising the student for sharing with other children and following rules when playing games with peers.

Punishment also has disadvantages or side effects. Melamed and Siegel (1980) noted that the procedure may produce unanticipated negative responses, including emotional reactions and avoidance behaviors. A child who is repeatedly reprimanded at school may become fearful of and purposely avoid the teacher who administers this punishment. As described previously, a consequence that decreases negative behaviors in one child (i.e., punishment) sometimes increases these behaviors in another (i.e., positive reinforcement). The verbal reprimands used to punish and eliminate misbehavior in some children provide attention and reinforce the same target behavior in others. Melamed and Siegel also noted that some children, through a process of observational learning (see Cognitive-Behavioral Theory later in this chapter), respond to punishment by engaging in the same behavior with others. For example, a child whose parents regularly use corporal punishment may become aggressive with peers.

Because of the interactional nature of operant procedures, parents are reinforced for using punishments that are effective with their children. Unfortunately, punishment often produces only temporary improvement in a child's behavior (Kazdin, 1994b), thereby creating a pattern of misbehavior-punishment-misbehavior. Consider a father who yells at his preschooler who resists sitting in her car seat during the drive to the day care center. After a brief struggle, the parent forces the child to comply. His application of a noxious consequence terminates the noncompliant behavior, if only for that day. Because he was reinforced for his actions, the father is likely to resort to this intervention, possibly at a more intense level, when the child resists in the future.

Extinction. Extinction involves a decrease in the rate of a target behavior after reinforcers are permanently removed. Punishment and extinction both result in a reduction of the behavior, but punishment involves the application of a negative stimulus or the temporary removal of positive stimuli. When extinction is used, the reinforcing stimulus is permanently eliminated in response to a child's negative target behavior. A common example is the use of inattention after an undesirable behavior. The parent in our supermarket example would use this technique if she ignored the child's crying and this behavior decreased over time.

Extinction is not the intervention of choice for very disruptive behaviors or those that are injurious to self or others. Extinction has other limitations. Some children exhibit what is called an "extinction burst" (Spiegler & Guevremont, 1998, p. 141) by increasing the frequency or intensity of the target behavior soon after extinction is administered. Comparable behavior sometimes occurs when a person repeatedly presses the buttons on a vending machine after inserting the correct change and receiving nothing in return. Likewise, a child who has learned that a parent will purchase candy if he misbehaves in public is likely to cry louder or longer when this behavior is ignored. Similar to punishment, extinction can cause emotional reactions, such as temper tantrums in children, that can complicate termination of the target behavior.

Ollendick and Cerny (1981) identified three factors that influence a child's response to extinction: the prior reinforcement schedule, the identification of relevant reinforcers, and the significant other's ability to withhold reinforcement. A child whose misbehavior was intermittently reinforced typically responds more slowly to extinction than does a child with a continuously reinforced behavior. Likewise, extinction is effective to the extent that relevant reinforcers are accurately identified and withheld from the child. If access to reinforcers is available through other persons, the procedure is compromised. A child's aggressive behavior, for example, frequently fulfills more than one function, such as gaining acceptance from friends, attention from teachers and parents, and dominance over selected peers. For extinction to be effective with this child, the parent or teacher must correctly identify the function of the aggression and exercise control over the reinforcers that maintain the behavior.

Cognitive-Behavioral Theory

The traditional focus of classical and operant conditioning has been overt or observable behaviors. Cognitive theorists have expanded this view to include covert behaviors, such as children's thoughts and attitudes. Cognitive-behavioral theorists have integrated behavioral and cognitive principles and thereby acknowledged the important role that cognitions play in the development and maintenance of children's behaviors and feelings. An important figure in the field of cognitive-behavioral theory is Albert Bandura, whose research on social learning theory provided significant child-related findings on observational learning, reciprocal determinism, and self-efficacy.

Social Learning Theory. According to Bandura (1969), children learn in ways other than direct reinforcement, punishment, or extinction of their behavior. In fact, much of the learning that takes place during a person's lifetime occurs through observation of others. A child can learn to thread a needle by having a parent teach and praise each step in the behavioral chain. A child also could develop this skill vicariously by observing the parent successfully thread a needle. According to Bandura (1969), vicarious influences can produce three outcomes: observational learning, behavioral inhibition or disinhibition, and response facilitation. A child who has never threaded a needle but does so after watching a parent model the behavior has experienced observational learning. Children also learn to increase or decrease their use of existing behaviors by observing others. An aggressive student who watches his teacher punish a classmate for hurting another child is less likely to hit other children. Response facilitation occurs when benign behaviors already present in the child's repertoire are exhibited in response to environmental cues. For example, a child who gazes around the classroom during a social studies test and observes other students intently answering items engages in this same behavior.

Observational Learning. Bandura and his colleagues demonstrated observational learning in their now classic studies of aggressive behavior in children. They found that nursery school students who observed aggressive models, either in vivo or on film, were more likely to exhibit aggression in a laboratory setting (Bandura, Ross, & Ross, 1961, 1963a). In other words, Bandura and his colleagues demonstrated that what children view in their environment affects their behavior. These findings are reason for concern because of the amount of violence in the programs that children watch on television (Murray, 1993) (see Contemporary Issues Box 10.1). Fortunately, the outcome of observational learning is more complex than a child's simple exposure to an aggressive model. For example, Bandura, Ross, and Ross (1963b) found that children who viewed a positive model or one punished for aggressive behavior exhibited significantly less aggression than did children who observed an aggressive model reinforced for these acts.

Observational learning is more than the unidirectional transmission of information from environment to child. Bandura (1977) addressed this issue when he proposed the concept of reciprocal determinism to describe the continuous interaction of overt behaviors, covert behaviors (e.g., thoughts, feelings), and environmental influences. As a young girl learns to ride a bicycle, her parents are there to encourage her. Their praise increases her self-confidence as a cyclist, so she works even harder to become skilled in this role. When her successful lesson ends, she smiles at her parents and reinforces them for their support and assistance. This example illustrates how a child's behavior is influenced by external events, such as a parent's praise, as well as internal stimuli, which include the child's attitude about herself and expectations for the future.

Self-efficacy. Child-centered theorists referred to self-concept or self-esteem when discussing children's view of self. Bandura (1977) also addressed this personal domain, but from a more cognitive point of view. His concept of self-efficacy refers to a person's belief that he or she "can successfully execute the behavior required to produce the outcomes" associated with a task (p. 79). Self-efficacy differs from a child's outcome expectations, which constitute the awareness of the consequences of a behavior. A child who is seated on a bicycle facing a downhill grade understands that releasing the brakes will cause her to coast down the winding street. Her belief in her ability to navigate the course ahead constitutes her self-efficacy as it relates to cycling. According to Bandura (1986), self-efficacy emerges from four primary sources of information: performance achievements, vicarious learning, verbal persuasion, and physiological arousal.

Bandura (1986) identified enactive or performance attainment as the most important source of self-efficacy information because the child has direct experience in mastering a given task. Success fosters self-efficacy, but failure decreases the child's expectations for a positive outcome. A child who repeatedly rides her bike down the street without falling experiences an increase in self-efficacy relative to this behavior. Vicarious learning also represents a source of self-efficacy information. Observing other children dive into a pool and successfully swim to the other side can enhance a child's belief in his ability to accomplish the same feat. Bandura also identified verbal persuasion as a potential source of self-efficacy. A

Contemporary Issues Box 10–1

Children, Television, and Video Games

Violence on television has been a controversial issue since the early development of this medium in the 1950s (Murray, 1993). Despite repeated calls for change during the intervening decades, there has been little progress in reducing the level of televised violence. Instead, the number of violent episodes has remained the same, and the nature of these events "has become more mean, more realistic, more random, and more sophisticated" (Jason, Hanaway, & Brackshaw, 1999, p. 135). Recently, violence has been integrated into the video games that children play. For example, Jason et al. described a game that contained the following scene:

> Three men burst into the bedroom of a young woman dressed only in a skimpy negligee. Unless the player makes the right moves, the men drag her off and plunge an electric drill into her neck, then hang her on a meat hook. (p. 136)

Mental health professionals and laypeople alike have expressed concern about children's exposure to such violent episodes. Of particular interest is the impact these scenes might have on children's behavior.

Albert Bandura's work on observation learning has been the foundation for many studies on the impact of television and video games. When Bandura conducted his research, television viewing was more likely to be a family activity instead of the "solitary enterprise" it has become for many children in the United States (Andreasen, 2001, p. 15). The single television in the typical 1950s home has been replaced by multiple outlets, sometimes in the child's bedroom, with cable channels that provide a diverse range of entertainment options. Because violent acts are relatively common on television (Murray, 1993), public concern about children's unsupervised access to these programs seems justified.

Anderson and Bushman (2001) concluded that evidence collected in correlational, experimental, and longitudinal studies points to a link between violence on television and aggressive behavior in children. But this relationship appears to be moderated by the child's developmental level and the nature of the violence portrayed on television. For example, Kromar and Cooke (2001) randomly assigned students from kindergarten to sixth grade to watch one of four videotaped segments of a popular television program. The plot involved the main character being provoked or not provoked to engage in violence and being punished or not punished for this act. The authors found that younger students who viewed the unpunished violence rated the character's aggressive behavior as more appropriate than did similar-age children who viewed punished violence and older participants from both experimental conditions. In other words, age and the nature of the violent episode appeared to moderate children's beliefs about the event.

Researchers have expanded their study of televised violence and children's behavior to include the impact of violent video games. Anderson and Bushman (2001) conducted a meta-analysis of studies on these games and found a significant relationship with aggressive thoughts, feelings, and behaviors in children, adolescents, and adults. In a related meta-analysis of 25 studies with children, adolescents, and adults, Sherry (2001) found that the correlation between playing violent video games and aggression was statistically significant, but the relationship was smaller than that reported for televised violence and aggressive behavior. Sherry reported that aggression was more likely to be associated with fantasy games involving human characters than it was with video games that depicted violence in sports activities.

The Anderson and Bushman (2001) and Sherry (2001) studies included participants of all ages. Although Anderson and Bushman did not report an effect for participants' age or gender, closer attention must be given to the relationship between violent video games and children's behavior. This appears to be especially true for boys' use of video games. When Funk, Buchman, and Germann (2000) surveyed fourth and fifth graders about their use of video games, they found that boys spent more time playing these games and were more

Contemporary Issues Box 10–1 *(cont.)*

likely to prefer games containing violence. Irwin and Gross (1995) assigned boys, ages 7 and 8 years, to 10 minutes of either aggressive or nonaggressive video game play. Participants were then taken to a playroom where they engaged in free play with an 8-year-old boy (a confederate of the experimenters) and a staged frustrating interaction with the child. Behavioral ratings revealed that boys who played the aggressive video exhibited significantly more physical and verbal aggression toward the play equipment and more verbal aggression toward the boy in free play and more physical aggression during the frustrating condition.

Two recent methods for controlling children's access to violence in the media are the V-chip or Violence-Chip and manufacturer ratings of video game content. Federally mandated on all television sets as of January 2000, the V-Chip allows parents to restrict access to programs they believe are inappropriate for their children. The chip is not a panacea for eliminating televised violence from the home. For example, Berk (2000) cautioned that it will require many years before this technology is in every television in the United States. And Andreasen (2001) stated that the chip and the accompanying codes used to classify program content have not improved the overall quality of programming.

Funk, Flores, Buchman, and Germann (1999) surveyed children in grades 4 and 6 and their parents to determine whether the violence ratings given to video games represent the views of study participants. The authors found that agreement was highest for the most and least violent games, with less agreement for videos that involved cartoon characters. Funk et al. concluded that the ratings of professional observers can be helpful to parents when purchasing video games, especially those containing more extreme levels of violence. But additional work is needed to devise a rating system for the full range of video games, including those that contain cartoon characters.

For the V-Chip and video game ratings to be useful, parents must become actively involved in monitoring their children's access to violent programming. Television sets equipped with the chip must be programmmed, and parents must evaluate the content of the video games their children play. Jason et al. (1999) pointed out that violence is part of everyday life and that children cannot be completely insulated from it. The challenge to parents, mental health professionals, and child advocates is to provide a developmentally appropriate introduction to this class of behaviors along with healthy ways of interpreting and responding to these events.

teacher who encourages a student to engage in a behavior that is within the child's repertoire can enhance the student's self-efficacy. The fourth source of information is a child's physiological state. A young musician who is extremely anxious before he walks on stage to perform may interpret this information as a sign of impending catastrophe. Likewise, a soccer player who is excited as she runs onto the field expects to perform well in the game.

Beck's Cognitive Model. Another important figure in the development of cognitive-behavioral theory is Aaron Beck, whose cognitive conceptualization of depression has had a major influence on the assessment and treatment of mood disorders. Central to Beck's cognitive model are the faulty belief systems that people develop over the course of their lives. A young child with loving and caring parents develops positive self-beliefs, such as "I am an important person" or "I am lovable." A preschooler whose parent berates and physically abuses him formulates very different beliefs about himself. According to Beck (1976), a person's belief system influences how the individual will behave and feel.

As children interact with their environment and develop beliefs about themselves, they organize these thoughts into cognitive schemas (Beck, 1967). A child's schemas can be positive or negative, are based on past experiences, and serve as the basis for expectations about the future. A child with positive schemas about popularity anticipates that other children will select her as a friend and view her as a good person. Conversely, a child with negative schemas expects rejection from his peers and a lonely existence. Cognitive schema also translate into behavioral and emotional responses. The child with positive schemas is more likely to feel self-confident, happy, and satisfied with life. Her belief system is also reflected in her behavior. She seeks out other children, smiles when talking to them, and participates in clubs or group activities. The child who processes information using negative schemas may feel depressed, anxious, or angry. He avoids interactions with other children, physically assaults his classmates, or breaks others' toys. Therefore, negative cognitive schemas are maladaptive because they create personal and interpersonal problems. The child with a depressed schema who withdraws from others is unlikely to develop friendships, which in turn reinforces the child's depressed affect and negative view of himself.

Cognitive schema translate into "automatic thoughts" (Beck, 1976, p. 33) that spontaneously emerge during the course of everyday life. When Beck (1976) had clients record their automatic thoughts, he discovered similarities. Thoughts were brief and personally meaningful statements (e.g., "I'm stupid") that appeared without logic or forethought. Although his clients accepted these idiosyncratic thoughts, other people sometimes had difficulty understanding them. According to Beck's model, distorted or self-defeating automatic thoughts (e.g., "I can't do this") are the basis for emotional and behavioral problems. Another cognitive source for these difficulties is the attributional style that a person uses to interpret life events.

Learned Helplessness. Martin Seligman (1975) introduced the concept of "learned helplessness" to explain the responses he observed in dogs who were exposed to an environmental stressor (i.e., electric shock) over which they had no control. Abramson, Seligman, and Teasdale (1978) applied the principles of learned helplessness to humans and described how a person's attributional style affects his or her emotional state. According to learned helplessness theory, a person attempts to explain an event using internal-external, stable-unstable, and specific-global attributions. For example, Katrina and her family move to a new town in February, and she enters a school where she is evaluated based on significantly higher academic standards. When she encounters problems in her math and science classes, she could attribute her difficulties to factors that are internal (e.g., "I can't do this work") or external (e.g., "My teacher expects way too much of me"). She would also make a temporal attribution by interpreting her problems as stable (e.g., "I'm never going to be able to do this work") or unstable (e.g., "I'll do better on the next text"). And she could limit the scope of her attributions to specific areas (e.g., "I'm no good in math and science") or make global self-judgments (e.g., "I'm a lousy student").

The three dimensions of the learned helplessness triad (i.e., internality, stability, globality) comprise a person's attributional style. If Katrina uses an external-unstable-specific style, she might explain her academic problems as follows: "Ms. Thomas gave us a really hard science test today, but I'll do better next time because all of my other grades this year have been higher." This adaptive attributional style for interpreting negative events differs significantly from the internal-stable-global depressive triad described by Abramson et al. (1978). If Katrina were to interpret her school problems in this manner, she might make a statement such as, "I am so dumb when it comes to school that I will never be able to get good grades in any of my classes." If her attributional style were to extend beyond the school setting, her internal-stable-global explanations for failure experiences could generalize to her relationships with her peers or her interactions with family members.

So far we have discussed how a child used the depressive triad to interpret negative events. Consider how Katrina would adopt a depressive attributional style to explain the high grade she received on a spelling test. Her success would be caused by factors that are external (e.g., "It was an easy test"), unstable (e.g., "I won't do this well next time"), and specific (e.g., "Just because I get an A on a spelling test doesn't mean I can do it in other subjects"). Metalsky, Laird, Heck, and Joiner (1995) described how the dimensions of learned helplessness interact with each other. A child's internal-unstable-specific attribution for a poor test grade can be adaptive. If Katrina had said, "I messed up on this math test, but I'll do better the next time and in all my other classes," her interpretation of the event could result in her studying harder in the future.

Seligman et al. (1984) applied the learned helplessness model to depression in children, ages 8 to 13 years. The authors found that children with depressed symptoms tended to interpret negative events using the internal-stable-global attributional style observed in adults with depression. These children were also likely to use the opposite attributional style (i.e., external-unstable-specific) to bring meaning to good events. Seligman et al. found that mothers' depressive symptomatology and attributional style for interpreting negative events were related to similar behaviors in their children. No relationship was found between fathers' and their children's depressive symptoms or attributional styles. Based on their findings, the authors concluded that "the child may learn attributional style and/or depressive symptoms from the mother, and these may then maintain each other" (p. 238). Therapists who treat children with depression should assess for like symptoms in parents as well as similarities in attributional style.

Rational-Emotive Behavior Theory

Albert Ellis discussed the role that cognitions play in human emotions and behaviors. In particular, he emphasized the importance of a person's belief system, which he defined as "that aspect of human cognition that is responsible for the mental health and the psychological well-being of the individual" (Ellis & Bernard, 1983, p. 11). Ellis (1977) described his A-B-C model of personality in which "A" represents an activating event, "B" is the person's belief system, and "C" is an emotional or behavioral consequence. Healthy personality development requires healthy or rational thoughts. For example, a student who receives a low grade on a math test (i.e., activating event) might think, "Well, one bad grade is not the end of the world." Although disappointed, the child remains hopeful and devotes additional effort when preparing for the next test.

If a child's beliefs are irrational, emotional and behavioral problems can result. Waters (1982) listed 10 common irrational beliefs in children:

1. It's awful if others don't like me.
2. I'm bad if I make a mistake.
3. Everything should always go my way; I should always get what I want.
4. Things should come easily to me.
5. The world should be fair, and bad people should be punished.
6. I shouldn't show my feelings.
7. Adults should be perfect.
8. There's only one right answer.
9. I must win.
10. I shouldn't have to wait for anything. (p. 572)

A child who holds the second irrational belief is likely to respond to a low test grade by invoking the belief that all his grades must be excellent. This belief might serve as the basis for feelings of frustration, anger, or even depression. Similarly, the child might engage in disruptive behaviors in class or refuse to study for future tests.

Ellis (1987) stated that humans beings are prone to irrational thinking, in part because of childhood experiences with significant others. A 7-year-old child who is constantly praised by parents for academic achievements, such as correctly reciting the 50 U.S. states and their capitals, learns that self-worth is contingent upon perfect performance of these feats. The irrational beliefs that children acquire early in life "tend to perpetuate and to sabotage their lives forever" (Ellis, 1972, p. 19). Fortunately, children can learn to think rationally and therefore live more fulfilling lives. Two methods for achieving this transition are rational-emotive education and rational-emotive behavior therapy, which are discussed in Chapter 11.

DEVELOPMENTAL CONSIDERATIONS

Behavioral and cognitive-behavioral theorists have focused on the role of learning in child development, and researchers have studied the relationship between overt and covert behavior and environmental stimuli. This section examines selected studies on early learning, including research on the role of prenatal experience. It also explores the development of thinking during childhood in a brief review of the work of Jean Piaget, Lev Vygostsky, and proponents of the information processing model. It concludes with a discussion of two related areas of development: children's use of narrative and the interests and preferences that are the foundation for career development.

Cognitive Development

When does learning first occur in children? The answer appears to be that classical and operant conditioning begin very early in life. Blass, Ganchrow, and Steiner (1984) found that classical conditioning even occurs in newborns, ages 2 to 48 hours. In an experimental group, the authors administered 18 learning trials of gentle stroking of the infants' forehead (CS) followed by oral delivery of a sucrose solution (UCS). Babies in the experimental and two control conditions were then exposed to nine extinction trials in which forehead stroking was not accompanied by sucrose delivery. During this phase, the experimental infants were significantly more likely to exhibit head orienting, sucking, and crying, which suggests they had learned to associate the conditioned and unconditioned stimuli.

DeCasper and Spence (1986) observed operant conditioning in newborns. The authors had mothers-to-be read aloud a target story twice each day during their final weeks of pregnancy. Within hours after birth, infants' sucking behavior was either followed by an audiotaped recording of the target story or a new story that mothers had not recited during pregnancy. Results revealed that babies responded to the target story, which served as a positive reinforcer for sucking behavior. When they tested babies whose mothers had not read the target story during pregnancy, DeCasper and Spence found no effect for target and novel stories on the infants' sucking behavior. The authors concluded that "the postnatal reinforcing value of a speech passage is increased by prenatal experience with the passage" (p. 148).

How children learn and think is an important consideration in the design and delivery of behavioral interventions, especially those based on cognitive-behavioral theories. For example, Kendall and Treadwell (1996) questioned whether cognitive-behavioral techniques can be effective with children under the age of 10 years whose cognitive skills are less sophisticated. Writers agree that thinking changes with maturity, but they differ in their description of the nature of this change, the ages when children attain various modes of thought, and the role of cultural influences (Berndt, 1997). This section examines models of cognitive development proposed by Jean Piaget, Lev Vygotsy, and the information processing theorists.

Piaget's Cognitive-Developmental Model. Piaget believed that children sequentially progress through four qualitatively different stages of thinking: sensorimotor intelligence (birth to 18 months), preoperational thinking (18 months to 6 years), concrete-operational thought (7 years to 11 years), and formal-operational thinking (12 years to adulthood). Although children interpret life events in a more sophisticated manner as they move from one level to the next, the age ranges for these stages should be considered estimates. Even Piaget (1972) revised his model and advanced the onset for formal-operational thinking to between ages 15 and 20 years. And other researchers (e.g., Tomlinson-Keasey, 1972) have questioned whether some adults ever achieve the ability to engage in the abstract thinking that characterizes this stage. We limit our discussion of Piaget's model to his preoperational and concrete operational stages because they are most relevant for children.

Preoperational thinkers use symbols, such as words and toys, to "represent something that is not physically present" (Feldman, 1998, p. 252). A preoperational child can use puppets to portray children at play or use words to describe recent events to a therapist. The preoperational stage also involves egocentric thought in which the child experiences "difficulty in seeing the world from another's outlook" (Kail, 1998, p. 148). Although children in this stage may seem selfish or stubborn, their behavior often reflects their inability to understand that other people have different views or opinions (Feldman, 1998). A therapist who tries to "reason" with a physically aggressive preschooler is confronted with this developmental challenge when this preoperational child is unable to understand the effect of his behavior on others.

Piaget believed that organized and logical thinking emerges during the concrete operational period (Feldman, 1998). A child's reasoning during this period is "an earthbound, concrete, practical-minded sort of problem-solving, one that persistently fixates on the perceptible and inferable reality right there in front of him" (Flavell, 1985, p. 98). Concrete operational children begin to recognize others' intentions, understand the predictable nature of the physical world, and use rules in games and sports (Cole & Cole, 1996). Thinking becomes more systematic and flexible as children become less egocentric, in part, because they are exposed to their playmates' views of the world (LeMare & Rubin, 1987). A child's progression from preoperational to concrete operational thinking is a gradual process that may involve uneven development across different cognitive domains (e.g., mathematical, social, artistic) (Mandler, 1983). In therapy, the transitional child may describe an event from another's perspective but have difficulty explaining why or how the event occurred, relying instead on a vague response such as, "Because." Or a mathematical genius may have difficulty processing social conflicts with other children. Although most children seem to develop at the same rate of speed across different cognitive domains (Marini & Case, 1994), therapists must be alert for clients who are more developed in certain areas.

The thinking of children in the concrete operational stage involves trial-and-error exploration of concrete objects and current events (Berndt, 1997; Hughes, Noppe, & Noppe, 1996). Therapists who work with these children typically incorporate toys and therapeutic games into the therapeutic process. Children in this stage become more skilled at detecting the relationship between their behavior and its consequences (Forehand & Wierson, 1993). As they acquire these skills, children develop and refine attributions for life events that affect their interpretations of and responses to these events. Licht and Dweck (1984) described how children's attributional styles can be categorized as either "mastery-oriented" or "helpless" (p. 628). The authors conducted a classroom study of students with these styles and found that mastery-oriented children were able to learn new material, regardless of its difficulty level (i.e., clearly written vs. confusing). When helpless students were presented with identical learning materials that were well written, their performance was comparable to that of mastery-oriented children. When the new material was presented in a confusing manner, the helpless children did significantly poorer. Based on these findings, Licht and Dweck proposed an interactional model containing children's attributional style and environmental demands. When presented with a challenge that seems to be achievable, mastery-oriented and helpless children are likely to respond in a similar manner. But when the challenge is unclear or confusing, helpless children may invoke negative attributions that hinder their performance.

The Information Processing Model. Therapists can overcome the cognitive- developmental divide that exists with children by remembering their earlier modes of thinking and solving problems of everyday life. This requires consideration of the qualitative transitions described by Piaget as well as the changes that information processing theorists have observed in children's use of "specific strategies, rules, and skills that affect memory, learning, and problem solving" (Berger & Thompson, 1996, p. 64). Proponents of the information processing model of cognitive development have adopted the analogy of "child-as-computer" (Cole & Cole, 1996, p. 356). According to this model, important environmental stimuli, such as colors and sounds, are registered via the body's senses and then transmitted to the brain where the information becomes part of short-term memory. These data are either forgotten or combined with information previously stored in long-term memory, a decision is made, and a response is activated (e.g., braking a car at a red traffic light, shoving books into a backpack when the class bell rings). Information processing theorists focus on both the hardware and software of thinking. These include the myelination of neural pathways and the rehearsal and coding strategies used to process information.

Therapists are often asked to help children develop more efficient information processing skills. Consider the role that attention span plays in children's thinking. For some students, environmental stimuli, such as music playing on a radio, inhibit information processing and result in unfinished homework and poor test grades. With these children, therapists should encourage parents to create learning environments that are relatively free of distractors. These include having a child complete all homework in a quiet setting. Attention span is also an important consideration if preschoolers are expected to participate in a 50-minute therapy session. Children's attention span in a free play setting increases between ages 1 and 5 years (Ruff & Lawson, 1990), but the clinician's interviewing style and the toys and manipulatives available to the child are also significant factors.

Information processing skills improve with age. Children become more efficient thinkers as they process information more rapidly (Kail, 1993), improve their problem-solving skills (Crowley & Siegler, 1993), gain better memory skills (Kail & Park, 1994), and acquire greater awareness and control of an expanded knowledge base (Keating, 1990). Therefore, therapists must adjust the pace of their questions and the timing of their interventions to the child's information processing speed. Consider the effect of a child's memory skills on the therapeutic process. Clinicians routinely ask children to describe events from the previous week or earlier times in life, all of which require the use of long-term memory.

Vygotsky's Sociocultural Model. When Piaget studied the development of thinking in children, he tended to focus on the individual child. As Kail

(1998) described it, "The child is seen as a solitary adventurer-explorer boldly forging ahead" (pp. 160–161). The Russian psychologist Lev Vygotsky (1896–1934) believed that cognitive development is a social process in which children learn to think as a result of their interactions with others. Vygotsky described a cultural model of development in which children learn to think and use the tools of their society through an apprenticeship with significant others who are more advanced in the use of these skills. As Rogoff (1990) noted, cognitive development "is embedded in the context of social relationships and sociocultural tools and practices" (p. 8). Depending on their surroundings and the tools of their elders, children learn to think using physical objects (e.g., shovels, computers) and symbols (e.g., pictures, the written word).

The symbols that are most central to cognitive development are those that comprise the child's native language (Berndt, 1997). Vygotsky (1934/1986) believed that children use speech to guide their activity. An important element of this process is private speech, which occurs when children speak aloud to direct or regulate their behavior. Berk (1992) reported that children are more likely to engage in private speech when they are confused, have made errors, or face a difficult challenge. As they become more proficient in handling a task or problem, children internalize private speech to a whisper or the silent movement of their lips (Berk & Landau, 1993). Therapists are sometimes treated to children's private speech when they use play techniques with young clients. As a child builds a house with wooden blocks, she may instruct herself during the placement of an important roof piece by saying, "Careful. Don't knock it down." A client who is adding detail to the face of a family member might utter, "Her eyes go here and here, and the nose is here." In fact, clinicians sometimes draw upon private speech, treating it as if it were initially verbalized as social speech intended to communicate meaning. The therapist for the house builder might respond, "So you want to be careful to not knock down the walls." To the young artist, the therapist might say, "So you're coloring the face to look just like your sister's."

Children's Narratives

An important source of clinical information is the stories that children tell. Young clients sometimes discuss uncomfortable events through the characters they create for their stories (Garbarino & Stott, 1989). Constructivist therapists recently adopted narrative as a technique for helping clients to make meaning out of their lives (see Chapter 16). To effectively use a child's stories in treatment, the clinician must adopt the developmental perspective of the client. This requires an understanding of adult–child differences in the structure, content, and complexity of the narratives that people tell.

Russell, van den Broek, Adams, Rosenberger, and Essig (1993) examined the therapist and child narratives that Gardner (1971) reported in his description of the Mutual Storytelling Technique (MST) (see Chapter 16). When they compared clients' initial stories with Gardner's retelling of these narratives, Russell et al. found that the parts or components of the therapist's stories were more structurally related than was true for the children's creations. In addition, there were fewer mistakes in the order in which events were presented in Gardner's retelling of the children's narratives. When the content of the stories was compared, results revealed that the therapist's corrective versions were more psychologically minded and more likely to contain personal characteristics, such as the protagonist's motivations and intentions. Gardner's stories were also more complex and redundant than were the children's original narratives. If the Russell et al. results are representative of therapists in general, we must question whether children benefit from reconstructed narratives that are beyond their developmental level. When using a procedure such as MST, clinicians should carefully listen to each child's story and provide a revised version that incorporates as much of the client's content, vocabulary, and grammatic structure as possible.

Vocational Development in Childhood

Vocational or career development begins early in life as children watch their parents leave home for work to provide financial support for the family. Children encounter their first structured work environment when they enter school and receive formal evaluations of their academic performance. Many young people have a similar experience at home where they receive a weekly allowance for successfully completing household tasks, such as cleaning their rooms or helping with mealtime activities. Adults intermittently orient children to the future when they ask, "What do you want to be when you grow up?" Although most vocational theorists and researchers have concentrated on adolescents and adults, important work has been done on the childhood foundations for career development.

Ginzberg, Ginsburg, Axelrad, and Herma (1951) presented a three-stage model of occupational choice. The authors' first stage, which coincides with the elementary school years, is characterized by fantasy choices that occur when children believe they can be whatever they want to be and select careers without taking into consideration their personal talents and job requirements. This does not mean that children necessarily choose fantasy occupations, such as a super hero or a fairy princess. On the contrary, Trice and King (1991) interviewed kindergarten students and found that most (74%) identified real careers, such as police officer and doctor. And the number of children who choose fantasy careers decreases with age. In a cross-sectional study of students in grades K through 6, Trice, Hughes, Odom, Woods, and McClellan (1995) reported that 21% of kindergartners gave a fantasy occupation as their first career choice. This figure compared with 6% of second graders, 3% of fourth graders, and none of the sixth grade students.

Donald Super dedicated his career to the formulation, testing, and revision of a five-stage theory of career development across the lifespan. The five stages in Super's model are growth (ages 4 to 13 years), exploration (ages 14 to 24 years), establishment (age 25 to 44 years), maintenance (ages 45 to 65 years), and disengagement (age 66 years and older) (Super, Savickas, & Super, 1996). The age ranges are estimates, and Super's stages are not invariant because he recognized that adults recycle through earlier stages when they change careers. Super's first stage is most relevant to our discussion because it is during this period that children acquire the necessary attitudes and rudimentary behaviors for career success. As Super et al. described, children learn to appreciate the value of achievement, they develop effective work habits, and they begin to think more about the future. Success during this developmental stage is believed to enhance a child's self-esteem and sense of personal autonomy. Although Super (1957) mentioned the growth stage in his famous text, *The Psychology of Careers*, he focused on adolescence through old age. And when Super and Overstreet (1960) conducted their famous Career Pattern Study, a longitudinal study of vocational development, they began with a sample of ninth grade boys.

Vocational research with children has been conducted on career interests or aspirations. A prominent figure in the study of career interests in adolescents and adults has been John Holland. His hexagonal model for the structure of career interests is the basis for both research and clinical applications. Holland's (1997) model is composed of six well-known personality and work environment types: realistic, investigative, artistic, social, enterprising, and conventional. Often referred to using the acronym, RIASEC, Holland's typology has been useful in studying the career interests of adolescents and adults (Tracey & Rounds, 1993), but Tracey and Ward (1998) questioned whether the model is appropriate for children.

Some researchers have reported similarities in the career interests of children, adolescents, and adults. For example, Trice et al. (1995) and Zbaracki, Clark, and Wolins (1985) used Holland's (1997) six types in organizing children's interests and aspirations, but they did not examine the validity of this model. Tracey and Ward (1998) studied elementary school, middle school, and university students and found that the interests of the two older groups, but not the elementary school children, were consistent with Holland's types. In addition, the structural relationships among the RIASEC categories differed in the youngest group. Tracey and Ward found that the interests of these elementary students were related to the gender typing and location of activities, rather than the two-dimensional structure of data/ideas and people/things that Prediger (1982) described for adults. Children's thinking about interests was apparently related to whether the activity was considered appropriate for boys or girls and whether the activity occurred in or outside of school.

If Tracey and Ward (1998) are correct in asserting that the structure of children's interests is different, researchers must conduct more detailed studies to uncover the change process that occurs from childhood to adolescence and adulthood. In other words, how does the relationship among the six Holland (1997) types change across time? A structural transition in interests has appeal, given other developmental changes that occur during childhood and adolescence. When compared to gender typing and location of activities, which are relatively concrete and observable criteria, choosing interests based on their involvement with data or ideas and people or things is likely to require the more abstract thinking that develops in adolescence and adulthood. Tracey

(2001) noted this relationship when he emphasized the need to study structural transitions in children and adolescents.

As an initial step in this direction, Tracey (2002) conducted a 1-year longitudinal study of interests with fifth and eighth grade students. In contrast to the earlier findings of Tracey and Ward (1998), he found that the interests of both groups could be categorized using the six Holland (1997) types. Similar to Tracey and Ward, he discovered that the structural relationship among these types was less integrated in his fifth grade sample, with little change taking place across a 1-year period. By contrast, the structure of interests in the older group resembled that of adolescents and adults. In addition, eighth graders' interests became more integrated across time. More longitudinal research is needed to study structural transitions across longer periods of time. Based on the results reported by Tracey, it appears that particular attention should be directed to the changes that occur during the late elementary and middle school years. The outcome of these studies can be used to design career education programs that take into account students' developmental levels. One component of these interventions should be information intended to enhance children's and parents' career awareness, which is examined later in the discussion of multicultural considerations for vocational development.

MULTICULTURAL CONSIDERATIONS

How children think, communicate, and plan for the future is influenced by their cultural surround. This section explores selected research on two of these topics. First, we examine variations in the narrative style of children from different ethnic groups. This includes a discussion of recent work on the clinical application of folktales with children of color. We then consider gender and ethnic influences on career development in childhood.

Ethnicity and Narrative Style

Chapter 5 discusses cultural influences on language development in children. Researchers have found that culture also seems to affect children's narrative style. To study this relationship, Michaels and Cazden (1986) analyzed the "Show and Tell" stories of African American and European American primary school students. The authors found that European American children use what the authors called a "topic-centered" approach to storytelling. Narratives for these children were temporally organized with "a marked beginning, middle, and end, with no shifts in time or space" (p.136). African American students were found to use a "topic-associating" approach characterized by "a series of implicitly associated personal anecdotes, often involving shifts in time, location, and key characters, with no explicit statement of an overall theme or point" (pp.136–137).

Michaels and Cazden (1986) provided the following example of a topic-associating narrative told by an African American first grade girl. The authors used forward slashes to indicate pauses (e.g., commas), double slashes for sentence closures (i.e., periods), and a colon for elongated vowels.

> I went to the beach Sunday / and to McDonald's / and to the park / and I got this for my birthday / (holds up purse) / my mother bought it for me / and I had two dollars for my birthday / and I put it in here / and I went to where my friend / named GiGi / I went over to my grandmother's house with her / and she was on my back / and I / and we was walkin' around / by my house / and she was HEA:VY // She was in the sixth or seventh grade// (p. 137)

Although the child begins her story in a topic-centered manner with temporal and physical organization, she quickly changes to a topic-associating style in which she ties together the personally relevant topics of a significant day (i.e., Sunday), a significant event (i.e., her birthday), and significant people in her life (i.e., mother, grandmother, friend).

Michaels and Cazden (1986) studied teachers' reactions to the students' narratives. They found that teachers, most of whom were European American, seemed to understand the topic-centered stories told by European American students, but they described the African Americans' narratives as rambling and in need of clarification. Michaels and Cazden presented the children's stories to a group of graduate students in education. The European American students restricted their positive ratings to topic-centered stories, but the African American students accepted topic-centered and topic-associating narratives, "noticing differences, but seeming to appreciate both" (p. 150). Narrative style is an important consideration when storytelling is used with children in therapy. Clinicians must recognize the role of cultural differences, especially when interventions such as Gardner's Mutual Storytelling Technique are used and children are expected to share a narrative containing a beginning, middle, and end (see Chapter 16).

Telling stories and fables is a common practice in many cultures. In an early comparison of folktales from different Native American groups (e.g., Navajo, Commanche), McClelland and Friedman (1952) found a relationship between parenting practices and the achievement orientation in the stories. The cultures that endorsed a more independent approach to child rearing were more likely to tell folktales with an achievement theme. Parents in these groups were less indulgent with their children, tended to emphasize independence at an earlier age, and were more likely to punish dependence in their children. The authors hypothesized that both child-rearing practices and folktales were reflections of a group's cultural beliefs. If folktales do represent these values, they appear to offer a useful therapeutic tool for children and families. Chapter 16 discusses one such application in an examination of work by Costantino, Malgady, and Rogler (1985, 1986) who explored the therapeutic use of folktales with Puerto Rican children in New York City.

Gender, Ethnicity, and Vocational Development

Psychologists have traditionally studied careers from the perspective of the individual, but vocational development occurs in the context of a person's cultural surround. For example, Hotchkiss and Borow (1996) described how wages are related to workers' gender and ethnic background. Gottfredson (1981, 1996) presented a theory of career development that takes into account sociological influences. Her work is relevant to our discussion because she recognized the importance of childhood experiences and the need to conceptualize career choice consistent with each child's developmental level.

Gottfredson's (1981, 1996) theory is based on two important constructs: circumspection and compromise. Circumspection is the process that occurs as children restrict their "zone of acceptable alternatives" (Gottfredson, 1996, p. 187) and reject career paths, even before they have an adequate understanding of these occupations. The child eliminates options believed to be less accessible and more incompatible with his or her image of self. Gottfredson described how premature rejection of a career path is irreversible unless a significant other, such as a parent or respected teacher, challenges the child's decision. Circumspection is thought to occur in four stages (Table 10.2). An important principle of Gottfredson's model is the progressive elimination of career options. Elementary school girls who reject heavy equipment operator because it is something boys should pursue will continue to do so, without appropriate intervention, during later stages. The gender typing that occurs between ages 6 to 8 years can also result in boys' elimination of traditionally female occupations, such as nurse and secretary.

Vocational compromise occurs as occupations previously identified as acceptable are eliminated, either because of anticipated environmental barriers or actual experience with these limits. As Gottfredson (1996) stated, "Compromise is adjusting aspirations to accommodate an external reality" (p. 195). Consider a child who wants to be a flutist in a symphony orchestra but rejects this career path as an adolescent when he realizes that very few jobs are available in this area. The classification criteria used during circumspection are also relevant to the compromise period. This includes the gender typing of occupations and the effect it has on access to various career paths.

Researchers have studied children's gender typing of activities and career interests. Looft (1971)

Table 10–2
Gottfredson's Stages of Circumspection

Stage	Age Range in Years	Characteristics
Orientation to size and power	3 to 5	Big vs. little
Orientation to sex roles	6 to 8	Own-gender vs. opposite-gender activities
Orientation to social valuation	9 to 13	Low-status vs. high-status careers
Orientation to the internal, unique self	14 and older	Personal abilities, values, and interests

Adapted from "Gottfredson's Theory of Circumspection and Compromise," by L. S. Gottfredson, 1996, pp. 191–195. In D. Brown & L. Brooks (Eds.), *Career choice and development* (3rd ed.) (pp. 179–232). San Francisco: Jossey-Bass. Copyright 1996 by Jossey-Bass, Inc.

questioned first and second graders about their career choices. He found that girls reported a lower number of occupational interests than did boys. Boys were more likely to select careers traditionally viewed as appropriate for men, and girls opted for female-stereotyped occupations. One of the girls in Looft's sample first indicated that she wanted to be a doctor, but upon further questioning said, "I'll probably have to be something else—maybe a store lady" (p. 366). Miller and Stanford (1987) reported similar results based on their study of African Americans in grades 1 through 5. Boys expressed a wider range of occupational choices, and students, in general, were likely to select gender-stereotyped careers.

More recently, Helwig (1998) reported an interesting age-by-gender interaction in his longitudinal study of elementary school students. The author followed a group of second graders through the sixth grade and found that with age, boys were significantly more likely to choose traditional male occupations. Girls, on the other hand, demonstrated a significant increase in their selection of opposite-gender careers. Although the results for boys are consistent with Gottfredson's (1981, 1996) theory, the pattern observed in girls raises questions about the irreversible effects of early career gender typing. Boys and girls in Helwig's study were more likely to choose traditional male careers in the sixth grade, an age when Gottfredson believed children engage in circumspection based on social valuations of careers. Interestingly, Helwig reported that sixth graders in his study were more likely to select socially valued professional, managerial, and technical careers. These students apparently considered status and prestige, which society has traditionally awarded to higher-paying jobs held by men. Helwig's results suggest that students' criteria for career selection do change and that older children are less restricted by gender stereotypes. Unfortunately, higher prestige and status in the United States generally equate with male-stereotyped occupations. Although children's movement into Gottfredson's Social Valuation Stage might expand the range of occupational considerations for girls, it appears to further restrict choices for boys.

Ginzberg et al. (1951) stated that during the fantasy stage, children learn that they will need to work when they are adults. Parents play an important role in transmitting this information. Reisman and Banuelos (1984) conducted an informal comparison of career fantasies in low-income Hispanic American and affluent European American kindergartners and first graders. When the authors interviewed these children, they found that socioeconomic status and parents' employment history were related to the sophistication level of students' career choices. Based on their results, Reisman and Banuelos recommended that parents should be involved in career guidance programs for elementary school children, especially those from low-income families.

If parents are to guide their children's vocational development, they must understand the educational requirements for different careers. In their study of low-income Mexican American and European American families, Azmitia, Cooper, Garcia, and Dunbar (1996) found that parents in both groups hoped their children would be very successful at school and work. But the Mexican American parents appeared to have limited knowledge of the educational pathways required for the professional careers (e.g., medicine and law) they wanted for their children. It is worth noting that whereas these parents had completed an average of 4 to 6 years of school, the mean educational level of European American parents was more than 13 years. The results of this study offer support for Reisman and Banuelos' (1984) recommendation to involve parents in career guidance programs. The adult component of these programs should include basic information about careers, including entry requirements, that could be presented to parents through classes and workbooks in a format similar to that of Kush and Cochran (1993) in their successful intervention for high school seniors and their parents. Of course, all written materials must be available at an appropriate reading level in a family's primary language.

The vocational implications of parent–child relationships must be considered in the context of the family's cultural surround. Cook et al. (1996) conducted a cross-sectional comparison of career aspirations among low- and middle-socioeconomic status boys enrolled in grades 2, 4, 6, and 8 at neighborhood schools. Ninety-nine percent of the inner-city schools was African American, but the majority (70%) of the comparison group was European American. Cook et al. found that inner-city students had lower career aspirations and expectations. Career aspirations were higher than expectations in both groups of students, but the gap was consistently wider among the inner-city children.

These findings suggest that ethnic background and where children are raised and educated are related to their occupational preferences and career self-efficacy. Cook et al. concluded that their results "conflict with the normative system of occupational stratification in the United States where all jobs are supposed to be open to everyone, irrespective of color, class, or residence" (p. 3381). The discrepancies observed in this study were apparent as early as the second grade. To counteract the effects of contextual influences, such as a neighborhood's socioeconomic level, therapists and educators must adopt an ecological perspective in the design and implementation of prevention programs for these children. Researchers need to give more attention to the career development of children from nondominant ethnic groups by conducting longitudinal studies to identify paths that predict success later in life.

Wahl and Blackhurst (2000) described a developmental and culturally sensitive approach to career guidance for elementary, middle, and high school students. In the elementary component of their program, the authors emphasized the need for activities designed to enhance students' career awareness. These activities should include developmentally appropriate information about careers, including educational requirements and challenges to cultural stereotypes. Wahl and Blackhurst recommended having representatives of nontraditional careers and nontraditional workers in traditional fields talk with students. One way of accomplishing this is a school-based career fair. Murrow-Taylor, Foltz, Ellis, and Culbertson (1999) described how they used a "multicultural career fair" (p. 241) to expand students' awareness of careers, ethnicity, and gender. Conducted as 45-minute in-class presentations, the program involved parents and other speakers of both genders and different ethnic backgrounds who spoke to students about their respective career choice and experiences. The authors informally evaluated their program, but there is a need for controlled research, including longitudinal studies to evaluate the developmental effects of this and other career awareness activities in schools.

SUMMARY

The theories presented in this chapter represent similar yet different perspectives on the human condition. All share a common interest in the learning process as it relates to children's interactions with their cultural surround. Theorists differ in the attention they devote to children's overt and covert behavior, but they share a common interest in the use of the scientific method to evaluate the outcomes of therapy. Considered as a whole, the theoretical principles presented here offer the foundation for diverse therapeutic techniques. Chapter 11 explores how these models have been used to design education/development, prevention, and remediation strategies for children.

11

Behavioral and Cognitive-Behavioral Interventions

■ ■ ■

Ten-year-old Antonio Henderson wets the bed almost every night. His mother first discussed the problem with her son's pediatrician when the boy was 5 years old. The pediatrician said that many young children are nocturnally incontinent and that most "eventually outgrow" this behavior. Since that time, Antonio has been dry for as long as 1 week at a time, but these episodes are rare. According to Ms. Henderson, Antonio achieved daytime urinary control at age 2 years, but he currently wets the bed an average of 6 nights every week. Both she and her son want him to become dry at night so he can begin to spend overnight visits with friends.

■ ■ ■

Nocturnal enuresis, or bed wetting, is a relatively common problem that is thought to affect approximately 2,000,000 children in the United States who are between the ages of 5 and 15 years (Wagner & Hicks-Jimenez, 1986). The most effective treatment for nocturnal incontinence is behavioral conditioning with a urine alarm (Houts, Berman, & Abramson, 1994). At the end of this chapter, we examine this technique in more detail. The chapter begins with a discussion of the unique approach that behavior therapists use to assess childhood problems. It then reviews various therapeutic applications of the behavioral and cognitive-behavioral principles described in Chapter 10.

ASSESSMENT

In contrast to the sign approach of psychodynamic assessment, behavior therapists view assessment results as a sample of a child's behavior under certain circumstances at a specific point in time. The two methods also differ in their timing of the assessment process. Behavior therapists do not limit themselves to the pretreatment and posttreatment assessments used by their psychodynamic colleagues. Instead, their assessments are ongoing and integrated into the intervention process in a repeating cycle of assessment, treatment, and evaluation of the target behavior. When it is discovered that a child who misbehaves at home receives attention from her parents only when she misbehaves (i.e., assessment), the father and mother are taught to positively reinforce appropriate behaviors (i.e., treatment), which is found to reduce the child's negative actions (i.e., evaluation). If the therapist discovers that the child continues to misbehave at school (i.e., assessment), the teacher is instructed to use a similar treatment that is then evaluated based on the child's response.

The foundation for behavioral assessment is the belief that environmental antecedents and consequences influence children's behavior. This has led some to conclude that behavioral assessment techniques are more useful than traditional methods in designing treatment interventions (Gresham & Lambros, 1998). For example, a therapist who discovers that a child's oppositional defiant behavior is prompted and reinforced by her parents can develop a problem-focused intervention that includes teaching the parents how to use more effective child-rearing skills. The integration of assessment and treatment means that data collected in a behavioral assessment have many purposes. They can be used to describe the problem, develop an intervention, and provide the basis for evaluating the effectiveness of treatment (Ciminero, 1986).

Behavioral assessment techniques include behavioral observation, behavior rating scales and questionnaires, psychophysiological measures, self-monitoring, and output samples. Observation is an integral part of any assessment, regardless of the therapist's theoretical orientation, but behavioral clinicians have developed the most systematic approach (see the descriptions of the Student Observation System and Direct Observation Form in Chapter 4). Behavioral observations are conducted in naturalistic (e.g., home, classroom, playground) and analogue (e.g., clinic playroom, research laboratory) settings. They are performed by clinicians, parents, teachers, and children. Observers sometimes focus on a single behavior that occurs in one setting, such as bed wetting, or they monitor multiple behaviors (e.g., being out of seat in class, hitting classmates) exhibited in one or more settings (e.g., math class, reading class, art class). The guidelines that observers adopt vary, depending on the nature of the target behavior or behaviors, the diversity of settings, and the observer's skills and experience.

An important step in the development of a behavioral observation system is the identification and operational definition of the target behaviors (Barrios, 1993). If a student's on-task behavior is the target, the therapist must specify what "on-task" actually means. This should be based on observable behaviors, such as "seated facing one's desk" and "performing paper-and-pencil mathematical calculations." Clinicians also must select the settings where the behavioral observations will be conducted (Barrios, 1993). A child's on-task behavior in school is influenced by a number of factors, including the quality of the learning environment and the child's interest and skills in each academic subject. Some children are on-task in all of their classes; but others exhibit this behavior in only one subject or with only one teacher. Although time constraints usually limit the frequency and duration of observation sessions, therapists must secure an adequate sampling of the child's behavior, especially when variability exists across settings (i.e., on task in math class, off task in language arts). Observers typically focus on a child's misbehavior, but they should also observe appropriate or prosocial acts. For example, a student who is on task in a structured reading class provides relevant information for improving compliance in an unstructured math class.

Once therapists have operationally defined the target behaviors and identified the observation settings, they must select the coding systems that will be used to observe and record the behaviors (Barrios, 1993). This includes consideration of the number of observation sessions, the length of each session, and the division of each session into observation and rating blocks. A popular coding method is interval recording, which sometimes involves the use of alternating time blocks, one for observation and another for data recording. Reynolds and Kamphaus (1992) used this method in their Student Observation System in which children's classroom behavior is alternately observed for 3 seconds and recorded in a 30-second interval over the course of a 15-minute observation period. Raters must always consider the impact of their presence on the behavior of the child and others in the observation setting. O'Leary and Johnson (1986) reported that the impact of this confound can be minimized "if there is an initial adaptation period for three to five days before actual data are obtained" (p. 427). Unfortunately, clinicians often lack the time or flexibility in their schedules to allow for an adaptation period of this length. Consequently, observers must understand how their presence can affect a child and result in an inaccurate sample of the target behavior.

Behavioral clinicians also administer questionnaires or rating forms to children, parents, or significant other adults. As discussed in Chapter 4, these measures can be used to obtain a global view of a child's functioning or an assessment of specific problems. A more recent addition to the behavioral approach is psychophysiological assessment, which King (1993) described as "one of the most challenging and rapidly growing" (p. 180) areas of child assessment. Although this method often requires special instrumentation (e.g., a physiograph), Geffken, Johnson, and Walker (1986) used inexpensive plastic urine collectors to measure the maximum functional bladder capacity of children entering treatment for nocturnal enuresis. This addition to the assessment battery was beneficial because the authors found that children who initially presented with a small bladder capacity and were treated with the urine alarm and daytime retention control training as well as clients who had a large capacity and received alarm treatment only became continent faster, had fewer nighttime wetting incidents, and were less likely to awaken and use the bathroom during the night. For these children, treatment appeared to improve their ability to retain fluids rather than helping them learn to awaken and empty their bladder during the night.

Sometimes children are asked to self-monitor their behavior using recording charts or wrist counters. To ensure accurate monitoring of overt (e.g., on-task behavior) and covert (e.g., suicidal ideation) behaviors, children must be involved in the definition of the target behavior. A major limitation of self-monitoring is its reactivity, or the tendency to produce behavioral change that is sometimes in the desired direction (Shapiro & Cole, 1993). When this occurs, self-monitoring is actually a form of treatment rather than a measure of the child's behavior before therapy. Children also are asked to produce output samples, our last behavioral assessment technique. A student diagnosed with attention-deficit hyperactivity disorder who does not finish his daily work could be assessed at the end of each day to determine the number of assignments he successfully completed in each class. The teacher would record these data on a monitoring chart to assess the daily rate and variability in the boy's output.

All of these assessment techniques can be used to perform what is called a functional assessment to identify the antecedents and consequences of a target behavior. O'Neill et al. (1997) identified three approaches to functional assessment: informant methods, direct observation, and functional analysis. Informant methods involve the use of interviews, questionnaires, and behavior rating forms to obtain the views of significant people (e.g., child, parents, teachers) regarding the child's behavior in different contexts (e.g., home, school). To collect more detailed information about a child's performance in a given setting, direct observations are conducted to assess the relationship between the target behavior and its environmental antecedents and consequences.

The third method identified by O'Neill et al. (1997) is functional analysis, which sometimes involves implementing the antecedents and consequences believed to cause the target behavior. This method is more likely to be used in schools and institutional settings where clinicians have more control over children's immediate surroundings. Consider a student who argues with and hits other children during recess. To test the hypothesis that misbehavior is more likely to occur during free play than in structured games, therapists would monitor the child's actions as they formally manipulate the two events (e.g., games—free play—games—free play). When functional analysis is used in conjunction with therapy, clinicians identify and control the specific environmental contingencies they believe will reduce the problem behavior.

During the past 50 years, the field of behavioral assessment moved beyond the analysis of overt behaviors as more attention was directed at children's thoughts and feelings. According to Reinecke, Datillio, and Freeman (1996), the starting point for cognitive-behavioral treatment is a thorough assessment of the child's thoughts and attitudes regarding the presenting problem. Clinicians must determine whether a child's problems are the result of cognitive deficiencies or cognitive distortions (Kendall, 1991). A deficiency in thinking exists when a child does not possess the information processing skills needed to solve the problem. Cognitive distortions occur when a child has the requisite skills but processes information in a dysfunctional manner. Kendall described how some problems involve cognitive deficiencies (e.g., impulsivity), others are the result of cognitive distortions (e.g., depression), and still others are characterized by a combination of cognitive deficiencies and distortions (e.g., aggressive behavior). In order to plan effective cognitive-behavioral interventions for a child, the therapist must assess whether the client needs to acquire cognitive skills, correct existing skills, or both.

DiGiuseppe (1990), writing about rational-emotive behavior therapy (REBT) approaches to child assessment, identified two important techniques for assessing irrational beliefs: inference chaining and deductive interpretation. The former involves having the child imagine that a negative belief is true (e.g., "I'm gonna fail this test"). DiGiuseppe described how the clinician then has the child imagine the chain of events that would follow:

THERAPIST: And what do you think would happen if you did fail it?
CHILD: Well, then I might fail all the tests.
THERAPIST: Well, let's suppose that would happen. What might you think then?
CHILD: I guess I would think that I'd be stupid or dumb.
THERAPIST: Well, what would it mean to you if you were not as smart as you would like?
CHILD: I'd be no good.
(p. 242)

Notice how the therapist directed the discussion from a feared behavior, (i.e., failing a test), to an irrational belief in which poor self-worth was based on the child's interpretation of negative performance.

If inference chaining is ineffective, DiGiuseppe (1990) recommended deductive interpretation in which the clinician formulates a hypothesis about the client's irrational beliefs and presents this as a possible explanation for the child's problems. For a gifted student who is unable to draw and paint as well as her friends, the examiner might respond, "It almost sounds like you think you should be great at everything." As DiGiuseppe indicated, the examiner must be careful to present hypotheses for what they are—*possible* explanations for a problem. Clinicians must accept this and be willing to revise their hypotheses based on feedback from the child.

EDUCATION/DEVELOPMENT AND PREVENTION

Although behavioral and cognitive-behavioral principles have often been used to design remedial interventions for children, they also serve as the theoretical foundation for many education/development and prevention programs. This section examines how these principles have been applied in schools and social environments, beginning with a discussion of behaviorally oriented utopian communities.

There are many examples of utopian societies in the United States, including the Oneida Community in Madison County, New York; the Amana Community near Davenport, Iowa; and the Harmony Society in Economy, Pennsylvania. Fundamental to many of these social experiments has been "the subordination of the individual's will to the general interest or the general will," which often involves "unquestioning obedience by the members toward the leaders, elders, or chiefs of their society" (Nordoff, 1961, p. 392). B. F. Skinner (1948/1969) challenged this hierarchical structure in his preface to *Walden Two*, a utopian community based on behavioral principles that was intended to "build a way of life in which people live together without quarreling, in a social climate of trust rather than suspicion, of love rather than jealousy, of cooperation rather than competition."

At Comunidad Los Horcones in Hermosillo, Sonora, Mexico, residents have applied Skinner's operant principles to everyday life. Established in 1973, Los Horcones was established to "promote altruistic, cooperative, sharing, and egalitarian behaviors" (Comunidad Los Horcones, 2001a). Members of the community have used behavior analysis in a decades-long study to develop "The Code of Communitarian Contingencies," which is designed to specify the antecedents and consequences for target behaviors that represent the values of the community (Comunidad Los Horcones, 2001b). Family life at Los Horcones is defined in communitarian terms (Comunidad Los Horcones, 2002). Although traditional family structure is recognized, the entire community assumes responsibility for raising children. Young people are taught to behave according to a "List of Behavioral Objectives for Children," which specifies the communitarian behaviors (e.g., sharing toys, cooperating with others) that are thought to contribute to a happy life (Comunidad Los Horcones, 2002). Education at Los Horcones is also based on behavioral principles. School children receive year-round, individualized instruction based on the Personalized System of Instruction described by Keller and Sherman (1982). Teachers rarely conduct lecture classes, and students are evaluated based on the number of instructional units they successfully complete each week.

The Comunidad Los Horcones involves a relatively small number of children compared with the millions of students in public schools, where teachers routinely use instructional and classroom management techniques based on operant principles. Skinner (1961) applied operant principles to the instructional process with his invention of the teaching machine, a rather primitive device for directing students through a sequence of learning activities.

Computer software designers have adopted the basic principles of the teaching machine to produce instructional materials that can be used to help students refine existing skills and learn new information. Educators have also used operant principles to manage children's behavior in school. Social reinforcers (e.g., smiles, praise), grades, and privileges have all been used to encourage appropriate student behavior and academic success.

Ellis (1972) discussed how rational-emotive behavior theory can be applied in what he called "the living school" (p. 19), where traditional academic subjects are combined with rational-emotive education to help children "achieve a higher percentage of their potential for fuller and more creative living" (p. 22). Vernon (1999) described a version of the latter involving introductory activities, such as games or art activities, followed by discussion periods during which students are questioned about the content of the lesson and challenged to apply this information to their everyday lives. Thompson and Rudolph (2000) reviewed the research on rational-emotive education and concluded that the approach appears to be helpful with some children.

Tucker (1999) described what she called a "self-empowerment" (p. 12) approach for enhancing the development of African American children. Her method includes attention to cognitive and behavioral factors that are thought to influence academic and social achievement. Included in the cognitive domain are self-motivation, self-control, and self-reinforcement. For example, a successful child is motivated to learn because she understands the connection between academic achievement and the attainment of life goals. Likewise, the child exercises self-control as she works toward these goals in a systematic manner. Teachers and parents are not always there to reward a student at each step, so the successful child engages in self-reinforcement, which Tucker believed "facilitates students' self-confidence and perseverance for goal attainment" (p. 236). In the behavioral component of her model, Tucker focused on the acquisition and performance of socialization, communication, and academic skills. With self-empowering cognitions and behaviors, African American children are able to capitalize on their strengths "under whatever external conditions exist" (p. 12).

Tucker (1999) offered practical suggestions for implementing her model with African American youths. First, she recommended that children, parents, teachers, clergy, and therapists collaborate to help students learn and exhibit adaptive behaviors, such as completing homework assignments and being on task in class. Parents of self-empowered children prepare preschoolers for success in school, and they reward their children for achievement and create home environments that are "learner friendly" (p. 290). This includes having a quiet location for home study and reserving evening hours for homework assignments. Effective teachers provide stimulating classroom environments and adjust to each student's learning style. Church leaders establish after-school tutoring and recreational activities and serve as positive African American role models for children. And Tucker stated that therapists must identify community-based resources (e.g., tutoring and mentoring programs), collaborate with significant other adults, and resist using "the disadvantages in a child's life . . . as excuses" (p. 344) for misbehavior or lack of improvement in therapy.

REMEDIATION

According to Ross (1981), child behavior therapy is "an empirical approach to psychological problems" (p. 1). Behavior therapists select interventions based on existing process and outcome research, and they systematically assess each child's problem and evaluate the impact of treatment by adapting the single-case experimental design (see Chapter 5) for clinical purposes. Behavioral interventions for childhood problems are many and varied, but they share a common allegiance to learning-based models of child development, the operational definition of problem behaviors, and ongoing evaluation of children's progress in therapy. We begin our discussion of this approach by examining classical and operant methods of behavioral conditioning. Later we turn our attention to more recent developments in cognitive-behavioral interventions for children.

Classical Conditioning

The most common application of the classical paradigm is systematic desensitization, which Wolpe (1958) used to treat anxiety disorders in adults. This procedure involves the pairing of a relaxed state in the client with increasing levels of anxiety related to the feared object or event. With older individuals, systematic desensitization typically involves three steps: relaxation training, development of an anxiety or fear hierarchy, and the pairing of hierarchy items with relaxation. When used with children, these steps are modified so they are more developmentally appropriate for young clients.

Koeppen (1974) described a program of 15-minute sessions scheduled two or three times a week in which children learn to tighten and relax various muscle groups in response to developmentally appropriate instructions. Here is the script he recommended to help children relax their hands and arms:

> Pretend you have a whole lemon in your left hand. Now squeeze it hard. Try to squeeze all the juice out. Feel the tightness in your hand and arm as you squeeze. Now drop the lemon. Notice how your muscles feel when they are relaxed. (p. 17)

Koeppen purposely made his directions more concrete than the relaxation scripts commonly used with adults (e.g., "By making a tight fist, I'd like you to tense the muscles in the right hand and lower arm"; Bernstein & Borkovev, 1973).

Concurrent with muscle relaxation training, the therapist helps the child construct an anxiety or fear hierarchy. This step requires having the child identify various levels of anxiety-producing stimuli, from the least to the most uncomfortable. As part of this process, the child is asked to use what are called subjective units of discomfort (SUD) by assigning numerical values (e.g., 0 to 100) to each anxiety-producing event (e.g., 0 = not at all, 100 = extremely anxiety producing). Stedman (1976) described how this procedure was used with a 9-year-old girl who became very anxious in school, especially in subjects in which she needed to perform in front of the class. When asked to provide SUDs ratings for different events, the child gave a "1" to being "at home at night thinking about sitting in music class watching the others play their recorders," but she awarded a "29" to actually reading a passage in front of her reading class, making mistakes, and having the other children laugh at her (p. 285).

When the client has acquired relaxation skills and constructed a hierarchy, the therapist uses techniques based on Wolpe's (1958) principle of reciprocal inhibition. For example, an anxious child is taught to pair muscle relaxation with imagining items on an anxiety hierarchy, beginning with the least uncomfortable item. Over the course of treatment sessions, the clinician gradually has the child imagine more uncomfortable items. The child is told to raise a finger if she experiences any anxiety after presentation of an item. If this occurs, the child is instructed to stop focusing on the item and turn her attention to muscle relaxation. When the child is able to imagine an item and not become anxious during three consecutive trials, the clinician moves to more uncomfortable items on the hierarchy, terminating treatment when the child remains relaxed when presented with the most uncomfortable item (Johnson et al., 1997).

Jones (1924) used systematic desensitization in her treatment of 2-year-old Peter, but she used food in place of relaxation training. Lazarus and Abramovitz (1962) described a another variation of systematic desensitization, which they called "emotive imagery" (p. 191). In emotive imagery, pleasant images are used in place of relaxation techniques. The child is asked to identify and imagine real or pretend hero figures as participants in "a sequence of events which is close enough to his everyday life to be credible" (p. 192). As the child imagines this story, the therapist introduces hierarchy items into the narrative. When Lazarus and Abramovitz used their technique to treat phobias in nine children, ages 7 to 14 years, they found that seven of the children improved after an average of about three sessions. During their initial meeting with a 10-year-old boy who was afraid of the dark, the authors learned that the child's heroes were Superman and Captain Silver. At the next session, emotive imagery was used, and the child was instructed to imagine his heroes as the therapist presented anxiety-producing scenes. Lazarus and Abramovitz described an early portion of this session:

> The child was asked to imagine that Superman and Captain Silver had joined forces and had appointed him their agent. After a brief discussion concerning the topography of his house he was given his first assignment. The therapist said, "Now I want you to close your eyes and imagine that you are sitting in the dining-room with your mother and father. It is night time. Suddenly, you receive a signal on the wrist radio that Superman has given you. You quickly run into the lounge because your mission must be kept a secret. There is only a little light coming into the lounge from the passage. Now pretend that you are all alone in the lounge waiting for Superman and Captain Silver to visit you. Think about this very clearly. If the idea makes you feel afraid, lift up your right hand." (p. 193)

When the boy indicated that he was feeling anxious, the therapist terminated the scene and revised it for later presentation to the child. After three sessions and at 11-month follow-up, the child no longer displayed a fear of the dark.

A technique that has recently gained attention is eye movement desensitization and reprocessing (EMDR), which incorporates systematic desensitization and cognitive restructuring, a technique sometimes used to modify children's maladaptive thoughts. Francine Shapiro (1995) developed EMDR to treat negative feelings, thoughts, and behaviors related to traumatic experiences. Her Accelerated Information Processing model represents a departure from traditional behavioral theory because psychological problems are thought to result from childhood experiences that "set in motion a continued pattern of affect, behavior, cognitions, and consequent identity structures" (Shapiro, 1995, p. 14). For example, a sexually abused girl's processing of information is compromised at the time of her abuse, and generalization of the cognitions and affect associated with this event limit her ability to process related information in the future.

The EMDR procedure is a complex intervention that requires more space than is available here. Readers who are interested in learning more about the use of EMDR with children should consult *Through the Eyes of a Child: EMDR with Children* by Tinker and Wilson (1999). We limit our discussion to the procedure's most characteristic phases, desensitization and installation. After the therapist has collected a client history, established a therapeutic relationship with the child, and assessed relevant information (e.g., the traumatic event and related thoughts and feelings), variants of an eye movement technique are used. Shapiro (1995) described the following procedure:

> Typically, the clinician holds two fingers upright, palm facing the client, approximately 12 to 14 inches from the client's face. . . . The clinician then demonstrates the direction of the eye movements by slowly moving her fingers horizontally from the extreme right to the extreme left (or the reverse) of the client's visual field, a distance of at least 12 inches. (p. 63)

The therapist uses eye movements in what are called sets, which initially include 24 right-left-right movements. After each set, the client is asked to rate negative and positive cognitions and the emotions (i.e., SUDs) associated with the traumatic image. When SUD ratings are either 0 or 1, the therapist begins the installation phase and instructs the client to pair a positive cognition with the traumatic image to reinforce the development of positive self-statements.

As Muris and Merckelbach (1999) stated, "Systematic research concerning EMDR and childhood psychopathology is sparse" (p. 8). Although controlled studies on EMDR are limited, numerous case reports with children have been published. Pellicer (1993), for example, achieved total remission of nightmares after one session of EMDR with a 10-year-old girl. On 5 of the 7 nights during baseline, the child had her usual nightmares about snakes crawling in her bed. The therapist had the child engage in rapid eye movement while visualizing the content of her nightmares. Pellicer reported that the girl experienced no additional nightmares after treatment during a 6-month follow-up period. Empirical studies on EMDR suggest that the technique may be more beneficial in changing children's cognitions than their behaviors. For example, in their studies on EMDR treatment of spider phobia in girls, ages 8 to 17 years, Muris and colleagues reported that EMDR and in vivo exposure produced similar reductions in self-reported fears, but in vivo exposure was more efficacious in reducing spider avoidance behavior (Muris, Merckelbach, Holdinet, & Sijsenaar, 1998; Muris, Merckelbach, van Haaften, & Mayer, 1997). Muris et al. (1998) acknowledged that EMDR may be useful in treating cognitive and affective aftereffects of trauma in children, but in vivo exposure seems to be the preferred intervention for phobic behaviors.

Operant Conditioning: Strategies for Increasing Desirable Behaviors

Operant conditioning methods represent some of the most commonly used child-rearing techniques. Parents and teachers use these interventions to increase appropriate behaviors and to reduce or eliminate maladaptive behaviors in children. This section examines how token economies, shaping, and chaining have been used to increase desirable behaviors in children.

Token Economies. Melamed and Siegel (1980) defined a token economy as "a highly systematic and highly complex reinforcement program" (p. 35) in which tokens, or relatively neutral reinforcers, can be exchanged for backup reinforcers that are meaningful to the child. Consider a dollar bill, which is basically a piece of paper with printing on it. This token is important only because children have learned that society recognizes money as legitimate tender for food, toys, and other backup reinforcers. It is worth noting that token reinforcers are rarely used in isolation. For example, children who meet a prearranged behavioral criterion often receive social reinforcement, including praise, along with their token.

As children mature and become more aware of the relationship between their behaviors and environmental consequences, therapists involve them more in the design of token economies (Forehand & Wierson, 1993). This means having children assist in the identification of tokens (e.g., stickers) and backup reinforcers (e.g., a trip to the park). Spiegler and Guevremont (1998) indicated that clinicians must consider the number of tokens the child will earn for each occurrence of the target behavior, and the number of tokens required for a reinforcer. Therapists must also determine when reinforcement will occur and who will administer the predetermined rewards. Of course, clinicians must involve the parents or teachers who will be responsible for awarding the tokens and backup reinforcers. If a token is meaningful to the parent but not the child, the intervention will undoubtedly have little therapeutic impact. Likewise, if the therapist and family do not specify how and when backup reinforcers are awarded, confusion and inconsistency will compromise the effectiveness of the program.

Some parents resist the use of token economies because they believe their children should behave without being "bribed" with rewards. In their study of medical compliance in two asthmatic children, Da Costa, Rapoff, Lemanek, and Goldstein (1997) described one mother who chose to not restore token reinforcement after its removal because she believed the strategy represented bribery. Interestingly, the child's compliance during the reinforcement phase was lower than that of the other client, which raises questions about the mother's compliance with the program throughout treatment. Da Costa et al. recommended that therapists prepare parents for token economies by describing the procedure as a temporary means of increasing the frequency of a target behavior. Clinicians should also compare the use of tokens with children to the remuneration systems that parents encounter at work when they receive a paycheck (i.e., a token) for duties performed.

Before a token economy is initiated, therapists must assess the parents' commitment to the program and educate them about the importance of dispensing tokens every time their child earns one. Therapists must ensure that parents have an adequate supply of tokens for the upcoming week. At follow-up appointments, the clinician determines whether the child received the tokens that were earned. If the tokens were awarded as planned, the therapist should determine if there was confusion regarding the exchange for backup reinforcers. For a token economy to work, all participants must be invested in the program and understand the expectations and consequences for the child's behavior. If these conditions are not met, the therapist should consider alternative interventions. Having a parent agree to administer tokens, only to fail when the child behaves as agreed upon, does little to effect positive behavioral change.

Da Costa et al. (1997) incorporated physiological measures into their study of a token reinforcement program designed to improve asthma inhalant usage in an 8-year-old girl and a 10-year-old boy. The authors combined a 2-hour, single-session educational program about pulmonary functioning and asthma treatment with a token economy in which the children received points, exchangeable for privileges, when they used their medications as prescribed. Adherence was measured using a chronolog that recorded when inhalants were used and a spirometer to evaluate each child's lung flow and volume. Results revealed increased usage in both children when the token economy was administered and a decline in compliance when reinforcement was withdrawn.

Carton and Schweitzer (1996) used a similar approach in their work with a 10-year-old boy who was verbally and physically resistant during hemodialysis sessions for end-stage renal disease. After a six-session baseline period when he was noncompliant during most of the 4-hour procedure, the child was informed that he would receive one token for each 30-minute period when he was compliant. At the end of each session, the boy was allowed to exchange his tokens for back-up reinforcers, including toys. Noncompliance declined dramatically when the token economy was in effect, increased when reinforcement was experimentally withdrawn, and declined again when tokens were reintroduced. Carton and Schweitzer provided evidence to support the interactional nature of operant conditioning (see Chapter 10) when they found that the reinforcing effects of their intervention were not limited to the child. Specifically, the attending physicians and nurses were reinforced by the boy's response to the token economy. As Carton and Schweitzer noted, the successful outcome with this child resulted in additional requests for behavioral interventions with other clients in the hemodialysis unit.

A special type of token economy is the home-based reinforcement program, which can be used to correct school-related problems. Children treated with this procedure are reinforced by their parents at home for appropriate behaviors at school. Consider a child who is failing to complete daily classwork. A home-based reinforcement program for this student would involve having the teacher monitor the number of assignments the child completes each day. School data are communicated to parents, either by telephone, electronic communication, or notes sent home with the child. Every evening, the parents review the day's information with the child and administer previously agreed upon reinforcers. Forehand and Wierson (1993) recommended that therapists not use this approach with students younger than third graders because these children tend to have more difficulty with delayed reinforcement programs such as this. If the approach is to be effective, the therapist, parents, and teachers must work as a team. If any member fails to implement the program in a consistent manner, the intervention's effectiveness is compromised.

Some token economies include the response cost procedure in which tokens are removed if the child exhibits an inappropriate behavior. This technique is actually an operant method for reducing undesirable behavior, but we examine it here because it frequently is combined with token reinforcement programs. A simple example of a token economy with a response cost component is the child who receives tokens for making his bed each morning but loses them when he hits his sister. Calculating the conditions for a response cost procedure requires consideration of the baseline frequency of the child's desirable and undesirable behaviors. If the boy in our example rarely completes his household tasks but hits his sister two or three times a day, he would encounter a "token deficit" in which he intermittently acquires a token for making his bed but loses many more for his aggressive behavior. Clinicians can avoid token deficits by selecting positive and negative target behaviors that allow children to accumulate tokens despite losses associated with the response cost procedure. When the inappropriate behavior is relatively benign in nature, therapists can postpone the procedure until the frequency of appropriate behaviors is significantly higher than the rate of negative behaviors.

Shaping. Complex behaviors, such as language, are acquired through shaping. The therapist begins with whatever behaviors exist in the child's repertoire and reinforces successive approximations toward the goal behavior (Kazdin, 1994b). Ollendick and Cerny (1981) reviewed the literature on shaping and recommended that therapists begin with a behavior that has a high probability of occurrence and apply meaningful reinforcers as the child's actions more closely resemble the desired outcome. Hagopian and Slifer (1993) described how shaping was used with Jennifer, a first grade student who cried and clung to her parents every morning to avoid going to school. Before treatment, the mother drove Jennifer to school and remained in class because Jennifer strongly resisted her departure. Hagopian and Slifer included a pre-baseline period during which the mother was to interact with her daughter as she had in previous weeks. During the regular baseline, she was to drive Jennifer to school but remain in class for only 1 hour. Treatment involved gradually removing one reinforcer (i.e., the mother in class) and introducing token reinforcement (i.e., daily stickers exchangeable for weekly prizes) when the child remained in class. Initially, the mother left the classroom for only 30 seconds, but as her daughter improved, she "went from standing outside the door, to walking down the hall, to sitting in her car, to driving to work, to not returning at all, and finally to not taking Jennifer to or from school" (p. 276). Hagopian and Slifer were able to disengage the mother from school and increase Jennifer's classroom attendance. At 2- and 9-month follow-up evaluations, the child was going to school on a regular basis without assistance from her mother.

Glasscock and MacLean (1990) combined classical and operant principles when they used contact desensitization and shaping to treat dog phobia in a 6-year-old girl who had been bitten by a dog. When she entered treatment, the child was reluctant to play outside and was fearful when a dog was near. After collecting baseline data, the therapists introduced contact desensitization in the home based on the girl's fear hierarchy that ranged from going outside in her yard (i.e., the least fearful step) to talking with and petting a dog for 3 minutes (i.e., the most fearful step). The therapist modeled these behaviors and praised the child for her performance of each step. The mother and siblings also shaped the child's behavior by reinforcing her for remaining outside for longer periods of time. Treatment resulted in a reduction in dog-related fears and an increase in outdoor play.

An important component in the Glasscock and MacLean (1990) hierarchy was the child's actual contact with a dog. To increase the probability of success, the authors chose the family's Labrador retriever, presumably because they decided the animal would not harm the child. This is an important consideration because the therapists had to ensure that the client's interactions with the dog were positive. They were also cautious when they tried to generalize progress to other dogs in the neighborhood. The therapists introduced the client to three additional dogs, presumably selected because of their positive temperaments. Although Glasscock and MacLean did not mention it, success in treatment would also include helping the child to discriminate between friendly and unfriendly dogs. Rather than having her acquire the incorrect belief that all dogs are safe and can be trusted, she could learn criteria (e.g., "Does the dog growl at you?") that will prepare her for contacts with animals that are threats to her safety.

Chaining. Chaining involves "combining simple behaviors into more global and more complex behaviors" (Ollendick & Cerny, 1981, p. 126). Unlike shaping, in which the goal behavior is reached through successive approximations, chaining is the combination or addition of acts that are easily recognized in the final behavior. Azrin, Sneed, and Foxx (1974) incorporated chaining into their treatment for childhood nocturnal enuresis. Before going to bed every night, children are required to perform 20 trials of what Azrin et al. called Positive Practice. This procedure is intended to teach children the chain of behaviors involved in getting up at night and voiding in a socially accepted manner. Specifically, the child is instructed to lie in bed and count to 50 before arising, walk to the bathroom and attempt to urinate, and then return to bed. Azrin et al. included Positive Practice in their program because each component of the chain is already present in the child's behavioral repertoire. Rather than acquiring an entirely new behavior as occurs with shaping, chaining produces an orderly sequence of preexisting behaviors. As part of their enuresis treatment program, Azrin et al. included another chaining procedure, which they called Cleanliness Training, that children perform when they wet the bed during the night. In our case example of Antonio at the end of this chapter, we will examine how Cleanliness Training is used as part of behavioral conditioning with the urine alarm to treat nocturnal incontinence in children.

Ollendick and Cerny (1981) described clinically relevant characteristics of chaining. Early links in a behavioral sequence are ultimately the weakest because they are furthest from the reinforcement the child receives upon completion of the chain. Therapists must ensure that adequate reinforcement exists throughout the chain. Although each link serves as a reinforcer for the previous behavior and a stimulus for the next, longer chains sometimes require the use of additional reinforcers, such as praise, to ensure that all links are performed. Failure to complete early links jeopardizes completion of the chain. Fortunately, premature termination of a chain does not appear to disrupt the performance of links performed to that point, so therapists can build upon the segments a child has learned to teach the entire sequence of behaviors.

Operant Conditioning: Strategies for Reducing Undesirable Behaviors

When children act inappropriately, caregivers sometimes use operant techniques to change these behaviors. If a child's actions represent a danger to self or others, parents and teachers are likely to apply negative consequences to eliminate the behavior. If an undesirable behavior is not overly disruptive or dangerous to the child or others, the caregiver may choose to ignore the behavior, thereby removing a reinforcer (e.g., social attention) that previously maintained the behavior. This section examines how differential reinforcement, aversion therapy and time out, and extinction have been used to decrease or eliminate undesirable behaviors in children.

Differential Reinforcement. Reinforcement can be used to decrease undesirable behaviors by rewarding acts other than the child's negative target behavior. This can be accomplished by differentially reinforcing 1) incompatible behaviors, 2) competing behaviors, 3) any acts other than the target behavior, and 4) low rates of the problem behavior (Spiegler & Guevremont, 1998). Differential reinforcement has been used to remediate certain behaviors in children with mental retardation. Nunes, Murphy, and Ruprecht (1977), for example, reinforced incompatible behaviors to treat self-injurious acts in a 12-year-old girl with this developmental disorder. After baseline, the authors used twice-daily sessions, 5 days a week, to reinforce the child with tactile stimulation from an electric back massager for assembling a puzzle, which was incompatible with hitting herself with her hands. The intervention resulted in a dramatic decline in inappropriate behaviors, which continued during the months immediately after termination of treatment.

When therapists are unable to identify an incompatible behavior, they sometimes resort to differential reinforcement of competing behaviors, even though children can simultaneously exhibit competing and target behaviors (Spiegler & Guevremont, 1998). Allyon, Layman, and Kandel (1975) incorporated this approach into a token economy with three students labeled as hyperactive. The children received tokens for correct answers in math and reading, and they exchanged these for a variety of backup reinforcers, including candy and special privileges at school. The intervention represents differential reinforcement of a competing rather than an incompatible behavior because the children were able to solve math problems while simultaneously engaging in hyperactive behaviors, such as walking around the room (Spiegler & Guevremont, 1998).

When they entered the study, all three children were receiving psychostimulants that seemed to control their hyperactive behavior but had little impact on academic performance. The authors evaluated the effect of reinforcement using a single-case experimental design that included a baseline while the children were taking medication, a second baseline after the removal of psychostimulants, reinforcement for math performance, and reinforcement for math and reading performance. As expected, hyperactive behaviors in all three children increased after termination of psychopharmacotherapy. When math performance was reinforced, hyperactivity declined and academic performance improved in math class only. When math and reading were reinforced, hyperactivity was low and academic performance better in both classes.

Later in this chapter, we discuss how Luiselli and Greenridge (1982) combined differential reinforcement of other behaviors and time out to treat aggressive behavior in a 12-year-old girl. But now we examine one of a series of studies by Dietz (1977) in which differential reinforcement of low rates of behavior was used to reduce a 6-year-old girl's disruptive comments in class. The child was told that whenever she interrupted class fewer than two times in each of a series of 5-minute intervals, she would receive a piece of candy. The change in her behavior was quick and dramatic, decreasing from an average of almost 10 interruptions in a 30-minute period during baseline to about two interruptions after treatment was initiated. To test the effectiveness of the intervention, Dietz withdrew reinforcement during a reversal period and found that the average number of disruptions returned to 10 per 30-minute period. When the reinforcement program was reintroduced, the child interrupted class fewer than two times per half-hour interval.

Aversion Therapy. Aversion therapy has the potential to produce a relatively quick change in a child's behavior. Based on a punishment paradigm in which the presentation of a consequence results in a decrease in the target behavior, this class of interventions should be used only after other procedures have been found to be ineffective (Gelfand & Hartmann, 1984). General exceptions to this rule include the treatment of behaviors that are either self-injurious or extremely disruptive for others. Otherwise, aversion techniques should be used sparingly; when used, they must be combined with positive reinforcement to help children learn healthy ways of handling the challenges of everyday life.

Therapists who use aversion techniques select a noxious stimulus, such as a sour tasting liquid, which is administered either during or immediately after the target behavior. Physical pain and electric shock have also been used for this purpose, so therapists face the challenge of devising interventions that are both effective and humane. Although electric shock treatment is an extreme and inappropriate consequence for a student's off-task behavior in reading class, this stimulus merits consideration in situations in which a behavior is life threatening and resistant to other interventions. Lang and Melamed (1969) described one such case when they used electric shock to control ruminative vomiting in a 9-month-old infant. Before the authors were consulted, the baby had received a number of treatments, including dietary changes, anti-nausea medications, and surgery. When Lang and Melamed were contacted, the infant weighed only 12 pounds, was fed through a nasogastric tube, and vomited within 10 minutes of being fed. Treatment involved 1-hour postfeeding sessions of "brief and repeated shock (approximately 1 sec. long with a 1-sec. interpulse interval)" to the baby's foot or calf every time regurgitation began. Shock was terminated when the vomiting ceased. Treatment resulted in dramatic improvements, with no in-session vomiting observed by the sixth session. One month after termination of treatment, the infant continued to progress and weighed 21 pounds.

Time Out. When a child is disruptive and violates the rights of others, clinicians sometimes use what Spiegler and Guevremont (1998) called "time out from generalized reinforcers" (p. 141). In this procedure, the child spends a brief period of time (e.g., 3 minutes) in a special location or time-out area that offers no access to the typical reinforcers of everyday life. Before the procedure is initiated, a responsible adult must inform the child of the target behavior and the consequence that will result every time the behavior occurs (e.g., "If you hit anyone, you will go to the time-out room for 3 minutes"). To leave time out, the child must behave appropriately for the specified period of time. Luiselli and Greenridge (1982) warned that when time out is used, an adult must supervise the procedure to ensure that children do not harm themselves. Additionally, Spiegler and Guevremont cautioned that time out itself must not serve as a reinforcer. It is counterproductive to use the procedure with children who misbehave in order to avoid unwanted tasks, such as completing classwork or household responsibilities.

Luiselli and Greenridge (1982) combined time out and differential reinforcement of other behaviors to treat aggressive behavior in a 12-year-old girl. The case is noteworthy because of the child's special needs. Specifically, she was legally blind, had severe bilateral hearing loss, and was diagnosed as severely retarded. After a baseline phase when teachers reinforced the child for nonaggressive behaviors (i.e., differential reinforcement), treatment was introduced in three increasingly restrictive levels of time out for aggressive behavior. Treatment #1 involved having the child sit calmly for 2 minutes in a chair located inside a partitioned area. Although the disruptive behavior declined, the teachers were unable to make the girl sit in the chair, so she was led to a small enclosure in her classroom (treatment #2). Aggressive behavior was again below baseline, but the child failed to sit calmly in the chair, so she was placed in a small room with the door closed and locked where she remained until she was calm for 2 minutes (treatment #3). This intervention proved to be effective and resulted in the child's aggressive behavior remaining under control during a 7-month follow-up period.

This use of time out and other aversive techniques raises critical questions about the ethical treatment of troubled children. For example, should clinicians ever recommend that children be locked in a room even if the intervention does control their disruptive behavior? Apparently, Luiselli and Greenridge (1982) were concerned about this issue. They used their most extreme level of time out only after less restrictive versions were found to be ineffective. The authors also obtained informed consent from the girl's parents and the professional staff to ensure that significant others understood and accepted the treatment program. Spiegler and Guevremont (1998) emphasized the need to use aversive consequences that are brief and to select stimuli based on an assessment of their costs and benefits. As noted earlier, administering electric shock for a relatively minor behavior is unacceptable and unethical. But if a child's behavior is life threatening, as was the case in the Lang and Melamed (1969) study, the benefits of keeping the child alive compensate for the physical pain of the stimulus.

Extinction. When a behavior is not self-injurious or overly disruptive for others, clinicians sometimes use extinction, which is the permanent removal of reinforcers for a negative behavior. In a classic study, Williams (1959) used extinction to eliminate nighttime tantrum behaviors in a 21-month-old boy whose parents had given him special attention during an extended illness. When the child was placed in bed at night, he cried or whined, and his parents remained with him, sometimes for as long as 2 hours, until he was asleep. The parents were instructed to place the boy in bed, leave his room, and not return. His tantrum behaviors declined from 45 minutes of crying on the first night to no tantrums on the tenth night. The impact of this intervention was unknowingly tested about 1 week later when the parents were away from home and the child's aunt put him to bed. The boy misbehaved, so the aunt remained in his room, thereby reinforcing his tantrum behaviors. When the parents re-initiated extinction, they again eliminated the misbehavior, with no additional tantrums observed over a 2-year follow-up period.

Williams' (1959) intervention was a relatively straightforward application of extinction for a low-risk behavior. He also pointed out the importance of consistency when using these interventions. As is true for other operant techniques intended to reduce undesirable behaviors, extinction is often combined with positive reinforcement to teach children more appropriate and effective replacements for the target behavior. Therapists must assess each situation to determine whether extinction is safe for the child. If it is decided that leaving a troubled child alone increases the likelihood of negative or self-injurious behavior, alternative interventions must be used.

Cognitive-Behavioral Interventions

Cognitive-behavioral therapists consider the behavioral effects of children's attitudes and thought processes. Meichenbaum (1977) emphasized the importance of both cognitions and behaviors when he stated that "focusing on only one side of the therapy equation is likely to prove less effective" (p. 81). Cognitive-behavioral interventions are based on laboratory research in cognitive psychology (e.g., modeling, self-instructional training), applications of self-control techniques, and cognitive therapies derived from clinical experience (e.g., reattribution training, coping skills training, rational-emotive behavior therapy) (Meyers & Craighead, 1984). This diverse background led Ronen (1998) to conclude that cognitive-behavioral therapy with children is "an umbrella term for different techniques that can be offered in many different sequences and permutations" (pp. 2–3). Often designed for and focused on the child, these techniques are also used with parents (e.g., Braswell & Bloomquist, 1991), families, (e.g., Robin & Foster, 1989; Turkewitz, 1984), and school personnel (e.g., Braswell & Bloomquist, 1991).

As is the case for psychodynamic and child-centered treatments, cognitive-behavioral interventions for children have been modeled after techniques designed for adults. Can these methods be adapted for children whose thinking and information processing skills are less sophisticated? In their meta-analysis of 64 studies on a variety of cognitive-behavioral therapies (e.g., social skills training, self-instructional training), Durlak, Fuhrman, and Lampman (1991) found that results were best for clients between the ages of 11 and 13 years. Durlak et al. emphasized that 5- to 11-year-old children seem to benefit from these techniques, but "they demonstrate only one half as much change as preadolescents" (p. 210). These findings are consistent with expected outcomes according to Piaget's theory of cognitive development in which younger children are believed to reason in concrete terms (see Chapter 10). Clinicians who use cognitive procedures must adapt these techniques to the child's developmental level. Ronen (1998), for example, stated that cognitive-behavioral therapists must use "simple, specific instructions" (p. 8) with children. Clinicians are also more likely to use strategies such as play (e.g., Knell, 1998), art activities and pictorial representations of thoughts and feelings (e.g., Kendall & Treadwell, 1996), and drama or roleplaying (e.g., Braswell & Bloomquist, 1991).

Therapists who use cognitive-behavioral interventions often incorporate these techniques into other treatment strategies. Van der Krol, Oosterbaan, Weller, and Koning (1998), for example, described a three-step model for treating children with ADHD. Before they introduced cognitive-behavioral interventions, the authors structured the child's environment and then used conditioning techniques to change overt behaviors. Van der Krol et al. believed that therapists must first ensure that a child lives in an organized and consistent environment before they use behavioral techniques to remediate misbehavior and cognitive-behavioral interventions to enhance the child's self-control or self-efficacy. The authors' model represents a logical approach to the sequencing of these procedures, but therapists must remember that ecological influences, thoughts, and behaviors are related to each other. Braswell and Bloomquist (1991) described how these factors can be combined and used to treat children diagnosed with ADHD.

In *Cognitive-Behavioral Therapy with ADHD Children: Child, Family, and School Interventions*, Braswell and Bloomquist (1991) conceptualized ADHD within the context of the child's cultural surround where the attitudes and behaviors of parents and teachers interact with the beliefs and actions of the child. The authors combined behaviorally oriented interventions (e.g., parenting skills training) with cognitive techniques (e.g., self-evaluation) in a comprehensive program that typically includes individual, group, or family therapy as well as consultation with teachers. They compensated for developmental differences by tailoring their treatment program for two age groups: children between age 8 and 12 years and adolescents between age 13 and 18 years. With younger clients, the authors were more likely to use formal reinforcement programs and games when presenting and practicing skills.

We now examine five cognitive-behavioral interventions that are used as either individual interventions or components of integrated treatment programs. These techniques are characterized by a focus on a child's attitudes and thought processes as they relate to a variety of childhood behavior problems. Notice how the strategies capitalize on children's observations of appropriate behavior (i.e., modeling), private speech (e.g., self-instructional training), modification of maladaptive thoughts (e.g., reattribution training), and development of problem-solving skills (e.g., self-instructional training, coping skills training).

Modeling. Bandura's work on observational learning is the theoretical and empirical foundation for many of the clinical applications of modeling with children. A commonly used technique is live modeling in which the therapist teaches adaptive behaviors by performing them for the client. This is often done through roleplaying in which the clinician demonstrates specific behaviors during a staged interaction with the child. Krop and Burgess (1993) described another approach, covert modeling, which they used with a profoundly deaf, sexually abused 7-year-old girl who was exhibiting temper tantrums and inappropriate sexual behaviors. The child was taught to imagine different scenes of a young girl acting in a manner incompatible with these negative behaviors. By invoking the images when she was prone to misbehaving, the client exhibited marked improvement by the fourth week of treatment and during a 9-week follow-up.

Symbolic modeling through videotapes has also been used with children. Park and Williams (1986) used videotapes of staged interactions between students and their school counselors to increase self-referral rates for services among children in grades 4 to 6. Webster-Stratton (1996) developed a series of videotapes for families with children, ages 3 to 8 years, who were diagnosed with either oppositional defiant disorder or conduct disorder. Three of Webster-Stratton's programs are intended to teach parents more effective child-rearing techniques, interpersonal skills, and strategies that could be used to improve their child's academic performance. She also developed videotapes for teachers to improve classroom management skills and for children to teach basic life skills, such as anger management, social skills, and problem-solving techniques. Webster-Stratton reported encouraging results based on extensive study of her programs. An important outcome of this research is a change in attitude about who should be the target of intervention. Although Webster-Stratton initially focused on parents and their child-rearing skills, she concluded that effective treatment requires the active participation of parents, teachers, and children.

An interesting therapeutic application of modeling is the self-as-model technique in which children serve as their own models of appropriate behavior. In this procedure, a child is videotaped, incidents of positive behaviors are selected and re-recorded as an edited version, and the positive videotape is then shown to the child. As Dowrick and Raeburn (1995) stated, children "see themselves not as they typically function but at a superior level of performance" (p. 26). Self-as-model videotapes have been found to offer a personally relevant and cost-effective method of treating a number of childhood problems, including elective mutism, disruptive behavior, and depression (see review by Clark, Kehle, Jenson, & Beck, 1992). Dowrick and Raeburn (1995) identified two methods of self-modeling: positive self-review and feedforward. The first technique involves filming and editing positive behaviors that are already part of the child's behavioral repertoire. A disruptive student, for example, is filmed in class, and only positive classroom behaviors are retained on the videotape and shown to the child.

Dowrick and Raeburn (1995) described the feedforward method as the use of self-as-model videotapes to illustrate behaviors that are not part of the child's repertoire. In their study of feedforward self-modeling for children with physical disabilities (e.g., spina bifida, muscular dystrophy), Dowrick and Raeburn edited 2-minute videotapes containing component skills of more advanced behaviors, such as climbing stairs. During filming, children were assisted by off-camera personnel and encouraged to do their best, received praise for their efforts, and were told that later they would have the chance to watch themselves on television. In their work with a 6-year-old girl with cerebral palsy who was videotaped while walking over an uneven surface, Dowrick and Raeburn used the following technique to produce a videotape to help the child acquire the skills needed to step over obstacles and curbs:

> The occupational therapist grasped her hand as she stepped over a block; at the same time the cameraperson . . . zoomed the recording onto her feet. This maneuver isolated the bended knee action otherwise missing from her attempts to step over objects. (p. 32)

Children viewed their 2-minute self-as-model videotapes a total of six times during a 2-week period. Results revealed that 14 of the 18 children improved relative to their self-modeled behavior, progress that continued 1 year after treatment was terminated. These results are particularly impressive because the authors helped these children acquire complex behaviors using videotapes containing only components of these behaviors.

Self-instructional Training. Ronen (1997) described self-instructional training as "one of the most popular cognitive techniques" (p. 78) for children. In this method, therapists use children's self-talk, which resembles the private speech described by Vygotsky (1934/1986) (see the Developmental Considerations section in Chapter 10). As Hinshaw (1996) described, the clinician "initially guides the child's actions with verbal commands and then fades such control (first to the child's overt speech, then to whispered speech, and finally to internalized verbalizations) as the child performs academic or social tasks" (p. 288). An example of self-instructional training is problem-solving skills training (PSST), which Braswell and Bloomquist (1991) incorporated into their cognitive-behavioral treatment program for children with ADHD.

When therapists use self-instructional training with children diagnosed as having ADHD, they typically focus on the child's impulsive behavior and difficulty sustaining attention on relevant tasks (Ervin, Bankert, & DuPaul, 1996). Braswell and Bloomquist (1991) described a five-step approach to PSST that can be used to help children handle everyday situations in a planful manner. Therapists who use this technique explain each step of the model to the child before roleplaying its use with the client (Table 11-1). Notice how the therapist uses roleplaying in the following example based on the work of Braswell and Bloomquist:

Table 11–1

A Five-Step Problem-Solving Skills Training Method for Children.

Step	Purpose
1. Stop! What is the problem?	Help the child specify the problem.
2. What are some plans?	Identify different courses of action.
3. What is the best plan?	Assess consequences and select a plan.
4. Do the plan.	Put the plan into action.
5. Did the plan work?	Evaluate the plan's effectiveness.

Adapted from *Cognitive-behavioral therapy with ADHD children: Child, family, and school interventions,* (p. 149), by L. Braswell and M. L. Bloomquist, 1991, New York: Guilford Publications, Inc. Copyright 1991 by Guilford Publications, Inc. Adapted with permission of the author.

> Now we are going to pretend that we are out on the playground and Tommy walks over to you and starts calling you names. (The therapist and client walk around the room and then approach each other.) OK, start calling me the names that Tommy uses with you. (The client calls the therapist a "sissy" and a "baby.") *Stop! What is the problem?* The problem is that Tommy is calling me names, and I am getting angry. *What are some plans?* I could hit him, I could call him names, or I could walk away and ignore him. *What is the best plan?* If I hit him, the teacher might see me, and I will be in trouble. If I call him names, he might get angry and hit me. If I walk away and ignore him, he might stop calling me names. OK, I will walk away and ignore him because that is my best plan. *Do the plan.* (The therapist models walking away and the name calling ceases.) *Did my plan work?* Yes, I found the problem, I made some plans, and I picked the best one. When I walked away and ignored him, he stopped calling me names.

After the therapist and client roleplay the five-step model, the child is trained to apply PSST in different problem situations, such as sibling rivalry and poor academic performance. Clinicians can use PSST to help children analyze problem situations, identify responses and potential consequences, and enact their best response as an alternative to maladaptive behaviors.

Parents play an important role in the use of child-focused techniques such as PSST. Cognitive-behavioral approaches to child management require observation of antecedents and consequences of a child's behavior. Many of these events directly involve parents who actively participate in effective and ineffective interactions with their children. Braswell and Bloomquist (1991) trained parents to record the times when they prompt their child to use cognitive strategies learned in treatment. Parents learn to encourage the child to follow the five-step PSST model and plan an appropriate response to the problem at hand. Parents record the nature of the problem, the name of the person (e.g., mother, child) who decided to use the plan, and a rating of the plan's effectiveness. Parents then incorporate positive reinforcement into treatment by rewarding the child for identifying and effectively implementing a quality plan.

Self-control Training. Karoly (1995) described self-control approaches to treatment as interventions in which the client assumes "much of the responsibility for program execution that previously fell to the clinician" (p. 260). One way that children can be more active in treatment is through their self-statements, which Meichenbaum and Goodman (1971) found to be beneficial in reducing impulsive behaviors. Helping children develop self-control involves three steps: self-monitoring, self-evaluation, and self-reinforcement (Kanfer & Gaelick-Buys, 1991). During the self-monitoring phase, clients attend to and record their behaviors. This sometimes involves the use of a behavioral diary in which children report the frequency, time, and intensity of the target behavior (Ronen & Wozner, 1995). During the self-evaluation stage, clients compare their actual behavior with the criterion for success. For example, a student who was completing no homework assignments before the outset of treatment compares each week's performance with weekly goals. Ronen and Wozner indicated that self-evaluation also involves an analysis of the types of goals that children set for themselves. Are their goals realistic or beyond or below their capabilities? During the self-reinforcement phase, children learn to react "cognitively and emotionally to the results of the self-evaluation" (Kanfer & Gaelick-Buys, 1991, p. 309) by praising themselves or exchanging tokens for backup reinforcers.

Children who receive self-control training are taught to replace maladaptive self-statements with more growth-enhancing responses. Kanfer, Karoly, and Newman (1975) studied the impact of three types of self-statements that 5- and 6-year-olds learned to invoke when they were afraid of the dark. Clients were taught to use one of three response types: competence (i.e., "I am a brave boy [girl]. I can take care of myself in the dark."), stimulus (i.e., "The dark is a fun place to be. There are many good things in the dark."), or a control condition (i.e., "Mary had a little lamb. Its fleece was white as snow.") (p. 253). When exposed to the dark, children trained to use the competence response performed better (e.g., they had longer tolerance of the dark) than did children in the stimulus response and control conditions. In this study, Kanfer et al. provided support for a central belief of the cognitive-behavioral approach. That is, changing children's thoughts about themselves can result in related changes in their behavior.

Ronen (1993) offered additional support for this conclusion when she described how a child's knowledge of thought processes can facilitate behavioral change. Ronen used self-control training to treat an 8-year-old academically talented girl with a chronic sleep disorder (e.g., awakening and crying during the night). Treatment involved modifying the girl's maladaptive thoughts, teaching her about sleep disorders, and training her to use self-control techniques to change her behavior. As part of the intervention, the author explained the relationship between thoughts and behaviors by telling the child that her brain was influencing her nighttime awakening. Specifically, Ronen told her that she had the ability "to change her brain's unwanted 'commands' (to wake up) into a better 'command' (to stay in bed)" (p. 59). The intervention was effective in eliminating the child's nightly crying and episodes of sleeping with her parents. There was also a marked decrease in the number of times she awoke each night. After her fourth and final treatment session, the child stated that she was able to "absolutely control her brain and find herself to be very good at it" (Ronen, 1993, p. 60).

Silverman and Kurtines (1996) described a transfer-of-control method for the treatment of children with internalizing disorders, such as anxiety and depression. According to this model, the therapist teaches behavior management skills to parents so they can establish a consistent and predictable environment for the child. Silverman and Kurtines also incorporated self-control training with the child by using the STOP model to reduce children's fears or anxieties. In this procedure, clients are first taught to recognize *S*cared or negative feelings and their associated *T*houghts. Then they learn to identify *O*ther or alternate thoughts that can be invoked and to use *P*raise when they are successful in controlling negative feelings. As children develop more self-control, parents gradually exert less external control, thereby increasing the child's level of autonomy to a developmentally appropriate level.

Reattribution Training. Reattribution training represents a therapeutic application of the principles of learned helplessness theory (Metalsky, Laird, Heck, & Joiner, 1995). Given the connection that some (see Abramson, Metalsky, & Alloy, 1989) have made between learned helplessness and depression, we might expect to find a wealth of studies on reattribution training with children who exhibit depressive symptoms. Unfortunately, this is not the case (Mufson & Moreau, 1997), although various authors have discussed how this technique can be incorporated into treatment programs for children with this problem. Schwartz, Kaslow, Racusin, and Carton (1998), for example, used reattribution training as one component of their 16-session family-based intervention. In the fifth and sixth sessions, the authors addressed "the negative cognitive triad, depressogenic attributional patterns, and faulty information processing" (p. 125) related to the child's depressive symptoms. Family members are trained to replace learned helplessness with learned optimism (Seligman, Reivich, Jaycox, & Gillham, 1995) so all of them are able to interpret and respond to positive and negative life events in a more accurate manner.

Schwartz et al. (1998) described their work with 12-year-old Julia and her mother who entered treatment after the child began to exhibit symptoms of depression when she received all A's and one B in English on her report card. The authors described the case as follows:

> Julia thought that the B was evidence that she was "dumb," a sentiment that was heightened by her mother's concern about implications of the B for Julia's future educational and occupational opportunities. Thus, Julia appeared to be making an internal-stable-global attribution for this perceived negative event, and her mother inadvertently was communicating a concern about the permanence of the cause of this event. Interventions therefore focused on providing attribution retraining to both Julia and her mother. Specific attention was paid to helping Julia take credit for her multiple successes and more realistically assess the causes and consequences of her English grade. Additionally, her mother was supported in praising Julia for her accomplishments and keeping her daughter's grade in perspective. (p. 140)

This is an excellent example of the therapeutic value of including parents in their child's treatment. If the authors had limited their attention to the girl's negative attributions, similar beliefs by the mother would have gone untreated and probably continued to be a negative influence on the child.

Braswell and Bloomquist (1991) also used reattribution training to modify parents' and teachers' attitudes about ADHD. When problematic beliefs are detected, the therapist distributes printed materials about the nature and treatment of ADHD and then addresses these attributions in session. If a parent or teacher believes a child is intentionally engaging in these behaviors, the therapist counters with a statement such as, "Many problems are out of this child's control" (p. 321). When a father has perfectionistic standards for his child-rearing skills, the therapist can help him revise this belief to: "I'm going to make mistakes. It's natural to make mistakes. This child is more challenging than others" (p. 321).

Coping Skills Training. Kendall and Treadwell (1996) developed a cognitive approach for treating children who are diagnosed with anxiety disorders. During the first half of the authors' 16- to 20-session program, therapists teach children to use a four-stage coping skills strategy the authors call their FEAR program. Children learn to identify anxious feelings (i.e., "*F*eeling frightened?") and related cognitions (i.e., "*E*xpecting bad things to happen?"); they use problem-solving skills to develop a coping plan (i.e., "*A*ctions and attitudes that help"); and they evaluate their progress and reward themselves for their progress (i.e., "*R*ate and reward") (p. 28). During the second half of treatment, children apply their FEAR plans, both in and out of session, as they are gradually exposed to imaginary and real anxiety-producing events.

The Kendall and Treadwell (1996) program is a developmentally based intervention that contains child-oriented techniques. For example, the authors used their *Coping Cat Workbook* (Kendall, 1992) to facilitate the disclosure of thoughts and feelings and the development of coping techniques for anxious situations. The workbook contains cartoon characters with empty message "bubbles" where children are to write or describe the character's thoughts and feelings. Children also become actively involved in the treatment process by producing "a videotaped commercial" to describe their use of the FEAR program with an anxiety-producing event. Kendall and Treadwell (1996) reported empirical support for the efficacy of their intervention. Compared with children on a waiting list, clients in the FEAR program improved significantly over the course of treatment. Kendall and his colleagues recently expanded their program to include parents in the treatment process, which Howard and Kendall (1996) found to have a favorable impact on treatment outcome.

Rational-Emotive Behavior Therapy

Based on his experiences in clinical practice, Albert Ellis developed REBT to teach clients the "principles of sane living" (Ellis, 1972, p. 20) so they could challenge the irrational beliefs that are thought to cause emotional and behavioral problems. When he formulated his therapeutic approach, Ellis expanded his A-B-C model of personality (see Chapter 10) to include an intervention level, called Disputation, and an outcome stage, which he labeled Effect (Ellis & Dryden, 1997). At the outset of treatment, the therapist develops rapport with the child and assesses the activating events that precipitate the client's beliefs and resulting emotions or behaviors. A crucial component of this process is the identification of irrational beliefs. A student who is repeatedly involved in fights at school may believe that other children should always do what he wants. When his classmates behave otherwise (i.e., activating event), this irrational belief causes him to feel angry and to hit other children.

When an irrational belief has been identified and its connection with activating events and consequences determined, the therapist introduces the client to the A-B-C model and disputes or challenges the child's irrational beliefs. Teaching REBT principles often requires the use of concrete activities, such as roleplaying and structured games. Vernon (1999) described how she helped a boy distinguish between assumptions and facts by having him juggle tennis balls. She reported that the child learned that it is normal for people to be talented in some areas and not others, and that even talented people make mistakes in their areas of expertise. The therapist introduced the boy to REBT principles, which were used to challenge his irrational belief of having to be perfect.

In the following therapist–client dialogue, Vernon (1999) described the use of questioning and teaching rational self-statements with a very young child who was afraid of the water:

CHILD: But I'm afraid to swim. The water is cold.

COUNSELOR: Have you gotten in? How do you know it is cold?

CHILD: Well, I just think it is.

COUNSELOR: Does it look as if the other children think it is too cold to have fun?

CHILD: I guess not.

COUNSELOR: Well, it must not be too bad or the other children would be shivering. What else is bothering you?

CHILD: What if I get in too deep and think that I will drown and no one is there to save me?

COUNSELOR: Well, let's look around. How many teachers and helpers are walking around supervising? Do you see the rope where some of the other children are standing? That rope comes up only to their waist. Do you see anyone going further? What do you suppose would happen if they did?

CHILD: I don't know. I suppose the teacher would make them get back. I still am sort of scared though.

COUNSELOR: It's okay to be scared, but as you can see, no one has drowned yet, the kids look like they are having fun, and you could get in and see for yourself what it's like, even if you're scared.

CHILD: Well, I guess I'll try it. (p. 151)

In this example, Vernon illustrated how a child's fear of the water and avoidance behavior were related to her beliefs about the discomfort and dangers of swimming. The therapist accepted or normalized the client's fear of the water (i.e., "It's okay to be scared") while challenging the cognitions underlying that feeling and the child's reluctance to enter the water.

The scope of REBT methods for childhood problems includes parent education programs. Joyce (1990) described the Rational Parenting Program, which can be used to alleviate parents' emotional problems that may be contributing to their child's misbehavior. Participants are taught REBT principles, either individually or in groups, which they use to manage their own thoughts and feelings and to use effective disciplinary techniques with their children. The goal of treatment is "to teach parents to think more rationally, so that they will *feel better* (less distressed), be *more effective problem solvers* in every day difficulties, and provide *healthier models for their children* in dealing with difficult, disappointing or frustrating events" (p. 312). In her research on the program, Joyce found the intervention to be effective in reducing parents' irrational beliefs and emotionality.

PLAY TECHNIQUES

Compared with psychodynamic and child-centered therapists, proponents of behavioral and cognitive-behavioral methods are less likely to use play interventions with children. But these clinicians have not completely overlooked play in their work with young clients. For example, some have combined behavioral interventions with other methods (see the discussion of parent–child interaction therapy in Chapter 16). Others devised group methods that can be used for skill development with children (see Schaefer, Jacobsen, & Ghahramanlou, 2000, later in this chapter). This section examines two individual behavioral play therapies, one developed during the 1970s and another of more recent origin.

Chapter 8 discusses gender identity disorder, which Rekers, Kilgus, and Rosen (1990) estimated to occur in 1 of every 100,000 to 200,000 children. This disorder and its treatment have been controversial topics. Neisen (1992), for example, questioned the value of diagnosing and treating behaviors that are considered pathological simply because they are inconsistent with prevailing cultural values. He cautioned against the use of a diagnostic category that represents "harmful, rigid gender role stereotypes" (p. 66). He also challenged clinicians to question the appropriateness of a treatment that is typically restricted to boys exhibiting what are traditionally thought to be feminine behaviors. Before therapists proceed with treatment for these children, they must consider Neisen's comments and ask themselves whether it is in the child's best interests to diagnose a young boy as having this disorder and provide therapy to decrease feminine and increase masculine interests and behaviors simply because parents have requested these changes.

Rekers (1983) described a behavioral intervention that he used to treat boys who engage in cross-gender play. Based on the results of a comprehensive assessment that includes observation of the child's behavior in the playroom (see Rekers & Kilgus, 1998), the therapist develops a treatment plan involving activities designed to reinforce traditional gender-typed play. Parents observe play sessions in which the clinician models techniques that can be used at home with the child. Although therapy often occurs in the clinician's playroom, Rekers did not restrict treatment to this setting. He described procedures that therapists can use with boys on the playground. These involve skills training in sports activities, such as football, basketball, and soccer. The clinician uses successive approximation to shape athletic behaviors, which are believed to facilitate relationship development with other boys.

In what Rekers (1983) described as "the first experimentally demonstrated effective treatment for cross-gender identification in children" (p. 379), Rekers and Lovaas (1974) used behavioral play therapy with a 4-year, 11-month-old boy who was engaging in cross-gender behaviors. These included cross-dressing since age 2 years and rejection of traditional masculine behaviors in favor of feminine activities, such as playing with cosmetics and preferring the role of "mother" when playing house with his female friends. In their playroom, Rekers and Lovaas trained the boy's mother to reinforce his use of traditionally masculine toys (e.g., a car, airplanes) and to ignore him when he played with toys thought to be feminine (e.g., a doll, toy dishes). The authors also taught the parents to use a token reinforcement system with a response cost condition to reward masculine behaviors and discourage cross-gender activities at home. The results of a single-case experimental design revealed a noticeable increase in masculine behaviors and a similar decline in feminine behaviors. When Rekers (1983) summarized this case, he reported that 10 years after treatment was terminated, the boy was observed to have " a normal gender identity as a male" (p. 379) and that he engaged in behaviors similar to those of his male peers. Rekers et al. (1990) reported similar long-term benefits of behavioral play therapy for boys diagnosed with gender identity disorder. Although his treatment is not appropriate for the normal variations that occur in children's gender-typed behavior, Rekers' method merits consideration with clients whose cross-gender behaviors are compromising their psychosocial development.

Knell (1998) developed a cognitive-behavioral play intervention that has been used to treat a variety of childhood problems, including encopresis (Knell & Moore, 1990) and sexual abuse (Knell & Ruma, 1996). Knell (2000) used this method to treat fears and phobias in children. Therapy sessions for these clients take place in the clinician's playroom or in the setting where the child's fears occur. Treatment for a student with school phobia might involve sessions at the therapist's office combined with meetings at the child's school, either after regular hours or when classes are in session. The purpose of cognitive-behavioral play therapy is to increase clients' sense of self-control over their fears through the successful use of behavioral and cognitive techniques.

Knell (2000) recommended that clinicians incorporate structured and unstructured play time into each session. During structured play, the therapist teaches the child to use fear control strategies. Unstructured or free play allows the client to disclose personally meaningful thoughts and feelings that might be overlooked during structured activities. Knell (2000) recommended such techniques as emotive imagery, positive reinforcement, and modeling. Playful use of these strategies can involve imaginary interactions of heroes and villains (see earlier example from Lazarus and Abramovitz, 1962). Therapists use puppets or other play materials to model effective responses to fear objects. Bibliotherapy also offers a model for appropriate behavior and can be used to transform clients' cognitive distortions into more effective beliefs. Knell recommended that therapists maintain contact with parents throughout treatment to ensure that appropriate contingencies are being used at home. When one or both parents are reinforcing a client's fears, the clinician must work with them to establish contingencies that encourage more independence in the child.

Knell (2000) provided four case examples of cognitive-behavioral play therapy with fearful children. A preschooler who was afraid of sleeping alone was given a container of spray that could be used to scare away the monsters in her bedroom. Another preschooler dictated and illustrated books about her fears and her successful attempts to deal with these feelings. With her therapist, she developed a list of coping statements that a bear puppet could use to control its fears. The clinician then used the puppet to model these statements for the child. As discussed in Chapter 3, Knell and Moore (1990) incorporated a bear puppet into their cognitive-behavioral play treatment for a 5-year-old boy diagnosed with encopresis. When it became apparent that the client was afraid of the toilet, the clinician used the puppet to model appropriate toileting and to reduce the child's toilet-related fears. By combining play and behavior management skills training for parents, Knell and Moore were successful in helping the boy to stop soiling and to use the toilet on a regular basis.

GROUP TECHNIQUES

Therapists who conduct behavioral and cognitive-behavioral groups with children are likely to focus on skills development. Some groups are designed to teach social skills, and others involve training in problem-solving strategies, anger management techniques, and the organizational and study skills needed to succeed in the classroom. Clinicians who conduct these groups assess clients' skills deficits, identify the behavioral components of each skill, model these behaviors for group members, and have children engage in supervised roleplaying or behavioral rehearsal to enhance skills development (Elias & Tobin, 1996). Group therapy offers a particular advantage over individual treatments in this regard. Whereas the therapist is the sole role model in individual therapy, the clinician and group members who behave appropriately and use the target skills effectively serve this function in group.

Before we discuss specific examples of behavioral and cognitive-behavioral groups, we need to discuss the general application of behavioral principles in group therapy with children. As discussed in Chapter 2, therapists must have sufficient control of the group process to ensure each member's safety. In addition, learning is more likely to occur in an environment in which children comply with social conventions, including listening to others and speaking one at a time. Clinicians can encourage these behaviors by using such techniques as positive reinforcement and punishment when the situation warrants. As Braswell and Bloomquist (1991) stated, "The use of behavioral contingencies is essential to running a group" (p. 146). Therapists can use both concrete and social reinforcers. The latter include smiling and verbal praise for clients' appropriate behavior. A popular concrete reinforcer for children is a brief snack at the end of each group session. Clinicians can make this activity contingent upon members' acceptable behavior during group therapy. By having children work toward this common goal, therapists can establish an environment in which members monitor, limit, and reinforce each other's behavior to obtain this reward.

Schaefer, Jacobsen, and Ghahramanlou (2000) described a social skills group for elementary school children that incorporates play activities. The authors' 10-session program is conducted by two co-therapists who meet with four to six children of the same gender and similar ages. Each 60-minute session has three parts: (1) a brief introduction to a specific skill (e.g., assertiveness, cooperation), (2) an extended practice period during which members engage in supervised structured activities, and (3) a snack to end the session. Activities include cooperative and competitive group games, a trust walk, and pairs interviews in which children learn about other members' hobbies and interests. The Schaefer et al. program also includes a group for parents to attend while children are in session. In this group, parents learn about social development and how to reinforce their child in the everyday use of the skills presented in children's group.

Schaefer et al. (2000) did not formally evaluate their method, but others have studied social skills training programs for children. Much of this research has involved treatment combinations based on different theories, including behavioral and cognitive-behavioral. In an early study, LaGreca and Santogrossi (1980) taught students in grades 3 to 5 to use a variety of social behaviors, including smiling, sharing, and basic conversation skills. Two co-therapists conducted four 90-minute weekly sessions with same-gender groups in which children viewed videotaped peer models demonstrating specific skills. Members were coached to use these behaviors during in-session roleplaying exercises, which were videotaped so clients could observe and evaluate their performance. The group leaders also asked children to practice these skills outside of session, and they reviewed these homework assignments at the next meeting. LaGraca and Santogrossi compared their four-session program with a waiting-list condition and a placebo-control group in which children met weekly to view videotapes of television programs, play games (e.g., charades), and complete nonsocial skills homework assignments. They found that clients in the social skills group exhibited significantly better knowledge and behavior than did their peers in the two control conditions, which were not significantly different from each other. Pfiffner and McBurnett (1997) replicated these findings with children, ages 8 to 10 years, who participated in eight 90-minute weekly sessions of a social skills training group. Similar to LaGreca and Santogrossi (1980), Pfiffner and McBurnett used two co-therapists who used modeling and roleplaying to teach a specific skill each week. The authors found that clients exhibited significantly more improvement in social skills knowledge and behaviors than did children assigned to a clinic waiting list.

Other researchers have used cognitive-behavioral group therapy to treat a variety of childhood problems, including anxiety (Toren et al., 2000) and behavior disorders (Larkin & Thyer, 1999). Sukhodolsky, Solomon, and Perine (2000) used this approach to help elementary school students control their anger. The authors' groups consisted of ten 45-minute sessions involving four to six children, ages 9 to 11 years. Treatment was divided into three stages: affective education, instruction in anger control techniques, and behavioral rehearsal of these strategies. During the first stage, children learned about emotions, including an emotional vocabulary they could use to describe their feelings in different situations. Anger control instruction included the use of relaxation techniques and self-instructional skills that were used when clients detected the physiological and cognitive signs of anger. In the last stage of treatment, students practiced these techniques in group by modeling and roleplaying appropriate responses to anger-provoking events.

Sukhodolsky et al. (2000) compared their intervention with an attention control condition in which children participated in play group sessions that included games (e.g., checkers) but none of the instructional components in the treatment program. The authors found that after treatment, clients in the cognitive-behavioral groups were rated by their teachers as less angry and less likely to engage in hostile behaviors. There was also some evidence to suggest that children in the treatment groups were more likely to report the use of anger control techniques. These results are encouraging and suggest that group therapy can be used to help children develop cognitive strategies for controlling negative feelings and behaviors. As mentioned earlier, group methods, in contrast to individual therapy, allow clients to practice new skills with peers in roleplaying situations that resemble their daily interactions with other children.

RESEARCH

Of the four major therapies presented in this text, the methods described in this chapter have the strongest empirical support. Researchers have used single-case and between-groups designs to evaluate behavioral and cognitive-behavioral strategies delivered as individual interventions or combined treatment programs. The empirical support that currently exists for behavioral and cognitive-behavioral methods has become the standard that is expected of all child interventions, regardless of their theoretical foundation. The progress made on these therapies has resulted in the delineation of criteria for empirically supported treatments (see Chapter 3).

The distinction that Messer & Wachtel (1997) made between treatment efficacy and treatment effectiveness merits consideration. As you will recall from Chapter 5, treatment efficacy is based on controlled studies in which children are recruited because they meet specific entrance criteria to receive manualized treatments delivered under experimental conditions (e.g., random assignment to treatment). In contrast, therapeutic effectiveness is determined in the real world of therapeutic practice where interventions must be tailored to the complex needs of each client. The standardized treatments used with specific problems in efficacy research are often modified or combined with each other in novel ways to design effective treatments. Investigators have studied behavioral and cognitive-behavioral treatments in real-life settings, including public school classrooms and residential treatment facilities for children. Many of these investigations have involved the use of single-case experimental designs (Barlow & Hersen, 1984). More effort is needed with alternative research methods to evaluate the outcome of behavioral and cognitive-behavioral interventions, individually or in combination with other treatments, in real-life settings with children whose problems are less specific in nature.

INTERVENTION TARGET

Role of the Parent

Parents' involvement in the treatment process ranges from being the sole participant in behavioral parent training (see Chapter 14) to limited or no involvement when cognitive-behavioral approaches, such as self-instructional training, are used with the child. Generally speaking, therapists have traditionally relied more on parents when behavioral conditioning is used and less when cognitive-behavioral interventions are adopted. When treatment is based on behavioral conditioning, parents are typically trained to use operant techniques with their children. This involves identifying, monitoring, and charting target behaviors; participating in the selection of reinforcers and the administration of behavioral consequences in a consistent manner; and structuring the child's environment to ensure the existence of appropriate antecedent conditions.

When clinicians rely on parents to implement operant procedures with their child, they must assess each parent's stage of therapeutic change and attitudes regarding behavioral techniques. As noted earlier in this chapter, the children of parents who are philosophically opposed to these methods are likely to gain little benefit from treatment. Although therapists are sometimes successful in changing parents' beliefs, alternative interventions (e.g., family systems therapy) merit consideration either as substitutes for or precursors to behavioral techniques. Some parents are "just too busy" to record and reinforce their child's behavior. Unfortunately, the therapist is often unaware of this until an intervention has been initiated and the parents and child return for their next session. Clinicians must determine whether a parent's inconsistent use of behavioral techniques represents a general pattern of interaction with the child. Inconsistent parents can sometimes be identified during a pretreatment assessment by asking them to describe previous attempts at remediating the target behavior. A therapist can learn, for example, how disagreements between a mother and father about child rearing or prematurely terminated interventions resulted in failed attempts to correct the child's behavior problems.

According to Ronen (1998), cognitive-behavioral therapists are likely to involve family members in the treatment process because of the situational, systems-oriented focus of this approach. Braswell and Boomquist (1991) discussed the value of having parents involved in treatment. First, parents are able to provide significant information about the nature, history, and scope of the child's presenting problem. They are significant agents of change because they control many of the reinforcers their children value. Toward the end of treatment, parents can maintain and generalize their child's progress as their role shifts from that of remediation to education/development and prevention.

In some cases, a parent's interpretation of a child's behavior is more significant than the child's actions. For example, parents who have limited knowledge of normal development sometimes have unrealistic expectations for their children. Consider two parents who are concerned about their 3-year-old son's inability to sit quietly and pay attention for extended periods. Clearly, the parents' expectations are unrealistic for a child this age, so the clinician should consider a psychoeducational intervention to teach the parents what constitutes a "normal" range of behaviors for preschool children. For some parents, the problem is not a lack of information but the manner in which they process information. For example, a father who catastrophizes about everyday events brings his first grader to therapy because he is worried that the B's she recently received on her report card mean she will be unable to attend a prestigious university. Treatment in this case would include individual sessions with the father to assess for cognitive distortions and to teach thinking skills for more healthy living.

Role of the Child

The typical preschool or primary school child in behavior therapy is the recipient of environmental changes performed by significant other adults. Although these clients are made aware of the target behavior and its consequences, they are less involved than older children in the development of behavioral interventions. As they age, children become more active participants in treatment, providing important information regarding the selection and delivery of reinforcers for appropriate behaviors. They also assume more responsibility for monitoring and recording their behaviors. But parents and teachers continue to retain control over relevant antecedents and consequences, which they manipulate to effect behavioral change in the child.

Children are more involved in the creation and implementation of cognitive-behavioral treatments, such as problem-solving skills or self-control training in which attention is directed at covert events (Kanfer & Gaelick-Buys, 1991). Ronen (1998) described the child in cognitive-behavioral therapy as "an active partner" (p. 3) who learns "how he or she behaves and how to acquire knowledge in order to change" (p. 9). Therapists impart this knowledge as they teach children how to use techniques such as self-instruction or self-monitoring. But it is the child who actually monitors, evaluates, and reinforces the application of these strategies outside of the therapy hour. When confronted with a decision during the week, the child is responsible for identifying the problem and developing a plan of action before responding. Homework is an important component of cognitive-behavioral treatment because it gives the child an opportunity to practice the skills learned in therapy.

Role of the Therapist

The traditional behavior therapist is often a psychoeducator who teaches parents and others to use effective child management skills. The first step in this process is the identification of a target behavior and an assessment of related antecedents and consequences. When parents seek therapy for their child, they sometimes describe the presenting problem as "trouble at school," "difficulty getting along with other children," or "angry with us all the time." The therapist's challenge is to help parents to develop an operational definition of the problem. For example, trouble at school sometimes translates into off-task behavior in the classroom and poor grades. Upon further investigation, the therapist learns that the child is receiving failing grades in English and social studies but grades of "B" and above in math, reading, and science. An important area for investigation in this case is any differences that exist in the environmental antecedents and consequences in these classes. If the therapist discovers that one teacher instructs English and social studies and another teaches the remaining subjects, she might explore such factors as the teachers' instructional styles and levels of experience, the physical quality of the classrooms, and the time of day when each class is taught.

With their assessment data in hand, behavior therapists design interventions that are consistent with existing empirical evidence. They use the single-case experimental design to monitor changes in the target behavior and to evaluate the effects of treatment. Weekly sessions with clients include a review of data collected on the child's behavior, a discussion of progress and problems encountered since the last meeting, and the specification of target behaviors and related consequences for the upcoming week. In a return session for a boy with encopresis, for example, the therapist reviews the client's monitoring chart and learns that the child soiled on four occasions, two fewer than the previous week. The parents awarded the previously agreed upon consequence (i.e., a trip to the zoo) and reported no unusual problems during the week. The therapist facilitates a discussion of progress and concludes the session by helping the family establish the criterion for success and the reward that will apply during the next week.

Kendall (1993) stated that cognitive-behavioral therapists fulfill a number of different functions in their work with children. As diagnosticians, they bring together relevant information about the child to develop appropriate treatments. They function as psychoeducators when they teach children and parents about the cognitive skills that are needed to make decisions that enhance emotional and behavioral development. Cognitive-behavioral clinicians consult with parents and teachers to correct distorted beliefs that are compromising interactions with the child.

An important step for behavior and cognitive-behavioral therapists is determining whether the focus for intervention should be the child, parents, family, school, or a combination thereof. Will the presenting problem respond best to direct intervention with the child using cognitive-behavioral self-control training? Is the client's misbehavior the result of inadequate child-rearing techniques the therapist can address with behavioral parent training? Will the problem respond to a family-based intervention in which family members are trained to identify and effectively use antecedents and consequences for constructive change? Or is the child's behavior a result of school-related problems that require therapist consultation with teachers or school counselors to create a more effective learning environment? Many childhood problems respond to collaborative interventions that are designed to address different causes. This often means that clinicians are adapting individual therapy to the child's developmental level, working with parents and motivating them to implement more effective child-rearing methods, and cooperating with school personnel to improve the client's classroom behavior.

Role of the School

Behavioral principles are an integral part of the educational process. The more questions a student correctly answers on an examination, the higher the child's letter grade. Children are reinforced for appropriate behaviors with smiles from teachers and good conduct grades on report cards. Behavior therapists also use a variety of school-based interventions to remediate students' misbehavior and poor academic progress. Forehand and Wierson (1993, p. 133) stated that teachers must be involved in treatment because they represent "significant sources of reinforcement" for students. Community-based clinicians must remember that teachers are more likely to implement an intervention if they have a sense of ownership in the treatment program (Bogat & Jason, 1997, p. 139). Therapists should invite teachers to share their impressions of the child and their knowledge of the school environment. With this information, clinicians can facilitate the development and implementation of behavioral treatments. Without it, they risk developing interventions that are impractical, empirically flawed, and of limited therapeutic value.

As suggested by Skinner (1954, 1961), the application of behavioral principles in the classroom creates a structured environment where children learn the skills needed to function in a democratic society. Kaplan (1991) described cognitive-behavioral interventions that can be used in schools to teach children how to manage stress, become better problem solvers, and be more effective modifiers of their behavior. The elementary school is a powerful setting for teaching students to use problem-solving and social skills. As Kaplan observed, "Teaching social skills is not very different from teaching other skills in school" (p. 187). The classroom becomes a laboratory where students learn the principles and techniques of interpersonal relationships and have the opportunity to roleplay social skills modeled by their instructors. Schools also provide an arena where children can practice the skills learned in therapy. When clinicians, teachers, and school counselors collaborate, they can facilitate the generalization and maintenance of these skills in the child's everyday life (Braswell & Bloomquist, 1991).

CONTRIBUTIONS AND LIMITATIONS

A major contribution of the behavioral approach is its application of the scientific method to clinical practice. Behavior therapists routinely evaluate the impact of their work using the single-case experimental design, which "fills the gap between the traditional, uncontrolled case-study method and the group-comparison approach to research that is rarely appropriate in a clinical setting" (Ross, 1981, p. 23). Controlled studies of behavioral and cognitive-behavioral techniques have produced many of the empirically supported therapies currently available for childhood problems. These treatments are of relatively brief duration and focused on the effects of the child's cultural surround on clearly defined overt and covert acts. Behavior therapists give little attention to intrapsychic forces. Instead, they help children, parents, and others to identify and control the environmental stimuli that bring about behavioral change. The brief nature of these methods, combined with their empirical support, makes them viable interventions in a managed mental health care environment (Fishman & Franks, 1997). They also fit the lifestyle of families who lack the time and financial resources to pursue more lengthy forms of therapy. As discussed in Chapter 3, the median number of sessions attended by adults and children is less than 10 (Garfield, 1994; Sowder, Burt, Rosenstein, & Milazzo-Sayre, 1981). Brief behavioral interventions match the limited resources of families who "vote with their feet" and terminate therapy according to their own schedules.

Critics have challenged the theoretical bases for behavioral treatments. Okun (1990) cautioned that therapists who limit their attention to overt behaviors run the risk of using an approach that is "reductionistic, simplistic, and mechanistic" (p. 183). Behavioral interventions have been described as superficial because they are used to treat symptoms, rather than the underlying cause of a child's problems. Critics once contended that these treatments would result in symptom substitution in which one negative behavior is brought under control, only to be replaced by another because the true cause of the problem was never addressed. Early researchers such as Baker (1969) responded to this challenge by empirically testing behavior therapy with children and finding therapeutic change without symptom substitution. But others have reported that improvement in the target behavior does not necessarily generalize to other areas. Shapiro and Bradley (1996), for example, described how self-instructional training for academic problems has been found to be effective with the specific concerns addressed in treatment, but the approach "once learned for one content area must be taught in others" (p. 349).

Another limitation of many behavioral and cognitive-behavioral interventions is their use of an external standard for acceptable behavior, which typically coincides with traditional European American values. Chapter 16 discusses how recent developments in constructivist therapies have contributed to an expanded view of treatment in which manipulation of the environment and teaching children the "correct" way to handle problems are being replaced with techniques (e.g., narrative reconstruction) designed to facilitate clients' personal understanding of themselves and their environment. The growth of cognitive-behavioral methods has brought about increased interest in children's thoughts and behaviors. Compared with the traditional behavioral approach, these techniques represent a more balanced treatment of behaviors, cognitions, and emotions. As Fishman and Franks (1997) observed, a positive outcome of these developments has been "the shift from a simplistic, mechanistic, S-R model to a nonlinear, multicausal but methodologically rigorous perspective" (p. 167). Based on this more holistic approach to intervention, a child's overt behavior is conceptualized relative to its reaction to and impact on the cultural surround. Consequently, the beliefs and expectations that parents, teachers, and the child have about the child's behavior and its causes merit consideration. The application of the scientific method to a multivariate interpretation such as this is considerably more complex than an evaluation of the consistent administration of a concrete reinforcer to a specific overt behavior.

BEHAVIORAL AND COGNITIVE-BEHAVIORAL INTERVENTIONS: A CASE EXAMPLE

We now return to the case of Antonio Henderson, a 10-year-old African American boy who wets the bed on a regular basis. There are various forms of childhood enuresis, as determined by the client's incontinence history and the timing of wetting episodes (Table 11-2). Although the majority of children diagnosed with enuresis are nighttime wetters only (i.e., nocturnal enuresis), some are incontinent both day and night (i.e., nocturnal/diurnal enuresis) but others wet only when they are awake (i.e., diurnal enuresis). Enuresis is also classified according to the length of time a child has been incontinent. Children who have wet since birth are classified as having primary enuresis, but those who have resumed wetting after a period of complete dryness (e.g., 12 consecutive months) are said to exhibit secondary enuresis. The combination of timing and wetting history results in six enuresis types. Because Antonio appears to be exhibiting primary nocturnal enuresis, we will focus our discussion on the causes and treatment of this disorder.

Organic dysfunction seems to be a logical cause for primary nocturnal enuresis, but the absence of "a general medical condition" is one of the diagnostic criteria for enuresis in the DSM-IV-TR (American Psychiatric Association, 2000, p. 118). An alternative explanation for this problem behavior is that nighttime wetting results from a learning deficit. That is, children are incontinent because they have not acquired the bladder control skills needed to retain fluids and void in an appropriate manner. Although this formulation constitutes the basis for behavioral treatments, other causes for nightly wetting have been proposed, including sleep disorders (Kolvin & Taunch, 1973), small functional bladder capacity (Doleys, Ciminero, Tollison, Williams, & Well, 1977;

Table 11–2
Subtypes of Functional Enuresis in Children

	THE CHILD'S WETTING HISTORY	
Time of Day When Wetting Occurs	Incontinent Since Birth	Incontinent After An Extended Dry Period
Daytime only	Primary diurnal enuresis	Secondary diurnal enuresis
Nighttime only	Primary nocturnal enuresis	Secondary nocturnal enuresis
Daytime and nighttime	Primary nocturnal/diurnal enuresis	Secondary nocturnal/diurnal enuresis

Zaleski, Gerrard, & Schokier, 1973), and emotional problems (Deutsch, 1953).

To identify children whose wetting is of organic origin, therapists must require parents to obtain a medical examination for their child before psychological intervention is initiated. The treatment of nocturnal enuresis has a rather picturesque history that dates back to at least 1550 B.C. when herbal remedies were used (Glicklich, 1951). More contemporary interventions have included psychopharmacotherapy (Wagner, Johnson, Walker, Carter, & Wittmer, 1982), behavioral conditioning with a urine alarm (Mowrer & Mowrer, 1938; Wagner, 1987b), traditional psychotherapy (DeLeon & Mandell, 1966; Werry & Cohrssen, 1965), and family therapy (Protinsky & Dillard, 1983). Of these, urine alarm treatment appears to be the intervention of choice for primary nocturnal enuresis (Houts et al., 1994).

More effective than psychopharmacotherapy (Wagner et al. 1982) and traditional psychotherapy (DeLeon & Mandell, 1966; Werry & Cohrssen, 1965), behavioral conditioning has been found to have initial cure rates ranging from 75% to 90% (Doleys, 1977; Johnson, 1980). A common problem with the urine alarm is relapse, with approximately 35% of successfully treated children experiencing a return of enuretic episodes within 1 year after termination of treatment (Morgan, 1978). Although the relapse rate for certain psychopharmacotherapies is much higher (e.g., 100% in Wagner et al., 1982), behavior therapists must prepare for this outcome if it occurs. One method of handling relapse is retreatment using the alarm, which Forsythe & Redmond (1970) found to produce lasting remission of wetting episodes. Another promising technique is self-control training, which Ronen and her colleagues developed and found to be as effective as the urine alarm in producing initial control of nighttime incontinence and better at preventing relapse (Ronen & Wozner, 1995; Ronen, Wozner, & Rahav, 1992).

Treatment for Antonio involves behavioral conditioning with a urine alarm (Wagner, 1987b) and self-control training that includes self-monitoring, self-evaluation, self-reinforcement, and positive self-talk (Kanfer & Gaelick-Buys, 1991; Ronen & Wozner, 1995). Antonio's pediatrician, Dr. Norton, recently examined him and found no organic causes for his wetting, so she encouraged his mother to seek therapy for the child. When Ms. Henderson indicated that she could not afford to pay for a private practitioner, Dr. Norton recommended that she seek help through an outpatient clinic at a nearby university in the southeastern United States. The clinic, operated in conjunction with graduate programs in counselor education and counseling psychology, provides a range of services and charges clients based on their income. Therapy for Antonio, for example, will cost $5 per session.

When Ms. Henderson telephones the clinic to schedule an appointment, her call is forwarded to Ms. Theresa Simpson, a fourth-year doctoral student with an interest in children and families. The mother describes the presenting problem, and Ms. Simpson schedules a meeting for 1 week later. Ms. Henderson agrees to use a calendar to record Antonio's wet and dry nights without his knowledge. These baseline data are an extremely important part of the single-case experimental design that Ms. Simpson will use to evaluate treatment outcome.

▪ ▪ ▪

During her first session with the boy and his mother, Ms. Simpson establishes rapport with the child and then says, "Antonio, I understand that we are here today because you want to stop wetting your bed." He nods his head in agreement, so Ms. Simpson asks the mother for the wetting calendar. She quickly studies the results and then shows the calendar to Antonio. "I asked your Mom to put an 'X' for each night you wet the bed," she explains. Both the mother and child agree that the 7 wet nights during the previous week are typical for Antonio.

Ms. Simpson asks about the techniques the family has used to control the bed wetting. Ms. Henderson describes how she limits her son's fluid intake after the evening meal and makes sure he uses the bathroom immediately before bedtime. Antonio says that he once placed stickers on a chart when he had dry nights. The parents mention that they recently tried a medication prescribed by Dr. Norton.

"Antonio had dry nights when he took the pills, but he started wetting again when he stop taking them," Ms. Henderson adds. "We tried waking him to go in the middle of the night, but that didn't help."

"You say, 'We tried to wake him,' " Ms. Simpson intervenes. "Who is 'we'?"

"Me and my sister," the mother answers. "She lives next door. Antonio sleeps with her when I work nights."

"Would your sister be able to meet with us here?"

"No, she has five kids of her own, but she'll do whatever you say."

Ms. Simpson plans to use the urine alarm with Antonio so she continues to explore this possible obstacle to therapy. Children in urine alarm treatment must use the apparatus every night, which means that Antonio and his caregivers will need to assemble the alarm on Antonio's bed wherever he sleeps. Although she is hesitant at first, Ms. Simpson decides to follow her plan after Ms. Henderson assures her that the aunt will cooperate.

When Ms. Simpson finishes her enuresis assessment, she asks Antonio and his mother if they have other concerns. Ms. Henderson states that she is worried about a recent deterioration in her son's academic performance. "Antonio is smart, but his grades fell from A's and B's to C's and a D last report card."

Antonio quickly interrupts, "If I'm so smart, how come I keep wetting my bed?"

Ms. Henderson appears surprised, "Baby, wetting the bed has nothing to do with your grades or how smart you are."

Ms. Simpson decides to explore this issue in an individual interview with the child, so she closes the family session and asks Ms. Henderson to return to the waiting room and complete the Child Behavior Checklist for Ages 6 to 18 (CBCL/6–18) and the Tolerance Scale for Enuresis, which Morgan and Young (1975) found to predict premature termination from urine alarm treatment. Ms. Simpson begins her individual meeting with Antonio by having the child complete the Piers-Harris Children's Self-Concept Scale, the Children's Depression Inventory, and the revised version of the Children's Manifest Anxiety Scale. When he finishes, the therapist asks him to elaborate on his earlier statement about wetting the bed.

"If I was smart like my Momma thinks I am, I wouldn't be wetting the bed. We've tried a lot of things, like she told you about, and I still keep wetting every night. I even took those pills and they didn't help."

Ms. Simpson acknowledges the boy's frustration but challenges his belief system by saying, "Being dry at night is something you learn with practice. When you were in first grade, did you know how to multiply and divide numbers like you do now?" He shakes his head as Ms. Simpson continues, "No, but you learned with practice, just like you can learn to stop wetting the bed." She proceeds to teach him about the physiology of continence by explaining how he will tell his brain to signal his bladder to retain fluids until he awakens and can void in an appropriate manner. She inflates a small balloon and says, "I need to hold my fingers together here in order to hold the air in the balloon, don't I? When we get together next week, I am going to teach you to use an alarm that will help you learn how to hold the water in your bladder."

Based on the information available to her, Ms. Simpson decides to collaborate with Antonio's pediatrician, teacher, and school counselor to treat his nocturnal enuresis and address his academic problems. When she presents her plan to the family, they agree, and sign assent and consent forms allowing her to contact Dr. Norton and the school. Because Antonio spends some nights with his aunt, Ms. Simpson also obtains assent and consent to discuss the boy's treatment with her. At the close of the session, she asks Ms. Henderson to use the Nightly Wetting Chart (Figure 11-1) to record Antonio's wet and dry nights during the upcoming week. She also asks the mother to indicate where the boy sleeps each night.

Parent and child responses to the inventories reveal a generally positive picture of a boy who is not exhibiting an excessive number of internalizing or externalizing behaviors. Ms. Henderson did report a significant number of academic problems on the Child Behavior Checklist Competence scales. She also indicated that Antonio was not involved in many out-of-home activities and had recently begun to resist age-appropriate tasks at home (e.g., cleaning his room). Ms. Henderson's responses to the

NAME: Antonio Henderson

Nightly Wetting Chart

Instructions:

In the first row below, please place a "W" in the appropriate box for each night your child wets the bed.

If your child does not wet, place a "D" in the box for that night. Use the row marked "Additional Information" to describe important events related to your child's wetting behavior.

This chart is for the week of March 1–7

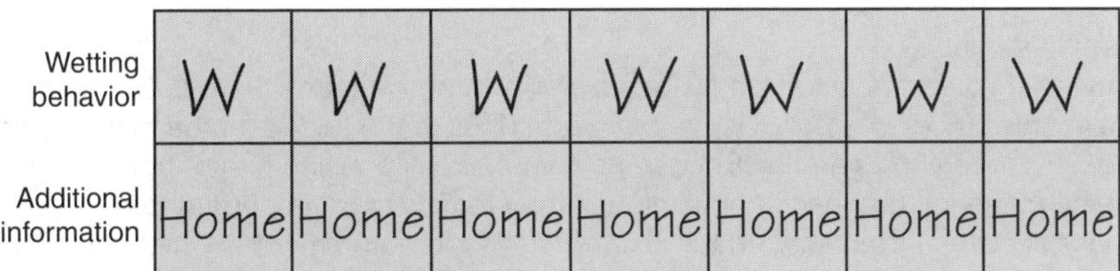

Wetting behavior	W	W	W	W	W	W	W
Additional information	Home	Home	Home	Home	Home	Home	Home

Figure 11–1. A Sample of a Nightly Wetting Chart.

Tolerance Scale for Enuresis reveal that she is tolerant of her son's bed wetting. The child's description of himself is positive but variable. He did not report a clinically significant number of depressive or anxious symptoms; his Piers-Harris total score is within the normal range, although he did indicate problems with his school work.

Between sessions, Ms. Simpson contacts Dr. Norton, who confirms that the boy's wetting is not of organic origin and that a 3-month trial of psychopharmacotherapy was ineffective. When she speaks with Ms. Tomlins, the school counselor, Ms. Simpson learns that Ms. Henderson is very supportive and actively involved in her son's education. Earlier in the school year, the mother asked Ms. Tomlins to meet with Antonio after he complained that fourth grade work was too difficult for him. He told the counselor that he was "dumb" because he was 10 years old and still wet the bed.

Mr. Green, Antonio's teacher, states that the boy submits all of his homework on time but rarely finishes his class work. Likewise, he does well on some tests but fails others. He agrees to provide Ms. Simpson with weekly summaries of Antonio's homework and test scores. Mr. Green also sends a copy of all grades for the previous 2-week period, which will serve as baseline data for interventions designed to improve the boy's school work. On the Teacher Report Form, he describes Antonio as a normal child whose only problem is a deterioration in his academic performance.

Table 11–3

Nighttime Training with the Urine Alarm: A Guide for Parents

The urine alarm we will be using with your child has been found to be a successful method for treating bed wetting for many children. The apparatus contains two elements: a water-sensitive pad that is placed on the mattress and a bedside alarm designed to ring when your child wets. If your alarm malfunctions at any time during treatment, please notify us as soon as possible so repairs can be made.

We ask that you take the following steps to increase the effectiveness of your alarm:

1. It is best if your child's bed is firm. This may require the use of a "bed board" beneath the mattress.
2. Make sure the water-sensitive pad is placed in the middle of the mattress where your child is most likely to wet.
3. Have your child cover the pad with a fitted sheet. Although younger children sometimes need help in placing the sheet on the bed, fitted sheets are preferable to the flat variety because they tend to prevent the pad from shifting on the mattress.
4. Every week before our session, check the strength of the battery in the alarm unit. Do this by turning the switch to "On" and placing the two metal clips in contact with each other. If the battery is weak, you must replace it immediately.
5. Turn on a dim night light every evening in your child's room.
6. Please have the following materials available every night in case your child wets the bed:
   a. a change of sheets
   b. a paper shopping bag for disposal of wet bed linens
   c. a towel for drying the water-sensitive pad
7. Immediately before your child goes to bed, make sure the metal clips are attached to the pad and the alarm unit is switched to "On."
8. With some children, it helps to have them lie face down on the mattress and to refrain from wearing their pajama bottoms.

We want your child to assume as much responsibility as possible for his or her treatment. If a wetting incident occurs, we ask that you supervise the performance of the nighttime steps but refrain from doing them yourself. During the early phase of the treatment program, it may be necessary for you to awaken your child before you supervise him or her in the following steps:

1. When the alarm rings, wake up and stand beside the bed before turning off the alarm.
2. Walk to the bathroom to finish urinating.
3. Go to the bathroom sink and splash water on your face to make sure you are awake.
4. Return to the bedroom, remove the wet sheets, and place them in the shopping bag.
5. Use the towel to dry the water-sensitive pad.
6. Place the pad on the bed, cover it with a dry fitted sheet, and replace the top sheet and blanket.
7. Turn the alarm switch to "On."
8. Return to bed and go back to sleep.

We have found that many children are fascinated with the alarm when we teach them how to use it during the training session. Children are not always as interested when the alarm rings in the middle of the night. Urine alarm treatment requires a lot of effort by children and parents. Encourage your child by praising him or her for performing the nighttime steps. Remember, at the outset of treatment, completion of the steps is more important than dry nights. We have observed that during the course of treatment, many children have more and more dry nights if they complete their steps after every wetting episode.

When Ms. Simpson telephones Ms. Henderson's sister, she learns that the aunt is raising her own five children, ages 2 to 11 years, as well as caring for Antonio and two other relatives. "I just like kids," she says. Ms. Simpson describes the urine alarm and says that she will mail a pamphlet outlining the treatment procedures (Table 11-3). "I'll get Antonio to show me how it works," the aunt replies. Ms. Simpson asks her to help the boy record information on the monitoring charts used in therapy. The two agree to maintain telephone contact during treatment to discuss Antonio's progress and solve problems that might arise.

At the beginning of the second session, Ms. Simpson inspects Antonio's wetting chart and learns that he again wet the bed every night. Knowing that his behavior was being recorded had no reactive effect on the boy's nighttime wetting. Ms. Simpson decides to proceed with urine alarm treatment but first asks Antonio to use a felt-tip marker to record his 2 weeks of wetting data on the Weekly Progress Chart (see Figure 11-2) that will serve as a record of his progress in treatment. With Ms. Henderson observing, Ms. Simpson teaches Antonio to assemble the urine alarm on her office floor. After the pad is attached to the alarm and covered with a standard bed sheet, she instructs him to turn on the alarm, lie on the sheet, and pretend he is asleep. She says that when he hears her make a buzzer sound, he is to stand up and turn off the alarm. She is silent for a few seconds before she makes the alarm sound and guides the boy through the Nightly Procedures Chart (Figure 11-3), which is a revised version of the steps Azrin et al. (1974) included in their Cleanliness Training procedure. Ms. Simpson completes the experiential component of the training by having Antonio lie down again on the sheet and pretend to be asleep. She then has him verbally repeat the steps in order until she is confident he has memorized them.

"It's important that you do the steps yourself," Ms. Simpson adds, "because when we're done, I want you to be able to say, 'I helped myself get dry.' " She emphasizes the importance of following the steps and gives him a Nightly Procedures Chart on which he is to write an "A" for each step he completes independently. If the mother or aunt performs or assists with a step, they are to record a "P" (i.e., adults only) or an "AP" (i.e., Antonio and adults) in the appropriate block. When Antonio has a dry night, he is to draw a straight line through the procedure blocks for that night. The family is to continue recording wet and dry nights on the Nightly Wetting Chart.

At the end of the session, Ms. Simpson meets with Antonio alone to help him use positive self-talk. She begins by asking, "So, what do you think about the alarm?"

"It's ok, but I don't think its going to work," he answers.

"You don't think you can use the alarm to help yourself become dry?"

NAME: Antonio Henderson

Weekly Progress Chart

Wet nights per week	B-1 *	B-2 *	1	2	3	4	5	6	7	8	9	10	11	12
7	X	X	X											
6	X	X	X	X										
5	X	X	X	X										
4	X	X	X	X										
3	X	X	X	X	X		X							
2	X	X	X	X	X	X	X							
1	X	X	X	X	X	X	X	X						
0	X	X	X	X	X	X	X	X	X					

Week of Treatment

Figure 11–2. A Sample of a Weekly Progress Chart.

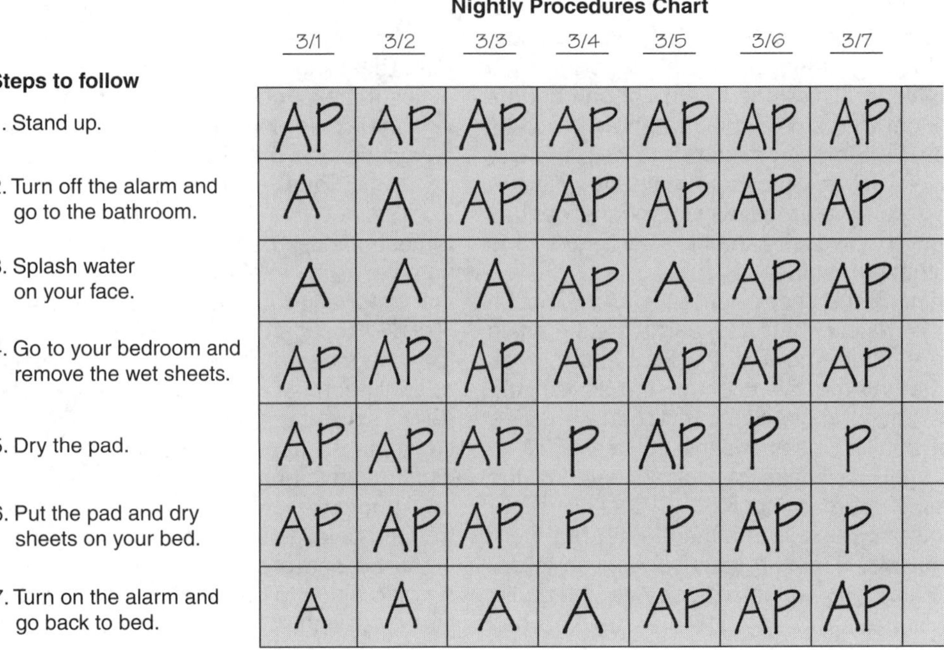

NAME: Antonio Henderson

Nightly Procedures Chart

Steps to follow	3/1	3/2	3/3	3/4	3/5	3/6	3/7	
1. Stand up.	AP	AP	AP	AP	AP	AP	AP	
2. Turn off the alarm and go to the bathroom.	A	A	AP	AP	AP	AP	AP	
3. Splash water on your face.	A	A	A	AP	A	AP	AP	
4. Go to your bedroom and remove the wet sheets.	AP	AP	AP	AP	AP	AP	AP	
5. Dry the pad.	AP	AP	AP	P	AP	P	P	
6. Put the pad and dry sheets on your bed.	AP	AP	AP	P	P	AP	P	
7. Turn on the alarm and go back to bed.	A	A	A	A	AP	AP	AP	

Figure 11–3. A Sample of a Nightly Procedures Chart.

"Nope. Nothing else worked, so why should this help?"

"Well, I believe if you practice your steps every time you wet the bed, you will have more and more dry nights until you are dry all the time. What can you say to yourself so you will begin to believe that practice can help you get dry?"

"Huh"

"Right now it sounds like you are telling yourself, 'Nothing is going to help.' What could you say instead that will help you believe that if you wake up and practice your steps, you will get dry at night?"

"I guess I could say, 'If I do steps, I'll get dry.'"

Ms. Simpson accepts this statement because she understands the empirical support for the urine alarm and the apparent absence of organic causes for the child's wetting. She asks Antonio to repeat his positive self-statement until he is able to do so without hesitation. The two of them practice having him say his usual negative self-statement and then replacing it with his positive alternative.

When the family returns the next week, they report that Antonio has wet every night, with the alarm sounding within 2 hours after bedtime. Ms. Simpson also learns that the boy spent the week with his mother because she did not work at night. As the child completes his Weekly Progress Chart, he says, "I'm not getting any better, am I?" Ms. Simpson agrees that his frequency of wet nights is unchanged, but she emphasizes that completing the steps is more important than dry nights at the outset of treatment. Unfortunately, most of his Nightly Procedures Chart contains "AP's," with a scattering of "A's" early in the week.

"Antonio just doesn't get up when the alarm rings," Ms. Henderson says. "He's a hard sleeper, and he won't do his steps by himself." Ms. Simpson mentions that many parents have observed the same initial reaction to the alarm but discovered that their children did awaken as treatment progressed.

When she questions the family about their response to each wetting episode, Ms. Simpson discovers a consistent pattern. Ms. Henderson arises when the alarm rings, enters Antonio's bedroom, and turns off the alarm before awakening him. Ms. Simpson describes how interrupting the chain of behaviors in the nightly procedures deprives Antonio of the chance to experience the crucial steps of awakening and standing beside his bed in response to the alarm. She encourages the mother to arouse her son and have him stand up and turn off the alarm. Because Antonio did not experience a complete learning trial during the week, Ms. Simpson conducts an abbreviated training session with the alarm, including rote recitation of the nightly procedures.

During her individual time with him, Ms. Simpson asks Antonio to evaluate his efforts during the previous week. As he looks at his procedures chart, he says, "I started out alright, but I stopped." Ms. Simpson reminds him of the need to perform the nightly procedures every time he wets so he will be able to help himself become dry. "Maybe something's wrong with me," he continues. "I mean, maybe I'm never gonna be dry." Ms. Simpson asks if he learned to ride a bike or kick a goal in soccer the first time he tried. "Nope, but I kept on trying," he answers. She asks if he used his positive self-statement during the week, and he indicates that he had not. She then has him repeat the statement and practice replacing his negative self-talk with the positive statement.

After the session, Ms. Simpson telephones Antonio's aunt to discuss the urine alarm procedures. She emphasizes the importance of having the boy stand beside his bed before he turns off the alarm. The aunt agrees and then states that Antonio would be staying with her at least 4 nights this week. Ms. Simpson reminds her of the need to maintain records of the boy's behavior.

At the outset of the fourth session, Ms. Henderson announces, "I don't know if this is worse on me or Antonio. I guess I'm looking for a quick end to Antonio's problem." When Ms. Simpson inspects Antonio's charts, she finds data for every night of the week. She discovers that he spent 5 nights with his aunt and had a total of 1 dry night, which occurred at home with his mother. More importantly, he performed most of the steps himself, including getting up and turning off the alarm. She praises the family for their efforts, especially Antonio, who completes his Weekly Progress Chart and announces, "This week I told myself that I can be dry if I do my steps."

During their individual time together, Ms. Simpson asks him to describe his hard work during the week. "I just got up and did my steps," he answers.

"What could you say to pat yourself on the back for your hard work?"

He smiles and then replies, "Atta boy."

Both of them laugh at this comment before Ms. Simpson says, "I like that, Antonio. You're right. You worked hard this week and you deserve an 'Atta boy.' " She encourages him to reinforce himself for his success with the alarm and in other areas of his life. At the end of the session, she asks him to discuss how he could improve his performance of the nightly procedures during the coming week.

Between sessions, Ms. Simpson reviews the information she received from Mr. Green. Antonio appears to be completing more of his class work, but his grades continue to be mostly B's and C's. Ms. Simpson contacts Ms. Tomlins, who says, "I know Antonio has the ability, but he just doesn't seem to believe he can do well in school anymore."

Antonio is noticeably excited when he and his mother arrive for the fifth session. He walks into Ms. Simpson's office with his wetting chart in hand and announces, "I had three dry nights and I did all my steps." Ms. Simpson praises him for his effort and progress. She also congratulates the mother for her support.

"Antonio is trying really hard," Ms. Henderson says. "I think he is going to beat this thing." Ms. Simpson agrees and then emphasizes how Antonio is helping himself become dry.

During her individual meeting with the child, she reinforces his use of positive self-talk, has him evaluate his performance of the nightly procedures, and encourages him to praise himself for his accomplishments to date. She then introduces the topic of school to help generalize his emerging self-confidence beyond his progress in urine alarm treatment. "How are things going for you at school?" she asks.

He hesitates and then answers, "I'm in gifted class."

"How does a student get into gifted class?"

"You've got to be real smart," he answers. "I'm smarter than the other kids in my class, because I get to go to gifted class and they don't."

"So both your Momma and your teachers think you are a pretty smart guy, huh? What do you think?"

Antonio shrugs his shoulders and then says, "I don't like school. Fourth grade's too hard." He describes how the homework requires too much time, the tests are too difficult, and his teacher dislikes him.

Ms. Simpson listens and then replies, "Do you remember how you used to tell yourself that you would never have any dry nights? And how you started to tell yourself that you could get dry? Maybe we need to come up with something you can say to help yourself believe you can do well at school."

Antonio nods his head in agreement and then suggests, "How about, 'I can get good grades if I try hard'?" Ms. Simpson has him repeat this statement and practice using it as an alternative for his negative self-statements about school. During subsequent weeks, his academic performance continues to improve. On one of his weekly grade reports, Mr. Green writes, "Antonio is doing much better in class."

As treatment progresses, Antonio has more dry nights. Ms. Simpson maintains regular contact with his aunt to ensure consistent use of the alarm. During the 2 weeks before the eighth session, he wets his bed only three times. His grades are all A's and B's, and he appears to have a more positive attitude about school. Ms. Henderson and her sister consistently follow the treatment procedures and make sure the urine alarm is on the boy's bed every night. When the mother completed the Child Behavior Checklist before therapy, she reported that Antonio was not involved in activities outside of the home and was no longer completing household tasks. Although these concerns may not require remediation, Ms. Simpson decides that they are appropriate targets for education/development and prevention.

In her work with the Hendersons, Ms. Simpson learns that Antonio wants to play youth soccer. She also knows that at age 10 years, he does not receive an allowance but is able to purchase toys and other items with money his mother gives him. In her eighth session with the family, she says, "A few weeks ago someone mentioned that Antonio would like to play soccer." She asks mother and son to discuss the issue and then helps them to devise a plan so Antonio can join the local soccer program. As an education/development strategy, this intervention will enable the child to interact with children outside of school and hopefully develop friendships to enhance his social self-esteem. Later in the tenth session, Ms. Simpson helps the family design a system for rewarding Antonio with a weekly allowance when he makes his bed, cleans his room, and empties the trash. Intended to prevent misunderstandings about the relationship between work and remuneration, the program involves charting his behavior and using money as tokens the boy may use to purchase items or activities of interest to him.

Antonio records his first string of 7 consecutive dry nights during his eighth week using the alarm. Ms. Simpson continues to divide each session into a family meeting to discuss weekly progress and an individual session to continue self-control training. By the tenth session, Antonio has been dry for 16 consecutive nights. Ms. Simpson asks him to evaluate his progress.

"The alarm really works," he says.

Ms. Simpson responds, "I think you did the work. You're the one who practiced all your steps when the alarm rang." Antonio smiles and nods his head. "I think it's time we took the alarm off your bed," she says. "How do you feel about that?"

Ms. Henderson interrupts, "I think that's a good idea because I heard Antonio go to the bathroom in the middle of the night instead of wetting his bed. I'm real proud of him."

Antonio agrees that removing the alarm is a good idea. Ms. Simpson tells him that practice now involves getting up and going to the bathroom whenever his bladder feels full. During their individual meeting, they revise his positive self-statement to reflect his progress: "If I get up in the night, I'll be dry." Ms. Simpson schedules a 2-week delay before the family's next appointment. She tells Antonio and his mother that the next session will be their last if he continues to do well. Antonio remains continent, so during the final session, Ms. Simpson again congratulates him for his hard work in therapy. She prepares him for the possibility of relapse by saying, "Sometimes kids have an accident at night. If that happens, don't think it means you are going to start wetting the bed again. Just tell yourself, 'That was an accident. If I get up in the night, I'll be dry.' "

She gives Antonio and his mother a 2-month supply of Nightly Wetting Charts to record his weekly progress. The mother agrees to mail the data to Ms. Simpson every week and says that she will contact her if the need arises. The Hendersons submit the charts, which reveal that Antonio continues to be continent. On the final chart, Ms. Henderson reports that Antonio is completing household tasks and beginning to understand the value of money. She also writes, "Antonio is still dry. He likes school and soccer. Thanks for your help."

▪ ▪ ▪

In this case example, the therapist's primary intervention was a commonly used behavioral conditioning approach for the treatment of nocturnal enuresis. Ms. Simpson also included a cognitive component to address Antonio's attitudes about his nighttime wetting and academic performance. She collaborated with his pediatrician and maintained regular contact with the school and the aunt who cared for the child when his mother was at work. Many children enrolled in urine alarm treatment sleep in the same bed every night. In families such as the Hendersons, members of the extended kinship system function as caregivers and must be involved in therapy to ensure consistent use of the alarm. It is worth noting that the pretreatment assessment revealed that Antonio was not exhibiting a significant number of internalizing and externalizing behaviors. These data are clinically relevant because Geffken et al. (1986) found that children who prematurely terminated urine alarm treatment were more likely to report lower self-esteem and be described by parents as having more behavior problems than were children who completed treatment.

Another important consideration in this case is that Antonio, his mother, and his aunt wanted him to stop wetting his bed. Ms. Henderson was tolerant of her son's enuresis, which Morgan and Young (1975) found to be associated with completion of urine alarm treatment. And the family had unsuccessfully used a number of techniques to eliminate the boy's wetting. Wagner and Johnson (1988) highlighted the importance of these factors when they found that more tolerant parents who had used more techniques with children who did not exhibit behavior problems were more likely to complete behavioral conditioning with the urine alarm. A child who is uncooperative or routinely misbehaves or whose parents are less tolerant or made few attempts to remediate the child's wetting may require alternative treatments for nocturnal enuresis.

The case of Antonio also illustrates the integration of education/development, prevention, and remediation in treatment. Ms. Simpson began with remedial interventions designed to address the family's presenting problems of nocturnal enuresis and declining academic performance. As these improved, she implemented her education/development and prevention strategies. Playing youth soccer facilitated the development of friendships and prevented future isolation from peers. This activity also gave Antonio another avenue to more positive self-efficacy. With Ms. Simpson's encouragement, the family was able to initiate systematic reinforcement for Antonio's completion of household tasks. This program became an introductory employment experience that served as a model for jobs and careers in adolescence and adulthood.

SUMMARY

Behavioral techniques are so integrated into our everyday lives that therapists cannot avoid using them in their interactions with children. All clinicians, regardless of their theoretical orientation, smile or praise clients for appropriate behaviors. Successful parents and teachers reinforce children for positive actions and penalize them when their misbehavior is thought to warrant punishment or termination of reinforcement. Unfortunately, techniques designed to increase desirable behaviors and decrease undesirable actions are not always used in an appropriate manner. Behavioral clinicians attend to the inconsistent and inappropriate ways these methods are used while helping clients to successfully apply behavioral principles in everyday life. The empirical orientation of this approach has contributed to the development of many behavioral and cognitive-behavioral techniques for children. Chapter 16 discusses recent developments in constructivist therapies that represent an expansion of existing cognitive principles and methods.

12

Family Systems Theory

Barbara Okun (1990) observed that when therapists are exposed to a systems model, their conceptualization of client problems is forever changed. Most of the theorists discussed so far in this text have focused on the child as an individual. Trait theorists, such as Freud, described biological and social factors that affect children's development. Proponents of the transactional perspective, such as Virginia Axline, emphasized the child's actualization of the self. Interactional theorists, including B. F. Skinner and J. B. Watson, studied how children's behaviors are affected by environmental events.

Family systems theorists transformed these intrapersonal and interactional versions of child development with their organismic conceptualization of development. According to this model, the child is the symptom bearer of dysfunction in the family system. As such, the focus of intervention is the family unit rather than the individual child. Family systems theory is relevant for all clinicians, even those who have limited contact with families. Lockhart and Keys (1998), for example, described how school counselors must understand the effects that family dynamics have on students' performance in the classroom.

This chapter explores the historical and theoretical development of family systems theory. It also considers how cultural differences and a child's developmental level can affect family functioning. Family systems theory can be viewed as a bridge between the linear and ecological interpretations of child development. For the most part, this approach was formulated during the second half of the 20th century, but families have existed across the millenia.

HISTORICAL BACKGROUND

This section examines two historical periods. The first is the development of the family and the many changes this system has undergone over the centuries, especially the past 200 years in the United States. The second is the emergence of family systems theory and therapy in the latter half of the 20th century. Family-based treatment was once considered controversial, but it became an accepted method of treating childhood problems as a result of the pioneering work of researchers and clinicians in the field.

The History of the Family

One characteristic that seems to describe families over the course of history is the structural dominance of fathers (Habenstein & Olson, 1992). For example, in upper-class families of the Roman Republic (509–77 B.C.), mothers were central to the operation of the home and nursing and bonding with their infants, but fathers were seen as being the ultimate authority in the family (Luepnitz, 1988). Fathers were also considered to be the head of household during the 16th and 17th century, but parents were more likely to share the responsibilities of rearing their children. As Ozment (1983) stated, "The bond between father and child was understood to be as intimate and as enduring as that between mother and child" (p. 132).

What we know as the modern family began with the emergence of the bourgeois class in mid-18th century Europe when fathers started to work outside of the home and mothers assumed responsibility for parenting children. According to Luepnitz (1988), it was at this point when "maternal guilt was born—or at least given a new lease on life" (p. 127) and mothers were held responsible for whatever their children became. Concurrent with this change was the ever-increasing detachment of fathers from everyday family life. According to Luepnitz, it was at this time when the foundation was set for contemporary family concepts such as "overinvolved mother," "disengaged father," and "triangulation" (p. 126).

Families in the United States have changed significantly over the past 200 years. Hernandez (1997) described six demographic factors related to this transformation: (1) the decline in agricultural employment, (2) a decrease in family size, (3) an increase in education, (4) mothers' participation in the labor force, (5) the increase in mother-only families, and (6) children's exposure to poverty. The rise in non-farm employment brought about a significant decline in the number of children living in families in which parents and children worked together on the land. Hernandez noted that in 1830, 70% of the children in the United States grew up in this environment. At the beginning of the 21st century, relatively few parents are employed on family farms.

Concurrent with this change was a decline in family size. Specifically, the median number of children per family declined from 7.3 in 1865 to 2.6 in 1930 (Hernandez, 1997). Although this figure fluctuated during later decades (e.g., the Baby Boom at the middle of the 20th century), the number of children per home in 1998 was 1.02 in European American families, 1.21 in African American families, and 1.46 in Hispanic American families (U.S. Bureau of the Census, 1999). The decline in family size was coupled with an increase in the number of years that children were enrolled in school. Hernandez reported that in 1870, 50% of 5- to 19-year-old children and young adults attended school. In 1998, approximately 83% of the U.S. population had completed at least high school (U.S. Bureau of the Census, 1999).

Beginning in 1940, there was an increase in mothers' employment outside the home. Hernandez (1997) noted that in 1940, 10% of children had a mother who was employed. By 1998, this figure had increased to 68% in married-couple families and 72% in mother-only homes (U.S. Bureau of the Census, 1999). During the second half of the 20th century, there was an increase in the number of children living in single-parent homes headed by their mothers. In 1980, 18% of U.S. children were in this group; by 1998, the figure had climbed to 23% (U.S. Bureau of the Census, 1999). Later in this chapter, we examine how the traditional family composed of two biological parents—one a resource provider and the other a rearer of children—has been replaced by a variety of structural arrangements. The financial well being of families in the United States has also changed. As we might expect, poverty rates for children were high during the Great Depression (e.g., 38% in 1939) (Hernandez, 1997). What is surprising are figures indicating that in 1997, approximately 20% of children in this country were still living in poverty (U.S. Bureau of the Census, 1999).

A History of Family Systems Theory

Family systems theory and therapies were developed in reaction to the traditional psychodynamic approach. Simply stated, researchers and practitioners discovered that traditional methods were not effective with all clients and presenting problems. When family therapies were first tried in the late 1940s and early 1950s, attention was focused on individual clients or identified patients. Because of what Okun (1990) described as "the strong taboos against involvement with clients' families" (p. 299), therapists were reluctant to practice or acknowledge their use of family-based techniques. As a result, early work in the area progressed at independent sites across the United States and with chronic client problems that did not respond to traditional therapies.

The initial work on family systems theory and therapy involved research with schizophrenic clients and their families. Before the development of psychotropic medications, schizophrenia was a significant mental health problem that was resistant to traditional interventions. Research groups were independently established at four locations in the United States: the Bateson group in Palo Alto, California; the Lidz group at Yale University; the Bowen group at the Menninger Clinic in Topeka, Kansas, and later at the National Institutes of Mental Health (NIMH) in Bethesda, Maryland; and the Wynn group that followed Bowen at the NIMH (Okun, 1990). Based on their study of communication in the families of schizophrenic patients, these pioneers in family therapy recognized the importance of the systemic influences but were unaware of each others' work until the late 1950s when the professional community was more accepting of this method (Okun, 1990).

Obviously, the roots of family therapy predate the work of these research groups. Sigmund Freud's treatment of Little Hans involved consultation with the boy's father rather than individual therapy with the child. Alfred Adler and his associates developed parent education groups to teach more effective child-rearing techniques. What distinguishes Freud and Adler from later family systems theorists is the attention that systems theorists gave to the family as a unit rather than to individual members. Interest in the family system led to the development of terms such as the *double bind* (i.e., Bateson group), *marital schism and skew* (i.e., Lidz group), *pseudomutuality* (i.e., Wynne group), and *undifferentiated family ego mass* (i.e., Bowen group). After researchers had the opportunity to communicate with each other, they borrowed and adapted concepts that they integrated into their respective theories. In this chapter and the next, we examine the theory and technique of seven family systems approaches: psychodynamic, multigenerational, humanistic, structural, behavioral, strategic, and solution focused. But first we explore the historical development of these methods.

Child psychiatrist Nathan Ackerman (1908–1971) incorporated psychoanalytic principles into his method of family therapy. Ackerman became interested in family dynamics when he practiced in a small mining town in Pennsylvania during the Depression. In his work with unemployed miners, Ackerman (1967) observed the systemic consequences of a father's loss of his job:

> The man who could no longer bring home his pay envelope was no longer the head of the family. He lost his position of respect and authority in the family; the woman drove him into the streets. Often, she turned for comfort to her first son. Mother and son then usurped the leadership position within the family. (p. 126)

Many readers will object to Ackerman's negative portrayal of mothers. His views of women were very traditional and based largely on his mother, who Bloch and Simon (1982, p. xv) described as the person who assumed responsibility for "nurturing, supporting, darning, cooking, counseling, and doing all those wise and wonderful things" for her family.

In 1935, Ackerman became a resident in neuropsychiatry at the Menninger Clinic in Topeka, Kansas, where he later practiced at the Southard School for problem children (Gurman & Kniskern, 1981). By the mid-1940s, he had begun to examine the intrapsychic and interpersonal concerns of the children and parents he treated together in family sessions (Sharf, 2000). Ackerman shared his model with others through workshops and books such as *The Psychodynamics of Family Life* (Ackerman, 1958), the first text published on family diagnosis and treatment (Sayger, 1992). Ackerman was also the founding editor for the journal *Family Process*. During his career, he taught at different institutions, including Columbia University and Yeshiva University. In 1960, he founded The Family Institute, a family therapy training center that was renamed the Ackerman Institute for Family Therapy after his death (Bloch & Simon, 1982).

Many of the early family theorists were trained in the use of psychoanalysis, so they adapted Freudian principles in their models of the family. Consider object relations family therapy, which Kilpatrick and Kilpatrick (1991) described as a modern "bridge between psychoanalysis—the study of individuals—and family theory, the study of social relationships" (p. 208). Building upon the work of Melanie Klein, Ronald Fairbairn, D. W. Winnicott, and Otto Kernberg, object relations family theorists have explored such issues as transference and countertransference within the context of the family system. Two contemporary writers in this field are psychiatrists David and Jill Scharff. David Scharff was trained in the United States and Jill Scharff was trained in Great Britain, but they followed a similar developmental path that included training and clinical experience in individual, group, and family interventions. In *Object Relations Family Therapy*, Scharff and Scharff (1987) articulated a family systems approach that is an integration of the intrapsychic and interpersonal realms.

Psychiatrist Murray Bowen became disenchanted with his psychoanalytic training and gradually rejected the techniques of individual psychoanalysis in favor of a method that conceptualized human behavior within the context of the family system (Bowen, 1966). According to Papero (1991), Bowen was committed to the scientific study of the family. Early in his career, he worked at the Menninger Clinic. From 1954 to 1959, he conducted research with the families of patients with schizophrenia at the NIMH. In publications such as "The Use of Family Theory in Clinical Practice" (Bowen, 1966) and a collection of his works titled *Family Therapy in Clinical Practice* (Bowen, 1978), he described the family as an emotional system and emphasized the role that multigenerational factors play in a child's development. Bowen was actively involved in the training of family therapists. In 1968, he helped establish the first postgraduate training program in family therapy at Georgetown University (Papero, 1991).

Virginia Satir (1916–1988) also had an interest in training family therapists. In 1955, she was instrumental in establishing at the Illinois State Psychiatric Institute what Leupnitz (1988) identified as the first training program for family therapists. Her fascination with family dynamics began at an early age. When she was 5 years old, she became what she called "a children's detective on parents" because "there was so much that went on between my parents that made little or no sense to me" (Satir & Bitter, 1991, p. 16). As an adult, Satir studied to be a teacher and worked in the classroom for 6 years. In order to better understand her students, she visited the homes of more than 200 children to learn more about their parents. These experiences helped her decide to enter graduate school to pursue a degree in social work.

During the years when she was a part-time instructor at the Illinois State Psychiatric Institute, Satir was also engaged in private practice. She became interested in multigenerational influences on the family as well as the work that Don Jackson and Gregory Bateson were conducting on family communications (Satir & Bitter, 1991). In *Conjoint Family Therapy*, Satir (1964) described how clinicians must establish a therapeutic relationship with the family in order to facilitate supportive communication within the system. Her work represents an integration of the Bateson group's communication model and the humanistic principles espoused by Carl Rogers, including his concept of the fully functioning person. Therefore, her approach is less oriented to the treatment of psychopathology and more focused on the optimal development of the family's potential.

Salvador Minuchin was born in rural Argentina, lived in Israel, and developed his structural approach to family therapy in the United States (Colapinto, 1991). In the early 1960s, Minuchin worked at the Wiltwyck School for Boys in New York. There he gained the material that he subsequently published in *Families of the Slums* (Minuchin, Montalvo, Guerney, Rosman, & Schumer, 1967). Minuchin's Wiltwyck experiences taught him that the therapeutic techniques used with middle-class clients were not effective with delinquent youth from dysfunctional and disadvantaged families. Minuchin eventually left the Wilwyck School to join the Philadelphia Child Guidance Clinic, where he developed a training program in family therapy and described his innovative structural approach in *Families and Family Therapy* (Minuchin, 1974). In collaboration with Children's Hospital of Philadelphia, Minuchin applied his structural family therapy to the treatment of children with various medical disorders, including asthma, juvenile onset diabetes, and anorexia nervosa (Colapinto, 1991). He discovered that traditional supportive therapies were not effective in treating these life-threatening conditions, so he devised a more directive method that challenged families to confront crises. His colleagues and he later presented the results of this work in *Psychosomatic Families* (Minuchin, Rosman, & Baker, 1978).

Strategic family systems theorists such as Jay Haley and Cloe Madanes were influenced by Bateson's work on family communication and Milton Erickson's use of hypnosis and creative techniques. In 1953, Bateson employed Haley as a member of his Palo Alto research team (Okun, 1990). Based on the group's work with the families of schizophrenic patients, Bateson and his associates integrated communications theory with systems theory (Schilson, 1991). They observed that family transactions are sometimes paradoxical because they contain contradictory messages (i.e., the double bind). The team's work in this area proved to be significant to Haley's professional development.

While at Palo Alto, Haley and colleague John Weakland made regular visits to Phoenix, Arizona, where Erickson had conducted private practice since 1948. Haley (1973) reflected on these visits with the master therapist:

> Despite his two attacks of polio and his need to walk awkwardly with a cane, he was vigorous and in good health. His office was in his home, a small room just off the dining room, and his living room was his waiting

> room. Several of his eight children were still small and at home in the 1950s, and so his patients mingled with his family. His home was a modest brick house on a quiet street, and I often wondered what patients from various parts of the country, who expected a leading psychiatrist to have a more pretentious office, must have thought. (pp. 9–10)

Haley (1973) described Erickson's approach in *Uncommon Therapy: The Psychiatric Techniques of Milton H. Erickson, M.D.*, and he integrated Erickson's techniques into his strategic family systems therapy.

In 1967, Haley moved from California to the East Coast, where he joined Salvador Minuchin and became director of family research at the Philadelphia Child Guidance Clinic. His experience in Philadelphia helped him expand his theoretical position to include elements of Minuchin's structural model (e.g., family boundaries) (Schilson, 1991). In 1976, Haley moved to Washington, D.C., where he joined the University of Maryland Medical School and established a training program based on his strategic model. Haley was joined there by Cloe Madanes, whom he had met while both were on staff at the Philadelphia Child Guidance Clinic. Similar to Minuchin, Madanes was born in Argentina. Her initial training was in psychoanalysis, but she became interested in Erickson's work while she was at Jackson's Mental Research Institute from 1965 to 1971 (Schilson, 1991). Similar to Haley, Madanes became active in training therapists through the Strategic Therapy Institute in Washington, D.C.

Brief-term family therapies have become more popular in recent years. According to De Shazer et al. (1986), Erickson's (1954) "Special Techniques of Brief Hypnotherapy" represents the first published work in brief therapies. In the 1960s, brief-term approaches to family therapy were studied at the Mental Research Institute in Palo Alto, leading to the publication of Weakland, Fisch, Watzlawick, and Bodin's (1974) "Brief Therapy: Focused Problem Resolution" and Haley's works on strategic interventions. Meanwhile in Milan, Italy, Mara Selvini-Palazzoli and her colleagues were exploring the use of innovative brief treatments for families (e.g., Selvini, 1988). In Milwaukee, Wisconsin, Steve De Shazer established the Brief Family Center, where his associates and he developed solution-focused brief family therapy (e.g., De Shazer, 1985; De Shazer, 1988). Brief family therapies are "not just less of the same" that is used in traditional treatments (De Shazer, 1985, p. 4). Instead, these methods require the use of unique techniques that are based on specific theoretical principles.

THEORETICAL FOUNDATIONS

The theoretical foundations for family systems therapy can be found in the works of writers such as Ludwig von Bertalanffy, Norbert Wiener, and Humberto Maturana. Bertalanffy, a biologist, believed that all systems share certain characteristics. According to his general systems theory, biological (e.g., living organisms) and social (e.g., families) systems are hierarchical, contain subsystems, and possess "interrelationships of parts to each other and to the whole system" (Sharf, 2000, p. 503). Translated into family theory, his view emphasizes how family members interact and relate to the family unit. Wiener, a mathematician, described a cybernetic model characterized by "circular information flow and homeostatic regulatory mechanisms" (Okun, 1990, p. 295). According to this view, the family is a system of interacting members who send and receive messages. Psychosocial symptoms or problems are interpreted relative to the function they serve in maintaining the status quo in the family.

Okun (1990) differentiated the models of Wiener and Bertalanffy from the constructivist theory of Humberto Maturana (Maturana & Varela, 1973/1980). Although the former are more mechanistic and reductionistic, Maturana's model takes into account the evolving and ever-changing nature of human social systems as well as the individual's role in constructing reality. According to this model, a child's behavior serves a function in the surrounding social environment; represents the complementary interaction of biological, intrapsychic, and interpersonal factors; and is influenced by the child's development and life history (O'Connor & Ammen, 1997). Children are viewed as active agents in this process who make meaning of their lives through their experiences.

Aspects of these models have been incorporated into different family systems theories. This section explores key concepts of various family therapies. Specifically, it examines constructs such as family identities and roles (Ackerman, 1958); differentiation, fusion, and emotional triangles (Bowen, 1966); self-esteem and communication patterns (Satir, 1972); family homeostasis, boundaries, and subsystems (Minuchin, 1974); and the family life cycle (Haley, 1973). Later the chapter explores the principles of brief therapies, but we begin with Nathan Ackerman's contributions to family systems theory.

Psychodynamic Family Systems Theory

Nathan Ackerman is important to the development of family therapy because in the 1940s, he worked with children and parents together rather than treating troubled children alone (Sharf, 2000). He expanded on the intrapsychic focus of traditional psychodynamic theories and described how the internal conflicts of family members are related to interactions within the family system. Therefore, the resolution of family problems requires consideration of the interpersonal aspects of intrapersonal conflicts. To explain the relationship between personal and interpersonal elements, Ackerman (1958) used concepts such as family identities, social roles, and role relationships to describe family functioning.

Each of us possesses a concept of self as well as identities associated with different social groups, including our families. According to Ackerman (1958), identity "qualifies a particular kind of person or persons, what they stand for, where they are going, their purpose and meaning in life" (p. 82). A child's identities of the self and family are interrelated and undergo transitions during the course of development. For example, Ackerman (1958) described parent–child relationships as follows:

> This relationship begins with the symbiosis of the child-mother pair; it is molded by processes of primary identification of child and parents; and it undergoes further change as the child gradually differentiates his separate self and expands his identification with other family members. (p. 83)

The family develops identities based on the roles of its members (e.g., disciplinarian) and the rules that govern family interactions (e.g., child-rearing practices).

How a family and the individuals within it develop is affected by members' role expectations for the mother, father, and children. In healthy families, parents assume responsibility for rearing their children. In larger families, older siblings have responsibilities different from those of younger brothers and sisters. But family roles extend beyond the family unit. In addition to being a parent within the family, a father or mother may have the roles of employee, school board member, and neighbor in the community. A child is a son or daughter as well as a student at school and a playmate in the neighborhood. Individual roles are established based on each person's goals for self-fulfillment and the familial and societal values that define acceptable behavior (Ackerman, 1958).

Ackerman (1958) discussed how family roles affect the stability and quality of family relationships. Families achieve stability in healthy and unhealthy ways. In some, familial rules are rigidly enforced to maintain control in response to conflict. In others, a more flexible style allows the family system and its members to grow and adapt to change. An important aspect of a family's reaction to conflict is its pattern of role complementarity, which Ackerman (1958) defined as "specific patterns of family role relations that provide satisfactions, avenues of solution of conflict, support for a needed self-image, and buttressing of crucial forms of defenses against anxiety" (p. 86). Complementarity can be positive or negative, and it involves intrapsychic and interpersonal elements. Families that exhibit positive complementarity handle conflict in a creative manner that facilitates personal and interpersonal growth. Negative complementarity may control family conflict, but personal and familial identities are compromised in the process.

Another psychodynamic model of the family is object relations family theory, which incorporates concepts such as anxiety, the unconscious, insight, and transference and countertransference. Chapter 6 discussed how interpersonal relationships, especially caregiver–infant interactions, are a significant component of object relations theory. Proponents of object relations family theory share this interest in family relationships, both within the family and with the external world (Scharff & Scharff, 1987). Object relations family theorists are interested in early childhood experiences, especially the young child's relationships with primary significant others. When early caregiver–child conflicts remain unresolved into adulthood, parents may rely on dysfunctional internal objects and project negative feelings onto their own children. As Scharff and Scharff (1987) noted, "When a couple has children, unmetabolized remnants of the repressed object relationships now pose a new threat to the family" (p. 19). Scharff and Scharff considered the marital relationship to be a significant force in a child's development of internal objects. If the parents are a loving couple who care for their child, the youngster will develop healthy object relations. If the marital relationship is conflicted and the child's physical and emotional needs are not met, the youngster will approach later relationships with apprehension.

Chapter 6 discussed the holding environment. Scharff and Scharff (1987) elaborated on this concept as it relates to the family when they differentiated centered and contextual holding. Centered holding occurs as a result of the primary caregiver's focused attention to the child's physical and emotional needs. Contextual holding is "an environmental extension of the mother's presence" (Scharff & Scharff, 1987, p. 60) that exists within the physical and social environment, which includes the spousal relationship, extended family, and neighborhood. When the mother is the primary caregiver, contextual holding can be provided by the father, grandparents or other members of the extended family, babysitters, and neighbors. Again, the parents' marital relationship is thought to be a significant influence. When a couple loves and cares for each other, the child can develop in a safe, stable, and secure environment. In healthy families, members are committed to the family as a unit (i.e., contextual holding) as well as the welfare of individual members (i.e., centered holding).

Multigenerational Family Systems Theory

Murray Bowen viewed the family as an emotional system that is the result of "the transmission of family patterns over multiple generations" (Bowen, 1966, p. 376). Bowen described multigenerational transmission as a process by which each spouse approaches the marital relationship in accordance with experiences gained in his or her family of origin. To describe this process, Bowen expanded on the work of Ackerman and the object relations theorists by developing concepts such as differentiation and fusion, undifferentiated family ego mass, and the emotional triangle.

Bowen (1966) described differentiation and fusion in terms of a person's emotional and intellectual functioning. When these two domains are sufficiently fused with each other, affect dominates and an inflexible approach to decision making emerges. The individual tends to be emotionally reactive. With increasing differentiation between emotion and intellect, decision making becomes more adaptive. How a person displays differentiation depends on the level of anxiety or tension in the surrounding social environment. As Bowen (1976) stated:

> People with the most fusion have most of the human problems, and those with the most differentiation, the fewest; but there can be people with intense fusion who manage to keep their relationships in balance, who are never subjected to severe stress, who never develop symptoms, and who appear normal. However, their life adjustments are tenuous, and, if they are stressed into dysfunction, the impairment can be chronic or permanent. (pp. 66)

Undifferentiated family ego mass is the emotional closeness that exists within families (Bowen, 1966). Problems develop when family members are so emotionally close (i.e., fusion) that the needs of the family supercede those of individual members. When fusion occurs across generational lines, the parents in a nuclear family are emotionally undifferentiated from their families of origin. When a mother and father remain fused to their parents, they have difficulty establishing and maintaining the emotional system within their nuclear family. The outcome can be unresolved disputes regarding spousal and parental roles and responsibilities. If the father was raised by authoritarian parents who used physical punishment and the mother was reared by authoritative parents who relied on reasoning and consistent limits for children, spousal conflicts can arise when the couple tries to rear their children. The more each parent is emotionally fused with his or her family of origin, the more difficult it is for the couple to develop a cooperative approach to parenting.

Bowen (1976) presented his concept of the emotional triangle to explain the family's response to conflict and tension. Described as "the basic building block of any emotional system" (Bowen, 1976, p. 76), triangles develop when unresolved stress in a two-person relationship (e.g., mother and father) is so uncomfortable that a third family member becomes involved. When the emotional relationships within a family are appropriately differentiated, triangulation can have positive outcomes. An adolescent who uses her problem-solving skills to help her younger siblings resolve a brief dispute is triangulating with these children in a healthy manner. The same cannot be said of triangulation that is emotionally driven and occurs repeatedly. In families in which the spousal relationship is conflicted, the parents may attempt to reduce their marital tension by involving the most vulnerable and least-differentiated family member. Typically a child, this third person becomes triangulated with the parents by misbehaving in order to direct attention away from the spousal conflict. Although triangulation may have the short-term benefit of reducing tension, it inhibits a child's differentiation from the parents and delays the parents' resolution of marital difficulties.

Bowen (1976) described how stressed families are composed of interlocking emotional triangles whose composition changes as family members realign to reduce tension. Consider a couple that is experiencing marital conflict. In an attempt to reduce tension, the parents triangulate with their 10-year-old son, whose academic performance has recently deteriorated. If this emotional triangle were to prove ineffective in reducing tension, the couple may triangulate with their 11-year-old daughter, who is unwilling to complete the household tasks assigned to her. Of course, repeated and extended triangulation is problematic because it enables the family to remain intact without addressing the familial conflict (e.g., marital discord) that precipitated this dysfunctional relationship pattern.

Humanistic Family Systems Theory

Known for her contributions to the communications approach to family therapy, Virginia Satir (1972) identified four problem areas in troubled families: self-worth or self-esteem, communication patterns, rules, and contact with society. Satir (1972) stated that a person with high self-worth exhibits "integrity, honesty, responsibility, compassion, love" (p. 22). People who have a low opinion of themselves experience anxiety and feelings of desperation, expect little from others, and try to conceal their feelings because they fear how others will react. According to Satir, parents play an important role in their children's development of self-worth. As she stated, "Every word, facial expression, gesture, or action on the part of the parent gives the child some message about his worth" (p. 25). In healthy families, parents believe their children are beautiful and noble persons, recognize each child's talents and accomplishments, communicate openly, and are flexible in implementing developmentally appropriate rules within the family.

Satir (1983) believed that problem families are more likely to have members with low self-esteem and that parents almost unconsciously seek affirmation of self-worth through a child because they are not being acknowledged by their spouse. In multisibling families in which marital conflict abounds, parents tend to focus their attention on one child, whom family theorists have called the *identified patient*. The stronger the parents' desire for approval, the more difficult it is for this child to respond to the pressure to side with one parent or the other. As Satir (1983) stated, "If the child seems to side with one parent, he runs the risk of losing the other parent. Since he needs both parents, making such a choice inevitably hurts him" (p. 38). Satir observed that some children become identified patients because their parents perceive them to be similar in appearance or temperament to another member of the nuclear family or a family of origin. Other children are thought to assume this role because of their birth order. The oldest child may be selected simply because he or she has been available the longest or was a member of the family during an early stressful period. The gender or age of the child may also play a role. A father may focus on his son because the boy will carry on the family name, but the mother may target the child because his behaviors resemble those of her husband.

In families with effective communication patterns, members interact in an open, genuine, and congruent manner. The verbal and nonverbal aspects of communication are consistent, such as the message a mother sends when she smiles and tells her child she is pleased with a recent success in school. Satir and Bitter (1991) contrasted effective communication and "double-bind messages" (p. 26) that often leave the listener feeling confused. If that same mother were to send one of these messages to her child, she might frown or appear distracted while she tells her child she is happy about the progress at school. Bateson, Jackson, Haley, and Weakland (1968) described three components of double-bind messages. The first is the verbal message that identifies the potential punishment for a behavior (e.g., "If your grades don't improve, you will be grounded"). A second and conflicting component frequently contains verbal (e.g., "Please don't make me do this to you") and nonverbal (e.g., smiling while describing the punishment) elements. The third aspect of the double-bind message is the listener's inability to escape from the situation. These messages are particularly troublesome for children, who depend on their parents for their everyday needs.

Satir (1972) observed that in dysfunctional families, members may respond to stress in one of four ways: placating, blaming, computing, or distracting. In their search for approval, placaters agree with others, appear helpless, and feel worthless. Blamers prefer the opposite approach, challenging or disagreeing with others while they feel lonely and unsuccessful. Computers, on the other hand, appear "calm, cool, and collected" (p. 68) and exhibit no signs of emotion, although they feel vulnerable inside. Finally, distracters send messages that are unrelated to the topic under discussion. These individuals are thought to have low opinions of themselves and tend to see others as uncaring. The result of these communication styles is a host of incongruent messages that fail to describe family members' true thoughts and feelings.

Satir (1972) believed that rules are "a vital, dynamic, and extremely important force" (p. 96) in the life of the family. As a society, we have developed formal rules such as speed limits to guide our interactions with each other. Some of the rules that exist in families are clearly stated. Some parents negotiate household chores with their children, who are then expected to perform specified tasks as prerequisites for their weekly allowance or other rewards. Many families follow rules that have never been articulated. For example, some families encourage open disclosure of thoughts and feelings, but others shun this practice. In certain families, parents are allowed to express themselves but children "are expected to be seen and not heard." Family rules may change unpredictably from one time to the next. A parent may spank or chastize a child for spilling milk on the kitchen floor on Monday but help the youngster clean the floor on Thursday. Satir encouraged families to examine spoken and unspoken rules, consider the function that each serves within the family, and take the risk of negotiating and following rules that enhance the self-worth of family members.

As Satir (1972) noted, families do not function in isolation from their cultural surround. Parents are typically the primary significant others in the lives of infants and very young children. But as children mature and begin to play with others in the neighborhood, watch television programs, or interact with teachers and fellow students at school, the attitudes and behaviors exhibited by these individuals become very important developmental influences. Satir described how some parents try to protect their children by insulating them from society, even though children learn important lessons through the interactions they have with their friends and teachers. As she stated, "No family could be expected to teach everything" (Satir, 1972, p. 292). If families are to grow and achieve their potential, communication within the family system must be clear and open in order to develop effective strategies for handling the ever-changing climate in the extrafamilial world.

Satir's work on family communication is an outgrowth of studies of communication patterns in the families of schizophrenic patients. An important concept in this research is family homeostasis, which is the status quo that occurs in families through "implicit rules governing who says what to whom and when and in what contexts" (Okun, 1990, pp. 300–301). As an interpersonal construct, homeostasis refers to the ways that members interact to maintain the family unit. Because the family is a system, the changes that occur in one member affect how others in the system behave and develop (Jackson, 1968a). As Jackson (1986b) elaborated:

> In a family we do not have just a linear system where A affects B who affects C and so on; nor do we have merely circuits in which A affects B who is affected by C which alignment augments or diminishes A's effects. Family interaction is a system in which A can also anticipate an effect on B, and this modifies his subsequent behavior; and B in turn modifies his response in anticipation of what he thinks A anticipates. When C and perhaps some little Ds and Es are thrown into the picture one is faced with a problem that Univac is unprepared to handle. (p. 188)

Through the dynamic relationships among these participants or forces, the family strives to maintain the status quo.

Structural Family Systems Theory

Salvador Minuchin focused on the structural aspects of the family system. He was less interested than was Bowen in multigenerational issues, but he shared Jackson's and Satir's interests in homeostasis and family rules. Minuchin (1974) identified different levels of power or authority in families. One of these is system maintenance, or family homeostasis, which refers to a family's efforts to continue the family unit as it has existed in the face of internal and external changes. A system's efforts to maintain itself may result in positive or negative outcomes. Some families react to change in a flexible manner, fluctuating between periods of disequilibrium and homeostasis as the system evolves in response to change (Minuchin, 1981). When sufficiently threatened by internal or external pressures, a family may become rigidly focused on maintaining the system, regardless of the costs to its members. Minuchin (1974) developed his structural theory to describe how families function in the face of everyday life transitions. In his model, he introduced terms such *subsystems, boundaries, alignments*, and *coalitions* to illustrate family members' relationships with each other and the outside world.

Minuchin (1974) described how family interactions occur within the context of subsystems, the most common of which are the spousal (i.e., husband and wife), parental (i.e., mother and father), and sibling (e.g., brother and sister) subsystems. It is possible for a person to be a member of more than one subsystem (e.g., spousal and parental) and for subsystems to include more than two members (e.g., sibling subsystem). With clients from nondominant ethnic groups, therapists must expand their definition of the family to include subsystems based on the extended kinships and community involvement found in these families. According to Minuchin (1974), subsystems are defined and differentiated by boundaries, which are the rules a family uses to dictate who interacts with whom and in what manner. The boundaries that exist between family subsystems can be either clear, diffuse, or rigid.

Minuchin (1974) believed that clear boundaries permit effective interaction between subsystems while allowing the members in each subsystem to perform their appropriate functions. When a clear boundary exists between parental and sibling subsystems, the mother and father are actively involved in child-rearing activities at the same time they are maintaining a healthy marital relationship with each other. The children experience developmentally appropriate limits that are consistently enforced by their parents. Likewise, parents and children assume responsibility for the decisions that are developmentally appropriate for each. For example, parents manage the family's finances and select child-rearing techniques, and children complete school work and play with their friends.

All families have boundaries that are somewhat rigid or diffuse, but most are able to maintain the family's identity and to adjust to change. Families in which boundaries are overly diffuse or rigid sacrifice members' autonomy for the sake of the family unit. When subsystem boundaries are diffuse, role distinctions between the parents and children become blurred and the children are at risk of becoming enmeshed in the parental or spousal subsystem. A husband and wife whose marital relationship is conflicted may develop a diffuse boundary with their 6-year-old son. The child becomes enmeshed with his parents and assumes at least partial responsibility for defining the limits on his behavior. He becomes triangulated with the spousal subsystem and begins to intervene when marital disputes arise. If his mother and father argue, he attempts to maintain family homeostasis by crying or throwing a temper tantrum to direct their attention to his misbehavior and away from their conflict. Unfortunately, this short-term solution to family tensions does not resolve the core problem of marital conflict, and it fails to enhance the child's developing sense of autonomy.

Rigid boundaries, by contrast, exist when there is disengagement between subsystems. If the 6-year-old boy lived in a disengaged family, we might expect to find his parents overinvolved with outside work activities and emotionally and socially detached from the family. He observes relatively little conflict between his parents because they spend little time together with him. Child care may be handled by a babysitter or a local day care center, or the boy might spend extended periods of time alone at home while his parents are away. The child is given the opportunity to become independent, albeit in a developmentally inappropriate manner, and he becomes emotionally detached from his parents.

Deal (1996) studied the impact of boundaries when he investigated the relationship between marital discord and the different ways that preschool and elementary school children are treated in families. He described how marital discord can result in differential treatment of siblings, with one child being scapegoated as the identified patient or becoming enmeshed with one parent in an alliance against the other. When Deal studied the impact of the marital relationship in approximately 100 nonclinical families, he found modest evidence to support the hypothesis that marital discord affects how children are treated. Specifically, he observed that "positive marital communication in an environment of mutual respect serves to lower the rate of differential treatment of siblings within the family" (p. 343). These findings provide some support for Minuchin's recommendation that therapists assess the quality of the marital relationship in their work with troubled families.

Sometimes the relationships between subsystems are more complex and require more involved graphic depictions than we have used thus far. Families frequently try to handle tension using dysfunctional transactions such as coalitions or detouring (Minuchin, 1974). Mr. and Mrs. Jones have been experiencing considerable marital conflict. When Mr. Jones is terminated from his job, he deals with this situation by arguing with his wife and becoming overinvolved with their 12-year-old son. The boy models his father's behavior and becomes oppositional with his mother, refusing to comply with her directives and undermining her parental authority. When she asks the father to intervene, he tells her that she expects too much of the boy. Subsystem boundaries in the Jones family are compromised as the father and son form a coalition against the mother. The child is enmeshed in the parental and spousal subsystems, serves as a buffer for the couple's marital discord, and is given child-rearing authority that is well beyond his developmental level.

According to Minuchin (1974), detouring involves the redirection of tension that exists within a subsystem. Consider the Jones family. When Mr. Jones loses his job, he and his wife try to handle their marital conflict by redirecting this anger toward their son. In order to avoid spending time alone with each other, the couple becomes increasingly involved in their child's daily activities. They focus on the boy's academic problems and his conflicted relationships with children in the neighborhood. Although detouring allows the couple to avoid their marital problems, maintaining family homeostasis in this manner compromises their son's ability to function as a child in the family system and in his extrafamilial environment.

Strategic Family Systems Theory

Drawing on the work of the late Milton Erickson, strategic family therapists such as Jay Haley (1976), Cloe Madanes (1981), and Mara Selvini Palazzoli (Selvini, 1988) are interested in helping families solve their problems. This requires little or no attention to past experiences and insight regarding the presenting problem. Instead, strategic family theory is based on a contextualized problem-oriented model. Haley (1976) defined a problem as "a type of behavior that is part of a sequence of acts between several people" (p. 2). This systemic perspective includes not only the members of the nuclear family but also the therapist and others in the extrafamilial system who are involved in a child's development. In this way, Haley expanded his vision beyond the family system to include ecological influences on the child. He offered the example of a boy of impoverished surroundings who was having difficulty in school. Haley's interpretation of the problem went beyond the child as an individual and the family as a system to include the impact of social, economic, and political influences. A strategic approach to this child's truancy and poor grades includes the search for contextual factors, such as a marginal school environment, that are related to the presenting problem.

Haley's theory is less developed than Minuchin's structural interpretation of the family (Sharf, 2000). He borrowed from other theorists, including concepts such as the double-bind message, family triangles, and homeostasis. On this foundation, he added his own special interest in the power hierarchies that exist in families and the metaphoric implications of the presenting problem. Strategic systems theorists recognize clients' power and control in their lives and in the therapeutic relationship. Haley (1973), for example, presented the following analogy of power, which he attributed to Milton Erickson:

> The analogy Erickson uses is that of a person who wants to change the course of a river. If he opposes the river by trying to block it, the river will merely go over and around him. But if he *accepts* the force of the river and diverts it in a new direction, the force of the river will cut a new channel. (p. 24)

To help the family cut this channel, the strategic systems therapist must understand the current direction and force of the family's homeostatic river. The clinician uses this information to design tasks intended to help family members try new relationship patterns and create a system that enhances the development of the family unit and its individual members.

In healthy families, parents have more power than their children. In troubled families, the power hierarchy is compromised when children assume more control than their developmental level warrants. A child's rise to power is often expressed through misbehavior, which is typically labeled using traditional diagnostic terminology. Strategic theorists believe that the children in these families function as protective links in the system's sequence of behaviors. Their misbehavior serves a positive purpose and actually represents "helpfulness and caring rather than conflict and strife" (Madanes, 1981, p. 66). This shift in the conceptualization of family functioning provides the foundation for interventions that offer family members alternative methods for achieving the purpose of the presenting problem. Madanes gave the following example:

> A child might develop a problem that will keep his mother at home to take care of him; consequently, the mother will not have to face the issue of looking for a job. The child's problem provides a convenient excuse to the parent for avoiding unpleasant situations. If a father comes home from work upset and worried and a child misbehaves, the father can then feel angry toward the child instead of feeling worried about his work. In this sense, the child's misbehavior is helpful to his father. Also, by making the father angry at him, he saves the mother from having to help her husband by sympathizing with him or quarreling with him. In this way, the child is helping both parents. (pp. 66–67)

When parents resolve their own difficulties, they no longer need their child's misbehavior to maintain the family system, and they are able to establish an appropriate power hierarchy in the family.

In the analogy cited earlier, Erickson used a river as a metaphor for the power and energy that exists within people and families. Chapter 16 discusses how children use metaphor to represent life experiences. Strategic theorists view metaphor as a relationship pattern that "develops around a situation and becomes an analogy for the deeper issue in the relationship" (Schilson, 1991, p. 154). Therefore, each person's behavior can be interpreted as a metaphor within the context of the family system. A child's misbehavior, for example, may be a metaphor for conflict in the parents' marital relationship, the family's problems adjusting to the recent loss of a loved one, or violence in the neighborhood. The symptom bearer's actions can bring temporary relief, but metaphoric handling of systemic problems does not result in long-term positive change (Madanes, 1981). To achieve this goal, family relationship patterns must change so the identified patient's metaphoric actions are no longer needed to maintain the "homeostatic stubbornness" that families use to handle stress (Minuchin & Fishman, 1981, p. 76).

Mara Selvini Palazzoli's model of the family is based on the metaphor of the game. As Satir (1972) and others have stated, families follow rules that define their system. The analogy of the game, therefore, seems appropriate, especially when family interactions are viewed as *"sequences of individual moves"* (Selvini, 1988, p. 17) similar to those practiced in games with rules. Each member of the family develops strategies that are used during intrafamilial and extrafamilial interactions. These strategies are reflected in members' communication styles and the psychological health of the family. As Selvini described, "Psychopathological behavior is treated as a *move*, and communicational confusions and ambiguities are seen, not as the crux of the problem, but as the direct result of a certain way of playing the social and family game" (p. 19).

Behavioral Family Theory

Behavioral family theory is based on the behavioral and cognitive-behavioral principles described in Chapter 10. Compared with other family theorists, the proponents of the behavioral viewpoint have given less attention to the family as a system (Nichols & Schwartz, 1998). Instead, they have focused on the interactions that occur between members of the family. As Forgatch and Patterson (1998) stated, behavioral family theorists believe that children's misbehavior is shaped by environmental contingencies, especially those under their parents' control. More specifically, Patterson and his colleagues observed that parents of disruptive children tend to ignore prosocial behaviors and fail to use appropriate responses for maladaptive behaviors. As Forgatch and Patterson stated, these parents should be trained to "maintain adequate levels of discipline, monitoring, family problem solving, and encouragement for prosocial development" (p. 86). One method that therapists use to achieve these goals is behavioral consultation in which parents are taught more effective child-rearing techniques (see Chapter 14).

Proponents of cognitive-behavioral family therapy are interested in how members' beliefs about the family and families in general affect family interactions (Schwebel & Fine, 1994). These family schemas are acquired, relatively stable, and mostly unconscious beliefs about other family members and relationships within the system (Dattilio, Epstein, & Baucom, 1998). Cognitive-behavioral theorists have recognized multigenerational influences on family life. For example, parents' family schemas have been shaped by experiences in their families of origin. How they expect a mother, father, or child to behave is influenced by models from their childhood. But family schemas also develop as a result of interactions in the nuclear family. If one parent typically performs certain household tasks, other family members are likely to expect this person to handle these responsibilities in the future. These shared beliefs then affect members' interpretation of each other's behaviors. A father who is viewed as "reliable" and "helpful" is likely to have others use these mental representations to interpret his actions in the future. Their thoughts and related behaviors about the father would be significantly different if their schema of him were to include "lazy" and "bitter."

Schwebel and Fine (1994) described four basic assumptions of the cognitive-behavioral family model. First, family members are viewed as scientists who study their world and organize the data obtained into a theory about the family and family life in general, which is then used to guide personal decision making. When family members are flexible and revise their theory in response to new or contradictory information, the family system develops a healthy response to change. When one or more members have a rigid theory of the family, problems arise. Schwebel and Fine's second assumption is that family schema have a profound impact on family relationships through members' expectations of others and explanations of family events. Families are thought to follow a healthy course of development unless their growth is interrupted by maladaptive theories of the family. For this reason, cognitive-behavioral family theorists also assume that is important for family members to recognize and understand the cognitions that comprise their theories.

Solution-Focused Family Systems Theory

Models for brief family therapy are intended to produce both first- and second-order change within the family system. That is, the clinician's goal is to effect timely change in the family's presenting problem while facilitating the overall development of family functioning. Early in the history of family systems therapies, pioneers in the brief-term approach at the Mental Research Institute (MRI) studied the role of family communication patterns. Others, such as Mara Selvini Palazzoli and her colleagues in the Milan school, devised systems-based treatments to help troubled families change with a minimum of therapeutic contacts. We examine another of these methods: the solution-focused approach developed by Steve De Shazer at the Brief Family Therapy Center in Milwaukee, Wisconsin.

Solution-focused family systems theory has a different perspective than most theoretical approaches, which focus on problems and psychopathology. Solution-focused theorists focus on a family's strengths and the ways the family uses these resources in a constructive manner. Because life is "a continuously changing process" (Berg, 1994, p. 10), proponents of solution-focused theory emphasize a family's capacity to grow and develop rather than its homeostatic tendencies. The positive orientation of this model translates into a positive perception of families in therapy. Specifically, families are thought to possess the resources needed to effect change and the motivation to find solutions for their problems.

De Shatzer et al. (1986) identified three concepts that are central to solution-focused theory: difficulties, complaints, and solutions. Difficulties are the day-to-day problems that families encounter, such as children disobeying family rules. Complaints are "a difficulty and a recurring, ineffective attempt to overcome that difficulty, and/or a difficulty plus the perception on the part of the client that the situation is static and nothing is changing" (De Shazer, 1986, p. 210). The distinction between difficulties and complaints is significant because it is complaints, not difficulties, that bring families to therapy. If a child was not completing homework and the parents intervened successfully, the family would be very unlikely to seek professional help. But if the parents were unable to change the child's behavior and believed that the youngster would never finish homework assignments, they might opt for therapy to find a solution for their problem.

Because solution-focused theory is a systems model, even minor change in a family member's behavior is capable of producing "profound and far-reaching differences" (De Shazer et al. 1986, p. 209) in the family. Consequently, first- and second-order change can occur as a result of brief-term interventions derived from this theory. Solution-focused theorists are less concerned about the history of a family's complaint and more interested in the family's goals and resources for change. De Shazer's model is a constructivist approach (see Chapter 16) because solving a family's complaints requires consideration of each member's view of the situation and the development of a different perspective or interpretation of the presenting problem that is acceptable to the family system. From this constructive viewpoint, the family experiences events surrounding the complaint in a new way and change occurs.

DEVELOPMENTAL CONSIDERATIONS

As discussed previously, the family is not a static system. Each family develops over time in response to internal and external change. In this section, we discuss the family life cycle, which Haley (1973) and others, such as Carter and McGoldrick (1988), have used to describe how these systems develop from courtship to old age. Another developmental consideration in families is the child-rearing method that parents use with their children. In the second part of this section, we explore this important topic by examining two well-known models of parenting and their effects on children.

Family Life Cycle

Developmental models with 5 to more than 20 stages have been proposed to describe the changes that families experience over time (Carter & McGoldrick, 1988). Haley (1973) included six stages in his model of the family life cycle: courtship, marriage, childbirth, middle marriage and child rearing, parents' individuation from their adult children, and retirement and old age. Movement from one stage to the next can be stressful. When a family has difficulty handling stage-related tasks, the growth of that system is compromised. Couples who learn to settle marital differences before the birth of their first child are less likely to triangulate with that child when conflict occurs later in the marriage. If a healthy spousal relationship does not exist during middle marriage, children can become enmeshed with their parents to maintain family homeostasis.

The family life cycle is a framework for understanding relationships across three generations: the nuclear family, the families of origin, and adult children who depart the nuclear family (Schilson, 1991). As Haley (1973) observed, "Man is the only animal with in-laws" (p. 45). The courtship stage that precedes marriage exposes a couple to values and practices that are sometimes radically different from those endorsed by each mate's family of origin. Marriage represents the merging of two families of origin into a more complex whole that must find novel solutions to the challenges of relationships, child rearing, money management, and social status. Haley observed that some families experience considerable stress when adult children begin leaving home. In a family in which the parents rely on an only child to maintain the marital relationship, the mother or father may develop physical or mental health problems so the child will remain at home to care for the ailing parent.

During retirement and old age, couples spend more time together because they no longer work outside of the home. Although many retirees successfully handle this life transition, some do not. Haley described a case in which the wife developed a psychosomatic complaint (i.e., the inability to open her eyes) after her husband retired. In the context of the family system, the wife's symptoms served the useful function of helping her husband adjust to his new lifestyle. As Haley stated:

> When his wife developed her problem, he had something important to do—help his wife recover. He took her from doctor to doctor, arranged their living situation so that she could function even though unable to see, and became extremely protective. (pp. 63–64)

The stages outlined by Haley (1973) have intuitive appeal, but they do not account for the development of all family systems. These include families with children born to unmarried parents and those whose parents divorce and remarry (see the Multicultural Considerations section of this chapter for additional examples). Carter and McGoldrick (1988) discussed marital transitions in terms of the changes that occur in family relationships as the system adjusts to the departure and arrival of its members. Haley, of course, recognized this dynamic when he discussed the birth of children and parents' individuation from their adult children. But Carter and McGoldrick suggested that at least one additional stage must be added to the family life cycle to account for the experiences related to divorce and remarriage. Divorce itself is not an event that takes place at a single point in time. Spouses think about this change, announce their decision to significant others, physically separate before the divorce is finalized, and then develop a new lifestyle. Peck and Manocherian (1988) elaborated on these experiences in what can be thought of as five substages (e.g., separation) occurring over a 2- to 3-year period of the life cycle of divorcing families. The systemic impact of these substages differs across families, depending on whether children are present and their ages at the time of the divorce.

Carter and McGoldrick (1988) adopted a multigenerational perspective in their discussion of the family life cycle. They recommended that therapists conceptualize families in the context of preceding and succeeding generations. Adult children who recently married have families of origin that are simultaneously facing individuation from their offspring. The newly married couple's development of the spousal relationship is affected by their parents' resolution of the challenges associated with their respective stage of the life cycle. Meanwhile, elderly grandparents on each side of the nuclear family are in retirement and old age and are at greater risk for physical decline and death, whose effects reverberate across generational boundaries.

Parenting Style

An important multigenerational influence in the life of a family is parenting style, which varies in terms of caregiver responsiveness and demands. Some parents attend to their children's needs; others devote little time and energy to the responsibilities of child rearing. Some parents demand a lot from their children, but others expect very little. Baumrind (1967) studied child-rearing styles and found that parents differ in their use of control and demands, verbal communication, and nurturance. Three patterns of parental authority emerged: authoritarian, permissive, and authoritative. Authoritarian parents tended to exert control over their children's behavior. They were also less affectionate and less likely to verbally interact with their child. Permissive parents were described as lax and moderately affectionate with their children. Authoritative parents were generally loving but firm, encouraged communication, and provided a rationale for the limits they set.

Maccoby and Martin (1983) described four styles of parenting based on their two-factor model of responsiveness and demands (Table 12-1). The authors divided Baumrind's (1967) permissive parenting into two categories: indulgent and uninvolved. Permissive-indulgent parents are tolerant, avoid the use of punishment, and establish few rules for children, but they do not ignore them as permissive-uninvolved parents do. Lamborn, Mounts, Steinberg, and Dornbusch (1991) provided empirical support for Maccoby and Martin's model. Based on their study of adolescents, ages 14 to 18 years, the authors found authoritative parenting to be the best method. Lamborn et al. found that adolescents who described their parents in this manner rated themselves as more competent, socially adept, and better adjusted behaviorally than did their peers from authoritarian, permissive-indulgent, and permissive-uninvolved homes. The differences were most obvious between adolescents of permissive-uninvolved parents and those from authoritative families. Permissive-uninvolved parents are more focused on themselves and have relatively little interest in rearing their children. Therapists must assess these families very carefully because extreme examples of this style of parenting constitute child neglect (Berk, 2000).

Parents must adapt their methods to the age and maturational level of the child (Maccoby, 1999). To prepare children for the complex decisions they will encounter during adolescence and adulthood, parents must provide structure and limits that are appropriate for a given age. Consider a child's daily selection of clothes for school. A 5-year-old child is given the choice of a red or a blue shirt to be worn with blue jeans, and an 8-year-old child may choose from four different shirts and two colors of pants, but a 12-year-old child selects from different items he chose during a recent shopping trip with his parents. Researchers have documented age-related changes in parenting style. Lytton, Watts, and Dunn (1988), for example, followed a sample of twin boys from age 2 to 9 years. When they examined mothers' disciplinary practices, they found a dramatic decline in physical punishment and a greater use of reasoning with children and removing their privileges.

Table 12–1
Maccoby and Martin's (1983) Two-factor Model of Parenting Styles

		RESPONSIVENESS	
		Responsive	Unresponsive
DEMANDS	Demanding	Authoritative	Authoritarian
	Permissive	Permissive-Indulgent	Permissive-Uninvolved

Adapted from "Socialization in the Context of the Family: Parent-child Interaction," by E. E. Macoby and J. A. Martin, 1983, pp. 39–51. In E. M. Hetherington (Ed.), *Handbook of Child Psychology: Vol. 4. Socialization, personality, and social development* (4th ed., pp. 1–101). New York: John Wiley. Copyright 1983 by John Wiley & Sons, Inc.

MULTICULTURAL CONSIDERATIONS

Earlier we discussed the work of Hernandez (1997) on the changing demographics of U.S. families. This evolution in family structure and purpose reflects political and economic developments occurring in society at large. The Great Depression, the Vietnam War, and the prosperity of the 1990s produced unique cohort-related challenges. Gradual but significant changes have occurred in social attitudes and practices related to the family. This section examines different family arrangements and the effects they can have on children. It also considers how ethnicity relates to family functioning and parenting style before turning to a discussion of feminist theory and gender considerations in therapy.

Diversity in Family Structure

The traditional two-parent family, with the father as financial provider and the mother as homemaker, has been replaced with diverse structural arrangements (Gottfried & Gottfried, 1994). In some families, children are raised by a single parent, typically the mother. In others, grandparents assume primary responsibility for rearing the child. In a small number of cases, children are parented by gay fathers or lesbian mothers and their partners. Researchers have studied the effects of family composition on child development and found that children respond positively to both traditional and nontraditional structures.

Even in homes where the biological parents' marriage is intact, major life transitions can alter the allocation of child-rearing responsibilities. Fathers in dual-career households sometimes become the primary caregiver after they are unemployed. In these families, parents and children must adjust to a system in which the father assumes responsibility for child rearing and household tasks. Researchers have found the father-as-caregiver model to be an appropriate method for raising children. As Radin (1994) stated, "There is no reason to believe that children's development is impaired as a result of being reared primarily by their fathers in two-parent homes, and there is some evidence that their growth is enhanced in desirable directions" (p. 46).

Gottfried, Bathurst, and Gottfried (1994) studied how families adapt when mothers are employed outside of the home. Based on their longitudinal investigation of children from ages 1 to 12 years, the authors found no significant difference in psychological adjustment between children of working mothers and those whose mothers were not employed. Based on their findings, the authors concluded, "It is truly time for researchers to discontinue their search for detriment caused by maternal employment" (p. 94). When both parents work outside the home, they face the challenge of finding quality child care services (Contemporary Issues Box 12-1). Lamb (1994) reviewed relevant research and reported that infants placed in day care are not significantly different from those raised at home. A factor that merits serious consideration is the quality of care received. Feldman (1998) noted that high-quality day care, which includes a low caregiver–child ratio, has not been found to have detrimental effects on children and may even foster development in certain domains, such as cooperative play. With approximately 70% of mothers employed outside of the home (U.S. Bureau of the Census, 1999), day care is a normal part of the lives of many children. The challenge for parents is to locate quality care provided by trained staff who are committed to fostering children's growth and development within a safe and happy environment (Feldman, 1998).

Shore and Hayslip (1994) studied custodial grandparents who have full-time responsibility for child-rearing activities. The authors reported that when children are raised apart from their parents, grandparents are the most likely relatives to care for them. In their study of custodial grandparents and traditional grandparents, Shore and Hayslip found that raising a grandchild was associated with lower satisfaction and feelings of well being and poorer attitudes about the grandparent–grandchild relationship. Raising a grandchild after weaning oneself of children creates developmental challenges that are inconsistent with the normal responsibilities of the later stages in Haley's (1973) family life cycle. As Shore and Hayslip stated, grandparents typically want "to enjoy their grandchildren without having responsibility for them" (p. 201). Therapists who treat these families must consider the needs of custodial grandparents in order to enhance the quality of life for children and their caregivers.

Patterson (1996) estimated that there are between 3 and 4 million gay and lesbian parents raising from 6 to 8 million children in the United States. Unfortunately, we know relatively little about these families. Falk (1994) reviewed the results of a growing body of

Contemporary Issues Box 12–1

The Challenge of Finding Quality Child Care Services in Working Families

Day care has become a normal part of life for many children in the United States. Based on data collected in the 1995 National Household Education Survey, Hofferth, Shauman, and Henke (1998) reported that 59% of children younger than age 6 years were involved in either formal or informal, nonparental child care. Those in informal care are supervised by relatives or nonrelatives in their own homes or the homes of others. Children enrolled in formal programs attend day care centers, preschools and prekindergartens, and Head Start programs. Many children attend day care while their parents are at work. This situation applies to 57% of families with dual-income married parents of children under age 6 years and 69% of single female-headed households (Bureau of Labor Statistics, 2001).

Working parents in dual-income and single-parent families face the challenge of finding affordable, quality care for their children. The financial cost of day care varies according to setting, with some children enrolled in free government-subsidized programs, such as Head Start, and others in privately owned centers where the average hourly rate was $2.39 in 1995 (Hofferth et al., 1998). For a working parent with one child in private care for 40 hours per week, this figure translates into an annual cost of approximately $4500.00. Clearly, nonparental child care represents a significant item in the monthly budgets of many families.

Ablon and Bemporad (2000) described quality child care as "responsive, attentive, and nurturing" (p. 14), but Shaffer (1999) concluded that much of the formal care for U.S. children is "woefully inadequate" (p. 586). Summarizing the work of others, Shaffer stated that child care settings should be safe and clean, the staff should be emotionally supportive and trained to meet the developmental needs of young children, and age-appropriate play materials and activities should be available. Care must be adapted to the needs of each child. Hofferth et al. (1998), for example, observed that very young children require more individual attention than do older children, who benefit from learning activities and social interactions with peers. Leslie, Ettenson, and Cumsille (2000) asked parents who were searching for child care services to report setting characteristics that were most important to them. After controlling for such factors as cleanliness, safety, and licensure, the authors found that different characteristics were important to the couples and single mothers in their sample. Although married mothers were most interested in the child-to-staff ratio, married fathers and single mothers were most concerned about the cost of care. Another factor that was important to all three groups was a convenient location for their child's day care setting.

Parents express concern about the developmental implications of nonparental child care, especially for infants and young children. Hungerford, Brownell, and Campbell (2000) stated that the question is more complex than the simple effect of day care services. Based on their review of recent studies, the authors concluded that child care must be evaluated from a broader perspective that includes characteristics of the child and the family. For example, low-quality child care might compromise the healthy development of children from high-functioning families, and might exacerbate the problems related to conflict and poor parenting in less healthy families. Hungerford et al. also cautioned that the type and duration of nonparental care are related to such factors as family income and parents' employment status. Therefore, the role of day care in children's lives must be evaluated in the context of other developmental influences. Although high-quality child care is clearly preferable to low-quality services, children's response to nonparental care varies depending on significant demographic and psychosocial factors.

research that suggests that, on average, lesbian and heterosexual mothers endorse similar child-rearing attitudes and practices. Likewise, children raised by lesbian mothers do not appear to be at greater risk for psychological problems, including gender identity confusion, although some may be negatively affected by the social stigma related to their mother's sexual orientation. Falk also cited research to counter the popular fear that lesbian mothers raise homosexual children. Barret and Robinson (1994) drew the same conclusion about children reared by gay fathers. Because we know considerably less about these families, Barret and Robinson emphasized the need for additional research in this area.

Ethnicity and the Family

McGoldrick (1988) described how ethnicity relates to the family life cycle. She observed that families differ in the number and beliefs of members involved at each developmental stage. Middle-class European American families, for example, tend to have fewer members than African American and Native American families, where community and extended kinships are embraced. McGoldrick described how ethnic rituals, such as bar and bat mitzvahs, weddings, and funerals, are used to celebrate different life stages. Childbirth is a particularly important stage because it is this transition in family life that highlights the child-rearing practices of different ethnic groups.

Comparisons of family structure in nondominant ethnic groups require consideration of between- and within-group differences. These families also share commonalities with European American families that must not be overlooked. For example, Lindahl and Malik (1999) found that overt marital conflict had similar effects on the behavioral adjustment of 7- to 11-year-old boys in Hispanic American, European American, and multiethnic (i.e., Hispanic and European American parents) families. Boyd-Franklin (1989) cautioned that any discussion of African American families must include recognition of its diversity because "there is no such entity as *the* Black family" (p. 6). Although African American families do not have the same structure, goals, and values, they tend to share a belief in kinship ties (Ho, 1987). Compared with their European American peers, African American children are more likely to derive emotional support from their parents, extended family, neighbors, and members of the community (e.g., pastors) (Boyd-Franklin, 1989). The reliance on extended family may reflect traditional African American values or a response to everyday societal pressures. In 1994, it was estimated that 59% of African American youths, ages 17 years and younger, were living in a female-headed household (U.S. Bureau of the Census, 1995). The extended family gives these children access to adult supervision provided by male and female role models in a familiar setting, as well as the opportunity to learn social skills that are needed to communicate with a variety of caregivers.

Therapists who work with Asian American families must understand the impact of acculturation and tailor their interventions to the needs of all family members. Ho (1987) described three levels of family acculturation: recent immigrants, families of immigrated parents and children born in the United States, and families that are second generation and beyond. Recently immigrated families tend to seek outside help for more basic needs, such as English language instruction, but second-generation families are more likely to request traditional forms of therapy. Interestingly, Ho described the families with foreign-born parents and children born in the United States as most in need of services designed to address culturally based generational conflicts. These problems are thought to arise, in part, from the differing rates at which family members adapt to their new culture (Huang & Ying, 1989).

The acculturation process can impact family dynamics in other ways. Asian American children have been traditionally taught to respect and obey their parents, and they are praised for actions that benefit the family but not necessarily them as individuals (Sue & Sue, 1991). Children raised in these families and formally educated in schools that endorse European American values of independence and self-determination sometimes experience confusion and stress as they attempt to balance their respect for parents with the desire to follow the values of the dominant culture. These opposing pressures sometimes result in children living what Yagi and Oh (1995) termed "double lives" (p. 68), where they speak the native language and obey their parents' wishes at home and converse in English and exhibit greater independence and assertive behavior at school.

Interestingly, parents who criticize their children for accepting dominant group values and pressure them to adhere to traditional beliefs might actually be pushing them away from their Asian American culture (Sodowsky, Kwan, & Pannu, 1995). Because of the central role of family in the life of these children, Kim (1985) recommended family therapy as the treatment of choice because the clinician is better able to mobilize constructive resources within the family. Kim suggested a combination of approaches, such as strategic and structural family therapies, in which problem-solving techniques are used to mobilize the family's energy and commitment to remediate the presenting problem.

Despite considerable within-group variability, Native Americans tend to conceptualize family within the context of community. LaFromboise and Low (1989) described the traditional family as a "system of collective interdependence, with family members responsible not only to one another but also to the clan and tribe to which they belong" (pp. 120–121). Therapy for Native American children should include the adults who are significant to the child's development. This often involves the participation of extended family members and the community. LaFromboise and Low, for example, described a mother who chose to avoid a confrontation with her daughter by discussing the child's behavior with the grandmother, who had assumed responsibility for handling the child. Because the girl's primary caretaker in this situation was the grandmother, the clinician should invite her to become involved in treatment.

Ethnicity and Parenting Style

Attitudes toward parenting vary considerably across and within cultures. For the purpose of comparison, we examine child-rearing practices used in African American, Hispanic American, and Asian American families. African American parents have been described as harsh and likely to use physical punishment with their children (Hines & Boyd-Franklin, 1996), but Kelley, Power, and Wimbush (1992) found that African American mothers actually used a range of child-rearing techniques. These included parent-oriented methods intended to enforce obedience and child-oriented strategies designed to enhance self-respect in children. When physical punishment is used, it may have different effects with African American children than it does with European American children. Deater-Deckard, Dodge, Bates, and Pettit (1996) studied mothers' use of physical punishment in a longitudinal study of European American and African American children from kindergarten to third grade. Results revealed that in kindergarten, African American boys living with single mothers in lower-income homes were more likely to receive physical punishment. But when children's school behavior in grades K through 3 was examined, aggression and conduct problems were related to the early use of physical punishment among European Americans only. Additional research is needed on parents' use of punishment with children of different ethnic groups. For example, Weiss, Dodge, Bates, and Pettit (1992) found that harsh discipline was related to externalizing behaviors in children. Did the African American mothers in the Deater-Deckard et al. sample punish their children in a way that communicated concern rather than anger and frustration? Compared with their European American peers, did these children interpret their mother's behavior in a different way?

Hispanic American parents are likely to emphasize children's respect for authority and family unity, but their child-rearing methods differ depending on the age of the child (Zayas & Solaris, 1994). This includes a more relaxed approach with young children (Falicov, 1998). Zayas and Solari (1994) described a 5-year-old Puerto Rican boy whose mother handled him much as she had when he was an infant. This included feeding the boy and allowing him to continue using a pacifier. The mother's rationale for this approach was that her extended family members endorsed indulgent parenting until a child was 5 years old. Now that her son had reached that age, family members were telling her to demand more of the boy in order to prepare him for school. When he did not respond immediately to this new approach, the mother sought therapy. Her clinician recommended a behavior management program that was consistent with the mother's desire for more control of the child's behavior. As the boy improved, the mother learned that his response to her new style of parenting would be gradual and positive.

Falicov (1998) described how Hispanic American parents sometimes combine physical punishment with shaming, which can involve "teasing and mocking, humiliation, threats, [and] ridicule" (pp. 220–221). Asian American parents also use shame to motivate their children in school and at work (Chung, 1997). European Americans tend to view this technique as inappropriate because of its potential for harming a child's self-esteem. But Chung observed that Asian American parents are unlikely to share this opinion because they are less concerned about emotional problems, which they believe children can use to avoid work and responsibility. Similar to parents from other nondominant ethnic groups, Asian Americans value education. They rear their children for success in school in ways that reflect their belief in hard work. Recent studies with Chinese American families have provided insight into the structured and demanding approach these parents use with their children.

When Chao (1994) studied the parenting style of immigrant Chinese mothers, she replicated the results of others, such as Lin and Fu (1990), who observed the high level of control that is characteristic of Baumrind's (1967) authoritarian approach. But Chao questioned whether Baumrind's model was appropriate for these mothers. She suggested that the use of control in immigrant families is culturally consistent with parents' care and concern for their children. Their approach to child rearing appears to have positive qualities that are not associated with the Western concept of authoritarian parenting. Chao cautioned against the universal application of Baumrind's model, suggesting instead that researchers and practitioners conceptualize parenting styles within the context of a family's cultural heritage.

Chao's (1994) hypothesis may help to explain the findings of Huntsinger, Jose, and Larson (1998), who conducted a 2-year longitudinal comparison of European American and immigrant Chinese American families. First tested when their children were in preschool or kindergarten, the Chinese American parents in this study were more likely to use formal and directive methods of instruction with their first and second grade children. Compared with their European American peers, these students spent more time in at-home structured learning activities and less time in free play with other children. One might expect this division of time to cause social adjustment problems for the Chinese American students, but Huntsinger et al. reported no such effect. Did these students recognize and appreciate the "parental care, concern, and involvement" described by Chao (p. 1112)? Will their social adjustment continue to parallel that of European American students when they enter adolescence and become more active in their peer group? Huntsinger et al. will hopefully offer insight into these questions as they conduct follow-up evaluations of these students.

Therapists must be sensitive to ethnic group differences in parenting techniques, but they should not condone the use of culturally sanctioned methods that are harsh or abusive. As McGoldrick and Giordano (1996) stated, "All cultural practices are not ethical" (p. 25). When clinicians encounter parents who rely on punitive methods to control their children, they must avoid debates about the merits of physical punishment. Instead, they should ask their parents to describe the child's response to this technique. Because families seek therapy for unresolved problems, the typical answer to this question is that physical discipline has produced no long-term improvement in the child's behavior. After parents volunteer this information, therapists can facilitate a discussion about alternative methods. When appropriate, they can teach parents to use more effective behavior management techniques with their children.

Feminist Theory and Family Therapy

Clinicians must consider the impact of gender when working with families. Feminist writers have criticized traditional theories and methods, especially those based on psychoanalytic principles, and focused attention on the male biases inherent in these approaches. For example, some have reconceptualized Freud's concept of penis envy as womb envy (Horney, 1967) or breast envy (Eichenbaum & Orbach, 1983) to counter the male-as-norm criterion of the original construct. Others have challenged the traditional emphasis that object relations theorists place on the mother–infant relationship, choosing instead to focus on the infant's interactions with male as well as female caregivers (Okun, 1990).

Compared with earlier theorists, feminist writers adopted a more social and multicultural perspective that addresses the empowerment of women in a male-dominated society. Conoley and Larson (1995) described "many parallels between women's issues and those of children and youth" (p. 202). In particular, the authors noted that the lives of women and children have traditionally been characterized by a lack of power. Therefore, feminist principles are relevant to the study of child development and the therapeutic interventions used with young clients (Dornbush & Strober, 1988). Of particular importance are the gender-stereotypic beliefs that parents have of their children.

Gender awareness precedes knowledge of gender-based differences. Berk (1996), for example, described how preschoolers use gender-related categories, such as toys and clothes, to construct their meaning of boys and girls before they understand the biological characteristics of the sexes. Children's gender awareness is influenced by the messages they receive from their parents, peers, teachers, and the media. Of these, parents have been a popular focus for researchers interested in the development of gender attitudes in children. When Pomerleau, Bolduc, Malcuit, and Cossette (1990) studied the toys given to infants and toddlers, they found that girls were more likely to receive dolls and that boys had more small toy vehicles. When they questioned parents about the donors of these items, they found that most of the toys (59%) were purchased by mothers and other women.

Eccles, Jacobs, and Harold (1990) suggested that parents' gender attitudes can have long-term implications for their children's development. The authors found that parents in two longitudinal studies held gender-stereotypic expectations of their children's competence in math, English, and athletics that were independent of students' actual performance in these areas. Eccles et al. described a self-fulfilling prophesy in which parents' beliefs shape their children's self-expectations, skill development, and career selection. Because society tends to reward performance in traditionally male careers, such as engineering, the authors suggested that parents' gender-stereotypic attitudes may place their daughters at risk for social and economic hardship later in life. Therapists must be alert to these beliefs and consider them in order to plan interventions that not only remediate existing problems but also enhance children's development throughout life.

Feminist therapists have been active in preventing and treating domestic violence, which includes the battering of spouses and the physical and sexual abuse of children (Contratto & Hassinger, 1995). Sternberg et al. (1993) underlined the importance of these efforts when they found that 8- to 12-year-old children exposed to various forms of violence, including physical abuse, were more likely to report externalizing and internalizing behaviors than were children from nonviolent families. According to Gelles (1998, p. 39), domestic violence has as its origin "the politics of gender," and women are judged in terms of their role as mothers in an unequal family system where traditional gender roles are reinforced. When evaluated in this manner, women are expected to nurture their children and remain dependent on the male head of household. All therapists, including child and adult specialists, can foster healthy growth and development in children by reducing the level of domestic violence and considering the effect of unequal spousal relationships in families.

Parents serve as marital and parental role models for their children. How they handle the responsibilities of child rearing and management of the home are, therefore, important. Unfortunately, mothers continue to assume more responsibility for completing household tasks, even in dual-income families. In their study of dual-earner couples, 91% of whom were parents, Barnett and Shen (1997) found that whereas women devoted significantly more time every week to domestic tasks, men spent more time in paid employment. In a 5-year longitudinal study of parents and their children, Aldous, Mulligan, and Bjarnason (1998) found that mothers were generally more involved than fathers in everyday child care activities. It is important to note that when fathers were actively involved with their children at a young age, they were likely to continue this pattern 5 years later. Although parents' work schedule had an effect on the amount of time they spent with their children, Aldous et al. observed that couples' decisions regarding domestic tasks were usually based on the father's work demands. Fathers were not completely unaware of these inequities, but they were apparently unwilling to change their behavior. As Aldous et al. stated, "There was little evidence that husbands, even though they recognized the unfairness of the division of child care, were prepared to make the effort needed to balance the load" (p. 818).

Luepnitz (1988) concluded that the traditional family has failed as "a social formation equally protective to all its members" (p. 9). She was referring specifically to how mothers' needs are too often viewed as less important than the needs of fathers and children. When therapists adopt this view of family, they are apt to provide treatment based on sexist assumptions. During family therapy sessions, for example, these clinicians run the risk of focusing on a mother's parenting deficits while supporting the disengaged father's willingness to participate in treatment. Clinicians who endorse feminist principles are aware of these obstacles as they attempt to engage their male and female clients in treatment designed to facilitate solutions to the complex decisions of everyday life. Therapy includes consideration of the ways in which the entire family can fulfill the developmental needs of children while enhancing the personal growth of each parent.

Consistent with their desire to empower women, feminist therapists are aware of the power differential that exists between the therapist as expert and the client who is seeking help. Conoley and Larson (1995) stated that therapists must be particularly aware of power-related issues when the client is a child. This includes an acceptance of the greater influence that external forces have on children's development. As Conoley and Larson stated, common childhood problems can be solved through systemic changes in the family, school, and community. Recent advances in child development and child assessment have challenged the traditional male-as-norm perspective. Researchers have given increased attention to gender-related influences on the developmental process, and many test developers are now providing norms for boys and girls so therapists can compare a client's adjustment with others of the same gender (see Chapter 4).

Conoley and Larson (1995) stated that feminist principles should be incorporated into child interventions because girls grow up and become women. The same can obviously be said for boys, many of whom later become husbands, fathers, and women's colleagues at work. To date, the contributions of feminist theory to child therapies are primarily theoretical in nature. Controlled studies are needed to evaluate the feminist treatments that will be developed for boys and girls. Additional research is needed on education/development and prevention programs designed to create more flexible gender attitudes and expectations.

SUMMARY

The theories examined in this chapter represent some of the most prominent models of the family developed during the 20th century. The field of child interventions has benefited from the emergence of family systems theory. Clinicians and clients are fortunate that pioneers in this area moved beyond their isolated research efforts to collaborate with others in the field. The problems that children encounter can no longer be considered the sole result of intrapsychic conflicts or stimulus–response learning. Rather, children and their development must be viewed in the context of their families and cultural surround.

13

Family Systems Interventions

▪ ▪ ▪

Mr. and Mrs. Lee and their 11-year-old son John are referred for family therapy by the Central County Child Abuse Multidisciplinary Team. Three weeks ago when Mr. and Mrs. Lee arrived home from work, they found John sitting at the kitchen table holding his report card. When Mr. Lee discovered that John failed math, English, and science, he became very angry and started yelling at the boy. At one point, he removed his leather belt and struck John repeatedly. Mrs. Lee intervened and restrained her husband while John ran out of the house and down the street to the home of his maternal grandparents.

▪ ▪ ▪

Giardino, Christian, and Giardino (1997) described child abuse and neglect as "a major threat to the health and well-being of children throughout the world" (p. 1). Some behaviors, such as intentional burns and rape, are clear examples of child maltreatment; others, including spanking, are more difficult to classify because they have become socially sanctioned methods for disciplining children. Wauchope and Straus (1990), for example, reported that between 47% and 79% of the parents of 3- to 12-year-old children use physical punishment, such as spanking, at least once in awhile. The psychological consequences of physical abuse are many and varied (Cole & Cole, 2001), and family therapy has been used to treat abused children and to prevent further maltreatment.

This chapter examines how the theories described in Chapter 12 have been translated into family-based treatments. As in previous chapters, this chapter considers assessment issues, intervention strategies, participants' roles, and the contributions and limitations of family systems therapies. At the end of the chapter, we return to the case of the Lee family to explore how family systems therapy can be used in the treatment of physically abused children.

ASSESSMENT

According to Brassard (1986), a child's referral for psychological services is "a systems event" (p. 401) in which parents or significant other adults have decided that professional assistance is needed. As a result, the assessment of a child's presenting problem requires consideration of the family system. Information about the family and the child's functioning within this system is collected during the family interview when the therapist observes family interactions and assesses clients' perceptions of the presenting problem and their expectations for treatment. But the family interview is not a substitute for individual meetings with the child or other family members (Sattler, 1998). Therapists sometimes meet with parents to collect information about the child's life history and topics that are inappropriate for discussion when children are present (e.g., marital conflict or impending divorce). Clinicians meet individually with children to obtain their impression of the presenting problem. When a combination of interview strategies is used, therapists should meet individually with the child after their interview with parents to dispel any fears that the interviewer will disclose the child's information to the parents.

Nathan Ackerman (1958) described a systems approach to assessment that involves consideration of "individual, role, family group, and their interrelationships" (p. 109). According to Ackerman, impaired family functioning results from individual members' problems, dysfunctional familial relationships, or a combination of the two. He believed that families are neither sick nor healthy but range from successful to unsuccessful in their ability to fulfill family functions. At the healthy end of this continuum are families that are able to address and solve their problems for the benefit of individual members as well as the family unit. At the unhealthy end are families that exhibit "increasing signs of emotional disintegration, which in some circumstances may culminate in disorganization of family ties" (Ackerman, 1958, p. 100). Between the two extremes are families that are unable to solve their problems so they "buy time" by controlling the problem or they identify a person within or outside of the family who is scapegoated as the identified patient. When a child is the scapegoat for family problems, his or her misbehavior "becomes the fulcrum or entering wedge" for treating the dysfunctional system (Ackerman, 1958, p. 305). Therapists must assess children's misbehavior in the context of the family system, recognizing the homeostatic function of this behavior.

Other family systems theorists have emphasized the importance of assessment. Jay Haley (1976), for example, noted that strategic family systems therapy begins with a careful assessment of the family's presenting problem. Before clinicians assign therapeutic tasks, they must have a clear idea of the nature and extent of the problem. Bowen's interests in multigenerational influences led him to develop the genogram to assess the impact of previous generations on the nuclear family. Brassard (1986) described the ecomap, which can be used as an ecological measure of the family's interactions with extrafamilial systems. Standardized questionnaires are also available for assessing family functioning. Here we examine the Family Environment Scale, which Moos and Moos (1994) designed to measure a family's goals, structure, and relationships. Finally, we discuss a very different approach to family assessment that Steve De Shazer and his colleagues developed based on the solution-focused brief therapy model.

Genogram

What Hartman (1979) described as an "assessment in time" (p. 51), the genogram enables therapists to examine a family's history. When collecting data for the measure, clinicians should "go back as many generations as possible" (Bowen, 1966, p. 366) and not limit themselves to the parents' immediate families of origin. Brassard (1986) suggested that therapists collect a comprehensive view of the family, including dates of birth, marriage, divorce, and death; places of birth, residence, and employment; medical and mental health history; and socioeconomic and cultural characteristics (Figure 13.1 is an abbreviated genogram of the Lee family). As this information is obtained, the therapist records it on a large piece of paper that is in full view of the family. Hartman (1978) recommended that males be represented by squares, females by circles, and ancestors whose gender is unknown by triangles. Relevant information about each person is recorded within the appropriate symbol. Deceased individuals are represented by an "X" drawn over their symbol. Relationships between family members are also graphically represented. Hartman (1978) suggested that a solid line be used to connect marital partners, children with their parents, and siblings with each other. To describe relationships within the family, McGoldrick and Gerson (1985) recommended a dotted line for "distant relationship," a zig-zag line to represent the "conflictual relationship," and a triple line for the "very close relationship" (p. 155). They also designated the identified patient using a double square or circle. McGoldrick and Gerson provided a detailed description of genogram format and its use with the families of famous figures, including Sigmund Freud and Harry Stack Sullivan.

Therapists must allow sufficient time to conduct the genogram. Some families have difficulty reporting information beyond the previous generation. Others, especially those from large families, disclose a considerable amount of material that cannot always be collected in a single interview. It is best to assess certain topics, such as legal problems, without children present. When using genograms with nondomi-

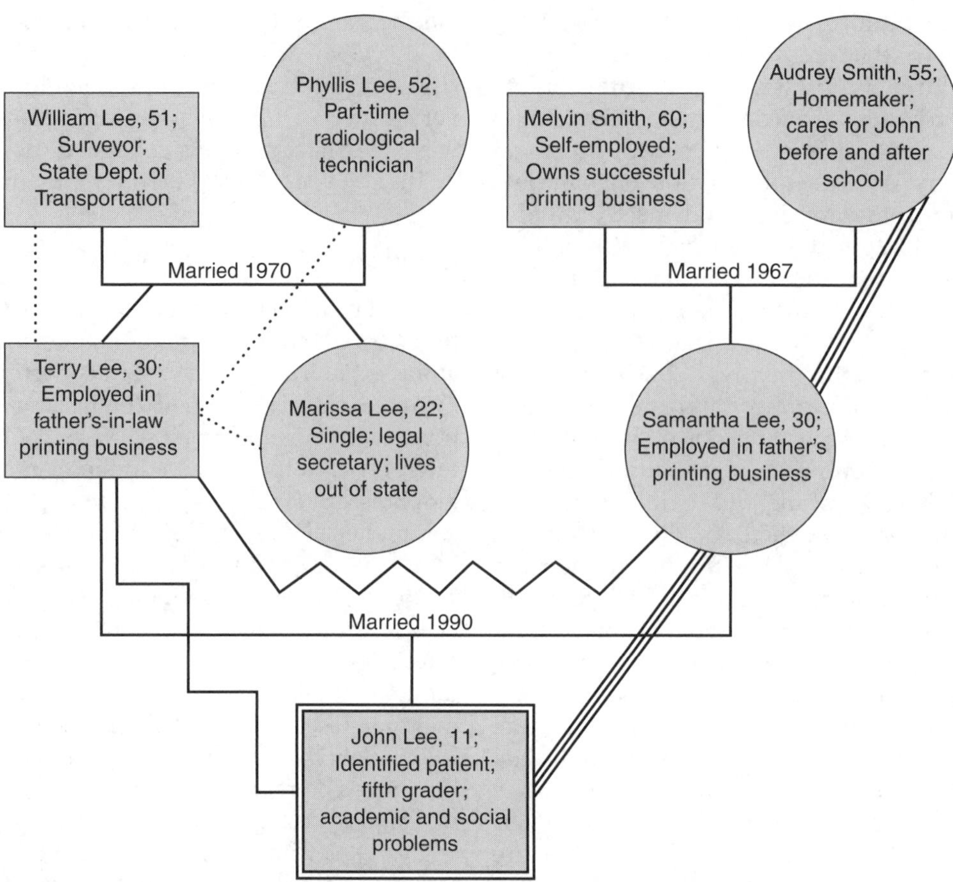

Other significant information: John and his parents lived in a 2-bedroom apartment in the Smith's home from 1990 to 1996, when the family moved into its own home.

Figure 13–1. A Genogram for the Lee Family.

nant ethnic groups, therapists must consider individuals from the community and extended family. Sutton and Broken Nose (1996) described how Native Americans' inclusive view of family sometimes results in clients' labeling the siblings of grandparents as grandparents on their genograms. And Hines and Boyd-Franklin (1996) recommended that clinicians use this technique to explore the extended kinship relationships in African American families that include members who are not relatives by blood. Despite the time and effort required, Brassard (1986) recommended that therapists use a genogram because the technique provides a more detailed view of "the complex and multifaceted world" (p. 412) of the family.

With Bowen's genogram, all family members of different generations are included in the same diagram. Satir and Bitter (1991) described two adaptations of this procedure: family maps and the Family Life Fact Chronology (FLFC). Family maps differ from genograms because they involve the development of three separate diagrams, one for the nuclear family and one each for the father's and mother's family of origin. The FLFC is a chronological and multigenerational listing of significant life events in the family, beginning with "the birth of the oldest grandparents" (Satir & Bitter, 1991, p. 32) and continuing to the nuclear family. Genograms, family maps, and the FLFC are tools that therapists can use to explore a family's history. The ecomap depicts the family's present interactions with their social environment.

Ecomap

Proponents of the ecological approach have emphasized the importance of extrafamilial systems, such as the neighborhood, school, and governmental agencies. Ecological assessment sets the stage for interventions that are very different from traditional individual or family therapy. Consider the public health implications of a town water system contaminated with harmful bacteria. Children who consume this water are likely to develop a gastrointestinal disorder. A child-focused assessment of the problem is likely to result in the use of antibiotics to treat each child's illness. A family-focused assessment might lead to family members boiling their water and ensuring that no one drinks untreated liquids. But an ecological assessment requires the identification of community-based causes. The outcome of this approach would be improvements to the town's water system, bringing benefits to a greater number of people for a longer period of time.

The ecomap is a tool that therapists have used to conduct an ecological assessment (see Figure13-2 for an ecomap of the Lee family). With this technique, clinicians can depict family members' contacts with their community, including neighbors, teachers, fellow employees, health care workers, and extended members of the family. Similar to the genogram, the ecomap involves the use of a large sheet of paper on which the therapist depicts the family's connection with extrafamilial systems (Hartman, 1978). At the center, the clinician draws a large circle to represent the nuclear family. Family members are then depicted with small circles containing the name and age of each female member and small squares with the name and age of each male member of the family. Lines are drawn to illustrate the relationships between the family members.

The family's extrafamilial systems are represented by circles drawn outside of the family circle. Members' relationships with these external systems are illustrated using connecting lines. If the entire family is affiliated with an external system, such as a house of worship, a line is drawn between the large circle and the circle representing that system. If one family member is connected with an external system, a line is drawn from that person's circle or square to the circle for that system. Hartman (1978) suggested that the nature of these connections can be illustrated using different types of lines: a solid line for "strong" connections, a dashed line for "tenuous" connections, and a

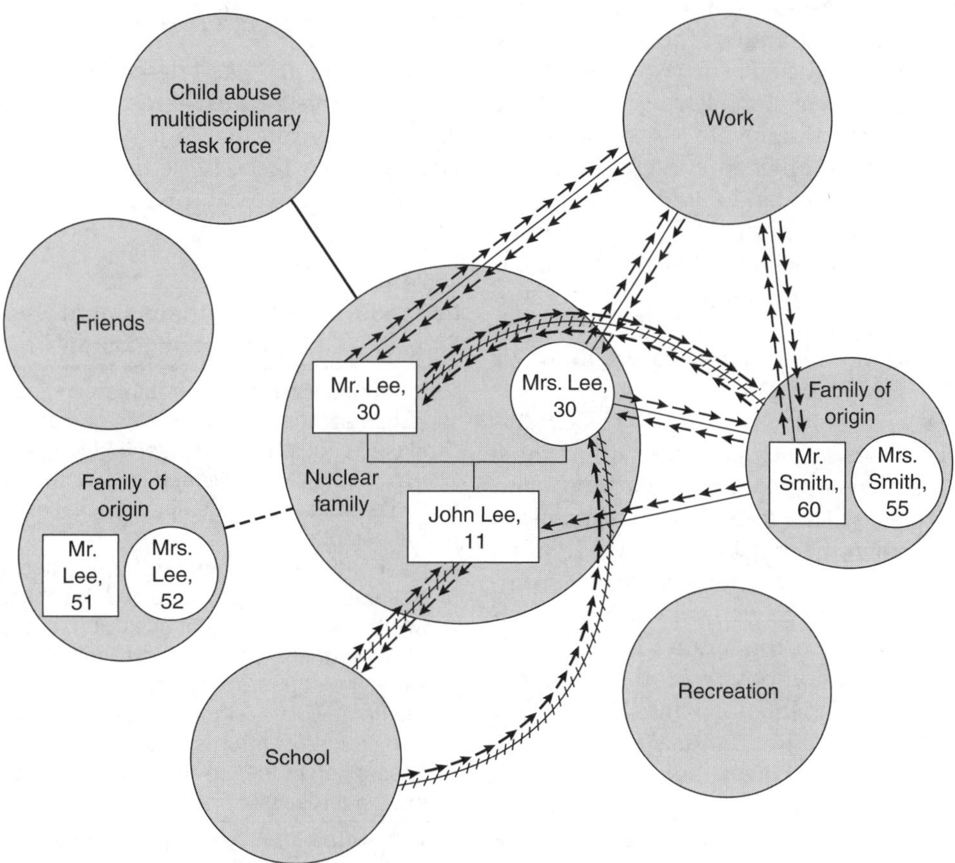

Figure 13–2. An Ecomap of the Lee Family.

hatched line for "stressful" connections (p. 469). She also recommended that therapists indicate the direction of energy flow with arrows included as part of each line. The ecomap can be used to help families identify social stressors and support networks or services that are relevant to their presenting problem.

Inspection of the Lees' ecomap reveals that the family's interactions with extrafamilial systems are limited. Although they have personal and work-related contacts, some conflicted, with John's maternal grandparents, the Lees have limited interaction with his paternal grandparents. They report having no friends and do not participate in recreational activities in the community. John attends school regularly, but his father has no contact with the teachers and school counselor and Mrs. Lee's limited interactions with the school have been negative.

Family Environment Scale

The Family Environment Scale (FES) (Moos & Moos, 1994) is a 90-item, forced-choice (i.e., true/false) inventory designed to assess family relationships, goals, and structure. The authors developed three forms of the FES: the Real Form (Form R), Ideal Form (Form I), and Expectations Form (Form E). As the names imply, one is designed to assess the family as it now exists, and the others are intended to provide pictures of the perfect family and a family's future, especially in cases in which change is anticipated (e.g., the birth of a child). Pino, Simons, and Slawinowski (1984) developed a pictorial version of the FES for children, but there is limited psychometric support for this measure. Therefore, we limit our discussion to the FES Form R.

Respondents' answers to Form R are scored and interpreted as 10 subscales organized within three dimensions: Relationship, Personal Growth, and System Maintenance. The Relationship dimension contains the Cohesion, Expressiveness, and Conflict subscales designed to assess family members' commitment to each other, their open expression of feelings, and disagreement in the family. The Personal Growth dimension is composed of the Independence, Achievement Orientation, Intellectual-Cultural Orientation, Active-Recreational Orientation, and Moral-Religious Emphasis subscales, which were included to assess a family's goals, decision-making style, and connection with extrafamilial systems. Finally, System Maintenance contains the Organization and Control subscales, which are intended to measure family structure and rules. Moos and Moos (1994) also described the procedure for calculating a Family Incongruence Score, which is intended to reflect members' level of agreement regarding the family environment.

Moos and Moos (1994) reported Form R subscale norms based on a diverse sample of 1432 normal families. Internal consistency for the 10 FES scales ranged from .61 to .78, with half above the .70 level. Test-retest reliability across a 12-month period ranged from .53 to .84, with seven scales above .70. Moos and Moos compared FES scores for families in the norm group with those obtained from 788 problem families. After controlling for socioeconomic factors and family background (e.g., educational level), the authors found that the problem families scored "lower on cohesion, expressiveness, independence, and intellectual and recreational orientation, and higher on conflict" (p. 18). In the FES manual, Moos and Moos summarized the results of additional validation studies in which the FES was found to be clinically relevant.

Solution-Focused Assessment

De Shazer et al. (1986) described a seven-step procedure therapists can use to develop treatment goals and identify alternative courses of action for their clients (Table 13-1). Little time is devoted to the history of the complaint. Instead, the family is asked to

Table 13–1
Procedures for the Assessment Session in De Shazer's Solution-focused Brief Family Therapy

1. Introduce the family to treatment model and setting (e.g., use of a treatment team and a one-way mirror or closed circuit audio or videotaping system).
2. Ask the family to describe its presenting complaint.
3. Invite the family to identify and describe exceptions to the complaint.
4. Have the family generate concrete goals for treatment.
5. Ask the family to generate and describe possible solutions or methods of achieving these goals.
6. The treatment team calls a 10-minute intermission when the counselor leaves the therapy room to develop the homework assignment for the family.
7. The counselor returns and gives the family a succinct description of the team's recommended tasks before ending the session.

Adapted from "Brief Therapy: Focused Solution Development," by S. De Shazer, I. K., Berg, E. Lipchik, E. Nunnally, A. Molnar, W. Gingerich, and M. Weiner-Davis, 1986, *Family Process, 25*, pp. 214–218. Copyright 1986 by Family Process, Inc.

provide a brief but detailed description of the presenting problem, similar to the way behavior therapists conduct a functional analysis of behavior (see Chapter 11). But solution-focused clinicians do not limit the discussion to the complaint. To help families view problems from a different and more positive perspective, the therapist asks them to identify exceptions when the complaint does not occur and to describe their typical actions at these times. This technique is intended to help family members realize that they are doing something right, at least part of the time. This information provides the foundation on which treatment goals are established.

Goals are constructed to communicate "the expectation that change is going to happen" (De Shazer et al., 1986, p. 215) because it is already happening under certain conditions (i.e., the exceptions). Throughout the session, the therapist avoids the traditional emphasis on psychopathology and focuses on "the absence of the complaint" (p. 216) to help the family develop alternative courses of actions. When this information is collected, a 10-minute intermission is called and the therapist leaves the room to consult with other professionals and develop homework tasks based on the family's strengths. De Shazer et al. (1986) offered the following example:

> If the parents are complaining about their bright child's failure to do his homework in spite of their nagging and joint lecturing, then the parents' homework task might be for them to toss a coin so that, randomly, one or the other gets a day off; or, if they want the child to be solely responsible for his own work, they might be asked to toss a coin to decide randomly which days neither of them would even mention homework to their child. (p. 217)

The therapist rejoins the family and presents the task for the coming week. The clients are instructed to observe and remember events they want to retain as part of family life. De Shazer's model is more similar to the behavioral than the traditional model of assessment because assessment and intervention activities are integrated into all treatment sessions.

Family Play Assessment

Play represents an important component in the assessment of families with young children. As mentioned previously, traditional adult methods of inquiry are less effective with young clients whose thinking processes are at a preoperational or concrete operational level. As a behavioral equivalent of the verbal metaphor used by adults, play provides the opportunity to explore clinically significant issues with children in a less threatening and developmentally appropriate manner. The role of play in family assessment differs from its use in individual methods in that children and parents are asked to participate together. This more inclusive approach provides a sample of parent–child interactions as family members playfully address significant life issues.

Gil and Sobol (2000) observed that family play assessment provides information about the content and process of family life. The authors stated that by having parents play with their children in session, interviewers are able to assess family cooperation, disciplinary techniques, family structure, and family members' ability to have fun with each other. Gil and Sobol described how puppetry, art, and sandtray can be used for assessment purposes. They also discussed a play adaptation of the family genogram that involves the use of a large sheet of paper, a magic marker, and sandtray miniatures. With the clinician's help, family members construct a traditional genogram and then individuals select miniatures to represent each other. A busy self-employed parent, for example, might be depicted using a car and a clock to symbolize the parent's absence from home and long hours at work. Gil and Sobol have clients place their miniatures at each member's spot on the genogram. They use this concrete information as a stimulus for family discussion about individual members and their relationships with each other. Creation of the genogram, discussion of symbols, and description of family relationships often require more than one session and sometimes involve a meeting dedicated to each stage of the procedure.

EDUCATION/DEVELOPMENT AND PREVENTION

Satir (1983) stated that therapists "can do a great deal of preventive work by including all the children in the therapy process" (p. 181). By helping families transform their rules and communication patterns, clinicians free the identified patient from the role of symptom bearer and decrease the probability that other children will fulfill this function. To enhance family functioning and prevent problems in the system, clinicians have devised a number of education/development and prevention programs. Many reflect experts' interests in the spousal relationship and the family life cycle and include marriage enrichment programs, childbirth and parent education, and premarital counseling (Levant, 1986). Here we discuss two examples of these programs: Parent Effectiveness Training and the Premarital Relationship Enhancement Program.

Gordon (1970) designed Parent Effectiveness Training (PET) to teach parents how to improve communication with their children and to resolve family conflicts. This 8-week didactic and experiential program is delivered to groups of parents who are taught to listen to their children, express their feelings in a genuine manner using "I" messages, and resolve conflicts by developing solutions that are acceptable to both the parent and child. As Gordon described:

> The parent asks the child to participate with him in a joint search for some solutions acceptable to both. One or both may offer possible solutions. They critically evaluate them and eventually make a decision on a final solution acceptable to both. (p. 196)

In their meta-analysis of 26 studies on PET, Cedar and Levant (1990) found support for the use of the program as a prevention technique. As the authors stated, "The effects of PET are not overwhelmingly large" (p. 382), but the method does seem to have merit and therefore warrants additional outcome studies.

Programs designed to prepare couples for marriage have included classroom instruction in family life education and the traditional premarital counseling offered by clergy members (Levant, 1986). Markman and Halhweg (1993) emphasized the importance of the premarital relationship. They found that how couples, especially the male partner, treated conflict before marriage was related to marital distress and divorce. As the authors stated, "It is not the differences between people so much that matters, but how those differences are handled" (p. 36). Markman and his colleagues developed the Premarital Relationship Enhancement Program (PREP) to improve couples' communication and conflict resolution skills. The program is delivered in a small group format in which three to five couples are taught how to effectively listen to their partner, express their feelings in a constructive manner, and identify and solve interpersonal problems. Markman, Renick, Floyd, Stanley, and Clements (1993) found that 4 years after couples completed the program, they were communicating and solving problems better than their counterparts in the control condition. Although the two groups were more similar at the 5-year follow-up, PREP participants were still significantly less likely to report being physically violent with their partner.

REMEDIATION

This section examines interventions developed by prominent family therapists. These techniques include the strategies commonly associated with traditional approaches to family-based treatment. For example, we discuss detriangulation (Bowen, 1966), family sculpting (Satir, 1983), reframing (Minuchin, Rosman, & Baker, 1978), and directives (Haley, 1976). We also examine family therapists' applications of the behavioral and cognitive-behavioral techniques described in Chapter 11. At the end of this section, we explore recently developed techniques for brief-term family treatment. We begin with an examination of psychodynamic approaches to family therapy.

Pyschodynamic Family Systems Therapy

Nathan Ackerman (1958) stated that family therapy is characterized by a transition in focus, from the problems of the symptom bearer to the conflicted relationships within the family and the emotional stress the symptom bearer experiences as a result of family conflict. Ackerman related intrapsychic functioning to interpersonal relationships to explain the purpose of a family member's behavior within the context of the family system. What at first seems to be dysfunctional behavior can be interpreted relative to its homeostatic function within the family. For example, a child's oppositional defiant behavior may have the adaptive purpose of redirecting attention from a conflicted spousal dyad even though the parents' use of punishment creates emotional turmoil for the child.

As discussed in Chapter 12, Ackerman was an early advocate of treating children with their families. Some of his techniques are considered nontraditional by today's standards. Bloch and Simon (1982), for example, reported that Ackerman sometimes treated children and adolescents by "playing ball with some in the park and sending others to do self-expressive work with artist friends of his" (p. xvi). And as someone who was known to challenge authority, Ackerman rejected the standard therapeutic hour in favor of sessions that could be as brief as 15 minutes or as long as 2 hours (Bloch & Simon, 1982).

Ackerman (1958) examined the therapeutic implications of family roles. This includes the very important change that occurs when a husband and wife become parents. In addition to maintaining and developing their marital relationship, the couple must now agree on parenting philosophy and techniques. Personal conflicts that compromise the marital relationship can be expected to have negative effects on the parents' interactions with their child. Ackerman recommended that therapists begin treatment by meeting with the parents and child together. The clinician can observe mother–child, father–child, and mother–father interactions, including each family member's attempts to resolve conflicts that arise during the session. The therapist's role is that of arbitrator and facilitator who encourages the discussion of clinically relevant information. As Ackerman stated, the clinician "stirs the process by leading questions, by challenging the behavior of one member, by checking with another, and at the same time he makes certain that each member has a chance to be heard and understood" (p. 192).

Therapists sometimes meet with parents apart from the child to discuss personal or marital issues that can not be handled appropriately in family sessions. They also conduct individual interviews with children to address both personal and familial concerns. According to Ackerman (1985), clinicians assume the roles of parent, teacher, and therapeutic agent in their interactions with children. The therapist-as-parent provides the emotional support the child is not receiving from the parents. In their educational role, clinicians help children learn socially appropriate behaviors and decision-making skills. As therapist, the clinician facilitates "the expression, relief, and fuller understanding of pathogenic conflict and anxiety in the child" (Ackerman, 1958, p. 287).

Scharff and Scharff (1987) described how object relations family therapists join with the family to provide members the "emotional space for a rediscovery of each other and of the lost parts of the self that have been put into each other" (p. 169). Clinicians use the therapeutic relationship to help clients establish the family environment that is required to meet the needs of the family system and its members. To accomplish this goal, therapists address transference issues and help members develop centered holding relationships to replace their projection of anxiety onto each other. Because the identified patient is expected to set aside personal needs to maintain stability in the family, clinicians facilitate the development of "a family holding environment that would support mature interdependence" (p. 194) within the system.

Object relations family therapists typically adopt a flexible format that includes individual, couple, and family techniques. When multiple formats are used, family treatment is sometimes offered along with individual sessions for one member and marital therapy for the couple. Clinicians often include very young children in family sessions because "the family is complete only when the young children—including infants—are present" (Scharff & Scharff, 1987, p. 288). The therapist focuses on the interactions between parents and children. Consider the benefit of involving a previously calm 4-year-old boy who jumps from his chair and begins to walk around the room in response to his father's loud and pointed rebuke of the mother. Having the child present, observing his actions, and then describing and discussing the behavior with the parents may be a significant transition point in treatment. Scharff and Scharff also described how therapists use play techniques with younger clients, either in individual sessions or during family meetings.

A central characteristic of object relations family systems therapy is the handling of transference and countertransference. In individual sessions, the focus of attention is the client's transference onto the therapist and the therapist's countertransference onto the client. In family sessions, transference-countertransference patterns are more complex. Consider the father's transference onto his wife (e.g., wife as the father's mother), who then exhibits countertransference onto her husband (e.g., husband as the wife's father). The father may also display transference with his young son, with whom he interacts as himself when he was a child. Families exhibit contextual transference with the therapist based on their expectations for treatment. In order to help the family and to avoid counterproductive countertransference, the clinician must be "emotionally equidistant from each of the family members" and "on the side of the family as a unit in its job of helping each of the members to grow, to love, and to work" (Scharff & Scharff, 1987, p. 72). This obviously requires considerable training and experience on the part of the therapist.

The Scharffs provided an example of transference and countertransference with the Jansen family in treatment. The father became angry with his son who was misbehaving when the two were discussing how the boy was being teased by other students. The father's provocative behavior appeared to be a transference reaction that was related to his own childhood experiences of being tormented by other children. The therapist analyzed his countertransference (i.e., feeling uncomfortable) to the father and realized that his discomfort was related to his own childhood problems with his peers. To himself, the clinician analyzed what the father might have done to provoke these fights and whether his current behavior at home and in session was in any way similar to his reactions as a child. The mother joined the discussion and reported that the father sometimes exhibited this type of behavior with her. Attention then turned to the father's provocative actions with the mother, his son, and the clinician. The therapist targeted the similarity of the father's and son's behavior by saying, "I wonder, Mr. Jansen, if you think you might want Tom to pick off a few of the tormenters for you, a sort of vicarious victory over the kids who used to beat on you?" (Scharff & Scharff, 1987, p. 222). In this case, the clinician was aware of how his reactions were grounded in his own experiences as a child, and he used this insight to help the family understand recurring relationship patterns.

Multigenerational Family Systems Therapy

Murray Bowen typically intervened with parents because he believed they were the individuals most responsible for family functioning. Bowen (1971) even defined "family" as "the two most responsible family members (both spouses) with the therapist as a 'potential' triangle person" (p. 192). To facilitate family members' differentiation from the family's undifferentiated ego mass, Bowen used a technique called detriangulation in which the therapist attempts to separate the emotional triangle of mother-father-child by working with the least vulnerable members of the triad, the parents. By remediating conflict in the spousal dyad, the therapist can increase the child's differentiation from his or her parents so the child no longer serves as a buffer in the marital dispute.

Bowen (1971) believed that behavioral change in any member of a family triangle transforms the operation of that triangle as well as related triangles. In families that have only one parent committed to the therapeutic process, the therapist works with that person alone to effect change in the family system. As Bowen stated, "If one member of a triangle can change, the triangle can change, an entire extended family can change" (p. 191). This approach differs from the traditional model of individual therapy because the client's presenting concern is conceptualized in terms of its function in the family system instead of a problem of intrapsychic origin. Bowen introduced clients to his concept of emotional triangles, and he encouraged family members to recognize their triangulated relationships and to monitor their emotional reactions to them.

Bowen (1971) acknowledged the challenges that clinicians encounter in effecting change in a family system. Working with both parents provides the therapist the opportunity to manipulate the emotional triangle in session. Early in the development of his approach, Bowen focused on intrapsychic processes, which included the use of dream analysis. Later he turned his attention to the family relationship system, especially interactions in the spousal dyad. Treatment involved having the mother and father share their thoughts and feelings to each other during session. Consistent with his concept of emotional triangles, Bowen believed clinicians have four primary functions:

1. Defining and clarifying the relationship between the spouses,
2. Keeping self de-triangled from the family emotional system,
3. Teaching the functioning of emotional systems,
4. Demonstrating differentiation by taking "I position" stands during the course of the therapy. (p. 193)

The therapist assumes a very active role in treatment, one that involves constant attention to clients' attempts to engage the clinician in the family's interlocking emotional triangles.

Therapists must understand how differentiated they are from their own nuclear families and families of origin in order to maintain an appropriate level of emotional distance from their clients and resist a family's invitations to ally with one spouse or the other. Although Bowen (1971) believed that clinicians must assess their emotional involvement in the mother-father-therapist triangle, he did not mean that therapists should be detached from their clients. To the contrary, the clinician assumes a central position in session by having the spouses direct all statements through the therapist rather than to each other. But overinvolved clinicians are unable to separate from their personal thoughts and feelings in order to understand the clients' emotional triangles. A therapist who has meaningful contact with a family is able to remain calm when conflict arises and to help clients develop a new understanding of their relationship patterns.

Bowen (1971) described the "I position" as the ability to express one's thoughts and feelings in a calm manner and to take appropriate action "without criticism of the beliefs of others and without becoming involved in emotional debate" (p. 197). For treatment to be effective, the clinician must be able to use the "I position" in session. The therapist serves as a model for clients by encouraging them to use this approach both in and out of session. Clients become more differentiated from the emotional systems of the nuclear family and their families of origin. A family's initial focus in therapy is symptom relief, usually the elimination of a child's misbehavior. But as treatment progresses, there is a shift to more in-depth discussion of family-of-origin issues, spousal conflicts, and concerns about self. Again, the "I position" provides a means of examining these issues in a calm and constructive manner.

Bowen (1971) developed what he called "multiple family therapy" (p. 198) as a more efficient method for communicating his theory to couples. He would bring together about four couples for 90-minute group sessions. Bowen observed that families treated with this approach seemed to progress very well, in part because they realized that other families had problems and learned from their attempts to bring about change. Later in this chapter, we will discuss recent developments in the use of multifamily therapy when we examine group techniques in family therapy. When Bowen first tested his multiple family method, he scheduled client appointments on a weekly basis. Later he found that families responded well to monthly sessions, and he made greater use of meetings at this interval with all of his clients, regardless of whether they were being seen in an individual or multiple family format. As he observed, "It takes a certain amount of time on the calendar for families to change, and the length of time necessary for change is not decreased by increasing the frequency of appointments" (p. 201). As discussed later in this chapter, Mara Selvini-Palazzoli came to the same conclusion when she adopted monthly sessions in her approach to family therapy.

Humanistic Family Systems Therapy

Humanistic family systems therapy represents a combination of the principles espoused by Carl Rogers and the family communications model of Gregory Bateson and Don Jackson. Therapists who use this approach encourage family members to be accepting and genuine with each other, to be open and honest about their feelings, and to resolve conflicts by communicating effectively and using the inherent strength in the family. The most recognized writer in this area is Virginia Satir, who believed that patterns of communication reveal the rules that operate within families.

At the outset of treatment, Satir (1983) recommended that clinicians question family members about their hopes for treatment. The therapist transitions to a discussion of communication patterns by stating, "Families operate by rules which they may not even know about. I want to know about the operation of this family" (p. 141). Progressively, the focus of attention moves from the identified patient to the family as a system. During the course of the interview, the therapist observes the family's communication patterns. For example, who takes the initiative and responds first to the therapist's questions? Do family members have the opportunity to express themselves without being interrupted or criticized by others? Who talks the most? The least? Do family members interact with each other, or do they direct their questions and comments through the therapist?

An important part of family rules is the approach that parents use to rear their children. As discussed in Chapter 12, parents in families with problems often disagree about child-rearing techniques. Satir (1983) described one such family in which the father withdrew when he was angry and the mother spanked the child. Children learn to recognize differences in parenting style and are often able to provide insightful observations in therapy. Satir summarized the comments of the children in this family:

> Oh, so Dad shuts up and won't talk to you? You know something is going on but maybe you aren't sure what. Mother tells you right out what she doesn't like. Are you sure what Dad is angry about? You seem to know what displeases Mother. (pp. 193–194)

After the children described what angered each parent, Satir turned her attention to the parents and asked them to discuss what angered their spouse.

She also gave family members the chance to disclose their reactions to others' behavior. Later Satir adopted a positive focus by asking family members to describe how they expressed pleasure when others treated them well. A family's communication patterns regarding positive feelings and actions provides the foundation for enhancing self-worth within the family. By turning the attention away from the presenting problems, the therapist can have family members discuss what children could do to please the parents, what the mother and father could do to please each other, and how the parents could praise and communicate love for their children.

Satir used a variety of experiential interventions to actively involve families in therapy. One method is the rope technique, which she used to illustrate family relationships (Satir & Baldwin, 1983). Members first tie one rope around their waist to represent themselves. To this rope, they attach one rope for each member of the family. These are given to others, who hold them to depict the relationships within the system. The rope procedure is a concrete method for illustrating how the behavior of one person affects the rest of the family. Consider the use of this technique with Mr. and Mrs. Smith and their two children. When the brother teases his sister, his relationship rope pulls on her, but his movement is also felt by the mother and father. The ropes are a metaphor for family interactions and offer a stimulus for discussing the interconnecting relationships in the system. An important part of this technique is having family members disclose the feelings that arise during the activity and how they resemble their emotional reactions to others' behavior outside of session.

Satir (1983) developed a dramatic technique that she called "sculpturing" (p. 250). Family members are asked to pose in the physical positions they previously assumed during significant family interactions. A critical husband may be asked to create a living picture of a recent disagreement with his wife. He stands beside his wife, points his finger at her, and glares as she portrays the posture she exhibited during the actual argument at home the previous day. Again, the therapist uses this experience to encourage disclosure of feelings. The procedure can be used with other family members to explore their emotional reactions to events and the unspoken rules that govern communication in the family. Satir and Baldwin (1983) believed that sculpturing "makes past experiences alive in the present" and is therefore "much more accurate in what it reflects about family communications than a verbal description" (p. 244). Clinicians must carefully plan their use of this technique, especially in families with a history of child or spouse abuse.

Structural Family Systems Therapy

Salvador Minuchin (1974) described his structural approach as a "therapy of action" (p. 14) that is oriented to the present. He indicated that the structure of a family system is not readily apparent to outside observers and that clinicians become aware of this information by joining the family. When a family enters treatment, the therapist becomes an active participant in the system as the family reorganizes itself in relation to this new member. As Minuchin and Fishman (1981) described, the therapist's questions and comments influence the process and content of a family session. An effective clinician is different from other members of the family because he or she carefully and temporarily joins and disengages with different family members or subsystems. This experience provides the opportunity to support or challenge the family and to observe the reactions of its members and subsystems.

One factor that complicates the joining process is clients' understanding of the presenting problem. A family, especially the parents, is likely to see the child's misbehavior as the focal issue in treatment. Therapists, on the other hand, tend to view the child's behavior as symptomatic of dysfunctional family relationships. As Minuchin and Fishman (1981) described, the clinician's view can mobilize a family's efforts to maintain homeostasis as the therapist pushes for structural change and the family resists. Overcoming this obstacle requires special therapeutic skills. As the newly designated leader of this system, the therapist "will have to accommodate, seduce, submit, support, direct, suggest, and follow in order to lead" (Minuchin & Fishman, 1981, p. 29).

One joining technique that clinicians use is mimesis, or "imitating the style and content of a family's communication" (Sharf, 2000, p. 515). The therapist adopts the family's interaction style, including members' speech volume, tempo, and pitch, as well as the language that parents and children use. When very young clients are present, Minuchin and Fishman (1981) recommended that clinicians use developmentally appropriate language to join with the child. Notice how Minuchin adapted his interviewing style with 4-year-old Patti, whose parents and 2-year-old sister Mimi were present in the session.

MINUCHIN: Hello, how are you?
PATTI: Fine. Can we play with toys?
MINUCHIN: We're going to get some toys. (*Kneels.*) You said that your name is Patti?
FATHER: Yeah.
MINUCHIN: Patti, what's the name of your sister?
PATTI: Mimi.
MINUCHIN: Mimi? (*Puts his thumb in his mouth like Mimi and engages her little finger with his.*) Hello, Mimi. (Minuchin & Fishman, 1981, p. 38)

In this brief interchange, we have the chance to see how Minuchin tailored his style to the child's developmental level. He adjusted to the adult–child height differential by kneeling on the floor to interview Patti. He acknowledged her as a person by addressing her by name and responding to her request for toys. Minuchin also displayed his ability to relate with children by mimicking Mimi's behavior and addressing her by name. The example provides another clinically significant characteristic of this family. Notice how the father spoke for Patti when Minuchin tried to confirm her name. Minuchin affirmed the child's importance as an individual by continuing his discussion with her rather than turning his attention to the father. The father's interruption provides information about the family's boundaries, which the therapist can address in treatment.

When family members interrupt others, as Patti's father did, structural family therapists address these intrusions. Minuchin and Fishman (1981) suggested that clinicians prepare family members for these interventions with the following admonition:

> In this room, I have only one rule. It is a small rule, but apparently very difficult for this family to follow. It is that no person should talk for another person, or tell another person how this person feels or thinks. People should tell their own story and own their own memory. (p. 149)

The therapist listens for interruptions and intervenes to ensure that each person is allowed to share his or her thoughts and feelings.

Minuchin and Fishman (1981) observed that where clients sit in sessions suggest the psychological distance that exists within a family. In psychologically enmeshed families, boundaries are vague and require strengthening; in disengaged families, boundaries must be made less rigid (Minuchin, 1974). When an 8-year-old boy is enmeshed with his parents, he might display this in session by sitting in the middle chair, with his father seated to the right and his mother to the left. Structural family therapists use a number of techniques, including spatial maneuvers, to change family boundaries. In this case, the clinician could challenge a father–son coalition against the mother by having the boy exchange seats with the mother in order to detriangulate him from his parents. The therapist would ask the parents to turn their chairs, face each other, and discuss a clinically relevant issue in order to strengthen the boundary between the parental and child subsystems.

Structural therapists combine verbal and nonverbal techniques to challenge family members to change their boundaries and move beyond the system's homeostasis. This sometimes involves having the clinician integrate hand gestures with comments to highlight dyadic communication. Consider the following case example from Minuchin and Fishman (1981):

THERAPIST: Mr. Karig, you seem to have a difference of opinion with your wife about that. Speak with her about your differences of opinion. (*General laughter from all four teenage children and the parents.*)
FATHER: That's funny, because we never talk to each other.
THERAPIST: Well. You need to now, to resolve this difference between you.
FATHER: (TO THERAPIST) I believe that Jerry—(*Therapist indicates that husband should talk to wife. Husband glances at his spouse and continues talking to the therapist. Several children begin making noises.*)
THERAPIST: No, speak to your wife. We will all listen, but you must speak with your wife. (*Makes a gesture that divides the parents from both himself and the rest of the family.*) (pp. 150–151)

Notice how the clinician combined hand gestures with verbal directives to delineate the boundary for the parental subsystem. We should suspect enmeshment in this family for a number of reasons. First, the children tried to rescue their parents by laughing and making noise in response to the therapist's statements. Second, the father reported that he and his wife "never talk to each other," which provides additional evidence of the children's involvement in the parents' marital conflict. If this family is to change, the therapist must strengthen the boundary between the parental and sibling subsystems. This sometimes involves direct intervention, such as the clinician's response to the father's attempt to triangulate (i.e., "No, speak to your wife").

When a family enters treatment, members have framed their own realities or beliefs about the presenting problem. The same is true for the clinician, who holds certain attitudes about the nature and purpose of therapy. Minuchin and Fishman (1981) indicated that the therapist's first challenge is to address these different frames of reference. As they stated:

> The family's framing is relevant for the continuity and maintenance of the organism more or less as it is; the therapeutic framing is related to the goal of moving the family toward a more differentiated and competent dealing with their dysfunctional reality. (p. 74)

A family's framing of reality includes its expectations of each member of the system. One child might be seen as energetic, dedicated, and intelligent. A sibling may be viewed as lazy, dishonest, and slow. Each child's behavior is interpreted relative to these expectations. In dysfunctional families, the identified patient has become the target for the family's problems. The therapist assumes the task of helping family members to reframe the presenting problem as a step toward modifying the system and detriangulating the child. Minuchin et al. (1978) described how reframing was used to alter a family's view of anorexia nervosa. When the Kaplans entered treatment, they described the daughter's eating disorder as a physical illness. Minuchin challenged this belief by saying, "She's not sick; she's involved in a struggle" (Minuchin et al., 1978, p. 178). By reframing the presenting problem in this manner, he provided a rationale for family systems therapy instead of surgery or medication.

Structural therapists also use enactment. In this technique, family members are instructed to act out their conflicts in session so the clinician can observe subsystem relationships and intervene to effect structural change. If Mr. and Mrs. Johnson, for example, avoid discussing their daughter's poor school work, the therapist might direct them to discuss how they plan to have the child complete homework assignments. When family members "enact instead of describe" their conflicts (Minuchin, 1974, p. 141), the therapist can observe family rules in action while turning attention from the identified patient to dysfunctional family relationships. Clinicians direct the enactment by systematically shifting their affiliation from one member to the next, entering into family coalitions and controlling the amount of time spent on different issues. As Minuchin and Fishman (1981) noted, "Enactment requires an active therapist who feels comfortable with engaging and mobilizing people whose responses cannot be predicted" (pp. 80–81). The clinician is definitely not an outside observer; he or she is a participant-observer who is actively involved in the family.

Minuchin and Fishman (1981) described three stages in enactment. The therapist first observes the family in session. When a significant pattern has been identified, the clinician directs the appropriate family members to enact this transaction. The therapist then suggests alternative ways the family could resolve the issue at hand. Enactment might involve the use of spatial manipulation in session (e.g., changes in seating arrangement), verbal directives to strengthen communication between members (e.g., Minuchin's directives to Mr. Karig in the case described previously), or withdrawing from the transaction (e.g., remaining quiet, gazing at the floor) to challenge family members to interact with each other.

Minuchin et al. (1978) described how they use a meal session with families of clients diagnosed with anorexia nervosa. When food is served during the meeting, the therapist watches the family members interact as they are likely to behave during mealtime at home. The clinician then issues a directive before leaving and observing the family from an adjacent room. In his session with the Kaplan family, Minuchin provided a dramatic example of enactment, beginning with the following instructions to the parents before his departure from the therapy room:

> I will be watching through the one-way mirror. I will come back shortly. I want you to negotiate with her. Otherwise she is going to die, the way she is eating. She is starving herself to death. I don't want that to happen. And she is your daughter. (p. 160)

Minuchin et al. (1978) described how the mother and father encouraged, negotiated, reasoned, pleaded, demanded, and threatened their daughter to try to get her to eat. Unfortunately, the parents were unsuccessful because they were not unified in their efforts.

Minuchin returns briefly to point out the parents' lack of cooperation: "The problem here is you two! You say, 'You should eat.' And Mother says, ' You shouldn't eat."' (Minuchin et al., 1978, p. 165). With this challenge, Minuchin relabels Deborah's eating disorder as a systems problem that has its roots in a conflicted spousal dyad. The parents continue to struggle as their daughter cries and criticizes their eating habits, which they in turn defend. When the father resorts to shoving food into his daughter's mouth, Minuchin intervenes and tells the parents they have failed but have done their best. He later ends the session by acknowledging the family's difficult situation but offers hope by recognizing Deborah's control over her life and telling the parents that he will help them work together in parenting their daughter. This example illustrates the powerful impact of enactment. It also serves as a warning of the potential risk of this technique, especially with families in which frustration and anger have reached the dangerous point where family members are likely to physically harm each other. Clinicians who use enactment must assess its risks in advance so the technique is a therapeutic tool that helps families move beyond rather than exacerbate their problems.

Strategic Family Systems Therapy

Strategic therapists have adopted a pragmatic approach in which the focus of treatment is the resolution of family problems, usually without providing insight about the presenting concerns (Sharf, 2000). Strategic therapists use tasks or directives to become a part of the family, collect information about relationship patterns, and precipitate change in members' behavior (Haley, 1976). By directing a family to discuss each day's events at the evening meal, for example, the clinician remains a part of family life outside of therapy sessions. The therapist also learns when the family dines, who attends, and the activities normally associated with the meal. When the family follows this directive, their behavior has changed as they meet, self-disclose, and learn about each other's experiences.

Chapter 12 discussed Haley's (1976) belief that a family's problem must be considered in the context of a sequence of behaviors between at least two members of the system. Madanes (1981, p. 21) stated that a primary goal of strategic therapy is "to prevent the repetition of sequences and to introduce more complexity and alternatives" into the family system. According to Madanes, the therapist's first step is to identify who is involved in this sequence and for what purpose. The clinician then devises an intervention that changes family members' relationships with each other and reorganizes the system. By directing the family to interact in new ways both in and out of session, the therapist helps them develop healthier strategies for fulfilling the function of the presenting problem.

Haley's definition of a directive is very broad. As he observed, "Whatever a therapist does is a message for the other person to do something, and in that sense he is giving a directive" (Haley, 1976, p. 50). Even a child-centered therapist who uses minimal encouragers, such as "Uh-huh," is directing the client to continue talking. Clinicians administer directives or tasks in either a straightforward or paradoxical manner. Straightforward tasks involve a therapist telling clients to do what he or she actually expects the family to do. Haley (1976) offered the following example of a straightforward task designed to strengthen the spousal dyad:

> A husband is asked to do something for his wife that she would not expect, and she is asked to receive it graciously. He cannot do something routine, which she would expect, and therefore he is encouraged to initiate something new in the marriage. He also must think about his wife carefully to decide on something she would not expect. (p. 60)

When clinicians assign straightforward tasks for homework, they set aside part of the following session to discuss the family's experience with the directive. A possible outcome is that the family performed the task, in which case the therapist offers congratulations and asks them to describe the experience. But some families will either partially finish or not complete their homework.

When a family partially completes a task, the therapist should explore the situation to determine the reasons behind this response. Haley (1976) advised against excusing families for incomplete effort because doing so would communicate that the task was not very important. Instead, the clinician should have the family discuss the events that limited their compliance in order to plan for better participation during the upcoming week. Haley recommended that therapists adopt a firm approach with families who make no effort to complete assigned tasks. This includes informing them that they have failed each other or have missed a valuable opportunity for growth. He also described another technique, the paradoxical task, that clinicians can use with families that do not respond to straightforward directives.

Paradoxical tasks are used when the therapist "wants the members to resist him so they will change" (Haley, 1976, p. 67). These tasks contain two messages: "change" and "don't change." By their very nature, paradoxical interventions are confusing for clients and therefore require considerable training and supervised experience on the part of the therapist. They are not to be used by novice clinicians. The theoretical foundation for this approach can be found in the concept of homeostasis. Although a family presumably enters treatment to bring about change, homeostatic forces resist such movement in order to maintain the present system. In paradoxical directives, change and the status quo are integrated into the same message.

Madanes (1981) described how paradoxical directives can be used to treat children's problems. She suggested that therapists adopt a flexible approach and use such techniques as having parents ask the child to exhibit the problem behavior, pretend to exhibit the problem, or pretend to help the parent. Madanes used a playful combination of these in her treatment of a 5-year-old boy who presented with temper tantrums. In session, the therapist asked the child to pretend to have a temper tantrum. The mother was instructed to respond as she typically acted when the boy misbehaved at home. The therapist then asked the child to have another tantrum and for the mother to pretend to walk her son to his bedroom, close the door, and hug and kiss the boy. The mother was then instructed to have a temper tantrum, and the child was to "hug the mother, kiss her, and calm her down" (p. 87). For homework, the therapist told the mother and son to perform each of these sequences before school and when the child returned home in the afternoon. Immediately after each pretend period, they were to have a snack of milk and cookies.

During the next session, the therapist learned that the mother and son had done their homework and that the boy had exhibited no "real" temper tantrums during the week. This improvement was maintained during a 6-month follow-up period. Madanes (1981) believed the paradoxical intervention was effective because the pretend play highlighted the power hierarchy in the mother–son relationship. That is, the boy's power over his mother was playfully illustrated by having the child discipline his mother; the alternate and more appropriate pattern was exhibited when the mother disciplined her son. The two also experienced positive and close contact during the snacks they had together after each pretend session.

Papp (1980) described three stages of paradoxical interventions: redefining the problem in systems terminology, prescribing the paradoxical task, and restraining growth to continue the paradoxical intervention. During the first stage, the therapist works with the family to develop a clear statement of the problem and specific goals for treatment (Madanes, 1981). Haley (1976) described problem redefinition with a 9-year-old boy for whom a year and a half of therapy had been ineffective in treating a long-standing pattern of compulsive masturbation. The treatment goal was redefined as "not to stop the boy from masturbating but from masturbating in public and without pleasure" (p. 72). Consistent with family systems theory, the masturbatory behavior was conceptualized relative to its role in maintaining family homeostasis and a systems-based intervention was developed.

In this case, Haley (1976) prescribed separate paradoxical tasks for the boy and his widowed mother. The child was encouraged to masturbate more often but to focus on the days when he enjoyed it the most. The mother was told she would feel upset when her son improved because she would need to find other activities for herself after she no longer had to spend her days trying to help the child. As Haley described, "A purpose in dealing this way with the mother is to encourage her to prove that she will not get upset when the boy improves" (p. 73). The therapist helped her explore other interests, including school and work, where she could focus her energy in the future.

By the fifth session, the child's masturbation began to diminish, so Haley used the following strategy to restrain growth:

> The therapist condemned him for not cooperating and, as punishment, required him to masturbate once each day in the living room in the presence of his mother and sisters. It had taken five weeks to arrange that the boy do exactly what he had been doing as a presenting problem. Now it was to be done as a punishment. (p. 74)

Haley noted how some therapists would have reservations about using punishment, especially this consequence, as part of a paradoxical task. He justified its use in this case because of the long-standing nature of the boy's problem and the fact that the punishment was identical to the behavior the child was exhibiting before treatment.

Mara Selvini Palazzoli and her associates in the Milan systemic school used the team approach to treatment, which involves having colleagues observe the therapist or co-therapists through a one-way mirror and confer with the clinicians during and after treatment. Although used by others (e.g., Minuchin), the team approach has been an integral part of the Selvini Palzzoli treatment program from its inception. This method offers more than emotional support for the therapists' efforts in session (Nichols & Schwartz, 1998). Team members provide interpretations of the family's verbal and nonverbal behaviors and recommend interventions to be used in session. Observers also can detect when a therapist becomes overinvolved in a family's dysfunctional patterns. Although it is sometimes used for traditional training and supervisory purposes, Selvini (1988) believed that the approach works best when it involves "a team of *equals*" (p. 91) who collaborate in the family's treatment.

Selvini Palazzoli, Boscolo, Cecchin, and Prata (1988a) indicated that members of the Milan school generally treat the entire family as a single unit. The only exceptions were situations when the child was under 5 years of age and when older children had "already been traumatized by numerous medical and psychiatric interventions and are therefore already labeled 'sick' " (p. 122). Selvini Palazzoli et al. initiate contact with the family via telephone. The therapist collects information about the presenting problem and decides who will be invited to the first session. Selvini Palazzoli (1988) described an approach to scheduling sessions that bears some resemblance to Bowen's (1971) method and the on-demand therapy recommended by Winnicott (1977). Although her meetings with a family are more regular than in Winnicott's approach, Selvini Palazzoli scheduled approximately 1 month between sessions to enable the family to respond to the therapist's interventions. As Selvini Palazzoli stated, "If after a therapeutic input we leave the family alone for too short a time, the change will not have developed enough to be observable" (p. 369).

During treatment, the clinician may use what Selvini Palazzoli, Boscolo, Cecchin, and Prata (1988b, p. 305) called the "ritualized prescription" in which the therapist challenges the family's typical relationship patterns by instructing them to engage in an alternative course of action. The clinician presents the ritualized prescription at the end of the session as a clear statement of the family's assignment before the next appointment. In one case, Selvini Palazzoli et al. (1988b) assigned the father responsibility for his son on Tuesdays, Thursdays, and Saturdays. The mother was to assume this job on Mondays, Wednesdays, and Fridays. On each of these days, the "unresponsible" parent was to act as if he or she were not present. Sundays were the day of the week when "everyone must behave spontaneously" (p. 308). Designed to alter the rules for the family game, the prescription specified the times when the parents were responsible for their son, but there was no clear indication of how the responsible parent was to act. According to Selvini et al., "When the family organization is not extremely rigid and dysfunctional, the prescription is followed with remarkable changes" (p. 313).

Behavioral Family Therapy

Nichols and Schwartz (1998) observed that behavioral family therapists adopt a different perspective on family-based interventions. Compared with their colleagues who view the family system as the problem, behavioral clinicians "accept the parents' view that the child is the problem" (p. 286). Treatment often involves the target child and one parent, usually the mother. The therapist typically functions as an educator who teaches parents how to successfully use behavioral techniques (e.g., positive reinforcement) with their children. Treatment characteristically involves a thorough assessment and identification of the problem behavior and related antecedents and consequences. Intervention is specific to the target behavior, and its effectiveness is evaluated throughout treatment using the single-case experimental method.

According to Nichols and Schwartz (1998), the most common behavioral techniques used in family-based treatments are operant conditioning and cognitive-behavioral interventions (see Chapter 11). An important question in any discussion of behavioral interventions with families is, "Who is the client?" When an assessment reveals that parents lack appropriate child-rearing skills, therapists often consult with them to teach effective child management techniques. Clinicians who use this intervention typically work only with parents. Because children are not directly involved in these sessions, we will examine this approach in Chapter 14 when we discuss parent consultation. Here we examine the use of behavioral and cognitive-behavioral techniques with children and their parents in family therapy.

Operant conditioning has been used in conjunction with other family systems therapies. Minuchin,

Rosman, and Baker (1978), for example, used behavioral techniques during the inpatient phase of their structural family systems treatment for youths with anorexia nervosa. When hospitalization is required, access to privileges is made contingent upon calorie consumption and weight gain. If a client fails to meet a preestablished daily weight gain, for example, she is restricted to bed rest or not allowed to receive visitors or mail. The authors found that most clients responded to this program, although all clients tested the limits set by hospital staff. The behavioral component of the program is brief and intended for clients most at risk for illness or death related to their eating disorder. After the behavioral program is successfully completed, structural family systems therapy is initiated.

Cognitive-behavioral family therapy is designed to explore "the cognitions that individuals hold about their own family life and about family life in general" (Schwebel & Fine, 1994, p. 50). Clients are often unaware of their personal theories of the family, so therapy involves helping them recognize these beliefs, assess their impact on daily life within and outside of the family, and restructure maladaptive beliefs into more healthy cognitions (Schwebel & Fine, 1994). Barton and Alexander (1981) described one version of this method, functional family therapy, which is based on the following assumption: *"Family members cannot change their behavior until they change their view of themselves and other family members"* (p. 421). To achieve this goal, clinicians must first confuse family members regarding their theories of the family and their beliefs about the presenting problem. When this is accomplished, therapists teach clients more healthy ways of fulfilling the functions served by the presenting problem.

According to Dattilio (1998), the first step in cognitive-behavioral family therapy is a meeting with the entire family to assess maladaptive family schema, and interactional patterns. This is followed by an explanation of the treatment program (e.g., descriptions of maladaptive thoughts) and an investigation of each member's theory of the family. As Dattilio stated:

> The trick here is to try to introduce the model in a creative way, so as to not bore the family with theories. Therefore, conveying this information is sometimes done in a playful manner, using jokes and making a potentially heavy situation more lively. Most importantly, this process of education helps family members cut through some of the bickering and blaming by providing them with tools and allowing them to become students of their own behavior. (p. 71)

Dattilio also assigns homework to families so they can apply what is learned in session. This might involve having family members record their maladaptive thoughts about everyday events and the use of constructive alternatives.

Solution-Focused Family Systems Therapy

When family systems therapies were first developed, treatment often continued for years. Bowen (1966), for example, reported that success with family therapy may require 4 years of weekly sessions. Treatment of this duration may have been acceptable at a time when lengthy psychodynamic interventions were the standard, but it is not viable in a practice environment that emphasizes brief therapies. Proponents of family systems therapies have responded to this change in mental health services by developing brief-term interventions that can be used with children and their families.

Segal (1991) identified different methods of brief-term family therapy, including those based on the strategic and behavioral models. Another brief approach is solution-focused family systems therapy, which is designed to help families find "solutions for their concerns in as few sessions as possible" (Lee, 1997, p. 6), typically between five and six meetings (De Shazer et al., 1986). Clinicians who use this model spend little time assessing for the causes of a family's complaint because they use therapy sessions to help clients devise solutions. This future-oriented approach is intended to help family members realize that their presenting complaints are not as pervasive as some might believe. For example, no child is disobedient or noncompliant with all people every minute of the day. Solution-focused therapists capitalize on the variability in children's behavior to instill hope for the future and to reframe the family's view of the situation.

Solution-focused therapists use various types of questions intended to help family members generate solutions for their complaints. Lee (1997) described five of these: exception, outcome, relationship, scaling, and coping questions. Exception questions are designed to change clients' perceptions of the presenting problem. De Shazer (1988) described how families develop absolute frames of reference for the difficulties they encounter. For example, a father believes that his daughter misbehaves because she is "a bad child." Because "reality is more what we make of it than what it might really be" (De Shazer, 1988, p. 100), this father's view of his child frames his interpretation of her broad and varied repertoire of behaviors. To help him reconstruct his view of the child, a clinician might use an exception question such as, "When do you not have these problems with Jane?" As the family generates exceptions to the father's rule (e.g., a sibling who mentions that Jane helped him with his homework yesterday), family perceptions of Jane begin to change as do their expectations for her future behavior.

Outcome questions relate to the future. If family members expect Jane to misbehave, they will probably notice these behaviors but overlook her appropriate actions. Lee (1997) described how outcome questions can be used to help the family focus on "small, observable, and concrete behaviors" (p. 5) in order to detect improvement in the child's behaviors. De Shazer (1988) described an outcome question that he termed "the miracle question" (p. 5). With the family we are discussing, the clinician might ask the following:

> If a miracle happened and you woke up tomorrow and your problem was solved, what would be the first small sign that tells you that a miracle has happened and your problems have been resolved, and what would be the first different thing that you would notice about yourself, your spouse, and your child? (Lee, 1997, p. 5)

The perceptual shift that family members experience as they ponder this question could result in a more positive and concrete orientation to the presenting complaint. The answers the family gives provide the basis for an intervention intended to make the miracle a reality.

Solution-focused therapists use relationship questions to obtain a client's perception of significant others' feelings and attitudes about the presenting problem. These questions prompt a person to adopt the perspective of another family member. For example, a therapist might ask a school-age child, "What would your parents think if they came home from work one day and your miracle had happened?" The child's answer to this question provides important information about the parents' reactions, which must be taken into account during treatment planning. If the child were to answer that the mother would be excited but the father would not notice the change, the therapist should consider ways of helping the father to recognize his child's accomplishments. Of course, clinicians must consider the child's ability to assume the other's perspective (see the Developmental Considerations section in Chapter 6) if relationship questions are to be of value with young clients.

Scaling questions are used to help family members quantify a host of treatment variables, such as pretreatment-posttreatment change in self-worth, on a multiple-point scale (e.g., 1 to 10, with 1 = worst and 10 = best) (Berg, 1994). Sometimes more than one scale is used to measure progress on different goals so family members are able to generalize their success with some goals to other areas of concern. Clinicians use scaling questions from the outset of therapy to assess clients' status relative to treatment goals. After a family has provided an initial rating, Selekman (1997) recommended that therapists ask the following question: "Let's say we get together in one week's time and you proceed to tell me that you took some steps and got to a 7 [the family was at a 6], what will you tell me that you did?" (p. 64). The clinician who listens carefully will learn possible interventions that can be used during the upcoming week.

The last type of question that Lee (1997) described is the coping question, which is designed to help clients overcome feelings of helplessness in dealing with the family's complaints. It is not unusual for clients to enter treatment believing that their situation could not be worse than it is. As a result, they often overlook areas they are handling in a competent manner. Selekman (1997) observed that coping questions are of particular value in working with families that believe they do not possess the skills needed to effect change. Consider a parent who remains triangulated with the family of origin and questions his or her ability to help an oppositional defiant child. The clinician might use the following intervention:

> Since you are the kind of person who believes what your mother said about you, I can see how discouraged you can become about yourself. So, tell me, how do you keep going, day after day, when there seems to be no hope? How do you even manage to get up in the morning? (Berg, 1994, p. 112)

The therapist communicates that the family situation could be worse and that the parent must have been doing something correct for the family to function as well as it has.

In an early paper on solution-focused therapy, De Shazer and Molnar (1984) described four dysfunctional client beliefs: (1) the presenting complaint is stable and destined to continue, (2) the family does not possess the resources needed to remedy the problem, (3) the family's current response is the only logical intervention, and (4) the complaint is beyond the family's control. De Shazer and Molnar provided examples to illustrate how a solution-focused therapist might intervene with these beliefs. In a family with an 8-year-old boy who was exhibiting temper tantrums at home and school, the parents found various forms of punishment (e.g., time-out, spanking) to be ineffective. They had begun to believe they lacked the skills needed to change their son's behavior.

With only the parents present, the therapist recommended that they respond to the boy's next temper tantrum in a different manner: "no matter how strange, or weird, or off the wall what you do might seem" (p. 301). The clinician was saying that there were a number of responses available, although the parents previously labeled most of them as so unusual to be of little benefit. They implemented the authors' directive in the following manner:

> During the next tantrum, father gave Jimmie a cookie without saying a word. The tantrum stopped. When mother next witnessed a tantrum, she danced circles around the boy while he kicked and screamed. The tantrum stopped. Subsequently, neither the parents nor the school reported any tantrums. The cookies and the dance seemed to have been effective because neither was "more of the same." (De Shazer & Molnar, 1984, p. 301)

When conceptualized in the context of family systems theory, a brief-term and focused intervention such as this produces other changes in the system. As a result of their success in remediating the temper tantrums, the parents would feel more confident and competent in their child-rearing role. Through their cooperation in the intervention, the couple could experience a closer marital relationship. And with these changes in the family, the child would become more individuated from the parents.

Many clinicians would treat this family by focusing on the problem behavior and using elimination of the problem as their sole measure of treatment outcome. De Shazer and Molnar (1984) noted that when families enter treatment, they typically believe they are limited to the ineffective technique (or techniques) they have been using. De Shazer et al. (1986) challenged therapists to expand the family's view of the complaint by having members focus on the future and generate a treatment goal that is positive in nature. As De Shazer et al. stated, "It seems commonsense that if you know where you want to go, then getting there is easier" (p. 213). By developing constructive goals for the future, the therapist asks the family to consider what the child might become rather than spending valuable time and energy discussing why the child is a problem.

Contextualized Family Treatments

Chapter 1 discussed how a child's cultural surround must be taken into consideration when planning treatment. Tharp (1991) described a continuum of contextualized treatments ranging from community-based interventions to individual therapy. He stated that the more contextualized alternatives, such as community-based strategies, network therapy, and home-based treatments, are the interventions of choice for children from nondominant ethnic groups. This section examines how network therapy and home-based treatments have been used with children of color.

Network therapy is designed to capitalize on what Speck and Attneave (1973) described as an "invisible, but at the same time a very real, structure in which an individual, nuclear family, or group is embedded" (p. 6). Network therapy involves not only the child and the nuclear family but also relatives, friends, neighbors, teachers, and any individual who is significant to the child's development. As you might expect, network therapy sessions can involve rather large groups (e.g., 50 participants) that are facilitated by as many as three therapists (Schoenfeld, Halevy-Martini, Hemley-van der Velden, & Ruhf, 1985). Schoenfeld, Halevy, Hemley-van der Velden, and Ruhf (1986) proposed three stages to be used in network therapy: (1) assessment of the family's presenting problem; (2) group discussion to inform participants of the presenting problem (or problems) and to enhance group cohesion; (3) and the network's active involvement in remediation of the presenting problem and the child's future care and development. Although Schoenfeld and colleagues (1985, 1986) studied the effectiveness of network therapy, they included very few children in their samples. But network therapy's effectiveness with adolescents suggests that this contextualized approach holds promise for troubled families from nondominant ethnic groups.

Juarez (1985) described a variant of network therapy that can be used with Hispanic American children. In this approach, the clinician serves as "an advocate or a direct mediator" (p. 445) between the family and the community. Juarez's approach does not necessarily involve non-family members directly in therapy. Instead, the clinician conducts treatment sessions with the family while establishing contact with significant others in extrafamilial systems. For example, a child's teachers and school counselor might not attend therapy sessions, but the clinician would have ongoing contact with these individuals if school-related problems were a focus of treatment. With low socioeconomic families, the therapist is likely to contact social service agencies, local houses of worship, or charitable organizations to help the family acquire financial assistance. Of course, clinicians who use this approach must uphold their ethical responsibility to obtain parents' consent to contact individuals who are not directly involved in treatment.

The Native Hawaiian practice of *ho'oponopono* is another example of network therapy (Tharp, 1991). Based on her interviews with five native Hawaiian faith healers, Mokuau (1990) described *ho'oponopono* as a "highly systematic and ritualized" (p. 610) practice that involves assessment and discussion of the presenting problem, family members' acceptance of responsibility for the problem and willingness to seek or offer forgiveness, and affirmation of the bonding of family members with each other and to the spiritual powers. The spiritual nature of *ho'oponopono* is also reflected in the prayers to God, family spirits, or both that are offered before and after the session. Likewise, food is offered to the spirits after the closing prayer when the family congregates for a meal. Mokuau noted that *ho'oponopono* is similar to traditional therapy with its structured approach to assessment, intervention, evaluation, and termination, but the approach differs with its "strong belief in spiritualism" (p. 610).

Compared with traditional family systems therapies, home-based treatments are "less insulated from the influences of home, family, and community" (Tharp, 1991, p. 806). They give therapists the opportunity to observe families in their everyday environment and to design contextualized interventions that are appropriate to the clients' needs. An interesting example of this approach is the Homebuilders program, which Kinney, Haapala, and Booth (1991) developed as an intensive home-based intervention for children at risk for out-of-home placement. Started in Tacoma, Washington, in 1974, the program capitalizes on family crises to bring about constructive change.

The Homebuilders therapist delivers services in the child's surroundings (e.g., home, school), averaging 8 to 10 hours of face-to-face contact each week for 4 to 6 weeks. To compensate for the time-intensive nature of this approach, clinicians have a caseload of only two families that are carefully selected based on program criteria, such as the impending removal of a child from the home. After a family is accepted, clinicians select from individual and family interventions, including training in child behavior management, communication and assertiveness skills, and time and money management. Therapists assist families in developing a daily routine to improve organization and consistency at home. They assign homework (e.g., recording the frequency of certain behaviors or events); contract with clients for behavioral change; encourage family members to view their problems as skills deficits rather than symptoms of psychopathology; and help families learn ways of meeting basic needs, including food and shelter. When appropriate, therapists advocate for clients or refer them for support services.

Homebuilders is a family preservation approach that merits serious consideration. Kinney et al. (1991) found that when out-of-home placement was imminent for at least one child, removal from the home was avoided in 73% to 91% of families for a period of 12 months after the Homebuilders services were initiated. Of particular importance to therapists who work with nondominant ethnic group families are results for the Bronx Homebuilders Program, where only 13 of 101 youths (56% Hispanic American, 30% African American, and 14% European American) had been formally placed out of their homes 3 months after termination of services. At first glance, some might consider Homebuilders to be an impractical method for preserving families. But Kinney et al. contended that their program is a cost-effective alternative to traditional out-of-home placements in group homes and residential treatment facilities. Although Homebuilders therapists do carry small caseloads, the cost of these family preservation efforts are similar to many of the traditional approaches currently in use. For example, a Homebuilders clinician will have brief-term intense contact with a small caseload, but therapists in group homes often have a larger clientele that is seen for a longer period of time. According to Kinney et al. (1991), the number of clients served per therapist during a 12-month period is similar, but the children treated in a Homebuilders program have the advantage of home-based interventions designed to mobilize the family's strengths amid crisis situations.

PLAY TECHNIQUES

Earlier in this chapter, we discussed how the family play assessment can be used to collect clinically relevant information about family members' interactions. Family systems therapists also have incorporated children's play into treatment. Scharff and Scharff (1987), for example, described the importance of play sessions with young clients:

> The natural vehicle of expression for the young child is play. Even the child who is verbally adept or precocious will find self-expression easier through play than words. It can be argued that an especially verbal child of 5 or 6 can manage with words in the family. But it is nevertheless true that even that child could say and reveal more of his or her internal world and observations of the family with the help of some extraverbal play material. (p. 307)

From a systems perspective, all family members, including young children, are important to the healthy development of the family (Hardaway, 2000). Therefore, clinicians must acquire the play skills needed to actively involve children in therapy.

Hardaway (2000) observed that children in family treatment are sometimes allowed to play as a diversionary activity while parents and older family members conduct the real work of therapy. Unfortunately, this approach deprives the clinician of valuable information that is available when parents play with their children in session. Hardaway believed that family play reveals the transference that occurs in everyday life between children and their primary attachment figures. Instead of relying on there-and-then reports about parent–child interactions, therapists who observe families at play can see actual examples of parents encouraging and disciplining their child, children defusing spousal conflict, and family members communicating or failing to communicate with each other. Hardaway divided each session of his short-term approach into two stages. During the first half of each hour-long meeting, parents are asked to play with their child as the clinician watches and provides guidance when needed. During the second half of the session, the therapist processes this experience with the parents while the child continues to play nearby. This discussion sometimes includes reviewing videotapes of the family's play to illustrate effective parent–child interactions. Hardaway believed that by having parents and children play in session, therapists can help family members understand the function of their behavior within the family system.

VanFleet (2000) described a brief family-based play therapy for children who either have a chronic illness or are from families with someone who has a condition that requires ongoing medical treatment. VanFleet adopted Guerney's (1964) filial therapy, which was originally designed to train small groups of parents in the use of child-centered play techniques. In his 10-session model of filial therapy, VanFleet worked with individual families to teach parents how to create a facilitative environment where children could disclose personally meaningful information. This method is thought to provide a developmentally appropriate mechanism (i.e., child-centered play) for supporting children in their exploration of the thoughts and feelings associated with chronic illness.

VanFleet (2000) recommended that clinicians begin filial therapy with an introductory meeting for parents to describe the purpose and format of treatment and to provide information about chronic illness. During the second session, the therapist meets with the family and demonstrates the use of child-centered techniques with each child between the ages of 3 and 12 years. Parents are given reading materials on filial therapy (see VanFleet, 1998) and asked to review them before the third session, when the clinician again meets with the parents to teach them how to structure play sessions, develop active listening skills, and set limits when playing with their child. VanFleet devoted the next three sessions to parent–child practice and feedback for parents in their use of these play skills. The focus of therapy then turns to the use of these techniques during scheduled play sessions at home. Although treatment is designed to last only 10 sessions, parents are encouraged to continue playing with their children and to expand their use of filial therapy skills to other aspects of family life.

Involving young children in family therapy requires the use of developmentally appropriate techniques, including play. Although some clinicians choose to adopt a more traditional approach by engaging in one-on-one play with these clients, family play sessions provide clinically relevant information that is otherwise unavailable to the therapist. Clinicians are able to observe actual interactions between parents and their children. The data collected in these sessions can be used to develop treatment plans and evaluate progress in therapy. Training parents to use facilitative play with their children also offers skills that can be used to enhance family functioning in general. A parent who learns to listen more effectively during play can apply this skill in everyday interactions and contribute to better communication within the family. This section examined two family play methods, one based on psychodynamic theory and the other on child-centered principles. Chapter 16 discusses parent–child interaction therapy (Eyberg, 1988) and a related treatment developed by McNeil, Bahl, and Herschell (2000), two integrated approaches in which play is used in the context of the family.

GROUP TECHNIQUES

Earlier in this chapter, we discussed Parent Effectiveness Training (Gordon, 1970) and the Premarital Relationship Enhancement Program (PREP) (Markman et al. 1993), two group methods designed to teach communication and conflict resolution skills. We reviewed network therapy (Speck & Attneave, 1973), a contextualized family intervention that involves the participation of significant others in a child's life. Group methods were also embraced by early contributors to the field of family therapy. As you will recall, Bowen (1971) used groups in his multiple family approach to intervention. For reasons of efficiency and outcome, group methods have continued to receive attention and constitute a treatment model that merits serious consideration. This section discusses recent group therapies that have been developed for use with troubled families.

In a preliminary study of family group therapy, Fristad, Gavazzi, and Soldano (1998) followed nine families enrolled in their multifamily psychoeducational group therapy program for children with mood disorders. The authors' six-session format included a family group at the outset of each meeting followed by separate groups for parents and children. Parent sessions provided information about depression and suicide, psychopharmacotherapy, and communication and problem-solving skills. Group sessions for children included the opportunity for social interaction, a factual discussion about mood disorders, and the development of effective social skills. After the sixth session, Fristad et al. collected consumer satisfaction data and found that clients rated the program as a positive learning experience. The authors also reported preliminary evidence to suggest that parents had more positive and fewer negative attitudes and behaviors toward their children at the end of treatment.

Meezan and O'Keefe (1998) described a multifamily approach designed to prevent child maltreatment in at-risk families. For their program, the authors used different methods, including structural family systems therapy, behavior and cognitive-behavioral therapies, and crisis intervention. Six to eight families participated in groups conducted by a team of four therapists. Weekly sessions scheduled over an 8-month period covered such topics as child and adult development, parenting techniques, and communication skills. Families also received the services of a case manager who helped them obtain public assistance for basic needs. Compared with clients randomly assigned to traditional family therapy, those in the multifamily condition were less likely to prematurely terminate treatment and appeared to have better parent–child interactions at the end of therapy.

Meezan and O'Keefe (1998) did not include a waiting list condition in their study, probably because they conducted their study in a clinic setting with documented cases of child maltreatment. As discussed in Chapter 5, researchers who work in these settings encounter a number of ethical and practical limitations, including those associated with assigning troubled families to waiting lists. Another confound in the Meezan and O'Keefe study is their use of different treatments, including multifamily group therapy and case management services. Although the Fristad et al. and Meezan and O'Keefe results are encouraging, additional research is needed to examine the benefits of multiple family treatments. These studies should include analyses of treatment components and comparisons with traditional family therapy. Investigators should consider recruiting families for whom a brief delay of treatment is not problematic, thereby providing the opportunity to incorporate a waiting list condition in their research design.

Barrett (1998) conducted a control-group treatment-components study in her evaluation of cognitive-behavioral group therapy with Australian children, ages 7 to 14 years, who were diagnosed with various anxiety disorders. Her 12-session program involved weekly 2-hour group meetings conducted by two co-therapists. Children were given an adaptation of Kendall's (1992) *Coping Cat Workbook*, which is discussed in Chapter 11. During the initial four sessions, clients were introduced to the techniques described in the workbook. These included relaxation training, positive self-talk for coping with anxiety, and self-evaluation and self-reward strategies. Barrett used two treatment formats: group sessions for children only and a family group for parents and children to facilitate parent–child teamwork. In the family group, the co-therapists, parents, and children completed the children's workbook together. Parents received a manual that covered problem-solving, communication, and child anxiety management skills, which parent–child dyads practiced in session. Parents were also trained to monitor their own feelings, including anxiety, to provide a more positive role model for their children.

Barrett (1998) found that her two therapy groups were comparable and more efficacious than assignment to a clinic waiting list. She also reported that the family group appeared to have a more positive impact over time. At 12-month follow-up, Barrett found that children in this group rated themselves as less fearful than did their peers in the child-only group. Children in the family group also exhibited significantly fewer internalizing and externalizing behaviors. Barrett pointed to systemic factors to account for clients' improvement after treatment ended. We can hypothesize that changes occurring in the parent–child relationship as a result of family group therapy transformed interactions in the system in a lasting and beneficial manner.

INTERVENTION TARGET

Role of the Parent

Parents are key figures in family systems therapy. Bowen (1971), for example, preferred to work only with parents because they are responsible for directing the life of the family. He recommended that clinicians explore family of origin issues and multigenerational influences on the presenting problem. Haley (1973) suggested that parent sessions be used to examine the family life cycle and developmental concerns that are relevant to treatment (Haley, 1973). Satir (1983) met with parents during the first few sessions to assess marital and parenting issues as they relate to the family's presenting problem. As she noted, "In dysfunctional families, the mates have usually despaired of or abandoned their marital roles and have become just parents, focused on their children because they dare not focus on one another" (p. 181). For treatment to be effective, the adults in the family must achieve a healthy integration of their roles as spouses and parents.

During family sessions, parents learn new ways of interacting with each other and their children. This sometimes involves participation in experiential activities, including enactment and family sculpting, to effect change in the family system. Parents are asked to complete or supervise homework assignments between treatment sessions. When a behavioral approach is used, they are expected to acquire and use specific child management skills with their children. They are also asked to monitor their child's behavior and maintain recording charts that are reviewed each week in therapy. Finally, parents are challenged to develop new and more positive views of the presenting problem. Instead of focusing on complaints, they generate solutions that capitalize on the strengths of the family.

Role of the Child

Family systems therapy offers the advantage of having all families members together at the same time. Although this allows the therapist to observe interactions as they occur instead of relying on clients' self-reports, children sometimes feel overwhelmed at the outset of treatment when their negative behavior is the focus of attention. For this reason, clinicians might encourage the identified patient to engage in therapeutic play during family sessions. Sometimes children are allowed to play in session, not as a source of clinical information but as a diversionary activity while the therapist works with other members of the family. Clinicians should not assume that a child at play is disengaged from the therapeutic process. It is not unusual for a young client to attend to the therapist's conversation with the family and to insert clinically relevant comments at appropriate times in the session.

Scharff and Scharff (1987) stated that very young children are often excluded from family sessions because therapists are uncomfortable working with this age group. Satir (1983), for example, warned that including these children "might spell anarchy to the therapy process" (p. 179). She was, of course, referring to the developmental differences between adults and children, who tend to be more distractible, lack verbal sophistication, and possess a more concrete and short-term view of the world. But Satir recommended that therapists involve all family members in at least some sessions to study family rules and communication styles. By observing parents and children interact, therapists can learn how the family handles conflict as it arises in session. For this reason, Satir (1983) suggested that therapists see the entire family for at least two sessions, although other meetings may involve only the parents when children are younger than 5 years. When children are older than this age, she included them as regular participants but reserved the right to schedule sessions for family subgroups, such as the mother and father.

Verbal children are encouraged to talk in family meetings. This can occur in response to the therapist's questions or during experiential activities. In behavioral family therapy, children sometimes monitor and record target behaviors under their parents' supervision. When appropriate, they implement cognitive-behavioral strategies to change negative self-statements or dysfunctional views of their cultural surround. In solution-focused family therapy, children are encouraged to participate with their family in developing new ways of conceptualizing the presenting problem.

Role of the Therapist

Family systems therapists are not independent of their clients (Minuchin & Fishman, 1981). They join each family in treatment and a become significant member of that system. The clinician's role varies on a continuum, from therapist as expert at one end to family members as experts at the other (Thayer, 1991). In the traditional approaches, such as structural, strategic, and behavioral family therapy, the clinician is viewed more as an expert who assumes responsibility for leading and directing treatment sessions. Solution-focused therapists tend toward the other end of the continuum because they see their role as that of facilitator for the family's self-exploration and discovery of alternative courses of action.

Scharff and Scharff (1987) described how therapists provide a holding environment that allows the family to examine the anxieties in the system and its individual members. Object relations family therapists attend to transference and countertransference in session to avoid becoming emotionally distant from clients, focusing on superficial issues, siding with one member, or interpreting the family's situation in overly simplistic or clinical terms. Minuchin et al. (1978) described a different role for the family therapist. They believed that clinicians direct treatment by "controlling the flow of transactions, organizing or unbalancing family dyads, supporting or stressing family members, and in general, exploring with family members their views of reality and offering alternatives which promise hope" (p. 94). Strategic therapists also adopt a directive stance in their efforts to help families solve problems. As Madanes (1981) has stated, the strategic model "assumes that all therapy is directive and that a therapist cannot avoid being directive, since even the issues he chooses to comment on and his tone of voice are directive" (pp. 23–24).

Satir (1983) discussed the therapist's role in directing family sessions when children are present. At the outset, the clinician states the rules that will apply in session. These typically include listening to others before speaking and no destruction of property or harming others. Satir cautioned that therapists should not discipline children in session. Rather, they should wait and watch how parents handle the misbehaving child. As she noted, "If I took over this role I would lose the very opportunity I am after, the opportunity to observe how the mother and father perform their parenting function" (p. 184). She believed that therapists function as teachers of effective communication who help families to become aware of relationship patterns and the roles (e.g., placater) of individual members. Behavioral family therapists also assume an educational function when they teach parents to use more effective child management techniques and to monitor and evaluate the effect that environmental manipulations have on their child's behavior.

Family systems therapists often abandon formal psychiatric diagnoses and instead focus on the definition and resolution of relationship problems in the family system (Madanes, 1981). Haley (1971) observed that the family is only one of a number of social systems in which family members are involved. Systems therapists are likely to interpret a presenting problem within the context of these overlapping social groups, which include the neighborhood, the child's school, and the parents' places of employment. According to Selvini (1988), clinicians translate their definition of the problem into a resolution of the family's complaints through a process of hypothesis formulation and testing. When a treatment strategy is not having the desired effect, the therapist reassesses the situation and adopts an alternative intervention. The direction of therapy is even changed during a single session when the clinician obtains information that requires rejecting existing treatment hypotheses and developing alternative formulations.

Solution-focused therapists enter into a cooperative relationship with their clients to unleash the family's constructive energies. Similar to their strategic colleagues, solution-focused therapists attend to the resolution of problems and give little attention to the causes of a family's complaints. They resemble structural family therapists in their use of questions (e.g., exception questions) intended to reframe the presenting problem and to convey hope for the future. Similar to behavioral family therapists, solution-focused clinicians help clients develop treatment goals that are both observable and measurable (Mostert, Johnson, & Mostert, 1997). They also encourage family members to "think small" (Lee, 1997, p. 6) when it comes to setting goals because they believe success in one aspect of family life cultivates positive change elsewhere. And their brief-term orientation requires that as therapists we "suspend our own therapeutic agendas, forget about what questions we might want to ask next, and concentrate deeply on the language, themes, and beliefs the clients use to describe their situations" (Selekman, 1997, p. 36).

Role of the School

Kraus (1998) stated that family therapy has traditionally been "a forbidden zone" (p. 14) for school counselors. But the artificial boundaries that professionals have imposed between the school and home are changing, and counselors are being asked to provide mental health services to families. Comprehensive services for troubled students require consideration of school and family influences on a child's problems. A trained counselor can distinguish between children who are in need of a school-based family intervention and those who require the services of a community-based family therapist. As Lockhart and Keys (1998) stated, school counselors must:

> understand basic family systems issues so they are able to conduct, at a minimum, a first interview with a family, help the school staff understand the family dynamics as they apply to the school scene, and interact appropriately with a therapist for the family. (p. 5)

Bilynsky and Vernaglia (1999) described a six-stage model for working with troubled children and their families. At the outset, the school counselor must determine whether a student's behavior at school is related to problems in the family. The counselor assesses the child's view of the situation before contacting the family and inviting them to become involved in an assessment of family functioning and the family's interpretation of the child's behavior. The counselor engages parents in the development of a treatment plan, which often includes home- and school-based interventions combined with community referrals for needed services. The last stage in the Bilynsky and Vernaglia model is ongoing contact with the family to evaluate the impact of treatment at home and in school. Central to this process is the establishment of a working relationship with the family, especially the parents.

Edwards and Foster (1995) discussed the challenges that counselors encounter when they try to bring together a family with school personnel. The authors indicated that a common obstacle is systems blaming in which parents hold teachers responsible for a student's problems and school staff members complain that the child's misbehavior or academic difficulties are the result of a dysfunctional home environment. Through telephone conversations and meetings with parents and their ongoing interaction with colleagues at school, counselors can facilitate communication and develop a cooperative effort on behalf of the child.

Sometimes students and their families require ongoing treatment services that are beyond the school counselor's training and supervised experience. Downing, Pierce, and Woodruff (1993) suggested that in these situations the counselor establish a collaborative effort among the parents, the school, and a community-based therapist. When counselors identify the need for specialized treatment, they can help parents locate a qualified service provider in the community. The counselor's involvement in a case does not end here. As Downing et al. noted, the school counselor has "the advantage of being part of the child's day-to-day life" (p. 105). After the parents have signed the appropriate releases of information, school counselors are able to capitalize on their unique position to coordinate the flow of information among the school, parents, and therapist and to develop and support multidisciplinary interventions for the child.

Most school counselors have limited or no training in systems theory and related therapies. Hinkle

(1993) emphasized the need for systems-based instruction in counselor education programs and the retraining of counselors currently in the schools. An important component of these programs is helping counselors to determine their competence in applying a systems approach. As Hinkle noted, school counselors can learn to conceptualize student problems in terms of experiences at school and home. They can acquire the knowledge and skills needed to work with parents and teach more effective child-rearing techniques. But counselors must be taught to identify families that require treatment from a specially trained therapist. When referrals are made to services providers in the community, school counselors can coordinate school- and community-based services by maintaining communication with the professionals involved with the case.

RESEARCH

Shadish, Ragsdale, Glaser, and Montgomery (1995) stated that the outcome research on systems therapies is "quite impressive;" (p. 346). Still, the history and scope of research on these methods is limited when compared with the studies on individual treatments for common childhood problems. According to Friedlander (1998), the existing work on family interventions has typically addressed questions that researchers such as Eysenck (1952) and Levitt (1957) were asking about individual therapies in the 1950s. Investigators have studied family therapy as a general approach to treatment and an intervention for specific problems. Pinsof, Wynne, and Hambright (1996) reviewed the results of empirical work in the area and concluded that family therapy is more effective than no treatment and that families are not harmed by these interventions. Based on their meta-analysis of 44 treatment studies, Shadish et al. (1995) also found that children treated with family-based interventions did better than clients who received no treatment. These results contrast with earlier observations by Hazelrigg, Cooper, and Borduin (1987), who concluded that there was "no clear consensus among reviewers regarding the effectiveness of family therapy" (p. 429).

Conducting controlled studies of family-based interventions is complicated by a variety of factors. Similar to psychodynamic approaches, the theoretical principles for family systems therapy are sufficiently diverse that researchers have difficulty studying the effectiveness of family therapy per se. Instead, investigators must be specific about the theoretical approach (e.g., strategic, structural) and the intervention strategies (e.g., paradoxical tasks, enactment) under investigation. Hazelrigg et al. (1987) cited the need for psychometrically sound measures that can be used to evaluate therapeutic process and outcome. The authors also observed that the focus of existing research has been the family system, with little or no attention given to the extrafamilial systems that play direct roles in children's development.

Pinsof et al. (1996) reported that research on family therapies has reached the point where treatment versus no-treatment comparisons should be reserved for presenting problems that have received little or no empirical scrutiny. The authors contended that for other childhood problems, researchers should examine the relative effectiveness of different interventions. Researchers sometimes forego the use of a no-treatment group for ethical reasons, especially in situations in which children present with life-threatening problems. Of course, a limitation of this method is the difficulty of interpreting results when no significant differences are found between the treatments under investigation. An example of this dilemma is the controlled comparison of behavioral family systems therapy and psychodynamic individual therapy that Robin et al. (1999) conducted with girls diagnosed with anorexia nervosa. Family therapy was found to be more effective in limited areas (e.g., change in body mass), but the general impression was that both treatments were equally effective when delivered over a 12- to 18-month period. Unfortunately, the lack of a no-treatment control condition makes it impossible to determine whether the interventions were therapeutic beyond what would be expected with the passage of time.

Controlled comparisons of family therapy and other treatments are in their infancy. Pinsof et al. (1996) identified a number of areas for improvement, including more specific definition of presenting problems and treatment methods. To facilitate comparison of the results obtained in different studies, Shadish et al. (1995) recommended that family researchers adopt common measures of treatment process and outcome. Both Pinsof et al. and Shadish et al. stated that research is needed on both treatment efficacy and effectiveness. The authors also agreed that more attention must be given to treatment efficiency to identify cost-effective family-based interventions for childhood problems. This includes studies based on treatment setting (e.g., inpatient vs. outpatient), theoretical orientation (e.g., structural vs. strategic), and intervention technique (e.g., family vs. individual).

CONTRIBUTIONS AND LIMITATIONS

A major contribution of family therapy is the attention given to the function of a child's behavior within the family system. Clinicians can no longer explain misbehavior as a personal deficit or a symptom of underlying psychopathology. Instead, a child's actions must be interpreted within the context of the family and remediation requires consideration of the relationships within the family. As Okun (1990) stated, family systems therapy offers "a holistic, logical, and efficient treatment format" (p. 360) that clinicians can use with a variety of presenting problems. The approach is grounded in the belief that families have the capacity to grow and that constructive change in any part of the system reverberates to benefit the family unit and its members.

Systems theorists have offered different ways of conceptualizing the family. Those who emphasized multigenerational effects have helped clinicians understand the impact of family of origin issues on the psychosocial development of the child. Structural theorists highlighted the ways that family members become isolated or enmeshed and maintain the status quo in the family at the expense of individual members. Family communication theorists described the relationship between family problems and dysfunctional communication patterns. Additionally, brief-term family theorists turned their attention to specific treatment goals that are addressed in a limited number of sessions to effect meaningful systemic change. As a group, family systems theorists developed the treatment team model of case conceptualization, which provided an impetus for training and research on family interventions (Okun, 1990).

Family systems theory has been limited by its oversight of genetic and physiological influences on children's development. Likewise, relatively little attention has been given to the role of extrafamilial systems, such as the school and community. Consider a child who walks to school carrying a concealed weapon for fear of being assaulted in a crime-ridden neighborhood. By restricting the scope of intervention to the family, the therapist overlooks some significant ecological factors. In this case, the clinician needs to expand the therapeutic horizon beyond the family system to include consideration of the role of local law enforcement, the neighborhood, the school, and city government in alleviating the conditions related to the child's decision to carry a weapon.

Critics of family systems therapies have questioned whether these interventions are a collection of techniques that lacks a strong theoretical foundation. As Okun (1990) stated, "This emphasis on techniques implies that family problems are technical and that there is a 'right' way to fix these problems" (p. 369), much like a plumber might search for a leaking pipe in need of resealing. Strategic and solution-focused strategies such as paradoxical directives, solution-focused questioning, and symptom prescription are very appealing, especially when presented in case studies that illustrate their effectiveness with families. Unfortunately, what appears to be simple and straightforward is actually a very involved therapeutic process. To successfully use these sophisticated methods, therapists must understand their rationale and technique. Clinicians who lack this awareness but try to implement these strategies are at risk of harming their clients.

In her feminist critique, Luepnitz (1988) expressed concern about the gender biases in traditional family therapies, including clinicians' tendency to identify mothers as the source of problems in dysfunctional families. She warned that gender and power are significant issues and that women should not be devalued when they participate in family therapy. Blaming mothers probably occurs for a variety of reasons, including clinicians' perception that mothers are more invested than fathers in the therapeutic process and are therefore less likely to terminate treatment when the therapist challenges them. The practical outcome of this belief system is the therapist's decision to focus on the mother's role in the family and to avoid challenging the father until he becomes more engaged in the treatment process.

Luepnitz (1988) placed the works of pioneers in family therapy under the lens of feminist principles. She criticized Bowen as being "responsible for some of the most politically conservative statements written anywhere in the family literature" (p. 38). Consider the gender bias inherent in Bowen's (1966) concept of undifferentiated family ego mass in which differentiation, which reflects the male value of independence, is viewed as preferable to fusion, which is thought to be more feminine and relationship oriented. Family theorists' oversight of extrafamilial systems has resulted in a lack of attention to sociopolitical influences, such as the different expectations that society holds for men and women. As Luepnitz stated, "Society, it might be said, actually schools females into undifferentiation by teaching them always to put others' needs first and by denying them the same degree of discretion as men with regard to their economic and physical fates" (p. 43). To move beyond these constraints, family therapists must become aware of their own gender biases and the impact these attitudes have on their interactions with women and men and boys and girls in therapy.

FAMILY SYSTEMS INTERVENTIONS: A CASE EXAMPLE

The abuse of children is an unfortunate but relatively common problem in the United States. In 1997, there were approximately 2,000,000 reported cases of child abuse and neglect, 750,000 of which were substantiated (U.S. Bureau of the Census, 1999). Child neglect represented the largest number of substantiated cases (n = 436,630), with physical abuse the second most common category (n = 195,517). Most children are abused by someone they know, often a parent or caregiver. There is no clear categorical distinction between socially accepted parenting techniques and abusive behavior (Contemporary Issues Box 13-1). In a controversial article, Besharov (1985) questioned the breadth and precision of the criteria used to define child abuse. He criticized the broadening of abuse and neglect reporting laws that states adopted after passage of the federal Child Abuse Prevention and Treatment Act of 1974. Besharov noted that the subsequent increase in child abuse reports has overwhelmed the public agencies responsible for protecting children.

Therapists must remember that child abuse and neglect constitute criminal behavior. Treating these families independent of the judicial and child protection systems poses many risks. In some cases, these include being responsible for the continued maltreatment of children whose abuse was not reported to the appropriate authorities. An alternative method is the child abuse multidisciplinary team that facilitates collaboration among the community-based professionals who investigate, prosecute, and treat these cases (Wagner, 1987a). We now return to the case example for this chapter to explore how a family-based intervention can be incorporated into the services provided by a multidisciplinary team.

As you will recall, John Lee ran to his grandparents' home after his father struck him with a belt. Upon hearing the details of the incident, John's grandfather telephoned Children's Protective Services (CPS) to report that his son-in-law had abused the boy. Lois Smithton, the CPS worker assigned to the case, visited the grandparents' home to interview John. The child told her that Mr. Lee had previously hit him with a ruler, a stick, and a belt for receiving poor grades in school. When Ms. Smithton visited the Lee residence to meet the parents, she encountered a remorseful father who accepted responsibility for his behavior. During her interview with the parents, she confirmed that Mr. Lee frequently shouts at John and has on occasions hit the boy.

The next day, Ms. Smithton telephoned John's pediatrician, who reported that the boy did not have a history of suspicious injuries. She also contacted Mr. Ferris, the school counselor, who indicated that John's teachers had never observed any unusual marks or bruises on the boy. The counselor said that John's problems at school are not of recent origin. As a first grader, he did not respond to teachers' directives and had difficulty getting along with other students. Now in the fifth grade, he continues to disobey his teachers and often fights with his classmates.

Ms. Smithton presented the results of her investigation to the community's child abuse multidisciplinary team. After she summarized the case, other members of the team expressed concern about the father's use of corporal punishment while in an angry state. They also recognized that Mr. Lee had acknowledged responsibility for his actions. It was decided that the district attorney would file charges against the father but defer prosecution and drop the charges if Mr. Lee complied with the team's plan for treatment. The father would be informed that he must successfully complete family therapy and be involved in no additional incidents of abusive behavior over the next 36 months. The Lees were referred to Dr. Michael Daley, a local family therapist with experience in treating the perpetrators and survivors of child abuse.

Before his initial meeting with the Lees, Dr. Daley reviewed Ms. Smithton's investigation report. He learned that following a brief courtship, Mr. and Mrs. Lee married during their senior year in high school after they learned they were to have what was to be their only child. Although both families of origin opposed the marriage, the maternal grandparents allowed the Lees to live in a two-bedroom

Contemporary Issues Box 13–1

Is Spanking An Appropriate Child-rearing Technique?

Should parents or teachers spank children for their misbehavior? Answers to this controversial question span the continuum from the popular translation of Proverbs 13:24, "Spare the rod and spoil the child," to laws prohibiting the use of this behavior (Straus, 1994). Spanking appears to be a relatively common practice among parents in the United States. Although it is more likely to occur with younger children, physical punishment is also used with adolescents. The results of national surveys suggest that more than 90% of U. S. parents have used physical punishment at least once with their 3- and 4-year-old children, a figure that remains at 33% for 15-year-old youths (Straus, 1991). Whether parents spank their children may be related to the geographical region where the family resides. Flynn (1994), for example, found that after controlling for the effects of such variables as race and family income, parents in the northeastern U.S. had less positive attitudes about spanking than did parents living in other areas of the country.

Kaplan (2000) contrasted the views of advocates and critics of spanking. The former see this behavior as a brief and immediate response to a child's misbehavior. Critics contend that corporal punishment teaches children to handle interpersonal conflict in an aggressive manner and intills the belief that "might makes right" (Kaplan, 2000, p. 360). Stormshak, Bierman, McMahon, and Lengua (2000) offered empirical support for this relationship when they found that parents' use of phyical punishment was related to aggressive behavior in their kindergarten-age children. But parents' use of physical punishment appears to one of a number of important influences. Bradley, Corwyn, Burchinal, McAdoo, and Coll (2001) analyzed data from the National Longitudinal Survey of Youth and found that spanking was one of a complex interaction of factors associated with behavior problems in children and adolescents. Specifically, the authors found that mothers' ratings of problem behaviors were related to ethnicity, poverty status, and children's age, as well as the use of spanking. As European American and poor African American children aged, the relationship between spanking and behavior problems became stronger. Although European American parents and those in poor African American families might use harsher measures in response to their children's misbehavior, it is also possible that children are more likely to exhibit behavior problems because of their parents' inclination to spank them. The correlational nature of these and other studies limits our ability to conclude a cause-and-effect relationship between spanking and children's development. For this reason, additional research is needed to evaluate the impact of the nature, frequency, and duration of spanking relative to children's behavior and other influences, including gender, ethnicity, and socioeconomic level (Kurz, 1991).

Baumrind (1996) argued that the impact of spanking and other punishment techniques is moderated by the parent–child relationship. For example, does an authoritative parent's use of these methods have different effects on children than the same response exhibited by an authoritarian parent? An important consideration is the parent's emotional state at the time punishment is administered. Do children respond differently to spanking administered in a controlled manner after a parent's rational decision versus an uncontrolled response that is an expression of the caregiver's frustration and anger? Dix, Reinhold, and Zambarano (1990) highlighted the importance of emotional state when they found that mothers who were angry were more likely to expect noncompliance from their children and to endorse sterner disciplinary action. How a parent perceives and responds to the child's actions may determine whether physical punishment remains at a level that many would consider to be an acceptable response or escalates to behavior that constitutes physical abuse of the child. As such, therapists must assess parents' emotional state during punishment episodes and recognize the potential for abuse when corporal punishment is applied in an uncontrolled manner.

In general, therapists should adopt an empirical approach when responding to parents' questions about spanking. To avoid unproductive debate that would jeopardize the therapist–client relationship, clinicians might ask, "How effective have you found spanking to be?" Some parents report short-term improvement in their child's behavior but then describe how these gains were temporary. Therapists should assess each situation as an interaction between the parent and child. For example, they must determine whether immediate improvement in the child's behavior reinforced the parent's use of spanking and increased the likelihood of future incidents of physical punishment. Another important consideration when responding to client questions about spanking is the concrete evidence that clinicians have to indicate that physical punishment was ineffective. The fact that parents sought professional help strongly suggests that physical punishment did not produce the desired outcomes. Considered in this context, the clinician's role then becomes one of helping parents to learn alternative and more effective methods of rearing their children.

apartment they remodeled in their home. After 6 years of this arrangement, the Lees purchased a small house nearby and Mrs. Lee worked with her husband at her father's printing company. On weekdays, Mrs. Lee's mother cared for John before and after school. Mrs. Lee appreciated this help, but her husband criticized his in-laws for "spoiling the kid instead of teaching him to respect his elders." The family has infrequent contact with Mr. Lee's parents, who live about 5 miles away but have never visited their son's home. Mr. Lee objects to his parents' treatment of his wife and child, but he often describes their strict discipline as the approach he and his sister needed as children.

▪ ▪ ▪

When the Lees arrive for their first session with Dr. Daley, he invites them to have a seat in his office. The family initially hesitates but then selects the arrangement illustrated in Figure 13-3. Dr. Daley indicates that he has read Ms. Smithton's report but he asks the family to describe their reasons for seeking therapy.

After a brief silence, Mrs. Lee says, "We are here because my husband got upset with John and . . . "

"What my wife really means," Mr. Lee interrupts, "is that I finally put my foot down and disciplined my son the way he should have been treated years ago. If her nosy parents hadn't . . . "

"Oh, it's my parents' fault that you abused John," Mrs. Lee retorts.

"Yes, if they would let us raise our son the right way, this whole thing never would have happened."

"I don't believe this. You beat the boy and you blame my parents."

"Mr. Lee," Dr. Daley intervenes, "I understand you told Ms. Smithton that you were responsible and you regret having struck John. I also read in her report that you have hit your son before." When the father acknowledges responsibility, Dr. Daley continues, "I imagine all of you have some pretty strong feelings about what happened that afternoon. If I am going to be of any help to you, I must learn how each of you views the situation. I want all of you to have the chance to tell me your story, so I want each person to share his or her thoughts and feelings without being interrupted. Is that OK with everyone?" When the family agrees to this condition, Dr. Daley turns to John and asks him to describe the recent events.

"My Dad expects too much out of me."

"John, that's a lie," Mr. Lee interrupts.

Dr. Daley turns to the father and reminds him of their agreement to not interrupt each other. "I want all of you to have the opportunity to speak. Right now, I'd like to hear from your son. John, please tell me about school."

"The teachers and the kids don't like me, and the work's too hard," he answers. Dr. Daley listens while John describes his father's threats to punish him for poor grades. "He tells me I'm not really trying. He says I could get good grades if I really wanted to."

Dr. Daley asks, "Are there classes where you do get good grades?"

<table>
<tr><th colspan="6">SESSION NUMBER</th></tr>
<tr><th colspan="3">Session #1</th><th colspan="3">Session #5</th></tr>
<tr><td></td><td>John</td><td></td><td></td><td>Mrs. Lee</td><td></td></tr>
<tr><td>Mr. Lee</td><td></td><td>Mrs. Lee</td><td>Mr. Lee</td><td></td><td>John</td></tr>
<tr><td></td><td>Dr. Daley</td><td></td><td></td><td>Dr. Daley</td><td></td></tr>
</table>

Figure 13–3. The Lee Family's Seating Selection During Therapy.

"Well, I guess so," John answers. "I got B's in reading and spelling and an A in art class."

Dr. Daley explores these exceptions to the family's perception of the boy. Mrs. Lee agrees that John does perform better in some classes, but her husband continues to focus on the boy's lack of academic effort and his oppositional behavior at home. Mr. Lee criticizes his wife and in-laws for not disciplining the boy.

"I can see how frustrated you must feel," Dr. Daley responds. He then asks the family, "If the three of you were to wake up tomorrow morning and all your problems were solved, how would you know this miracle had happened and how would each of you be different?"

A brief silence follows before John announces, "I'd get all A's and everybody at school would like me." Unable to explain how he would be different, he adds that his parents would be happy and his father would stop yelling at him.

Mr. and Mrs. Lee do not answer Dr. Daley's miracle question, so he again asks, "If tomorrow morning, the two of you had solved all of these problems, what would have happened to cause that and how would each of you be different?"

"I guess I'm a practical person and just don't expect things to change all that much," Mr. Lee says.

"But if there was a change and your problems were solved by tomorrow morning, how would you know that a miracle had happened? And in what ways would you be different?"

"That's really hard for me to say," answers Mr. Lee.

Mrs. Lee agrees, "I guess we've become so accustomed to the way things are that we can't think about life without all these problems."

Dr. Daley closes the clinical interview by asking each of the Lees to rate their present situation on a scale of 1 to 10, with 10 being the best it could be. No one offers a rating higher than 3. As Mrs. Lee stated, "I'd give us a 1. John is not doing well in school, and my husband and I disagree all the time."

Dr. Daley has the parents complete the BASC Parent Rating Scales and the Family Environment Scale in his waiting room while he administers the BASC Self-Report of Personality to John. At the close of the session, Dr Daley obtains the parents' written consent and the boy's assent to contact Ms. Smithton and John's teachers and school counselor. He asks that Mr. and Mrs. Lee attend the next appointment without their son.

After the session, Dr. Daley telephones Ms. Smithton to notify her of the family's participation in therapy and Mr. Lee's somewhat reluctant admission of responsibility for his behavior. When he phones Mr. Ferris, Dr. Daley learns that the counselor had attempted to use a home-based reinforcement system to reward John for positive behavior at school. When he presented the idea to Mrs. Lee, she rejected it and said that the teachers are responsible for handling problems at school. Dr. Daley contacts John's teacher and discovers that the boy rarely completes homework assignments and never seems to be prepared for tests. The teacher agrees to complete the BASC Teacher Rating Scales.

When Dr. Daley scores the parent-, child-, and teacher-report measures, he learns that Mr. and Mrs. Lee rated their family in a similar manner. Both reported significant problems in the Relationship, Personal Growth, and System Maintenance dimensions of the Family Environment Scale. The general picture was that of a system characterized by conflict, a lack of cohesion, limited independence for its members, and a lack of organization despite a high degree of control. Their BASC results were less consistent, with Mr. Lee reporting a significant number of externalizing behaviors (e.g., conduct problems) and Mrs. Lee describing her son as having social skills deficits. John's teacher also rated him as having poor social relationships. In addition, he reported that the child had poor study skills and exhibited aggressive behavior at school. John's BASC responses indicated that he had a poor attitude toward school and his teachers and relationship problems with his parents and others.

With the information available to him, Dr. Daley develops a treatment plan based on De Shazer's solution-focused approach and principles espoused by Bowen, Haley, Minuchin, and Satir. During the second and third sessions, the parents complete a genogram to examine multigenerational influences on the family's presenting problem (see Figure 13-1). As he conducts this exercise with the couple, they begin to discuss family of origin issues. At one point in the session, Dr. Daley says, "It sounds like your parents used very different child-rearing techniques. So much of what we learn about being a parent comes from our own parents. I am starting to understand why it has been so difficult for the two of you to develop a consistent approach with John." Based on the results of the genogram, Dr. Daley hypothesizes that John is enmeshed with his mother, who is in turn enmeshed with her mother. Triangulation related to diffuse boundaries seems to exist across at least three generations in this family. For example, when Mrs. Lee was a preschooler, her father spent 60 to 70 hours a week away from home building his printing business. During this period, her mother met her own social and emotional needs through her daughter.

Dr. Daley also interprets the Lees' situation from the perspective of the family life cycle. Although their courtship lasted almost 1 year, Mr. and Mrs. Lee skipped to the childbirth period before they had the opportunity to establish their relationship as husband and wife. In treatment, Dr. Daley will attempt to have the couple remediate this deficit by encouraging them to engage in marital activities, including going to the movies as a couple, to complement their parental interactions with each other.

When Mr. and Mrs. Lee return for the fourth session, Dr. Daley asks if they have thought about the miracle question he posed during their first meeting. Mrs. Lee answers by saying that "mornings would be calmer and more organized, and we would get along better."

"Does that include the two of you?" Dr. Daley asks.

"Yes," Mr. Lee responds, "my wife and I would agree about how we want to raise John and we would have breakfast as a family without her mother telephoning to find out when John will be at her house."

"Why do you always blame everything on my parents? If it weren't for them, neither of us would have a job." Mrs. Lee says.

Despite Dr. Daley's attempts to have them address the miracle question, the couple continues to argue about which grandparents' child-rearing techniques are more effective. He decides to address these multigenerational issues to help the couple achieve more individuation from their families of origin. He asks them to discuss a time when the two of them agreed on an effective response to their son's behavior.

Mrs. Lee describes how they recently watched John throw a rock at their neighbor's garage. "We made him go to his room right away. My husband and I talked about it, and we decided we would take away his bicycle for the weekend. John was really upset with us, but we stuck to it. I mean, he's going to hurt someone throwing rocks like that."

"My parents would have done a lot worse to me if I'd have been in John's shoes," Mr. Lee adds, "but I guess we did the right thing because I haven't seen him throwing any rocks lately."

Dr. Daley congratulates the parents on their collaborative effort. He asks them if there are other behaviors they want to address with their son. Mr. Lee immediately identifies the boy's academic performance as his biggest concern. Dr. Daley admits that this is a very important issue, but he encourages the parents to "think smaller at first, something that happens at home where the two of you have much more control over John's behavior." During this part of the session, he carefully chooses his words to emphasize the parents' cooperation (e.g., "the two of you") and their ability to assume greater control of their son's upbringing.

Dr. Daley asks the couple to sit facing each other and to discuss their goals. They manage to communicate about relevant issues but are unable to identify a specific goal for the next week. Based on his observations of the couple's interactions, he assigns them the task of meeting for no more than 1 hour during the week to select their next child-rearing goal. He then asks them to identify any obstacles that might prevent them from setting aside this time.

"Nothing," they answer in unison.

"What about your parents?" Dr. Daley asks.

"My parents?" Mrs. Lee.

"I'm referring to both of your parents," he answers.

Appearing somewhat confused, Mr. Lee asks, "My parents? What have they got to do with it? We never see them."

"But they seem to have a presence in your home," Dr. Daley says. "We have talked a lot about how your in-laws' attitudes toward child rearing have influenced your wife's interactions with John. The same can be said for your family and you."

Turning to her husband, Mrs. Lee says, "I think he's saying that both of us are trying to raise John the way we were raised. Maybe we need to find out what works best for us."

When Mr. Lee agrees, Dr. Daley asks the parents to bring John to the next appointment so the four of them can discuss the family's goals for therapy.

During the fifth session, the family's seating arrangement has changed (see Figure 13-3). The parents select chairs adjacent to each other, and John sits next to his mother. The parents announce that they want their son to make his bed every morning before he goes to his grandparents' house. Dr. Daley facilitates a discussion between the parents and child to explore avenues for achieving this goal. During subsequent sessions, the family addresses more complex parenting issues, including John's problems at school. The parents are asked to set aside time every week to discuss their goals for John. Through his contacts with the boy's teacher and school counselor, Dr. Daley is able to gain the parents' cooperation with the home-based reinforcement program the counselor had previously suggested.

During the eighth session with Mr. and Mrs. Lee, Dr. Daley focuses on the couple's relationship with Mr. Lee's parents. The Lees describe their limited contacts with John's paternal grandparents. Mr. Lee says, "I think my wife was right a few weeks ago when she said that my parents play an important part in all this. I disagreed at first because I figured we never saw them, so how could they be important? But the more I thought about it, the more I realized that I want them to be part of our life." He describes two recent telephone conversations with his parents and a visit he and John made to their house. With Dr. Daley's help, the Lees discuss how they want both sets of grandparents to have meaningful contact with their family.

Toward the end of the session, Dr. Daley changes the topic to the Lees' marital relationship by focusing on the couple's recent achievements in parenting their son. "We've talked a lot about rewarding John for appropriate behavior. How do the two of you want to reward yourselves for your success as parents during the past few weeks?"

"The two of us? What do you mean?" Mrs. Lee asks.

"You have worked together very well, and you have been successful in improving John's behavior. I think it would be a good idea for you to do something as a couple to reward yourselves for your efforts."

"You mean, go out and do something without John? Like go on a date?" Mrs. Lee asks.

"Yes," Dr. Daley answers.

Mr. Lee anxiously shifts in his chair and says, "We aren't rich, you know. With the money it's costing us for these sessions, we can't afford a sitter. Plus the price of dinner. I don't know."

"Yes," adds Mrs. Lee, "if we were to do anything like you're suggesting, we'd have to ask my parents to watch John. I thought we were supposed to be avoiding my parents and living our own lives."

Dr. Daley listens to the parents' objections and then intervenes, "Our goal is not for you to be totally independent of your parents. What we probably want to develop is more interdependence that enables you to assume primary responsibility for raising John while giving both of your parents the chance to be grandparents. You know, let them spoil John before they return to the peace and quiet of their own home." The parents laugh at this thought, and Dr. Daley turns to Mr. Lee, "What do you think would happen if you asked your parents to watch John while the two of you went out for a few hours?"

"Based on what they've said lately, I think they would really like that."

"I think it's time we did that," Mrs. Lee adds. "John needs to spend time with all of his grandparents."

The couple decides to ask Mr. Lee's parents to watch John on Saturday night so they can take a walk and get ice cream, something they enjoyed before they married. Eventually, they no longer need the discussion of child-rearing issues as an "excuse" to be together. By capitalizing on their success as parents, Dr. Daley helps them devote more time and attention to their marital relationship. As this relationship improves, Mr. and Mrs. Lee enjoy each other more and become more consistent in raising their son.

When John and his parents return for the ninth session, he sits in the chair next to his father and proudly shows his report card to Dr. Daley. The lowest grade is a "C" in math, and his teacher had written the following comment: "John has handed in all his homework and been better prepared for tests." Mr. Lee describes how he and his son spend time each night reviewing class assignments and studying for tests. Dr. Daley turns to John and says, "Your teacher told me that you have been getting along with the kids in class." The boy smiles and nods his head in agreement. Dr. Daley conducts 11 weekly sessions with the Lees before moving to biweekly and then monthly follow-up appointments during the 36-month period specified by the multidisciplinary team. No additional incidents of abusive behavior by the father were reported, so the district attorney dropped the original charges filed against Mr. Lee.

▪ ▪ ▪

Family therapy for the Lees included consideration of multigenerational, developmental, and structural issues. The therapist determined that Mr. and Mrs. Lee's marital and parenting problems were caused partly by a lack of differentiation from their families of origin. Before they entered treatment, the Lees had never developed their own approach to parenting because each of them remained enmeshed with his or her family of origin. Although most visible between Mrs. Lee and her parents, Mr. Lee was also emotionally fused with his parents, whom he respected for their child-rearing efforts and resented for abandoning him and his family.

The Lee family did not follow the normal course of development described by Haley (1973). The couple moved rather abruptly from the courtship stage to the birth of their son. Consequently, they were unable to develop their roles as husband and wife before assuming the responsibilities of father and mother. As you observed in this example, Dr. Daley used the couple's interactions as parents to strengthen the marital relationship. This involved accepting the Lees' child-rearing conflicts as the starting point for communication and cooperation, which was subsequently used to remediate developmental deficits resulting from the couple's lack of a marriage stage. Specifically, the therapist encouraged Mr. and Mrs. Lee to engage in activities as husband and wife, without their son or extended family members present. By scheduling time for themselves, the Lees were able to interact as a spousal dyad and establish a marital relationship that did not rely on the identified patient for survival.

Dr. Daley used clients' seat selection in therapy as a dependent measure of structural change in the family. The Lees' initial seating arrangement reflected the parents' triangulation with their son (see Figure 13-3). By the fifth session, the parents sat next to each other, with John beside his mother. Although this arrangement may suggest continued mother–son enmeshment, the parents' seating selection suggests that structural change was occurring. Support for this hypothesis comes from two sources. First, the parents were beginning to exhibit increased cooperation with their child-rearing responsibilities. Second, John sat next to his father in the ninth session. This occurred when he showed the therapist his most recent report card, which covered a time period when he and his father had been working together on homework assignments.

When the Lees first entered treatment, their extrafamilial interactions were limited to work, the maternal grandparents, and John's attendance at school. During therapy, the parents' collaboration with the child's teacher and school counselor resulted in the implementation of a successful home-based reinforcement program. As the Lees' marital relationship improved, the couple joined their community's physical fitness program where they gradually developed a small group of friends. By relying more on the paternal grandparents for child care, the Lees began to balance their interactions with the families of origin. Less isolated, John and his parents were able to benefit both individually and as a family from their increased involvement with extrafamilial systems.

A family-based intervention was appropriate for the Lee family because the father had acknowledged responsibility for his abusive behavior and therapy was provided as part of a coordinated treatment plan developed by a multidisciplinary team. Mr. Lee had accepted the district attorney's offer for deferred prosecution of the charges filed against him. Because all family members were in agreement regarding the abusive event, dual relationships between the therapist and individual family members did not pose an ethical dilemma. Dr. Daley incorporated education/development, prevention, and remediation strategies into treatment. He taught the parents to implement a home-based reinforcement program to improve John's behavior at school. He capitalized on the Lees' success as parents to facilitate development of their marital relationship. The resulting improvements in spousal communication created a consistent and supportive home environment where John could acquire the decision-making skills and a self-image needed for success later in life.

SUMMARY

Family systems therapy represents a diverse set of techniques based on different theoretical principles. By capitalizing on the strengths that exist within families, clinicians can effect structural changes that remediate existing problems, prevent the development of similar or related problems in the future, and support optimal functioning among all members of the family system. Because children depend on their parents for basic needs and psychosocial development, family therapies represent an efficient method of bringing together a child's primary significant others in a collaborative approach to intervention.

Part 3

Multidimensional Interventions with Children: Other Therapeutic Strategies

The four schools of therapy described in Part 2 are the most commonly used psychosocial interventions with children, but they are not the only methods available. This section considers other treatments that have been developed for children. The theoretical foundation for some of these methods can be found in the principles described in previous chapters. Other approaches are based on different belief systems, such as the biological model, which serves as the basis for psychopharmacotherapy. Many of the treatments described in earlier chapters involve direct therapist contact with children and families, but some clinicians work indirectly with children by consulting with parents, teachers, or significant other adults. Therapists who use the traditional model of treatment typically help children one at a time or in small groups. Consultants simultaneously affect the lives of many children (e.g., students in an elementary classroom) by working with a third party (e.g., a teacher) who is responsible for their development. Some of the techniques used with children have been popular despite empirical evidence to the contrary. These controversial methods, which include dietary restrictions, are of questionable value but continue to be used with children. Therapists must be aware of these methods and the research on their benefits and liabilities if they are to respond informatively to clients' questions about these techniques.

This section begins with a discussion of consultation as it is used with parents and other adults in various settings, such as schools and the courts (see Chapter 14). Then it examines other interventions for children, including psychopharmacotherapy, hypnotherapy, and controversial treatments (see Chapter 15). It concludes with a discussion of our ultimate goal—integrated treatments for children (see Chapter 16). As you will learn, the concept of integrated treatment can be explored from differerent perspectives. Two important components—theoretical integration and the integrated delivery of treatment services—are examined. The discussion of the former revisits the transtheoretical model (see Chapter 5) and considers other approaches, including recent developments in constructivist therapy for children. This section also explores integrated treatment delivery, which is sometimes called the "wraparound" approach, to show how the multidisciplinary component of the multidimensional model can be used with children and families.

14

Consultation

■ ■ ■

Jerome is a fourth grade student of Ms. Pernella Hollison, a first-year teacher at Elmwood Elementary School. Since the beginning of the school year, Jerome has exhibited a number of disruptive behaviors, such as getting out of his seat without permission and showing off in class. Ms. Hollison has tried different interventions, including private talks with the boy, but she has been unable to change his behavior. When she realized that Jerome was interfering with other students' learning, she met with Mr. Thompson, the school counselor, to ask that he assign the child to another teacher.

■ ■ ■

The traditional method of treating students such as Jerome has been direct interventions, such as individual and group therapy. An indirect approach to helping these children is consultation, during which clinicians have little or no contact with the child. Consultation has been used for many purposes in settings as diverse as hospitals, courts, and schools (Fritz, Mattison, Nurcombe, & Spirito, 1993). This chapter discusses different methods of consultation that are used in these settings and then examines an integrated approach with Jerome's mother and teacher.

MENTAL HEALTH CONSULTATION

Gerald Caplan, a psychiatrist and pioneer in the field of mental health consultation, described this method as "a process of interaction between two professionals—the consultant, who is a specialist, and the consultee, who invokes the consultant's help in a current work problem that he believes is within the consultant's area of specialized competence" (Caplan & Caplan, 1993, p. 11). Caplan (1970) described four types of consultation that are used in mental health settings. The focus of consultation is either the consultee, a client, or a program (Table 14-1). Its content or purpose is an improvement in administrative operations or personal growth for the consultee or client. Consultation is often compared with therapy and supervision. The triadic relationship of consultant, consultee, and client differs from the interactions that occur in therapy, where the clinician has direct contact with the child. Consultation also has a different focus than therapy. Therapists ask themselves, "What can I do to help this child?" Consultants want to know, "What can I do to help this therapist (parent, teacher or physician) help this child?" Consultant-consultee interactions also differ from the hierarchical relationship that exists in supervision. Supervisors direct and evaluate the work of supervisees. Consultants usually lack this authority and, in Caplan's (1970) words, the consultee is "free to ac-

Table 14–1
The Four Types of Mental Health Consultation Described by Caplan (1970)

Type	Primary Goal
Client-centered case consultation	Assess the client's presenting problem and recommend more effective interventions the consultee can use to meet the client's needs
Consultee-centered case consultation	Improve the consultee's knowledge, skills, self-confidence, and objectivity so he or she can meet the client's needs
Program-centered administrative consultation	Assess an administrative issue and recommend solutions for concerns such as the development or improvement of agency programs
Consultee-centered administrative consultation	Improve the consultee's knowledge, skills, self-confidence, and objectivity so he or she can design and implement programs consistent with the mission of the agency

Adapted from *The Theory and Practice of Mental Health Consultation* (pp. 30–34), by G. Caplan, 1970, New York: Basic Books. Copyright 1970 by Basic Books, Inc.

cept or reject all or part" (p. 20) of the recommendations or decisions given during consultation.

When Caplan (1970) presented his model, he described the consultant as an expert who is recruited from outside the administrative structure of the consultee's work environment. Caplan, Caplan, and Erchul (1995) contrasted this approach with mental health collaboration, which involves experts within the consultee's agency or school. Sometimes called collaborative consultation, this method is similar to the multidisciplinary treatment model discussed throughout this book. Collaborative consultation requires the formation of a treatment team whose members consult with each other and contribute their special knowledge and skills (Rosenfield & Gravois, 1996). In contrast to traditional mental health consultation, clinicians who use the collaborative model have direct contact with clients and share responsibility for each child's progress.

Consultation is an important tool for education/development, prevention, and remediation with children. Many support services are provided by non–mental health professionals, such as teachers and members of the clergy, who can benefit from a consultative relationship designed to impart knowledge, enhance skills, or facilitate the development and coordination of program activities. The impact of consultation is exponential. As Caplan (1963) stated, a very small number of consultants can train many consultees, who provide direct service to a very large number of children and families. Consider a therapist who instructs 20 teachers in the use of classroom management techniques. This consultant has an indirect effect on hundreds of students who benefit from improved learning environments. The consultant's impact is even more obvious when we realize that many of these children will never receive direct care from a mental health clinician.

Consultation has a long history and was used by physicians before it was introduced to the mental health field (Dougherty, 1995). Marks (1995) described the changes that occurred in the second half of the 20th century, beginning with Caplan's (1970) model, the behavioral and problem-solving methods of Bergan (1977) and D'Zurilla & Goldfried (1971), and the process consultation of Schein (1969). The emergence of family therapy resulted in the development of consultation methods based on systems theory (Davis & Sandoval, 1991). More recently, Schmuck (1990) described how consultants can use the principles of organizational development to change the social structure in schools, and Marks (1995) discussed a holistic approach designed to address the needs of students and teachers within the educational system. The scope of theory and research on this important intervention has reached the point at which books are needed to describe its use for specific purposes (see Dyer, 1999). We now turn our attention to the use of consultation as a change process for childhood problems at home and in schools, hospitals, and courts.

CONSULTATION WITH PARENTS

Sigmund Freud (1909/1956) used consultation in the case of Little Hans when he had a brief meeting with the child but relied on the father to implement treatment (see Chapter 7). Brown, Pryzwansky, and Schulte (1995) observed that parent consultation has been slow to develop, in part because of Caplan's (1970) definition of consultation as an "interaction between two professional persons" (p. 19). Still, many therapists adopt the consultation model with parents when they teach child-rearing techniques to indirectly remediate behavior problems in children. The distinction between therapist and consultant in these cases can be illustrated with the following examples.

In therapy, a clinician would focus on the needs of the parent as client. Consider the following session with a mother whose 7-year-old daughter is exhibiting behavior problems after her recent molestation by a neighbor.

MOTHER: I just don't know what to do when she won't listen to me. I mean, I really feel bad for her because I know what it's like to be abused. My Dad did it to me.

THERAPIST: Your Dad abused you?

MOTHER: Uh-huh. I don't think about it much anymore, but when all this happened to Mary, I guess it all started coming back to me.

THERAPIST: Started coming back to you. Can you tell me more about that?

In this case, the clinician focused on the parent's needs rather than the impact of the mother's abuse on the parent–child relationship.

As a consultant, the clinician would be sensitive to the mother's abuse but treat this experience as it relates to present interactions with her daughter. The focus of intervention is significantly different.

MOTHER: I just don't know what to do when she won't listen to me. I mean, I really feel bad for her because I know what it's like to be abused. My Dad did it to me.

CONSULTANT: Your Dad abused you?

MOTHER: Uh-huh. I don't think about it much anymore, but when all this happened to Mary, I guess it all started coming back to me.

CONSULTANT: How do you think this might be affecting your relationship with Mary?

MOTHER: Oh, I don't know. (*Pause.*) I guess I feel sorry for her because I see me in her shoes. When she misbehaves, I ask myself, "After all she's been through, how can you expect her to do her homework every night?"

CONSULTANT: So you're not sure how you can help her through this difficult period.

Notice how the needs of the child, not the parent, were the focus of intervention. When the mother disclosed her abuse, the clinician related this experience to the mother's current child-rearing practices. If the consultant ever decided that the mother needed therapy for her personal problems, the appropriate response would be referral to another clinician for this service.

Brown et al. (1995) identified Adlerian consultation and behavioral consultation as the two most common methods used with parents. Alfred Adler used the triadic consultation model in his parent education groups (see Chapter 7). Sweeney (1998) indicated that Adlerian consultants help parents to solve problems and resolve conflicts with their children. Clinicians teach a more democratic approach to parenting and encourage consultees to believe in themselves as they use new techniques. In Chapter 7, we discussed Systematic Training for Effective Parenting (STEP) (Dinkmeyer & McKay, 1976). This structured program is designed for use in groups to help parents set aside autocratic methods of child rearing. Through their participation in STEP, parents acquire basic communication skills as they learn to apply the Adlerian principles of encouragement and natural and logical consequences.

Behavioral consultants also function as educators in their work with parents. Again, the clinician attempts to indirectly remediate a child's misbehavior by teaching the parents to use behavior management techniques. Consultants use the scientific method to promote behavioral change, beginning with a detailed examination of the environmental antecedents and consequences of a child's actions. Unlike behavior therapy in which the clinician has direct contact with the child, behavioral consultation involves training parents to monitor and change behaviors using empirically supported techniques. Through this process, consultees become more observant and aware of positive and negative behaviors in their children. Parents also learn to identify relevant environmental stimuli as they become more proficient in the use of a functional analysis of their child's behaviors (see Chapter 11).

The most common behavioral approach to parent training is operant conditioning, which includes the techniques of positive reinforcement, punishment, and extinction with children. Gerald Patterson and his colleagues have devoted considerable time and energy to the development and evaluation of behavioral parent training. Central to Patterson's method is the belief that children's actions change in response to parents' manipulation of environmental contingencies (Forgatch & Patterson, 1998). Consultants focus on training parents to effectively use behavior management techniques with their children. The ultimate goal of treatment is to improve the child's behavior, but these methods also have been found to produce positive change in parents' behavior, affect, and attitudes (Estrada & Pinsof, 1995).

Danforth (1998a) developed the Behavior Management Flow Chart to teach parents a step-by-step procedure for reducing noncompliance in their children. This method offers a decision-making tree of parent responses for child behaviors (e.g., praise for compliance; reprimands, warnings, and time out for noncompliance). Consultees are trained to use the flow chart as a guide for managing their child's actions in a consistent, immediate, and reasoned manner. Danforth has organized common behavioral techniques into a planned approach to parenting that specifies when and how each component of the flow chart is used. When he used the program to train mothers of children with oppositional defiant disorder (ODD) and attention-deficit hyperactivity disorder (ADHD), Danforth (1998b) found significant improvements in parenting behaviors and significant declines in mothers' stress and children's inappropriate behavior. Danforth (1999) reported similar outcomes when he used the approach with the mother of 4-year-old twin boys diagnosed with ODD and ADHD.

A crucial step in behavioral parent training is the identification of effective reinforcers for appropriate behaviors. As discussed in Chapter 11, children and parents often respond to different reinforcers. When consultants use operant techniques with families, they must identify specific reinforcers for the child, mother, father, siblings, and members of the extended family who are involved in the child's development. If clinicians consider only the child, they compromise the effectiveness of their intervention by failing to recognize the behaviors and needs of significant others in the child's life.

CONSULTATION IN SCHOOLS

Consultation is an accepted role for elementary school counselors who endorse the developmental approach (Myrick, 1997). The challenge of serving large numbers of children, sometimes in more than one school, has required counselors to reconsider the traditional methods of delivering therapeutic services. Through their consultation with teachers and other school personnel, counselors have been able to address the needs of a larger and more diverse student body. Community-based therapists who consult in elementary schools offer a variety of services, including the identification of children with psychosocial problems, development of programs to prevent school violence (Contemporary Issues Box 14-1, and research and service in school-based health clinics (Mattison & Spirito, 1993).

Meyers (1995) adapted Caplan's model in his description of three school-based approaches to consultation: student-centered, teacher-centered, and system-centered. The first involves direct and indirect services for the child, and the others resemble Caplan's consultee- and program-centered methods. Meyers recommended an approach similar to the model Tharp (1991) described for treating children of color. Although Tharp cited community-based interventions as preferable to family or individual therapy, Meyers suggested that consultants begin with a system- or teacher-centered approach. When asked to assist in the remediation of a student's misbehavior, the consultant would first determine whether school officials have adopted a disciplinary policy that teachers are consistently implementing. Only then would the consultant consider child-centered interventions. As Meyers indicated, school-based consultation often involves the use of more than one method. For example, a consultant might train teachers to use more effective classroom management techniques (i.e., teacher centered) while facilitating students' access to psychological evaluation and therapeutic services (i.e., student centered).

Consultation involves a number of stages, which Dougherty (1995) described as entry, diagnosis, implementation, and disengagement. Marks (1995) discussed how these unfold in schools. First, the consultant establishes a working relationship with the consultee and develops a formal contract to specify the purpose and length of consultation. The consultant and consultee then define and assess the problem in order to establish their goals for intervention. The consultant facilitates the implementation of the intervention plan and the evaluation of its effect on the consultation target, which may be the student, teacher, or school administrators. Marks described the final stage as the institutionalization of the intervention to facilitate program maintenance and development in the future without the consultant's assistance. The process of consultation involves multiple contacts between the consultant and consultee, who

Contemporary Issues Box 14–1

Preventing School Violence

Incidents of students shooting and killing other students in school are the material for newspaper headlines and lead stories on the evening news. As tragic as these events are, the media attention they receive distorts the fact that school is one of the safest places for a child to be. Snyder and Sickmund (1999, p. 31) reported figures that revealed that in-school murder of children in the United States is an "extraordinarily rare" event. Although these findings are of little comfort to the family and friends of deceased students, they offer a counterpoint to the attention that school murders have received in the media. They also document that violent acts, some very serious, do occur in schools. For example, Kachur et al. (1996) identified a total of 76 students who died as a result of school violence between 1992 and 1994. These deaths were followed by others in locations as geographically diverse as Littleton, Colorado; Jonesboro, Arkansas; Springfield, Oregon; and Paducah, Kentucky.

Therapists typically become involved after violent events occur and the school and community decide that mental health services are needed. Given the tragic outcome of these incidents, we must consider what the clinician's role is in preventing violence in schools. A common question that is asked after a school shooting is, "Why didn't someone see this coming?" Mulvey and Cauffman (2001) described the difficulty involved in predicting students' behavior, especially when the focus is a low-rate occurrence such as murder. They indicated that one method of identifying students who have a potential for violent acts is to expand the definition of violence to include such behaviors as physical fights, bullying, and teasing. But Mulvey and Cauffman cautioned that this approach has limitations because different forms of violence, including murder and teasing, are then treated as if they have the same etiology.

Mulvey and Cauffman (2001) recommended that communities approach school violence as a risk management issue. They suggested using available sources of data, including students' sociometric ratings of their classmates, to identify children who are at risk for violating the rights of others. Teachers and administrators should create supportive schools where students feel comfortable sharing their concerns about classmates who have problems dealing with the stressors of everyday life. Mulvey and Cauffman reasoned that when students know that school personnel will not react in a punitive manner, they are more likely to disclose information related to impending violence.

School counselors are an important part of any school violence prevention program (Sandhu, 2000). Their services include classroom presentations to prevent violent behavior in students. An intervention designed for this purpose is the Good Behavior Game (Barrish, Saunders, & Wolf, 1969; Dolan et al., 1993) in which students are divided into groups and receive rewards for exhibiting low rates of aggressive behaviors. Because reinforcers are awarded to groups, not individuals, children have been found to encourage members of their groups to act appropriately. Kellam, Rebok, Ialongo, and Mayer (1994) conducted a 6-year follow-up of first graders assigned to a 2-year trial of either the Good Behavior Game, an attention-placebo intervention designed to foster academic achievement, or a no-treatment control condition. When they evaluated their participants in middle school, the authors found that the game was especially helpful in reducing aggression in boys who were rated as more aggressive in first grade. These results suggest that early intervention programs, such as the Good Behavior Game, can have long-term benefits for troubled children and represent one method of preventing violence in schools.

School counselors provide other services, including the development of peer mentoring programs, conflict resolution skills training for students, and educational programs to inform teachers and staff about school violence (Hanish & Guerra, 2000; Riley & McDaniel, 2000). In their work with teachers and administrators, counselors promote the humane treatment of children by facilitating the development of policies and procedures intended to protect the rights of individuals. This includes the design and consistent implementation of school-wide standards for student behavior. In consultation with teachers, counselors assist those in need of classroom management skills to promote safer and more supportive learning environments. School counselors are also in a position to identify children at risk for violent behavior and to obtain appropriate intervention services for these students before they harm themselves or others.

Programs to prevent violence in schools must be part of community-wide efforts to improve the lives of children and families. A program to control violent behavior within a school located in a high-crime area is likely to fall short of its goals unless a more comprehensive effort is made to create a safer community. McElhaney and Effley (1999) described how schools, government, and community agencies can work together to develop and implement violence prevention programs. This includes sharing resources and the collaboration of personnel from schools, mental health and law enforcement agencies, community planners, and religious groups. Violence prevention programs represent an important component of a community's efforts to improve the quality of life for its citizens. As McElhaney and Effley stated, "By recognizing the power of prevention, it is possible to take an optimist's view in believing that violence can and will be reduced" (p. 297).

design the intervention according to the needs of students, parents, teachers, administrators, and the community.

Research on consultation in the schools includes studies on consultee- and client-related outcomes. A popular method has been school-based behavioral consultation, which Wilkinson (1997) found to be effective in reducing disruptive behavior in students. Wilkinson used a single-case experimental design to study a behavioral intervention with the teachers of three students, ages 6 to 9 years, who were exhibiting significant externalizing behaviors in the classroom. The consultant met with the three teachers to specify the target behaviors and initiate collection of baseline data. Another meeting was held to jointly analyze these results and develop a reinforcement program to decrease students' disruptive behavior. The consultant maintained informal contact with the teachers while they implemented the intervention, and a formal meeting was scheduled at the end of the program to analyze teachers' classroom observation data and pretreatment-posttreatment scores on Achenbach's (1991c) Teacher Report Form. Although Wilkinson reported less disruptive behavior from students after consultation, his results must be interpreted with caution because the teachers in the study both delivered and evaluated the intervention program.

Meyers, Freidman, and Gaughan (1975) addressed this design problem in their single-case experimental study of consultee-centered consultation with three elementary school teachers. The authors trained uninformed observers to rate teachers' classroom behaviors on a daily basis. After baseline, the consultant met with each teacher for three 1-hour conferences during the first week of intervention and once weekly thereafter. Consultation sessions were based on Rogerian principles and intended "to help the teacher express and clarify her attitudes and feelings related to teaching" (p. 291). Consultants used basic attending skills (e.g., empathy) and verbal reinforcement. Meyers et al. observed an abrupt consultation-related decline in the negative classroom behaviors of two teachers, although improvement was observed during baseline for the third teacher. The authors concluded that consultee-centered consultation appears to have merit in modifying the behaviors of at least some teachers.

In a related study, Meyers (1975) described an interesting combination of Caplan's (1970) client- and consultee-centered consultation with a third grade teacher whose students were misbehaving in class. Meyers initially used a single-case experimental design to evaluate the effectiveness of client-centered consultation for two problem students. The teacher was instructed to use positive reinforcement for appropriate behaviors and inattention or reprimands for misbehavior with one child and to delay intervention with the second student. Meyers reported that the target child responded to the behavioral intervention, but the rest of the students, including the other problem child, continued to disrupt the learning process. Three sessions of consultee-centered consultation were conducted to help the teacher explore her discomfort in the role of authority figure in the classroom. Although client-centered consultation appeared to be effective in improving the behavior of one child, Meyers observed that the consultee-centered approach seemed to have a positive impact on the entire class. As he noted, helping the teacher feel more at ease as the class disciplinarian resulted in "less inappropriate talking, more in-seat behavior, fewer fights, and generally more orderly behavior" (p. 118) in the classroom.

Additional research is needed on the process and outcome of consultation in schools. Behavioral approaches have been found to be helpful, and Meyers and his colleagues reported that Rogerian techniques can be used to benefit teachers and their students. Additional research is needed with these and other methods, including Systematic Training for Effective Teaching (STET) (Dinkmeyer, McKay, & Dinkmeyer, 1980), which was designed to help teachers apply Adlerian principles in the classroom (see Chapter 7). Consultation appears to be an effective and efficient method of delivering psychological services in schools. By collaborating with teachers and administrators, consultants can remediate students' problems and enhance their development through improved learning environments in schools.

CONSULTATION IN HOSPITALS

Fritz (1993) estimated that 4 million youths are hospitalized each year. Although the reason for admission is likely to be a physical illness, children admitted to pediatric units frequently require mental health interventions. Consultants to these facilities are asked to evaluate patients' psychological development, help children and families cope with serious medical problems and complex treatment procedures, and increase patients' compliance with treatment and ward policies.

Fritz (1993) stated that success in this environment depends on the consultant's knowledge of hospital systems, including the supervisory hierarchy of the institution and the reaction of pediatric staff to so-called "outside experts." A number of questions merit consideration. Is the hospital a large university-affiliated institution that supports clinical training and research, or is it a small community hospital whose sole purpose is patient care? In the former, consultants typically work with a number of physicians on each case. They must maintain communication with a treatment team in order to develop and implement an effective intervention for the child. In the small hospital, a consultant is more likely to interact with a single physician, so treatment outcome can hinge on the quality of a single professional relationship. In both large and small hospitals, consultants must assess the willingness of the medical staff to support mental health interventions. This involves consideration of the hospital's power hierarchy and its effect on the consultation process. Physicians are ultimately responsible for patient care, but nurses have more direct contact with children. Consultants must have the physician's support in order to perform their jobs. They also need the cooperation of the nursing staff that is usually responsible for implementing the consultation plan.

Pediatric consultation is a brief-term endeavor because most children are hospitalized for a relatively short period. The consultant's work is compressed into hours or days rather than the weeks or months available in schools. Fritz and Spirito (1993) offered a six-stage model of pediatric consultation: intake, preinterview data collection, parent interview, child assessment, initial recommendations, and the consultation report. The consultation intake gives the pediatric staff an opportunity to request assistance and report basic information, including patient demographic data. Before the parent interview, the consultant conducts a more detailed assessment of the situation. This involves contact with the referring physician and other staff members to clarify the consultation request and determine whether the child and family have been informed of the consultant's participation in the case.

Fritz and Spirito (1993) recommended that consultants meet with parents before they see the child. Although this may not be possible in crisis situations, the parent interview allows the consultant to correct any misunderstandings about his or her role and to collect a history of the child's development. At the outset of the child assessment, the clinician should give a developmentally appropriate explanation of the consultation process. When the patient's medical condition permits, the assessment should be conducted in a private setting to facilitate development of rapport and the administration of standardized measures. With younger children and those reluctant to talk, consultants should use toys and other manipulatives. Fritz and Spirito described how one consultant used this approach with a 7-year-old girl who refused to talk after surgical repair of her bladder:

> The consultant engaged the child with a display of syringes, intravenous equipment, splints, and a stethoscope. The child vengefully gave injections to the consultant, immobilized a doll, and prescribed painful

procedures that conveyed her anger at what she experienced as undeserved punishment. (p. 34)

When the assessment is completed, the consultant offers initial recommendations to the staff. These include specific interventions required for patients who are a danger to themselves or others. Before leaving the unit, the consultant records each contact in the patient's medical record. As discussed previously, hospitalization for most children lasts a few days. For this reason, consultants must prepare and submit their formal reports to the referring physician in a timely manner. Fritz and Spirito (1993) described the consultation report as a "succinct, understandable, and practical" (p. 40) presentation of the patient's history and current status, the purpose of the consultation, and realistic suggestions for the staff to implement with the child. These might include preparing children for surgery (Campbell, Kirkpatrick, Berry, & Lamberti, 1995), behavioral conditioning (Minuchin, Rosman, & Baker, 1978), and hypnotherapy (see Chapter 15). Fritz and Spirito recommended that the summary be one or two pages in length because brevity and specificity increase the probability that pediatric staff will read the report.

CONSULTATION IN COURTS

Forensic consultants must understand the relationship between psychology and the law. They must recognize the importance of the consultant–attorney relationship, know how to behave in court, and understand the difference between fact and expert witnesses. Many clinicians feel uncomfortable in the adversarial environment of the courtroom, where the purpose and standards are significantly different from those found in the typical therapeutic setting. But with proper training and experience, therapists can develop the knowledge and skills needed to overcome their anxiety and become effective consultants on legal matters.

Mental health consultants serve as either expert or fact witnesses. An expert witness is someone deemed sufficiently competent, through education and experience, to offer an opinion on matters before the court. A clinician who has published extensively on the effects of physical abuse might serve as an expert to assist a judge or jury in the determination of guilt or innocence for an alleged perpetrator. An expert witness is different from a fact witness, whose testimony is limited to information obtained through direct experience, such as therapy sessions with children and their families. In general, clinicians who have had previous contact with a child can serve as fact witnesses but should not give expert testimony on issues related to the case.

Nurcombe (1993a) described expert witnesses as informants, not advocates. Consultants are to give an unbiased presentation of relevant information to the court. In contrast, attorneys advocate for their client's best interests, and the courts render decisions. The consultant's job as expert witness begins at the pretrial conference with the attorney who requests the clinician's services. Lawyers hire forensic consultants when they need specialized knowledge to argue their cases, so clinicians should provide information about the training and experience that qualify them as experts (Nurcombe, 1993b). A consultant also must determine whether he or she is competent to serve as an expert on matters before the court (Committee on Ethical Guidelines for Forensic Psychologists, 1991). As Miller and Allen (1998) noted, a consultant's client is the attorney. The pecuniary nature of this relationship presents clinicians with special ethical dilemmas. Although employed by the client-attorney, the consultant must testify based on existing empirical evidence and not misrepresent these findings to benefit the attorney's case.

At the pretrial meeting, the consultant and attorney discuss questions that are likely to arise during expert testimony. Consultants prepare for the court appearance by organizing notes, reviewing case materials and relevant research reports, and preparing charts or graphs when needed. The Committee on Ethical Guidelines for Forensic Psychologists (1991) highlighted other issues that merit consideration. When consultants are asked to interview or assess a child, parent, or family, they ensure that these individuals understand the nature and purpose of the forensic consultation. This includes a developmentally appropriate explanation for children regarding confidentiality, privileged communication, and how test results will be used. When conducting an assessment, consultants must develop alternative hypotheses, collect data to test these explanations, and present their results to the court in a fair manner.

Expert testimony can be given through deposition or an actual court appearance. Melton, Petrila, Poythress, and Slobogin (1997) defined a deposition as "sworn testimony, given out of court but transcribed as a formal record" (p. 527). Depositions are often conducted in the office of the attorney or consultant. The process resembles the procedures used during a regular court appearance: the witness is sworn in, examined, cross-examined by opposing counsel, and then reexamined by both attorneys. Nurcombe (1993b) described how the atmosphere of the deposition may appear relaxed, even congenial, but he warned clinicians to maintain a serious attitude because their answers can have a significant impact on the outcome of the case.

For an unseasoned expert, a courtroom appearance is anything but relaxing. The formal and argumentative nature of judicial proceedings is very different from the atmosphere of a clinician's office. Before they take the witness stand, experts need to be aware of acceptable courtroom behavior, which they should discuss with their client-attorney before the court appearance. Nurcombe (1993b) stated that consultants should dress in a professional manner and avoid clothing or jewelry that distracts attention from their testimony. Although procedures can vary from one court to the next, Blau (1984) stated that upon entering the courtroom, the consultant should walk to the front, nod to the judge, stop at the corner of the witness box, turn and face the court reporter, and raise the right arm. As Blau stated, "Do not hesitate. Nothing can be done until the witness is sworn. Following these procedures without hesitation announces to all present that this expert understands courtroom procedure and is, indeed, an expert" (p. 223).

When giving testimony, witnesses should avoid speculation and answer questions based on the evidence available to them. If opposing counsel challenges the consultant during cross-examination, the expert should remain calm, listen carefully to each question, and pause and formulate a response before answering. When confused by an attorney's question, the witness should ask for clarification. When unable to answer a question, the consultant should say, "I don't know" rather than fabricate an inaccurate response that opposing counsel can use to challenge the expert's credibility. Blau (1984) recommended that witnesses prepare a notebook of special reference materials before they testify. During cross-examination, the consultant can refer to the notebook for detailed information on relevant state statutes, the psychometric properties of tests, and the results of empirical studies on topics related to the case. Direct and cross-examination are followed by reexamination when both attorneys again question the witness to clarify, highlight, or challenge the consultant's earlier statements. When testimony is completed and the witness is excused, the consultant should nod to the judge, step down from the witness box, nod to the jury, and depart through the door used to enter the courtroom (Blau, 1984).

Clinicians have served as expert witnesses on a number of child-related issues. Chapter 2 discusses some of the legal and ethical issues involved in child custody evaluations. Consultants have also given expert testimony in cases pertaining to the termination of parental rights and the abuse and neglect of children. Terminating a parent's rights to his or her child can be a lengthy and complex legal process. When parents abuse, neglect, or are unable to care for their children, the courts are often asked to determine whether the relationship between the parent and child should be legally severed. Consultants who serve as expert witnesses in these cases offer their professional opinions about the psychological effects of maltreatment and out-of-home placement on the child. They conduct evaluations of survivors and perpetrators to assist the court in its deliberations. Clinicians are also asked to offer recommendations regarding appropriate interventions for abused and neglected children as well as treatments that can be used to rehabilitate parents (American Psychological Association, 1999).

Berliner (1998) discussed the expert's role in child sexual abuse cases. She stated that expert witnesses can inform judges and juries about the growing body of scientific evidence about child survivors and the perpetrators of these crimes against children. Berliner cautioned that experts should present evidence "in a complete and accurate fashion, prevent the misuse of research findings, not testify beyond their expertise, and resist the pressures to become partisans" (p. 21). This is no easy task within the adversarial environment of the courtroom. The consultant must prepare for each deposition or court appearance by reviewing research that is relevant to the case. Nurcombe (1993b) offered an example to illustrate this point:

COUNSEL: Dr. Smith, are you familiar with an article by D. L. Rosenhan published in 1983, entitled "On Being Sane in Insane Places"?
WITNESS: Yes.
COUNSEL: Do you agree that the article is an authoritative one?
WITNESS: No.
COUNSEL: Why not?

WITNESS: Because the article is based on poorly performed research, and its conclusions are unjustified. (p. 286)

Consultants who are not prepared to handle this type of cross-examination should not offer expert testimony. Remember that opposing counsel is likely to call its own experts.

Miller and Allen (1998) described an expert witness as an educator to the judge, jury, and client-attorney. Because of the complexities involved in forensic consultation, clinicians who serve as expert witnesses must acquire the knowledge and skills needed to function within the judicial system. Clinicians can begin to educate themselves by reading books, such as *Psychological Evaluations for the Courts: A Handbook for Mental Health Professionals and Lawyers* (2nd ed.) (Melton et al., 1997); *Psychological Consultation in Parental Rights Cases* (Dyer, 1999); and *Expert Witnesses in Child Abuse Cases: What Can and Should Be Said in Court* (Ceci & Hembrooke, 1998). With this knowledge and appropriate training, clinicians can overcome obstacles to effective consultant-attorney communication, which include the use of professional jargon and ignorance of the legal field (Melton et al., 1997). Forensic consultants must become students of the law who understand the implications and complications that might arise from their expert testimony. They also accept the fact that no clinician can be an expert on all aspects of child development, so they limit their testimony to areas where they are indeed experts.

AN INTEGRATED APPROACH TO CONSULTATION FOR SCHOOL-RELATED PROBLEMS: A CASE EXAMPLE

Edens (1998, p. 337) described elementary schools as "an ideal setting" for consultation to enhance children's development, prevent problems, and remediate existing concerns. As discussed previously, helping teachers to become more effective in the classroom is an indirect and very powerful way of helping students. Teachers' willingness to seek outside assistance has been found to be related to the types of behavior problems that children exhibit in the classroom. Alderman and Gimpel (1996), for example, reported that approximately 75% of the teachers surveyed in their study indicated that they would request help with students who were exhibiting aggressive behavior. But fewer than 15% of the teachers would ask for assistance with children who were withdrawn, inattentive, or talked excessively. The outcome of school-based consultation depends, in part, on the level of cooperation between school and home. Consultants can facilitate teacher–parent collaboration by conceptualizing each case in the context of the transtheoretical model described by Prochaska and Norcross (1994).

As discussed in Chapter 5, Prochaska and Norcross (1994) identified stages, levels, and processes of therapeutic change. These elements must be assessed at the outset of every consultation with parents and teachers. Edens (1998) described how the Prochaska and Norcross model relates to the five phases of his school-home approach to consultation: entry, problem identification, problem analysis, treatment implementation, and evaluation. During the entry phase, consultants contact and engage teachers and parents in the consultation process. It is at this time when clinicians must assess each consultee's stage of change and adapt their interventions accordingly.

In our case example, Jerome's teacher appears to be in the preparation stage because she recognizes that a problem exists, has attempted to intervene, and recently decided to seek help to remediate the situation. The consultant in this case must conduct a similar assessment with Jerome's mother, who has raised the boy since the parents divorced 2 years ago. The initial direction of consultation and the techniques used will differ depending on whether the mother denies that a problem exists (i.e., precontemplation); recognizes that there is a problem but has difficulty describing its causes or solutions (i.e., contemplation); or, similar to Jerome's teacher, is open to outside assistance.

The consultant also needs to consider the levels and processes of therapeutic change. It is worth noting that Ms. Hollison's parents divorced when she was in elementary school. The consultant must determine whether the teacher is experiencing what Caplan (1970, p. 144) called "theme interference" related to unresolved concerns about this childhood experience. If such interference exists, Ms. Hollison may be responding to Jerome as if he were she as a child. Consequently, she does not apply the classroom management skills that are already part of her instructional repertoire and used with other students. Training her to use behavior management techniques would not address the therapeutic level at which change is needed. Using a theme interference reduction technique, such as Caplan's (1970) parable, is probably a more appropriate starting point for intervention.

The parable is a narrative technique that Caplan (1970) used to help consultees indirectly address unresolved conflicts from the past. The consultant first assesses the consultee's emotional connection with matters related to the current problem situation. When these ties are thought to be excessive, the consultant collects information about specific aspects of the case that are particularly distressing for the consultee. These data are used to identify the personally meaningful theme that is impeding the consultee's ability to objectively handle the present situation. The consultant also assesses the consultee's expectations about the outcome of the case. As Caplan stated, theme interference "always constitutes some form of doom or bad end" (p. 160) as the consultee displaces unresolved personal conflicts onto the present situation. Consider a therapist who was sexually abused as a child and is having difficulty treating a young survivor of sexual assault. The consultant in this situation must determine if the clinician's problems are caused by a knowledge or skills deficit or the result of theme interference related to early childhood experiences. The more extreme a consultee's thoughts, feelings, and behaviors are in connection with the present case, the more consideration the consultant must give to theme interference reduction techniques.

Consultants who use the parable with consultees draw narrative material from the assessment to refocus the consultee's conscious attention away from the present situation to a case that is superficially different but contains thematic elements central to the current problem (Caplan, 1970). Consultants who are effective in their use of this technique possess the storytelling skills needed to deliver a narrative that is both cognitively and emotionally meaningful. Consultees are not informed that material for the parable has been drawn from fantasy or the "average" case the consultant has treated with a similar presenting problem. With our sexually abused therapist, the consultant might offer the description of a fourth grade teacher who was a below-average student in school and had difficulty dealing with the underachieving pupils in her class. The parable would contain themes parallel to those expressed by the consultee, such as the fear of being unable to help these students (i.e., sexually abused clients). Not all consultants are prepared to use this technique. Crafting a parable that indirectly touches personally meaningful themes for the consultee requires training and supervised experience.

Maital (1996) described another method that consultants can use to address consultees' theme interference. As an alternative to Caplan's parable, Maital recommended cognitive restructuring to modify the thoughts and feelings that limit a consultee's ability to respond effectively. Consultants use this technique to help clients identify and change dysfunctional automatic thoughts and cognitive schemas. These include the belief that the consultee is a failure as a parent or teacher because he or she has been unable to solve a child's problems without assistance from others. Consultants who address these schemas and their related thoughts can reduce consultees' theme interference and prepare them to become agents of therapeutic change. Whether they select a psychodynamic or cognitive alternative for theme interference reduction, consultants share the same purpose of countering the thoughts and feelings that interfere with a consultee's interactions with the child.

In his integrated approach to consultation, Edens (1998) involved parents and teachers in a collaborative effort using interventions appropriate to the consultees' stage and level of change. Consultees are asked to identify and analyze the problem and then implement and evaluate treatment developed under the consultant's guidance. To be successful in these efforts, the consultant must establish a working relationship with the consultees. This requires a careful assessment of the reasons behind a consultee's request for help. For example, the therapist should determine if the consultee has voluntarily entered the consultation relationship or if participation has been mandated by someone else, such as a principal or spouse. The reason for entering consultation is both a reflection and an indication of a consultee's motivation to participate in the process. When consultation has been mandated, the consultant should carefully assess the consultee's attitudes and feelings to determine the level on which change must begin.

Edens (1998) stated that consultants must actually meet with their consultees. The ideal situation is one in which the teacher and parents attend a joint conference at the school or the clinician's office. When this is not possible, the consultant must consider alternatives, such as meeting with the teacher at school and conducting a home visit with the parents. To engage consultees, the consultant should treat them as experts who know valuable information about the child, family, and school environment. For example, parents can identify behavioral consequences that are reinforcing or rewarding for their child, and teachers are able to describe problem behaviors the student exhibits in the classroom. Consultants then use their knowledge of developmental psychology and the principles of human behavior to help consultees combine these data into a behavior management program for the child.

Consultants who use an integrated approach for school-based problems must get parents and teachers "playing off the same page" by having them develop a shared conceptualization of the situation as a common foundation for handling the presenting problem. Edens (1998) recommended that consultants empower consultees by inviting teachers and parents to describe their primary concerns and then generate treatment hypotheses and intervention strategies. Edens suggested specific strategies for motivating and involving consultees in treatment. If a consultee makes negative attributions about him- or herself or the child, the consultant should consider using the parable (Caplan, 1970) or cognitive techniques (Maital, 1996) to address theme interference or distorted thoughts. To move consultees into the action stage, Edens recommended training teachers and parents to use behavior management skills to refocus their attention from intrapsychic causes to environmental stimuli.

When the consultees have developed a joint treatment plan that the consultant deems appropriate, treatment is implemented and monitored. Every treatment plan should be viewed as a starting point for intervention, which consultant and consultees revise based on the child's response. Edens (1998) recommended that treatment be practical and straightforward; involve the use of charts to record progress; and include ongoing support from the consultant, who reinforces successful efforts and provides help in revising the treatment plan when needed. Edens indicated that when complications are thought to be the result of a consultee's theme interference or skills deficits, the consultant intervenes using confrontation, a theme interference strategy, or simplification of the treatment plan combined with additional behavioral training. Consultants must remember that confrontation involves a broad range of techniques, from direct and critical responses that induce guilt in consultees to more facilitative strategies that involve the juxtaposition of conflicting thoughts, feelings, and behaviors. An example of the latter is: "I suspect you had some important reasons for not praising Terry's behavior in math class this week. Can we talk about them?" If the consultee responds by saying that it is impossible to monitor and reinforce one child's actions in a class of 25 to 30 students, the consultant should consider revising the treatment plan to make it more practical. The teacher might benefit from additional training in the classroom management skills used in treatment. It is also possible that the consultee is having difficulty implementing treatment because of intrapsychic conflicts or cognitive distortions. If this is the case, the consultant should use an appropriate technique, such as the parable, to reduce this interference.

Edens (1998) stated that consultants must assume responsibility for evaluating the outcomes of treatment. Consistent with the principles of behavioral assessment (see Chapter 11), consultation should be routinely evaluated. When an intervention is not working, evaluation results provide data that can be used to revise the treatment plan. When an intervention is effective, both the consultant and the consultees acquire valuable information that can be used to handle similar child behavior problems in the future.

Lavelle (1998) indicated that teachers consistently identify classroom management techniques as an area for growth. Teachers who model and consistently reinforce appropriate behaviors facilitate the development of self-control in children. As a result, early intervention with disruptive students can be conceptualized in educational/developmental, preventive, and remedial terms. Because these children currently exhibit a clinically significant level of externalizing behaviors, consultants intervene in an attempt to eliminate these problems. McMahon (1994) described how preschoolers and young elementary school students who exhibit these behaviors appear to be at risk for conduct problems later in life. Consultation designed to remediate these behaviors at an early age can prevent conduct disorders in adolescence and adulthood while enhancing children's academic and psychosocial development through improved classroom performance and more acceptance from their peers, parents, teachers.

Webster-Stratton (1993) estimated that every year, teachers typically have at least two students in class who exhibit a high rate of externalizing behavior problems. These include children similar to our case example of Jerome, who is disrupting the learning environment by getting out of his seat and displaying attention-seeking behaviors in class.

Webster-Stratton proposed that treatment of children with these problem behaviors requires what she called a "home-school partnership" (p. 437) in which parents and teachers work together for the benefit of the child. With this integrated approach, consultants are able to remediate a student's misbehavior, prevent future problems, and develop the child's potential in a broader ecological context than is offered in the home or school alone. We now return to our case example and examine how such a program can be implemented.

▪ ▪ ▪

As Miss Hollison tells Mr. Thompson about her attempts to change Jerome's behavior, she becomes increasingly distraught and says, "Maybe teaching isn't for me." Mr. Thompson responds by asking Miss Hollison to describe the trouble she is having with other students in her class. "Oh, the other kids are fine," she answers, "I guess it's really Jerome who's causing all the problems. I just don't know what to do with him."

Mr. Thompson describes a new program the school psychologist has established to help beginning teachers. He explains that every school counselor in the district has been trained to use a consultation model with the parents and teachers of disruptive students. Although all teachers are allowed to participate, the program is designed to help first-year teachers make the transition to the public school classroom. "We want you to be successful," he says, "so we are offering this program on a voluntary basis to help teachers improve their classroom management skills. We also ask parents to work with us in developing and implementing a treatment plan with the child."

"Well, I need to do something," Ms. Hollison answers. "The program sounds like a good idea. I just don't understand why I can't correct the situation on my own. I was so excited when I got this job, but now I dread getting up and going to work each day."

As Mr. Thompson listens, he realizes that Ms. Hollison is engaging in some of the cognitive distortion techniques he learned in his consultation in-service program. She believes she must be perfect and solve every student's problem by herself. She magnifies her errors with Jerome while overlooking her effectiveness with the other students. Later Mr. Thompson learns that Ms. Hollison also experiences theme interference related to unresolved issues from her childhood.

"I didn't act like this when I was in school," Ms. Hollison continues, referring to Jerome's disruptive behavior. "You mentioned something about getting Jerome's mother involved. I've talked to Mrs. Martain on the phone once. I tried to get her to say something to Jerome, but she didn't seem all that interested. If my mother had gotten a call about me having problems at school, she would have stepped in right away and made sure I behaved."

Later that afternoon, Mr. Thompson telephones Mrs. Martain to invite her to attend an after-school meeting with him and Ms. Hollison. "I work until 5:00," the mother says. "Anyways, I don't know what I can do to help. I mean, if Jerome is causing problems at school, his teacher should make him behave. That's what she's getting paid to do."

"I believe you'll be able to contribute some valuable information that all of us can use to help Jerome," Mr. Thompson answers. He eventually convinces the mother to attend a 5:15 meeting in his office the next week. The next morning, he discusses this with Ms. Hollison, who also agrees to attend. As he plans for the first consultation session, Mr. Thompson realizes that his consultees are at two different stages of change. Ms. Hollison appears to be in the preparation stage because she recognizes that a problem exists but has been unable to change Jerome's behavior. In contrast, Ms. Martain seems to be a contemplator who realizes there is a problem but does not understand her role in remediating her son's disruptive behavior.

When the consultant and his two consultees meet, Mr. Thompson begins by saying, "I'm glad the three of us are here to discuss how we can help Jerome. By sharing what we know about him, I believe we'll be able to find a way to improve his behavior." He adds that no one is to blame for the boy's current problems and that treatment will be effective to the extent that the three of them cooperate on Jerome's behalf.

"Like I said yesterday," Ms. Hollison says, "I feel bad that I haven't been able to help Jerome do better in class."

Mr. Thompson adopts a solution-focused approach and treats the mother as an "expert" when he asks, "Ms. Martain, what kinds of things have you found to be helpful with Jerome at home?"

"I don't really know," she answers, "He kinda takes care of himself. When I get home from work, I'm pretty tired, so I like to relax and watch TV. Jerome, he just plays in his room or in the backyard."

Mr. Thompson uses active listening to facilitate disclosure from his consultees. He learns that Ms. Martain was uncomfortable before and during the first half of the meeting. "I hated school," she says, "I never got good grades, so I dropped out when I was in 10th grade. School just wasn't my thing."

"Well, I'm really glad you're here," the consultant responds, "because you know so much more about Jerome than we do. Without your help, we won't be able to change his behavior."

"I was a little unsure about this meeting too," Ms. Hollison says. "I've spent so much time thinking about how I can help Jerome. It's hard to admit that you don't know what to do. Jerome's third grade teacher told me that you and his Dad are divorced. My parents got divorced when I was in second grade, so I know how hard it can be on a child."

By the end of their hour-long meeting, Mr. Thompson and his consultees have agreed to meet next week to discuss a home-based reinforcement program the teacher and mother can use to reward Jerome for proper classroom behavior. As preparation for their next meeting, he asks Ms. Hollison to rank order the behaviors that are of concern to her. He asks Ms. Martain to prepare a list of rewards that can be used to reinforce Jerome for "good days" at school.

As he writes his progress notes after the session, Mr. Thompson decides to address the cognitive distortions and theme interference he detects in his consultees. To counter the mother's school-related attitudes and feelings, he will continue to emphasize her role as expert in the school's efforts to improve Jerome's behavior. Although he plans to use Caplan's parable with Ms. Hollison in the next session, the opportunity presents itself the next day when she visits him in his office.

"One thing we didn't discuss yesterday was moving Jerome to another room," Ms. Hollison says.

"Oh, I forgot," Mr. Thompson answers. The two of them discuss the mechanics of such a change for a few minutes, and then he continues, "You know, I'm not sure that's the best thing for Jerome. A number of years ago, I saw a child who was having problems here and at home. Her Mom and Dad were good people, but they just didn't know how to be parents. I talked with them a couple times, but it didn't do any good."

"What happened to the student?" she asks.

"Thanks to her teacher, she did fine. About 10 years later, I saw her in the grocery store. We talked a bit and then she said, 'I really gave Ms. Porter a rough time, but she's the best teacher I ever had.' Kids really are amazing, aren't they?" Ms. Hollison smiles, nods her head, and says she will be at the next consultation meeting.

When the consultees return the next week, Ms. Hollison brings a list of six problem behaviors. The most serious is hitting other students in class, which has happened twice this year, and the two least disruptive behaviors are Jerome's mumbling to himself and talking to his neighbors. Mr. Thompson asks Ms. Martain if Jerome exhibits any of these behaviors at home and learns that fights with neighborhood children have been infrequent. He also discovers that before the parents' divorce and the mother's subsequent return to outside employment, Ms. Martain spent time with Jerome every day after school, working together around the house, shopping, or visiting nearby friends and relatives. Although she does not bring her list of reinforcers, she says she thought about the assignment and decided that two good rewards would be hot dogs and ice cream for dinner and allowing Jerome to stay up an extra half hour to watch television.

Mr. Thompson spends the majority of the session designing a home-based reinforcement program involving a daily token for good classroom behavior. Every night, Jerome can decide whether he wants to use his token to delay bedtime or add it to others until he has the required five needed for his special meal. The consultant works with Ms. Hollison to define "good classroom behavior." They decide that Jerome will receive a token every day he remains in his seat during class. The criterion will be adjusted to include other behaviors on the teacher's list as progress is made in treatment. Mr. Thompson capitalizes on Ms. Hollison's concern for the boy by having her routinely praise him when he acts appropriately. The mother and teacher are to communicate with each other using a notebook that Jerome carries with him every day. The consultant also encourages them to maintain telephone contact to discuss the boy's behavior at home and school.

Two additional consultation sessions are scheduled to evaluate progress in treatment and to revise the criteria for tokens. During the first week of the reinforcement program, there was a noticeable improvement in Jerome's classroom behavior. In subsequent weeks, change was more gradual and positive, albeit uneven at times. A significant intervention appeared to be the prescribed telephone contact between the teacher and parent. Unlike the pre-consultation conversation that was difficult and unproductive, the two of them now call each other at least once each week to discuss Jerome's progress.

The mother and son now spend more time together, in part because of their joint participation in the rewards used as part of the reinforcement program. These have included trips to the park and regular visits to the local library, where they select children's books to read before bedtime. Ms. Martain recently made arrangements for one of Jerome's classmates to spend a Sunday afternoon at their house. As his classroom behavior has improved, so have his relationships with other students. Jerome and his mother now work together on his homework, and he is getting better grades at school. Ms. Hollison recently mentioned that Jerome was selected by the class to serve as hall monitor for the week. Although she continues to have a special interest in his welfare, Ms. Hollison now uses the same classroom management techniques with him that she uses with her other students.

▪ ▪ ▪

The success of this consultation effort is probably caused by several factors. First, the consultant conceptualized his work in the context of the transtheoretical model (Prochaska & Norcross, 1994). After assessing each consultee's stage of change, he realized that the teacher was more prepared to take action than was the mother. His early work with Ms. Martain included establishing the need for treatment and emphasizing her contribution to the effort. As a result, he initially focused on the helping relationship to develop rapport with the mother. Although the consultant and teacher had a professional relationship before she sought help with Jerome, Mr. Thompson realized that their interactions as consultant and consultee would be unique; therefore, he also attended to the development of this new relationship.

When Ms. Hollison first contacted the consultant, she asked that he assign Jerome to another teacher. Mr. Thompson acknowledged this request but turned his attention to what he believed was the theme interference that impeded the consultee's work with the child. He chose Caplan's (1970) parable to address Ms. Hollison's thoughts and feelings about her parents' divorce. With his description of a troubled student who benefited from a persistent and caring teacher, Mr. Thompson communicated the importance of maintaining Jerome's current assignment to a teacher who would devote the time and energy he needed. Ms. Hollison was able to reconstruct her interpretation of the situation and to successfully implement the behavior management skills she was using with other students. By helping her to interact with Jerome as she did with his classmates, he established the foundation for a successful home-based reinforcement program.

The positive change in Jerome's behavior is undoubtedly the result of improved communication between his mother and teacher. Before treatment, the teacher and parent had one telephone contact; after consultation, they had weekly conversations that both of them initiated. The consultant's success in developing this partnership enabled the ongoing revision and implementation of a reinforcement program that was consistent with the child's changing behavior. Mr. Thompson was able to effect a change in the teacher–parent relationship that developed and endured without his direct and ongoing participation. Because of the indirect nature of consultation, he was able to enter and depart from the therapeutic relationship without disrupting the progress of treatment. In the process, Ms. Hollison and Ms. Martain learned to overcome past experiences and work together for the benefit of the child.

The integrated approach used here had educational/developmental, preventive, and remedial outcomes. First, the home-based reinforcement program appeared to have a positive impact on the boy's disruptive behavior. Consultation also had educational/developmental benefits, including Jerome's friendships with other students, a growing interest in reading, and a healthier parent–teacher relationship. Likewise, the consultant's use of theme interference reduction and cognitive restructuring is likely to prevent Ms. Hollison from having similar difficulties with students of divorced parents and Ms. Martain from having conflicted relationships with other teachers in the future.

SUMMARY

Consultation can be a meaningful and effective way of providing education/development, prevention, and remediation services for children. Some clinicians avoid this intervention because they prefer direct therapeutic contacts with children and families, but consultation is an important addition to the techniques used in a multidimensional approach to treatment. Through their consultative relationships with parents and significant other adults, clinicians are able to effect positive change in a child's environment and indirectly bring about therapeutic change in the child.

15

Psychopharmacotherapy and Other Interventions for Children

The treatments discussed to this point are the most commonly used interventions with children, but they are not the only methods available. Others range from traditional psychopharmacotherapy to controversial dietary restrictions for children. This chapter examines some of these techniques. After a discussion of drug therapies, the chapter reviews bibliotherapy, therapeutic board games, and hypnotherapy, which clinicians sometimes use in treatment. We then turn our attention to dietary methods that have been used with children.

PEDIATRIC PSYCHOPHARMACOTHERAPY

Psychopharmacotherapy with children was once considered "the back ward of drug research" (Gadow, 1991, p. 842), but significant advances have occurred in the past 3 decades. Economic considerations may have stimulated recent developments in the field. As growth in the demand for psychoactive drugs, such as antidepressants, has slowed among adults, pharmaceutical companies have initiated treatment trials with children. Tanouye (1997) questioned whether these studies were conducted because of manufacturers' desire to expand sales in this population. The use of psychoactive drugs with children has been a controversial topic, leading some experts to question whether these medications are being overprescribed (Contemporary Issues Box 15-1).

Gadow (1991) stated that empirical evidence for the effectiveness of psychopharmacotherapy has not been a prerequisite for its use with children. Research is sorely needed to correct this problem because many of the psychoactive drugs approved by the U.S. Food and Drug Administration are not indicated for use with juveniles. If a physician determines that a child needs one of these medications, he or she may prescribe the drug under a procedure known as "off-label use" (McLeer & Wills, 2000, p. 223). Because of the lack of research on pediatric psychopharmacology, many of the prescriptions written for these drugs probably fall into this category.

Werry (1999) described how psychoactive medications are currently classified according to their therapeutic applications (e.g., antidepressants) and then subclassified, first by clinical action (e.g., tricyclics) and then by chemical

Contemporary Issues Box 15–1

Are Psychoactive Medications Overprescribed for Children?

Tanouye (1997) questioned whether psychoactive drugs are overprescribed for children with emotional and behavioral problems. Researchers have studied this issue by examining drug utilization rates in various locations and at different points in time. Zito et al. (2000) studied preschoolers' prescription records and found that the use of psychoactive drugs was low (i.e., approximately 1%) compared with utilization rates in older children and adolescents. Still, the authors found a 1.7- to 3.1-fold increase in prescription rates from 1991 to 1995. The most commonly prescribed drugs were psychostimulants and antidepressants. Coyle (2000, p. 1060) reviewed these findings and described what he believed to be "a growing crisis in mental health services to children" in which psychoactive medications are used with very young children in the absence of controlled studies designed to evaluate the safety and effectiveness of these drugs.

Safer, Zito, and Fine (1996) studied the use of psychostimulants and found "a fairly consistent pattern of a sizable rate of increase of methylphenidate treatment for ADD youths in the 1990s" (p. 1086). The authors offered possible explanations for this increase, including the long-term use of psychostimulants beyond the elementary school years and an increase in the number of girls prescribed methylphenidate. Although Safer et al. were unable to determine whether psychostimulants were being overprescribed for school-age children, they suggested that utilization rates may differ from one region of the country to the next. LeFever, Morrow, and Dawson (1999) provided evidence to support this explanation. The authors examined psychostimulant use among second to fifth graders in the schools of two Virginia cities during the 1995 to 1996 academic year. Based on school nursing records, LeFever et al. found that in-school administration of psychostimulants ranged from 8% to 10%, with methylphenidate prescribed most often. Although these figures exceed commonly accepted ADHD prevalence estimates of 3% to 7% among school children (American Psychiatric Association, 2000), the more alarming finding is that 18% to 20% of European American fifth-grade boys in both cities were given psychostimulants during the school day.

Jensen et al. (1999) offered another perspective on the use of psychostimulants with children. Based on their study of prescription rates for 1992 in four communities in the Continental United States and Puerto Rico, the authors concluded that these drugs may be both overprescribed and underprescribed based on "region-, community-, and provider-specific" differences (p. 802). Jensen et al. found that only 1.4% of the 9- to 17-year-old youths in their sample received psychostimulants. Although this figure does not suggest that physicians were overprescribing these drugs, there were children asymptomatic for ADHD who were administered these medications. Jensen et al. also reported that only 12.1% of those diagnosed with ADHD were receiving psychostimulants. This finding suggests that psychopharmacotherapy may be underused with some children who could benefit from these drugs. The authors emphasized the need for accurate assessment and diagnosis to identify the children who require a combined treatment that involves psychostimulants and psychosocial interventions. As Jensen et al. observed, "Given the widespread concern about presumed inappropriate use of medications, better education appears warranted for parents, physicians, and the media about the appropriate assessments and treatments for ADHD" (p. 803).

grouping (e.g., imipramine). Drugs also are known by their trade or brand name. For example, the trade name for the tricyclic antidepressant (TCA) imipramine is Tofranil. Table 15-1 contains a summary of the therapeutic use, clinical action, chemical grouping, and trade name for psychoactive medications that have been used with children. Relatively little is known about the mechanisms behind the action of these agents with young people. The rationale for using them has been drawn from research trials with adults. It is tempting to assume that medications used to treat disorders in

Table 15–1
Classification of Psychoactive Medications for Children

Therapeutic Use	Clinical Action	Chemical Grouping (Trade Name)
Anxiolytics	Benzodiazepines	clonazepam (Klonopin, Rivotril)
Antimanics	Lithium salts	lithium carbonate (e.g., Lithane)
Anticonvulsants		carbamazepine (Tegretol)
Neuroleptics	Phenothiazines	chlorpromazine (e.g., Thorazine)
	Butyrophenones	haloperidol (e.g., Haldol)
Antidepressants	TCAs	imipramine (Tofranil)
		clomipramine (Anafranil)
		desipramine (Norpramin, Pertofrane)
	SSRIs	fluoxetine (Prozac)
	Serotonin-norepinephrine dual reuptake inhibitors	venlafaxine (Effexor)
Psychostimulants	Amphetamines	dextroamphetamine (Dexedrine)
		dextroamphetamine/amphetamine (Adderall)
	Amines and other analogs	methylphenidate (Ritalin)
		pemoline (Cylert)

Adapted from *Practitioner's Guide to Psychoactive Drugs for Children and Adolescents* (2nd ed.), by J. S. Werry and M. G. Aman, 1999, New York: Plenum Medical Book Co. Copyright 1999 by Plenum Publishing Corporation.

adults are also effective for the same purposes with children, but researchers have suggested otherwise. For example, TCAs were enthusiastically embraced during the 1980s to treat depressed youths, but Gadow (1991) noted the lack of empirical support for their use with these children.

Counselors, social workers, and psychologists are prohibited from prescribing medications for their clients. Because they lack the competence and legal authority, therapists must collaborate with physicians, especially board-certified child psychiatrists, when psychoactive drugs are deemed necessary. This collaborative approach sometimes originates with the child's pediatrician or the family physician, who refers the client for psychological services to be provided instead of or in combination with psychopharmacotherapy. But therapists also encounter children who require medical treatment. Clinicians must be able to identify clients for whom psychosocial intervention alone is inadequate or inappropriate. Chapter 4 examined the five criteria that Strayhorn (1987) recommended for identifying children whose behavioral or emotional problems have organic causes. In his review of psychopharmacotherapy with children, Bukstein (1993) recommended that therapists consider the severity of a child's symptoms and the prior response to psychosocial treatments when assessing the need for medical treatment.

Pediatric psychopharmacotherapy differs from drug therapies with adults because physicians must consider the child's age and physical development to determine the dosage required to produce therapeutic benefits without causing negative side effects. Compared with adults, children typically require different weight-adjusted doses of a drug, and they are susceptible to unique toxic reactions, such as growth retardation related to the use of psychostimulants (Bukstein, 1993). In his discussion of the toxic effects of pediatric psychoactive medications, Gadow (1991) concluded that "drug therapy is relatively safe" (p. 847) compared with other potentially dangerous childhood activities, such as climbing trees and riding bicycles or all-terrain vehicles. Still, side effects are an important consideration in psychopharmacotherapy. Gadow described how untoward effects range from the relatively benign, such as nausea and a change in appetite, to death which can occur at therapeutic levels or after ingestion of large amounts of certain drugs, such as TCAs. Iatrogenic effects, or those related to contact with a physician, also have been cited. Gadow described how the use of psychoactive medications may lead some children to conclude that the solution to their problems can be found in a pill. He also stated that the symptomatic relief obtained through drug therapy can delay a child's acquisition of adaptive behaviors, such as problem-solving skills.

Methodological problems limit the interpretation and clinical application of the results of many studies on pediatric psychopharmacotherapies. Some researchers have treated samples that contain both children and adolescents. Although some (e.g., Emslie et al., 1997) reported no age-related difference in patients' response to drug therapies, the developmental differences between children and adolescents merit serious consideration in the design of these studies. Another issue that warrants attention is the criteria used to evaluate treatment outcome. Researchers have routinely used a reduction in symptoms, rather than elimination of the problem behaviors, as a dependent variable. Although a drug may perform significantly better than placebo, total remission of symptoms often occurs in only a minority of patients.

Two disorders that have received considerable attention in regard to psychopharmacotherapies are attention-deficit hyperactivity disorder (ADHD) and childhood nocturnal enuresis. Numerous controlled studies are available on the use of psychostimulants for children with ADHD and TCAs for bed wetting. Before we examine the research on these disorders, we begin with a discussion of three childhood problems that have received limited empirical scrutiny: anxiety disorders, depression, and aggressive behavior.

Childhood Anxiety Disorders

McLeer and Wills (2000) identified three classes of drugs that are used to treat anxiety disorders in children and adolescents: anxiolytics, TCAs, and selective serotonin reuptake inhibitors (SSRIs). As discussed in Chapter 4, children exhibit a variety of anxiety disorders, including separation anxiety disorder, generalized anxiety disorder, and obsessive-compulsive disorder (OCD). Although these share the common feature of heightened anxiety, each disorder is unique in its behavioral and contextual qualities. For example, separation anxiety disorder is characterized by excessive distress upon separation from a significant other or familiar environment, and generalized anxiety disorder involves heightened tension and discomfort across different people, places, and times. Because of the diverse nature of childhood anxiety disorders, therapists must carefully assess each client to determine the child's specific problem.

Benzodiazepines are sedative-hypnotic drugs that have frequently been used to treat anxiety disorders in adults (Kendall & Treadwell, 1993). Few controlled studies exist on the use of these medications for childhood anxiety disorders. Werry and Aman (1999) concluded that the efficacy of benzodiazepines has not been established in controlled trials that include random assignment to drug or placebo. Milner, Rizzotto, and Klein (1994), for example, compared clonazepam with placebo in a sample of 15 children, ages 7 to 13 years, most of whom were diagnosed with separation anxiety disorder. Although patients seemed to improve while taking the drug, the difference was not statistically significant. McLeer and Wills (2000) warned against prolonged use of benzodiazepines because of the risk of tolerance and dependence for these drugs.

The effectiveness of TCAs with childhood anxiety has not been established (Wilens et al., 1998). Gittelman-Klein and Klein (1971, 1973) reported positive results for imipramine therapy with 35 children, ages 6 to 14 years, who exhibited separation anxiety and were afraid of or refused to attend school. But the results of later studies have raised questions about the use of TCAs with childhood anxiety disorders (Bernstein & Shaw, 1993). Klein, Koplewicz, and Kanner (1992), for example, conducted a controlled comparison of imipramine and placebo with 20 patients, ages 6 to 15 years, who were in behavior therapy for their anxiety. The addition of a 6-week trial of drug or placebo resulted in no significant improvement for patients in the imipramine group.

Tricyclic antidepressants have been found to be of value in controlling OCD. Flament et al. (1985) compared clomipramine with placebo in a sample of 19 patients, ages 6 to 18 years. Although they reported positive results for the drug, the authors used numerous statistical analyses with this small sample, thereby limiting the interpretation of their findings. Leonard et al. (1989) studied a larger group of 7- to 18-year-old patients. They found that clomipramine was better than desipramine in reducing the symptoms of OCD. DeVeaugh-Geiss et al. (1992) also used a larger sample in their comparison of clomipramine and placebo. In a controlled study with 54 youths, ages 10 to 17 years, the authors found the drug to be significantly better in reducing the symptoms of this disorder.

Investigators recently turned their attention to a new class of antidepressants, SSRIs. Research on pediatric applications of SSRIs is in its infancy, but Wilens et al. (1998) noted that these drugs appear to have less serious side effects than do TCAs. Although studies with children are limited, McLeer and Wills (2000) indicated that SSRIs seem to be helpful in treating childhood anxiety disorders. In an uncontrolled study, Birmaher et al. (1994) reported a decrease in symptoms after the use of fluoxetine in a sample of 21 children and adolescents diagnosed with various anxiety disorders, including separation anxiety and overanxious disorders. Based on a retrospective review of client records, Geller, Biederman, Reed, Spencer, and Wilens (1995) reported that fluoxetine was effective in treating OCD in children. The authors found no significant difference between children's and adolescents' responses to the medication.

Childhood Depression

McLeer and Wills (2000) described the controversy surrounding the use of antidepressants in children. They noted that psychiatrists continue to prescribe these drugs despite the lack of empirical support for their use with depressed youths. When Puig-Antich et al. (1987) conducted a controlled study of imipramine and placebo in a sample of prepubertal depressed children, they found no significant effect for the drug. The results of other controlled studies are generally consistent with the findings of Puig-Antich et al. Based on their meta-analysis of 12 randomized trials of these drugs, Hazell, O'Connell, Heathcote, Robertson, and Henry (1995) reported that TCAs were no better than placebo in controlling depression in young people. Both Kutcher (1999) and Viesselman (1999) concluded that TCAs should not be considered the treatment of choice for depression in children because of their disappointing results and toxic side effects.

Recent studies on the use of SSRIs with depressed children have produced some encouraging findings (Ambrosini, 2000). Emslie et al. (1997) reported a significantly better response for fluoxetine compared with placebo. Although the authors included children and adolescents in their controlled study, they found no significant age effect on patients' response to treatment. Not all recently developed drugs have been found to be helpful with children. Mandoki et al. (1997), for example, studied children's uses of another new class of antidepressants, the serotonin-norepinephrine dual reuptake inhibitors. The authors compared a combination of venlafaxine and cognitive-behavioral therapy with placebo and cognitive-behavioral therapy in a sample of 33 patients, ages 8 to 17 years. They found no significant effect for the drug during a 6-week trial.

Aggressive Behavior

Aggressive behavior is an important feature of disruptive behaviors in children (American Psychiatric Association, 2000). Although oppositional defiant disorder (ODD) is more likely to involve verbal aggression, conduct disorder may include physical aggression toward others. Adults often respond negatively to either form of aggressive behavior in children. Sometimes these acts represent a danger to the self or others. It is not surprising that various drug therapies have been used to treat children with these problem behaviors.

Psychostimulants are commonly used in the treatment of children with ADHD (see discussion later in this chapter). These drugs have been found to reduce aggressive behavior in children diagnosed with this disorder (Gadow, Nolan, Sverd, Sprafkin, & Paolicelli, 1990; Hinshaw, Henker, Whalen, Erhardt, & Dunnington, 1989). Klein, Abikoff, Klass, Ganeles, Seese, and Pollack (1997) compared methylphenidate with placebo in 83 youths, ages 6 to 15 years, who were diagnosed with conduct disorder and with or without ADHD. The authors randomly assigned patients to a 5-week trial of either drug or placebo and found methylphenidate to be significantly better in reducing aggressive behaviors, such as physical attacks on others and destruction of property. The benefits of drug therapy were similar for patients with and without ADHD.

Waslick, Werry, and Greenhill (1999) described other drug therapies for children's disruptive behaviors, including the use of neuroleptics and antimanics. Research on the use of neuroleptics with aggressive children is limited. Campbell and her colleagues (1984) reported the results of a 6-week controlled comparison of haloperidol, lithium, and placebo with 61 aggressive inpatients, ages 5 to 12 years. The authors found that children in the medication groups behaved significantly better than did patients in the placebo condition. There was no significant difference in treatment outcome for the drug therapies, although negative side effects were more likely to occur with haloperidol. Campbell, Cueva, and Adams (1999) cautioned that extended use of neuroleptic agents has been found to cause what are called "extrapyramidal effects." A common form is tardive dyskinesia, which involves uncontrolled physical movements, most frequently in the muscles of the face and upper body. Although these problems seem to be less severe in children than older adults, they represent a significant limitation for these drugs.

According to Campbell et al. (1999), the antimanic drug lithium has been used for more than 25 years to control aggression in children. In a controlled comparison of lithium with placebo, Campbell et al.

(1995) reported positive results for the drug in a sample of 50 hospitalized aggressive children, ages 5 to 12 years. To be included in the study, patients must have responded negatively to prior psychosocial and psychopharmacological treatments. Although a number of the children in the placebo group improved during the 6-week treatment period, Campbell et al. (1995) reported significantly better results for the patients who received lithium.

Carbamazepine is an anticonvulsant drug with antimanic properties that has been used to treat aggressive children (Evans, Clay, & Uualtieri, 1987). In an uncontrolled study with 10 hospitalized aggressive patients, ages 5 to 10 years, Kafantaris et al. (1992) reported a significant decline in aggressive behaviors during 3 to 5 weeks of carbamazepine therapy. To date, controlled studies of the drug have not established its efficacy in reducing aggression in children. Cueva et al. (1996), for example, randomly assigned hospitalized aggressive children to either 6 weeks of carbamazepine therapy or placebo. Results for the 22 children who completed the study revealed no significant benefits for the drug in these 5- to 11-year-old patients.

The use of any drug requires a thorough assessment of the child, family, and environment. It is inappropriate and unethical to use any of these drugs to control negative behaviors that are within the range of normal development. When a child's actions exceed these limits and are a threat to personal safety or the welfare of others, medication warrants consideration. As Waslick et al. (1999) noted in their discussion of neuroleptic treatments for children with aggressive behavior, the side effects of psychopharmacotherapy must be balanced against the threat that a child's behavior represents to self and others.

Attention-Deficit Hyperactivity Disorder

Manos, Short, and Findling (1999) stated that "psychostimulants are the mainstays of pharmacotherapy for attention-deficit hyperactivity disorder (ADHD) in children" (p. 813). These medications are apparently prescribed for more than a million U.S. children each year (Safer, Zito, & Fine, 1996) and are effective in reducing ADHD symptoms in approximately 70% to 80% of those diagnosed with the disorder (DuPaul, Barkley, & Connor, 1998). A number of different psychostimulants have been studied, including dextroamphetamine, methylphenidate, pemoline, and an amphetamine combination marketed under the name Adderall. The most commonly prescribed of these is methyphenidate, which has been found to decrease impulsive and disruptive behaviors, improve attention span, increase on-task behavior, and decrease physical aggression (Barkley, 1997; Gadow et al., 1990).

Despite these therapeutic benefits, DuPaul et al. (1998, p. 510) warned that psychostimulants are "no panacea" for ADHD symptoms and related problems. Whalen and Henker (1991) noted that the behavioral gains observed in children taking methylphenidate do not necessarily translate into better grades. This may be the result of what could be termed "learning voids" that developed before the child was placed on medication. Consider a fifth grade student for whom methylphenidate was prescribed after a recent diagnosis of ADHD. Although the child may be more on task and less disruptive in the classroom, he continues to have difficulty with complex division problems because his ADHD symptoms limited his mastery of basic math facts (e.g., subtraction, division) in the earlier grades. This child will require a comprehensive treatment, such as that recommended by Kronenberger and Meyer (1996), in which psychostimulants are combined with other interventions (e.g., tutoring, behavior modification) to address the behavioral, emotional, and learning problems related to ADHD.

Further evidence for comprehensive treatment can be found in studies of the long-term effectiveness of psychostimulants. DuPaul et al. (1998) described these medications as having brief-term benefits but relatively little enduring effects after termination of the drug (see Chapter 16 for additional information). Psychostimulants have also been found to produce various side effects, including decreased appetite, headaches, stomachaches, and insomnia (Barkley, McMurray, Edelbrock, & Robbins, 1990). One side effect that merits serious consideration is the appearance or exacerbation of tics and Tourette's disorder in children treated with psychostimulants. Although Sverd, Gadow, Nolan, Sprafkin, and Ezor (1992) found no drug-related increase in tics among boys comorbid for ADHD and tic disorder, DuPaul et al. (1998) recommended that clinicians assess for a family history of tics and Tourette's disorder and remain vigilant for their appearance during treatment. To monitor these and other psychostimulant-related behaviors, Barkley et al. developed the Stimulant Drug Side Effects Rating Scale, which parents and teachers can use before and during children's treatment.

Nocturnal Enuresis

The most commonly used drugs for treating nighttime urinary incontinence in children are imipramine and desmopressin (Rushton, 1993). As with other drugs, researchers have evaluated these medications using two outcome criteria: a reduction in the child's wetting episodes and the elimination of this troublesome behavior. Moffatt, Harlos, Kirshen, and Burd (1993) concluded that the second criterion is more clinically meaningful. Consequently, a child's wetting frequency must be monitored during baseline, treatment, and a sufficient follow-up period to determine whether psychopharmacotherapy has a lasting effect. Rushton emphasized the importance of posttreatment monitoring to evaluate whether the drug simply controlled incontinence during therapy or actually cured the enuretic behavior.

Imipramine has been found to be better than placebo in controlling nighttime wetting but less effective than behavioral conditioning with a urine alarm (Houts, Berman, & Abramson, 1994; Johnson, 1980; Wagner, Johnson, Walker, Carter, & Witmer, 1982). As you will recall from the discussion in Chapter 11, relapse has been a problem with urine alarm treatment. The same is true for imipramine, leading Rushton (1993) and Wagner (1987b) to suggest that the drug offers symptom management but relatively few cures. When taken as prescribed, imipramine has been found to cause minor side effects such as dry mouth, constipation, irritability, and insomnia. Taken in large doses, the drug can be fatal, so parents must carefully monitor its use with children.

Desmopressin, an antidiuretic hormone, is another medication that has been used to treat nighttime urinary incontinence in children. Administered in either oral or nasal form, the drug has been found to produce relatively few side effects (Rushton, 1993). Moffatt et al. (1993) analyzed the results of controlled studies with desmopressin and found that the drug significantly reduced the frequency of wetting episodes. The authors also reported relatively high relapse rates after termination of the drug, with 20% or fewer children remaining dry in two studies in which patients were systematically monitored. Wille (1986) compared desmopressin with the urine alarm and found more immediate improvement for children taking the drug. Although both groups had significantly fewer wet nights at termination of treatment, results were significantly better for children in the alarm group. Relapse was also significantly higher for clients who received drug therapy. Similar to imipramine, desmopressin appears to be "a symptomatic treatment" (Moffatt et al., 1993, p. 424), albeit more expensive than its TCA alternative (Rushton, 1993).

Summary

According to Bukstein (1993), "Drug therapy should never be the sole treatment modality in children" (p. 22). This does not mean that psychoactive medications should never be used in treating children's disorders. In writing about the use of psychostimulants for the treatment of children with ADHD, DuPaul et al. (1998) stated the following:

> Although the issue of controlling the behavior of children with psychotropic drugs is highly controversial, the difficulties these youngsters present to others who must live, work, or attend school with them must not be overlooked.... If stimulants can temporarily ameliorate these difficulties, while reducing the level of ostracism, censure, and punishment that children with ADHD receive, they seem certainly worthwhile. (p. 542)

Many authors, including Bernstein and Shaw (1993) and Werry (1999), have recommended that when psychoactive drugs are used to treat children's disorders, they should be combined with psychosocial interventions. The challenge for therapists and physicians is identifying children in need of psychopharmacotherapy and establishing the collaborative relationships required to design and deliver integrated treatments.

BIBLIOTHERAPY

Chapter 10 discussed developmental and multicultural aspects of children's narratives, which are sometimes used for therapeutic purposes (see Chapter 16). A related intervention is bibliotherapy, which Schrank and Engels (1981) defined as "guided reading that helps individuals gain understanding of the self and environment, learn from others, or find solutions to problems" (p. 143). Pardeck (1990) believed that a story's characters and plot enable children to explore personally relevant thoughts or feelings and to learn how others handle common experiences. Although the research on bibliotherapy is limited, this technique has been used to address a number of childhood concerns, including parental alcoholism, child abuse, parents' marital transitions, and adjustment to the death of a loved one (Krickeberg, 1991).

Therapists use bibliotherapy in different ways. With younger children, they sometimes read with clients in therapy. Clinicians also recommend books for children to read at home. In certain cases, they teach parents how to achieve therapeutic benefits by reading books and stories with their children. Training is sometimes required because the purpose of bibliotherapy is different from that of the bedtime stories that many parents read to their children. As Schrank and Engels (1981) suggested, the therapeutic use of stories involves three processes: identification, catharsis, and insight. Therapists and parents must select books that are developmentally appropriate and contain characters and action relevant to the child's situation. The reader's vicarious experience of a character's response to a problem then provides the opportunity for insight into personal problems.

Pardeck and Pardeck (1986) noted that bibliotherapy can be used for education/development, prevention, and remediation with children. For example, books can be used to help all children thrive and surmount normal challenges inherent in the developmental process. Krickeberg (1991) noted that as a prevention tool, bibliotherapy can provide information and problem-solving strategies for at-risk children. When used as a remedial intervention, the technique can facilitate disclosure and the generation of possible solutions for children's problems (Pardeck, 1995; Watson, 1980). Learning how a character experiences and overcomes challenges serves as a model for the child. The goal is to have children translate cognitive, emotional, and behavioral aspects of the character's experience into personal solutions for their problems. Pardeck (1990) recommended the use of follow-up activities to facilitate this process. Therapists can encourage clients' self-disclosure and self-examination by having children discuss, roleplay or draw pictures of personally significant episodes, or write a diary from a character's point of view (Pardeck, 1995).

Different authors have discussed the effectiveness of bibliotherapy. Riordan and Wilson (1989) and Schrank and Engels (1981), in reviews of studies with children and adults, reported varying outcomes for bibliotherapy. Mikulas, Coffman, Dayton, Frayne, and Maier (1985) evaluated the approach with young children who were afraid of the dark. The authors used a specially prepared 85-page book, *Uncle Lightfoot,* which is a story about a young boy who fears the dark and visits his Native American uncle's farm. Mikulas et al. trained parents to combine readings of the book, social reinforcement of their children, and games related to the content of the story. The program, therefore, matches Pardeck's (1990) description of bibliotherapy as an adjunctive intervention, not "a single approach to treatment" (p. 1048). In preliminary studies, Mikulas and his colleagues observed a significant decline in children's fears and significant improvement in their tolerance of the dark. Additional research is needed to evaluate components of the Mikulas et al. program (e.g., bibliotherapy, social reinforcement) and to compare the intervention with a waiting list condition.

Incorporating literature into the therapeutic process can facilitate the development of rapport between the therapist and child, thereby enabling exploration of client concerns through the use of traditional techniques, such as open questions and reflection of feeling. Clinicians must prepare for each session by selecting literature that is appropriate to the child's presenting problem (Krickeberg, 1991; Pardeck, 1990). If a client is to benefit from bibliotherapy, the books and stories used in therapy must be relevant and developmentally appropriate for the child. Ginns-Gruenberg and Zacks (1999) added that the materials should be current and culturally accurate. Table 15-2 contains the early criteria that Gillespie and Conner (1975) recommended for selecting literature for young children.

Literature based on the cultural backgrounds and experiences of nondominant ethnic groups is commercially available (see Beaty, 1997, for a listing of these resources). An example is the Japanese story called "The Old Man Who Made the Trees Bloom" (McAlpine & McAlpine, 1958), about an aging farmer and his wife who help their neighbor overcome his greedy behavior. Another story is the Native American tale *Children of the Sun* (Carew, 1980), in which spirituality is intermingled with family dy-

Table 15–2
The Gillespie and Conner (1975) Criteria for Selecting Bibliotherapy Resources for Preschoolers and Primary School Children

1. The illustrations complement the content of the story and are appealing to the child.
2. The story has interesting and believable characters (e.g., other children, animals).
3. The information in the story is presented in a developmentally appropriate manner.
4. The humor in the story must be obvious to the young child.
5. The plot of the story contains an element of surprise.
6. The story contains recurring phrases or verse that are pleasing to see and hear.

Adapted from *Creative Growth Through Literature for Children and Adolescents*, by M. C. Gillespie and J. W. Conner, 1975, Columbus, OH: Merrill. Copyright 1975 by Merrill.

namics to teach a lesson of cooperative and helpful behavior. Various writers (e.g., Cecil & Roberts, 1992; Ginns-Gruenberg & Zacks, 1999; Pardeck, 1995) have developed or reviewed bibliographies of children's literature that therapists can use to select appropriate books for young clients. In 1999, the National Education Association developed a list of 100 favorite children's books based on the organization's survey of more than 1000 members. Table 15-3 contains the top 10 books along with their authors and suggested age ranges for each.

Dorr and Rabin (1995) reported that children spend more time watching television than any other activity except sleeping. Television programs, videotapes, and the Internet offer electronic alternatives to the traditional literary approach to bibliotherapy. Programs such as *Mister Rogers' Neighborhood* have been found to foster positive behaviors, such as task persistence and compliance with rules, in preschool children (Friedrich & Stein, 1973). The use of electronic media for psychological purposes merits empirical investigation. Pardeck (1990) stated that bibliotherapy is appropriate for children who enjoy reading. When clients do not respond to this method, videotherapy merits consideration. Unfortunately, therapists must proceed with caution because controlled studies on the effectiveness of this method are currently unavailable.

THERAPEUTIC BOARD GAMES

Schaefer and Reid (1986) described therapeutic games with children as enjoyable, rule-governed, and challenging activities that involve at least two participants. Compared with the self-directed play activities used in child-centered treatment (see Chapter 9), therapeutic games are more structured and are sometimes competitive in nature. The latter quality makes them well suited for children ages 7 years and older who have developed an interest in games with rules (Cole & Cole, 2001). A special technique for these children is therapeutic board games, which often incorporate the elements of chance and strategy in therapist–child interactions intended to explore clinically significant topics,

Table 15–3
The Top 10 Children's Books According to Members of the National Education Association

Book Title	Author	Suggested Age Range
Charlotte's Web	E. B. White	9–12 years
The Polar Express	Chris Van Allsburg	4–8 years
Green Eggs and Ham	Dr. Seuss	4–8 years
The Cat In the Hat	Dr. Seuss	4–8 years
Where the Wild Things Are	Maurice Sendak	4–8 years
I'll Love You Forever	Robert N. Munsch	4–8 years
The Giving Tree	Shel Silverstein	All ages
The Very Hungry Caterpillar	Eric Carle	Baby–preschool
Where the Red Fern Grows	Wilson Rawls	Young adult
The Mitten	Jan Brett	4–8 years

Adapted from *Give the Gift of Reading for Valentine's Day, Teachers Announce Top 100 Favorite Children's Books* [News release], by National Education Association, 1999, Washington, DC: Author. Copyright 1999 by the National Education Association.

such as friendships and social skills, problem-solving skills, and adjustment to divorce and sexual abuse.

Therapists frequently use games that are familiar to children. For example, checkers or chess and Candyland or Chutes and Ladders can be incorporated into the therapy hour as an "ice-breaker" to develop rapport with a child or as a background activity for facilitating client disclosure about clinically relevant topics. In these applications, board games are not intended to teach skills or impart information. Instead, their primary purpose is that of enhancing the therapeutic relationship to enable the child to explore more sensitive issues. Therapists also use games that are psychoeducational in nature and related to important life experiences. This section examines three games intended for these purposes: The Ungame (Zakich, 1975), The Talking, Feeling, and Doing Game (Gardner, 1973), and My Two Homes (The Center for Applied Psychology, 1992).

The Ungame and The Talking, Feeling, and Doing Game are designed to facilitate clients' general self-disclosure about attitudes and feelings. Both games are played by rolling dice, advancing a game piece on the board, and responding to questions that appear on cards the therapist and child draw at designated spaces. The two methods differ in that The Ungame is noncompetitive, with no predetermined termination point and no designation of a winner. In The Talking, Feeling, and Doing Game, players collect chips for responding to questions or acting out the instructions contained on game cards. The person who has the most chips upon arriving at "Finish" is declared the winner.

Frey (1986) recommended that therapists consider The Ungame to establish rapport with children because its questions are of a general nature and are therefore "less threatening" (p. 35). The Talking, Feeling and Doing Game is designed to facilitate the timely discussion of uncomfortable topics in children, ages 4 to 12 years (Gardner, 1973). Gardner recommended that therapists capitalize on children's responses by encouraging them to elaborate on clinically relevant issues. Both the therapist and child have the option of not responding to individual cards, although no reinforcer is awarded when this occurs. Gardner (1986) indicated that when he played the game with children, he rarely avoided answering questions because he believed that clinicians can selectively model self-disclosure by giving responses that are therapeutic and appropriate for the child's developmental level. Despite the lack of controlled studies on these games with children, the anecdotal information that appears in clinical reports suggests that The Ungame and The Talking, Feeling and Doing Game have therapeutic potential.

Chapter 9 discusses Burroughs, Wagner, and Johnson's (1997) controlled comparison of traditional play therapy and My Two Homes (The Center for Applied Psychology, 1992), a competitive game intended to help children process their parents' divorce. Players move a game piece around the board and draw cards of a factual and situational nature about "Mom's House, Dad's House, or Me." Factual questions, which have a true-or-false or multiple-choice format, are designed to teach children the facts about divorce (e.g., prevalence, legal aspects). Situation cards prompt players to discuss challenges encountered by children of divorce (e.g., visitation experiences). When players respond to a situation card or correctly answer a factual card, they receive two chips. The first person with at least 10 chips to reach a designated point on the board is declared the winner.

Although many therapeutic games are commercially available, some clinicians decide to develop their own. Chapter 5 reviewed the research on one example, the Child Sexual Abuse Board Game designed by Fowler and Wagner (1993). Shapiro (1994/1996) offered guidelines for therapists to follow when designing therapeutic games for children. He stated that the game must be fun and developmentally appropriate if it is to appeal to young clients. Shapiro also indicated that the therapists must design each game according to its intended purpose. For example, a board game for enhancing self-esteem could include questions designed to facilitate client disclosure about personal skills and successful life experiences. A social skills development game might involve the use of roleplaying to help children practice basic communication techniques. A format common to many games is the use of a board and cards containing relevant questions. Clinicians who adopt this strategy should develop a large sample of questions, from which they can select the most appropriate items. They should consult with their colleagues to ensure that the content and wording of questions are appropriate to the child's developmental level. Finally, the game board should be visually appealing, with colors, figures, and designs that interest children.

HYPNOTHERAPY

Benson (1989) described hypnotherapy as the combination of hypnosis and other therapeutic strategies. Hypnosis dates back to ancient Greece, although modern applications originated with the work of Franz Anton Mesmer in the 1700s (Watson, 1978). Benson defined this technique as "a replication of any one of a number of trance-like states or 'altered states of consciousness' which are part of most people's everyday experiences" (p. 114). Hypnotherapy, in contrast, is *"a treatment modality* in which the patient is in the altered state of hypnosis at least part of the time" (Olness & Kohen, 1996, p. xi). Benson believed that hypnotherapy is well suited for young clients because of their imaginative skills. This intervention has been used to treat a variety of common childhood problems, including thumb sucking, nail biting, enuresis, encopresis, phobias, sleep disorders, and physical disorders such as headaches and asthma (LaBaw & LaBaw, 1990).

Olness and Kohen (1996) described four phases of hypnotherapy: the pre-induction interview, induction, hypnotherapeutic intervention, and arousal upon termination of the hypnotic state. During the pre-induction interview, the therapist explains hypnosis to the child and provides a developmentally appropriate rationale for using the technique for the client's presenting problem. Before proceeding to the induction phase, the hypnotherapist must develop a therapeutic relationship with the child and explore any reservations the client has about the procedure.

The induction phase involves the introduction of the trance-like state. Olness and Kohen (1996) suggested that clinicians avoid words such as "sleepy" or "tired" when describing the hypnotic state because some children resist going to sleep. Strong directives, such as "Your hands and arms are feeling heavy," should be dropped in favor of statements resembling, "Just think about how you feel when you are building a house with Legos at home; just let yourself feel that way now" (p. 54). Hypnotherapists select from a number of induction strategies, including visual or auditory imagery, ideomotor techniques, progressive relaxation, and eye fixation techniques. Sometimes induction involves having the child imagine pleasant visual (e.g., a favorite place or activity) or auditory (e.g., a favorite piece of music) images. Ideomotor techniques include procedures such as hand levitation in which children are encouraged to imagine an arm being lifted by helium-filled balloons. Hypnotherapists also use progressive relaxation techniques (see Chapter 11) and eye fixation procedures that include having the child hold a coin or place it in the paws of a favorite animal. The child then stares at the coin as the therapist says:

> After a while the fingers [or paws] begin to get a little tired of holding it, and after a while the coin can slip down to the floor [or sofa or bed]. It will be safe there. You can get it later. When it falls, that is your signal to yourself to just let those eyes close by themselves. That's right. (p. 69)

When the induction is completed, the therapist moves to the intervention stage. During this phase, the clinician uses developmentally appropriate suggestions to alter the child's experience of the presenting problem. Hypnotherapy with children is delivered in different ways. The traditional format is the therapist using hypnotic techniques with the child, but clinicians also teach self-hypnosis to clients and train parents to use the procedure with their children. Basic to all of these methods is the arousal phase, which often involves informal instructions, such as "Do that a little longer and, when you're ready, go back [or return] to what you were doing before we began this practice" (Olness & Kohen, 1996, p. 75). When the child is no longer in the trancelike state, Kohen (1997) recommended that therapists ask the client to describe their hypnotic experience. When self-hypnosis is used, he emphasized the importance of having children practice the procedure between therapy sessions.

Hypnotic techniques have often been used as adjunctive treatment for children undergoing medical procedures. Jacknow, Tschann, Link, and Boyce (1994) studied self-hypnosis to treat chemotherapy-related emesis and nausea in children and adolescents between the ages of 6 and 18 years. The authors used visual imagery, such as the child's favorite place, to induce the hypnotic state in the younger patients. Children were instructed "to use their imaginations to transport themselves experientially to a special place or adventure" (p. 260). When they trained the clients to perform self-hypnosis, the therapists also gave patients suggestions about "feeling safe and well" and shutting down their brain's "vomiting-control center" (p. 260). Children were instructed to practice the intervention twice a day. Compared with patients in a control group, those trained in self-hypnosis used significantly fewer antiemetic drugs and reported significantly less anticipatory nausea in advance of subsequent chemotherapy sessions. No differences were found in actual treatment-related nausea and vomiting.

The outcome of hypnotherapy has been associated with children's hypnotizability or suggestibility. Although formal measures are available, LaBaw and LaBaw (1990) suggested that therapists test suggestibility levels in children through actual clinical trials. Smith, Barabasz, and Barabasz (1996) studied the role of hypnotizability in children, ages 3 to 8 years, who were receiving painful medical procedures (e.g., venipuncture, bone marrow aspirations) for diseases such as leukemia. Patients were identified as either high or low hypnotizable children and then randomly assigned to different orders of parent-administered hypnotherapy and a distraction task. The latter involved the child's use of a favorite toy to distract the patient's attention during the medical procedure. Hypnotherapy involved the parent's use of the favorite place induction technique. During medical treatment, the parent expanded on the visual imagery by telling the child a story related to the favorite place. Smith et al. found that with the hypnotizable children, the hypnotic intervention was more effective than the distraction technique in reducing pain and anxiety. Children who were identified as having low hypnotizability did not seem to respond better to one intervention or the other.

There is some evidence to suggest that hypnosis may be helpful in treating some children with nighttime urinary incontinence. Banarjee, Srivastav, and Palan (1993) compared hypnosis with psychopharmacotherapy with imipramine and reported comparable cure rates (i.e., 72% vs. 76%) after 3 months of treatment, but significantly better results for hypnosis (i.e., 68% vs. 24%) at the end of a 6-month follow-up period. The authors used visual imagery and progressive relaxation to induce the hypnotic state. Intervention involved general suggestions that the child could become dry and specific suggestions related to effective nighttime awakening and voiding of the bladder. Children were taught self-hypnosis, which they were told to use every night at bedtime. Banarjee et al. reported that the hypnosis group practiced self-hypnosis on at least 80% of the nights in the follow-up period, which probably contributed to the more positive outcome among these clients.

Therapists who want to provide hypnotherapy must obtain the training needed to become competent with the technique. Olness and Kohen (1996) recommended that clinicians consider courses sponsored by the Society for Developmental and Behavioral Pediatrics, Society for Clinical and Experimental Hypnosis, and American Society of Clinical Hypnosis. These organizations offer workshops and conferences on general issues related to hypnotherapy as well as specialized training in the application of this method with children.

CONTROVERSIAL TREATMENTS

Any discussion of alternative interventions for children would be incomplete without considering the "controversial therapies" (Golden, 1984, p. 459) that have been used to treat chronic childhood problems, such as ADHD and learning disabilities. Table 15-4 contains Golden's criteria for these treatments. In general, controversial methods are often described as "natural," have been recommended for a range of childhood problems, and lack empirical support for their effectiveness. They include patterning (Ameri-

Table 15–4
Golden's Six Characteristics of Controversial Therapies

1. The theories on which these therapies are based are novel and not completely consistent with modern scientific knowledge.
2. The new treatment is presented as being effective for a broad range of problems that are often not rigorously defined.
3. As the treatment usually relies on the use of 'natural' substances such as vitamins, or is based on dietary therapy, exercises, or simple manipulations of the body, it is stated that there is no possibility of adverse effects.
4. The initial presentation is often, but not always, in a medium other than a peer-reviewed scientific journal.
5. Controlled studies that do not support the new treatment are discounted as being improperly performed or biased because of the unwillingness of the medical establishment to accept novel ideas.
6. Lay organizations develop and support the use of the treatment, proselytize new members, and become socially active in attempting to develop special interest legislation and regulations.

From "Controversial Therapies," by G. S. Golden, 1984, *Pediatric Clinics of North America, 31*, p. 459. Copyright 1984 by W. B. Saunders Company. Reprinted with permission of the author.

can Academy of Pediatrics, 1982; Cummins, 1988; Delacato, 1974), megavitamin therapy (Cott, 1972; Haslam, 1992), and optometric vision therapy (American Academy of Ophthalmology, American Academy of Pediatrics, & American Association for Pediatric Ophthalmology and Strabismus, 1998; Beauchamp, 1986; Cohen, 1988). One of the most common and controversial techniques used with children is dietary restrictions. As many as 80% of the parents of children with ADHD have tried this method (Stubberfield, Wray, & Parry, 1999; Varley, 1984), so therapists must be prepared to answer clients' questions about this approach.

As discussed in Chapter 3, increasing the fiber content in a child's diet is an accepted part of therapy for clients with retentive encopresis. Much of the controversy surrounding dietary restrictions with children has centered on the treatment of children with ADHD (Baumgaertel, 1999). A significant stimulus for this debate was the 1975 publication of Benjamin Feingold's book, *Why Your Child Is Hyperactive*. Feingold suggested that some children are genetically predisposed to exhibit hyperactive behaviors in response to certain chemicals in their food. To remediate these problems, he developed the Kaiser-Permanente (K-P) diet as an alternative to psychostimulant medication for children diagnosed with ADHD. The K-P diet requires the elimination of foods with additives, such as artificial colors and flavorings, as well as those containing natural salicylates (see Table 15-5 for examples).

When a child is prescribed this diet, the entire family should participate in order to reduce infractions. Feingold (1975) warned that children must adhere to all aspects of the program because "a single bite or a single drink can cause an undesired response which may persist for seventy-two hours or more" (p. 176). He claimed that his treatment was effective for about 50% of hyperactive children, with an additional 25% exhibiting sufficient improvement to allow termination of psychostimulant therapy (p. 71). Although some question these figures based on controlled studies of the K-P diet, its popularity increased and so did the number of local chapters of the Feingold Association of the United States. More information about the Association and the K-P diet can be found at www.feingold.org.

Researchers use cross-over and specific challenge designs to study the effects of dietary restrictions. The cross-over design involves a controlled comparison of different diets. For example, children are randomly assigned to one of two diets and then reassigned to the other after a specified period without participants' knowledge. Specific challenge designs are used with children whose parents have identified them as "responders" to determine whether elevated levels of a food or additive actually cause a change in behavior. In these studies, children follow the Feingold diet and periodically consume foods containing the suspected substances. Both designs have practical limitations. First, it is very difficult for investigators to manipulate dietary restrictions without a family's knowledge. If tomatoes are thought to cause a certain behavior, the researcher must restrict and introduce tomato-based foods unbeknownst to the participants. As Feingold (1975) indicated, investigators must ensure that family members adhere to the assigned diet and avoid restricted foods. Dietary studies should also include the use of multiple methods and informants, such as neurological testing of children, teacher ratings of classroom performance, and parent ratings of behavior in the home.

Table 15–5
Examples of Foods Restricted on the Kaiser-Permanente Diet

Group I: Foods That Contain Salicylates	Group II: Foods That Contain Artificial Colors and Flavors
Apples, apricots, oranges, peaches	Cereals with artificial colors and flavors
Tomatoes, tomato-based products (e.g., ketchup, spaghetti sauce), cucumbers	Commercial candies and bakery items (e.g., cakes, pies)
Grapes, grape-based products (e.g., grape juices and jellies)	Processed meats (e.g., bologna, hot dogs)
Aspirin and aspirin-based products	Soft drinks, commercial chocolate milk, chocolate flavorings
	Margarine
	Toothpaste, cough drops
	Vitamins and medications containing artificial colors and flavors

Adapted from *Why Your Child Is Hyperactive*, by B. F. Feingold, 1975, New York: Random House. Copyright 1975 by Random House.

Despite the many obstacles, researchers have conducted empirically sound studies on the effects of dietary restrictions with children. In what Johnson et al. (1997, p. 251) called "the most elaborate and highly controlled series of studies on the Feingold hypothesis," Harley et al. (1978) examined the effects of the K-P diet with 36 boys exhibiting ADHD symptoms. The authors used a cross-over design with 3 to 4 weeks of either the Feingold or a placebo diet. Children were rated by their parents and teachers, observed in their classrooms, and administered various neuropsychological tests (e.g., intelligence, reaction time) on three occasions: immediately before the first diet, after completing the K-P diet, and after the placebo condition.

To ensure compliance, members of the research team met with families at the outset to stress the need for everyone to follow the program. Harley et al. (1978) removed existing foods from each home and delivered supplies on a weekly basis. Extra precautions were taken in the preparation of food items, including "identically packaged chocolate bars and specialty cakes, with one containing standard ingredients and the other free of artificial flavors and colors" (p. 821). A dietician visited the home every week to encourage compliance and remove foods that violated the diet. The authors' efforts paid off because at posttest, no family was able to correctly identify when they were assigned to each diet.

Harley et al. (1978) were unable to provide conclusive support for the Feingold diet. Mothers' and fathers' ratings of their children suggested behavioral improvements while using the diet, but these results were not replicated in the teachers' ratings, classroom observations, and laboratory testing. Based on their findings, the authors concluded:

> While there may well exist a subset of hyperactive children whose behavior is adversely affected by artificial food colors, the results of the present study of boys aged 6 to 12 suggest that such a subset is very small or that the relationship of diet manipulation to behavioral change is much less dramatic and predictable than has been described in anecdotal clinical reports. (p. 826)

How large that subset of children is remains unclear, although Waksman (1983) suggested that the K-P diet might be helpful with 5% to 10% of children diagnosed with ADHD.

To learn more about responders, researchers conducted specific-challenge studies of the K-P diet. Mattes and Gittelman (1981), for example, studied the effects of Feingold's restrictions on 11 children whose parents had reported significant improvement while their child was using the diet. When participants were exposed to a 1-week challenge of cookies containing artificial colorings, no significant change was observed in their behavior. In related studies, Weiss et al. (1980) and Adams (1981) also failed to support parents' endorsement of dietary restrictions. These findings are important because the K-P diet, although not physically harmful to children receiving nutritious meals (Golden, 1984), does require considerable effort from the entire family. Another limitation is children's dislike for the diet, which Gross et al. (1987) described as "distasteful to the typical American child" (p. 55). Parents face the challenge of enforcing dietary restrictions at home and elsewhere. Some are willing to make this commitment, even when the diet is of little help (Wender, 1986). The therapist's role in these cases involves training parents to objectively monitor their child's behavior. Data are then collected to challenge unfounded allegiance to the diet and to identify the relatively small number of children who benefit from the program.

The debate over dietary effects has not been limited to food additives and natural salicylates. Many parents believe that sugar causes their children to misbehave. Researchers have studied a variety of sugars and sugar substitutes: sucrose (e.g., cane sugar, sugar beets), glucose (e.g., fruits), fructose (e.g., honey), and saccharin and aspartame. Despite popular opinion, there is no empirical evidence that sugars cause disruptive behavior. In one study, Wolraich et al. (1994) examined the effects of sucrose, aspartame, and saccharin on the behavioral and cognitive performance of 25 normal preschoolers, ages 3 to 5 years, and 23 children between the ages of 6 and 11 years whose parents had identified them as sugar responders. Participants were prescribed a different diet (i.e., high sucrose/no artificial sweetener, low sucrose/aspartame, low sucrose/saccharin) during each of three succeeding 3-week periods. The authors controlled each family's diet using procedures similar to those used by Harley et al. (1978). Data collected from the children, parents, teachers, and project examiners revealed no behavioral or cognitive effects for the sweeteners, even among children identified as sugar responders.

Based on his review of the research, Kinsbourne (1994) concluded that "there is no evidence that sugar alone can turn a child with normal attention into a hyperactive child" (p. 355). Wolraich, Wilson, and White (1995) agreed after they conducted a meta-analysis of 16 studies on the subject. Wolraich et al. cautioned that subtle effects have been observed, which might explain the reports of sugar reactivity in some children. But they suggested that parents' expectations may play a role. Hoover and Milich (1994) examined this factor when they studied 31 boys, ages 5 to 7 years, whose mothers identified them as sugar responders. All boys consumed an aspartame-based drink, but their mothers were told that the drink contained either sugar or aspartame. After a 25-minute play session with their child, the mothers who thought their sons had consumed sugar rated the boys significantly higher on a hyperactivity subscale. When Hoover and Milich examined children's wrist actometer scores, they found that these boys were actually less active than the children in the aspartame group.

So how should clinicians respond when questioned about the benefits of dietary restrictions? Based on the empirical evidence available, they can say that special diets are not a panacea for disruptive behaviors but may help a small number of children. Therapists should anticipate the psychosocial implications of dietary restrictions by having families discuss the practical challenges associated with the use of the K-P diet and sugar restrictions. Clinicians should adopt a serious attitude toward parents' questions and emphasize the importance of a healthy diet for all children (Baumgaertel, 1999). In cases in which dietary causes are suspected, parents can be trained to evaluate the effects of a brief-term elimination diet using a single-case experimental design that includes behavioral ratings from different informants. But Baumgaertel cautioned that parents who decide to use dietary restrictions with their child should first consult with their pediatrician or family physician.

SUMMARY

This chapter examined a variety of interventions that have been used to address childhood problems. These methods range from traditional approaches, such as psychopharmacotherapy, to controversial dietary restrictions with children. Clinicians sometimes use bibliotherapy, therapeutic board games, and hypnotherapy with young clients. Empirical support for these methods is limited; however anecdotal and some data-based evidence suggests that these techniques can be effectively incorporated into therapy with children. Clinicians must obtain the training required to become competent in the use of methods such as hypnotherapy. When clients need psychopharmacotherapy, clinicians must collaborate with the medical practitioners who are competent to provide this service. Many of the interventions described in this chapter can be used as components of the integrated treatments that are addressed in Chapter 16.

16

Integrated Approaches to Intervention

■ ■ ■

Seven-year-old Joseph was evaluated for overactivity, impulsivity, and inattention at home and in school. Based on the results of medical, psychological, and educational assessments, the boy was diagnosed with attention-deficit hyperactivity disorder (ADHD), combined type (American Psychiatric Association, 2000). Joseph appears to be of average intelligence, but his school work has been inconsistent, as reflected in grades ranging from A's to F's. The assessment also revealed other problems, including rejection by his peers, who apparently avoid him because of his negative behavior.

■ ■ ■

The treatment of children with ADHD often involves the combination of different therapeutic methods and the collaboration of the therapist, parents, and teachers. This chapter explores how clinicians intervene using what the American Psychological Association (1994b, p. 7) has called "comprehensive and integrated" treatments that are consistent with the multidimensional model presented in this book. The chapter discusses two important aspects of integrated therapies: theoretical considerations and practical issues related to the delivery of treatment services. At the end of the chapter, we return to the case of Joseph described in Chapter 4 to examine the use of an integrated approach to intervention.

INTEGRATED INTERVENTIONS: THEORETICAL CONSIDERATIONS

Children typically present for therapy with problems that are both complex and multidetermined. As Kamphaus and Frick (1996) stated, "It is clear that comorbidity is the rule, rather than the exception, in children with psychological difficulties" (p. 53). Because of the nature of these problems, clinicians must avoid simplistic case conceptualizations in favor of multidimensional interpretations that serve as the basis for integrated treatments. An important aspect of these interventions is the combination of principles and techniques chosen from the systems of child therapy described in previous chapters. Researchers and practitioners have developed integrated treatments using four methods: the transtheoretical model, theoretical integration, technical eclecticism, and constructivism.

Chapter 5 examines the transtheoretical model of Prochaska and Norcross (1994), who described psychotherapy in terms of the stages, levels, and processes of change. Clinicians who use this approach consider clients' readiness for treatment, the nature of the presenting problem, and the use of intervention strategies that are appropriate for these stages and levels of change. Theoretical integration, as the term implies, is the combination of principles from at least two theories of therapy that results in a new method that is more than the two theories taken individually. A clinician who uses this approach might combine the developmental aspects of psychodynamic theory with the environmental focus of behavioral theory to create an intervention that recognizes the interaction of early childhood experiences and contemporary influences on a child's behavior.

Proponents of technical eclecticism adopt a more empirical approach to the combination of therapeutic strategies by selecting interventions that have been found to be effective in treating children with the presenting problem. These therapists treat children diagnosed with ADHD using empirically supported therapies, such as behavioral parent training and behavioral interventions in the classroom (Pelham, Wheeler, & Chronis, 1998). Constructivism represents an integration of principles from the major systems of psychotherapy. Proponents of this approach recognize "the active role of the human mind in organizing and creating meaning—in literally inventing rather than discovering reality" (Lyddon, 1995, p. 69). Constructivist therapists are less interested in applying external standards to evaluate a child's behavior than they are in obtaining the client's personal and unique view of self and his or her cultural surround.

The Transtheoretical Model

Chapter 5 discusses the stages, levels, and processes of change that Prochaska and Norcross (1994) described in their transtheoretical model. We now examine how the authors combined these elements into an empirical approach to the study of change within and outside of therapy. Prochaska and Norcross wanted an integrated model that therapists can use to devise innovative treatments across a broad range of presenting problems. They did this by highlighting processes common to different theories of therapy while preserving the unique contributions of each.

The search for common factors across theoretical perspectives is not a recent development. When Rosenzweig (1936) observed that different therapies can have similar outcomes, he reasoned that these treatments may be equally effective because they share common therapeutic factors. Based on their study of articles, book chapters, and books on psychotherapy, Grencavage and Norcross (1990) estimated that there may be as few as one or as many as 20 of these factors. The most frequently cited factor was the therapeutic alliance, although theorists also believed that therapeutic change occurs as a result of cathartic experiences and the acquisition of new behaviors. The most common client characteristic was a hope for the future, and the most frequently cited therapist qualities were the ability to relate with clients in a positive manner and to foster hope.

Studies of common factors in child therapies are lacking, but theorists and therapists seem to share a belief in the importance of the therapeutic relationship, the client's developmental level, and language. Although traditional theorists have given relatively little attention to multicultural considerations, culture can be added to the list of important transtheoretical factors. If multiculturalism is indeed the "fourth force" in therapy, as proposed by Pederson (1991, p. 6), theorists and practitioners must give more attention to the role of cultural influences in the development and delivery of child treatments.

The therapeutic relationship is as important with child clients as it is with adults in therapy, but treatments for these groups differ in that child therapy also requires the development of a working relationship with parents and significant other adults. Family therapists work with parents and children together to address systemic factors. Behavioral clinicians collaborate with parents to implement behavior management techniques in the home. The therapist–child relationship gives young clients the opportunity to test their beliefs and expectations about themselves and their cultural surround. Shirk (1998) identified this relationship as an important agent of change for clients' interpersonal schemas. As an abused child interacts with a caring and supportive therapist, he or she must evaluate and revise negative beliefs about relationships with significant others when the clinician does not respond as expected.

The process of therapy differs for adults and children. Most theorists believe that children should be allowed to express their thoughts and feelings and to learn new behaviors in therapy. But clinicians often encounter developmental challenges when they try to help young clients become aware of the causes and effects of their behavior. As discussed previously, children rarely refer themselves for therapy, so it is not unusual for them to have little interest in examining a problem they either fail to understand or accept as their own. The preceding chapters explore how a child's developmental level impacts the therapeutic process. Therefore, development itself constitutes a common factor in child therapies. From the early psychodynamic writers to modern family systems theorists, therapeutic techniques have been designed to take into account developmental differences in children. Sigmund Freud used consultation, Melanie Klein developed play analysis, and Alfred Adler used parent education groups. Virginia Axline reformulated Carl Rogers' client-centered theory as the basis for her child-centered play therapy. Behaviorists recognized the role of parents and teachers in shaping children's behavior through the use of operant conditioning. And family systems theorists explored the impact of generational boundaries on family functioning. All of these writers realized that children and adults hold qualitatively different views of themselves and the world and therefore require interventions appropriate to their developmental level.

Another common factor across theories and therapies is language, the tool we use to make meaning of our world (Russell, 1998). Language is obviously a central component of traditional talk therapies, but linguistic ability is also important when play interventions are used with children. Klein's interpretations of children's behavior, Axline's use of active listening, and Knell's cognitive-behavioral play therapy are all examples of the integration of language and play with children. Language development involves the acquisition of expressive and receptive abilities. A quiet and withdrawn child may not talk during play therapy, but we generally assume that clients can at least listen to and understand what the clinician says. As discussed in Chapter 5, children's ability to understand and use language improves during the elementary school years. Clinicians must adapt their interventions to these changes to ensure that treatment matches the child's developmental level.

A transtheoretical assessment of childhood problems requires consideration of the stages, levels, and processes of change as they relate to the child, parents, and significant other adults. It is not unusual for these individuals to be at different stages of change at the outset of treatment. As discussed in Chapter 5, clinicians must assess each person's readiness for therapy and not assume that all of them are prepared to actively engage in treatment. The therapist's selection of intervention strategies is also influenced by each participant's level of change. When symptomatic or situational and systemic problems are identified, treatment is more likely to include parent consultation to teach effective child-rearing skills and couples or family therapy to address marital discord and multigenerational boundary issues. Based on an assessment of the family with these problems, the therapist is likely to develop a treatment plan that involves a number of change processes, including the helping relationship and contingency management.

Prochaska and Norcross (1994) based their transtheoretical model on empirical studies of the stages, levels, and processes of change in adults. Similar research is needed to examine the levels and processes of change at different stages of treatment for children and their families. Nelson (1994) provided some insight into transtheoretical factors when she compared the behavioral (Fraser, Pecora, & Haapala, 1991) and family systems (Nelson, Emlen, Landsman, & Hutchinson, 1988) approaches to preserving troubled families. Although the methods differed in regard to clinicians' focus on family history (i.e., family systems) and education and advocacy efforts (i.e., behavioral), therapists in both programs relied on listening, encouragement, goal setting, attention to present behavior, and problem solving. If we examine the theoretical origins of these techniques, we find that whereas listening and encouragement are generally associated with child-centered theory, goal setting is characteristic of Adlerian, behavioral, and some family systems approaches. A focus on present behavior is typical of behavioral approaches, and problem solving is characteristic of cognitive-behavioral and certain family systems therapies. At this point, the study of transtheoretical factors in child therapy is in its infancy, so more work such as Nelson's is needed to promote the use of this model with children. At the end of this chapter, we discuss an application of the transtheoretical model with our sample case of Joseph Morris.

Theoretical Integration

As Goldfried (1998) stated, "The field of psychotherapy has been characterized by competing schools of thought, each with its own jargon, concepts, and techniques" (p. 49). This state of theoretical diversity and adversity probably reflects the stage of development of child therapies. To establish their respective position, the proponents of different theories have tried to distinguish their approach from other belief systems. The resulting focus on "different from" as opposed to "similar to" has contributed to a variety of methods, each with acknowledged experts and professional journals endorsing their own principles and techniques. A transition to integrated treatments requires the acceptance of different theoretical perspectives and the recognition that each system can contribute to effective interventions for children.

Theoretical Considerations. Theoretical integration involves more than common therapeutic factors and the simple addition of principles selected from different theories. By integrating two or more perspectives, clinicians create a unique method for conceptualizing and treating childhood problems. Consider how the combination of object relations theory and cognitive-behavioral principles would affect the techniques used in therapy. The psychodynamic emphasis on early childhood experiences and associated mental representations of interpersonal relationships could be conceptualized in the context of the child's learning history. The client's social anxiety is seen as having its origins in an authoritarian parent–child relationship in which little consideration was given to the emotional needs of the child. The dysfunctional cognitive schemas that were learned during early childhood can be unlearned. In therapy, reattribution training could be used to revise the mental maps the client has been using to interpret and predict relationships with peers and adults. The therapeutic relationship itself becomes the emotional holding environment that was unavailable early in life. Through the combination of principles and procedures, the child's clinician attempts to remediate cognitive, emotional, and behavioral problems while establishing the foundation for healthy psychosocial development.

Assessment. Theoretically integrated treatment begins with an integrated assessment. Coonerty (1993) identified the multidetermined nature of children's behavior as justification for this approach. As she stated:

> Although one may conceive of a problem as having a specific starting point, this does not by any means infer that the starting point is the essential source of the problem. Rather, the emotional illness or crisis has spread to other aspects of functioning while difficulties in other areas have, in turn, modified or increased emotional stress overall. (p. 416)

To adequately assess a child, the clinician must consider the interactional effect of personal (e.g., physiological predisposition, cognitions, affect), interpersonal (e.g., peer relationships), familial, and sociopolitical (e.g., prejudice, socioeconomic level) factors. Through the use of a multiaxial approach, therapists collect information from the child and significant others, such as parents and teachers, to better understand how these factors mutually affect each other. Coonerty described how the assessment of a 4-year-old aggressive boy revealed that he needed language therapy and medical treatment for a chronic ear infection. When problems were identified in the child's relationship with his nursery school teacher, the examiner encouraged the parents to find a more appropriate educational setting. An integrated assessment consists of more than the identification and description of problems. The examiner must also consider how the child's and parents' strengths can be used to effect constructive change. For example, the therapist in the Coonerty case might capitalize on the client's interest and talent in soccer or swimming by encouraging the parents to involve the child in this activity to enhance motor coordination, social cooperation, and self-esteem.

O'Connor and Ammen (1997) outlined a comprehensive assessment approach based on biological, developmental, intrapsychic, interpersonal, and ecological factors. The authors combined the child orientation of psychodynamic and child-centered theories with the systems focus of family and ecological theories. O'Connor and Ammen identified the child as the primary focus for assessment and treatment, but they stated that the meaning of a client's thoughts, feelings, and behaviors are apparent only when they are considered in relation to the child's cultural surround. Children begin to develop interpersonal schemas based on their early interactions with primary significant others. The emotional concomitants of these mental representations affect how a child interacts with significant others, who then respond based on their perception of the child's behavior, their own intrapsychic perspectives, and other environmental influences. In their workbook, *Play Therapy Treatment Planning and Interventions: The Ecosystemic Model and Workbook*, O'Connor and Ammen provided sample assessment forms and case examples to illustrate the use of their approach.

In contrast to the case study format of O'Connor and Ammen (1997), Schuhman, Foote, Eyberg, Boggs, and Algina (1998) used a standardized, empirically based approach to integrated assessment. The authors' method is based on behavioral and child-centered theories, which provide the foundation for their parent–child interaction therapy (see discussion later in this chapter). Schuhman et al. used an extensive battery of psychometrically sound measures to assess the child, parents, and the parent–child relationship. They screened clients for intellectual abilities using the Wonderlic Personnel Test (Dodrill, 1981) for parents and the Peabody Picture Vocabulary Test (Dunn & Dunn, 1981) for children. Parents were asked to complete the Dyadic Adjustment Scale (Spanier, 1976) to assess their marital relationship and the Beck Depression Inventory (Beck & Steer, 1987), the Parenting Stress Index (Abidin, 1995), and the Parental Locus of Control Scale (Campis, Lyman, & Prentice-Dunn, 1986) to evaluate their psychosocial adjustment. Schuhman et al. assessed the child's adjustment based on parents' responses to the DSM-III-R Structured Interview (McNeil, Eyberg, Eisenstadt, Newcomb, & Funderburk, 1991) and the Eyberg Child Behavior Inventory (Eyberg, 1992). Trained raters used the Dyadic Parent-child Interaction Coding System II (Eyberg, Bessmer, Newcomb, Edwards, & Robinson, 1994) to rate actual parent–child interactions in a laboratory setting. Finally, parents' satisfaction with therapy was evaluated at the end of treatment using the Therapy Attitude Inventory (Eyberg, 1993).

Clinicians determine the starting point for treatment based on the assessment results. Coonerty (1993) observed that there are no clear rules to define this process. Parents often provide direction for the therapist when they specify their reasons for seeking treatment for their child. The clinician's challenge is to not adopt a restricted view of the situation at the outset of therapy. A child may indeed be exhibiting angry outbursts at home, but this inappropriate behavior may be related to ineffective parenting, tension in the marital relationship, or school-related stress. It is not unusual for treatment to involve more than one point of origin. For example, the clinician may opt for family therapy in cases in which the child is triangulated with the parents in conflict. The treatment plan could also include consultation with teachers when the assessment reveals systems-related problems at school.

Treatment. Writers have described a variety of theoretically integrated treatments for children. A popular component of these therapies has been psychodynamic theory, possibly because of its developmental focus and its historical and conceptual foundation for other methods. Ellen Wachtel (1994) integrated psychodynamic, family systems, and behavioral theories in her "child-in-family approach" (p. 282) to treatment. She described how clinicians must consider intrapsychic and interpersonal factors in order to identify possible causes and cures for a child's problems. For example, the oppositional defiant behavior of a 6-year-old may be a reflection of both the parents' and child's inner world and the family's interactions with each other and those in the outside world. The child's interpersonal schemas may reflect insecure attachment during infancy when caregivers were physically or emotionally unavailable. The parents' current emotional problems may compromise parent–child and mother–father interactions, resulting in ineffective parenting and the maintenance of misbehavior in the child.

Wachtel (1994) stated that the focus of therapy is not the child's past, but "*current* interactions that maintain (and are maintained by) unconscious concerns" (p. 16). Her integrated treatment involves the use of psychodynamic techniques to address the child's unconscious anxiety, behavioral strategies to help parents modify the child's inappropriate behavior, and family-based interventions to alter the ways that family members interact. Wachtel used an interesting adaptation of psychodynamic narrative methods when she taught parents to become more effective storytellers with their children. She instructed parents to focus on the feelings that are significant to the child, such as fear of peer rejection, or self-disclose experiences and related feelings from their past. She also used traditional play activities with children and behavioral interventions with parents to teach effective behavior change strategies.

As discussed previously, clinicians are sometimes asked to treat a child without having parents in therapy. Wachtel (1994) described one such experience involving 4.5 year-old Sara, whose behavior had deteriorated during her parents' marital separation. The child was very close with her father, but she no longer had contact with him after he moved out of town. Neither the mother nor the daughter discussed the father or their feelings about his absence. Wachtel theorized that Sara misbehaved because of the mother's parenting style, the child's use of inappropriate behaviors to test the mother's love, and the anxiety she experienced in connection with her father's departure. Wachtel incorporated psychodynamic principles by having the mother establish a holding environment for Sara, giving her permission to talk about her father. Wachtel also taught the mother to use behavior management techniques and to express her love for the child. The father never participated in therapy, but Wachtel relied on family systems theory to help the mother examine how her roles as mother, daughter to her own parents, and worker and family provider affected her intrapsychic and interpersonal functioning. The mother eventually accepted help from her parents and granted Sara's request for daily telephone contact with her father. Wachtel was also in contact with Sara's teacher, which proved to be beneficial in improving the child's behavior at school.

Kirschner and Kirschner (1993) considered individual and systemic factors in their integration of object relations, family systems, and cognitive-behavioral theories. An important aspect of Kirschner and Kirschner's model is the belief that the power for growth and dysfunction in a family rests in the marital relationship. The authors focused on what they called a couple's "marital, rearing, and independent (or career)" (p. 401) transactions. To be effective, therapists must consider the interactional effects these transactions have on the family. When a conflicted marital relationship restricts the parents' ability to rear their children and pursue lives outside of the home, the clinician must address these difficulties while focusing on the family's presenting problem, which is the child's negative behaviors.

Kirschner and Kirschner (1993) described a three-phase model of treatment designed to address the interaction of individual and systemic factors. During the first phase of treatment, the clinician assesses family relationships, develops a rapport with the family, explores family of origin issues, and initiates systemic changes to help parents work as a team in rearing their child. Treatment includes fostering insight and facilitating behavioral change. For example, the therapist can help the parents understand how family of origin issues are affecting their interactions with the child. Treatment may also involve training parents to use effective child-rearing strategies. Kirschner and Kirschner observed that phase one interventions typically result in some improvement in the child's behavior.

During the first and second phases of treatment, the clinician combines family sessions with individual and conjoint meetings with parents. As the child's behavior improves and rearing transactions are strengthened during the second phase, the therapist monitors the child's behavior while turning his or her attention to the spousal relationship. During individual sessions with each spouse, the clinician facilitates disclosure of personal thoughts and feelings regarding themselves and the marriage. The remedial focus of this phase is transformed into education/development and prevention strategies during the third phase, when the therapist helps the husband and wife "become more active growth agents for each other" (Kirschner & Kirschner, 1993, p. 408). Individual meetings are replaced by conjoint sessions with the couple, and attention turns to the independent transactions component of the authors' tripartite model. The therapist helps the husband and wife develop their own sense of self, which provides the basis for meaningful and supportive marital and rearing transactions. The Kirschner and Kirschner model is characterized by a gradual change of focus from the child's misbehavior to problems in the marital relationship and then to the parents' extrafamilial relationships.

Coonerty (1993) described an integrated approach based on psychodynamic, behavioral, cognitive-behavioral, and systemic principles. Therapists who use this approach must consider each dimension as it relates to the child. Because of its systemic component, the model is thought to be effective to the extent that the child, parents, and significant others actively participate in treatment. Coonerty integrated developmentally appropriate interventions based on psychodynamic (e.g., play therapy), behavioral and cognitive-behavioral (e.g., parent training, cognitive restructuring), and family systems (e.g., family sessions) theories. She described how parent- and teacher-based techniques could be combined with individual play therapy to treat the 4-year-old aggressive boy mentioned earlier. Although behavioral and systems interventions facilitated change in significant others' interactions with the boy, play was effective in helping the child to express his feelings of anger, fear, and shame.

For decades, behavioral and child-centered theories have been treated as distinctly different belief systems of therapy and human development. Carl Rogers and B. F. Skinner (1956) articulated these differences when they presented their conflicting views on the importance of personal and environmental factors. Reflecting on the Rogers–Skinner debate in the context of contemporary practice, Goldfried (1998) stated, "It is fascinating to see how these seemingly incompatible approaches might be used in a complementary way" (p. 52). An example of the integration of behavioral and child-centered principles is the parent-child interaction therapy developed by Sheila Eyberg and her colleagues.

Eyberg (1988) recognized the value of two traditions in child treatment: child-centered therapists' emphasis on the therapeutic relationship and behaviorists' contributions to parent training and behavior management programs. She combined the principles and techniques of these methods to create parent–child interaction therapy, a brief-term intervention that can be used to empower parents and improve behavior and self-esteem in children. Eyberg's method is based on the assumption that parents have a significant influence on a child's development. Hembree-Kigin and McNeil (1995) emphasized this point when they stated that "any therapeutic work done with a child of preschool or early elementary school age directly involves the child's caregivers" (p. 3).

Eyberg (1988) divided her 9- to 12-session program into two stages: child-directed interaction and parent-directed interaction. In the first phase, parents are taught to use the skills that child-centered clinicians use in play therapy with children. These include observing, describing, and imitating the child's play as it occurs. For example, when a child uses wooden blocks to construct a building, the parent might say, "You're making a big building" while adding blocks to the structure or constructing a similar building nearby. Parents also learn to use paraphrase and praise. If the child were to say, "That's a big building," the parent might respond, "That really is a big, tall building. You're doing a great job." When these skills are part of the parent's behavioral repertoire, the therapist introduces parent-directed interactions.

In this second stage of treatment, parents learn behavior management techniques during play sessions with their child. These methods include recognizing and praising appropriate actions, ignoring minor infractions, and punishing severe misbehavior (Hembree-Kigin & McNeil, 1995). Parent–child interaction therapy is different from many other parenting methods in that the parent and child interact during treatment sessions so clinicians can train parents to combine child-centered active listening with behavioral management skills. As they become more attentive, parents are able to recognize and appreciate their child's appropriate behaviors. They learn to administer consistent praise for positive actions and developmentally appropriate punishment for negative behavior, thereby creating a more predictable environment for the child.

Evidence for the effectiveness of most integrated treatments is limited to case studies. Arkowitz (1997) described empirical research on these methods as "disappointingly low" (p. 257). Although this may be a result of the field's early stage of development, general acceptance of theoretically integrated treatments requires supporting research using a variety of research designs. Despite the formidable task of investigating these multidimensional interventions, some researchers have embraced the challenge and evaluated the efficacy of theoretically integrated treatments for children. One example is the work of Schuhmann and colleagues (1998) on the impact of parent–child interaction therapy in families with conduct disordered preschoolers. The authors found that after treatment, mothers and fathers were more likely to use positive techniques, such as praise, with their children. Parents reported feeling more in control of their children, who were better behaved. Other data-based studies of parent–child interaction therapy have revealed positive changes in parents' interactional style and children's behavior (Eisenstadt, Eyberg, McNeil, Newcomb, & Funderburk, 1993) and students' performance at school (McNeil, Eyberg, Eisenstadt, Newcomb, & Funderburk, 1991). Another encouraging outcome of these studies is the finding by Brestan, Eyberg, Boggs, and Algina (1997) that improvement generalized to the siblings of children enrolled in treatment. Later in this chapter we examine an adaptation of parent–child interaction therapy that emphasizes therapeutic play rather than parent training.

The data-based methods used to evaluate parent–child interaction therapy must be applied to other theoretically integrated treatments to address the criticisms that some writers have leveled against these interventions. Lazarus and Beutler (1993), for example, warned that theoretical integration can produce a jumble of principles and techniques that are difficult to evaluate because they lack a consistent rationale. As an alternative, the authors recommended that clinicians embrace technical eclecticism, a systematic approach to integration that is "built on empirical demonstrations of the conditions, problems, and clients with whom different procedures are effective" (p. 383).

Technical Eclecticism

Theoretical Considerations. Introduced by Arnold Lazarus in 1967, technical eclecticism involves the use of empirically tested treatments. Less attention is given to theoretical considerations because clinicians choose interventions based on the efficacy or effectiveness of the techniques rather than their theoretical principles. Therapists who adhere to the principles of technical eclecticism may have a preferred theory, but their approach to treatment selection is "more actuarial than theoretical" (Arkowitz, 1997, p. 249). The term "eclecticism" has sometimes had negative connotations in the mental health field. This is caused partly by the unsystematic way that some clinicians have integrated techniques in practice. As Lazarus and Beutler (1993) indicated, this "ragtag, shotgun collection of miscellaneous methods" (p. 381) does little to promote the effectiveness of therapeutic interventions because clinicians ignore existing research and deliver treatments that are difficult to replicate and evaluate. Lazarus (1976) described the use of technical eclecticism in his multimodal behavior therapy, which is composed of seven modes represented by the BASIC ID acronym: Behavior, Affect, Sensation, Imagery, Cognition, Interpersonal relations, and Drugs or physiological considerations.

Assessment. Keat (1978, 1979, 1990) applied the Lazarus model to psychological interventions with children when he translated the BASIC ID acronym into his HELPING model: Health; Emotions-Feelings; Learning-School; People-Personal Relationships; Imagination-Interests; Need to Know-Think; and Guidance of Acts, Behaviors, and Consequences. Keat (1990) described his model as a map for assessment and a guide for facilitating therapeutic change in children. Clinicians who use this method are able to obtain a more complete picture of the client based on reports obtained from parents, teachers, and the child. Before the initial clinic visit, parents and teachers complete referral forms designed to assess the child's functioning across the seven domains. Keat (1990) recommended that therapists have them rank order their concerns relative to the seven HELPING modes. This information is then used to individualize treatment to the parents' presenting concerns. In some families, assessment results are translated into interventions designed to address Health and People-Personal Relationships concerns, such as exercise programs or family therapy. In others, the clinician focuses on concerns related to Learning-School and Guidance of Actions, Behaviors and Consequences through the use of token reinforcement programs or parenting groups.

Keat (1990) noted that a comprehensive assessment must include information obtained directly from the child. Starr and Raykovitz (1990) used the HELPING model to develop the Multimodal Child Interview Schedule (MCIS). Because the MCIS contains a number of questions for each mode, the therapist selects items that are relevant to the child's presenting problem. Child-report information is summarized according to the seven modes, combined with information collected from the parents and significant others, and a multimodal treatment plan is developed.

Treatment. To date, most of the support for Keat's multimodal therapy can be found in case reports (Keat, 1990). Still, the model offers a conceptual framework that clinicians can use to identify specific areas that warrant clinical intervention. Whether treatment represents unsystematic eclecticism or technical eclecticism depends on the clinician's selection of intervention strategies. When empirically supported therapies are available, therapists combine and adapt these treatments to the specific needs of the child. This approach was used in the Multimodal Treatment Study of Children with ADHD Cooperative Group, US (1999a) in which psychopharmacotherapy was combined with behavioral interventions for children with ADHD. We will examine this method in more detail when we return to our case example of Joseph Morris at the end of this chapter.

Sometimes clinicians are confronted with presenting problems that have received insufficient empirical scrutiny. In these situations, the therapist is likely to select techniques previously found to be effective with related problems and to evaluate the effectiveness of treatment using the single-case experimental design. Martin-Causey and Hinkle (1995) described a case of this type when they used the BASIC ID model with a 9-year-old aggressive girl in residential treatment. The authors used all of the Lazarus modes, with the exception of Sensation, which they replaced with School. Based on daily behavioral ratings completed by the child and professional staff, Martin-Causey and Hinkle found that their multimodal intervention was effective in improving the girl's affect, cognitions, and academic performance. Later in this chapter, we examine Multisystemic Therapy, developed by Henggeler and his colleagues, which is another example of technical eclecticism as defined by Lazarus and Beutler (1993).

Constructivism

Theoretical Considerations. Constructivist theory is a relatively recent addition to the psychotherapy literature. Lyddon (1993) described it as an integrated approach that includes principles and techniques drawn from psychodynamic, behavioral, cognitive, client-centered, and existential theories. Proponents of constructivism consider human beings to be "active agents who, individually and collectively, co-constitute the meaning of their experiential world" (Neimeyer, 1993, p. 222). Accordingly, there is no single external reality or standard that can be used to evaluate a client's mental health status. Each child's thoughts, feelings, and behaviors are considered meaningful and are conceptualized within the context of his or her cultural surround. To date, the primary focus for constructivist writers has been adults, although Epting (1984) noted that work with children is "very much needed" (p. 192).

A major figure in the development of constructivism is George Kelly (1905–1967), who was the only child of farming parents in rural Kansas who expanded his horizons through imagination and educational pursuits, including earning a Ph.D. in psychology at the University of Iowa (Neimeyer & Jackson, 1997). Although he devoted much of his later career to the development of personal construct theory, Kelly "spent a great deal of his early years" working with children (Fransella, 1995, p. 127). During his 12 years as a faculty member at Fort Hays Kansas State College, Kelly founded the Psychological Clinic, where he and his students evaluated problem children from local schools. While working at Fort Hays and later at Ohio State University, he developed his theory, which he published as a two-volume text, *The Psychology of Personal Constructs* (Kelly, 1955). According to Kelly's person-as-scientist model, individuals "devise conceptual templates (personal constructs) that permit them to interpret, anticipate, and appropriately respond to events with which they are confronted" (Neimeyer, 1985, p. 2). Kelly believed this process of meaning making to be a life-long activity. Although children and adults differ in the ways they think (see Chapter 10), they share the desire to make meaning out of their world.

Kelly (1955) believed that human beings are active construers, not passive recipients of meaning in the world around them. People are viewed as scientists who formulate, test, and revise personal theories about themselves and their environment (Epting, 1984). With the personal constructs that constitute their theory of themselves and the world, they predict the future based on their past experiences. As Kelly (1955) stated, "A person's processes are psychologically channelized by the ways in which he anticipates events" (p. 129). This perspective resembles, in some ways, Adler's socioteleological theory in which behavior is viewed as purposive or goal-directed. But personal construct theorists have a particular interest in the unique belief system that each person develops in order to bring meaning to life.

To understand another person's view of self and the world requires insight into the individual's personal constructs, which Kelly (1955) described as idiosyncratic, dichotomous, ever changing, and organized. These characteristics can be illustrated by the personal construct "strong." Although many people use this term as part of their meaning-making process, each person's definition of this construct is uniquely different from that of anyone else. Personal constructs are bipolar or dichotomous, and the personal meaning of a construct emerges when attention is directed at the individual's contrast or antonym for the construct of interest. For example, a mother may use "unreliable" as her contrast for "strong," and the father may use "needy." These parents' respective construct–contrast pairs translate into different interpretations of healthy development for their child. The mother in our example is likely to view a strong child as one who follows through on assigned tasks, but the father would tend to prefer an independent child who has relatively little "need" of others.

People refine their personal constructs as they apply them to everyday experiences and retain relevant aspects while revising their meaning to integrate new life experiences. Personal constructs are also organized into a system of overlapping and fragmented terms. For example, a boy who is confronted by a bully on the playground will construe the event based on construct–contrast pairs such as safe–dangerous, strong–weak, and dumb–smart. His response and its consequences will modify his personal construct system and affect the meaning he makes of similar events in the future. Ravenette (1977) noted that personal constructs in children lack the level of sophistication found in adults. As he stated:

> It is part of the growth process that the child is able to make progressively finer levels of discrimination and to develop a greater hierarchy of abstractions, both of which, over time, lead to richer and more complex construct systems. (p. 260)

The everyday language of children tends to be concrete, so therapists must remember to limit their use of abstract terminology with young clients.

Constructivist theory is also a structural-developmental approach because consideration is given to children's early attachment to primary significant others, typically the mother and father (Neimeyer, 1993). Chapter 6 examined the work of Main and Cassidy (1988) and Sroufe and colleagues (e.g., Egeland, Carlson, & Sroufe, 1993; Sroufe, Carlson, & Shulman, 1993) who reported evidence for the stability of infant–caregiver attachment patterns from age 6 months through childhood and adolescence. This combination of psychodynamic and cognitive-behavioral principles has resulted in a constructivist perspective that contains both a developmental focus and an interactional conceptualization of a person's here-and-now thoughts, feelings, and behaviors.

Another variant of constructivist theory is narrative reconstruction. Chapter 10 discusses developmental and multicultural considerations in the use of storytelling with children. Neimeyer (1993) summarized narrative theories as follows: "The common assumption of these 'literary' approaches to psychological phenomena is that the structure of human lives is inherently narrative in form; people constitute and are constituted by the stories that they live and the stories that they tell" (p. 226). From this perspective, narrative constitutes a lifelong vehicle for communication and meaning making. Consequently, the stories children tell provide clinicians with vehicles for understanding clients' personal points of view on themselves and others.

Rosen (1996) indicated that "good" stories are coherent, have meaning, and contain a plot and characters that capture the listener. When Mary tells her father about her day at school, she includes experiences (e.g., interactions with friends, a high grade on a test) as they relate to a theme (i.e., success). She relates her story in a form she believes will be interesting to her father. What she includes in her narrative is as important as the information she excludes. For example, she does not mention being sent to the end of the cafeteria line for a minor infraction, either because she expects a negative response from her father or because the event is insignificant within the overall context of her successful day at school. If the cafeteria experience were another incident in a very difficult day, Mary's exclusion of this event from her narrative would be therapeutically relevant. Freeman, Epston, and Lobovits (1997) observed that children often avoid direct discussion of their problems, opting instead for metaphor or play. Because we have addressed the therapeutic benefits of play elsewhere, we direct our attention here to children's communication through metaphor.

Mills and Crowley (1986) defined metaphor as "a form of symbolic language that has been used for centuries . . . to convey an idea in an indirect yet paradoxically more meaningful way" (p. 7). One person might describe a difficult work day as one in which he "worked like a dog," but another might say she had her "nose to the grindstone." Metaphor can be used to objectify a child's problem so it can be challenged as an external entity (Neimeyer, 1993). A volatile temper might be called "the demon" or off-task behavior "the dreamer." By expressing the problem in metaphoric terms, the child has an opponent that can be confronted in a direct manner. Freeman et al. (1997) observed that when children "realize that the problem, instead of them, is going to be put on the spot or under scrutiny, they enthusiastically join in the conversation" (p. 10).

Assessment. Various constructivist techniques have been developed for assessing children. An approach based on Kelly's (1955) theory is "a process in which *elicitation* of constructs comes first, and the *operationalisation*, or use, of constructs comes second" (Ravenette, 1977, p. 256) Therapists assess the latter by using a series of interview questions or a developmentally appropriate version of Kelly's Role Construct Repertory Test. Central to this method is the belief that children are experts on their life experiences, use idiosyncratic language to describe these events, and consequently provide information about their personal construct system.

Ravenette (1977) described how drawings of everyday school situations containing a troubled child can be used to assess a client's personal constructs. For each picture, the child is asked the following questions:

1. What do you think is happening?
2. Who might be troubled and why?
3. How did this come about?
4. If you were there, what would you do and why?
5. What difference would that make?
6. What kind of boy is the one picked out? (pp. 272–273)

The meaning that children make of these pictures provides insight into the constructs they use in everyday life.

The Role Construct Repertory Test, often referred to as the Rep Grid, was designed to assess personal constructs in adults (Epting, 1984). Clients provide the names of significant people in their lives, which are called elements, and then compare and contrast these individuals as three-person groups. By identifying the two people who are similar to each other and different from the third, clients reveal the personal constructs that are most important to them. The adult format for the Rep Grid is too complicated for children, so Jones (1997) devised a developmentally appropriate version for elementary school students. Her School Behaviour Game (SBG) is a board game that therapists and clients play by rolling a die and moving a game piece around a game board. Children "capture" spaces on the board by describing activities at school, such as their favorite class and playground activities, which serve as the Rep Grid elements. Each response is written on a game card that is placed on the captured space. The therapist "steals" cards by landing on spaces held by the child, who then recaptures them three at a time by describing how the activities that appear on two cards are similar to each other and different from the third (i.e., the personal constructs).

Jones (1997) described how she used this method with 10-year-old John, who was chronically truant from school. The boy stated that the behaviors listed on two cards were similar (i.e., fighting on the playground, whistling during a school assembly) because they were something that Jesus would not want children to do. Both differed from the behavior on the third card (i.e., never wanting to do math again in school) because this was not of concern to Jesus. Clearly, John drew a moral distinction between social and academic behaviors, so he could refuse to attend school and complete class assignments without compromising his religious values.

Treatment. Compared with traditional cognitive-behavioral interventions, constructivist therapy is more likely to focus on the developmental process (e.g., infant–caregiver attachment), personal constructs, and narratives. These characteristics have resulted in a therapeutic approach that is "more creative than corrective" and "more exploratory then directive" (Neimeyer, 1993, p. 224). The cognitive-behavioral approach to treating depressed children tends to be a corrective and directive intervention intended to modify the child's view of himself and the world so it approximates an external standard. Constructivists are more likely to collaborate with the child to help the client discover the meaning he makes of himself and the world around him.

Much of the work on constructivist psychotherapies has been conducted with adults. While still in its infancy, child constructivist therapy has created a renewed interest in traditional interventions, such as play therapy and storytelling, as well as new developments in family treatments. Writers have emphasized the importance of the developing mind in children's interpretation of life events (see Rosen, 1996). Consequently, therapeutic applications of constructivist theory involve the use of play and narrative techniques that are tailored to the developmental level of young clients. An intervention that has potential as a constructivist procedure is sandplay, which is discussed as a psychodynamic method in Chapter 7.

Dale and Lyddon (2000) described how the Jungian approach to sandplay can be modified for use as a constructivist technique with children. Similar to their Jungian colleagues, constructivist therapists have clients select miniatures, construct a sand world, and then tell a story about their creation. But the two groups differ in the way they interpret the meaning of children's sand pictures. When constructivists use this technique, the child rather than the therapist construes the meaning of the sand world. Because there is no single external standard for reality, constructivists emphasize the idiosyncratic meaning that each child gives to the sand creation. As Dale and Lyddon stated, the sand world provides a concrete stimulus that children can use to express their inner thoughts and feelings. The child engages in a process of self-organization that involves the assimilation of new information into existing personal constructs as well as the accommodation of existing constructs in response to novel life experiences.

Constructivists have expanded the framework of family therapy. Hoffman (1988) described her transformation to constructivist family therapist from what she called the role of "repairman-social engineer" (p. 111) that is characteristic of traditional family systems therapies. Instead of identifying and treating the clinician's conception of a family's problems, constructivists focus on the meaning that clients make of their situations. The application of externally defined diagnostic categories is replaced with a search for the theories that clients use to understand their world and their place in it. This includes the examination of shared beliefs or constructs that define what a family is and how it responds to changes within and outside of the family. Rather than being "at war with the family" (p. 121) in a mission to find and eliminate the family's "problem," the constructivist therapist collaborates with clients to empower the family system to discover "the meaning behind even the most repugnant actions or events" (p. 125).

Nichols and Schwartz (1998) described constructivist theory as "the crowbar that pried family therapy away from its belief in objectivity—the belief that what one *sees* in families is what *is* in families" (p. 318). As a result, family therapists are challenged to understand how their own attitudes and feelings affect their formulation of the presenting problem and the role of individual family members. As Nichols and Schwartz indicated, constructivism has given family therapists reason to pause when they "know" the causes of a family's presenting concern and are prepared to use directive techniques. As the authors stated, "These ideas inject a note of humility into the clinical discourse" (p. 319).

The focus of constructivist family therapy is the examination of ways that family members "negotiate a common reality" (Neimeyer, 1993, p. 227). Therapists recognize that they bring idiosyncratic beliefs to treatment. Their understanding of a family and its problems differs from the family members', constructions or beliefs about themselves. Consequently, they must use techniques that minimize therapist direction and encourage family members to construct a shared view of self. Neimeyer described two methods that constructivist therapists use with families: therapeutic rituals and circular questioning.

Prescription of therapeutic rituals can be used when family members differ in their interpretation of the presenting problem (Neimeyer, 1993). Consider a family's views on ADHD. Some members may believe the problem to be the response of a defiant, undisciplined child, but others may see it as a physiological disorder. Using an approach similar to that of Selvini Palazzoli, Boscolo, Cecchin, and Prata (1988b), a constructivist therapist who elicits these differing views could encourage the family to interpret the child's behavior as a physiological problem on Monday, Wednesday, and Friday and adopt the alternate view on Tuesday, Thursday, and Saturday. Sunday "might be left for each family member to construe the problem as he or she pleased" (Neimeyer, 1993, p. 228).

Chapter 13 discusses De Shazer's (1985, 1988) solution-focused brief family systems therapy. The questions used in this method are consistent with the emphasis on meaning making found in constructivist theory. Tomm (1988) described how a clinician's view of the family is manifested in the questions posed to clients in session. Tomm identified four question types: lineal, strategic, circular, and reflexive. Therapists typically use lineal and circular questions to improve their understanding of a family's problem. Whereas lineal inquiries are intended to identify cause-and-effect relationships (e.g., "When is Tony most likely to misbehave?"), circular questions are used to assess patterns within the family system (e.g., "How does the rest of the family respond when Tony misbehaves?"). Strategic and reflexive questions are used to change family members' understanding of the presenting problem. Therapists use strategic questions to indirectly effect change in the family (e.g., "Why don't the rest of you just ignore Tony when he misbehaves?") and reflexive questions to mobilize the family's ability to solve its own problems (e.g., "If all of you were to describe your feelings when Tony misbehaves, what do you think he would think or do?"). Tomm emphasized the relationship between therapists' questions and clients' responses. As he stated, "To ask a particular question, then, is to invite a particular answer" (p. 14).

Dozier, Hicks, Cornille, and Peterson (1998) conducted an analog study to investigate the therapeutic impact of these question. Forty families viewed one of four videotaped family sessions in which therapists used one of the question types described by Tomm (1988). The authors found that families who watched a therapist using circular or reflexive questions were more likely to describe themselves as connected or joined with the clinician. It appears that inquiries intended to foster clients' understanding of their family system were more likely to be perceived as therapeutic. Each of Tomm's question types has a purpose in therapy (e.g., lineal questions for information gathering), but circular and reflexive inquiries appear to have a more positive effect on the development of the relationship between the therapist and family.

Many therapists have used narrative approaches with children. Gardner (1971), for example, described storytelling as "a time-honored practice in child psychotherapy" (p. 17). To effectively use narratives, therapists must be able to reconnect with their childhood. As Mills and Crowley (1986) stated, they must connect with the "*child within* by recapturing pleasant memories and playful fantasies, or by observing children playing at parks, beaches, and schoolyards" (p. 27). Although storytelling is frequently combined with other therapeutic activities, such as art or puppetry, it is also used alone in the form of autogenic stories with children in therapy (Brandell, 1988).

Children are asked to tell autogenic stories independent of other therapeutic stimuli. Clinicians use these narratives to help clients discuss personal issues without external pressure to conform to socially sanctioned rules of acceptability. A popular method is Gardner's (1971) Mutual Storytelling Technique (MST), a psychodynamic procedure in which children are instructed to tell a story with a beginning, middle, and end, followed by a moral for the narrative. For example, Antoine tells the story of a dog who leaves home one day and gets lost in the forest. The dog asks the other animals for directions, but no one is willing to help. When asked for the moral of the story, Antoine replies, "Don't expect anybody to help you."

When the child's resolution of a story is thought to be problematic, the MST therapist retells the story in a positive manner using the characters, setting, and emotional context in the child's story to formulate "a healthier resolution or a more mature adaptation than the one used by the child" (Gardner, 1971, p. 29). The retelling of Antoine's story might include the introduction of a friendly bear who offers food to the dog and provides a map indicating the way home. According to Friedberg (1994), MST can be considered a cognitive intervention that is designed to correct a child's errors of thinking. Because therapists using MST are responsible for telling the "healthier" version of the story, the procedure is more of a traditional cognitive-behavioral intervention than a constructivist technique.

Friedberg used a variation of MST with a 4-year-old boy who was exhibiting separation anxiety. The child had difficulty separating from his mother at preschool, and he was abused by the other students. In response to the boy's story of a kitten that scratches other kittens at school, Friedberg told of a skunk named "Stinky" who felt lonely and afraid at school, so he hit and bit the other skunks in class. In the therapist's positive resolution to the story, Stinky's parents and teachers taught him to make friends so he would feel comfortable away from his mother. As Friedberg stated, "The lesson, of course, was skunks could learn to be away from their moms and still be safe" (p. 213).

Mills and Crowley (1986) described a treatment session with an 8-year-old girl who was experiencing chronic sleep problems that were caused by "monsters" in her room. The therapist listened carefully to the child's narrative of her scary world, then told the girl that "monsters were really make-believe disguises for unhappy children who had no friends" (p. 31). Armed with this conceptual shift, the child left a cupcake for her monsters every night, and the girl experienced significant improvement in her sleeping behavior.

Kestenbaum (1985) described a less directive variant of therapeutic storytelling in which children create a book containing the stories they tell in therapy. As clients dictate their narratives, the clinician writes them in the book. This collaborative effort enables the child to maintain the flow of the story without having to tackle spelling and grammatical challenges. The therapist can ask the child to elaborate on the characters and to describe their thoughts and feelings relative to events in the story. Kestenbaum recommended that clinicians record this information elsewhere for later reference. This procedure differs from MST in that the child's telling of a story is of primary importance, without modifications provided by the therapist.

Constructivist therapists use a technique called narrative reconstruction in which children reformulate and retell their own stories. One aspect of this approach is the use of therapeutic metaphors, which are used "to offer new choices, show different ways of perceiving a situation, and tap a variety of dormant beliefs, attitudes, and values of the child" (Frey, 1993, p. 223). When used in combination with other therapeutic techniques, metaphors offer a means of helping children develop new ways of handling problem situations. As Frey described in the case of a 5-year-old girl who was grieving the loss of significant others, metaphor can facilitate discussion of very difficult topics. Using a board game the child had developed containing various medieval figures (e.g., king, princess, flying horse), the girl used metaphors that:

> had a theme of the princess on a quest on the flying horse to find the mother, aunts, and grandmother in heaven. It was an arduous quest inasmuch as the princess had a difficult time finding them. When she found them, they assured her that they were doing well and were fine. She informed them that she wanted to join them . . . but the relatives told her she could not do that, that it was not in her control or their control. (p. 237)

This client used metaphor to reprocess personally relevant themes (e.g., the inability to rejoin loved ones) that were difficult for her to discuss in a direct manner.

As discussed earlier, narrative therapists often use a linguistic technique called externalization to separate children from their problems. Clinicians who use this approach do not ignore the child's difficulties. Instead, the problem behavior is given a label and attention is focused on the child's relationship with the problem. Consider the parents of a 7-year-old boy who describe their son as an angry child who has no friends. If the boy also states that he hates his fellow students, the therapist could externalize the problem by using the label "Mr. Temper" and helping the child devise techniques to "show Mr. Temper who's in charge here."

Freeman et al. (1997) illustrated this approach when they described how a therapist used the term "Squirmies" (p. 38) to externalize the fidgety behavior of 9-year-old Leon. To capitalize on the boy's creative skills, the clinician asked, "Have you ever used your talent of inventing games to put the Squirmies in their place?" (p. 38). The boy responded with the following:

> If the Squirmies "got me in the classroom," ten points went to the Squirmies and zero to Leon. If Leon held off the Squirmies in class . . . he got more and more points, up to a maximum of ten, for putting the Squirmies where they belonged—on the playground during recess. (Freeman et al., pp. 38–39)

In this example, the therapist separated the child from his problem and then challenged the boy to use his imagination to design a self-control technique.

Freidberg (1994) noted the lack of controlled studies on the effectiveness of narrative approaches with children. An exception is the work of Costantino, Malgady, and Rogler (1985, 1986), who developed *cuento* therapy as a storytelling technique for Puerto Rican children. *Cuentos* are culturally based stories derived from Puerto Rican folktales. Costantino et al. believed that ethnic stories motivate children of nondominant groups and provide constructive models for their behavior, beliefs, and interpersonal relationships. In session with small groups of mother–child dyads, the authors had a male and a female therapist alternate with mothers in the bilingual presentation of two *cuentos*. The clinicians led a discussion about the moral of each *cuento* and the behavior of the characters in the story. Each mother–child dyad was videotaped as the clients portrayed the behaviors described in the *cuentos*. Therapists played the videotapes and conducted a group discussion of the positive and negative consequences of these behaviors. Costantino et al. provided empirical support for their method when they found that *cuento* therapy was preferable to client-centered therapy and a control condition in the treatment of 210 Puerto Rican children in kindergarten to grade 3.

Summary

The theories and techniques of the major systems of child therapy have both common and unique characteristics. All share a commitment to remediating problems in a manner consistent with a child's developmental level, but each system is recognized for a particular emphasis, whether that is an intrapsychic formulation of personality or a systems-based interpretation of the function of behavior within the family. Recent efforts to integrate the major theories have resulted in four important methods: the transtheoretical model, theoretical integration, technical eclecticism, and constructivism. These approaches allow clinicians to combine different theories and select empirically supported interventions appropriate to each child's needs.

INTEGRATED PLAY TECHNIQUES

Eyberg (1988) demonstrated that traditional play therapy can be combined with other treatment methods. She chose to focus on parents by teaching them to use child-centered techniques to improve the quality of the parent–child relationship and to facilitate development of children's self-esteem. This is an integrated approach because Eyberg also recognized the need to train parents in the use of child management strategies developed by proponents of behavioral treatments for children. Other writers have incorporated play into their work with children and families. Hardaway (2000), for example, described a brief family play therapy based on the principles of psychodynamic and family systems theories. As discussed in Chapter 13, he asked parents to play with their children in session so he could observe and interpret transference as it occurred between the child and these primary attachment figures.

Therapists must recognize that children, even those of preschool age, are active members of their family and therefore have important information to contribute to treatment. Evidence to support this claim comes from the fact that families typically enter treatment to remediate the behavior problems exhibited by an identified patient—the child. Clinicians must realize that younger clients are less likely to possess the verbal skills needed to communicate their thoughts and feelings in a language that most adults understand. To involve a preschool child or early elementary school student in therapy, clinicians must be prepared to use play. As discussed in other chapters, therapists of different theoretical orientations have devised developmentally appropriate play methods for working with children. Therefore, clinicians who adopt an integrated approach to treatment have a wealth of techniques that can be used to communicate with the young client. Although play is not a therapist's only technique in an integrated treatment, it represents an important therapeutic strategy for helping troubled children.

Play constitutes a central activity in the brief therapy developed by McNeil, Bahl, and Herschell (2000). The authors' primary theoretical orientation is child centered, but they incorporated behavioral techniques to manage clients' behavior in session. McNeil et al. viewed children's disruptive behavior as an impediment to brief therapy. In this sense, their method differs from traditional psychodynamic and child-centered play treatments in which a client's misbehavior is thought to provide "rich therapeutic material" (p. 233). The authors organized their sessions through consistent application of rules for behavior and a standard session format in which structured activities preceded free play. They also used selective inattention for children's disruptive behavior and reinforced clients for behaving in an appropriate manner.

The McNeil et al. (2000) method consists of 12 sessions designed to improve the parent–child relationship, remediate children's disruptive behaviors, and develop self-esteem and anger control in children. During the first seven sessions, the therapist conducts child-centered therapy to develop rapport with the child and to create a fun atmosphere in the playroom. During the last five meetings, the clinician teaches and coaches parents to use child-centered techniques with their child. These include the strategies that Eyberg (1988) used in parent–child interaction therapy. For example, parents learn to imitate the child's play and to paraphrase statements made in session. They are assigned weekly homework that involves home-based play sessions with the child to facilitate development of the skills learned in treatment.

McNeil et al. (2000) divided each of their sessions into a 10-minute check-in period to discuss treatment progress, 20 minutes of what they called Child's Work, 20 minutes of Child's Play, and a 10-minute check-out period to discuss homework tasks. The Child's Work phase is structured and involves the use of bibliotherapy, therapeutic games, and play materials consistent with the clinician's objectives for each session. McNeil et al. described their work with an 8-year-old boy who was exhibiting sexualized behaviors, including masturbating in public. During the sixth session, the clinician used a dollhouse and dollhouse figures to indicate rooms where masturbation would be acceptable and locations where this behavior would be socially inappropriate. McNeil et al. followed their structured play period with free play when the therapist sets aside the day's agenda for Child's Work and follows the client's lead. This child-centered experience is intended to facilitate development of the therapist–client relationship and to allow clients to explore personally meaningful issues.

Earlier in this chapter, we discussed the assessment model that O'Connor and Ammen (1997) developed for ecosystemic play therapy. This treatment approach involves the application of developmental, psychodynamic, family systems, and ecological principles to conceptualize children and their behavior in the context of their cultural surround (O'Connor, 1993). Proponents of this model assess the child's intrapsychic functioning, interactions with significant others, and environmental conditions that influence the child's development. Treatment occurs at various levels, including direct interaction with the child, interviews with family members, consultation with teachers, and community-based child advocacy. O'Connor and Ammen (1997) stated that ecosystemic play therapy is intended:

> to resolve children's psychopathology, that is, to enable children to get their needs met consistently and in ways that do not interfere with the ability of others to get their needs met. A secondary goal is to facilitate the assumption or resumption of optimal developmental functioning and growth. (p. 11)

Similar to Kirschner and Kirschner (1993), O'Connor and Ammens (1997) adopted a stage model for their ecosystemic approach that progresses from Introduction and Exploration to Tentative Acceptance, Negative Reaction, Growing and Trusting, and Termination. The authors described intervention strategies that therapists can use to address the challenges of each stage. These include the use of art activities at the outset of treatment to establish the therapeutic relationship. O'Connor and Ammen described an Introduction and Exploration activity in which the child lies on a large sheet of paper while the therapist outlines his or her body. The client then completes the picture by drawing in characteristics to define him- or herself.

During the Tentative Acceptance stage, clinicians can use the "Simon Says" game, alternating between directions from the therapist and client. The same game can be adapted for use during the Negative Reaction stage "so the child either does the opposite of what Simon says or only follows the directions that are not preceded by the phrase 'Simon says . . . ' " (O'Connor & Ammen, 1997, p. 142). The clinician begins to focus on the child's problem-solving abilities during the Growing and Trusting stage. Although treatment is intended to help children solve specific problems, its main purpose is that of teaching problem-solving strategies (see Chapter 11 for Braswell & Bloomquist's five-step approach) that clients can use throughout life. Therapists sometimes use competitive games to help children become more resilient by having them reassess a losing strategy before returning to the game. The ultimate goal of all therapies is successful termination. Because of the interpersonal nature of ecosystemic play therapy, O'Connor and Ammen (1997) recommended that clinicians not lose sight of this important stage. Therapists can prepare children for termination in various ways, such as having them write a book about their therapeutic experience to take with them at the end of treatment.

INTEGRATED INTERVENTIONS: SERVICE DELIVERY CONSIDERATIONS

Integrated treatments are more than the combination of theoretical principles or therapeutic techniques. They represent comprehensive and coordinated services offered by collaborating professionals who are willing to consider innovative ways of meeting the needs of children and families in the least restricted environment appropriate to the presenting problem (Henggeler, 1994). Integrated treatment requires a transformation of the traditional service delivery system. Systems-level change includes the dissolution of artificial boundaries that separate professionals in their work with children. Traditional treatments are provided in individual locations, such as community mental health clinics, schools, hospitals, and social service agencies. Eliminating territorial boundaries not only facilitates collaboration among the professionals employed at these sites, but it also prompts a reevaluation of the way treatment is delivered.

The literature on child therapies is based primarily on services provided in traditional settings. Friedman (1994) described how this situation is the result of outdated assumptions about children and families. The developers of these programs expected that relatively few children would require professional help. They also believed that families:

> would almost always include two parents and would receive support from neighbors and extended family. We also expected that most children who were not in need of special service would have clearly configured problems that would respond well to discrete, single-system, and often unidimensional interventions. (p. 41)

These assumptions do not apply to the complex problems that children currently experience. Therapists must revise each of these beliefs if they are to develop innovative and effective interventions for troubled children. This includes the use of less traditional service venues, such as the child's home, school, and community (e.g., Friedman, 1994).

Nelson and Landsman (1992) described the characteristics of family-based services designed to reduce out-of-home placements for children. Clinicians who use these methods emphasize the family's role in the child's development, work to preserve the integrity of the family, and provide "time-limited, intensive and comprehensive services including therapeutic, concrete and supportive services" (Nelson & Landsman, 1992, p. 5). Treatment according to this model might include traditional family therapy delivered in the home as well as information or referral for needed resources, such as food or medical care.

Nelson (1994) described two family-based interventions: intensive family preservation services (IFPS) and intensive family services (IFS). Chapter 13 discusses a commonly used IFPS method, the behaviorally oriented Homebuilders program (Kinney, Haapala, & Booth, 1991). Homebuilders is an intensive, time-limited, crisis-oriented intervention delivered in the home. In contrast, IFS services are provided in the home or at the therapist's office. The cornerstone of this model is family therapy, although program recipients also may receive parent training, financial assistance, and medical care. According to Nelson (1994), evaluations of IFPS and IFS programs have revealed that both are "a great advance in child welfare services away from child placement and toward family preservation services" (p. 29). Although the two methods are based on different theoretical principles, both actively engage families in treatment planning by helping clients develop alternative means of achieving treatment goals, focusing on here-and-now concerns, and providing support and encouragement for program participants.

The delivery of integrated treatment also involves the participation of school personnel. Duchnowski (1994) discussed recent developments in the delivery of educational and psychological services to troubled children. School-based services for these students have traditionally been provided in self-contained classrooms with limited effectiveness (Knitzer, Steinberg, & Fleisch, 1990). Duchnowski contrasted these services with integrated programs in which professionals collaborate for the benefit of the child. The Positive Education Program (PEP) in Cleveland, Ohio, is one such example. This community-based multidisciplinary program was started in the early 1970s to train teachers who worked with students who have academic and behavioral problems (Hobbs, 1982). Teachers learn basic attending skills and are responsible for establishing therapeutic relationships with the children. The PEP staff also includes a case manager who maintains contact with families to assess systemic needs and to encourage parents' participation in the program.

Reorganization of the current system of care is an important first step in the delivery of effective integrated treatments. Henggeler (1994) described additional changes that are needed in the types of interventions used with children. He indicated that clinicians must be flexible so they can devise treatments that are appropriate to the individual needs of children and families. Therapists must adopt a comprehensive approach and consider the multidetermined nature of each child's problems. Treatment also requires the active collaboration of parents to address both intrafamilial and extrafamilial influences on the child's development. Although a number of innovative programs have been developed, we focus on three: Multisystemic Therapy, Vermont's statewide New Directions Program, and the Fort Bragg Child and Adolescent Mental Health Demonstration Project.

Multisystemic Therapy

Henggeler and Borduin (1990) developed Multisystemic Therapy (MST) to treat children and adolescents with behavior problems. Used primarily with adolescent offenders, the principles of MST (Table16-1) are consistent with Bronfenbrenner's (1979) ecological model. As Schoenwald, Borduin, and Henggeler (1998) described, children are viewed as "nested within a complex of interconnected systems that encompass individual (e.g., biological, cognitive), family, and extrafamilial (peer, school, neighborhood) factors" (p. 487). A child's behavior is therefore viewed as multidetermined, rather than the result of a single cause. Henggeler and Borduin (1990), for example, described the aggressive behavior of an 11-year-old boy as related to poor behavior management skills by his mother and teacher, peer support for the child's negative behaviors, the mother's inadequate after-school supervision of the boy, and the child's low intelligence and high impulsivity.

When assessing children and their families, clinicians who adopt the MST model do not limit themselves to correlates of a child's misbehavior. They also identify individual, familial, and extrafamilial strengths that can be used to facilitate therapeutic change. Treatment is designed to reduce or eliminate problem behaviors while strengthening positive attributes in the child and family. In their assessment of the aggressive 11-year-old boy, Henggeler and Borduin (1990) found that the mother, the teacher, and the boy's siblings were concerned about him. They also discovered that the mother had a social support network and the boy had the respect of his

Table 16–1
The Principles of Multisystemic Therapy

Principle 1.	The primary purpose of assessment is to understand the fit between the identified problems and their broader systemic context.
Principle 2.	Therapeutic contacts emphasize the positive and use systemic strengths as levers for change.
Principle 3.	Interventions are designed to promote responsible behavior and decrease irresponsible behavior among family members.
Principle 4.	Interventions are present focused and action oriented, targeting specific and well-defined problems.
Principle 5.	Interventions target sequences of behavior within and between multiple systems that maintain the identified problems.
Principle 6.	Interventions are developmentally appropriate and fit the developmental needs of the youth.
Principle 7.	Interventions are designed to require daily or weekly effort by family members.
Principle 8.	Intervention effectiveness is evaluated continuously from multiple perspectives with providers assuming accountability for overcoming barriers to successful outcomes.
Principle 9.	Interventions are designed to promote treatment generalization and long-term maintenance of therapeutic change by empowering caregivers to address family members' needs across multiple systemic contexts.

From *Multisystemic Treatment of Antisocial Behavior in Children and Adolescents* (p. 23), by S. W. Henggeler, S. K. Schoenwald, C. M. Borduin, C. M. Rowland, and P. B. Cunningham, 1998, p. 23 New York: Guilford Press. Copyright 1998 by Guilford Press. Reprinted with permission of the author.

peers, possibly because of his sense of humor and athletic skills. Treatment in this case would involve the collaboration of the parent, child, and significant others to instill hope, solve problems in a step-by-step manner, and acknowledge progress in therapy (Henggeler, Schoenwald, Borduin, Rowland, & Cunningham, 1998).

As Schoenwald et al. (1998) described, MST is delivered in a manner similar to the family preservation model. Therapists handle a limited number of cases in an intensive, comprehensive, and brief manner. Schoenwald et al. reported that MST clinicians typically have a caseload of four to six families, who are in treatment for about 3 to 5 months. Therapists individualize services to the needs of the child and family, but they are held accountable and are expected to provide evidence for the outcome of their work. According to Schoenwald et al., MST practitioners draw from empirically supported psychopharmacological, behavioral, cognitive behavioral, and family systems approaches. Treatment may include couples therapy to address marital conflict, behavior management training for parents, self-control or assertiveness training for the child, and systemic changes at the child's school or in the community.

Although the bulk of Henggeler's empirical support for MST was collected from adolescents and their families, Brunk, Henggeler, and Whalen (1987) conducted a randomized study of MST and parent training with the families of abused and neglected children. Consistent with MST principles, the authors adopted an ecological model that involved consideration of "the background of the parent, family relations, family transactions with extrafamilial systems, and cultural variables that support maltreatment" (p. 171). Therapists in the parent training groups taught parents to use behavior modification techniques with their children. The MST families were often treated in their homes with interventions, such as family therapy and advocacy, designed to address family members' strengths and areas for growth. The MST and parent training interventions were equally effective in certain domains, including parent reports of problem severity. But at the termination of treatment, the MST group exhibited more positive parent–child interactions, which should reduce the risk of maltreatment (Henggeler et al., 1998).

Henggeler, Smith, and Schoenwald (1994) identified four factors related to the outcome of MST. First, the authors believed that MST has been effective because treatment principles and procedures are consistent with the empirical literature on antisocial behavior in youth. Second, MST is a family preservation approach in which services are typically delivered in the child's home and school environments. Third, successful therapists have maintained the integrity of the treatment model because they were trained and supervised in its use. Finally, MST proponents recognize the importance of multidisciplinary collaboration and the development of working relationships with professionals in different agencies and settings. In short, MST appears to be effective because it is empirically grounded, delivered in clients' environment, and provided by well-trained and supervised clinicians who cooperate with other professionals.

The New Direction Program

Vermont's New Directions Program is a statewide effort designed to provide multidimensional services to children and adolescents with serious emotional problems. Interventions are comprehensive and systems oriented, individualized to the child's needs, and delivered in the least restrictive environment (Santarcangelo, Bruns, & Yoe, 1998). An important component of the program is collaboration among the professionals who coordinate the delivery of services. These include intensive home-based family preservation techniques to reduce out-of-home placement for troubled children. Community mental health care centers offer crisis management and coordinate respite care for children in need of temporary separation from their families. The Vermont model also includes the participation of local schools where children receive therapy and specialized educational experiences. Parents also have access to a variety of services, including support groups offered throughout the state.

According to Santarcangelo et al. (1998), the program's therapeutic case managers are "the glue that holds the system together" (p. 121). Case managers coordinate care for an average of four to seven clients. Their responsibilities include the formation of treatment teams composed of professionals and other adults significant to a child's development. Case managers provide what Burchard and Clarke (1990) called a "wraparound" (p. 50) approach that:

> involves working with the people who are most influential in the life of the child and family, agreeing on what that particular child and family most need to live a stable and productive life, devising and implementing individualized, positive ways to meet those needs, and never giving up on the child and family. (Burchard & Bruns, 1998, pp. 363–364)

The authors stated that wraparound service requires a commitment to serve troubled children in the least restricted environment appropriate to their behavior, flexible approaches to funding treatment, and a collaborative approach to intervention.

The New Directions Program has been evaluated at two levels: the service delivery system (e.g., program costs, cooperation among child care professionals) and clinical outcome (e.g., children's behavioral adjustment, consumer satisfaction). One goal of the Vermont initiative was to reduce expensive out-of-state placements for seriously emotionally disturbed youths. Santarcangelo et al. (1998) cited studies on the comparative cost of services, which was lower for the individualized, community-based approach. Children served by the program were significantly less likely to be living in more restrictive, residential treatment programs 1 year after they had been referred to the program (Bruns, Burchard, & Yoe, 1995; Yoe, Santarcangelo, Atkins, & Burchard, 1996). Santarcangelo et al. (1998) also reported information from the Vermont Department of Mental Health and Mental Retardation that revealed a high level of collaboration across agencies in the state.

Youths enrolled in the program exhibited a decline in inappropriate behaviors (Bruns et al., 1995). Clients were satisfied with program services, including the help they received from their case managers (Rosen, Heckman, Carro, & Burchard, 1994; Santarcangelo, 1998). This finding is particularly important because of the central role of these professionals in the coordination and individualization of treatment. When Bruns et al. (1995) analyzed data for a sample of 27 participants, they found that the annual cost per client of $43,440 was less than the average price of $59,000 for the children and adolescents in Vermont who were placed in residential treatment facilities.

The Fort Bragg Demonstration Project

The Fort Bragg Child and Adolescent Mental Health Demonstration Project is an $80 million multi-year project that DeLeon and Mandell (1997) described as "the most desirable, seamless, and up-to-date treatment regime possible while disregarding costs" (p. 551). The Vermont and Fort Bragg programs were similar in many ways, including their use of case managers or treatment teams to coordinate a broad range of community-based services. Unlike the New Directions Program, the Fort Bragg initiative involved a comparison of community-based service delivery systems. Specifically, the comprehensive continuum-of-care approach provided to 547 families of U. S. military personnel in Fayetteville, North Carolina, was compared with the more traditional system used with 410 children and their families at other military installations in the state. Fayetteville families had access to a full range of services, including traditional inpatient and outpatient care and intermediate-level interventions, such as "in-home therapy, after-school group treatment services, day treatment services, therapeutic homes, specialized group homes, and 24-hour crisis management teams" (Bickman, 1996a, p. 10). Services in the comparison group were funded through the Civilian Health and Medical Program of the Uniformed Services (CHAMPUS). Children in this group had access to traditional clinical interventions, which included a maximum of "45 days of inpatient or hospital care, 150 days of residential treatment, and 23 outpatient visits per year" (Hoagwood, 1997, p. 546).

Program evaluators found that 12 and 18 months after the outset of treatment, children in both groups had improved significantly from baseline, with no significant difference between families at the Fayetteville and comparison sites (Bickman, 1996b; Hamner, Lambert, & Bickman, 1997). The overall effectiveness of the continuum-of-care and traditional programs was impressive, with 84% of the Fayetteville group and 88% of the comparison children showing improvement during treatment (Saxe & Cross, 1997). As Saxe and Cross suggested, the Fort Bragg findings may indicate that all participants in the study had access to quality mental health care. This may not be the case for the children of civilian families whose access to treatment services is often limited because of financial or geographical factors. In fact, Fayetteville families entered treatment more quickly, received more types of services, and remained in treatment longer than did comparison group clients, possibly because they had access to unlimited services at no out-of-pocket expense (Bickman, 1996b; Hamner et al., 1997).

Quantity and quality of treatment services are not synonymous terms. The latter is reflected in the effectiveness of individual treatment strategies and clients' satisfaction with the services received. Heflinger, Sonnichsen, and Brannan (1996) noted that consumer satisfaction was higher in the Fort Bragg group. Although the program's unlimited access to services may have contributed to this outcome, it is also possible that families liked the continuum-of-care approach used in Fayetteville. Similar to children and families in Vermont's New Directions Program, Fort Bragg participants may have appreciated professionals' collaboration in the delivery of individualized services. The Fort Bragg study was an evaluation of "a system, not individual services" (Weisz, Han, & Valeri, 1997, p. 541), so we are unable to draw conclusions about the effectiveness of specific components of this integrated treatment. Still, the overall effect of this continuum-of-care approach was positive, leading us to conclude that at least some of the program's interventions were effective.

Based on the results for MST, the New Directions Program, and the Fort Bragg initiative, we can draw a number of tentative conclusions. First, empirically supported therapies can be integrated and used effectively with children and their families. Second, collaboration among service providers appears to be effective in developing treatments that children and their families appreciate. And the number of services provided to clients may be less important than the effectiveness of individual treatment components. Therapists now face the challenge of developing empirically sound methods for delivering multidisciplinary treatments to children and their families. To accomplish this goal, practitioners and researchers must work together to design and evaluate integrated methods for treating the various problems these clients bring to therapy.

INTEGRATION OF THEORETICAL PRINCIPLES AND DELIVERY OF SERVICE: A CASE EXAMPLE

Attention-deficit hyperactivity disorder is a relatively common presenting problem, so therapists can expect to encounter these clients and their families. As you will recall from Chapter 4, the disorder is thought to occur in 3% to 7% of school-age children and is characterized by unusually high levels of activity, inattention, and impulsivity. Because ADHD is so troublesome to children, parents, and teachers, many treatments have been tried. These include controversial therapies, such as those described in Chapter 15, in addition to the traditional methods of psychopharmacotherapy, behavioral parent training, bibliotherapy, social skills training, individual therapy, classroom-based behavior modification programs, and family therapy (Abikoff & Hechtman, 1996; Brown, 2000). Of these, only three have been found to meet the criteria for empirically supported treatments: psychopharmacotherapy, behavioral parent training, and behavior modification in the classroom (Pelham et al., 1998). Although methods such as traditional individual therapy and bibliotherapy may be appropriate for certain children, the existing body of empirical evidence suggests that these interventions should not be first-line treatment for children with ADHD.

Drawing from more than 3 decades of outcome research, clinicians have developed multimodal and multidisciplinary approaches for the treatment of children with ADHD. The multimodal component of these programs involves remediation (e.g., psychostimulants to control behavior), education/development (e.g., classroom management for teachers to improve the quality of the classroom learning environment), and prevention (e.g., social skills training to minimize clients' isolation from peers). Treatment is multidisciplinary to the extent that the therapist, parents, teachers and significant other adults collaborate and contribute their expertise and energy to an integrated approach to intervention. Early work by Satterfield and his colleagues offered support for this method (Satterfield, Cantwell, & Satterfield, 1979; Satterfield, Satterfield, & Cantwell, 1981). The Satterfield et al. program included psychopharmacotherapy, educational interventions, traditional individual therapy, parent training, and family therapy individualized to the needs of the child. The authors reported positive outcomes for this method, but their project was not a controlled study involving random assignment of children to different treatment conditions. It is only recently that a multimodal and multidisciplinary approach has been examined in controlled studies, the most prominent of which is the multisite investigation supported by the National Institute of Mental Health (NIMH) (Richters et al., 1995).

Pelham et al. (1998) described this important study as "the largest clinical trial ever conducted by the NIMH, and it comprises the largest, most intensive, and longest treatment study of a childhood disorder that has ever been conducted" (p. 201). This 14-month project involved 579 children, ages 7 to 9 years, who met the diagnostic criteria for ADHD—combined type. Clients were randomly assigned to either psychopharmacotherapy with methylphenidate; behavioral treatment; a combination of methylphenidate and behavioral interventions; or community care in which children were treated by their regular physician, who typically prescribed various forms of psychopharmacotherapy (Multimodal Treatment Study of Children with ADHD Cooperative Group, US, 1999a).

The behavioral treatment used in this study involved manualized interventions with children, parents, and the school. Children participated in an 8-week summer camp that involved the use of token reinforcement programs, time out, social skills and problem-solving training, modeling, and social reinforcement. Parents participated in family sessions and parenting groups where they learned behavior management techniques described by Barkley (1987b). School-based treatments involved consultation with teachers to teach classroom management skills, the preparation of behaviorally trained aides who worked directly with students, and the use of daily report cards as part of a home-based reinforcement program.

The authors reported positive results for children in their study (Multimodal Treatment Study of Children with ADHD Cooperative Group, US, 1999a, 1999b). Children in all groups showed improvement over the course of treatment, but those who received psychopharmacotherapy and the combined treatment exhibited a greater reduction in ADHD symptoms than did children in behavioral treatment only and the community care condition. Although the combined treatment was not significantly better than medication alone in reducing ADHD behaviors, it was the only method that performed better than community care in reducing problems related to academic achievement, parent–child relationships, social skills, and disruptive behaviors. The combination of psychosocial interventions and medication has been found to have additional benefits. Vitiello et al. (2001) reported that children treated with the combined approach required a lower therapeutic dose of methylphenidate than did patients who received drug therapy only.

As noted earlier, Pelham et al. (1998) identified behavioral parent training and behavior modification in the classroom as the psychosocial interventions that meet the criteria for empirically supported therapies. Pelham et al. (1993) described the classroom-based behavior modification program they used as part of their summer camp for children with ADHD. This treatment included token reinforcement, time out, the posting of class rules, social reinforcement, and a home-based reinforcement program. The authors found that the behavioral approach was better than traditional classroom procedures in reducing students' disruptive behaviors and improving their compliance with classroom rules. When Pelham et al. combined psychopharmacotherapy and behavioral treatment, they obtained results similar to those reported in the Multimodal Treatment Study of Children with ADHD. That is, the combined treatment was better than behavior modification only but offered limited benefits beyond those found with medication only.

These findings offer important data that can be used to develop more effective and efficient treatments for children with ADHD. If reduction in core ADHD symptoms is the goal, psychostimulant therapy merits serious consideration because it is a relatively low-cost method for controlling these behaviors in some children. But parents are sometimes reluctant to use medications because of potential side effects, and not all children exhibit a positive response to psychostimulants. Likewise, medications have not been found to remediate academic deficits, improve peer relationships, or resolve family problems (Pelham et al., 1998). As a result, multimodal treatments are sometimes needed to adequately address the needs of these children.

Many studies are available on school-based psychosocial interventions for students with ADHD. DuPaul and Ekert (1997) conducted a meta-analysis of 63 outcome studies and found that behavior management techniques and academic interventions were more effective than cognitive-behavioral methods in improving students' classroom behaviors. DuPaul, Ervin, Hook, and McGoey (1998) studied the effects of peer tutoring as an educational intervention for students, ages 6 to 10 years, who were not receiving psychopharmacotherapy for ADHD. The authors used a classwide peer tutoring (CWPT) approach in which children formed dyads and alternated roles as tutor and student. When DuPaul et al. examined the results obtained using a single-case experimental design, they found that on-task behaviors for students with ADHD fluctuated from 29% during baseline to 80% for CWPT and from 21% during a return to baseline to 83% when tutoring was reintroduced.

Recent studies using cognitive-behavioral interventions have suggested that these methods are helpful for some children with ADHD. Miranda and Presentación (2000) described the benefits of a self-control program that included the use of problem-solving skills training, modeling, and behavioral contingencies. The authors treated 32 children with ADHD using 22 1-hour group sessions over a 3-month period. They observed positive changes in the students' behavior but no improvement in school grades. Sheridon, Dee, Morgan, McCormick, and Walker (1996) used manualized social skills training with student and parent groups. They used modeling, behavioral rehearsal, and homework assignments to teach children how to establish relationships, interact in a cooperative manner, and use self-control and problem-solving techniques to resolve interpersonal conflicts. Parent groups involved the use of bibliotherapy, group discussion, and videotaped models to help parents support their children's everyday application of skills learned in therapy. Teachers and parents reported general improvement in students' behavior, although there were some problems noted in the long-term generalization of these skills to interpersonal relationships.

We now return to the case of Joseph Morris, whose evaluation for ADHD was presented in Chapter 4. The multimodal and multidisciplinary treatment used with this child involves the collaboration of Joseph's therapist, school counselor and psychologist, teacher, family, and co-leaders for a parenting group. Services are provided in a community mental health center, the boy's home, and his school. Notice how behavioral, cognitive-behavioral, and family systems interventions are integrated with psychopharmacotherapy and educational tutoring to address the various problems that brought about Joseph's referral for therapy.

As you will remember from the multidimensional assessment described in Chapter 4, Dr. Pellegrini determined that Joseph met the diagnostic criteria for ADHD—combined type (DSM-IV-TR: 314.01). His problems with inattention and hyperactivity-impulsivity occur in different settings, are of longstanding duration, and have negatively affected the boy's academic and social development. Because Mr. and Mrs. Morris disagreed about child-rearing techniques and the use of medication for Joseph, Dr. Pellegrini scheduled her first therapy session with the parents. She decides to explore these differences from the perspective of multigenerational family systems theory.

▪ ▪ ▪

About 5 minutes into the session, Dr. Pellegrini says, "Last time we talked about the different parenting techniques you use with your boys. I was wondering how the two of you chose these methods."

"Well, I think we have to be strict with Joseph, like my parents were with me when I was a kid," Mr. Morris answers. "I mean, I didn't always like the way they raised me, but I guess they knew what they were doing."

"What would your parents suggest you do with Joseph?" Dr. Pellegrini asks.

"I know what they'd say because they've told me. They think we need to spank him and not let him get his way all the time." The father elaborates on the many discussions he has had about Joseph with his parents.

The father's comments about physical punishment cause Dr. Pellegrini to question whether he has abused his son. When she asks him to describe his use of physical measures, he answers, "I only spanked him twice, once when he rode his bike into the street without watching for traffic and another time when he threw his toys all over the living room and wouldn't put them away when his mother asked." As his wife nods her head in agreement, he adds, "I'm not sure it really did any good."

"That's what I've been trying to tell you," Mrs. Morris says. "Spanking may have worked with you as a kid, but it's not the answer for Joseph."

When Mr. Morris does not respond, the therapist turns to the mother and asks, "How do you typically discipline the boys?"

"Oh, I don't know. I guess I try to reason with them. I mean, my parents never spanked me . . . "

"They never had to," Mr. Morris interrupts. "You always did what your parents said. You still do."

"Tom, that's not true. They don't think Joseph needs that medicine."

"Well, that's one thing they're right about," he responds.

Dr. Pellegrini decides to follow this change of topic. "It sounds like Dr. Rahmed encouraged you to consider medication for Joseph."

"I know, but I just don't like the idea of my son taking a pill to fix his problems," the father answers. "And what about the side effects of this drug?"

"Have the two of you talked with Dr. Rahmed about this?" the therapist asks.

"I have, but Tom hasn't," the mother answers.

Mr. Morris describes the many discussions he has had with his parents, who strongly oppose the use of medication. "I just think my wife needs to be firmer with the boy."

Dr. Pellegrini says, "It's been my experience that some children benefit from medication, especially kids like Joseph who are very active and have problems staying on task. How do you feel about meeting together with Dr. Rahmed?"

"Oh, I'll do it if you think it would help," Mr. Morris answers in a reluctant tone.

As the parents discuss the arrangements for their meeting with Dr. Rahmed, Dr. Pellegrini ponders the father's enmeshment with his parents. She decides to focus the couple's attention on their successes in parenting Joseph. She opts for a solution-focused exception question. "When do you not have problems with Joseph?"

"Never," the father answers.

"That's not true," Mrs. Morris responds. "I think we do better on weekends."

The mother explains how her husband is more involved with both boys on weekends, especially Sunday afternoon, when he often takes them to the park or plays games with them. Dr. Pellegrini turns to the father, "It sounds like you are an important influence on Joseph. Let's talk about how both of you can work together to help your sons." When the parents immediately revert to a disagreement about their differences, Dr. Pellegrini asks a miracle question. "If you were to wake up tomorrow morning and Joseph's problems were cured, how would you know this had happened, and what would you notice different about yourselves and the boys?"

Mrs. Morris says that Joseph would be less active and more compliant with her requests. The father describes how his son would have a productive day at school. "And he would arrive home happy," the mother adds, "and talk about the fun he had with the other children." When they describe how the two of them would be different, they state that they would have fewer disagreements and work together in parenting their sons.

As Dr. Pellegrini listens to them talk about their child-rearing strategies, she realizes that neither parent understands the principles of effective behavior management. She encourages them to join the mental health center's parenting group. "The next group begins in 2 weeks and lasts for 10 sessions," she says. "The program helps parents work together and use behavior management techniques with their children." Mr. and Mrs. Morris ask a number of questions about the group and then agree to attend. They sign consent forms allowing the therapist to contact the co-leaders for the group.

Dr. Pellegrini schedules a family session with Joseph and his parents for the following week. During the intervening period, she contacts Dr. Rahmed and Mr. Johnson, Joseph's teacher, having obtained the necessary parent consent and child assent during the assessment session. When she speaks with Dr. Rahmed by telephone, she learns that he plans to give the parents an information pamphlet on the use of psychostimulants for ADHD and to answer their concerns about drug therapies. Dr. Pellegrini explains that she plans to routinely evaluate the boy's behavior in school and at home. Dr. Rahmed requests copies of these data to analyze for drug-related effects if the parents decide to use medication.

Dr. Pellegrini travels to Joseph's school one afternoon to meet with Mr. Johnson. He tells her that the boy's grades have not improved nor has his completion of classwork and homework assignments. "He does his homework, but he rarely has it with him when he gets to school. I think Joseph needs some help getting organized. He always seems to be losing things. It wouldn't surprise me if his homework ends up on the bus or somewhere else before he even gets to school."

When Dr. Pellegrini asks about Joseph's relationships with other students, Mr. Johnson says there has been no change. He suggests that the boy join the weekly social skills group run by Ms. Chester, the school counselor. The program is designed to help unpopular students learn techniques for establishing and maintaining positive peer relationships. "I don't know why I never thought about it before," he says. "Could you recommend it to the parents the next time you see them?"

Dr. Pellegrini agrees and then discusses a variety of interventions that could be used to improve Joseph's academic performance. The therapist and teacher decide to initiate a home-based reinforcement program. Dr. Pellegrini will work with Joseph and his parents to purchase and prepare a special notebook the child can use to record each night's homework assignments. Mr. Johnson will check and sign the notebook at the end of the school day to ensure that Joseph has recorded all of his assignments. Every morning, Mr. Johnson will record the child's completion of his homework. At her next meeting with the family, Dr. Pellegrini will have Joseph and his parents devise a token reinforcement system in which Joseph receives points for bringing home the signed notebook and materials needed to complete his homework. Points will also be awarded for daily submission of completed class assignments. At the end of each week, Joseph will be allowed to exchange his points for privileges or tangible rewards agreed upon in advance during therapy sessions.

"A few weeks ago, your school psychologist mentioned that he was developing a peer tutoring program," Dr. Pellegrini tells Mr. Johnson.

"Yes, I've thought about using it in my class, but I just haven't had the time to talk with Dr. Shuttersworth," he answers.

"I think this might be good for Joseph. If we were able to pair him with a talented and understanding student, I think we might see improvement in his academic and social functioning."

Mr. Johnson says that he will contact the school psychologist to arrange training sessions for his students. The therapist and teacher also implement structural changes in the classroom. Based on the data collected as part of Dr. Shuttersworth's assessment of Joseph's behavior, they decide to move the boy's desk next to the teacher's and to surround him with students who will model appropriate behaviors and successful academic performance. Although Mr. Johnson has discussed class rules with his students, he has never posted them. He decides to make a poster of the rules, which he will display in front of the room. To assist in the evaluation of treatment, he agrees to complete the ADHD Rating Scale—IV (DuPaul, Power, et al., 1998) and the Academic Performance Rating Scale (DuPaul, Rapport, & Perriello, 1991) on a regular basis.

"You know something that really concerns me?" Mr. Johnson asks. "Has Joseph told you that he hates school?"

"Yes," Dr. Pellegrini answers.

"Maybe I've been too hard on him. You know, he always seems to be the one who's causing problems. He never has his homework or class assignments finished. Except for the time Dr. Shuttersworth had me put tokens on his desk, I don't think I've ever praised Joseph when he's done what he was supposed to do."

The two of them spend the remainder of their meeting discussing the importance of a positive learning environment for all children, including those diagnosed with ADHD. Dr. Pellegrini praises the teacher's concern for Joseph and helps him devise a social reinforcement plan he can implement with the boy. "I think having him close to my desk will help because I'll be more likely to notice when he's on task," Mr. Johnson says. "And I'll be able to praise him without singling him out and interrupting the other students."

Dr. Pellegrini contacts the co-leaders of the clinic's parenting group and provides a brief description of Joseph and her plans for treatment. When she says she intends to use a home-based reinforcement program, the leaders indicate that they address this technique in group sessions. They also teach parents to use a variety of behavior management techniques, including social reinforcement, time out, and attending skills to increase parents' observation of positive behaviors in their children. Early sessions are devoted to an educational program that provides information about common childhood problems, including ADHD.

When Joseph and his parents return for their family session with Dr. Pellegrini, Mr. Morris announces that he and his wife met with Dr. Rahmed and decided to try psychostimulant therapy for their son. "He told us he would start with a low dose and gradually increase it so he can decide how much medicine Joseph needs each day. I felt a little better about the idea after we had a chance to talk with him."

"When does Joseph start on the medicine?" As Dr. Pellegrini asks this question, the child stands and starts to walk across the room.

"Joseph, please sit down," Mrs. Morris says before answering the therapist's question. "He has an appointment with Dr. Rahmed tomorrow, so I guess he'll start then."

As Joseph returns to his chair, Dr. Pellegrini realizes that she has made little effort to develop a therapeutic relationship with the boy. For the next 10 minutes, she directs her complete attention to the child, continuing the discussion they had during the pretreatment assessment. She notices that when she focuses her attention on him, he remains in his chair and answers her questions. She remembers Mr. Johnson's comment that the child finishes class assignments if the teacher stands beside his desk and keeps him on task. Joseph has no difficulty talking with Dr. Pellegrini. Again, he describes how he dislikes school and then adds that his parents give preferential treatment to his older brother. "I'm just dumb," he says.

Before the parents have the chance to intervene, Dr. Pellegrini draws on Dr. Shuttersworth's test results to firmly challenge the child's statement. "Joseph, I think you are a pretty smart guy, and I want to do whatever I can to help make things better for you." She hesitates for a moment and then returns to the discussion of drug treatments. "How do you feel about taking the medicine?"

"OK, I guess." The boy hesitates and then asks, "He's not going to give me a shot, is he?"

"No," the father answers. "He's just going to talk with you and give us some pills you can take."

When this discussion ends, Dr. Pellegrini presents her plan for treatment. In addition to psychostimulants for Joseph, Mr. and Mrs. Morris will attend the clinic's parenting group, and Mr. Johnson and Dr. Shuttersworth will institute the peer tutoring program at school. She also presents the idea of having Joseph join the school counselor's social skills training group. Both parents encourage their son to participate. Joseph initially resists the idea but then asks for more information about the group.

"Ms. Chester has about four or five students come to her office each week," Dr. Pellegrini says. "They talk about what a friend is. They play games to learn how to make friends."

The child seems unsure about the idea, so the therapist adds, "Joseph, you told me that the other kids make fun of you."

"Uh-huh," he answers.

"I think Ms. Chester's friends group might be a good idea. Let's give it a try."

"I guess," he answers.

Throughout the session, Joseph exhibits the same level of overactivity that was present during the pretreatment assessment. Dr. Pellegrini is careful to observe and praise Joseph when his behavior is appropriate. During their discussion of the social skills group, she says, "Joseph, I'm happy to see you sitting in your chair right now." Mr. and Mrs. Morris continue to respond as they did before, with the mother asking the boy to behave and his father threatening to punish him. When the therapist introduces the home-based reinforcement program, she directs her attention to the child and asks him about his class work and homework assignments.

"How do you carry your books and papers back and forth to school?" she asks. Joseph seems puzzled by the question. "I mean, do you use a backpack?"

"No, I just carry them," he answers.

"We bought him a backpack, but he lost it," the father adds.

"I think we need to get organized," Dr. Pellegrini says with a smile. She asks the family to talk with each other about how they can help Joseph get his homework assignments to and from school. Although somewhat hesitant at first, they eventually decide to go shopping after the session and purchase a notebook and another backpack for Joseph. As the therapist listens, she realizes that the family has avoided any discussion of the boy's behavior.

"How might we increase the chances that Joseph will bring home his assignments every evening and turn in his work to Mr. Johnson the next day?" she asks.

"Well," the father responds, "I think if we go to the trouble of buying him these things, he should be responsible enough to hold onto them and get his homework to school."

As Dr. Pellegrini listens to this solution, she again realizes that the parents can benefit from the clinic's parenting group. She responds with a brief explanation of the home-based reinforcement program she plans to implement. "When Joseph turns in his homework every morning, Mr. Johnson will sign the daily log in the front of the notebook. At the end of the day, Mr. Johnson will sign the log a second time if Joseph has listed all of his assignments and has the books and papers he needs to finish his homework." Every day when Joseph comes home, his mother will check the daily log, praise him for successes, and award a sticker for each signature. Joseph will place his stickers on a weekly chart posted on the kitchen refrigerator. When his father arrives, he will check the chart and praise his son for his accomplishments. Dr. Pellegrini then asks Joseph and his parents to decide how the tokens will be exchanged for back-up reinforcers. She encourages them to work for success and to consider privileges and material objects as reinforcers.

At the end of the session, Dr. Pellegrini asks the parents to complete the ADHD Rating Scale—IV (DuPaul et al., 1998). She plans to re-administer this measure at various points in treatment to evaluate the impact of therapy on Joseph's behavior at home. She also has Joseph and his parents complete assent and consent forms allowing her to speak with Ms. Chester about the boy's participation in the social skills group. She concludes the session by scheduling another family meeting for the following week.

Joseph's behavior improves over the next 2 months. As Dr. Rahmed increases the dosage of psychostimulants, the boy's activity level gradually declines to more normal levels. He also exhibits more on-task behaviors at school and during nightly homework sessions. Results for the weekly charts also reveal a slow but steady increase in the number of tokens awarded. To date, Joseph has used the stickers he earned to go to the movies with his brother, purchase additions to his collection of sports cards, and take a weekend hike in the country with his family. Although his performance on tests continues to vary, the distribution of his grades has narrowed to A's, B's, and C's. The parents seem to have a better understanding of ADHD, and they are beginning to use a more consistent team approach with both of their sons.

Joseph enjoys his friendship group at school. In her regular contacts with Ms. Chester, the therapist learns that the boy's use of social skills continues to improve as his activity level declines. Dr. Shuttersworth and Mr. Johnson match Joseph with a male classmate who is an excellent student. Although this child seems frustrated with Joseph at the outset of their peer tutoring relationship, Mr. Johnson recently observed the two boys playing together at recess. "This is the first time I've seen Joseph not fighting or arguing with a child on the playground," he tells Dr. Pellegrini.

▪ ▪ ▪

In this case, the clinician served as both therapist and case manager. To address her client's social skills deficits, she elicited the help of the teacher, school counselor, and school psychologist. She also asked the parents and the teacher to assist in improving Joseph's completion of class work and nightly assignments. She relied on fellow clinicians at the mental health center to teach the parents to use more effective child-rearing techniques. She also collaborated with the family physician to administer and evaluate a successful trial of psychostimulants. Her regular summaries of parent- and teacher-report measures provided objective data the physician used to select the appropriate level of medication for the child.

Through her family meetings with Joseph and his parents, the therapist was able to identify problems and make appropriate adjustments to the treatment plan. One such incident occurred when Joseph received his second report card. Most of his grades were C or above, with the exception of mathematics. When she consulted with Mr. Johnson, Dr. Pellegrini learned that the child was having extreme difficulty completing tests in a timely manner. "I'm afraid Joseph just doesn't know his basic math facts well enough," he observed. Dr. Pellegrini discussed this with the parents, and they decided to remediate this deficit by enrolling their son in after-school tutoring at a local learning center.

When Mrs. Morris completed the Beck Depression Inventory (Beck & Steer, 1987) during the pretreatment assessment, she scored in the mild to moderate range of depression. After the family's fourth visit with Dr. Pellegrini, the mother telephoned the therapist to schedule individual therapy for herself. The clinician explained the ethical dilemmas associated with this request and encouraged Mrs. Morris to meet with another therapist at the mental health center. The mother followed this suggestion and met briefly with a clinician who helped her address family of origin issues that seemed to be affecting her marriage and relationships with her children.

The therapist's approach to treatment represents the use of the transtheoretical model described by Prochaska and Norcross (1994). She was especially aware of stage-related issues at the outset of treatment when the mother appeared to be in the preparation stage and the father and son could best be described as contemplator and precontemplator, respectively. Meanwhile, significant other adults had attempted to initiate change. Mr. Johnson, the boy's teacher, had made some effort to modify Joseph's classroom behavior and was probably in the preparation stage. Based on his assessment and diagnosis, Dr. Rahmed recommended psychopharmacotherapy, but his action-oriented response was thwarted by the father, who resisted the use of medication for his son.

We must also consider the therapist's application of the levels of therapeutic change. Although much of her treatment plan was devoted to the remediation of the ADHD symptoms using empirically supported therapies, she also addressed problems related to maladaptive thoughts, interpersonal conflict, and systemic conflicts. As an example, she challenged Joseph's belief that he was dumb by saying that she thought he was "a pretty smart guy." She worked with the child, the parents, and the school to initiate a peer tutoring program in the classroom and have Joseph join the school counselor's social skills training group to improve his relationships with the other students. Dr. Pellegrini also addressed family systems conflicts when she attempted to strengthen the spousal and parental dyad and decrease the father's enmeshment with his family of origin.

To accomplish these goals, the therapist used a number of change processes. In particular, she developed a treatment plan that represented an integration of the helping relationship, consciousness raising, stimulus control, and contingency management. It is worth noting that she selected treatments that were either identified as empirically supported therapies for children with ADHD or had been found to have some empirical evidence to justify their use with these clients. First, she was careful to develop a helping relationship with Joseph and his parents. She used stimulus control in the classroom when she advised Mr. Johnson to move the boy's desk close to his and surround the child with students who would model appropriate behaviors. Dr. Pellegrini integrated contingency management in the home and at school with her home-based reinforcement program and the recommendation that Mr. and Mrs. Morris join the clinic's parenting group. She also combined referral to the group and the family physician with her own efforts in session to raise the parents' awareness or consciousness of ADHD-related issues.

The collaborative treatment used in this case included education/development, prevention, and remediation strategies. In a chapter on integrated treatments, it is appropriate to consider how individual techniques simultaneously address different goals. For example, the school psychologist's peer tutoring program is itself a multimodal strategy. Designed to remediate academic deficits, the program also facilitates students' development by giving them a foundation for long-term success in the classroom, which prevents them from dropping out of school with only marginal job skills. Similar multimodal benefits would be expected from the therapist's home-based reinforcement program. Likewise, participation in the counselor's social skills group could correct dysfunctional peer relationships (i.e., remediation), minimize social isolation during adolescence and adulthood (i.e., prevention), and enhance friendships through better skills and an understanding of interpersonal relationships (i.e., education/development).

Children with ADHD typically present for therapy with a diverse set of problems. For this reason, they are ideal candidates for a multimodal and multidisciplinary approach to intervention. The therapist in this case met with the Morris family for 11 sessions over an 8-month period, but the parents also received clinic-based group therapy, and Joseph had regular visits with Dr. Rahmed and school-based experiences in a social skills training group and peer tutoring program. Dr. Pellegrini had neither the time nor expertise to provide all of these services, so she collaborated with other professionals to implement a treatment that was both effective and efficient. Children who enter therapy for other problems may not require the participation of as many professionals as were involved in this case. The number of service providers and treatment modalities used with a child varies according to the nature and severity of the presenting problem.

SUMMARY

This chapter examined theoretical and practical considerations for developing and implementing therapeutic services for children. By collaborating with other professionals, clinicians can devise interventions that use the expertise of each member of the multidisciplinary team. The therapist functions as both a treatment provider and the case manager who coordinates the delivery of services. In their work with clients, clinicians must develop treatment plans that meet the unique needs of the child. To accomplish this, they often draw on the theoretical principles and intervention techniques of various systems of child therapy. As indicated by Prochaska and Norcross (1994), this requires an understanding of the stages, levels, and processes of therapeutic change and how these apply to the child, the family, and significant others.

The practice of child therapy at the turn of the 21st century is quite different from the methods used 50 or 100 years ago. The emergence of brief treatments has increased the pressure on clinicians to resolve clients' presenting problems in a time-limited fashion. The criteria for empirically supported treatments provide an external standard that can be used to evaluate therapists' work with clients. Clinicians must adopt a method of evaluation to document the effectiveness of the individualized interventions they provide to children and families. Therapists must also expand on the traditional model of treatment by collaborating with significant others in the child's life and developing integrated methods for dealing with childhood problems. This challenge requires consideration of the multidetermined nature of each client's presenting problem and the implementation of multimodal and multidisciplinary services for children and families of different cultural backgrounds.

References

Abidin, R. R. (1995). *Parenting Stress Index-Manual* (3rd ed.). Odessa, FL: Psychological Assessment Resources.

Abidin, R. R. (1995). *Parenting Stress Index: Professional manual.* (3rd ed.). Odessa, FL: Psychological Assessment Resources.

Abikoff, H. B., & Hechtman, L. (1996). Multimodal therapy and stimulants in the treatment of children with attention-deficit hyperactivity disorder. In E. D. Hibbs & P. S. Jensen (Eds.), *Psychosocial treatments for child and adolescent disorders: Empirically based strategies for clinical practice* (pp. 341–369). Washington, DC: American Psychological Association.

Aboud, F. (1988). *Children and prejudice.* New York: Basil Blackwell.

Abramson, L. Y., Metalsky, G. I., & Alloy, L. B. (1989) Hopelessness depression: A theory-based subtype of depression. *Psychological Review, 96,* 358–372.

Abramson, L. Y., Seligman, M. E., & Teasdale, J. O. (1978). Learned helplessness in humans: Critique and reformulation. *Journal of Abnormal Psychology, 87,* 49–74.

Achenbach, T. M. (1990). Conceptualization of developmental psychopathology. In M. Lewis & S. M. Miller (Eds.), *Handbook of developmental psychopathology* (pp. 3–14). New York: Plenum.

Achenbach, T. M. (1991a). *Manual for the Child Behavior Checklist/4–18 and 1991 Profile.* Burlington, VT: University of Vermont, Department of Psychiatry.

Achenbach, T. M. (1991b). *Manual for the Youth Self-Report and 1991 Profile.* Burlington, VT: University of Vermont, Department of Psychiatry.

Achenbach, T. M. (1991c). *Manual for the Teacher's Report Form and 1991 Profile.* Burlington, VT: University of Vermont, Department of Psychiatry.

Achenbach, T. M. (1992). *Manual for the Child Behavior Checklist/2–3 and 1992 profile.* Burlington, VT: University of Vermont, Department of Psychiatry.

Achenbach, T. M., & Edelbrock, C. S. (1978). The classification of child psychopathology: A review and analysis of empirical efforts. *Psychological Bulletin, 85,* 1275–1301.

Achenbach, T. M., & Edelbrock, C. S. (1983). *Manual for the Child Behavior Checklist and Revised Child Behavior Profile.* Burlington, VT: University of Vermont, Department of Psychiatry.

Achenbach, T. M., Edelbrock, C. S., & Howell, C. T. (1987). Empirically based assessment of the behavioral/emotional problems of 2- and 3-year-old children. *Journal of Abnormal Child Psychology, 15,* 629–650.

Achenbach, T. M., & McConaughy, S. H. (1997). *Empirically based assessment of child and adolescent psychopathology: Practical applications* (2nd ed.). Thousand Oaks, CA: Sage.

Achenbach, T. M., McConaughy, S. H., & Howell, C. T. (1987). Child/adolescent behavioral and emotional problems: Implications of cross-informant correlations for situational specificity. *Psychological Bulletin, 101,* 213–232.

Achenbach. T. M., & Rescorla, L. A. (2001a). *Manual for the ASEBA School-Age Forms and Profiles.* Burlington, VT: University of Vermont, Research Center for Children, Youth, and Families.

Achenbach. T. M., & Rescorla, L. A. (2001b). *Manual for the ASEBA Preschool Forms and Profiles.* Burlington, VT: University of Vermont, Research Center for Children, Youth, and Families.

Ackerman, N. W. (1958). *The psychodynamics of family life.* New York: Basic Books.

Ackerman, N. W. (1967). The emergence of family diagnosis and treatment: A personal view. *Psychotherapy: Theory, Research, and Practice, 4(3),* 125–129.

Ackley, D. C. (1997). *Breaking free of managed care: A step-by-step guide to regaining control of your practice.* New York: Guilford.

Acosta, F., & Cristo, M. (1981). Development of a bilingual interpreter program: An alternative model for Spanish-speaking services. *Professional Psychology Research and Therapy, 12,* 474–482.

Acting alone, Mississippi settles suit with 4 tobacco companies. (1997, July 4). *The New York Times,* p. 1A.

Adams, W. (1981). Lack of behavioral effects from Feingold diet violations. *Perceptual and Motor Skills, 52,* 307–313.

Adelman, H. S., Kaser-Boyd, N., & Taylor, L. (1984). Children's participation in consent for psychotherapy and their subsequent response to treatment. *Journal of Clinical Child Psychology, 13,* 170–178.

Adler, A. (1927/1954). *Understanding human nature.* Greenwich, CT: Fawcett.

Ainsworth, M. D. S. (1979). Infant-mother attachment. *American Psychologist, 34,* 932–937.

Ainsworth, M. D. S., Blehar, M. C., Waters, E., & Wall, S. (1978). *Patterns of attachment: A psychological study of the strange situation.* Hillsdale, NJ: Lawrence Erlbaum.

Albee, G. W. (1990). The futility of psychotherapy. *Journal of Mind and Behavior, 11,* 369–384.

Albee, G. W. (1992). Saving children means social revolution. In G. W. Albee, L. A. Bond, & T. V. C. Monsey (Eds.), *Improving children's lives: Global perspectives on prevention* (pp. 311–329). Newbury Park, CA: Sage.

Alderman, G. L., & Gimpel, G. A. (1996). The interaction between type of behavior problem and type of consultant: Teachers' preferences for professional assistance. *Journal of Educational and Psychological Consultation, 7,* 305–313.

Aldous, J., Mulligan, G. M., & Bjarnason, T. (1998). Fathering over time: What makes the difference? *Journal of Marriage and the Family, 60,* 809–820.

Allan, J. (1988). *Inscapes of the child's world: Jungian counseling in schools and clinics.* Dallas, TX: Spring.

Allen, F. H. (1934). Therapeutic work with children. *American Journal of Orthopsychiatry, 4,* 193–202.

Allyon, T., Layman, D., & Kandel, H. J. (1975). A behavioral-educational alternative to drug control of hyperactive children. *Journal of Applied Behavior Analysis, 8,* 137–146.

Altman, I., & Rogoff, B. (1987). World views in psychology: Trait, interactional, organismic, and transactional perspectives. In D. Stokols & I. Altman (Eds.), *Handbook of environmental psychology* (pp. 7–40). New York: John Wiley.

Ambrosini, P. J. (2000). A review of pharmacotherapy of major depression in children and adolescents. *Psychiatric Services, 51*, 627–633.

American Academy of Child and Adolescent Psychiatry. (1994). *The American Academy of Child and Adolescent Psychiatry mission statement*. Retrieved on May 24, 2002, from http://www.aacap.org/about/mission.htm.

American Academy of Family Physicians. (1996). *Family practice residency programs*, July 1996. Kansas City, MO: Author.

American Academy of Ophthalmology, American Academy of Pediatrics, & American Association for Pediatric Ophthalmology and Strabismus. (1998). *Policy statement: Learning disabilities, dyslexia, and vision*. San Francisco: American Academy of Ophthalmology.

American Academy of Pediatrics. (1982). Policy statement: The Doman-Delacato treatment of neurologically handicapped children. *Pediatrics, 70*, 810–812.

American Academy of Pediatrics. (1995). *Pediatrics specialty profile fact sheet*. Elk Grove, IL: Author.

American Academy of Pediatrics. (1998). *Pediatric nutrition handbook* (4th ed.). Elm Grove Village, IL: Author.

American Academy of Pediatrics Committee on Bioethics. (1999). Informed consent, parental permission, and assent in pediatric practice. *Pediatrics, 95*, 314–317.

American Academy of Pediatrics, Committee on Nutrition. (1976). Megavitamin therapy for childhood psychoses and learning disabilities. *Pediatrics, 58*, 910–912.

American Association for Marriage and Family Therapy. (2001). *AAMFT code of ethics*. Retrieved on May 24, 2002, from http://www.aamft.org/resources/lrmplan/ethics/ ethicscode2001.htm.

American Counseling Association. (1995). *Code of ethics and standards of practice*. Alexandria, VA: Author.

American Counseling Association. (1999). *Ethical standards for Internet on-line counseling*. Retrieved January 17, 2002, from http://www.counseling.org/gc/cybertx.htm

American Psychiatric Association. (1980). *Diagnostic and statistical manual of mental disorders* (3rd ed.) Washington, DC: Author.

American Psychiatric Association. (1987). *Diagnostic and statistical manual of mental disorders* (3rd ed., rev.) Washington, DC: Author.

American Psychiatric Association. (1994). *Diagnostic and statistical manual of mental disorders* (4th ed.) Washington, DC: Author.

American Psychiatric Association. (2000). *Diagnostic and statistical manual of mental disorders* (5th ed.), (Text revision). Washington, DC: Author.

American Psychological Association. (1992). Ethical principles of psychologists and code of conduct. *American Psychologist*, 47, 1597–1611.

American Psychological Association. (1993a). Record keeping guidelines. *American Psychologist*, 48, 984–986.

American Psychological Association. (1993b). Guidelines for providers of psychological services to ethnic, linguistic, and culturally diverse populations. *American Psychologist, 48*, 45–48.

American Psychological Association. (1994a). Guidelines for child custody evaluations in divorce proceedings. *American Psychologist*, 49, 677–680.

American Psychological Association. (1994b). *Comprehensive and coordinated psychological services for children: A call for service integration*. Washington, DC: Author.

American Psychological Association. (1997, November 5). *APA statement on services by telephone, teleconferencing, and Internet*. Retrieved January 17, 2002, from http://www.apa.org/ethics/stmnt01.html

American Psychological Association. (1999). Guidelines for psychological evaluations in child protection matters. *American Psychologist, 54*, 586–593.

American Psychological Association. (2001). Accredited doctoral programs in professional psychology: 2001. *American Psychologist, 56*, 1136–1149.

American School Counselor Association. (1990). *Rule statement: The school counselor*. Alexandria, VA: Author.

American School Counselor Association. (1998). *Ethical standards for school counselors*. Alexandria, VA: Author. Retrieved on May 13, 2002, from http://www.schoolcounselor.org/library/ethics.pdf.

Anderson, C. A., & Bushman, B. J. (2001). Effects of violent video games on aggressive behavior, aggressive cognition, aggressive affect, physiological arousal, and prosocial behavior: A meta-analytic review of the scientific literature. *Psychological Science, 12*, 353–359.

Andreasen, M. (2001). Evolution in the family's use of television: An overview. In J. Bryant & J. A. Bryant (Eds.), *Television and the American family* (2nd ed.) (pp. 3–30). Mahwah, NJ: Lawrence Erlbaum.

Andrews, L. B. (1999). *The clone age: Adventures in the new world of reproductive technology*. New York: Henry Holt.

Anonymous. (1995). Hidden benefits of managed care. *Professional Psychology: Research and Practice, 26*, 235–237.

Ansbacher, H. L. & Ansbacher, R. (Eds.). (1956). *The individual psychology of Alfred Adler*. New York: Basic Books

Ansbacher, H. L. & Ansbacher, R. (Eds.). (1964). *Superiority and social interest: A collection of later writings*. Evanston, IL: Northwestern University Press.

Anti-smoking funds sparse despite a $250 billion tobacco lawsuit windfall, only a few states are using the money to fight teen smoking. However, those that try are coming up big. (2001, January 30). *USA Today*, p. 1A.

Arkowitz, H. (1997). Integrative theories of therapy. In P. L. Wachtel & S. B. Messer (Eds.), *Theories of psychotherapy: Origins and evolution* (pp. 227–288). Washington, DC: American Psychological Association.

Arnold, L. E., Christopher, J., Huestis, R. D., & Smeltzer, D. J. (1978). Megavitamins for minimal brain dysfunction: A placebo-controlled study. *Journal of the American Medical Association, 240*, 2642–2643.

Arredondo, P., Toporek, R., Brown, S. P., Jones, J., Locke, D. C., Sanchez, J., & Stadler. H. (1996). Operationalization of the multicultural counseling competencies. *Journal of Multicultural Counseling and Development, 24*, 42–78.

Ashbaugh, R., & Peck, S. M. (1998). Treatment of sleep problems in a toddler: A replication of the faded bedtime with response cost protocol. *Journal of Applied Behavior Analysis, 31*, 127–129.

Aspy, D. N., & Roebuck, F. N. (1977). *Kids don't learn from people they don't like*. Amherst, MA: Human Resource Development Press.

Atkinson, D. R., Morten, G., & Sue, D. W. (1993). *Counseling American minorities: A cross-cultural perspective* (4th ed.). Madison, WI: Brown & Benchmark.

Averhart, C. J., & Bigler, R. S. (1997). Shades of meaning: Skin tone, racial attitudes, and constructive memory in African American children. *Journal of Experimental Child Psychology, 67*, 363–388.

Axline, V. M. (1944). Morale on the school front. *Journal of Educational Research, 37*, 521–533.

Axline, V. M. (1947). *Play therapy: The inner dynamics of childhood*. New York: Houghton Mifflin.

Axline, V. M. (1948). Play therapy and race conflict in young children. *Journal of Abnormal and Social Psychology, 43*, 300–310.

Axline, V. M. (1950). Entering the child's world via play experiences. *Progressive Education, 27*, 68–75.

Axline, V. M. (1950a). Play therapy experiences as described by child participants. *Journal of Consulting Psychology, 14*, 53–63.

Axline, V. M. (1964). *Dibs: In search of self*. Boston: Houghton Mifflin.

Aymard, L. L. (1999). Therapeutic applications of computers with children. In C. E. Schaefer (Ed.), *Innovative psychotherapy techniques in child and adolescent therapy* (2nd ed.) (pp. 271–314). New York: John Wiley.

Azmitia, M., Cooper, C. R., Garcia, E. E., & Dunbar, N. D. (1996). The ecology of family guidance in low-income Mexican-American and European-American families. *Social Development, 5*, 1–23.

Azrin, N., Sneed, T., & Foxx, R. (1974). Dry-bed training: Rapid elimination of childhood enuresis. *Behavior Research and Therapy, 12(3)*, 147–156.

Bagarozzi, D. A. (1996). *The couple and family in managed care: Assessment, evaluation, and treatment*. New York: Brunner/Mazel.

Bajt, T. R., & Pope, K. S. (1989). Therapist-patient sexual intimacy involving children and adolescents. *American Psychologist, 44,* 455.

Baker, B. (1969). Symptom treatment and symptom substitution in enuresis. *Journal of Abnormal Psychology, 74,* 42–49.

Ballou, M. (1995). Naming the issue. In E. J. Rave & C. C. Larsen (Eds.), *Ethical decision making in therapy: Feminist perspectives* (pp. 42–56). New York: Guilford.

Bandura, A. (1969). *Principles of behavior modification.* New York: Holt, Rinehart, & Winston.

Bandura, A. (1977). *Social learning theory.* Englewood Cliffs, NJ: Prentice-Hall.

Bandura, A. (1986). *Social foundations of thought and action: A social cognitive theory.* Englewood Cliffs, NJ: Prentice-Hall.

Bandura, A. (1997). *Self-efficacy: The exercise of control.* New York: W. H. Freeman.

Bandura, A., Ross, D., & Ross, S. A. (1961). Transmission of aggression through imitation of aggressive models. *Journal of Abnormal Social Psychology, 63,* 575–582.

Bandura, A., Ross, D., & Ross, S. A. (1963a). Imitation of film-mediated aggressive models. *Journal of Abnormal Social Psychology, 66,* 3–11.

Bandura, A., Ross, D., & Ross, S. A. (1963b). Vicarious reinforcement and imitative learning. *Journal of Abnormal Social Psychology, 67,* 601–607.

Banerjee, S., Srivastav, A., & Palan, B. M. (1993). Hypnosis and self-hypnosis in the management of nocturnal enuresis: A comparative study with imipramine therapy. *American Journal of Clinical Hypnosis, 36(2),* 113–119.

Barker, P. (1990). *Clinical interviews with children and adolescents.* New York: W.W. Norton & Co.

Barkley, R. A. (1987). *Defiant children: A clinician's manual for parent training.* New York: Guilford.

Barkley, R. A. (1995). *Taking charge of ADHD: The complete, authoritative guide for parents.* New York: Guilford.

Barkley, R. A. (1997a). Attention-deficit hyperactivity disorder. In E. J. Mash & L. G. Terdal (Eds.), *Assessment of childhood disorders* (3rd ed.) (pp. 71–129). New York: Guilford.

Barkley, R. A. (1997b). *Defiant children (2nd ed.): A clinician's manual for assessment and parent training.* New York: Guilford.

Barkley, R. A., McMurray, M. B., Edelbrock, C. S., & Robbins, K. (1990). Side effects of methylphenidate in children with attention deficit hyperactivity disorder: A systematic, placebo-controlled evaluation. *Pediatrics, 86,* 184–192.

Barlow, D. H., & Hersen, M. (1984). *Single case experimental designs: Strategies for studying behavior change* (2nd ed.). New York: Pergamon.

Barlow, K., Strother, J., & Landreth, G. (1985). Child-centered play therapy: Nancy from baldness to curls. *School Counselor, 32,* 347–356.

Barnett, R. C., & Shen, Y. (1997). Gender, high- and low-schedule-control housework tasks, and psychological distress: A study of dual-earner couples. *Journal of Family Issues, 18,* 403–428.

Barret, R. L., & Robinson, B. E. (1994). Gay dads. In A. E. Gottfried & A. W. Gottfried (Eds.), *Redefining families: Implications for children's development* (pp. 157–170). New York: Plenum Press.

Barrett, C. L., Hampe, I. E., & Miller, L. C. (1978). Research on child psychotherapy. In S. L. Garfield & A. E. Bergin (Eds.), *Handbook of psychotherapy and behavior change: An empirical analysis* (2nd ed.) (pp. 411–435). New York: John Wiley.

Barrett, P. M. (1998). Evaluation of cognitive-behavioral group treatments for childhood anxiety disorders. *Journal of Clinical Child Psychology, 27,* 459–468.

Barrett, P. M., Dadds, M. R., & Rapee, R. M. (1996). Family treatment of childhood anxiety: A controlled trial. *Journal of Consulting and Clinical Psychology, 64,* 333–342.

Barrios, B. A. (1993). Direct observation. In T. Ollendick & M. Hersen (Eds.), *Handbook of child and adolescent assessment* (pp. 140–164). Boston: Allyn & Bacon.

Barrish, H. H., Saunders, M., & Wolf, M. M. (1969). Good behavior game: Effects of individual contingencies for group consequences on disruptive behavior in a classroom. *Journal of Applied Behavior Analysis, 2,* 119–124.

Barton, C., & Alexander, J. F. (1981). Functional family therapy. In A. S. Gurman & D. P. Kniskern (Eds.), *Handbook of family therapy* (pp. 403–443). New York: Brunner/Mazel.

Baruth, L. G., & Manning, M. L. (2003). *Multicultural counseling and psychotherapy: A lifespan perspective* (3rd ed.). Upper Saddle River, NJ: Prentice-Hall.

Bass, L. J. (1996). Future trends. In L. J. Bass, S. T. DeMers, J. R. P. Ogloff, C. Peterson, J. L. Pettifor, R. P. Reaves, T. Retfalvi, N. P. Simon, C. Sinclair, & R. M. Tipton (Eds.), *Professional conduct and discipline in psychology* (pp. 143–155). Washington, DC: American Psychological Association.

Bateson, G., Jackson, D. D., Haley, J., & Weakland, J. H. (1968). Toward a theory of schizophrenia. In D. D. Jackson (Ed.), *Communication, family, and marriage: Human communication.* (Vol. 1) (pp. 31–54). Palo Alto, CA: Science and Behavior Books.

Battle, J. (1992). *Culture-free self-esteem inventories: Examiner's manual* (2nd ed.). Austin, TX: PRO-ED.

Baumgaertel, A. (1999). Alternative and controversial treatments for attention-deficit/hyperactivity disorder. In A. M. Morgan (Ed.), *The pediatric clinics of North America: Attention-deficit/hyperactivity disorder* (pp. 977–992). Philadelphia: W. B. Saunders.

Baumrind, D. (1967). Child care practices anteceding three patterns of preschool behavior. *Genetic Psychology Monographs, 75,* 43–88.

Baumrind, D. (1971). Current patterns of parental authority. *Developmental Psychology Monographs, 4,* (1, Part 2).

Baumrind, D. (1996). The discipline controversy revisited. *Family Relations, 45,* 405–414.

Beaty, J. J. (1997). *Building bridges with multicultural picture books for children 3–5.* Upper Saddle River, NJ: Prentice-Hall.

Beauchamp, G. R. (1986). Optometric vision training. *Pediatrics, 77,* 121–124.

Beck, A. T. (1967). *Depression: Clinical, experimental, and theoretical aspects.* New York: Harper & Row.

Beck, A. T. (1976). *Cognitive therapy and the emotional disorders.* New York: International Universities Press.

Beck, A., & Steer, R. (1987). *BDI: Beck Depression Inventory Manual.* New York: The Psychological Corporation.

Bee, H. (1997). *The developing child* (8th ed.). New York: Longman.

Behrman, R. E. (1992). The field of pediatrics. In R. E. Behrman & R. M. Kliegman (Eds.), *Nelson textbook of pediatrics* (14th ed.) (pp. 1–5). Philadelphia, PA: W. B. Saunders Co.

Behrman, R. E., Kliegman, R. M., Nelson, W. E., & Vaughan III, V. C. (1992). *Nelson textbook of pediatrics* (14th ed.). Philadelphia: W. B. Saunders Co.

Belar, C. D. (2000). Ethical issues in managed care: Perspectives in evolution. *The Counseling Psychologist, 28,* 237–241.

Bellak, L. (1954). *The Thematic Apperception Test and the Children's Apperception Test in clinical use.* New York: Grune & Stratton.

Bellak, L., & Bellak, S. S. (1949). *The Children's Apperception Test.* New York: CPS.

Benedetto, A. E., & Olisky, T. (2001). Biracial youth: The role of the school counselor in racial identity development. *Professional School Counseling, 5,* 66–69.

Benson, G. (1989). Hypnosis as a therapeutic technique for use by school psychologists. *School Psychology International, 10,* 113–119.

Berg, I. K. (1994). *Family-based services: A solution-focused approach.* New York: W. W. Norton.

Bergan, J. R. (1977). *Behavioral consultation.* Columbus, OH: Charles Merrill.

Bergen, D. (1988). Stages of play development. In D. Bergen (Ed.), *Play as a medium for learning and development: A handbook of thery and practice* (pp. 49–66). Portsmouth, NH: Heinemeann.

Berger, K. S., & Thompson, R. A. (1996). *The developing person through childhood.* New York: Worth.

Bergin, J. J. (1999). Small-group counseling. In A. Vernon (Ed.), *Counseling children and adolescents* (2nd ed.) (pp. 299–332). Denver, CO: Love Publishing Co.

Berk, L. E. (1992). Children's private speech: An overview of theory and the status of research. In R. M. Diaz & L. E. Berk (Eds.), *Private speech: From social interaction to self-regulation* (pp. 17–53). Hillsdale, NJ: Erlbaum.

Berk, L. E. (1996). *Infants and children: Prenatal through middle childhood* (2nd ed.). Boston: Allyn and Bacon.

Berk, L. E. (2000). *Child development* (5th ed.). Boston: Allyn and Bacon.

Berk, L. E., & Landau, S. (1993). Private speech of learning disabled and normally achieving children in classroom academic and laboratory contexts. *Child Development, 64*, 556–571.

Berliner, L. (1998). The use of expert testimony in child sexual abuse cases. In S. J. Ceci & H. Hembrooke (Eds.), *Expert witnesses in child abuse cases: What can and should be said in court* (pp. 11–27). Washington, DC: American Psychological Association.

Bernal, M. E., Knight, G. P., Garza, C. A., Ocampo, K. A., & Cota, M. K. (1990). The development of ethnic identity in Mexican-American children. *Hispanic Journal of Behavioral Sciences, 12(1)*, 3–24.

Bernard-Bonnin, A. C., Haley, N., Belanger, S., & Nodeau, D. (1993). Parental and parent perceptions about encopresis and its treatment. *Journal of Developmental and Behavioral Pediatrics, 14*, 397–400.

Berndt, J. J. (1992). *Child development*. Fort Worth, TX: Harcourt Brace Jovanovich.

Berndt, T. J. (1997). *Child development* (2nd ed.). Madison, WI: Brown & Benchmark.

Bernstein, D. A., & Borkovec, T. D. (1973). *Progressive relaxation training: A manual for the helping professions*. Champaign, IL: Research Press.

Bernstein, G. A., & Shaw, K. S. (1993). Practice parameters for the assessment and treatment of anxiety disorders. *Journal of the American Academy of Child and Adolescent Psychiatry, 32*, 1089–1098.

Besharov, D. J. (1985). "Doing something" about child abuse: The need to narrow the grounds for state intervention. *Harvard Journal of Law and Public Policy, 8*, 539–589.

Bickman, L. (1996a). The evaluation of a children's mental health managed care demonstration. *Journal of Mental Health Administration, 23*, 7–15.

Bickman, L. (1996b). A continuum of care: More is not always better. *American Psychologist, 51*, 689–701.

Bickman, L. (1997). Resolving issues raised by the Fort Bragg evaluation: New directions for mental health services research. *American Psychologist, 52*, 562–565.

Bigelow, B. J. (1977). Children's friendship expectations: A cognitive-developmental study. *Child Development, 48*, 246–253.

Bigler, R. S., & Liben, L. S. (1990). The role of attitudes and interventions in gender-schematic processing. *Child Development, 61*, 1440–1452.

Bigler, R. S., & Liben, L. S. (1992). Cognitive mechanisms in children's gender stereotyping: Theoretical and educational implications of a cognitive-based intervention. *Child Development, 63*, 1351–1363.

Bills, R. (1950). Nondirective play therapy with retarded readers. *Journal of Consulting Psychology, 14*, 140–149.

Bilynsky, N. S., & Vernaglia, E. R. (1999). Identifying and working with dysfunctional families. *Professional School Counseling, 2*, 305–313.

Birmaher, B., Waterman, G. S., Ryan, N., Cully, M., Balach, L., Ingram, J., & Brodsky, M. (1994). Fluoxetine for childhood anxiety disorders. *Journal of the American Academy of Child and Adolescent Psychiatry, 33*, 993–999.

Birnbrauer, J. S. (1978). Some guides to designing behavioral programs. In D. Marholin, II (Ed.), *Child behavior therapy* (pp. 37–81). New York: Gardner Press.

Bjork, D. W. (1993). *B. F. Skinner: A life*. New York: Basic Books.

Blanck, R., & Blanck, G. (1996). *Beyond ego psychology: Developmental object relations theory*. New York: Columbia University Press.

Blass, E. M., Ganchrow, J. R., & Steiner, J. E. (1984). Classical conditioning in newborn humans 2–48 hours of age. *Infant Behavior and Development, 7*, 223–235.

Blau, T. H. (1984). *The psychologist as expert witness*. New York: John Wiley.

Blick, L. C., & Porter, F. S. (1982). Group therapy with female adolescent incest victims. In S. Sgroi (Ed.), *Handbook of clinical intervention in child sexual abuse* (pp. 147–176). Lexington, MA: Lexington Books.

Bloch, D., & Simon, R. (Eds.). (1982). *The strength of family therapy: Selected papers of Nathan W. Ackerman*. New York: Brunner/Mazel.

Blumberg, M. (1981). Depression in abused and neglected children. *American Journal of Psychotherapy, 35*, 342–355.

Boat, B. W., & Everson, M. D. (1986). Using anatomical dolls: Guidelines for interviewing young children in sexual abuse investigations. Chapel Hill, NC: Department of Psychiatry, University of North Carolina.

Boat, B. W., & Everson, M. D. (1993). The use of anatomical dolls in sexual abuse evaluations: Current research and practice. In G. S. Goodman & B. L. Bottoms (Eds.), *Child victims, child witnesses: Understanding and improving testimony* (pp. 47–69). New York: Guilford.

Bogat, G. A., & Jason, L. A. (1997). Interventions in the school and community. In R. T. Ammerman & M. Hersen (Eds.), *Handbook of prevention and treatment with children and adolescents: Intervention in the real world context* (pp. 134–154). New York: John Wiley.

Bonner, B., & Everett, F. (1982). Influence of client preparation and therapist prognostic expectations on children's attitudes and expectations of psychotherapy. *Journal of Clinical Child Psychology, 11*, 202–208.

Bountress, N. G. (1980). Attitudes and training of public school clinicians providing services to speakers of Black English. *Language, Speech, and Hearing Services in Schools, 11*(1), 41–49.

Boutwell, D., & Myrick, R. D. (1992). The Go For It Club. *Elementary School Guidance and Counseling, 27(1)*, 65–72.

Bowen, M. (1966). The use of family therapy in clinical practice. *Comprehensive Psychiatry, 7*, 345–374.

Bowen, M. (1971). Principles and techniques of multiple family therapy. In J. Bradt & C. Moynihan (Eds.), *Systems therapy, Selected papers: Theory, technique, research* (pp. 187–203). Washington, DC: Bradt & Moynihan.

Bowen, M. (1976). Theory in the practice of psychotherapy. In P. J. Guerin, Jr. (Ed.), *Family therapy: Theory and practice* (pp. 42–90). New York: Gardner.

Bowen, M. (1978). *Family therapy in clinical practice*. New York: Jason Aronson.

Boyd-Franklin, N. (1989). *Black families in therapy: A multisystems approach*. New York: Guilford Press.

Brack, C. F., Orr, D. P., & Ingersoll, G. (1988). Pubertal maturation and self-esteem. *Journal of Adolescent Health Care, 9*, 280–285.

Bradley, R. H., Corwyn, R. F., Burchinal, M., McAdoo, H. P., & Coll, C. G. (2001). The home environments of children in the United States. Part II: Relations with behavioral development through age thirteen. *Child Development, 72*, 1868–1886.

Brandell, J. R. (1988). Storytelling in child psychotherapy. In C. E. Schaefer (Ed.), *Innovative interventions in child and adolescent therapy* (pp. 9–42). New York: John Wiley & Sons.

Brassard, M. A. (1986). Family assessment approaches and procedures. In H. M. Knoff (Ed.), *The assessment of child and adolescent personality* (pp. 399–449). New York: Guilford Press.

Braswell, L. (1991). Involving parents in cognitive-behavioral therapy with children and adolescents. In P. C. Kendall (Ed.), *Child and adolescent therapy: Cognitive behavioral procedures* (pp. 316–351). New York: Guilford.

Braswell, L. & Bloomquist, M. L. (1991). *Cognitive-behavioral therapy with ADHD children: Child, family, and school interventions*. New York: Guilford.

Braverman, A. M. (1997). When is enough, enough? Abandoning medical treatment for infertility. In S. R. Leiblum (Ed.), *Infertility: Psychological issues and counseling strategies* (pp. 209–229). New York: John Wiley.

Bray, J. H., & McDaniel, S. H. (1998). Behavioral health practice in primary care settings. In L. VandeCreek, S. Knapp, & T. L. Jackson (Eds.), *Innovations in clinical practice: A source book (Vol. 16)* (pp. 313–323). Sarasota, FL: Professional Resource Press.

Brazelton, T. B. (1962). A child-oriented approach to toilet training. *Pediatrics, 29*, 121–128.

Brestan, E. V., Eyberg, S. M., Boggs, S. R., & Algina, J. (1997). Parent-child interaction therapy: Parents' perceptions of untreated siblings. *Child and Family Behavior Therapy, 19(3)*, 13–28.

Bretherton, I. (1989). Pretense: The form and function of make-believe play. *Developmental Review, 9*, 383–401.

Broderick, C. B., & Schrader, S. S. (1981). In A. S. Gurman & D. P. Kniskern (Eds.), *Handbook of family therapy* (pp. 5–35). New York: Brunner/Mazel.

Brody, V. A. (1997). Developmental play therapy. In K. O'Connor & L. M. Braverman (Eds.), *Play therapy theory and practice: A comparative presentation* (pp. 160–183). New York: John Wiley.

Bronfenbrenner, U. (1979). *The ecology of human development*. Cambridge, MA: Harvard University Press.

Brooke, S. L. (1995). Critical analysis of the Culture-Free Self-Esteem Inventories. *Measurement and Evaluation in Counseling and Development, 27*, 248–252.

Brooks, R. B. (1994). Children at risk: Fostering resilience and hope. *American Journal of Orthopsychiatry, 64*, 545–553.

Brooks-Gunn, J. (1988). Antecedents and consequences of variations in girls' maturational timing. *Journal of Adolescent Health Care, 9*, 365–373.

Brown v. Board of Education, 347 U.S. 483 (1954).

Brown, D., Pryzwansky, W. B., & Schulte, A. C. (1995). *Psychological consultation: Introduction to theory and practice* (3rd ed.). Boston: Allyn and Bacon.

Brown, M. B. (2000). Diagnosis and treatment of children and adolescents with attention-deficit/hyperactivity disorder. *Journal of Counseling and Development, 78*, 195–203.

Bruck, M., & Ceci, S. J. (1999). The suggestibility of children's memory. *Annual Review of Psychology, 50*, 419–439.

Bruck, M., Melnyk, L., & Ceci, S. J. (2000). Draw it again Sam: The effect of drawing on children's suggestibility and source monitoring ability. *Journal of Experimental Child Psychology, 77*, 169–196.

Bruening, C. C., Wagner, W. G., & Johnson, J. T. (1997). The impact of rater knowledge on sexually abused and non-abused girls' scores on the Draw-A-Person: Screening Procedure for Emotional Disturbance (DAP:SPED). *Journal of Personality Assessment, 68*, 665–677.

Brunk, M., Henggeler, S. W., & Whalen, J. P. (1987). Comparison of multisystemic therapy and parent training in the brief treatment of child abuse and neglect. *Journal of Consulting and Clinical Psychology, 55*, 171–178.

Bruns, E. J., Burchard, J. D., & Yoe, J. T. (1995). Evaluating the Vermont system of care: Outcomes associated with community-based wraparound services. *Journal of Child and Family Studies, 4*, 321–339.

Buchanan, W. L. (1997). Children's mental health services and managed care. In S. R. Sauber (Ed.), *Managed mental health care: Major diagnostic and treatment approaches* (pp. 187–215). New York: Brunner/Mazel.

Buck, J. N. (1948). The H-T-P technique; A qualitative and quantitative scoring manual. *Journal of Clinical Psychology, 4*, 317–396.

Bukatko, D., & Daehler, M. W. (1995). *Child development: A thematic approach* (2nd ed.). Boston: Houghton Mifflin.

Bukowskyj, M., Nakatsu, K., & Munt, P. W. (1984). Theophylline reassessed. *Annals of Internal Medicine, 101*, 63–73.

Bukstein, O. G. (1993). Overview of pharmacological treatment. In V. B. Van Hasselt & M. Hersen (Eds.), *Handbook of behavior therapy and pharmacotherapy for children: A comprehensive analysis* (pp. 13–32). Boston: Allyn and Bacon.

Bullock, M. (1985). Animism in childhood thinking: A new look at an old question. *Developmental Psychology, 21*, 217–225.

Burchard, J. D., & Bruns, E. J. (1998). The role of the case study in the evaluation of individualized services. In M. H. Epstein, K. Kutash, & A. Duchnowsli (Eds.), *Outcomes for children and youth with emotional and behavioral disorders and their families* (pp. 363–383). Austin, TX: Pro-Ed.

Burchard, J. D., & Clarke, R. (1990). The role of individualized care in a service delivery system for children and adolescents with severely maladjusted behavior. *Journal of Mental Health Administration, 17*, 48–60.

Bureau of Labor Statistics. (2001). *Employment characteristics of family summary*. Washington, DC: U.S. Department of Labor. Retrieved February 9, 2002, from www.bls.gov/news.release/famee.nr0.htm.

Burns, R. C., & Kaufman, S. H. (1972). *Actions, styles and symbols in kinetic family drawings (K-F-D): An interpretive manual*. New York: Brunner/Mazel.

Burroughs, M. S., Wagner, W. G., & Johnson, J. T. (1997). Treatment with children of divorce: A comparison of two types of therapy. *Journal of Divorce and Remarriage, 27*, 83–99.

Calkins, S. D., & Fox, N. A. (1992). The relationship among infant temperament, security of attachment, and behavioral inhibition at twenty-four months. *Child Development, 63*, 1456–1472.

Campbell, J. (1995). *Understanding John Dewey: Nature and cooperative intelligence*. Chicago: Open Court Publishing.

Campbell, L. A., Kirkpatrick, S. E., Berry, C. C., & Lamberti, J. J. (1995). Preparing children with congenital heart disease for cardiac surgery. *Journal of Pediatric Psychology, 20*, 313–328.

Campbell, M., Adams, P. B., Small, A. M., Kapantaris, V., Silva, R. R., Shell, J., Perry, R., & Overall, J. E. (1995). Lithium in hospitalized aggressive children with conduct disorder: A double-blind and placebo-controlled study. *Journal of the American Academy of Child and Adolescent Psychiatry, 34*, 445–453.

Campbell, M., Cueva, J. E., & Adams, P. B. (1999). Pharmacotherapy of impulsive-aggressive behavior. In C. R. Cloninger (Ed.), *Personality and psychopathology* (pp. 431–455). Washington, DC: American Psychiatric Press.

Campbell, M., Small, A. M., Green, W. H., Jennings, S. J., Perry, R., Bennett, W. G., & Anderson, L. (1984). Behavioral efficacy of haloperidol and lithium carbonate: A comparison in hospitalized aggressive children with conduct disorder. *Archives of General Psychiatry, 41*, 650–656.

Campis, L. K., Lyman, R. D., & Prentice-Dunn, S. (1986). The parental locus of control scale: Development and validation. *Journal of Clinical Child Psychology, 15*, 260–267.

Canter, M. B., Bennett, B. E., Jones, S. E., & Nagy, T. F. (1994). *Ethics for psychologists: A commentary on the APA Ethics Code*. Washington, DC: American Psychological Association.

Cantor, D. W. (1982). The psychologist as child advocate with divorcing families. In E. O. Fisher & M. S. Fisher (Eds.), *Therapists, lawyers, and divorcing families* (pp. 77–86). New York: Haworth Press.

Caplan, G. (1963). Types of mental health consultation. *American Journal of Orthopsychiatry, 33*, 470–481.

Caplan, G. (1970). *The theory and practice of mental health consultation*. New York: Basic Books.

Caplan, G., & Caplan, R. B. (1993). *Mental health consultation and collaboration*. San Francisco: Jossey-Bass.

Caplan, G., Caplan, R. B., & Erchul, W. P. (1995). A contemporary view of mental health consultation: Comments on "Types of mental health consultation" by Gerald Caplan (1963). *Journal of Educational and Psychological Consultation, 6*, 23–30.

Carew, J. (1980). *Children of the sun*. Boston: Little Brown and Company.

Carey, S. (1985). *Conceptual change in childhood*. Cambridge, MA: MIT Press.

Carpenter, S. L., King-Sears, M. E., & Keys, S. G. (1998). Counselors + educators + families as a transdisciplinary team = More effective inclusion for students with disabilities. *Professional School Counseling, 2(1)*, 1–9.

Carter, B., & McGoldrick, M. (1988). Overview: The changing family life cycle—A framework for family therapy. In B. Carter & M. McGoldrick (Eds.), *The changing family life cycle: A framework for family therapy* (2nd ed.) (pp. 3–28). New York: Gardner Press.

Carter, D. B., & Levy, G. D. (1988). Cognitive aspects of children's early sex-role development: The influence of gender schemas on preschoolers' memories and preferences for sex-typed toys and activities. *Child Development, 59*, 782–792.

Carter, R. T., & Qureshi, A. (1995). A typology of philosophical assumptions in multicultural counseling and training. In J. G. Ponterotto, J. M. Casas, L. A. Suzuki, & C. M. Alexander (Eds.), *Handbook of multicultural counseling* (pp. 239–262). Thousand Oaks, CA: Sage.

Carton, J. S., & Schweitzer, J. B. (1996). Use of a token economy to increase compliance during hemodialysis. *Journal of Applied Behavior Analysis, 29*, 111–113.

Carver, V., Reinert, B., Range, L. M., & Campbell, C. (2000). *How antitobacco training and curriculum impact elementary teachers and children.* Manuscript submitted for publication.

Casey, R. J., & Berman, J. S. (1985). The outcome of psychotherapy with children. *Psychological Bulletin, 98*, 388–400.

Castaneda, A. McCandless, B. R., & Palermo, D. S. (1956). The children's form of the manifest anxiety scale. *Child Development, 27*, 317–326.

Ceci, S. J., & Bruck, M. (1993). Suggestibility of the child witness: A historical review and synthesis. *Psychological Bulletin, 113*, 403–439.

Ceci, S. J., & Hembrooke, H. (1998). *Expert witnesses in child abuse cases: What can and should be said in court.* Washington, DC: American Psychological Association.

Cecil, N. L., & Roberts, P. L. (1992). *Developing resiliency through children's literature: A guide for teachers and librarians, K–8.* Jefferson, NC: McFarland & Company.

Cedar, B., & Levant, R. F. (1990). A meta-analysis of the effects of parent effectiveness training. *American Journal of Family Therapy, 18*, 373–384.

Cervantes, J. M., & Ramirez, O. (1992). Spirituality and family dynamics in psychotherapy with Latino children. In L. A. Vargas & J. D. Koss-Chioino (Eds.), *Working with culture; Psychotherapeutic interventions with ethnic minority children and adolescents* (pp. 103–128). San Francisco: Jossey-Bass.

Chamberlin, R. W. (1987). Anticipatory guidance: The role of the physician in parent education about child development. In R. A. Hoekelman, S. Blatman, S. B. Friedman, N. M. Nelson, & K. M. Seidel (Eds.), *Primary pediatric care* (pp. 148–153). St. Louis: C. V. Mosby.

Chambers v. State, 628 S.W.2d 306 (Ark. 1982).

Chambless, D. L., Baker, M. J., Baucom, D. H., Beutler, L. E., Calhoun, K. S., Crits-Christoph, P., Daiuto, A., DeRubeis, R., Detweiler, J., Haaga, D. A. F., Johnson, S. B., McCurry, S., Mueser, K. T., Pope, K. S., Sanderson, W. C., Shoham, V., Stickle, T., Williams, D. A., Woody, S. R. (1998). Update on empirically validated therapies, II. *The Clinical Psychologist, 51(1)*, 3–16.

Chambless, D. L., Sanderson, W. C., Shoham, V., Johnson, S. B., Pope, K. S., Crits-Christoph, P., Baker, M. Johnson, B., Woody, S. R., Sue, S., Beutler, L., Williams, D. A., & McCurry, S. (1996). An update on empirically validated therapies. *The Clinical Psychologist, 49(2)*, 5–16.

Chao, R. K. (1994). Beyond parental control and authoritarian parenting style: Understanding Chinese parenting through the cultural notion of training. *Child Development, 65*, 1111–1119.

Chapman, A. H. (1978). *The treatment techniques of Harry Stack Sullivan.* New York: Brunner/Mazel.

Chesler, P. (1988). *Sacred bond: The legacy of Baby M.* New York: Times Books.

Child Abuse Prevention and Treatment Act, Pub. L. No. 93–247, 88 Stat. 5 (1974).

Chodorow, N. (1989). *Feminism and psychoanalytic theory.* New Haven, CT: Yale University Press.

Choney, S. K., Berryhill-Paapke, E., & Robbins, R. R. (1995). The acculturation of American Indians: Developing frameworks for research and practice. In J. G. Ponterotto, J. M. Casas, L. A. Suzuki, & C. M. Alexander (Eds.), *Handbook of multicultural counseling* (pp.73–92). Thousand Oaks, CA: Sage.

Christophersen, E. R., & Mortweet, S. L. (2001). *Treatments that work with children: Empirically supported strategies for managing childhood problems.* Washington, DC: American Psychological Association.

Chung, W. (1997). Asian American children. In E Lee (Ed.), *Working with Asian Americans: A guide for clinicians* (pp. 165–174). New York: Guilford.

Ciminero, A. R. (1986). Behavioral assessment: An overview. In A. R. Ciminero, K. S. Calhoun, & H. E. Adams (Eds.), *Handbook of behavioral assessment* (2nd ed.) (pp. 3–11). New York: John Wiley.

Clark, A. J. (1995). The organization and implementation of a social interest program in the schools. *Individual Psychology, 51*, 317–331.

Clark, E., Kehle, T. J., Jenson, W. R., & Beck, D. E. (1992). Evaluation of the parameters of self-modeling interventions. *School Psychology Review, 21*, 246–254.

Clark, K. B., & Clark, M. K. (1958). Racial identification and preference in Negro children. In E. E. Maccoby, T. M. Newcomb, & E. L. Hartley (Eds.), *Readings in social psychology* (3rd ed.) (pp. 602–611). New York: Holt, Rinehart, & Winston.

Clark, R. A. (1953). *Six talks on Jung's psychology.* Pittsburgh, PA: Boxwood Press.

Cohen, A. H. (1988). The efficacy of optometric vision therapy. *Journal of the American Optometric Association, 59*, 95–105.

Cohen, R. J., & Swerdlik, M. E. (1999). *Psychological testing and assessment: An introduction to tests and measurement* (4th ed.). Mountain View, CA: Mayfield Publishing Company.

Colapinto, J. (1991). Structural family therapy. In A. M. Horne & J. L. Passmore (Eds.), *Family counseling and therapy* (2nd ed.) (pp. 77–106). Itasca, IL: F. E. Peacock Publishers.

Colby, A., Kohlberg, L., Gibbs, J., & Lieberman, M. (1983). A longitudinal study of moral judgment. *Monographs of the Society for Research in Child Development, 48* (Serial No. 200), 1–124.

Cole, C. G. (1988). The school counselor: Image and impact, counselor role and function, 1960s to 1980s and beyond. In G. R. Walz (Ed.), *Research and counseling: Building strong school counseling programs* (pp. 127–149). Alexandria, VA: American Association of Counseling and Education.

Cole, C. L. (1985). A group design for adult female survivors of childhood incest. *Women & Therapy, 4*, 71–82.

Cole, D. A. (1991). Change in self-perceived competence as a function of peer and teacher evaluation. *Developmental Psychology, 27*, 682–688.

Cole, M., & Cole, S. R. (1996). *The development of children* (3rd ed.). New York: W. H. Freeman & Co.

Cole, M., & Cole, S. R. (2001). *The development of children* (4th ed.). New York: Worth Publishers.

Cole, P. A., & Taylor, O. L. (1990). Performance of working class African-American children on three tests of articulation. *Language, Speech, and Hearing Services in the School, 21*, 171–176.

Cole, P. M., Barrett, K. C., & Zahn-Waxler, C. (1992). Emotion display in two-year-olds during mishaps. *Child Development, 63*, 314–324.

Coleman, S. R. (1997). B. F. Skinner: Maverick, inventor, behaviorist, critic. In W. G. Bringmann, H. E. Lueck, R. Miller, & C. E. Early (Eds.), *A pictorial history of psychology* (pp. 206–213). Chicago: Quintessence Publishing.

Coles, R. (1970). *Erik H. Erikson: The growth of his work.* Boston: Little, Brown.

Commission on Accreditation of Marriage and Family Therapy Education. (2002, May 17). *Directory of MFT training programs.* Retrieved on May 24, 2002, from http://www.aamft.org/resources/Online_Directories/coamfte.htm.

Committee on Ethical Guidelines for Forensic Psychologists. (1991). Specialty guidelines for forensic psychologists. *Law and Human Behavior, 15*, 655–665.

Comunidad Los Horcones. (2001a). Brief history of Los Horcones. Retrieved on June 7, 2002, from http://www.loshorcones.org.mx/briefhistory.html.

Comunidad Los Horcones. (2001b). Code of communication contingencies: Behavior code. Retrieved on June 7, 2002, from http://www.loshorcones.org.mx/code.html.

Comunidad Los Horcones. (2002). Walden-communitarian family. Retrieved on June 7, 2002, from http://www.loshorcones.org.mx/family.html.

Conception in a watch glass. (1937). *New England Journal of Medicine, 217*, 678.

Conoley, J. C., & Conoley, C. W. (1991). Collaboration for child adjustment: Issues for school-based and clinic-based child psychologists. *Journal of Consulting and Clinical Psychology, 59*, 821–829.

Conoley, J. C., & Larson, P. (1995). Conflicts in care: Early years of the lifespan. In E. J. Rave & C. C. Larsen (Eds.), *Ethical decision making in therapy: Feminist perspectives* (pp. 202–222). New York: Guilford.

Conte, J., & Schuerman, J. (1987). Factors associated with an increased impact of child sexual abuse. *Child Abuse and Neglect, 11*, 201–211.

Contratto, S. & Hassinger, J. (1995). Violence against women. In E. J. Rave & C. C. Larsen (Eds.), *Ethical decision making in therapy: Feminist perspectives* (pp. 124–152). New York: Guilford.

Cook, T. D., Church, M. B., Ajanaku, S., Shadish, W. R., Jr., Kim, J., & Cohen, R. (1996). The development of occupational aspirations and expectations among inner-city boys. *Child Development, 67*, 3368–3385.

Coonerty, S. (1993). Integrative child therapy. In G. Stricker & J. R. Gold (Eds.), *Comprehensive handbook of psychotherapy integration* (pp. 413–425). New York: Plenum.

Cooper, C. C., & Gottlieb, M. C. (2000). Ethical issues with managed care. *The Counseling Psychologist, 28*, 179–236.

Coopersmith, S. (1967). *The antecedents of self-esteem*. San Francisco: W. H. Freeman.

Corey, M. S., & Corey, G. (2002). *Groups: Process and practice* (6th ed.). Pacific Grove, CA: Brooks/Cole.

Corr, C. A. (1995). Entering into adolescent understandings of death. In E. A. Grollman (Ed.), *Bereaved children and teens: A support guide for parents and professionals* (pp. 21–35). Boston: Beacon Press.

Costantino, G., & Malgady, R. G. (1996). Development of TEMAS, a multicultural thematic apperception test: Psychometric properties and clinical utility. In G. R. Sodowsky & J. C. Impara (Eds.), *Multicultural assessment in counseling and clinical psychology*, (pp. 85–136). Lincoln, NE: Buros Institute of Mental Measurements.

Costantino, G., Malgady, B. G., & Rogler, L. H. (1988). *TEMAS (Tell-Me-A-Story)*. Los Angeles, CA: Western Psychological Services.

Costantino, G., Malgady, R. G., & Rogler, L. H. (1985). *Cuento therapy: Folktales as a culturally sensitive psychotherapy for Puerto Rican children* (Hispanic Research Center, Fordham University, Monograph No. 12). Maplewood, NJ: Waterfront Press.

Costantino, G., Malgady, R. G., & Rogler, L. H. (1986). Cuento therapy: A culturally sensitive modality for Puerto Rican children. *Journal of Consulting and Clinical Psychology, 54*, 639–645.

Costantino, G., Malgady, R. G., Rogler, L. H., & Tsui, E. C. (1988). Discriminant analysis of clinical outpatients and public school children by TEMAS: A thematic apperception test for Hispanics and Blacks. *Journal of Personality Assessment, 52*, 670–678.

Costantino, G., Malgady, R. G., Colon-Malgady, G., & Bailey, J. (1992). Clinical utility of the TEMAS with nonminority children. *Journal of Personality Assessment, 59*, 433–438.

Costello, E. J. (1989). Developments in child psychiatric epidemiology. *Journal of the American Academy of Child and Adolescent Psychiatry, 28*, 836–841.

Cott, A. (1972). Megavitamins: The orthomolecular approach to behavioral disorders and learning disabilities. *Academic Therapy, 7*, 245–258.

Cott, A. (1977). *The orthomolecular approach to learning disabilities*. San Rafael, CA: Academic Therapy Publications.

Council for the Accreditation of Counseling and Related Educational Programs. (2002). *Directory of accredited programs—2002*. Retrieved on May 24, 2002, from http://www.counseling.org/cacrep/directory.htm.

Council on Social Work Education. (2002). *Most recent action taken by the commission on accreditation*. Retrieved on May 20, 2002, from http://www.cswe.org.

Cowen, E. L., Hightower, A. D., Pedro-Carroll, J. L., Work, W. C., Wyman, P. A., & Haffey, W. G. (1996). *School-based prevention for children at risk: The primary mental health project*. Washington, DC: American Psychological Association.

Cox, M. J., Owen, M. T., Henderson, V. K., & Margand, N. A. (1992). Prediction of infant-father and infant-mother attachment. *Developmental Psychology, 28*, 474–483.

Coyle, J. T. (2000). Psychotropic drug use in very young children. *Journal of the American Medical Association, 283*, 1059–1060.

Craighead, W. E., Kazdin, A. E., & Mahoney, M. J. (1976). *Behavior modification: Principles, issues, and applications*. Boston: Houghton Mifflin.

Crain, W. (2000). *Theories of development: Concepts and applications* (4th ed.). Upper Saddle River, NJ: Prentice-Hall.

Cross, R. W., & Huberty, T. J. (1993). Factor analysis of the State-Trait Anxiety Inventory for children with a sample of seventh- and eighth-grade students. *Journal of Psychoeducational Assessment, 11*, 232–241.

Cross, W. E., Jr. (1978). The Thomas and Cross models of psychological nigrescence: A review. *The Journal of Black Psychology, 5(1)*, 13–31.

Crossman, E. K. (1991). Schedules of reinforcement. In W. Ishaq (Ed.), *Human behavior in today's world* (pp. 133–138). New York: Praeger.

Crowley, K., & Siegler, R. S. (1993). Flexible strategy use in young children's tic-tac-toe. *Cognitive Science, 17*, 531–561.

Cueva, J. E., Overall, J. E., Small, A. M., Armenteros, J. L., Perry, R., & Campbell, M. (1996). Carbamazepine in aggressive children with conduct disorder: A double-blind and placebo-controlled study. *Journal of the American Academy of Child and Adolescent Psychiatry, 35*, 480–490.

Cummins, R. A. (1988). *The neurologically-impaired child: Doman-Delacato techniques reappraised*. London, UK: Croom Helm.

D'Amato, R. C., & Dean, R. S. (1989). The past, present, and future of school psychology in nontraditional settings. In R. C. D'Amato & R. S. Dean (Eds.), *The school psychologist in nontraditional settings: Integrating clients, services, and settings* (pp. 185–209). Hillsdale, NJ: Lawrence Erlbaum.

Da Costa, I. G., Rapoff, M. A., Lemanek, K., & Goldstein, G. L. (1997). Improving adherence to medication regimens for children with asthma and its effect on clinical outcome. *Journal of Applied Behavior Analysis, 30*, 687–691.

Dalakar, J. (2001). *Poverty in the United States: 2000*. Washington, DC: U. S. Census Bureau.

Dale, M. A., & Lyddon, W. J. (2000). Sandplay: A constructivist strategy for assessment and change. *Journal of Constructivist Psychology, 13*, 135–154.

Daly, S. L., & Glenwick, D. S. (2000). Personal adjustment and perceptions of grandchild behavior in custodial grandmothers. *Journal of Clinical Child Psychology, 29*, 108–118.

Damon, W. (1977). *The social world of the child*. San Francisco: Jossey-Bass.

Damon, W., & Hart, D. (1982). The development of self-understanding from infancy through adolescence. *Child Development, 53*, 841–864.

Dana, R. H. (1993). *Multicultural assessment perspectives for professional psychology*. Needham Heights, MA: Allyn and Bacon.

Danforth, J. S. (1998a). The Behavior Management Flow Chart: A component analysis of behavior management strategies. *Clinical Psychology Review, 18*, 229–257.

Danforth, J. S. (1998b). The outcome of parent training using the Behavior Management Flow Chart with mothers and their children with oppositional defiant disorder and attention-deficit hyperactivity disorder. *Behavior Modification, 22*, 443–473.

Danforth, J. S. (1999). The outcome of parent training using the Behavior Management Flow Chart with a mother and her twin boys with oppositonal defiant disorder and attention-deficit hyperactivity disorder. *Child and Family Behavior Therapy, 21(4)*, 59–80.

Daniel, J. E., & Daniel, J. L. (1998). Preschool children's selection of race-related personal names. *Journal of Black Studies, 28*, 471–490.

Daniels, J. A. (2001). Managed care, ethics, and counseling. *Journal of Counseling and Development, 79*, 119–122.

Dattilio, F. M. (1998). Cognitive-behavioral family therapy. In F. M. Dattilio (Ed.), *Case studies in couple and family therapy: Systemic and cognitive perspectives* (pp. 62–84). New York: Guilford.

Dattilio, F. M., Epstein, N. B., & Baucom, D. H. (1998). An introduction to cognitive-behavioral therapy with couples and families. In F. M. Dattilio (Ed.), *Case studies in couple and family therapy: Systemic and cognitive perspectives*. (pp. 1–36). New York: Guilford.

Davidson, M., & Range, L. M. (2000). Age appropriate no-suicide agreements: Professionals' ratings of appropriateness and effectiveness. *Education and Treatment of Children, 23*, 143–155.

Davidson, M., Wagner, W., & Range. L. (1995). Clinicians' attitudes toward no-suicide agreements. *Suicide and Life Threatening Behavior, 25*, 410–414.

Davis, J. M., & Sandoval, J. (1991). A pragmatic framework for systems-oriented consultation. *Journal of Educational and Psychological Consultation, 2*, 201–216.

Davis, S. R., & Meier, S. T. (2001). *The elements of managed health care: A guide for helping professionals*. Belmont, CA: Brooks/Cole.

Deal, J. E. (1996). Marital conflict and differential treatment of siblings. *Family Process, 35*, 333–346.

Deater-Deckard, K., Dodge, K. A., Bates, J. E., & Pettit, G. S. (1996). Physical discipline among African American and European American mothers: Links to children's externalizing behaviors. *Developmental Psychology, 32*, 1065–1072.

DeCasper, A. J., & Spence, M. J. (1986). Prenatal maternal speech influences newborns' perception of speech sounds. *Infant Behavior and Development, 9*, 133–150.

Deck, A. F. (1995). The challenge of evangelical/pentecostal Christianity to Hispanic Catholicism. In D. G. Hackett (Eds.), *Religion and American culture* (pp. 461–477). New York: Routledge.

Delacato, C. H. (1974). *The ultimate stranger: The autistic child*. Novato, CA: Arena Press.

DeLeon, G. & Mandell, W. (1966). A comparison of conditioning and psychotherapy in the treatment of functional enuresis. *Journal of Clinical Psychology, 22*, 326–330.

DeLeon, P. H., & Williams, J. G. (1997). Evaluation research and public policy formation: Are psychologists collectively willing to accept unpopular findings? *American Psychologist, 52*, 551–552.

Denham, S. A. (1998). *Emotional development in young children*. New York: Guilford.

Dennis, S. (1991). Stage and structure in the development of children's spatial representations. In R. Case (Ed.), *The mind's staircase: Exploring the conceptual underpinnings of children's thought and knowledge* (pp. 229–245). Hillsdale, NJ: Lawrence Erlbaum.

Depner, C. E. (1994). Revolution and reassessment: Child custody in context. In A. E. Gottfried & A. W. Gottfried (Eds.), *Redefining families: Implications for children's development* (pp. 99–129). New York: Plenum.

De Shazer, S. (1985). *Keys to solution in brief therapy*. New York: W. W. Norton.

De Shazer, S. (1988). *Clues: Investigating solutions in brief therapy*. New York: W. W. Norton.

De Shazer, S., Berg, I. K., Lipchik, E., Nunnally, E., Molnar, A., Gingerich, W., & Weiner-Davis, M. (1986). Brief therapy: Focused solution development. *Family Process, 25*, 207–221.

De Shazer, S., & Molnar, A. (1984). Four useful interventions in brief family therapy. *Journal of Marital and Family Therapy, 10*, 297–304.

Deutsch, F. (1953). *The psychosomatic concept in psychoanalysis*. New York: International University Press.

DeVeaugh-Geiss, J., Moroz, G., Biederman, J. Cantwell, D., Fontaine, R., Greist, J. H., Reichler, R., Katz, R., & Landau, P. (1992). Clomipramine hydrochloride in childhood and adolescent obsessive-compulsive disorder—A multicenter trial. *Journal of the American Academy of Child and Adolescent Psychiatry, 31*, 45–49.

Dewey, J. (1934). *Art as experience*. New York: Minton, Balch & Co.

Dial, T. H., Tebbutt, R., Pion, G. M., Kohout, J., VandenBos, G., Johnson, M., Shervish, P. H., Whiting, L. Fox, J. G., & Merwin, E. I. (1990). Human resources in mental health. In R. W. Mandersheid & M. A. Sonnenshein (Eds.), *Mental Health, United States, 1990* (pp. 196–215). (DHHS Publication No. ADM 90-1708). Washington, DC: U.S. Government Printing Office.

Dietz, S. M. (1977). An analysis of programming DRL schedules in educational settings. *Behaviour Research and Therapy, 15*, 103–111.

DiGiuseppe, R. (1990). Rational-emotive assessment of school aged children. *School Psychology Review, 19*, 287–293.

Di Leo, J. H. (1977). *Child development: Analysis and synthesis*. New York: Brunner/Mazel.

DiLorenzo, T. M. (1987). Standardized and projective tests. In C. L. Frame & J. L. Matson (Eds.), Handbook of assessment in childhood psychopathology: Applied issues in differential diagnosis and treatment evaluation. *Applied Clinical Psychology* (pp. 63–78). New York: Plenum.

Dimick, K. M., & Huff, V. E. (1970). *Child counseling*. Dubuque, IA: W. C. Brown Co.

Dinkmeyer, D., & Dinkmeyer, D. (1979). A comprehensive and systematic approach to parent education. *American Journal of Family Therapy, 7(2)*, 46–50.

Dinkmeyer, D. & Dinkmeyer, D., (1982). *Developing understanding of self and others, DUSO-1 Revised, DUSO-2 Revised*. Circle Pines, MN: American Guidance Service.

Dinkmeyer, D., & McKay, G. (1973). *Raising a responsible child: Practical steps to successful family relationships*. New York: Simon and Schuster.

Dinkmeyer, D., & McKay, G. (1976). *Systematic training for effective parenting*. Circle Pines, MN: American Guidance Service.

Dinkmeyer, D., Dinkmeyer, D., & Sperry, L. (1987). *Adlerian counseling and psychotherapy* (2nd ed.). Colombus, OH: Merrill.

Dinkmeyer, D., McKay, G., & Dinkmeyer, D. (1980). *Systematic training for effective teaching*. Circle Pines, MN: American Guidance Service.

Dinkmeyer, D., McKay, G., & Dinkmeyer, D. (1990). Inaccuracy in STEP research reporting. *Canadian Journal of Counseling, 24*, 103–105.

Dix, T., Reinhold, D. P., & Zambarano, R. J. (1990). Mothers' judgment in moments of anger. *Merrill-Palmer Quarterly, 36*, 465–486.

Dodrill, C. B. (1981). An economical method for the evaluation of general intelligence in adults. *Journal of Consulting and Clinical Psychology, 49*, 668–673.

Dolan, L. J., Kellam, S. G., Brown, C. H. & Werthamer-Larsson, I. (1993). The short-term impact of two classroom-based preventive interversions on aggressive and shy behaviors and poor achievement. *Journal of Applied Developmental Psychology, 14*, 317–345.

Doleys, D., Ciminero, A., Tollison, J., Williams, C. & Wells, K. (1977). Dry-bed training and retention control training: A comparison. *Behavior Therapy, 8*, 541–548.

Doleys, D. M. (1989). Enuresis and encopresis. In T. H. Ollendick & M. Hersen (Eds.), *Handbook of child psychopathology* (2nd ed.) (pp. 291–314). New York: Plenum.

Dolgin, J. L. (1997). *Defining the family: Law, technology, and reproduction in an uneasy age*. New York: New York University Press.

Dorfman, E. (1951). Play therapy. In C. R. Rogers, *Client-centered therapy* (pp. 235–277). Boston: Houghton Mifflin.

Dorfman, E. (1958). Personality outcomes of client-centered therapy. *Psychological Monographs, 72(3)*, (Whole No. 456), 1–22.

Dornbush, S. M., & Strober, M. H. (1988). Our perspective. In S. M. Dornbush & M. H. Strober (Eds.), *Feminism, children, and the new family* (pp. 3–24). New York: Guilford.

Dorr, A., & Rabin, B. E. (1995). Parents, children, and television. In M. H. Bornstein (Ed.), *Handbook of parenting* (Vol. 4) (pp. 323–353). Hillsdale, NJ: Erlbaum.

Dougherty, A. M. (1995). *Consultation: Practice and perspectives in school and community settings* (2nd ed.). Pacific Grove, CA: Brooks/Cole.

Douglas, C. (1995). Analytical psychotherapy. In R. J. Corsini & D. Wedding (Eds.), *Current Psychotherapies* (5th ed.) (pp. 95–127). Itasca, IL: F. E. Peacock.

Downing, J., Pierce, K. A., & Woodruff, P. (1993). A community network for helping families. *The School Counselor, 41*, 102–108.

Dowrick, P. W., & Raeburn, J. M. (1995). Self-modeling: Rapid skill training for children with physical disabilities. *Journal of Developmental and Physical Disabilities, 7*, 25–37.

Doyle, A. B., & Aboud, F. E. (1995). A longitudinal study of white children's racial prejudice as a social-cognitive development. *Merrill-Palmer Quarterly, 41*, 209–228.

Dozier, R. M., Hicks, M. W., Cornille, T. A., & Peterson, G. W. (1998). The effect of Tomm's therapeutic questioning styles on therapeutic alliance: A clinical analog study. *Family Process, 37*, 189–200.

Dreikurs, R. (1948). *The challenge of parenthood*. New York: Duell, Sloan, and Pearce.

Dreikurs, R. (1964). *Children: The challenge*. New York: Hawthorn Books.

Dreikurs, R., & Grey, L. (1968). *Logical consequences: A new approach to discipline*. New York: Hawthorn.

Dreikurs, R., Gould, S., & Corsini, R. J. (1974). *Family council: The Dreikurs technique for putting an end to war between parents and children (and between children and children)*. Chicago: Henry Regnery.

Dreikurs, R., Grunwald, B. B., & Pepper, F. C. (1982) *Maintaining sanity in the classroom: Classroom management techniques* (2nd ed.). New York: Harper and Row.

Dressler, W. W. (1991). *Stress and adaptation in the context of culture: Depression in a southern Black community*. Albany, NY; State University of New York Press.

Dressler, W. W. (1991). *Stress and adaptation in the context of culture: Depression in a southern Black community*. Albany: State University of New York Press.

Dryden, W. (1987). Theoretically consistent eclecticism: Humanizing a computer "addict." In J. C. Norcross (Ed.), *Casebook of eclectic psychotherapy* (pp. 221–237). New York: Brunner/Mazel.

Dryden, W. (1989). Albert Ellis: An efficient and passionate life. *Journal of Counseling and Development, 67*, 539–546.

Dryfoos, J. G. (1997). School-based youth programs: Exemplary models and emerging opportunities. In R. J. Illback, C. T. Cobb, & H. M. Joseph, Jr. (Eds.), *Integrated services for children and families: Opportunities for psychological practice* (pp. 23–52). Washington, DC: American Psychological Association.

Dubow, E. F., Schmidt, D., McBride, J., Edwards, S., & Merk, F. L. (1993). Teaching children to cope with stressful experiences: Initial implementation and evaluation of a primary prevention program. *Journal of Clinical Child Psychology, 22*, 428–440.

Duchnowski, A. J. (1994). Innovative service models: Education. *Journal of Clinical Child Psychology, 23 (suppl.)*, 13–18.

Duff, R. S., Rowe, D. S., & Anderson, F. P. (1973). Patient care and student learning in a pediatric clinic. *Pediatrics, 50*, 839–846.

Dunn, L. M., & Dunn, L. M. (1981). *Peabody Picture Vocabulary Test-Revised: Manual*. Circle Pines, MN: American Guidance Service.

Dunn, J., & Hughes, C. (1998). Young children's understanding of emotions within close relationships. *Cognition and Emotion, 12*, 171–190.

DuPaul, G. J., Barkley, R. A., & Connor, D. F. (1998). Stimulants. In R. A. Barkley (Ed.), *Attention-deficit hyperactivity disorder: A handbook for diagnosis and treatment* (pp. 510–551). New York: Guilford.

DuPaul, G. J., & Ekert, T. (1997). School-based interventions for students with attention-deficit hyperactivity disorder: A meta-analysis. *School Psychology Review, 26*, 5–27.

DuPaul, G. J., Ervin, R. A., Hook, C. L., & McGoey, K. E. (1998). Peer tutoring for children with attention deficit hyperactivity disorder: Effects on classroom behavior and academic performance. *Journal of Applied Behavior Analysis, 31*, 579–592.

DuPaul, G. J., Power, T. J., Anastopoulos, A. D., & Reid, R. (1998). *ADHD Rating Scale–IV: Checklists, norms, and clinical interpretation*. New York: Guilford.

DuPaul, G. J., Rapport, M. D., & Perriello, L. M. (1991). Teacher ratings of academic skills: The development of the Academic Performance Rating Scale. *School Psychology Review, 20*, 284–300.

Durlak, J. A., Fuhrman, T., & Lampman, C. (1991). Effectiveness of cognitive-behavioral therapy for maladapting children: A meta-analysis. *Psychological Bulletin, 110*, 204–214.

Dyer, F. J. (1999). *Psychological consultation in parental rights cases*. New York: Guilford.

D'Zurilla, T. J., & Goldfried, M. R. (1971). Problem solving and behavior modification. *Journal of Abnormal Psychology, 78*, 107–126.

Easson, W. M. (1960). Encopresis: Psychogenic soiling. *Canadian Medical Association Journal, 82*, 624–628.

Eaves, L. J., Silberg, J. L., Maes, H. H., Simonoff, E., Pickles, A., Rutter, M., Neale, M. C., Reynolds, C. A., Erikson, M. T., Heath, A. C., Loeber, R., Truett, K. R., & Hewitt, J. K. (1997). Genetics and developmental psychopathology: 2. The main effects of genes and environment on behavioral problems in the Virginia Twin Study of Adolescent Behavioral Development. *Journal of Child Psychology and Psychiatry and Allied Disciplines, 38*, 965–980.

Eccles, J. S., Jacobs, J., & Harold, R. D. (1990). Gender-role sterotypes, expectancy effects, and parents' role in the socialization of gender differences in self-perceptions and skill acquisition. *Journal of Social Issues, 46*, 183–201.

Edens, J. F. (1998). School-based consultation services for children with externalizing behavioral problems. In L. VandeCreek, S. Knapp. & T. L. Jackson (Eds.), *Innovations in clinical practice: A source book* (Vol. 16) (pp. 337–353). Sarasota, FL: Professional Resource Press.

Eder, R. A. (1989). The emergent personologist: The structure and content of 3½-, 5½-, and 7½-year-olds' concepts of themselves and other persons. *Child Development, 60*, 1218–1228.

Edmunds, M., Frank, R., Hogan, M., McCarty, D., Robinson-Beale, R., & Weisner, C. (Eds.). (1997). *Managing managed care: Quality improvement in behavioral health*. Washington, DC: National Academy Press.

Edwards, D. J. A. (1996). Case study research: The cornerstone of theory and practice. In M. A. Reineke, F. M. Dattilio, & A. Freeman (Eds.), *Cognitive therapy with children and adolescents: A casebook for clinical practice* (pp. 10–37). New York: Guilford.

Edwards, D. L., & Foster, M. A. (1995). Uniting the family and school systems: A process of empowering the school counselor. *The School Counselor, 42*, 277–282.

Egeland, B. R., Carlson, E., & Sroufe, L. A. (1993). Resilience as process: Special issue: Milestones in the development of resilience. *Development and Psychopathology, 5*, 517–528.

Eichenbaum, L., & Orbach, S. (1983). *Understanding women: A feminist psychoanalytic approach*. New York: Basic Books.

Eisenberg, N. (1988). The development of prosocial and aggressive behavior. In M. H. Bornstein & M. E. Lamb (Eds.), *Social, emotional and personality development. Part III of Developmental psychology: An advanced textbook* (2nd ed.) (pp. 461–486). Hillsdale, NJ: Lawrence Erlbaum.

Eisenberg, N., & Fabes, R. A. (1998). Prosocial development. In W. Damon & N. Eisenberg (Eds.), *Handbook of child psychology (5th ed.) Vol. 3: Social, emotional, and personality development* (pp. 701–778). New York: John Wiley.

Eisenberg, N., Martin, C. L., & Fabes, R. A. (1996). Gender development and gender effects. In D. C. Berliner & R. C. Calfee (Eds.), *Handbook of educational psychology* (pp. 358–396). New York: Macmillan.

Eisenstadt, T. H., Eyberg, S., McNeil, C. B., Newcomb, K., & Funderburk, B. (1993). Parent-child interaction therapy with behavior problem children: Relative effectiveness of two stages and overall treatment outcome. *Journal of Clinical Child Psychology, 22*, 42–51.

Elementary and Secondary Education Act of 1965, Vol. 79 *United States Statutes at Large* (1966).

Elias, M. J., & Tobias, S. E. (1996). *Social problem solving: Interventions in the schools*. New York: Guilford.

Elkins, D. N., Hedstrom, L. J., Hughes, L. L., Leaf, J. A., & Saunders, Toward a humanistic-phenomenological spirituality: Definition, description, and measurement. *Journal of Humanistic Psychology, 28*(4), 5–18.

Ellinwood, C. G., & Raskin, N. J. (1993). Client-centered/humanistic psychotherapy. In T. R. Kratochwill & R. J. Morris (Eds.), *Handbook of psychotherapy with children and adolescents* (pp. 258–287). Needham Heights, MA: Allyn and Bacon.

Ellis, A. (1962). *Reason and emotion in psychotherapy*. Secaucus, NJ: Lyle Stuart.

Ellis, A. (1972). Emotional education in the classroom: The living school. *Journal of Clinical Child Psychology, 1*, 19–22.

Ellis, A. (1977). The basic clinical theory of rational-emotive therapy. In A. Ellis & R. Greiger (Eds.), *Handbook of rational-emotive therapy* (pp. 3–34). New York: Springer.

Ellis, A. (1987). The impossibility of achieving consistently good mental health. *American Psychologist, 42*, 364–375.

Ellis, A., & Bernard, M. E. (1983). An overview of rational-emotive approaches to the problems of childhood. In A. Ellis & M. E. Bernard (Eds.), *Rational-emotive approaches to the problems of childhood* (pp. 3–43). New York: Plenum.

Ellis, A., & Dryden, W. (1997). *The practice of rational emotive behavior therapy* (2nd ed.). New York: Springer Publishing Co.

Ellis, A., & Wilde, J. (2002). *Case studies in rational emotive behavior therapy with children and adolescents.* Upper Saddle River, NJ: Pearson Education.

Emery, R. E. (1988). *Marriage, divorce, and children's adjustment.* Thousand Oaks, CA: Sage.

Emslie, G. J., Rush, A. J., Weinberg, W. A., Kowatch, R. A., Hughes, C. W., Carmody, T., & Rintelmann, J. (1997). A double-blind, randomized, placebo-controlled trial of fluoxetine in children and adolescents with depression. *Archives of General Psychiatry, 54*, 1031–1037.

Enright, R. D., Gassin, E. A., & Wu, C. (1992). Forgiveness: A developmental view. *Journal of Moral Education, 21 (2)*, 99–114.

Enright, R. D., Santos, M. J. D., & Al-Mabuk, R. (1989). The adolescent as forgiver. *Journal of Adolescence, 12*, 95–110.

Epstein, L. H., Valoski, A., Wing, R. R., & McCurley, J. (1994). Ten-year outcomes of behavioral family-based treatment for childhood obesity. *Health Psychology, 13*, 373–383.

Epting, F. R. (1984). *Personal construct counseling and psychotherapy.* New York: John Wiley.

Erickson. M. H. (1954) Special techniques of brief hypnotherapy. *Journal of Clinical and Experimental Hypnosis, 2*, 109–129.

Erikson, E. (1950). *Childhood and society.* New York: W.W. Norton & Co.

Erikson, E. (1968). *Identity: Youth and crisis.* New York: W. W. Norton & Co.

Ermer, D. J. (1999). Experience with a rural telepsychiatry clinic for children and adolescents. *Psychiatric Services, 50*, 260–261.

Ervin, R. A., Bankert, C. L. & DuPaul, G. J. (1996). Treatment of attention-deficit/hyperactivity disorder. In M. A. Reineoke, F. M. Datfilio, & A. Freeman (Eds.). *Cognitive Therapy with children and adolescents: A casebook for clinical practice* (pp. 38–61). New York: Guilford.

Estrada, A. U., & Pinsof, W. M. (1995). The effectiveness of family therapies for selected behavioral disorders of childhood. *Journal of Marital and Family Therapy, 21*, 403–440.

Etzel, B. C., & Gewirtz, J. L. (1967). Experimentation model of caretaker-maintained heart-rate operant crying in a six and a twenty week old infant: Extinction of crying with reinforcement of eye contact and smiling. *Journal of Experimental Child Psychology, 5*, 303–317.

Evans, R. W., Clay, T. H., & Gualtieri, C. T. (1987)). Carbamazepine in pediatric psychiatry. *Journal of the American Academy of Child and Adolescent Psychiatry*, 26, 2–8.

Evers-Szostak, M. (1998). Psychological practice in pediatric primary care settings. In L. VandeCreek, S. Knapp, & T. L. Jackson (Eds.), *Innovations in clinical practice: A source book* (Vol. 16) (pp. 325–335). Sarasota, FL: Professional Resource Press.

Eyberg, S. M. (1988). Parent-child interaction therapy: Integration of traditional and behavioral concerns. *Child and Family Behavior Therapy, 10*, 33–46.

Eyberg, S. M. (1992). Parent and teacher behavior inventories for the assessment of conduct problem behaviors in children. In L. VandeCreek, S. Knapp, & T. L. Jackson (Eds.), *Innovations in clinical practice: A source book* (Vol. 11) (pp. 261–270). Sarasota, FL: Professional Resource Press.

Eyberg, S. M. (1993). Consumer satisfaction measures for assessing parent training programs. In L. VandeCreek, S. Knapp, & T. L. Jackson (Eds.), *Innovations in clinical practice: A source book* (Vol. 12) (pp. 377–382). Sarasota, FL: Professional Resource Press.

Eyberg, S. M., Bessmer, J., Newcomb, K., Edwards, D., & Robinson, E. A. (1994). Dyadic Parent-child Interaction Coding System-II: A manual. *Social and behavioral sciences documents* (Ms. No. 2897). San Rafael, CA: Select Press.

Eyberg, S. M., Boggs, S. R., & Algina, J. (1995). Parent-child interaction therapy: A psychosocial model for the treatment of young children with conduct problem behavior and their families. *Psychopharmacology Bulletin, 31*, 83–91.

Eysenck, H. (1952). The effects of psychotherapy: An evaluation. *Journal of Consulting Psychology, 16*, 319–324.

Fagan, T. K. (1986). School psychology's dilemma: Reappraising solutions and directing attention to the future. *American Psychologist, 41*, 851–861.

Falicov, C. J. (1998). *Latino families in therapy: A guide to multicultural practice.* New York: Guilford.

Falk, P. J. (1994). The gap between psychosocial assumptions and empirical research in lesbian-mother child custody cases. In A. E. Gottfried & A. W. Gottfried (Eds.), *Redefining families: Implications for children's development* (pp. 131–156). New York: Plenum Press.

Family Educational Rights and Privacy Act. (1974). 20 U.S.C.A. Sec. 1232g with implementing regulations set down in 34 C.F.R. 99.3 Fed. Reg. 65, No. 130, 41853.

Feingold, B. F. (1975). *Why your child is hyperactive.* New York: Random House.

Feldman, E., & Dodge, K. A. (1987). Social information processing and sociometric status: Sex, age, and situational effects. *Journal of Abnormal Child Psychology, 15*, 211–227.

Feldman, R. S. (1998). *Child development.* Upper Saddle River, NJ: Prentice Hall.

Feldman, S. (1997). The Fort Bragg demonstration and evaluation. *American Psychologist, 52*, 560–561.

Field, T. M., Woodson, R., Cohen, D., Greenberg, R., Garcia, R., & Collins, K. (1983). Discrimination and imitation of facial expressions by term and preterm neonates. *Infant Behavior and Development, 6*, 485–489.

Field, T. M., Woodson, R., Greenberg, R., & Cohen, D. (1982). Discrimination and imitation of facial expressions by neonates. *Science, 218*, 179–181.

Finkelhor, D., Hotaling, G., Lewis, I. A., & Smith, C. (1990). Sexual abuse in a national survey of adult men and women: Prevalence, characteristics, and risk factors. *Child Abuse and Neglect, 14*, 19–28.

Finkelhor, D., & Russell, D. E. H. (1984). Women as perpetrators. In D. Finkelhor (Ed.), *Child sexual abuse: New theory and research* (pp. 171–187). New York: Free Press.

Fischer, L., & Sorenson, G. P. (1996). *School law for counselors, psychologists, and social workers* (3rd ed.). New York: Longman.

Fishman, D. B., & Franks, C. M. (1997). The conceptual evolution of behavior therapy. In P. L. Wachtel & S. B. Messer (Eds.), *Theories of psychotherapy: Origins and evolution* (pp. 131–180). Washington, DC: American Psychological Association.

Flament, M. F., Rapoport, J. L., Berg, C. J., Sceery, W., Kilts, C., Mellstrom, B., Linnoila, M. (1985). Clomipramine treatment of childhood obsessive-compulsive disorder: A double-blind controlled study. *Archives of General Psychiatry, 42*, 977–983.

Flavell, J. H. (1985). *Cognitive development* (2nd ed.). Englewood Cliffs, NJ: Prentice-Hall.

Flynn, C. P. (1994). Regional differences in attitudes toward corporal punishment. *Journal of Marriage and the Family, 56*, 314–324.

Fonagy, P. (1999). Psychodynamic psychotherapy. In S. W. Russ & T. H. Ollendick (Eds.), *Handbook of psychotherapies with children and families* (pp. 87–106). New York: Kluwer Academic/Plenum Publishers.

Fonseca, A. C., Yule, W., & Erol, N. (1994). Cross-cultural issues. In T. H. Ollendick, N. J. King, & W. Yule (Eds.), *International handbook of phobic and anxiety disorders in children and adolescents* (pp. 67–84). New York: Plenum.

Fontaine, J. H. (1998). Evidencing a need: School counselors' experiences with gay and lesbian students. *Professional School Counseling, 1(3)*, 8–14.

Forehand, R., & Wierson, M. (1993). The role of developmental factors in planning behavioral interventions for children: Disruptive behavior as an example. *Behavior Therapy, 24*, 117–141.

Forgatch, M. S., & Patterson, G. R. (1998). Behavioral family therapy. In F. M. Dattilio (Ed.), *Case studies in couple and family therapy: Systemic and cognitive perspectives* (pp. 85–107). New York: Guilford.

Forsythe, W., & Redmond, A. (1970). Enuresis and the urine alarm: Study of 200 cases. *British Medical Journal, 1*, 211–213.

Fortier, L. M., & Wanslass, R. L. (1984). Family crisis following the diagnosis of a handicapped child. *Family Relations, 33*, 13–24.

Fowler, W. E., & Wagner, W. G. (1993). Preference for and comfort with male vs. female counselors among sexually abused girls in individual treatment. *Journal of Counseling Psychology, 40*, 65–72.

Fowler, W. E., Wagner, W. G., Iachini, A., & Johnson, J. T. (1992). The impact of sex of psychological examiner on sexually abused girls' preference for and anticipated comfort with male versus female counselors. *Child Study Journal, 22*, 1–10.

Fox, P. D. (1996). An overview of managed care. In P. R. Kongstvedt (Ed.), *The managed health care handbook* (3rd ed.) (pp. 3–15). Gaithersburg, MD: Aspen Publishers.

Fransella, F. (1995). *George Kelly*. London: Sage.

Fraser, M. W., Pecora, P. J., & Haapala, D. A. (1991). *Families in crisis: The impact of intensive family preservation services*. New York: Aldine De Gruyter.

Freedheim, D. K., & Russ, S. R. (1983). Psychotherapy with children. In C. E. Walter & M. C. Roberts (Eds.), *Handbook of clinical child psychology* (pp. 978–994). New York: John Wiley.

Freeman, J., Epston, D., & Lobovits, D. (1997). *Playful approaches to serious problems: Narrative therapy with children and their families*. New York: W. W. Norton.

Freitas, A. L., & Downey, G. (1998). Resilience: A dynamic perspective. *International Journal of Behavioral Development, 22*, 263–285.

French, J. L. (1990). History of school psychology. In T. B. Gutkin & C. R. Reynolds (Eds.), *The handbook of school psychology* (2nd ed.) (pp. 3–20). New York: John Wiley.

Freud, A. (1927/1965). The theory of children's analysis. In A. Freud, *The psycho-analytical treatment of children: Technical lectures and essays* (pp. 53–64). New York: International Universities Press, Inc.

Freud, A. (1928). *Introduction to the technic of child analysis*. New York: Arno Press.

Freud, A. (1936/1966). *The writings of Anna Freud, Vol. II: The ego and the mechanism of defense*. New York: International Universities Press.

Freud, A. (1946). *The psycho-analytical treatment of children*. New York: International Universities Press.

Freud, A. (1956/1969). *The assessment of borderline cases*. In *The writings of Anna Freud* (Vol. V) (pp. 301–314). New York: International Universities Press.

Freud, A. (1962/1969). Assessment of pathology in childhood: Part I. In *The writings of Anna Freud* (Vol. V) (pp. 26–37). New York: International Universities Press.

Freud, A. (1965). *The writings of Anna Freud, Vol. VI: Normality and pathology in childhood: Assessments of development*. New York: International Universities Press.

Freud, A., & Burlingham, D. T. (1943). *War and children*. Westport, CT: Greenwood Press.

Freud, S. (1904/1956). On psychotherapy. In E. Jones (Ed.), *Sigmund Freud: Collected papers* (Vol. 1) (pp. 249–263). London: Hogarth Press.

Freud, S. (1909/1956). Analysis of a phobia in a five-year-old boy. In E. Jones (Ed.), *Sigmund Freud: Collected papers* (Vol. 3) (pp.149–287). London: Hogarth Press.

Freud, S. (1915/1953). Instincts and their vicissitudes. In E. Jones (Ed.), *Sigmund Freud: Collected papers* (Vol. 4) (pp. 60–83). London: Hogarth Press.

Freud, S. (1920). *A general introduction to psychoanalysis*. New York: Boni and Liveright.

Freud, S. (1922/1953). Two encyclopedia articles. In E. Jones & J. Strachey (Eds.), *Sigmund Freud: Collected papers* (Vol. 5) (pp. 107–135). London: Hogarth Press.

Freud, S. (1922/1956). Postscript. In E. Jones (Ed.), *Sigmund Freud, Collected papers* (Vol. 3) (pp. 288–289). London: Hogarth Press.

Freud, S. (1925/1953). Some psychological consequences of the anatomical distinction between the sexes. In E. Jones & J. Strachey (Eds.), *Sigmund Freud: Collected papers* (Vol. 5) (pp. 186–197). London: Hogarth Press.

Freud, S. (1933/1964a). Lecture XXXIV—Explanations, applications, and orientations. In J. Strachey (Ed.), *The standard edition of the complete psychological works of Sigmund Freud* (Vol. 22) (pp. 136–157). London: Hogarth Press.

Freud, S. (1933/1964b). Lecture XXXI—The dissection of the psychical personality. J. Strachey (Ed.), *The standard edition of the complete works of Sigmund Freud* (Vol.22) (pp. 57–80). London: Hogarth Press.

Frey, D. E. (1986). Communication boardgames with children. In C. E. Schaefer & S. E. Reid (Eds.), *Game play: Therapeutic use of childhood games* (pp. 21–39). New York: John Wiley.

Frey, D. E. (1993). Learning by metaphor. In C. E. Schaefer (Ed.), *The therapeutic powers of play* (pp. 223–239). Northvale, NJ: Jason Aronson.

Friedberg, R. D. (1994). Storytelling and cognitive therapy with children. *Journal of Cognitive Psychotherapy: An International Quarterly, 8*, 209–217.

Friedlander, M. L. (1998). Family therapy research: Science into practice, practice into science. In M. P. Nichols & R. C. Schwartz (Eds.), *Family therapy: Concepts and methods* (4th ed.). Boston: Allyn and Bacon.

Friedman, R. M. (1994). Restructuring of systems to emphasize prevention and family support. *Journal of Clinical Child Psychology, 23(Suppl.)*, 40–47.

Friedrich, L., & Stein, A. (1973). Aggressive and prosocial television programs and the natural behavior of preschool children. *Monographs of the Society for Research in Child Development*, 38(4, Serial No. 151.

Fristad, M. A., Gavazzi, S. M., & Soldano, K. W. (1998). Multi-family psychoeducational groups for childhood mood disorders: A program description and preliminary efficacy data. *Contemporary Family Therapy, 20*, 385–402.

Fritz, G. K. (1993). The hospital: An approach to consultation. In G. K. Fritz, R. E. Mattison, B. Nurcombe, & A. Spirito (Eds.), *Child and adolescent mental health consultation in hospitals, schools, and courts* (pp. 7–24). Washington, DC: American Psychiatric Press.

Fritz, G. K., & Spirito, A. (1993). The process of consultation on a pediatric unit. In G. K. Fritz, R. E. Mattison, B. Nurcombe, & A. Spirito (Eds.), *Child and adolescent mental health consultation in hospitals, schools, and courts* (pp. 25–46). Washington, DC: American Psychiatric Press.

Fritz, G. K., Mattison, R. E., Nurcombe, B., & Spirito, A. (1993). *Child and adolescent mental health consultation in hospitals, schools, and courts*. Washington, DC: American Psychiatric Press.

Fuchs, N. R. (1957). Play therapy at home. *Merrill-Palmer Quarterly, 3*, 89–95.

Funk, J. B., Buchman, D. D., & Germann, J. N. (2000). Preference for violent electronic games, self-concept, and gender differences in young children. *American Journal of Orthopsychiatry, 70*, 233–241.

Funk, J. B., Flores, G., Buchman, D. D., & Germann, J. N. (1999). Rating electronic games: Violence is in the eye of the beholder. *Youth and Society, 30*, 283–312.

Gadow, K. D. (1991). Clinical issues in child and adolescent psychopharmacology. *Journal of Consulting and Clinical Psychology, 59*, 842–852.

Gadow, K. D., Nolan, E. E., Sverd, J., Sprafkin, J., & Paolicelli, L. M. (1990). Methylphenidate in aggressive-hyperactive boys: I. Effects on peer aggression in public school settings. *Journal of the American Academy of Child and Adolescent Psychiatry, 29*, 710–718.

Gaines, E. J. (1993). *A lesson before dying*. New York: A. A. Knopf.

Garbarino, J., & Stott, F. M. (1989). *What children can tell us: Eliciting, interpreting, and evaluating information from children*. San Francisco: Jossey-Bass.

Gardner, R. A. (1970). *The boys and girls book about divorce*. New York: Science House.

Gardner, R. A. (1971). *Therapeutic communication with children: The mutual storytelling technique*. New York: Science House.

Gardner, R. A. (1973). *The Talking, Feeling, and Doing Game*. Creskill, NJ: Creative Therapeutics.

Gardner, R. A. (1986). The Talking Feeling, and Doing Game. In C. E. Schaefer & S. E. Reid (Eds.), *Game play: Therapeutic use of childhood games* (pp. 41–72). New York: John Wiley.

Garfield, S. L. (1965). Historical introduction. In B. B. Wolman, G. F. Derner, M. Harrower, R. R. Holt, J. G. Miller, O. H. Mowrer, H. A. Murray, & S. S. Tomkins (Eds.), *Handbook of clinical psychology* (pp. 125–140). New York: McGraw-Hill.

Garfield, S. L. (1989). *The practice of brief psychotherapy*. New York: Pergamon.

Garfield, S. L. (1994). Research on client variables in psychotherapy. In A. E. Bergin & S. L. Garfield (Eds.), *Handbook of psychotherapy and behavior change* (4th ed.) (pp. 190–228). New York: John Wiley.

Garfield, S. L., & Bergin, A. E. (1994). Introduction and historical overview. In A. E. Bergin & S. L. Garfield (Eds.), *Handbook of psychotherapy and behavior change* (4th ed.) (pp. 3–18). New York: John Wiley.

Garrison, W. T., Bailey, E. N., Garb, J., Ecker, B., Spencer, P., & Sigelman, D. (1992). Interactions between parents and pediatric primary care physicians about children's mental health. *Hospital and Community Psychiatry, 43*, 489–493.

Garska v. McCoy, 167 W.Va. 59, 278 S.E.2d357 (1981).

Garven, S., Wood, J. M., & Malpass, R. S. (2000). Allegations of wrongdoing: The effects of reinforcement on children's mundane and fantastic claims. *Journal of Applied Psychology, 85*, 38–49.

Garven, S., Wood, J. M., Malpass, R. S., & Shaw, III, J. S. (1998). More than suggestion: The effect of interviewing techniques from the McMartin Preschool case. *Journal of Applied Psychology, 83*, 347–359.

Geffken, G., Johnson, S. B., & Walker, D. (1986). Behavioral interventions for childhood nocturnal enuresis: The differential effect of bladder capacity on treatment process and outcome. *Health Psychology, 5*, 261–272.

Gelfad, D. M., & Hartmann, D. P. (1968). Behavior therapy with children: A review and evaluation of research methodolgy. *Psychological Bulletin, 69*, 204–215.

Geller, D. Biederman, J., Reed, E. D., Spencer, T., & Wilens, T. E. (1995). Similarities in response to fluoxetine in the treatment of children and adolescents with obsessive compulsive disorder. *Journal of the American Academy of Child and Adolescent Psychiatry, 34*, 36–44.

Gelles, R. J. (1998). The youngest victims: Violence toward children. In R. K. Bergen (Ed.), *Issues in intimate violence* (pp. 5–24). Thousand Oaks, CA: Sage.

Gelman, S. A. (1989). Children's use of categories to guide biological inferences. *Human Development, 32*, 65–71.

Gelso, C. J., & Fretz, B. R. (1992). *Counseling psychology*. Fort Worth, TX: Harcourt Brace Jovanovich.

Gergen, K. J. (1971). *The concept of self*. New York: Holt, Rinehart, & Winston.

Geroski, A. M., & Rodgers, K. A. (1998). Collaborative assessment and treatment of children with enuresis and encopresis. *Professional School Counseling, 2*, 128–134.

Gerstein, M., & Lichtman, M. (1990). *The best for our kids: Exemplary elementary guidance and counseling programs*. Alexandria, VA: American School Counselor Association.

Giardino, A. P., Christian, C. W., & Giardino, E. R. (1997). *A practical guide to the evaluation of child physical abuse and neglect*. Thousand Oaks, CA: Sage.

Gibbs, J. T. (1989). Biracial adolescents. In J. T. Gibbs & L. N. Huang (Eds.), *Children of color: Psychological interventions with minority youth* (pp. 30–66). San Francisco: Jossey-Bass.

Gibson, R. L., Mitchell, M. H., & Basile, S. K. (1993). *Counseling in the elementary school: A comprehensive approach*. Boston: Allyn and Bacon.

Gil, E., & Sobol, B. (2000). Engaging families in therapeutic play. In C. E. Bailey (Ed.), *Children in therapy: Using the family as a resource* (pp. 341–382). New York: W. W. Norton.

Gillespie, M. C., & Conner, J. W. (1975). *Creative growth through literature for children and adolescents*. Columbus, OH: Merrill.

Gilligan, C. (1982). *In a different voice: Psychological theory and women's development*. Cambridge, MA: Harvard University Press.

Gilligan, C., & Attanucci, J. (1988). Two moral orientations: Gender differences and similarities. *Merrill-Palmer Quarterly, 34*, 223–237.

Ginns-Gruenberg, D., & Zacks, A. (1999). Bibliotherapy: The use of children's literature as a therapeutic tool. In C. E. Schaefer (Ed.), *Innovative psychotherapy techniques in child and adolescent therapy* (2nd ed.) (pp. 454–489). New York: John Wiley.

Ginott, H. G., & Lebo, D. (1961). Play therapy limits and theoretical orientation. *Journal of Consulting Psychology, 25*, 337–340.

Ginzberg, E., Ginsburg, S. W., Axelrad, S., & Herma, J. L. (1951). *Occupational choice: An approach to a general theory*. New York: Columbia University Press.

Gittelman-Klein, R., & Klein, D. F. (1971). Controlled imipramine treatment of school phobia. *Archives of General Psychiatry, 25*, 204–207.

Gittelman-Klein, R., & Klein, D. F. (1973). School phobia: Diagnostic considerations in light of imipramine effects. *Journal of Nervous and Mental Disease, 156*, 199–215.

Gleason, T. R., Sebanc, A. M., & Hartup, W. W. (2000). Imaginary companions of preschool children. *Developmental Psychology, 36*, 419–428.

Glenwick, D. S., & Neuhaus, S. M. (1985). A system-oriented, community-based training model for clinical child psychology: Implications for role development and skill acquisition. In J. M. Tuma (Ed.), *Proceedings: Conference on training clinical child psychologists* (pp. 43–46). Washington, DC: American Psychological Association.

Glicklich, L. B. (1951). An historical account of enuresis. *Pediatrics, 8*, 859–876.

Glionna, J. M. (2001, August 11). Twins rejected, surrogate birth mother sues. *Los Angeles Times*, p. B10.

Glosoff, H. L., Benshoff, J. M., Hosie, T. W., & Maki, D. R. (1995). The 1994 ACA model legislation for licensed professional counselors. *Journal of Counseling and Development, 74*, 209–220.

Glosoff, H. L., & Rockwell, P. J. (1997). The counseling profession: A historical perspective. In D. Capuzzi & D. Gross (Eds.), *Introduction to the counseling profession* (2nd ed., pp. 3–47). Needham Heights, MA: Allyn and Bacon.

Gold, J. R. (1992). An integrative-systemic treatment approach to severe psychopathology of children and adolescents. *Journal of Integrative and Eclectic Psychotherapy, 11*, 58–63.

Golden, G. S. (1984). Controversial therapies. *Pediatric Clinics of North America, 31*, 459–469.

Goldenberg, I., & Goldenberg, H. (1991). *Family therapy: An overview* (3rd ed.). Pacific Grove, CA: Brooks/Cole.

Goldfried, M. R. (1998). A comment on psychotherapy integration in the treatment of children. *Journal of Clinical Child Psychology, 27*, 49–53.

Goldman, J., Stein, C. L., & Guerry, S. (1990). *Psychological methods of child assessment*. New York: Brunner/Mazel.

Goldman, L. (2000). *Helping the grieving child in school*. Bloomington, IN: Phi Delta Kappa Educational Foundation.

Goldman, S., & Beardslee, W. R. (1999). Suicide in children and adolescents. In D. G. Jacobs (Ed.), *The Harvard Medical School guide to suicide assessment and intervention* (pp. 417–442). San Francisco: Jossey-Bass.

Golombok, S., Cook, R., Bish, A., & Murray, C. (1995). Families created by the new reproductive technologies: Quality of parenting and social and emotional development of the children. *Child Development, 66*, 285–298.

Golombok, S., MacCallum, F., & Goodman, E. (2001). The "test-tube" generation: Parent-child relationships and the psychological well-being of in vitro fertilization children at adolescence. *Child Development, 72*, 599–608.

Gordon, T. (1970). *P.E.T.: Parent effectiveness training*. New York: Peter H. Wyden.

Gordon, T. (1974). *T.E.T.: Teacher effectiveness training*. New York: Peter H. Wyden.

Gordon, T., Grumm, D. L., Rogers, C. R., & Seeman, J. (1954). Developing a program of research in psychotherapy. In C. R. Rogers & R. F. Dymond (Eds.), *Psychotherapy and personality change: Co-ordinated research studies in the client-centered approach* (pp. 12–34). Chicago: University of Chicago Press.

Gottfredson, L. S. (1981). Circumscription and compromise: A developmental theory of occupational choice. *Journal of Counseling Psychology, 28*, 545–579.

Gottfredson, L. S. (1996). Gottfredson's theory of circumspection and compromise. In D. Brown & L. Brooks (Eds.), *Career choice and development* (3rd ed.) (pp. 179–232). San Francisco: Jossey-Bass.

Gottfried, A. E., Bathurst, K., & Gottfried, A. W. (1994). Role of maternal and dual-earner employment status in children's development: A longitudinal study from infancy through early adolescence. In A. E. Gottfried & A. W. Gottfried (Eds.), *Redefining families: Implications for children's development* (pp. 55–97). New York: Plenum.

Gottfried, A. E., & Gottfried, A. W. (1994). Impact of redefined families on children's development: Conclusions, conceptual perspectives, and social implications. In A. E. Gottfried & A. W. Gottfried (Eds.), *Redefining families: Implications for children's development* (pp. 221–229). New York: Plenum Press.

Graae, F., Milner, J., Rizzotto, L., & Klein, R. G. (1994). Clonazepam in childhood anxiety disorders. *Journal of the American Academy of Child and Adolescent Psychiatry, 33*, 372–376.

Graham, J. A., & Cohen, R. (1997). Race and sex as factors in children's sociometric ratings and friendship choices. *Social Development, 6*, 355–372.

Graham, J. A., Cohen, R., Zbikowski, S. M., & Secrist, M. E. (1998). A longitudinal investigation of race and sex as factors in children's classroom friendship choices. *Child Study Journal, 28*, 245–265.

Green, R. (1987). *The "Sissy Boy Syndrome" and the development of homosexuality*. New Haven, CT: Yale University Press.

Greenberg, J. R., & Mitchell, S. A. (1983). *Object relations in psychoanalytic theory*. Cambridge: Harvard University.

Greenberg, L. S., & Pinsof, W. M. (1986). Process research: Current trends and future perspectives. In L. S. Greenberg & W. M. Pinsof (Eds.), *The psychotherapeutic process: A research handbook*. (pp. 3–20). New York: Guilford.

Greene, L., Kamps, D., Wyble, J., & Ellis, C. (1999). Home-based consultation for parents of young children with behavioral problems. *Child and Family Behavior Therapy, 21(2)*, 19–45.

Grencavage, L. M., & Norcross, J. C. (1990). Where are the commonalities among therapeutic common factors? *Professional Psychology: Research and Practice, 21*, 372–378.

Gresham, F. M. (1989) Review of the Revised Children's Manifest Anxiety Scale. In J. C. Conoley & J. J. Kramer (Ed.), *Tenth Mental Measurements Yearbook* (pp. 695–697). Lincoln, NE: Buros Institute of Mental Measurements.

Gresham, F. M., & Lambros, K. M. (1998). Behavioral and functional assessment. In T. S. Watson & F. M. Gresham (Eds.), *Handbook of child behavior therapy* (pp. 3–22). New York: Plenum Press.

Gross, M. D., Tofanelli, R. A., Butzirus, S. M., & Snodgrass, E. W. (1987). The effect of diets rich in and free from additives on the behavior of children with hyperkinetic and learning disorders. *Journal of the American Academy of Child and Adolescent Psychiatry, 26*, 53–55.

Guerney, B. G., Jr. (1964). Filial therapy: Description and rationale. Journal of *Consulting Psychology, 28*, 304–310.

Guerney, L. (1997). Filial therapy. In K. O'Connor & L. M. Braverman (Eds.), *Play therapy theory and practice: A comparative presentation* (pp. 131–159). New York: John Wiley.

Gurman, A. S., & Kniskern, D. P. (1981). *Handbook of family therapy*. New York: Brunner/Mazel.

Gushue, G. V., & Schiarra, D. T. (1995). Culture and families: A multidimensional approach. In J. G. Ponterotto, J. M. Casas, L. A., Suzuki, & C. M. Alexander (Eds.), *Handbook of multicultural counseling* (pp. 586–606). Thousand Oaks, CA: Sage.

Gysbers, N. C. (1990). A model comprehensive guidance program. In N. C. Gysbers (Ed.), *Comprehensive guidance programs that work* (pp. 1–25). Ann Arbor, MI: ERIC Counseling and Personal Services Clearinghouse.

Habenstein, R., & Olson, R. A. (1992). Families and children in history. In C. E. Walker & M. C. Roberts (Eds.), *Handbook of clinical child psychology* (2nd ed.) (pp. 3–17). New York: John Wiley.

Hagopian, L. P., & Ollendick, T. H. (1997). Anxiety disorders. In R. T. Ammerman & M. Hersen (Eds.), *Handbook of prevention and treatment with children and adolescents: Intervention in the real world context* (pp. 431–454). New York: John Wiley.

Hagopian, L. P., & Slifer, K. J. (1993). Treatment of separation anxiety disorder with graduated exposure and reinforcement targeting school attendance: A controlled study. *Journal of Anxiety Disorders, 7*, 271–280.

Haley, J. (1971). *Changing families: A family therapy reader*. New York: Grune & Stratton.

Haley, J. (1973). *Uncommon therapy: The psychiatric techniques of Milton H. Erickson, M.D.* New York: W. W. Norton.

Haley, J. (1976). *Problem-solving therapy*. San Francisco: Jossey-Bass.

Hamner, K. M., Lambert, E. W., & Bickman, L. (1997). Children's mental health in a continuum of care: Clinical outcomes at 18 months for the Fort Bragg Demonstration. *Journal of Mental Health Administration, 24*, 465–471.

Hanish, L. D., & Guerra, N. G. (2000). Children who get victimized at school: What is known? What can be done? *Professional School Counseling, 4*, 113–119.

Hardaway, T. G. (2000). Family play therapy and child psychiatry in an era of managed care. In H. G. Kaduson & C. E. Schaefer (Eds.), *Short-term play therapy for children* (pp. 256–265). New York: Guilford.

Hardesty, P. H., & Dillard, J. M. (1994). The role of elementary school counselors compared with their middle and secondary school counterparts. *Elementary School Guidance and Counseling, 29*, 83–91.

Harley, J. P., Ray, R. S., Tomasi, L., Eichman, P. L., Matthews, C. G., Chun, R., Cleeland, C. S., & Traisman, E. (1978). Hyperkinesis and food additives: Testing the Feingold hypothesis. *Pediatrics, 61*, 818–828.

Harris, J. R., & Liebert, R. M. (1991). *The child: A contemporary view of development* (3rd ed.). Upper Saddle River, NJ: Prentice Hall.

Harter, S. (1982). The Perceived Competence Scale for Children. *Child Development, 53*, 87–97.

Harter, S. (1983a). Developmental perspectives on the self-system. In E. M. Hetherington (Ed.), P. M. Mussen (Series Ed.), *Handbook of child psychology: Vol. 4, Socialization, personality, and social development* (pp. 275–385). New York: John Wiley.

Harter, S. (1983b). Cognitive-developmental considerations in the conduct of play therapy. In C. E. Schaefer & K. J. O'Connor (Eds.), *Handbook of play therapy* (pp. 95–127). New York: John Wiley.

Harter, S. (1985). *Manual for the Self-Perception Profile for Children*. Denver, CO: University of Denver.

Harter, S. (1986). Cognitive-developmental processes in the integration of concepts about emotions and the self. *Social Cognition, 4*, 119–151.

Harter, S. (1998). The development of self-representations. In W. Damon & N. Eisenberg (Eds.), *Handbook of child psychology. Social, emotional, and personality development* (5th ed.) (Vol. 3) (pp. 553–617). New York: John Wiley.

Harter, S., & Buddin, B. J. (1987). Children's understanding of the simultaneity of two emotions: A five-stage developmental acquisition sequence. *Developmental Psychology, 23*, 388–399.

Harter, S., & Pike, R. (1984). The pictorial scale of Perceived Competence and Social Acceptance for Young children. *Child Development, 55*, 1969–1982.

Hartman, A. (1978). Diagrammatic assessment of family relationships. *Social Casework, 59*, 465–476.

Hartman, A. (1979). *Finding families: An ecological approach to family assessment in adoption*. Beverly Hills, CA: Sage.

Hartup, W. W. (1996). The company they keep: Friendships and their developmental significance. *Child Development, 67*, 1–13.

Haslam, R. H. A. (1992). Is there a role for megavitamin therapy in the treatment of attention deficit hyperactivity disorder? In T. N. Chase, A. J. Friedhoff, & D. J. Cohen (Eds.), *Tourette syndrome: Genetics, neurobiology, and treatment. Advances in neurology.* (Vol. 58) (pp. 303–310). New York: Raven Press.

Haslett, B. B. (1997). The development of language. In B. B. Haslett & W. Samter (Eds.), *Children communicating: The first 5 years* (pp. 57–92). Mahwah, NJ: Lawrence Erlbaum.

Haviland-Jones, J., Gebelt, J. L., & Stapley, J. C. (1997). The questions of development in emotion. In P. Salovey & D. J. Sluyter (Eds.), *Emotional development and emotional intelligence* (pp. 223–253). New York: Basic Books.

Hayes, S. C. (1981). Single case experimental design and empirical clinical practice. *Journal of Consulting and Clinical Psychology, 49*, 193–211.

Hayghe, H. V. (1990). Family members in the work force. *Monthly Labor Review, 113(3)*, 14–19.

Hazell, P. O'Connell, D., Heathcote, D., Robertson, J., & Henry, D. (1995). Efficacy of tricyclic drugs on treating child and adolescent depression: A meta-analysis. *British Medical Journal, 310*, 897–901.

Hazelrigg, M. D., Cooper, H. M., & Borduin, C. M. (1987). Evaluating the effectiveness of family therapies: An integrative review and analysis. *Psychological Bulletin, 101*, 428–442.

Hazzard, A., King, H. E., & Webb, C. (1986). Group therapy with sexually abused adolescent girls. *American Journal of Psychotherapy, 40*, 213–223.

Heflinger, C. A., Sonnichsen, S. E., & Brannan, A. M. (1996). Parent satisfaction with children's mental health services in a children's mental health managed care demonstration. *Journal of Mental Health Administration, 23*, 69–79.

Heinicke, C. M., & Ramsey-Klee, D. M. (1986). Outcome of child psychotherapy as a function of frequency of session. *Journal of the American Academy of Child Psychiatry, 25*, 247–253.

Hektner, J. M., August, G. J., & Realmuto, G. M. (2000). Patterns and temporal changes in peer affiliation among aggressive and nonaggressive children participating in a summer school program. *Journal of Clinical Child Psychology, 29*, 603–614.

Helms, J. E., & Talleyrand, R. M. (1997). Race is not ethnicity. *American Psychologist, 52*, 1246–1247.

Helwig, A. A. (1998). Occupational aspirations of a longitudinal sample from second to sixth grade. *Journal of Career Development, 24*, 247–265.

Hembree-Kigin, T., & McNeil, C. (1995). *Parent-child interaction therapy: A step-by-step guide for clinicians.* New York: Plenum Press.

Hendrix, D. H. (1991). Ethics and intrafamily confidentiality in counseling with children. *Journal of Mental Health Counseling,* 13, 323–333.

Henggeler, S. W. (1994). A consensus: Conclusions of the APA task force report on innovative models of mental health services for children, adolescents, and their families. *Journal of Clinical Child Psychology, 23(Suppl.)*, 3–6.

Henggeler, S. W., & Borduin, C. M. (1990). *Family therapy and beyond: A multisystemic approach to treating the behavior problems of children and adolescents.* Pacific Grove, CA: Brooks/Cole.

Henggeler, S. W., Melton, G. B., Brondino, M. J., Scherer, D. G., & Hanley, J. H. (1997). Multisystemic therapy with violent and chronic juvenile offenders and their families: The role of treatment fidelity in successful dissemination. *Journal of Consulting and Clinical Psychology, 65*, 821–833.

Henggeler, S. W., Schoenwald, S. K., Borduin, C. M., Rowland, C. M., & Cunningham, P. B. (1998). *Multisystemic treatment of antisocial behavior in children and adolescents.* New York: Guilford.

Henggeler, S. W., Smith, B. H., & Schoenwald, S. K. (1994). Key theoretical and methodological issues in conducting treatment research in the juvenile justice system. *Journal of Clinical Child Psychology, 23*, 143–150.

Herlihy, B. (1998). Mandy: Out in the world. In L. B. Golden (Ed.), *Case studies in child and adolescent counseling* (2nd ed.) (pp. 60–69). Upper Saddle River, NJ: Merrill.

Hernandez, D. J. (1997). Child development and the social demography of childhood. *Child Development, 68*, 149–169.

Hersen, M., & Barlow, D. H. (1976). *Single case experimental design: Strategies for studying behavior change.* New York: Pergamon.

Hershenson, D. B., & Power, P. W. (1987). *Mental health counseling: Theory and practice.* London: Pergamon.

Hetherington, E. M., Cox, M., & Cox, R. (1979). Play and social interaction in children following divorce. *Journal of Social Issues, 35(4)*, 26–49.

Hetherington, E. M., Stanley-Hagan, M., & Anderson, E. R. (1989). Marital transitions: A child's perspective. *American Psychologist, 44*, 303–312.

Hibbs, E. D., & Jensen, P. S. (1996). Analyzing the research: What this book is about. In E. D. Hibbs & P. S. Jensen (Eds.), *Psychosocial treatments for child and adolescent disorders: Empirically based strategies for clinical practice* (pp. 3–8). Washington, DC: American Psychological Association.

Hines, P. M., & Boyd-Franklin, N. (1996). African American families. In M. McGoldrick, J. Giordano, & J. K. Pearce (Eds.), *Ethnicity and family therapy* (2nd ed.) (pp. 66–84). New York: Guilford.

Hinkle, J. S. (1993). Training school counselors to do family counseling. *Elementary School Guidance and Counseling, 27*, 252–257.

Hinshaw, S. P. (1996). Enhancing social competence: Integrating self-management strategies with behavioral procedures for children with ADHD. In E. D. Hibbs & P. S. Jensen (Eds.), *Psychosocial treatments for child and adolescent disorders: Empirically based strategies for clinical practice* (pp. 285–309). Washington, DC: American Psychological Association.

Hinshaw, S. P., Henker, B., Whalen, C. K., Erhardt, D., & Dunnington, R. E., Jr. (1989). Aggressive, prosocial, and nonsocial behavior in hyperactive boys: Dose effects of methylphenidate in naturalistic settings. *Journal of Consulting and Clinical Psychology, 57*, 636–643.

Ho, M. K. (1987). *Family therapy with ethnic minorities.* Newbury Park, CA: Sage.

Hoagwood, K. (1997). Interpreting nullity: The Fort Bragg experiment—A comparative success or failure? *American Psychologist, 52*, 546–550.

Hoagwood, K., Jensen, P. S., Petti, T., & Burns, B. J. (1996). Outcomes of mental health care for children and adolescents: I. A comprehensive conceptual model. *Journal of the American Academy of Child and Adolescent Psychiatry, 35*, 1055–1063.

Hoagwood, K., & Rupp, A. (1994). Mental health service needs, use, and costs for children and adolescents with mental disorders and their families: Preliminary evidence. In R. W. Mandersheid & M. A. Sonnenshein (Eds.), *Mental Health, United States, 1994* (pp. 52–64). (DHHS Publication N. SMA 94–3000). Washington, DC: U.S. Government Printing Office.

Hobbs, N. (1982). *The troubled and troubling child.* San Francisco, CA: Jossey-Bass.

Hodges, K. (1990). Depression and anxiety in children: A comparison of self-report questionnaires to clinical interviews. *Psychological Assessment, 2*, 376–381.

Hofferth, S. L., Shauman, K. A., & Henke, R. R. (1998). *Characteristics of children's early care and education programs: Data from the 1995 National Household Education Survey.* Washington, DC: U. S. Department of Education.

Hoffman, K. S. (1992). Should we support the continuum in social work education? Yes! *Journal of Social Work Education, 28*, 6–10.

Hoffman, L. (1988). A constructivist position for family therapy. *The Irish Journal of Psychology, 9*, 110–129.

Hoffman, L. R. (1991). Developmental counseling for prekindergarten children: A preventive approach. *Elementary School Guidance and Counseling, 26*, 56–66.

Holaday, M. Callahan, K., Fabre, L., Hall, C., MacDonald, N., Mundy, M., Owens, B., & Plappert, H. (1996). A comparison of culture-free self-esteem scale norms from different child and adolescent groups. *Journal of Personality Assessment, 66*, 540–554.

Holden, G., Bearison, D. J., Rode, D. C., Kapiloff, M. F., Rosenberg, G. (2000). The effects of a computer network on pediatric pain and anxiety. *Journal of Technology in Human Services, 17*, 27–47.

Holden, W. (1991). Prevention of child psychopathology. *The Child, Youth, and Family Services Quarterly, 14(l)*, 1–2.

Holland, J. L. (1997). *Making vocational choices: A theory of vocational personalities and work environments* (3rd ed.). Odessa, FL: Psychological Assessment Resources.

Holt, S. (2001). *The 18 ways (and then some)*. Retrieved from http://www.pbs. org/wgbh/nova/baby/18ways.html on February 14, 2002.

Hoover, D. W., & Milich, R. (1994). Effects of sugar ingestion expectancies on mother-child interactions. *Journal of Abnormal Child Psychology, 22*, 501–515.

Horney, K. (1967). *Feminine psychology*. New York: Norton.

Hotchkiss, L., & Borow, H. (1996). Sociological perspective on work and career development. In D. Brown & L. Brooks (Eds.), *Career choice and development* (3rd ed.) (pp. 281–334). San Francisco: Jossey-Bass.

House, A. E. (1999). *DSM-IV diagnosis in the schools*. New York: Guilford.

Houts, A. C., Berman, J. S., & Abramson, H. (1994). Effectiveness of psychological and pharmacological treatments for nocturnal enuresis. *Journal of Consulting and Clinical Psychology, 62*, 737–745.

Houts, A. C., & Peterson, J. K. (1986). Treatment of a retentive encopretic child using contingency management and diet modification with stimulus control. *Journal of Pediatric Psychology, 11*, 375–383.

Howard, B. L., & Kendall, P. C. (1996). Cognitive-behavioral family therapy for anxiety-disordered children: A multiple-baseline evaluation. *Cognitive Therapy and Research, 20*, 423–443.

Huang, L. N., & Ying, Y. (1989). Chinese American children and adolescents. In J. T. Gibbs & L. N. Huang (Eds.), *Children of color: Psychological interventions with minority youth* (pp. 30–66). San Francisco: Jossey-Bass.

Hudson, L. M., Forman, E. R., & Brion-Meisels, S. (1982). Role-taking as a predictor of prosocial behavior in cross-age tutors. *Child Development, 53*, 1320–1329.

Hudziak, J. J. (1998). *DSM-IV Checklist for Childhood Disorders*. Burlington, VT: University of Vermont, Research Center for Children, Youth, and Families.

Huesmann, L. R., Eron, L. D., Lefkowitz, M. M., & Walder, L. O. (1984). Stability of aggression over time and generations. *Developmental Psychology, 20*, 1120–1134.

Hug-Hellmuth, H. von. (1921). On the technique of child analysis. *International Journal of Psychoanalysis, 2*, 287–305.

Hughes, F. P., Noppe, L. D., & Noppe, I. C. (1996). *Child development*. Upper Saddle River, NJ: Prentice Hall.

Hughes, J. N., & Baker, D. B. (1990). *The clinical child interview*. New York: Guilford.

Hundley, R. J., & Cohen, R. (1999). Children's relationships with classmates: A comprehensive analysis of friendship nominations and liking. *Child Study Journal, 29*, 233–246.

Hungerford, A., Brownell, C. A., & Campbell, S. B. (2000). Child care in infancy: A transactional perspective. In C. H. Zeanah, Jr. (Ed.), *Handbook of infant mental health* (2nd ed.) (pp. 519–532). New York: Guilford.

Huntsinger, C. S., Jose, P. E., & Larson, S. L. (1998). Do parent practices to encourage academic competence influence the social adjustment of young European American and Chinese American children? *Developmental Psychology, 34*, 747–756.

Huston, A. C. (1983). Sex-typing. In E. M. Hetherington (Ed.), *Handbook of child psychology* (4th ed.) (Vol. 4) (pp. 387–469). New York: John Wiley.

Huston, A. C., McLoyd, V. C., & Garcia Coll, C. (1994). Children and poverty: Issues in contemporary research. *Child Development, 65*, 275–282.

Ibrahim, F., Ohnishi, H., & Sandhu, D. S. (1997). Asian American identity development: A culture specific model for South Asian Americans. *Journal of Multicultural Counseling and Development, 25*, 34–50.

Ingoldsby, E. M., Shaw, D. S., & Garcia, M. M. (2001). Intrafamily conflict in relation to boys' adjustment at school. *Development and Psychopathology, 13*, 35–52.

In re Gault, 387 U.S. 1 (1967).

Irwin, A. R., & Gross, A. M. (1995). Cognitive tempo, violent video games, and aggressive behavior in young boys. *Journal of Family Violence, 10*, 337–350.

Isabella, R., & Belsky, J. (1991). Interactional synchrony and the origins of infant-mother attachment: A replication study. *Child Development, 62*, 373–384.

Isabella, R., Belsky, J., von Eye, A. (1989). Origins of infant-mother attachment: An examination of interactional synchrony during the infant's first year. *Developmental Psychology, 25*, 12–21.

Ivey, A., & Simek-Downing, L. (1980). *Counseling and psychotherapy: Skills, theories, and practice*. Englewood Cliffs, NJ: Prentice-Hall.

Izard, C. E., & Malatesta, C. Z. (1987). Perspectives on emotional development I: Differential emotions theory of early emotional development. In J. D. Osofsky (Ed.), *Handbook of infant development* (2nd ed.) (pp. 494–554). New York: John Wiley.

Jacknow, D. S., Tschann, J. M., Link, M. P., & Boyce, W. T. (1994). Hypnosis in the prevention of chemotherapy-related nausea and vomiting in children: A prospective study. *Journal of Developmental and Behavioral Pediatrics, 15*, 258–264.

Jackson, D. D. (1968a). The question of family homeostasis. In D. D. Jackson (Ed.), *Communication, family, and marriage: Human communication*. (Vol. 1) (pp. 1–111). Palo Alto, CA: Science and Behavior Books.

Jackson, D. D. (1968b). Family interaction, family homeostasis and some implications for conjoint family psychotherapy. In D. D. Jackson (Ed.), *Therapy, communication, and change: Human communication*. (Vol. 2) (pp. 185–203). Palo Alto, CA: Science & Behavior Books.

Jacobs, J. H. (1992). Identity development in biracial children. In M. P. P. Root (Ed.), *Racially mixed people in America* (pp. 190–206). Newbury Park, CA: Sage.

Jacobson, S. W., & Frye, K. F. (1991). Effects of maternal support on attachment: Experimental evidence. *Child Development, 62*, 572–582.

James, R. K., & Myer, R. (1987). Puppets: The elementary school counselor's right or left arm. *Elementary School Guidance and Counseling, 21*, 292–299.

Jason, L. A., Hanaway, L. K., & Brackshaw, E. (1999). Television violence and children: Problems and solutions. In T. P. Gullotta & S. J. McElhaney (Eds.), *Violence in homes and communities: Prevention, intervention, and treatment* (pp. 133–156). Thousand Oaks, CA: Sage.

Jensen, P. S., Kettle, L., Roper, M. T., Sloan, M. T., Dulcan, M. K., Hoven, C., Bird, H. R., Bauermeister, J. J., & Payne, J. D. (1999). Are psychostimulants overprescribed? Treatment of ADHD in four U.S. communities. *Journal of the American Academy of Child and Adolescent Psychiatry, 38*, 797–804.

Jeske, R. J. (1985). Review of Piers-Harris Children's Self-Concept Scale (The Way I Feel About Myself). In J. V. Mitchell, Jr. (Ed.), *The Ninth Mental Measurements Yearbook, Vol. II*. (1169–1170). Lincoln, NE: The University of Nebraska Press.

Johnson, J. H., Rasbury, W. C., & Siegel, L. J. (1997). *Approaches to child treatment: Introduction to theory, research, and practice (2nd ed.)*. Boston: Allyn and Bacon.

Johnson, L. M., & Schwartz, R. C. (2000). Internal family systems work with children and families. In C. E. Bailey (Ed.), *Children in therapy: Using the family as a resource* (pp. 73–111). New York: W. W. Norton.

Johnson, L., McLeod, E. H., & Fall, M. (1997). Play therapy with labeled children in the schools. *Professional School Counseling, 1*, 31–34.

Johnson, R. C., & Nagoshi, C. T. (1986). The adjustment of offspring of within-group and interracial/intercultural marriage: A comparison of personality factor scores. *Journal of Marriage and the Family, 48*, 279–284.

Johnson, S. B. (1980). Enuresis. In R. Daitzman (Ed.), *Clinical behavior therapy and behavior modification* (pp. 81–142). New York: Garland Press.

Johnson, S. B. (1981). The behavioral assessment. In S. Gabel (Ed.), *Behavioral problems in childhood: A primary care approach* (pp. 51–66). New York: Grune & Stratton.

Johnson, S. B. (1994). Counseling with children: Comments from a child psychologist. *The Counseling Psychologist, 22,* 458–461.

Jones, E. (1955). Contributions to theory. *The life and work of Sigmund Freud* (Vol. 2) (pp. 310–331). New York: Basic Books.

Jones, M. C. (1924). A laboratory study of fear: The case of Peter. *The Pedagogical Seminary, 31,* 308–315.

Jones, R. A. (1997). The School Behaviour Game: Making "human sense" of the repertory grid in research with children. *British Journal of Guidance and Counselling, 25,* 399–407.

Jordan, D. R. (1998). *Attention deficit disorder: ADHD and ADD syndromes* (3rd ed.). Austin, TX: Pro-Ed.

Joyce, M. R. (1990). Rational-emotive parent consultation. *School Psychology Review, 19,* 304–314.

Juarez, R. (1985). Core issues in psychotherapy with the Hispanic child. *Psychotherapy, 22,* 441–448.

Jung, C. G. (1921/1971). *Psychological types: The collected works of C.G. Jung* (Vol. 6). Princeton, NJ: Princeton University Press.

Jung, C. G. (1928/1954). Child development and education. In *The Development of Personality, The collected works of C. G. Jung* (Vol. 17) (pp. 47–62). Princeton, NJ: Princeton University Press.

Jung, C. G. (1931/1969). Analytical psychology and *Weltauschauung.* In *The structure and dynamics of the psyche (2nd ed.), The collected works of C.G. Jung* (Vol. 8) (pp. 358–381). Princeton, NJ: Princeton University Press.

Jung, C. G. (1935/1976). The Tavistock lectures. In *The symbolic life, The collected works of C.G. Jung* (Vol. 18) (pp. 5–182). Princeton, NJ: Princeton University Press.

Jung, C. G. (1948/1969). Instinct and the unconscious. In *The structure and dynamics of the psyche, The collected works of C.G. Jung* (2nd ed.) (Vol. 8) (pp. 129–138). Princeton, NJ: Princeton University Press.

Jung, C. G. (1954/1969). Archetypes of the collective unconscious. In *The archetypes and the collective unconscious, The collected works of C.G. Jung* (Vol. 9, pt. 1) (pp. 3–41). Princeton, NJ: Princeton University Press.

Jung, C. G. (1956). *Symbols of transformation: An analysis of the prelude to a case of schizophrenia, The collected works of C.G. Jung (Vol. 5).* Princeton, NJ: Princeton University Press.

Jung, C. G. (1963). *Memories, dreams, and reflections.* New York: Pantheon Books.

Kachur, S. P., Stennies, G. M., Powell, K. E., Modzeleski, W., Stephens, R., Murphy, R., Kresnow, M., Sleet, D., & Lowry, R. (1996). School-associated violent deaths in the United States, 1992 to 1994. *Journal of the American Medical Association, 275,* 1729–1733.

Kaczkowski, H., & Patterson, C. H. (1975). *Counseling and psychology in elementary schools.* Springfield, IL: Charles C. Thomas.

Kaczmarek, P. G., & Wagner, W. G. (1994). Future training requirements for counseling psychologists: Competence with children. *The Counseling Psychologist, 22,* 426– 443.

Kafantaris, V., Campbell, M., Padron-Gayol, M. V., Small, A. M., Locascio, J. J., & Rosenberg, C. R. (1992). Carbamazepine in hospitalized aggressive conduct disorder children: An open pilot study. *Psychopharmacology Bulletin, 28,* 193–199.

Kagan, J. (1965). The new marriage: Pediatrics and psychology. *American Journal of Diseases of Childhood, 110,* 272–278.

Kail, R. (1991). Developmental change in speed of processing during childhood and adolescence. *Psychological Bulletin, 109,* 490–501.

Kail, R. V. (1998). *Children and their development.* Upper Saddle River, NJ: Prentice Hall.

Kail, R. V., & Park, Y. (1994). Processing time, articulation time, and memory span. *Journal of Experimental Child Psychology, 57,* 281–291.

Kalff, D. M. (1980). *Sandplay: A psychotherapeutic approach to the psyche.* Boston, MA: Sigo Press.

Kalichman, S. C., Craig, M. E., & Follingstad, D. R. (1989). Factors influencing the reporting of father-child sexual abuse: Study of licensed practicing psychologists. *Professional Psychology: Research and Practice, 20,* 84–89.

Kamphaus, R. W., & Frick, P. J. (1996). *Clinical assessment of child and adolescent personality and behavior.* Needham Heights, MA: Allyn and Bacon.

Kanfer, F. H., & Gaelick-Buys, L. (1991). Self-management techniques. In F. H. Kanfer & A. P. Goldstein (Eds.), *Helping people change: A textbook of methods* (pp. 305–360). New York: Pergamon.

Kanfer, F. H., Karoly, P., & Newman, A. (1975). Reduction of children's fear of the dark by competence-related and situational threat-related verbal cues. *Journal of Consulting and Clinical Psychology, 43,* 251–258.

Kaplan, J. S. (1991). *Beyond behavior modification: A cognitive-behavioral approach to behavior management in the school* (2nd ed.). Austin, TX: Pro-Ed.

Kaplan, L. (1986). *Working with multiproblem families.* New York: Lexington Books.

Kaplan, P. S. (2000). *A child's odyssey* (3rd ed.). Belmont, CA: Wadsworth.

Karcher, M. J., & Nakkula, M. J. (1997). Multicultural pair counseling and the development of expanded worldviews. In R. L. Selman, C. L. Watts, & L. H. Schultz (Eds.), *Fostering friendship: Pair therapy for treatment and prevention* (pp. 207–227). New York: De Gruyter.

Karoly, P. (1995). Self-control theory. In W. O'Donohue & L. Krasner (Eds.), *Theories of behavior therapy: Exploring behavior change* (pp. 259–285). Washington, DC: American Psychological Association.

Kaser-Boyd, N., Adelman, H. S., Taylor, L., & Nelson, P. (1986). Children's understanding of risks and benefits of psychotherapy. *Journal of Clinical Child Psychology, 15,* 165–171.

Kashani, J., & Simonds, J. F. (1979). The incidence of depression in children. *American Journal of Psychiatry, 136,* 1203–1205.

Katz, E. R., Kellerman, J., & Ellenberg, L. (1987). Hypnosis in the reduction of acute pain and distress in children with cancer. *Journal of Pediatric Psychology, 12,* 379–394.

Katz, P. A., & Kofkin, J. A. (1997). Race, gender, and young children. In S. S. Luthar, J. A. Burack, D. Cicchetti, & J. R. Weisz (Eds.), *Developmental psychopathology: Perspectives on adjustment, risk, and disorder* (pp. 51–74). New York: Cambridge University Press.

Kazdin, A. E. (1982). *Single-case research design: Methods for clinical and applied settings.* New York: Oxford University Press.

Kazdin, A. E. (1993). Psychotherapy for children and adolescents: Current progress and future research directions. *American Psychologist, 48,* 644–657.

Kazdin, A. E. (1994a). Psychotherapy for children and adolescents. In A. E. Bergin & S. L. Garfield (Eds.), *Handbook of psychotherapy and behavior change* (4th ed.) (pp. 543–594). New York: John Wiley.

Kazdin, A. E. (1994b). *Behavior modification in applied settings* (5th ed.). Pacific Grove, CA: Brooks/Cole.

Kazdin, A. E., Bass, D., Ayers, W. A., & Rodgers, A. (1990). Empirical and clinical focus of child and adolescent psychotherapy research. *Journal of Consulting and Clinical Psychology, 58,* 729–740.

Kazdin, A. E., Siegel, T. C., & Bass, D. (1990). Drawing upon clinical practice to inform research on child and adolescent psychotherapy: A survey of practitioners. *Professional Psychology: Research and Practice, 21,* 189–198.

Keat, D. B. (1978). Multimodal evolution. *Elementary School Guidance and Counseling, 13,* 12–15.

Keat, D. B. (1979). *Multimodal therapy with children.* New York: Pergamon.

Keat, D. B. (1990). *Child multimodal therapy.* Norwood, NJ: Ablex.

Keating, D. P. (1990). Adolescent thinking. In S. Feldman & G. R. Elliott (Eds.), *At the threshold: The developing adolescent* (pp. 54–89). Cambridge, MA: Harvard University Press.

Kellam, S. G., Rebok, G. W., Ialongo, N., & Mayer, L. S. (1994). The course and malleability of aggressive behavior from early first grade into middle school: Results of a developmental epidemiologically-based preventive trial. *Journal of Child Psychology and Psychiatry and Allied Disciplines, 35,* 259–281.

Keller, A., Ford, L. H., & Meacham, J. A. (1978). Dimensions of self-concept in preschool children. *Developmental Psychology, 14,* 483–489.

Keller, F. S., & Sherman, J. G. (1982). *The PSI handbook: Essays on personalized instruction.* Lawrence, KS: TRI Publications.

Keller, M., & Wood, P. (1989). Development of friendship reasoning: A study of interindividual differences and intraindividual change. *Developmental Psychology, 25,* 820–826.

Kelley, M. L., Power, T. G., & Wimbush, D. D. (1992). Determinants of disciplinary practices in low-income black mothers. *Child Development, 63,* 573–582.

Kellogg, R. (1955). *What children scribble and why.* Palo Alto, CA: N-P Publications.

Kelly, F. D. (1999). Adlerian approaches to counseling with children and adolescents. In H. T. Prout & D. T. Brown (Eds.), *Counseling and psychotherapy with children and adolescents: Theory and practice for school and clinical settings* (3rd ed.). (pp. 108–154). New York: John Wiley.

Kelly, G. A. (1955). *The psychology of personal constructs.* New York: Norton.

Kendall, P. C. (1991). Guiding theory for treating children and adolescents. In P. C. Kendall (Ed.), *Child and adolescent therapy: Cognitive-behavioral procedures* (pp. 3–24). New York: Guilford Press.

Kendall, P. C. (1992). *Coping cat workbook.* Ardmore, PA: Workbook Publishing.

Kendall, P. C. (1993). Cognitive-behavioral therapies with youth: Guiding theory, current status, and emerging developments. *Journal of Consulting and Clinical Psychology, 61,* 235–247.

Kendall, P. C. (1994). Treating anxiety disorders in children: Results of a randomized clinical trial. *Journal of Consulting and Clinical Psychology, 62,* 100–110.

Kendall, P. C. (1998). Empirically supported psychological therapies. *Journal of Consulting and Clinical Psychology, 66,* 3–6.

Kendall, P. C., & Treadwell, K. R. H. (1993). Overanxious disorders. In R. T. Ammerman, C. G. Last, & M. Hersen (Eds.), *Handbook of prescriptive treatments for children and adolescents* (pp. 159–177). Boston: Allyn and Bacon.

Kendall, P. C., & Treadwell, K. R. H. (1996). Cognitive-behavioral treatment for childhood anxiety disorders. In E. D. Hibbs & P. S. Jensen (Eds.), *Psychosocial treatments for child and adolescent disorders: Empirically based strategies for clinical practice* (pp. 23–41). Washington, DC: American Psychological Association.

Kernberg, P. F., & Chazan, S. E. (1991). *Children with conduct disorders: A psychotherapy manual.* New York: Basic Books.

Kerwin, C., Ponterotto, J. G., Jackson, B. C., & Harris, A. (1993). Racial identity in biracial children: A qualitative investigation. *Journal of Counseling Psychology, 40,* 221–231.

Kestenbaum, C. (1985). The creative process in child psychotherapy. *American Journal of Psychotherapy, 39,* 479–489.

Kilpatrick, A. C., & Kilpatrick, Jr., E. G. (1991). Object relations family therapy. In A. M. Horne & J. L. Passmore (Eds.), *Family counseling and therapy* (2nd ed.) (pp. 207–234). Itasca, IL: F. E. Peacock Publishers.

Kim, S. C. (1985). Family therapy for Asian Americans: A strategic structural framework. *Psychotherapy, 22,* 342–348.

Kimmel, S. R., & Chessare, J. (1994). Selected problems of infancy and childhood. In R. B. Taylor (Ed.), *Family medicine: Principles and practice* (4th ed.) (pp. 152–161). New York: Springer-Verlag.

King, H. E. (1992). The reactions of children to divorce. In C. E. Walker & M. C. Roberts (Eds.), *Handbook of clinical child psychology* (2nd ed.) (pp. 1009–1023). New York: John Wiley.

King, N. J. (1993). Physiological assessment. In T. H. Ollendick & M. Hersen (Eds.), *Handbook of child and adolescent assessment* (pp. 180–191). Needham Heights, MA: Allyn and Bacon.

Kinney, J., Haapala, D., & Booth, C. (1991). *Keeping families together: The homebuilders model.* New York: Aldine de Gruyter.

Kinsbourne, M. (1994). Sugar and the hyperactive child. *The New England Journal of Medicine, 330,* 355–356.

Kirschner, S., & Kirschner, D. A. (1993). Couples and families. In G. Stricker & J. R. Gold (Eds.), *Comprehensive handbook of psychotherapy integration* (pp. 401–412). New York: Plenum.

Kistner, J., Metzler, A., Gatlin, D., & Risi, S. (1993). Classroom racial proportions and children's peer relations: Race and gender effects. *Journal of Educational Psychology, 85,* 446–452.

Kizner, L. R., & Kizner, S. R. (1999). Small group counseling with adopted children. *Professional School Counseling, 2,* 226–229.

Klein, M. (1921/1975). The development of a child. In M. Klein, *Love, guilt, and reparation and other works 1921–1945* (pp. 1–53). London: Hogarth Press.

Klein, M. (1927/1975). Symposium on child-analysis. In M. Klein, *Love, guilt, and reparation and other works 1921–1945* (pp. 139–169). London: Hogarth Press.

Klein, M. (1932/1959). *The psycho-analysis of children.* London: Hogarth Press.

Klein, M. (1955/1975). The psycho-analytic play technique: Its history and significance. In M. Klein, *Envy and gratitude and other works 1921–1945* (pp. 122–140). London: Hogarth Press.

Klein, M. (1984). *Narrative of a child analysis: The conduct of psycho-analysis of children as seen in the treatment of a ten-year-old boy.* New York: The Free Press.

Klein, R. G., Abikoff, H., Klass, E., Ganeles, D. Seese, L. M., Pollack, S. (1997). Clinical efficacy of methylphenidate in conduct disorder with and without attention deficit hyperactivity disorder. *Archives of General Psychiatry, 54,* 1073–1080.

Klein, R. G., Koplewicz, H. S., & Kanner, A. (1992). Imipramine treatment of children with separation anxiety disorder. *Journal of the American Academy of Child and Adolescent Psychiatry, 31,* 21–28.

Kleinpeter, C. H., & Hohman, M. M. (2000). Surrogate motherhood: Personality traits and satisfaction with service providers. *Psychological Reports, 87,* 957–970.

Kline, P. (1984). *Psychology and Freudian theory: An introduction.* London: Methuen.

Knell, S. M. (1998). Cognitive-behavioral play therapy. *Journal of Clinical Child Psychology, 27,* 28–33.

Knell, S. M. (2000). Cognitive-behavioral play therapy for childhood fears and phobias. In H. G. Kaduson & C. E. Schaefer (Eds.), *Short-term play therapy for children* (pp. 3–27). New York: Guilford.

Knell, S. M., & Moore, D. J. (1990). Cognitive-behavioral play therapy in the treatment of encopresis. *Journal of Clinical Child Psychology, 19,* 55–60.

Knell, S. M., & Ruma, C. D. (1996). Play therapy with a sexually abused child. In M. A. Reinecke, F. M. Dattilio, & A. Freeman (Eds.), *Cognitive therapy with children and adolescents: A casebook for clinical practice* (pp. 367–393). New York: Guilford.

Knitzer, J., Steinberg, Z., & Fleisch, B. (1990). *At the schoolhouse door: An examination of programs and policies for children with behavioral and emotional problems.* New York: Bank Street College of Education.

Knoff, H. M. (1986). *The assessment of child and adolescent personality.* New York: Guilford.

Koeppen, A. S. (1974). Relaxation training for children. *Elementary School Guidance and Counseling, 9,* 14–21.

Kohen, D. P. (1997). Teaching children with asthma to help themselves with relaxation/mental imagery. In W. J. Matthews & J. H. Edgette (Eds.), *Current thinking and research in brief therapy: Solutions, strategies, narratives* (Vol. 1) (pp. 169–191). New York: Brunner/Mazel.

Kohlberg, L. (1976). Moral stages and moralization: The cognitive-developmental approach. In T. Lickona (Ed.), *Moral developmental and behavior* (pp. 31–53). New York: Holt, Rinehart & Winston.

Kolevzon, M. S., & Green, R. G. (1985). *Family therapy models: Convergence and divergence.* New York: Springer Publishing Co.

Kolvin, I., & Taunch, J. (1973). A dual theory of nocturnal enuresis. In I. Kolvin, R. C. Mac Keith, & S. R. Meadow (Eds.), *Bladder control and enuresis. Clinics in developmental medicine* Nos. 48/49 (pp. 156–172). Philadelphia: J. B. Lippincott.

Konarski, E. A., & Spruill, J. (1987). Theoretical approaches to assessment and treatment. In C. L. Frame & J. L. Matson (Eds.), *Handbook of assessment in childhood psychopathology: Applied issues in differential diagnosis and treatment evaluation* (pp. 13–32). New York: Plenum Press.

Kongstvedt, P. R. (Ed.). (1997). *Essentials of managed health care* (2nd ed.). Gaithersburg, MD: Aspen Publishers.

Koocher, G. P. (1995). Managed care: Hidden benefits or delusional thinking? *Professional Psychology: Research and Practice, 26*, 630–631.

Koocher, G. P., & Keith-Spiegel, P. (1998). *Ethics in psychology: Professional standards and cases* (2nd ed.). New York: Oxford University Press.

Koppitz, E. M. (1968). *Psychological evaluation of children's human figure drawings*. New York: Grune & Stratton.

Koppitz, E. M. (1983). Projective drawings with children and adolescents. *School Psychology Review, 12*, 421–427.

Koss, M. P., & Shiang, J. (1994). Research on brief psychotherapy. In A. E. Bergin & S. L. Garfield (Eds.), *Handbook of psychotherapy and behavior change* (4th ed.) (pp. 664–700). New York: John Wiley.

Kovacs, M. (1992). *Children's Depression Inventory manual*. North Tonawanda, NY: Multi-Health Systems, Inc.

Kramer, D. T. (1994) *Legal rights of children* (2nd ed.) (Vol. I). New York: McGraw- Hill.

Kraus, I. (1998). A fresh look at school counseling: A family-systems approach. *Professional School Counseling, 1(4)*, 12–17.

Krcmar, M., & Cooke, M. C. (2001). Children's moral reasoning and their perceptions of television violence. *Journal of Communication, 51*, 300–316.

Krickeberg, S. K. (1991). Away from Walton Mountain: Bibliographies for today's troubled youth. *The School Counselor, 39*, 52–56.

Kronenberger, W. G., & Meyer, R. G. (1996). *The child clinician's handbook*. Boston: Allyn and Bacon.

Krop, H., & Burgess, D. (1993). The use of covert modeling in the treatment of a sexual abuse victim. In J. R. Cautela & A. J. Kearney (Eds.), *Covert conditioning casebook* (pp. 153–158). Pacific Grove, CA: Brooks/Cole.

Kupersmidt, J. B., DeRosier, M. E., & Patterson, C. P. (1995). Similarity as the basis for children's friendships: The roles of sociometric status, aggressive and withdrawn behavior, academic achievement and demographic characteristics. *Journal of Social and Personal Relationships, 12*, 439–452.

Kurdek, L. A., & Krile, D. (1982). A developmental analysis of the relation between peer acceptance and both interpersonal understanding and perceived social self-competence. *Child Development, 53*, 1485–1491.

Kurz, D. (1991). Corporal punishment and adult use of violence: A critique of "Discipline and deviance." *Social Problems, 38*, 155–161.

Kush, K., & Cochran, L. (1993). Enhancing a sense of agency through career planning. *Journal of Counseling Psychology, 40*, 434–439.

Kutcher, S. P. (1999). Pharmacotherapy of depression: A review of current evidence and practical clinical directions. In C. A. Essau & F. Petermann (Eds.), *Depressive disorders in children and adolescents: Epidemiology, risk factors, and treatment* (pp. 437–458). Northvale, NJ: Jason Aronson.

LaBaw, J. L., & LaBaw, W. L. (1990). Self-hypnosis and hypnotherapy with children. In R. P. Zahourek (Ed.), *Clinical hypnosis and therapeutic suggestion in patient care* (pp. 127–153). New York: Brunner/Mazel.

Lachar, D. (1982). *Personality Inventory for Children (PIC) revised format manual supplement*. Los Angeles, CA: Western Psychological Services.

Ladd, G. W. (1990). Having friends, keeping friends, making friends, and being liked by peers in the classroom: Predictors of children's early school adjustment? *Child Development, 61*, 1081–1100.

Ladd, G. W., Kochenderfer, B. J., & Coleman, C. C. (1996). Friendship quality as a predictor of young children's early school adjustment. *Child Development, 67*, 1103–1118.

LaFromboise, T. D., & Low, K. G. (1989). American Indian children and adolescents. In J. T. Gibbs & L. N. Huang (Eds.), *Children of color: Psychological interventions with minority youth* (pp. 114–147). San Francisco: Jossey-Bass.

LaGreca, A. M. (1985). Rules and responsibilities of clinical child psychologists: Boundary issues. In J. M. Tuma (Ed.), *Proceedings: Conference on training clinical child psychologists* (pp. 38–39). Washington, DC: American Psychological Association.

LaGreca, A. M., & Santogrossi, D. A. (1980). Social skills training with elementary school students: A behavioral group approach. *Journal of Consulting and Clinical Psychology, 48*, 220–227.

Lamb, M. (1994). Infant care practices and the application of knowledge. In C. B. Fisher & R. M. Lerner (Eds.), *Applied developmental psychology* (pp. 23–45). New York: McGraw-Hill.

Lamb, M. E. (Ed.). (1987). *The father's role: Cross-cultural perspectives*. Hillsdale, NJ: Lawrence Erlbaum.

Lamborn, S. D., Mounts, N. S., Steinberg, L., & Dornbusch, S. M. (1991). Patterns of competence and adjustment among adolescents from authoritative, authoritarian, indulgent, and neglectful families. *Child Development, 62*, 1049–1065.

Landisberg, S., & Snyder, W. U. (1946). Nondirective play therapy. *Journal of Clinical Psychology, 2*, 203–214.

Landreth, G. (1991). *Play therapy: The art of the relationship*. Muncie, IN: Accelerated Development.

Landreth, G. (2000). *Play therapy training directory* (4th ed.). Denton, TX: Center for Play Therapy.

Landreth, G., & Sweeney, D. (1997). Child-centered play therapy. In K. O'Connor & L. M. Braverman (Eds.), *Play therapy theory and practice: A comparative presentation* (pp. 17–45). New York: John Wiley.

Landsman, T. (1974). The humanizer. *American Journal of Orthopsychiatry, 44*, 345–352.

Lang, P. J., & Melamed, B. C. (1969). Case report: Avoidance conditioning therapy of an infant with chronic ruminative vomiting. *Journal of Abnormal Psychology, 74*, 1–8.

Langs, R. (Ed.). (1981). *Classics in psychoanalytic technique*. New York; Jason Aronson.

Lansford, J. E., & Parker, J. G. (1999). Children's interactions in triads: Behavioral profiles and effects of gender and patterns of friendship among members. *Developmental Psychology, 35*, 80–93.

Larkin, R., & Thyer, B. A. (1999). Evaluating cognitive-behavioral group counseling to improve elementary school students' self-esteem, self-control, and classroom behavior. *Behavioral Interventions, 14*, 147–161.

Lavelle, L. (1998). *Practical charts for managing behavior*. Austin: Pro-ed.

Lazar, A., & Torney-Purta, J. (1991). The development of the subconcepts of death In young children: A short-term longitudinal study. *Child Development, 62*, 1321–1333.

Lazarus, A. A. (1967). In support of technical eclecticism. *Psychological Reports, 21*, 415–416.

Lazarus, A. A. (Ed.). (1976). *Multimodal behavior therapy*. New York: Springer.

Lazarus, A. A., & Abramovitz, A. (1962). The use of "emotive imagery" in the treatment of children's phobias, *Journal of Mental Science, 108*, 191–195.

Lazarus, A. A., & Beutler, L. E. (1993). On technical eclecticism. *Journal of Counseling and Development, 71*, 381–385.

Lebo, D. (1952). The relationship of response categories in play therapy to chronological age. *Journal of Child Psychiatry, 2*, 330–336.

Lebo, D. (1953). The present status of research on nondirective play therapy. *Journal of Consulting Psychology, 17*, 177–183.

Lecanuet, J.-P., Granier-Deferre, C., & Busnel, M.-C. (1995). Human fetal auditory perception. In J.-P. Lecanuet, W. P. Fifer, N. A. Krasnegor, & W. P. Smotherman (Eds.), *Fetal development: A psychobiological perspective* (pp. 239–262). Hillsdale, NJ: Lawrence Erlbaum.

Lechtenberg, R. (1984). *Epilepsy and the family*. Cambridge, MA: Harvard University Press.

Lee, C. C. (1995). School counseling and cultural diversity: A framework for effective practice. In C. C. Lee (Ed.), *Counseling for diversity: A guide for school counselors and related professionals* (pp. 3–17). Boston: Allyn and Bacon.

Lee, E. (1997). Overview: The assessment and treatment of Asian American families. In E. Lee (Ed.), *Working with Asian Americans: A guide for clinicians* (pp. 3–36). New York: Guilford.

Lee, M-Y. (1997). A study of solution-focused brief family therapy: Outcomes and issues. *The American Journal of Family Therapy, 25(1),* 3–17.

Lee, R. E., & Sturkie, K. (1997). The national marital and family therapy examination program. *Journal of Marital and Family Therapy, 23,* 255–269.

Lee, W. M. L. (1999). *An introduction to multicultural counseling.* Philadelphia, PA: Accelerated Development.

LeFever, G. B., Morrow, A., & Dawson, K. (1999). The extent of drug therapy for attention deficit-hyperactivity disorder among children in public schools. *American Journal of Public Health, 89,* 1359–1364.

Lefkowitz, M. M., & Tesiny, E. P. (1985). Depression in children: Prevalence and correlates. *Journal of Consulting and Clinical Psychology, 53,* 647–656.

Leiblum, S. R. (1997). Introduction. In S. R. Leiblum (Ed.), *Infertility: Psychological issues and counseling strategies* (pp. 3–19). New York: John Wiley.

LeMare, L. J., & Rubin, K. H. (1987). Perspective taking and peer interaction: Structural and developmental analyses. *Child Development, 58,* 306–315.

Leonard, H. L., Swedo, S. E., Rapoport, J. L., Koby, E. V., Lenane, M. C., Cheslow, D. L., & Hamburger, S. D. (1989). Treatment of obsessive-compulsive disorder with clomipramine and desipramine in children and adolescents: A double-blind crossover comparison. *Archives of General Psychiatry, 46,* 1088–1092.

Lepore, S. J., & Sesco, B. (1994). Disturbing children's reports and interpretations of events through suggestion. *Journal of Applied Psychology, 79,* 108–120.

Leslie, L. A., Ettenson, R., & Cumsille, P. (2000). Selecting a child care center: What really matters to parents? *Child and Youth Care Forum, 29,* 299–322.

Lester, E. P. (1975). Language behavior and child psychotherapy. *Canadian Psychiatric Association Journal, 20,* 175–181.

Levant, R. F. (Ed.). (1986). *Psychoeducational approaches to family therapy and counseling.* New York: Springer.

Levine, M., & Levine, A. (1992). *Helping children: A social history.* New York: Oxford University Press.

Levitt, E. E. (1957). The results of psychotherapy with children: An evaluation. *Journal of Consulting Psychology, 21,* 189–196.

Levitt, E. E., & French, J. (1992). Projective testing with children. In C. E. Walker & M. C. Roberts (Eds.), *Handbook of clinical child psychology* (2nd ed.) (pp. 149–162). New York: John Wiley.

Levitt, E. E., Beiser, H. R., & Robertson, R. E. (1959). A follow-up evaluation of cases treated at a community child guidance clinic. *American Journal of Orthopsychiatry, 29,* 337–349.

Lewis, M., & Brooks, J. (1974). Self, other, and fear: Infants' reactions to people. In H. Lewis & L. Rosenblum (Eds.), *The origins of fear: The origins of behavior* (Vol. 2) (pp. 195–227). New York: John Wiley.

Lewis, M., & Brooks-Gunn, J. (1979). *Social cognition and the acquisition of self.* New York: Plenum.

Licht, B. G., & Dweck, C. S. (1984). Determinants of academic achievement: The interaction of children's achievement orientations with skill area. *Developmental Psychology, 20,* 628–636.

Lieberman, E. J. (1985). *Acts of will: The life and work of Otto Rank.* New York: Free Press.

Light, P., & Barnes, P. (1995). Development in drawing. In V. Lee & P. das Gupta (Eds.), *Children's cognitive and language development* (pp. 231–268). Oxford, UK: Blackwell Publishers.

Likierman, M. (1995). The debate between Anna Freud and Melanie Klein: An historical survey. *Journal of Child Psychotherapy, 21,* 313–325.

Lin, C. C., & Fu, V. R. (1990). A comparison of child-rearing practices among Chinese, immigrant Chinese, and Caucasian-American parents. *Child Development, 61,* 429–433.

Lindahl, K. M., & Malik, N. M. (1999). Marital conflict, family processes, and boys' externalizing behavior in Hispanic American and European American families. *Journal of Clinical Child Psychology, 28,* 12–24.

Linehan, M. M., Goodstein, J. L., Neilsen, S. L., & Chiles, J. A. (1983). Reasons for staying alive when you are thinking about killing yourself: The Reasons for Living Inventory. *Journal of Consulting and Clinical Psychology, 51,* 276–286.

Lobovits, D. A., & Handal, P. J. (1985). Childhood depression: Prevalence using DSM-II criteria and validity of parent and child depression scales. *Journal of Pediatric Psychology, 10,* 45–54.

Lockhart, E. J., & Keys, S. G. (1998). The mental health counseling role of school counselors. *Professional School Counseling, 1(4),* 3–6.

Lonigan, C. J., Elbert, J. C., & Johnson, S. B. (1998). Empirically supported psychosocial interventions for children: An overview. *Journal of Clinical Child Psychology, 27,* 138–145.

Looft, W. R. (1971). Sex differences in the expression of vocational aspirations of elementary school children. *Developmental Psychology, 5,* 366.

Loving v. Virginia, 388 U.S. 1 (1967).

Lowery v. Collins, 988 F.2d 1364 (5th Cir. 1993).

Lubin, B., Larsen, R. M., & Matarazzo, J. D. (1984). Patterns of psychological test usage in the United States: 1935–1982. *American Psychologist, 39,* 451–454.

Luck, H. E. (1997). Psychoanalysts in caricatures. In W. G. Bringmann, H. E. Luck, R. Miller, & C. E. Early (Eds.), *A pictorial history of psychology* (pp. 413–415). Chicago: Quintessence Publishing.

Luepnitz, D. A. (1988). *The family interpreted: Feminist theory in clinical practice.* New York: Basic Books.

Luiselli, J. K., & Greenridge, A. (1982). Behavioral treatment of high-rate aggression in a rubella child. *Journal of Behavior Therapy and Experimental Psychiatry, 13,* 152–157.

Lundervold, D. A., & Belwood, M. F. (2000). The best kept secret in counseling: Single-case (N = 1) experimental designs. *Journal of Counseling and Development, 78,* 92–102.

Lyddon, W. J. (1993). Developmental constructivism: An integrative framework for psychotherapy practice. *Journal of Cognitive Psychotherapy, 7,* 217–224.

Lyddon, W. J. (1995). Forms and facets of constructivist psychology. In R. A. Neimeyer & M. J. Mahoney (Eds.), *Constructivism in psychotherapy* (pp. 69–92). Washington, DC: American Psychological Association.

Lytton, H., Watts, D., & Dunn, B. E. (1988). Continuity and change in child characteristics and maternal practices between ages 2 and 9: An analysis of interview responses. *Child Study Journal, 18(1),* 1–15.

Maccoby, E. E. (1992). The role of parents in the socialization of children: An historical overview. *Developmental Psychology, 28,* 1006–1017.

Maccoby, E. E. (1998). *The two sexes: Growing up apart, coming together.* Cambridge, MA: Harvard University Press.

Maccoby, E. E. (1999). The uniqueness of the parent-child relationship. In W. A. Collins & B. Laursen (Eds.), *Relationships as developmental contexts* (pp. 157–175). Mahwah, NJ: Lawrence Erlbaum.

Maccoby, E. E., & Martin, J. A. (1983). Socialization in the context of the family: Parent-child interaction. In E. M. Hetherington (Ed.), *Handbook of Child Psychology: Socialization, personality, and social development* (4th ed., pp. 1–101). New York: John Wiley.

MacFarlane, J. W., Allen, L, & Honzik, M. P. (1954). *A developmental study of the behavior problems of normal children between 21 months and 14 years.* Berkeley CA: University of California Press.

MacGregor, R. R., Nelson, J. R., & Wesch, D. (1997). Creating positive learning environments: The school-wide student management program. *Professional School Counseling, 1,* 33–35.

MacLean, G. (1986). Hermine Hug-Hellmuth: A neglected pioneer in child psychoanalysis. *Journal of the American Academy of Child Psychiatry, 25,* 579–580.

Madanes, C. (1981). *Strategic family therapy.* San Francisco: Jossey-Bass.

Main, M., & Cassidy, J. (1988). Categories of response to reunion with the parent at age 6: Predictable from attachment classifications and stable over a 1-month period. *Developmental Psychology, 24,* 415–426.

Main, M., & Solomon, J. (1986). Discovery of an insecure-disorganized/disoriented attachment pattern. In T. B. Brazelton & M. Yogman (Eds.), *Affective development in infancy* (pp. 95–124). Norwood, NJ: Ablex.

Maital, S. L. (1996). Integration of behavioral and mental health consultation as a means of overcoming resistance. *Journal of Educational and Psychological Consultation, 7,* 291–303.

Major, B., Barr, L., Zubek, J., & Babey, S. H. (1999). Gender and self-esteem: A meta-analysis. In W. B. Swann, Jr., J. H. Langlois, & L. A. Gilbert (Eds.), *Sexism and stereotypes in modern society: The gender science of Janet Taylor Spence* (pp. 223–253). Washington, DC: American Psychological Association.

Malgady, R. G., Costantino, G., & Rogler, L. H. (1984). Development of a Thematic Apperception Test (TEMAS) for urban Hispanic children. *Journal of Clinical and ConsultingPsychology, 52,* 986–996.

Malina, R. M. (1990). Physical growth and development during the transitional years (9–16). In R. Montemayer, G. R. Adams, & T. P. Gullotta (Eds.), *From childhood to adolescence: A transitional period* (pp. 41–62). Newbury Park, CA: Sage.

Mandler, J. (1983). Representation. In P. H. Mussen (Ed.), *Handbook of child psychology: Vol. 3. Cognitive development* (pp. 420–494). New York: John Wiley.

Mandoki, M. W., Tapia, M. R., Tapia, M. A., Sumner, G. S., & Parker, J. L. (1997). Venlafaxine in the treatment of children and adolescents with major depression. *Psychopharmacology Bulletin, 33,* 149–154.

Mannarino, A., & Cohen, J. (1986). A clinical-demographic study of sexually abused children. *Child Abuse and Neglect, 10,* 17–23.

Manos, M. J., Short, E. J., & Findling, R. L. (1999). Differential effectiveness of methylphenidate and Adderall in school-age youths with attention-deficit hyperactivity disorder. *Journal of the American Academy of Child and Adolescent Psychiatry,* 38, 813–819.

Marans, S. (1989). Psychoanalytic psychotherapy with children: Current research trends and challenges. *Journal of the American Academy of Child and Adolescent Psychiatry, 28,* 669–674.

Marcia, J. E. (1980). Identity in adolescence. In J. Adelson (Ed.), *Handbook of adolescent psychology* (pp. 159–187). New York: John Wiley.

Marini, Z., & Case, R. (1994). The development of abstract reasoning about the physical and social world. *Child Development, 65,* 147–159.

Markman, H. J., & Hahlweg, K. (1993). The prediction and prevention of marital distress: An international perspective. *Clinical Psychology Review, 13,* 29–43.

Markman, H. J., Renick, M. J. H., Floyd, F. J., Stanley, S. M., & Clements, M. (1993). Preventing marital distress through communication and conflict management training: A 4- and 5-year follow-up. *Journal of Consulting and Clinical Psychology, 61,* 70–77.

Marks, E. S. (1995). *Entry strategies for school consultation.* New York: Guilford.

Marshall, C., & Rossman, G. B. (1999). *Designing qualitative research* (3rd ed.). Thousand Oaks, CA: Sage.

Marshall, S. (1995). Ethnic socialization of African American children: Implications for parenting, identity development, and academic achievement. *Journal of Youth and Adolescence, 24,* 377–396.

Martin, C. L., Eisenbud, L., & Rose, H. (1995). Children's gender-based reasoning about toys. *Child Development, 66,* 1453–1471.

Martin, N. K., & Baldwin, B. (1996). Helping beginning teachers foster healthy classroom management: Implications for elementary school counselors. *Elementary School Guidance and Counseling, 31,* 106–113.

Martin, R. P. (1988). *Assessment of personality and behavior problems: Infancy through adolescence.* New York: Guilford.

Martin-Causey, T., & Hinkle, J. S. (1995). Multimodal therapy with an aggressive preadolescent: A demonstration of effectiveness and accountability. *Journal of Counseling and Development, 73,* 305–310.

Maryland v. Craig, 110 S. Ct. 3157 (1990).

Maslow, A. H. (1954). *Motivation and personality.* New York: Harper & Row.

Maslow, A. H. (1968). *Toward a psychology of being* (2nd ed.). New York: Van Nostrand Reinhold.

Mather, J. H., & Lager, P. B. (2000). *Child welfare: A unifying model of practice.* Belmont, CA: Brooks/Cole.

Mattes, J. A., & Gittelman, R. (1981). Effects of artificial food colorings in children with hyperactive symptoms: A critical review and results of a controlled study. *Archives of General Psychiatry, 38,* 714–718.

Mattison, R. E., & Spirito, A. (1993). Current consultation needs of school systems. In G. K. Fritz, R. E. Mattison, B. Nurcombe, & A. Spirito (Eds.), *Child and adolescent mental health consultation in hospitals, schools, and courts* (pp. 161–183). Washington, DC: American Psychiatric Press.

Maturana, H. R., & Varela, F. J. (1973/1980). *Autopoiesis and cognition: The realization of the living.* Boston: Reidel.

McAlpine, H., & McAlpine, W. (1958). *Japanese tales and legends.* Oxford, UK: Oxford University Press.

McClelland, D. C., & Friedman, G. A. (1952). A cross-cultural study of the relationship between child-training practices and achievement motivation appearing in folk tales. In G. E. Swanson, T. M. Newcomb, & E. L. Hartley (Eds.), *Readings in social psychology* (2nd ed.) (pp. 243–249). New York: Holt.

McConaughy, S. H., & Achenbach, T. M. (1990). *Guide for the Semistructured Clinical Interview for Children Aged 6–11.* Burlington: University of Vermont, Department of Psychiatry.

McConaughy, S. H. & Achenbach. T. M. (2001). *Manual for the Semistructured Clinical Interview for Children and Adolescents* (2nd ed.). Burlington, VT: University of Vermont, Research Center for Children, Youth, and Families.

McConaughy, S. H., Achenbach, T.M., & Gent, C. L. (1988). Multiaxial empirically based assessment: Parent, teacher, observational, cognitive, and personality correlates of child behavior profile types for 6- to 11-year-old boys. *Journal of Abnormal Child Psychology, 16,* 485–509.

McElhaney, S. J., & Effley, K. M. (1999). Community-based approaches to violence prevention. In T. P. Gullotta & S. J. McElhaney (Eds.), *Violence in homes and communities: Prevention, intervention, and treatment* (pp. 269–299). Thousand Oaks, CA: Sage.

McGoldrick, M. (1998). Ethnicity and the family life cycle. In B. Carter & M. McGoldrick (Eds.), *The changing family life cycle: A framework for family therapy* (2nd ed.), pp. 69–90). New York: Gardner Press.

McGoldrick, M., & Gerson, R. (1985). *Genograms in family assessment.* New York: W. W. Norton.

McGoldrick, M., & Giordano, J. (1996). Overview: Ethnicity and family therapy. In M. McGoldrick, J. Giordano, & J. K. Pearce (Eds.), *Ethnicity and family therapy* (2nd ed.) (pp. 1–27). New York: Guilford.

McGrath, M. L., Mellon, M. W., & Murphy, L. (2000). Empirically supported treatments in pediatric psychology: Constipation and encopresis. *Journal of Pediatric Psychology, 25,* 225–254.

McLeer, S. V., & Wills, C. (2000). Psychopharmacological treatment. In M. Hersen & R. T. Ammerman (Eds.), *Advanced abnormal child psychology* (2nd ed.) (pp. 219–250). Mahwah, NJ: Lawrence Erlbaum.

McLoyd, V. C. (1989). Socialization and development in a changing economy: The effects of paternal job and income loss on children. *American Psychologist, 44,* 293–302.

McLoyd, V. C. (1998). Socioeconomic disadvantage and child development. *American Psychologist, 53,* 185–204.

McMahon, R. J. (1994). Diagnosis, assessment, and treatment of externalizing problems in children: The role of longitudinal data. *Journal of Consulting and Clinical Psychology, 5,* 901–917.

McNeil, C. B., Bahl, A., & Herschell, A. D. (2000). Involving and empowering parents in short-term play therapy for disrupted children. In H. G. Kaduson & C. E. Schaefer (Eds.), *Short-term play therapy for children* (pp. 228–255). New York: Guilford.

McNeil, C. B., Eyberg, S., Eisenstadt, T. H., Newcomb, K., & Funderburk, B. W. (1991). Parent-child interaction therapy with behavior problem children: Generalization of treatment effects to the school setting. *Journal of Clinical Child Psychology, 20,* 140–151.

McNeish, T. J., & Naglieri, J. A. (1993). Identification of individuals with serious emotional disturbance using the Draw-A-Person: Screening Procedure for Emotional Disturbance. *Journal of Special Education, 27,* 115–121.

Mead, M. A., Hohenshil, T. H., & Singh, K. (1997). How the DSM system is used by clinical counselors: A national study. *Journal of Mental Health Counseling, 19,* 383–401.

Meezan, W., & O'Keefe, M. (1998). Multifamily group therapy: Impact on family functioning and child behavior. *Families in Society, 79,* 32–44.

Meichenbaum, D. (1977). *Cognitive-behavioral modification: An integrative approach.* New York: Plenum Press.

Meichenbaum, D. H., & Goodman, J. (1971). Training impulsive children to talk to themselves: A means of developing self-control. *Journal of Abnormal Psychology, 77,* 115–126.

Melamed, B. G., & Siegel, L. J. (1980). *Behavioral medicine: Practical applications in health care.* New York: Springer.

Melton, G. B. (1991). Preserving the dignity of children around the world: The U.N. Convention on the Rights of the Child. *Child Abuse and Neglect, 15,* 343–350.

Melton, G. B., & Ehrenreich, N. S. (1992). Ethical and legal issues in mental health services for children. In C. E. Walker & M. C. Roberts (Eds.), *Handbook of clinical child psychology* (pp. 1035–1055). New York: John Wiley.

Melton, G. B., Petrila, J., Poythress, N. G., & Slobogin, C. (1997). *Psychological evaluations for the courts: A handbook for mental health professionals and lawyers* (2nd ed.). New York: Guilford.

Meltzer, M. L. (1975). Insurance reimbursement: A mixed blessing. *American Psychologist, 30,* 1150–1156.

Menzies, R. G., & Clarke, J. C. (1993). A comparison of *in vivo* and vicarious exposure in the treatment of childhood water phobia. *Behaviour Research and Therapy, 31,* 9–15.

Merrell, K. W. (1999). *Behavioral, social, and emotional assessment of children and adolescents.* Mahwah, NJ: Lawrence Erlbaum.

Mertens, D. M. (1998). *Research methods in education and psychology: Integrating diversity with quantitative and qualitative approaches.* Thousand Oaks, CA: Sage.

Messer, S. B., & Wachtel, P. L. (1997). The contemporary psychotherapeutic landscape: Issues and prospects. In P. L. Wachtel & S. B. Messer (Eds.), *Theories of psychotherapy: Origins and evolution* (pp. 1–38). Washington, DC: American Psychological Association.

Metalsky, G. I., Laird, R. S., Heck, P. M., & Joiner, T. E. (1995). Attribution theory: Clinical applications. In W. O'Donohue & L. Krasner (Eds.), *Theories of behavior therapy: Exploring behavior change* (pp. 385–413). Washington, DC: American Psychological Association.

Meyers, A. W., & Craighead, W. E. (1984). Cognitive behavior therapy with children: A historical, conceptual, and organizational overview. In A. W. Meyers & W. E. Craighead (Eds.), *Cognitive behavior therapy with children* (pp. 1–17). New York: Plenum.

Meyers, J. (1975). Consultee-centered consultation as a technique in classroom management. *American Journal of Community Psychology, 3,* 111–121.

Meyers, J. (1995). A consultation model for school psychological services: Twenty years later. *Journal of Educational and Psychological Consultation, 6,* 73–81.

Meyers, J., Freidman, M. P., & Gaughan, E. J., Jr. (1975). The effects of consultee-centered consultation on teacher behavior. *Psychology in the Schools, 12,* 288–295.

Michaels, S., & Cazden, C. B. (1986). Teacher/child collaboration as oral preparation for literacy. In B. B. Schieffelin & P. Gilmore (Eds.), *The acquisition of literacy: Ethnographic perspectives* (pp. 132–154). Norwood, NJ: Ablex Publishing.

Mikulas, W. L., Coffman, M. G., Dayton, D., Frayne, C., & Maier, P. L. (1985). Behavioral bibliotherapy and games for treating fear of the dark. *Child and Family Behavior Therapy, 7,* 1–7.

Miller, J. S., & Allen, R. J. (1998). The expert as educator. In S. J. Ceci & H. Hembrooke (Eds.), *Expert witnesses in child abuse cases: What can and should be said in court* (pp. 137–155). Washington, DC: American Psychological Association.

Miller, L. C. (1967). Louisville Behavior Checklist for males, 6–12 years of age. *Psychological Reports, 21,* 885–896.

Miller, M. C. (1999). Suicide-prevention contracts: Advantages, disadvantages, and an alternative approach. In D. G. Jacobs (Ed.), *The Harvard Medical School guide to suicide assessment and intervention* (pp. 463–481). San Francisco: Jossey-Bass.

Miller, M. J., & Stanford, J. T. (1987). Early occupational restriction: An examination of elementary school children's expression of vocational preferences. *Journal of Employment Counseling, 24,* 115–121.

Milling, L., & Carey, M. P. (1994). Adolescent and preadolescent suicide: Assessing suicidal behavior in adolescents and preadolescents. In R. A. Olson, L. L. Mullins, J. B. Gillman, & J. M. Chaney (Eds.), *The sourcebook of pediatric psychology* (pp. 395–404). Boston: Allyn and Bacon.

Milling, L., & Martin, B. (1992). Depression and suicidal behavior in preadolescent children. In C. E. Walker & M. C. Roberts (Eds.), *Handbook of clinical child psychology* (2nd ed.) (pp. 319–339). New York: John Wiley.

Mills, J. C., & Crowley, R. J. (1986). *Therapeutic metaphors for children and the child within.* New York: Brunner/Mazel.

Minuchin, S. (1974). *Families and family therapy.* Cambridge, MA: Harvard University Press.

Minuchin, S., & Fishman, H. C. (1981). *Family therapy techniques.* Cambridge, MA: Harvard University Press.

Minuchin, S., Montalvo, B., Guerney, Jr., B. G., Rosman, B. L., & Schumer, F. (1967). *Families of the slums: An exploration of their structure and treatment.* New York: Basic Books.

Minuchin, S., Rosman, B. L., & Baker, L. (1978). *Psychosomatic families: Anorexia nervosa in context.* Cambridge, MA: Harvard University Press.

Miranda, A., & Presentación, M. J. (2000). Efficacy of cognitive-behavioral therapy in the treatment of children with ADHD, with and without aggressiveness. *Psychology in the Schools, 37,* 169–182.

Mishne, J. M. (1993). *The evolution and application of clinical theory: Perspectives from four psychologies.* New York: The Free Press.

Mississippi Department of Public Health. (2000). *Mississippi 2000 Youth Tobacco Survey.* Jackson, MS: Author.

Moffatt, M. E. K., Harlos, S., Kirshen, A. J., & Burd, L. (1993). Desmopressin acetate and nocturnal enuresis: How much do we know? *Pediatrics, 92,* 420–425.

Mogul, K. M. (1982). Overview: The sex of the therapist. *American Journal of Psychiatry, 139,* 1–11.

Mokuau, N. (1990). A family centered approach In Native Hawaiian culture. *Families In Society: The Journal of Contemporary Human Services, 71,* 607–613.

Moline, M. E., Williams, G. T., & Austin, K. M. (1998). *Documenting psychotherapy: Essentials for mental health practitioners.* Thousand Oaks, CA: Sage.

Money-Kryle, R. E. (1975). Introduction. In M. Klein, *Love, guilt, and reparation and other works (1921–1945)* (pp. ix–xi). London: Hogarth Press.

Moon, L. T., Wagner, W. G., & Kazelskis, R. (2000). Counseling sexually abused girls: The impact of sex of counselor. *Child Abuse and Neglect, 24,* 753–765.

Moore, H. B., Presbury, J. H., Smith, L. W., & McKee, J. E. (1999). Person-centered approaches. In H. T. Prout & D. T. Brown (Eds.), *Counseling and psychotherapy with children and adolescents: Theory and practice for school and clinical settings* (3rd ed.) (pp. 155–202). New York: John Wiley.

Moos, R. H., & Moos, B. S. (1994). *Family Environment Scale manual: Development, applications, research* (3rd ed.). Palo Alto, CA: Consulting Psychologists Press.

Morgan, R. T. T. (1978). Relapse and therapeutic response in the conditioning treatment of enuresis: A review of recent findings on the intermittent reinforcement, overlearning, and stimulus intensity. *Behavior Research and Therapy, 16*, 273–279.

Morgan, R. T. T., & Young, G. (1975). Parental attitudes and the conditioning treatment of childhood enuresis. *Behavior Research and Therapy, 13*, 197–199.

Morland, J. K. (1958). Racial recognition by nursery school children in Lynchburg, Virginia. *Social Forces, 37*, 132–137.

Morrill, W. H., Oetting, E. R., & Hurst, J. C. (1974). Dimensions of counselor functioning. *Personnel and Guidance Journal, 52*, 354–359.

Morris, R. J., & Nicholson, J. (1993). The therapeutic relationship in child and adolescent psychotherapy: Research issues and trends. In T. Kratochwill & R. Morris (Eds.), *Handbook of psychotherapy with children and adolescents* (pp. 405–425). Needham Heights, MA: Allyn and Bacon.

Morrison, J. K. (1979). A consumer-oriented approach to psychotherapy. *Psychotherapy: Theory, Research and Practice, 16*, 381–384.

Morrison, J., & Anders, T. F. (1999). *Interviewing children and adolescents: Skills and strategies for effective DSM-IV diagnosis*. New York: Guilford.

Mosak, H. H. (1995). Adlerian psychotherapy. In R. J. Corsini & D. Wedding (Eds.), *Current psychotherapies* (5th ed., pp. 51–94). Itasca, IL: F. E. Peacock.

Mostert, D. L., Johnson, E., & Mostert, M. P. (1997). The utility of solution-focused, brief counseling in schools: Potential from an initial study. *Professional School Counseling, 1(1)*, 21–24.

Moustakas, C. E. (1953). *Children in play therapy: A key to understanding normal and disturbed emotions*. New York: McGraw-Hill.

Moustakas, C. E. (1955). Emotional adjustment and the play therapy process. *Journal of Genetic Psychology, 86*, 79–99.

Moustakas, C. E. (1959). *Psychotherapy with children: The living relationship*. New York: Harper & Brothers.

Moustakas, C. E., & Schalock, H. D. (1955). An analysis of therapist-child interaction in play therapy. *Child Development, 26*, 143–157.

Mowrer, O. H. & Mowrer, W. M. (1938). Enuresis: A method for its study and treatment. *American Journal of Orthopsychiatry, 8*, 436–459.

Mufson, L. & Moreau, D. (1997). Depressive disorders. In R. T. Ammerman & M. Hersen (Eds.), *Handbook of prevention and treatment with children and adolescents* (pp. 403–430). New York: John Wiley.

Multimodal Treatment Study of Children with ADHD Cooperative Group, US. (1999a). A 14-month randomized clinical trial of treatment strategies for attention-deficit/hyperactivity disorder. *Archives of General Psychiatry, 56*, 1073–1086.

Multimodal Treatment Study of Children with ADHD Cooperative Group, US. (1999b). Moderators and mediators of treatment response for children with attention-deficit/hyperactivity disorder: The multimodal treatment study of children with attention-deficit/hyperactivity disorder. *Archives of General Psychiatry, 56*, 1088–1096.

Mulvey, E. P., & Cauffman, E. (2001). The inherent limits of predicting school violence. *American Psychologist, 56*, 797–802.

Muris, P., & Merckelbach, H. (1999). Eye movement desensitization and reprocessing. *Journal of the American Academy of Child and Adolescent Psychiatry, 38*, 7–8.

Muris, P., Merckelbach, H., Holdrinet, I., & Sijsenaar, M. (1998). Treating phobic children: Effects of EMDR versus exposure. *Journal of Consulting and Clinical Psychology, 66*, 193–198.

Muris, P., Merckelbach, H., van Haaften, H., & Mayer, B. (1997). Eye movement desensitization and reprocessing versus exposure in vivo: A single-session crossover study of spider-phobic children. *British Journal of Psychiatry, 171*, 82–86.

Murray, H. A. (1943). *Thematic Apperception Test manual*. Cambridge, MA: Harvard University Press.

Murray, J. P. (1993). The developing child in a multimedia society. In G. L. Berry & J. K. Asamen (Eds.), *Children and television: Images in a changing sociocultural world* (pp. 9–22). Newbury Park, CA: Sage.

Murrow-Taylor, C., Foltz, B. M., Ellis, M. R., & Culbertson, K. (1999). A multicultural career fair for elementary school students. *Professional School Counseling, 2*, 241–243.

Myrick, R. D. (1997). *Developmental guidance and counseling: A practical approach* (3rd ed.). Minneapolis, MN: Educational Media Corporation.

Myrick, R., & Haldin, W. (1971). A study of play process in counseling. *Elementary School Guidance and Counseling, 5*, 256–265.

Nagin, D., & Tremblay, R. E. (1999). Trajectories of boys' physical aggression, opposition, and hyperactivity on the path to physically violent and nonviolent juvenile delinquency. *Child Development, 70*, 1181–1196.

Naglieri, J. A., McNeish, T. J., & Bardos, A. N. (1991). *DAP:SPED Draw A Person: Screening Procedure for Emotional Disturbance examiner's manual*. Austin, TX: Pro-Ed.

Naglieri, J. A., & Pfeiffer, S. L. (1992). Performance of disruptive behavior disordered and normal samples on the Draw-A-Person: Screening Procedure for Emotional Disturbance. *Psychological Assessment, 4*, 156–159.

National Association of Social Workers. (1999). *Code of ethics of the National Association of Social Workers*. Washington, DC: Author. Retrieved on May 10, 2002, from http://www.naswdc.org/pubs/code/code.aps.

National Clearinghouse on Child Abuse and Neglect Information. (2000a). *Child abuse and neglect state statutes elements. Crimes. Number 37. Religious exemptions to criminal child abuse and neglect*. Washington, DC: Author. Retrieved on May 14, 2002, from http://www.calib. com/nccanch/pubs/stats00/relig.pdf.

National Clearinghouse on Child Abuse and Neglect Information. (2000b). *Child abuse and neglect state statutes series. Child witnesses. Number 28. Special procedures In criminal child abuse cases*. Washington, DC: Author. Retrieved on May 14, 2002, from http://www.calib.com/nccanch/pubs/stats00/special.pdf.

National Clearinghouse on Child Abuse and Neglect Information. (2000c). *Child abuse and neglect state statutes elements. Child witnesses. Number 20. The use of closed-circuit television testimony*. Washington, DC: Author. Retrieved on May 14, 2002, from http://www.calib. com/nccanch/pubs/stats00/cctv.pdf.

National Clearinghouse on Child Abuse and Neglect Information. (2001a). *Child abuse and neglect state statutes elements. Reporting laws. Number 2. Mandatory reporters of child abuse and neglect*. Washington, DC: Author. Retrieved on May 14, 2002, from http://www.calib.com /nccanch/pubs/stats01/mandrep.pdf.

National Clearinghouse on Child Abuse and Neglect Information. (2001b). *Child abuse and neglect state statutes elements. Reporting laws. Number 6. Reporting procedures*. Washington, DC: Author. Retrieved on May 14, 2002, from http://www.calib.com/nccanch/pubs /stats01/report.pdf.

National Clearinghouse on Child Abuse and Neglect Information. (2001c). *Child abuse and neglect state statutes elements. Reporting laws. Number 4. Penalties for failure to report*. Washington, DC: Author. Retrieved on May 14, 2002, from http://www.calib.com/nccanch/ pubs/stats01/ failrepo.pdf.

National Defense Education Act of 1958, Vol. 72, *United States Statutes at Large* (1959).

National Education Association. (1999). *Give the gift of reading for Valentine's Day, Teachers announce top 100 favorite children's books* [News release]. Washington, DC: Author.

Needlman, R. D. (1996). Growth and development. In N. E. Nelson, R. E. Behrman, R. M. Kliegman, & A. M. Arvin (Eds.), *Nelson textbook of pediatrics* (15th ed.) (pp. 30–72). Philadelphia: W. B. Saunders Co.

Neill, A. S. (1960). *Summerhill: A radical approach to child rearing*. New York: Hart Publishing.

Neimeyer, R. A. (1985). *The development of personal construct psychology*. Lincoln, NE: University of Nebraska Press.

Neimeyer, R. A. (1993). An appraisal of constructivist psychotherapies. *Journal of Consulting and Clinical Psychology, 61*, 221–234.

Neimeyer, R. A., & Jackson, T. T. (1997). George A. Kelly and the development of personal construct theory. In W. G. Bringmann, H. E. Lueck, R. Miller, & C. E. Early (Eds.), *A pictorial history of psychology* (pp. 364–372). Chicago: Quintessence Publishing.

Neisen, J. (1992). Gender identity disorder of childhood: By whose standard and for what purpose? A response to Rekers and Morey. *Journal of Psychology and Human Sexuality, 5*(3), 65–67.

Nelson, K. E. (1994). Innovative delivery models in social services. *Journal of Clinical Child Psychology, 23(suppl.)*, 26–31.

Nelson, K. E., Emlen, A., Landsman, M. J., & Hutchinson, J. (1988). *Factors contributing to success and failure in family-based child welfare services.* Iowa City, IA: The University of Iowa, National Resource Center on Family Based Services.

Nelson, K. E., & Landsman, M. J. (1992) *Alternative models of family preservation: Family-based services in content.* Springfield, Il: Charles C. Thomas.

Nemiroff, M. A., & Annunziata, J. (1990). *A child's first book about play therapy.* Washington, DC: American Psychological Association.

Neukrug, E. (1999). *The world of the counselor: An introduction to the counseling profession.* Pacific Grove, CA: Brooks/Cole.

Neukrug, E. S., Barr, C. G., Hoffman, L. R., & Kaplan, L. S. (1993). Developmental counseling and guidance: A model for use in your school. *The School Counselor, 40*, 356–362.

Nichols, M. P., & Schwartz, R. C. (1998). *Family therapy: Concepts and methods* (4th ed.). Boston: Allyn and Bacon.

Njiokiktjien, C. (1988). *Pediatric behavioral neurology, Vol. 1, Clinical principles.* Amsterdam: Suyi Publicaties.

Nordby, V. J., & Hall, C. S. (1974). *A guide to psychologists and their concepts.* San Francisco: W. H. Freeman.

Nordhoff, C. (1961). *The communistic societies of the United States.* New York: Hillary House Publishers.

Nunes, D. L., Murphy, R. J., & Ruprecht, M. L. (1977). Reducing self-injurious behavior of severely retarded individuals through withdrawal-of-reinforcement procedures. *Behavior Modification, 1*, 499–516.

Nurcombe, B. (1993a). The forensic evaluation. In G. K. Fritz, R. E. Mattison, B. Nurcombe, & A. Spirito (Eds.), *Child and adolescent mental health consultation in hospitals, schools, and courts* (pp. 257–273). Washington, DC: American Psychiatric Press.

Nurcombe, B. (1993b). Giving testimony as an expert witness. In G. K. Fritz, R. E. Mattison, B. Nurcombe, & A. Spirito (Eds.), *Child and adolescent mental health consultation in hospitals, schools, and courts* (pp. 275–289). Washington, DC: American Psychiatric Press.

Nystul, M. S. (1982). The effects of systematic training for effective parenting on parental attitudes. *Journal of Psychology, 112*, 63–66.

Nystul, M. S. (1993). *The art and science of counseling and psychotherapy.* New York: Merrill/Macmillan.

O'Brien, S., Ross, L. V., & Christophersen, E. R. (1986). Primary encopresis: Evaluation and treatment. *Journal of Applied Behavior Analysis, 19*, 137–145.

Oclander, S. (1993). Brief work with children of divorcing parents. *Psychoanalytic Psychotherapy, 9(1)*, 59–72.

O'Connor, K. J. (1993). Ecosystemic play therapy. In K. J. O'Connor & C. E. Schaefer (Eds.), *Handbook of play therapy: Advances and innovations* (Vol. 2) (pp. 61–84). New York: John Wiley.

O'Connor, K. J., & Ammen, S. (1997). *Play therapy treatment planning and interventions: The ecosystemic model and workbook.* San Diego, CA: Academic Press.

O'Connor, K., & Braverman, L. M. (1997). *Play therapy theory and practice: A comparative presentation.* New York: John Wiley.

O'Leary, K. D., & Johnson, S. B. (1979). Assessment and assessment of change. In H. C. Quay & J. S. Werry (Eds.), *Psychopathological disorders of childhood* (2nd ed.) (pp. 210–246). New York: John Wiley.

O'Leary, K. D., & Johnson, S. B. (1986). Assessment and assessment of change. In H. C. Quay & J. S. Werry (Eds.), *Psychopathological disorders of childhood* (3rd ed.) (pp. 423–453). New York: John Wiley.

O'Malley, P. (1998). Raising Martin. In L. B. Golden (Ed.), *Case studies in child and adolescent therapy* (2nd ed.) (pp. 92–102). Upper Saddle River, NJ: Merrill.

O'Neill, R. E., Horner, R. H., Albin, R. W., Sprague, J. R., Storey, K., & Newton, J. S. (1997). *Functional assessment and program development for problem behavior: A practical handbook* (2nd ed.). Pacific Grove, CA: Brooks/Cole.

Okun, B. F. (1990). *Seeking connections in psychotherapy.* San Francisco: Jossey- Bass.

Ollendick, T. H. (1983). Reliability and validity of the Revised Fear Survey Schedule for Children (FSSC-R). *Behaviour Research and Therapy, 21*, 685–692.

Ollendick, T. H., & Cerny, J. A. (1981). *Clinical behavior therapy with children.* New York: Plenum.

Ollendick, T. H., King, N. J., & Frary, R. B. (1989) Fears in children and adolescents: Reliability and generalizability across gender, age and nationality. *Behaviour Research and Therapy, 27*, 19–26.

Ollendick, T. H., & Russ, S. W. (1999). Psychotherapy with children and families: Historical traditions and current trends. In S. W. Russ & T. H. Ollendick (Eds.), *Handbook of psychotherapies with children and families* (pp. 3–13). New York: Kluwer Academic/Plenum Publishers.

Olness, K., & Kohen, D. P. (1996). *Hypnosis and hypnotherapy with children* (3rd ed.). New York: Guilford.

Oppel, W. C., Harper, P. A., & Rider, R. V. (1968). The age of attaining bladder control. *Pediatrics, 42*, 614–626.

Osborne, J. L., & Collison, B. B. (1998). School counselors and external providers: Conflict or complement. *Professional School Counseling, 1*(4), 7–11.

Otwell, P. S., & Mullis, F. (1997). Counselor-led staff development: An efficient approach to teacher consultation. *Professional School Counseling, 1*, 25–30.

Ozment, S. (1983). *When fathers ruled: Family life in reformation Europe.* Cambridge, MA: Harvard University Press.

Page v. Rotterdam-Mohonasen Central School District, 441 N.Y.S.2d 323 (Sup. Ct. 1981).

Pagliocca, P. M., Melton, G. B., Weisz, V., & Lyons, Jr., P. M. (1995). Parenting and the law. In M. H. Bornstein (Ed.), *Handbook of parenting, Vol. 3: Status and social conditions of parenting* (pp. 437–457). Hillsdale, NJ: Lawrence Erlbaum.

Paisley, P. O., & Peace, S. D. (1995). Developmental principles: A framework for school counseling programs. *Elementary School Guidance and Counseling, 30*, 85–93.

Papay, J. P., & Hedl, J. J. (1978). Psychometric characteristics and norms for disadvantaged third and fourth grade children on the State-Trait Anxiety Inventory for children. *Journal of Abnormal Child Psychology, 6*, 115–120.

Papay, J. P., & Spielberger, C. D. (1986). Assessment of anxiety and achievement in kindergarten and first- and second grade children. *Journal of Abnormal Child Psychiatry, 14*, 279–286.

Papero, D. V. (1991). The Bowen theory. In A. M. Horne & J. L. Passmore (Eds.), *Family counseling and therapy* (2nd ed.) (pp. 47–75). Itasca, IL: F. E. Peacock Publishers.

Papp, P. (1980). The Greek chorus and other techniques of paradoxical therapy. *Family Process, 19*, 45–57.

Pardeck, J. A., & Pardeck, J. T. (1986). *Books for early childhood: A developmental perspective.* New York: Greenwood Press.

Pardeck, J. T. (1990). Using bibliotherapy in clinical practice with children. *Psychological Reports, 67*, 1043–1049.

Pardeck, J. T. (1995). Bibliotherapy: An innovative approach for helping children. *Early Child Development and Care, 110*, 83–88.

Park, W. D., & Williams, G. T. (1986). Encouraging elementary school children to refer themselves for counseling. *Elementary School Guidance and Counseling, 21*, 8–14.

Parten, M. (1932). Social play among pre-school children. *Journal of Abnormal and Social Psychology, 27*, 243–269.

Patterson, C. J. (1996). Lesbian and gay parents and their children. In R. C. Savin-Williams & K. M. Cohen (Eds.), *The lives of lesbians, gays, and bisexuals: Children to adults* (pp. 274–304). Fort Worth, TX: Harcourt Brace.

Patton, M. Q. (1990). *Qualitative evaluation and research methods* (2nd ed.). Thousand Oaks, CA: Sage.

Pauling, L. (1968). Orthomolecular psychiatry. *Science, 160*, 265–271.

Peck, J. S., & Manocherian, J. R. (1988). Divorce in the changing family life cycle. In B. Carter & M. McGoldrick (Eds.), *The changing family life cycle: A framework for family therapy* (2nd ed.) (pp. 335–369). New York: Gardner Press.

Pedersen, P. B. (1991). Multiculturalism as a generic approach to counseling. *Journal of Counseling and Development, 70*, 6–12.

Pedersen, P. B., & Carey, J. C. (1994). *Multicultural counseling in schools: A practical handbook*. Boston: Allyn and Bacon.

Pedro-Carroll, J. L., Cowen, E. L., Hightower, A. D., & Guare, J. C. (1986). Preventive intervention with latency-aged children of divorce: A replication study. *American Journal of Community Psychology, 14*, 277–290.

Peled, E., & Davis, D. (1995). *Groupwork with children of battered women: A practitioner's guide*. Thousand Oaks, CA: Sage.

Pelham, W. E., Carlson, C., Sams, S. E., Vallano, G., Dixon, M. J., & Hoza, B. (1993). Separate and combined effects of methylphenidate and behavior modification on boys with attention-deficit hyperactivity disorder in the classroom. *Journal of Consulting and Clinical Psychology, 61*, 506–515.

Pelham, W. E., Wheeler, T., & Chronis, A. (1998). Empirically supported psychosocial treatments for attention deficit hyperactivity disorder. *Journal of Clinical Child Psychology, 27*, 190–205.

Pellicer, X. (1993). Eye movement desensitization treatment of a child's nightmares: A case report. *Journal of Behavior Therapy and Experimental Psychiatry, 24*, 73–75.

Pennington, J. A. T. (1998). *Bowes and Church's food values of portions commonly used* (17th ed.). Philadelphia, PA: Lippincott-Raven.

Peters, V. H. (1985). *Anna Freud: A life dedicated to children*. New York: Schocken Books.

Peterson, C., & Bell, M. (1996). Children's memory for traumatic injury. *Child Development, 67*, 3045–3070.

Peterson, D. R. (1961). Behavior problems of middle childhood. *Journal of Consulting Psychology, 25*, 205–209.

Pfeffer, C. R. (1986). *The suicidal child*. New York: Guilford Press.

Pfeffer, C. R. (2000). Suicidal behaviour in children: An emphasis on development influences. In K. Hawton & K. van Heeringen (Eds.), *The international handbook of suicide and attempted suicide* (pp. 237–248). New York: John Wiley.

Pfeffer, C. R., Conte, H. R., Plutchik, R., & Jerrett, I. (1979). Suicidal behavior In latency-age children: An empirical study. *Journal of the American Academy of Child Psychiatry, 18*, 679–692.

Pfeffer, C. R., Conte, H. R., Plutchik, R., & Jerrett, I. (1980). Suicidal behavior In latency-age children: An empirical study: An outpatient population. *Journal of the American Academy of Child Psychiatry, 19*, 703–710.

Pfeffer, C. R., Zuckerman, S., Plutchik, R., & Mizruchi, M. S. (1984). Suicidal behavior in normal school children: A comparison with child psychiatric inpatients. *Journal of the Academy of Child Psychiatry, 23*, 416–423.

Pfiffner, L. J., & McBurnett, K. (1997). Social skills training with parent generalization: Treatment effects for children with attention deficit disorder. *Journal of Consulting and Clinical Psychology, 5*, 749–757.

Phares, V. (1996). *Fathers and developmental psychopathology*. New York: John Wiley.

Phelps, R., Eisman, E. J., & Kohut, J. (1998). Psychological practice and managed care: Results of the CAPP practitioner survey. *Professional Psychology: Research and Practice, 29*, 31–36.

Phillips, R., & Landreth, G. (1995). Play therapists on play therapy I.: A report of methods, demographics, and professional practices. *International Journal of Play Therapy, 1(4)*, 1–26.

Phillips, S., Sarles, R. M., & Friedman, S. B. (1987). Behavioral consultation and referral. In R. A. Hoekelman, S. Blatman, S. B. Friedman, N. M. Nelson, & K. M. Seidels (Eds.), *Primary pediatric care* (pp. 780–784). St. Louis: C. V. Mosby.

Phillis P. v. Clairmont Unified School District (86 Daily Journal D.A.R. 2795, July 30, 1986).

Phinney, J. S. (1989). Stages of ethnic identity development in minority group adolescents. *Journal of Early Adolescence, 9*, 34–49.

Phinney, J. S. (1990). Ethnic identity in adolescents and adults: Review of research. *Psychological Bulletin, 108*, 499–514.

Phinney, J. S. (1996). When we talk about American ethnic groups, what do we mean? *American Psychologist, 51*, 918–927.

Phinney, J. S., Romero, I., Nava, M., & Huang, D. (2001). The role of language, parents, and peers in ethnic identity among adolescents in immigrant families. *Journal of Youth and Adolescence, 30*, 135–153.

Piaget, J. (1926). *The language and thought of the child* (M. Worden, Trans.). New York: Harcourt Brace Jovanovich.

Piaget, J. (1929). *The child's conception of the world* (J. Tomlinson & A. Tomlinson, Trans.). New York: Harcourt Brace Jovanovich.

Piaget, J. (1972). Intellectual evolution from adolescence to adulthood. *Human Development, 15*, 1–12.

Piaget, J., & Inhelder, B. (1969). *The psychology of the child*. New York: Basic Books.

Pick, I., & Segal, H. (1978). Melanie Klein's contribution to child analysis; Theory and technique. In J. Glenn & M. A. Scharfman (Eds.), *Child analysis and therapy* (pp. 425–449). New York: Jason Aronson.

Piers, E. V. (1984). *Piers-Harris Children's Self-Concept Scale: Revised manual 1984*. Los Angeles, CA: Western Psychological Services.

Piers, E. V., & Harris, D. B. (1969). *Manual for the Piers-Harris Children's Self Concept Scale*. Nashville, TN: Counselor Recording and Tests.

Pino, C. J., Simons, N., & Slawinowski, M. J. (1984). *The Children's Version of the Family Environment Scale manual*. East Aurora, NY: Slosson Educational Publications.

Pinsof, W. M., Wynne, L. C., Hambright, A. B. (1996). The outcomes of couple and family therapy: Findings, conclusions, and recommendations. *Psychotherapy, 33*, 321–331.

Pollin, R., & Luce, S. (2000). *The living wage: Building a fair economy*. New York: The New Press.

Pomerleau, A., Bolduc, D., Malcuit, G., & Cossette, L. (1990). Pink or blue: Environmental gender stereotypes in the first two years of life. *Sex Roles, 22*, 359–367.

Ponec, D. L., Poggi. J. A., & Dickel, C. T. (1998). Unity: Developing relationships between school and community counselors. *Professional School Counseling, 2*, 95–102.

Poole, D. A., & White, L. T. (1991). Effects of question repetition on the eyewitness testimony of children and adults. *Developmental Psychology, 27*, 975–986.

Pope, K. S., & Vasquez, M. J. T. (1991). *Ethics in psychotherapy and counseling: A practical guide for psychologists*. San Francisco: Jossey-Bass.

Popple, P. R., & Leighninger, L. (1996). *Social work, social welfare, and American society* (3rd ed.). Boston: Allyn and Bacon.

Porter, R., Wagner, W. G., Johnson, J. T., & Cox, L. (1996). Sexually abused girls' verbalizations in counseling: An application of the client behavior system. *Journal of Counseling Psychology, 43*, 383–388.

Powell-Hopson, D., & Hopson, D. S. (1992). Implications of doll color preferences among Black preschool children and White preschool children. In A. K. H. Burlew, W. C. Banks, H. P. McAdoo, & D. A. Azibo (Eds.), *African American psychology: Theory, research, and practice* (pp. 183–189). Newbury Park, CA: Sage.

Power, T. J., & DuPaul, G. J. (1996). Implications of DSM-IV for the practice of school psychology: Introduction to the mini-series. *School Psychology Review, 25*, 255–258.

Poynter, W. L. (1998). *The textbook of behavioral managed care: From concept through management to treatment*. New York: Brunner/Mazel.

Prediger, D. J. (1982). Dimensions underlying Holland's hexagon: Missing link between interests and occupations? *Journal of Vocational Behavior, 21*, 259–287.

Prediger, D. J. (1994). Multicultural assessment standards: A compilation for counselors. *Measurement and Evaluation in Counseling and Development, 27*, 68–73.

Premack, D. (1959). Toward empirical behavior laws: I. Positive reinforcement. *Psychological Review, 66*, 219–233.

Prochaska, J. O., & Norcross, J. C. (1994). *Systems of psychotherapy: A transtheoretical analysis* (3rd ed.). Pacific Grove, CA: Brooks/Cole.

Protection of Human Research Subjects. Title 45, C.F.R. Part 46. 66 F.R. 3878 (1991).

Protinsky, H., & Dillard, C. (1993). Enuresis: A family therapy model. *Psychotherapy: Theory, Research and Practice, 20*, 81–89.

Prout, H. T., & Brown, D. T. (1999). *Counseling and psychotherapy with children and adolescents: Theory and practice for school and clinical settings* (3rd ed.). New York: John Wiley.

Prout, S. M., DeMartino, R. A., & Prout, H. T. (1999). Ethical and legal issues In psychological interventions with children and adolescents. In H. T. Prout & D. T. Brown (Eds.), *Counseling and psychotherapy with children and adolescents: Theory and practice for school and clinical settings* (3rd ed.) (pp. 26–48). New York: John Wiley.

Puig-Antich, J., Perel, J. M., Lupatkin, W. Chambers, W. J., Tabrizi, M. A., King, J., Goetz, R., Davies, M., & Stiller, R. L. (1987). Imipramine in prepubertal major depressive disorders. *Archives of General Psychiatry, 44*, 81–89.

Quintana, S. M., & Vera, E. M. (1999). Mexican American children's ethnic identity, understanding of ethnic prejudice, and parental ethnic socialization. *Hispanic Journal of Behavioral Sciences, 21*, 387–404.

Rabian, B. (1994). Revised Children's Manifest Anxiety Scale. In D. J. Keyser & R. C. Sweetland (Eds.), *Test critiques* (Vol. X) (pp. 593–600). Austin, TX: Pro-Ed.

Radin, N. (1994). Primary-caregiving fathers in intact families. In A. E. Gottfried & A. W. Gottfried (Eds.), *Redefining families: Implications for children's development* (pp. 11–54). New York: Plenum Press.

Rae, W. A., & Fournier, C. J. (1999). Ethical and legal issues In the treatment of children and families. In S. W. Russ & T. H. Ollendick (Eds.), *Handbook of psychotherapies with children and families* (pp. 67–83). New York: Kluwer Academic/Plenum Publishers.

Rae, W. A., Worchel, F. F., Upchurch, J., Sanner, J. H., & Daniel, C. A. (1989). The psychosocial impact of play on hospitalized children. *Journal of Pediatric Psychology, 14*, 617–627.

Rank, O. (1936). *Will therapy and truth and reality*. New York: Knopf.

Rapin, L., & Keel, L. (1998). Association for Specialists in Group Work Best Practice Guidelines. *Journal for Specialists in Group Work, 23*, 237–244.

Ravenette, A. T. (1977). Personal construct theory: An approach to the psychological investigation of children and young people. In D. Bannister (Ed.), *New perspectives in personal construct theory* (pp. 251–280). London: Academic Press.

Reaves, R. P., & Ogloff, J. R. P. (1996). Liability for professional misconduct. In L. J. Bass, S. T. DeMers, J. R. P. Ogloff, C. Peterson, J. L. Pettifor, R. P. Reaves, T. Retfalvi, N. P. Simon, C. Sinclair, & R. M. Tipton (Eds.), *Professional conduct and discipline in psychology* (pp. 117–142). Washington, DC: American Psychological Association.

Reed, G. M., McLaughlin, C. J., & Milholland, K. (2000). Ten interdisciplinary principles for professional practice in telehealth: Implications for psychology. *Professional Psychology: Research and Practice, 31*, 170–178.

Reed, L. J., Carter, B. D., & Miller, L. C. (1992). Fear and anxiety in children. In C. E. Walker & M. C. Roberts (Eds.), *Handbook of clinical child psychology* (pp 237–260). New York: John Wiley.

Reed, M. L., & Edelbrock, C. S. (1983). Reliability and validity of the Direct Observation Form of the Child Behavior Checklist. *Journal of Abnormal Child Psychology, 11*, 521–530.

Reinecke, M. A., Dattilio, F. M., & Freeman, A. (1996). General issues. In M. A. Reinecke, F. M. Dattilio, & A. Freeman (Eds.), *Cognitive therapy with children and adolescents: A casebook for clinical practice* (pp. 1–9). New York: Guilford.

Reinert, D. R. (1998). A look at the challenges facing gay, lesbian, bisexual, and transgender youth [Special issue]. *Professional School Counseling, 1(3)*, 2–3.

Reisinger, K. S., & Bires, J. A. (1980). Anticipatory guidance in pediatric practice. *Pediatrics, 66*, 889–892.

Reisman, B. L., & Banuelos, D. (1984). Career fantasy in the barrio. *Journal of Non-White Concerns in Personnel and Guidance, 12(3)*, 99–104.

Rekers, G. A. (1983). Play therapy with cross-gender identified children. In C. E. Schaefer & K. J. O'Connor (Eds.), *Handbook of play therapy* (pp. 369–385). New York: John Wiley.

Rekers, G. A., & Kilgus, M. D. (1998). Diagnosis and treatment of gender identity disorders in children and adolescents. In L. VandeCreek, S. Knapp, & T. L. Jackson (Eds.), *Innovations in clinical practice: A source book* (Vol. 16) (pp. 127–141). Sarasota, FL: Professional Resource Press.

Rekers, G. A., Kilgus, M., & Rosen, A. C. (1990). Long-term effects of treatment for gender identity disorder of childhood. *Journal of Psychology and Human Sexuality, 3*, 121–153.

Rekers, G. A., & Lovaas, O. I. (1974). Behavioral treatment of deviant sex-role behaviors in a male child. *Journal of Applied Behavior Analysis, 7*, 173–190.

Remley, T. P. Jr., & Herlihy, B. (2001). *Ethical, legal, and professional issues in counseling*. Upper Saddle River, NJ: Prentice-Hall.

Reschly, D. J., & Wilson, M. S. (1997). Characteristics of school psychology graduate education: Implications for the entry-level discussion and doctoral-level specialty definition. *School Psychology Review, 26*, 74–92.

Resnick, M. D., Bearman, P. S., Blum, R. W., Bauman, K. E., Harris, K. M., Jones, J., Tabor, J., Beuhring, T., Sieving, R. E., Shew, M., Ireland, M., Bearinger, L. H., & Udry, J. R. (1997). Protecting adolescents from harm: Findings from the National Longitudinal Study on Adolescent Health. *Journal of the American Medical Association, 278*, 823–832.

Reyna v. State, 797 S.W.2d 189 (Tex. Ct. App. 1990).

Reynolds, C. R. (1980). Concurrent validity of "What I Think and Feel": The Revised Children's Manifest Anxiety Scale. *Journal of Consulting and Clinical Psychology, 48*, 774–775.

Reynolds, C.R. (1981). Long-term stability of scores on the Revised Children's Manifest Anxiety Scale. *Perceptual and Motor Skills, 53*, 702.

Reynolds, C. R., & Kamphaus, R. W. (1992). *BASC: Behavior Assessment System for Children manual*. Circle Pines, MN: American Guidance Services.

Reynolds, C. R., & Paget, K. D. (1983). National normative and reliability data for the Revised Children's Manifest Anxiety Scale. *School Psychology Review, 12*, 324–336.

Reynolds, C. R., & Richmond, B. O. (1978). What I Think and Feel: A revised measure of children's manifest anxiety. *Journal of Abnormal Child Psychology, 6*, 271–280.

Reynolds, C. R., & Richmond, B. O. (1985). *Revised Children's Manifest Anxiety Scale (RCMAS) manual*. Los Angeles, CA: Western Psychological Services.

Rhoden, B. L., Kranz, P. L., & Lund, N. L. (1981). Current trends in the use of limits in play therapy. *The Journal of Psychology, 107*, 191–198.

Richards, D. D., & Siegler, R. S. (1984). The effects of task requirements on children's life judgments. *Child Development, 55*, 1687–1696.

Richards, D. D., & Siegler, R. S. (1986). Children's understandings of the attributes of life. *Journal of Experimental Child Psychology, 42*, 1–22.

Richardson, B. L. (1989). Attitudes of Black clergy toward mental health professionals: Implications for pastoral care. *Journal of Pastoral Care, 43*, 33–39.

Richardson, B. L. (1991). Utilizing the resources of the African American church: Strategies for counseling professionals. In C. C. Lee & B. L. Richardson (Eds.), *Multicultural issues in counseling: New approaches to diversity* (pp. 65–75). Alexandria, VA: American Counseling Association.

Richters, J. E., Arnold, L. E., Jensen, P. S., Abikoff, H., Conners, C. K., Greenhill, L. L., Hechtman, L., Hinshaw, S. P., Pelham, W. E., &

Swanson, J. M. (1995). National Institute of Mental Health collaborative multisite, multimodal treatment study of children with attention deficit hyperactivity disorder (MTA): Part 1. Background and rationale. *Journal of the American Academy of Child and Adolescent Psychiatry, 34*, 987–1000.

Ridgeway, D., Waters, E., & Kuczaj, S. A. (1985). Acquisition of emotion-descriptive language: Receptive and productive vocabulary norms for ages 18 months to 6 years. *Developmental Psychology, 21*, 901–908.

Riley, P. L., & McDaniel, J. (2000). School violence prevention, intervention, and crisis response [Special issue: School violence and counselors]. *Professional School Counseling, 4*, 120–125.

Riordan, R. J., & Wilson, L. S. (1989). Bibliotherapy: Does it work? *Journal of Counseling and Development, 67*, 506–508.

Ritterband, L. M., Cox, D. J., Kovatchev, B. P., Borowitz, S. M., Ling, W. D., & Marshall, B. (2001). A telecommunication monitoring system for clinical and research practice. *Professional Psychology: Research and Practice, 32*, 636–641.

Roberts, M. C. (1986). *Pediatric psychology: Psychological interventions and strategies for pediatric problems.* New York: Pergamon.

Roberts, R. G. (1994). *Practice of family medicine. In R. B. Taylor (Ed.), Family medicine: Principles and practice* (4th ed.) (pp.1017–1020). New York: Springer.

Roberts, W., & Strayer, J. (1996). Empathy, emotional expressiveness, and prosocial behavior. *Child Development, 67*, 449–470.

Robin, A. & Foster, S. (1989). *Negotiating parent adolescent conflict: A behavioral-family systems approach.* New York: Guilford Press.

Robin, A. L., Bedway, M. Siegel, P. T., & Gilroy, M. (1996). Therapy for adolescent anorexia nervosa: Addressing cognitions, feelings, and the family role. In E. D. Hibbs & P. S. Jensen (Eds.), *Psychosocial treatments for child and adolescent disorders: Empirically based strategies for clinical practice* (pp. 239–284). Washington, DC: American Psychological Association.

Robin, A. L., Siegel, P. T., Moye, A. W., Gilroy, M., Dennis, A. B., & Sikand, A. (1999). A controlled comparison of family versus individual therapy for adolescents with anorexia nervosa. *Journal of the American Academy of Child and Adolescent Psychiatry, 38*, 1482–1489.

Robinson, J. L., Zahn-Waxler, C., & Emde, R. N. (1994). Patterns of development In early empathic behavior: Environmental and child constitutional influences. *Social Development, 3*, 125–145.

Rodwin, M. A. (1995). Conflicts in managed care. *New England Journal of Medicine, 332*, 604–607.

Rogers, C. R. (1931). *Measuring personality adjustment in children nine to thirteen years of age.* New York: Teachers College, Columbia University, Bureau of Publications.

Rogers, C. R. (1939). *The clinical treatment of the problem child.* Boston: Houghton Mifflin.

Rogers, C. R. (1942a). *Counseling and psychotherapy.* Boston: Houghton Mifflin.

Rogers, C. R. (1942b). The psychologist's contributions to parent, child, and community problems. *Journal of Consulting Psychology, 6*, 8–18.

Rogers, C. R. (1942c). Mental health problems in three elementary schools. *Educational Research Bulletin, 21*, 69–79.

Rogers, C. R. (1943). Therapy in guidance clinics. *Journal of Abnormal and Social Psychology, 38*, 284–289.

Rogers, C. R. (1946). Psychometric tests and client-centered counseling. *Educational and Psychological Measurement, 6*, 139–144.

Rogers, C. R. (1951). *Client-centered therapy: Its current practice, implications, and theory.* Boston: Houghton Mifflin.

Rogers, C. R. (1957). The necessary and sufficient conditions of therapeutic personality change. *Journal of Consulting Psychology, 21*, 95–103.

Rogers, C. R. (1961). *On becoming a person.* Boston: Houghton Mifflin.

Rogers, C. R. (1969). *Freedom to learn.* Columbus, OH: Merrill Publishing.

Rogers, C. R. (1970). *Carl Rogers on encounter groups.* New York: Harper & Row.

Rogers, C. R., & Dymond, R. F. (1954). *Psychotherapy and personality change: Co-ordinated research studies in the client-centered approach.* Chicago: University of Chicago Press.

Rogers, C. R., & Skinner, B. R. (1956). Some issues concerning the control of human behavior: A symposium. *Science, 124*, 1057–1066.

Rogler, L. H., Malgady, R. G., Costantino, G., & Blumenthal, R. (1987). What do culturally sensitive mental health services mean? The case of Hispanics. *American Psychologist, 42*, 565–570.

Rogoff, B. (1990). *Apprenticeship in thinking: Cognitive development in social context.* Oxford, UK: Oxford University Press.

Ronen, T. (1993). Self-control training in the treatment of sleep disorder: A case study. *Child and Family Behavior Therapy, 15*, 53–63.

Ronen, T. (1997). *Cognitive developmental therapy with children.* Chichester, UK: John Wiley.

Ronen, T. (1998). Linking developmental and emotional elements into child and family cognitive-behavioural therapy. In P. Graham (Ed.), *Cognitive-behaviour therapy for children and families* (pp. 1–17). Cambridge, England: Cambridge University Press.

Ronen, T., & Wozner, Y. (1995). A self-control intervention package for the treatment of primary nocturnal enuresis. *Child & Family Behavior Therapy, 17*, 1–20.

Ronen, T., Wozner, Y., & Rahav, G. (1992). Cognitive intervention in enuresis. *Child & Family Behavior Therapy, 14*, 1–14.

Root, M. P. P. (1992). Within, between, and beyond race. In M. P. P. Rott (Ed.)., *Racially mixed people in America* (pp. 3–11). Newbury Park, CA: Sage.

Rorschach, H. (1921). *Psychodiagnostik.* Bern: Bircher (Trans. Hans Huber Verlag, 1942).

Rose, A. J., & Asher, S. R. (1999). Children's goals and strategies in response to conflicts within a friendship. *Developmental Psychology, 35*, 69–79.

Rosen, H. (1996). Meaning-making narratives: Foundations for constructivist and social constructionist psychotherapies. In H. Rosen & K. Kuehlwein (Eds.), *Constructing realities: Meaning-making perspectives for psychotherapists* (pp. 3–54). San Francisco, CA: Jossey-Bass.

Rosen, L. D., Heckman, T., Carro, M. G., & Burchard, J. D. (1994). Satisfaction, involvement and unconditional care: The perceptions of children and adolescents receiving wraparound services. *Journal of Child and Family Services, 3*, 55–67.

Rosenfield, S. A., & Gravois, T. A. (1996). *Instructional consultation teams: Collaborating for change.* New York: Guilford.

Rosenzweig, S. (1936). Some implicit common factors in diverse methods of psychotherapy. *American Journal of Orthopsychiatry, 6*, 412–415.

Ross, A. O. (1958). Confidentiality in child guidance treatment. *Mental Hygiene, 42*, 60–66.

Ross, A. O. (1959). *The practice of clinical child psychology.* New York: Grune and Stratton.

Ross, A. O. (1980). *Psychological disorders of children: A behavioral approach to theory, research and therapy* (2nd ed.). New York: McGraw-Hill.

Ross, A. O. (1981). *Child behavior therapy: Principles, procedures, and empirical basis.* New York: John Wiley & Sons.

Ross, A. O. (1985). A (brief) look back. In J. M. Tuma (Ed.), *Proceedings: Conference on training clinical child psychologists* (pp. 31–33). Washington, DC: American Psychological Association.

Rubin, K. H., Fein, G. G., & Vandenberg, B. (1983). Play. In P. H. Mussen (Ed.), *Handbook of child psychology: Vol. 4. Socialization, personality and social development* (pp. 693–774). New York: John Wiley.

Ruble, D. N., & Martin, C. L. (1998). Gender development. In W. Damon (Series Ed.) & N. Eisenberg (Vol. Ed.), *Handbook of child psychology: Social, emotional, and personality development* (5th ed.) (Vol. 3) (pp. 933–1016). New York: John Wiley.

Ruff, H. A., & Lawson, K. R. (1990). Development of sustained, focused attention in young children during free play. *Developmental Psychology, 26*, 85–93.

Rushton, H. G. (1993). Older pharmacologic therapy for nocturnal enuresis. *Clinical Pediatrics* (Special Edition), *32*, 10–13.

Russ, S. W., & Ollendick, T. H. (1999). Epilogue. In S. W. Russ & T. H. Ollendick (Eds.), *Handbook of psychotherapies with children and families* (pp. 553–555). New York: Kluwer Academic/Plenum Publishers.

Russell, R. L. (1998). Linguistic psychotherapy research: New directions and promising findings. *Journal of Clinical Child Psychology, 27*, 17–27.

Russell, R. L., van den Broek, P., Adams, S., Rosenberger, K., & Essig, T. (1993). Analyzing narratives in psychotherapy: A formal framework and empirical analyses. *Journal of Narrative and Life History, 3*, 337–360.

Ryan, C., & Futterman, D. (1998). *Lesbian and gay youth: Care and counseling*. New York: Columbia University Press.

Safer, D. J., Zito, J. M., & Fine, E. M. (1996). Increased methylphenidate usage for attention deficit disorder in the 1990s. *Pediatrics, 98*, 1084–1088.

Sammons, M. T. (2001). Trends in telehealth. *The Register Report, 27*, 21–25.

Sandhu, D. S. (2000). Special issue: School violence and counselors. *Professional School Counseling, 4*, iv–v.

Sandler, J., Holder, A., Kawenoka, M., Kennedy, H. E., & Neurath, L. (1981). Notes on some theoretical and clinical aspects of transference. In R. Langs (Ed.), *Classics in psychoanalytic technique* (pp. 37–49). New York: Jason Aronson.

Santarcangelo, S., Bruns, E. J., & Yoe, J. T. (1998). New Directions: Vermont's statewide model of individualized care. In M. H. Epstein, K. Kutash, & A Duchnowski (Eds.), *Outcomes for children and youth with emotional and behavioral disorders and their families: Programs and evaluation best practices* (pp. 117–139). Austin, TX: Pro-Ed.

Santosky v. Kramer, 455 U.S. 745 (1982).

Santrock, J. W. (1995). *Children* (4th ed.). Madison, WI: Brown & Benchmark.

Santrock, J. W. (2000). *Children* (6th ed.). New York: McGraw-Hill.

Satir, V. (1964). *Conjoint family therapy*. Palo Alto, CA: Science and Behavior Books.

Satir, V. (1972). *Peoplemaking*. Palo Alto, CA: Science & Behavior Books.

Satir, V. (1983). *Conjoint family therapy* (3rd ed.). Palo Alto, CA: Science and Behavior Books.

Satir, V., & Baldwin, M. (1983). *Satir: Step by step*. Palo Alto, CA: Science and Behavior Books.

Satir, V., & Bitter, J. R. (1991). The therapist and family therapy: Satir's human validation process model. In A. M. Horne & J. L. Passmore (Eds.), *Family counseling and therapy* (2nd ed.) (pp. 13–45). Itasca, IL: F. E. Peacock Publishers.

Satterfield, J. H., Cantwell, D. P., & Satterfield, B. T. (1979). Multimodality treatment. *Archives of General Psychiatry, 36*, 965–974.

Satterfield, J. H., Satterfield, B. T., & Cantwell, D. P. (1981). Three-year multimodality treatment study of 100 hyperactive boys. *Journal of Pediatrics, 98*, 650–655.

Sattler, J. M. (1998). *Clinical and forensic interviewing of children and families: Guidelines for the mental health, education, pediatric, and child maltreatment fields*. San Diego, CA: Jerome M. Sattler, Publisher, Inc.

Sauber, S. R. (1997). Introduction to managed mental health care: Provider survival. In S. R. Sauber (Ed.), *Managed mental health care: Major diagnostic and treatment approaches* (pp. 1–39). New York: Brunner/Mazel.

Savin-Williams, R. C. (1996). Memories of childhood and early adolescent sexual feelings among gay and bisexual boys: A narrative approach. In R. C. Savin-Williams & K. M. Cohen (Eds.), *The lives of lesbians, gays, and bisexuals: Children to adults* (pp. 94–109). Fort Worth, TX: Harcourt Brace.

Saxe, L., & Cross, T. P. (1997). Interpreting the Fort Bragg Children's Mental Health Demonstration Project: The cup is half full. *American Psychologist, 52*, 553–556.

Sayger, T. V. (1992). Family psychology and therapy. In C. E. Walker & M. C. Roberts (Eds.), *Handbook of clinical child psychology* (2nd ed.) (pp. 783–807). New York: John Wiley.

Schaefer, C. E., Jacobsen, H. E., & Ghahramanlou, M. (2000). Play group therapy for social skills deficits in children. In H. G. Kaduson & C. E. Schaefer (Eds.), *Short-term play therapy for children* (pp. 296–344). New York: Guilford.

Schaefer, C. E., & Reid, S. E. (1986). *Game play: Therapeutic use of childhood games*. New York: John Wiley.

Scharff, D. E., & Scharff, J. S. (1987). *Object relations family therapy*. Northvale, NJ: Aronson.

Schein, E. H. (1969). *Process consultation: Its role in organization development*. Reading, MA: Addison–Wesley.

Scherer, M. W., & Nakamura, C. Y. (1968). A fear survey schedule for children (FSS-FC): A factor analytic comparison with manifest anxiety (CMAS). *Behaviour Research and Therapy, 6*, 173–182.

Schilson, E. A. (1991). Strategic therapy. In A. M. Horne & J. L. Passmore (Eds.), *Family counseling and therapy* (2nd ed.) (pp. 141–178). Itasca, IL: F. E. Peacock Publishers.

Schmuck, R. A. (1990). Organization development in schools: Contemporary concepts and practices. In T. B. Gutkin & C. R Reynolds (Eds.), *The handbook of school psychology* (pp. 899–919). New York: John Wiley.

Schoenfeld, P., Halevy, J., Hemley-van der Velden, E., & Ruhf, L. (1986). Long-term outcome network therapy. *Hospital and Community Psychiatry, 37*, 373–376.

Schoenfeld, P., Halevy-Martini, J., Hemley-van der Velden, E., & Ruhf, L. (1985). Network therapy: An outcome study of twelve social networks. *Journal of Community Psychology, 13*, 281–287.

Schoenwald, S. K., Borduin, C. M., & Henggeler, S. W. (1998). Multisystemic therapy: Changing the natural and service ecologies of adolescents and families. In M. H. Epstein, K. Kutash, & A. Duchnowski (Eds.), *Outcomes for children and youth with emotional and behavioral disorders and their families: Programs and evaluation best practices* (pp. 485–511). Austin, TX: Pro-Ed.

Schouten, R., & Duckworth, K. S. (1999). Medicolegal and ethical issues in the pharmacological treatment of children. In J. S. Werry & M. G. Aman (Eds.), *Practitioner's guide to psychoactive drugs for children and adolescents* (2nd ed.) (pp. 165–181). New York: Plenum.

Schrank, F. A., & Engels, D. W. (1981). Bibliotherapy as a counseling adjunct: Research findings. *The Personnel and Guidance Journal, 60*, 143–147.

Schuhmann, E. M., Foote, R. C., Eyberg, S. M., Boggs, S. R., & Algina, J. (1998). Efficacy of parent-child interaction therapy: Interim report of a randomized trial with short-term maintenance. *Journal of Clinical Child Psychology, 27*, 34–45.

Schwartz, J. A. J., Kaslow, N. J., Racusin, G. R., & Carton, E. R. (1998). Interpersonal family therapy for childhood depression. In V. B. Van Hasselt & M. Hersen (Eds.), *Handbook of psychological treatment protocols for children and adolescents* (pp. 109–151). Mahwah, NJ: Lawrence Erlbaum.

Schwebel, A. I., & Fine, M. A. (1994). *Understanding and helping families: A cognitive-behavioral approach*. Hillsdale, NJ: Lawrence Erlbaum.

Sealander, K. A., Schwiebert, V. L., Oren, T. A., & Weekley, J. L. (1999). Confidentiality and the law. *Professional School Counseling, 3*, 122–127.

Sedlak, A. J., & Broadhurst, D. D. (1996). *Executive summary of the Third National Incidence Study of Child Abuse and Neglect*. Washington, DC: National Center on Child Abuse and Neglect.

Segal, L. (1991). Brief family therapy. In A. M. Horne & J. L. Passmore (Eds.), *Family counseling and therapy* (2nd ed.) (pp. 179–205). Itasca, IL: F. E. Peacock.

Seifert, K. L., & Hoffnung, R. J. (1997). *Child and adolescent development*. Boston: Houghton Mifflin.

Selekman, M. D. (1997). *Solution-focused therapy with children: Harnessing family strengths for systemic change*. New York: Guilford.

Seligman, M. E. (1975). *Helplessness: On depression, development, and death*. New York: W. H. Freeman.

Seligman, M. E., Peterson, C., Kaslow, N. J., Tanenbaum, R. L., Alloy, L. B., & Abramson, L. Y. (1984). Attributional style and depressive symptoms among children. *Journal of Abnormal Psychology, 2*, 235–238.

Seligman, M. P., Reivich, K., Jaycox, L., & Gillham, J. (1995). *The optimistic child: A revolutionary program that safeguards children against depression and builds lifelong resilience*. Boston: Houghton Mifflin.

Selman, R. L. (1976). Social-cognitive understanding: A guide to educational and clinical practice. In T. Lickona (Ed.), *Moral development and behavior: Theory, research, and social issues* (pp. 299–316). New York: Holt, Rinehart and Winston.

Selman, R. L., & Byrne, D. F. (1974). A structural-developmental analysis of levels of role taking in middle childhood. *Child Development, 45*, 803–806.

Selman, R. L., Watts, C. L., & Schultz, L. H. (1997). *Fostering friendship: Pair therapy for treatment and prevention*. New York: De Gruyter.

Selvini, M. (Ed.). (1988). *The work of Mara Selvini Palazzoli*. Northvale, NJ: Jason Aronson.

Selvini Palazzoli, M. (1988). Why a long interval between sessions? In M. Selvini Palazzoli (Ed.), *The work of Mara Selvini Palazzoli* (pp. 363–378). Northvale, NJ: Jason Aronson.

Selvini Palazzoli, M., Boscolo, L., Cecchin, G., & Prata, G. (1988a). The treatment of children through brief therapy of their parents. In M. Selvini (Ed.), *The work of Mara Selvini Palazzoli* (pp. 121–144). Northvale, NJ: Jason Aronson.

Selvini Palazzoli, M., Boscolo, L., Cecchin, G., & Prata, G. (1988b). A ritualized prescription in family therapy: Odd days and even days. In M. Selvini (Ed.), *The work of Mara Selvini Palazzoli* (pp. 305–322). Northvale, NJ: Jason Aronson.

Seymour, H. N., & Ralabate, P. K. (1985). The acquisition of a phonologic feature of Black English. *Journal of Communication Disorders, 18*, 139–148.

Shackford, K. (1984). Interracial children: Growing up healthy in an unhealthy society. *Interracial Books for Children Bulletin, 15(6)*, 4–6.

Shadish, W. R., Ragsdale, K., Glaser, R. R., & Montgomery, L. M. (1995). The efficacy and effectiveness of marital and family therapy: A perspective from meta-analysis. *Journal of Marital and Family Therapy, 21*, 345–360.

Shaffer, D. R. (1999). *Developmental psychology: Childhood and adolescence (5th ed.)* . Pacific Grove, CA: Brooks/Cole.

Shapiro, E. S., & Bradley, K. L. (1996). Treatment of academic problems. In M. A. Reinecke, F. M. Dattilio, & A. Freeman (Eds.), *Cognitive therapy with children and adolescents: A casebook for clinical practice* (pp. 344–366). New York: Guilford Press.

Shapiro, E. S., & Cole, C. L. (1993). Self-monitoring. In T. H. Ollendick & M. Hersen (Eds.), *Handbook of child and adolescent assessment* (pp. 124–139). Boston: Allyn and Bacon.

Shapiro, F. (1995). *Eye movement desensitization and reprocessing: Basic principles, protocols, and procedures*. New York: Guilford Press.

Shapiro, L. E. (1994). *Short-term therapy with children*. King of Prussia, PA: The Center for Applied Psychology.

Shapiro, L. E. (1994/1996). *Short-term therapy with children: Make-a-game instructions*. King of Prussia, PA: The Center for Applied Psychology.

Shapiro, T. (1985). Developmental considerations in psychopharmacology: The interaction of drugs and development. In J. M. Weiner (Ed.), *Diagnosis and psychopharmacology of childhood and adolescents disorders* (pp. 51–68). New York: John Wiley.

Sharf, R. S. (2000). *Theories of psychotherapy and counseling: Concepts and cases* (2nd ed.). Pacific Grove, CA: Brooks/Cole.

Sheridon, S. M., Dee, C. C., Morgan, J. C., McCormick, M. E., & Walker, D. (1996). A multimethod intervention for social skills deficits in children with ADHD and their parents. *School Psychology Review, 25*, 57–76.

Sherry, J. L. (2001). The effects of violent video games on aggression: A meta-analysis. *Human Communication Research, 27*, 409–431.

Shirk, S. R. (1998). Interpersonal schemata in child psychotherapy: A cognitive-interpersonal perspective. *Journal of Clinical Child Psychology, 27*, 4–16.

Shirk, S. R., & Saiz, C. C. (1992). Clinical, empirical, and developmental perspectives on the therapeutic relationship in child psychotherapy. *Development and Psychopathology, 4*, 713–728.

Shore, R. J., & Hayslip, B., Jr. (1994). Custodial grandparenting: Implications for children's development. In A. E. Gottfried & A. W. Gottfried (Eds.), *Redefining families: Implications for children's development* (pp. 171–218). New York: Plenum Press.

Siegal, M. (1991). *Knowing children: Experiments In conversation and cognition*. Hillsdale, NJ: Lawrence Erlbaum.

Sigelman, C. K., & Mansfield, K. A. (1992). Knowledge and receptivity to psychological treatment in childhood and adolescence. *Journal of Clinical Child Psychology, 21*, 2–9.

Silverman, W. K., & Kurtines, W. M. (1996). Transfer of control: A psychosocial intervention model for internalizing disorders in youth. In E. D. Hibbs & P. S. Jensen (Eds.), *Psychosocial treatments for child and adolescent disorders: Empirically based strategies for clinical practice* (pp. 63–81). Washington, DC: American Psychological Association.

Singer, D. G., & Singer, J. L. (1992). *The house of make-believe: Children's play and the developing imagination*. Cambridge, MA: Harvard University Press.

Skinner, B. F. (1948). *Walden two*. New York: Macmillan.

Skinner, B. F. (1953). *Science and human behavior*. New York: Free Press.

Skinner, B. F. (1954). The science of learning and the art of teaching. *Harvard Educational Review, 24*, 86–97.

Skinner, B. F. (1961). Teaching machines. *Scientific American, 205*(5), 90–102.

Sloves, R., & Peterlin, K. B. (1993). Where in the world is . . . my father? A time-limited play therapy. In T. Kottman & C. Schaefer (Eds.), *Play therapy in action: A casebook for practitioners* (pp. 301–346). Northvale, NJ: Jason Aronson.

Smead, R. (1995). *Skills and techniques for group work with children and adolescents*. Champaign, IL: Research Press.

Smilansky, S. (1968). *The effects of sociodramatic play on disadvantaged preschool children*. New York: John Wiley.

Smith, E. J. (1981). Cultural and historical perspectives in counseling Blacks. In D. W. Sue (Ed.), *Counseling the culturally different: Theory and practice* (pp. 141–185). New York: John Wiley.

Smith, E. M. J., & Vasquez, M. J. T. (Eds.). (1985). Cross-cultural counseling. [Special issue]. *The Counseling Psychologist, 13*, 531–536.

Smith, J. T., Barabasz, A., & Barabasz, M. (1996). Comparison of hypnosis and distraction in severely ill children undergoing painful medical procedures. *Journal of Counseling Psychology, 43*, 187–195.

Smith-Acuna, S., Durlak, J. A., & Kaspar, C. J. (1991). Development of child psychotherapy process measures. *Journal of Clinical Child Psychology, 20*, 126–131.

Smyrnios, K. X., & Kirkby, R. J. (1993). Long-term comparison of brief versus unlimited psychodynamic treatments with children and their parents. *Journal of Consulting and Clinical Psychology, 61*, 1020–1027.

Snyder, H., & Sickmund, M. (1999). *Juvenile offenders and victims: 1999 national report*. Washington, DC: Office of Juvenile Justice and Delinquency Prevention.

Sodowsky, G. R., Kwan, K. K., & Pannu, R. (1995). Ethnic identity of Asians in the United States. In J. G. Ponterotto, Casas, J. M., Suzuki, L. A., & Alexander, C. M. (Eds.), *Handbook of multicultural counseling* (pp. 123–154). Thousand Oaks, CA: Sage.

Sonuga-Barke, X., & Edmund, J. S. (1998). Categorical models of childhood disorder: A conceptual and empirical analysis. *Journal of Child Psychology and Psychiatry and Allied Disciplines, 39*, 115–133.

Sowder, B. J., Burt, M. R., Rosenstein, M. J., & Milazzo-Sayre, L. J. (1981). *Use of psychiatric facilities by children and youth. United States 1975* (DHHS Publication No. ADM 81-1142). Washington, DC: National Institute of Mental Health.

Spaide, D. (1995). *Teaching your kids to care: How to discover and develop the spirit of charity in your children*. New York: Citadel Press.

Spanier, G. B. (1976). Measuring dyadic adjustment: New scales for assessing the quality of marriage and similar dyads. *Journal of Marriage and the Family, 38*, 15–28.

Speck, R., & Attneave, C. (1973). *Family networks: Retribalization and healing*. New York: Pantheon.

Spiegler, M D., & Guevremont, D. C. (1998). *Contemporary behavior therapy* (3rd ed.). Pacific Grove, CA: Brooks/Cole.

Spielberger, C. D. (1973). *Manual for the State-Trait Anxiety Inventory for Children*. Palo Alto, CA: Consulting Psychologists Press.

Spielberger, C. D., Gorsuch, R. L., & Lushene, R. E. (1970). *Manual for the State-Trait Anxiety Inventory*. Palo Alto, CA: Consulting Psychologists Press.

Sroufe, L. A., Carlson, E., & Shulman, S (1993). Individuals in relationships: Development from infancy to adolescence. In D. C. Funder, R. D. Parke, C. Tomlinson-Keasey, & K. Widaman (Eds.), *Studying lives through time: Personality and development* (pp. 315–342). Washington, DC: American Psychological Association.

St. Clair, M. (1996). *Object relations and self psychology: An introduction*. Pacific Grove, CA: Brooks/Cole.

Stadler, H. A. (1989). Balancing ethical responsibilities: Reporting child abuse and neglect. *The Counseling Psychologist, 17*, 102–110.

Stanley v. Illinois, 405 U.S. 645 (1972).

Stark, L. J., Opipari, L. C., Donaldson, D. L., Danovsky, M. B., Rasile, D. A., & DelSanto, A. F. (1997). Evaluation of a standard protocol for retentive encopresis: A replication. *Journal of Pediatric Psychology, 22*, 619–633.

Stark, L. J., Owens-Stively, J., Spirito, A., Lewis, A., & Guevremont, D. (1990). Group behavioral treatment of retentive encopresis. *Journal of Pediatric Psychology, 15*, 659–671.

Starr, J., & Raykovitz, J. (1990). A multimodal approach to interviewing children. In D, B. Keats (Ed.), *Child multimodal therapy* (pp. 33–38). Norwood, NJ: Ablex.

State v. Brotherton, 384 N.W.2d 375 (Iowa 1986).

State v. St. John, 410 A.2d 1126 (N.H. 1980).

Stedman, J. M. (1976). Family counseling with a school-phobic child. In J. D. Krumboltz & C. E. Thoreson (Eds.), *Counseling methods* (pp. 280–288). New York: Holt, Rinehart, & Winston.

Stein, T. J. (1998). *Child welfare and the law* (rev. ed.). Washington, DC: CWLA Press.

Stephenson, J. (1995). Sick kids find help in a cyberspace world. *Journal of the American Medical Association, 274*, 1899–1901.

Sternberg, K. J., Lamb, M. E., Greenbaum, C., Cicchetti, D., Dawud, S., Cortes, R. M., Krispin, O., & Lorey, F. (1993). Effects of domestic violence on children's behavior problems and depression. *Developmental Psychology, 29*, 44–52.

Stevenson, H. W. (1991). The development of prosocial behavior In large-scale collective societies: China and Japan. In R. A. Hinde & J. Groebel (Eds.), *Cooperation and prosocial behavior* (pp. 89–105). Cambridge, UK: Cambridge University Press.

Stillion, J. M., & McDowell, E. E. (1996). *Suicide across the life span* (2nd ed.). Washington DC: Taylor & Francis.

Stockdale, D. F., Hegland, S. M., & Chiaromonte, T. (1989). Helping behaviors: An observational study of preschool children. *Early Childhood Research Quarterly, 4*, 533–543.

Stormshak, E. A., Bierman, K. L., McMahon, R. J., & Lengua, L. J. (2000). Parenting practices and child disruptive behavior problems in early elementary school. *Journal of Clinical Child Psychology, 29*, 17–29.

Straus, M. A. (1991). Discipline and deviance: Physical punishment of children and violence and other crime in adulthood. *Social Problems, 38*, 133–154.

Straus, M. A. (1994). *Beating the devil out of them: Corporal punishment in American families*. New York: Lexington Books.

Strauss, C. C., Last, C. G., Hersen M., & Kazdin, A. E. (1988). Association between anxiety and depression in children and adolescents with anxiety disorders. *Journal of Abnormal Child Psychology, 16*, 57–68.

Strayhorn, J. M. (1987). Medical assessment of children with behavioral problems. In M. Hersen & V. B. Van Hasselt (Eds.), *Behavior therapy with children and adolescents: A clinical approach* (pp. 50–74). New York: John Wiley.

Stubberfield, T. G., Wray, J. A., & Parry, T. S. (1999). Utilization of alternative therapies in attention-deficit hyperactivity disorder. *Journal of Paediatrics and Child Health, 35*, 450–453.

Sue, D. W., Arredondo, P., & McDavis, R. J. (1992) Multicultural counseling competencies and standards: A call to the profession. *Journal of Counseling and Development, 70*, 477–486.

Sue, D., & Sue, D. W. (1991). Counseling strategies for Chinese Americans. In C. C. Lee & B. L. Richardson (Eds.), *Multicultural issues in counseling: New approaches to diversity* (pp. 79–90). Alexandria, VA: American Association of Counseling and Development.

Sue, S. (1998). In search of cultural competence in psychotherapy and counseling. *American Psychologist, 53*, 440–448.

Sue, S., Fujino, D. C., Ho, L., Takeuchi, D. T., & Zane, N. W. S. (1991). Community mental health services for ethnic minority groups: A test of the cultural responsiveness hypothesis. *Journal of Consulting and Clinical Psychology, 59*, 533–540.

Sukhodolsky, D. G., Solomon, R. M., & Perine, J. (2000). Cognitive-behavioral, anger-control intervention for elementary school children: A treatment-outcome study. *Journal of Child and Adolescent Group Therapy, 10*, 159–170.

Super, D. E. (1957). *The psychology of careers: An introduction to vocational development*. New York: Harper.

Super, D. E., & Overstreet, P. L. (1960). *The vocational maturity of ninth-grade boys*. New York: Teachers College Press.

Super, D. E., Savickas, M. L., & Super, C. M. (1996). The life-span, life-space approach to careers. In D. Brown & L. Brooks (Eds.), *Career choice and development* (3rd ed.) (pp. 121–178). San Francisco: Jossey-Bass.

Sutton, C. T., & Broken Nose, M. A. (1996). American Indian families: An overview. In M. McGoldrick, J. Giordano, & J. K. Pearce (Eds.), *Ethnicity and family therapy* (2nd ed.) (pp. 31–44). New York: Guilford.

Sverd, J., Gadow, K. D., Nolan, E. E., Sprafkin, J., & Ezor, S. N. (1992). Methylphenidate in hyperactive boys with comorbid tic disorder: I. Clinic evaluations. In T. N. Chase, A. J. Friedhoff, & D. J. Cohen (Eds.), *Tourette syndrome: Genetics, neurobiology, and treatment. Advances In neurology* (Vol. 58) (pp. 271–281). New York: Raven Press.

Sweeney, T. J. (1998). *Adlerian counseling: A practitioner's approach* (4th ed.). Philadelphia, PA: Accelerated Development.

Tabor v. Doctors Memorial Hospital, 563 So. 2d 233 (1990).

Taft, J. (1927/1962). The function of a mental hygienist in a children's agency. In V. P. Robinson (Ed.), *Jesse Taft: Therapist and social work educator* (pp. 108–118). Philadelphia: University of Pennsylvania Press.

Taft, J. (1930). A changing psychology in child welfare. *The Annals of the American Academy of Political and Social Sciences, 151*, 121–129.

Taft, J. (1933/1962). *The dynamics of therapy in a controlled relationship*. New York: Dover Publications.

Tanner, J. M. (1978). *Foetus into man: Physical growth from conception to maturity* (2nd ed.). Cambridge, MA: Harvard University Press.

Tanouye, E. (1997, April 4). Antidepressant makers study kids' market. *The Wall Street Journal*, pp. B1, B6.

Tarasoff v. Board of Regents of the University of California, 551 P.2d 334 (Cal. Sup. Ct. 1976).

Task Force on Promotion and Dissemination of Psychological Procedures. (1995). Training in and dissemination of empirically-validated psychological treatments. *The Clinical Psychologist, 48*, 3–23.

Taylor, L., & Adelman, H. S. (1989). Reframing the confidentiality dilemma to work in children's best interests. *Professional Psychology: Research and Practice, 20*, 79–83.

Taylor, L., Adelman, H. S., & Kaser-Boyd, N. (1983). Perspectives of children regarding their participation in psychoeducational decisions. *Professional Psychology: Research and Practice, 14*, 882–894.

Taylor, L., Adelman, H. S., & Kaser-Boyd, N. (1984). Attitudes toward involving minors in decisions. *Professional Psychology: Research and Practice, 15*, 436–449.

Taylor, R. B. (1994). Family medicine principles: Current expressions. In R. B. Taylor (Ed.), *Family medicine: Principles and practice* (5th ed.) (pp. 1–4). New York: Springer-Verlag.

Tharp, R. G. (1989). Psychocultural variables and constants: Effects on teaching and learning in schools. *American Psychologist, 44*, 349–359.

Tharp, R. G. (1991). Cultural diversity and treatment of children. *Journal of Consulting and Clinical Psychology, 59*, 799–812.

Thayer, L. (1991). Toward a person-centered approach to family therapy. In A. M. Horne & J. L. Passmore (Eds.), *Family counseling and therapy* (2nd. ed.) (pp. 301–346). Itasca, IL: F. E. Peacock Publishers.

The Center for Applied Psychology. (1992). *My Two Homes* [Game]. King of Prussia, PA: Author.

The Health Insurance Association of America. (1999). *Fundamentals of health insurance: Part A*. Washington, DC: Author.

The Ungame Company. (1983). *The Ungame*. Anaheim, CA: Author.

Thomas, J. L., & Cummings, J. L. (Eds.). (2000). *The value of psychological treatment: The collected papers of Nicholas A. Cummings* (Vol. I). Phoenix, AZ: Zeig, Tucker, & Co.

Thomas, M. B., & Danby, P. G. (1985). Black clients: Family structure, therapeutic issues, and strengths. *Psychotherapy, 22*, 398–407.

Thompson, C. L., & Rudolph, L. B. (2000). *Counseling children* (5th ed.). Belmont, CA: Wadsworth Publishing.

Thorne, B. (1992). *Carl Rogers*. London: Sage.

Thornton, M. C., Chatters, L. M., Taylor, R. J., & Allen, W. R. (1990). Sociodemographic and environmental correlates of racial socialization by Black parents. *Child Development, 61*, 401–409.

Tinker v. Des Moines Independent Community School District, 393 U.S. 503 (1969).

Tinker, R. H., & Wilson, S. A. (1999). *Through the eyes of a child: EMDR with children*. New York: Norton.

Tomlinson-Keasey, C. (1972). Formal operations in females from 11 to 54 years of age. *Developmental Psychology, 6*, 364.

Tomm, K. (1988). Interventive interviewing: Part III. Intending to ask lineal, circular, strategic, or reflexive questions? *Family Process, 27*, 1–15.

Tong, L., Oates, K., & McDowell, M. (1987). Personality development following sexual abuse. *Child Abuse and Neglect, 11*, 371–383.

Toren, P., Wolmer, L., Rosental, B., Eldar, S., Koren, S., Lask, M., Weizman, R., & Loar, N. (2000). Case series: Brief parent-child group therapy for childhood anxiety disorders using a manual-based cognitive-behavioral technique. *Journal of the American Academy of Child and Adolescent Psychiatry, 39*, 1309–1312.

Toth, S. L., & Cicchetti, D. (1999). Developmental psychopathology and child psychotherapy. In S. W. Russ & T. H. Ollendick (Eds.), *Handbook of psychotherapies with children and families* (pp. 15–44). New York: Kluwer Academic/Plenum Publishers.

Tracey, T. J. (2001). The development of structure of interests in children: Setting the stage. *Journal of Vocational Behavior, 59*, 89–104.

Tracey, T. J. (2002). Development of interests and competency beliefs: A 1-year longitudinal study of fifth- to eighth-grade students using the ICA-R and structural equation modeling. *Journal of Counseling Psychology, 49*, 148–163.

Tracey, T. J., & Rounds, J. B. (1993). Evaluating Holland's and Gati's vocational interest models: A structural meta-analysis. *Psychological Bulletin, 113*, 229–246.

Tracey, T. J., & Ward, C. C. (1998). The structure of children's interests and competence perceptions. *Journal of Counseling Psychology, 45*, 290–303.

Trice, A. D., Hughes, M. A., Odom, C., Woods, K., & McClellan, N. C. (1995). The origins of children's career aspirations: IV. Testing hypotheses from four theories. *Vocational Guidance Quarterly, 43*, 307–322.

Trice, A. D., & King, R. (1991). Stability of kindergarten children's career aspirations. *Psychological Reports, 68*, 1378.

Troiden, R. R. (1989). The formation of homosexual identities. *Journal of Homosexuality, 17*, 43–73.

Truax, C. B., Altmann, H., Wright, L., & Mitchell, K. M. (1973). Effects of therapeutic conditions in child therapy. *Journal of Community Psychology, 1*, 313–318.

Tucker, C. M. (1999). *African American children: A self-empowerment approach to modifying behavior problems and preventing academic failure*. Boston: Allyn and Bacon.

Tuma, J. M., & Pratt, J. M. (1982). Clinical child psychology practice and training: A survey. *Journal of Clinical Child Psychology, 11*, 27–34.

U.S. Bureau of the Census. (1995). *Statistical abstract of the United States* (115th ed.). Washington, DC: Government Printing Office.

U.S. Bureau of the Census. (1999). *Statistical abstract of the United States: 1997* (119th ed.). Washington, DC: Author.

U.S. Bureau of the Census. (2000). Profile of general demographic characteristics for the United States: 2000. Retrieved December 13, 2001, from http://www.olemiss.edu/ depts/sdc/profiles/unitedstates.pdf

U.S. Department of Agriculture. (1981). *Nutritive value of food*. Washington, DC: U.S. Government Printing Office.

Ullmann, R., Sleator, E., & Sprague, R. (1984). A new rating scale for diagnosis and monitoring of ADD children. *Psychopharmacology Bulletin, 20*, 160–164.

United Nations Convention on the Rights of the Child, U.N. Doc. A/Res/44/25 (1989).

Vacc, N. A. & Loesch, L. A. (1994). *A professional orientation to counseling* (2nd ed.). Muncie, IN: Accelerated Development Inc.

VandenBos, G. R., & Williams, S. (2000). The Internet versus the telephone: What is telehealth, anyway? *Professional Psychology: Research and Practice, 31*, 490–492.

Van der Krol, R. J., Oosterbaan, H., Weller, S. D., & Koning, A. E. (1998) Attention-deficit disorder. In P. Graham (Ed.), *Cognitive-behaviour therapy for children and families* (pp. 32–44). Cambridge, England: Cambridge University Press.

VanFleet, R. (1998). A parent's guide to filial therapy. In L. Vandecreek, S. Knapp, & T. L Jackson (Eds.), *Innovations in clinical practice: A source book* (Vol. 16) (pp. 457–463). Sarasota, FL: Professional Resource Press.

VanFleet, R. (2000). Short-term play therapy for families with chronic illness. In H. G. Kaduson & C. E. Schaefer (Eds.), *Short-term play therapy for children* (pp. 175–193). New York: Guilford.

Van Horn, S. M., & Myrick, R. D. (2001). Computer technology and the 21st century school counselor. *Professional School Counseling, 5*, 124–130.

Varley, C. K. (1984). Diet and the behavior of children with attention deficit disorder. *Journal of the American Academy of Child Psychiatry, 23*, 182–185.

Vasquez, C., & Javier, R. A. (1991). The problem with interpreters: Communicating with Spanish-speaking patients. *Hospital and Community Psychiatry, 42*, 163–165.

Vaughn, B., Egeland, B., Sroufe, L.A., & Waters, E. (1979). Individual differences in infant-mother attachment at twelve and eighteen months: Stability and change in families under stress. *Child Development, 50*, 971–975.

Venable, W. M., & Thompson, B. (1998). Caretaker psychological factors predicting premature termination of children's counseling. *Journal of Counseling and Development, 76*, 286–293.

Vernon, A. (Ed.), (1999). *Counseling children and adolescents* (2nd ed.). Denver, CO: Love Publishing Co.

Vernon, A. (1999). Applications of rational-emotive behavior therapy with children and adolescents. In A. Vernon (Ed.), *Counseling children and adolescents* (2nd ed.) (pp. 139–157). Denver, CO: Love Publishing.

Viesselman, J. O. (1999). Antidepressant and antimanic drugs. In J. S. Werry & M. G. Aman (Eds.), *Practitioner's guide to psychoactive drugs for children and adolescents* (2nd ed.) (pp. 249–296). New York: Plenum Medical Book Co.

Vitiello, B., Severe, J. B., Greenhill, L. L., Arnold, L. E., Abikoff, H. B., Bukstein, O. G., Elliott, G. R., Hechtman, L., Jensen, P. S., Hinshaw, S. P., March, J. S., Newcorn, J. H., Swanson, J. M., & Cantwell, D. P.

(2001). Methylphenidate dosage for children with ADHD over time under controlled conditions: Lessons from the MTA. *Journal of the American Academy of Child and Adolescent Psychiatry, 40,* 188–196.

Vontress, C. E. (1986). Social and cultural foundations. In M. D. Lewis, R. L. Hayes, & J. A. Lewis (Eds.), *An introduction to the counseling profession* (pp. 215–250). Itasca, IL: F.E. Peacock Publishers.

Vygotsky, L. S. (1934/1986). *Thought and language* (A. Kozulin, Trans.). Cambridge, MA: MIT Press.

Wachtel, E. F. (1994). *Treating troubled children and their families.* New York: Guilford.

Wachtel, P. L., & Messer, S. B. (1997). *Theories of psychotherapy: Origins and evolution.* Washington, DC: American Psychological Association.

Wagner, W. G. (1987a). Child sexual abuse: A multidisciplinary approach to case management. *Journal of Counseling and Development, 65,* 435–439.

Wagner, W. G. (1987b). The behavioral treatment of childhood nocturnal enuresis. *Journal of Counseling and Development, 65,* 262–265.

Wagner, W. G. (1991). Brief-term psychological adjustment of sexually abused children. *Child Study Journal, 21,* 263–276.

Wagner, W. G. (1994). Counseling with children: An opportunity for tomorrow. *The Counseling Psychologist, 22,* 381–401.

Wagner, W. G. (1996). Optimal development in adolescence: What is it and how can it be encouraged? *The Counseling Psychologist, 24,* 360–399.

Wagner, W. G., & Hicks-Jimenez, K. (1986). Clinicians' knowledge and attitudes regarding the treatment of childhood nocturnal enuresis. *The Behavior Therapist, 4,* 77–78.

Wagner, W. G., Johnson, S. B., Walker, D., Carter, R., & Wittmer, J. (1982). A controlled comparison of two treatments for nocturnal enuresis. *Journal of Pediatrics, 101,* 302–307.

Wagner, W. G., Kilcrease-Fleming, D., Fowler, W. E., & Kazelskis, R. (1993). Brief-term counseling with sexually abused girls: The impact of sex of counselor on clients' therapeutic involvement, self-concept, and depression. *Journal of Counseling Psychology, 40,* 490–500.

Wagner, W. G., Stern, M., & Kaczmarek, P. G. (1994). Counseling with children. [Special issue] *The Counseling Psychologist, 22,* 379–380.

Wahl, K. H., & Blackhurst, A. (2000). Factors affecting the occupational and educational aspirations of children and adolescents. *Professional School Counseling, 3,* 367–374.

Waksman, S. A. (1983). Diet and children's behavior disorders: A review of the research. *Clinical Psychology Review, 3,* 201–213.

Walker, C. E., Kaufman, K. (1984). State-Trait Anxiety Inventory for Children. In D. J. Keyser & R. C. Sweetland (Eds.), *Test Critiques* (Vol. I) (pp. 633–640). Kansas City, MO: Test Corporation of America.

Walker, L. J. (1991). Sex differences in moral development. In W. M. Kurtines & J. Gewirtz (Eds.), *Handbook of moral behavior and development. Vol. 2: Research* (pp. 333– 364). Hillsdale, NJ: Lawrence Erlbaum.

Walker, L. J., & Taylor, J. H. (1991). Family interactions and the development of moral reasoning. *Child Development, 62,* 264–283.

Wallender, J. L. (1993). Special section editorial: Current research on pediatric chronic illness. *Journal of Pediatric Psychology, 18,* 7–10.

Warren, C. S., & Messer, S. B. (1999). Brief psychodynamic therapy with anxious children. In S. W. Russ & T. H. Ollendick (Eds.), *Handbook of psychotherapies with children and families* (pp. 219–237). New York: Kluwer Academic/Plenum Publishers.

Waslick, B., Werry, J. S., & Greenhill, L. L. (1999). Pharmacotherapy and toxicology of oppositional defiant disorder and conduct disorder. In H. C. Quay & A. E. Hogan (Eds.), *Handbook of disruptive behavior disorders* (pp. 455–474). New York: Kluwer Academic/Plenum.

Waters, V. (1982). Therapies for children: Rational-emotive therapy. In C. R. Reynolds & T. B. Gutkin (Eds.), *Handbook of school psychology* (pp. 570–579). New York: John Wiley.

Watson, J. (1980). Bibliotherapy for abused children. *The School Counselor, 27,* 204–208.

Watson, J. B. (1913). Psychology as the behaviorist views it. *Psychological Review, 20,* 158–177.

Watson, J. B. (1925). *Behaviorism.* New York: People's Institute.

Watson, J. B. (1928). *Psychological care of infant and child.* New York: Norton.

Watson, J. B., & Raynor, R. (1920). Conditioned emotional reactions. *Journal of Experimental Psychology, 3,* 1–14.

Watson, R. I. (1978). *The great psychologists* (4th ed.). Philadelphia: J. B. Lippincott Co.

Wauchope, B., & Straus, M. A. (1990). Physical punishment and physical abuse of American children: Incidence rates by age, gender, and occupational class. In M. S. Straus & R. J. Gelles (Eds.), *Physical violence in the American family* (pp. 133–148). New York: Doubleday/Anchor.

Weakland, J. H., Fisch, R., Watzlawick, P., & Bodin, A. M. (1974). Brief therapy: Focused problem resolution. *Family Process, 13,* 141–168.

Webster-Stratton, C. (1993). Strategies for helping early school-aged children with oppositional defiant and conduct disorders: The importance of home-school partnerships. *School Psychology Review, 22,* 437–457.

Webster-Stratton, C. (1996). Early intervention with videotape modeling: Programs for families of children with oppositional defiant disorder or conduct disorder. In E. D. Hibbs & P. S. Jensen (Eds.), *Psychosocial treatments for child and adolescent disorders: Empirically based strategies for clinical practice* (pp. 435–474). Washington, DC: American Psychological Association.

Weikel, W. J., & Palmo, A. J. (1989). The evolution and practice of mental health counseling. *Journal of Mental Health Counseling, 11,* 7–25.

Weiner, D. N. (1988). *Albert Ellis: Passionate skeptic.* New York: Praeger.

Weiss, B., Catron, T., Harris, V., & Phung, T. M. (1999). The effectiveness of traditional child psychotherapy. *Journal of Consulting and Clinical Psychology, 67,* 82–94.

Weiss, B., Dodge, K. A., Bates, J. E., & Pettit, G. S. (1992). Some consequences of early harsh discipline: Child aggression and a maladaptive social information processing style. *Child Development, 63,* 1321–1335.

Weiss, B., Weiss, J. R., Politano, M., Carey, M., Nelson, N. M., & Finch, A. J. (1991). Developmental differences in the factor structure of the Children's Depression Inventory. *Psychological Assessment, 3,* 38–45.

Weiss, B., Williams, J. H., Margen, S., Abrams, B., Caan, B., Citron, L. J., Cox, C., McKibben, J., Ogar, D., & Schultz, S. (1980). Behavioral responses to artificial food colors. *Science, 207,* 1487–1489.

Weisz, J. R., Han, S. S., & Valeri, S. M. (1997). More of what? Issues raised by the Fort Bragg study. *American Psychologist, 52,* 541–545.

Weisz, J. R., & Weiss, B. (1989). Assessing the effects of clinic-based psychotherapy with children and adolescents. *Journal of Consulting and Clinical Psychology, 57,* 741–746.

Weisz, J. R., Weiss, B., Alicke, M. D., & Klotz, M. L. (1987). Effectiveness of psychotherapy with children and adolescents: A meta-analysis for clinicians. *Journal of Consulting and Clinical Psychology, 55,* 542–549.

Weisz, J. R., Weiss, B., & Donenberg, G. R. (1992). The lab versus the clinic: Effects of child and adolescent psychotherapy. *American Psychologist, 47,* 1578–1585.

Weisz, J. R., Weiss, B., Han, S. S., Granger, D. A., & Morton, T. (1995). Effects of psychotherapy with children and adolescents revisited: A meta-analysis of treatment outcome studies. *Psychological Bulletin, 117,* 450–468.

Weithorn, L. A., & Grisso, T. (1987). Psychological evaluations in divorce custody: Problems, principles, and procedures. In L. A. Weithorn (Ed.), *Psychology and child custody determinations: Knowledge, rules, and expertise* (pp. 157–181). Lincoln, NE: University of Nebraska Press.

Wells, K. C., & Egan, J. (1988). Social learning and systems family therapy for childhood oppositional disorder: Comparative treatment outcome. *Comprehensive Psychiatry, 29,* 138–146.

Wells, L. E. & Maxwell, G. (1976) *Self-esteem*. Beverly Hills, CA: Sage.

Wenar, C. (1982a). Developmental psychopathology: Its nature and models. *Journal of Clinical Child Psychology, 11*, 192–201.

Wenar, C. (1982b). *Psychopathology from infancy through adolescence: A developmental approach*. New York: Random House.

Wender, E. H. (1986). The food additive-free diet In the treatment of behavior disorders: A review. *Journal of Developmental and Behavioral Pediatrics, 7*, 35–42.

Werry, J. S. (1999). Introduction: A guide for practitioners, professionals, and public. In J. S. Werry & M. G. Aman (Eds.), *Practitioner's guide to psychoactive drugs for children and adolescents* (2nd ed.) (pp. 3–22). New York: Plenum Medical Book Co.

Werry, J. S., & Aman, M. G. (1999). Anxiolytics, sedatives, and miscellaneous drugs. In J. S. Werry & M. G. Aman (Eds.), *Practitioner's guide to psychoactive drugs for children and adolescents* (2nd ed.) (pp. 433–469). New York: Plenum Medical Book Co.

Werry, J. S., & Cohrssen, J. (1965). Enuresis: An etiologic and therapeutic study. *Journal of Pediatrics, 67*, 423–431.

West, J. D., Hosie, T. W., & Mackey, J. A. (1987). Employment and roles of counselors in mental health agencies. *Journal of Counseling and Development, 66*, 135–138.

Whalen, C. K., & Henker, B. (1991). Therapies for hyperactive children: Comparisons, combinations, and compromises. *Journal of Consulting and Clinical Psychology, 59*, 126–137.

Wheeler, M. E., & Hess, K. W. (1976). Treatment of juvenile obesity by successive approximation control of eating. *Journal of Behavior Therapy and Experimental Psychiatry, 7*, 235–241.

Whiteley, B. E. (1996). *Principles of research in behavioral science*. Mountain View, CA: Mayfield.

Wick, D. T., Wick, J. K., & Peterson, N. (1997). Improving self-esteem with Adlerian adventure therapy. *Professional School Counseling, 1*, 53–56.

Wigfield, A., & Eccles, J. S. (1994). Children's competence beliefs, achievement values, and general self-esteem: Changes across elementary and middle school. *Journal of Early Adolescence, 14*, 107–138.

Wilens, T. E., Spencer, T. J., Frazier, J., & Biederman, J. (1998). Child and adolescent psychopharmacology. In T. H. Ollendick & M. Hersen (Eds.), *Handbook of child psychopathology* (3rd ed.) (pp. 603–636). New York: Plenum Press.

Wilkinson, L. A. (1997). School-based behavioral consultation: Delivering treatment for children's externalizing behavior in the classroom. *Journal of Educational and Psychological Consultation, 8*, 255–276.

Wille, S. (1986). Comparison of desmopressin and enuresis alarm for nocturnal enuresis. *Archives of Diseases In Children, 61*, 30–33.

Williams, C. D. (1959). The elimination of tantrum behaviors by extinction procedures. *Journal of Abnormal and Social Psychology, 59*, 269.

Williams, C. L., Bollella, M., & Wynder, E. L. (1995). A new recommendation for dietary fiber in childhood. *Pediatrics, 96*, 985–988.

Winn, N. N., & Priest, R. (1993). Counseling biracial children: A forgotten component of multicultural counseling. *Family Therapy, 20*, 29–36.

Winnicott, D. W. (1957). *Mother and child: A primer of first relationships*. New York: Basic Books.

Winnicott, D. W. (1965) *The maturational process and the facilitating environment: Studies in the theory of emotional development*. New York: International Universities Press.

Winnicott, D. W. (1971). *Therapeutic consultations in child psychiatry*. New York: Basic Books.

Winnicott, D. W. (1977). *The piggle: An account of the psychoanalytic treatment of a little girl*. New York: International Universities Press.

Winnicott, D.W. (1987). *Babies and their mothers*. Reading, MA: Addison-Wesley.

Winnicott, D.W. (1993). *Talking to parents*. Reading, MA: Addison Wesley.

Wirt, R. D., Lachar, D., Klinedinst, J. K., & Seat, P. D. (1977). *Multidimensional description of child personality: A manual for the Personality Inventory for Children*. Los Angeles: Western Psychological Services.

Wirt, R. D., Lachar, D., Klinedinst, J. K., & Seat, P. D. (1990). *Personality inventory for children—1990 edition*. Los Angeles, CA: Western Psychological Services.

Witmer, H. L. (1935). A comparison of treatment results in various types of child guidance clinics. *American Journal of Orthopsychiatry, 5*, 351–360.

Witmer, H. L., and Students. (1933). The outcome of treatment in a child guidance clinic: A comparison and an evaluation. *Smith College Studies in Social Work, 3*, 339–399.

Wohlford, P. (1991). Trends in NIMH support for clinical training for ethnic minorities. In H. F. Myers, P. Wohlford, L. P. Guzman, & R. J. Echemendia (Eds.), *Ethnic minority perspectives on clinical training and services in psychology* (pp. 13–21). Washington, DC: American Psychological Association.

Wolfe, V. V., Sas, L., & Wilson, S. K. (1987). Some issues in preparing sexually abused children for court testimony. *Behavior Therapist, 10*, 107–113.

Wolin, S. J., & Wolin, S. (1993). *The resilient self: How survivors of troubled families rise above adversity*. New York: Villard Books.

Wolitzky, D. L., & Eagle, M. N. (1997). Psychoanalytic theories of psychotherapy. In P. L. Wachtel & S. B. Messer (Eds.), *Theories of psychotherapy: Origins and evolution* (pp. 39–96). Washington, DC: American Psychological Association.

Wolpe, J. (1958). *Psychotherapy by reciprocal inhibition*. Stanford, CA: Stanford University Press.

Wolraich, M. L., Lindgren, S. D., Stumbo, P. J., Stegink, L. D., Appelbaum, M. I., & Kiritsy, M. C. (1994). Effects of diets high in sucrose or aspartame on the behavior and cognitive performance of children. *The New England Journal of Medicine, 330*, 301–307.

Wolraich, M. L., Wilson, D. B., & White, J. W. (1995). The effect of sugar on behavior or cognition in children: A meta-analysis. *Journal of the American Medical Association, 274*, 1617–1621.

World Health Organization. (1991). *International statistical classification of diseases and health related diseases* (10th revision). Geneva: Author.

World Health Organization. (1996). *Multiaxial classification of child and adolescent psychiatric disorders: The ICD-10 classification of mental and behavioural disorders in children and adolescents*. Cambridge: Cambridge University Press.

Wozniak, R. H. (1997). Behaviorism. In W. G. Bringmann, H. E. Luck, R. Miller, & C. E. Early (Eds.), *A pictorial history of psychology* (pp. 198–205). Chicago: Quintessence Publishing Co.

Wright, L., Truax, C. B., & Mitchell, K. M. (1972). Reliability of process ratings of psychotherapy with children. *Psychology in the Schools, 9*, 64–66.

Wynn, K. (1992). Addition and subtraction by human infants. *Nature, 358*, 749–750.

Wynn, K. (1995). Infants possess a system of numerical knowledge. *Current Directions in Psychological Science, 4*, 172–177.

Yagi, D. T., & Oh, M. Y. (1995). Counseling Asian American students. In C. C. Lee (Ed.), *Counseling for diversity: A guide for school counselors and related professionals* (pp. 61–83). Boston: Allyn and Bacon.

Yin, R. K. (1993). *Applications of case study research*. Newbury Park, CA: Sage.

Yin, R. K. (1994). *Case study research design methods* (2nd ed.). Thousand Oaks, CA: Sage.

Yoe, J. T., Santarcangelo, S., Atkins, M., & Burchard, J. D. (1996). Wraparound care in Vermont: Program development, implementation, and evaluation of a statewide system of individualized services. *Journal of Child and Family Studies, 5*, 23–37.

Young, G. C. (1973). The treatment of childhood encopresis by conditioned gastro-ileal reflex training. *Behaviour Research and Therapy, 11*, 499–503.

Young-Bruehl, E. (1988). *Anna Freud: A biography*. New York: Summit Books.

Yuille, J. C., Hunter, R., Joffe, R., & Zaparniuk, J. (1993). Interviewing children in sexual abuse cases. In G. S. Goodman & B. L. Bottoms (Eds.), *Child victims, child witnesses: Understanding and improving testimony* (pp. 95–115). New York: Guilford.

Yura, M.T., & Galassi, M.D. (1974). Adlerian usage of children's play. *Journal of Individual Psychology, 30*, 194–201.

Zahner, G., Pawelkiewicz, W., De Francesco, J. J., & Adnopoz, J. (1992). Children's mental health service needs and utilization patterns in an urban community: An epidemiological assessment. *Journal of the American Academy of Child and Adolescent Psychiatry, 31*, 951–960.

Zakich, R. (1975). *The Ungame*. Anaheim, CA: The Ungame Company.

Zaleski, A., Gerrard, J. W., & Schokier, M. H. K. (1973). Nocturnal enuresis: The importance of a small bladder capacity. In I. Kolvin, R. C. Mac Keith, & S. R. Meadow (Eds.), *Bladder control and enuresis. Clinics in developmental medicine* Nos. 48/49 (pp. 95–101). Philadelphia: J. B. Lippincott.

Zarbatany, L., Van Brunschot, M., Meadows, K., & Pepper, S. (1996). Effects of friendship and gender on peer group entry. *Child Development, 67*, 2287–2300.

Zayas, L. H., & Solari, F. (1994). Early childhood socialization in Hispanic families: Context, culture, and practice implications. *Professional Psychology: Research and Practice*, 25, 200–206.

Zbaracki, J. U., Clark, S. G., & Wolins, L. (1985). Children's interests inventory, grades 4–6. *Educational and Psychological Measurements, 45*, 517–521.

Zito, J. M., Safer, D. J., dosReis, S., Gardner, J. F., Boles, M., & Lynch, F. (2000). Trends in the prescribing of psychotropic medications to preschoolers. *Journal of the American Medical Association, 283*, 1025–1030.

Zucker, K. J. (2000). Gender identity disorder. In A. J. Sameroff, M. Lewis, & S. M. Miller (Eds.), *Handbook of developmental psychopathology* (2nd ed.) (pp. 671–686). New York: Kluwer Academic/Plenum.

Zuckerman, M. (1990). Some dubious premises in research and theory on racial differences. *American Psychologist, 45*, 1297–1303.

Appendix A
ACA Code of Ethics

ACA CODE OF ETHICS PREAMBLE

The American Counseling Association is an educational, scientific, and professional organization whose members are dedicated to the enhancement of human development throughout the life-span. Association members recognize diversity in our society and embrace a cross-cultural approach in support of the worth, dignity, potential, and uniqueness of each individual.

The specification of a code of ethics enables the association to clarify to current and future members, and to those served by members, the nature of the ethical responsibilities held in common by its members. As the code of ethics of the association, this document establishes principles that define the ethical behavior of association members. All members of the American Counseling Association are required to adhere to the Code of Ethics and the Standards of Practice. The Code of Ethics will serve as the basis for processing ethical complaints initiated against members of the association.

Section A: The Counseling Relationship

A.1. Client Welfare.

a. Primary Responsibility. The primary responsibility of counselors is to respect the dignity and to promote the welfare of clients.
b. Positive Growth and Development. Counselors encourage client growth and development in ways that foster the clients' interest and welfare; counselors avoid fostering dependent counseling relationships.
c. Counseling Plans. Counselors and their clients work jointly in devising integrated, individual counseling plans that offer reasonable promise of success and are consistent with abilities and circumstances of clients. Counselors and clients regularly review counseling plans to ensure their continued viability and effectiveness, respecting clients' freedom of choice. (See A.3.b.)
d. Family Involvement. Counselors recognize that families are usually important in clients' lives and strive to enlist family understanding and involvement as a positive resource, when appropriate.
e. Career and Employment Needs. Counselors work with their clients in considering employment in jobs and circumstances that are consistent with the clients' overall abilities, vocational limitations, physical restrictions, general temperament, interest and aptitude patterns, social skills, education, general qualifications, and other relevant characteristics and needs. Counselors neither place nor participate in placing clients in positions that will result in damaging the interest and the welfare of clients, employers, or the public.

A.2. Respecting Diversity.

a. Nondiscrimination. Counselors do not condone or engage in discrimination based on age, color, culture, disability, ethnic group, gender, race, religion, sexual orientation, marital status, or socioeconomic status. (See C.5.a., C.5.b, and D.1.i.)
b. Respecting Differences. Counselors will actively attempt to understand the diverse cultural backgrounds of the clients with whom they work. This includes, but is not limited to, learning how the counselor's own cultural/ethnic/racial identity impacts her or his values and beliefs about the counseling process. (See E.8. and F.2.i.)

A.3. Client Rights.

a. Disclosure to Clients. When counseling is initiated, and throughout the counseling process as necessary, counselors inform clients of the purposes, goals, techniques, procedures, limitations, potential risks, and benefits of services to be performed, and other pertinent information. Counselors take steps to ensure that clients understand the implications of diagnosis, the intended use of tests and reports, fees, and billing arrangements. Clients have the right to expect confidentiality and to be provided with an explanation of its limitations, including supervision and/or treatment team professionals; to obtain clear information about their case records; to participate in the ongoing counseling plans; and to refuse any recommended services and be advised of the consequences of such refusal. (See E5.a. and G.2.)
b. Freedom of Choice. Counselors offer clients the freedom to choose whether to enter into a counseling relationship and to determine which professional(s) will provide counseling. Restrictions that limit choices of clients are fully explained. (See A.1.c.)
c. Inability to Give Consent. When counseling minors or persons unable to give voluntary informed consent, counselors act in these clients' best interests. (See B.3.)

A.4. Clients Served by Others. If a client is receiving services from another mental health professional, counselors, with client consent, inform the professional persons already involved and develop clear agreements to avoid confusion and conflict for the client. (See C.6.c.)

A.5. Personal Needs and Values.

a. Personal Needs. In the counseling relationship, counselors are aware of the intimacy and responsibilities inherent in the counseling relationship, maintain respect for clients, and avoid actions that seek to meet their personal needs at the expense of clients.

b. Personal Values. Counselors are aware of their own values, attitudes, beliefs, and behaviors and how these apply in a diverse society, and avoid imposing their values on clients. (See C.5.a.)

A.6. Dual Relationships.

a. Avoid When Possible. Counselors are aware of their influential positions with respect to clients, and they avoid exploiting the trust and dependency of clients. Counselors make every effort to avoid dual relationships with clients that could impair professional judgment or increase the risk of harm to clients. (Examples of such relationships include, but are not limited to, familial, social, financial, business, or close personal relationships with clients.) When a dual relationship cannot be avoided, counselors take appropriate professional precautions such as informed consent, consultation, supervision, and documentation to ensure that judgment is not impaired and no exploitation occurs. (See F.1.b.)

b. Superior/Subordinate Relationships. Counselors do not accept as clients superiors or subordinates with whom they have administrative, supervisory, or evaluative relationships.

A.7. Sexual Intimacies With Clients.

a. Current Clients. Counselors do not have any type of sexual intimacies with clients and do not counsel persons with whom they have had a sexual relationship.

b. Former Clients. Counselors do not engage in sexual intimacies with former clients within a minimum of 2 years after terminating the counseling relationship. Counselors who engage in such relationship after 2 years following termination have the responsibility to examine and document thoroughly that such relations did not have an exploitative nature, based on factors such as duration of counseling, amount of time since counseling, termination circumstances, client's personal history and mental status, adverse impact on the client, and actions by the counselor suggesting a plan to initiate a sexual relationship with the client after termination.

A.8. Multiple Clients. When counselors agree to provide counseling services to two or more persons who have a relationship (such as husband and wife, or parents and children), counselors clarify at the outset which person or persons are clients and the nature of the relationships they will have with each involved person. If it becomes apparent that counselors may be called upon to perform potentially conflicting roles, they clarify, adjust, or withdraw from roles appropriately. (See B.2. and B.4.d.)

A.9. Group Work.

a. Screening. Counselors screen prospective group counseling/therapy participants. To the extent possible, counselors select members whose needs and goals are compatible with goals of the group, who will not impede the group process, and whose well-being will not be jeopardized by the group experience.

b. Protecting Clients. In a group setting, counselors take reasonable precautions to protect clients from physical or psychological trauma.

A.10. Fees and Bartering (See D.3.a. and D.3.b.).

a. Advance Understanding. Counselors clearly explain to clients, prior to entering the counseling relationship, all financial arrangements related to professional services including the use of collection agencies or legal measures for nonpayment. (See A.11.c.)

b. Establishing Fees. In establishing fees for professional counseling services, counselors consider the financial status of clients and locality. In the event that the established fee structure is inappropriate for a client, assistance is provided in attempting to find comparable services of acceptable cost. (See A.10.d., D.3.a., and D.3.b.)

c. Bartering Discouraged. Counselors ordinarily refrain from accepting goods or services from clients in return for counseling services because such arrangements create inherent potential for conflicts, exploitation, and distortion of the professional relationship. Counselors may participate in bartering only if the relationship is not exploitative, if the client requests it, if a clear written contract is established, and if such arrangements are an accepted practice among professionals in the community. (See A.6.a.)

d. Pro Bono Service. Counselors contribute to society by devoting a portion of their professional activity to services for which there is little or no financial return (pro bono).

A.11. Termination and Referral.

a. Abandonment Prohibited. Counselors do not abandon or neglect clients in counseling. Counselors assist in making appropriate arrangements for the continuation of treatment, when necessary, during interruptions such as vacations, and following termination.

b. Inability to Assist Clients. If counselors determine an inability to be of professional assistance to clients, they avoid entering or immediately terminate a counseling relationship. Counselors are knowledgeable about referral resources and suggest appropriate alternatives. If clients decline the suggested referral, counselors should discontinue the relationship.

c. Appropriate Termination. Counselors terminate a counseling relationship, securing client agreement when possible, when it is reasonably clear that the client is no longer benefiting, when services are no longer required, when counseling no longer serves the client's needs or interests, when clients do not pay fees charged, or when agency or institution limits do not allow provision of further counseling services. (See A.10.b. and C.2.g.)

A.12. Computer Technology.

a. Use of Computers. When computer applications are used in counseling services, counselors ensure that (1) the client is intellectually, emotionally, and physically capable of using the computer application; (2) the computer application is appropriate for the needs of the client; (3) the client understands the purpose and operation of the computer applications; and (4) a follow-up of client use of a computer application is provided to correct possible misconceptions, discover inappropriate use, and assess subsequent needs.

b. Explanation of Limitations. Counselors ensure that clients are provided information as a part of the counseling relationship that adequately explains the limitations of computer technology.

c. Access to Computer Applications. Counselors provide for equal access to computer applications in counseling services. (See A.2.a.)

Section B: Confidentiality

B.1. Right to Privacy.

a. Respect for Privacy. Counselors respect their clients' right to privacy and avoid illegal and unwarranted disclosures of confidential information. (See A.3.a. and B.6.a.)

b. Client Waiver. The right to privacy may be waived by the client or his or her legally recognized representative.

c. Exceptions. The general requirement that counselors keep information confidential does not apply when disclosure is required to prevent clear and imminent danger to the client or others or when legal requirements demand that confidential information be revealed. Counselors consult with other professionals when in doubt as to the validity of an exception.

d. Contagious, Fatal Diseases. A counselor who receives information confirming that a client has a disease commonly known to be both communicable and fatal is justified in disclosing information to an identifiable third party, who by his or her relationship with the client is at a high risk of contracting the disease. Prior to making a disclosure the counselor should ascertain that the client has not already informed the third party about his or her disease and that the client is not intending to inform the third party in the immediate future. (See B.1.c and B.1.f.)

e. Court-Ordered Disclosure. When court ordered to release confidential information without a client's permission, counselors request to the court that the disclosure not be required due to potential harm to the client or counseling relationship. (See B.1.c.)

f. Minimal Disclosure. When circumstances require the disclosure of confidential information, only essential information is revealed. To the extent possible, clients are informed before confidential information is disclosed.

g. Explanation of Limitations. When counseling is initiated and throughout the counseling process as necessary, counselors inform clients of the limitations of confidentiality and identify foreseeable situations in which confidentiality must be breached. (See G.2.a.)

h. Subordinates. Counselors make every effort to ensure that privacy and confidentiality of clients are maintained by subordinates including employees, supervisees, clerical assistants, and volunteers. (See B.1.a.)

i. Treatment Teams. If client treatment will involve a continued review by a treatment team, the client will be informed of the team's existence and composition.

B.2. Groups and Families.

a. Group Work. In group work, counselors clearly define confidentiality and the parameters for the specific group being entered, explain its importance, and discuss the difficulties related to confidentiality involved in group work. The fact that confidentiality cannot be guaranteed is clearly communicated to group members.

b. Family Counseling. In family counseling, information about one family member cannot be disclosed to another member without permission. Counselors protect the privacy rights of each family member. (See A.8., B.3., an B.4.d.)

B.3. Minor or Incompetent Clients. When counseling clients who are minors or individuals who are unable to give voluntary, informed consent, parents or guardians may be included in the counseling process as appropriate. Counselors act in the best interests of clients and take measures to safeguard confidentiality. (See A.3.c.)

B.4. Records.

a. Requirement of Records. Counselors maintain records necessary for rendering professional services to their clients and as required by laws, regulations, or agency or institution procedures.

b. Confidentiality of Records. Counselors are responsible for securing the safety and confidentiality of any counseling records they create, maintain, transfer, or destroy whether the records are written, taped, computerized, or stored in any other medium. (See B.1.a.)

c. Permission to Record or Observe. Counselors obtain permission from clients prior to electronically recording or observing sessions. (See A.3.a.)

d. Client Access. Counselors recognize that counseling records are kept for the benefit of clients, and therefore provide access to records and copies of records when requested by competent clients, unless the records contain information that may be misleading and detrimental to the client. In situations involving multiple clients, access to records is limited to those parts of records that do not include confidential information related to another client. (See A.8., B.1.a, and B.2.b.)

e. Disclosure or Transfer. Counselors obtain written permission from clients to disclose or transfer records to legitimate third parties unless exceptions to confidentiality exist as listed in Section B.1. Steps are taken to ensure that receivers of counseling records are sensitive to their confidential nature.

B.5. Research and Training.

a. Data Disguise Required. Use of data derived from counseling relationships for purposes of training, research, or publication is confined to content that is disguised to ensure the anonymity of the individuals involved. (See B.1.g. and G.3.d.)

b. Agreement for Identification. Identification of a client in a presentation or publication is permissible only when the client has reviewed the material and has agreed to its presentation or publication. (See G.3.d.)

B.6. Consultation.

a. Respect for Privacy. Information obtained in a consulting relationship is discussed for professional purposes only with persons clearly concerned with the case. Written and oral reports present data germane to the purposes of the consultation, and every effort is made to protect client identity and avoid undue invasion of privacy.

b. Cooperating Agencies. Before sharing information, counselors make efforts to ensure that there are defined policies in other agencies serving the counselor's clients that effectively protect the confidentiality of information.

Section C: Professional Responsibility

C.1. Standards Knowledge. Counselors have a responsibility to read, understand, and follow the Code of Ethics and the Standards of Practice.

C.2. Professional Competence.

a. Boundaries of Competence. Counselors practice only within the boundaries of their competence, based on their education, training, supervised experience, state and national professional credentials, and appropriate professional experience. Counselors will demonstrate a commitment to gain knowledge, personal awareness, sensitivity, and skills pertinent to working with a diverse client population.

b. New Specialty Areas of Practice. Counselors practice in specialty areas new to them only after appropriate education, training, and supervised experience. While developing skills in new specialty areas, counselors take steps to ensure the competence of their work and to protect others from possible harm.

c. Qualified for Employment. Counselors accept employment only for positions for which they are qualified by education, training, supervised experience, state and national professional credentials, and appropriate professional experience. Counselors hire for professional counseling positions only individuals who are qualified and competent.

d. Monitor Effectiveness. Counselors continually monitor their effectiveness as professionals and take steps to improve when necessary. Counselors in private practice take reasonable steps to seek out peer supervision to evaluate their efficacy as counselors.

e. Ethical Issues Consultation. Counselors take reasonable steps to consult with other counselors or related professionals when they have questions regarding their ethical obligations or professional practice. (See H.1.)

f. Continuing Education. Counselors recognize the need for continuing education to maintain a reasonable level of awareness of current scientific and professional information in their fields of activity. They take steps to maintain competence in the skills they use, are open to new procedures, and keep current with the diverse and/or special populations with whom they work.

g. Impairment. Counselors refrain from offering or accepting professional services when their physical, mental, or emotional problems are likely to harm a client or others. They are alert to the signs of impairment, seek assistance for problems, and, if necessary, limit, suspend, or terminate their professional responsibilities. (See A.11.c.)

C.3. Advertising and Soliciting Clients.

a. Accurate Advertising. There are no restrictions on advertising by counselors except those that can be specifically justified to protect the public from deceptive practices. Counselors advertise or represent their services to the public by identifying their credentials in an accurate manner that is not false, misleading, deceptive, or fraudulent. Counselors may only advertise the highest degree earned which is in counseling or a closely related field from a college or university that was accredited when the degree was awarded by one of the regional accrediting bodies recognized by the Council on Postsecondary Accreditation.

b. Testimonials. Counselors who use testimonials do not solicit them from clients or other persons who, because of their particular circumstances, may be vulnerable to undue influence.

c. Statements by Others. Counselors make reasonable efforts to ensure that statements made by others about them or the profession of counseling are accurate.

d. Recruiting Through Employment. Counselors do not use their places of employment or institutional affiliation to recruit or gain clients, supervisees, or consultees for their private practices. (See C.5.e.)

e. Products and Training Advertisements. Counselors who develop products related to their profession or conduct workshops or training events ensure that the advertisements concerning these products or events are accurate and disclose adequate information for consumers to make informed choices.

f. Promoting to Those Served. Counselors do not use counseling, teaching, training, or supervisory relationships to promote their products or training events in a manner that is deceptive or would exert undue influence on individuals who may be vulnerable. Counselors may adopt textbooks they have authored for instruction purposes.

g. Professional Association Involvement. Counselors actively participate in local, state, and national associations that foster the development and improvement of counseling.

C.4. Credentials.

a. Credentials Claimed. Counselors claim or imply only professional credentials possessed and are responsible for correcting any known misrepresentations of their credentials by others. Professional credentials include graduate degrees in counseling or closely related mental health fields, accreditation of graduate programs, national voluntary certifications, government-issued certifications or licenses, ACA professional membership, or any other credential that might indicate to the public specialized knowledge or expertise in counseling.

b. ACA Professional Membership. ACA professional members may announce to the public their membership status. Regular members may not announce their ACA membership in a manner that might imply they are credentialed counselors.

c. Credential Guidelines. Counselors follow the guidelines for use of credentials that have been established by the entities that issue the credentials.

d. Misrepresentation of Credentials. Counselors do not attribute more to their credentials than the credentials represent, and do not imply that other counselors are not qualified because they do not possess certain credentials.

e. Doctoral Degrees From Other Fields. Counselors who hold a master's degree in counseling or a closely related mental health field, but hold a doctoral degree from other than counseling or a closely related field, do not use the title "Dr." in their practices and do not announce to the public in relation to their practice or status as a counselor that they hold a doctorate.

C.5. Public Responsibility.

a. Nondiscrimination. Counselors do not discriminate against clients, students, or supervisees in a manner that has a negative impact based on their age, color, culture, disability, ethnic group, gender, race, religion, sexual orientation, or socioeconomic status, or for any other reason. (See A.2.a.)

b. Sexual Harassment. Counselors do not engage in sexual harassment. Sexual harassment is defined as sexual solicitation, physical advances, or verbal or nonverbal conduct that is sexual in nature, that occurs in connection with professional activities or roles, and that either (1) is unwelcome, is offensive, or creates a hostile workplace environment, and counselors know or are told this; or (2) is sufficiently severe or intense to be perceived as harassment to a reasonable person in the context. Sexual harassment can consist of a single intense or severe act or multiple persistent or pervasive acts.

c. Reports to Third Parties. Counselors are accurate, honest, and unbiased in reporting their professional activities and judgments to appropriate third parties including courts, health insurance companies, those who are the recipients of evaluation reports, and others. (See B.1.g.)

d. Media Presentations. When counselors provide advice or comment by means of public lectures, demonstrations, radio or television programs, prerecorded tapes, printed articles, mailed material, or other media, they take reasonable precautions to ensure that (1) the statements are based on appropriate professional counseling literature and practice; (2) the statements are otherwise consistent with the Code of Ethics and the Standards of Practice; and (3) the recipients of the information are not encouraged to infer that a professional counseling relationship has been established. (See C.6.b.)

e. Unjustified Gains. Counselors do not use their professional positions to seek or receive unjustified personal gains, sexual favors, unfair advantage, or unearned goods or services. (See C.3.d.)

C.6. Responsibility to Other Professionals.

a. Different Approaches. Counselors are respectful of approaches to professional counseling that differ from their own. Counselors know and take into account the traditions and practices of other professional groups with which they work.

b. Personal Public Statements. When making personal statements in a public context, counselors clarify that they are speaking from their personal perspectives and that they are not speaking on behalf of all counselors or the profession. (See C.5.d.)

c. Clients Served by Others. When counselors learn that their clients are in a professional relationship with another mental health professional, they request release from clients to inform the other professionals and strive to establish positive and collaborative professional relationships. (See A.4.)

Section D: Relationships With Other Professionals

D.1. Relationships With Employers and Employees.

a. Role Definition. Counselors define and describe for their employers and employees the parameters and levels of their professional roles.

b. Agreements. Counselors establish working agreements with supervisors, colleagues, and subordinates regarding counseling or clinical relationships, confidentiality, adherence to professional standards, distinction between public and private material, maintenance and dissemination of recorded information, work load, and accountability. Working agreements in each instance are specified and made known to those concerned.

c. Negative Conditions. Counselors alert their employers to conditions that may be potentially disruptive or damaging to the counselor's professional responsibilities or that may limit their effectiveness.

d. Evaluation. Counselors submit regularly to professional review and evaluation by their supervisor or the appropriate representative of the employer.

e. In-Service. Counselors are responsible for in-service development of self and staff.

f. Goals. Counselors inform their staff of goals and programs.

g. Practices. Counselors provide personnel and agency practices that respect and enhance the rights and welfare of each employee and recipient of agency services. Counselors strive to maintain the highest levels of professional services.

h. Personnel Selection and Assignment. Counselors select competent staff and assign responsibilities compatible with their skills and experiences.

i. Discrimination. Counselors, as either employers or employees, do not engage in or condone practices that are inhumane, illegal, or unjustifiable (such as considerations based on age, color, culture, disability, ethnic group, gender, race, religion, sexual orientation, or socioeconomic status) in hiring, promotion, or training. (See A.2.a. and C.5.b.)

j. Professional Conduct. Counselors have a responsibility both to clients and to the agency or institution within which services are performed to maintain high standards of professional conduct.

k. Exploitative Relationships. Counselors do not engage in exploitative relationships with individuals over whom they have supervisory, evaluative, or instructional control or authority.

l. Employer Policies. The acceptance of employment in an agency or institution implies that counselors are in agreement with its general policies and principles. Counselors strive to reach agreement with employers as to acceptable standards of conduct that allow for changes in institutional policy conducive to the growth and development of clients.

D.2. Consultation (See B.6.).

a. Consultation as an Option. Counselors may choose to consult with any other professionally competent persons about their clients. In choosing consultants, counselors avoid placing the consultant in a conflict of interest situation that would preclude the consultant being a proper party to the counselor's efforts to help the client. Should counselors be engaged in a work setting that compromises this consultation standard, they consult with other professionals whenever possible to consider justifiable alternatives.

b. Consultant Competency. Counselors are reasonably certain that they have or the organization represented has the necessary competencies and resources for giving the kind of consulting services needed and that appropriate referral resources are available.

c. Understanding With Clients. When providing consultation, counselors attempt to develop with their clients a clear understanding of problem definition, goals for change, and predicted consequences of interventions selected.

d. Consultant Goals. The consulting relationship is one in which client adaptability and growth toward self-direction are consistently encouraged and cultivated. (See A.1.b.)

D.3. Fees for Referral.

a. Accepting Fees From Agency Clients. Counselors refuse a private fee or other remuneration for rendering services to persons who are entitled to such services through the counselor's employing agency or institution. The policies of a particular agency may make explicit provisions for agency clients to receive counseling services from members of its staff in private practice. In such instances, the clients must be informed of other options open to them should they seek private counseling services. (See A.10.a., A.11.b., and C.3.d.)

b. Referral Fees. Counselors do not accept a referral fee from other professionals.

D.4. Subcontractor Arrangements. When counselors work as subcontractors for counseling services for a third party, they have a duty to inform clients of the limitations of confidentiality that the organization may place on counselors in providing counseling services to clients. The limits of such confidentiality ordinarily are discussed as part of the intake session. (See B.1.e. and B.1.f.)

Section E: Evaluation, Assessment, and Interpretation

E.1. General.

a. Appraisal Techniques. The primary purpose of educational and psychological assessment is to provide measures that are objective and interpretable in either comparative or absolute terms. Counselors recognize the need to interpret the statements in this section as applying to the whole range of appraisal techniques, including test and nontest data.

b. Client Welfare. Counselors promote the welfare and best interest of the client in the development, publication, and utilization of educational and psychological assessment techniques. They do not misuse assessment results and interpretations and take reasonable steps to prevent others from misusing the information these techniques provide. They respect the client's right to know the results, the interpretations made, and the bases for their conclusions and recommendations.

E.2. Competence to Use and Interpret Tests.

a. Limits of Competence. Counselors recognize the limits of their competence and perform only those testing and assessment services for which they have been trained. They are familiar with reliability, validity, related standardization, error of measurement, and proper application of any technique utilized. Counselors using computer-based test interpretations are trained in the construct being measured and the specific instrument being used prior to using this type of computer application. Counselors take reasonable measures to ensure the proper use of psychological assessment techniques by persons under their supervision.

b. Appropriate Use. Counselors are responsible for the appropriate application, scoring, interpretation, and use of assessment instruments, whether they score and interpret such tests themselves or use computerized or other services.

c. Decisions Based on Results. Counselors responsible for decisions involving individuals or policies that are based on assessment results have a thorough understanding of educational and psychological measurement, including validation criteria, test research, and guidelines for test development and use.

d. Accurate Information. Counselors provide accurate information and avoid false claims or misconceptions when making statements about assessment instruments or techniques. Special efforts are made to avoid unwarranted connotations of such terms as IQ and grade equivalent scores. (See C.5.c.)

E.3. Informed Consent.

a. Explanation to Clients. Prior to assessment, counselors explain the nature and purposes of assessment and the specific use of results in language the client (or other legally authorized person on behalf of the client) can understand, unless an explicit exception to this right has been agreed upon in advance. Regardless of whether scoring and interpretation are completed by counselors, by assistants, or by computer or other outside services, counselors take reasonable steps to ensure that appropriate explanations are given to the client.

b. Recipients of Results. The examinee's welfare, explicit understanding, and prior agreement determine the recipients of test results. Counselors include accurate and appropriate interpretations with any release of individual or group test results. (See B.1.a. and C.5.c.)

E.4. Release of Information to Competent Professionals.

a. Misuse of Results. Counselors do not misuse assessment results, including test results, and interpretations, and take reasonable steps to prevent the misuse of such by others. (See C.5.c.)

b. Release of Raw Data. Counselors ordinarily release data (e.g., protocols, counseling or interview notes, or questionnaires) in which the client is identified only with the consent of the client or the client's legal representative. Such data are usually released only to persons recognized by counselors as competent to interpret the data. (See B.1.a.)

E.5. Proper Diagnosis of Mental Disorders.

a. Proper Diagnosis. Counselors take special care to provide proper diagnosis of mental disorders. Assessment techniques (including personal interview) used to determine client care (e.g., locus of treatment, type of treatment, or recommended follow-up) are carefully selected and appropriately used. (See A.3.a. and C.5.c.)

b. Cultural Sensitivity. Counselors recognize that culture affects the manner in which clients' problems are defined. Clients' socioeconomic and cultural experience is considered when diagnosing mental disorders.

E.6. Test Selection.

a. Appropriateness of Instruments. Counselors carefully consider the validity, reliability, psychometric limitations, and appropriateness of instruments when selecting tests for use in a given situation or with a particular client.

b. Culturally Diverse Populations. Counselors are cautious when selecting tests for culturally diverse populations to avoid inappropriateness of testing that may be outside of socialized behavioral or cognitive patterns.

E.7. Conditions of Test Administration.

a. Administration Conditions. Counselors administer tests under the same conditions that were established in their standardization. When tests are not administered under standard conditions or when unusual behavior or irregularities occur during the testing session, those conditions are noted in interpretation, and the results may be designated as invalid or of questionable validity.

b. Computer Administration. Counselors are responsible for ensuring that administration programs function properly to provide clients with accurate results when a computer or other electronic methods are used for test administration. (See A.12.b.)

c. Unsupervised Test Taking. Counselors do not permit unsupervised or inadequately supervised use of tests or assessments unless the tests or assessments are designed, intended, and validated for self-administration and/or scoring.

d. Disclosure of Favorable Conditions. Prior to test administration, conditions that produce most favorable test results are made known to the examinee.

E.8. Diversity in Testing. Counselors are cautious in using assessment techniques, making evaluations, and interpreting the performance of populations not represented in the norm group on which an instrument was standardized. They recognize the effects of age, color, culture, disability, ethnic group, gender, race, religion, sexual orientation, and socioeconomic status on test administration and interpretation and place test results in proper perspective with other relevant factors. (See A.2.a.)

E.9. Test Scoring and Interpretation.

a. Reporting Reservations. In reporting assessment results, counselors indicate any reservations that exist regarding validity or reliability because of the circumstances of the assessment or the inappropriateness of the norms for the person tested.

b. Research Instruments. Counselors exercise caution when interpreting the results of research instruments possessing insufficient technical data to support respondent results. The specific purposes for the use of such instruments are stated explicitly to the examinee.

c. Testing Services. Counselors who provide test scoring and test interpretation services to support the assessment process confirm the validity of such interpretations. They accurately describe the purpose, norms, validity, reliability, and applications of the procedures and any special qualifications applicable to their use. The public offering of an automated test interpretations service is considered a professional-to-professional consultation. The formal responsibility of the consultant is to the consultee, but the ultimate and overriding responsibility is to the client.

E.10. Test Security. Counselors maintain the integrity and security of tests and other assessment techniques consistent with legal and contractual obligations. Counselors do not appropriate, reproduce, or modify published tests or parts thereof without acknowledgment and permission from the publisher.

E.11. Obsolete Tests and Outdated Test Results. Counselors do not use data or test results that are obsolete or outdated for the current purpose. Counselors make every effort to prevent the misuse of obsolete measures and test data by others.

E.12. Test Construction. Counselors use established scientific procedures, relevant standards, and current professional knowledge for test design in the development, publication, and utilization of educational and psychological assessment techniques.

Section F: Teaching, Training, and Supervision

F.1. Counselor Educators and Trainers.

a. Educators as Teachers and Practitioners. Counselors who are responsible for developing, implementing, and supervising educational programs are skilled as teachers and practitioners. They are knowledgeable regarding the ethical, legal, and regulatory aspects of the profession, are skilled in applying that knowledge, and make students and supervisees aware of their responsibilities. Counselors conduct counselor education and training programs in an ethical manner and serve as role models for professional behavior. Counselor educators should make an effort to infuse material related to human diversity into all courses and/or workshops that are designed to promote the development of professional counselors.

b. Relationship Boundaries With Students and Supervisees. Counselors clearly define and maintain ethical, professional, and social relationship boundaries with their students and supervisees. They are aware of the differential in power that exists and the student's or supervisee's possible incomprehension of that power differential. Counselors explain to students and supervisees the potential for the relationship to become exploitive.

c. Sexual Relationships. Counselors do not engage in sexual relationships with students or supervisees and do not subject them to sexual harassment. (See A.6. and C.5.b)

d. Contributions to Research. Counselors give credit to students or supervisees for their contributions to research and scholarly projects. Credit is given through coauthorship, acknowledgment, footnote statement, or other appropriate means, in accordance with such contributions. (See G.4.b. and G.4.c.)

e. Close Relatives. Counselors do not accept close relatives as students or supervisees.

f. Supervision Preparation. Counselors who offer clinical supervision services are adequately prepared in supervision methods and techniques. Counselors who are doctoral students serving as practicum or internship supervisors to master's level students are adequately prepared and supervised by the training program.

g. Responsibility for Services to Clients. Counselors who supervise the counseling services of others take reasonable measures to ensure that counseling services provided to clients are professional.

h. Endorsement. Counselors do not endorse students or supervisees for certification, licensure, employment, or completion of an academic or training program if they believe students or supervisees are not qualified for the endorsement. Counselors take reasonable steps to assist students or supervisees who are not qualified for endorsement to become qualified.

F.2. Counselor Education and Training Programs.

a. Orientation. Prior to admission, counselors orient prospective students to the counselor education or training program's expectations, including but not limited to the following: (1) the type and level of skill acquisition required for successful completion of the training, (2) subject matter to be covered, (3) basis for evaluation, (4) training components that encourage self-growth or self-disclosure as part of the training process, (5) the type of supervision settings and requirements of the sites for required clinical field experiences, (6) student and supervisee evaluation and dismissal policies and procedures, and (7) up-to-date employment prospects for graduates.

b. Integration of Study and Practice. Counselors establish counselor education and training programs that integrate academic study and supervised practice.

c. Evaluation. Counselors clearly state to students and supervisees, in advance of training, the levels of competency expected, appraisal methods, and timing of evaluations for both didactic and experiential components. Counselors provide students and supervisees with periodic performance appraisal and evaluation feedback throughout the training program.

d. Teaching Ethics. Counselors make students and supervisees aware of the ethical responsibilities and standards of the profession and the students' and supervisees' ethical responsibilities to the profession. (See C.1. and F.3.e.)

e. Peer Relationships. When students or supervisees are assigned to lead counseling groups or provide clinical supervision for their peers, counselors take steps to ensure that students and supervisees placed in these roles do not have personal or adverse relationships with peers and that they understand they have the same ethical obligations as counselor educators, trainers, and supervisors. Counselors make every effort to ensure that the rights of peers are not compromised when students or supervisees are assigned to lead counseling groups or provide clinical supervision.

f. Varied Theoretical Positions. Counselors present varied theoretical positions so that students and supervisees may make comparisons and have opportunities to develop their own positions. Counselors provide information concerning the scientific bases of professional practice. (See C.6.a.)

g. Field Placements. Counselors develop clear policies within their training program regarding field placement and other clinical experiences. Counselors provide clearly stated roles and responsibilities for the student or supervisee, the site supervisor, and the program supervisor. They confirm that site supervisors are qualified to provide supervision and are informed of their professional and ethical responsibilities in this role.

h. Dual Relationships as Supervisors. Counselors avoid dual relationships such as performing the role of site supervisor and training program supervisor in the student's or supervisee's training program. Counselors do not accept any form of professional services, fees, commissions, reimbursement, or remuneration from a site for student or supervisee placement.

i. Diversity in Programs. Counselors are responsive to their institution's and program's recruitment and retention needs for training program administrators, faculty, and students with diverse backgrounds and special needs. (See A.2.a.)

F.3. Students and Supervisees.

a. Limitations. Counselors, through ongoing evaluation and appraisal, are aware of the academic and personal limitations of students and supervisees that might impede performance. Counselors assist students and supervisees in securing remedial assistance when needed, and dismiss from the training program supervisees who are unable to provide competent service due to academic or personal limitations. Counselors seek professional consultation and document their decision to dismiss or refer students or supervisees for assistance. Counselors ensure that students and supervisees have recourse to address decisions made to require them to seek assistance or to dismiss them.
b. Self-Growth Experiences. Counselors use professional judgment when designing training experiences conducted by the counselors themselves that require student and supervisee self-growth or self-disclosure. Safeguards are provided so that students and supervisees are aware of the ramifications their self-disclosure may have on counselors whose primary role as teacher, trainer, or supervisor requires acting on ethical obligations to the profession. Evaluative components of experiential training experiences explicitly delineate predetermined academic standards that are separate and do not depend on the student's level of self-disclosure. (See A.6.)
c. Counseling for Students and Supervisees. If students or supervisees request counseling, supervisors, or counselor educators provide them with acceptable referrals. Supervisors or counselor educators do not serve as counselor to students or supervisees over whom they hold administrative, teaching, or evaluative roles unless this is a brief role associated with a training experience. (See A.6.b.)
d. Clients of Students and Supervisees. Counselors make every effort to ensure that the clients at field placements are aware of the services rendered and the qualifications of the students and supervisees rendering those services. Clients receive professional disclosure information and are informed of the limits of confidentiality. Client permission is obtained in order for the students and supervisees to use any information concerning the counseling relationship in the training process. (See B.1.e.)
e. Standards for Students and Supervisees. Students and supervisees preparing to become counselors adhere to the Code of Ethics and the Standards of Practice. Students and supervisees have the same obligations to clients as those required of counselors. (See H.1.)

Section G: Research and Publication

G.1. Research Responsibilities.

a. Use of Human Subjects. Counselors plan, design, conduct, and report research in a manner consistent with pertinent ethical principles, federal and state laws, host institutional regulations, and scientific standards governing research with human subjects. Counselors design and conduct research that reflects cultural sensitivity appropriateness.
b. Deviation From Standard Practices. Counselors seek consultation and observe stringent safeguards to protect the rights of research participants when a research problem suggests a deviation from standard acceptable practices. (See B.6.)
c. Precautions to Avoid Injury. Counselors who conduct research with human subjects are responsible for the subjects' welfare throughout the experiment and take reasonable precautions to avoid causing injurious psychological, physical, or social effects to their subjects.
d. Principal Researcher Responsibility. The ultimate responsibility for ethical research practice lies with the principal researcher. All others involved in the research activities share ethical obligations and full responsibility for their own actions.
e. Minimal Interference. Counselors take reasonable precautions to avoid causing disruptions in subjects' lives due to participation in research.
f. Diversity. Counselors are sensitive to diversity and research issues with special populations. They seek consultation when appropriate. (See A.2.a. and B.6.)

G.2. Informed Consent.

a. Topics Disclosed. In obtaining informed consent for research, counselors use language that is understandable to research participants and that (1) accurately explains the purpose and procedures to be followed; (2) identifies any procedures that are experimental or relatively untried; (3) describes the attendant discomforts and risks; (4) describes the benefits or changes in individuals or organizations that might be reasonably expected; (5) discloses appropriate alternative procedures that would be advantageous for subjects; (6) offers to answer any inquiries concerning the procedures; (7) describes any limitations on confidentiality; and (8) instructs that subjects are free to withdraw their consent and to discontinue participation in the project at any time. (See B.1.f.)
b. Deception. Counselors do not conduct research involving deception unless alternative procedures are not feasible and the prospective value of the research justifies the deception. When the methodological requirements of a study necessitate concealment or deception, the investigator is required to explain clearly the reasons for this action as soon as possible.
c. Voluntary Participation. Participation in research is typically voluntary and without any penalty for refusal to participate. Involuntary participation is appropriate only when it can be demonstrated that participation will have no harmful effects on subjects and is essential to the investigation.
d. Confidentiality of Information. Information obtained about research participants during the course of an investigation is confidential. When the possibility exists that others may obtain access to such information, ethical research practice requires that the possibility, together with the plans for protecting confidentiality, be

explained to participants as a part of the procedure for obtaining informed consent. (See B.1.e.)

e. Persons Incapable of Giving Informed Consent. When a person is incapable of giving informed consent, counselors provide an appropriate explanation, obtain agreement for participation, and obtain appropriate consent from a legally authorized person.
f. Commitments to Participants. Counselors take reasonable measures to honor all commitments to research participants.
g. Explanations After Data Collection. After data are collected, counselors provide participants with full clarification of the nature of the study to remove any misconceptions. Where scientific or human values justify delaying or withholding information, counselors take reasonable measures to avoid causing harm.
h. Agreements to Cooperate. Counselors who agree to cooperate with another individual in research or publication incur an obligation to cooperate as promised in terms of punctuality of performance and with regard to the completeness and accuracy of the information required.
i. Informed Consent for Sponsors. In the pursuit of research, counselors give sponsors, institutions, and publication channels the same respect and opportunity for giving informed consent that they accord to individual research participants. Counselors are aware of their obligation to future research workers and ensure that host institutions are given feedback information and proper acknowledgment.

G.3. Reporting Results.

a. Information Affecting Outcome. When reporting research results, counselors explicitly mention all variables and conditions known to the investigator that may have affected the outcome of a study or the interpretation of data.
b. Accurate Results. Counselors plan, conduct, and report research accurately and in a manner that minimizes the possibility that results will be misleading. They provide thorough discussions of the limitations of their data and alternative hypotheses. Counselors do not engage in fraudulent research, distort data, misrepresent data, or deliberately bias their results.
c. Obligation to Report Unfavorable Results. Counselors communicate to other counselors the results of any research judged to be of professional value. Results that reflect unfavorably on institutions, programs, services, prevailing opinions, or vested interests are not withheld.
d. Identity of Subjects. Counselors who supply data, aid in the research of another person, report research results, or make original data available take due care to disguise the identity of respective subjects in the absence of specific authorization from the subjects to do otherwise. (See B.1.g. and B.5.a.)
e. Replication Studies. Counselors are obligated to make available sufficient original research data to qualified professionals who may wish to replicate the study.

G.4. Publication.

a. Recognition of Others When conducting and reporting research, counselors are familiar with and give recognition to previous work on the topic, observe copyright laws, and give full credit to those to whom credit is due. (See F.1.d. and G.4.c.)
b. Contributors. Counselors give credit through joint authorship, acknowledgment, footnote statements, or other appropriate means to those who have contributed significantly to research or concept development in accordance with such contributions. The principal contributor is listed first and minor technical or professional contributions are acknowledged in notes or introductory statements.
c. Student Research. For an article that is substantially based on a student's dissertation or thesis, the student is listed as the principal author. (See F.1.d. and G.4.a.)
d. Duplicate Submission. Counselors submit manuscripts for consideration to only one journal at a time. Manuscripts that are published in whole or in substantial part in another journal or published work are not submitted for publication without acknowledgment and permission from the previous publication.
e. Professional Review. Counselors who review material submitted for publication, research, or other scholarly purposes respect the confidentiality and proprietary rights of those who submitted it.

Section H: Resolving Ethical Issues

H.1. Knowledge of Standards. Counselors are familiar with the Code of Ethics and the Standards of Practice and other applicable ethics codes from other professional organizations of which they are members, or from certification and licensure bodies. Lack of knowledge or misunderstanding of an ethical responsibility is not a defense against a charge of unethical conduct. (See F.3.e.)

H.2. Suspected Violations.

a. Ethical Behavior Expected. Counselors expect professional associates to adhere to the Code of Ethics. When counselors possess reasonable cause that raises doubts as to whether a counselor is acting in an ethical manner, they take appropriate action. (See H.2.d. and H.2.e.)
b. Consultation. When uncertain as to whether a particular situation or course of action may be in violation of the Code of Ethics, counselors consult with other counselors who are knowledgeable about ethics, with colleagues, or with appropriate authorities.
c. Organization Conflicts. If the demands of an organization with which counselors are affiliated pose a conflict with the Code of Ethics, counselors specify the nature of such conflicts and express to their supervisors or other responsible officials their commitment to the Code of Ethics. When possible, counselors work toward change within the organization to allow full adherence to the Code of Ethics.
d. Informal Resolution. When counselors have reasonable cause to believe that another counselor is violating an ethical standard, they attempt to first resolve the issue informally with the other counselor if feasible, providing that such action does not violate confidentiality rights that may be involved.

e. Reporting Suspected Violations. When an informal resolution is not appropriate or feasible, counselors, upon reasonable cause, take action such as reporting the suspected ethical violation to state or national ethics committees, unless this action conflicts with confidentiality rights that cannot be resolved.
f. Unwarranted Complaints. Counselors do not initiate, participate in, or encourage the filing of ethics complaints that are unwarranted or intend to harm a counselor rather than to protect clients or the public.

H.3. Cooperation With Ethics Committees. Counselors assist in the process of enforcing the Code of Ethics. Counselors cooperate with investigations, proceedings, and requirements of the ACA Ethics Committee or ethics committees of other duly constituted associations or boards having jurisdiction over those charged with a violation. Counselors are familiar with the ACA Policies and Procedures and use it as a reference in assisting the enforcement of the Code of Ethics.

ACA STANDARDS OF PRACTICE

All members of the American Counseling Association (ACA) are required to adhere to the Standards of Practice and the Code of Ethics. The Standards of Practice represent minimal behavioral statements of the Code of Ethics. Members should refer to the applicable section of the Code of Ethics for further interpretation and amplification of the applicable Standard of Practice.

Section A: The Counseling Relationship

Standard of Practice One (SP-1): Nondiscrimination. Counselors respect diversity and must not discriminate against clients because of age, color, culture, disability, ethnic group, gender, race, religion, sexual orientation, marital status, or socioeconomic status. (See A.2.a.)

Standard of Practice Two (SP-2): Disclosure to Clients. Counselors must adequately inform clients, preferably in writing, regarding the counseling process and counseling relationship at or before the time it begins and throughout the relationship. (See A.3.a.)

Standard of Practice Three (SP-3): Dual Relationships. Counselors must make every effort to avoid dual relationships with clients that could impair their professional judgment or increase the risk of harm to clients. When a dual relationship cannot be avoided, counselors must take appropriate steps to ensure that judgment is not impaired and that no exploitation occurs. (See A.6.a and A.6.b.)

Standard of Practice Four (SP-4): Sexual Intimacies With Clients. Counselors must not engage in any type of sexual intimacies with current clients and must not engage in sexual intimacies with former clients within a minimum of 2 years after terminating the counseling relationship. Counselors who engage in such relationship after 2 years following termination have the responsibility to examine and document thoroughly that such relations did not have an exploitative nature.

Standard of Practice Five (SP-5): Protecting Clients During Group Work. Counselors must take steps to protect clients from physical or psychological trauma resulting from interactions during group work. (See A.9.b.)

Standard of Practice Six (SP-6): Advance Understanding of Fees. Counselors must explain to clients, prior to their entering the counseling relationship, financial arrangements related to professional services. (See A.10. a.–d. and A.11.c.)

Standard of Practice Seven (SP-7): Termination. Counselors must assist in making appropriate arrangements for the continuation of treatment of clients, when necessary, following termination of counseling relationships. (See A.11.a.)

Standard of Practice Eight (SP-8): Inability to Assist Clients. Counselors must avoid entering or immediately terminate a counseling relationship if it is determined that they are unable to be of professional assistance to a client. The counselor may assist in making an appropriate referral for the client. (See A.11.b.)

Section B: Confidentiality

Standard of Practice Nine (SP-9): Confidentiality Requirement. Counselors must keep information related to counseling services confidential unless disclosure is in the best interest of clients, is required for the welfare of others, or is required by law. When disclosure is required, only information that is essential is revealed and the client is informed of such disclosure. (See B.1.a.–f.)

Standard of Practice Ten (SP-10): Confidentiality Requirements for Subordinates. Counselors must take measures to ensure that privacy and confidentiality of clients are maintained by subordinates. (See B.1.h.)

Standard of Practice Eleven (SP-11): Confidentiality in Group Work. Counselors must clearly communicate to group members that confidentiality cannot be guaranteed in group work. (See B.2.a.)

Standard of Practice Twelve (SP-12): Confidentiality in Family Counseling. Counselors must not disclose information about one family member in counseling to another family member without prior consent. (See B.2.b.)

Standard of Practice Thirteen (SP-13): Confidentiality of Records. Counselors must maintain appropriate confidentiality in creating, storing, accessing, transferring, and disposing of counseling records. (See B.4.b.)

Standard of Practice Fourteen (SP-14): Permission to Record or Observe. Counselors must obtain prior consent from clients in order to record electronically or observe sessions. (See B.4.c.)

Standard of Practice Fifteen (SP-15). Disclosure or Transfer of Records. Counselors must obtain client consent to disclose or transfer records to third parties, unless exceptions listed in SP-9 exist. (See B.4.e.)

Standard of Practice Sixteen (SP-16): Data Disguise Required. Counselors must disguise the identity of the client when using data for training, research, or publication. (See B.5.a.)

Section C: Professional Responsibility

Standard of Practice Seventeen (SP-17): Boundaries of Competence. Counselors must practice only within the boundaries of their competence. (See C.2.a.)

Standard of Practice Eighteen (SP-18): Continuing Education. Counselors must engage in continuing education to maintain their professional competence. (See C.2.f.)

Standard of Practice Nineteen (SP-19): Impairment of Professionals. Counselors must refrain from offering professional services when their personal problems or conflicts may cause harm to a client or others. (See C.2.g.)

Standard of Practice Twenty (SP-20): Accurate Advertising. Counselors must accurately represent their credentials and services when advertising. (See C.3.a.)

Standard of Practice Twenty-One (SP-21): Recruiting Through Employment. Counselors must not use their place of employment or institutional affiliation to recruit clients for their private practices. (See C.3.d.)

Standard of Practice Twenty-Two (SP-22): Credentials Claimed. Counselors must claim or imply only professional credentials possessed and must correct any known misrepresentations of their credentials by others. (See C.4.a.)

Standard of Practice Twenty-Three (SP-23): Sexual Harassment. Counselors must not engage in sexual harassment. (See C.5.b.)

Standard of Practice Twenty-Four (SP-24): Unjustified Gains. Counselors must not use their professional positions to seek or receive unjustified personal gains, sexual favors, unfair advantage, or unearned goods or services. (See C.5.e.)

Standard of Practice Twenty-Five (SP-25): Clients Served by Others. With the consent of the client, counselors must inform other mental health professionals serving the same client that a counseling relationship between the counselor and client exists. (See C.6.c.)

Standard of Practice Twenty-Six (SP-26): Negative Employment Conditions. Counselors must alert their employers to institutional policy or conditions that may be potentially disruptive or damaging to the counselor's professional responsibilities, or that may limit their effectiveness or deny clients' rights. (See D.1.c.)

Standard of Practice Twenty-Seven (SP-27): Personnel Selection and Assignment. Counselors must select competent staff and must assign responsibilities compatible with staff skills and experiences. (See D.1.h.)

Standard of Practice Twenty-Eight (SP-28): Exploitative Relationships With Subordinates. Counselors must not engage in exploitative relationships with individuals over whom they have supervisory, evaluative, or instructional control or authority. (See D.1.k.)

Section D: Relationship With Other Professionals

Standard of Practice Twenty-Nine (SP-29): Accepting Fees From Agency Clients. Counselors must not accept fees or other remuneration for consultation with persons entitled to such services through the counselor's employing agency or institution. (See D.3.a.)

Standard of Practice Thirty (SP-30): Referral Fees. Counselors must not accept referral fees. (See D.3.b.)

Section E: Evaluation, Assessment and Interpretation

Standard of Practice Thirty-One (SP-31): Limits of Competence. Counselors must perform only testing and assessment services for which they are competent. Counselors must not allow the use of psychological assessment techniques by unqualified persons under their supervision. (See E.2.a.)

Standard of Practice Thirty-Two (SP-32): Appropriate Use of Assessment Instruments. Counselors must use assessment instruments in the manner for which they were intended. (See E.2.b.)

Standard of Practice Thirty-Three (SP-33): Assessment Explanations to Clients. Counselors must provide explanations to clients prior to assessment about the nature and purposes of assessment and the specific uses of results. (See E.3.a.)

Standard of Practice Thirty-Four (SP-34): Recipients of Test Results. Counselors must ensure that accurate and appropriate interpretations accompany any release of testing and assessment information. (See E.3.b.)

Standard of Practice Thirty-Five (SP-35): Obsolete Tests and Outdated Test Results. Counselors must not base their assessment or intervention decisions or recommendations on data or test results that are obsolete or outdated for the current purpose. (See E.11.)

Section F: Teaching, Training, and Supervision

Standard of Practice Thirty-Six (SP-36): Sexual Relationships With Students or Supervisees. Counselors must not engage in sexual relationships with their students and supervisees. (See F.1.c.)

Standard of Practice Thirty-Seven (SP-37): Credit for Contributions to Research. Counselors must give credit to students or supervisees for their contributions to research and scholarly projects. (See F.1.d.)

Standard of Practice Thirty-Eight (SP-38): Supervision Preparation. Counselors who offer clinical supervision services must be trained and prepared in supervision methods and techniques. (See F.1.f.)

Standard of Practice Thirty-Nine (SP-39): Evaluation Information. Counselors must clearly state to students and supervisees in advance of training the levels of competency expected, appraisal methods, and timing of evaluations. Counselors must provide students and supervisees with periodic performance appraisal and evaluation feedback throughout the training program. (See F.2.c.)

Standard of Practice Forty (SP-40): Peer Relationships in Training. Counselors must make every effort to ensure that the rights of peers are not violated when students and supervisees are assigned to lead counseling groups or provide clinical supervision. (See F.2.e.)

Standard of Practice Forty-One (SP-41): Limitations of Students and Supervisees. Counselors must assist students and supervisees in securing remedial assistance, when needed, and must dismiss from the training program students and supervisees who are unable to provide competent service due to academic or personal limitations. (See F.3.a.)

Standard of Practice Forty-Two (SP-42): Self-Growth Experiences. Counselors who conduct experiences for students or supervisees that include self-growth or self-disclosure must inform participants of counselors' ethical obligations to the profession and must not grade participants based on their nonacademic performance. (See F.3.b.)

Standard of Practice Forty-Three (SP-43): Standards for Students and Supervisees. Students and supervisees preparing to become counselors must adhere to the Code of Ethics and the Standards of Practice of counselors. (See F.3.e.)

Section G: Research and Publication

Standard of Practice Forty-Four (SP-44): Precautions to Avoid Injury in Research. Counselors must avoid causing physical, social, or psychological harm or injury to subjects in research. (See G.1.c.)

Standard of Practice Forty-Five (SP-45): Confidentiality of Research Information. Counselors must keep confidential information obtained about research participants. (See G.2.d.)

Standard of Practice Forty-Six (SP-46): Information Affecting Research Outcome. Counselors must report all variables and conditions known to the investigator that may have affected research data or outcomes. (See G.3.a.)

Standard of Practice Forty-Seven (SP-47): Accurate Research Results. Counselors must not distort or misrepresent research data, nor fabricate or intentionally bias research results. (See G.3.b.)

Standard of Practice Forty-Eight (SP-48): Publication Contributors. Counselors must give appropriate credit to those who have contributed to research. (See G.4.a. and G.4.b.)

Section H: Resolving Ethical Issues

Standard of Practice Forty-Nine (SP-49): Ethical Behavior Expected. Counselors must take appropriate action when they possess reasonable cause that raises doubts as to whether counselors or other mental health professionals are acting in an ethical manner. (See H.2.a.)

Standard of Practice Fifty (SP-50): Unwarranted Complaints. Counselors must not initiate, participate in, or encourage the filing of ethics complaints that are unwarranted or intended to harm a mental health professional rather than to protect clients or the public. (See H.2.f.)

Standard of Practice Fifty-One (SP-51): Cooperation With Ethics Committees. Counselors must cooperate with investigations, proceedings, and requirements of the ACA Ethics Committee or ethics committees of other duly constituted associations or boards having jurisdiction over those charged with a violation. (See H.3.)

Appendix B
American Psychological Association Code of Ethics

PREAMBLE

Psychologists work to develop a valid and reliable body of scientific knowledge based on research. They may apply that knowledge to human behavior in a variety of contexts. In doing so, they perform many roles, such as researcher, educator, diagnostician, therapist, supervisor, consultant, administrator, social interventionist, and expert witness. Their goal is to broaden knowledge of behavior and, where appropriate, to apply it pragmatically to improve the condition of both the individual and society. Psychologists respect the central importance of freedom of inquiry and expression in research, teaching, and publication. They also strive to help the public in developing informed judgments and choices concerning human behavior. This Ethics Code provides a common set of values upon which psychologists build their professional and scientific work.

This Code is intended to provide both the general principles and the decision rules to cover most situations encountered by psychologists. It has as its primary goal the welfare and protection of the individuals and groups with whom psychologists work. It is the individual responsibility of each psychologist to aspire to the highest possible standards of conduct. Psychologists respect and protect human and civil rights, and do not knowingly participate in or condone unfair discriminatory practices.

The development of a dynamic set of ethical standards for a psychologist's work-related conduct requires a personal commitment to a lifelong effort to act ethically; to encourage ethical behavior by students, supervisees, employees, and colleagues, as appropriate; and to consult with others, as needed, concerning ethical problems. Each psychologist supplements, but does not violate, the Ethics Code's values and rules on the basis of guidance drawn from personal values, culture, and experience.

GENERAL PRINCIPLES

Principle A: Competence

Psychologists strive to maintain high standards of competence in their work. They recognize the boundaries of their particular competencies and the limitations of their expertise. They provide only those services and use only those techniques for which they are qualified by education, training, or experience. Psychologists are cognizant of the fact that the competencies required in serving, teaching, and/or studying groups of people vary with the distinctive characteristics of those groups. In those areas in which recognized professional standards do not yet exist, psychologists exercise careful judgment and take appropriate precautions to protect the welfare of those with whom they work. They maintain knowledge of relevant scientific and professional information related to the services they render, and they recognize the need for ongoing education. Psychologists make appropriate use of scientific, professional, technical, and administrative resources.

Principle B: Integrity

Psychologists seek to promote integrity in the science, teaching, and practice of psychology. In these activities psychologists are honest, fair, and respectful of others. In describing or reporting their qualifications, services, products, fees, research, or teaching, they do not make statements that are false, misleading, or deceptive. Psychologists strive to be aware of their own belief systems, values, needs, and limitations and the effect of these on their work. To the extent feasible, they attempt to clarify for relevant parties the roles they are performing and to function appropriately in accordance with those roles. Psychologists avoid improper and potentially harmful dual relationships.

Principle C: Professional and Scientific Responsibility

Psychologists uphold professional standards of conduct, clarify their professional roles and obligations, accept appropriate responsibility for their behavior, and adapt their methods to the needs of different populations. Psychologists consult with, refer to, or cooperate with other professionals and institutions to the extent needed to serve the best interests of their patients, clients, or other recipients of their services. Psychologists' moral standards and conduct are personal matters to the same degree as is true for any other person, except as psychologists' conduct may compromise their professional responsibilities or reduce the public's trust in psychology and psychologists. Psychologists are concerned about the ethical compliance of their colleagues' scientific and professional conduct. When appropriate, they consult with colleagues in order to prevent or avoid unethical conduct.

Principle D: Respect for People's Rights and Dignity

Psychologists accord appropriate respect to the fundamental rights, dignity, and worth of all people. They respect the rights of individuals to privacy, confidentiality, self-determination, and autonomy, mindful that legal and other obligations may lead to inconsistency and conflict with the exercise of these rights. Psychologists are aware of cultural, individual, and role differences, including those due to age, gender, race, ethnicity, national origin, religion, sexual orientation, disability, language, and socioeconomic status. Psychologists try to eliminate the effect on their work of biases based on those factors, and they do not knowingly participate in or condone unfair discriminatory practices.

Principle E: Concern for Others' Welfare

Psychologists seek to contribute to the welfare of those with whom they interact professionally. In their professional actions, psychologists weigh the welfare and rights of their patients or clients, students, supervisees, human research participants, and other affected persons, and the welfare of animal subjects of research. When conflicts occur among psychologists' obligations or concerns, they attempt to resolve these conflicts and to perform their roles in a responsible fashion that avoids or minimizes harm. Psychologists are sensitive to real and ascribed differences in power between themselves and others, and they do not exploit or mislead other people during or after professional relationships.

Principle F: Social Responsibility

Psychologists are aware of their professional and scientific responsibilities to the community and the society in which they work and live. They apply and make public their knowledge of psychology in order to contribute to human welfare. Psychologists are concerned about and work to mitigate the causes of human suffering. When undertaking research, they strive to advance human welfare and the science of psychology. Psychologists try to avoid misuse of their work. Psychologists comply with the law and encourage the development of law and social policy that serve the interests of their patients and clients and the public. They are encouraged to contribute a portion of their professional time for little or no personal advantage.

ETHICAL STANDARDS

1. General Standards

These General Standards are potentially applicable to the professional and scientific activities of all psychologists.

1.01 Applicability of the Ethics Code. The activity of a psychologist subject to the Ethics Code may be reviewed under these Ethical Standards only if the activity is part of his or her work-related functions or the activity is psychological in nature. Personal activities having no connection to or effect on psychological roles are not subject to the Ethics Code.

1.02 Relationship of Ethics and Law. If psychologists' ethical responsibilities conflict with law, psychologists make known their commitment to the Ethics Code and take steps to resolve the conflict in a responsible manner.

1.03 Professional and Scientific Relationship. Psychologists provide diagnostic, therapeutic, teaching, research, supervisory, consultative, or other psychological services only in the context of a defined professional or scientific relationship or role. (See also Standards 2.01, Evaluation, Diagnosis, and Interventions in Professional Context, and 7.02, Forensic Assessments.)

1.04 Boundaries of Competence.

a. Psychologists provide services, teach, and conduct research only within the boundaries of their competence, based on their education, training, supervised experience, or appropriate professional experience.
b. Psychologists provide services, teach, or conduct research in new areas or involving new techniques only after first undertaking appropriate study, training, supervision, and/or consultation from persons who are competent in those areas or techniques.
c. In those emerging areas in which generally recognized standards for preparatory training do not yet exist, psychologists nevertheless take reasonable steps to ensure the competence of their work and to protect patients, clients, students, research participants, and others from harm.

1.05 Maintaining Expertise. Psychologists who engage in assessment, therapy, teaching, research, organizational consulting, or other professional activities maintain a reasonable level of awareness of current scientific and professional information in their fields of activity, and undertake ongoing efforts to maintain competence in the skills they use.

1.06 Basis for Scientific and Professional Judgments. Psychologists rely on scientifically and professionally derived knowledge when making scientific or professional judgments or when engaging in scholarly or professional endeavors.

1.07 Describing the Nature and Results of Psychological Services.

a. When psychologists provide assessment, evaluation, treatment, counseling, supervision, teaching, consultation, research, or other psychological services to an individual, a group, or an organization, they provide, using language that is reasonably understandable to the recipient of those services, appropriate information beforehand about the nature of such services and appropriate information later about results and conclusions. (See also Standard 2.09, Explaining Assessment Results.)
b. If psychologists will be precluded by law or by organizational roles from providing such information to particular individuals or groups, they so inform those individuals or groups at the outset of the service.

1.08 Human Differences. Where differences of age, gender, race, ethnicity, national origin, religion, sexual orientation, disability, language, or socioeconomic status significantly affect psychologists' work concerning particular individuals or groups, psychologists obtain the training, experience, consultation, or supervision necessary to ensure the competence of their services, or they make appropriate referrals.

1.09 Respecting Others. In their work-related activities, psychologists respect the rights of others to hold values, attitudes, and opinions that differ from their own.

1.10 Nondiscrimination. In their work-related activities, psychologists do not engage in unfair discrimination based on age, gender, race, ethnicity, national origin, religion, sexual orientation, disability, socio-economic status, or any basis proscribed by law.

1.11 Sexual Harassment.

a. Psychologists do not engage in sexual harassment. Sexual harassment is sexual solicitation, physical advances, or verbal or nonverbal conduct that is sexual in nature, that occurs in connection with the psychologist's activities or roles as a psychologist, and that either: (1) is unwelcome, is offensive, or creates a hostile workplace environment, and the psychologist knows or is told this; or (2) is sufficiently severe or intense to be abusive to a reasonable person in the context. Sexual harassment can consist of a single intense or severe act or of multiple persistent or pervasive acts.
b. Psychologists accord sexual-harassment complainants and respondents dignity and respect. Psychologists do not participate in denying a person academic admittance or advancement, employment, tenure, or promotion, based solely upon their having made, or their being the subject of, sexual harassment charges. This does not preclude taking action based upon the outcome of such proceedings or consideration of other appropriate information.

1.12 Other Harassment. Psychologists do not knowingly engage in behavior that is harassing or demeaning to persons with whom they interact in their work based on factors such as those persons' age, gender, race, ethnicity, national origin, religion, sexual orientation, disability, language, or socioeconomic status.

1.13 Personal Problems and Conflicts.

a. Psychologists recognize that their personal problems and conflicts may interfere with their effectiveness. Accordingly, they refrain from undertaking an activity when they know or should know that their personal problems are likely to lead to harm to a patient, client, colleague, student, research participant, or other person to whom they may owe a professional or scientific obligation.
b. In addition, psychologists have an obligation to be alert to signs of, and to obtain assistance for, their personal problems at an early stage, in order to prevent significantly impaired performance.
c. When psychologists become aware of personal problems that may interfere with their performing work-related duties adequately, they take appropriate measures, such as obtaining professional consultation or assistance, and determine whether they should limit, suspend, or terminate their work-related duties.

1.14 Avoiding Harm. Psychologists take reasonable steps to avoid harming their patients or clients, research participants, students, and others with whom they work, and to minimize harm where it is foreseeable and unavoidable.

1.15 Misuse of Psychologists' Influence. Because psychologists' scientific and professional judgments and actions may affect the lives of others, they are alert to and guard against personal, financial, social, organizational, or political factors that might lead to misuse of their influence.

1.16 Misuse of Psychologists' Work.

a. Psychologists do not participate in activities in which it appears likely that their skills or data will be misused by others, unless corrective mechanisms are available. (See also Standard 7.04, Truthfulness and Candor).
b. If psychologists learn of misuse or misrepresentation of their work, they take reasonable steps to correct or minimize the misuse or misrepresentation.

1.17 Multiple Relationships.

a. In many communities and situations, it may not be feasible or reasonable for psychologists to avoid social or other nonprofessional contacts with persons such as patients, clients, students, supervisees, or research participants. Psychologists must always be sensitive to the potential harmful effects of other contacts on their work and on those persons with whom they deal. A psychologist refrains from entering into or promising another personal, scientific, professional, financial, or other relationship with such persons if it appears likely that such a relationship reasonably might impair the psychologist's objectivity or otherwise interfere with the psychologist's effectively performing his or her functions as a psychologist, or might harm or exploit the other party.
b. Likewise, whenever feasible, a psychologist refrains from taking on professional or scientific obligations when pre-existing relationships would create a risk of such harm.
c. If a psychologist finds that, due to unforeseen factors, a potentially harmful multiple relationship has arisen, the psychologist attempts to resolve it with due regard for the best interests of the affected person and maximal compliance with the Ethics Code.

1.18 Barter (With Patients or Clients). Psychologists ordinarily refrain from accepting goods, services, or other nonmonetary remuneration from patients or clients in return for psychological services because such arrangements create inherent potential for conflicts, exploitation, and distortion of the professional relationship. A psychologist may participate in bartering only if (1) it is not clinically contraindicated, and (2) the relationship is not exploitative. (See also Standards 1.17, multiple Relationships, and 1.25, Fees and Financial Arrangements.)

1.19 Exploitative Relationships.

a. Psychologists do not exploit persons over whom they have supervisory, evaluative, or other authority such as students, supervisees, employees, research participants, and clients or patients. (See also Standards 4.05–4.07 regarding sexual involvement with clients or patients.)

b. Psychologists do not engage in sexual relationships with students or supervisees in training over whom the psychologist has evaluative or direct authority, because such relationships are so likely to impair judgment or be exploitative.

1.20 Consultations and Referrals.

a. Psychologists arrange for appropriate consultations and referrals based principally on the best interest of their patients or clients, with appropriate consent, and subject to other relevant considerations, including applicable law and contractual obligations. (See also Standards 5.01, Discussing the Limits of Confidentiality, and 5.06, Consultations.)
b. When indicated and professionally appropriate, psychologists cooperate with other professionals in order to serve their patients or clients effectively and appropriately.
c. Psychologists' referral practices are consistent with law.

1.21 Third-Party Requests for Services.

a. When a psychologist agrees to provide services to a person or entity at the request of a third party, the psychologist clarifies to the extent feasible, at the outset of the service, the nature of the relationship with each party. This clarification includes the role of the psychologist (such as therapist, organizational consultant, diagnostician, or expert witness), the probable uses of the services provided or the information obtained, and the fact that there may be limits to confidentiality.
b. If there is a foreseeable risk of the psychologist's being called upon to perform conflicting roles because of the involvement of a third party, the psychologist clarifies the nature and direction of his or her responsibilities, keeps all parties appropriately informed as matters develop, and resolves the situation in accordance with this Ethics Code.

1.22 Delegation to and Supervision of Subordinates.

a. Psychologists delegate to their employees, supervisees, and research assistants only those responsibilities that such persons can reasonably be expected to perform competently, on the basis of their education, training, or experience, either independently or with the level of supervision being provided.
b. Psychologists provide proper training and supervision to their employees or supervisees and take reasonable steps to see that such persons perform services responsibly, competently, and ethically.
c. If institutional policies, procedures, or practices prevent fulfillment of this obligation, psychologists attempt to modify their role or to correct the situation to the extent feasible.

1.23 Documentation of Professional and Scientific Work.

a. Psychologists appropriately document their professional and scientific work in order to facilitate provision of services later by them or by other professionals, to ensure accountability, and to meet other requirements of institutions or the law.
b. When psychologists have reason to believe that records of their professional services will be used in legal proceedings involving recipients of or participants in their work, they have a responsibility to create and maintain documentation in the kind of detail and quality that would be consistent with reasonable scrutiny in an adjudicative forum. (See also Standard 7.01, Professionalism, under Forensic Activities.)

1.24 Records and Data. Psychologists create, maintain, disseminate, store, retain, and dispose of records and data relating to their research, practice, and other work in accordance with law and in a manner that permits compliance with the requirements of this Ethics Code. (See also Standard 5.04, Maintenance of Records.)

1.25 Fees and Financial Arrangements.

a. As early as is feasible in a professional or scientific relationship, the psychologist and the patient, client, or other appropriate recipient of psychological services reach an agreement specifying the compensation and the billing arrangements.
b. Psychologists do not exploit recipients of services or payors with respect to fees.
c. Psychologists' fee practices are consistent with law.
d. Psychologists do not misrepresent their fees.
e. If limitations to services can be anticipated because of limitations in financing, this is discussed with the patient, client, or other appropriate recipient of services as early as is feasible. (See also Standard 4.08, Interruption of Services.)
f. If the patient, client, or other recipient of services does not pay for services as agreed, and if the psychologist wishes to use collection agencies or legal measures to collect the fees, the psychologist first informs the person that such measures will be taken and provides that person an opportunity to make prompt payment. (See also Standard 5.11, Withholding Records for Nonpayment.)

1.26 Accuracy in Reports to Payors and Funding Sources. In their reports to payors for services or sources of research funding, psychologists accurately state the nature of the research or service provided, the fees or charges, and where applicable, the identity of the provider, the findings, and the diagnosis. (See also Standard 5.05, Disclosures.)

1.27 Referrals and Fees. When a psychologist pays, receives payment from, or divides fees with another professional other than in an employer–employee relationship, the payment to each is based on the services (clinical, consultative, administrative, or other) provided and is not based on the referral itself.

2. Evaluation, Assessment, or Intervention

2.01 Evaluation, Diagnosis, and Interventions in Professional Context.

a. Psychologists perform evaluations, diagnostic services, or interventions only within the context of a defined professional relationship. (See also Standards 1.03, Professional and Scientific Relationship.)
b. Psychologists' assessments, recommendations, reports, and psychological diagnostic or evaluative statements are based on information and techniques (including per-

sonal interviews of the individual when appropriate) sufficient to provide appropriate substantiation for their findings. (See also Standard 7.02, Forensic Assessments.)

2.02 Competence and Appropriate Use of Assessments and Interventions.

a. Psychologists who develop, administer, score, interpret, or use psychological assessment techniques, interviews, tests, or instruments do so in a manner and for purposes that are appropriate in light of the research on or evidence of the usefulness and proper application of the techniques.
b. Psychologists refrain from misuse of assessment techniques, interventions, results, and interpretations and take reasonable steps to prevent others from misusing the information these techniques provide. This includes refraining from releasing raw test results or raw data to persons, other than to patients or clients as appropriate, who are not qualified to use such information. (See also Standards 1.02, Relationship of Ethics and Law, and 1.04, Boundaries of Competence.)

2.03 Test Construction. Psychologists who develop and conduct research with tests and other assessment techniques use scientific procedures and current professional knowledge for test design, standardization, validation, reduction or elimination of bias, and recommendations for use.

2.04 Use of Assessment in General and With Special Populations.

a. Psychologists who perform interventions or administer, score, interpret, or use assessment techniques are familiar with the reliability, validation, and related standardization or outcome studies of, and proper applications and uses of, the techniques they use.
b. Psychologists recognize limits to the certainty with which diagnoses, judgments, or predictions can be made about individuals.
c. Psychologists attempt to identify situations in which particular interventions or assessment techniques or norms may not be applicable or may require adjustment in administration or interpretation because of factors such as individuals' gender, age, race, ethnicity, national origin, religion, sexual orientation, disability, language, or socioeconomic status.

2.05 Interpreting Assessment Results. When interpreting assessment results, including automated interpretations, psychologists take into account the various test factors and characteristics of the person being assessed that might affect psychologists' judgments or reduce the accuracy of their interpretations. They indicate any significant reservations they have about the accuracy or limitations of their interpretations.

2.06 Unqualified Persons. Psychologists do not promote the use of psychological assessment techniques by unqualified persons. (See also Standard 1.22, Delegation to and Supervision of Subordinates.)

2.07 Obsolete Tests and Outdated Test Results.

a. Psychologists do not base their assessment or intervention decisions or recommendations on data or test results that are outdated for the current purpose.
b. Similarly, psychologists do not base such decisions or recommendations on tests and measures that are obsolete and not useful for the current purpose.

2.08 Test Scoring and Interpretation Services.

a. Psychologists who offer assessment or scoring procedures to other professionals accurately describe the purpose, norms, validity, reliability, and applications of the procedures and any special qualifications applicable to their use.
b. Psychologists select scoring and interpretation services (including automated services) on the basis of evidence of the validity of the program and procedures as well as on other appropriate considerations.
c. Psychologists retain appropriate responsibility for the appropriate application, interpretation, and use of assessment instruments, whether they score and interpret such tests themselves or use automated or other services.

2.09 Explaining Assessment Results. Unless the nature of the relationship is clearly explained to the person being assessed in advance and precludes provision of an explanation of results (such as in some organizational consulting, pre-employment or security screenings, and forensic evaluations), psychologists ensure that an explanation of the results is provided using language that is reasonably understandable to the person assessed or to another legally authorized person on behalf of the client. Regardless of whether the scoring and interpretation are done by the psychologist, by assistants, or by automated or other outside services, psychologists take reasonable steps to ensure that appropriate explanations of results are given.

2.10 Maintaining Test Security. Psychologists make reasonable efforts to maintain the integrity and security of tests and other assessment techniques consistent with law, contractual obligations, and in a manner that permits compliance with the requirements of this Ethics Code. (See also Standard 1.02, Relationship of Ethics and Law.)

3. Advertising and Other Public Statements

3.01 Definition of Public Statements. Psychologists comply with this Ethics Code in public statements relating to their professional services, products, or publications or to the field of psychology. Public statements include but are not limited to paid or unpaid advertising, brochures, printed matter, directory listings, personal resumes or curriculum vitae, interviews or comments for use in media, statements in legal proceedings, lectures and public oral presentations, and published materials.

3.02 Statements by Others.

a. Psychologists who engage others to create or place public statements that promote their professional practice, products, or activities retain professional responsibility for such statements.
b. In addition, psychologists make reasonable efforts to prevent others whom they do not control (such as employers, publishers, sponsors, organizational clients, and representatives of the print or broadcast

media) from making deceptive statements concerning psychologists' practice or professional or scientific activities.

c. If psychologists learn of deceptive statements about their work made by others, psychologists make reasonable efforts to correct such statements.
d. Psychologists do not compensate employees of press, radio, television, or other communication media in return for publicity in a news item.
e. A paid advertisement relating to the psychologist's activities must be identified as such, unless it is already apparent from the context.

3.03 Avoidance of False or Deceptive Statements.

a. Psychologists do not make public statements that are false, deceptive, misleading, or fraudulent, either because of what they state, convey, or suggest or because of what they omit, concerning their research, practice, or other work activities or those of persons or organizations with which they are affiliated. As examples (and not in limitation) of this standard, psychologists do not make false or deceptive statements concerning (1) their training, experience, or competence; (2) their academic degrees; (3) their credentials; (4) their institutional or association affiliations; (5) their services; (6) the scientific or clinical basis for, or results or degrees of success of, their services; (7) their fees; or (8) their publications or research findings. (See also Standards 6.15, Deception in Research, and 6.18, Providing Participants With Information About the Study.)
b. Psychologists claim as credentials for their psychological work, only degrees that (1) were earned from a regionally accredited educational institution or (2) were the basis for psychology licensure by the state in which they practice.

3.04 Media Presentations. When psychologists provide advice or comment by means of public lectures, demonstrations, radio or television programs, prerecorded tapes, printed articles, mailed material, or other media, they take reasonable precautions to ensure that (1) the statements are based on appropriate psychological literature and practice, (2) the statements are otherwise consistent with this Ethics Code, and (3) the recipients of the information are not encouraged to infer that a relationship has been established with them personally.

3.05 Testimonials. Psychologists do not solicit testimonials from current psychotherapy clients or patients or other persons who because of their particular circumstances are vulnerable to undue influence.

3.06 In-Person Solicitation. Psychologists do not engage, directly or through agents, in uninvited in-person solicitation of business from actual or potential psychotherapy patients or clients or other persons who because of their particular circumstances are vulnerable to undue influence. However, this does not preclude attempting to implement appropriate collateral contacts with significant others for the purpose of benefiting an already engaged therapy patient.

4. Therapy

4.01 Structuring the Relationship.

a. Psychologists discuss with clients or patients as early as in feasible in the therapeutic relationship appropriate issues, such as the nature and anticipated course of therapy, fees, and confidentiality. (See also Standards 1.25, Fees and Financial Arrangements, and 5.01, Discussing the Limits of Confidentiality.)
b. When the psychologist's work with clients or patients will be supervised, the above discussion includes that fact, and the name of the supervisor, when the supervisor has legal responsibility for the case.
c. When the therapist is a student intern, the client or patient is informed of that fact.
d. Psychologists make reasonable efforts to answer patients' questions and to avoid apparent misunderstandings about therapy. Whenever possible, psychologists provide oral and/or written information, using language that is reasonably understandable to the patient or client.

4.02 Informed Consent to Therapy.

a. Psychologists obtain appropriate informed consent to therapy or related procedures, using language that is reasonably understandable to participants. The content of informed consent will vary depending on many circumstances; however, informed consent generally implies that the person (1) has the capacity to consent, (2) has been informed of significant information concerning the procedure, (3) has freely and without undue influence expressed consent, and (4) consent has been appropriately documented.
b. When persons are legally incapable of giving informed consent, psychologists obtain informed permission from a legally authorized person, if such substitute consent is permitted by law.
c. In addition, psychologists (1) inform those persons who are legally incapable of giving informed consent about the proposed interventions in a manner commensurate with the persons' psychological capacities, (2) seek their assent to those interventions, and (3) consider such persons' preferences and best interests.

4.03 Couple and Family Relationships.

a. When a psychologist agrees to provide services to several persons who have a relationship (such as husband and wife or parents and children), the psychologist attempts to clarify at the outset (1) which of the individuals are patients or clients and (2) the relationship the psychologist will have with each person. This clarification includes the role of the psychologist and the probable uses of the services provided or the information obtained. (See also Standard 5.01, Discussing the Limits of Confidentiality.)
b. As soon as it becomes apparent that the psychologist may be called on to perform potentially conflicting roles (such as marital counselor to husband and wife, and then witness for one party in a divorce proceeding), the psychologist attempts to clarify and adjust, or

withdraw from, roles appropriately. (See also Standard 7.03, Clarification of Role, under Forensic Activities.)

4.04 Providing Mental Health Services to Those Served by Others. In deciding whether to offer or provide services to those already receiving mental health services elsewhere, psychologists carefully consider the treatment issues and the potential patient's or client's welfare. The psychologist discusses these issues with the patient or client, or another legally authorized person on behalf of the client, in order to minimize the risk of confusion and conflict, consults with the other service providers when appropriate, and proceeds with caution and sensitivity to the therapeutic issues.

4.05 Sexual Intimacies With Current Patients or Clients. Psychologists do not engage in sexual intimacies with current patients or clients.

4.06 Therapy With Former Sexual Partners. Psychologists do not accept as therapy patients or clients persons with whom they have engaged in sexual intimacies.

4.07 Sexual Intimacies With Former Therapy Patients.

a. Psychologists do not engage in sexual intimacies with a former therapy patient or client for at least two years after cessation or termination of professional services.
b. Because sexual intimacies with a former therapy patient or client are so frequently harmful to the patient or client, and because such intimacies undermine public confidence in the psychology profession and thereby deter the public's use of needed services, psychologists do not engage in sexual intimacies with former therapy patients and clients even after a two-year interval except in the most unusual circumstances. The psychologist who engages in such activity after the two years following cessation or termination of treatment bears the burden of demonstrating that there has been no exploitation, in light of all relevant factors, including (1) the amount of time that has passed since therapy terminated, (2) the nature and duration of the therapy, (3) the circumstances of termination, (4) the patient's or client's personal history, (5) the patient's or client's current mental status, (6) the likelihood of adverse impact on the patient or client and others, and (7) any statements or actions made by the therapist during the course of therapy suggesting or inviting the possibility of a post-termination sexual or romantic relationship with the patient or client. (See also Standard 1.17, Multiple Relationships.)

4.08 Interruption of Services.

a. Psychologists make reasonable efforts to plan for facilitating care in the event that psychological services are interrupted by factors such as the psychologist's illness, death, unavailability, or relocation or by the client's relocation or financial limitations. (See also Standard 5.09, Preserving Records and Data.)
b. When entering into employment or contractual relationships, psychologists provide for orderly and appropriate resolution of responsibility for patient or client care in the event that the employment or contractual relationship ends, with paramount consideration given to the welfare of the patient or client.

4.09 Terminating the Professional Relationship.

a. Psychologists do not abandon patients or clients. (See also Standard 1.25e, under Fees and Financial Arrangements.)
b. Psychologists terminate a professional relationship when it becomes reasonably clear that the patient or client no longer needs the service, is not benefiting, or is being harmed by continued service.
c. Prior to termination for whatever reason, except where precluded by the patient's or client's conduct, the psychologist discusses the patient's or client's views and needs, provides appropriate pretermination counseling, suggests alternative service providers as appropriate, and takes other reasonable steps to facilitate transfer of responsibility to another provider if the patient or client needs one immediately.

5. Privacy and Confidentiality

These Standards are potentially applicable to the professional and scientific activities of all psychologists.

5.01 Discussing the Limits of Confidentiality.

a. Psychologists discuss with persons and organizations with whom they establish a scientific or professional relationship (including, to the extent feasible, minors and their legal representatives) (1) the relevant limitations on confidentiality, including limitations where applicable in group, marital, and family therapy or in organizational consulting, and (2) the foreseeable uses of the information generated through their services.
b. Unless it is not feasible or is contraindicated, the discussion of confidentiality occurs at the outset of the relationship and thereafter as new circumstances may warrant.
c. Permission for electronic recording of interviews is secured from clients and patients.

5.02 Maintaining Confidentiality. Psychologists have a primary obligation and take reasonable precautions to respect the confidentiality rights of those with whom they work or consult, recognizing that confidentiality may be established by law, institutional rules, or professional or scientific relationships. (See also Standard 6.26, Professional Reviewers.)

5.03 Minimizing Intrusions on Privacy.

a. In order to minimize intrusions on privacy, psychologists include in written and oral reports, consultations, and the like, only information germane to the purpose for which the communication is made.
b. Psychologists discuss confidential information obtained in clinical or consulting relationships, or evaluative data concerning patients, individual or organizational clients, students, research participants, supervisees, and employees, only for appropriate scientific or professional purpose and only with persons clearly concerned with such matters.

5.04 Maintenance of Records. Psychologists maintain appropriate confidentiality in creating, storing, accessing, transferring, and disposing of records under their control, whether these are written, automated, or in any other medium. Psychologists maintain and dispose of records in accordance with law and in a manner that permits compliance with the requirements of this Ethics Code.

5.05 Disclosures.

a. Psychologists disclose confidential information without the consent of the individual only as mandated by law, or where permitted by law for a valid purpose, such as (1) to provide needed professional services to the patient or the individual or organizational client, (2) to obtain appropriate professional consultations, (3) to protect the patient or client or others from harm, or (4) to obtain payment for services, in which instance disclosure is limited to the minimum that is necessary to achieve the purpose.
b. Psychologists also may disclose confidential information with the appropriate consent of the patient or the individual or organizational client (or of another legally authorized person on behalf of the patient or client), unless prohibited by law.

5.06 Consultations. When consulting with colleagues, (1) psychologists do not share confidential information that reasonably could lead to the identification of a patient, client, research participant, or other person or organization with whom they have a confidential relationship unless they have obtained the prior consent of the person or organization or the disclosure cannot be avoided, and (2) they share information only to the extent necessary to achieve the purposes of the consultation. (See also Standard 5.02, Maintaining Confidentiality.)

5.07 Confidential Information in Databases.

a. If confidential information concerning recipients of psychological services is to be entered into databases or systems of records available to persons whose access has not been consented to by the recipient, then psychologists use coding or other techniques to avoid the inclusion of personal identifiers.
b. If a research protocol approved by an institutional review board or similar body requires the inclusion of personal identifiers, such identifiers are deleted before the information is made accessible to persons other than those of whom the subject was advised.
c. If such deletion is not feasible, then before psychologists transfer such data to others or review such data collected by others, they take reasonable steps to determine that appropriate consent of personally identifiable individuals has been obtained.

5.08 Use of Confidential Information for Didactic or Other Purposes.

a. Psychologists do not disclose in their writings, lectures, or other public media, confidential, personally identifiable information concerning their patients, individual or organizational clients, students, research participants, or other recipients of their services that they obtained during the course of their work, unless the person or organization has consented in writing or unless there is other ethical or legal authorization for doing so.
b. Ordinarily, in such scientific and professional presentations, psychologists disguise confidential information concerning such persons or organizations so that they are not individually identifiable to others and so that discussions do not cause harm to subjects who might identify themselves.

5.09 Preserving Records and Data. A psychologist makes plans in advance so that confidentiality of records and data is protected in the event of the psychologist's death, incapacity, or withdrawal from the position or practice.

5.10 Ownership of Records and Data. Recognizing that ownership of records and data is governed by legal principles, psychologists take reasonable and lawful steps so that records and data remain available to the extent needed to serve the best interests of patients, individual or organizational clients, research participants, or appropriate others.

5.11 Withholding Records for Nonpayment. Psychologists may not withhold records under their control that are requested and imminently needed for a patient's or client's treatment solely because payment has not been received, except as otherwise provided by law.

6. Teaching, Training Supervision, Research, and Publishing

6.01 Design of Education and Training Programs. Psychologists who are responsible for education and training programs seek to ensure that the programs are competently designed, provide the proper experiences, and meet the requirements for licensure, certification, or other goals for which claims are made by the program.

6.02 Descriptions of Education and Training Programs.

a. Psychologists responsible for education and training programs seek to ensure that there is a current and accurate description of the program content, training goals and objectives, and requirements that must be met for satisfactory completion of the program. This information must be made readily available to all interested parties.
b. Psychologists seek to ensure that statements concerning their course outlines are accurate and not misleading, particularly regarding the subject matter to be covered, bases for evaluating progress, and the nature of course experiences. (See also Standard 3.03, Avoidance of False or Deceptive Statements.)
c. To the degree to which they exercise control, psychologists responsible for announcements, catalogs, brochures, or advertisements describing workshops, seminars, or other non-degree-granting educational programs ensure that they accurately describe the audience for which the program is intended, the educational objectives, the presenters, and the fees involved.

6.03 Accuracy and Objectivity in Teaching.

a. When engaged in teaching or training, psychologists present psychological information accurately and with a reasonable degree of objectivity.
b. When engaged in teaching or training, psychologists recognize the power they hold over students or super-

visees and therefore make reasonable efforts to avoid engaging in conduct that is personally demeaning to students or supervisees. (See also Standards 1.09, Respecting Others, and 1.12, Other Harassment.)

6.04 Limitation on Teaching. Psychologists do not teach the use of techniques or procedures that require specialized training, licensure, or expertise, including but not limited to hypnosis, biofeedback, and projective techniques, to individuals who lack the prerequisite training, legal scope of practice, or expertise.

6.05 Assessing Student and Supervisee Performance.

a. In academic and supervisory relationships, psychologists establish an appropriate process for providing feedback to students and supervisees.
b. Psychologists evaluate students and supervisees on the basis of their actual performance on relevant and established program requirements.

6.06 Planning Research.

a. Psychologists design, conduct, and report research in accordance with recognized standards of scientific competence and ethical research.
b. Psychologists plan their research so as to minimize the possibility that results will be misleading.
c. In planning research, psychologists consider its ethical acceptability under the Ethics Code. If an ethical issue is unclear, psychologists seek to resolve the issue through consultation with institutional review boards, animal care and use committees, peer consultations, or other proper mechanisms.
d. Psychologists take reasonable steps to implement appropriate protections for the rights and welfare of human participants, other persons affected by the research, and the welfare of animal subjects.

6.07 Responsibility.

a. Psychologists conduct research competently and with due concern for the dignity and welfare of the participants.
b. Psychologists are responsible for the ethical conduct of research conducted by them or by others under their supervision or control.
c. Researchers and assistants are permitted to perform only those tasks for which they are appropriately trained and prepared.
d. As part of the process of development and implementation of research projects, psychologists consult those with expertise concerning any special population under investigation or most likely to be affected.

6.08 Compliance With Law and Standards. Psychologists plan and conduct research in a manner consistent with federal and state law and regulations, as well as professional standards governing the conduct of research, and particularly those standards governing research with human participants and animal subjects.

6.09 Institutional Approval. Psychologists obtain from host institutions or organizations appropriate approval prior to conducting research, and they provide accurate information about their research proposals. They conduct the research in accordance with the approved research protocol.

6.10 Research Responsibilities. Prior to conducting research (except research involving only anonymous surveys, naturalistic observations, or similar research), psychologists enter into an agreement with participants that clarifies the nature of the research and the responsibilities of each party.

6.11 Informed Consent to Research.

a. Psychologists use language that is reasonably understandable to research participants in obtaining their appropriate informed consent (except as provided in Standard 6.12, Dispensing with Informed Consent). Such informed consent is appropriately documented.
b. Using language that is reasonably understandable to participants, psychologists inform participants of the nature of the research; they inform participants that they are free to participate or to decline to participate or to withdraw from the research; they explain the foreseeable consequences of declining or withdrawing; they inform participants of significant factors that may be expected to influence their willingness to participate (such as risks, discomfort, adverse effects, or limitations on confidentiality, except as provided in Standard 6.15, Deception in Research); and they explain other aspects about which the prospective participants inquire.
c. When psychologists conduct research with individuals such as students or subordinates, psychologists take special care to protect the prospective participants from adverse consequences of declining or withdrawing from participation.
d. When research participation is a course requirement or opportunity for extra credit, the prospective participant is given the choice of equitable alternative activities.
e. For persons who are legally incapable of giving informed consent, psychologists nevertheless (1) provide an appropriate explanation, (2) obtain the participant's assent, and (3) obtain appropriate permission from a legally authorized person, if such substitute consent is permitted by law.

6.12 Dispensing With Informed Consent. Before determining that planned research (such as research involving only anonymous questionnaires, naturalistic observations, or certain kinds of archival research) does not require the informed consent of research participants, psychologists consider applicable regulations and institutional review board requirements, and they consult with colleagues as appropriate.

6.13 Informed Consent in Research Filming or Recording. Psychologists obtain informed consent from research participants prior to filming or recording them in any form, unless the research involves simply naturalistic observations in public places and it is not anticipated that the recording will be used in a manner that could cause personal identification or harm.

6.14 Offering Inducements for Research Participants.

a. In offering professional services as an inducement to obtain research participants, psychologists make clear the nature of the services, as well as the risks, obligations, and limitations. (See also Standard 1.18, Barter [With Patients or Clients].)

b. Psychologists do not offer excessive or inappropriate financial or other inducements to obtain research participants, particularly when it might tend to coerce participation.

6.15 Deception in Research.

a. Psychologists do not conduct a study involving deception unless they have determined that the use of deceptive techniques is justified by the study's prospective scientific, educational, or applied value and that equally effective alternative procedures that do not use deception are not feasible.
b. Psychologists never deceive research participants about significant aspects that would affect their willingness to participate, such as physical risks, discomfort, or unpleasant emotional experiences.
c. Any other deception that is an integral feature of the design and conduct of an experiment must be explained to participants as early as is feasible, preferably at the conclusion of their participation, but no later than at the conclusion of the research. (See also Standard 6.18, Providing Participants With Information About the Study.)

6.16 Sharing and Utilizing Data. Psychologists inform research participants of their anticipated sharing or further use of personally identifiable research data and of the possibility of unanticipated future uses.

6.17 Minimizing Invasiveness. In conducting research, psychologists interfere with the participants or milieu from which data are collected only in a manner that is warranted by an appropriate research design and that is consistent with psychologists' roles as scientific investigators.

6.18 Providing Participants With Information About the Study.

a. Psychologists provide a prompt opportunity for participants to obtain appropriate information about the nature, results, and conclusions of the research, and psychologists attempt to correct any misconceptions that participants may have.
b. If scientific or humane values justify delaying or withholding this information, psychologists take reasonable measures to reduce the risk of harm.

6.19 Honoring Commitments. Psychologists take reasonable measures to honor all commitments they have made to research participants.

6.20 Care and Use of Animals in Research.

a. Psychologists who conduct research involving animals treat them humanely.
b. Psychologists acquire, care for, use, and dispose of animals in compliance with current federal, state, and local laws and regulations, and with professional standards.
c. Psychologists trained in research methods and experienced in the care of laboratory animals supervise all procedures involving animals and are responsible for ensuring appropriate consideration of their comfort, health, and humane treatment.
d. Psychologists ensure that all individuals using animals under their supervision have received instruction in research methods and in the care, maintenance, and handling of the species being used, to the extent appropriate to their role.
e. Responsibilities and activities of individuals assisting in a research project are consistent with their respective competencies.
f. Psychologists make reasonable efforts to minimize the discomfort, infection, illness, and pain of animal subjects.
g. A procedure subjecting animals to pain, stress, or privation is used only when an alternative procedure is unavailable and the goal is justified by its prospective scientific, educational, or applied value.
h. Surgical procedures are performed under appropriate anesthesia; techniques to avoid infection and minimize pain are followed during and after surgery.
i. When it is appropriate that the animal's life be terminated, it is done rapidly, with an effort to minimize pain, and in accordance with accepted procedures.

6.21 Reporting of Results.

a. Psychologists do not fabricate data or falsify results in their publications.
b. If psychologists discover significant errors in their published data, they take reasonable steps to correct such errors in a correction, retraction, erratum, or other appropriate publication means.

6.22 Plagiarism. Psychologists do not present substantial portions or elements of another's work or data as their own, even if the other work or data source is cited occasionally.

6.23 Publication Credit.

a. Psychologists take responsibility and credit, including authorship credit, only for work they have actually performed or to which they have contributed.
b. Principal authorship and other publication credits accurately reflect the relative scientific or professional contributions of the individuals involved, regardless of their relative status. Mere possession of an institutional position, such as Department Chair, does not justify authorship credit. Minor contributions to the research or to the writing for publications are appropriately acknowledged, such as in footnotes or in an introductory statement.
c. A student is usually listed as principal author on any multiple-authored article that is substantially based on the student's dissertation or thesis.

6.24 Duplicate Publication of Data. Psychologists do not publish, as original data, data that have been previously published. This does not preclude republishing data when they are accompanied by proper acknowledgment.

6.25 Sharing Data. After research results are published, psychologists do not withhold the data on which their conclusions are based from other competent professionals who seek to verify the substantive claims through reanalysis and who intend to use such data only for that purpose, provided that the confidentiality of the participants can be protected and unless legal rights concerning proprietary data preclude their release.

6.26 Professional Reviewers. Psychologists who review material submitted for publication, grant, or other research proposal review respect the confidentiality of and the proprietary rights in such information of those who submitted it.

7. Forensic Activities

7.01 Professionalism. Psychologists who perform forensic functions, such as assessments, interviews, consultations, reports, or expert testimony, must comply with all other provisions of this Ethics Code to the extent that they apply to such activities. In addition, psychologists base their forensic work on appropriate knowledge of and competence in the areas underlying such work, including specialized knowledge concerning special populations. (See also Standards 1.06, Basis for Scientific and Professional Judgments; 1.08, Human Differences; 1.15, Misuse of Psychologists' Influence; and 1.23, Documentation of Professional and Scientific Work.)

7.02 Forensic Assessments.

a. Psychologists' forensic assessments, recommendations, and reports are based on information and techniques (including personal interviews of the individual, when appropriate) sufficient to provide appropriate substantiation for their findings. (See also Standards 1.03, Professional and Scientific Relationship; 1.23, Documentation of Professional and Scientific Work; 2.01, Evaluation, Diagnosis, and Interventions in Professional Context; and 2.05, Interpreting Assessment Results.)
b. Except as noted in (c), below, psychologists provide written or oral forensic reports or testimony of the psychological characteristics of an individual only after they have conducted an examination of the individual adequate to support their statements or conclusions.
c. When, despite reasonable efforts, such an examination is not feasible, psychologists clarify the impact of their limited information on the reliability and validity of their reports and testimony, and they appropriately limit the nature and extent of their conclusions or recommendations.

7.03 Clarification of Role. In most circumstances, psychologists avoid performing multiple and potentially conflicting roles in forensic matters. When psychologists may be called on to serve in more than one role in a legal proceeding—for example, as consultant or expert for one party or for the court and as a fact witness—they clarify role expectations and the extent of confidentiality in advance to the extent feasible, and thereafter as changes occur, in order to avoid compromising their professional judgment and objectivity and in order to avoid misleading others regarding their role.

7.04 Truthfulness and Candor.

a. In forensic testimony and reports, psychologists testify truthfully, honestly, and candidly and, consistent with applicable legal procedures, describe fairly the bases for their testimony and conclusions.
b. Whenever necessary to avoid misleading, psychologists acknowledge the limits of their data or conclusions.

7.05 Prior Relationships. A prior professional relationship with a party does not preclude psychologists from testifying as fact witnesses or from testifying to their services to the extent permitted by applicable law. Psychologists appropriately take into account ways in which the prior relationship might affect their professional objectivity or opinions and disclose the potential conflict to the relevant parties.

7.06 Compliance With Law and Rules. In performing forensic roles, psychologists are reasonably familiar with the rules governing their roles. Psychologists are aware of the occasionally competing demands placed upon them by these principles and the requirements of the court system, and attempt to resolve these conflicts by making known their commitment to this Ethics Code and taking steps to resolve the conflict in a responsible manner. (See also Standard 1.02, Relationship of Ethics and Law.)

8. Resolving Ethical Issues

8.01 Familiarity With Ethics Code. Psychologists have an obligation to be familiar with this Ethics Code, other applicable ethics codes, and their application to psychologists' work. Lack of awareness or misunderstanding of an ethical standard is not itself a defense to a charge of unethical conduct.

8.02 Confronting Ethical Issues. When a psychologist is uncertain whether a particular situation or course of action would violate this Ethics Code, the psychologist ordinarily consults with other psychologists knowledgeable about ethical issues, with state or national psychology ethics committees, or with other appropriate authorities in order to choose a proper response.

8.03 Conflicts Between Ethics and Organizational Demands. If the demands of an organization with which psychologists are affiliated conflict with this Ethics Code, psychologists clarify the nature of the conflict, make known their commitment to the Ethics Code, and to the extent feasible, seek to resolve the conflict in a way that permits the fullest adherence to the Ethics Code.

8.04 Informal Resolution of Ethical Violations. When psychologists believe that there may have been an ethical violation by another psychologist, they attempt to resolve the issue by bringing it to the attention of that individual if an informal resolution appears appropriate and the intervention does not violate any confidentiality rights that may be involved.

8.05 Reporting Ethical Violations. If an apparent ethical violation is not appropriate for informal resolution under Standard 8.04 or is not resolved properly in that fashion, psychologists take further action appropriate to the situation, unless such action conflicts with confidentiality rights in ways that cannot be resolved. Such action might include referral to state or national committees on professional ethics or to state licensing boards.

8.06 Cooperating With Ethics Committees. Psychologists cooperate in ethics investigations, proceedings, and resulting requirements of the APA or any affiliated state psychological association to which they belong. In doing so, they make reasonable efforts to resolve any issues as to confidentiality. Failure to cooperate is itself an ethics violation.

8.07 Improper Complaints. Psychologists do not file or encourage the filing of ethics complaints that are frivolous and are intended to harm the respondent rather than to protect the public.

History and Effective Date

This version of the APA Ethics Code was adopted by the American Psychological Association's Council of Representatives during its meeting, August 13 and 16, 1992, and is effective beginning December 1, 1992. Inquiries concerning the substance or interpretation of the APA Ethics Code should be addressed to the Director, Office of Ethics, American Psychological Association, 750 First Street, NE, Washington, DC 20002-4242.

This Code will be used to adjudicate complaints brought concerning alleged conduct occurring after the effective date. Complaints regarding conduct occurring prior to the effective date will be adjudicated on the basis of the version of the Code that was in effect at the time the conduct occurred, except that no provisions repealed in June 1989, will be enforced even if an earlier version contains the provision. The Ethics Code will undergo continuing review and study for future revisions; comments on the Code may be sent to the above address.

The APA has previously published its Ethical Standards as follows:

American Psychological Association. (1953). Ethical standards of psychologists. Washington, DC: Author.

American Psychological Association. (1958). Standards of ethical behavior for psychologists. *American Psychologist, 13,* 268–271.

American Psychological Association. (1963). Ethical standards of psychologists. *American Psychologist, 18,* 56–60.

American Psychological Association. (1968). Ethical standards of psychologists. *American Psychologist, 23,* 357–361.

American Psychological Association. (1977, March). Ethical standards of psychologists. *APA Monitor,* 22–23.

American Psychological Association. (1979). Ethical standards of psychologists. Washington, DC: Author.

American Psychological Association. (1981). Ethical principles of psychologists. *American Psychologist, 36,* 633–638.

American Psychological Association. (1990). Ethical principles of psychologists (Amended June 2, 1989). *American Psychologist, 45,* 390–395.

Request copies of the APA's Ethical Principles of Psychologists and Code of Conduct from the APA Order Department, 750 First Street, NE, Washington, DC 20002-4242, or phone (202) 336-5510.

Note: Professional materials that are most helpful in this regard are guidelines and standards that have been adopted or endorsed by professional psychological organizations. Such guidelines and standards, whether adopted by the American Psychological Association (APA) or its Divisions, are not enforceable as such by this Ethics Code, but are of educative value to psychologists, courts, and professional bodies. Such materials include, but are not limited to, the APA's General Guidelines for Providers of Psychological Services (1987), Specialty Guidelines for the Delivery of Services by Clinical Psychologists, Counseling Psychologists, Industrial/Organizational Psychologists, and School Psychologists (1981), Guidelines for Computer Based Tests and Interpretations (1987), Standards for Educational and Psychological Testing (1985), Ethical Principles in the Conduct of Research With Human Participants (1982), Guidelines for Ethical Conduct in the Care and Use of Animals (1986), Guidelines for Providers of Psychological Services to Ethnic, Linguistic, and Culturally Diverse Populations (1990), and Publication Manual of the American Psychological Association (3rd ed., 1983). Materials not adopted by APA as a whole include the APA Division 41 (Forensic Psychology)/American Psychology—Law Society's Specialty Guidelines for Forensic Psychologists (1991).

Appendix C
NASW Code of Ethics

PREAMBLE

The primary mission of the social work profession is to enhance human well-being and help meet the basic human needs of all people, with particular attention to the needs and empowerment of people who are vulnerable, oppressed, and living in poverty. A historic and defining feature of social work is the profession's focus on individual well-being in a social context and the well-being of society. Fundamental to social work is attention to the environmental forces that create, contribute to, and address problems in living.

Social workers promote social justice and social change with and on behalf of clients. "Clients" is used inclusively to refer to individuals, families, groups, organizations, and communities. Social workers are sensitive to cultural and ethnic diversity and strive to end discrimination, oppression, poverty, and other forms of social injustice. These activities may be in the form of direct practice, community organizing, supervision, consultation, administration, advocacy, social and political action, policy development and implementation, education, and research and evaluation. Social workers seek to enhance the capacity of people to address their own needs. Social workers also seek to promote the responsiveness of organizations, communities, and other social institutions to individuals' needs and social problems.

The mission of the social work profession is rooted in a set of core values. These core values, embraced by social workers throughout the profession's history, are the foundation of social work's unique purpose and perspective:

- service
- social justice
- dignity and worth of the person
- importance of human relationships
- integrity
- competence.

This constellation of core values reflects what is unique to the social work profession. Core values, and the principles that flow from them, must be balanced within the context and complexity of the human experience.

PURPOSE OF THE NASW CODE OF ETHICS

Professional ethics are at the core of social work. The profession has an obligation to articulate its basic values, ethical principles, and ethical standards. The *NASW Code of Ethics* sets forth these values, principles, and standards to guide social workers' conduct. The *Code* is relevant to all social workers and social work students, regardless of their professional functions, the settings in which they work, or the populations they serve.

The *NASW Code of Ethics* serves six purposes:

1. The *Code* identifies core values on which social work's mission is based.
2. The *Code* summarizes broad ethical principles that reflect the profession's core values and establishes a set of specific ethical standards that should be used to guide social work practice.
3. The *Code* is designed to help social workers identify relevant considerations when professional obligations conflict or ethical uncertainties arise.
4. The *Code* provides ethical standards to which the general public can hold the social work profession accountable.
5. The *Code* socializes practitioners new to the field to social work's mission, values, ethical principles, and ethical standards.
6. The *Code* articulates standards that the social work profession itself can use to assess whether social workers have engaged in unethical conduct. NASW has formal procedures to adjudicate ethics complaints filed against its members.* In subscribing to this *Code*, social workers are required to cooperate in its implementation, participate in NASW adjudication proceedings, and abide by any NASW disciplinary rulings or sanctions based on it.

*For information on NASW adjudication procedures, see *NASW Procedures for the Adjudication of Grievances*.

The *Code* offers a set of values, principles, and standards to guide decision making and conduct when ethical issues arise. It does not provide a set of rules that prescribe how social workers should act in all situations. Specific applications of the *Code* must take into account the context in which it is being considered and the possibility of conflicts among the *Code*'s values, principles, and standards. Ethical responsibilities flow from all human relationships, from the personal and familial to the social and professional.

Further, the *NASW Code of Ethics* does not specify which values, principles, and standards are most important and ought to outweigh others in instances when they conflict. Reasonable differences of opinion can and do exist among social workers with respect to the ways in which values, ethical principles, and ethical standards should be rank ordered when they conflict. Ethical decision making in a given situation must apply the informed judgment of the individual social worker and should also consider how the issues would be judged in a peer review process where the ethical standards of the profession would be applied.

Ethical decision making is a process. There are many instances in social work where simple answers are not available to resolve complex ethical issues. Social workers should take into consideration all the values, principles, and standards in this *Code* that are relevant to any situation in which ethical judgment is warranted. Social workers' decisions and actions should be consistent with the spirit as well as the letter of this *Code*.

In addition to this *Code*, there are many other sources of information about ethical thinking that may be useful. Social workers should consider ethical theory and principles generally, social work theory and research, laws, regulations, agency policies, and other relevant codes of ethics, recognizing that among codes of ethics social workers should consider the *NASW Code of Ethics* as their primary source. Social workers also should be aware of the impact on ethical decision making of their clients' and their own personal values and cultural and religious beliefs and practices. They should be aware of any conflicts between personal and professional values and deal with them responsibly. For additional guidance social workers should consult the relevant literature on professional ethics and ethical decision making and seek appropriate consultation when faced with ethical dilemmas. This may involve consultation with an agency-based or social work organization's ethics committee, a regulatory body, knowledgeable colleagues, supervisors, or legal counsel.

Instances may arise when social workers' ethical obligations conflict with agency policies or relevant laws or regulations. When such conflicts occur, social workers must make a responsible effort to resolve the conflict in a manner that is consistent with the values, principles, and standards expressed in this *Code*. If a reasonable resolution of the conflict does not appear possible, social workers should seek proper consultation before making a decision.

The *NASW Code of Ethics* is to be used by NASW and by individuals, agencies, organizations, and bodies (such as licensing and regulatory boards, professional liability insurance providers, courts of law, agency boards of directors, government agencies, and other professional groups) that choose to adopt it or use it as a frame of reference. Violation of standards in this *code* does not automatically imply legal liability or violation of the law. Such determination can only be made in the context of legal and judicial proceedings. Alleged violations of the *Code* would be subject to a peer review process. Such processes are generally separate from legal or administrative procedures and insulated from legal review or proceedings to allow the profession to counsel and discipline its own members.

A code of ethics cannot guarantee ethical behavior. Moreover, a code of ethics cannot resolve all ethical issues or disputes or capture the richness and complexity involved in striving to make responsible choices within a moral community. Rather a code of ethics sets forth values, ethical principles, and ethical standards to which professionals aspire and by which their actions can be judged. Social workers' ethical behavior should result from their personal commitment to engage in ethical practice. The *NASW Code of Ethics* reflects the commitment of all social workers to uphold the profession's values and to act ethically. Principles and standards must be applied by individuals of good character who discern moral questions and, in good faith, seek to make reliable ethical judgments.

ETHICAL PRINCIPLES

The following broad ethical principles are based on social work's core values of service, social justice, dignity and worth of the person, importance of human relationships, integrity, and competence. These principles set forth ideals to which all social workers should aspire.

Value: *Service*

Ethical Principle: *Social workers' primary goal is to help people in need and to address social problems.*

Social workers elevate service to others above self-interest. Social workers draw on their knowledge, values, and skills to help people in need and to address social problems. Social workers are encouraged to volunteer some portion of their professional skills with no expectation of significant financial return (pro bono service).

Value: *Social Justice*

Ethical Principle: *Social workers challenge social injustice.*

Social workers pursue social change, particularly with and on behalf of vulnerable and oppressed individuals and groups of people. Social workers' social change efforts are focused primarily on issues of poverty, unemployment, discrimination, and other forms of social injustice. These activities seek to promote sensitivity to and knowledge about oppression and cultural and ethnic diversity. Social workers strive to ensure access to needed information, services, and resources; equality of opportunity; and meaningful participation in decision making for all people.

Value: *Dignity and Worth of the Person*

Ethical Principle: *Social workers respect the inherent dignity and worth of the person.*

Social workers treat each person in a caring and respectful fashion, mindful of individual differences and cultural and ethnic diversity. Social workers promote clients' socially responsible self-determination. Social workers seek to enhance clients' capacity and opportunity to change and to address their own needs. Social workers are cognizant of their dual responsibility to clients and to the broader society. They seek to resolve conflicts between clients' interests and the broader society's interests in a socially responsible manner consistent with the values, ethical principles, and ethical standards of the profession.

Value: *Importance of Human Relationships*

Ethical Principle: *Social workers recognize the central importance of human relationships.*

Social workers understand that relationships between and among people are an important vehicle for change. Social workers engage people as partners in the helping process. Social workers seek to strengthen relationships among people in a purposeful effort to promote, restore, maintain, and enhance the well-being of individuals, families, social groups, organizations, and communities.

Value: *Integrity*

Ethical Principle: *Social workers behave in a trustworthy manner.*

Social workers are continually aware of the profession's mission, values, ethical principles, and ethical standards and practice in a manner consistent with them. Social workers act honestly and responsibly and promote ethical practices on the part of the organizations with which they are affiliated.

Value: *Competence*

Ethical Principle: *Social workers practice within their areas of competence and develop and enhance their professional expertise.*

Social workers continually strive to increase their professional knowledge and skills and to apply them in practice. Social workers should aspire to contribute to the knowledge base of the profession.

ETHICAL STANDARDS

The following ethical standards are relevant to the professional activities of all social workers. These standards concern (1) social workers' ethical responsibilities to clients, (2) social workers' ethical responsibilities to colleagues, (3) social workers' ethical responsibilities in practice settings, (4) social workers' ethical responsibilities as professionals, (5) social workers' ethical responsibilities to the social work profession, and (6) social workers' ethical responsibilities to the broader society.

Some of the standards that follow are enforceable guidelines for professional conduct, and some are aspirational. The extent to which each standard is enforceable is a matter of professional judgment to be exercised by those responsible for reviewing alleged violations of ethical standards.

1. Social Workers' Ethical Responsibilities to Clients

1.01 Commitment to Clients. Social workers' primary responsibility is to promote the well-being of clients. In general, clients' interests are primary. However, social workers' responsibility to the larger society or specific legal obligations may on limited occasions supersede the loyalty owed clients, and clients should be so advised. (Examples include when a social worker is required by law to report that a client has abused a child or has threatened to harm self or others.)

1.02 Self-Determination. Social workers respect and promote the right of clients to self-determination and assist clients in their efforts to identify and clarify their goals. Social workers may limit clients' right to self-determination when, in the social workers' professional judgment, clients' actions or potential actions pose a serious, foreseeable, and imminent risk to themselves or others.

1.03 Informed Consent.

a. Social workers should provide services to clients only in the context of a professional relationship based, when appropriate, on valid informed consent. Social workers should use clear and understandable language to inform clients of the purpose of the services, risks related to the services, limits to services because of the requirements of a third-party payer, relevant costs, reasonable alternatives, clients' right to refuse or withdraw consent, and the time frame covered by the consent. Social workers should provide clients with an opportunity to ask questions.
b. In instances when clients are not literate or have difficulty understanding the primary language used in the practice setting, social workers should take steps to ensure clients' comprehension. This may include providing clients with a detailed verbal explanation or arranging for a qualified interpreter or translator whenever possible.
c. In instances when clients lack the capacity to provide informed consent, social workers should protect clients' interests by seeking permission from an appropriate third party, informing clients consistent with the clients' level of understanding. In such instances social workers should seek to ensure that the third party acts in a manner consistent with clients' wishes and interests. Social workers should take reasonable steps to enhance such clients' ability to give informed consent.
d. In instances when clients are receiving services involuntarily, social workers should provide information about the nature and extent of services and about the extent of clients' right to refuse service.
e. Social workers who provide services via electronic media (such as computer, telephone, radio, and television) should inform recipients of the limitations and risks associated with such services.
f. Social workers should obtain clients' informed consent before audiotaping or videotaping clients or permitting observation of services to clients by a third party.

1.04 Competence.

a. Social workers should provide services and represent themselves as competent only within the boundaries of their education, training, license, certification, consultation received, supervised experience, or other relevant professional experience.
b. Social workers should provide services in substantive areas or use intervention techniques or approaches that are new to them only after engaging in appropriate study, training, consultation, and supervision from people who are competent in those interventions or techniques.
c. When generally recognized standards do not exist with respect to an emerging area of practice, social workers should exercise careful judgment and take responsible steps (including appropriate education, research, training, consultation, and supervision) to ensure the competence of their work and to protect clients from harm.

1.05 Cultural Competence and Social Diversity.

a. Social workers should understand culture and its function in human behavior and society, recognizing the strengths that exist in all cultures.
b. Social workers should have a knowledge base of their clients' cultures and be able to demonstrate competence in the provision of services that are sensitive to clients' cultures and to differences among people and cultural groups.

c. Social workers should obtain education about and seek to understand the nature of social diversity and oppression with respect to race, ethnicity, national origin, color, sex, sexual orientation, age, marital status, political belief, religion, and mental or physical disability.

1.06 Conflicts of Interest.

a. Social workers should be alert to and avoid conflicts of interest that interfere with the exercise of professional discretion and impartial judgment. Social workers should inform clients when a real or potential conflict of interest arises and take reasonable steps to resolve the issue in a manner that makes the clients' interests primary and protects clients' interests to the greatest extent possible. In some cases, protecting clients' interests may require termination of the professional relationship with proper referral of the client.
b. Social workers should not take unfair advantage of any professional relationship or exploit others to further their personal, religious, political, or business interests.
c. Social workers should not engage in dual or multiple relationships with clients or former clients in which there is a risk of exploitation or potential harm to the client. In instances when dual or multiple relationships are unavoidable, social workers should take steps to protect clients and are responsible for setting clear, appropriate, and culturally sensitive boundaries. (Dual or multiple relationships occur when social workers relate to clients in more than one relationship, whether professional, social, or business. Dual or multiple relationships can occur simultaneously or consecutively.)
d. When social workers provide services to two or more people who have a relationship with each other (for example, couples, family members), social workers should clarify with all parties which individuals will be considered clients and the nature of social workers' professional obligations to the various individuals who are receiving services. Social workers who anticipate a conflict of interest among the individuals receiving services or who anticipate having to perform in potentially conflicting roles (for example, when a social worker is asked to testify in a child custody dispute or divorce proceedings involving clients) should clarify their role with the parties involved and take appropriate action to minimize any conflict of interest.

1.07 Privacy and Confidentiality.

a. Social workers should respect clients' right to privacy. Social workers should not solicit private information from clients unless it is essential to providing services or conducting social work evaluation or research. Once private information is shared, standards of confidentiality apply.
b. Social workers may disclose confidential information when appropriate with valid consent from a client or a person legally authorized to consent on behalf of a client.
c. Social workers should protect the confidentiality of all information obtained in the course of professional service, except for compelling professional reasons. The general expectation that social workers will keep information confidential does not apply when disclosure is necessary to prevent serious, foreseeable, and imminent harm to a client or other identifiable person. In all instances, social workers should disclose the least amount of confidential information necessary to achieve the desired purpose; only information that is directly relevant to the purpose for which the disclosure is made should be revealed.
d. Social workers should inform clients, to the extent possible, about the disclosure of confidential information and the potential consequences, when feasible before the disclosure is made. This applies whether social workers disclose confidential information on the basis of a legal requirement or client consent.
e. Social workers should discuss with clients and other interested parties the nature of confidentiality and limitations of clients' right to confidentiality. Social workers should review with clients circumstances where confidential information may be requested and where disclosure of confidential information may be legally required. This discussion should occur as soon as possible in the social worker-client relationship and as needed throughout the course of the relationship.
f. When social workers provide counseling services to families, couples, or groups, social workers should seek agreement among the parties involved concerning each individual's right to confidentiality and obligation to preserve the confidentiality of information shared by others. Social workers should inform participants in family, couples, or group counseling that social workers cannot guarantee that all participants will honor such agreements.
g. Social workers should inform clients involved in family, couples, marital, or group counseling of the social worker's, employer's, and agency's policy concerning the social worker's disclosure of confidential information among the parties involved in the counseling.
h. Social workers should not disclose confidential information to third-party payers unless clients have authorized such disclosure.
i. Social workers should not discuss confidential information in any setting unless privacy can be ensured. Social workers should not discuss confidential information in public or semipublic areas such as hallways, waiting rooms, elevators, and restaurants.
j. Social workers should protect the confidentiality of clients during legal proceedings to the extent permitted by law. When a court or other legally authorized body orders social workers to disclose confidential or privileged information without a client's consent and such disclosure could cause harm to the client, social workers should request that the court withdraw the order or limit the order as narrowly as possible or maintain the records under seal, unavailable for public inspection.
k. Social workers should protect the confidentiality of clients when responding to requests from members of the media.
l. Social workers should protect the confidentiality of clients' written and electronic records and other sensitive information. Social workers should take reasonable steps to ensure that clients' records are stored in a

secure location and that clients' records are not available to others who are not authorized to have access.

m. Social workers should take precautions to ensure and maintain the confidentiality of information transmitted to other parties through the use of computers, electronic mail, facsimile machines, telephones and telephone answering machines, and other electronic or computer technology. Disclosure of identifying information should be avoided whenever possible.
n. Social workers should transfer or dispose of clients' records in a manner that protects clients' confidentiality and is consistent with state statutes governing records and social work licensure.
o. Social workers should take reasonable precautions to protect client confidentiality in the event of the social worker's termination of practice, incapacitation, or death.
p. Social workers should not disclose identifying information when discussing clients for teaching or training purposes unless the client has consented to disclosure of confidential information.
q. Social workers should not disclose identifying information when discussing clients with consultants unless the client has consented to disclosure of confidential information or there is a compelling need for such disclosure.
r. Social workers should protect the confidentiality of deceased clients consistent with the preceding standards.

1.08 Access to Records.

a. Social workers should provide clients with reasonable access to records concerning the clients. Social workers who are concerned that clients' access to their records could cause serious misunderstanding or harm to the client should provide assistance in interpreting the records and consultation with the client regarding the records. Social workers should limit clients' access to their records, or portions of their records, only in exceptional circumstances when there is compelling evidence that such access would cause serious harm to the client. Both clients' requests and the rationale for withholding some or all of the record should be documented in clients' files.
b. When providing clients with access to their records, social workers should take steps to protect the confidentiality of other individuals identified or discussed in such records.

1.09 Sexual Relationships.

a. Social workers should under no circumstances engage in sexual activities or sexual contact with current clients, whether such contact is consensual or forced.
b. Social workers should not engage in sexual activities or sexual contact with clients' relatives or other individuals with whom clients maintain a close personal relationship when there is a risk of exploitation or potential harm to the client. Sexual activity or sexual contact with clients' relatives or other individuals with whom clients maintain a personal relationship has the potential to be harmful to the client and may make it difficult for the social worker and client to maintain appropriate professional boundaries. Social workers—not their clients, their clients' relatives, or other individuals with whom the client maintains a personal relationship—assume the full burden for setting clear, appropriate, and culturally sensitive boundaries.
c. Social workers should not engage in sexual activities or sexual contact with former clients because of the potential for harm to the client. If social workers engage in conduct contrary to this prohibition or claim that an exception to this prohibition is warranted because of extraordinary circumstances, it is social workers—not their clients—who assume the full burden of demonstrating that the former client has not been exploited, coerced, or manipulated, intentionally or unintentionally.
d. Social workers should not provide clinical services to individuals with whom they have had a prior sexual relationship. Providing clinical services to a former sexual partner has the potential to be harmful to the individual and is likely to make it difficult for the social worker and individual to maintain appropriate professional boundaries.

1.10 Physical Contact. Social workers should not engage in physical contact with clients when there is a possibility of psychological harm to the client as a result of the contact (such as cradling or caressing clients). Social workers who engage in appropriate physical contact with clients are responsible for setting clear, appropriate, and culturally sensitive boundaries that govern such physical contact.

1.11 Sexual Harassment. Social workers should not sexually harass clients. Sexual harassment includes sexual advances, sexual solicitation, requests for sexual favors, and other verbal or physical conduct of a sexual nature.

1.12 Derogatory Language. Social workers should not use derogatory language in their written or verbal communications to or about clients. Social workers should use accurate and respectful language in all communications to and about clients.

1.13 Payment for Services.

a. When setting fees, social workers should ensure that the fees are fair, reasonable, and commensurate with the services performed. Consideration should be given to clients' ability to pay.
b. Social workers should avoid accepting goods or services from clients as payment for professional services. Bartering arrangements, particularly involving services, create the potential for conflicts of interest, exploitation, and inappropriate boundaries in social workers' relationships with clients. Social workers should explore and may participate in bartering only in very limited circumstances when it can be demonstrated that such arrangements are an accepted practice among professionals in the local community, considered to be essential for the provision of services, negotiated without coercion, and entered into at the client's initiative and with the client's informed consent. Social workers who accept goods or services from clients as payment for professional services assume the full burden of demonstrating that this arrangement will not be detrimental to the client or the professional relationship.

c. Social workers should not solicit a private fee or other remuneration for providing services to clients who are entitled to such available services through the social workers' employer or agency.

1.14 Clients Who Lack Decision-Making Capacity. When social workers act on behalf of clients who lack the capacity to make informed decisions, social workers should take reasonable steps to safeguard the interests and rights of those clients.

1.15 Interruption of Services. Social workers should make reasonable efforts to ensure continuity of services in the event that services are interrupted by factors such as unavailability, relocation, illness, disability, or death.

1.16 Termination of Services.

a. Social workers should terminate services to clients and professional relationships with them when such services and relationships are no longer required or no longer serve the clients' needs or interests.
b. Social workers should take reasonable steps to avoid abandoning clients who are still in need of services. Social workers should withdraw services precipitously only under unusual circumstances, giving careful consideration to all factors in the situation and taking care to minimize possible adverse effects. Social workers should assist in making appropriate arrangements for continuation of services when necessary.
c. Social workers in fee-for-service settings may terminate services to clients who are not paying an overdue balance if the financial contractual arrangements have been made clear to the client, if the client does not pose an imminent danger to self or others, and if the clinical and other consequences of the current nonpayment have been addressed and discussed with the client.
d. Social workers should not terminate services to pursue a social, financial, or sexual relationship with a client.
e. Social workers who anticipate the termination or interruption of services to clients should notify clients promptly and seek the transfer, referral, or continuation of services in relation to the clients' needs and preferences.
f. Social workers who are leaving an employment setting should inform clients of appropriate options for the continuation of services and of the benefits and risks of the options.

2. Social Workers' Ethical Responsibilities to Colleagues

2.01 Respect.

a. Social workers should treat colleagues with respect and should represent accurately and fairly the qualifications, views, and obligations of colleagues.
b. Social workers should avoid unwarranted negative criticism of colleagues in communications with clients or with other professionals. Unwarranted negative criticism may include demeaning comments that refer to colleagues' level of competence or to individuals' attributes such as race, ethnicity, national origin, color, sex, sexual orientation, age, marital status, political belief, religion, and mental or physical disability.
c. Social workers should cooperate with social work colleagues and with colleagues of other professions when such cooperation serves the well-being of clients.

2.02 Confidentiality. Social workers should respect confidential information shared by colleagues in the course of their professional relationships and transactions. Social workers should ensure that such colleagues understand social workers' obligation to respect confidentiality and any exceptions related to it.

2.03 Interdisciplinary Collaboration.

a. Social workers who are members of an interdisciplinary team should participate in and contribute to decisions that affect the well-being of clients by drawing on the perspectives, values, and experiences of the social work profession. Professional and ethical obligations of the interdisciplinary team as a whole and of its individual members should be clearly established.
b. Social workers for whom a team decision raises ethical concerns should attempt to resolve the disagreement through appropriate channels. If the disagreement cannot be resolved, social workers should pursue other avenues to address their concerns consistent with client well-being.

2.04 Disputes Involving Colleagues.

a. Social workers should not take advantage of a dispute between a colleague and an employer to obtain a position or otherwise advance the social workers' own interests.
b. Social workers should not exploit clients in disputes with colleagues or engage clients in any inappropriate discussion of conflicts between social workers and their colleagues.

2.05 Consultation.

a. Social workers should seek the advice and counsel of colleagues whenever such consultation is in the best interests of clients.
b. Social workers should keep themselves informed about colleagues' areas of expertise and competencies. Social workers should seek consultation only from colleagues who have demonstrated knowledge, expertise, and competence related to the subject of the consultation.
c. When consulting with colleagues about clients, social workers should disclose the least amount of information necessary to achieve the purposes of the consultation.

2.06 Referral for Services.

a. Social workers should refer clients to other professionals when the other professionals' specialized knowledge or expertise is needed to serve clients fully or when social workers believe that they are not being effective or making reasonable progress with clients and that additional service is required.
b. Social workers who refer clients to other professionals should take appropriate steps to facilitate an orderly transfer of responsibility. Social workers who refer clients to other professionals should disclose, with

clients' consent, all pertinent information to the new service providers.

c. Social workers are prohibited from giving or receiving payment for a referral when no professional service is provided by the referring social worker.

2.07 Sexual Relationships.

a. Social workers who function as supervisors or educators should not engage in sexual activities or contact with supervisees, students, trainees, or other colleagues over whom they exercise professional authority.

b. Social workers should avoid engaging in sexual relationships with colleagues when there is potential for a conflict of interest. Social workers who become involved in, or anticipate becoming involved in, a sexual relationship with a colleague have a duty to transfer professional responsibilities, when necessary, to avoid a conflict of interest.

2.08 Sexual Harassment. Social workers should not sexually harass supervisees, students, trainees, or colleagues. Sexual harassment includes sexual advances, sexual solicitation, requests for sexual favors, and other verbal or physical conduct of a sexual nature.

2.09 Impairment of Colleagues.

a. Social workers who have direct knowledge of a social work colleague's impairment that is due to personal problems, psychosocial distress, substance abuse, or mental health difficulties and that interferes with practice effectiveness should consult with that colleague when feasible and assist the colleague in taking remedial action.

b. Social workers who believe that a social work colleague's impairment interferes with practice effectiveness and that the colleague has not taken adequate steps to address the impairment should take action through appropriate channels established by employers, agencies, NASW, licensing and regulatory bodies, and other professional organizations.

2.10 Incompetence of Colleagues.

a. Social workers who have direct knowledge of a social work colleague's incompetence should consult with that colleague when feasible and assist the colleague in taking remedial action.

b. Social workers who believe that a social work colleague is incompetent and has not taken adequate steps to address the incompetence should take action through appropriate channels established by employers, agencies, NASW, licensing and regulatory bodies, and other professional organizations.

2.11 Unethical Conduct of Colleagues.

a. Social workers should take adequate measures to discourage, prevent, expose, and correct the unethical conduct of colleagues.

b. Social workers should be knowledgeable about established policies and procedures for handling concerns about colleagues' unethical behavior. Social workers should be familiar with national, state, and local procedures for handling ethics complaints. These include policies and procedures created by NASW, licensing and regulatory bodies, employers, agencies, and other professional organizations.

c. Social workers who believe that a colleague has acted unethically should seek resolution by discussing their concerns with the colleague when feasible and when such discussion is likely to be productive.

d. When necessary, social workers who believe that a colleague has acted unethically should take action through appropriate formal channels (such as contacting a state licensing board or regulatory body, an NASW committee on inquiry, or other professional ethics committees).

e. Social workers should defend and assist colleagues who are unjustly charged with unethical conduct.

3. Social Workers' Ethical Responsibilities in Practice Settings

3.01 Supervision and Consultation.

a. Social workers who provide supervision or consultation should have the necessary knowledge and skill to supervise or consult appropriately and should do so only within their areas of knowledge and competence.

b. Social workers who provide supervision or consultation are responsible for setting clear, appropriate, and culturally sensitive boundaries.

c. Social workers should not engage in any dual or multiple relationships with supervisees in which there is a risk of exploitation of or potential harm to the supervisee.

d. Social workers who provide supervision should evaluate supervisees' performance in a manner that is fair and respectful.

3.02 Education and Training.

a. Social workers who function as educators, field instructors for students, or trainers should provide instruction only within their areas of knowledge and competence and should provide instruction based on the most current information and knowledge available in the profession.

b. Social workers who function as educators or field instructors for students should evaluate students' performance in a manner that is fair and respectful.

c. Social workers who function as educators or field instructors for students should take reasonable steps to ensure that clients are routinely informed when services are being provided by students.

d. Social workers who function as educators or field instructors for students should not engage in any dual or multiple relationships with students in which there is a risk of exploitation or potential harm to the student. Social work educators and field instructors are responsible for setting clear, appropriate, and culturally sensitive boundaries.

3.03 Performance Evaluation. Social workers who have responsibility for evaluating the performance of others should fulfill such responsibility in a fair and considerate manner and on the basis of clearly stated criteria.

3.04 Client Records.

a. Social workers should take reasonable steps to ensure that documentation in records is accurate and reflects the services provided.
b. Social workers should include sufficient and timely documentation in records to facilitate the delivery of services and to ensure continuity of services provided to clients in the future.
c. Social workers' documentation should protect clients' privacy to the extent that is possible and appropriate and should include only information that is directly relevant to the delivery of services.
d. Social workers should store records following the termination of services to ensure reasonable future access. Records should be maintained for the number of years required by state statutes or relevant contracts.

3.05 Billing. Social workers should establish and maintain billing practices that accurately reflect the nature and extent of services provided and that identify who provided the service in the practice setting.

3.06 Client Transfer.

a. When an individual who is receiving services from another agency or colleague contacts a social worker for services, the social worker should carefully consider the client's needs before agreeing to provide services. To minimize possible confusion and conflict, social workers should discuss with potential clients the nature of the clients' current relationship with other service providers and the implications, including possible benefits or risks, of entering into a relationship with a new service provider.
b. If a new client has been served by another agency or colleague, social workers should discuss with the client whether consultation with the previous service provider is in the client's best interest.

3.07 Administration.

a. Social work administrators should advocate within and outside their agencies for adequate resources to meet clients' needs.
b. Social workers should advocate for resource allocation procedures that are open and fair. When not all clients' needs can be met, an allocation procedure should be developed that is nondiscriminatory and based on appropriate and consistently applied principles.
c. Social workers who are administrators should take reasonable steps to ensure that adequate agency or organizational resources are available to provide appropriate staff supervision.
d. Social work administrators should take reasonable steps to ensure that the working environment for which they are responsible is consistent with and encourages compliance with the NASW Code of Ethics. Social work administrators should take reasonable steps to eliminate any conditions in their organizations that violate, interfere with, or discourage compliance with the Code.

3.08 Continuing Education and Staff Development. Social work administrators and supervisors should take reasonable steps to provide or arrange for continuing education and staff development for all staff for whom they are responsible. Continuing education and staff development should address current knowledge and emerging developments related to social work practice and ethics.

3.09 Commitments to Employers.

a. Social workers generally should adhere to commitments made to employers and employing organizations.
b. Social workers should work to improve employing agencies' policies and procedures and the efficiency and effectiveness of their services.
c. Social workers should take reasonable steps to ensure that employers are aware of social workers' ethical obligations as set forth in the NASW Code of Ethics and of the implications of those obligations for social work practice.
d. Social workers should not allow an employing organization's policies, procedures, regulations, or administrative orders to interfere with their ethical practice of social work. Social workers should take reasonable steps to ensure that their employing organizations' practices are consistent with the NASW Code of Ethics.
e. Social workers should act to prevent and eliminate discrimination in the employing organization's work assignments and in its employment policies and practices.
f. Social workers should accept employment or arrange student field placements only in organizations that exercise fair personnel practices.
g. Social workers should be diligent stewards of the resources of their employing organizations, wisely conserving funds where appropriate and never misappropriating funds or using them for unintended purposes.

3.10 Labor-Management Disputes.

a. Social workers may engage in organized action, including the formation of and participation in labor unions, to improve services to clients and working conditions.
b. The actions of social workers who are involved in labor-management disputes, job actions, or labor strikes should be guided by the profession's values, ethical principles, and ethical standards. Reasonable differences of opinion exist among social workers concerning their primary obligation as professionals during an actual or threatened labor strike or job action. Social workers should carefully examine relevant issues and their possible impact on clients before deciding on a course of action.

4. Social Workers' Ethical Responsibilities as Professionals

4.01 Competence.

a. Social workers should accept responsibility or employment only on the basis of existing competence or the intention to acquire the necessary competence.
b. Social workers should strive to become and remain proficient in professional practice and the performance

of professional functions. Social workers should critically examine and keep current with emerging knowledge relevant to social work. Social workers should routinely review the professional literature and participate in continuing education relevant to social work practice and social work ethics.

c. Social workers should base practice on recognized knowledge, including empirically based knowledge, relevant to social work and social work ethics.

4.02 Discrimination. Social workers should not practice, condone, facilitate, or collaborate with any form of discrimination on the basis of race, ethnicity, national origin, color, sex, sexual orientation, age, marital status, political belief, religion, or mental or physical disability.

4.03 Private Conduct. Social workers should not permit their private conduct to interfere with their ability to fulfill their professional responsibilities.

4.04 Dishonesty, Fraud, and Deception. Social workers should not participate in, condone, or be associated with dishonesty, fraud, or deception.

4.05 Impairment.

a. Social workers should not allow their own personal problems, psychosocial distress, legal problems, substance abuse, or mental health difficulties to interfere with their professional judgment and performance or to jeopardize the best interests of people for whom they have a professional responsibility.
b. Social workers whose personal problems, psychosocial distress, legal problems, substance abuse, or mental health difficulties interfere with their professional judgment and performance should immediately seek consultation and take appropriate remedial action by seeking professional help, making adjustments in workload, terminating practice, or taking any other steps necessary to protect clients and others.

4.06 Misrepresentation.

a. Social workers should make clear distinctions between statements made and actions engaged in as a private individual and as a representative of the social work profession, a professional social work organization, or the social worker's employing agency.
b. Social workers who speak on behalf of professional social work organizations should accurately represent the official and authorized positions of the organizations.
c. Social workers should ensure that their representations to clients, agencies, and the public of professional qualifications, credentials, education, competence, affiliations, services provided, or results to be achieved are accurate. Social workers should claim only those relevant professional credentials they actually possess and take steps to correct any inaccuracies or misrepresentations of their credentials by others.

4.07 Solicitations.

a. Social workers should not engage in uninvited solicitation of potential clients who, because of their circumstances, are vulnerable to undue influence, manipulation, or coercion.
b. Social workers should not engage in solicitation of testimonial endorsements (including solicitation of consent to use a client's prior statement as a testimonial endorsement) from current clients or from other people who, because of their particular circumstances, are vulnerable to undue influence.

4.08 Acknowledging Credit.

a. Social workers should take responsibility and credit, including authorship credit, only for work they have actually performed and to which they have contributed.
b. Social workers should honestly acknowledge the work of and the contributions made by others.

5. Social Workers' Ethical Responsibilities to the Social Work Profession

5.01 Integrity of the Profession.

a. Social workers should work toward the maintenance and promotion of high standards of practice.
b. Social workers should uphold and advance the values, ethics, knowledge, and mission of the profession. Social workers should protect, enhance, and improve the integrity of the profession through appropriate study and research, active discussion, and responsible criticism of the profession.
c. Social workers should contribute time and professional expertise to activities that promote respect for the value, integrity, and competence of the social work profession. These activities may include teaching, research, consultation, service, legislative testimony, presentations in the community, and participation in their professional organizations.
d. Social workers should contribute to the knowledge base of social work and share with colleagues their knowledge related to practice, research, and ethics. Social workers should seek to contribute to the profession's literature and to share their knowledge at professional meetings and conferences.
e. Social workers should act to prevent the unauthorized and unqualified practice of social work.

5.02 Evaluation and Research.

a. Social workers should monitor and evaluate policies, the implementation of programs, and practice interventions.
b. Social workers should promote and facilitate evaluation and research to contribute to the development of knowledge.
c. Social workers should critically examine and keep current with emerging knowledge relevant to social work and fully use evaluation and research evidence in their professional practice.
d. Social workers engaged in evaluation or research should carefully consider possible consequences and should follow guidelines developed for the protection of evaluation and research participants. Appropriate institutional review boards should be consulted.
e. Social workers engaged in evaluation or research should obtain voluntary and written informed consent

from participants, when appropriate, without any implied or actual deprivation or penalty for refusal to participate; without undue inducement to participate; and with due regard for participants' well-being, privacy, and dignity. Informed consent should include information about the nature, extent, and duration of the participation requested and disclosure of the risks and benefits of participation in the research.

f. When evaluation or research participants are incapable of giving informed consent, social workers should provide an appropriate explanation to the participants, obtain the participants' assent to the extent they are able, and obtain written consent from an appropriate proxy.

g. Social workers should never design or conduct evaluation or research that does not use consent procedures, such as certain forms of naturalistic observation and archival research, unless rigorous and responsible review of the research has found it to be justified because of its prospective scientific, educational, or applied value and unless equally effective alternative procedures that do not involve waiver of consent are not feasible.

h. Social workers should inform participants of their right to withdraw from evaluation and research at any time without penalty.

i. Social workers should take appropriate steps to ensure that participants in evaluation and research have access to appropriate supportive services.

j. Social workers engaged in evaluation or research should protect participants from unwarranted physical or mental distress, harm, danger, or deprivation.

k. Social workers engaged in the evaluation of services should discuss collected information only for professional purposes and only with people professionally concerned with this information.

l. Social workers engaged in evaluation or research should ensure the anonymity or confidentiality of participants and of the data obtained from them. Social workers should inform participants of any limits of confidentiality, the measures that will be taken to ensure confidentiality, and when any records containing research data will be destroyed.

m. Social workers who report evaluation and research results should protect participants' confidentiality by omitting identifying information unless proper consent has been obtained authorizing disclosure.

n. Social workers should report evaluation and research findings accurately. They should not fabricate or falsify results and should take steps to correct any errors later found in published data using standard publication methods.

o. Social workers engaged in evaluation or research should be alert to and avoid conflicts of interest and dual relationships with participants, should inform participants when a real or potential conflict of interest arises, and should take steps to resolve the issue in a manner that makes participants' interests primary.

p. Social workers should educate themselves, their students, and their colleagues about responsible research practices.

6. Social Workers' Ethical Responsibilities to the Broader Society

6.01 Social Welfare. Social workers should promote the general welfare of society, from local to global levels, and the development of people, their communities, and their environments. Social workers should advocate for living conditions conducive to the fulfillment of basic human needs and should promote social, economic, political, and cultural values and institutions that are compatible with the realization of social justice.

6.02 Public Participation. Social workers should facilitate informed participation by the public in shaping social policies and institutions.

6.03 Public Emergencies. Social workers should provide appropriate professional services in public emergencies to the greatest extent possible.

6.04 Social and Political Action.

a. Social workers should engage in social and political action that seeks to ensure that all people have equal access to the resources, employment, services, and opportunities they require to meet their basic human needs and to develop fully. Social workers should be aware of the impact of the political arena on practice and should advocate for changes in policy and legislation to improve social conditions in order to meet basic human needs and promote social justice.

b. Social workers should act to expand choice and opportunity for all people, with special regard for vulnerable, disadvantaged, oppressed, and exploited people and groups.

c. Social workers should promote conditions that encourage respect for cultural and social diversity within the United States and globally. Social workers should promote policies and practices that demonstrate respect for difference, support the expansion of cultural knowledge and resources, advocate for programs and institutions that demonstrate cultural competence, and promote policies that safeguard the rights of and confirm equity and social justice for all people.

d. Social workers should act to prevent and eliminate domination of, exploitation of, and discrimination against any person, group, or class on the basis of race, ethnicity, national origin, color, sex, sexual orientation, age, marital status, political belief, religion, or mental or physical disability.

Note: Approved by the 1996 NASW Delegate Assembly and revised by the 1999 NASW Delegate Assembly. National Association of Social Workers, 750 First Street NE, Suite 700, Washington, DC 20002-4241, 202-408-8600/800-638-8799.

Name Index

Subject Index